Let's

Central

GW00792367

"...ghthearted and sophisticated, informative and fun to read. *[Let's Go]* helps the novice traveler navigate like a knowledgeable old hand."
—*Atlanta Journal-Constitution*

"The guides are aimed not only at young budget travelers but at the independent traveler, a sort of streetwise cookbook for traveling alone."
—*The New York Times*

▨ Let's Go writers travel on your budget.

"Retains the spirit of the student-written publication it is: candid, opinionated, resourceful, amusing info for the traveler of limited means but broad curiosity." —*Mademoiselle*

"The writers seem to have experienced every rooster-packed bus and lunar-surfaced mattress about which they write." —*The New York Times*

"All the dirt, dirt cheap." —*People*

▨ Great for independent travelers.

"A world-wise traveling companion—always ready with friendly advice and helpful hints, all sprinkled with a bit of wit." —*The Philadelphia Inquirer*

"Lots of valuable information for any independent traveler."
—*The Chicago Tribune*

▨ Let's Go is completely revised each year.

"Unbeatable: good sight-seeing advice; up-to-date info on restaurants, hotels, and inns; a commitment to money-saving travel; and a wry style that brightens nearly every page." —*The Washington Post*

"Its yearly revision by a new crop of Harvard students makes it as valuable as ever." —*The New York Times*

▨ All the important information you need.

"Enough information to satisfy even the most demanding of budget travelers...*Let's Go* follows the creed that you don't have to toss your life's savings to the wind to travel—unless you want to."
—*The Salt Lake Tribune*

"Value-packed, unbeatable, accurate, and comprehensive."
—*The Los Angeles Times*

Let's Go Publications

Let's Go: Alaska & the Pacific Northwest 1998
Let's Go: Australia 1998 **New title!**
Let's Go: Austria & Switzerland 1998
Let's Go: Britain & Ireland 1998
Let's Go: California 1998
Let's Go: Central America 1998
Let's Go: Eastern Europe 1998
Let's Go: Ecuador & the Galápagos Islands 1998
Let's Go: Europe 1998
Let's Go: France 1998
Let's Go: Germany 1998
Let's Go: Greece & Turkey 1998
Let's Go: India & Nepal 1998
Let's Go: Ireland 1998
Let's Go: Israel & Egypt 1998
Let's Go: Italy 1998
Let's Go: London 1998
Let's Go: Mexico 1998
Let's Go: New York City 1998
Let's Go: New Zealand 1998 **New title!**
Let's Go: Paris 1998
Let's Go: Rome 1998
Let's Go: Southeast Asia 1998
Let's Go: Spain & Portugal 1998
Let's Go: USA 1998
Let's Go: Washington, D.C. 1998

Let's Go Map Guides

Berlin	New Orleans
Boston	New York City
Chicago	Paris
London	Rome
Los Angeles	San Francisco
Madrid	Washington, D.C.

Coming Soon: Amsterdam, Florence

**Let's Go
Publications**

LET'S GO
Central
America
1998

Paula Nikia Bergan
Editor

Allyson Vanessa Hobbs
Associate Editor

Macmillan

HELPING LET'S GO

If you want to share your discoveries, suggestions, or corrections, please drop us a line. We read every piece of correspondence, whether a postcard, a 10-page email, or a coconut. Please note that mail received after May 1998 may be too late for the 1999 book, but will be kept for future editions. **Address mail to:**

> **Let's Go: Central America**
> **67 Mount Auburn Street**
> **Cambridge, MA 02138**
> **USA**

Visit Let's Go at **http://www.letsgo.com,** or send email to:

> **fanmail@letsgo.com**
> **Subject: "Let's Go: Central America"**

In addition to the invaluable travel advice our readers share with us, many are kind enough to offer their services as researchers or editors. Unfortunately, our charter enables us to employ only currently enrolled Harvard-Radcliffe students.

Published in Great Britain 1998 by Macmillan, an imprint of Macmillan General Books, 25 Eccleston Place, London SW1W 9NF and Basingstoke.

Map revisions pp. 61, 69, 71, 87, 113, 121, 125, 133, 155, 173, 182, 183, 187, 195, 207, 221, 233, 239, 243, 249, 275, 277, 285, 307, 326, 327, 337, 339, 347, 349, 355, 375, 383, 397, 409, 437, 453 by Let's Go, Inc.

Published in the United States of America by St. Martin's Press, Inc.

ADVERTISING DISCLAIMER

About Let's Go

Back in 1960, a few students at Harvard University banded together to produce a 20-page pamphlet offering a collection of tips on budget travel in Europe. This modest, mimeographed packet, offered as an extra to passengers on student charter flights to Europe, met with instant popularity. The following year, students traveling to Europe researched the first, full-fledged edition of *Let's Go: Europe,* a pocket-sized book featuring honest, irreverent writing and a decidedly youthful outlook on the world. Throughout the 60s, our guides reflected the times; the 1969 guide to America led off by inviting travelers to "dig the scene" at San Francisco's Haight-Ashbury. During the 70s and 80s, we gradually added regional guides and expanded coverage into the Middle East and Central America. With the addition of our in-depth city guides, handy map guides, and extensive coverage of Asia and Australia, the 90s are also proving to be a time of explosive growth for Let's Go, and there's certainly no end in sight. The first editions of *Let's Go: Australia* and *Let's Go: New Zealand* hit the shelves this year, expanding our coverage to six continents, and research for next year's series has already begun.

We've seen a lot in 38 years. *Let's Go: Europe* is now the world's bestselling international guide, translated into seven languages. And our new guides bring Let's Go's total number of titles, with their spirit of adventure and their reputation for honesty, accuracy, and editorial integrity, to 40. But some things never change: our guides are still researched, written, and produced entirely by students who know first-hand how to see the world on the cheap.

HOW WE DO IT

Each guide is completely revised and thoroughly updated every year by a well-traveled set of over 200 students. Every winter, we recruit over 140 researchers and 60 editors to write the books anew. After several months of training, Researcher-Writers hit the road for seven weeks of exploration, from Anchorage to Adelaide, Estonia to El Salvador, Iceland to Indonesia. Hired for their rare combination of budget travel sense, writing ability, stamina, and courage, these adventurous travelers know that train strikes, stolen luggage, food poisoning, and marriage proposals are all part of a day's work. Back at our offices, editors work from spring to fall, massaging copy written on Himalayan bus rides into witty yet informative prose. A student staff of typesetters, cartographers, publicists, and managers keeps our lively team together. In September, the collected efforts of the summer are delivered to our printer, who turns them into books in record time, so that you have the most up-to-date information available for your vacation. And even as you read this, work on next year's editions is well underway.

WHY WE DO IT

We don't think of budget travel as the last recourse of the destitute; we believe that it's the only way to travel. Living cheaply and simply brings you closer to the people and places you've been saving up to visit. Our books will ease your anxieties and answer your questions about the basics—so you can get off the beaten track and explore. Once you learn the ropes, we encourage you to put *Let's Go* down now and then to strike out on your own. As any seasoned traveler will tell you, the best discoveries are often those you make yourself. When you find something worth sharing, drop us a line. We're Let's Go Publications, 67 Mount Auburn Street, Cambridge, MA 02138, USA (email fanmail@letsgo.com).

HAPPY TRAVELS.

Contents

HONDURAS 211

NICARAGUA 263

COSTA RICA 324

PANAMÁ 419

APPENDIX 483
INDEX 489

Maps

Acknowledgments

Shout-outs go first and foremost to our stellar research squad: rock on to the break o dawn. Nick Corman, what can we say? Thanks for keepin' it real (touch). Props to our running crew, Team Latin America—Robin, Nick, Joanna, Marnie, Krzys and Sha kira—summer wouldn't have been half as fun without you. Nick, thanks for the crunch; you rule. Luis, your editing prowess and bell-ringing savvy are where it's at. Meera Deean and Alice Liu, your help was invaluable. Adam Stein and Ryan (Cito) Bradley, here's to four-square. To the receptionists, Laurie, Emily, Katherine, and Chuck:, thanks for keeping things in line and transferring Krzys's calls to us. Thanks to Janna, Jane, and Margo for putting up with constant talk of page counts; we'll miss you. Jake, Anne, Mel, and Dave: we *really* couldn't have done it without you. —**US**

Allyson, the ultimate butt-dance goes to you. Your sense of humor, Spanish-language smarts, and amazingly easy spirit held us together. Just remember who got you started... Big (huge) thanks to Laura, Vic, Sam, and Alexa for keeping me off the streets. I'll miss you more than you know. Amir, to you I leave my Archives film pass (oops, I didn't buy one) and my Kierkegaard Reader. Lucy, thanks for good times, good food. Bruce, Eric, Ethan, and Andrew: thanks for the email sewing tips, ladies. Jen Rhodes, I'll see *you* in Genoa. Mom, Dad, Alex and Joshy, thanks for taking me on good faith; as always, you are ever-missed, ever-loved. —**PNB**

Muchísimas gracias to Nikia, editrice extraordinaire, for your sparkling wit and fine Spanish-speaking skills (Me llamo Nikia Bergan...). Aw shucks, I'll miss you. Thanks to the amazing women (and man) of Walker, Katherine, Lucy, Laurie, Bruce, Margo and Emily, for an awesome summer of knee-slappin' impersonations, delicious strawberry shortcake, mistaken identities, and great talks. Propers to Ryan. Love to my favorite globe-trotter, Becky, my fellow salty-fry lover, Margot, and Liz, who helped me escape Cambridge on the weekends. Most of all, much love and many thanks to all my family, especially Mommy, Daddy, Greg, Verinda, Sharon and Carl. —**AVH**

Editor	Paula Nikia Bergan
Associate Editor	Allyson Vanessa Hobbs
Managing Editor	Nicholas Corman
Publishing Director	John R. Brooks
Production Manager	Melanie Quintana Kansil
Associate Production Manager	David Collins
Cartography Manager	Sara K. Smith
Editorial Manager	Melissa M. Reyen
Editorial Manager	Emily J. Stebbins
Financial Manager	Krzysztof Owerkowicz
Personnel Manager	Andrew E. Nieland
Publicity Manager	Nicholas Corman
Publicity Manager	Kate Galbraith
New Media Manager	Daniel O. Williams
Associate Cartographer	Joseph E. Reagan
Associate Cartographer	Luke Z. Fenchel
Office Coordinators	Emily Bowen, Chuck Kapelke
	Laurie Santos
Director of Advertising Sales	Todd L. Glaskin
Senior Sales Executives	Matthew R. Hillery, Joseph W. Lind
	Peter J. Zakowich, Jr.
President	Amit Tiwari
General Manager	Richard Olken
Assistant General Manager	Anne E. Chisholm

Researcher-Writers

Ken Blazejewski   *Panamá, Costa Rica*

Instead of touring Central America with his band, Vlemin Lava Brotiv, Ken opted to travel for *Let's Go* instead. Perhaps the only traveler to Central America deathly allergic to beans, Ken spent much of the summer trying to dodge the nefarious pine nut. From the surliest bus driver to the most accommodating hotel owner, few in Panamá escaped Ken's god-given charm. Ken survived a swim with blood-thirsty sharks, a misplaced money pouch, and a three-day hike from hell to pen some of the sharpest, wittiest prose this side of the border. Way to go, Carmen Sandiego!

Sean Coar   *El Salvador, Honduras, Guatemala*

If you want to travel like a prince on a pauper's purse, Sean Coar can show you how. With a keen eye for bargains, Sean enjoyed the cheapest meals on the finest menus, while staying in the finest rooms in the cheapest hotels. Sean happily immersed himself in Latin American life, infusing every page of his copy with insightful cultural observations. He rallied through a power outage in Trujillo, a crazed soccer mob in Utila, and the aftermath of a crazy fourth of July celebration in San Salvador to gracefully complete a difficult itinerary in record time.

Andrew Mitchell   *Guatemala, Belize*

Cow. Turkey. Deer. Armadillo. Rabbit. A nature tour of Central America? No, just some of the many dishes Andrew sampled as he traversed Guatemala and Belize. Andrew was hungry for adventure: he discovered two new towns, saw three movies (his favorite was *Last Tango in Paris*), wrote crisp new copy like it was going out of style, worshiped San Simón, and still remembered to call his parents on their anniversary. With characteristic perseverance and pluck, Andrew gobbled up every opportunity to explore new sites and sank his teeth into Central America's meatiest offerings.

Scott Newstrom   *Nicaragua, Costa Rica*

Scott did it the way it was meant to be done: every map sparkled, every fact checked, and every line of prose shone. Scott's lifelong interest in Nicaraguan politics translated into scrupulous copy chock-full of pensive musings (and sometimes even a poem). After five grueling weeks in wild, wonderful Nicaragua, Scott's enthusiasm never flagged—his last copybatch was as perfect as his first. All work and no play? Not quite. Like his kindred spirit, poet Rubén Darío, Scott broke a few hearts along the way. He hardly caught his breath before jetting off to Ireland. Look out, ladies.

Maureen Schad   *Costa Rica*

Maureen loved every moment she spent in Costa Rica, and her lively copybatches made us love it too. In a mere seven weeks, she set off metal detectors at the tourist agency, cut a rug in *salsa* clubs, got a bad haircut, was accosted by the police for flashing her Swiss army knife in the park, and fended off multiple marriage proposals. She ran, she swam, she hiked—she saw what Costa Rica has to offer, she liked what she saw, and she wrote it all down for you. Maureen's good humor and spunk, combined with thorough researching and fact-finding, left us begging for more.

Elena Schneider   *Belize, Honduras, Guatemala*

Elena's derring-do did it. After a few trying first days, Elena found her Garifuna groove and never looked back. Her copy sparkled like the blade of the machete she used to chop open coconuts in Belize. Elena met every challenge head on. Whether she was chasing down the thief who stole her watch, researching despite a bout of *turista*, or attempting to elude persistent suitors, her copybatches just got better and better. Elena's exuberance took her far beyond the world of researching; look for her in an upcoming movie on Garifuna culture.

Sandrine Goffard   *Yucatán Peninsula, Mexico*

How to Use This Book

Gentle reader, you are about to embark on the journey of your life, and our mission to help you enjoy it. Along with the expected assortment of torrid rains, blisterin suns, poisonous beasties, perilous buses, pristine beaches, halcyon sunsets, untran meled rain forests, and that-can't-be-lave-it's-been-extinct-for-centuries volcanos, w hope to show you the intricate details of what we believe is one of the earth's mo interesting, historically rich, culturally diverse regions. While whimsical jaunts can b the most thrilling, thoughtfully planned journeys are usually the most successful. Th beginning **Essentials** section is chock-full of information. We help you decide whe and how to travel, and demystify the intricacies of passports and customs; exchang rates and currency; traveler's checks; and credit cards. We offer helpful hints on hov to keep safe and healthy while traveling, whether you're hiking the moors or shakin, it down in clubs. This section contains a host of money-saving tips, too; read it *befor* you venture out and then relax in informed bliss while on the road.

Of course travel is about more than practicalities. It involves immersing yourself ir a culture different from your own. Be savvy and peruse the **Life and Times** introduc tions to Central America and each country therein. They contain brief essays on his tory and politics, literature, music, food, language, and festivals. While these presentations are by no means exhaustive, they provide some necessary backgrouno for an informed perspective on traveling in the region.

Our individual treatments of towns, cities, and national parks follow an established format. Large cities and parks begin with impressionistic introductions, followed by an **Orientation** section to help you get around. The **Practical Information** provides hard data on tourist offices, financial services, bus and train stations, bike rental, laun-derettes, hospitals, emergency numbers, police, post offices, postal codes (for the listed post office), and telephone codes—with sundry services like taxis and book-stores thrown in where appropriate. **Accommodations** and **Food** feature ranked list-ings; those establishments we feel provide the highest quality for the best price can be found at the top. **Sights** highlights places you might wish to visit, while **Entertain-ment** is your guide to where to see the booty and where to shake your booty. Small towns are not subdivided, and the text flows roughly in the opposite direction—Introduction followed by Sights and Entertainment, Accommodations and Food, Practical Information, and Transport.

Finally, a note on **how *not* to use this book.** Navigating through a new region can be overwhelming, but resist the temptation to let our guide be your pilot. Don't allow *Let's Go* to substitute for your personal travel exploits; rather, let it help you head off on your own adventures. Have fun, explore, respect those around you, and write us and let us know how it went.

A NOTE TO OUR READERS

The information for this book is gathered by *Let's Go*'s researchers from late May through August. Each listing is derived from the assigned researcher's opinion based upon his or her visit at a particular time. The opinions are expressed in a candid and forthright manner. Other travelers might disagree. Those traveling at a different time may have different experiences since prices, dates, hours, and conditions are always subject to change. You are urged to check beforehand to avoid inconvenience and surprises. Travel always involves a certain degree of risk, especially in low-cost areas. When traveling, especially on a budget, always take particular care to ensure your safety.

Let's Go Picks

We offer these picks as appetizers to whet your palette for the full menu of options which follows. These are some of our favorites, but don't trust our judgment—one of the attractions of Central America is that its jungles still hide unsullied spots quietly waiting to be discovered and enjoyed by intrepid travelers like you.

Best Wildlife: First prize goes to the *gringo* bar scene in Antigua. When we tired of that, we watched ancient green turtles lay their eggs on the beaches of **Tortuguero National Park,** Costa Rica (p. 400), jogged with jaguars at the **Belize Zoo** (p. 139), and listened to the yowls of the howler monkeys at the nearby **Community Baboon Sanctuary** (p. 139). We tiptoed around porcupines in El Salvador's **Montecristo Wilderness Preserve** for a while (p. 198), and then headed back to Costa Rica to chase butterflies at the **Finca de Mariposas** (p. 354) and to search out the famous golden toads in the **Monteverde Cloud Forest Reserve** (p. 370).

Best Ruins: First we went to **Tikal,** Guatemala, where we scaled the Temple of the Two-Headed Serpent and played a fierce game of *pok-ta-pok* on the Maya ballcourt (p. 119). Then we were off to **Copán,** Honduras, to decipher the 63 steps of the Hieroglyphic Stairway, take a quick gander at the Plaza of Jaguars, and to play a double-or-nothing round of *pok-ta-pok* in the Great Plaza (p. 232). At exactly sunrise on the vernal equinox, we joined the throngs at **Chichén Itzá,** Mexico, to watch the serpent's shadow descend the stairs of the giant El Castillo pyramid on its way to a sudden-death match of *pok-ta-pok* (p. 475). In Belize, we couldn't stay away from the ruins at **Lamanai** and the Mew River Lagoon that surrounds them; there was no ball court there, so we hiked, took a river safari, and hung out with the howler monkeys. Finally, we followed the *Camino Real* and ended up, as Spanish traders always used to, at awe-inspiring **Panamá Viejo,** Panamá (p. 437).

Best Watersports: First over the waves, then under. In **surfing** capital **La Libertad,** El Salvador, we caught the big one (p. 189), but it wasn't big enough, so we took our boards to the famous **La Roca Loca** ("the crazy rock") off the coast of **Jacó,** Costa Rica (p. 366). After a quick, cheap, but thorough **scuba** certification course in **Utila,** Honduras (p. 255), we dove deep beneath **Peter's Place** in nearby Roatán (p. 259), and then capped off our underwater days exploring the hemisphere's largest **barrier reef** near **Caye Caulker,** Belize (p. 145). We found divine snorkeling off Ambergris Caye at the **Hol Chan Marine Reserve** (p. 150). Having had our fill of petting sharks, rays and fluorescent fish, we headed south to watch the waters rise and fall under the ocean liners in the **Gatún Locks** of the **Panama Canal** (p. 436). The steaming springs that feed the **Banas de Payexú,** near Xela, Guatemala (p. 90), started to soothe our tired muscles, and a day spent lazing on the beaches of the **Corn Islands,** Nicaragua, finished the job (p. 322).

Best Meals: We started things off Hungarian-style at **El Hungaro** in Chinandega, Nicaragua (p. 290), and later enjoyed sweet waffles at the **Deli Restaurant** in Panajachel, Guatemala (p. 77). The next day, the vegetarians among us reveled in the plethora of options at **Café la Fuente** in Antigua, Guatemala (p. 72), and everyone enjoyed the name and the food of the **Pasteleria y Cafeteria Whipping Cream** in San José, Costa Rica (p. 341). We loved the homemade cooking of our Maya hosts at the **Village Guest House Program** in Belize (p. 164), and we praised gods we don't even worship after dining at the **Garifuna Restaurant** in Tela, Honduras (p. 246).

Best Nightlife by a Long Shot: We cut the rug in Central America. We mastered the *salsa* and the *merengue.* We learned the *bachata.* But nowhere did the jam pump louder than **Ubafu Life Music** in Livington, Guatemala (p. 110). We even made our own drums and beat them along with the best.

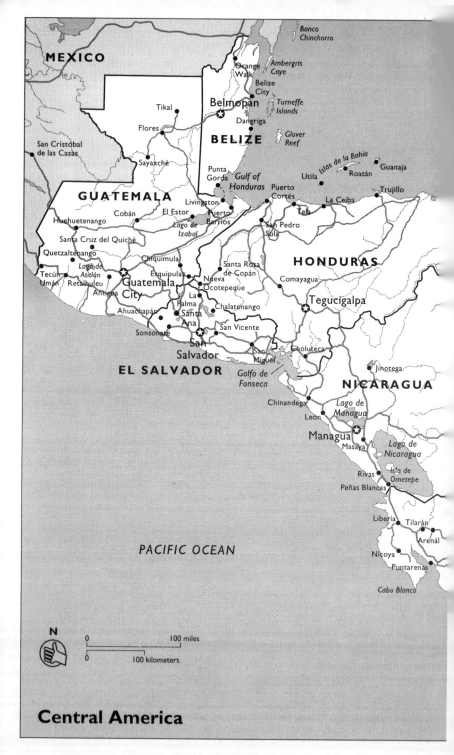

MEXICO

Banco Chinchorro

Orange Walk

Ambergris Caye

Belize City

Belmopan

Turneffe Islands

Tikal

Flores

Dangriga

BELIZE

San Cristóbal de las Casas

Sayaxché

Glover Reef

Punta Gorda

Gulf of Honduras

Islas de la Bahía

Utila

Roatán

Guanaja

GUATEMALA

Livingston

Puerto Cortés

La Ceiba

Trujillo

Cobán

El Estor

Puerto Barrios

Tela

Huehuetenango

Lago de Izabal

San Pedro Sula

HONDURAS

Santa Cruz del Quiché

Chiquimula

Santa Rosa de Copán

Comayagua

Quetzaltenango

Esquipulas

Lago de Atitlán

Nueva Ocotepeque

Tegucigalpa

Tecún Umán

Retalhuleu

Guatemala City

Antigua

La Palma

Chalatenango

Ahuachapán

Santa Ana

San Vicente

Sonsonate

San Salvador

San Miguel

Choluteca

Jinotega

EL SALVADOR

Golfo de Fonseca

NICARAGUA

Chinandega

Lago de Managua

León

Managua

Masaya

Lago de Nicaragua

Isla de Ometepe

Rivas

Peñas Blancas

PACIFIC OCEAN

Liberia

Tilarán

Arenál

Nicoya

Puntarenas

Cabo Blanco

N

0   100 miles

0   100 kilometers

Central America

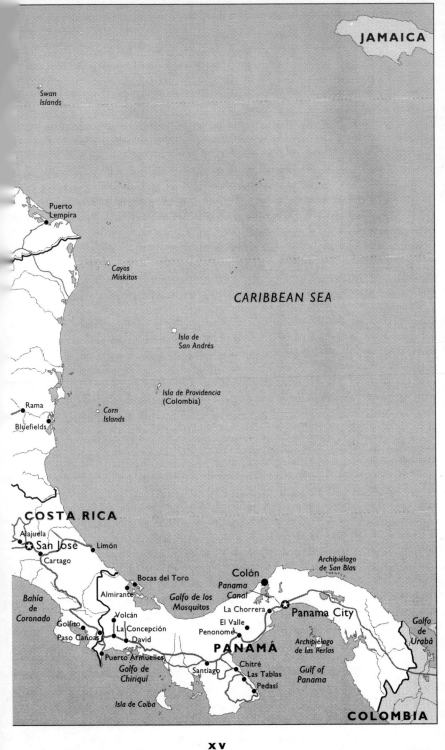

JAMAICA

Swan
Islands

Puerto
Lempira

Cayos
Miskitos

CARIBBEAN SEA

Isla de
San Andrés

Isla de Providencia
(Colombia)

Rama

Corn
Islands

Bluefields

COSTA RICA

Alajuela

San José   Limón

Cartago

Archipiélago
de San Blas

Colón

Bocas del Toro   Panama
Canal

Bahía
de
Coronado

Almirante   Golfo de los
Mosquitos   La Chorrera   Panama City

Volcán   El Valle
                                                   Golfo
Golfito   La Concepción   de
                                   Penonomé   Urabá
Paso Cañoas   David

PANAMÁ   Archipiélago
de las Perlas

Puerto Armuelles
                Santiago   Chitré   Gulf of
Golfo de   Las Tablas Panama
Chiriquí   Pedasí

Isla de Coiba

COLOMBIA

ESSENTIALS

PLANNING YOUR TRIP

Travelers to Central America thrive on adventure, but few anticipate the challenging labyrinth sometimes posed by the region's sluggish bureaucracies. Expect long waits for visa processing, get used to delays on buses and airplanes, don't be surprised when the bank you've been desperately searching for shuts down early for a local festival, and never expect to reach someone by telephone. In short, sit back and summon oodles of patience. For more information on individual countries, see each chapter's **Essentials** section.

◼ When to Go

The weather in Central America varies wildly from region to region, but altitude, rather than latitude, is the main determinant. In the lowlands (from sea level to 3,000 ft.), daytime temperatures average about 90°F, but a few thousand feet up, both days and nights can get downright chilly, with nighttime temperatures falling to 50°F. The coastal areas also tend to be more humid, and though breezes sometimes cool the moisture, travelers new to the tropics will sweat as never before.

The rainy season falls between May and November, with the highest probability of hurricanes from August to October, the "low season." Note that this season is often called *invierno* (winter), the opposite of what a traveler from the northern hemisphere would expect. The rain usually will be more intense and longer-lasting in the highlands, and keep in mind that the Caribbean side of the isthmus gets twice as much rain as the Pacific side. Otherwise, things are sunny and dry; only about 15 percent of the rain on the Pacific Coast falls between November and April. Even during the rainy season, though, the sun usually rears its happy head for part of the day, with the majority of rainstorms occurring in the afternoon. Unless your sole objective is getting that deep, dark tan, the rainy season can be pleasant; temperatures never reach extremes, and rain renders only a few dirt roads entirely inaccessible.

Still, it's not surprising that the "high season" for tourism in Central America coincides with the drier weather. Along with better weather, expect the high season to bring larger crowds and boosted prices, particularly around Christmas vacation. *Semana Santa,* the festival associated with Easter week, marks the most happening parties in the region. Central Americans and tourists alike flock to traditionally festive destinations. If traveling during this time of year, try to book rooms in advance.

◼ Useful Information

TRAVEL ORGANIZATIONS

Council on International Educational Exchange (CIEE), 205 East 42nd St., New York, NY 10017-5706 (tel. (888)-COUNCIL (268-6245); fax (212) 822-2699; http://www.ciee.org). A private, not-for-profit organization, Council administers work, volunteer, academic, internship, and professional programs around the world. They also offer identity cards (including the ISIC and the GO25) and a range of publications, among them the useful magazine *Student Travels* (free).

Federation of International Youth Travel Organizations (FIYTO), Bredgade 25H, DK-1260 Copenhagen K, Denmark (tel. (45) 33 33 96 00; fax 33 93 96 76; email mailbox@fiyto.org; http://www.fiyto.org), is an international organization promoting educational, cultural and social travel for young people. Member organizations include language schools, educational travel companies, national tourist boards, accommodation centers, and other suppliers of travel services to youth and students. FIYTO sponsors the GO25 Card (http://www.go25.org).

International Student Travel Confederation, Herengracht 479, 1017 BS Amsterdam, The Netherlands (tel. (31) 20 421 2800; fax 20 421 2810; email istcinfo@istc.org; http://www.istc.org). The ISTC is a nonprofit confederation of student travel organizations whose focus is to develop, promote, and facilitate travel among young people and students. Member organizations include International Student Surface Travel Association (ISSA), Student Air Travel Association (SATA), IASIS Travel Insurance, and the International Association for Educational and Work Exchange Programs (IAEWEP).

USEFUL PUBLICATIONS

The publishers and mail-order bookstores listed below offer detailed maps and information on everything in Central America from restaurants to festivals. You can order most of these books directly from the publishers. For official **United States Department of State travel advisories,** including crime and security information, call their 24-hour hotline at (202) 647-5225 or check out their web site at http://www.state.gov.

Adventurous Traveler Bookstore, P.O. Box 1468, Williston, VT 05495 (tel. (801) 282-3963; fax 677-1821; email books@atbook.com; http://www.AdventurousTraveler.com). Free 40-page catalogue upon request. Specializes in outdoor adventure travel books and maps for the U.S. and abroad.

Bon Voyage!, 2069 W. Bullard Ave., Fresno, CA 93711-1200 (tel. (800) 995-9716, from abroad (209) 447-8441; fax 266-6460; email 70754.3511@compuserve.com). Annual mail order catalogue offers a range of products, including books, travel accessories, luggage, electrical converters, maps, and videos.

The Latin American Travel Advisor, P.O. Box 17-17-908, Quito, Ecuador (fax (593) 2-562-566; email: latc@pi.pro.ec; http://www.amerispan.com/latc). Focuses on public safety, health, weather and natural phenomena, travel costs, and the politics and economy of each country. Offers Spanish immersion programs in 25 different cities in 12 Latin American countries. Annual subscriptions to the newsletter US$39, single issue $15.

South American Fiesta, 4936 Chalden Lane, Marietta, GA 30066 (tel. (800) 334-3782; fax (770) 516-5753). Tours and stays throughout Latin America.

Specialty Travel Index, 305 San Anselmo Ave., #313, San Anselmo, CA 94960 (tel. (415) 459-4900; fax 459-4974; email spectrav@ix.netcom.com; http://www.spectrav.com). Published twice yearly, this is an extensive listing of "off the beaten track" and specialty travel opportunities. One copy US$6, one-year subscription (2 copies) US$10.

Superintendent of Documents, P.O. Box 371954, Pittsburgh, PA 15250-7954 (tel. (202) 512-1800; fax 512-2250; email gpoaccess@gpo.gov; http://www.access.gpo.gov/su_docs). Open Mon.-Fri. 7:30am-4:30pm. Publishes *Your Trip Abroad* (US$1.25), *Health Information for International Travel* (US$14), and "Background Notes" on all countries ($1 each). Postage included in the prices.

Transitions Abroad, P.O. Box 1300, 18 Hulst Rd., Amherst, MA 01004-1300 (tel. (800) 293-0373; fax 256-0373; email trabroad@aol.com; http://transabroad.com). Invaluable magazine lists publications and resources for overseas study, work, and volunteering (US$25 for 6 issues, single copy $6.25). Also publishes *The Alternative Travel Directory,* a comprehensive guide to living, learning, and working overseas (US$20; postage $4).

■ Internet Resources

Along with everything else in the 90s, budget travel is moving rapidly into the information age, and the **Internet** is becoming a leading travel resource. In addition to connecting personally with others abroad, people can make their own airline, hotel, hostel, and car rental reservations on the Internet. **NetTravel: How Travelers Use the Internet,** by Michael Shapiro, is a very thorough and informative guide which lists useful web sites and describes the different ways travelers can use the Internet (US$25). With many Central American businesses, language schools, and individuals now online, it offers a cheap and accessible alternative to pricey phone calls and the less-than-reliable Central American mail system. For information on specific countries, check out the Bureau of Consular Affairs' web site at http://travel.state.gov. It is possible to access the **Internet** through popular commercial services, such as **America Online** (tel. (800) 827-6364) and **CompuServe** (tel. (800) 433-0389).

THE WORLD WIDE WEB

Increasingly the Internet forum of choice, the **World Wide Web** provides its users with a plethora of interactive, specialized web pages (individual sites within the World Wide Web). **Search engines** (services that hunt for web pages about specific subjects) can significantly aid the search process. **Lycos** (http://a2z.lycos.com), **Infoseek** (http://guide.infoseek.com), and **HOTBOT** (http://www.hotbot.com) are among the most popular. **Yahoo!** is a slightly more organized search engine; check out its travel links at http://www.yahoo.com/Recreation/Travel. Also search for Yahoo! for travel links specific to Central America that provide information on businesses, culture, and health issues. **City.Net** (http://www.city.net) offers many resources for travelers, including travel bulletin boards, access to travel guides, weather reports, and links to newspapers and magazines. Check out *Let's Go's* **web site** (http://www.letsgo.com) and find our newsletter, information about our books, and an always-current list of links. *Let's Go* lists relevant web sites throughout the Essentials chapter. Try some of our favorite sites directly:

Green Arrow Guide to Central America (http://www.greenarrow.com/welcome.htm) includes information on Spanish language study programs, regional news, ecotourism, and volunteer opportunities.

Foreign Language for Travelers (http://www.travlang.com) can help you brush up on your Spanish.

Rent-A-Wreck's Travel Links (http://www.rent-a-wreck.com/raw/travlist.htm) is a very complete list of excellent links.

Big World Magazine (http://www.paonline.com/bigworld), a budget travel magazine, has a web page with a great collection of links to travel pages.

The CIA World Factbook (http://www.odci.gov/cia/publications/nsolo/wfb-all.htm) has vital statistics on the country you want to visit. Check out an overview of a country's economy or an explanation of their system of government.

Shoestring Travel (http://www.stratpub.com) is a budget travel e-zine, with feature articles, links, user exchange, and accommodations information.

The Student and Budget Travel Guide (http://asa.ugl.lib.umich.edu/chdocs/travel/travel-guide.html) gives info on accommodations, transport, and packing.

TravelHUB (http://www.travelhub.com) is a great site for cheap travel deals.

Cybercafe Guide (http://www.cyberiacafe.net/cyberia/guide/ccafe.htm) can help you find cybercafes worldwide.

NEWSGROUPS

Usenet newsgroups are electronic forums carrying publicly-readable dialogues on virtually every imaginable topic. One user "posts" a written question or thought, which other users read and respond to in kind. Anyone with a connection can post which might make you wade through piles of nonsense to come to useful information. Despite this, there are still a number of useful newsgroups for travelers to Central America, including **rec.travel.air** and **rec.travel.latin-america.**

▓ Documents and Formalities

Keep in mind that it often takes government agencies much longer than you expect to process applications. File all applications several weeks or months in advance of your planned departure date. Demand for passports is highest between January and

August, so apply as early as possible. When you travel, always carry two or more forms of identification, including at least one photo ID. A passport combined with a driver's license or birth certificate usually serves as adequate proof of your identity and citizenship. Many establishments, especially banks, require several IDs before cashing traveler's checks. Never carry all your forms of ID together; you risk being left entirely without ID or funds in case of theft or loss. Make two sets of photocopies of your essential documents—leave one at home and carry one with you. Carry several extra passport size photos to attach to the additional IDs you may acquire. If you plan an extended stay, register your passport with the nearest embassy or consulate.

U.S. citizens can request the booklet *A Safe Trip Abroad* (US$1.25) from the **Superintendent of Documents,** U.S. Government Printing Office, P.O. Box 371954, Pittsburgh, PA 15250-7954 (tel. (202) 512-1800; fax (202) 512-2250).

ENTRANCE REQUIREMENTS AND VISAS

Citizens of Australia, Canada, Ireland, New Zealand, South Africa, the U.K., and the U.S. all need valid **passports** to enter most countries and to re-enter their own country. Some countries do not allow entrance if the holder's passport expires in under six months; returning home with an expired passport is illegal, and may result in a fine. Some countries also require a **visa,** an endorsement that a foreign government stamps into a passport that allows the bearer to stay in that country for a specific purpose and period of time. Most visas cost US$10-70 and allow about a month in a country, within six months to a year from the date of issue. For more information, send for *Foreign Entry Requirements* (US$0.50) from the **Consumer Information Center,** Pueblo, CO 81009 (tel. (719) 948-4000; http://www.pueblo.gsa.gov). This service also offers over 200 federal publications about health and travel.

Upon entering a country, you must declare certain items from abroad and pay a duty on the value of those articles that exceed the allowance established by that country's **customs** service. Keeping receipts for purchases made abroad will help establish values when you return. It is wise to make a list, including serial numbers, of any valuables that you carry with you from home; if you register this list with customs before your departure and have an official stamp it, you will avoid import duty charges and ensure an easy passage upon your return. Be especially careful to document items manufactured abroad.

As you enter a country, dress neatly and carry **proof of your financial independence,** such as a visa to the next country on your itinerary, an airplane ticket to depart, and/or enough money to cover the cost of your living expenses. Admission as a visitor does not include the right to work, which is authorized only by a **work permit.** Certain countries require special visas for study; immigration officers may want to see proof of acceptance from a school and proof that you can support yourself.

PASSPORTS

Again, before you leave, photocopy the page of your passport that contains your photograph, passport number, and other identifying information. Carry one photocopy in a safe place apart from your passport, and leave another copy at home. These measures will help prove your citizenship and facilitate the issuing of a new passport if you lose the original document. Consulates also recommend that you carry an expired passport or an official copy of your birth certificate in a part of your baggage separate from other documents. Request a duplicate birth certificate from the **Bureau of Vital Records and Statistics.**

If you do lose your passport, immediately notify the local police and the nearest embassy or consulate of your home government. To expedite its replacement, you will need to know all information previously recorded and show identification and proof of citizenship. A replacement may take weeks to process, and it may be valid only for a limited time. Some consulates can issue new passports within 24 hours if you give them proof of citizenship. Any visas stamped in your old passport will be irretrievably lost. In an emergency, ask for immediate temporary traveling papers that will permit you to reenter your home country.

Your passport is a public document belonging to your nation's government. You may have to surrender it to a foreign government official, but if you don't get it back in a reasonable amount of time, inform the nearest mission of your home country.

Australia Citizens must apply for a passport in person at a post office, a passport office, or an Australian diplomatic mission overseas. An appointment may be necessary. A parent may file an application for a child who is under 18 and unmarried. Adult passports cost AUS$120 (for a 32-page passport) or AUS$180 (64 page), and a child's is AUS$60 (32 page) or AUS$90 (64 page). For more info, call toll-free (in Australia) 13 12 32.

Canada Citizens may apply in person at any 1 of 28 regional Passport Offices across Canada. Children under 16 may be included on a parent's passport. Passports cost CDN$60, are valid for 5 years, and are not renewable. For additional info, contact the Canadian Passport Office, Department of Foreign Affairs and International Trade, Ottawa, ON, K1A 0G3 (tel. (613) 994-3500; http://www.dfait-maeci.gc.ca/passport). Travelers may also call (800) 567-6868 (24hr.).

Ireland Citizens can apply for a passport by mail to either the Department of Foreign Affairs, Passport Office, Setanta Centre, Molesworth St., Dublin 2 (tel. (01) 671 1633), or the Passport Office, Irish Life Building, 1A South Mall, Cork (tel. (021) 272 525). Obtain an application at a local Garda station or request one from a passport office. Passports cost IR£45 and are valid for 10 years. Citizens under 18 or over 65 can request a 3-year passport that costs IR£10.

New Zealand Application forms for passports are available in New Zealand from travel agents and Department of Internal Affairs Link Centres in the main cities and towns. If you are overseas, forms and passport services are provided by New Zealand embassies, high commissions, and consulates. Applications may also be forwarded to the Passport Office, P.O. Box 10526, Wellington, New Zealand. Fee for an adult is NZ$80, child NZ$40. Children's names can no longer be endorsed on a parent's passport—they must apply for their own, which are valid for up to 5 years. An adult's passport is valid for up to 10 years.

South Africa Citizens can apply for a passport at any Home Affairs Office or South African Mission. Tourist passports, valid for 10 years, cost SAR80. Children under 16 must be issued their own passports, valid for 5 years, which cost SAR60. Turnaround time is usually 2 weeks. For further information, contact the nearest Department of Home Affairs Office.

United Kingdom British citizens, British Dependent Territories citizens, British Nationals (overseas), and British Overseas citizens may apply for a full passport, valid for 10 years (5 years if under 16). Apply in person or by mail to one of the passport offices, located in London, Liverpool, Newport, Peterborough, Glasgow, or Belfast. The fee is UK£18. Children under 16 may be included on a parent's passport. Every traveler over 16 needs a 10 yr., standard passport. The U.K. Passport Agency can be reached by phone at (0990) 21 04 10, and information is available on the Internet at http://www.open.gov.uk/ukpass.

United States Citizens may apply for a passport at any federal or state **courthouse** or **post office** authorized to accept passport applications, or at a **U.S. Passport Agency,** located in Boston, Chicago, Honolulu, Houston, Los Angeles, Miami, New Orleans, New York, Philadelphia, San Francisco, Seattle, Stamford, or Washington, D.C. Refer to the "U.S. Government, State Department" section of the telephone directory or the local post office for addresses. Parents must apply in person for children under age 13. You must apply in person if this is your first passport, if you're under age 18, or if your current passport is more than 12 years old or was issued before your 18th birthday. Passports are valid for 10 years (5 years if under 18) and cost US$65 (under 18 US$40). Passports may be **renewed** by mail or in person for US$55. Given proof of citizenship, a U.S. embassy or consulate abroad can usually issue a new passport. Report a passport lost or stolen in the U.S. in writing to Passport Services, 1425 K St., N.W., U.S. Department of State, Washington D.C., 20524 or to the nearest passport agency. For more info, contact the U.S. Passport Information's **24 hr. recorded message** (tel. (202) 647-0518).

ESSENTIALS

CUSTOMS: GOING HOME

Upon returning home, you must declare all articles you acquired abroad and pay a **duty** on the value of those articles that exceed the allowance established by your country's customs service. Goods and gifts purchased at **duty-free** shops abroad are not exempt from duty or sales tax at your point of return; you must declare these items as well. "Duty-free" merely means that you need not pay a tax in the country of purchase.

Australia Citizens may import AUS$400 (under 18 AUS$200) of goods duty-free, in addition to 1.125L alcohol and 250 cigarettes or 250g tobacco. For information, contact the Regional Director, Australian Customs Service, GPO Box 8, Sydney NSW 2001 (tel. (02) 9213 2000; fax 9213 4000).

Canada Citizens who remain abroad for at least 1 week may bring back up to CDN$500 worth of goods duty-free any time. Citizens or residents who travel for a period between 48 hours and 6 days can bring back up to CDN$200. For more information, write to Canadian Customs, 2265 St. Laurent Blvd., Ottawa, Ontario K1G 4K3 (tel. (613) 993-0534), phone the 24 hr. Automated Customs Information Service at (800) 461-9999, or visit Revenue Canada at http://www.revcan.ca.

Ireland Citizens must declare everything in excess of IR£142 (IR£73 per traveler under 15 years of age) obtained outside the EU or duty- and tax-free in the EU. Goods obtained duty and tax paid in another EU country up to a value of IR£460 (IR£115 per traveler under 15) will not be subject to additional customs duties. For more information, contact The Revenue Commissioners, Dublin Castle (tel. (01) 679 27 77; fax 671 20 21; email taxes@iol.ie; http://www.revenue.ie) or The Collector of Customs and Excise, The Custom House, Dublin 1.

New Zealand Citizens may import up to NZ$700 worth of goods duty-free if they are intended for personal use or are unsolicited gifts. For more information, contact New Zealand Customs, 50 Anzac Ave., Box 29, Auckland (tel. (09) 377 35 20; fax 309 29 78).

South Africa Citizens may import varying amounts of the following items duty-free: cigarettes, cigars, tobacco, wine, spirits, toilet water, perfume, and other consumable items up to a value of SAR500. Goods up to a value of SAR10,000 over and above this duty-free allowance are dutiable at 20%; such goods are exempted from payment of VAT. Items acquired abroad and sent to the Republic as unaccompanied baggage do not qualify for any allowances. You may not export or import South African bank notes in excess of SAR2000. For more information, consult the free pamphlet *South African Customs Information,* available in airports or from the Commissioner for Customs and Excise, Private Bag X47, Pretoria 0001 (tel. (12) 314 99 11; fax 328 64 78).

United Kingdom Citizens or visitors arriving in the U.K. from outside the EU are subject to duties on cigarettes, tobacco, liquor, perfume, and UK£136 worth of all other goods including gifts and souvenirs. Goods obtained duty and tax paid for personal use (regulated according to set guide levels) within the EU do not require any further customs duty. For more information, contact Her Majesty's Customs and Excise, Custom House, Nettleton Road, Heathrow Airport, Hounslow, Middlesex TW6 2LA (tel. (0181) 910-3744; fax 910-3765).

United States Citizens may import US$400 worth of accompanying goods duty-free and must pay a 10% tax on the next US$1000. You must declare all purchases, so have sales slips ready. If you mail home personal goods of U.S. origin, you can avoid duty charges by marking the package "American goods returned." For more information, consult the brochure *Know Before You Go,* available from the U.S. Customs Service, Box 7407, Washington D.C. 20044 (tel. (202) 927-6724), or visit the Web (http://www.customs.ustreas.gov).

YOUTH, STUDENT, & TEACHER IDENTIFICATION

The **International Student Identity Card (ISIC)** is the most widely accepted form of student identification. Flashing this card can procure you discounts for sights, theaters, museums, accommodations, meals, train, ferry, bus, airplane transportation, and other services. Present the card wherever you go, and ask about discounts even when none are advertised. It also provides insurance benefits, including US$100 per day of in-hospital sickness for a maximum of 60 days, and US$3000 accident-related medical reimbursement for each accident. In addition, cardholders have access to a toll-free 24hr. ISIC helpline whose multilingual staff can provide assistance in medical, legal, and financial emergencies overseas.

Many student travel agencies around the world issue ISICs, including STA Travel in Australia and New Zealand; Travel CUTS in Canada; USIT in Ireland and Northern Ireland; SASTS in South Africa; Campus Travel and STA Travel in the U.K.; Council Travel, Let's Go Travel, and STA Travel in the U.S.; and any of the other organizations under the auspices of the International Student Travel Confederation (ISTC). When you apply for the card, request a copy of the *International Student Identity Card Handbook*, which lists by country some of the available discounts. You can also write to Council for a copy. The card is valid from September to December of the following year and costs US$19 or CDN$15. Applicants must be at least 12 years old and degree-seeking students of a secondary or post-secondary school. Because of the proliferation of phony ISICs, many airlines and some other services require other proof of student identity, such as a signed letter from the registrar attesting to your student status and stamped with the school seal or your school ID card. The US$20 **International Teacher Identity Card (ITIC)** offers the same insurance coverage, and similar, but limited discounts. For more information on these cards, consult the organization's web site (http:\\www.istc.org; email isicinfo@istc.org).

Federation of International Youth Travel Organizations (FIYTO) issues a discount card to travelers who are under 26 but not students. Known as the **GO25 Card,** this one-year card offers many of the same benefits as the ISIC, and most organizations that sell the ISIC also sell the GO25 Card. A brochure that lists discounts is free when you purchase the card. To apply, you will need a passport, valid driver's license, or copy of a birth certificate, and a passport-sized photo with your name printed on the back. The fee is US$19, CDN$15, or UK£5. Information is available on the web at http://www.fiyto.org or http://www.go25.org, or by contacting Travel CUTS in Canada, STA Travel in the U.K., Council Travel in the U.S., or FIYTO headquarters in Denmark (see **Useful Information,** p. 1).

INTERNATIONAL DRIVER'S PERMIT

Acquiring an **International Driver's Permit (IDP)** is recommended for travelers to Central America, although it is not mandatory. It may be a good idea to get one anyway, in case you're in a position (such as an accident or stranded in a smaller town) where the police may not read or speak English. In Belize, your U.S., British, or Canadian license is valid. In Panamá, Nicaragua, and Guatemala, your foreign license is valid for 90 days. Carry your registration papers and proof of ownership at all times. In Mexico, an international driver's permit is not required, but a **vehicle permit** is. Requirements for these permits have changed rapidly; they usually include two proofs of ownership of your car and a credit card or cash to pay a financial guarantee for temporary importation. Contact a Mexican consulate for up-to-date info.

Your IDP, valid for one year, must be issued in your own country before you depart. A valid driver's license from your home country must always accompany the IDP. An application for an IDP usually needs to be accompanied by one or two photos, a current local license, an additional form of identification, and a fee. Australians can obtain an IDP by contacting their local **Royal Automobile Club (RAC),** or the **National Royal Motorist Association (NRMA)** if in NSW or the ACT, where a permit can be obtained for AUS$12. Canadian license holders can obtain an IDP (CDN$10) through any **Canadian Automobile Association (CAA)** branch office in Canada, or by writing to CAA Central Ontario, 60 Commerce Valley Drive East, Thornhill, Ontario L3T 7P9 (tel. (416) 221-4300). Citizens of Ireland should drop into their nearest **Automobile Association (AA)** office where an IDP can be picked up for IR£4, or phone (1) 283 3555 for a postal application form. In New Zealand, contact your local **Automobile Association (AA),** or their main office at 99 Albert

Street, PO Box 5, Auckland (tel. (09) 377 4660; fax 309 4564), IDPs cost NZ$8 ĜNZ$2 for return postage. In South Africa visit your local **Automobile Association of South Africa** office, where IDPs can be picked up for SAR25, or for more information phone (011) 466 6641, or write to P.O. Box 596, 2000 Johannesburg. In the U.K. IDPs are UK£4 and you can either visit your local **AA Shop,** or call (01256) 49 39 32 and order a postal application form (allow 2-3 weeks). U.S. license holders can obtain an IDP (US$10) at any **American Automobile Association (AAA)** office or by writing to AAA Florida, Travel Agency Services Department, 1000 AAA Drive (mail stop 28), Heathrow, FL 32746-5080 (tel. (407) 444-4245; fax 444-4247).

Most credit cards cover standard **insurance.** If you rent, lease, or borrow a car, you will need a **green card,** or **International Insurance Certificate,** to prove that you have liability insurance. Obtain it through the car rental agency; most include coverage in their prices. If you lease a car, you can obtain a green card from the dealer.

■ Money Matters

CURRENCY AND EXCHANGE

Approximate currency values are listed in each country's **Essentials** section. Expect to spend anywhere from US$5-50 per person per day, depending on the local cost of living and your needs. Don't sacrifice your health or safety for a cheaper tab. Also, no matter how low your budget, you'll need to keep handy a larger amount of cash than usual. Carrying it around with you, even in a money belt, is risky but necessary; personal checks from home will almost never be accepted no matter how many forms of identification you have.

As a rule you should convert money after arriving at your destination to save on conversion fees. However, converting some money before you go will allow you to zip through the airport while others languish in exchange lines. To avoid getting stuck with no money after banking hours or on a holiday, it's a good idea to bring enough foreign currency to last for the first 24-72 hours of a trip. In the U.S. you can get foreign currency easily at home; contact **Capital Foreign Exchange** on the East Coast (toll-free (888) 842-0880; fax (202) 842-8008), or on the West Coast, **International Currency Express** (toll-free (888) 278-6628; fax (310) 278-6410).

The instability of Central American economies often makes it impossible to exchange the currencies of one country in the banks of another; such transactions must be made at the border. **U.S. dollars** are as good as gold in almost all of Central America, except perhaps in the remotest areas, where the national cash is preferred. However, avoid using Western money when you can. Throwing dollars around to gain preferential treatment is offensive and attracts theft. It also labels you as a foreigner and invites spontaneous price increases.

Black-market exchange is a popular option in Latin America, since money can be exchanged during banks' closing hours. The traders aren't hard to find; they're the guys with huge wads of cash in one hand and a calculator in the other. While convenient, these transactions are riskier than exchange at banks.

Since every exchange transaction means losing some money, convert in large sums (unless the currency is depreciating rapidly), but don't change more than you will need for the country you're in, and only as much as you feel safe carrying. Carry some traveler's checks or bills in small denominations for times when exchange must be made at disadvantageous rates.

TRAVELER'S CHECKS

Traveler's checks are one of the safest and least troublesome means of carrying funds, as they can be refunded if stolen. Several agencies and many banks sell them, usually for face value plus a 1% commission. In small towns, traveler's checks are less readily accepted than in cities with large tourist industries, but at least one place in every town should be willing to exchange them for local currency. In Central America, businesses rarely exchange traveler's checks, but many banks perform the service for a small fee. If you are ordering checks, do so well in advance, especially if large sums are being requested.

Each agency provides refunds **if your checks are lost or stolen,** and many provide additional services. (Note that you may need a police report verifying the loss or theft.) When you purchase your checks, inquire about toll-free refund hotlines, emergency message services, and stolen card assistance in the countries you are visiting. Expect a fair amount of red tape and delay if your traveler's checks are lost or stolen; to expedite the refund process, keep your check receipts separate from your checks and store them in a safe place or with a traveling companion. Record check numbers when you cash them. Leave a list of check numbers with someone at home, and ask for a list of refund centers when you buy your checks. American Express and Bank of America have over 40,000 centers worldwide. Keep a separate supply of cash or traveler's checks for emergencies. Be sure never to countersign your checks until you're prepared to cash them, and have your passport with you when you use the checks.

American Express: Call (800) 25 19 02 in Australia; in New Zealand (0800) 44 10 68; in the U.K. (0800) 52 13 13; in the U.S. and Canada (800) 221-7282). Elsewhere, call U.S. collect (801) 964-6665. AmEx traveler's checks are widely recognized in Central America and the easiest to replace if lost or stolen. Checks can be purchased for a small fee (1-4%) at AmEx Travel Service Offices, banks, and American Automobile Association offices (AAA members can buy the checks commission-free). Cardmembers can also purchase checks at American Express Dispensers at Travel Service Offices at airports and by ordering them via phone (tel. (800) ORDER-TC/673-3782). American Express offices usually cash their checks commission-free, although at slightly worse rates than banks. *Cheques for Two* can be signed by either of two people traveling together. Visit their online travel offices (http://www.aexp.com).

Citicorp: Call (800) 645-6556 in the U.S. and Canada; in Europe, the Middle East, or Africa (44) 171 508 7007; from elsewhere call U.S. collect (813) 623-1709. Sells both Citicorp and Citicorp Visa traveler's checks in a variety of currencies. Commission is 1-2% on check purchases. Checkholders are automatically enrolled for 45 days in the Travel Assist Program (hotline tel. (800) 250-4377 or collect (202) 296-8728) which provides travelers with English-speaking doctor, lawyer, and interpreter referrals as well as check refund assistance and general travel information. Citicorp's World Courier Service guarantees hand-delivery of traveler's checks when a refund location is not convenient. Call 24 hr. per day, 7 days per week.

Thomas Cook MasterCard: For 24-hour cashing or refund assistance, call (800) 223-9920 in the U.S. and Canada; elsewhere call U.S. collect (609) 987-7300; from the U.K. call (0800) 622 101 free or (1733) 502 995 collect or (1733) 318 950 collect. Offers checks in U.S., Canadian, and Australian dollars, British and Cypriot pounds, French and Swiss francs, German marks, Japanese yen, Dutch guilders, Spanish pesetas, South African rand, and ECUs. Commission 1-2% for purchases. Thomas Cook offices may sell checks for lower commissions and will cash checks commission-free. Thomas Cook MasterCard Traveler's Checks are also available from **Capital Foreign Exchange** in U.S. or Canadian dollars, French and Swiss francs, British pounds, and German marks.

Visa: Call (800) 227-6811 in the U.S.; in the U.K. (0800) 895 492; from anywhere else in the world call (01733 318 949) and reverse the charges. Any of the above numbers can tell you the location of their nearest office. Any type of Visa traveler's checks can be reported lost at the Visa number.

CREDIT CARDS

Although the overwhelming majority of businesses in Central America still demand cash, more and more are willing to accept credit cards as a direct form of payment. Banks sometimes give cash advances in local currency on major credit cards—**Visa** is by far the most accepted—often at the wholesale exchange rate, which is generally 5% better than the retail rate used by banks.

Using your cards through **Automatic Teller Machines (ATMs)** requires having and knowing a **Personal Identification Number (PIN),** which credit cards in the United States do not usually carry. You must ask American Express, MasterCard, or Visa to assign you a PIN before you leave. Keep in mind that MasterCard and Visa have different names elsewhere ("EuroCard" or "Access" for MasterCard and "Carte Bleue" or "Barclaycard" for Visa); some cashiers may not know this until they check.

Credit cards are also invaluable in an emergency—an unexpected hospital bill or ticket home or the loss of traveler's checks—which may leave you temporarily without other resources. Furthermore, credit cards offer an array of other services, from insurance to emergency assistance, which depend completely on the issuer.

American Express (tel. (800) 554-2639 in U.S. and Canada; from abroad call U.S. collect (301) 214-8228), **MasterCard** (tel. (800) 999-0454), and **Visa** (tel. (800) 336-8472) are issued in cooperation with individual banks and some other organizations; ask the issuer about services which go along with the cards.

CASH CARDS

ATM machines get the same wholesale exchange rate as credit cards, but are rare in much of Central America. Do some research before relying too heavily on automation; we list the few ATMs that exist in the major cities. There is often a limit on the amount of money you can withdraw per day (usually about US$500, depending on the type of card and account), and computer network failures are not uncommon. Be sure to memorize your PIN code in numeral form since machines outside the U.S. and Canada often don't have letters on the keys. Also, if your PIN is longer than four digits, ask your bank if the first four digits will work, or if you need a new number.

The two major international money networks are **Cirrus** (U.S. tel. (800) 4-CIRRUS / 424-7787) and **PLUS** (U.S. tel. (800) 843-7587). Cirrus now has international cash machines in 80 countries and territories. It charges US$3-5 to withdraw non-domestically depending on your bank. PLUS is not quite as extensive, only covering 51 countries. If you can do it, carrying two cards, one linked to each network, should leave you covered.

GETTING MONEY FROM HOME

One of the easiest ways to get money from home is to bring an **American Express** card. AmEx allows green-card holders to draw cash from their checking accounts at any of its major offices and many of its representatives' offices, up to US$1000 every 21 days (no service charge, no interest). AmEx also offers an Express Cash service. Express Cash withdrawals are automatically debited from the cardmember's checking account or line of credit. To enroll in Express Cash, cardmembers may call (800) CASH NOW/227-4669. Outside the U.S. call collect (904) 565-7875. Unless using the AmEx service, avoid cashing checks in foreign currencies; they usually take weeks and a US$30 fee to clear.

Money can also be wired abroad through international money transfer services operated by **Western Union** (tel. (800) 325-6000). In emergencies, U.S. citizens can have money sent via the State Department's **Overseas Citizens Service, American Citizens Services,** Consular Affairs, Room 4811, U.S. Department of State, Washington, D.C. 20520 (tel. (202) 647-5225; nights, Sundays, and holidays (202) 647-4000; fax (on demand only) (202) 647-3000; http://travel.state.gov). For a fee of US$15, the State Department will forward money within hours to the nearest consular office, which will then disburse it according to instructions. The office serves only Americans in the direst of straits abroad; non-American travelers should contact their embassies for information on wiring cash.

BARGAINING AND TIPPING

Bargaining for rooms works best in the low season, and it's not hard to get prices lowered at markets or from street vendors. While many locals do not tip for food and other services, a little something extra is often expected from foreigners, who are

> ### Bargaining Basics
> Part of the allure of traveling to Central America is that it's possible to get by on next to nothing. For some travelers, living on a microscopic budget becomes a sort of competition, and they seek boasting rights about having gone two months on US$10 a day or less. Too often, though, this strategy interferes with enjoyment of the region. Many scrimp and save until they get home, when they regret not having lived it up more. There are also those who incessantly try to **bargain** in places where haggling isn't custom; shouting at a farmer that he should sell you some bananas for $.07 instead of $.10 is not only insulting, it's akin to robbery, especially since many assume that foreigners must have a decent amount of money to be traveling in the first place. It's easy to lose perspective on prices, so appreciate the low costs, bring enough money, and don't push unless you know that bargaining is acceptable or that a price is too high.

assumed to be relatively affluent. There are no set values for gratuities, as in the U.S., but 10-15% should be fine; leaving too small a tip is worse than leaving no tip. Even if you're not used to tipping for services such as guided tours, be aware that these people count on a small bonus.

■ Packing

Plan your packing according to the type of travel you'll be doing (multi city backpacking tour, week-long stay in one place, etc.) and the area's high and low temperatures. If you don't pack lightly, your back and wallet will suffer. Before you leave, pack your bag, strap it on, and imagine yourself walking uphill on hot asphalt for the next three hours. A good rule is to lay out only what you absolutely need, then take half the clothes and twice the money.

LUGGAGE

Backpack: Almost all travelers to Central America ride a lot of buses and cover a lot of ground by foot, for which a sturdy backpack is the best sort of baggage. Many packs are designed specifically for travelers, while others are for hikers; consider how you will use the pack before purchasing one or the other. In any case, get a pack with a strong, padded hip belt to transfer weight from your shoulders to your hips. Don't sacrifice quality; good packs cost between US$150 and US$420.

Daypack, rucksack, or courier bag: Bringing a smaller bag in addition to your pack allows you to leave your big bag behind while you go sight-seeing. It can be used as an airplane carry-on to keep essentials with you.

Moneybelt or neck pouch: Guard your money, passport, and other important articles in either one of these, available at any camping store, and *always* keep it with you. The moneybelt should tuck inside the waist of your pants or skirt; you want to hide your valuables, not announce them with a colorful fanny-pack. For more information on protecting you and your valuables, see **Safety and Security,** p. 12.

CLOTHING AND FOOTWEAR

The original Easy Rider Peter Fonda said, "Pack less than you'd ever imagine...there are always laundromats." Although Fonda never made it to Central America, where there are very few public places to do laundry, his advice to pack lightly is right on. One solution to the laundry dilemma is to give your clothes to a hotel cleaning person. Make sure that whoever you approach is a permanent employee of the hotel, and establish a price in advance. Another possibility is to carry laundry soap and wash by hand in hotel sinks.

Clothing: When choosing your travel wardrobe, aim for versatility and comfort, and avoid fabrics that wrinkle easily (to test a fabric, hold it tightly in your fist for 20 seconds). Solid colors absorb the most dirt and grime without looking dirty. Always have a jacket or wool sweater, especially if you'll be in the mountains; natural fibers and lightweight cottons are the best clothing materials for hot weather. Packing lightly does not mean dressing badly. Bring something besides the basic shorts, t-shirts, and jeans, because **dress codes** are stricter (especially for women) in Central America. Remember that clothing can make you stand out as a tourist, either because it is too flashy, culturally inappropriate, or even offensive, particularly in rural areas. Travelers are advised not to wear clothing specific to a culture of Central America; stash it in your bag until you're out of the country, as some people are offended when foreigners "buy" their cultural traditions. Similarly, do not wear camouflage clothing, or anything else associated with the military. Most Latin American **men** do not wear short pants, donning slacks or trousers on even the hottest days. Loose khaki pants and short-sleeve dress shirts do not look out of place, nor do shorts if worn with a nice shirt. **Women** should avoid dressing scantily; shorts, short skirts, or anything that shows too much skin might be interpreted in the wrong way, especially since foreigners are already perceived to be "loose." Long skirts with t-shirts is an ideal combination, and always wear a bra.

Rain gear: A **waterproof jacket** and a backpack cover will take care of you and your stuff at a moment's notice. Gore-Tex® is a miracle fabric that's both waterproof and breathable; it's all but mandatory if you plan on hiking. During the rainy season, avoid cotton as outer-wear for hiking.

Walking shoes: Well-cushioned **sneakers** are good for walking, though you may want to consider a good pair of water-proof **hiking boots.** A double pair of socks—light silk or polypropylene inside and thick wool outside—will cushion feet, keep them dry, and help prevent blisters. Bring a pair of flip-flops for protection in the shower. Talcum powder in your shoes and on your feet can prevent sores, and moleskin is great for blisters. *Break in your shoes before you leave!*

MISCELLANEOUS

Only Noah had a complete list. However, you will find the following items valuable:

Sleepsacks: If you plan to stay in **youth hostels,** don't pay the linen charge; make the requisite sleepsack yourself. Fold a full size sheet in half the long way, then sew it closed along the open long side and one of the short sides. Sleepsacks can also be used along with hotel bedding if the sheets are less-than-clean.

Other useful items: umbrella; sealable plastic bags (for damp clothes, soap, food, shampoo, and other spillables); alarm clock; waterproof matches; sun hat; moleskin (for blisters); needle and thread; safety pins; sunglasses; spare glasses or contact lenses; a personal stereo (Walkman) with headphones; pocketknife; plastic water bottle; compass; string (makeshift clothesline and lashing material); towel; padlock; whistle; rubber bands; toilet paper; flashlight; cold-water soap; cold-water detergent; earplugs; insect repellant; electrical tape (for patching tears); clothespins; maps and phrasebooks; camera film packed in a lead-lined film case (available at camera shops); tweezers; garbage bags; sunscreen; vitamins. Some items not always readily available or affordable on the road: deodorant; razors; condoms; tampons; your favorite contact lens solutions. Always have a **first-aid kit.**

■ Safety and Security

PERSONAL SAFETY

Tourists are particularly vulnerable to crime for two reasons: they often carry large amounts of cash and they are not as street savvy as locals. To avoid unwanted attention, try to **blend in** as much as possible. Respecting local customs and dressing more conservatively may placate would-be hecklers. The gawking camera-toter is a more obvious target than the low-profile traveler. Look over your map before setting out or check it inside a shop or cafe rather than on a street corner.

When exploring a new **city,** extra vigilance is wise, but no city should force you to turn precautions into panic. Find out about unsafe areas from tourist information offices, from the manager of your hotel or hostel, or from a local whom you trust. Especially if you travel alone, be sure that someone at home knows your itinerary.

Never say that you're traveling alone. You may want to carry a small **whistle** to scare off attackers or attract attention. Memorize the emergency number of the city or area.

When walking at night, stick to busy, well-lit streets. Do not attempt to cross through parks, parking lots or other large, deserted areas. Whenever possible, *Let's Go* warns of unsafe neighborhoods and areas, but exercise your own judgment about the safety of your environs. A district can change character drastically between blocks. Awareness of the flow of people can reveal a great deal about the relative safety of the area; look for children playing, women walking in the open, and other signs of an active community. If you feel uncomfortable, leave as quickly and directly as you can, but don't allow fear of the unknown to turn you into a hermit. Careful, persistent exploration will build confidence and make your stay in an area that much more enjoyable.

If you are using a **car,** learn local driving signals. Be sure to park your vehicle in a garage or well-traveled area. Wearing a seatbelt is law in many areas. If you plan on spending a lot of time on the road, you may want to bring spare parts and knowledge of what to do with them if you need them. Study route maps before you hit the road; some roads have poor (or nonexistent) shoulders, few gas stations, and roaming animals. In many regions, road conditions necessitate driving more slowly and more cautiously than you would at home.

Sleeping in your car is extremely dangerous (and often illegal). If your car breaks down, wait for the police to assist you. If you must sleep in your car, do so as close to a police station or 24-hour service station as possible. *Let's Go* does not recommend **hitchhiking,** particularly for women.

A good self-defense course will give you more concrete ways to react to different types of aggression, but it often carries a steep price tag. **Impact, Prepare, and Model Mugging** can refer you to local self-defense courses in the United States (tel. (800) 345-KICK). Course prices vary from $50-400. Women's and men's courses are offered. Community colleges frequently offer inexpensive self-defense courses.

For official **United States Department of State** travel advisories, call their 24-hour hotline at (202) 647-5225 or check their web site (http://travel.state.gov), which provides travel information and publications. Order publications, including a free pamphlet entitled *A Safe Trip Abroad,* by writing to Superintendent of Documents, U.S. Government Printing Office, Washington, D.C. 20402, or by calling them at (202) 512-1800. Official warnings from the **United Kingdom Foreign and Commonwealth Office** are on-line at http://www.fco.gov.uk; you can also call the office at (0171) 238-4503. The **Canadian Department of Foreign Affairs and International Trade** (DFAIT) offers advisories and travel warnings at its web site (http://www.dfait-maeci.gc.ca) and at its phone number ((613) 944-6788 in Ottawa, (800) 267-6788 elsewhere in Canada). Their free publication, *Bon Voyage, But....*, offers travel tips to Canadian citizens; you can receive a copy by calling them at (613) 944-6788 from Ottawa or abroad, or at (800) 267-6788 from Canada.

FINANCIAL SECURITY

Don't put a wallet with money in your back pocket. Never count your money in public and carry as little as possible. If you carry a purse, buy a sturdy one with a secure clasp, and carry it crosswise on the side away from the street with the clasp against you. Secure packs with small combination padlocks which slip through the two zippers. A **money belt** or a nylon, zippered pouch with belt that sits inside the waist of your pants or skirt is the most convenient and secure the best way to carry cash; you can buy one at most camping supply stores. A **neck pouch** is equally safe, although far less accessible. Refrain from pulling out your neck pouch in public; if you must, be very discreet. Avoid keeping anything precious in a fanny pack (even if it's worn on your stomach): your valuables will be highly visible and easy to steal.

In city crowds and especially on public transportation, pick-pockets are amazingly deft at their craft. If someone stands uncomfortably close, move away and hold your bags tightly. Also, be alert in public telephone booths. If you must say your calling-card number, do so very quietly; if you punch it in, make sure no one can look over your shoulder. **Photocopies** of important documents allow you to recover them in case they are lost or filched. Carry one copy separate from the documents and leave another copy at home. Keep some money separate to use in an emergency or in case of theft. Label every piece of luggage both inside and out.

Beware of fast-talkers; many Central American cities and towns have their share of hustlers. Con artists and hustlers often work in groups, and children are among the most effective. Don't trust anyone to "watch your bag for a second."

Travel Assistance International by Worldwide Assistance Services, Inc. provides its members with a 24-hour hotline for assistance. Their year-long frequent traveler package ($235-295) includes medical and travel insurance, financial assistance, and help in replacing lost documents. Call (800) 821-2828 or (202) 828-5894, fax (202) 828-5896, or write them at 1133 15th St. NW, Suite 400, Washington, D.C. 20005-2710. The **American Society of Travel Agents** provides extensive informational resources, both at their web site (http://www.astanet.com) and in their free brochure, *Travel Safety.* You can obtain a copy by sending a request and self-addressed, stamped envelope to 1101 King St., Alexandria, VA 22313.

DRUGS AND ALCOHOL

Laws vary from country to country, but needless to say, **illegal drugs** are best avoided. The average sentence for possession outside the U.S. is about seven years. Some countries do not differentiate between "hard" drugs and more mainstream ones such as marijuana. Buying or selling *any* type of drug may lead to anything from a prison sentence to the death penalty. A meek "I didn't know it was illegal" will not suffice. Remember that you are subject to the laws of the country in which you travel, and it is your responsibility to familiarize yourself with these laws before leaving. If you carry **prescription drugs** while you travel, it is vital to have a copy of the prescriptions readily accessible at country borders.

The specific laws in each Central American country regarding **illegal drugs** are different; don't risk having to learn them the hard way. Drug users and handlers are never treated leniently, so expect the worst. Similarly, don't bring drugs back into your home country; customs agents and their perceptive K-9s are not to be taken lightly. For the free pamphlet *Travel Warning on Drugs Abroad,* send a SASE to the Bureau of Consular Affairs, Public Affairs #6831, Dept. of State, Washington, D.C. 20520-4818 (tel. (202) 647-1488; fax (202) 647-3000; email travel-advisories-REQUEST@stolaf.edu; http://travel.state.gov).

Public drunkenness is against the law in many countries. It can also jeopardize your safety and earn the disdain of locals. **Drinking** in any part of Latin America is not for amateurs; bars are strongholds of machismo. When someone calls you *amigo* and orders you a beer, bow out quickly unless you want to match him glass for glass in a challenge lasting several days.

■ Health

Before you can say "pass the *jalapeños,*" your vacation can turn into a study of the wonders of a Central American country's health care system. Local pharmacies can give shots and dispense other remedies for mild illnesses; a sterile, disposable needle is crucial. Wherever possible, *Let's Go* lists pharmacies open for extended hours. If there is no listing, ask a policeman or cab driver. If you have an emergency and the door is locked, knock loudly; someone may be inside.

Common sense is the simplest prescription for good health while you travel: eat well, drink and sleep enough, and don't overexert yourself. Travelers complain most often about their feet and their guts, so take precautionary measures. Drinking lots of fluids can often prevent dehydration and constipation; wearing sturdy shoes, clean socks and talcum powder can help keep your feet dry.

BEFORE YOU GO

Though no amount of planning can guarantee an accident-free trip, preparation can help minimize the likelihood of contracting a disease and maximize the chances of receiving effective health care in the event of an emergency.

For minor health problems, bring a compact first-aid kit, including bandages, aspirin or other pain killer, antibiotic cream, a thermometer, a Swiss Army knife with tweezers, moleskin, a decongestant for colds, a motion sickness remedy, medicine for diarrhea or stomach problems, sunscreen, insect repellent, and burn ointment.

In your passport, write the names of any people you wish to be contacted in case of a medical emergency, and also list any allergies or medical conditions you would want doctors to be aware of. If you wear glasses or contact lenses, carry an extra prescription and pair of glasses or arrange to have your doctor or a family member send a replacement pair in an emergency. Allergy sufferers should find out if their conditions are likely to be aggravated in the regions they plan to visit, and obtain a full supply of any necessary medication before the trip—matching a prescription to a foreign equivalent is not always easy, safe, or possible. Carry up-to-date, legible prescriptions or a statement from your doctor, especially if you use insulin, a syringe, or a narcotic. While traveling, keep all medication with you in carry-on luggage.

Take a look at your **immunization** records before you go; some countries require visitors to carry vaccination certificates. A booster of Tetanus-diptheria (Td) is recommended once every 10 years, and adults traveling to Central America should consider an additional dose of Polio vaccine if they have not already had one during their adult years. A Hepatitis A vaccine and/or Immune Globulin (IG) is also recommended. If you will be spending more than four weeks in a developing country, you should consider the typhoid vaccine as well. Check with a doctor for guidance through this maze of injections, and try to remember that no matter how bad the needles are, they're better than the diseases they prevent.

For up-to-date information about which vaccinations are recommended for your destination, and region-specific health data, try these resources: The **United States Centers for Disease Control and Prevention** (based in Atlanta, Georgia), an excellent source of information for travelers around the world, maintains an international travelers' hotline (tel. (404) 332-4559; fax 332-4565; http://www.cdc.gov). The CDC publishes the booklet "Health Information for International Travelers" (US$20), an annual global rundown of disease, immunization, and general health advice, including risks in particular countries. This book may be purchased by sending a check or money order to the Superintendent of Documents, U.S. Government Printing Office, P.O. Box 371954, Pittsburgh, PA, 15250-7954. Orders can be made by phone (tel. (202) 512-1800) with a credit card (Visa Mastercard, Discover). The **United States State Department** compiles Consular Information Sheets on health, entry requirements, and other issues for all countries of the world. For quick information on travel warnings, call the **Overseas Citizens' Services** (tel. (202) 647-5225; fax (202) 642-3000). If you are HIV positive, call (202) 647-1488 for country-specific entry requirements or write to the Bureau of Consular Affairs, #6831, Department of State, Washington, D.C. 20520. For more general health information, contact the **American Red Cross (ARC)**. The ARC publishes a First-Aid and Safety Handbook (US$5) available for purchase by calling or writing to the American Red Cross, 285 Columbus Ave., Boston, MA 02116-5114 (tel. (800) 564-1234).

Those with medical conditions (e.g. diabetes, allergies to antibiotics, epilepsy, heart conditions) may want to obtain a stainless steel **Medic Alert** identification tag (US$35 the first year, and $15 annually thereafter), which identifies the disease and gives a 24-hour collect-call information number. Contact Medic Alert at (800) 825-3785, or write to Medic Alert Foundation, 2323 Colorado Ave., Turlock, CA 95382. Diabetics can contact the **American Diabetes Association,** 1660 Duke St., Alexandria, VA 22314 (tel. (800) 232-3472) to receive copies of the article "Travel and Diabetes" and a diabetic ID card, which carries messages in 18 languages explaining the carrier's diabetic status.

If you are concerned about being able to access medical support while traveling, contact one of these two services: **Global Emergency Medical Services (GEMS)** has products called *MedPass* that provide 24-hour international medical assistance and support coordinated through registered nurses who have on-line access to your medical information, your primary physician, and a worldwide network of accredited English-speaking doctors and hospitals. Subscribers also receive a personal medical record that contains vital information in case of emergencies. For more information call (800) 860-1111, fax (770) 475-0058, or write: 2001 Westside Drive, #120, Alpharetta, GA 30201. The **International Association for Medical Assistance to Travelers (IAMAT)** offers a membership ID card, a directory of English-speaking doctors around the world who treat members for a set fee schedule, and detailed charts on immunization requirements, various tropical diseases, climate, and sanitation. Membership is free, though donations are appreciated and used for further research. Contact chapters in the **U.S.,** 417 Center St., Lewiston, NY 14092 (tel. (716) 754-4883; fax (519) 836-3412; email iamat@sentex.net; http://www.sentex.net/ ~iamat), **Canada,** 40 Regal Road, Guelph, Ontario, N1K 1B5 (tel. (519) 836-0102) or 1287 St. Clair Avenue West, Toronto, M6E 1B8 (tel. (416) 652-0137; fax (519) 836-3412), or **New Zealand,** P.O. Box 5049, Christchurch 5.

PREVENTING DISEASE

Avoid animals with open wounds, and beware of touching any animal at all in developing countries. Often dogs are not given shots, so that sweet-faced pooch at your feet might very well be a disease-ridden deathtrap. If you are bitten, be concerned about **rabies**—clean your wound thoroughly and seek medical help immediately.

Many diseases are transmitted by insects—mainly mosquitoes, fleas, ticks, and lice. Be aware of insects in wet or forested areas, while hiking, and especially while camping. **Mosquitoes** are most active from dusk to dawn. Wear long pants and long sleeves (fabric need not be thick or warm; tropic-weight cottons can keep you comfortable in the heat) and buy a bednet for camping. Wear shoes and socks, and tuck long pants into socks. Use insect repellents; DEET can be bought in spray or liquid form, but use it sparingly, especially on children. Soak or spray your gear with permethrin, which is licensed in the U.S. for use on clothing. Calamine lotion or topical cortisones (like Cortaid) may stop insect bites from itching, as can a bath with a half-cup of baking soda or oatmeal.

Malaria is transmitted by Anopheles mosquitoes which bite during the night. These pesky bloodsuckers are present in almost all tropical and subtropical regions. Preliminary symptoms include fever, chills, aches, and fatigue. Since early stages resemble the flu, you should see a doctor for any flu-like sickness that occurs after travel in a risk area. If left untreated, malaria can cause anemia, kidney failure, coma, and death. Malaria poses an especially serious threat to pregnant women and their fetuses. If hiking or staying overnight in certain areas (whether camping or not), you may want to take weekly anti-malarial drugs. Contact your doctor for a prescription. For travel in eastern Panamá, travelers are given mefloquine; elsewhere, chloroquine.

Dengue Fever is an "urban viral infection" transmitted by Aedes mosquitoes, which bite during the day rather than at night. Dengue has flu-like symptoms and is often indicated by a rash three to four days after the onset of fever; see a doctor immediately if you come down with these symptoms. Dengue Fever causes death in about 5% of cases, and there is no vaccine. To treat the symptoms, rest, drink lots of water, and take fever-reducing medication such as acetaminophen (but avoid aspirin).

Other insect diseases present in some parts of Central America include the following: **filariasis** is a round worm infestation transmitted by mosquitoes. Infection causes enlargement (elephantiasis) of extremities; there is no vaccine. **Leishmaniasis,** a parasite transmitted by sand flies, can also occur. There is a treatment, but no vaccine. **American Trypanomiasis/CHAGAS Disease** is another fairly common parasite. Transmitted by the reduviid bug, a cone nose or kissing bug, which infests mud, adobe, and thatch, the symptoms are fever, heart disease, and later, an enlarged intestine. There is no vaccine and limited treatment. If you contract these or any diseases, see a doctor immediately, as they can be fatal.

FOOD- AND WATER-BORNE DISEASES

To ensure that your food is safe, make sure that everything is completely cooked (deep-fried is good, for once), and be positive the **water** you drink is clean. Never drink unbottled water which you have not treated yourself—the risk of contracting traveler's diarrhea or other diseases is high. To purify your own water, bring it to a rolling boil (simmering isn't enough), or treat it with iodine drops or tablets. Don't brush your teeth with tap water, and don't even rinse your toothbrush under the faucet. Keep your mouth closed in the shower. Don't be fooled by the clever disguise of impure water—the ice-cube. Stay away from salads: uncooked vegetables (including lettuce and coleslaw) are full of untreated water. Other culprits are raw shellfish, unpasteurized milk, and sauces containing raw eggs. Peel all fruits and vegetables yourself, and beware of watermelon, which is often injected with impure water. Watch out for food from markets or street vendors that may have been washed in dirty water or fried in rancid cooking oil, such as juices, peeled fruits, and exposed coconut slices. Always wash your hands before eating. Your bowels will thank you.

Cholera is an intestinal disease caused by a bacteria found in contaminated food; the disease has recently reached epidemic stages in Central America. The first severe symptoms of cholera are lots of watery diarrhea, dehydration, vomiting, and muscle cramps. Untreated, cholera can cause death very quickly. Antibiotics are available, but the most important treatment is rehydration. Consider getting a (50% effective) vaccine if you have stomach problems (e.g. ulcers), or if you will be camping a good deal or living where water is not always reliable.

Typhoid Fever is common in villages and rural areas. While mostly transmitted through contaminated food and water, it may also be acquired by direct contact with another person. Symptoms include fever, headaches, fatigue, loss of appetite, constipation, and a rash on the abdomen or chest; antibiotics treat typhoid fever. The Center for Disease Control and Prevention recommends (70-90% effective) vaccinations if you will be going off the "usual tourist itineraries," that is, to small cities or rural areas.

Parasites (tapeworms, etc.) also hide in unsafe water and food. *Giardia,* for example, is acquired by drinking untreated water from streams or lakes. It can stay with you for years. Symptoms of parasitic infections in general include swollen glands or lymph nodes, fever, rashes or itchiness, digestive problems, eye problems, and anemia. Boil your water, wear shoes, avoid bugs, and eat cooked food.

Hepatitis A (distinct from B and C) is a high risk in Central America. Hep. A, a viral infection of the liver, acquired primarily through contaminated water, ice, shellfish, unpeeled fruits, and vegetables (as well as from sexual contact). Symptoms include fatigue, fever, loss of appetite, nausea, dark urine, jaundice, vomiting, aches and pains, and light stools. Ask your doctor about a vaccine called "Harvix," or ask to get an injection of immune globulin (IG; formerly called Gamma Globulin). Risk is highest in rural areas, but is also present in urban areas.

Hepatitis B is a viral infection of the liver transmitted by sharing needles, having unprotected sex, or coming into direct contact with an infected person's lesioned skin. If you think you may be sexually active while traveling or if you are working or living in rural areas, you are typically advised to get a Hepatitis B. Note: vaccination must begin six months before traveling.

Hepatitis C is like Hepatitis B, but the methods of transmission are different. At risk are intravenous drug users, those with occupational exposure to blood, hemodialysis patients, or recipients of a blood transfusion; doctors aren't sure if you can get it through sexual contact.

TRAVELER'S DIARRHEA

Traveler's diarrhea, known as *turista,* is the dastardly consequence of ignoring the warnings against drinking untreated water in Latin America. The illness can last from three to seven days, and symptoms include diarrhea, nausea, bloating, urgency, and-

malaise. If the nasties hit, have quick-energy, non-sugary foods with protein and carbohydrates to keep your strength up. Over-the-counter remedies (such as Pepto-Bismol or Immodium) may counteract the problems, but they can complicate serious infections. Avoid anti-diarrheals if you suspect you have been exposed to contaminated food or water, which puts you at risk for other diseases. The most dangerous side effect of diarrhea is dehydration; the most effective anti-dehydration formula is 8 oz. of (clean) water with a ½ tsp. of sugar or honey and a pinch of salt. Also good are soft drinks without caffeine, and salted crackers. Down several of these remedies a day, rest, and wait for the disease to run its course. If you a fever or your symptoms don't go away after four or five days, consult a doctor. Also consult a doctor if children develop traveler's diarrhea, since treatment is different.

HOT AND COLD

Common sense goes a long way toward preventing **heat exhaustion:** relax in hot weather, drink lots of non-alcoholic fluids, and lie down inside if you feel awful. Continuous heat stress can eventually lead to **heatstroke,** characterized by rising body temperature, severe headache, and cessation of sweating. Victims must be cooled off with wet towels and taken to a doctor as soon as possible.

Always drink enough liquids to keep your urine clear. Alcoholic beverages are dehydrating, as are coffee, strong tea, and caffeinated sodas. If you sweat a lot, be sure to eat enough salty food to prevent electrolyte depletion, which causes severe headaches. Less debilitating, but still dangerous, is **sunburn.** If you're prone to sunburn, bring sunscreen with you (it's more expensive and hard to find when traveling), and apply it liberally and often. If you get sunburned, drink more fluids than usual.

Don't underestimate how cold Central American nights can be. Extreme cold is just as dangerous as heat—overexposure to cold brings the risk of **hypothermia.** Warning signs are easy to detect: body temperature drops rapidly, resulting in the failure to produce body heat. You may shiver, have poor coordination, feel exhausted, or have slurred speech, feel sleepy, hallucinate, or suffer amnesia. Do not let hypothermia victims fall asleep if they are in the advanced stages—their body temperature will drop more, and if they lose consciousness they may die. Seek medical help as soon as possible. To avoid hypothermia, keep dry and stay out of the wind. In wet weather, wool and most synthetics, such as pile, will keep you warm, but most other fabrics, especially cotton, will make you colder.

Travelers to **high altitudes** must allow their bodies a couple of days to adjust to lower oxygen levels before exerting themselves. Also be careful about alcohol, especially if you're used to U.S. standards for beer—many foreign brews and liquors pack more punch, and where the air has less oxygen, any alcohol will do you in quickly.

WOMEN'S HEALTH

Women traveling in unsanitary conditions are vulnerable to urinary tract and bladder infections, common and severely uncomfortable bacterial diseases which cause a burning sensation and painful, and sometimes frequent, urination. Drink tons of vitamin-C-rich juice, plenty of clean water, and urinate frequently, especially right after intercourse. Untreated, these infections can lead to kidney infections, sterility, and even death. If symptoms persist, see a doctor. If you often develop vaginal yeast infections, take along enough over-the-counter medicine, as treatments may not be readily available in Central America. Women may also be more susceptible to vaginal thrush and cystitis, two treatable but uncomfortable illnesses that are likely to flare up in hot and humid climates. Wearing loosely fitting trousers or a skirt and cotton underwear may help. When traveling, your preferred brands of tampons and pads may be hard to find; take enough supplies along, especially if you're picky. Refer to the *Handbook for Women Travellers* by Maggie and Gemma Moss (published by Piatkus Books) or to the women's health guide *Our Bodies, Our Selves* (published by the Boston Women's Health Collective) for more extensive information specific to women's health on the road.

BIRTH CONTROL

Contraceptive devices may be difficult to find on the road. Women on the pill should bring enough to allow for possible loss or extended stays. Bring a prescription, since forms of the pill vary a good deal. Women who use a diaphragm should have enough contraceptive jelly on hand. Though condoms are usually available, you might want to bring your favorite brand along with you; availability and quality vary.

Abortion is completely illegal in all of Central America, except in Belize, Costa Rica, Honduras, and Panamá, where it is only legal under specific circumstances. For information on contraception, condoms, and abortion worldwide, contact the **International Planned Parenthood Federation,** European Regional Office, Regent's College Inner Circle, Regent's Park, London NW1 4NS (tel. (0171) 487 7900, fax (0171) 487 7950).

AIDS, HIV, STDS

Acquired Immune Deficiency Syndrome (AIDS) is a growing problem around the world. The World Health Organization estimates that there are around 13 million people infected with the HIV virus. Well over 90% of adults newly infected with HIV acquired their infection through heterosexual sex; women now represent 50% of all new HIV infections.

The easiest mode of HIV transmission is through the exchange of blood with an HIV+ person; *never* share intravenous drug, tattooing, or other needles. The most common mode of transmission is sexual intercourse. Health professionals recommend the use of latex condoms. Since it isn't always easy to buy condoms when traveling, take a supply with you before you depart for your trip. Casual contact (including drinking from the same glass or using the same eating utensils as an infected person) is not believed to pose a risk.

For more information on AIDS, call the **U.S. Center for Disease Control's** 24 hour hotline at (800) 342-2437. In Europe, write to the **World Health Organization,** attn: Global Program on AIDS, 20 Avenue Appia, 1211 Geneva 27, Switzerland (tel. (22) 791-2111), for statistical material on AIDS internationally. Or write to the **Bureau of Consular Affairs,** #6831, Department of State, Washington, D.C. 20520. Check council Travel's *Travel Safe: AIDS and International Travel.*

Sexually transmitted diseases (STDs) such as gonorrhea, chlamydia, genital warts, syphilis, and herpes are a lot easier to catch than HIV, and can be just as deadly. *Look* at your partner's genitals before sex. Warning signs for STDs include: swelling, sores, bumps, or blisters on sex organs, rectum, or mouth; burning and pain during urination and bowel movements; itching around sex organs; swelling or redness in the throat, flu-like symptoms with fever, chills, and aches. If these symptoms develop, see a doctor immediately. When having sex, condoms may protect you from certain STDs, but oral or even tactile contact can lead to transmission.

■ Alternatives to Tourism

STUDY

Foreign study programs vary tremendously in expense, academic quality, living conditions, degree of contact with local students, and exposure to local culture and languages. There is a plethora of exchange programs for high school students. Most American undergraduates enroll in programs sponsored by U.S. universities, and many colleges have offices that give advice and information on study abroad. Local libraries and bookstores are also helpful sources for current information on study abroad, and the Internet has a study abroad web site at **www.studyabroad.com.**

American Field Service (AFS), 198 Madison Ave., 8th Fl., New York, NY 10016 (Students tel. (800) AFS-INFO (237-4636); administration (800) 876-2376; fax (503) 241-1653; email afsinfo@afs.org; http://www.afs.org/usa). AFS offers summer,

semester, and year-long homestay international exchange programs for high school students and recent high school graduates. Financial aid available. Exchanges in Costa Rica, Honduras, and Panamá.

Amerispan, P.O Box 40513, Philadelphia, PA, 19106-0513 (tel. (800) 879-6640; worldwide (215) 751-1100; fax (215) 751-1986; email info@amerispan.com; http://www.amerispan.com). Spanish immersion programs in Costa Rica, El Salvador, Guatemala, Honduras, Panamá, and Nicaragua. Classes one-on-one or in small groups; homestay, travel insurance, and meals included. US$350-2000 plus a US$100 registration fee to cover expenses.

Institute for Central American Development Studies (ICADS), Dept. 826, P.O. Box 025216, Miami, FL 33102-5216 or **Instituto de Estudios de Desarrollo Centroamericano,** Apdo. 3-2070, Sabanilla, San José, Costa Rica (tel. (506) 225-0508; fax (506) 234-1337; email icads@netbox.com). Semester abroad programs in Costa Rica, Nicaragua, and Belize aimed at students who wish to work for social justice in Central America. Areas of study include women's studies, environmental/ecological studies, biology, public health, education, and agriculture. 30-day intensive Spanish program US$1225, including classes, homestay, breakfasts and dinners, field trips, and afternoon volunteer opportunities. Field courses in resource management and sustainable development.

Institute of International Education (IIE), 809 United Nations Plaza, New York, NY 10017-3580 (tel. (212) 984-5413; fax 984-5358). For book orders: IIE Books, Institute of International Education, P.O. Box 371, Annapolis Junction, MD 20701 (tel. (800) 445-0443; fax (301) 206-9789; email iiebooks@pmds.com). A nonprofit, international and cultural exchange agency, IIE's library of study abroad resources is open to the public Tues.-Thurs. 11am-3:45pm. Publishes *Academic Year Abroad* (US$43, US$5 postage) and *Vacation Study Abroad* (US$37, US$5 postage). Write for a complete list of publications.

World Learning, Inc., Summer Abroad, Kipling Rd., P.O. Box 676, Brattleboro, VT 05302 (tel. (800) 345-2929 or (802) 257-7751; fax (802) 258-3248; http://www.worldlearning.org). Offers 3-5-week-long high school programs to study, travel and live abroad in Belize and Costa Rica. Positions as group leaders are available world-wide if you are over 24, have previous in-country experience, are applicably fluent, and have experience with high school students.

WORK

There's no better way to immerse yourself in a Central American country than to become part of its economy. Unfortunately, the leaders of developing nations aren't about to give up precious paid jobs to *gringos* when many of their own people are unemployed. If you find a **temporary job,** it will rarely be glamorous and may not even pay for your plane fare or your accommodations. Officially, you can hold a job in most countries only with a **work permit.** Your employer must obtain this document, usually by demonstrating that you have skills that locals lack—not always the easiest of tasks. Friends in your destination country can help expedite work permits or arrange work-for-accommodations swaps. Advertise to teach English. Many permitless agricultural workers go untroubled by local authorities. Students can check with their universities' foreign language departments, which may have connections to jobs abroad. Call the consulate or embassy of the country in which you wish to work to get more information about work permits.

If you are a **U.S. citizen** and a full-time student at a U.S. university, the simplest way to get a job abroad is through work permit programs run by **Council on International Educational Exchange (Council)** and its member organizations. For a US$225 application fee, Council can procure three- to six-month work permits (and a handbook to help you find work and housing) for Costa Rica. Council offices help with finding accommodations, openings, and connections. Contact Council for more information (see **Travel Organizations,** p. 1). **Vacation Work Publications** publishes *Work Your Way Around the World* (UK£11, UK£ 2.50 postage, UK£1.50 within U.K) to help you along the way (see below).

The Archaeological Institute of America, 656 Beacon St., Boston, MA 02215-2010 (tel. (617) 353-9361; fax 353-6550; email aia@bu.edu; http://csa.brynmawr.edu/web2/aia.html), puts out the *Archaeological Fieldwork Opportunities Bulletin* (US$11 non-members) which lists over 300 field sites throughout the world.

Office of Overseas Schools, A/OS Room 245, SA-29, Dept. of State, Washington, D.C. 20522-2902 (tel. (703) 875-7800; http://www.state.gov/www/about_state/schools/). Keeps a list of schools abroad and agencies that arrange placement for Americans to teach abroad.

Transitions Abroad Publishing, Inc., 18 Hulst Rd., P.O. Box 1300, Amherst, MA 01004-1300 (tel. (800) 293-0373; fax (413) 256-0373; email trabroad@aol.com; http://www.transabroad.com). Publishes *Transitions Abroad*, a bi-monthly magazine listing all kinds of opportunities and printed resources for those seeking to study, work, or travel abroad.

VOLUNTEERING

Volunteer jobs are readily available in many locations. Some programs may provide room and board in exchange for your labor; the work can be fascinating. You can sometimes avoid the high application fees charged by the organizations that arrange placement by contacting the individual programs directly; check with the organizations. Listings in **Vacation Work Publications's** *International Directory of Voluntary Work* (UK£10; postage UK£2.50, £1.50 within U.K.) can be helpful (see above).

Central Bureau for Educational Visits and Exchanges, 10 Spring Gardens, London SW1A 2BN (tel. (0171) 389-4004; fax (0171) 389-4426; e-mail 101472.2264@compuserve.com). Publishes *Working Holidays 1997, Volunteer Work, Teach Abroad, A Year Between,* and *Home from Home.* All books are UK£8.99. Distributed in North America by IIE Books.

Conservation International, Attn. Eco-Escuela de Español, 2501 M St. NW, Suite 200, Washington, D.C., 20037 (tel. (202) 973-2264; fax (202) 331-9328; email ecoescuela@conservation.org; http://www.conservation.org/web/fieldact/ecoescue.hfm). Eco-Escuela de Español offers Spanish language instruction, environmental education, and volunteer opportunities in Guatemala.

Global Volunteers, 375 E. Little Canada Rd., St. Paul, MN 55117-1628 (tel. (800) 487-1074 or (612) 482-1074; fax (612) 482-0915; email: email@globalvlntrs.org; http://www.globalvlntrs.org). Facilitates approximately 120 teams of North Americans on short-term social and economic development projects in Costa Rica and 15 other countries in Europe, Asia and Africa.

Peace Corps, 1990 K St. NW, Room 8508, Washington, D.C. 20526 (tel. (800) 424-8580; fax (202) 606-4469; email msaucier@peacecorps.gov; http://www.peacecorps.gov). Volunteers must be U.S. citizens, age 18 and over, and willing to make a 2-year commitment. A bachelor's degree is usually required.

Volunteers for Peace, 43 Tiffany Rd., Belmont, VT 05730 (tel. (802) 259-2759; fax 259-2922; email vfp@vfp.org; http://www.vfp.org). A nonprofit organization that arranges speedy placement in 2-3 week workcamps comprised of 10-15 people.

WorldTeach, Harvard Institute for International Development, 1 Eliot St., Cambridge, MA 02138-5705 (tel. (617) 495-5527; fax 495-1599; email info@worldteach.org; http://www.igc.org/worldteach). Volunteers teach English, math, science, and environmental education to students of all ages in developing countries, including Costa Rica, Ecuador, Lithuania, Mexico, Thailand, and Vietnam. Bachelor's degree required for most programs. Room, board, and a small stipend are provided during the period of service, but volunteers must pay a program fee which covers health insurance, airfare, and training. Rolling admission.

▓ Specific Concerns

WOMEN TRAVELERS

Women travelers to Central America are often surprised by the unwanted attention they receive. Men commonly insist on joining women, who should also expect to

hear whistles and propositions while walking down the street. Offer no response and make no eye contact; any kind of answer could be interpreted as a come-on. If need be, turn to an older woman for help in an uncomfortable situation; her stern rebukes will usually be enough to embarrass the most persistent jerks. Should a situation become threatening, however, do not hesitate to lash out with a scream or even physical force. The extremely persistent can sometimes be dissuaded by a firm, loud, and very public "Go away!" in the appropriate language. Creating a loud fuss is often publicly humiliating for the menacer, who may shrink back in defeat. Carry a whistle on your keychain, and don't hesitate to use it in an emergency. **Hitching** is never safe for women. A **Model Mugging** course will raise your level of awareness and increase your confidence in your ability to defend yourself.

Being aware of Latin American social norms can also prevent unpleasant confrontations. Bars are all-male institutions; the only women working there are servers or prostitutes. If you are traveling with a male friend, it may help to pose as a couple; this will assuage any misgivings hotel proprietors have about letting you share rooms and may chill the blood of your Central American admirers. Women traveling alone should consider preparing a story of an "uncle" or other male who is "supposed to show up any minute." Some women wear a "wedding ring" on their left hand to discourage unwanted attention. Consider staying in hostels that offer single rooms that lock from the inside or in religious organizations with women-only rooms; avoid any hostel with "communal" showers. Finally, be aware that some of the worst offenders you encounter may be fellow travelers who interpret the atmosphere described above as a mandate for harassment and misogyny. Women traveling alone should not attempt to challenge custom or assert strong feminist beliefs.

For general information, contact the **National Organization for Women (NOW),** which boasts branches across the country that can refer women travelers to rape crisis centers and counseling services, and provide lists of feminist events. Main offices are located at 22 W. 21st St., 7th Fl., **New York,** NY 10010 (tel. (212) 260-4422); 1000 16th St. NW, 7th Fl., **Washington, D.C.** 20004 (tel. (202) 331-0066); and 3543 18th St., **San Francisco,** CA 94110 (tel. (415) 861-8960; fax 861-8969; email sfnow@sirius.com; http://www.sirius.com/~sfnow/now.html.

Handbook For Women Travellers by Maggie and Gemma Moss (UK£9). Encyclopedic and well-written. Available from Piatkus Books, 5 Windmill St., London W1P 1HF (tel. (0171) 631 07 10).

A Journey of One's Own, by Thalia Zepatos (US$17). Full of valuable advice, with a bibliography of books and resources. **Adventures in Good Company,** on group travel by the same author, costs US$17. Available from The Eighth Mountain Press, 624 Southeast 29th Ave., Portland, OR 97214 (tel. (503) 233-3936; fax 233-0774; email eightmt@aol.com).

Gutsy Women: Travel Tips and Wisdom for the Road by Marybeth Bond (US$7.95). An indispensable and inspirational travel guide for women on road. Available from O'Reilly and Associates, 101 Morris St., Sebastopol, CA 95472 (tel. (800) 889-8969).

Women Going Places is a women's travel and resource guide geared towards lesbians which emphasizes women-owned enterprises. Advice appropriate for all women. US$15 from Inland Book Company, 1436 W. Randolph St., Chicago, IL 60607 (tel. (800) 243-0138; fax (800) 334-3892) or a local bookstore.

LESBIAN, BISEXUAL, AND GAY TRAVELERS

Until recently, the strength of the Catholic church in Central America hindered the gay rights movement; today the region's countries accept homosexuality to varying degrees. In general, Central Americans disapprove of public displays of homosexual affection, though people in cities are bound to be more tolerant than in rural areas. Honduras has been cited as the most liberal country in Central America for gays, although Costa Rica also has a supportive community. Homosexuality is legal (or not mentioned in the laws) in Belize, Costa Rica (at 17 years), El Salvador, Guatemala (at

ESSENTIALS

18 years), Honduras, and Panamá. In Nicaragua, "sodomy" is illegal and punishable with prison sentences, particularly for those who work with children.

Ferrari Guides, P.O. Box 37887, Phoenix, AZ 85069 (tel. (602) 863-2408; fax 439-3952; email ferrari@q-net.com; http://www.q-net.com). Gay and lesbian travel guides: *Ferrari Guides' Gay Travel A to Z* (US$16), *Ferrari Guides' Men's Travel in Your Pocket* (US$16), *Ferrari Guides' Women's Travel in Your Pocket* (US$14), *Ferrari Guides' Inn Places* (US$16), *Ferrari Guides' Gay Paris* (Spring 1997). Available in bookstores or by mail order (postage/handling US$4.50 for the first item, US$1 for each additional item mailed within the U.S. Overseas, call or write for shipping cost).

Giovanni's Room, 345 S. 12th St., Philadelphia, PA 19107 (tel. (215) 923-2960; fax 923-0813; email giolphilp@netaxs.com). An international feminist, lesbian, and gay bookstore with mail-order service which carries many useful publications.

International Gay and LesbianTravel Association, P.O. Box 4974, Key West, FL 33041 (tel. (800) 448-8550; fax (305) 296-6633; email IGTA@aol.com; http://www.rainbow-mall.com/igta). An organization of over 1300 companies serving gay and lesbian travelers worldwide. Call for lists of travel agents, accommodations, and events.

Spartacus International Gay Guides (US$33), published by Bruno Gmunder, Postfach 61 01 04, D-10921 Berlin, Germany (tel. (30) 615 00 3-42; fax (30) 615 91 34). Lists bars, restaurants, hotels, and bookstores around the world catering to gays. Also lists hotlines for gays in various countries and homosexuality laws for each country. Available in bookstores and in the U.S. by mail from Lambda Rising, 1625 Connecticut Ave. NW, Washington D.C., 20009-1013 (tel. (202) 462-6969).

DISABLED TRAVELERS

Central America is not tremendously amenable to disabled travelers. Rainforests, volcanoes, and beaches rarely have smooth paths, and wheelchair-accessible buildings are rare. Still, there are exceptions, and the region is not entirely off-limits to disabled tourists. Those with disabilities should inform airlines and hotels of their disabilities when making arrangements for travel; some time may be needed to prepare special accommodations. If you give sufficient notice, some major car rental agencies offer hand-controlled vehicles at select locations. Travelers with seeing eye dogs should inquire about the specific quarantine policies of the countries that they are visiting. At the very least, dogs will need certificates of immunization against rabies. The following organizations provide helpful information, and some arrange tours or trips for disabled travelers.

American Foundation for the Blind, 11 Penn Plaza, 300, New York, NY 10011 (tel. (212) 502-7600), open Mon.-Fri. 8:30am-4:30pm. Provides information and services for the visually impaired. For a catalogue of products, contact Lighthouse, Enterprises, 36-20 Northern Boulevard, Long Island City, NY 11101 (tel. (800) 829-0500).

Directions Unlimited, 720 N. Bedford Rd., Bedford Hills, NY 10507 (tel. (800) 533-5343; in NY (914) 241-1700; fax 241-0243). Specializes in arranging individual and group vacations, tours, and cruises for the physically disabled. Group tours for blind travelers.

Flying Wheels Travel Service, 143 W. Bridge St., Owatonne, MN 55060 (tel. (800) 535-6790; fax 451-1685). Arranges trips in the U.S. and abroad for groups and individuals in wheelchairs or with other sorts of limited mobility.

The Guided Tour Inc., Elkins Park House, 114B, 7900 Old York Rd., Elkins Park, PA 19027-2339 (tel. (800) 783-5841 or (215) 782-1370; fax 635-2637). Organizes travel programs for persons with developmental and physical challenges and those requiring renal dialysis. Call, fax, or write for a free brochure.

Mobility International, USA (MIUSA), P.O. Box 10767, Eugene, OR 97440 (tel. (514) 343-1284 voice and TDD; fax 343-6812; email info@miusa.org; http://miusa.org). International Headquarters in Brussels, rue de Manchester 25 Brussels, Belgium, B-1070 (tel. (322) 410-6297, fax 410 6874). Contacts in 30 countries.

Information on travel programs, international work camps, accommodations, access guides, and organized tours for those with physical disabilities. Membership US$30 per year.

Society for the Advancement of Travel for the Handicapped (SATH), 347 Fifth Ave., #610, New York, NY 10016 (tel. (212) 447-1928; fax 725-8253; email sath-travel@aol.com; http://www.sath.org). Publishes a quarterly color travel magazine *OPEN WORLD* (free for members or on subscription US$13 for nonmembers). Also publishes a wide range of information sheets on disability travel facilitation and accessible destinations. Annual membership US$45, students and seniors US$30.

DIETARY CONCERNS

San José, Costa Rica; Tegucigalpa, Honduras; and Panama City, Panamá all have size-able Jewish communities. For lists of **kosher** restaurants, plus synagogues and Jewish institutions in over 80 countries, consult **The Jewish Travel Guide.** Available from Ballantine-Mitchell Publishers, Newbury House 890-900, Eastern Ave., Newbury Park, Ilford, Essex, U.K. IG2 7HH (tel. (0181) 599 88 66; fax 599 09 84). It is available in the U.S. from Sepher-Hermon Press, 1265 46th St., Brooklyn, NY 11219 (tel. (718) 972-9010; US$15 plus US$2.50 shipping).

Vegetarians are often frustrated by the heavy emphasis on chicken in Central American cuisine, but rice, beans, and a variety of fresh fruits and vegetables offer other options. *Let's Go* often notes restaurants with good vegetarian selections in listings. For more tips, check out the **The International Vegetarian Travel Guide** (UK£2) last published in 1991. Order back copies from the Vegetarian Society of the UK (VSUK), Parkdale, Dunham Rd., Altringham, Cheshire WA14 4QG (tel. (0161) 928 0793). VSUK also publishes other titles, including *The European Vegetarian Guide to Hotels and Restaurants.* Call or send a self-addressed stamped envelope.

OLDER TRAVELERS

Senior citizens are eligible for a wide range of discounts on transportation, museums, movies, theaters, concerts, restaurants, and accommodations. If you don't see a senior citizen price listed, ask, and you may be delightfully surprised. Agencies for senior group travel (like **Eldertreks,** 597 Markham St., Toronto, Ontario, CANADA, M6G 2L7, tel. (416) 588-5000, fax 588-9839, email passages@inforamp.net, and **Walking the World,** P.O. Box 1186, Fort Collins, CO 80522, tel. (970) 225-0500, fax 225-9100, email walktworld@aol.com; travel to North America, Europe, New Zealand, and Central America) are growing in enrollment and popularity. Senior travelers should bring a medical record that includes updates on conditions and prescriptions, the name, phone number, and address of a regular doctor, and a recent medical history. For more tips, write to the tourism offices of the countries you plan to visit. The following organizations and publications can also be helpful:

AARP (American Association of Retired Persons), 601 E. St. NW, Washington, D.C. 20049 (tel. (202) 434-2277). Members 50 and over receive benefits and services including the AARP Motoring Plan from AMOCO (tel. (800) 334-3300), and discounts on lodging, car rental, cruises, and sight-seeing. Annual fee US$8 per couple; $20 for three years; lifetime membership US$75.

Elderhostel, 75 Federal St., 3rd Fl., Boston, MA 02110-1941 (tel. (617) 426-7788, fax 426-8351; email Cadyg@elderhostel.org; http://www.elderhostel.org). For those 55 or over (spouse of any age). Programs at colleges, universities, and other learning centers in over 70 countries on varied subjects lasting 1-4 weeks.

National Council of Senior Citizens, 8403 Colesville Rd., Silver Spring, MD 20910-31200 (tel. (301) 578-8800; fax 578-8999). Memberships cost US$13 per year, US$33 for 3 years, or US$175 for a lifetime. Information on hotel and auto rental discounts, a senior citizen newspaper, and use of a discount travel agency.

Unbelievably Good Deals and Great Adventures That You Absolutely Can't Get Unless You're Over 50, by Joan Rattner Heilman. After you finish reading the title page, check inside for some great tips on senior discounts. US$10 from Contemporary Books.

FOXY OLD WOMEN TRAVELERS

A Foxy Old Woman's Guide to Traveling Alone, by Jay Ben-Lesser (Crossing Press, US $11). Info, informal advice, and a resource list on solo travel on a low-to-medium budget.

MINORITY TRAVELERS

Though a recent **Travel Industry Association of America (TIA)** study was published under the title "Minority Travelers: A Large and Growing Market" (find it at http://www.travelleader.com/tlpr/tia/minority.html), resources on the subject are extremely hard to come by. Since each Central American country, and sometimes each region within a country, has its own history of race relations, it is impossible to generalize about how minority travelers will be treated. The populations of most Central American nations are comprised primarily of people of Spanish, native, and *mestizo* (mixed ancestry) descent. Travelers of other ethnicities may find themselves the object of stares, especially from children in small villages, but most stares of curiosity, not animosity. In many cases, your status as a foreigner will make you stand out more than your ethnicity, but one can never rule out the occasional racist remark. Be aware that terms such as *negro* have different connotations in Spanish than in English-speaking countries.

TRAVELING ALONE

There are many benefits to traveling alone, among them greater independence, challenge, and an opportunity to see the world through a lens unfiltered by others. As a lone traveler, you have greater opportunity to meet and interact with natives. Lone travelers need to be well-organized and look confident at all times. Maintain regular contact with someone at home who knows your itinerary. A number of organizations can find travel companions for solo travelers.

Travel Companions, P.O. Box 833, Amityville, NY 11701 (tel. (516) 454-0880). Monthly newsletter with listings and helpful tips; subscription US$48.

Traveling On Your Own, by Eleanor Berman (US$13). Lists information resources for "singles" (old and young) and single parents. Crown Publishers, Inc., 201 East 50th St., New York, NY 10022.

GETTING THERE

■ Budget Travel Agencies

Students and people under 26 with proper ID qualify for enticing reduced "youth" airfares. These are rarely available from airlines or travel agents, but from student travel agencies which negotiate special reduced-rate bulk purchase with the airlines, then resell them to the youth market. Return-date change fees also tend to be low (around US$35 per segment through **Council** or **Let's Go Travel**). Most flights are on major airlines, though in peak season some agencies may sell seats on less reliable chartered aircraft. Student travel agencies can also help non-students and people over 26, but probably won't be able to get the same low fares.

Campus Travel, 52 Grosvenor Gardens, London SW1W 0AG (http://www.campus-travel.co.uk). Student and youth fares on plane, train, boat, and bus travel. Skytrekker, flexible airline tickets. Discount and ID cards for students and youths, travel insurance for students and those under 35, and maps and guides. Puts out travel suggestion booklets. Telephone booking service: worldwide call (0171) 730 81 11.

Council Travel (http://www.ciee.org/travel/index.htm), the travel division of Council, is a full-service travel agency specializing in youth and budget travel. They offer discount airfares on scheduled airlines, hosteling cards, low-cost accommodations, budget tours, travel gear, and international student (ISIC), youth (GO25), and teacher (ITIC) identity cards. U.S. offices include: 2000 Guadalupe, **Austin,** TX 78705 (tel. (512) 472-4931); 1153 N. Dearborn, **Chicago,** IL 60610 (tel. (312) 951-0585); 10904 Lindbrook Dr., **Los Angeles,** CA 90024 (tel. (310) 208-3551); 205 E. 42nd St., **New York,** NY 10017 (tel. (212) 822-2700); 3300 M St. NW, **Washington, D.C.** 20007 (tel. (202) 337-6464). **For U.S. cities not listed,** call 800-2-COUNCIL/226-8624. Also 28A Poland St. (Oxford Circus), **London,** W1V 3DB (tel. (0171) 287 3337).

Let's Go Travel, Harvard Student Agencies, 17 Holyoke St., Cambridge, MA 02138 (tel. (617) 495-9649; fax 495-7956; email travel@hsa.net; http://hsa.net/travel). Railpasses, HI-AYH memberships, ISICs, ITICs, FIYTO cards, guidebooks (including every *Let's Go*), maps, bargain flights, and a complete line of budget travel gear. All items available by mail; call or write for a catalogue (or see the catalogue in center of this publication).

STA Travel, 6560 Scottsdale Rd. #F100, Scottsdale, AZ 85253 (tel. (800) 777-0112 nationwide; fax (602) 922-0793; http://sta-travel.com). A student and youth travel organization with over 150 offices worldwide offering discount airfares, railpasses, accommodations, tours, insurance, and ISICs for young travelers. Call for a list of offices in the U.S. and abroad.

Travel CUTS (Canadian Universities Travel Services Limited), 187 College St., Toronto, Ont. M5T 1P7 (tel. (416) 979-2406; fax 979-8167; email mail@travelcuts). Canada's national student travel bureau and equivalent of Council, with 40 offices across Canada. Also in the U.K., 295-A Regent St., **London** W1R 7YA (tel. (0171) 637 31 61). Discounted domestic and international airfares open to all; special student fares to all destinations with valid ISIC. Issues ISIC, FIYTO, GO25, and HI hostel cards, as well as railpasses. Offers free *Student Traveller* magazine, as well as information on the Student Work Abroad Program (SWAP).

■ By Plane

The first challenge of the budget traveler is getting there. Call every toll-free number and ask about discounts. Allow knowledgeable **travel agents** to guide you; better yet, have an agent who specializes in Central America guide you.

Seniors and youth can also get great deals. Sunday newspapers often have travel sections that list bargain fares from the local airport. More accessible is Michael McColl's *The Worldwide Guide to Cheap Airfare* (US$15), an incredibly useful guide for finding cheap airfare. Outsmart airline reps with the phone-book-sized *Official Airline Guide* (check your local library; at US$359/yr, the tome costs as much as some flights), a monthly guide listing nearly every scheduled flight in the world and toll-free numbers for all the airlines, allowing you to call in reservations directly.

There is also a steadily increasing amount of travel information to be found on the Internet. The *Official Airline Guide* now also has a web site (http://www.oag.com) which allows access to flight schedules. (One-time hook-up fee US$25 and a user's fee (17¢-47¢/min). The site also provides information on hotels, cruises, and rail and ferry schedules. **TravelHUB** (http://www.travelhub.com) will help you search for travel agencies on the web. The **Air Traveler's Handbook** (http://www.cis.ohio-state.edu/hypertext/faq/usenet/travel/air/handbook/top.html) is an excellent source of general information on air travel. Marc-David Seidel's **Airlines of the Web** (http://www.itn.net/airlines) provides links to pages and 800 numbers for most of the world's airlines. The newsgroup **rec.travel.air** is a good source of tips on current bargains.

COMMERCIAL AIRLINES

The commercial airlines' lowest regular offer is the **Advance Purchase Excursion Fare (APEX);** specials advertised in newspapers may be cheaper, but have more restrictions and fewer available seats. APEX fares provide you with confirmed reservations and allow "open-jaw" tickets (landing in and returning from different cities). Generally, reservations must be made seven to 21 days in advance, with seven- to 14-

day minimum, up to 90-day maximum stay limits, and hefty cancellation and change penalties (fees rise in summer). Book APEX fares early during peak season; by May you will have a hard time getting the departure date you want. Even if you pay an airline's lowest published fare, you may waste hundreds of dollars. For the adventurous or the bargain-hungry, there are other, perhaps more inconvenient or time-consuming options, but before shopping around it is a good idea to find out the average commercial price in order to measure just how great a "bargain" you are offered.

TICKET CONSOLIDATORS

Ticket consolidators resell unsold tickets on commercial and charter airlines at unpublished fares. The consolidator market is by and large international; domestic flights, if they do exist, are typically for cross-country flights. Consolidator flights are the best deals if you are traveling on short notice; you bypass advance purchase requirements because you aren't tangled in airline bureaucracy); on a high-priced trip; to an offbeat destination; or in the peak season, when published fares are sky-rocket. Fares sold by consolidators are generally as much as 30-40% cheaper. There are rarely age constraints or stay limitations, but unlike tickets bought through an airline, you won't be able to use your tickets on another flight if you miss yours, and you will have to go back to the consolidator to get a refund, rather than the airline. Keep in mind that these tickets are often for coach seats on connecting (not direct) flights on foreign airlines, and that frequent-flyer miles may not be credited. Decide what you can and can't live with before shopping.

Consolidators come in three varieties: wholesale only; specialty agencies (both wholesale and retail); and **bucket shops** (discount retail agencies). As a private customer, you only come in contact with the last; you have access to a larger market if you use a travel agent who can get tickets from wholesale consolidators. Look for bucket shops' tiny ads in the travel section of weekend papers; in the U.S., the *Sunday New York Times* is a good source. In London, a call to the **Air Travel Advisory**

Bureau (tel. (0171) 636 50 00) can provide names of reliable consolidators and discount flight specialists.

Be a smart shopper; check out the competition. Among the many reputable and trustworthy companies are, unfortunately, some shady wheeler-dealers. Contact your local **Better Business Bureau** to find out how long the company has been in business and its track record. It is preferable to deal with consolidators close to home so you can visit in person. Ask to receive your tickets as quickly as possible so you have time to fix any problems. Get the company's policy in writing: insist on a **receipt** that gives full details about the tickets, refunds, and restrictions, and record who you talked to and when. It may be worth paying with a credit card (despite the 2-5% fee) so you can stop payment if you never receive your tickets.

For destinations **worldwide,** try **Airfare Busters,** (offices in Washington, D.C. (tel. (202) 776-0478), Boca Raton, FL (tel. (561) 994-9590), and Houston, TX (tel. (800) 232-8783); **Cheap Tickets,** offices in Los Angeles, CA, San Francisco, CA, Honolulu, HI, Seattle, WA, and New York, NY, (tel. (800) 377-1000); or **Moment's Notice,** New York, NY (tel. (718) 234-6295; fax 234-6450; http://www.moments-notice.com) offers air tickets, tours, and hotels; US$25 annual fee. **Travel Avenue,** Chicago, IL (tel. (800) 333-3335; fax (312) 876-1254; http://www.travelavenue.com) will search for the lowest international airfare available, including consolidated prices, and will even give you a rebate on fares over US$300.

Kelly Monaghan's *Consolidators: Air Travel's Bargain Basement* (US$7 plus US$2 shipping), from the Intrepid Traveler, P.O. Box 438, New York, NY 10034 (email intreptrav@aol.com), is a valuable source for more information and lists of consolidators by location and destination. Cyber-resources include **World Wide** (http://www.tmn.com/wwwanderer/WWWa) and Edward Hasbrouck's incredibly informative **Airline ticket consolidators and bucket shops** (http://www.gnn.com/gnn/wic/wics/trav.97.html). A few of the many consolidators that offer flights to Central America are **Air Travel Discounts** (tel. (800) 888-2621) in New York; **Embassy Tours** (tel. (800) 299-5284) in Dallas, TX; **Holiday Tours** (tel. (800) 393-1212) in California; and **Mena Tours** (tel. (800) 937-6362) in Chicago, IL.

STAND-BY FLIGHTS

Airhitch, 2641 Broadway, 3rd Floor, New York, NY 10025 (tel. (800) 326-2009 or (212) 864-2000, fax 864-5489) and Los Angeles, CA (tel. (310) 726-5000), will add a certain thrill to deciding when you will leave and where exactly you will end up. Complete flexibility is necessary; flights cost US$175 each way when departing from the Northeast, $269 from the West Coast or Northwest, $229 from the Midwest, and $209 from the Southeast. The snag is that you buy not a ticket, but the promise that you will get to a destination near where you're intending to go within a window of time (usually 5 days) from a location in a region you've specified. You call in before your date-range to hear all of your flight options for the next seven days and your probability of boarding. You then decide which flights you want to try to make and present a voucher at the airport which grants you the right to board a flight on a space-available basis. This procedure must be followed again for the return trip. Be aware that you may only receive a monetary refund if all available flights which departed within your date-range from the specified region are full, but future travel credit is always available.

Air-Tech, Ltd., 588 Broadway #204, New York, NY 10012 (tel. (212) 219-7000, fax 219-0066) offers a very similar service. Their travel window is one to four days. Upon registration and payment, Air-Tech sends you a flight pass with a contact date falling soon before your Travel Window, when you are to call them for flight instructions. You must go through the same procedure to return—and that no refunds are granted unless the company fails to get you a seat before your travel window expires. Air-Tech also arranges courier flights and regular confirmed-reserved flights at discounts.

Be sure to read all the fine print in your agreements with either company. Be warned that it is difficult to receive refunds, and that clients' vouchers will not be honored if an airline fails to receive payment in time.

CHARTER FLIGHTS

Charters are flights a tour operator contracts with an airline (usually one specializing in charters) to fly extra loads of passengers to peak-season destinations. Charters are often cheaper than flights on scheduled airlines, especially during peak seasons, although fare wars, consolidator tickets, and small airlines can beat charter prices. Some charters operate nonstop, and restrictions on minimum advance-purchase and minimum stay are more lenient. However, they fly less frequently than major airlines, and are almost always fully booked. Schedules and itineraries may also change or be cancelled at the last moment (as late as 48 hours before the trip, and without a full refund), and check-in, boarding, and baggage claim are often much slower. As always, pay with a credit card if you can; consider traveler's insurance against trip interruption. Try **Interworld** (tel. (305) 443-4929, fax 443-0351); **Travac** (tel. (800) 872-8800; fax (212) 714-9063; email mail@travac.com; http://www.travac.com) or **Rebel,** Valencia, CA (tel. (800) 227-3235; fax (805)-294-0981; http://rebeltours.com; e-mail travel@rebeltours.com) or Orlando, FL (tel. (800) 732-3588).

COURIER COMPANIES AND FREIGHTERS

Those who travel lightly should consider flying internationally as a **courier.** The company hiring you will use your checked luggage space for freight; you're only allowed to bring carry-ons. You are responsible for the safe delivery of the baggage claim slips (given to you by a courier company representative) to the representative waiting for you when you arrive—don't screw up or you will be blacklisted as a courier. You will probably never see the cargo you are transporting—the company handles it all—and airport officials know that couriers are not responsible for the baggage checked for them. There are some restrictions: you must be over 21 (18 in some cases), have a valid passport, and procure your own visa (if necessary); most flights are round-trip only with short fixed-length stays (usually one week); only single tickets are issued (but a companion may be able to get a next-day flight). Most flights are from New York. For an annual fee of $45, the **International Association of Air Travel Couriers,** 8 South J St., P.O. Box 1349, Lake Worth, Florida 33460 (tel. (561) 582-8320) informs travelers of courier opportunities worldwide. **NOW Voyager,** 74 Varick St. #307, New York, NY 10013 (tel. (212) 431-1616; fax 334-5243); email info@nowvoyagertravel.com; http://www.nowvoyagertravel.com), acts as an agent for many courier flights, as well as a consolidator, worldwide primarily from New York. Other agents to try are **Halbart Express,** 147-05 176th St., Jamaica, NY 11434 (tel. (718) 656-5000; fax 917-0708) and **Discount Travel International** (tel. (212) 362-3636).

■ By Bus or Train

All overland routes to Central America from the U.S. necessarily go through Mexico. **Greyhound** serves many U.S.-Mexico border towns, including El Paso and Brownsville, TX. Buses tend not to cross the border, but you can always pick up Mexican bus lines on the other side. **Tres Estrellas de Oro, Estrella Blanca,** and **Transportes Del Norte** provide service from the border. It is also possible to travel by **Amtrak** to San Antonio or El Paso (US$318-518 round-trip from New York) and bus to the border towns or, from El Paso, walk across the border to Ciudad Juárez.

Follow whichever bus route suits your fancy to get through Mexico (see *Let's Go: Mexico* for detailed information). **Omnibus de México** (tel. (5)567-67-56 or (5)567-72-86) buses run to and from most major destinations through their hub in Mexico City. **Cristóbal Colón** (tel. 916-2-61-22) is the major bus line in Chiapas, and goes right to the Guatemalan border. The **Batty Brothers** line goes from Chetumal, Mexico to Belize, if that's your preferred entry point.

For wild adventures of another kind, **Green Tortoise Adventure Travel,** 494 Broadway, San Francisco, CA 94133 (tel. (800) 867-8647 or (415) 956-7500; fax (415) 956-4900; email info@greentortoise.com; http://www.greentortoise.com), maintains a fleet of old diesel coaches, dubbed "hostels on wheels," complete with foam mattresses, sofa seats, and dinettes. Travelers can expect communal cooking and frequent jaunts off the road for hikes, swims, and explorations including "The Southern Migration" runs from San Francisco, California to Antigua, Guatemala, takes 23 days, and costs US$900 (includes food). There are also trips which provide *en route* language instruction. Green Tortoise will also help arrange low-cost air travel for your return. Book ahead, as trips fill up *fast*.

Traveling through Mexico by train takes longer, but is considerably less expensive than by bus. The government-run Mexican railroads operate under the name of **Ferrocarriles Nacionales de Mexico**. Trains run from the U.S. border at Nogales, Piedras Negras, Nuevo Laredo, Matamoros, and Mexicali.

■ By Car

Cruising to Central America from the U.S. with a car can be an inexpensive way to get through Mexico, but it could easily turn into a nightmarish tale of mayhem. Be prepared for the worst, make sure your shock-absorbers are primed, and come up with several ways to ensure your car's security; someone will likely try to break into it. In the United States, the **American Automobile Association (AAA)** offers emergency road, travel, and auto insurance services (free for members, for a fee if not). For emergency road services, call (800) 222-4357; to become a member, call (800) 926-4222. Check out their web site at www.aaa.com. Once in Mexico, the AAA-affiliated **Asociación Mexicana Automovilística, A.C. (AMA)** (for emergency road service, call (5) 58-89-355 or (5) 58-87-055) provides information about car travel in Mexico, up-to-date road maps, publications, and emergency road assistance.

All non-Mexican **car insurance** is invalid in Mexico, no matter what your policy says. You will probably be able to buy insurance at the border from one of many small insurance offices located next door to immigration offices. **Sanborn's,** Home Office, 2009 South 10th Street, McAllen, TX 78503 (tel. (210) 686-0711; fax (210) 686-0732) offers Mexican and Central American insurance with all the trimmings, including road maps, newsletters, a ride board, a mile-by-mile guide to Mexico and Central America, 24 hour medical emergency hotline, legal assistance, towing and roadside aid, and "Mexico Mike," a researcher for travel guides. Write to Mike care of Dept. N at the McAllen address for up-to-date information on driving in Mexico, or check out his web page at www.mexicomike.com. Remember that if you are in an accident, the police might hold you in jail until everything is sorted out and all claims are settled. If you can prove your ability to pay, they will release you.

ONCE THERE

■ Getting Around

BY PLANE

Flights between Central American cities are usually cheap (compared to domestic fares in the U.S.) and are considerably more time-efficient than long, winding bus routes. Single-, and twin-engine planes travel within countries, offering unique flying experiences; some planes are so small that one lucky passenger actually sits up front with the pilot. Make sure a line is reputably safe before boarding; some are not, hence the ominous "In God We Trust" signs hanging over the doors of some planes.

BY BUS

Most budget visitors to Central America get from place to place by bus. Direct, first-class trips are often available between major cities, but otherwise, expect a few harrowing adventures on the legendary Central American chicken buses. Don't expect to get to your destination on time. Worn shocks let passengers feel every bump in the rough roads, and drivers have few qualms about putting it into high gear on windy downhills. It's usually best to snag a window seat (unless you're tall) to enjoy the view and for cool, fresh air. Getting the shadier side is an even better bonus. Traveling by bus at night is often unsafe; check with authorities before doing so. Be particularly careful about your luggage.

BY CAR

If driving in a **taxi,** be sure to tell the driver where you want to go before you get in. If he agrees to take you, always ask how much the trip will cost. If you think he's asking too much, you can either bite the bullet, try to bargain him down, or simply find another cab. Beware the higher-than-normal *gringo* rate. Taxi drivers don't like it when pedestrians or other drivers ask them for directions, and often have no problems with leading someone astray. Women are advised to always sit in the back of a taxi to avoid unwanted physical attention.

If you have your own **car,** the durability and security of your car are of unspeakable importance for successful travel through Central America. Parts, gas, and trust-worthy service stations are all hard to come by, so be prepared for every possible occurrence. Come equipped with spare parts and thorough know-how. Hide baggage in the trunk, although savvy thieves can tell if a car is heavily loaded by the way it is settled on its tires. Park your vehicle in garages or well-traveled areas. Unleaded gas is no longer as hard to get as in years past, but even if you do find an unleaded pump, it may be filled with leaded gasoline. Mechanically inclined drivers might want to order a "test" pipe from a specialty parts house to replace the catalytic converter so that the car can process regular.

Be careful driving during the rainy season (May-Oct.), when roads are often in poor condition, potholes become craters, and landslides are common. At night, pedestrians and livestock pop up on the roadway at the darndest times. This doesn't seem to bother the locals, many of whom drive without headlights. If you can help it, don't drive at night. When approaching a one-lane bridge, labeled *puente angosto* or *solo*

carril, the first driver to flash headlights has the right of way. Lanes are narrow, so if a truck tries to pass your car on a two-lane road, you might need to pull off onto the gravel or dirt in order to give it enough room. Highway drivers increasingly have become victims of **assaults** and **robberies.** Be especially careful when traveling alone.

BY THUMB

> *Let's Go* urges you to use common sense if you decide to hitch and to seriously consider all possible risks before you make that decision. The information listed below and throughout the book is not intended to recommend hitchhiking; *Let's Go* does not recommend hitchhiking as a means of transportation.

The Central Americans who pick up tourists are commonly friendly, offering meals, tours, or other extras, but suspicion is often warranted. Those who hitch should find out where the driver is going before they get in and think twice if he or she opens the door quickly and offers to drive anywhere. Do not accept a ride if any cause for concern arises; make an excuse and wait for another car to come along. Women should never hitchhike alone. Never accept a ride without sizing up the driver. On many highways, *banditos* are common.

Before getting in, make sure the passenger window or door opens from inside. If there are several people in the car, do not sit in the middle. Avoid the back seat of a two-door car. Keep backpacks and other baggage easily accessible—don't let the driver store them in the trunk. If you have trouble getting out for any reason, affecting the pose of someone about to vomit works wonders.

It's said that those who appear neat and travel light have a better chance of getting a ride. Some drivers may ask for payment for the ride, especially in areas where no public transportation exists. Truck drivers often earn extra revenue by taking on passengers. Riders should always ask what a ride in a truck will cost before getting in; though it may be costly, the truckers' prices are usually based on expenses.

■ Accommodations

HOTELS

Every large city in Central America offers a wide range of hotels, from the dirt-cheap (where the dirt comes cheaply) to the ultra-ritzy. The smaller the town, the narrower the selection. Usually located within a block or two of the main town square, the cheapest hotels rarely provide private bathrooms or other amenities. Slightly more expensive, better equipped hotels usually exist in the same district. Before accepting any room, ask to see it, and always ask if the price includes any meals. Also, don't forget to consider whether there are fans or air-conditioning, and beware of the potential for nerve-wracking noise (usually based on the room's proximity to the street or bus station). If the hotel looks like it hasn't seen a customer in several days, bargaining may work wonders, especially if you offer to stay a number of days. For a room with one bed, request *un cuarto con una cama*. If bedding down with a fellow wayfarer, ask for one *con dos camas* (with two beds). Some proprietors might not allow unmarried mixed-sex couples to share a bed, so be prepared to settle for separation or to pose as newlyweds.

Hotels in Central America often lock their doors at night, and small-town establishments may do so surprisingly early. A locked door doesn't necessarily mean "closed for the night," as someone usually is on duty. By arriving early in small towns or calling ahead if you can't avoid arriving late, and by checking with the hotel desk before going out for a late night on the town, you'll save yourself some anxiety and the proprietor some sleep.

Prepare yourself for toilets without flush mechanisms; before using the john, look for a bucket and fill it with water. When you're done, quickly pour the water in the bowl and watch in amazement as the laws of lavatory gravity do their magical stuff.

HOSTELS

In Central America many hostels are independently owned and not part of large umbrella organizations, but Hosteling International (HI) does have a few member-hostels there, particularly in Costa Rica. Check out the **Internet Guide to Hosteling** (http://hostels.com). Prices range from US$5 to US$25 per night, but those that belong to hostel associations often have lower rates for members. Reservations for over 300 HI hostels (see listing below) may be made via the International Booking Network (IBN), a computerized system, allowing you to book HI hostels in advance for a nominal fee (tel. (202) 783-6161). Every country has its own Hosteling International office. In the **U.S.,** call (202) 783-6161; in **Canada,** call (613) 237-7884; in **England and Wales,** call (01727) 855215; in **Ireland,** call (01232) 324733 or 315435; in **New Zealand,** call (03) 379 9970; and in **South Africa,** call (021) 24 2511.

■ Camping & the Outdoors

CAMPING AND HIKING EQUIPMENT

Purchase **equipment** before you leave. Whether buying or renting, finding sturdy and light equipment is a must.

    Sleeping bags: Most good **sleeping bags** are rated by "season," or the lowest outdoor temperature at which they will keep you warm. Sleeping bags are made of down (warmer and lighter, but more expensive, and miserable when wet) or of synthetic material (heavier, more durable, and warmer when wet). Keep the climate in mind as the dry lowlands require different gear than the humid tropics.

    Tents: Just as when selecting a mate, your major considerations in selecting a tent should be size and shape. The best **tents** are free-standing, with their own frames and suspension systems; they set up quickly and require no staking (except in high winds). Low profile dome tents are the best all-around, with little unnecessary bulk. Seal the seams of your tent with waterproofer, and make sure it has a rain fly.

    Backpacks: see **Luggage,** p. 11.

    Other necessities: Rain gear should come in two pieces, a jacket and pants, rather than a poncho. Synthetics, like polypropylene tops, socks, and long underwear, along with a pile jacket, will keep you warm even when wet. When camping in autumn, winter, or spring, bring along a "space blanket," which helps you to retain your body heat and doubles as a groundcloth (US$5-15). Plastic canteens or water bottles keep water cooler than metal ones do, and are virtually shatter- and leak-proof. Bring water-purification tablets for when you can't boil water. Most campgrounds provide campfire sites, but you may want to bring a small metal grate or grill of your own. A first aid kit, swiss army knife, insect repellent, calamine lotion, and waterproof matches or a lighter are essential camping items. Other items include: a battery-operated lantern, a plastic groundcloth, a nylon tarp, a waterproof backpack cover (although you can also store your belongings in plastic bags inside your backpack), and a stuff sack or plastic bag to keep your sleeping bag dry.

The mail-order companies listed below offer lower prices than those you'll find in many stores, but shop around to determine what items actually look like and weigh.

    Eastern Mountain Sports (EMS), One Vose Farm Rd., Peterborough, NH 03458 (tel. (603) 924-9591), has stores throughout the U.S. Though slightly higher-priced, they provide excellent service and guaranteed customer satisfaction on most items sold. They don't have a catalogue, and they generally don't take mail or phone orders; call the above number for the store nearest you.

    L.L. Bean, Freeport, ME 04033-0001 (tel. (800) 441-5713 in Canada or the U.S.; (0800) 962 954 in the U.K.; (207) 552-6878 elsewhere; fax (207) 552-3080; http://www.llbean.com). This monolithic equipment and outdoor clothing supplier offers high quality and loads of information. Call or write for their free catalogue.

Mountain Designs, P.O. Box 1472, Fortitude Valley, Queensland 4006, Australia (tel. (07) 3252 8894; fax (07) 3252 4569) is a leading Australian manufacturer and mail order retailer of camping and climbing gear.

WILDERNESS AND SAFETY CONCERNS

Never pitch a tent in Central America without first asking local authorities. Sleeping near a town risks attracting thieves and hostile property owners; heading into the wild to camp is equally dangerous. Regardless of whether you're venturing out on a day trip to Maya ruins or embarking on a full-fledged camping expedition in the rain forest, be safety-conscious at all times.

The three most important things to remember when hiking or camping are: **stay warm, stay dry, stay hydrated.** The vast majority of life-threatening wilderness problems stem from a failure to follow this advice. On any hike, however brief, you should pack enough equipment to survive should disaster befall. This includes **rain gear, hat** and **mittens,** a **first-aid kit, high energy food,** and **water.** Dress in warm layers of **synthetic materials** designed for the outdoors, or wear **wool.** Pile fleece jackets and Gore-Tex® raingear are excellent choices (see above). Never rely on **cotton** for warmth; this "death cloth" will be absolutely useless should it get wet. Be sure to wear supportive hiking boots appropriate for the terrain. Your boots should be sized so that they fit snugly and comfortably over two wool socks and a thin liner sock.

Don't underestimate how cold it can get at night in Central America, especially in the highlands. If possible, let someone know where you are going hiking. Above all, do not attempt a hike beyond your ability. See **Health** (p. 14) for information about outdoor ailments such as giardia, rabies, and insects, as well as basic medical concerns and first-aid. A good guide to outdoor survival is *How to Stay Alive in the Woods,* by Bradford Angier (Macmillan, US$8).

ENVIRONMENTALLY RESPONSIBLE TOURISM

Future tourists should be able to appreciate Central America's natural wonders, too, so try to leave the wilderness as you found it. At the very least, practice responsible **"minimum impact"** techniques. Leave no trace of your presence when you leave a site. Don't unnecessarily trample vegetation by walking off established paths; do not clear new campsites. Because firewood is scarce in popular areas, campers are asked to make small fires using only dead branches or brush; using a campstove is the more cautious (and efficient) way to cook. Make sure your campsite is at least 150 feet from any water source. If there are no toilet facilities, bury human waste (but not paper) at least four inches deep and above the high-water line 150 feet or more from any water supplies and campsites. Always pack your trash in a plastic bag and carry it with you until you reach a trash can.

Responsible tourism means more than picking up your litter, however. Growing numbers of "ecotourists" are asking hard questions of resort owners and tour operators about how their policies affect local ecologies and local economies. Some try to give something back to the regions they enjoy by volunteering for environmental organizations at home or abroad. Above all, responsible tourism means being aware of your impact on the places you visit, and taking responsibility for your actions.

If you want to know more about "ecotourism" or responsible travel in a particular region, these organizations are good places to start:

Center for Responsible Tourism, P.O. Box 827, San Anselmo, CA 94979 (tel. (415) 258-6594).

Ecotourism Association of Australia, P.O. Box 3839, Alice Springs, Northern Territory 0871, Australia (tel. (011) 61-89-528-308).

Ecumenical Coalition on Third World Tourism, P.O. Box 24, Chokrakhebua, Bangkok 10230, Thailand (tel. (011) 66-2-510-7287).

■ Keeping in Touch

MAIL

Central American mail service ranges from slow and erratic to speedy and reliable, depending on the country and fate's whims. (See the "Keeping in Touch" sections for each country for more specific information.)

Sending mail to Central America

You can have letters sent to you in Central America through **Lista de Correos** (a.k.a. *Entrega General* or *Poste Restante),* a letter-holding service similar to General Delivery in the U.S. Mark the envelope "HOLD" and address it, for example, "Nikia BERGAN, Poste Restante, City, Country." The letter should also be marked *Favor de retener hasta la llegada* ("Please hold until arrival"). Mail sent to *Lista de Correos* should be addressed to a first and last name only, capitalizing and underlining the name under which the item should be filed. Keep names as simple as possible. Because Latin American *apellidos* (paternal last names) fall in the middle of the written name, confusion arises for foreigners with more than a simple first and last name, or in the case of mail addressed to more than one person.

The mail will go to a special desk in the central post office, unless you specify a post office by street address or postal code. When picking up mail sent to you via *Lista de Correos,* look for a list posted in the post office. Check it carefully for any possible misspellings or confusions. If there is no list posted, ask the attendant, "¿Está la lista de hoy?" (Is today's list here?) Letters and packages will be held for varying lengths of time, but count on two weeks. Bring a passport or other ID to pick up your mail. It's wise to use the Spanish abbreviations or names for countries (EEUU or EUA for the U.S.). Write *Por Avión* on all postcards and letters not otherwise marked, unless you don't mind it arriving in the next millennium.

American Express offices throughout the world will act as a mail service for cardholders if you contact them in advance. Under this free **"Client Letter Service,"** they will hold mail for 30 days, forward upon request, and accept telegrams. Just like *Poste Restante,* the last name of the person to whom the mail is addressed should be capitalized and underlined. Some offices will offer these services to non-cardholders (especially those who have purchased AmEx *travelers' cheques*), but you must call ahead to make sure. Check the **Practical Information** section of the countries you plan to visit; *Let's Go* lists AmEx office locations for most large cities. A list is available from AmEx (tel. (800) 528-4800) in *Traveler's Companion.*

Sending mail from Central America

Airmail often reaches the U.S. in as few as six days, but can just as easily take a month or more. It takes even longer (at least two weeks) to Europe and other destinations, since mail is usually routed through U.S. mail. Official estimates average 40 days by boat, but it may take months. Anything important should be sent registered mail, or duplicates should be sent. Never deposit anything important in the black holes known euphemistically as mailboxes.

While it is often possible to send packages from smaller towns, post offices in large cities provide more reliable service. In order to send packages, you must provide a list of contents including estimated value and nature of the package ("gift" works best), address, and return address. In a trade office, you may need to show receipts for each item purchased.

TELEPHONES

Calling Central America

Patience is the key to success when trying to call Central America from another country, or even when calling town to town within a country. Don't be surprised if no one picks up right away when you call information. To call Central America from the

United States, dial the universal international access code (011) followed by the country code, the city code, and the local number. Country codes and city codes may sometimes be listed with a zero in front (e.g. 502-09), but when using 011, drop successive zeros (e.g., dial 011-502-9). In some areas, you will have to have an operator place the call. Country-specific **telephone codes** are listed in each chapter's Essentials section. In some cases, **city codes** are listed under Telephones in the applicable Practical Information sections.

Calling Home

Many public phones are out of service, and others only accept rare low-denomination coins. Few have access to international lines. If you speak Spanish and can't reach an international operator, call a national or local operator, who will connect you. The term for a **collect call** is *llamada por cobrar* or *llamada con cobro revertido*. Calling from hotels is usually faster, but can mean hefty surcharges. Fortunately, service from AT&T and other companies is improving, and collect calls with English-speaking operators are available from more and more central telephone offices. It's sometimes cheaper to access an international line, deposit just enough money to be able to say "Call me," and give your number.

A **calling card** is another, cheaper alternative; your local long-distance phone company will have a number for you to dial while traveling (either toll-free or charged as a local call) that connects instantly to an operator in your home country. For more info, call **AT&T** about its **USADirect** and **World Connect** services (tel. (800) 331-1140, from abroad (412) 553-7458), **Sprint** (tel. (800) 877-4646), or **MCI World-Phone** and **World Reach** (tel. in the U.S. (800) 996-7535). MCI's WorldPhone also provides access to MCI's Traveler's Assist, which gives legal and medical advice, exchange rate information, and translation services. In Canada, contact Bell Canada **Canada Direct** (tel. (800) 565 4708); in the U.K., British Telecom **BT Direct** (tel. (800) 34 51 44); in Ireland, Telecom Éireann **Ireland Direct** (tel. (800) 250 250); in Australia, Telstra **Australia Direct** (tel. 13 22 00); in New Zealand, **Telecom New Zealand** (tel. 123); and in South Africa, **Telkom South Africa** (tel. 09 03).

FAXES AND TELEGRAMS

A surprisingly large number of Central American businesses have fax machines; even low-tech enterprises like laundromats seem convinced that capitalistic legitimacy means owning one. As a result, it can be easier to reach some people by fax than by telephone. Public faxes are often available at telephone offices, for both sending and receiving. International telegrams can also be faster and cheaper than using the phone; most post or telephone offices provide telegram services.

CENTRAL AMERICA: LIFE AND TIMES

■ History

Like misfit pieces of an unsolvable jigsaw puzzle, the countries of Central America seem to have been doomed to permanent political fragmentation. Bound together by geography, language, culture, and history, the modern Central American nations have still never successfully attained the isthmian unity for which many leaders have struggled. The political turbulence of the last few decades has received unprecedented attention from the international press, but the region has had a long history of division and turmoil. Modern visitors who enjoy Central America for its unique heterogeneity often aren't aware that the region's current status is the result of a historical roller coaster with more downs than ups.

Some archaeologists speculate that humans inhabited the area as many as 40,000 years ago, but evidence suggests the actual development of civilizations around 3000 years ago, when Mesoamerican, South American, and Caribbean populations spread over the area and began to exchange ideas. Though the Maya maintained the most developed **Pre-Columbian civilization** in Central America (see **Maya Marvels,** p. 41), they were by no means the area's only natives when Columbus arrived. The Chibcha inhabited Panamá and Costa Rica after migrating from the South, the Pipil and Nicarao groups lived in modern day El Salvador and Nicaragua, and the Miskito, Sumo, and Rama tribes filled the **Mosquitia** of Honduras, where they still live today, a particularly impressive feat given the brute swiftness with which the Spanish conquered and absorbed many other indigenous groups after 1500.

The first Europeans to come to Central America, **Rodrigo de Bastidas** and **Christopher Columbus,** were merely interested in exploration; they bypassed settlement of the area, perhaps not recognizing the region's economic potential. But the value of the area's riches was not lost on **Vasco Núñez de Balboa,** who not only settled in Panamá, but also fostered relations with the Indians and found his way through to the Pacific. Until 1517, the Indians' Spanish-induced suffering was limited to the diseases the Europeans brought with them, but following the execution of Balboa and the ascension of **General Pedrarias Dávila,** a period of enslavement and genocide began. In a few years, Pedrarias had all but conquered the southern part of Central America; meanwhile, **Hector Cortés's** forces headed south from Mexico, spreading the Spanish brutality to the rest of the land bridge. The Spanish forces killed millions of Indians, and, under the **Spanish New Laws** of 1542, enslaved millions more; simultaneously establishing a tradition of oppressing the *indígenas* with lasting ramifications.

Using the wealth of precious metals taken from the region, strong Spanish leaders like **Pedro de Alvarado** helped form the **Kingdom of Guatemala,** which consisted of Chiapas, Mexico, and Costa Rica. Meanwhile, Panamá grew steadily as the trans-isthmian crossing point for riches stripped from the Peruvian Incas. As wealth increased, so did the divisions within the class system, in which Creole landholders and Spanish administrators ruled Indian workers. Haughty municipal councils competed for riches, blocking unification of the region. As wealth from exports increased during the next centuries, so did regionalistic sentiment; no ruler was willing to let his profits slip into his neighbors' coffers. By the 19th century, European wars had weakened Spain's hold on the isthmus, and finally, the Spanish allowed the installation of the **Cadíz Constitution** of 1812, which increased the colonies' representation in the national Parliament. Soon thereafter, the constitution was annulled, a royal act which divided Conservatives from Liberals.

Spain's Liberal Revolution of 1820 set the stage for Central America's most successful attempt at union. In 1823, an assembly officially decreed the independence of the **United Province of Central America,** which included Guatemala, El Salvador, Honduras, Nicaragua, and Costa Rica (Belize was under British control and Panamá was a part of Colombia). However, though the states were granted a great deal of autonomy, state leaders refused to adhere to the federation's constitutional laws, and before long, jealousies and self-interest frustrated the attempt at unity. Conservatives (royalists), pushing to centralize power, fought the reforming ideals of Liberal (republican) leaders such as Honduras' **Francisco Morazan,** and by 1840, the states were fragmented anew.

The year 1847 marked the start of the formation of the Central American nations as we know them today. The four recently divided republics joined forces briefly against Nicaragua's (American) "president" **William Walker,** but his defeat did not lead to the renewed unity for which many liberals had hoped. After defeating Walker, the other four states instituted liberal policies like those the American had implemented; only in scarred Nicaragua did liberalism take longer to initiate. Simultaneously, leaders such as **Justo Rufino Barrios** of Guatemala made countless efforts to reinstall the federation, but could not overcome the lack of unity and infrastructure within the individual countries themselves, where local community spirit was becoming more deeply entrenched. Walker's bizarre reign in Nicaragua was an ominous hint of what the countries could expect from the next 150 years—heavy-handed U.S. intervention in Central American affairs, first to satiate economic interests and later to pursue political objectives. For the next 80 years, "liberals" throughout Central America tried to hammer their nations into shape, supporting the development of export crops such as coffee and bananas, but found that the U.S. was having more and more influence on their policies. U.S. President **Teddy Roosevelt** sent down a warship to settle disputes between El Salvador and Guatemala; Nicaragua and Panamá competed to be the site of the U.S. trans-continental bridge; and, most importantly, American fruit producers such as the **United Fruit Company** (known as *El Pulpo*, or "the Octopus") became increasingly formidable influences and exacerbated the class divisions between land owners and laborers.

The political turbulence of the last few decades has received unprecedented attention from the international press.

This lengthy period of inequality and injustice to workers reached its pinnacle during the Great Depression, after which unrest and revolution were inevitable. Most Central American nations resorted to harsh dictatorial rule throughout the Second World War, when all five countries joined the side of the Allies. Following the war, Central America was drawn into the **Cold War.** Today, following a century of bloody revolt, stern governmental rule, and constant upheaval, Central American unity seems unimaginable. But despite strict borders between the countries, all share the heavy burdens common to developing nations, including poverty and illiteracy. Some idealists seek another attempt at unification; the formation of the **Organization of Central American States** in 1951 was a step in this direction, as is the **Central American Common Market.** Proponents of unity theorize that the combined economies of Central America could rise above the often desperate situations in which the countries independently find themselves. Others worry that such a move will only compound an already severe problem. Either way, the nations of Central America have developed distinct personalities and are unlikely to erase their borders anytime soon.

▓ Maya Marvels

Mesoamerica has long lured scores of amateur and professional anthropologists and archaeologists. The **Aztecs** of Mexico, **Incas** of Peru, and other ancient civilizations indigenous to Latin America left behind intriguing remnants, but Central America holds the most copious and impressive selection of artifacts—the most incredible of those of the Ancient Maya.

"Incredible" can be taken literally in the case of early European explorers' interpretation of the ruins they discovered. Stumbling upon the towering remains of temples, structures covered with alien and complex hieroglyphics, the first wave of *conquistadores* found it impossible to imagine that these monumental artifacts could have sprung from the hands and minds of the region's natives. Even as they were laying waste to the postclassic outposts of high Maya civilization, Cortés and his soldiers undermined its greatest achievements by assuming them to be the result of some previous Old World expedition to the Americas. Today, archaeological evidence shows soundly that the indigenous inhabitants of the Americas, including the Maya, were profoundly original.

Of all the New World cultures, the Maya were the most artistically and intellectually developed, although neither their political nor economic systems ever matched those of the Aztecs and Incas. Still, the binding cultural unity of the various Maya city-states survived until 1697, when the Guatemalan city of **Tayasal** fell to siege. Some Maya, the **Lacandón,** were able to resist subjugation during the entire colonial period, waging a guerilla war from jungled highlands throughout the Spanish rule.

If it weren't for the Maya's distinctive cultural legacy, we would probably perceive the ruins as coming from several competing tribes and not from one vast, varying civilization. The diversity and originality that boggles the minds of anthropologists is even more astounding considering just how disjointed the civilization actually was. At different times, the ancient Maya are thought to have inhabited **Chiapas** and **Yucatán,** the southernmost parts of Mexico, as well as all of Guatemala and Belize, most of El Salvador and Honduras, and even parts of Nicaragua. That's not to mention the area populated by related groups such as the **Olmec** and central Mexican **Nahautl.** Still, the civilization never covered the whole region at one time. In fact, just as culture set the Maya apart from other New World Civilizations, so did it define different periods in Maya history, commonly divided into three eras—the preclassic, the classic, and the postclassic periods.

The onset of the preclassic period is difficult to determine, but is generally thought to coincide with the development of several highland cities near the Pacific coast of the isthmus around 500 BC. The central metropolis was **Kaminaljuyú,** in southern Guatemala; other remains, such as **Tazumal** and **San Andrés,** stand in modern El Salvador. The preclassic Maya of the north experimented with agriculture, but not until the classic period, in the first millennium AD, did scientific and cultural centers begin to descend into the hotter and more humid land of Belize, northern Guatemala, the Atlantic coast of Honduras, and the Yucatán Peninsula. By then, the Maya had already started to develop their systems of writing, time-keeping, and math. The highland regions remained populated, but the truly cutting-edge Maya culture pressed on

Cutting-edge Maya culture pressed on toward Atlantic jungles, where the richest ruins have been found.

toward Atlantic jungles, where archaeologists have found the richest and most famous ruins. The most famous Maya architecture dates back to this period, and it's for their majestic temples and **stelae** (carved and marked altars) that colossal cities such as Tikal and Copán are so popular as tourist sites. Nearby, less spectacular remains hint that suburban sprawl is hardly a new trend; thousands of inhabitants were connected to the larger cities by extensive "suburban" networks and miles of paved highway. Meanwhile, the elite removed themselves more and more, keeping their heads in the stars and gaining insights into **astronomy** leaps and bounds ahead of their European contemporaries.

Over the next several hundred years, Maya civilization fell into decline. Residents of the great focal points of the classical culture mysteriously migrated into the outlying jungle and into what is now Mexico, where they constructed the cities of the postclassic period. The most visible of these, **Chichén Itzá, Mayapán, Tulum,** and **Uxmal,** are all quite popular among ruin-seeking travelers, but less so among archaeologists, since most other aspects of the Maya culture had significantly diminished.

Heads Up: Pok-ta-pok, Anyone?

Drawings found by archaeologists reveal that the Maya played a challenging game at the courts, in which players had to keep a **hefty rubber ball** aloft without using their hands or feet. This team sport might have resembled basketball more than **Hot Potato;** bouncing the ball from body to body, gleeful pok-ta-pok-kers did their damnedest to pop the puck into one of the two circular stone goals mounted at either end of the enclosed court. They kept score with macaw-shaped markers. In some ways, the event was more like a Roman gladiatorial contest than an NBA game—according to hieroglyphic records, the captain of the winning team won a **robe** from each spectator in the audience, right off their backs, while the losing captain was **ceremonially beheaded.**

These newer locations also made them more susceptible to outside influences. Whereas previous generations of Maya had traded ideas and inventions among themselves, the postclassic inhabitants fell prey to the expanding Toltec culture of central Mexico; their eventual defeat at the hands of the unified Aztecs punctuated their decline. As to the mystery of why the classic age of Maya civilization ever came to an end in the first place, theories abound; none is especially satisfying. Perhaps drawing from our own environmental woes, some suggest that ecological abuses caused the lowlanders to flee; others suggest overpopulation, unbridled social stratification, or even extraterrestrial intervention as reasons for the Maya's end.

Other rich riddles linger along with the question of decline. We remember the Maya best for their amazingly precise artistic and scientific practices, many of which matched those of Europe and the Far East. The well-known arched and columned buildings are just a few of the traditional visual forms of art that date from at least as long ago as the establishment of the first highland cities, as we can tell from dated remnants of paintings, ceramics, weavings, and sculpture. In the sciences, Maya scholars produced complex arithmetical, algebraic, and geometrical calculations and records. The mathematics also employed a "zero" character of the sort that Europeans adopted from Arabic mathematicians. Maya math was tightly related to the calendar system, which played a fundamental role in shaping the culture's agricultural cycle and religious beliefs. The indigenous Americans had also developed a working **sidereal calendar** (a calendar that measures years by gauging the earth's revolution relative to stars other than the Sun), a method much closer to the modern calendar's than was Europe's at the time.

Given this scientific sophistication, the Maya's technological limitations were remarkable and may have contributed to the civilization's inability to impress the *conquistadores*. Literate Maya were often remarkable carvers and used tools of flint, obsidian, and fire-hardened wood to carve dates and pictures into solid blocks of stone. They also were able to transport these enormous monoliths across hundreds of miles of hilly jungle. But astonishingly, the Maya never employed the **wheel** in any practical context (it was used in children's games, however). They never domesticated animals, yet nonetheless managed to develop an extremely efficient system for irrigating and cultivating crops. Maya social structure was sophisticated, but the pyramidal division of labor left small, elite groups of scientists and priests to delegate responsibilities to their inferiors within a city government, and for these delegates to further pass the buck to the bottom (and most populous) rung, who bent over to pull up the corn, beans, and **manioc** (cassava melon).

By the time Cortés arrived, the real damage to the ancient Maya civilization had already been wrought by a combination of internal corrosion and external pressure from trading with non-Maya populations. Still, the decentralized city-states, usually buried deep within humid, insect-infested jungles, were able to resist European subjugation for much longer than were the more militaristic Aztecs and Incas. As the binding cultural ties faded, though, so too did any sense of a "Maya nation." Following rampant disease and economic exploitation, only a fragmented jumble of cultural odds and ends and an equally crumbled string of ruined temples remained. Today, even those ruins are in danger of irrevocable damage and dispersal. Visitors to the ruins can sense the structures' intrinsic worth, but only by looking deep into the fascinating lives behind their construction can one grasp the culture's full value.

■ Ecotourism

As recently as a decade ago, Central American tourism destroyed natural resources as quickly as any other industry. Cruise ships brought littering foreigners to beaches, where they bought ornaments fashioned from the shells of endangered tortoises. Developers paved roads through the jungles, and scuba resorts encouraged divers to feed the fish and fondle the coral. Since then, countries around the world, particularly in Central America, have faced strong demands for more responsible, sustainable tourism. "Ecotourism" is the pop name for this trend.

The fastest-growing sector of the tourist industry, ecotourism is intended to be environmentally friendly, encouraging enjoyment and appreciation of nature while simultaneously contributing to its continued existence. With more than 500 million people traveling as tourists throughout the world each year, few can object to the goal of encouraging respect for the environment. Still, ecotourism has garnered its share of criticism. Some say "eco" has come to mean economics rather than ecology, pointing to greedy entrepreneurs who lead ecotours with little or no concern for nature; others warn that increased traffic in natural settings, no matter how "low-impact," can only do harm.

Since the early days of the movement, ecotourists have flocked to Central America for its bevy of natural beauties. Since the 60s, the average number of international tourists to Belize has increased 250%, and the tourism industry now brings in nearly 30% of the country's GNP. Costa Rica, perhaps the world's model for successful ecotourism, has dedicated 20% of its land to the national park system; in 1994, tourists pumped US$650 million into Costa Rica's economy, the greater part of which came from ecotourists. Such numbers tantalize entrepreneurs and experienced tour leaders alike, who readily grasp that tagging their services as "eco" could yield huge profits. However, the most concerned tour leaders actually encourage limiting the number of visitors to popular destinations, even at the cost of losing money. True eco-devotees should seek out organizations that actively support conservation efforts and strive to minimize their impact on the environment.

Resurging interest in native cultures has led to organizations which manage to please visitors and repay the local community at the same time.

Unfortunately, some ecotourism efforts have forgotten about the native peoples who inhabit the environments on which they focus. For example, the success of **Monteverde, Costa Rica** has imposed an unpredicted strain on the local community. Villagers, who face higher costs of living after tourism hits, can no longer farm the land once it is set aside as a national park and often have to leave altogether. Environmentalists who worry about the state of indigenous cultures as well as prospering biodiversity urge that affected communities be paid directly for the use of their land. A resurgence of interest in native cultures has led to stellar organizations such as Belize's **Maya Village Guesthouse Program,** which manages to please visitors and repay the local community at the same time (see **Meet the Maya,** p. 164).

Although progress may occur slowly and sporadically, environmental awareness is on the rise. More and more, companies are realizing that economics and ecotourism can go hand in hand, especially in the long term. Businesses ensure profits later by minimizing visitation now and supporting efforts to conserve nature, gaining an improved reputation among travelers and still providing "unspoiled nature." Overall, the new wave of environmentally conscious tourism has been immensely rewarding—to the countries' economies, to tourists with a thirst for adventure and immersion in nature, and, most importantly, to the environment itself.

■ Flora and Fauna

The isthmus of Central America hosts an unbelievably diverse range of plants and animals, especially given the region's relatively compact size. In the rain forests along the eastern lowlands, this variety is packed into just a hundred square miles. Activists around the world have recently stepped up efforts to protect the biodiversity of these forests, where tall, enveloping trees form a several-story-high canopy under which smaller ferns, palms, and other plants grow. Thousands of animal species thrive within the confines of the forest, from deer, squirrels, and bats to agoutis, capybaras, and coatimundis. The palm-lined coasts, meanwhile, are a dream come true for fishermen and divers alike, and bird-watchers will delight at the tropical species found in the coastal woodlands and savanna. The endangered quetzal, a bird worshipped by the Maya for its brilliant plumage, can sometimes be spotted today in cloud forests. Found in high-altitude regions, these forests are remarkable for their strange combinations of cool, moist air and fairy-tale flora. Wizened trees are covered in bright moss and colorful mushrooms, and one can't help thinking that area must be home to at least a few gnomes or pixies.

■ Festivals and Holidays

Semana Santa, the week before Easter, occasions the most parties in Central America. Most countries have special party-meccas for the festival (e.g. Chitré, Panamá and Antigua, Guatemala), and you should arrange accommodations well in advance at the more popular destinations. The Semana Santa festivities aren't isolated to the hotspots, though—you're bound to find something going on wherever you are.

Always keep your eyes and ears peeled for local fiestas wherever you are, as they can be fascinating and exceptionally fun. Spend enough time in El Salvador, for example, and you might witness the Indians' unusual celebration of the **Historia de Moros y Cristianos,** a party with elaborate dances and costumes from Spanish lore. Even familiar holidays are given a new twist; unlike the hyper-commercialized **Father's** and **Mother's Day** celebrations common to the United States, there is no gift-giving or flower-sending in Central America. Instead, mothers and fathers simply get to take the day off from work to relax or party with other mothers or fathers. Regional festivals, such as those dedicated to patron saints of local communities, are another common reason to cut loose, and are usually celebrated by drinking, dancing to local music, and sometimes a beauty pageant or two. For more information, see the **When To Go** section for each country.

■ The People

Most modern Central Americans are *mestizos,* people of mixed Indian and Spanish ancestry. The rest are predominantly *indígenas,* native Indians, although each country has its own distinct composition, and the groups are not evenly distributed throughout the isthmus. An overwhelming majority of the extant Indian population lives in Guatemala, from where it is thought most other tribes migrated outward within the last millennium. More than 40% of Belize's population is of African descent (compared to 6% for the rest of the region), and the majority of Costa Ricans are of direct European descent. Within this isthmus-wide melting pot, traditions have meshed to create a rich pattern of cultural diversity. One common thread amid this diversity comes from the other American melting pot—no matter where you go, you'll find fast food, clothes, and movies from the United States. For many Central Americans, U.S. products are often associated with high status, and North American corporations have capitalized on this attitude.

The cult of commercialism, however, still doesn't compare to the deep religiosity of almost all Central Americans. Probably the most lasting influence of the Spanish conquest was the conversion of the natives to Roman Catholicism; even those Indians who didn't fully convert still combined aspects of the European religion with their own. Today, only one out of seven Central Americans isn't Catholic, and those in the minority are usually Protestant, converted by more recent evangelical sects. While the Catholic Church has lost much of the political strength it once clenched, the Pope's decisions are still immensely influential in people's lives here, and thousands of Central Americans make annual devotional pilgrimages to sacred shrines.

■ Language

Central America is situated in the heart of Latin America, so it's not surprising that Spanish is the official language of six of the seven Central American countries. Brushing up on your *me gusta*'s and other *vocabularios* before arriving will make things considerably easier (see **Glossary,** p. 485). Still, in many places, Spanish is of secondary importance. The official language of Belize is English, which is also frequently spoken in many other Caribbean towns throughout the region. In some places, English has blended with mixed African languages into a funky-sounding Creole that's just barely intelligible to native English speakers. Fun phrases include "Weh path yu gwine?" (Where are you going?) and "Weh de gwane?" (What's going on?). Elsewhere, particularly in Guatemala, Indian languages continue to thrive.

Even primed Spanish speakers find Central American dialects shocking. "S" is often left off the end of words or omitted completely. To add to the confusion, different dialects (with different vocabulary words) are spoken from country to country, so keep an open ear. In Honduras, for example, *pisto* (not *dinero*) means money, and *polo* isn't a cologne; it means drunk, pissed, wasted, *borracho*.

Also be aware that each country has its own terms for the citizens of other countries. To a Honduran, for example, a Guatemalan is a *chapine,* a Nicaraguan is a *muco,* a Salvadoran is a *guanaco,* a Costa Rican is a *tico,* a Panamanian is a *canalero,* and a Honduran is a *catracho.* These names vary from country to country and may be interpreted as insulting in certain situations, so use tact.

■ Sports

There's no question about which sport dominates the isthmus in terms of popularity—*fútbol!* Few Latin Americans would dare to admit to not being a soccer fan, and although the nations of Central America are too small to consistently compete on an international level, the people are still unabashedly devoted to the game. When, as in the 1994 World Cup, no Central American countries compete, Argentina, Colombia, Mexico, and Brazil became the teams of choice. From children to grandparents, watching and playing the world's sport is a daily source of distraction and pleasure.

Contrary to popular belief, however, soccer is not the only sport in the world, nor is it the only game with which Central Americans concern themselves. Baseball is actually the national sport of Nicaragua, Belizeans enjoy a good game of cricket, and boxing, softball, and basketball are becoming more popular every year. In rural areas, cockfights and bullfights satisfy more bestial urges.

GUATEMALA

A bus ride through Guatemala often feels like a bumpy journey through time. A few hours will take you from the menacing frenzy of Guatemala City, with its modern theaters, orchestra, and ritzy *salsa* discos, to the rolling western highlands, where indigenous Maya Indians fire tortillas in thatched homes, weave their native *huipiles* clothing, and live in villages on the volcanic shores of Lake Atitlán just as their ancestors did 500 years ago. This overwhelming contrast—and the violence that sometimes erupts from it—are reminders that Guatemala has not yet seen all the consequences of its colonial past. It remains the least developed country in the region and is prone to political instability.

For adventure-hungry budget travelers, these conditions promise a wealth of quetzales—the country's currency—to spend while visiting and a wealth of stories to bring home. Travel here is often the least expensive in Central America; visitors can find excellent meals for about US$2.25. The markets overflow with spectacular local clothing, leather, pottery, and woven blankets and rugs, all ridiculously inexpensive. Since tourism is the second-largest source of foreign exchange (behind coffee), *gringos* are eagerly courted at the markets and elsewhere.

Most visitors, however, come for more than cheap eats and urban discos. Beyond the cities and mountains, the ruins of the Maya city of Tikal are among the most compelling archaeological sites in the Americas, and the dense leaves of the surrounding jungle in El Petén can be parted to reveal peacocks, wild parrots, lizards, and the rarely seen sacred jaguar. The chance to relax on picturesque beaches, climb steaming volcanoes, and become one of the many devotees of San Simón, the patron saint of partying, only rarely converge within one nation's borders.

ESSENTIALS

▩ When to Go

CLIMATE

Temperature varies widely across Guatemala's irregular terrain. The coastal regions can reach 100°F, while the highlands get down to freezing. In arid areas, the nights can be cool any time of the year. The rainy season lasts from May to October and is characterized by clear morning skies and afternoon or early-evening showers. The middle of the Motagua River valley is dominated by near-desert conditions, while the volcanos facing the Pacific are pummeled by as much as 4m of rain each year. In other words, come prepared for everything.

FESTIVALS AND HOLIDAYS

Guatemalans are hard-core about their festivals; patron saints' days include eardrum-pounding firecrackers and wacky parades and, while Indian influence on Christian traditions is discouraged by the church, festivals often sport the traits of several cultures' customs. **Antigua** hoots it up particularly loud for **Semana Santa,** when billowing trains of floats (carried by men, not cars) fill the streets. **Christmas** celebrations actually begin Dec. 7 with **The Burning of the Devil;** every household sets a heap of trash on fire to purge evil vibes and clear the way for processions during the rest of the month. The closer it gets to Christmas in Quetzaltenango, the harder it is to see and breathe, as the entire Central Park area becomes enshrouded in smoke. And on the Thursday after Easter in Panajachel, all hell breaks loose during the celebration of

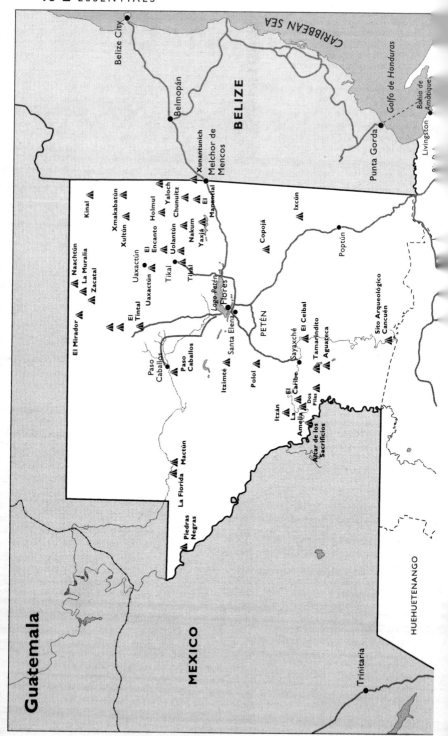

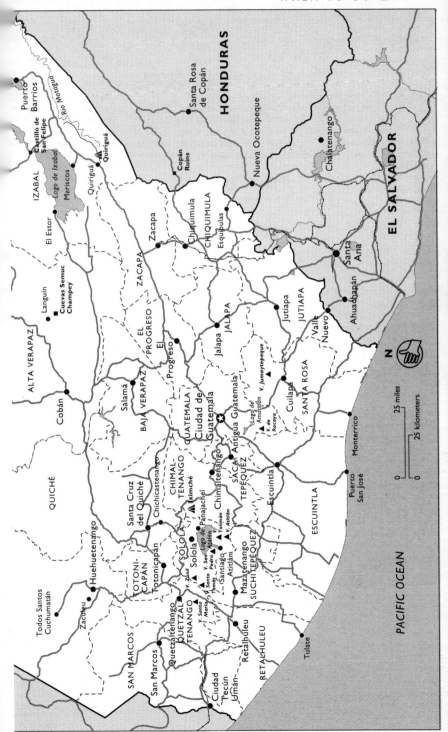

the festival of **Corpus Cristi,** a Catholic holiday which nominally commemorates the Eucharist, but has been heavily infused with Indian tradition. Snag a seat early on as the moving theater works its way through the town streets—men in elaborate masks pummel each other with huge bags of soccer balls while women dance around cawing out bird sounds.

Pick up a copy of the *Directorio de Fiestas,* available at INGUAT offices, for semi-comprehensive and up-to-date info on village and Market Days across the country.

Expect banks and post offices to close down on national holidays, which include: **January 1** (New Year's Day); **March-April** (Easter Week); **May 1** (Labor Day); **June 30** (Army Day); **August 15** (Our Lady of the Assumption); **September 15** (Independence Day); **October 20** (Revolution Day); **November 1** (All Saints' Day); **December 24-25** (Christmas Eve/Christmas); and **December 31** (New Year's Eve).

■ Useful Information

For publications and organizations of general interest, see **Useful Information,** p. 1.

Guatemala Tourist Commission, 299 Alhambra Circle, Suite 510, Coral Gables, FL 33134 (tel. (800) 742-4529; fax (305) 442-1013). Write for loads of glossy brochures and maps, posters, information on Spanish schools and on the Mundo Maya project, plus a list of rates charged by all major hotels in the country.

■ Documents and Formalities

EMBASSIES AND CONSULATES

Embassy of Guatemala, U.S., 2220 R St. NW, Washington, DC 20008 (tel. (202) 745-4952; fax 745-1908). Open to the public Mon.-Fri. 9am-12:30pm. **U.K.,** 13 Fawcett St., London, SW 10 9HN (tel. (0171) 351-3042; fax 376-5708).

Consulate of Guatemala, 57 Park Ave., New York, NY 10016 (tel. (212) 686-3837; fax 447-6947). Open Mon.-Fri. 9:30am-12:30pm for document processing. Guatemala also maintains consulates in Washington, Los Angeles, San Francisco, Miami, New Orleans, Houston, and Chicago.

U.S. Consulate in Guatemala, Av. La Reforma 7-01, Zona 10, Guatemala City (tel. (502) 331-1541; fax 331-0564) publishes *Helpful Hints for Americans in Guatemala,* which includes safety and practical info for travelers of all nationalities.

PASSPORTS, VISAS, AND CUSTOMS

All visitors to Guatemala need a valid **passport** and either a **visa** or a **tourist card.** A tourist card can be purchased at the border or at the airport departure gate for US$5, but you can save the fiver by obtaining a free visa at a consulate instead. When your card is issued, Guatemalan officials will decide how long you may stay; authorized stays range from one to three months. An extension on your tourist card can sometimes be obtained at an immigration office. Visas are free at Guatemalan consulates in Britain, Canada, and the U.S.; citizens of Ireland, South Africa, and New Zealand must pay US$10. Obtain a visa several weeks before leaving home or at consulates in Comitán, Tapachula, or Chetumal (all in Mexico) if coming from the north. Citizens of most Western European nations need only a valid passport to enter the country. All visitors should carry identification at all times. Visitors departing from the Guatemala City airport must pay a small **exit tax.**

Drivers in Guatemala must carry a valid foreign driver's license, a title, and registration. When driving across the border, visitors receive a 30 to 90 day driving permit. After that, get a license at the Departmental de Tránsito, 6 Avenida and 14 Calle, Zona 1 in Guatemala City. The whole process sounds innocuous enough, but is actually a bureaucratic nightmare. Insurance is not required for driving in Guatemala.

▓ Money Matters

CURRENCY AND EXCHANGE

US$1 = 5.96 quetzales	Q1 = US$0.17
CDN$1 = Q4.35	Q1 = CDN$0.23
UK£1 = Q9.73	Q1 = UK£0.10
IR£1 = Q8.67	Q1 = IR£0.12
AUS$1 = Q4.43	Q1 = AUS$0.23
NZ$1 = Q3.87	Q1 = NZ$0.26
SARand = Q1.29	Q1 = SARand 0.77
DM1 = Q3.26	Q1 = DM0.31

The Guatemalan unit of currency is the quetzal, named for the colorful bird and abbreviated with a "Q." U.S. dollars are the only directly exchangeable currency. For other currencies, use **BanQuetzal,** which has a branch at the airport in Guatemala City. They will first change your currency into U.S. dollars, then into quetzales.

There seems to be little rhyme and less reason to which banks accept which kinds of traveler's checks. The **Thomas Cook MasterCard** home office in Guatemala is at Unitours S.A., 7A Avenida 7-91, Zona 4, Guatemala City 01004 (tel. (502) 334-1003). **American Express** is at Edificio Banco del Café, Av. La Reforma 9-30, Zona 9, Guatemala City (tel. (502) 331-1311).

Bargaining is expected in markets and handicrafts shops, but not in urban shopping centers. When bargaining, aim for 20 to 30% off the original price. **Tipping** is not customary in *comedores*. Many restaurants will include a 10% tip in your bill.

▓ Safety

Crime is a problem in many parts of Guatemala. Pickpockets and purse snatchers constitute a perennial hazard in Guatemala City, especially in the central market. Protect yourself by keeping money in a moneybelt (*not* in a pocket or a fanny pack) and by holding on to your bags tightly; remember, most robberies are of the unarmed snatch-and-dash variety. Even Antigua, which had been considered one of the safest areas in the country, has seen an increasing number of armed robberies and rapes.

In the summer of 1996, travel between cities after sunset was considered very unsafe. **Armed bandits** stopped city buses and tour buses along highways at night, but their intended victims reportedly escaped injury by following their assailants' directions, exiting the bus in a calm fashion, and not attempting to flee. Many travelers and locals consider daylight bus rides to be relatively safe. Also, travelers should be aware that in 1994, several tourists were attacked as a result of rumors about foreigners abducting Guatemalan children for organ transplants. Visitors are advised to avoid interacting with Guatemalan children.

Those driving from Guatemala City to Lake Atitlán should take the Interamerican Hwy. (CA-1) through Chimaltenango and Tecpan to the crossroads at Los Encuentros, and then either CA-1 to Solola and Panajachel or CA-15 to Chichicastenango. Other routes to Lake Atitlán are more dangerous. In the summer of 1996, bandits were most active on the road between Tikal and the Guatemala-Belize border at Melchor de Mencos, as well as at the stretch between Sayaxché and La Libertad. As of the summer of 1997 saftey had improved, though tourists should only drive along this road at their own risk.

Climbing **volcanos** in Guatemala is also particularly risky. The volcanos are prime spots for robberies and assaults; even travelers in groups have been pulled off the path to be robbed and raped. The U.S. Consulate in Guatemala recommends not only traveling in groups, but with *armed tour leaders*. Also, check up on the safety of an area before venturing out.

GUATEMALA

Do *not* carry drugs in Guatemala. Under a 1992 anti-narcotics law, anyone caught in the possession of even small amounts of illegal drugs can spend several months in jail—before their case is decided. Those convicted face serious jail sentences.

U.S. citizens should register with the Consular Section of the U.S. Embassy in Guatemala City upon arrival. This means filling out an application and providing two photos and proof of citizenship. Informal registration may be accomplished by mail or fax; include local address and telephone, planned itinerary, emergency contact in the U.S., and intended length of stay.

In an emergency, call the **police** (120) or **fire department** (122 or 123).

■ Health

Diarrhea strikes many foreigners traveling in Guatemala, and local amoebas love to induce cases of **amoebic dysentery,** transmitted by drinking or cleaning with impure water, by eating improperly cleaned foods, or simply by handling currency. Bottled water is a prudent investment in cities and absolutely necessary in smaller villages. It might be a good idea to carry a small bottle of iodine; add a few drops to your water and wait 15 minutes before drinking. Preventive pills are handy, but don't forget to let nature take its course. As always, avoid dehydration. **Cholera** was a presence in Guatemala in 1995, but seems to have died down somewhat; **malaria** is always a risk in the rural areas of the country. Those venturing off the beaten trail should bring a supply of chloroquine tablets; take one tablet a week, starting one week before you leave home. **Dengue fever,** also big in Guatemala, is also transmitted by mosquitoes, so slap on that repellent. **Typhoid fever** is common, and vaccinations are recommended for campers and visitors to rural areas. **Hepatitis A** is another hazard common to rural areas, although it's also spread in cities. For more information, see **Health,** p. 14. According to the U.S. State Department, many public hospitals outside of Guatemala City are ill-equipped to handle some emergencies, suffering from a lack of money and supplies.

■ Alternatives to Tourism

If you somehow manage to land a **job** in Guatemala, contact the Ministerio de Trabajo for a **work permit.** These are granted to resident foreigners who do not have a Guatemalan spouse or children but who do have a written offer of employment and other documents. Expect 15 to 20 days for processing.

Guatemala is full of **language institutes** where you can pick up or polish Spanish skills. Antigua is particularly full of schools. Indigenous languages are also taught at a number of institutions. Most schools offer individual instruction at flexible times (usually 4-7hr., 5 days per week). Schools encourage potential students to make written reservations well in advance, but it is often possible and even advisable to arrive without arrangements and then shop around. Tuition may be US$40 to US$80 for a week of instruction (5 days, 4hr. per day). You can avoid commissions and middlemen by arranging study directly through the schools. Virtually all schools can arrange homestays with Guatemalan families. Room and board costs about US$50 to 100 per week.

Keep in mind that speaking Spanish will only get you so far in Guatemala, especially as you travel farther off the *gringo*-beaten track into the smaller *pueblos.* Twenty-three Indian languages are spoken, the most complete and widespread of which is Quiché. To know it when you hear it, imagine a percussive stream of roof-of-the-mouth clicks and back-of-the-throat clucks. Those who study the language report having to chew lozenges in order to numb their raw, tickled tonsils.

Antigua is the center of the language study universe, but schools are also located in Guatemala City, Petén, Huehuetenango, Quetzaltenango, and elsewhere. The following list includes some of the available schools, as well as local volunteer organizations. For more information, see **Alternatives to Tourism,** p. 19.

Amerispan, 6 Avenida Norte #40A, Antigua (tel./fax 832-0164). Language courses with homestays and meals, 1 week or longer. Offers information and services for pre-registered students and travelers just arriving, discount one-way airfares from Guatemala to just about anywhere, and a discount card (US$5) good at locations in Guatemala and Honduras.

Centro de Español Don Pedro de Alvarado, 1 Calle Pte. #24, Antigua (tel. 832-4180; fax 832-0082). The only school in Antigua authorized to give the ACTFL and FSI foreign proficiency exams, which may qualify students for college credit in the U.S. Rates as low as US$78 per week for 4hr. per day.

Centro de Estudios de Español Pop Wuj, Apdo. 68, Quetzaltenango, Guatemala (tel./fax 761-8286). This cooperatively-owned Spanish school donates its profits to scholarships, community construction efforts, and health and nutritional programs. Students learn Spanish while participating in projects to help Guatemala's poor. In the U.S., write to P.O. Box 43685, Washington, D.C. 20011-9685.

Conservation International, Attn: Eco-Escuela de Español, 1015-18th St. NW, Suite 1000, Washington, D.C., 20036 (tel. (202) 973-2264; fax 331-9328; email ecoscuela@conservation.org; http://www.conservation.org/). Offers placement in a school in the Petén, combining language instruction and environmental work.

Desarrollo Del Pueblo Instituto de Español, Apdo. Postal 41, 19 Av. 0-34, Zona 3, Quetzaltenango (tel./fax 961-6754). For more information, write to Stacy Smith, 2325 Highland Ave., Everett, WA 98201; or call Jeff Rubracht in the U.S. (tel. (208) 733-2700; fax (208) 733-2700). One-on-one instruction 5hr. per day US$105-130 per week, homestay and meals included. Students are encouraged to perform service work, assisting in vaccination drives, rural clinics, and local construction.

Proyecto Lingüístico Francisco Marroquín, 7 Calle Pte. #31, Apdo. 237, Antigua 03901 (tel. (800) 552-2051; fax (9) 832-2886). The oldest, largest school in Antigua. A nonprofit foundation whose revenue goes toward preserving Maya languages. Organizes regular *fiestas* for its students and excursions to many parts of Guatemala. 6hr. per day of one-on-one instruction. 2-week minimum stay during summer. Make reservations 8-10 weeks in advance.

▓ Getting There

La Aurora International Airport in Guatemala City is served by many major airlines. **American, Aviateca, British Airways, Continental, Mexicana, Copa, Lacsa, Taca,** and **Tapsa** are among the carriers serving the city.

When entering Guatemala **by land,** arrive at the border as early in the day as possible, both to facilitate transportation connections and to avoid delay should the border close at an unofficially early hour (as has been known to happen). Make sure you have enough time to reach a town from the border before sunset.

Overland **bus** service connects Guatemala City and the interior to all major border crossings from Mexico, El Salvador, and Honduras.

BORDER CROSSINGS

Those entering Guatemala **by car** from **Mexico** usually cross the border at either Tecún Umán (Highway CA-2) on the Pacific coast or at La Mesilla (Highway CA-1) in the highlands. The La Mesilla border crossing was closed during the January 1994 uprising in Chiapas, Mexico. Travelers are advised to exercise caution in this still unstable region, and U.S. citizens may want to check with a consulate and the U.S. State Department before attempting to cross at La Mesilla. The border crossing between Las Chinamas, **El Salvador** and Valle Nuevo, Guatemala is preferred for connections between those two countries (open daily 8am-5pm). When going to **Honduras,** go through El Florido or Agua Caliente, or take the Jungle Route. The Petén region of Guatemala borders **Belize,** but the bus route across the border, though popular, poses special risks; see the applicable **warning** (p. 158).

■ Once There

The government tourist bureau is the **Instituto Guatemalteco de Turismo** (INGUAT). There are INGUAT offices in Guatemala City, Antigua, Quetzaltenango, Panajachel, and Flores. For information about goings-on in Antigua and Guatemala City, check *The Revue*, an English-language publication. For the most current information on 24 hr. pharmacies, consult a local paper and look for the *"Farmacias, servicio 24 horas"* listing.

TRANSPORTATION

Travel **by air** within Guatemala is not particularly cheap, but it may be worth avoiding the hassles of bus travel during the rainy season (see **Practical Information,** p. 60). **Common buses,** cursed by some as "mobile chicken coops," are converted school buses that sit three to a bench. Many travelers have reported getting overcharged on Guatemalan buses at a special *"gringo* rate." Inquire about authorized tariffs ahead of time, and whenever possible, pay in exact change, so the drivers don't give themselves a little bonus. **Driving** your own vehicle in Guatemala can be a hazardous experience. Road conditions are generally poor. Those involved in accidents can be put in jail regardless of who is at fault, and armed car thefts are very common. The safest strategy if cornered by armed bandits on the road is to surrender your car without resistance. For more information, see **Safety,** p. 51.

ADDRESSES

Many streets in Guatemalan cities are numbered but not named. This can be confusing because addresses typically also include building-numbers. The name or number of the *avenida* or *calle* always comes first. For example, "6 Av. 25" refers to #25 on Sixth Avenue. You will also see "6a Av. 25," which means the same thing ("6a" short for *sexta*). In cities that are divided into zones, we designate the zone with "Zona #," e.g. 6 Av. 25 Zona 1. A building with the address 12 Calle 6-14, is on 12 Calle between 6 and 7 Avs. at #14.

Buildings can also be specified without any number; in this case, the two closest cross streets are used instead. For example, an address could be 6 Av., 1 Calle, meaning at the intersection of Sixth Avenue and First Street. In a further permutation, addresses can specify the street and the *two* cross streets. For example, 6 Av., 1/2 Calles, means on Sixth Avenue between First and Second Streets.

KEEPING IN TOUCH

Guatemala's **postal service** is plagued by strikes and poor management, but a letter only costs Q0.40. If necessary, packages can be sent to the U.S. using **UPS** or **DHL** (tel. 334-3038), but it's very expensive (about US$20 per lb.). **First-class air mail** ought to take 10-14 days to reach the U.S., but it's not uncommon for a letter to take several months. You can receive mail general delivery at most post offices through the *lista de correos* (see Keeping in Touch, p. 38). Mail should be addressed:

Andrew <u>MITCHELL</u>
a/c Lista de Correos
Antigua [city], Guatemala
Central America

If mailing from the U.S., omit the last line (Central America) and move "Guatemala" down, since the computers that sort mail can only recognize names of countries.

Telephones are erratically handled by **Guatel,** the national communications network. Phoning can be difficult, even from Guatel *cabinas,* so try the more expensive hotels when placing international or domestic calls. Local calls cost Q0.10 per minute; inter-city, in-country calls cost Q1-3. Collect calls and credit-card calls can be made from pay phones free of charge by dialing 190 for AT&T, 189 for MCI, 195 for

Sprint, or 171 for an international operator. Some cities (like Antigua, for example) have limited direct dial and international operator service, and many public phones do not offer long-distance service. Some phones require money to make a calling-card call; others do not. Listen for the amazing Guatemalan feedback effect; most conversations are spent listening to your own echo, and then awkwardly waiting for a response to "Hello? Can you hear me?" If you place coins in a phone's slot and they don't drop when you pick up the receiver, the phone is "full": use another one and don't expect to get your change back. Guatemala's **country code** is 502.

GUATEMALA: LIFE AND TIMES

■ History

Conquest and oppression of indigenous populations is a disturbing and familiar part of every Central American country's past, but in Guatemala it continues even today. The Guatemalans write the annals of their difficult history in 23 *indígena* languages and dialects, as well as in Spanish. About half of Guatemala's nine million citizens are descended from the Quiché (Toltec) Indians, who conquered the Guatemalan arm of the Maya Empire in AD 1000 to become the dominant force in the land. In 1524, one of **Cortés'** lieutenants, **Pedro de Alvarado,** claimed the whole country with that uncanny ease characteristic of Spanish explorers—his army of 635 men and four cannons sustained only six casualties. The Spanish leader defeated the last king of the Quiché, **Tecún Umán,** in hand-to-hand combat; to this day, the highland Indians claim that their fallen king will one day rise from the dead and rule his people justly. It is understandable that the Indians still look to mythical sources for hope, as the Guatemalan government has given them little else on which to rely. Guatemalan history since the Spanish conquest traces countless efforts by the Indians to protect their culture and free themselves from governmental oppression.

Spanish rule, based in modern day Antigua until 1773, when it moved to Guatemala City, lasted 300 years. Like many other Central American countries, Guatemala first gained independence from Spain on September 15, 1821 as part of the Mexican Empire and then as the center of the **United Provinces of Central America** (which eventually collapsed in 1841). Guatemala was subsequently governed by a succession of military and civilian dictators, all members of the quasi-ethnic, quasi-socioeconomic group Guatemalans call **ladinos,** people of predominantly wealthy, European descent. The first of these dictators, **Rafael Carrera,** implemented a nationalistic policy and declared Guatemala a sovereign nation in 1847; his Conservative successor was overthrown by Liberals, who ruled nearly continuously until 1944. Traditionally, the Liberals have tried to transform the country's socioeconomic situation through political progress, while the Conservatives have centralized power in the church and the government. The most notable Liberal leader, **Justo Rufino Barrios,** introduced sweeping reforms in 1872, creating a new constitution and laying out a solid infrastructure of roads and industry. The next few presidents enacted fewer reforms, and one of them was ousted when the assembly declared him insane. **General Jorge Ubico** was the first dictator to address the problems of the Indians directly, for which they pledged allegiance to him. However, his leadership was still too restrictive for many students and workers, who organized the **October Revolution** to overthrow his dictatorship in 1944.

Guatemala experimented with a socialist government under President **Juan José Arévalo Bermejo,** who implemented liberal labor laws and showed governmental concern for the Indians' situation. In 1952, the fully communist regime under **Jacobo Arbenz** tried in vain to implement land reform, unnerving many groups, including the United Fruit Company, which controlled the banana crop. The U.S. government helped to instigate a successful military coup in order to safeguard the economic well-being of the massive fruit-exporting conglomerate. A procession of military dictators followed, each opposed by sundry marauding guerrilla rebel forces. A massive earthquake in 1976 caused widespread famine and disease, which in turn heightened Indian unrest. By 1982, a series of Indian revolts seemed to have successfully secured a foothold for Guatemala's indigenous population. Soon thereafter, however, the government seized the reins again. The regime of **General García** was characterized by brutal death squads; his successor, **General Ríos Montt,** who moderated the institutional cruelty somewhat, nonetheless attempted to squelch Indian unrest by burning villages and "civilizing" the *indígena*s through intense Christian evangelism. In the face of such assaults, native culture has gradually but steadily disappeared. In the past three decades it is estimated that the army has conducted 100,000 political *extrajudicia* killings, making Guatemala's human rights record one of the worst in the world.

After effectively pardoning itself for earlier atrocities, the government made a superficial transition to democracy. The country became more stable after 1985, when civilian president **Vinicio Cerezo** was elected. New and powerful civil rights groups formed, and Marxist rebels were politically weakened to the extent that a sane selection of Cerezo's successor was possible. The constitution of 1986 paved the way for the election of a civilian, democratic government. The Guatemalan government has implemented economic reforms in return for financial assistance from the World Bank, but in so doing has often hurt small-scale agriculture. The private watch-dog organization, *Americas Watch,* announced in 1990 that human rights abuses had dishearteningly returned to the levels of the old military regimes, and Cerezo's government acquired a reputation for corruption and indifference. In May 1993, President Serrano suspended parts of the Constitution as civil unrest escalated. The **Unidad Revolucionaria Nacional Guatemalteca (URNG),** the main guerrilla group, withdrew from peace negotiations in 1994, citing persistent human rights violations by the government. Serrano was ousted after trying to gather what little control he could through force, leaving his successor, **President De León Carpio,** to rein in both the national army and the guerillas.

The government is still mired in problems. Eighty percent of Guatemalan children under five are malnourished, half the population is either unemployed or underemployed, and 20 families control 80% of the nation's land. Guatemala is posted on the U.S. State Department's "drug problem list" in honor of its work in the transportation of cocaine and the manufacture of opium. And the nation is still trying to reclaim Belize, which it says was unjustly granted independence by Great Britain. Meanwhile, the historical discrimination against the large *indígena* population continues, albeit with heightened awareness on the part of outsiders and the Guatemalan government. In an effort to escape its bad reputation, Guatemala hosted the international conference of indigenous peoples, *Majawil Q'ij:* 500 Years of Indigenous and Popular Resistance. *Indígenas* gathered in October 1991 to commemorate the tragic side of Columbus's discovery of the Americas, and to proclaim the "New Dawn" of an era to claim the social, economic, and political respect they deserve. Perhaps as a sign of change, exiled activist for indigenous peoples in Guatemala and Nobel Peace Prize laureate, **Rigoberta Menchú,** was allowed to return to participate in the conference. Her autobiography, *I, Rigoberta Menchú*, is a horrifying account of life on a small Guatemalan farm.

■ The Arts

Guatemala's literary tradition dates back to the *Popol Vuh*—the Maya Holy Book—an ancient document whose existence was first recorded by the Spanish in Chichicastenango in 1701. Since then, Guatemalan writers have continuously forged the gap between Indian myth and European literary forms; magic recurs in Guatemalan literature, coloring even modern writing with traces of native religions. The country has produced few notable playwrights, though **Vicenta Laparra de La Cerda** (1834-1905) movingly portrayed the plight of women in *Angel caído (Fallen Angel,* 1880) and *Hija maldita (Accursed Girl,* 1895). The modern poet **Rafael Arévalo Martínez** (1884-1975) is said to have led the way towards "magical realism"—famously characteristic of much Latin American fiction—in short stories such as *El hombre que parecía un caballo* (*"The Man Who Resembled a Horse,"* 1915). But Guatemala is most proud of the work of **Miguel Angel Asturias** (1899-1974), who won the 1967 Nobel Prize and whose novels penetrate the deep political realities of this century. Most notable among his writings are *El señor Presidente* (1946), *Maladrón* (1969), and the more highly charged *Banana Trilogy* from the 1950s. His *Hombres de maiz* (*Men of Corn*, 1949) expresses the conflict between European and native ways of life through a poetic reflection on the sacred seed of the Maya and its commercial use by outsiders. Also critical of the sociopolitical conditions of the Indians are the novels of **Mario Monteforte Toledo,** who was forced into exile in Mexico for his work.

Traveling around, you're likely to hear the *marimba,* a large, mellow-toned xylophone that could easily be considered the national instrument of Guatemala. Marimba players often band together to create haunting (or happy) melodies to accompany dancing.

Fruit Loops of the Loom

Famous the world over, Guatemalan indigenous clothing is a rich tapestry of intricate woven patterns and colors fit for a **toucan's** beak. The natural dyes are fashioned from *clavel* and *heraño* flowers and then mixed with the crushed bodies of **mosquitoes** to keep the dye from running. The bugs themselves are often depicted in the resulting patterns, which are woven on huge, unwieldy looms and are specific to each village. The clothing, each piece of which can take up to six months to make, is nearly always produced and worn by women.

Travelers in search of genuine **hand-made clothing** in the tourist-saturated markets will be courted with machine-made replicas; shop carefully. An easy way to tell a fake is if **gold** or **silver** synthetic fibers are woven into the fabric, if the stitching on the back is suspiciously neat, or if the prices seem too good to be true. Q50 will not buy you six months' labor. Be cautious about wearing the clothing in Guatemala; to some Indians, a foreigner in native dress reeks of **blasphemy** (it's especially insulting when women tourists wear traditionally male garments).

■ Food and Drink

Chicken rules supreme in Central American *típico* fare; don't be surprised if the bird is occasionally served with the feet still attached. But as the meat's the treat, meals are weighed down with rice, beans, eggs, and stick-to-your-ribs tortillas. There is good reason why tortillas in Guatemala are all made out of corn—according to Quiché traditional myths, humans *came* from the corn, and the grain is our essence.

Along the coasts, seafood is more common, usually peppered with Caribbean Creole flare. Despite the fruit's thorny, green exterior, the *guanába's* juicy, pulpy white core is definitely worth trying. If restaurant grub isn't your thing, have no fear— nearly every town has its own tent-strewn market, stocked with tons of fruits, vegetables, and other food. Caution, though—the fruit is often washed in dirty water.

■ Media

In both circulation and sheer mass, *Prensa Libre* is the biggest Guatemalan daily newspaper, followed by *Siglo XXI.* The biweekly news journal *Crónica* is like the U.S. magazine *Time* in name as well as in format, providing in-depth analysis of national and international events. *Crítica* comes out once a month, and provides a tempestuous forum for Guatemalan intellectuals.

Guatemala is hardly a 3.2 televisions-per-household country, so TV-watching is a deeply communal activity. Locals assemble in bars and restaurants to watch their favorite shows on cable, often clogging the doorways during soccer games.

■ Recent News

That Guatemala has a history of human rights violations is well known, but the extent of these transgressions has only recently surfaced. Allegedly, at the height of Guatemala's 36-year civil war, some passengers traveling in rural areas without proper documents attracted the attention of soldiers, were pulled out of vehicles by members of the notoriously ruthless Guatemalan army, and were never seen again. In the spring of 1997, archaeologists digging for Maya antiquities unexpectedly unearthed mass burial pits. Investigators now believe that the bodies buried in these plots—some still wearing tattered jeans and tennis shoes—are the remains of the locals and tourists who disappeared while traveling in the countryside. Some of the unearthed bodies still have their arms bound behind them and rope marks around their necks—testimony to the ways in which they died. Relatives of the dead, as well as various human-rights organizations within Guatemala, hope to use this evidence of torture to press charges against Guatemala's military leaders of the early 80s, General Romeo Lucas Garcia and General Efrain Rios Montt.

Fear not, gentle travelers, the worst is over. On December 29, 1996, under United Nations supervision, an armistice was signed officially ending the civil war. By March 3, soldiers and guerilla forces alike were demobilized, leaving Maya ruins and market towns—once conflict zones too dangerous to visit—accessible again to tourists. The Guatemalan government, in an attempt to draw in revenue from tourism, has been particularly amenable to the needs of travelers, even paving roads to key ruins sites and placing tourist policemen at international borders to help travelers cross smoothly. Although the number of foreign visitors to Guatemala dropped in 1996, the government is expecting up to a 10% increase in foreign visitors over the next two years. The U.S. State Department, in response to the changes effected within the country, has significantly reduced its travel warning, calling most of Guatemala essentially safe for tourists.

Guatemala City

Guate (GUAH-tuh), as Guatemalans affectionately (or not so affectionately) call it, offers quite a few gems to the intrepid traveler. Few tourists, however, are hardy enough to brave the city's sprawling and sometimes frightening thicket of poverty and pollution in search of the attractions buried in its midst. Elsewhere in the country, tin-roofed shacks and sprawling markets blend almost seamlessly into the jungles and adjoining farmlands of the Pueblos; in Guatemala City, poverty is laid bare, and stands in particularly harsh contrast to the antiseptic shopping malls and guard-patrolled, fortress-like mansions in the nation's wealthiest neighborhoods. The city teems with vendors, business people, and beggars whose primary goals do not include coddling the pleasure traveler. Even though it is virtually impossible to journey through Guatemala without passing through its capital city, the vast majority of tourists hightail it out of Guate as soon as they can. After replacing a lost passport or frantically changing buses at one of the terminals, most visitors opt to flee the smog-belching buses of the city for the verdant volcanos of the western highlands.

Don't leave the city the first chance you get—Guatemala City (pop. 3 million) is a force to be reckoned with. After camping in the countryside and hiking through jungles, you may actually appreciate the hot showers and in-room television sets offered by Guatemala City's quality budget accommodations. In addition, Guate's museums provide a good introduction to indigenous history and culture, and an electric nightlife keeps the city convulsing long after sunset. Shaking and rocking is nothing new to Guatemala City, which was dubbed the new capital in 1775 after an earthquake in Antigua left the government scrambling for a safer haven. Although city leaders' sense of security was dashed by quakes in 1917, 1918, and 1976, Guatemala City has

COLONIA MONTE REAL

BETHANIA

COLONIA VILLA LINDA

EL ZAPOTE

Puente Ing. Martín Prado Velez

5a C. (C. Marti)

LOS CIPRESALES

PROVECTO 4-10

LAVARREDA

14 Calle

2a Calle

Carretera Interamericana

COLONIA JARDINES DE TIKAL II

8a C.

13 C.

18 C.

JARDINES DE LA ASUNCIÓN

SABANA ARRIBA

LAS VACAS

Area Arqueológica Kaminaljuyú

COLONIA PÉREZ GUISASOLA

Calzada Roosevelt

Anillo Periférico

COLONIA MIRAFLORES

13 Calle

Av. Bolivar

26 C.

28 C.

COLONIA SARAVIA

COLONIA VIVIBIÉN

SANTA ROSITA

COLONIA TRINIDAD

COLONIA TECÚN UMÁN

2a C.

5a C.

8a C.

10a C.

Ciudad San Cristóbal

LAS CHARCAS

COLONIA EL CARMEN

Ciudad Universitaria

Diagonal 17

Hipódromo Nacional

Aeropuerto Internacional La Aurora

20 C.

COLONIA VISTA HERMOSA II

COLONIA SAN LÁZARO

COLONIA MONTE MARÍA

COLONIA LAS CONCHAS

Rio Pinula

18 C.

COLONIA SAN RAFAEL

Guatemala City Overview

COLONIA ELGIN

LA LIBERTAD

LA CUCHILLA DEL CARMEN

GUATEMALA

swollen ceaselessly, spreading into the surrounding valleys to become the largest urban amalgamation in Central America.

■ Orientation

When you first look at a map of Guate, you may be intimidated by the city's seemingly overwhelming scale. Never fear. Although the enormous capital is divided into 21 zones, nearly all sights and services of interest are in Zonas 1, 4, 9, 10, and 13. A line drawn from the airport (in Zona 13) to the **Plaza Mayor** (the city's main plaza in Zona 1) would pass first along **Avenida de la Reforma** (the border between Zonas 9 and 10), then through Zona 4, and finally through Zona 1. Walking at night is not recommended anywhere in the city. Taxi cabs should be hired only from clearly marked stands at the airport, at major hotels, at major intersections, and at certain parks. Make sure that your cab has a number painted on its side and a license plate that begins with "A."

Zona 1, the city's downtown and oldest section, houses all the budget hotels and restaurants. It is considered unsafe for after-dark perambulation. Be on guard during daylight hours as well. *Calles* run east to west, with street numbers increasing as you move southward. *Avenidas* run north to south, with numbers increasing as you move eastward. The major thoroughfare is **6 Avenida,** which passes the Plaza Mayor in the northern part of Zona 1 and continues south through Zonas 4 and 9.

Zona 4 lies immediately to the south of Zona 1. An industrial area, Zona 4 boasts few tourist attractions, with the exception of Guate's essential **INGUAT** office. A series of northeast-to-southwest *vías* and northwest-to-southeast *rutas* (with numbers increasing north to south) replace the street pattern established in Zona 1. Fortunately, Zona 4 is too small for you to lose your bearings.

Zonas 9 and **10** are realms unto themselves—expect to see exclusive boutiques, fancy restaurants, five-star hotels, and the homes of the elite. The southern portion of Zona 10 is the **Zona Viva** (Lively Zone), where the bulk of the city's most happening (and expensive) nightclubs and discos provide entertainment into the wee hours. These two *zonas* are both relatively safe and pickpocket-free. They are divided by the tree-lined, north-south Av. de la Reforma; Zona 9 is to the west and Zona 10 to the east. *Avenidas* run parallel to La Reforma and increase eastward, starting at 1 Av. in each *zona*. *Calles* run perpendicular to them and increase southward.

Zona 13 is south of Zona 9 and contains museums, parks, and the international airport. Lucky 13 is removed from the hubbub of the center, and is generally secure.

Some possible causes for confusion: 1a Avenida of Zona 1 is different from the 1a Avenida of Zona 5. Also, some streets are nameless for a block or two, and some *calles* in Zona 1 have secondary names.

Dilapidated, crowded *camionetas* (buses) go almost everywhere in the city for Q0.90. Bus #82 follows perhaps the most useful route, from 10 Av. in Zona 1, through Zona 4, and down Av. Reforma between Zonas 9 and 10. Returning, it travels north on Av. de la Reforma, through Zona 4, and up 9 Av. in Zona 1. Bus #83 goes from 10 Av. in Zona 1 to the airport and the Zona 13 attractions and returns to 9 Av. in Zona 1. Bus #85 follows a similar route. *Micros* (vans or smaller buses) charge Q0.90 and course the same routes as *camionetas,* plus many additional ones. Keep in mind that there is no *camioneta* schedule: you'll have to read windshields, ask drivers, or guess. Wave to the driver to get on; otherwise, the buses might just puff on by.

Guatemala City has no central **bus terminal;** instead, dozens of bus companies maintain separate offices throughout the city. Many buses leave from 19 Calle between 7 and 10 Avs. (near the train station in Zona 1). Several others leave from the huge combined terminal/market in Zona 4, between 1 and 4 Avs. and 1 and 7 Calles. Though a few companies have offices in these areas, most buses simply idle in one of the two enormous parking lots while crews call out their destinations.

■ Practical Information

Tourist Office: Instituto Guatemalteco de Turismo (INGUAT), 7 Av. 1-17, Zona 4 (tel. 331-1333), in the Centro Cívico just south of the Zona 1 border. Helpful, knowledgeable, and bilingual staff. Maps (Q5.50) of the city and surrounding areas and free, invaluable lists of bus destinations, terminals, and schedules. Open Mon.-Fri. 8am-4pm, Sat. 8am-1pm.

Currency Exchange: There is a **BanQuetzal** at the airport (tel. 334-7508), open Mon.-Fri. 7am-8pm, Sat.-Sun. 8am-6pm. **Banco Agro,** 7 Ave 16-57, Zona 1 (tel. 232-7433), is open Mon.-Fri. 9am-6pm, Sat. 10am-2pm. **Lloyd's Bank International,** 11 Calle 8-20, Zona 1 (tel. 230-2950), and 6 Av. 9-51, Zona 9 (tel. 332-7580), and **Banco Internacional,** 7 Av. 11-20, Zona 1 (tel. 251-8066), are open Mon.-Fri. 9am-3pm.

American Express: Av. La Reforma 9-30, Zona 9 (tel. 331-1311), in the Banco del Café building. Holds mail for card holders and traveler's check holders. Issues card holders traveler's checks in exchange for personal checks. Open Mon.-Fri. 8:30am-4:30pm.

Telegrams: At the main post office (see below).

Embassies: U.S., Av. de la Reforma 7-01, Zona 10 (tel. 331-1541). Open Mon.-Fri. 8am-noon and 1-3pm. Emergency assistance after hours (tel. 332-3347) at the embassy Marine Guard. **Canada,** 13 Calle 8-44, Zona 10, Edyma Plaza Niv. 8 (tel. 333-6102). Open Mon.-Fri. 8am-2pm. **U.K.,** 7 Av. 5-10, Zona 4 (tel. 334-1984), 7th floor of the Centro Financiero Torre II. Open Mon.-Thurs. 9am-noon and 2-4pm, Fri. 8am-12pm. **Mexico,** 15 Calle 3-20, Zona 10 (tel. 333-7258), on the 7th floor of the Edifico Centro. Mon.-Fri. 9am-1pm and 3pm-6pm. **Belize** is represented by the U.K. embassy. **Costa Rica,** Av. Reforma 8-60, Zona 9 (tel. 331-9604), #320 in Edificio Galerías Reforma. Open Mon.-Fri. 8:30am-2pm. **Honduras,** 13 Calle 12-33, Zona

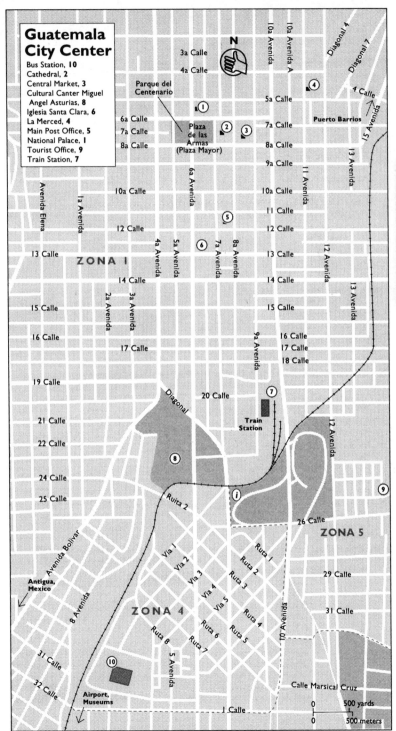

Guatemala City Center

Bus Station, 10
Cathedral, 2
Central Market, 3
Cultural Canter Miguel
 Angel Asturias, 8
Iglesia Santa Clara, 6
La Merced, 4
Main Post Office, 5
National Palace, 1
Tourist Office, 9
Train Station, 7

Parque del Centenario

Plaza de las Armas (Plaza Mayor)

Puerto Barrios

ZONA 1

Train Station

ZONA 4

ZONA 5

Antigua, Mexico

Airport, Museums

Calle Marsical Cruz

0   500 yards
0   500 meters

10, Colonia Oakland (tel. 337-4344). Open Mon.-Fri. 8:30am-1:30pm. **Nicaragua,** 10 Av. 14-72, Zona 10 (tel. 368-0785). Open Mon.-Fri. 9am-1pm. **Panamá,** 5 Av. 15-45, Zona 10 (tel. 333-7182). Open Mon.-Fri. 8:30am-1:30pm. Consult the phone book for other embassy and consulate listings.

Consulates: Mexico, 13 Calle 7-30, Zona 9, ½ block from Av. Reforma. Get your **Mexican tourist card** here. Open Mon.-Fri. 8:30-11:30am and 12:30-2:30pm. there are often lines, so arrive as early as possible. **U.S.,** Av. de la Reforma 7-01, Zona 10 (tel. 331-1541). A slew of different business hours, depending on what your business is (a lost visa, someone seeking a visa, or other). **Canada,** 13 Calle 8-44, Zona 10 (tel. 333-6102). **U.K.,** 7 Av. 5-10, Zona 4 (tel. 332-1601). Open Mon.-Thurs. 9am-noon and 2-4pm. **El Salvador,** 18 Calle 14-30, Zona 13 (tel. 332-2449). Open Mon.-Fri 8am-2pm. Consult the blue section of the phone book for other consulates. If you are a foreigner traveling in Guatemala, register with your country's consulate (rather than the adjacent embassy) upon entering the country.

Immigration Office: 41 Calle 17-36, Zona 8 (tel. 471-4670). Open Mon.-Fri. 8am-3pm. Catch bus #71 from 10 Av. (Q0.90). Phone is often busy.

Airport: La Aurora International Airport (tel. 331-8392), about 7km south of downtown, in Zona 13. Served by **American** (tel. 334-7379), **British Airways** (tel. 332-7402), **Continental** (tel. 335-3341), **Mexicana** (tel. 331-2697), and other domestic and international carriers. **Tikal Jets** (tel. 332-5070, 334-6855), **Tapsa** (tel. 331-9180), and **Aviateca** (tel. 331-8222, 334-7722) fly to Flores—rates fluctuate wildly. Call for rates and hours, and check at hotels and INGUAT offices for special fares. Bus #83 shuttles passengers between Zona 1 and the airport for Q0.90. Taxis charge Q40 for the same route.

Buses: There is a plethora of different terminals and lines, with each destination served by its own company. Consult the tourist office for a free list, but be aware that inaccuracies are common. Terminals are clustered in three fairly distinct areas. **AREA 1:** Located in the southwest corner of Zona 4, 7a Calle, and 4a Av. Serves all points to the west and southwest of Guatemala City. Be particularly wary of muggers as you navigate this confusing, crowded, and street-vendor-choked area. Buses to: **Chichicastenengo** (every 30min, 5am-6pm, 3hr., Q9); **La Democracia** (every 30min., 6am-4:30pm, 2hr., Q6); the **Pacific Coast (Reserve)** (at 10:30am, 12:30pm, and 2:30pm, 4½hr., Q7); and **San Salvador,** Melva Internacional (tel. 331-0874), from nearby 3 Av. 1-38, Zona 9 (every hr., 5:30am-4:30pm, 5hr., Q32). **AREA 2:** Centered around the corner of 10a Av. and 16 Calle, this terminal includes several well-organized lines. Los Halcones (tel. 238-1929) goes to **Huehuetenango** from 7a Av. 15-27 Zona 1 (7am, 2pm, 5hr., Q19). The Escobar y Monja Blanca line (tel. 238-1409), 8 Av. 15-16, Zona 1 provides buses to **Cobán** (every hr., 4am-5pm, 4hr., Q17.10, call to reserve seats) and **Biotopo del Quetzal** (every hr., 4am-5pm, 3 hr., Q13.10, tel. 251-1878, 253-7282). Galgos (tel. 232-3661) takes passengers to **Quetzaltenango,** from 7 Av. 19-44, Zona 1 (7 per day, 5:30am-7pm, 4hr., Q16.50) and to **Talisman** and the Mexican border crossing at **El Carmen** (5 daily, 6am-5:30pm, 5hr., Q24.15). To **Esquipulas,** try Rutas Orientales (tel. 253-6714, 251-2160), 19 Calle 8-18, Zona 1 (every 30 min., 4am-6pm, 4hr., Q24); change to Buses Vilma in Chiquimula for **El Florido** and **Copán, Honduras** (7, 10am, and 12:30pm, 2hr.). Buses to **Puerto Barrios** on Litegua (tel. 253-8169) leave from 15 Calle 10-42, Zona 1 (8 per day, 7am-3pm, 5hr., Q32). Try Fuentes del Norte (tel. 238-3894), 17 Calle 8-46, Zona 1, to **Río Dulce** (5hr., Q40). Look for the spotless, safe terminal with cafeteria, waiting area, and efficient service. Transportes Fortaleza (tel. 230-3390), 19 Calle 8-70, Zona 1, provides buses to **Retalhuleu** and **Tecún Umán** (4 per day, 1:30am-5:30pm, 5hr, Q20). Another clean, safe terminal with indoor seating and free luggage storage for bus travelers, with a receipt and everything. **AREA 3:** At 20 Calle and Simon Bolívar Av., just west of the Centro Cultural Asturias in Zona 1. Buses to **Tecpan,** near Iximché (every 20 min., 5:30am-7pm, 2hr., Q4.50); Transporte Velazquez leaves for **La Mesilla** at the Mexican border (8:30am every day, 8hr., Q30). To **Panajachel,** Rebulli (tel. 251-3521) departs from 21 Calle 1-34, Zona 1 (every hr., 6am-4pm, 3hr., Q10). Tourist authorities warn that thieves are often at work here, so beware. Finally, buses to **Puerto San José** depart from Frebol, Zona 12 (every 10 min., 5am-8pm, 1hr., Q3). At 20 Calle and 2a Avenida, catch a bus to **Amatitlán** (every 30 min., 7am-7pm, 30 min.,

Q1.60). Buses to **Antigua** leave from a spot outside of the three areas listed above, Transportes Unidos (tel. 232-4949, 253-6929), 15 Calle, between 3 and 4 Av., Zona 1 (every 30 min., 7am-8pm, 1hr., Q2.50).

Taxis: Always be sure that the car is marked as a taxi and that the license plate number begins with an "A." Although airport security has improved recently, there have been incidents of tourists being picked up by bogus cabs, taken to secluded destinations, and mugged. **Biltmore y Camino Real,** Zona 10 (tel. 333-5613); **Reforma,** Zona 10 (tel. 368-1354); and **Infantil Colón,** Zona 1 (tel. 253-9304) are cab companies. Many hotels work with cab drivers who have documented and reliable track records. Fare between Zona 1 and Zona Viva Q35. 24hr. service.

Car Rental: Tally, 7 Av. 14-60, Zona 1 (tel. 251-4113), open daily 7am-9pm; at the airport (tel. 334-5925), open daily 6am-9pm. Small cars Q202 per day (Q0.40 each additional km), including taxes, insurance, and 100km free. **Dollar,** at Av. La Reforma 6-14, Zona 9 (tel. 334-8285), open Mon.-Fri. 7am-9pm, Sat. 7am-7pm; at the airport (tel. 331-7185), open Mon.-Sat. 6am-9pm, Sun. 7am-8pm. Small cars, including taxes, insurance, and unlimited mileage, Q242 per day.

Market: Central Market, 6/8 Calles, 8/9 Avs. Open Mon.-Sat. 6am-6pm, Sun. 8am-noon. Virtually ignored by tourists, the whole market is in a big, cement, underground garage and boasts a good selection of indigenous wares at more sensible prices than at Chichi or Panajachel. There is also a big **food vendors' market** surrounding the bus terminal in Zona 4, but it's crowded, not very clean, and can be dangerous. Open daily 7am-6pm. **Supermarket: Paiz,** 18 Calle 6-85, Zona 1 (tel. 253-5674). Open Mon.-Sat. 9am-8pm, Sun. 9am-6pm.

Laundromat: El Siglo, 4 Av. 13-09 (tel. 232-1469). Q7 per wash, Q7 per dry. Other locations around the city. Open Mon.-Fri. 8am-6pm, Sat. 8am-1pm.

English Bookstores: Arnel, 9 Calle, 7 Av., Edificio el Centro 108, Zona 1 (tel. 232-4631). Large selection of books. Mon.-Fri. 11am-12:30pm and 3:30-7pm, Sat. 11am-12:30pm. Best selection of U.S. magazines is at **Book Nook,** Av. Reforma 14-30, Zona 9 (tel. 333-4633), in the Camino Real Hotel. The latest bestsellers Q20-35. Open daily 7am-9pm.

Pharmacy: Farmacia Sinai Centro, 4 Av. 12-74, Zona 1 (tel. 251-5276). **Farmacia Osco,** 16 Calle 4 Av., Zona 10 (tel. 337-1566). Both open 24hr.

Ambulance: tel. 128 (24hr. service).

Red Cross: 3 Calle 8-40, Zona 1 (tel. 125). 24-hr. emergency service.

Police: 6 Av. 13-71, Zona 1 (tel. 120).

Central Post Office: 7 Av. 11-67, Zona 1, in the enormous pink building (tel. 232-6101). Open Mon.-Sat. 7:30am-6:30pm. *Lista de correos* in Room 110 (ext. 106). Open Mon.-Fri. 8am-4:30pm. **United Parcel Service,** 2 Calle 6-40, Zona 9 (tel. 331-2094). Open Mon.-Sat. 8am-8pm. **DHL,** 7 Av. 2-42, Zona 9 (tel. 332-3023). Open Mon.-Fri. 8am-7:30pm, Sat. 8am-1pm. **Postal code:** 01001.

Telephones: Guatel, main office at 12 Calle 8-42, Zona 1 (tel. 253-1399). Open 24hr. **Phone, fax,** and **radiogram** service. Long-distance calls can also be made from any of the Guatel branches located throughout the city, including 7 Av. 3-34, Zona 4, and 8 Av., 12 Calle, Zona 1. Open daily 7am-midnight. **Telephone code:** 2.

▥ Accommodations

Budget accommodations are concentrated in Zona 1, the city's aging downtown area. Like most of Guatemala City, Zona 1 is plagued by muggings and robberies. Even if it costs a bit extra, make safety a top consideration in choosing a hotel—windows should be barred, balconies secure, locks functional, and management conscientious. Call hotels ahead of time to make reservations or arrive in the city early enough to ensure you'll find lodging before dusk—this ain't a great town in which to wander at night. All hotels listed here have hot water showers. Note: many hotels and restaurants won't notice your presence until you ring a service bell by the door (it usually looks like a light switch).

Pensión Meza, 10 Calle 10-17, Zona 1 (tel. 232-3177). This 85-year-old happy hippie hangout is both in a good location, *and* perhaps the best place for travel tips. Play ping-pong or chill in the shady courtyard. Warm, friendly service and a gregarious atmosphere combine with free filtered water (a real bonus!) to complete the Meza mystique. In addition, the management here speaks English *and* has a phone. Local calls can be made at the desk for a reasonable fee. Open 24hr. Dorm beds Q15 (bring a small padlock for your bags and be prepared to sleep in an unlocked room); singles Q33; doubles and triples Q45; triples with private bath Q55.

Lessing House, 12 Calle 4-35, Zona 1 (tel. 238-1881). Bathrooms could be cleaner, but at least each room has its own. Some of the Art Deco nightstands could fetch a pretty penny in a U.S. antique shop. Big wooden front doors are locked at night. Shared TV. Singles Q48; doubles Q84; triples Q120. Prices include taxes.

Hoteles Centroamérica, 9 Av. 16-38, Zona 1 (tel. 251-8160). The bubbling fountain in the spacious lobby seems to mumble of happier times seen here. Echoed footsteps lead to small rooms (some with tortilla-thin walls), and dirt lurks in bath corners. Nevertheless, the TV is color, foreign currency is exchanged, and restaurant, taxi, and fax services are all provided. There are 52 rooms, but unkempt discountseekers should know that few come with a bath. Singles Q64, with bath Q74, with bath and TV Q84; doubles Q98, with bath Q111; triples Q142, with bath Q160.

Hotel Colonial, 7 Av. 14-19, Zona 1 (tel. 232-6722; fax 232-8671). Colonial Guatemala City was destroyed by earthquakes, but a bit of its flavor survives here. Dark, polished antique beds and heavy wardrobes and nightstands adorn each room. Bathrooms are very clean, and most rooms have sitting areas. Restaurant serves breakfast. *Agua purificada* on sale at the desk. Very friendly staff. Singles Q108, with bath Q198. Larger rooms are available up to a whopping six beds Q396.

El Aeropuerto Guest House, 15 Calle "A" 7-32, Zona 13 (tel. 332-3086). Location, location, location—only 150m from the airport. Immaculate rooms and bathrooms (mostly communal) in a homey, friendly atmosphere. Cable TV in the living room. Includes breakfast and free transportation to and from the airport (versus Q40 for a taxi or a 30min. bus ride). Call when you arrive at the airport for a free pickup. Singles US$25, with private bath US$30; doubles US$30, with private bath US$35; triples US$35, with private bath US$40.

Hotel Mayestic, 5a Av. 11-23, Zona 9 (tel. 331-0824). The cheapest hotel close to Zona 10 nightlife and amenities. The 14 carpeted rooms, though not large, all have a private bath, hot water, TV, furniture, and complimentary art-deco-ish architecture. Singles Q120; doubles Q144; triples Q168.

■ Food

Eat cheap or eat chic—whatever your style, Guatemala City has a place for you. Sidewalk vendors always offer the cheapest grub (not necessarily for the faint of stomach). Plenty of side street eateries in Zona 1 sell full *típico* meals for Q6-12. In Zonas 4, 9, and 10 you'll find many moderately priced restaurants with dishes for US$4-5. More often than not you won't be seated: either order at the counter or seat yourself.

Delicadezas Hamburgo, 15 Calle 5-34, Zona 1 (tel. 238-1627), at the south side of Parque Centenario. Street performers and political activists bark at the doorstep. Chicken sandwich Q8.50, spaghetti Q16.50. Roasted ½ chicken with fries Q25, filet mignon with potatoes Q38. Open daily 7am-10pm.

Productos Integrales Rey Sol, 8 Calle 5-36, Zona 1 (tel. 251-2588), on the south side of Parque Central and at 12 Calle 0-66, Zona 9 (tel. 331-7607). The lunch crowd packs into this unconventional *comedor* for whole-grain cakes (Q3.50) and vegetarian soy dishes that change every day (Q8). Indulge in a luscious fruit *licuado* without fear—the fruit is washed in purified water (Q 4.50). Friendly staff, airy, and well lit. Burning incense offers an olfactory refuge from the carbon-monoxide of traffic outside. Open Mon.-Sat. 7am-9pm.

Restaurant Los Tecomates, 6 Av. 15-69, Zona 1 (tel. 251-2886). A bit of the sleepy western highlands in the heart of Zona 1. Pine needles blanket the floor and colored streamers hang from the ceiling, evoking the feel of many an *indígena* church. As always, real Quiché don't eat quiche—*carnes asadas* Q20, tacos Q2.75-Q3, and soups Q4-8. Open daily noon-10pm.

Patsy, 6a Calle 5-13, Zona 1 (tel. 232-4235) and Av. de la Reforma 8-01, Zona 10 (tel. 331-2435). When your desire to go native is drowned in the brackish water of the street vendors' wash pails, this is the place to recuperate. Typical Guatemalan fare served under a full-service/fast food concept. *Menú del día* lunch with soup and *refresco* Q13.90. Submarine sandwiches range from Q9.95-Q23.45. Avoid the noon-2pm lunch rush. Open daily 8:30am-9:30pm.

La Spaghetteria, Av. Reforma, 11 Calle (tel. 331-3893), across from the American Express office in Zona 10. Popular, clean, outdoor cafe serves great cappuccino, pizza (Q32), and ravioli (Q26). Extensive menu includes many toothsome desserts. Open daily 9am-8pm.

Las Tertulias, Av. Reforma 10-31, Zona 10 (tel. 332-0057). Despite the extensive menu, its main attraction is the super bargainous *super lunch ejecutivo,* with soup, an entree, salad, and dessert for Q20—it's not just for CEOs anymore. Live music after 5pm. Open Mon.-Thurs. 7am-midnight, Fri.-Sat. 7am-1am, Sun. 7am-7pm.

Cafetería San Martín, 10 Av. 10-11, Zona 1, (tel. 253-1314). Although this dim *comedor* is patronized by many a loyal housefly, its convenient location (near Pensión Meza) and large portions of above-average quality fare make up the difference. A standard breakfast costs Q8. Open daily 7am-8pm.

▓ Sights

Zona I

La Plaza Mayor (also called *Parque Central*) consists of two large plazas—**Parque de Centenario** and **Plaza de las Armas,** bounded on the west and east by 6 and 7 Avs., and on the north and south by 6 and 8 Calles. Permanently animated by persistent *limpiabotas* (shoe-shine boys), and often beseiged by the political demonstrators, Plaza Mayor never bores. It's been called "the center of all Guatemala," and on Sundays it is easy to understand why, as *indígenas* from all regions pour in to sell their textiles or just to take their afternoon strolls.

To the east of the plaza rises the beautiful, Neoclassical **Catedral Metropolitana,** constructed between 1782 and 1868 (open Mon.-Sat. 7am-6pm, Sun. 7am-8pm). To the north lies the **Palacio Nacional** (tel. 221-4444), built between 1928 and 1943 under the orders of president Jorge Ubico. Dozens of camouflaged, gun-toting soldiers guard the seat of the Republic's troubled government, but they allow the public to visit two spectacular rooms of the palace's 350—**La Sala de Recepción** and **La Sala de Banquetes.** The Sala de Recepción awes visitors with its massive Bohemian crystal chandelier, decorated with graceful *quetzales* in brass and gold. The parquet floor was sliced from the tropical hardwoods of Petén, and the elaborate reception table was carved in Spain from a single piece of wood. Stained glass windows depict Guatemala's pre-Hispanic and colonial history, coloring book style. The Sala de Banquetes features another chandelier in Bohemian crystal and 18-karat gold. Behind this elegance, however, lurks bitter irony and political turmoil. Fifteen years ago, the stained glass windows which had depicted the 10 virtues of a good nation were shattered by a bomb (free tours in Spanish or English Mon.-Fri. 8am-4:30pm).

Behind the cathedral, between 8 and 9 Avs. and 6 and 8 Calles, is the underground **Mercado Central,** which boasts a fantastic selection of food, crafts, and flowers. Though great deals abound, this market still caters primarily to locals (open Mon.-Sat. 6am-6pm, Sun. 8am-noon).

The **Miguel Angel Asturias Cultural Center** is at the south end of Zona 1, located in the Civic Center. It houses the National Theater, a chamber theater, and an open-air theater. The oldest church in the Ermita Valley, **Cerrito del Carmen** (finished in 1620), rests peacefully at 12 Av., 2 Calle. The first public clock in the city ticks away in one of the two towers of the **Santo Domingo Church,** 12 Av., 10 Calle. But the church most often praised for its elaborate paintings, sculptures, woodcarvings, and mosaics is **La Merced,** which stands at 11 Av. and 5 Calle.

GUATEMALA

Zona 2

The **Mapa en Relieve** (tel. 251-1156) is an enormous horizontal relief map of Guatemala, which was designed and built in the early 1900s. The vertical scale of the map is twice the horizontal scale, contributing to an overwhelming sense of vertigo. Viewers mount towers on either side of the map to look down upon a precise representation of the mountainous country. If you bring binoculars, you can watch a tiny replica of yourself looking at the map. The *mapa* is at the end of 6 Av., about 2km north of the plaza. Open daily 8:30am-5pm; admission Q1.50. (Take buses #1, 2, 45, or 46 from 5 Av. or #47, 49 or 50 from 3a Av. in Zona 1.)

Zonas 4, 9, and 10

Iglesia Yurrita (tel. 331-2514), a funky vermilion castle on the corner of Ruta 6 and Vía 9 in Zona 4, will catch your eye every time you take a bus between Zona 1 and Zonas 9 or 13 (open Tues.-Sun., 7am-noon, 4-6pm). Nearby, on the border between Zonas 4 and 9, lies a smaller version of the Eiffel Tower named **La Torre del Reformador** after Justo Rufino Barrio, the man who attempted to unite Central America and whose face graces the Q5 bill. A block east and across from Av. de la Reforma in Zona 10 is the **Jardín Botanico** (tel. 334-6064). Come here for a quiet picnic in lush surroundings or for details about Guatemala's natural history and geography (open Mon.-Fri. 7am-3pm).

The very fabric of indigenous life is on display at the above-mentioned **Museo Ixchel del Traje Indígena,** 6 Calle Final, Zona 10 (tel. 331-3739), on the campus of the Universidad Francisco Marroquín. Don't miss this museum, which offers a richly textured introduction to the weaving and textile traditions of the Guatemalan highlands. A 20-minute video (in English and Spanish) spins the story of indigenous dress from pre-Hispanic times to the present. The galleries exhibit antique cloth and paintings of indigenous costumes, all accompanied by English text (open Mon.-Fri. 8am-4:50pm, Sat. 9am-12:50pm, admission Q10, with student ID Q3).

This building also hosts the famous **Popol Vuh** museum. Named after the sacred Maya text, a cyclical cosmological epic, the museum houses a large collection of pre-Columbian Maya pottery. There are no signs in the museum, but the admission charge of Q10 includes a guidebook in English or Spanish.

Zona 13

Only a 20-minute walk from the airport, Zona 13 is full of tourist attractions and provides a great way to while away the hours until your flight. The **Mercado de Artesanías,** Blvd. Aeropuerto, 6 Calle, Zona 13, is your last chance to shop for traditional textiles, ceramics, and jewelry from each region of the country (open Mon.-Fri. 9am-6pm, Sat.-Sun. 8am-noon). The zoo next door, also called **Parque Aurora** (tel. 472-0507), offers a chance to stare long and hard at all those animals and birds of which you caught only fleeting glimpses in the jungle of Tikal or down the Río Dulce. If their small cement cells will turn your stomach, spare yourself the visit (open Tues.-Fri. 9am-5pm, Sat.-Sun. 9am-5:30pm; admission Q5). Behind the market and the zoo is the **Museo de Arte Moderno** (tel. 720-467), a solid collection which features the works of contemporary Guatemalan artists such as Carlos Mérida and Humberto Garavito (open Mon.-Fri. 9am-4pm; admission Q0.25). **Museo Nacional de Arqueología y Etnología** (tel. 720-489) primarily traces Maya preclassic, classic, and postclassic history in a display of hundreds of Maya artifacts from all over Guatemala; an excellent scale model of the ancient city at Tikal; and a large collection of ceremonial mastodont apparel, both pre-Hispanic and modern. There is also a reconstructed grave site of a Maya ruler. (Open Tues.-Fri. 9am-4pm, Sat.-Sun. 9am-noon and 2-4pm; the Jade room is open only Tues.-Fri. 9am-4pm; admission Q1.) **Museo de Historia Natural** (tel. 720-468) is home to a stuffed effigy of the sacred bird of the Maya. To get to any of these destinations catch bus #83 from 10 Av. or #63 and #85 (red) from 4 Av.

■ Entertainment

For a current listing of cultural events and movies, check **La Prensa Libre** (Q1.75) or any of the other local newspapers. Theater and opera performances in both English and Spanish are staged at **Teatro IGA,** 1 Ruta 4-05, Zona 4 (tel. 331-0022), on Friday and Saturday nights. Sometimes there are free showings of movies at the theater; call the office for information. Performances in Spanish are also presented at the **Teatro Nacional,** 24 Calle 3-81, Zona 1 (tel. 253-1743), the **Teatro La Universidad Popular,** 10 Calle 10-32, Zona 1, and in several other theaters throughout the city. The **Conservatorio Nacional de Música,** 5 Calle, 3 Av., Zona 1, organizes musical performances.

Guatemala City's nightlife gets pretty active, particularly in the newly developed **Zona Viva** (Zona 9). It's best to bar-hop in cabs, since the city isn't safe to wander through at night. The pace picks up at 11pm and winds down around 3am. The **Tropical Room** (between the Sheraton and a strip joint on 6 Av., Zona 4) is the best place to practice your *salsa,* while grown-up wannabes swarm to **Dash** (tel. 232-6030), in the Geminis commercial complex on 10 Calle, Zona 10. It's a modern disco: Thursday nights feature *música en vivo* (live music). Next on the city's "hot spots" list comes **Le Pont,** 13 Calle 0-48, Zona 10, decorated in a French Caribbean theme. The newest nightlife mecca is **La Terraza,** on the fourth floor of the Centro Commercial Los Próceres. The elevator opens onto a security checkpoint, beyond which throb four discos and 10 bars—some of the hippest bars and clubs in Guatemala.

■ Near Guatemala City

VOLCÁN PACAYA

Guatemala's volcanos have been plagued with robberies, rapes, and murders, and the Pacaya Volcano has been at the center of these troubles. In the summer of 1994, a group of sixteen Americans was assaulted by three armed men, who robbed them and raped one of the women in the group. As of the summer of 1996, the volcano was considered safer than in the past, as guards have been stationed around the mountain, and it is possible to make the ascent in groups (often with an armed guide). Travel agencies in Guatemala City or Antigua will be able to procure guides for volcano-climbing. Tours from Antigua run around US $15 per person. For updated information on the safety of traveling to the volcanoes, check with the INGUAT office in Guatemala City or Antigua and the U.S. embassy in Guatemala City (see Practical Information, above). Buses leave Guatemala City from the terminal in Zona 4 to San Viciente Pacaya, El Cedro, and San Francisco de Salle. Some climbers stay the night at one of these villages and start the two-hour ascent early the next morning, in order to catch the early afternoon bus back to Guatemala City. Climb at your own risk.

SAN JUAN DE COMALAPA

Comalapa is a small Cakchiquel village famed for its indigenous "primitivist" art. It is 40km from the capital, in the province of Chimaltenango. In fact, most of the works of indigenous art in the Museum of Modern Art in Guatemala City come from Comalapa; many more can be seen on a trip to the village. Seven art galleries line the **Calle Principal** and sell excellent pieces of art depicting the traditional folk rituals which are still a way of life in Comalapa.

Plan to visit Comalapa during the week of June 20-26, when the local *feria* in honor of the patron saint of the village, San Juan, takes place. Everyone turns out to strut their stuff in daily processions—*marimba* orchestras, masked dancers, hot air balloons, and a dancing, fireworks-spewing *torre.* **Buses** to Comalapa leave Guatemala City from the terminal at 20 Calle, 1 Av., Zona 1 (every hr. 7am-5:30pm, 2hr.). It's also possible to take any bus that passes through Chimaltenango and change there for one of the buses that leaves hourly for San Juan. The last bus leaves San Juan around 3 or 4pm, so plan ahead; there are no hotels and few restaurants.

WESTERN HIGHLANDS

■ Antigua

Antigua was improvidently built at the base of the magnificent Volcán de Agua in 1527. Within two decades, the volcano wiped the city off the map. Unfazed, the Spaniards re-built Antigua in the Valley of Panchoy, and it grew to become the political capital of the region. Alas, in the 1770s another natural disaster, this time a gargantuan earthquake, destroyed the city and jostled it from its position as a center of political power in the process.

Set amid rugged green mountains, today's Antigua is a tourist magnet. Restaurants and hotels catering to international travelers have cropped up everywhere and have lent the city a cosmopolitan air. Ironically, in a city famed for its Spanish language schools, knowledge of Spanish is rather unnecessary—English is everywhere. At times, Antigua can feel a bit too cozy; some feel the narrow streets aren't meant to hold as many *gringos* as they do. Through it all, however, the tourists (and the Guatemalans who cater to them) have respected Antigua's colonial charm, which remains unobscured. The cobblestone streets are kept spotless, and earthquakes have limited the construction of awkward, oversized buildings. Hanging signs or advertisements is strictly forbidden in Antigua; a rule which enhances the city's mystique (though it does make most everything damn hard to find). Year after year, Antigua continues to embrace the hearts of most visitors as it did Aldous Huxley's, who deemed the town one of the most romantic in the world.

ORIENTATION

While Antigua (altitude 1500m) is only 45km southwest of Guatemala City, the trip over winding mountain roads can consume an hour and a half. Frequent-running, converted school buses connect the cities. **Transportes Unidos, América Preciosa,** and several other lines leave Guatemala City every half hour (see **Practical Information,** p. 60) and arrive in Antigua at *el mercado* on Alameda Santa Lucía, three blocks west of the central plaza (Q3.50).

Though compact, Antigua is often tricky to navigate. Few of its *calles* and *avenidas* are marked, street numbers follow no obvious plan, and many streets look alike. *Avenidas* run north to south; numbers increase from east to west. North of 5 Calle, *avenidas* are all designated **Norte** (Nte.); south of it, **Sur.** *Calles* run east to west; numbers increase from north to south. East of 4 Av., *calles* are named **Oriente** (Ote.); west of it, **Poniente** (Pte.). The **Parque Central (park)** is bounded by 4 and 5 Calles on the north and south, respectively, and by 4 and 5 Av. on the east and west.

PRACTICAL INFORMATION

Tourist Office: INGUAT (tel. 832-0763) is on the south side of park, kitty-corner with the cathedral. The office has brochures and an excellent map. English is spoken. Open daily 8am-6pm. Guides roam the park looking to show tourists around for a hefty price (4hr. through Antigua and San Antonio Aguas Calientes, US$35).

Currency Exchange: Ban Quetzal, on the north side of the park, usually exchanges traveler's checks at a superior rate. Open Mon.-Fri. 8:30am-7pm, Sat. 9am-1pm. **Banco del Agro** (tel. 832-0793), on the north side of the park, always exchanges dollars. Open Mon.-Fri. 9am-8pm, Sat. 9am-6pm. **Banco Industrial,** 5 Av. Sur 4 (tel. 832-0958), has a 24hr. **ATM** and gives cash advances on Visa cards (and supposedly on PLUS System ATM cards). Open Mon.-Fri. 8:30am-1pm, Sat. 10am-2pm.

Telegrams: Alameda de Santa Lucía at 4 Calle Pte. (tel. 832-0485), next door to the post office. Open daily 8am-7pm. **Western Union,** inside Banco Agrícola, 5a Av. Norte #8, just west of the park (tel. 832-3822). Open Mon.-Fri. 9am-4:30pm.

Buses: The "terminal" is located behind the market on 5 Calle Pte. To find your bus, ask your way through the labyrinthine parking lot; there is no main office. To:

GUATEMALA

Western Highlands

ALTA VERAPAZ
BAJA VERAPAZ
EL PROGRESO
JALAPA
SANTA ROSA
GUATEMALA
CHIMALTENANGO
SACATEPÉQUEZ
SANTA CRUZ del QUICHÉ
HUEHUETENANGO
TOTONICAPÁN
SOLOLÁ
QUEZALTENANGO
SAN MARCOS
SUCHITEPÉQUEZ
RETALHULEU
MEXICO
PACIFIC OCEAN

El Progreso
Salamá
Rabinal
Cubulco
Chuarrancho
Ciudad de Guatemala
Mixco
San Juan Sacatepéquez
Villa Nueva
Villa Canales
S. Vicente Pacaya
Amatitlán
Lago de Amatitlán
Volcán de Pacaya
Palín
Escuintla
Ciudad Vieja
Antigua
Chimaltenango
S. Antonio Aguas Calientes
Volcán de Agua
Volcán Acatenango
Volcán de Fuego
Sta. Lucia Cotzumalguapa
Tecpán
Iximché
Panajachel
San Lucas Tolimán
Volcán Tolimán
Volcán Atitlán
Lago de Atitlán
Sololá
San Pablo La Laguna
S. Pedro La Laguna
Volcán San Pedro
Mazatenango
Retalhuleu
Pueblo Nuevo Tiquisate
San Martín Jilotepeque
Chichicastenango (Sto. Tomás)
Zacualpa
San Bartolomé Jocotenango
Sta. Lucia la Reforma
San Pedro Jocopilas
Sacapulas
Nebaj
Momostenango
San Cristóbal Totonicapán
Totonicapán
Cuatro Caminos Junction
Olintepeque
Quezaltenango (Xela)
Zunil
Volcán Siete Orejas
Volcán Sta. Maria
Colomba
Coatepeque
Ciudad Tecún Umán
Pampas El Guamuchal
La Libertad
Ciudad Hidalgo
Frontera Hidalgo
Malacatán
San Pablo
San Marcos
El Carmen
Concepción Tutuapa
Tejutla
Ixchiguán
Tajumulco
Volcán Tajumulco
Volcán Tacaná
Tacaná
Unión Juárez
Cacahoatán
Tuxtla Chico
San Miguel Ixtahuacán
Cuilapa
El Cuchillo Junction
El Tablón Junction
Codie Junction
N

Guatemala City (every 15min., 5am-7pm, 55min., Q3.25); **Chimaltenango** (every 15min., 5am-7pm, Q1.75); **San Antonio Aguas Calientes** (every hr., 7am-7pm, 30min., Q0.75); **Ciudad Vieja** (every 30min., Q0.50); to **Santa María de Jesús** (every hr., 7am-7pm, 2hr., Q1.25); **Puerto San José** (6, 7am, and 2pm, 1½hr., Q3). Hotels and travel agencies advertise various shuttles to the **airport** (US$7-10) and to **Panajachel** (US$12).

Taxis: (tel. 832-0526), lined up along the east side of Parque Central. To Ciudad Vieja Q25-35. Negotiable fares.

Car Rental: Avis (tel. 832-2692), 5 Av. Nte 22, rents small Chevrolets for US$50 per day, including insurance and unlimited mileage (you must be at least 21 years old).

Travel Agency: Turansa, 5 Calle Pte. 11B (tel. 832-3316). Makes ticket reservations and organizes tours to Panajachel, Chichicastenango, Copán, Quiriguá, and Esquipulas. Open Mon.-Sat. 8am-1pm and 2-6pm. **Servicios Turísticos Atitlán,** 6 Av. Sur 8 (tel. 832-0648), also offer tours. Shop around for tour packages since prices vary widely and change frequently.

Tattoo Parlor: The perfect crazy thing to do while traveling and then regret for the rest of your life. **Colliers Art Studio,** 5a Av. Nte. #14, just off the park inside Casa de las Gargoles. Make sure needles are sterile.

Market: On the west side of Alameda de Sta. Lucía, 1/5 Calles Pte. Batteries, socks, and buckets of fruit—all under a colossal tent. Open daily 7am-6pm.

Laundromat: Lavandería Guatemala, 4 Calle Pte. 30., washes and hangs for 1 load for Q13.50. Additionally, many hotels have their own washing machines.

Pharmacy: Farmacia Santa María, 5 Av. Nte. (tel. 832-0572), on the west side of Parque Central. Open daily 8am-10pm. Rotating schedule for 24hr. pharmacies; all are required to post the name of the *farmacia de turno* on their door.

Hospital: Hospital Pedro de Betancur, 6 Calle Ote. 20, 3/4 Avs. (tel. 832-0883), in a big yellow building with few windows. English is spoken. Open daily 7am-8pm.

Emergency: Los Bomberos (tel. 832-0234), on the north side of the bus station.

Police: Policía Nacional (tel. 832-0251), on the south side of Parque Central in the Palacio de los Capitanes Generales. 24hr. emergency service.

Internet: Tecni Camaras, 3 Calle Pte. 21. Charges US$2 for email and US$0.25 per min. for other services. **Villa San Francisco,** 1 Av. Sur 15 (tel./fax 832-3383), also offers email services. (See **Accommodations,** below).

Post Office: Alameda de Santa Lucía at 4 Calle Pte. (tel. 832-0485), across the street from the market. Open Mon.-Fri. 9am-5:30pm. **DHL,** on the corner of 6 Calle Pte. and 7 Av. Sur (tel. 832-3718), has no maximum weight restriction on packages. Open Mon.-Fri. 8am-noon and 2-6pm, Sat. 8am-noon. **Postal code:** 3001.

Telephones: Use pay phones on the south and west sides of the park for direct-dial international calls. **Guatel,** on 5 Av. Sur 2 (tel. 832-2498), just south of the southwest corner of the park, will place both domestic and pricey international calls and is often crowded. Open daily 7am-10pm. Private telecommunications services may offer better rates and advertise all over the city.

ACCOMMODATIONS

In every crack of Antigua's cobblestone streets sprouts a budget hotel. Unfortunately, these cracks also tend to be filled with budget travelers. Yet with perseverance—or the help of one of the suspiciously eager, yet free, guides who comb the streets—you will find a deal worthy of your low means. Many families provide room and board to Spanish language students for about US$40 per week. Such homestays can be a great deal; your belongings are secure, the food is safer than street grub, and you can practice your Spanish over dinner. Contact one of the language schools in Antigua (for more information, see **Alternatives to Tourism,** p. 52). Inquire at travel agencies for information on willing families.) Prices quoted below do not include taxes (which can be 17% or more). Do not be ashamed to test the hot water before you pay.

Posada Ruíz #2, 2 Calle Ote. 24. Look for the rock-studded, arched doorway. There are no exotic plants or peacocks in the courtyard, but the hotel's cleanliness, price, and smiling service leave nothing to be desired. Rooms are adequate, campy, and

Antigua

Agencia de Viajes Travel, 1
Alianza Francesca, 2
Biblioteca Francisco
  Antonio de Fuentes
  y Guzmán, 3
Biblioteca Rafael Landívar
  y Caballero Monumento, 4
Convento de la
  Orden Belemita, 5
Guardía de Hacienda, 6

Hospital Nacional Pedro de
  Betancur, 7
Museo Colonial, 8
Museo del Libro; Museo de
  Armas, 9
Office of Tourism, 10
Palacio de la Real Audencia, 11
Palacio del Ayuntamiento
  Alcaldía Municipal; Museo de
  Santiago, 12

quiet—and often booked solid. Expansive and appealing common area. Common bathroom and laundry machine. Singles Q17; doubles Q30.

Villa San Francisco, 1 Av. Sur 15 (tel./fax 832-3383). This technological avant-garde of hotels has fax, long-distance phone, and email services. Behind the big wooden colonial doors stretches a long, thin courtyard. Some rooms have tapestries and wrought-iron light fixtures. Clean bathrooms and unbeatable views from the roof-top terrace. Singles Q40, with bath Q65; doubles Q55, with bath Q80. Open 24hr.

Posada Landívar, 5 Calle Pte. 23 (tel. 832-2962), ½ block southeast of the *mercado*. Visible from Alameda Santa Lucía. Small but hygienic surroundings; red tiling rules. Hot water flows freely in clean bathrooms. Gulp from jugs of *agua purificada* in the halls. Singles and doubles Q50, with bath Q60.

Hospedaje El Pasaje, Santa Lucía Sur 3 (tel. 832-3149), south of the bus stop. Big, white, basic rooms and hardwood furniture recalls the days before mushy beds and synthetic, worn linens. Nevertheless, hot water is hot. Simple roof-top terrace bedecked with droopy horticulture. Free purified water. Checkout 11am. Singles Q20; doubles Q30, with bath Q40.

El Refugio, 4a Calle Pte. 30. Smallish rooms vary a great deal; ask to see several before making a decision. Tiny, mediocre bathrooms, iffy beds, and cracked mirrors are all compensated for by the courtyard and the outstanding views from the rooftop terrace. Kitchen available for guests' use. Singles Q20, with bath Q25 or Q30; doubles Q35, with bath Q45.

FOOD

Some only half-jokingly call Antigua "the capital of international budget cuisine"— incredibly enough, there are more restaurants here than there are ruined churches.

In Antigua, everything is possible and nothing is forbidden: chow down on burgers, *chiles rellenos,* fresh pasta, and all the culinary madness which lies in between. Most fare pleases your papillae without breaking your budgetary back. Meals that would cost US$40 in Miami cost only $5 here. The eateries are often cafes where *gringos* talk, and sometimes study, all afternoon; many establishments cultivate a polished, cultured, "Spanish-colonial" ambience.

Cafetería de Doña Luisa, 4 Calle Ote. 12 (tel. 832-2578), in 2 floors of a 17th-century house. *Everyone* goes here. Sit in the sunny courtyard with fellow *gringos,* gawk at the naturalistic wall art, or peruse the floor-to-ceiling bulletin board for the latest travelers' info, including houses for rent and personal ads. Use the phone booth to make local calls or slip into your favorite superhero costume. Eggs with frijoles Q11, sandwiches Q16. Breaking Mesoamerican tradition, the second cup of coffee is *gratis.* Traveler's checks accepted. Open daily 7am-9:30pm.

La Cenicienta, 5 Av. Nte. 7. This plush, polished cafe offers the most seductive desserts in town. Brownies (Q3), chunks of choco-banana cake (Q4.50), and cheese and fruit *postres* (Q4.50) seduce passersby. Open daily 8:30am-8pm.

Café la Fuente, 4 Calle Ote. 14., next to Doña Luisa's. Mull over the lengthy menu of vegetarian cuisine, as you listen to the fountain gurgle in the beautiful Andalucian courtyard. Tofu with beans and fruit Q22, falafel Q22. Open daily 7am-7pm.

Restaurante San Carlos, on the west side of Parque Central. Relish people-watching in the park out front. Ask for the special and they'll show you a little leg (roast leg of pork Q20)—and they're not shy. Open daily 8am-10pm.

Quesos y Vino, 5 Av. Nte. 31A, just past the arch. When the rooms are poorly lit, the tables are low, and the seats are stools, you know it's gourmet. Fresh homemade pasta and wines from France, Italy, Chile, and Argentina will not disappoint. *Pasta con ricotta y tomate* Q25, medium pizza Q28, cup o' wine Q13. Open Wed.-Mon. 8:30am-11am, 1:30-4pm, and 5:30-10pm.

Café El Jardín, 5 Av. Nte., on the west side of Parque Central. Breakfast for backpackers. Coffee, cornflakes, yogurt, and a big plate of fruit Q16.50, waffles with honey and juice Q18. Open daily 8:30am-8pm.

SIGHTS

Travelers come to Antigua not for any particular "sights" but for the combined effect of the city's broad, peaceful streets, melancholy colonial ruins, and green mountains. Antigua's charms are best absorbed on a leisurely, day-long walking tour.

The city's centerpiece is the **Parque Central,** now a tranquil park, but for most of its history a muddy hubbub of markets and public hangings. Today, foreigners practice their *español* with long-suffering locals around the 250-year-old central fountain, **La Llamada de las Sirenas** (The Sirens' Call). The stony babes enthrall with their charmingly leaky breasts. On the north side of the plaza is the **Palacio del Noble Ayuntamiento,** built in 1743. Unlike most of Antigua's other buildings, the Palacio, well braced by its meter-thick walls, survived the earthquakes of 1773 and 1776. Once a jail, the building now houses two museums. The small **Museo de Santiago** exhibits colonial furniture, art, and weapons aplenty (open Tues.-Fri. 9am-4pm, Sat.-Sun. 9am-noon and 2-4pm; admission Q0.25, or whatever you care to drop in the contributions box). Also in the *Ayuntamiento* (city hall) is the **Museo del Libro Antiguo** (Old Book Museum), which displays a reproduction of the first printing press in Central America, brought to Antigua in 1660. Some of the fruits of that old press are displayed nearby, including an 18th-century lexicon of Guatemala's indigenous languages (open Tues.-Fri. 9am-4pm, Sat.-Sun. 9am-noon and 2-4pm; admission Q10).

The main **cathedral** stands on the east side of the park. This structure is but a shadow of its former self. Once the most spectacular of its kind in Spanish America, the cathedral was begun in 1670 and was renowned for its five naves, 18 chapels, towering dome, and silver-and-pearl inlaid altar. Unfortunately, the earthquake of 1773 leveled the awesome edifice, and only two partially restored and entirely unremarkable chapels remain. The rest of the old cathedral lies in ruins behind the modern church. A small crypt at the east end of the ruins houses a much venerated, completely charred, 313-year-old **black Christ** (site open daily 9am-noon and 1:30-4:45pm; admission Q2). Unfortunately, during the summer of 1997, the Savior was closed for repairs.

On the south side of Parque Central is the **Palacio de los Capitanes Generales,** rebuilt after the 1773 earthquake. The Palacio was the political nerve center of colonial Guatemala, which included Chiapas and all of Central America, minus Panamá. The most powerful men between Mexico and the Andes once ruled from this building, surrounded by bureaucrats, law courts, tax offices, and a mint. Today, the building's purpose is more prosaic—it houses the police.

Half a block east of Plaza Mayor on 5 Calle Ote. is the old building of the **University of San Carlos de Borromeo.** Founded in 1676, San Carlos was the third university in all of Latin America. Today it holds the **Museo de Arte Colonial** and temporary exhibits of contemporary Guatemalan art. The large canvasses by Thomas de Merlo are especially impressive; each depicts a scene from the life of Saint Francis. The university is among the finest of colonial Antigua's architectural survivors—cast your eyes heavenward to see the graceful *mudéjar* arches of the central patio, or the colonial wooden ceilings and baroque mouldings of its large gallery (open Tues.-Fri. 9am-4pm, Sat.-Sun. 9am-noon and 2-4pm; Q0.25).

Just northwest of San Francisco are the ruins of **Santa Clara,** 2 Av. Sur 27, at 6 Calle Ote. This massive convent, founded in 1699, was a popular place for aristocratic women to take the veil. Overgrown with flowers, the ruins are among the most beautiful in the city. Get thee there in the early morning or in late evening, when the play of light and shadow dapples the courtyard (open daily 9am-5pm; Q10).

Round out your tour of Antigua's churches with a visit to **La Merced,** on 1 Calle Nte. at the northern end of 5 Av. Originally built in 1548, the church survived the 1760 earthquake, only to collapse in the 1773 quake. Although the rebuilt interior is not spectacular, the yellow facade offers the best extant example of Antigua's baroque style (open daily 7am-noon and 3-7pm; free).

To the west of Santa Clara lies the **Parque de la Unión.** This sun-bleached, unkempt patch of palm trees has long served as the local laundromat. Although scrubbing clothes by hand has become a dwindling practice, the queued stone basins still get their fair share of use.

Farther north on 2 Av. is **Las Capuchinas,** 2 Calle Ote. and 2 Av. Nte., built in 1736, destroyed 37 years later. The **Torre de Retiro** (Tower of Retreat) towers on its north side and marks the site where nuns used to cloister themselves for months of meditation. To compensate for their deprivation, they had one luxury of the flesh—private baths with running water. Today, mannequin nuns pray in fiberglass eternity. The chambers with dripping water (not the private baths, the other ones) were used for corporal and psychological punishment (open daily 9am-5pm; Q10).

One of Antigua's most interesting attractions is **Casa K'ojom,** Recoletos 55, a museum dedicated to the traditional song and dance of Guatemala's *indígenas.* To reach the Casa, follow 5 Calle Pte. west to the outskirts of town, turning right just before the road ends at the cemetery; it's the third entrance on the left. The director is concerned that western pop and the increasing popularity of Christian evangelical denominations are squelching *indígena* music and dance by prohibiting traditional dancing and singing among their converts. Casa K'ojom attempts to document these waning traditions. A program of slides and music is shown at 10, 11am, 2 and 3pm, followed by a guided tour of the two exhibit halls. At other times, exhibits are still open and a less-than-spectacular videotape is available (open Mon.-Fri. 9:30am-12:30pm and 2-5pm, Sat. 9:30am-12:30pm and 2-4pm; Q5).

Proyecto Cultural el Sitio, at 5 Calle Pte. 15 (tel. 832-3037), exhibits and sells paintings (open Tues.-Sun. 11am-7pm. Prices hover around Q1000). **Los Naza Renos,** 6 Calle Pte. 3, exhibits paintings by local artists of local attractions, from the lovely Parque Central to fuming volcanos. Prices range from Q150 to 2000. The synthesizers lying around are for music classes offered to children on Saturdays.

To shed Antigua's sultry air, a short jaunt by bus or by foot brings you to the perch of a volcano and to the largest local *pueblo,* **San Antonio Agua Caliente,** known for its regal church and handmade fabrics. A textile store halfway to San Antonio has an unbeatable selection at better prices than you'll ever see in Antigua. A room in back displays the village's finest ceremonial robes, which take over six months to complete and are not for sale.

ENTERTAINMENT

Tune in to the local scene by picking up a free copy of *The Revue* (in English) at INGUAT or any of the more touristy establishments. For food, flicks, and fun, try **Cinemala,** 2 Calle Ote. 4, inside the Spanish Academy. Shows two different films a day at 3:30, 6, and 8pm on VCRs. Bring your own popcorn; shows cost Q10. **Cinema Bistro,** 5a Av. Norte #8, features shows at 3:30, 6, and 8:30pm and at 1pm on weekends. **Mistral Bar,** 2a Av. Norte #6B, rolls'em at 5:30 and 8pm (Q8).

The tourist office tells visitors to go to bed early to keep you off Antigua's dark and empty nighttime streets, where muggings have been known to occur. If you go out in a group, though, you can enjoy a small but lively bar scene; just be careful. Also, bear in mind Guatemala's *Ley Seca* which forbids the sale of alcoholic beverages past midnight. The haunt of choice for most is **La Chimenea,** 7 Av. Norte #7, where hordes of foreigners chatter in several tongues, sip down brews (Q8), and lounge on sofas, caught in the sway of live musical performances (open daily noon-1am).

For classical concerts and dramatic productions in both English and Spanish, head to the **Proyecto Cultural el Sitio,** at 5 Calle Pte. 15 (tel. 832-3037), open Tuesday through Sunday 11am-7pm. Ticket prices vary from Q10 to Q30. On Sundays, check out mid-morning *fútbol* games on the field near the bus stop. **Macondo,** 5 Calle Pte. 28, is a classy drinking establishment that somehow keeps its prices low. A mahogany staircase leads to three spacious tiers, and rock and jazz bounce off lavender tiles and framed pictures of Charlie Chaplin and the Blues Brothers. This is *serious* pop culture (beer Q6; open 6pm-1am). On the same block, just past the Arc, lies **La Casbah,** 5 Av. Norte #30 (tel. 832-2640), the hot place for jet-setters to bootie-shake to Latin and Anglo hits while sipping pricey potables (beer Q10). There is no cover on Thursdays, Fridays, and Saturdays, the cover is Q25 and the crowds are quite thick.

Come to **Rainbow Café,** at 7 Av. Sur 8, where wanna-be intellectuals ruminate alone or find connections with each other, borrow books from the library, stare into an open fire, or gaze at the stars above while sipping their beverages. Poetry readings on Thursdays, local musicians on Fridays, deep thoughts and cosmopolitan chatter at all times. Vegetarian menu includes pasta or falafel for Q23, beer for Q8. (Open Thurs.-Tues. 9am-11pm.) **Riki's Bar,** in La Escudilla at 4 Av. Norte #4, is low-key and never crowded, but it plays chillin' music and gives two drinks for Q6 from 8-9pm nightly (open 8am-1am). There is a small group of bars on 7 Av. Nte., where the action starts to pick up around 10pm. **Latinos Bar,** 7 Av. Nte. 16, has live music most nights and a lively ambience at all times. Guatemalan rock as well as standard Latin music. (No cover; open Mon.-Sat. 6pm-1am; happy hour 6-9pm; 3 beers Q16.) **Picasso's,** down the block a bit at 7 Av. Nte. 3, is always packed with travelers and students (open daily 6pm-midnight).

■ Panajachel and Lago Atitlán

According to Quiché belief, Lago Atitlán was one of the four lakes which demarcated the corners of the world. For tourists visiting Guatemala, magnificent Lago Atitlán is simply the center of the universe. Hugged on all sides by the green-checkered hillsides of farmland dotted with grazing cattle, the lake emanates endless natural beauty. In the late afternoon, rays of sun tango seductively in the sloping hills around the lake. When an electrical storm blows in and lingers wet and heavy, the squall lights up the ridge in silhouettes and illuminates the whole expanse of water, purging evening shadows. Atitlán is ringed by a coterie of 12 small villages inhabited mainly by *indígena* of Cakchiquel and Tzutuhil descent. Today, many villagers proudly wear the traditional dress that distinguishes each town from its neighbors.

Panajachel, the thirteenth town on Atitlán, is also a rowdy ringleader for its 12 cousins, replete with beach-side belly dancers, mellow market-lovin' hippies, and a large number of retirees who peacefully while away the days in expensive hotels. Perhaps because of its eclectic spirit and individuality, "Pana," as locals have affectionately dubbed it (they also not-so-affectionately call it *Gringotenango*), is the most touristed town in the area. While indigenous fishermen cast off from their villages in wooden skiffs, *gringos* set out in rented kayaks and launches to drink their fill of Atitlán's scenery. Though hardly the most authentic town on the lake, Panajachel is a convenient place to run errands, savor waffles with fruit and honey, or just take a hot shower. The town is home to an amiable group of international expatriates whose shops, restaurants, and bars line the streets. This *gringo* outpost and way-station has become increasingly popular with prosperous weekenders from Guatemala City who are eager to escape the congestion of the capital. Many Guatemalans have begun building vacation homes in town and along the lake, and their incoming capital supports a good selection of video salons and vegetarian restaurants. After a meal and a flick, however, consider ferrying across the lake to a less expensive village.

ORIENTATION AND PRACTICAL INFORMATION

Panajachel is small enough that addresses and street names are not often used, but many signs point the way to various accommodations off the main street. Buses pull into Panajachel along its **Calle Principal** (the "Main Street" on INGUAT's English-language map) and stop at or near its most important intersection, at **Calle Santander,** about 30m from the tourist office. A useful map that includes most budget lodgings is posted right by the bus stop. Calle Santander begins here and stretches southward to the lakefront; **Calle Rancho Grande** lies to the east of Santander and runs parallel to it. Going north from the main intersection, Calle Principal forks. Its name lives on to the right side of the fork, while **Avenida Los Árboles** rises to the left. All services and most hotels are on Calle Principal, Calle Santander, and Av. Los Árboles. The public beach is at the end of Calle Santander and to the left.

Tourist Office: (tel. 762-2337 or 762-1392), located on Calle Santander. Friendly, English-speaking staff gives away free maps of the town and the lake. Safety updates on tourist excursions. Open Mon-Sat 8am-1pm and 2-6pm. During the high season, a beachfront extension office operates Tues., Wed., Fri., Sun. 9am-4pm.

Currency Exchange: Banco Inmobilario (tel. 762-1056), on Av. Los Árboles, 2 blocks from Calle Principal. Open for exchange Mon.-Fri. 9am-8pm, Sat. 10am-1pm. **Banco Agrícola Mercantil** (tel. 762-1145), on Calle Principal at Calle Santander. Open Mon.-Fri. 9am-7pm, Sat. 9am-1pm. **Banco Industrial,** on Calle Santander near Mario's Rooms, has a 24hr., Visa-friendly ATM.

Buses: Normally, buses arrive at and depart from Calle Principal, near the Banco Agrícola Mercantil, to **Guatemala City** (8 per day, 3½hr., Q10.50) and to **Chichicastenango** (10 per day, 1hr., Q5). Take any bus to Guatemala City, disembark at Los Encuentros, then board buses to **Quetzaltenango** (4 per day, 2hr., Q8) or to **Antigua** (10:45am, 2½hr., Q10). Alternatively, take any Guatemala City-bound bus to **Chimaltenango,** then change to an Antigua-bound bus to **Cocales** on the Pacific Highway (4 per day, 1½hr., Q6). To reach the **Mexican border,** take any Guatemala City bus to Los Encuentros, then change to a "Galgos" or "El Condor" bus to **La Mesilla, El Carmen,** or **Tecún Umán.** Buses from Pana also leave for **San Antonio** and **Santa Catarina** (5, 8:30, and 10:30am, 30min., Q2).

Ferries: Join commuters on the beautiful ferry rides around the lake; from the docks in front of Hotel del Lago to **Santiago** (8 per day, 5:45am-4pm, 1hr., Q10) and to **San Pedro** (7 per day, 8:20am-12:45pm, 1½hr., Q10). Irregular ferry service runs to Santa Catarina, San Antonio, and San Lucas Tolimán. Some San Pedro ferries stop at Santa Clara, San Marcos, and Santa Cruz. **Tours** of the lake (Q40) leave the docks at 8:30am and stop at San Antonio, Santiago, and San Pedro, returning at 3:30pm.

Taxis: (tel. 762-2028). Call, or look for one in front of Restaurante Vegetariano Hsieh on Calle Los Arboles.

Car Rental: Daiton Rent-a-Car, represented by BIGSA Moto Rent (tel. 762-1253), on Av. Los Árboles, between Circus Bar and Restaurante El Chisme. Small Nissan US$45 per 24hr., including unlimited mileage and insurance, with US$800 deductible (covered with a credit card impression or a deposit). Open daily 9am-6pm.

Bike/Motorcycle Rental: Moto Servicio Quiché (tel. 762-2089), at the corner of Av. Los Árboles and Calle Principal. For motorcycles, Q35 per hr. or Q110 per 8hr., including unlimited mileage and insurance. Q800 deposit and copy of passport required. For bikes, Q10 per hr. or Q40 per day. Bikes can also be rented from a nameless hole in the wall by the bus stop for Q5 per hr. or Q30 per day.

Boat Rental: Diversiones Balam, on the beach inside the main lifeguard tower. Kayaks available, individual Q10 per hr. or double Q20 per hr. Canoes Q20 per hr. Water bicycles Q20 per hr. Open daily 7:30am-6pm. Ferry and launch companies also hire out private launches (Q175 for 1-5 people).

English Bookstore: Delante, turn off Calle Santander at La posada de Don Rodrigo. English paperbacks Q6-15. Open Mon., Wed., Fri., Sat. noon-5pm.

Internet: At **c@fe.net,** next to Guatel. All services Q1 per minute.

Market: At the north end of Calle Principal. Open daily 7am-6pm.

Laundromat: Lavandería, 1½ blocks from Calle Santander, down the street which branches off to the left (facing the lake) after Guatel, inside Sevananda Restaurant. Up to 10 pounds for Q20; add Q5 for same-day service. Open 9am-6pm.

Pharmacy: Farmacia La Unión (tel. 762-2041), Calle Santander 2-19. Home delivery. Open daily 8am-11pm.

Medical Emergency: Dr. Eduardo Hernández (tel. 762-1068), on Calle Principal near the fire department. He speaks some English.

Police: (tel. 762-1120), at the end of Calle Principal in the municipal building. No English spoken.

Post Office and Telegrams: Up Calle Principal and behind the Catholic church. Post office open Mon.-Fri. 9am-5:30pm; national telegram office open 24hr. **Postal code:** 07010.

Telephones: Guatel, halfway down Calle Santander. Long-distance calls. Open daily 7am-10pm.

ACCOMMODATIONS

Pana is more expensive than the surrounding villages. Practically none of the available budget rooms has much personality, but a few of the places make up for it with gorgeously tended gardens and courtyards. Alternatively, stay in San Pedro for US$2 per night. There's a public campground at the east end of the public beach, on the other side of the Panajachel River, but it has no services or security. More here than most places, it pays to look around before you pay; prices tend to fluctuate on the owner's whim. Remember that while many places promise hot water, few deliver; clarify hot water availability (hours and fees if any) before accepting your room.

Hospedaje Pana Rooms, up Av. Los Árboles and left (west) at the dirt road just past the natural foods store. Small rooms with low ceilings. Clean shared bathrooms have 24hr. hot water. A wall around the courtyard and locked doors make the place relatively secure. Weights and boxing gloves in the exercise room; if pugilism isn't for you, try fattening up on snacks from the adjoining store. Singles Q15; doubles Q30; triples Q36.

Hotel Panajachel, on Calle Principal just before the market. Clean, basic rooms around a courtyard brightened by ruby-red trim and Maya-style paintings. A snappy little restaurant below serves bread and drinks. The service is very warm; the water sometimes isn't. Shared bathrooms are in good shape. Q20 per person. Ask for a discount (Q5-10) if business is slow.

Hospedaje Santa Elena, Calle Monterey off Calle Santander. Baby turkeys skitter while parrots and doves eye you from the ubiquitous tangles of vines. The owners living on the first floor are friendly and quite vigilant. Public bathrooms have adequate, stone-built showers. Singles Q18; doubles Q25; hot water Q2 per use. Hearty partiers beware: at the stroke of midnight the doors close and your magical beer gut turns back into a pumpkin.

Dos Mercedes, across from Hospedaje Eli. A tiny, 6-room alternative to Eli and Hotel Pana. A cracked cement courtyard supports a few plants—nothing fancy, but service is friendly, and you don't have to own two luxury cars to stay here. Extra beds available. Singles Q15; doubles Q25; quads Q40.

FOOD

If *plátanos* and peanuts don't tempt your tastebuds, fear not—Panajachel's gourmet restaurants are sure to pleasure the palate. The large tourist population has made its influence felt, so many foreign and expatriate owners have geared their menus towards a healthier, more cosmopolitan milieu. Prices are higher than in other parts of Guatemala, and are out of control in the lakeside restaurants. Alimentary options are more limited, but much less expensive in the smaller towns. At some point during your stay on the lake, you'll probably stare a fried black bass in the eye or cut open a **pitalla,** a bizarre-looking object which resembles a red and green artichoke on the outside but holds a beautiful and delicious purple fruit on the inside.

Deli Restaurant, on Calle Principal, next to Hotel Galindo. Look for the small green sign. One of the best breakfast places in town. Makes homemade waffles with fruit and syrup or honey (Q15). Serves oatmeal with raisins, nuts, and banana (Q8.50). Papaya *licuados* are thick and delicious, but they run up the tab. Complete breakfasts with pancakes, eggs, or omelettes (Q14-19). Homemade *fettucine alfredo* Q22. Bagels! Open daily 7:00am-5:45pm.

Restaurante Vegetariano Hsieh, on Calle Los Árboles, just after the intersection with Calle Principal. *Típico* atmosphere, health-conscious menu: crepes (Q6), granola (Q9), or the special of the day (lasagna, pizza, pasta, or *chile relleno* with soup, salad, and whole-wheat bread Q20). Open Tues.-Sun. 9am-10pm.

Mario's Restaurant, on Calle Santander halfway between the intersection with Calle Principal and the lakefront. A cheap joint popular with the backpacker brigade. Cinderblock walls enlivened by windows and funky contemporary art; slap your ham and cheese sandwich (Q6) up alongside it and see if anyone makes you an offer. Spaghetti Q15, omelettes Q8-12, chicken dinner with pasta, salad, and bread Q21. Open daily 8am-8:30pm.

Bombay Pub and Café, Calle de los Árboles under El Cine next to Ubu's. Trash novels galore and many English-language magazines, from *Vogue* to *Time* to *The New Yorker.* Watch out for slivers when you make your selection; the shelves are a carpenter's nightmare. Rest for hours tucked away from the streets in a verdant, shady courtyard. Burritos Q5, coffee Q4.

ENTERTAINMENT

Panajachel offers more amusements than its cheaper neighbors on the lake. A popular pastime is to dodge the treacherous obstacle course of *artesanía* vendors between your hotel and the lakefront. Try saying *"no estoy de compras, gracias"* ("I'm not shopping, thanks"). For a bit of high culture before diving head-first into the bar scene, **The Art Gallery** on Calle Río Grande displays the spiritual pastels of world-renowned artist Nan Cruz, as well as the work of other artists (open 9am-noon and 2-6pm, closed Tues.). The **Grapevine,** by Cafe Sicodelico on Calle Santander, shows a few movies each night (admission Q10). **The Carrot Chic,** across from the natural foods store on Av. Los Árboles, shows the movie of your choice (of 100) at the time of your choice (Q6 per person). **Ubu's Cosmic Cantina,** behind Restaurant Sevananda, occasionally shows free movies, though it's polite to have a drink or two.

Cowboys rearin' for a foot-stompin', heart-stoppin' good time can head over to **The Circus Bar and Pizzeria,** on Av. Los Árboles. Swing through the saloon doors as the clunky piano and dusty sound system boom flamenco and gypsy, starting at 9pm nightly. Faded circus posters are ghosts of the owner's crushed dream to start a three-ringer in Panajachel. Roll the dice and double your drink (Sun.-Thurs.). Have a beer (Q9) with your imported Italian pasta in an egg cream sauce (Q24), or try *bürek,* Turkish pizza, for only Q9 (open daily noon-midnight). Ubu's Cosmic Cantina, behind Restaurant Sevananda, opens when the owner gets there and closes when the guests go home (approximately noon-4am). The owner is gracefully ignorant of the clock but thorough with his entertainment, offering the best live rhythm and reggae Panajachel has to offer. Addicts, rejoice! *The Simpsons* and *The X-Files* are shown religiously on a gigantic TV. Plump, well-loved couches and chairs beckon for intimacy as Christmas lights twinkle above among the flags and *piñatas.* The adjoining room has ping-pong and pool tables (English spoken; beer Q8).

■ Around Lago Atitlán

The cafe-filled streets of *Gringotenango* can't compete with the necklace of *indígena* villages hung around Lake Atitlán. All the villages are accessible as daytrips from Panajachel, and it's possible to visit two or three in a single, leisurely day. Alternatively, you could work your way around the lake gradually, stopping to spend the night in whatever village seems most comfortable. The hyperadventurous skip the boat entirely and make the circuit on foot. There are several trails that wind around the water and over the volcanoes; the trip takes at least a week, so adequate preparation and a solid foundation of safety information are absolute prerequisites for this journey. The only areas not recommended are: the town of San Lucas Tolimán, the road connecting it to Santiago Atitlán, and the road between Santiago and San Pedro la Laguna that snakes behind San Pedro Volcano, away from the lake. In these areas, there have been problems with crime and assault. Check with the tourist office about safety at other destinations before hitting the trail or jumping on a bus or boat.

A Special Sort of Saint

Some distance from Santiago's church, lost among the houses near the edge of town, hides a sacred, alternative center of worship, one of the more **bizarre** examples of **religious syncretism** in a country known for its folk Catholicism. For a few *quetzals,* local kids will show you to the shrine dedicated to **Maximón,** or San Simón in his Christian incarnation, a wooden figure dressed in European garb and associated with vices such as smoking and drinking. Maximón, ever a consummate enemy of the church, is quite popular in Santiago. The incense-choked **shrine** is full of devotees praying, playing the guitar, and making offerings of liquor and cigarettes. The saint's specialty is **casting curses,** so beware. On the Wednesday of Semana Santa, a Maximón idol is paraded through the village, and worshipers stand chomping on unlit stogies as the procession passes. Newcomers can experience the ritual themselves. For Q10 the head counter will **mummify** you and solemnly spit alcohol in your face. Or just let him bum a cig or some of whatever else you have on you.

SANTIAGO DE ATITLÁN

The largest and most touristed of the *pueblos* is Santiago de Atitlán, nestled between the San Pedro and Tolimán volcanoes. **Launches,** or *lanchas,* run from Panajachel to Santiago (8 per day, 5:45am-4pm, 1½hr., Q10). Santiago is home to the Tzutuhil people, who were Pedro de Alvarado's allies in subduing the Cakchiquel of Panajachel. Santiago was the most influential of the Atitlán villages until its former rival Panajachel took sweet revenge and reclaimed the title of largest Atitlán village.

In today's Santiago, indigenous cultural forms have become somewhat obscured. Few women still sport the *xocop,* the extraordinary, 10-meter-long red strap worn wrapped around the head. However, on July 25 (the feast of Santiago) or during Semana Santa, the *xocops* are out in full force. Even the men get funky during the feast, donning their multi-colored trousers and cowboy hats. Aside from colorful garb, Santiago is known for its paintings of the lake and its woodcarvings of St. James. If you're looking for relief from the *artesanía* of Panajachel, you've come to the wrong place.

The **post office** is in front of the market, near the municipal building (open Mon.-Sat. 8am-2pm). For **phone** calls, **Guatel** is on the main street, behind the church (open 7am-8pm). **Buses** leave from one end of the market for: **Guatemala City** (every hr., 2:30-7:30am and 11am-2pm, Q12) and **Esquintla** via San Lucas at 1:30pm (Q6). **Launches** leave from Santiago to Panajachel (7 per day, 6am-5pm, 1hr., Q7.50) and to towns along the lake's western edge. The local **doctors** are Francisco Pulo and Juan Carlos Perez; both have offices in the center of town. The huge, purple creature in the village center is the **art gallery,** where local paintings are displayed and sold.

If you like Santiago enough to stay, **Chi Nim Ya,** just above the dock, offers acceptable rooms and laundry service at Q1 per item. Rooms are Q20 per person, with private bath Q30. But you may as well go the whole nine yards and head straight from Maximón's shrine to one of the smaller, cheaper towns on the lake.

SAN PEDRO LA LAGUNA

To escape the bustle of Pana, you might join the relaxed crowd at San Pedro La Laguna, the San Pedro volcano, and the nearby beach. The town has gotten bigger in the last few years, so it's not as cute. Frugality, however, is cute in its own way. If you're lookin' to spend, however, stick around on a Sunday, the prime market day, and especially **June 19,** when it's party time. **Launches** from Pana to San Pedro leave from the docks in front of Pana's Hotel del Lago (9 per day, 1½hr., Q7.50).

Guatel phones are on the main street up from the dock (open daily 7am-10pm). **Launches** leave San Pedro for **Pana** (9 per day, 5am-5pm, 1¼hr., Q7.50) and for **Santiago** (8 per day, 6am-3pm, 45min., Q7.50). Some launches to Pana stop at the towns on the western shore of the lake and, though scenic, take much longer than an hour. Be aware that the last boat to Pana does not leave from the main dock in front of Villa

Sol, but from the one in front of Restaurante Johana, about 1km away. The trail between the two docks winds through the village and branches several times, but one of the local kids can lead you through for a small tip. San Pedro's **post office** is tucked behind the church (open Mon.-Fri. 8am-4pm, Sat. 8am-noon).

Past El Fondeatero, **Hotel Valle Azul** has balconies overlooking its rocky, clean portion of the shore. Communal baths sport hot water, private ones don't (singles Q10, with bath Q20; doubles Q20, with bath Q30). Behind Nick's Place is **Hospedaje Puerto Bello.** Friendly expatriate family supplies hot water, a rooftop view, beverages at good prices, and maybe even a free tour of the town (singles Q10; doubles Q18; triples Q26). The road past Puerto Bello leads to other neat stuff. If you turn at the sign for Hospedaje El Balneario and walk around the Bethel school, you'll pass **Comedor El Amigo Viajero** (Q7) and the ultra-hip **Thermal Waters,** whose name doesn't do it justice. The **hot water baths** are solar-heated (Q25 per person), and they are only one of many services which include kayak rental and **gourmet veggie meals** made from home-grown materials (soups Q12, omelettes Q16, spaghetti Q18, pizza Q38). If you head onward, your reward is the large hammocks of the **Hospedaje Ti-Kaaj,** whose basic cement rooms surround a leafy garden. Communal bathrooms have dirt-strewn floors and water streaks in the showers. There *is* hot water, just ask for the key to the hidden shower. Checkout is at noon, and quiet time begins at 10pm (singles Q10; doubles Q18; triples Q26; get an extra bed for Q8). Nicer rooms *sans* views are had at **Hotel San Pedro,** onward and up the next main road (singles Q20, with bath Q36; doubles Q30, with bath Q42). Stuff grub at **El Fondeatero Restaurant** (entrees at Q12 per plate) and set up house rentals with Pedro (Q15) while you're there. An alternative, particularly for its yogurt, fruit and granola breakfast (Q12), is **Nick's Place** across the street, which has a romper room upstairs for games and night-time movies.

The **beach** here is much nicer than Pana's, and the town sits at the foot of the San Pedro volcano, making it a good jumping-off point for ascents. Locals rent **horses** (Q15 per hr.), which can take you part-way up the volcano and to other destinations. Possible trips with or without horse include the **weaving center** of San Juan, the **rope-making** village of San Pablo, or the simple beach **Cristalina,** whose waters are squeaky clean. It's also possible to rent kayak-like boats much more cheaply here than in Pana (1-person boat Q3 per hr., 2-person boat Q5 per hr.). After hours, **Restaurant Ti Kaaj** cranks rock to the bone. Look for the hotel with the huge mural of volcanoes, and follow the power cords emanating from there (assorted pastas Q7-11, beer Q6). For tamer fun, walk uphill to the surprisingly large Catholic church and check out the reclining Jesus **tanning salon** inside.

SAN MARCOS AND SANTA CRUZ

Tucked away in the escarpments of Atitlan's western shore, the not-so-twin villages of **San Marcos La Laguna** and **Santa Cruz La Laguna** are pleasantly isolated by their lack of road access. In San Marcos, dirt trails wind upward to the center of town, a panorama of gardens, patios, and basketball courts, and an **amphitheater** hosts plays and concerts on holidays. Where you can afford to stay depends almost entirely on the size of your group. **Posada Schumann** (tel. 360-4049), on the shore, is a solo traveler's dream. A flat Q60 per person rate applies to the two- or four-person houses complete with furbished kitchens, manicured gardens, and cold water showers. You may want to call and reserve, though, since not all rooms have kitchens. If you are in a larger group, try **La Paz,** where nature clamors at your window while electric stoves and televisions purr inside. Each four-person bungalow is an architectural wonder with its own courtyard and richly furnished sitting room. As a finishing touch, a tree-branch ladder leads to the loft. Cold-water bathrooms are communal, but immaculate (Q100 for 4 people). In front, the prestigious La Paz vegetarian cuisine is cooked with finesse and served generously for Q25. At neighboring **Manuela's,** luscious loaves of Italian bread (Q5.75) bake in clay ovens. **Hotel San Marcos** takes you away from it all. The tiny establishment peeks out from an orchard of orange trees, but offers the contemporary comfort of new toilets. Big beds have extra blankets, and everything is clean. Showers are cold (singles Q20; doubles Q40).

Nearby **Santa Cruz La Laguna** boasts a 16th-century church surrounded by colonial homes and the cleanest shore water on the lake. There's a **post office** next to the church. None of the existing accommodations has hot water. **La Iguana Perdida** offers an assortment of glorified bamboo huts among the lush trails of its backyard. There is the "birdcage," a Q20 double with charmingly understated walls, as well as a room of Q15 dorm beds. Otherwise, it's Q35 for a single or Q50 for a double. La Iguana also offers **scuba diving certification courses** for US$150 and two-tank dives on the lake for US$40. **El Arca de Noé** boasts rock walls and Maya textile decor, plus a bottle of water, in each of its charming rooms. Superb multicourse dinners (Q45) are served on the lakeside porch (reservations required for non-guests), as are breakfasts and lunches (Q20; singles Q40, with bath Q105; doubles Q60, with bath Q120). **Hotel García,** next to the Iguana, sports clean cement cells with beds and a dark, but spotless bathroom (singles Q25; doubles Q41).

From both Santa Cruz and San Marcos, trails along the coast offer breathtaking views of the azure Lake Atitlán. The lake is deep right up to the shoreline, and the water on the other side of the docks has nary a ripple.

■ Hiking and Volcanoes

Don't let the tranquil beauty of the lake lull you into complacency about safety. The region around Lake Atitlán has a history of muggings, so check with the INGUAT office in Panajachel before setting out (see Panajachel and Lago Atitlán, p. 74).

Three volcanos dominate the south shore of Atitlán. **Volcán Atitlán,** at 3535m (11,604ft.), is the tallest of the three, while **Volcán Tolimán,** standing at a height of 3158m (10,360ft.), is the only active one. Ascending Tolimán and Atitlán is not recommended due to the high incidences of theft and violence. **Volcán San Pedro** (3020m or 9908ft.) is considered safer and easier to climb. It's usually necessary to spend the night prior to the climb in San Pedro, since the guides who take groups along the volcano's poorly marked trails set out around 6am, long before the first launch from Pana arrives. The group usually returns to San Pedro well before dinnertime. Guides can be found around town or at the Hospedaje Ti-Kaaj. Prices are never high, but exact amounts vary with demand. Alternatively, get your hands on a free ascent map at El Balneario Hospedaje (guests only). Two-thirds of the way up the volcano, you reach a false summit (a wooded, park-like clearing). At this point veer to the left, and you'll find the correct trail again.

■ Godinez and San Antonio Palopó

One spectacular hike descends a trail from the hilltop town of **Godinez,** on the east side of the lake, to the shore town of San Antonio. Access Godinez from Pana by bus (Q3, but infrequent), taxi (Q60), or the every ready *picop* (pickup) truck. Before you reach Godinez, you'll come across something of a Lover's Leap vista point. If you decide not to end your honeymoon abruptly, head down the narrow and steep (though not dangerous) trail on the left. An hour's hike leads to **San Antonio Palopó,** a Cakchiquel town whose inhabitants make reed mats and maguey fiber products. It's often included in the three-town tour of the lake offered by the launch companies.

■ Iximché

Iximché was the ancient capital of the Cakchiquel people and the first capital of Guatemala. The city was founded in 1470 under governors **Juntoh, Vukubatz,** and **Ho Evets,** who freed the Cakchiquel from the Quiché, only to fall to the Spaniards in 1524. The city surrendered peacefully to Pedro de Alvarado, but abuses and the cruel extraction of tribute caused two bloody rebellions in 1526 and 1532. That period of conflict ended in 1535 with the death of Cakchiquel governors of the city.

GUATEMALA

Iximché is a naturally fortified city, surrounded on all sides by deep ravines. The present **archaeological site** encompasses the palaces and temples of the governors. The huge stone edifices rise out of the earth as if in deep slumber, some fully uncovered, some caked in grass and trees. In contrast, the ruins' natural surroundings seem tame, more like a picnic area than a site of sanguineous seizure (open daily 7:30am-4pm; admission Q1). There is also a **museum** exhibiting pictures and objects from the excavation project (open daily 8am-noon and 1-4pm). There are no guides, but a brochure (in Spanish) summarizes the significance of the artifacts on display.

Iximché is located about 5km from the pitstop village of **Tecpán.** To get to Tecpán, catch a **bus** from the Panajachel bus terminal in Guatemala City on Calle 20, Zona 1 (every 30min., 2hr.). If coming from elsewhere, take a Guatemala City-bound bus to Los Encuentros, and there change to Tecpán (1hr.). From Tecpán to Iximché, either walk the 5km or hire a taxi (Q25 one way). If you plan to take a taxi, do so right where the bus drops you off, because there are few in town.

■ Chichicastenango

The town of Chichicastenango is, without question, the most popular destination in the Department of El Quiché. Its Sunday and Thursday markets attract droves of tourists from Guatemala City, Panajachel, and Antigua. But there's more to the region than brightly colored tapestries, wooden figurines, and *rebajas* (bargains). The soot from charcoal cookfires, the lilt of spoken Maya-Quiché, and the haze of devotional incense remind visitors that Chichicastenango is still very much an authentic *indígena* town, despite its stature as a tourist mecca.

Chichicastenango was built by the Spaniards in the 16th century as a home for refugees from Utatlán, the Quiché capital they had brutally leveled. In the centuries following the Conquest, El Quiché has witnessed countless abuses of human rights. During the 19th century, the Guatemalan government used forced-labor laws written during the colonial era to pull Quiché workers down from the mountains to work on coffee plantations. In the 1970s, Chichicastenango became a center of guerrilla activity, but the guerrillas have since been driven north into rain forests far from town. Remarkably, the region's *indígena* strain of Catholicism survives here in an atmosphere of official tolerance, despite years of repression and persecution.

ORIENTATION

Chichicastenango rests on a hill 37km north of Panajachel. The town is laid out in a grid. *Avenidas* run north to south and are numbered from west to east. *Calles* run east to west and are numbered from north to south. Street addresses are not very useful, since most street signs display Maya-Quiché names and locals tend to give directions in terms of place names and landmarks. The main street through town is **5 Av.**, which is where the buses stop. A large green arch with Maya-style decoration crouches over this *avenida;* most everything of interest is on the south side, except for the bus stop, which is slightly north of the arch.

PRACTICAL INFORMATION

There is no **tourist office,** but registered guides loiter at the bus terminal. For **currency exchange** and all accredited travelers' checks, try **Banco del Ejército** (tel. 756-1201), 6 Calle between 5 and 6 Avs. (open for exchange Tues.-Fri. 9am-noon and 2-5pm, Sat. 9am-3pm, Sun. 9am-8pm). Phone home from **Guatel,** 7 Av. 8-21 (tel. 756-1398), near the post office. There's also a public **fax** (open daily 7am-8pm). **Buses** leave from 5 Av., between 2 and 3 Calles, for **Guatemala City** (30 per day, 3am-6pm, 3hr., Q9); **Quetzaltenango** (7 per day, 6am-3pm, 2½hr., Q8); **Santa Cruz del Quiché** (every hr., 30min., Q2); and **Panajachel** (6 per day, 6am-2:30 pm, 1hr., Q4). The **police station,** 8 Calle between 5 and 6 Avs., in a blue building to the left of the church, posts a map of town and cheerful officers answer questions (open 24hr.).

The famed **market** is on the plaza in front of the church. There's also an enclosed produce market in the building to the left of the plaza, facing the front of the church. **Shoe repair,** 6 Av., 3 Calle A, a relative rarity in rural Guatemala, can be found down from the arch and to the left, around the corner from Ferretería El Martillo; ask for Sr. Disraeli (minor repairs Q2). **Farmacia San Ignacio,** 4 Av. 6-65, is open daily 8am-9pm. There is a rotating schedule for 24-hour pharmacies, but it is rarely observed here. The **Centro de Salud** (tel. 756-1356) is at the edge of town on 2 Av. and 2 Calle. The **Clínica Médica Dr. Bonilla** (tel. 756-1309) is a private institution on 5 Calle 6-30 (open Mon.-Fri. 8am-noon and 3-7pm, Sun. 8am-noon). In an emergency, call **Los Bomberos** (tel. 756-1066)—they have the only ambulance. The **post** and **telegraph** office, at 7 Av. 8-47, is open Monday-Friday 9am-5:30pm. Warning: in June 1997, the telegraph service was "temporarily" out of service.

ACCOMMODATIONS

Like any self-respecting indigenous village, Chichicastenango has several luxury hotels, but a flock of recently built budget hotels tips the balance in frugality's favor. If frugality is a prime concern, however, beware of the "guides" that appear when you arrive. Once you tell a kid where you are going, he will make like a barnacle until you arrive at the hotel. There, you will be charged a per-urchin tax for your room. **Hotel Posada Belén,** 12 Calle 5-55, Zona 1 has rooms with *two* views: the *pueblos* on one side, the town on the other. Sprawl out to snooze on cushy beds. The private bathrooms are immaculate, but the communal one is not so good. Warm water is available 24 hours, but the front door is not (curfew 10pm). Towel and toilet paper are provided. (Laundry service Q1 per piece. Singles Q35, with bath Q50; doubles Q50, with bath Q70; triples Q75, with bath Q90.) **Hospedaje El Salvador** coruscates on 5 Av., two blocks beyond the church (tel. 756-1329). The street drops down a hill, then rises again; the hotel is on the right on the upward slope. Eccentric staircases lead to clean rooms arranged along balconies. Bougainvillea and hibiscus complement stucco walls, and the upper floors enjoy wonderful views of town. The private bathrooms are spotless, though the communal facilities are more water-streaked and gritty in the corners. If the hot water's not running, insist! (Singles Q25, with bath Q66; doubles Q40, with bath Q70; triples Q55, with bath Q75.) **Hotel Giron,** 6 Calle 4-52 (tel. 756-1156), just off 5 Av., between the bus stop and the church. Lusciously decorated rooms (with matching oak furniture) are arranged around a patio that doubles as a parking lot. Bathrooms are spotless and the beds are magnificently comfortable. Both private and communal bathrooms have hot water. The market couldn't be closer. (Singles Q35, with bath Q55; doubles Q60, with bath Q90.) Slightly more expensive rooms have TVs.

FOOD

For the cheapest fare, plunge into the heart of the market, where tent-swaddled *comedores* await. Tortillas sizzle on every grill, and dogs slither beneath your feet looking for scraps. Fight your way through the ring of *artesanía* stalls that surround them; on non-market days these *comedores* serve as the local hangouts. Additionally, inexpensive sit-down restaurants surround the plaza. **Restaurante Tziguan Tinamit,** 5 Av. 5-67 (tel. 056-1144), 1½ blocks from the plaza, lets you watch the telly while you enjoy what may be the best meal in town. The place is super-saturated with tourists on market days. Breakfasts cost Q10-17, lunches run Q30, and come complete with soup, salad, potatoes or rice, dessert, and coffee or tea. They serve pizza, too. All vegetables are rinsed in *agua purificada* (sandwiches Q10-15. Open daily 7am-9pm.) **Café-Restaurante La Villa de los Cofrades** is on the small arcade on the north side of the market. Turn right as you enter the plaza from 5 Av. The people-watching is better here than anywhere else in town, and breakfast is a bargain (Q7-13.50), as are the full meals. A lunch of *pollo asado* (roast chicken) with soup, salad, rice or potatoes, and vegetables goes for Q22. (Soups Q8 and sandwiches Q10. Open daily 7am-about 10pm.) **Restaurante La Fonda del Tzijdaj** (tel. 756-1013) jactitates on the second floor of the same arcade as Café-Restaurante La Villa de los Cofrades. The balcony offers a bird's eye view of the market below *(chuchitos* Q5, sandwiches Q9-20, *chiles rellenos* Q20). **Las Brasas** (tel. 756-1006) can be found on top of Hotel Giron, though it's not well-marked. Its quiet setting provides escape from the maniacal shop-o-rama below. Known best for their beef steak and aspic (Q25), they also serve coffee, alcohol, and fruit juice.

SIGHTS

On Sundays and Thursdays, Chichicastenango is host to one of the most famous indigenous **handicraft markets** in Latin America. What is otherwise a quiet town swells with *artesanía* vendors from the nearby highlands and tourists from all over the world. Prices, however, are by no means the lowest in the country. To get real deals, some collectors venture out into the highlands where many items are made. Caution: the U.S. State Department has periodically issued warnings against such ventures, so check with the State Department before setting out on an outback shopping expedition (tel. (202) 647-5225). In Chichicastenango, your best bet is to buy on the afternoon before market day, or after 3pm on the day of the market, when the balance of bargaining power tips decisively in the buyer's favor; expect to get 30-50% off the asking price. If you don't get a little thorny about the initial price, the vendor will look at you funny; some bargaining is expected. Beware of "antique" wooden masks which have very often spent less time "aging" in a hole than you've spent in Guatemala. Authentic antique masks are available in the country, but they are much more expensive than those you see in the markets. Be sure to shop carefully; quality merchandise is sometimes lost among piles of more mediocre wares. Large, woolly blankets can cost Q220, hammocks generally sell at Q150-200, and wooden masks go for Q30-80. Most vendors don't speak English well, but they've learned to make do with what vocabulary they've got—all of them know how to deal with numbers.

The market is by no means Chichicastanango's only attraction. The **Iglesia de Santo Tomás** rises above the southeast corner of the central market plaza. On market days it is a scene of sacred ritual; an incense fire is kept burning at the base of the church's steps and brightly dressed indigenous women blanket one side of the stairs with hibiscus, lilies, roses, and gladiolas, selling the blooms as offerings to churchgoers. The church steps are considered to be an extension of the chapel and as sacred as the interior, especially when the fire is burning. This is not a place to sit and chat.

The structure of the church provides a fascinating glimpse into the hybrid folk Catholicism of the Maya-Quiché. The church is built on an ancient Maya-Quiché holy site, and has been sacred to local indigenous communities since Father Francisco Jiménez, an 18th-century parish priest, began re-copying the Popol Vuh, a cosmogony and collection of *indígena* legends. Jiménez's work introduced the outside world to the Popol Vuh, and his respect for indigenous beliefs drew many to worship once again at their ancient sacred site. *Indígenas* today make an elaborate ritual of ascending the steps, repeatedly kneeling, and waving incensiaries. Respectful visitors are welcome, but they should use the side entrance, to the right. Clouded by a haze of incense, the interior buzzes with mumbled prayers. Candles flicker on low platforms between the pews, reflecting off the glass cases which house statues of saints. The devout gather around the platforms, lighting candles, murmuring prayers, and strewing flower petals. Do *not* take photographs.

On the opposite side of the plaza stands the chapel of **El Calvario,** which is reserved exclusively for *indígenas.* Next to it and open to everyone are some pleasant gardens. Also, facing the plaza is the ramshackle **Rossbach Museum,** containing a small collection of pre-Hispanic artifacts, most of them donated by local families (open Tues.-Wed. and Fri.-Sat. 8am-noon and 2-4pm, Thurs. and Sun. 8am-1pm and 2-4pm; admission Q1). Beyond the plaza, 9 Calle, the street lining the south side of the square, leads down the hill to the town's **cemetery,** where monuments surround another *indígena* shrine.

For more insight into the particulars of indigenous worship, a 20-minute walk from town leads to the shrine of **Pascual Abaj.** Take the road to the right of Santo Tomás

Church downhill; at 9a Calle, make another right. Continue down the cement molded road until you see signs for the shrine, which sits atop a wooded hill. Watch *indígenas* and *ladinos* alike pray to a stony face as they feed the sacrificial bonfire with everything from live chickens to Orange Crush. The ceremonies usually take place on market days before noon, and taking photographs is tolerated if you are unobtrusive. If you want to see the ceremonies, and avoid the hassle of finding the hill, hire one of many willing street folk to take you there for a small fee.

■ Santa Cruz del Quiché

The village of Santa Cruz del Quiché is located about 30km north of Panajachel. Though small, unattractive, and offering virtually nothing to do, it serves as the primary launching point for tourists on their way to the undeveloped ruins of Utatlán.

Santa Cruz del Quiché is built in the familiar grid of north to south *avenidas* and east to west *calles*. The **police** make their nest at 0 Av. and 3 Calle, Zona 1 (tel. 120; open 24hr.). Change **traveler's checks** at **Banco Industrial,** 2 Av. and 3 Calle (tel. 755-1079; open Mon.-Fri. 8:30am-5:30pm, Sat. 8:30am-12:30pm). The **post office** is hidden in a building with no sign, on 3a Calle, 0/1 Av., Zona 5 (tel. 755-1085), and is open Monday through Friday 8am-4:30pm. The **postal code** is 14501. The **telegraph office** is next door to the post office and is open 24 hours. Knock on the door if it appears locked. **Guatel,** 1 Av., 2 Calle, Zona 5, is open daily 7am-midnight. The **bus station,** 1 Av. and 10 Calle has service to: **Guatemala City** (every 15min., 2:30am-6pm, 4hr., Q10); **Panajachel** (every hr., 6am-5pm, 2hr., Q5); **Quetzaltenango** (4 per day, 4am-8:30pm, 3hr., Q8); and **Nebaj** (9, 10am, and 2pm, 4½hr., Q12). For medical **emergencies** contact the **Los Bomberos** (tel. 755-1122) on 2 Calle 0-11, Zona 1.

The best place to spend the night is **Hotel San Pascual,** 7 Calle, ½ Av, (tel. 755-1107). Rooms are huge and comfortable and the communal baths well-kept. Hot water runs from 6:30-7:30am only. (Singles Q24, Q26 with bath; doubles Q36, with bath Q60; triples Q48, with bath Q82.) Somewhat darker and lacking private showers, but nonetheless comfortable and immaculately clean, are the rooms in the **Posada Calle Real,** 2 Av. 7-36, Zona 1 (tel. 755-1438; Q21 per person). If you just need a place to crash, then the **Hospedaje Tropicales,** 1 Av., 9 Calle 5, right up from the bus stop, does the job. Communal bathrooms may give travelers pause. The bus stop clamor rings through the indoor courtyard (singles Q9; doubles Q14). For cheap, reliable eats, check **Restaurante Las Rosas,** 1 Av. 1-28, Zona 1 (tel. 755-1504), one block away from the park (complete breakfast Q10; open daily 6:30am-9:30pm). Though it isn't super clean, the **Musi Café,** 1 Av. 1-24, (tel. 755-1156), offers cheap food, mostly burgers and sandwiches. Breakfast isn't on the menu, but if you ask for it, you'll get a nice big one (Q10.50; open 7am-8pm).

Near Santa Cruz lies **K'umarkaaj,** a.k.a. **Utatlán,** capital of the Quiché Kingdom, which formed during the postclassic period (AD 1000-1523) of Maya civilization. Under the rule of Q'uk'ab, the Quiché domain extended from the Pacific almost to the Atlantic, encompassing nine different nations. Two of these, the Tzutuhil and Cakchiquel, are the two major indigenous groups around Lago Atitlán today. The name *K'umarkaaj* has been translated as "Houses of Old Reeds" (not to be confused with "The House of the Rising Sun"). The official **archaeological site** covers an area of eight square kilometers, but the few discernible structures are located around a single plaza. Most everything consists in mounds of grass, the regular shapes of which suggest underlying buildings. Perhaps the most interesting element in all of this is a **small cave,** only 100m from the plaza and along an indicated trail, where the past and the present come together in the living tradition of the *indígenas*. The cave is still used by locals for religious and healing ceremonies, as it was 500 years ago. If you smell incense and see smoke coming out of its entrance, don't hesitate to enter, just be considerate and keep your camera in your bag. You need a flashlight to enter the cave, and if you have not brought your own, you can rent one at the museum (Q2). The **museum** has posters explaining the social and political structures of the Quiché

Kingdom, as well as its history (all signs are in Spanish). This site is open daily 8am-4:30pm, and admission is Q0.25.

To get to K'umarkaaj, either walk the 5km or hire a taxi from the bus station at 1 Av., 10 Calle, Zona 5, which takes you there, waits, and brings passengers back for Q40. **Camping** in the parking lot is free, and is an excellent alternative to paying for hotel rooms in Santa Cruz. There are no services, except for the museum's outside toilets, and travelers may want to bring a little extra food for the site's 24-hour guard.

■ Quetzaltenango

Quetzaltenango is full of monuments to what might have been. In 1823, when the Central American Federation broke away from Mexico, Quetzaltenango boldly declared itself the capital of the independent state of Los Altos, which encompassed much of Guatemala's western highlands. Seventeen years later, dreams of independence were smothered by the emergence of Guatemalan dictator Rafael Carrera. With the coffee boom of the 19th century, Quetzaltenango flourished anew, drawing boatloads of German capital and immigrants to its extraordinarily rich land. But alas, Quetzaltenango's aspirations crumbled again in 1902, when a devastating earthquake leveled the city. Somehow still full of ambition, the city leaders rebuilt the city, scattering numerous Neoclassical buildings throughout the small metropolis. However, by the 1930s Guatemala City had outpaced its rival for the title of national capital. Quetzaltenango remains something of a provincial might-have-been with bigger dreams. City leaders recently constructed the **Pasaje Enrique,** a glass-ceilinged, European-style concourse on the plaza intended to be a sophisticated shopping center. Instead, it sits nearly vacant. In failing to rise to the top, Quetzaltenango has avoided many of the urban problems that plague Guatemala City. Namely, it is far safer, friendlier, and less polluted than Guate.

Don't be surprised if you never hear the name "Quetzaltenango" mentioned in town. Locals are more likely to refer to their city as **Xela** (SHEH-lah), an abbreviation of the Quiché name Xelajú, which means "under the ten," a reference to the ten mountain-dwelling gods of the Quiché. Xela has long been a center of Quiché culture; its teeming market and busy Parque Central draw *indígenas* from all over the western highlands. Xela proper won't detain you for more than a day or two; though its markets are among the best in the country, most visitors come to commune with the surrounding countryside and to soak in the hot sulfuric springs in nearby Zunil and Fuentes Georgina.

ORIENTATION

Quetzaltenango's *avenidas* run north to south and the *calles* run east to west. *Avenida* numbers increase to the west, *calle* numbers to the south. The **Parque Centroamérica** is at the center of town in Zona 1 and is bordered by 11 Avenida on the east, 12 Avenida on the west, 4 Calle to the north, and 7 Calle to the south. Most services are located in Zona 1. The second-class bus station and the main market are in Zona 3, northwest of the city center. If you arrive at this station, the **Terminal La Minerva,** walk though the market to its south side. Any of the buses going left (east) on 4 Calle or 6 Calle will take you to the Parque (Q0.50). If you arrive on a first-class pullman, you can walk to the park in the time it would take to wait for a bus.

PRACTICAL INFORMATION

Tourist Office: INGUAT, 7 Calle, 12 Av.#11-35 (tel. 761-4931), at the south side of the park. Free city maps. Some English. Open Mon.-Fri. 8am-1pm and 2-5pm.

Currency Exchange: Banco Immobilario, 12 Av., 4 Calle, on the west side of the park (tel. 761-4161). Open Mon.-Sat. 9am-8pm. **Banco Industrial,** on the east side of the park (tel. 761-2258). Home to a 24hr., Visa-friendly **ATM.** Open Mon.-Fri. 9:30am-7:30pm, Sat. 9:30am-1:30pm.

TO TERMINAL
LA MINERVA

N

Quetzaltenango

Banco Inmobilario, **7**
Banco Industrial, **13**
Café Bavaria, **11**
Casa Kaehler/Pensión Radar, **6**
Deli-Crepe, **4**
Farmacia Nueva, **12**
Hotel Horiana, **1**
Hotel Río Azul, **2**
La Polonesa, **9**
Library/Casa de la Cultura, **15**
Museo de Arte, **14**
Museo de
  Ciencias Naturales, **16**
Pensión Altense, **17**
Pizza Ricca, **3**
Restaurant Utz Hua, **5**
Ricca Burger, **10**
Supermercado La Selecta, **8**

GUATEMALA

la Calle
2a Calle
3a Calle
4a Calle
5a Calle
6a Calle
7a Calle
8a Calle
9a Calle
10a Calle
11a Calle

14a Avenida
14 Avenida
12a Avenida
15a Avenida
13a Avenida
10a Avenida
11a Avenida
9a Avenida
8a Avenida
7a Avenida
6a Avenida
5a Avenida

Parque
Centroamerica

0   100 yards

0   100 m

Buses: Most buses leave from **Terminal La Minerva** at the northwest end of Zona 3. To get to the terminal, take any city bus, since all routes eventually pass through the station; buses on 14 Av. go directly there. The #6, from 8 Calle, 12 Av., Zona 1 (Q0.50), is particularly direct. Most buses from La Minerva pass though La Rotonda on Calzada Independencia in Zona 2, which is a 15min. walk or a Q7 taxi ride away from Zona 1. From Terminal La Minerva, buses leave for **Tecún Umán** (3½hr., Q11). Buses also run to: **La Mesilla** (8 per day, 6hr., Q12); **Guatemala City** (every 15min., 5am-5:30pm and at 8pm, 4½hr., Q14); **Huehuetenango** (every 30min., 5am-5pm, 2hr., Q8); **San Andres Xecul** (every 30min., 6:30am-6:30pm, 45min., Q2); **San Francisco El Alto** (6 per day, 1hr., Q2); **Momostenango** (5 per day, 2hr., Q5); **Panajachel** (4 per day, 2½hr., Q10); and **Chichicastenango** (4 per day, 2½hr., Q8). Since direct buses to Panajachel and Chichicastenango run infrequently, it's often easier to take a bus to Los Encuentros in Guatemala City instead; buses to Panajachel and Chichicastenango wait there. Buses to **Retalhuleu** leave every hr. (7am-5pm, 2hr., Q5). **Galgos,** Calle Rodolfo Robles 17-43 (tel. 761-2931), runs 1st-class pullmans to Guatemala City (7 per day, 4½hr., Q18).
Public Transportation: City buses run 6:30am-8pm (Q0.50 per trip).
Taxis: (tel. 761-4085), lined up along the east side of the park. To Terminal La Minerva Q15, to La Rotonda Q7.
Market: At Terminal La Minerva, Zona 3. Open Mon.-Sat. 6am-6pm. To get there, catch bus #6 from 8 Calle, 12 Av., Zona 1, or any bus to the terminal.
Supermarket: La Selecta, 4 Calle 13-16, Zona 1 (tel. 761-2004). Open Mon.-Sat. 9am-1pm and 3-7pm, Sun. 9am-1pm. As of June 1997, the supermarket was still at this location, but appeared to be closed indefinitely.
Laundromat: Lavandería Mini-max, 14 Av. C-47, Zona 1 (tel. 761-2952). Wash and dry Q13 per load. Open Mon.-Sat. 7:30am-7:30pm.

Red Cross: (tel. 125), 8 Av. 6-62, Zona 1. Open 24hr.
Pharmacy: Farmacia Nueva, 10 Av., 6 Calle (tel. 761-4531). Open Mon.-Fri. 9am-1pm and 2pm-8pm. There is a rotating schedule for 24hr. pharmacies; the name of the current *farmacia de turno* should be posted near the entrance of every pharmacy.
Medical Services: Hospital San Rafael, 9 Calle 10-41, Zona 1 (tel. 761-4414), is the closest to downtown. English spoken. Open 24hr.
Police: (tel. 120), 10 Calle 12-21, Zona 1. Open 24hr.
Post Office: 4 Calle 15-07, Zona 1 (tel. 761-2671). Open Mon.-Fri. 8am-4:30pm.
Telephones: Guatel, 4 Calle, 15 Av. (tel. 761-6200). **Phone, fax,** and **telegram** service. Open daily 8am-8pm.

ACCOMMODATIONS

Quetzaltenango is sprinkled with bargain hotels and guest houses, most of them within a few blocks of the Parque Centroamérica. The city's altitude makes it quite cool (the average temperature is 65°F/18°C), but the air is not exactly clear. Indeed, most hotels barely fend off the emissions from the armies of smog-spewing, gas-belching, pollution-puking, exhaust-exhaling, fume-farting autos that plague Xela's streets. Bathrooms in all hotels have "hot water," but "hot" sometimes means scalding hot and sometimes means "lukewarm"—be sure to check before checking in.

Hotel Horiami, 2 Calle, 12 Av., Zona 1 (tel. 763-0815). The tile floors are well swept and the rooms brightly lit by large windows. The communal bathrooms are irreproachable, and the place takes unusual safety precautions—you have to ring a bell to get in. Well worth the low price. Singles Q20. Less spacious doubles Q35.
Casa Kaehler, 13 Av. 3-33, Zona 1 (tel. 761-2091). Most rooms are on the 2nd floor balcony of this refurbished, colonial-style house with hardwood floors. The 19th-century rockers cozify chilly Xela nights. The front door is locked 24hr.; guests have keys. The communal bathrooms are perfectly adequate, and the management is very friendly. Singles Q42, with bath Q48. Doubles Q48, with bath Q60. Each additional person only costs an extra Q6, so bring the whole herd. All taxes included, so it's not quite as pricey as it sounds.
Pensión Altense, 9 Calle 8-48, Zona 1 (tel. 761-2811). This hotel, although a bit farther from the Parque Centroamérica than many, offers spacious rooms around a courtyard bursting with geraniums. Large windows with safety bars look out onto the street or the courtyard. Some rooms and bathrooms are cleaner than others; check first. All rooms have a private bath. Singles Q30-40; doubles Q60.
Pensión Radar 99, 13 Av. 3-27, Zona 1. Next to Casa Kaehler. Not posh, but low-cost. Clean bathrooms. Singles Q18, with bath Q25; doubles Q25, with bath Q30.

FOOD

If you haven't tried *típico* cuisine, start here. It's affordable, it's delicious, and if your nerve (or stomach) fails, cheap *gringo* food abounds. Many restaurants are within blocks of the Parque Central, particularly on 14 Av.

Ricca Burger, 4a Calle 13-25, Zona 1 (tel. 765-3328). Full-service, plentiful eats in fast-food style cleanliness. Sundry breakfast combinations with coffee Q9. Burgers Q4.50. Full meals with *naranjada*, Q9-15. Salad bar is Q8.50. Holy Good News, Batman! All vegetables are washed in purified water. Open daily 7am-10:30pm.
Café Baviera, 5 Calle 12-50, Zona 1. Popular hangout for the Spanish-school crowd, decorated with nostalgic pictures of Xela in the good old days. Pineapple pie (Q6), sandwiches Q8.50, and quiche Q8.50. Used books for sale. Open daily 8am-8pm.
Restaurante Deli-Crepe, 14 Av. 3-11, Zona 1. A small, tavern-like, crepe-like place, Deli-Crepe is probably the only crepe place in Xela where you'll find crepes; crepes with ham and cheese (Q12.50), or crepes with your choice of dessert topping, including strawberries or more crepes (Q12.50). They also serve other American food like crepes, hamburgers (Q4), and crepes. Open daily 9am-9pm. Crepes!

Restaurant Utz-Hua, (Gesundheit), 12 Av. 3-02, Zona 1. Family-run place which serves mmm-good, mmm-cheap Guatemalan food. Try the *típico* platter with a steak and spicy sausage (Q15), or the *carne asada* in tangy tomato sauce (Q15). *Comida corridente* Q12, fresh fruit with honey and yogurt Q4. Watch your favorite *telenovela* on the 19-inch TV. No crepes whatsoever. Open daily 7am-10pm.

Pizza Ricca, 14 Av. 2-42, Zona 1 (tel. 761-8162). Brick-oven pizzas made fresh in a fast-foodish environment. Locals (even *indígenas*) dig into personal pizzas (Q13-22). Spaghetti Q25. Vegetarians' best bet is their tasty cheese pizza. Delivery available. Open daily 11:30am-10pm.

La Polonesa, 14 Av. "A" 4-45, Zona 1. Small and friendly family place serve some of the cheapest meals in town. *Comida económica* Q12, pancakes Q7, one-quarter chicken with fries Q12. Make it a ½ chicken with potatoes, salad, soup, rice, and dessert for Q22., whole chicken and a Coke Q30. Open Mon.-Sat. 7:30am-8:30pm.

SIGHTS AND ENTERTAINMENT

Xela's biggest attraction is its vibrant produce **market** at Terminal Minerva, which is one of the major commercial centers of the western highlands—you might be the only one there who doesn't speak Quiché. Woolly blankets and hammocks go for about Q60 each. Bargaining is expected—most vendors don't speak English but they know the numbers well from having clashed wills with tourists for generations. Prices can drop 30% in the blink of an eye. Ask before taking any photographs, and beware of pickpockets. To reach the market, take any bus on 14 Av. (Q0.50). (Open Mon.-Sat. 8am-6pm, Sun. 8am-noon.)

Aside from the market, Xela offers few diversions. The **Casa de Cultura,** 7 Calle 11-27, Zona 1 (tel. 761-6427), next to the tourist office on the south side of Parque Centroamérica, presents a swirl of Maya artifacts, taxidermy, old manuscripts, and local herbology (open Mon.-Fri. 8am-noon and 2-6pm, Sat. 9am-1pm; admission Q6). The Casa de Cultura is also an unparalleled source for information on current cultural events. Nearby is the **Museo de Arte,** corner of 12 Av. and 7 Calle. Traditional scenes alternate with modernist paintings and metallurgical sculpture—don't miss the mechanical Maximón statue (open Mon.-Fri., 8am-1pm, 3-7pm; admission Q6). On the first Sunday of each month, the Parque Centroamérica hosts an important handicrafts market, accompanied by outdoor concerts and performances of traditional music. The city's main **festival** takes place September 12-18. The **Municipal Theater,** 1 Calle, 14 Av., Zona 1 (tel. 761-2218), usually houses ballet, *marimba*, orchestra, and theater performances (every other Fri. and Sat., Q3-25)—though as of June 1997 it was under construction. **Salón Tecún** (tel. 761-2832), inside Pasaja Enrique by the park, hosts an international backpacking clientele as well as many locals. *Indígena* attire labeled with village of origin decorates the walls (beers Q5; open 5:30pm-midnight).

■ Near Quetzaltenango

The town of **Zunil,** about 7km from Xela toward the coast, is home to yet another shrine to the Maya God *Maximón,* also known by his Christian name of **San Simón.** For more information, see Santiago de Atitlán (p. 79). Offerings of any kind may be made to San Simón; the seedier, the better (admission Q2; if you buy good-luck candles for San Simón, entrance is free). A **shaman** also occasionally frequents the shrine. If you're lucky, you might even get to see the morning installation of Simón in his throne (around 8:30am). To leave Xela, head down to the *parque central,* then over and down a few blocks to the gas station where buses leave about every twenty minutes (Q1.50). Buses to Zunil also leave from Terminal Minerva.

About 9km from Zunil on a narrow dirt road bubble the hot springs of **Fuentes Georgina.** Set in a forested notch part of the way up a volcano, Fuentes Georgina is a peaceful place to come and purge the cool, wet weather of Quetzaltenango (open daily 8am-6pm, admission Q5). Cabins with fireplaces for overnight stays are available for Q42 for one person and Q12 for each additional person; additionally, there is a small restaurant by the pool. There is no bus to Fuentes Georgina, but trucks lined up in front of the church in Zunil will take four to six people there for Q25. Unless you plan to walk back (a very manageable and picturesque 9km downhill) or stay overnight, you'll have to pay the taxi an additional Q40 (Q25 for the trip back and Q15 for the hour the driver waits while you frolic in the springs).

If neither the shaman nor Fuentes Georgina cured your boils and blisters, you could head over to **El Recreo,** just after Almolonga on the way to Zunil. Ask the bus driver to be let off at the hot springs. Other destinations for daytrips include a number of towns specializing in *artesanía*. **Salcajá** (9km from Xela, on the way to Cuatro Caminos) is known for its embroidered textiles and is home to the oldest church in Guatemala (according to some historians). **San Francisco El Alto** (17km from Xela) sits atop a hill overlooking Quetzaltenango. On Fridays, the central plaza bustles with vendors; catch a bird's eye view of this gigantic market from the church roof (Q1). If you decide to spend the night, **Hotel Vista Herma** (tel. 766-1060) has single rooms for Q7, Q6 for each additional person. Some of the rooms have beautiful views of Xela. **Buses** for San Francisco leave from Terminal Minerva every 30 minutes (Q1.50).

Also quite close to Xela, but placed in wonderful isolation among cornfields, is the *indígena* village of **San Andrés Xecul.** The canary yellow church, with its technicolor collage of angels, icons, and adornments, stands in razor-sharp contrast to the town's mud-brick houses. Hike uphill 15 minutes to the chapel for views of the whole town and the farmland. Buses leave from Xela (every ½hr., 1hr., Q2); you can also catch them at the Xecul turn-off, about 1km toward Xela from Cuatro Caminos.

Two hours away from Xela, in the heart of Guatemala's wool-growing region, lies **Momostenango.** Here, you'll find popular Wednesday and Sunday markets with produce aplenty and (you guessed it) cheap woolen goods (blankets of all sizes, designs and patterns Q70-110, hooded pullovers Q80). Ask for directions to the Mars-like *riscos*, heavily eroded clay formations reminiscent of a Star Trek set—it's only about a 12-minute walk. Another 20-minute walk on the road to the left as you face the church will take you alongside a forested ravine with waterfalls and down a steep-staired path to the **Baños de Payexú,** where water literally bursts out boiling next to the river. Watch respectfully as whole *indígena* families bathe in the steaming water, diluted with cooler river water to avoid poaching the locals like so many eggs. To bathe without the crowds, try coming early in the morning, late in the afternoon, or on a non-market day. Lukewarm water and lukewarm service characterize **Casa Palcom,** a bland, dark, but clean lodge (Q15 per person). **Hospedaje Roxana** is your only other choice; tired beds in small rooms that share a minute, but blossom-filled, courtyard and a bathroom (Q6 per person). The culinary situation is similarly confining; **Cafetería Flipper's** *licuados* are a world full of wonder for parched throats, but otherwise, Momo is a true street-stall and *comedor* town. Given the dearth of comfortable accommodations and eating establishments, it's probably best to view Momo as a day trip from Xela. **Buses** leave about every 90 minutes from Xela's Terminal Minerva (2hr., Q4). Leaving Momo, hourly buses pass Cuatro Caminos (1hr., Q2.50) regardless of final destination.

The nearby **Volcán Santa María** towers over Xela and is a popular destination for visitors to Quetzaltenango. The tourist office says that there have been no robberies or assaults on the volcano, and INGUAT considers Santa María to be one of the safest climbs in Guatemala. **Buses** to **Llanos de Pinal,** leaving from Terminal Minerva (8am-5:30pm, Q3), pass near the trailhead for the volcano. Ask the bus driver to let you off at the crossroads near the trailhead (Say this: *¿Podría dejarme cerca del camino que sube el volcán?*). Following the road toward the volcano about 200m on the left, you'll pass a plaque dedicated to the Guatemalan Mountaineering Club. From here the road veers to the right, while the trail continues straight. The first section of the trail is wide and strewn with many small boulders. Rising up through a small valley dotted with cornfields, the trail gently curves to the left of the cave (visible if it's not cloudy). Black arrows painted on boulders indicate the appropriate trail.

After an hour's hike, the trail arrives at a flat, grassy area about 50m in length. One trail skirts the edge of the meadow, but the trail up the volcano cuts directly through it. If the weather is clear, the top of the cone can be seen from here. It looks tantalizingly close, but don't be fooled; you're not even a third of the way up. From here, the trail becomes much narrower and steeper, leaving the farmland and proceeding up the mountain surrounded by pine trees and undergrowth. From the meadow, the climb is two to three hours of unspeakable misery. The trail is steep, irregular, and poorly maintained—going down is almost as hard as going up. At this point, the trail is more diligently marked with frequent beer cans, graffiti, and many notches in the trees, but it's still easy to get lost.

If you're lucky, the view at the summit is spectacular, with the Cuchumatanes to the north and volcanos to the east and west; then again, the view might be nothing at all, as the summit is frequently suffocated by clouds, especially in the afternoon. The best way to catch a view is to head up at dawn; Xela is usually covered by an early morning layer of fog, but the summit is almost always clear. To accomplish this requires that you camp near the summit. There are a number of sites and **camping** is permitted, but only do so if you are adequately prepared with food, water, and especially warm clothing. For more information, see Camping & the Outdoors (p. 36). Otherwise, the climb up Santa María makes a rigorous daytrip. Hikers who attempt this climb should be in good shape and well-acclimated to the elevation. The round trip takes five to seven hours. If you're hiking during the rainy season (May-Oct.), leave early in the day, as afternoon rains can make the trip down hellish.

■ Huehuetenango

Huehuetenango has fewer than 40,000 inhabitants, but successfully melds small-town charm and cleanliness with some of the frenzied activity of larger urban centers. As local *indígenas* hustle and bustle in the marketplace, the predominantly *ladino* population scoots about on mopeds and in little cars. The central plaza, replete with a Neoclassical church, manicured gardens, and a *pink* bandstand, brings a mix of serenity and gaudy accoutrements. For more serenity, visit the attractive public library (Spanish books only).

Just big enough to supply passers-through with necessities and a little taste of the good life, today's "Huehue" began its life as a suburb of **Zaculeu,** the nearby Maya ruin. Since the Spanish conquest, the area has borne witness to a couple of minor silver rushes and the region-wide coffee boom; the mineral has since petered out, but the beany-brew still runs strong. The Interamerican Highway doesn't go through here, but for a prime pit stop on the way to Mexico or simply amiable headquarters for exploring nearby ruins, this way (way) cool town should not be overlooked.

ORIENTATION

Huehuetenango lies 226km northwest of the capital and about 90km north of Xela. *Avenidas* run north to south, increasing numerically as you go west. East to west running *calles* increase numerically as you go south. The **main square** is in Zona 1, bounded by 2 Calle and 4 Calle on the north and south and by 4 Av. and 5 Av. on the east and west, respectively. The main market is just east of the central square.

First- and second-class buses pull into the terminal, which is about 1km west of El Centro. City buses leave for the center about every 15 minutes (Q0.50). Taxis run to the central square for about Q15. The main plaza and surrounding areas provide most practical essentials.

PRACTICAL INFORMATION

Consulate: Get your tourist card at the **Mexican Consulate** inside Farmacia del Cid, on 5 Av., between 4 and 5 Calles. Open Mon.-Fri. 8am-12pm and 2-8pm.
Currency Exchange: Bancor, 2 Calle at 3 Av. (tel. 764-2606; fax 764-1487). Gives money in exchange for traveler's checks. Open Mon.-Fri. 9am-7pm, Sat. 9am-1pm.
Bancafe, 3 Calle at 6 Av. (tel. 764-1557), also accepts traveler's checks. Open Mon.-Fri. 8:30am-8pm, Sat. 10am-2pm.

Buses: Buses arrive and depart from the orderly terminal just off 6 Calle, about 1km west of the plaza. Most municipal buses pass through the terminal, and there are stops along 5 Calle near the plaza. From the terminal, buses leave for **La Mesilla** and the Mexican border (every 30min., 4am-7pm, 2hr., Q5); for **Quetzaltenango/Xela** (every 30-45min., 9am-6pm, 2hr., Q6); and for **Guatemala City** (every hr., 7am-4pm, 5½hr., Q15). For service to **Panajachel** or **Chichicastenango**, it's easiest to take a bus to Guatemala City and then transfer at Los Encuentros. Velasquez runs first-class pullmans from the terminal to **Guatemala City** (every 2hr. from 7:30am-5:30pm, Q24). To **Todos Santos Cuchumatán** (4 and 11am, 3hr.).

Public Transportation: Fares within town are Q0.50. Buses to the terminal run along 5 and 6 Calles. Buses to **Zaculeu** leave from 2 Calle and 7 Av. every hr., Q0.50; to **Chiantla**, they run every 20min. from 1 Calle and 1 Av., Q1.

Taxis: Line up along 5 Av. in front of the church. To the terminal Q15.

Video Games: Get some bang for your buck (over 20 games!) at **Juegos Eléctricos Intergalácticas**, down 2a Calle from **Hotel Mary** (see below).

Market: Along 2 Av. between 2 and 3 Calles; sells some food and snappy souvenirs along with loads of practical stuff. Open daily 6am-6pm. Try supermercado **Casa Saenz**, 4 Calle and 5 Av. Open Mon.-Sat. 8:30am-12:30pm and 2:30-6:30pm.

Pharmacy: Farmacia Del Cid, 4 Calle and 5 Av. Open daily 8am-noon and 2-8pm. Near the central square, you're never more than a block from a pharmacy. Check the rotating schedule of 24hr. pharmacies posted in front of every pharmacy.

Medical Services: National Hospital (tel. 764-1414 for **emergencies**), Las Lagunas, Zona 10. Available 24hr. Very little English spoken.

Police: Policía Nacional, 5 Av. between 6 and 7 Calles (emergency tel. 764-1150).

Post Office: Mail away at 2 Calle between 4 and 3 Avs. Open Mon.-Fri. 8am-4:30pm.

Telephones: Guatel, 4 Av. 6-54. Open daily 7am-midnight.

ACCOMMODATIONS

Even though Huehuetenango is not a major tourist attraction, cheap (and not coincidentally, shoddy) hotels abound, concentrated mostly to the immediate north and west of the central square. All hotels listed here have hot water.

Hotel Viajero, 2 Calle 5-32, Zona 1 (tel. 764-2655), one block west of the central square. The ceilings are low, the mattresses stiff, and the single, nude lightbulb a sickly yellow. But the place feels generally safe and at Q15 for singles and Q30 for doubles, the prices are hard to beat.

Hotel Mary, 2 Calle 3-52 (tel. 764-1618). The rooms are narrow and small, but the pink, stuccoed walls and lacquered wooden doors—all centered around a well-lit, multi-story atrium—lend an air of sophistication to this inexpensive hotel. The collective baths are clean and odorless. Singles Q35; doubles Q45; with bath and cable TV Q70. Reservations welcome.

Todos Santos Inn, 2 Calle 6-64, between 6a/7a Avs (tel. 764-1241). A peek through the whitewashed concrete entrance reveals polished tile floors and rich blue bedspreads, all in color-coordinated rooms. Situated on the quiet end of the square, some rooms have views of the beautiful surrounding countryside. Make friends with Polly the parrot. *Ella habla inglés.* Singles Q30, with bath Q45; doubles Q55, with bath Q70. TV is Q12 extra.

FOOD

Huehue may not be the culinary capital of Guatemala, but the food comes cheap. There are a number of *comedores* just east of the church in and around the marketplace. Most mid-range hotels also have their own (mid-range) restaurants.

Villa Flor, 7 Av. 3-41, Zona 1 (tel./fax 764-2586), located in Hotel Casa Blanca. The hotel devotes its entire Spanish courtyard to the restaurant, a placid oasis from polluted streets. Dine to the gentle gurgling of the fountain while you sip a glass of Guatemalan wine (yes, Guatemalan wine) for Q4. Reasonable prices; hamburgers Q8-10, omelette with ham Q20. Open daily 6am-10pm.

Pizza Hogareña, 2a Calle, just east of the square, across from Guatel. The colorblind may well love the interior; faux gold baroque mirrors, bright green drapes, and tangerine stucco surround the hungry-eña. The food is mega-good, though, and vegetarians will do back flips over the large cheese pizza (Q28). Open Tues.-Sun. 9:30am-9pm.

Jardín Cafe Restaurante, on the corner of 6a Av. and 4a Calle. Feeling Grecian? Come for hanging ferns, industrious ceiling fans, and late-night Mediterranean dinners. Situated on a noisy street corner, the Jardín sports a large menu with both local and American-style food. *Chile relleno con sopa y ensalada* Q20.50, hamburgers Q8. Open daily 2:15pm-10:30pm.

Restaurante Bougainvilia, 5 Av., facing the church. This 4-story restaurant, heavily patronized by locals, sticks out like a concrete thumb in this mostly 1-story town. On the street level is the kitchen, open to the public, and on the upper 3 floors are tables with breezy views. The *comida típica* (Q13) changes from day to day, but generally runs heavy on the flesh: *carne asada, chorizo* (sausage), or some sort of chicken. Open daily 7am-10pm.

■ Near Huehuetenango

About 4km west of Huehuetenango lies the ancient Maya site of **Zaculeu,** the former capital and cultural center of the Mam tribe from AD 600. The Mam reached all the way to Todos Santos, and their language continues in the area today. Ruled by the Quiché until the 15th century, the tribe finally managed to escape oppression by their fellow Indians, but fell right out of the frying pan and into a Spanish fire. When an army led by Gonzalo de Alvarado met the Mam on a battlefield, the Indians took a look at the fearsome Iberians and retreated to their base at Zaculeu. Their home had been built to protect them; the temples, plaza, and ball court that comprise the present site were fortified on three sides. Instead of wasting resources on a pointless attack, the Spanish simply waited a few months until hunger set in, and the weakened Mam were forced to surrender.

The United Fruit Company, already notorious for sticking its nose in places it shouldn't (see History, p. 40), sponsored an overzealous restoration of Zaculeu earlier this century. Today, few of the original stones aren't slathered in stucco, and Zaculeu is not what you'd expect from ancient ruins; no jungly vines envelop the area, and nary a temple is strewn with toppled towers or relics. The site exudes some of the sterility of a mini-golf course, but while perhaps not the best place to explore Maya mysteries, Zaculeu tells us plenty about another odd culture, that of compulsive, overimaginative archaeologists. Bus #2 leaves Huehuetenango from the mini-plaza at 2 Calle and 7 Av. every hour. The walk takes 30 to 45 minutes. Head west on 2 Calle out of town, past the soccer stadium, and from there signs point the way to the ruins; look for the 17m temple (site open daily 8am-4pm; admission Q1).

■ Nebaj

The town of Nebaj has its origins in the early days of Maya civilization, when Mam Indians migrated to the Western Highlands. Known as the **Ixil** (ee-SHEEL), they developed a distinct culture and lived unobtrusively as farmers and weavers for centuries. But in the 1970s and 80s, Guatemala's civil war hit Nebaj full force and the quiet village became a battleground between the government and guerillas, sustaining almost irreparable damage. Since the mid-80s, Nebaj has been recovering—what was once a desolate square is now a thriving market, and the town is now considered safe for tourism. Though difficult to reach, Nebaj is worth the effort; besides being a friendly, clean, and uncommercialized town, it provides a wonderful base for exploring a distinctive, ancient culture and the mountains that host it. Many cite the town as their favorite in Guatemala.

Buses disembark in the **parque central.** The church is at the south end of the park, and the town has the usual grid, with *avenidas* running north to south and *calles* east to west. **Bancafe,** one block east and two blocks north of the northeast corner of the park, changes traveler's checks and gives cash advances on Visa (open Mon.-Fri. 9am-4pm, Sat. 8am-1pm). The only regular **buses** leave from the northeast corner of the park to: **Santa Cruz del Quiché** (daily 10pm and 1am, sometimes 3 and 6am; occasional afternoon buses, 4½ hr.); **Sacapulas** and the junction to **Cobán** (daily 7am); **Huehuetenango** (daily 1:30am, 5½ hr.). Try to find the bus drivers earlier in the day to validate departure times. The daily **market** appears one block east of the park and is especially large on Thursdays and Sundays. **Farmacia Beth-El** is at the west end of the park (open daily 7am-7:30pm).

Do not let the hordes of children that aim to show you to a hotel carry your bags; they have been known to run off with luggage. To reach **Hotel Ixil**, walk up the stairs to the church plaza. (Take a look at the Nebajanese Santa among the holy moments, known by no one in particular as "San Santa.") Cross the plaza and walk down 5 Av., keeping the church on your left, until you reach Calle 10. **Ixil** has clean rooms, a pleasant courtyard (with hammocks!), comfortable beds, and semi-hot water (singles Q18; Q12 per additional person). **Hospedaje Los Tres Hermanos** is located one block north of the *parque central*, and one block to the left. It is unmarked; look for the big open doorway on the corner. This joint, which seems as old as the octogenarian who runs it efficiently and provides guard service, has dark rooms, thin mattresses, and a very public shower, but it's clean and cheap (Q7 per person). To reach **La Casa de Juana,** take the main road south from the park. At the edge of town, take a right on Av. 0a when you see Funereria Merida on your left; then, take the first left onto a small dirt road. Juana's house is the last one on your left. It's not actually a restaurant, just the home of a warm family that serves heaps of Maya food for Q10. They serve lunch at around 1pm and dinner at about 6pm; try to stop by a couple of hours beforehand to let them know you're coming. **Comedor Delicias** is located on a corner two blocks downhill from the church, and sells dinner for Q8.

The more sophisticated residents of Nebaj refer to its surrounding countryside as the "Alps of Guatemala," a rather appropriate comparison. One particularly pleasant walk goes through the Swiss cheese producing village of **Acul**. Walk down the main road to Chajul (north from the park) for a couple of kilometers until you reach a fork marked by a small yellow turret. Go left, and at the next fork, several kilometers later, go left again on the small dirt road. Follow the small river up to Acul. The cheese joint is the group of five or six white buildings on your right. To return to Nebaj, continue on the road through town, then climb for what seems like an eternity (actually about an hour) on a steep, red-clay path that ascends the mountain separating Acul and Nebaj. From the top, you'll see Nebaj on the other side; simply follow the same road back to town. The entire trip should take about six hours.

A less intense hike (about 1½hr.) leads to a waterfall outside the town: facing away from the church, take the road ahead of you to your left out of town until you reach a bridge. Follow the path that veers off to the left before the bridge to the waterfall.

Nebaj and the surrounding area, especially the villages of **Chajul** and **Cotzal,** are also well known for **traditional clothing.** Merchandise is available almost everywhere; consider buying used clothes, and don't feel pressured into making unwanted purchases. Juana (see above) also gives **weaving lessons** for Q5 per hour, if you're interested in learning to make your own garb. Juana also sells garments of her own making and offers a sauna (Q20) by reservation.

■ Todos Santos Cuchumatán

If you're lucky enough to get a left side window seat on the bus (or to sit on top), the ride to Todos Santos is one of the most spectacular in Guatemala. Ascending skyward over 1000m from Huehuetenango, the road snakes around sharp ravines; with each turn, the road below looks smaller, narrower—and the low ground much more alluring than before. After a brief passage through a high plateau, the road dives into a valley at dizzying speeds before arriving safely (knock on wood) at Todos Santos. Those prone to carsickness may want to bring along a baggie just in case.

The spectacular, if arduous, three-hour trek is well worth the prize waiting at the end. The small village of Todos Santos Cuchumatán, nestled between two towering bridges, evokes a pre-Columbian lifestyle. In fact, some of the folks here (men decked out in crazy, red-striped, bell-bottom pants and tall cowboy hats, and women dressed in bright red *huipiles* and dark blue *cortes*) might very well have lost track of time as we know it. After all, Todos Santos is one of the few villages left that still uses the 260-day Maya calendar for religious events. Don't worry, though; nobody around here forgets when there's a holiday coming up, especially the **All Saint's Day** celebration from October 31 to November 5 (see **Hold On to Your Horses!**, below). While the core population of Todos Santos is composed of only about a thousand people, thousands more depend on the town, particularly farmers who come down from their mountains for trade and services.

Hold On to Your Horses!

Todos Santos' residents kick off their out-of-control, outrageously fun All Saint's Day revelry with one of the wildest customs around. For the cost of a few quetzales, locals rent horses and enter a no-holds-barred, last-one-standing-wins race through the village. There's **no finish line** to the course, though its length is finite. Whenever a rider makes it to either of the two ends, he has to take a shot of the specially prepared moonshine; each successful lap incurs another two shots. Thanks to the time-honored tradition of using **chickens to whip the horses** into gear, the race starts off at break-neck speeds—until riders start to break their own necks, which usually doesn't take very long. Even so, ardent contestants tie themselves onto their horses in order to keep from toppling, and the race's winner is anybody still mounted and conscious at the end. Afterwards, back in town, the **marimbas** belt out everyone's favorite hits while villagers hold a different "no-bars-barred" competition of a similar sort, *sin* chickens.

There are few services in Todos Santos, and there's no way to get really lost. It might be hard to get directions anywhere, though, since Mam (and not Spanish) is most locals' native tongue. There is a **post office** in the center of town (open Mon.-Fri. 8am-4:30pm). **Buses** back to Huehue leave at 4:30am, 5am, and 12:30pm (3hr., Q8). There used to be a museum in town, but the building has collapsed.

Recent spurts of construction have markedly improved local lodgings. **Hospedaje Casa Familiar,** the nicest of the town's three hotels, is just up the street from the museum: signs point the way (singles Q20; doubles Q30). Enjoy views of the mountain from their terraces while you break the fast with oatmeal just like the Mom used to make (Q3.50). Hot water costs Q6 per (communal) shower. A block before the museum lurks **Hotel Tres Olguitas,** which has divided up a whole floor into a dozen airplane-lavatory-sized but bright rooms (only singles Q6 or Q10 per person). As a last resort (without any other element of "resort" attached), there's **Hospedaje La Paz,** also a block before the museum. Rooms are dark, spartan, but super cheap. No hot water (Q6 per person). After the bus ride makes you spill your guts, fill them up again at **Comedor Katy,** adjacent to Casa Familiar. Vegetarians delight! Pay Q10 for chicken and rice or eggs and beans; breakfast includes *mush,* and dinner a choice of soup (open 7am-9pm).

■ Near Todos Santos

Photographically inclined early-risers may want to consider taking the 4:30am bus back to Huehue and asking to be dropped off at **La Ventosa.** The morning light endows this semi-arid hamlet, situated just past the head of Todos Santos' valley, with a gilt lining. Various trails from the main road lead you through stark but captivating countryside, or even to the pine forests and high peaks of the Cuchumatanes. Stick to marked trails and be sure to be back on the road by 2pm when the last buses pass by; otherwise, it's a three-hour walk downhill to Todos Santos. Another six-hour hike from Todos Santos takes you to the beyond-traditional agricultural village of **Tzunul.**

Ask locals in Todos Santos for directions. Or, for a less demanding hike, follow the road uphill from Casa Familiar for 20 minutes to the Maya ruins of **Tecun-manchún**, a secluded place to enjoy a picnic or an afternoon nap.

THE PACIFIC SLOPE

The Pacific coast offers something quite different from the striking Maya temples, gorgeous mountain vistas, and ever-bright native costumes familiar to the nearby highland region—namely, a sweltering, generally unattractive plain of coffee and banana plantations and diesel trucks on their way to someplace else. Still, *La Costa Sur,* as Guatemalans call the area, is worth a gander, if only to check out the bracing contrasts between these black sand beaches and Central America's more stereotypical, postcard-worthy stretches of sand.

■ Retalhuleu

Reu (RAY-oo), as Retalhuleu is concisely nicknamed, has managed to carve itself a liveable—even likeable—patch out of an area where the muggy swamp usually wards off tourists like your DEET does mosquitoes. Spared the truck-emitted pollution from the distant CA-2 Highway, the road into colonial Retalhuleu is lined with majestic royal palms and the homes of the town's rich. The central square is a testament to plantain plantation pretensions: the appropriately banana-colored city hall is built in a stately neoclassical style, and the snow-white colonial church is flanked by even *more* royal palms. It's not a bad place to spend a day or so, perhaps by sipping cups of the locally produced coffee and sugar—especially if you stop by on June 12th or June 24th, when the town paints itself red in celebration of its patron saints.

ORIENTATION AND PRACTICAL INFORMATION

Avenidas in Retalhuleu run north-south and *Calles* run east-west. The central square is bounded by 5 and 6 Calles on the north and south sides, respectively, and by 4 and 6 Avs. on the east and west. Retalhuleu's bus terminal is about seven blocks north of the central square, but buses can be caught at 8 Av. and 8 Calle.

Banks line the central square, though only a few accept traveler's checks. **Banco Agrícola Mercantil** (tel. 771-0176), on the east end of the square, is one of these proud and brave few (open Mon.-Fri. 8:30am-8pm, Sat. 9am-1pm). The **post office** is on the other end of the square (open Mon.-Fri. 8am-4:30pm), and **Guatel** roosts just around the corner, on 5 Calle (open daily 7am-10pm).

Because the town's just off the CA-2 highway, **buses** traveling between the capital and the border crossing at **Tecún Umán** pull into the terminal all day long. Buses to **Tecún Umán** (2hr., Q6) leave via **Coatepeque** (1hr., Q3) every 30 minutes. Buses to **Guatemala City** (4hr., Q20) via **Esquintla** (3hr., Q15) also leave every 30 minutes. Buses leave for **Quetzaltenango** every hour from 7am to 5pm (2hr., Q5). There are taxis lined up in front of the church that charge Q5 to the terminal, but the distance is definitely short enough to walk. Snag a snack right on the square at the **supermarket, Comisariato Central,** open Mon.-Sat. 8:30am-7:30pm, Sun. 9am-1pm. There are a number of **pharmacies** within a few blocks of the central square, including **Farmacia San Antonio** (tel 771-0853), at 5 Av. just north of 6 Calle (open daily 7:30am-8pm), and **Farmacia La Salad,** 5 Av 6-45, open Mon.-Sat. 7am-7pm, Sun. 7am-noon. **Cine Condor,** 6 Calle 6-27, shows American action flicks on video for Q3 (shows at 6pm and 9pm and on Sun. at 10:30am and 3, 5, 7, 9pm). **Cine Moran,** on the square, shows movies (Q5) in English with subtitles on a big screen.

ACCOMMODATIONS AND FOOD

Retalhuleu is not geared for tight budgets, and the choices are bleak for a place to stay. Your best shot is **Hotel Hilman** on 7Av. between 7 and 8 Calles. All rooms have private baths, and most have a fan (singles Q25; doubles Q48). On the cheap side, there's **Hotel Pacífico** (tel. 771-1178), on 7 Av. between 9 and 10 Calles, which charges Q15 per person for dim, fanless rooms and a smudgy communal bath. If you can convince the owner of **Hospedaje San Fransisco** that you *are* looking for windowless, cell-like rooms, he'll graciously let you stay (also Q15 per person). From there the prices jump significantly. **Hotel Modelo,** 5 Calle 4-53 (tel 771-0256), isn't exactly a model; dark but large, well-kept rooms have ceiling fans and private baths (singles Q54; doubles Q78).

Pack that grumbly stomach full at **Cafetería La Luna,** located on 5 Calle in front of the church. **Carne** and **pollo** both go for Q20 in this classy and clean joint. Thrifty, but still nifty, are the hamburgers (Q8) and super-authentic "clud" sandwiches (Q10). South of the square at 7 Calle 4-36 is **Pizza Rondinella,** (tel. 771-0567) serving pizza for about Q23 in a restaurant that seems more a *comedor* than a fast food joint. Across the street from Hotel Hilman is **Comedor Mary.** Though apt to fill up quickly and not overly clean, this place sells **pollo** and **bistek** for Q12 a pop, and the **menú del día** (the only option, Q8) comes with **mosh**, veggies in the eggs, and a small pitcher of coffee. **Pizza de Ciro,** across the street from La Luna, serves portions for Q2.25 and very large, tasty pizzas (Q22-60; open daily 8am-8:30pm). **Pollo Llamero** offers an unexciting menu at unexciting prices, but it's clean and located conveniently between Hotels Hilman and Pacífico. **Hamburgues Especial** (Q12) serves fast food that is cooked *after* you order it.

■ Near Retalhuleu

Situated on a narrow black dune and separated from the mainland by a slender channel, **Tulate** is home to one of the nicest beaches on Guatemala's Pacific Coast; many locals consider it Guatemala's best-kept secret. The sand is black, of course, and it lacks the development, garbage, and pollution of other nearby coastal towns. There are no direct **buses** from Retalhuleu to Tulate but it's still an easy daytrip from Reu. Take a bus headed to **Mazatenango** (they leave every 30min.), and transfer at **Cuyotenango** (30min., Q2). From there the ride is about two hours (Q7). The bus route ends at a strait which must be crossed by boat (Q2); the skiff also does sea jaunts for Q30. Run the gauntlet of **comedores** (all seafood joints) and frolic for hours—more precisely, until 4pm, when the last bus leaves. If you miss it, you'll have to stay in Tulate's lone *hospedaje,* **Rancho de Xelaju,** which is located on the main drag and is something of a drag. Q20 buys one or two reed-stuffed cots under a thatched roof, replete with swirling bats and communal bath (with fresh water).

CROSSING THE BORDER TO MEXICO

Two hours west of Retahuleu is the border town of **Tecún Umán.** Like most border towns, Tecún Umán is rather unattractive, with the added disadvantage of being along the broiling Pacific Coast. As Guatemala's main entry point from Mexico, however, the crossing is busy 24 hours. The spanning bridge symbolically links the two nations. **Tourist cards** from Guatemala can be had at the border for Q10; the more intelligent you look, the less border guards will add to this price. There are a number of cheap hotels in Tecún, but there is no reason to linger; **buses** for Guatemala City and other destinations in between leave every 30 minutes from 5am-10pm. When planning, expect to lose some time to road construction.

■ Puerto San José

Puerto San José sits right in the middle of the black-sand *costa sur* (southern coast) which stretches from Mexico to El Salvador. Because the Pacific Highway connects Puerto San José to Guate, the town swells with ocean-hungry city dwellers on weekends. Puerto San José is a port town, complete with sailors and prostitutes, and the stifling heat of the southern coast. Convenience is the key to the town's popularity; folks with time to spare might do better traveling onward.

The town's two parallel main drags are **Avenida 30 de Junio** and **Avenida del Comercio.** The park and bus depot are sandwiched between them. The only place to **exchange currency** is **Banco G&T,** Av. del Comercio, Calles 8/9 (open Mon.-Fri. 9am-3pm, Sat. 10am-2pm). **Telephones** await at **GUATEL,** Av. 30 de Junio, which allows cash and collect calls only (open daily 7am-10pm). **Buses to Guatemala City** from Puerto San José almost invariably stop in **Escuintla. Transporte Trans-pacifico** and **Transporte Esmerelda** follow this route (every 20min., 5am-6pm, Q12 to Guate, Q5 to Escuintla). Trans-pacifico also goes a little farther down the coast to **Iztapa** (every ½hr., 6am-8pm, Q1). **Taxis** line up next to the park on Av. del Comercio. **Police** wait in the station on the left on the way from the bus depot to Av. 30 de Junio.

Surprisingly, Puerto San José's weekend retreat popularity does not translate into a good variety of places to stay. The best deal around is probably **Casa San José Hotel,** Av. del Comercio and Calle 1a. The mattresses can't quite be called plump, but this small hotel (7 rooms) has a good location—close to buses, the market, and the beach. There's even a pool and a restaurant (singles Q60; doubles Q90; triples Q120; add Q10 for TV). A step up in price, though not necessarily in quality, are the **Posada Quetzal II** and the **Hotel Papillon.** The **Hotel Papillon,** Barrio Miramar (tel. 084-10-64), offers ocean view rooms with fans. Up to eight can stay in a suite (Mon.-Fri. doubles Q100; quads Q125; 6 or 8 Q150; Sat.-Sun. doubles Q125; quads 150; 6 or 8 Q180). Dune buggies are rented out for Q100 per hour.

■ Monterrico

After a lengthy trek by boat or bus, the first question to cross a visitor's mind might be, "Why on earth is this place so highly recommended?" You'll soon find out. Blessed with beautiful black sand beaches and crashing waves, Monterrico is an excellent place to lounge away the days. The nights are equally beautiful, with frequent lightning storms. A sand shelf protects Monterrico from the rain, but allows visitors to watch the storms a few kilometers off the shore. Finally Monterrico's southward orientation lets you admire the sun as it rises and sets on the water, an incredible sight to behold. Surprisingly, the city has not developed much of a tourist industry, so you won't be overwhelmed by fellow travelers, but you will need to bring a flashlight and mosquito net. You'll be happy to find that Monterrico offers pristine Guatemalan wildlife in the form of huge flocks of birds, nesting sea turtles, and bioluminescent waves. Grab a drink, watch a spectacular sunset, and be mellow.

Orientation and Practical Information Situated on a narrow strip of land separated from the mainland by 2km of mangrove swamp, Monterrico is accessible by two routes. The faster is to proceed by bus from **Escuintla** to **Taxisco.** From there, **buses** leave for **La Avellana** (every hr., 6am-5pm, 1hr., Q2.50), whence goeth a quick ferry to Monterrico (45min., Q2.50). The whole process takes about four hours from the capital. An alternate route is to take the bus due south to **Iztapa,** cross the channel to **Puerto Viejo** (10min., Q20), then take a bus over a slow, bumpy, dirt road 15km to Monterrico. Four buses leave daily from Puerto Viejo to Monterrico (11:30am, 1:30, 4, and 6pm, 2½hr., Q6). There is also an express Micro-bus from the Alm School (next to the San Gregorio Hotel) in Antigua on Saturday, which returns to **Antigua** and **Guate** on Sun. at 2pm (US$12, 4hr.).

Aside from arriving, departing, or checking out some of the eateries on the Calle Principal, the only reasons to head into town are the **SuperMonterrico** and the **Farmacia Carolina.** The SuperMonterrico (three-quarters of the way to the beach) is the town's version of a supermarket (open Mon.-Fri. 8am-6pm, Sat. 8am-10pm). The Farmacia (half way to the beach) sells vitamins, tonics, and over-the-counter antibiotics (open daily 7am-6pm).

Accommodations and Food Monterrico's accommodations are very reasonable. The spot for after-hours entertainment, **Pig Pen,** has expanded to include a hotel. Despite the name, the rooms are clean and relatively safe (singles 20Q; doubles

25Q; 6Q for a hammock). Run by a former Peace Corps volunteer, **Hotel Baule Beach** (tel. 873-6196, call after 7:30pm), located on the beach about 100m to the left of the main street, offers private baths, comfortable beds, and **mosquito netting** (singles Q48; doubles Q82; prices decrease if you stay 3 nights or more). A bit newer and funkier, **Kaiman Inn,** adjacent to Baule Beach, offers similar amenities (Q55 per person; Q60 on weekends). The Kaiman also has a good, if pricey, Italian **restaurant** (Q30-80). Service and quality are reportedly better on weekends when the owner comes from town with a sharp eye and fresh supplies. For fresh seafood, head to the main road and enjoy the fine dining at the *comedores* which have the same fish as Kaiman, just at half the price. **Turicentro Doble "L,"** located on the beach about 20m to the right of where the main street ends, is one of many cheap *pensiones* with dark rooms and cockroach-infested public baths, but the only one to have mosquito nets, a must in the rainy season (Q15 per person, Q20 in summer; Q3 net rental).

Sights Set up as a reserve for sea turtles to lay eggs, **Biotopo Monterrico** also preserves one of the last remaining mangrove swamps on Guatemala's Pacific coast and is home to thousands of birds. Local fishermen give tours on their boats (Q20 per hour). If arriving or departing by launch from La Avellana, however, the tour is redundant, unless you must quench a burning desire to name every bird and plant. The magnificent **sea turtles** hide from poachers and predators, but patient visitors can often spot them coming ashore to lay their eggs early in the morning during the summer months.

Next door to the Baule Beach Hotel is the **Tortuguero,** a university-run zoo/education center. Tours are offered on Sundays, but anyone can easily pick their own way through the scant, random exhibits. Especially interesting are the iguana and *caiman* (crocodile) tanks. Don't get too close; they're not fed during the week.

ALTA Y BAJA VERAPAZ

For years, the Kekchí Indians of this area successfully resisted the Spanish conquest, which gave rise to the Kekchí name for the region, *Tuzuntohil,* or "Land of War." But thanks to Fray Bartolomé de las Casas and the Franciscan friars, the region has earned its present, Spanish name, **Verapaz,** or "true peace." When the Fray organized a powerful campaign in defense of the *indígenas,* the Spanish empire actually halted its military conquest and granted him five military-free years for the peaceful and "humane" conversion of the Kekchí. He and the friars learned Kekchí and composed gospel songs in it. They passed the tunes on to a few merchants who frequently visited the warring areas, and the visitors sang the songs while introducing mirrors, knives, and other European objects to the area. The chiefs, assured that the friars were not interested in their gold and land, finally let them in, and a peaceful conversion followed shortly thereafter. Since then, Verapaz has been more a land of war than one of peace, serving as a base for guerilla activity in the last decades, but the recent peace agreement of 1996 has given its citizens hope that it may be free from war for generations to come.

▓ Cobán

Once the center of *Tuzuntohil,* Cobán was overrun by the Spanish conquistadors and later by German coffee plantation lords, who were driven out by American troops during WWII. Today the Land of War is on a coffee break, catching a breath as a sultry tourist town with natural parks and scattered *balnearios* (scenic bathing pools), ideal for dawdling in the clean mountain air. Mother Nature is always nearby in Cobán, but paved roads and modern conveniences keep your feet firmly planted in civilization while some of the best coffee in the world keeps your veins surging.

ORIENTATION AND PRACTICAL INFORMATION

Primera Avenida (north to south) and **1 Calle** (east to west) divide the city into four quadrants. The northwest is labeled Zona 1, the southwest Zona 2, the southeast Zona 3, and the northeast Zona 4. The central park is framed by 1 and 2 Avs. and 1 and 2 Calles in Zona 2. Get your tourist info at **Hostal de Doña Victoria,** 3a Calle 2-38, Zona 3, which has a map, and at **Hostal Casa de Acuña,** 4 Calle 3-11, Zona 2, which has information on trips in and outside Cobán.

Cobán may be your only chance to **exchange currency** in this part of the country. **Banco del Café,** 1 Av. 2-66, Zona 2 (tel. 952-1011), changes traveler's checks (open Mon.-Fri. 8:30am-8pm, Sat. 10am-2pm). **Banco Industrial,** 2 Av., 1 Calle, Zona 1, has a 24hr., Visa- and PLUS-friendly **ATM** and exchanges traveler's checks (open Mon.-Fri. 8:30am-7pm, Sat. 8:30am-5:30pm).

Transportes Escobar y Monja Blanca, 2 Calle 3-77, Zona 4 (tel. 952-1952), sends **buses** to **Guatemala City** (every hr., 2am-4pm, 4hr., Q25). All other buses leave from the bus terminal at the end of 2 Calle, Zona 4, to: **San Cristóbal** (11 per day, 6am-7pm, 45min., Q1.50); **Lanquín** (6am, 1, 1:30, and 3pm, 3hr., Q7; the 6am bus leaves from 3 Av. and 1 Calle, Zona 4, in front of Hospedaje Maya); **Tactic** (every 30min., 6am-6pm, 45min., Q2); **Carcha** (every 10min., 6am-7pm, 15min., Q0.75). Pick-up trucks to **Playa Grande** and **Cantabal** (6-8hr., Q30) via **Parque Nacional Laguna Lachuá** (5-7hr., Q25) leave the bus station between 2 and 5am daily. Inquire the previous afternoon for departure times. **Taxis** (tel. 952-1897) line up on the north side of the park, by the cathedral, and in front of the post office. Clean clothes at **Lavandería La Providencia,** Diagonal 4, 2-43, Zona 2, on the south side of the park (7lb. wash Q5, dry Q10; open Mon.-Sat. 8am-noon and 2-5pm). **Farmacia Carvi** sits at 1 Calle 4-53, Zona 3; open 24hr.). In a **medical emergency,** try **Los Bomberos** (tel. 952-3094), 3 Av. and 3 Calle, Zona 4 (open 24hr.) or the **Red Cross,** 2 Calle 2-13, Zona 13 (tel. 125). The **police** are at 1 Calle 5-12, Zona 1 (tel. 952-1225; open 24hr.). The **post** and **telegraph office** is at 3 Calle 2-00, Zona 3 (tel. 952-1140); the post office is open Monday through Friday 7am-5:30pm; in June 1997, telegraphs were temporarily closed. The **postal code** is 16001. **Email** services are available at **Access,** la Calle 3-13, Zona 1. Send for Q5, receive for Q2, and copy for Q1. **Guatel** has **telephones** at 2 Av. and 1 Calle, Zona 1, but the office has moved to 3 Av., Zona 2 (open daily 7am-10pm).

ACCOMMODATIONS AND FOOD

Accommodations in Cobán are chock-full of tourists year-round, so finding a room may take a little wandering. The lucky and frugal get into **Hospedaje Maya** on 1a Calle 2-33, Zona 4 (tel. 952-2380). Basic, uneventful rooms have comfy beds, and the public bathrooms smell like a leaky barn. Modern refurbishments such as a washer, dryer, and leather reclining chairs make up for it (Q10 per person, with bath Q12). **Hostal de Acuña,** 4 Calle 3-11, Zona 2 (tel. 952-1547), provides an interesting gamble for the solo traveler: your Q30 goes toward a two-person room which may or may not be filled with another guest. Pine wood bunkbeds are arranged in homey, antiseptic two- or four-person rooms. Hot water pours from the gleaming showers, and each guest gets a locked drawer for belongings. The small, lush courtyard garden rings with jazz or classical music. If you do stay, clarify how long you have the room for, since the place does fill up quickly (Q30 per person). **Pensión Familiar,** Diagonal 4, 2-49, Zona 2, has large, bright, nice-smelling rooms. Toucans and doves spruce up a drab lounge. The hot water shower is on the ground floor (Q16 per person). **Hotel Nuevo Monterrey** (tel. 952-1131), 6 Av. and 1 Calle, Zona 1, connected to the Hotel Cobán Imperial, has well-maintained rooms and decent communal baths with cold water (singles Q15, with bath Q16; doubles Q25, with bath Q31; triples Q35, with bath Q45). **Hotel La Paz,** 6 Av. 2-19, Zona 1 (tel. 952-1358), has slightly worn, but tidy rooms and baboon statues shouldering potted plants. Bathrooms dribble hot water (singles Q24, with bath Q30; doubles Q40, with bath Q48). The cafeteria offers cheap chow and toiletries (breakfast Q8, lunch Q12). The **Hostal de Doña Victoria** offers colorful, clean, furnished rooms with model private baths. Cross your fingers; if the "backpacker special" (Q30 per person) is in effect (the standard price is Q103 for singles), you'll get the best deal in town, complete with hammocks, a garden, and little library. Otherwise, you'll just have to loiter in the **restaurant** and pretend (breakfast Q10-20, sandwiches Q13).

An enticing tunnel entrance leads to **Café El Tirol,** 1 Calle 3-13, Zona 1, a great place to bring a book—or borrow one from the baby library of paperbacks—and murmur sweet, intellectual nothings over a wide selection of rich coffees, teas, and chocolate drinks, hot or cold—not to mention the rare strawberry *licuado* (Q6.50 with milk, coffee Q2.75-10, sandwiches Q8-10; open Mon.-Sat. 7am-8:30pm). **Hostal de Acuña** also hosts a cozy restaurant with higher prices. Budget travelers can chomp on a sandwich cubano (Q19) or slurp the soup of the day (Q25) while tapping the owners' wealth of regional travel tips or gazing at the budding art gallery (open daily 8am-9pm). **Cafetería Santa Rita** (tel. 952-1842), 2 Calle, Zona 2, next to the large spider-like structure in the main park, speedily serves *típico* dishes in large portions (breakfast Q10.50, lunch or dinner Q13; open Mon.-Fri. 7am-9pm, Sat. 7:30am-9pm). A hard-rockin' action flick or the latest cup game distracts customers and employees at **Restaurant El Refugio,** 2 Calle 1-34, Zona 4 (tel. 952-2380). Privacy is no problem, as tables are spaced light-years apart (*spaghuetti a la crema* Q23, *chile relleno* with rice and beans Q17, *taco cobanero* Q8; open daily 11am-11pm). **Comedor Rosita,** 1 Calle 314, Zona 3, has a big menu with small prices (lunch Q9, snacks Q4.50, cakes Q2.50; open daily 8am-10pm). **Restaurant Kam-mun,** 1 Calle 8-12, Zona 1, serves traditional Chinese fare.

SIGHTS AND ENTERTAINMENT

No matter how hot and hectic it gets on the baking streets of Cobán, tranquility always awaits at **Parque Las Victorias,** seven blocks west and two blocks north of Parque Central (open daily 8am-4:30pm). As you hike the trails, swing by the **Bajaritos,** a thatch-roofed village of swings, slides, and exercise equipment as innovative in its construction as the residences on *Gilligan's Island.* Nearby, the foliage breaks into a sunny clearing, where a garden coddles the region's endangered plants and flowers. The Q1 admission fee may be your best-spent quetzal in Guatemala. The Q10 camping fee is more of a gamble, but camping's always a gamble. Next to the park, but farther up the hill, **Iglesia Calvario** provides a wonderful view of Cobán from on high. Near the Hostal de Acuña is the **Dieseldorff** coffee company, 3 Calle 4-12. The Q6 tour is unspectacular, especially during the wet season, but if you play your cards right, you may get a free cup of coffee. Otherwise, you'll have to buy by the pound (Q16; open Mon.-Fri. 8am-12:30pm and 1:30-5pm).

■ Near Cobán

Cobán just can't seem to get enough of *balnearios,* scenic swimming pools often built alongside rivers. The most lovely example is **Las Islas,** where water bounces through a rocky riverbed into a natural pool surrounded by picnic bungalows. To get there, take a bus to Carchá from the Cobán terminal. From Carchá, take a taxi (Q5) or walk 20 minutes; admission is Q1. Also try **Hermanas del León,** 20 minutes down Diagonal 4 (free camping). To get to **La Colonia,** take a bus to Carchá, get off at the bridge, and walk 30 minutes east. If you *still* haven't had enough swimming, **Balneario de Camché,** near Tactic, 31km south of Cobán, is a local favorite, as well. Another option is Vivero Verapaz, an orchid farm which is filled with a great multitude of orchids. The place is in bloom, but your Q5 is still well spent on a leisurely and detailed tour during the wet season. Take the diagonal out of town (the "old road") and walk one km or so past the Hermanas del León balneario.

■ Lanquín

Seventy kilometers north of Cobán, the little village of Lanquín possesses two of the most spectacular jewels in Guatemala's crown—the natural bridge and cascades of

Samuc Champey and the enormous **Grutas de Lanquín,** some of Guatemala's most beautiful caves. The caves are 2km before the village, but first go into town and look for the policeman who can open the doors and turn on the electricity (Q10 per person); he works in the municipal building in the center of town daily, 7:30am-noon and 1:30-5pm. However, the cave works 24 hours a day; arrive at dusk to witness the soul-shaking flocks of bats. Bring a flashlight or two, as being caught lightless could lead to calamity. The lovely, blue-green Lanquín river springs forth from beneath the cave's entrance, making a good swimming spot. Visiting Samuc Champey is more of a challenge. It's a long, two-and-a-half-hour, 10km walk from Lanquín. **Hotel El Recreo,** 1½km past the cave and ½km before town, organizes tours for Q20 per person during the high season, but it's much cheaper to ask around in the village and find out if there's a pick-up (Q3). Mondays, Thursdays, and Sundays are market or church days, and it is recommended to save Samuc for one of these days when rides are cheaper and more easily available. A hired ride at other times during the week will wait for you while you swim, but will also charge Q125, making it cheaper to go in large group. The ride takes about 45 minutes, and admission is Q5. Pray for good weather—while the disappearance of the Cahabón river into the earth's bowels is spectacular anytime, the natural bridge and its crystalline swimming pool are best enjoyed in the midday sun.

Only four **buses** go to Lanquín (6am, 1, 1:30, and 3:30pm from Cobán, 3hr., Q7) and only four leave it (2 at 6am, one at 7am, and one at 3pm to Cobán). Times are not exact, so be there half an hour early, ready to wait as long as an hour. Limited transportation makes Lanquín difficult as a daytrip, so spend the night at **Pensión la Providencia,** on the main street, which has spacious rooms, hammocks, and exclusive boasting rights to hot water (heated by firewood; Q10 per person). Nearby **Lugar el Turista** offers a more delapidated option, with springy beds stuffed into an airy loft. If the coils get to you, try the hammocks (Q10 per person). Both places have attached restaurants where beans, eggs, and steak go for about Q10. **Hotel El Recreo** (see above) glitters with its own pool and wildlife kingdom. Immaculate bungalow rooms go for Q40 per person, and carpeted chambers for much more (singles Q106; doubles Q150; triples Q180). Lavish multi-course meals include soup, steak, *frijoles,* and tortillas (Q24); you can also order breakfast (Q18). It's easiest to arrive in Lanquín on the early bus so you can hop into bed before the electricity goes out at 9pm.

■ Near Lanquín: Biotopo Quetzal Mario Dary

Some of the last remaining *quetzales,* the bright green-and-red birds emblematic of Guatemala, hang out at this reserve, 160km north of Guatemala City on the highway to Cobán. The reserve is set in a cloud-strewn highland forest with twisting trails throughout. Due to repeated muggings along its trails, the Biotopo was closed for several months early in 1996. It has now reopened, and all visitors are required to use the free police escorts on the trails. These escorts arrive at 7:30am, but the long-plumed quetzals (whose tail feathers can reach a yard in length and were once used to adorn the headdresses of Maya royalty) are usually only seen from 5:30am-7:30am. Never fear, the easiest places to see the quetzals at dawn are the roadsides in front of the *biotopo* and the Hospedaje Randieto del Quetzal, neither of which requires the accompaniment of an escort. The *hospedaje* is on the other side of the street, down the road to Cobán, on its own patch of forest complete with a private trail which can be safely explore unescorted. Viewing these noble birds in a zoo is not an option, as they cannot survive in captivity. The *hospedaje* has private cabins and rooms in the woods (singles Q25, with bath Q40; doubles Q40, with bath Q55—all not including 17% tax). Be sure to ask the staff to point out the most popular trees the evening before. An attached restaurant serves eggs and beans for Q8 and coffee for Q2 (open daily 7am-8pm).

EASTERN GUATEMALA

Want to lose the crowds in *Gringotenango* and the western highlands? Go east, young person. The eastern *biotopos* (wildlife reserves), ruins, and *aguas bonitas* offer diversions unparalleled in the west, and everything's served in the sauce of a hang-loose, come-as-you-are atmosphere. The well-maintained Atlantic Highway offers access to some of the eastern hot spots. Buses between Guatemala City and Puerto Barrios usually make stops at **Quiriguá** and near **Lago Izabal;** just ask beforehand to be let off at your destination. To head south to **Chiquimula** and **Esquipulas,** get off at Río Hondo or head toward Zacapa.

■ Chiquimula

Set among the rounded peaks of the Eastern Highlands, Chiquimula occupies a truly spectacular location. From the town proper, however, all views of the surrounding countryside are obscured by the ramshackle and monotonous buildings that line the streets. Although it is the area's commercial and financial center, Chiquimula offers tourists little more than a springboard to Honduras, especially Copán.

The town is built on a hill, and its layout is a simple grid. *Avenidas* run across the hill, while *calles* follow the fall line down. *Avenida* numbers increase as you head downhill and, facing downhill, *calle* numbers increase from left to right. The **bus station** is at 10 Av., 1/2 Calles, and the plaza sits at 7 Av. and 3 Calle. **Banco del Agro** (tel. 942-0765), on Calle 3, 6/7 Av., directly across from the plaza, changes cash and AmEx traveler's checks (open Mon.-Fri. 9am-8pm). **Guatel** (tel. 942-0299), just downhill from the plaza, offers **telephone** and **fax** service from 7am-10pm. **Buses** leave from the station at about 30-minute intervals to: **Guatemala City** (3½hr., Q18); **Puerto Barrios** (3hr., Q15); and **Esquipulas** (1hr.). To reach the **Honduran border** near **Copán Ruinas,** catch a bus for El Florido (6am-2pm, 2½hr., Q12), but start early; the price of the last truck from the border to Copán is a lot higher than that of earlier buses (1 hr., about L15). Two **markets** appear daily (6am-6pm) at the terminal and the plaza. On Thursdays and Sundays they swell to the bursting point, as Chiquimula hosts the largest market in the region. Drugs may be purchased at **Farmacia America**

That's Quite a Quetzal!

For centuries, the quetzal has been known by a variety of cultures under many names: he is *kukul* to the Mayans, *quetzaltototl* to the Aztecs, and *Pharomachus mocinnus* to international bird nerds. No matter what they call him, however, people have a **universal respect** for the quetzal—particularly for the metallic-green plumage of the colorful male. It's always been **illegal to kill** the now-endangered bird, and the offense was punished by death in pre-colonial times. Quetzal feathers were powerful bartering tools until the arrival of the *conquistadores* who quickly followed the native lead in incorporating the plumes in to robes, headgear, and other **adornments.** The quetzal's flashy beauty hoisted him to a godly altitude in the years of early Mesoamerica. The "quetzal-serpent" makes cameo appearances in artwork in Tikal, Guatemala and Palenque, Mexico, and many major players of the ancient world, such as Quetzalcoatl, proudly wore its feathers. The quetzal is truly respected not for its looks, but for its special brand of **supernatural spunk.** Although only pigeon-sized, the plucky duck fought valiantly as the *nahual* (animal spirit) of the heroic, but doomed, Tecún Umán. Legend has it that after the battle of Xela—another **killing spree** at the hands of Pedro de Alvarado—quetzals descended to the blood-stained field overnight, thus gaining their bright red breasts. Yet for all its gumption (which has earned it the status of national bird, symbol of independence and autonomy), today's quetzal seems rather timid; to catch a glimpse of it at the Biotopo, you'll need a lot of time and patience.

GUATEMALA

(tel. 942-0856), just downhill from the plaza (open 7:30am-10pm). For more hands-on medical care, the **Hospital Central Clínico de Especialidades** (tel. 942-2053), 9 Av. and 4 Calle, has a good reputation (available 24 hr.). The larger hospital may be reached at 942-0363. The **police** (tel. 942-0256) hang out at 14 Calle, 6 Av., Zona 1. Call **120** for **emergency, 122** in case of **fire**. You'll find the **post office** is directly across from the bus station (open Mon.-Fri. 9am-5:30pm); its **postal code** is 20001.

Inexpensive accommodations are easy to find in Chiquimula; just make sure you take a good look at the room before putting down your quetzales. The best deal is probably the **Hotel Hernandez** (tel. 942-0708), 3 Calle, 7-8 Av., just down the street from the park. The front door is locked at midnight, but the hotel's *piscina* (swimming pool) is open 24 hours (singles Q20, with private bath and cable TV Q48; doubles Q40, with the works Q60). A considerable step down in price, but an even greater leap down in quality, is the **Hotel Dario** (tel. 942-0192), 8 Av., 4/5 Calles (singles Q18, with private bath Q16; doubles Q25, with private bath Q32; add Q2 for fan). If you feel inexplicably drawn to the bus station area, the only choice is the **Hotel Victoria**, 2 Calle, 10 Av. (tel. 942-2179) across from the terminal, with smallish but clean rooms, private baths, cable TVs, and fans (singles Q35; doubles Q60; each additional person Q25).

If you're not weary of the Central American hat-trick of tortilla, beans, and meat, eating won't be a problem here. Many *comedores* line the streets around the plaza. Two newcomers, **Jimena María** and **Albita,** are particularly well-liked; they're right next to each other on 8 Av., 3/4 Calle. Most meals cost less than Q10. More elaborate cuisine along the same theme is served just down the avenue at **Restaurant El Lugar de Paso;** locals recommend the *lomito* (Q25; open daily 7am-10pm).

If you're stuck in Chiquimula during the day, the town has one sight to offer. The remains of a **colonial church,** destroyed in the 18th century by an earthquake, have been left to erode on the edge of town. To get there, walk down 3 Calle until you're nearly at the highway. Take a right at the abandoned railroad tracks and keep walking for about five minutes until you see the church on your left. As night falls, Chiquimula goes to sleep. The only formal option for nighttime entertainment is the **Cine Liv,** across from the plaza, which shows second rate, year-old American flicks dubbed in Spanish. Films start at 6:30 and 8pm (Q2-3).

■ Esquipulas

Sniff carefully: the crystal mountain air of Esquipulas smells of tourists, but a different breed than you may have encountered elsewhere. A major pilgrimage sight for all of Central America, the town's chief industry is the reception and diversion of the 1¼ million visitors who stream through yearly, giving it the aura of a religious theme park. Pilgrims come to worship and make offerings to **El Cristo Negro**, a mahogany carving of Christ on the cross that was delivered by Spanish missionaries (see **"El Cristo Negro?"** below). Ever since its arrival in 1595, the figure has been revered for its miraculous healing powers, which supposedly cured Archbishop Figueroa of his ailments in 1737. El Cristo Negro hovers in the cloud-white **Basílica de Esquipulas,** which towers majestically over the town's other buildings and vendors' tents. The church's interior shimmers with candles and the murmurs of mumbled prayers; some devotees crouch in pews, while others kneel at the entrance or join the queue that stretches through the side entrance to shuffle past the holy statue. For those not among the faithful, Esquipulas offers an intriguing glimpse of the region's ardent religiosity, as well as a mountain-high springboard into nearby Honduras.

ORIENTATION AND PRACTICAL INFORMATION

Buses deposit pilgrims on Doble Vía, the main east-west drag which crosses in front of the basilica and the **Parque Central. 3a Avenida,** the *calle principal,* heads north from Doble Vía at the basilica. With your back to the church, avenidas increase in number from left to right, calles count up as they approach the park. **Banco del Café**

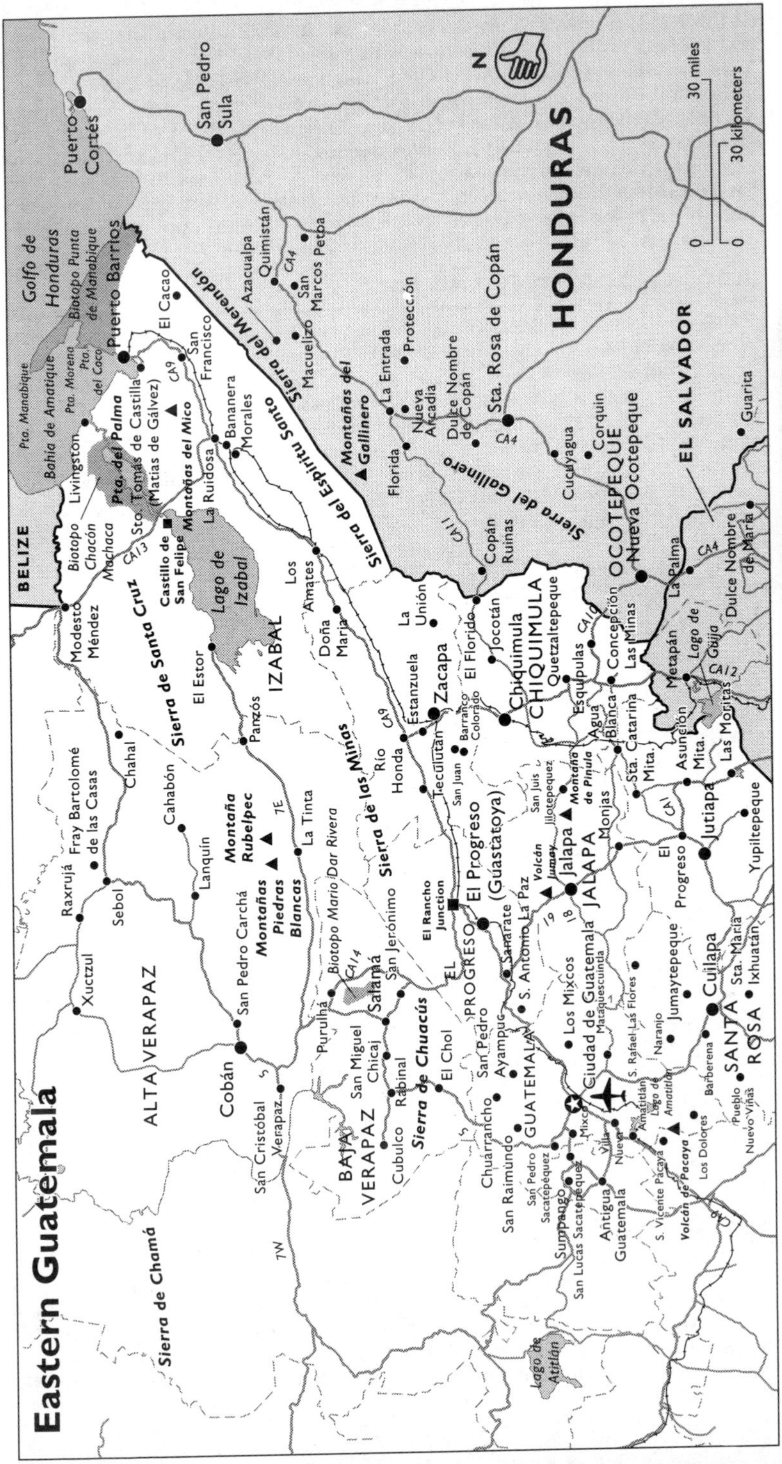
Eastern Guatemala
BELIZE
HONDURAS
EL SALVADOR
Golfo de Honduras
Biotopo Punta de Manabique
Pta. Manabique
Bahía de Amatique
Pta. Morena
Pta. del Cacao
Puerto Barrios
Puerto Cortés
San Pedro Sula
Livingston
Biotopo Chacón Machaca
Pta. del Palma
Sto. Tomás de Castilla (Matías de Gálvez)
Montañas del Mico
Castillo de San Felipe
Lago de Izabal
IZABAL
El Cacao
San Francisco
Bananera
Morales
La Ruidosa
Sierra del Merendón
Sierra del Espíritu Santo
Montañas del Gallinero
Sierra del Gallinero
Azacualpa
Quimistán
San Marcos
Petoa
Macuelizo
Protección
La Entrada
Nueva Arcadia
Florida
Dulce Nombre de Copán
Sta. Rosa de Copán
Cucuyagua
Corquín
Copán Ruinas
OCOTEPEQUE
Nueva Ocotepeque
La Palma
Dulce Nombre de María
Guarita
Modesto Méndez
Sierra de Santa Cruz
El Estor
Los Amates
Doña María
La Unión
Zacapa
Estanzuela
El Florido
Jocotán
Chiquimula
CHIQUIMULA
Quetzaltepeque
Esquipulas
Concepción Las Minas
Metapán
Lago de Güija
Las Moritas
Asunción Mita
Sta. Catarina Mita
Agua Blanca
Chahal
Fray Bartolomé de las Casas
Raxruhá
Sebol
Cahabón
Lanquín
Panzós
Montaña Rubelpec
Montañas Piedras Blancas
La Tinta
Biotopo Mario Dary Rivera
Sierra de las Minas
Río Hondo
Teculután
San Juan
Barranco Colorado
El Rancho Junction
El Progreso (Guastatoya)
EL PROGRESO
Sanarate
San Juis Jilotepeque
Montaña de Pínula
Volcán Jumay
Jalapa
JALAPA
Monjas
El Progreso
Jutiapa
Yupiltepeque
Xucuzul
ALTA VERAPAZ
San Pedro Carchá
Cobán
San Cristóbal Verapaz
Purulhá
Salamá
San Jerónimo
San Miguel Chicaj
Rabinal
Cubulco
BAJA VERAPAZ
Sierra de Chuacús
El Chol
San Pedro Ayampuc
S. Antonio La Paz
Los Mixcos
Ciudad de Guatemala
Mataquescuintla
S. Rafael Las Flores
Naranjo
Jumaytepeque
Cuilapa
Sta. María Ixhuatán
SANTA ROSA
Barberena
Chuarrancho
GUATEMALA
San Raimundo
San Pedro Sacatepéquez
Mixco
Villa Nueva
Amatitlán
Lago de Amatitlán
Pueblo Nuevo Viñas
Los Dolores
Volcán de Pacaya
S. Vicente Pacaya
Antigua Guatemala
Sumpango
San Lucas Sacatepéquez
Lago de Atitlán
Sierra de Chamá
CA1
CA4
CA9
CA10
CA12
CA13
CA14
7E
7W
N
30 miles
30 kilometers

(tel. 943-1439), 4 blocks down 3a Av. from the basilica, changes money and accepts the widest array of traveler's checks (open Mon.-Fri. 8:30am-7pm, Sat. 9am-1pm). **Guatel telephones** sit on 5 Av., 9 Calle, Zona 1 (tel. 943-1121; fax 943-1299; open 8am-8pm). **Buses** leave for: **Guatemala City** (every 30min., 2:30am-5:30pm, Q21.50), **Chiquimula** (minivans every 30min., 5am-5pm, 1hr., Q6), where connections can be made to **Quiriguá, Puerto Barrios**, and other stops along the Atlantic Highway. One of many **pharmacies** sits on 3 Av. 26, Zona 1 (open 7am-10pm). The **post office** is at the northern end of 6a Av. (open Mon.-Sat. 9am-5pm), and its **postal code** is 9002. The **police** (tel. 943-1207) may be found at the opposite end of 3a Av. from the basilica between 2/3 calles (available 24hr.).

ACCOMMODATIONS AND FOOD

Esquipulas treats its wealthier visitors well; several 4-star hotels and expensive restaurants welcome wayfarers with open arms. Unfortunately, most of the cheapest places are not as attractive or friendly: prices can as much as double on Saturdays and during festivals, as the crowds descend on the town. **Casa Norman** (tel. 943-1503), 3 Av., 9-20, zone 1 (or, 1½ blocks down from the basilica), has 4 sparkling, spacious rooms with private baths and hot water. American owner Gerardo has spent 38 years in the area and consequently has a lot to share (Q30 per person). **Hotel San Francisco**, 2 Av., 11-22, Zona 1 (tel. 943-1402), enjoys the constant roar of buses arriving at the terminal and the communal bathrooms could use some tender loving cleaning. But the price is right and the owner likeable (singles Q15; doubles Q30, with bath Q50). In **Hotel Paris**, 10 Calle, 2 Av. 1-99 (tel. 943-1276), rooms are less homely and more homey, though it's built around a parking lot. Stalwart, firm mattresses, clean, shared bathrooms and hot water make this motor lodge quite comfortable (singles Q20; doubles Q40). Prices *double* on Saturdays and during festivals.

Most budget restaurants in town are connected to hotels and offer identical fare: if you've eaten anything since you arrived in Guatemala, you won't be surprised by your choice of *pollo, carne asado*, or *huevos con frijoles*. Prices are more reasonable the farther you stray from the basilica's holy aura. **Restaurant Villa Edelmira**, 2½ blocks down 3a Av., is run by an amiable family with quite a horse fetish. Munch on *pollo dorado* (Q15). **Restaurant Santa María,** at the corner of 2a Av. and 10, trades its standard breakfasts for a low Q7.

SIGHTS AND ENTERTAINMENT

Of the several sights in the area, all are—not surprisingly—of the religious variety. In front of the church, visitors enjoy picnics in the **Parque Central,** while the more rambunctious among them light firecrackers to commemorate their arrival. Vendors in the market next door peddle a rainbow assortment of candles and religious paraphernalia: Mother Mary keychains go for Q2-3, straw hats decked with ornaments and Christ figurines for about Q15. Before heading off to less holy ground, take a look at the **cemetery** behind the basilica. The collection of pastel mausoleums are particularly striking against the whitewashed church in the background.

For a sweet panorama of Esquipulas, climb up to the Franciscan convent on the opposite end of town. Follow 3a Av. to its base, turn left, and after two blocks charge 1 km. up the rocky road to your right. The convent, halfway up, hangs a large collection of Byzantine, gold-ground icons, and a little chapel at the top, replete with a requisite Cristo Negro of its own, affords ample photo ops of Esquipulas below.

■ Near Esquipulas: Crossing into Honduras

From the center of town, *colectivo* drivers can take you to **Agua Caliente,** the site of the border crossing (5:30am-6pm, Q5). Another colectivo will whisk you the 2km from Guatemalan to Honduran immigration (Q2). Though money can be exchanged in Esquipulas, better rates can be had at the border. Ask around among the many wad-flashing, calculator-toting money-changers for the best rate; they can even cash

¡¡El Cristo Negro?

El Cristo Negro, a 16th century mahogany carving of Christ on the cross, is all the rage in Esquipulas and has sparked a rash of replicas and imitations throughout the New World. It owes its inspiration to the Chortí natives living in the area, who by the mid-16th century had been converted to **Catholicism** by Spanish missionaries. One memorable day, a group of natives working in the cotton fields had a **mass vision of Christ** on the cross, which they promptly interpreted as a call to worship. Upon the natives' request, a chapel was built and the famed Spaniard Quirio Cataño commissioned to carve an emblem of their vision. El Cristo Negro has forever been Cristo, but not always negro: decades of the devout burning candles and incense and rubbing their hands over the carving turned this **chameleon Christ** from brown to black. Among some indígenos, popular legend has it that the mahogany miracle worker was not man-made, but birthed directly by the black earth of the caves in the mountains just above Esquipulas. Reigning supreme in the newer 18th-century basilica, El Cristo Negro is now untouchable, carefully enclosed in glass-case comfort. On festival days marking the arrival of El Cristo Negro (January 15th) and the commencement of construction on the newer basilica (March 9th), El Cristo's more modest replica, who sports a towel around his waist and calls the old Church home, is **paraded through the streets** before thousands of eager on-lookers.

Mastercard, Visa, and Citicorps traveler's checks. Dollars and AmEx traveler's checks can be changed at **Banco de Occidente** or **Banco Mercantil,** but you'll get fewer lempiras for your money (open Mon.-Fri. 8am-noon, 2-4pm and Sat. 8-11:30am).

The immigration office in Agua Caliente is open daily from 4am to 9pm. Your passport will be marked with a 30-day tourist stamp (L20). If you're driving across the border, go to the *tránsito* office around the corner from immigration. The form you fill out and the fee you pay depend on your plans.

Buses go to **San Pedro Sula** daily at 7:15, 9:30, 11:30am, 1:30 and 3:30pm (5-6hrs., 45L); look for the brilliant blue schoolbuses of the **Sonotran** line. **Congolan** keeps the same schedule, with an 8:30am run as well. These buses crawl as slowly as a slug over the misty hills and stop at **Santa Rosa de Copán** (2-3hr., 22L) and **La Entrada,** (3-3½hr., 30L) where you can catch other buses to **Copán Ruínas.**

■ Quiriguá

While Quiriguá cannot compare in size with other sites on *la Ruta Maya,* it contains some of the grandest and best preserved stelae yet uncovered. Quiriguá's beginnings have been traced back to around 300 AD, though its exact origins are unknown. The community remained subservient to the nearby empire of Copán for several centuries, and was probably valued for its strategic position on the River Motagua.

This relatively peaceful coexistence was shattered about 15 years after **Cauac Sky** ("two-legged sky") ascended to the throne. By 737 AD, he had defeated Copán and captured its ruler, 18 Rabbit. Under Cauac Sky, Quiriguá's power continued to grow, as evidenced by an aggressive building campaign that continued under his immediate successors. Among the monuments erected during that time are the spectacular stelae, many of which bear Cauac Sky's now crumbling visage.

Thatched roofs abate the wear and tear on the seven stelae (designated with letters of the alphabet). Stela E, at a towering 12m, is the tallest in Mesoamerica. Look for it on the 10-centavo Guatemalan coin. The archaeological site consists of the **Plaza Central,** where the stelae are located, the **stadium** for the Maya ball game at the southwest end of the plaza, and the **Acropolis,** the residence quarters of the elite, to the south of the plaza. The surrounding forest provides a beautiful green backdrop, but try to go early in the day to avoid the heat and humidity, and lather up with mosquito repellent (open daily 7:30am-5pm; admission Q25 for *extranjeros*). Sadly, there are no guides to interpret the glyphs that line many of the monuments, though an informative history of the site may be bought back at the entrance's shady kiosk (Q6, both Spanish and English).

To reach Quiriguá, take any bus travelling the Atlantic Highway line and ask to be let off at Quiriguá Ruínas. A regular bus zips visitors 4km through a Del Monte banana plantation to the site (every 30min., 7:30am-5:30pm, Q1); the road is well-traveled, and many passing trucks will also let you hop in the back for Q1 or nothing at all.

Pickings are slim for food and hotels; Quiriguá is best as a stop en route to somewhere else along the Atlantic Highway. The pleasant banana company town of **Quiriguá** is about 1.5km west of the turnoff for the ruins. At the sign for Quiriguá, turn left, and walk about 700m into town. There is one **public telephone** by the Hotel Royal and another back at the turnoff from the main road, where **buses** may be caught to: **Guatemala City** (every 5min., 3am-7pm, 4hr., Q35); **Puerto Barrios** (every 30min., 5am-5pm, 2hr., Q10); and **Chiquimula** (every 30min., 6am-6pm, 2hr., Q10). Across the street from the Hotel Royal is the **post** and **telegram** office (open Mon.-Fri. 7am-6pm). You can make your way from the ruins to the town more directly by walking along the railroad tracks 3 km through the banana fields. The only place to stay is the **Hotel Royal,** itself a fine place to rest your inscription-filled head; the large, clean rooms pass the white-glove test (singles Q22, with private bath Q33; doubles Q33, with private bath Q55). The **restaurant** in front serves ample, full-course meals (Q30), while a **billiard table** next door lets you ruin a rack or two.

RÍO DULCE

A conduit between Lago Izabal and Amatique Bay on the Caribbean, the Río Dulce offers some of the most scenic boat rides in the country, occasional manatee sightings, and the unique Caribbean culture of Livingston at its mouth. It also makes a marvelous diversion, well worth inserting into the formidable capital-to-Tikal trek.

A bridge spans the Río Dulce where it begins at the northeastern end of Lago Izabal. To the south of the bridge sprawls the town **El Relleno;** to the north lies **Fronteras,** where you can spend the night. Four kilometers upstream on the Fronteras bank is the fortress/town of **Castillo San Felipe.** Two bus lines travel to Fronteras: **Fuente del Norte** buses from Guatemala City to Flores and **Litegua** bus to Puerto Barrios. On the Liegua bus, get off at **La Ruidosa,** the highway junction nearest the Río Dulce bridge. From there, take one of the infrequent local buses the remaining 34km. Launches beneath the bridge will shuttle passengers to and from nearby sights (see Livingston, below, for details).

▓ Livingston

Where the Río Dulce tickles the waves of the Atlantic, life is oh-so-sweet—Livingston is Guatemala's riff on the laid-back Caribbean. It boasts the country's largest population of Garifuna, African slaves brought to the New World who mixed with Carib Indians to form a distinct language and culture. Once the largest port in Central America, Livingston now fritters away its hours with all-week partying and the shuttling of tourists to an array of nearby beautiful sites including the cascades of the **Seven Altars** and the effervescent **aguas calientes** (hot springs). In town, steady infusions of coconut bread, fresh fish, and mellifluous reggae and punta rock refine *tranquilo* to unheard-of levels. Don't let the town's laid-back style lull you to sleep, though; hotel thefts and muggings on the beach are disturbingly common. Be sure to ask locals about appropriate precautions.

ORIENTATION AND PRACTICAL INFORMATION

Livingston only has two main streets, and they run perpendicular to each other. Each is parallel to a different beach, however, because the town basks along a promontory.

The largest street (known as the "principal street") leads directly up a hill from the main dock, and the other ("secondary street") branches left at the public school.

Tourist information: The **Exotic Travel Agency** more than fills INGUAT's shoes in town. They have one office on the street to the left of the dock, across from Banco Comercial and another in Bahía Azul restaurant, halfway up Main St. Free maps and extensive advice.

Embassies and Consulates: Get your exit stamp at the immigration office in Livingston, across from the Guatel sign. Open daily 8am-6pm.

Traveler's checks: Exchange at **Banco Comercio,** down the street to the left of the launch; open Mon.-Fri. 9am-4pm. **Bancafé,** up Main St. past Bahía Azul restaurant, has American Express moneygram service as well. Open Mon.-Fri. 9am-5pm, Sat. 9am-1pm. Beware of high transaction fees at the many establishments on the main drag that advertise this service in English.

Telephones: Guatel telephones are on the hill leading up from the dock. Open daily 7am-9pm.

Buses: Nowhere to be found; Livingston is accessible only by water.

Ferries: They leave for **Puerto Barrios** (daily, 5am and 2pm, 1½hr., Q8). Private *lanchas* leave from the same dock as soon as 5 or 6 people gather (30min., Q20 per person). To get to the **Río Dulce bridge** and **Fronteras** (to connect with the road to Flores, Tikal, or Guatemala City), you must take a private *lancha,* which usually stops along the way at the hot springs, the biotopo, and **Castillo San Felipe** (9am, 3½hr., Q50 per person). Add Q25 for the return leg. The same trip may be arranged through Exotic Travel for a similar price (10% discount with ISIC). Watercraft go to **Siete Alteras** waterfalls for about Q150 round-trip for 4 people. You can also hire a lancha to **Punta Gorda, Belize,** (1hr., 6-8 people, Q75 per person). Choose a boat with two big motors: they cost the same as their weaker, one-engined cousins. Tues.-Fri. Exotic sends a boat to **Puerto Omoa, Honduras** (8am, 2hr., US$35); additionally, their directions for the jungle border crossing between Puerto Barrios and **Puerto Cortés, Honduras** are so explicit they even provide a virtual reality video segment upon request.

Pharmacy: Livingston, on the main street about 50m. after the split with the secondary street. Feminine products and a good stock of over-the-counter remedies. Open daily 9am-9pm.

Hospital: The **Centro de Salud,** above Playa la Capitanilla. Head uphill about 200m from the Guatel sign, go right after the Restaurant Jaguar, and look for the large yellow building at the end of the street on the left. Open 24hr.

Police: On the main street leading up from the dock, right after the Guatel sign. Open 24hr.; knock if the door is closed.

Post office: Right behind the Guatel office. Open Mon.-Fri. 9am-5pm.

Postal code: 18002.

ACCOMMODATIONS

A sturdy lock makes for a happy guest; take security seriously when choosing a place to stay. All the better, if you smile and ask politely (and trust him), maybe the manager will store your valuables. Budget lodging in central Livingston has its bright spots, but perhaps even brighter are several new bungalows opening along the beach outside of town. **Salvador Giavotta's** have manicured, palm-dotted lawns, thatched roofs, private baths, and kitchen facilities for around Q25 per person. Inquire at Exotic Travel Agency (see **Tourist Information**) for contacts. Here are some choicer choices within "downtown" Livingston:

African Place, at the end of secondary street. More of a palace than a place, with a drawbridge and untamed jungle licking its doormat, this hotel takes you beyond the Caribbean back to regal Moorish roots. The rooms overwhelm with high ceilings, inlaid tile, and a leaf-crackling tropical breeze wafting in the window while fans buzz below. Rooms with baths also come with newer, thicker, softer mattresses. The owner sells English books. Singles Q25, with bath Q50; doubles Q40, with bath Q70; triples Q50, with bath Q90.

Hotel Caribe, 50m left from the dock, the first hotel you see. Many travelers never go farther. Rooms are basic and clean, and the sound of ocean waves will soothe your soul. Private bathrooms sparkle, though communal facilities are gloomier. The waterless rooms have no fans. Lockout at midnight. Doubles Q24, with private bath Q33.

Hotel Garifuna, down the secondary street away from town, turn right at the sign. Though not in a great part of town, the Garifuna itself is a fortress. Spacious, comfortable rooms come with clean private baths and large, looming ceiling fans. Singles Q35; doubles Q50.

FOOD

Livingston's two main streets are lined with Garifuna eateries that lavish their *plato típico* with things exotic. It's better to avoid the English-signed tourist traps. *Tapado,* a local favorite consisting of seafood and plantains drenched in a spicy coconut broth, can be so complicated to make that it sometimes has to be ordered several hours in advance—but it's worth the wait. For dessert, the Caribbean *pan de coco* and *pie de pina* will leave you wobbling back to your hammock, woozy with ecstasy. For a quick, heaping plateful of savory local food (Q10), join the *lancha* drivers at the cart by the dock (between 10am and 5pm).

African Place (see **Accommodations,** above). A beacon amid the tin roof diners, with a menu that charms. Some tables overlook the jungle. Chicken *a la nigeri-aner* Q20 and crab soup Q15. Open Mon.-Sat. 7am-3pm and 5-9pm.

Restaurant Tiburón Gato, halfway up the principal street. Tasty typical offerings at kinder prices. Begging *gatitos* that frequent the place know best: the very smell of the *tapado* (Q25) can send them into paroxysms of meowing. Generous portions of seafood and spaghetti dishes as well. Open daily 7am-10pm.

Restaurant Margoth, 50m down the secondary street. The Margoth may be a bit more pricey, but its seafood is fresh and bountiful. Shrimp ceviche Q15. Ice made from boiled water makes drinking *licuados* and *refrescos* a cool, usually safe experience. Open daily 9am-3pm and 6:45-10pm.

Cafetín Lili, just after the town's main intersection, walking away from the dock. From her tiny kitchen, Lili serves traditional Garifuna food to locals and a few lucky visitors. Her specialty is eggs with beans and plantains (Q10); many great seafood items as well. Open daily 8am-9pm.

SIGHTS AND ENTERTAINMENT

On the Caribbean side of Livingston cascade the cascades, **Siete Altares.** The pools may be reached by a 90-minute walk down the beach, though this stretch has not been kind to tourists past. Robberies are common, and assaults against tourists are not unknown. Consider hiring a launch or going with a guide. If you choose to make the trek unaided, go in a sizeable group and leave your cameras and bags behind. The trip is well worth it, as the crisp, clear pools dribbling with sunlight are light years better than Livingston's beaches. Climb and clamber up the rocks—the third pool proffers the most refreshing swimming. Flail furiously against the current at the base of the falls or scale the left side for an exhilarating jump in. If you're dead set on making it to the top, a sturdy pair of shoes will facilitate hiking the jungle trails.

A mellow village by day, Livingston pumps up the jam at night, in a clatter of live Garifuna music. Bongo drums, tortoise shells, and maracas pound out frenetic, hollow rhythms while couples do the vertical dirty on the floor after downing sweet rum punch. Bars and beachside discos, however, have a bad reputation for drug and alcohol problems, robberies, and fights; watch your step and your wallet. The Garifuna music scene begins and ends with **Ubafu Life Music,** 50m down the secondary street. Painted to resemble a pack of Life-Savers on its exterior, plastered on the inside with Bob Marley's inspirational visage, the live music here is truly *alive* (open daily until 1am). Have your own drum handmade (starting at Q400) and beat it along with the best; inquire with the endearing family that owns Ubafu. And after converting wholeheartedly to the Rasta mode, there's the chance to make travels that much easier with some **dredlocks.** Get them at one of the two locations on the principal street (look for the sign depicting a person's head; Q50 and up).

■ Near Livingston: Río Dulce

Thirty minutes down the Río Dulce through the looming escarpments lie the **aguas calientes** (hot springs). Boat drivers can take you to them, but travelers with decent nasal skills may be able to sniff out these sulfuric springs on their own. The piping-hot waters form a natural jacuzzi beneath the encroaching jungle.

Chug up the river another half hour to the **Biotopo Chocon Machacas,** which supposedly protects manatees (open daily 7am-6pm). Your 15-minute jaunt along the jungle path in the *biotopo* will only flush out a jaguar or a tapir when the moon is blue, and the shy sea cows do a great job of hiding in the river. Still, the *biotopo* is worthwhile—if not for the giant tree ferns and butterflies on the walk, then for the eclectic collection in the "museum" (donations accepted), from a manatee skeleton to "white tail deer legs donated by a hunter." The aquatic part of the *biotopo* includes several scenic lagoons; ply your boat driver to take you through them. The *biotopo* has a free camping area with bathrooms, kitchen facilities, and well-trained mosquito squadrons. Most boats continue up river to **Castillo San Felipe.** While few of the destinations on the Río Dulce tour are spectacular, the trip is worthwhile for the boat ride itself. The beginning of the river winds through a towering chasm, and long-necked white herons are easy to spot gliding above the water.

Castillo San Felipe itself is a 17th-century Spanish fortress built to stave off plundering pirates. It still roosts in all its cannon-bristling splendor at the mouth of the Río Dulce, at one end of Lake Izabal. Bring a flashlight if you've got one—it'll help you through the maze of tunnels leading through the dungeons. A cartoon history of the oft-plundered castle (in Spanish or English) is included with the Q5 entrance fee. The Castillo grounds also include a pool (Q3), bathrooms, picnic facilities, and a **restaurant** (fried chicken Q23, burgers Q12; open daily 7am-6pm). Hordes of Guatemalan weekenders flock to the castle for family outings (open daily 8am-5pm). A cheaper, fun alternative to swimming in the pool is swimming in the lake at **Playa La Cabaña,** 300m west. A five-minute's walk north from the castle, the **Hotel and Restaurant Don Humberto** lies in the charming little village of San Felipe, a peaceful place to plop down for the night. Humberto's small cement rooms have royal beds and private baths (singles Q36; doubles Q66; triples Q96). Park your RV at the **Tienda Glendy,** next to Don Humberto, or your tent at **Hotel La Cabaña del Viajero,** a seven-minute walk down the road to Fronteras (Q10). San Felipe can also be reached by private *lancha* from the Río Dulce bridge (one way Q40). A 4km road and a fleet of pick-ups also link Fronteras and San Felipe (every 30min., 6am-6pm, Q2): packed-in "standees" have ample time for intimate sharing with their 5 closest neighbors. Some may find that passing vehicles give rides along this road.

■ Puerto Barrios

At the end of the highway from Guatemala to the Caribbean, Puerto Barrios was once the nation's most important port. Recently, however, the city's significance has faded as commerce has moved to Guatemala's Pacific ports. Still, a handful of lingering sailors haunt the bars and stagger through the streets in a vigorous effort to keep the town rowdy. When it's hot, the streets of Puerto Barrios whirl with blinding dust clouds. Because it's not much more pleasant when the weather's bearable, most travelers use Puerto Barrios only as a stepping stone to Honduras or Belize.

Change currency at **Banco Industrial,** 7 Av. and 7 Calle (tel. 9480-241; Mon.-Fri. 8:30am-5pm, Sat. 10am-2pm). **ATM** offers cash back on Visa cards and Plus system ATM cards. A different **Banco Industrial,** at 8 Calle, 6 Av. (tel. 9480-105, fax 9482-351), has **Western Union** as well (open Mon.-Fri. 9am-8pm, Sat. 9am-1pm). **Telephones** and a **fax** are available at **Guatel,** 13 Calle (tel. 948-2198; open daily 7am-11pm, Sun. until 10pm). **Litegua buses,** 6 Av., 9/10 Calles (tel. 948-1172), go to **Guatemala City** (18 per day, 5-6hr., Q35). To get to **Tikal** ask for the proper transfer:

buses leave for the north from La Ruidosa, which is about 45 minutes from Puerto Barrios. Just hop on a (non-direct) bus headed for Guatemala City and ask for the transfer. The **ferry** to **Livingston** docks at 1 Av. and 12 Calle (10:30am and 5pm, 1½-2hr., Q8.50). **Lanchas** also make the trip (when enough people gather, 6:30am-5pm, 30min.). Lanchas go to **Punta Gorda, Belize** (10am daily except Tues. and Fri. at 8am, 50min., Q70). All lanchas leave from directly next to the ferry. For late-night medicine, try **Farmacia Americana,** 9 Calle, 6/7 Avs. (tel. 948-0842; open Mon.-Fri. 7am-9pm, Sat. 7am-8pm, Sun. 7am-noon). In a **medical emergency,** call on **Los Bomberos**—any time, day or night—at 5 Av., 5/6 Calles (tel. 122). The **police** are available around the clock at 6 Av. and 5 Calle (tel. 120 or 385). The **post office,** 6 Av. and 6 Calle (tel. 948-0748), is open Monday through Friday from 9am to 5:30pm. The **postal code** is 18001.

If you decide to spend the night in Puerto Barrios, you'll find the most luxury at **Caribbean Hotel and Restaurant Calypso,** 7 Calle, 6/7 Avs. (tel. 948-0494). Cable TV is an added perk (singles Q70, with A/C Q92; doubles Q105, with A/C Q133; triples Q140, with A/C Q160). The 24-hour restaurant attached to the hotel features mellow indoor-outdoor dining and live *merengue* Tuesdays through Sundays. Specialties include conch with coconut milk (Q46.50) and a seafood shishkebab (Q46.50). The **Hotel La Caribeña** (tel. 948-0860) is decidedly cheaper and closest to the dock at 4 Av., 10/11 Calles. Simple square rooms boast clean bathrooms, a lovely view of the parking lot, and powerful fans. Checkout is at 1pm (singles Q25, with private bath Q40; doubles Q40, with private bath Q55; triples and quads with private baths Q65 and Q80). The attached restaurant has a *menú del día* for Q13. Puerto Barrios has a number of restaurants, as well as an excellent market with enough fruit to satiate even the most seasoned Central American traveler. English-speaking nightlife *sans* the prostitutes lights up at **Bar/Restaurant/Hotel Patty,** a converted brothel at 6 Av. and 6/7 Calles (tel. 948-0394). Small but sparkling clean rooms upstairs for those who can't quite wobble home (singles Q40; doubles Q60). American movies with Spanish subtitles play at the **movie theater** around the corner (Mon. and Tues. 8:30pm; Q5).

■ Near Puerto Barrios: The Honduran Border

Citizens of certain countries may need Honduran visas to cross the border (see **Documents and Formalities,** p. 212). If this applies to you, then visit the **Honduran Consulate** in Puerto Barrios (tel. 948-0050), 22 Calle and 15 Av. (open Mon.-Fri. 8am-noon and 2-5pm). Ask for Gilma Magali Nuñez. Visas cost US$10 and may also be acquired at the **Libreria Norte,** 7 Calle, 6/7 Avs. (tel. 948-0467), next to the Hotel Caribbean. Ask for David Vargas during the hours when the consulate is open.

If you're coming from Belize and want to go to Copán or take a well-traveled route into Honduras, go to **Chiquimula.** Carmencita Buses head that way from 6 Av. and 9 Calle at the corner of the market, every 15 minutes starting at 4am (Q15). From there, connecting buses run to **El Florido** at the Honduran border. If you want a direct ride and are willing to get up godawful early, a **Bargas** bus leaves daily at 4:40am and goes directly to **Esquipulas,** on the Honduran border (5hr., Q20). Keep in mind that the ride from Esquipulas to San Pedro Sula takes about six hours. A **taxi** from Puerto Barrios to the border will set you back about Q300; split the price with some new "friends." If you have aquatic aspirations, some **boats** in Puerto Barrios will run to Puerto Cortés; be forewarned, this form of transport is quite costly.

There is another, more adventurous way to get to Honduras. Allow some time for the journey, be sure to get your exit visa before you leave, and then ask around in Puerto Cortés for more specific directions for this trip because details will change: at the bus terminal, snag a bus headed for **Río Motagua** to the towns of **Entre Ríos, Chinok,** or **El Cinchado** (every hr., 9:45am-6pm, 2hr., Q6). The only legal border crossing is at El Cinchado, and though it's possible to get an exit stamp here, you shouldn't count on it. Launches will take you to the border (Q25). After what usually amounts to a few hours on boat, walk 15 minutes along the river where another launch on the Honduran side takes you on to **Cuyamel** for 10 lempiras. From there, buses run to **Puerto Cortés** (1½hr., 5 lempiras). Otherwise, ask directions for getting to Corinto,

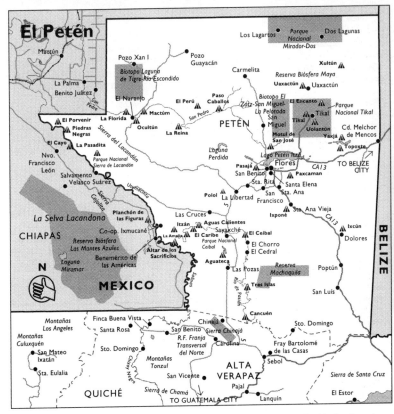

which also has buses to Puerto Cortés. Come adequately prepared with food, water, cash, and adequate supplies should you have to camp. Some advise that this trip should only be attempted during the dry season and only by Spanish speakers.

EL PETÉN

Anyone taking a glance at a map of Guatemala for the first time can't help but be puzzled by the vast, intimidating, and seemingly deserted northern region known as El Petén. Such bewilderment is justified, especially since the southern and western parts of the country are so densely populated in comparison to this northern monster. The looming Petén region has not been particularly welcoming to humans ever since the Maya mysteriously abandoned their power center at Tikal. Early Spanish settlers quickly found the jungle too dense and the soil too poor for serious mining or farming. Despite a brief resurrection of *homo sapien* interest following the discovery of the masticatory potential of *chicle,* only a tough-as-nails group of Guatemalans known as *Peteneros* continues to live there, in both geographical and cultural isolation from the rest of the country. Meanwhile, countless non-human species flourish in the thick jungles, from giant rodents to tiny butterflies and skulking jaguars. In fact, although virtually no travelers would ever make the journey to El Petén were it not for the resplendence of Tikal and other nearby ruins, most visitors who've actually gotten there agree that the pure air, rustic setting, and tantalizing jungles provide more than enough reason to stick around.

■ Poptún

Though considerably less spectacular than the Tikal area, the south Petén is a vital part of Guatemala's archaeological record. Unfortunately, its sites remain largely undeveloped. The real reason to visit Poptún, the largest town in the south Petén, is **Finca Ixobel,** a traveler's Eden close to fascinating caves and gorgeous rainforests.

ORIENTATION AND PRACTICAL INFORMATION

Buses arrive and depart from the gas station on the main street, 4 Calle "A." If you stand in front of the restaurant Fonda Ixobel and face the station, you are looking roughly northward. **Exchange currency** at **BanOro,** one block west (toward decreasing avenues) and one block south. **Guatel** is one block north and 2½ west (open daily 7am-7pm). **Fuente del Norte** (tel. 927-7347) operates first-class buses to **Guatemala City** (6 per day, Q45-70) and to **Flores** (6 per day, Q15; Q20 for *gringos*). A second-class bus goes to **Guatemala City** at 5am (Q40). The **market,** a block west of the gas station, is busy from 6am to 6pm daily. **Farmacia Hermano Pedro** (tel. 927-7218) is east on 4 Calle "A" (open daily from 7am-9pm), as is the **Centro de Salud** (tel. 927-7347), open 24 hours for emergencies. The **police** (tel. 927-7201) have an office next to the municipal building, two blocks west of the gas station (open 24hr.). The **post office** (open Mon.-Fri. 8am-4:30pm) and **telegraph office** (open 24hr.) is in front of Salón de Usos Múltiples, beyond the pharmacy.

ACCOMMODATIONS AND FOOD

Consider spending a night and a day at **Finca Ixobel** (see below), but if you are set on sleeping in town, there are several good places to do so. Try **Posada de los Castellanos,** in front of the market, one block west and half a block south of the bus drop-off point. Spotless rooms have no hot water, but all have private baths and fans (singles Q30; doubles Q36).

The best food around is at **Restaurante La Fonda Ixobel,** in front of the gas station. This place is run by the same people as the finca, so ask here for information about the finca and make your plans to visit it. All food (including bread, granola, yogurt, etc.) is homemade and delicious. *Chimichangas* (big tortillas with meat, beans, cheese, and onions) go for Q13.50, granola with fruit for Q11.50. The banana bread of your dreams is Q3 (open daily 7:30am-11pm).

SIGHTS AND ENTERTAINMENT

Finca Ixobel (tel./fax 927-7363), 3km south of Poptún, has become notorious for the spell it casts upon travelers, who plan to come for a day but end up staying for several days, weeks, or even months. Owner Carol Divine gained international attention recently after going on a hunger strike to motivate the U.S. government to investigate the murder of her husband. For those who want to conquer or commune with nature, a four-day trip plunges you into the spectacular jungle, where you'll ride horses, sleep in a cave, and swing from the trees in hammocks. Do it all for Q550 (including horseback riding). Also available are inner-tubing trips on the Machiquila River (Q60) and horseback riding (Q45 for 2hr.). One daytrip which is almost guaranteed to go out each day—and to please you as much as it has past travelers—is a thrilling cave excursion. Participants swim and do a bit of rock-climbing, all the while balancing candles and flashlights, and then take what is literally a leap of faith into a dark pool dozens of feet below (Q30; bring sturdy shoes and a flashlight, or buy one for Q12). Other activities include self-guided tours to two nearby caves (25min. and 45min. walks), a swim-friendly pond with a scenic background, soccer, volleyball, ping-pong, frisbee, and the friendly company of other travelers. Gluttony and piracy are the order of the day amongst the finca's Noah's Ark of animals—during the day, the macaws wrestle food from under your nose while sneaky spider monkeys go through your luggage, and at night, the energetic kinkajou raids the dessert plates.

Sleep in a hammock or a sleeping bag (Q15; bag or hammock rental add Q3), a dorm bed (Q21), or an adult-size tree house (singles Q40; doubles Q50; triples Q60). You can also camp (Q11) or take a comfortable private room (singles Q36; doubles Q50). The cook is a virtuoso and everything is homemade—from the bread and granola to the unforgettable family-style buffet dinners (Q30), enormous sandwiches (Q12-15), and five-star banana, apple, or carrot bread (Q3.25).

To get there, ask the man who drives the bus out of town to drop you off at the sign for Finca Ixobel, then walk the remaining 1.5km; or take the pick-up cab that hangs out in front of the Fonda Ixobel in Poptún. Walking to the Finca at night is unsafe and *not* advised.

The archaeological sights of **Poxté** (40km), **Ixtupu** (30km), and **Dolores** (28km), all north of Poptún, are partially developed, though still very small. Dolores has the most to offer enthusiasts. The contact person is Sr. Dacio Castellanos, an inspector of national monuments (ask locals for his whereabouts). He will gladly take you for free to and through the ruins of **Ixcun**, 8km north of Dolores, or to **Ixtonton,** 1.5km northeast. Both sprout stelae and small temples and are accessible only by hoof (rent horses for Q10 per day). The tour and entrances are free. If Sr. Castellanos is unavailable, ask for Sr. Ronnie Aldana. If you have a hammock or a sleeping bag, you can also stay at the guardian's house for free. All Flores-bound buses pass through Dolores from Poptún (45min., Q3).

■ Sayaxché

As you take the ferry across the muddy La Pasión river toward slumberous Sayaxché in the southwest Petén and gaze at the decay on the riverfront, you may ask yourself whether there's *anything* to do here. There isn't, except leave, perhaps: the main reason travelers come to this drowsy hamlet is to arrange boat trips to the nearby ruins at Ceibal and several other virtually untapped archaeological sites. Sayaxché is also the last place to stock up if you're heading south toward Cobán and Alta Verapaz.

Everything you'll need is within blocks of the waterfront. An easy point of reference is the eye-catching **Hotel Guayacán,** which sits right by the river. **BanOro** (tel. 928-6143), one block up from the hotel, changes currency and traveler's checks (open Mon.-Fri. 9am-5pm, Sat. 9am-1pm). There are no **public phones;** in a pinch, ask if there are private phones "to rent." **Buses** depart across the river to: **Santa Elena/ Flores** (5:30am, 12:30 and 1pm, 2½hr., Q10); **Raxrujá** (6am, 5hr., Q25) via **Cruce del Pato** (3hr., Q15); and **Playita** (7am, 4hr., Q20) via **Cruce del Pato** and **Rubelsanto.** From Rubelsanto, you can catch the buses or pick-ups to **Cantabal,** which pass **Laguna de Lachuá National Park** (1½hr., Q10).

Sayaxché is the best place to hire **boats** to Maya sites on the backwaters. **Servicio de Lanchas Don Pedro** (tel. 928-6109) has the best prices among organized operators, offering trips to: **Ceibal** (up to 5 people, 4-5hr., 2hr. at the site, Q250); **Aguateca** (up to 5 people, 6hr., Q300); and **Dos Pilas** (up to 5 people, Q400; trek and overnight stay required). **Restaurant La Montaña** (tel. 928-6114) also arranges boat tours to **Ceibal** (1-3 people, Q300; 3-6 people, Q385). Finally, **native commercial boats** often take passengers for Q20-40. Most boats are going downstream, and the tips of their bows have big, curved "horns"; those few going upstream (toward Ceibal) have smaller, straighter tips, and are usually smaller overall. **Farmacia Arteaga** has the best hours in town (open daily 7am-8pm). There is no police force, but the **army** is stationed a few blocks from BanOro toward Ceibal (available 24hr.). The **post office** is by the soccer field, three blocks from the Guayacán away from the shore (open Mon.-Fri. 9am-5pm, Sat. 9am-1pm).

Hospedaje Margot, three blocks up and one block right from the Guayacán, has small, quiet rooms, a communal bath, and a leafy courtyard (Q15 per person, fan rental Q10). **Hospedaje Mayapan,** one block up from Guayacán and to the left, offers rooms with fans included (singles Q15; doubles Q25; triples Q35). The rich, famous, and weary stay at **Hotel Guayacán** (tel./fax 928-6111), where a lofty, breezy terrace affords views of the busy river, and spotless rooms come with firm beds, fans, and private baths (singles Q40; doubles Q60). **Restaurante Yaxkin,** near Hospedaje Maya-pan, serves abundant *típico* meals in a fan-cooled, mosquito-screened environment, has the most up-to-date road map of the Petén you'll find anywhere, and stores patrons' luggage for free (breakfast Q10, veggie plate Q15, full meal with fried chicken or beef Q22; open daily 7am-8pm).

■ Near Sayaxché

CEIBAL

Though certainly no match for Tikal's grandeur, the ruins at Ceibal provide their own mystique, especially if you arrive by boat. The river journey from Sayaxché takes you by shrubs, pastures, and *indígena* hamlets for an hour or two, until you reach the jungly shore of Ceibal National Park. The footpath from the landing leads you through dark rain forest, as you hike up an escarpment toward the main camp (40min.). Pay the admission fee (Q25) and get your bearings here. **Group A** contains a restored pyramid and a profusion of stelae. Don't miss **stelae 9 and 10,** whose depictions of mustached rulers lead archaeologists to believe that Ceibal may have been ruled by the Toltecs of Mexico. Much farther afield lies restored **structure 79,** which has a table-like altar depicting a jaguar. But magnificent stelae are scattered everywhere; look carefully, as many are nearly obscured by vines and vegetation. **Camping** is free, and the early morning is a great time to see the site come alive with tropical birds and howler monkeys. Bring mosquito repellent, water, and some extra food for the park rangers.

For information on reaching Ceibal by boat, see Sayaxché, p. 115. By land, take any bus or pick-up from Sayaxché to **El Paraíso** (30min., Q4), and then walk 8km through pastures and rain forest to the site.

THE TRANSVERSAL DEL NORTE REGION

Head this way only if you're ready for adventure, discomfort, improvisation, and *very* flexible time frames. The Transversal del Norte region, comprised of the southern-most Petén and northernmost Alta Verapaz, is full of karst landscapes, mammoth caves, and humid rain forests. Oil was discovered here 20 years ago, and the region's first road (the Transversal del Norte) and thousands of *kekchí* from the war-torn high-lands soon followed. Today, it remains a sparsely populated agricultural frontier criss-crossed by a baffling web of roads built by the oil industry. Its magnificent natural sites, the **Candelaria Caves** and **Parque Nacional Laguna de Lachuá,** remain unknown to tourists, but are worth the hassles involved in reaching them.

Anyone traveling in this region eventually passes through a ring of towns domi-nated by **Cobán** to the southwest. Proceeding east and north from Cobán, you'll pass Pájul (the junction to Lanquín), Sebol, and **Raxrujá**—also spelled Raxujá or Raxuhá—the smaller, northern ringleader. Raxrujá is the region's transportation hub. Daily buses arrive there from Flores via Sayaxché and Cruce del Pato and from San Pedro Carchá/Cobán (leaves Carchá at 6am, arrives in Raxujá at 1pm; Q25). **Bus service** to the smaller towns is becoming more common in the region, but the most prevalent form of public transportation is still the pick-up truck. Be very careful *not to hitch rides with empty cargo trucks* (however tempting it may be), as the drivers carry cash to buy cargo and are therefore frequent targets of assaults.

The mighty **Candelaria Caves** are part of an underground system said to be over 40km long. Its tunnels and chambers once were inhabited by an ancient Maya tribe which settled next to the underground section of the Candelaria River. Cathedral-sized vaults open up to the rain forest above, sunlight flooding in to illuminate the peculiar rock formations. French archaeologist Daniel Dreux explored the site in the 70s. Now, the old archaeological camp near the town of **Mucbilhá** is **Candelaria,** a deluxe hotel managed by locals (lodging US$40 per night, dinner, breakfast, and tour included) who also act as guides to the cave (tour costs Q25 for a guide and Q15 per person, 2hr.; camp closed Sat. 3pm-Mon. 7am). To get there, take the daily 5am pick-up from Raxrujá to Chisec and ask to be let off at Mucbilhá (1hr., Q6). Pass the corral on your left and the red house on the hill on your right. Follow the small trail off the road to the left; enter the doors and take the stone path to this well-hidden hotel. The pick-up heads back from Chisec at 10am, passing Mucbilhá at around noon.

Parque Nacional Laguna de Lachuá is the undiscovered gem of the Guatemalan park system, all ready for visitors that haven't shown up yet. Eons ago, a giant meteor landed on this remote stretch of rain forest, creating a clear, deep, limestone-ringed lagoon. A single river feeds the lagoon, and two drain it. The 14 square km park borders the road to Cantabal on the north and includes headwaters in the mountains to the south. Approaching by road, watch in disbelief as slashed-and-burned, ecologically sabotaged land gives way to pristine jungle, and enormous billboards welcome you enthusiastically to the park. From the billboards, it is a 2.4km walk on a wide footpath to the lagoon shore and another 2km to base camp. Bathe and commune with abundant fish, admire the coral-like rock formations, and ask how on earth this slice of the Caribbean became trapped in the dark wilderness. Admission is Q1, aluminum **canoes** rent for Q5 per hour, and **camping** or hanging a hammock under a thatched roof is Q10 per person. There are rustic cooking facilities, but bring your own food and water (or, if you have no bottled water, purify water from the camp's well). To get there, a somewhat unreliable daily **bus** (that starts, believe it or not, in Guatemala City) hits Raxujá at 11:30am, passing through Cruce del Pato (1:30pm) and west through Cruce Rubelsanto (3pm) before reaching the park entrance at 4:30pm, from which it continues on to Cantabal. The return bus leaves Cantabal at 4am and passes the park entrance at 6am. Alternately, **pick-ups** from Cantabal pass Lachuá until 8am as they head eastward to Cruce de Rubelsanto, Chisec, and Cobán. Pick-ups heading north from Cobán pass Lachuá at irregular times starting at about 9am. To reach the park from Sayaxché, take the daily bus to Playita, get off at Cruce de Rubelsanto, and catch a pick-up there.

■ Flores and Santa Elena

Amid the dense wilderness, sprawling cattle ranches, and winding dirt roads of the Petén lie Santa Elena and the island city of Flores, isolated splotches of civilization in perpetual combat with nature. On one side, the jungle and its nasty beasts encroach on Santa Elena's sprawl of shacks, banks, and *comedores;* across the causeway the water of **Lago Itzá** threatens to engulf the fringes of Flores even as authorities work to siphon it off. The history of the towns is also marked by struggle: tiny Flores, along with nearby Tayasal (now in ruins), was the last city of independent Maya. Finally, the governor of Yucatán, Martín de Urzúa, captured the city in 1697 and—in his own act of defiance—razed the temple and built a church on top. Despite the rigors of survival (and contemporary worries that new roads through the Petén will re-route travelers away from Flores completely), the towns still stand and vie to remain pleasant refueling stops for travelers who just want to survive the night in the Petén and get to Tikal the next day.

ORIENTATION AND PRACTICAL INFORMATION

Flores's main street, **Avenida Central America,** is round, like the island. Buses stop in Santa Elena's dusty market, just a few hundred meters across the causeway. Stock up for long hauls here, then head across the lake to Flores.

Tourist Office: INGUAT has offices in Santa Elena's airport and in Flores on the Parque Central (atop the hill, by the church and the basketball court). Get a map at **CINCAP**—the Center of Information, Culture and Handicrafts of Petén—across the square. Information is also available at **Información Turística El Tucán** (tel. 926-1380), on Av. Central America, near the intersection with Calle 30 de Junio. Open Mon.-Fri. 8am-4pm.

Currency Exchange: Banco de Guatemala is at the end of Calle 30 de Junio in Flores (tel. 926-1363). Open Mon.-Thurs. 8:30am-2pm, Fri. 8:30am-2:30pm.

Bandesa, 0 Av. and 2 Calle, is open Mon.-Fri. 8am-4pm. If you need cash after-hours, go beyond the causeway, walk left on Av. Central America and bear right at the end of the street; **Hotel Petén** (tel. 926-0692), on the left, changes traveler's checks until 9pm or later.

Airport: Planes leave Santa Elena's airport for: **Guatemala City** (7 per day, US$45-94); **Belize City** (Mon.-Fri. 9am and 3pm, US$63); and **Cancún, Mexico** (1 per day except Thurs., US$140). Make reservations at any travel agency. For a deal, contact **Agencia de Viajes Arco Iris** (tel. 926-7086), on Av. Central America in Flores. They'll drive you to the airport for half the price of other services, or for free if you buy the tickets from them. Open Mon.-Sat. 8am-noon and 2-6pm, Sun. 8am-noon.

Buses: All buses leave from Santa Elena's market. Travelers intending to head to Belize from Santa Elena or Flores should read the applicable **warning** (p. 158). Second-class **Fuentes del Norte** buses (tel. 926-0517) leave Santa Elena from a white building on the right, 3 blocks through the market—buy tickets in advance to **Guatemala City** (daily 9:30am, 14hr., Q50) via **Río Dulce** (Q35). **First-class buses** to Guatemala City also leave daily (8, 11:30am, 3:30, 5, 7, and 8pm, 12hr., Q70) via **Poptún** (Q10), **Río Dulce** (Q40), and **Quiriguá** (Q45). **Tikal Express** (tel. 250-0517), next door to Fuentes del Norte, also runs second-class buses to the capital (3, 4, 6, and 8pm, Q50). **Pinita** buses (tel. 926-0562) leave daily to: **Melchor de Mencos** and the **Belizean border** (5, 8, and 10am, 3hr., Q15); **Poptún** (5, 10am, 1, and 4pm, 3hr., Q15); **Sayaxché** (6am and 1pm, 2hr., Q10); **El Naranjo** near the **Mexican border** (4, 5, 8, 11am, and 1pm, 5hr., Q25); and **Tikal** (6am and 1pm, 2hr., Q10; the 1pm bus goes on to **Uaxactún** for an extra Q5). **Del Rocío** buses serve **El Naranjo** (4:45, 8, 10:30am, and 1:30pm, Q25) via **Sayaxché** (Q7). Numerous **express vans** also go to **Tikal** (1hr., one-way Q20, round-trip Q30). Sign up for a van at any of the travel agencies and at most hotels in Flores and Santa Elena. Vans from **Travel Agency San Juan** (tel. 926-0042), in Hotel San Juan, off the causeway in Santa Elena, are the best. Their tickets have the most possible departures and are valid for 15 days (daily 4, 6, 8, and 10am, returning at 2, 4, 5, and 8pm).

Taxis: (tel. 926-0034), near the market in Santa Elena. From Flores to Santa Elena should cost Q10 or less, to the airport Q15.

Laundromat: Lavandería Petenchel, on Av. Central America in Flores, lovingly washes and dries with modern appliances for Q20 per load. Open daily 8am-8pm.

Pharmacy: Next to Las Puertas. Open daily 8:30am-1pm and 2-8:30pm.

Post Office: In the center of Flores on Pasaje Progreso, just east of the park. Open Mon.-Fri. 9am-noon and 2-4pm.

Internet: Tikal Net, near the monolithic Hotel Itzá No. 2, down a few doors from Refresquería La Jícara. Send a message of any length from their address for Q12. Print received messages for Q7. Use telnet or surf for Q1 per min.

Telephones: Guatel (tel. 926-1299), is on the extension of the causeway into Santa Elena. Don't confuse it with its old location across the street. No booths, so calls can be hectic. Open daily 7am-10pm.

ACCOMMODATIONS

Both cities offer an array of budget accommodations. Flores is the more expensive of the two, but it's also cleaner and nicer. In Flores, **El Tucán** (tel. 926-0536), at the far end of Av. Central America on the water, has a gorgeous lake view; sunlight bounces off the spacious rooms and bathrooms have hot water (doubles Q42; triples Q60—no singles, but a lone ranger may get the double for Q30). **Doña Goya,** on the other side of the island, has the region's cleanest common baths. Rooms are spotless and airy (singles Q30, with bath Q40; doubles Q40, with bath Q50). It's a bird, it's a plane, it's a hotel! **Hotel Itzá,** on Calle Principal along the lake shore, won't earn rave reviews for its decor, but the rooms do have private baths and fans. Pricing is a very personal process. Rooms with 2 beds tend to be Q30 for 1 person or 2; a sob story may lower the price to Q15 for a single or even Q20 for a double. Rooms for 3 present countless possible arrangements (approximately Q60).

In Santa Elena, the best-run place is **Hotel Alonzo,** near Guatel. Downstairs bathrooms have hot water, and fans spin at hair-mussing velocities. The Alonzo changes traveler's checks and stays open 24 hours (singles Q20, with bath Q30; doubles Q30, with bath Q60). The cheap *comedor* in front is open from 7am to 9:30pm. The **Hotel San Juan,** on 2a Calle, one block from the causeway, offers spiffy rooms with private baths (singles Q50; doubles Q60; triples Q70), as well as basic rooms sharing a communal bath (singles Q20; doubles Q30).

FOOD

In Flores, **Las Puertas,** around the bend from Picasso and off the main drag, has cornered the health food market: Q20 gets you carrot juice, yogurt *licuados,* and a mountain of fresh fruit and natural yogurt over pancakes. Don't worry; even the ice is pure. The classical and jazz music is free (open 8am-midnight). For the Italian-starved, **Pizzería Picasso,** on Av. Central America, serves *tortellini* (Q22), *antipasti* (Q14), and of course, cubist pizza (Q28; open daily 9:30am-10pm). For a bit more culinary personality, **La Mesa de los Mayas** (tel. 926-1240) serves atypical *típico* fare: grilled deer (Q40), armadillo (Q40), wild turkey (the beast, not the beverage, Q40), and tongue (Q25; open daily 7am-10pm). **Refresquería La Jícara,** near Hotel Itzá No. 2, dishes out the cheapest grub on the island. (Full breakfasts Q10, spaghetti Q10, steak with fries and a salad Q22; open 7am-2pm and 6-9pm, Sun. 7am-2pm.)

In Santa Elena, cheap (sometimes unsanitary) *comedores* are the rule, offering standard eggs and beans for Q10, chicken or meat for Q15.

SIGHTS AND ENTERTAINMENT

Tikal overshadows the diversions of Flores and Santa Elena; still, the Lago Itzá's attractions manage to keep travelers busy. Near the park in Flores, an **art museum** displays a good selection of local work. On the lakeshore opposite Flores is the **Petencito,** a small zoo with dishearteningly small cages. Nearby, homemade **waterslides** whip the foolhardy around rickety corners at Mach speeds. Launches leave any time if you just want to **cruise** around the lake (up to 5 people, 1½hr., Q60); check at the Santa Elena side of the causeway. Swimming in the lake is not recommended because of pollution. Instead, swim in the little lakeside pool at the **Yum Kax** hotel (Q10 per non-guest or Q5 for Hotel Itzá patron) or visit the **Actun Can Cave,** 2km south of Santa Elena. The cave has 300m of well-illuminated paths with signs pointing to imaginative natural shapes, as well as several kilometers of unilluminated paths, which have outlets as far north as Santa Elena (bring your own flashlight). To get to the cave, follow the street that is a continuation of the causeway; bear left at the sign for the caves and then turn right at the little red arrow marked "Actun Can" (open daily 8am-5pm; admission Q7). The **nocturnal** crowd's only refuge is **Las Puertas** (see **Food,** above), which cranks jazz, Latin, and Brazilian tunes most nights.

▓ Tikal

Tikal is probably the most fascinating archaeological site in the Americas. Situated in the north Petén, 670km north of Guatemala City, the ruins encompass over 3000 Maya stone constructions, including six large pyramids (two of which are entirely excavated). While other ruins, such as those at Copán, Honduras, are in pristine condition and often more useful to scholars, most travelers agree that viewing Tikal's immense pyramids jutting out of the merciless jungle is an experience that goes right to the gut. As a bonus, the surrounding **Parque Nacional Tikal** (222 sq. mi.) is nearly as intriguing as the temples. Falling fruit is a tell-tale sign of spider monkeys overhead; remote paths hide parrots, peacocks, iguanas, and buzzcocks; and lucky early risers may spot a sacred jaguar slinking through the undergrowth.

GETTING THERE

Not all roads lead to Tikal; in fact, it's pretty hard to get there. Most bus connections are made through **Flores,** one hour outside Tikal. Overland routes connect Tikal with **Tenosique, Mexico, Guatemala City,** and **Belize City.** The Belize route is popular, but is considered unsafe (see Sights, p. 158). Buses to **Flores** leave the border between 3am and 2pm (3hr.,Q10). Get off at the intersection two-thirds of the way to Flores at **El Cruce** (Ixlu crossing) and catch either of the **Pinita** buses that run to Tikal (6am and 1pm, 2½hr., Q10). You can also wave down the Tikal-bound microbuses listed below. Few cars go to Tikal, so hitching is virtually impossible and not recommended. Consult either the U.S. State Department or the U.S. Consulate in Guatemala City about the safety of overland routes to Tikal (see Safety, p. 51). Aside from the Pinita buses, **microbuses** leave Flores directly for Tikal daily at 4, 6, 8, and 10am, and noon during high season. You can catch these from any hotel (one way Q20, round-trip Q30). You get the most flexibility with San Juan Travel minibuses (p. 117).

Four **airlines** shuttle daily between Guatemala City and Santa Elena, which is just across the lake from Flores and is served by the same buses and microbuses. Buy your ticket in Flores or Santa Elena and book at least a day in advance (p. 117). **Buses** from Guatemala City are cheaper than planes, but by land, you'll suffer through 280km of jarring dirt roads between Morales and Santa Elena. (see On the Highway to Hell, p. 120). Should you decide to brave the bus, take the first-class Pullman, which has shock absorbers and doesn't make rest stops to relieve the chickens (12hr., Q70). The regular bus takes at least 15 hours on a good day (Q50). The best buses to take are the 6:30 and 8pm **Fuentes del Norte** buses, which leave the capital from 17 Calle 8-46, Zona 1 (tel. 238-3894). You'll arrive in Santa Elena the next morning in time for the 8 or 10am vans to Tikal.

To keep up with the Indiana Joneses, take the wildest and most cinematic alternative: a boat and bus odyssey from Tenosique, Mexico. This involves a four-hour cruise up the Río San Pedro to **El Naranjo, Guatemala** (Q75). From El Naranjo, you'll bounce five hours east over dirt roads to Santa Elena (Q25).

On the Highway to Hell

Although many tourists travel to Tikal from Guatemala City quickly and painlessly by airplane, others opt for the 15-hour bus ride, a journey that has gained legendary status among travelers around the world. To help you decide, here's an hour-by-hour account of what you're getting into when you go with the bus:

Hour 1: Giddy with optimism, you take your seat, self-assuredly chuckling about the chickens in the overhead compartment and the "Jesus is my Co-Pilot" stickers plastering the driver's window.

Hour 3: The driver's miraculous whipping by other vehicles on blind, uphill roads is convincing enough that yes, Jesus really must be on his side.

Hour 4: A bitter, fowl stench wafts from above, as chickens cease to seem cute.

Hour 5: At Río Dulce, more people get on, and now you're packed in three to a seat. Miserable souls in the aisle don't stand so much as they lean on each other. For lack of room, two *gringos* are placed on the roof.

Hour 7: Bug-eyed and nauseous, you quickly learn to anticipate the biggest bumps by that extra split-second in which the bus hovers in mid-air before crashing down; that tickling in your tailbone bursts into raw pain.

Hour 9: The road narrows and the universe shakes. Your bus squeezes past another as grating metal shrieks and glass cracks. Acrobatically shifting your tailbone onto its least painful spot, you wonder if the guys on top have fallen off yet.

Hour 12: Just past Poptún, the bus slows and everyone peers out the window to gawk down the 150m cliff at The Bus That Didn't Make It, overturned and half-concealed in the foliage. You gulp and murmur a quick prayer.

Hour 15: Your butt feels like it was brutally spanked by the Hand of God for all the sins you ever thought of committing, but the bus has pulled into Santa Elena—home free. A vendor at the terminal sells "I took the bus to Tikal and survived" t-shirts, and the frazzled duo from the top of the bus wave *quetzales* at him like born-again lunatics. As the sound of a jet overhead reminds you that the last 15 hours were a self-induced hardship, granting you passage into the budget travel elite, you waddle toward that vendor, too.

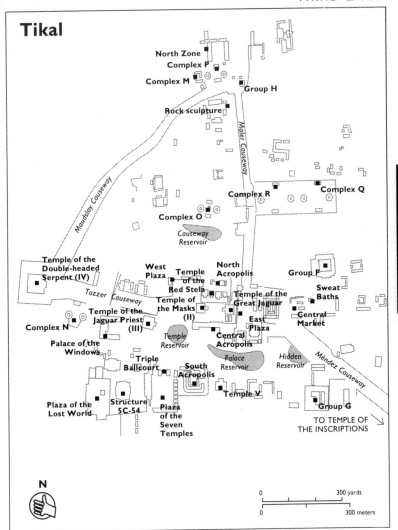

Tikal

North Zone
Complex P
Complex M
Group H
Rock sculpture
Maler Causeway
Maudslay Causeway
Complex R
Complex Q
Complex O
Causeway Reservoir
Temple of the Double-headed Serpent (IV)
West Plaza
Temple of the Red Stela
North Acropolis
Group F
Tozzer Causeway
Temple of the Masks (II)
Temple of the Great Jaguar
Sweat Baths
Temple of the Jaguar Priest (III)
East Plaza
Central Market
Complex N
Temple Reservoir
Central Acropolis
Palace of the Windows
Triple Ballcourt
South Acropolis
Palace Reservoir
Hidden Reservoir
Méndez Causeway
Plaza of the Lost World
Structure 5C-54
Plaza of the Seven Temples
Temple V
Group G

TO TEMPLE OF
THE INSCRIPTIONS

N

| 0 | | | 300 yards |
| 0 | | | 300 meters |

GUATEMALA

In the park, but 17km from the site itself, is a checkpoint where passengers disembark and are attacked by blood-sucking bureaucrats (admission Q50, must be renewed each day). Tickets can also be bought at the site; the checkpoint is there probably so that visitors pay before they can see how easy it is to sneak in. The park is open from 5am to 5pm. Those wishing to enter early or linger after hours (particularly to see the sunset from Mundo Perdido) are now required to hire a "guide," or armed guard, for about US$20.

PRACTICAL INFORMATION

As befits a small jungle outpost, Tikal offers few services. There is a small **visitors center,** in the large building next to **Café Restaurant del Parque,** that has a scale model of the site and sells maps (Q5) and guidebooks (Q65). **Change money** before you get there; the exchange rate in hotels here is 10% worse than in Flores. There are **public** bathrooms in the visitors center and throughout the archaeological site. For **medical emergencies,** go to Flores; the clinic at Tikal has minimal resources (open Mon.-Fri. 7am-noon and 2-5pm).

ACCOMMODATIONS AND FOOD

Tikal has one good campground and three expensive hotels. Single rooms are most expensive, and it is wise to travel to Tikal in groups of two or three to cut costs. The camping complex, set in a vast, grassy field, consists of large, concrete platforms with thatched roofs. The mosquito squads and occasional scorpions and tarantulas signifi-cantly detract from one's enjoyment of the great outdoors. Communal baths have showers; lockers are not available. Camping costs Q30 per person (hammock Q10, mosquito net Q5, 2-person tent Q20). Sleeping in the ruins is illegal and this rule is strictly enforced by patrolling guards. Another way to cut costs is to return to nearby **El Remate** each night (see **Near Tikal,** below).

Hotel Jaguar Inn (tel. 926-0002) serves three meals a day and offers expensive, well-furnished bungalows with private bathrooms. Electricity only runs from 6 to 9pm. (Singles US$47; doubles US$81; triples US$115; without meals US$24; US$30; and US$48 respectively.) A few hammocks with *mosquiteros* are rented for Q40 each. **The Jungle Lodge** (tel. 777-0570; fax 476-0294 or 476-8775) has basic bunga-lows, a pool, and a restaurant in the main lodge (electricity runs 5-7am, 9am-3pm and 6-11pm; singles US$20, with bath US$48; doubles US$25, with bath US$60). If bunga-lows drive you bonkers and splurging sounds splendid, **Tikal Inn** has pretty little rooms set around a palatial garden and pool (volts flow from 6pm to 9am). The meal plan is optional (singles US$25, 35 or 45; doubles US$55; triples US$82).

The four fly-infested *comedores* facing the visitors center have identical menus: eggs and beans (Q12), chicken and beans (Q15), and beef and beans (Q15). All are open daily 5am-9pm. **Comedor Tikal** offers the best selection for budget travelers (sandwiches Q8-20, vegetarian dishes Q15, spaghetti Q12; open daily 6:30am-8pm). **Restaurant Jaguar Inn** serves a full breakfast (pancake, eggs, homemade bread, and coffee) for Q15. Complete lunches and dinners go for Q36 (open daily 6am-9pm).

SIGHTS

How cool is this place? George Lucas considered it worthy to be a setting for *Star Wars,* in which the ruins are part of the rebel base near the planet Javin. The ancient Maya settled Tikal at least as early as 600 BC, and seashells from the Pacific Coast and jade from the highlands testify to Tikal's extensive role in the Mesoamerican trade network. Architectural details and artifacts from several tombs suggest that residents of Tikal even communicated with distant **Teotihuacán,** near modern Mexico City. Most of the temples and other constructions at Tikal date from the late classic period (AD 550-900), when Tikal may have had anywhere from 20,000 to 70,000 inhabit-ants. It thrived longer than any other ancient metropolis, but collapsed mysteriously at the end of the classic era. Theories as to the details of its downfall include war with the Aztecs, a plague, and a catastrophic rebellion.

While postclassic descendants of the original population continued to live and wor-ship at Tikal, they did little of lasting significance other than pillage the tombs of the classical period. By AD 1000, the jungle had engulfed the city. The modern world did not rediscover Tikal until a commercial expedition in search of chewing-gum stum-bled across the site in 1848. Guatemalans **Modesto Mendez** and **Ambrosio Tut** orga-nized an official excavation 58 years later.

Begin your tour at the **Great Plaza,** Tikal's geographic and ceremonial heart, 2km west of the entrance. The terraced **North Acropolis** lies ahead, facing north into the plaza. To its right and left are **Temples I** and **II;** the **Central Acropolis** is behind it.

Temple I, a.k.a. the Temple of the Great Jaguar, towers 45m (145ft.) above the Grand Plaza. Built around AD 700, this structure, the modern-day symbol of Tikal, has nine sharply ascending terraces that support a three-chambered temple on top. The first seven steps have been restored to their original state, but due to ongoing restoration work, this temple and Temple V are still off-limits to visitors. Its westward orientation (toward the setting sun) and the fact that the other temples face it emphasize the temple's importance.

Across the plaza, **Temple II,** or the Temple of the Masks, is shorter and easier to scale. Excavations at the **North Acropolis,** a partially restored complex of temples, revealed at least 10 levels of construction. Archeologists peeled away the outer layers of the front-center building, an Early Classic temple which hoists two large gruesome faces over the plaza. Grab your torch and squeeze into the passageway by the lower face—there you'll find the best mug of all, of which nary a stone has been restored.

Across from the north acropolis is the **Central Acropolis.** In Court 2, ancient graffiti at **Maler's Place** illustrates the Maya practice of squeezing the head of a ruling-class infant between two boards to create the high-status flattened skull. Join archeologists in trying to guess the use of these buildings. East of this subcomplex is Court G, another cluster of palace-like buildings. **Temple III,** to the west, is called Temple of the Jaguar Priest for the scene depicted on its well-preserved hardwood lintels. After a stony climb up, emulate your favorite action-thriller hero by edging around the narrow catwalk for a view of **Temple IV,** one kilometer west of the Great Plaza on Tozzer Causeway. Temple IV, or the Temple of the Two-Headed Serpent, dates from AD 741 and is the tallest pre-Columbian construction in the Americas. Seventy meters (212ft.) from base to roof, the pyramid is almost totally cloaked by the jungle.

Temple V faces east, 500m south of the Great Plaza. The 57m (190ft.) temple is temporarily closed to the public due to restorations. Ornate glyphs cover the looming roof comb of the **Temple of the Inscriptions,** 2km southeast of the Great Plaza. Most visible at dawn, the monumental symbols record the Maya date 9.16.15.0.0 (AD 766). Southwest of the Great Plaza is **Mundo Perdido** (Lost World). Rumor has it that the name derives from a depiction of two men making love, found in one of the tunnels in the complex. Teotihuacán's architectural influence shines through in hulking structures such as the **Temple of the Warriors.**

The best stelae (event monuments) can be found in **Complex Q** (en route to the Gran Plaza via Maler Causeway), and in **Complex N,** on the way to temple IV, although the original stela and altar of this complex are in the visitors center. Another sideshow attraction is the **ballcourt** between Temple I and the Central Acropolis. (See Heads Up: Pok-ta-pok, Anyone? p. 43).

The small **Museum of Tikal,** at the entrance to the site, displays a collection of ceramics, stelae, jade, and carved and painted bones. Richly detailed Stela 31 depicts Stormy Sky, a 5th-century governor of Tikal. Peer down at the reconstruction of Tomb 116, which contains a full skeleton accompanied by shells and ceramics, as well as 16 lbs. of jade (admission Q10). The **Litico Museum of Stelae** at the visitors center is free; there you'll see stelae inscribed with legible hieroglyphics (both museums open Mon.-Fri. 9am-5pm, Sat.-Sun. 9am-4pm).

Climb Temple IV at **sunrise** for a breath-taking view of the jungle coming alive and the soaring pyramids breaking the forest canopy. Keel-billed toucans, parrots, and howler monkeys frolic atop the trees right under your perch. Leave from the campground or the hotels by 5:30am to arrive on time. The Mundo Perdido pyramid is great for viewing the **sunset,** although hiring a heavy is now required. Bring mosquito repellent and a flashlight.

To view Tikal intelligently, invest in a handbook to the ruins or hire a guide; a quick study of the scale model by the museum provides a good introduction, but it doesn't suffice. Tikal's major attractions are dispersed over a 4 sq. km area, and few signs point the way. Tour guides are available at both the hotels and the entrance to the site. Tours that include the ruins, flora, and fauna last three hours (Q150-250).

NEAR TIKAL: UAXACTUN AND EL REMATE

Twelve kilometers north of Tikal on a dirt road, Uaxactún is an old-time Petén town. **Group E** is the more interesting of Uaxactún's two sets of ruins. It contains a pyramid decorated on all sides with enormous carved faces. If you climb to the top of the pyramid, look west. You'll see three smaller pyramids, placed exactly at the point where

GUATEMALA

the sun sets during the winter solstice, both equinoxes, and the summer solstice, respectively. Admission to the sites is free, and a tour takes about two hours (you can hire a local kid to guide you for about Q5).

El Remate sits on Lake Petén Itzá, but it's close enough to Tikal to serve as a base of budget archaeological expeditions. Local buses from Flores to Tikal pass through the town, which can be reached from the east by switching buses at "El Cruce" in Ixlú. The **Biotopo Cerro Cahuí** and local wood carvings distract visitors. There are a number of hostels; single rooms can be found for as little as Q30.

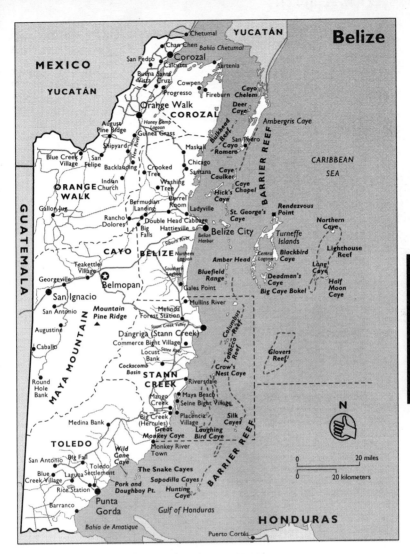

BELIZE

Peopled with a wildly heterogeneous population (pop. a meager 30,000) and graced with a nearly untouched natural beauty, the tiny nation of Belize fills a unique role in Central America. More Caribbean than Latin, this peaceful eye of the storm of Central American politics is anomalous in nearly every way. Apart from being more expensive than its neighbors, the country is otherwise extremely accessible to tourists. English is the official language, transportation is a relative piece of cake, and few other places in the world offer such mind-boggling diversity packed into such a small space (8867 sq. mi., or about the size of Massachusetts). Ten years ago, many travelers viewed Belize as a stop-over between Mexico and Guatemala;

the boom in ecotourism since then has increased the number of yearly visitors ten-fold, and the tourist industry has become the nation's leading money-maker. Fortunately, development of the tourist industry has been kept far below the leviathan proportions of places like Cancún in Mexico, but even so, the country's infrastructure is being pushed to its limits by the recent influx. Its most popular destinations are still the national parks, nearly 20 of which have been set aside for preservation.

There's an amazing array of things to do in Belize; in one day, a hyperactive traveler could snorkel at the largest barrier reef in the hemisphere, scale Maya temples, and slide down waterfalls in a pine forest, along the way stopping in at a jaguar preserve or a baboon sanctuary. The country also offers plenty of opportunity to do nothing, as well. Many travelers don't want to budge an inch once they find themselves on one of Belize's countless idyllic beaches along the crystalline Caribbean, chomping inexpensive lobster and sipping smooth Belikin beers. It's hard not to fall in with this crowd, especially after meeting a few of the amiable, ultra-mellow Creoles along the coast. Regardless of their motivation, thousands more tourists arrive each year to explore the country's natural wonders and affirm the tourist bureau's catchy slogan, "You've got to see it to Belize it."

ESSENTIALS

■ When to Go

CLIMATE

A brisk prevailing wind from the Caribbean cools this sub-tropical climate. The humid summer rarely sizzles at more than 95°F; winter cools rarely dip below 60°F. The rainy season extends from June to August.

FESTIVALS AND HOLIDAYS

Public holidays and local festivals are derived from Catholic, indigenous, and British sources; as a result, a party can pop up at any given moment. Some public holidays (when banks, post offices, and government offices shut down) include: **January 1** (New Year's Day); **February 13-15** (San Pedro Carnival); **March 9** (Baron Bliss Day); **March or April** (Holy Week); **May 1** (Labor Day); **May 24** (Commonwealth Day); **September 10** (St. George's Caye Day); **September 21** (National Independence Day); **October 12** (Pan-American Day); **November 19** (Garifuna Settlement Day); **December 25** (Christmas Day); and **December 26** (Boxing Day).

■ Useful Information

For publications and travel organizations of general interest, see **Essentials,** p. 1. When dialing direct from the U.S. or Canada, remember to drop the first zero of the Belizean phone number; dial 011-501 plus the last six digits.

Belize Tourist Board, 421 7th Ave., Suite 1110, New York, NY 10001 (tel. (800) 624-0686 or (212) 563-6011; fax 563-6033). Exhaustive information sheet available. In **Belize,** 83 N. Front St., P.O. Box 325, Belize City (tel. 027-72-13; fax 027-74-90). Detailed maps of Belize (BZ$15), helpful and friendly staff, and loads of loose info.

Belize Audobon Society, 12 Fort St., Belize City (tel. 023-50-04; email base@btl.net; http://www.bas.org). Information about all national parks and wildlife, as well as where to find the biggest bounty of beauteous birds in Belize. Sells a guide to Belize's wildlife (BZ$8). Open Mon.-Fri. 8:30am-5pm.

Belize Center for Environmental Studies, Box 666, 55 Eve St., Belize City (tel. 023-41-53; fax 023-23-47). The center also has an office in Punta Gorda (tel. 072-21-11). Promotes sustainable management of Belize's natural resources; conducts research on social and environmental issues; disseminates information on both international and local conservation. Accepts volunteers/interns as positions become available.

Department of Archaeology, Independence Hill, Belmopan, Belize (tel. 082-21-06; fax 082-33-45). Provides information on ruins and archaeological sites.

Jungle Drift Lodge and Tours, P.O. Box 1442, Belize City (tel. 014-95-78; fax 027-81-60; email jungled@bpl.net; http://www.belizemall.com/jungled). Offers guided canoe and kayak trips US$30, excursions to Altun Ha US$50. Lodging: singles and doubles US$20-50; camping US$5.

Laughing Heart Adventures, P.O. Box 669, Willow Creek, CA 95573 (tel./fax (916) 629-3516; http://www.tecwaves.com/laughingheart/adventures). Tours include snorkeling, jungle canoeing, and trips to Maya ruins. Open Mon.-Fri. 10am-3pm.

Glover's Atoll Resort and Marine Biology Station, P.O. Box 563, Belize City (tel. 014-83-51). US$95 week packages include boat trip, snorkeling, fishing, and marine science lectures. Boat leaves on Sun. Cabins have toilets and kitchens. Camping US$75 per week. Inexpensive diving from the beach also available.

Triton Tours, 812 Airline Park Blvd., Metairie, LA 70003 (tel. (504) 464-7964; fax 464-7965). Airfare and accommodations organized for diving and ecotourism in Belize. Open Mon.-Fri. 9am-5pm.

▓ Documents and Formalities

EMBASSIES AND CONSULATES

Embassy of Belize, 2535 Massachusetts Ave. NW, Washington, D.C. 20008 (tel. (202) 332-9636; fax 332-6888). Open to the public Mon.-Fri. 9am-5pm.

Consulate of Belize, 862 NE 2nd Ave., Miami, FL 33138 (tel. (305) 751-5655). Open Mon.-Fri. 9am-noon. Belize also has consulates in New York (tel. (212) 599-0233), Washington, Chicago, New Orleans, San Francisco, Houston, and other cities.

PASSPORTS, VISAS, AND CUSTOMS

Passports are required of all visitors to Belize. Visits are limited to one month and travelers must demonstrate that they have sufficient funds for their visit and a ticket to their next destination. Extensions beyond 30 days (for up to 90 days) are granted by the immigration office in Belize City.

Visas are not required for citizens of the U.S., Canada, Australia, New Zealand, or European Community countries. Others, such as citizens of Israel and South Africa, may need visas; inquire at an embassy or consulate.

You will be charged an **airport departure and security tax** (roughly US$15) upon leaving Belize. **Third-party insurance,** required of everyone driving into Belize, can be purchased at the border from the Belize International Insurance Company (Belinsco) for around BZ$40. Belize will not let you in if an immigration officer suspects you of drug use, and you won't be allowed out if you're carrying fish, coral, or shells. Overzealous beachgoers be warned: Belize protects its natural treasures, so attempting to take certain marine species home could land you in jail.

▓ Money Matters

CURRENCY AND EXCHANGE

US$1 = BZ$2	BZ$1 = US$0.5
CDN$1 = BZ$1.46	BZ$1 = CDN$0.68
UK£1 = BZ$3.26	BZ$1 = UK£0.31
IR£1 = BZ$2.91	BZ$1 = IR£0.34
AUS$1 = BZ$1.49	BZ$1 = AUS$0.67
NZ$1 = BZ$1.30	BZ$1 = NZ$0.77
SARand = BZ$0.43	BZ$1 = SARand 2.31
DM1 = BZ$1.09	BZ$1 = DM0.92

The Belizean dollar is tied directly to the U.S. dollar, so exchange rates are guaranteed for Americans. The official rate is fixed at US$1=BZ$2, but actual rates at banks are slightly below two for one. Most banks will only change British pounds and U.S. and Canadian dollars. Many accept traveler's checks, but you'll have to show a passport and a return plane ticket out of Belize to change more than US$250 of them. Barclay's Bank is usually a good choice for cashing traveler's checks and getting cash advances, as it doesn't charge service fees. Strangely, you can often find better-than-bank rates at local businesses willing to exchange traveler's checks.

If you are coming from Mexico or Guatemala, it's best to exchange all your pesos or quetzales for Belizean dollars at the border. The BZ$0.25 coin is known as a "shilling." Though American paper currency is good just about everywhere, U.S. coins are unwelcome and usually unaccepted.

■ Safety

The non-medical hazards of Belize come in three flavors—the inebriated rowdy, the on-the-make male, and the anxious-to-sell-drugs heavy—and a few Belizeans manage to wear all three hats. Particularly in English-speaking areas (along the coast), expect hustlers and self-appointed "guides" to confront you at every step. Firmly and immediately refuse their services and make it clear that you won't give them money, but don't be rude (the problem could escalate). Public drunkenness is not infrequent in Belize, and women should take more than the usual precautions. Even the most careful may not be able to avoid being approached by a representative of the recently-intensified drug trade. To avoid a confrontation in these situations, some try saying no thanks, you've already gotten yours elsewhere. Remember that the nearest **police** station can be reached anywhere in Belize by dialing 911.

■ Health

Don't bumble blithely into that Belizean scuba vacation—prepare yourself, or you might find yourself in deep water, medically speaking. **Malaria** is a hazard everywhere in Belize except the central coastal district. **Dengue fever** has also been reported across the country, as have **typhoid fever, cholera,** and **hepatitis A.** Sunscreen is almost impossible to obtain in Belize, so stock up before you leave in order to avoid a painful sunburn. As for water, "if it ain't bottled, you hadn't better," especially in rural areas. For more information, see **Health,** p. 14.

■ Once There

TRANSPORTATION

The **international airport** is located 16km northwest of Belize City, on the northern highway. Try to share a cab to Belize City, as the fare could run you BZ$30, but make all arrangements *before* approaching a driver, as they strongly discourage the practice. The **municipal airport** in Belize City offers flights to points within Belize, including Ambergris Caye and Caye Chapel, and other parts of Central America. Flying from the smaller airport is cheaper than from the international, enough so to cover the BZ$7.50 bus ride between them.

Travel is often over water, rather than land. Water routes connect Belize City to Caye Caulker and Ambergris Caye; from Punta Gorda catch a ferry to Puerto Barrios, Guatemala. (For details, see the Practical Information sections of the corresponding areas.) Belizean **buses** are cheap (roughly US$20 to cross the country the long way, north to south). Bus seats are often reserved, but often as not, someone will take your reserved seat. Be persistent about reclaiming it and ask the driver for help.

KEEPING IN TOUCH

The **mail** system is fairly reliable. It costs BZ$0.60 to mail a letter from Belize to the U.S., BZ$0.30 for a postcard. To Europe, letters are BZ$0.75 and postcards are BZ$0.40. First-class airmail takes about 10-15 days to travel between the U.S. and Belize. Pharmacies sell stamps and have mailboxes. You can have mail sent to you in Belize through general delivery. Address letters:

Elena SCHNEIDER
Poste Restante
Orange Walk (city)
BELIZE

Belizean **telephone** offices generally provide cheap and reliable service. Calls to the U.S. cost BZ$9.60 for the first three minutes, and BZ$3.20 per minute after that. Calls to Europe cost BZ$6 per minute. Collect calls are free in Belize. **Direct-dial service** is available between Belize and the U.S. and Canada. To dial Belize from either country, dial 011-501, drop the first zero from the local number, then dial the remaining numbers. For example, to reach 021-23-45, dial 011-501-21-23-45. **Collect calls** and **AT&T credit card calls** can be made to the U.S. through an operator in Belize (dial 115). Belize operates on U.S. Central Standard Time, and daylight-savings time is not observed. **Country code:** 501.

BELIZE: LIFE AND TIMES

■ History

Belize's unusual status in Central America stems partly from Spain's choice not to settle in the area back in the 16th century. Frustrated by the area's lack of natural minerals and the Maya's unwillingness to convert to Christianity, the Spanish moved on to greener pastures. Meanwhile, shipwrecked English sailors discovered another use for Belize; they settled the area (which was still under Spanish sovereignty) and took large quantities of precious mahogany and logwood, used for dyes, to finance their buccaneering ventures. After the 1655 capture of Jamaica from Spain, British soldiers (known as **"baymen"**) and their families joined the growing settlement. The white settlers imported slaves from Jamaica and other English territories to log the wood. Meanwhile, British pirates frequently took booty from the Spanish Navy, finding protection behind the shallow coral reef. After 200 years of skirmishes with Spain, England won decisive control over Belize at the **Battle of St. George's Caye** in 1798. British Honduras became an official colony in 1862, but by then, the supply of wood was thinning out and thousands of Creole workers were left in poverty.

Belize's modern hodgepodge population results from the immigration of various groups in the late 19th century. Although Belize considers English its official language, only the most talented polyglots will feel fluent in all regions of the country. Refugees from the **Caste War** of 1847-48 and from more recent fighting in Guatemala, Nicaragua, Honduras, and El Salvador add a heavy infusion of Spanish, especially in the Cayo, Orange Walk, and Corozal districts. Maya people flourished here between 300 and 1000 BC, and **Cuello,** one of the earliest settlements, may date from as far back as AD 2500. In about the 10th century AD, the Maya abandoned the ceremonial sites of **Altun Ha** and **Xunantunich,** but no one knows why. The settlement at **Lamanai** lasted until colonial times. The **Ketchi** and **Mopan-Mayan** speaking descendants of the Maya still dwell in Belize. In the Stann Creek and Toledo districts to the south live the **Garifuna,** descendants of a race created when survivors of an African slave shipwreck intermixed with so-called Red Caribe natives, forming a new culture unique to Belize and the Bay Islands of Honduras. East Indian and Chinese laborers who came looking for work at the beginning of this century, a few expatriate Americans, and several thousand German **Mennonite** farmers even out the cultural melange. Nearly a third of Belizeans are Protestant, as evangelism was facilitated by the population's familiarity with English.

Recent Belizean politics have not been quite as heterogeneous. Since the 1950s, a two-party democratic system has gradually developed, characterized by the domination of the centrist **People's Unity Party** (PUP), which is headed by the cautious liberal George Price. On June 30, 1993, in an early election called by the PUP, the United Democratic Party (UDP), headed by **Manuél Esquivel,** broke the PUP rule for only the second time in nearly 30 years in a fantastically close election. Belize did not achieve full independence from Great Britain until September 21, 1981, and Guatemala has only recently and reluctantly relented their long-standing claim that Belize actually belongs to it.

Despite, or perhaps because of, U.S. efforts to transform Belize into a prosperous, fully democratic nation, the country is still struggling economically. Agriculture and tourism are the most important chunks of Belize's economy; the timber industry fell drastically after English colonists stripped the land of wood. Illiteracy is high, a hindrance made worse by tariffs on book imports high enough to make bookstores nearly obsolete. **Slash-and-burn farmers** are starting to accept ecotourism as an efficient source of income, but in the short term they still feel beleaguered by the new restrictions on how they can use their land. Nevertheless, the people seem unfazed, and national pride runs high. Most Belizeans cite their 53 cable channels as proof that the country isn't underdeveloped, and residents sport t-shirts with the resounding phrase "Belize da fu we" ("Belize, there for us!").

■ The Arts

The artistic tradition of Belize reflects the nation's unique blend of cultures and the daily lives and struggles of its people. A growing body of Belizean **literature** includes **Zee Edgell's** *In Times Like These,* which explores one woman's struggle for self-definition, and **Zoila Elli's** bright collection of short stories, *On Heroes, Lizards, and Passion.* Poetry also has a strong tradition in Belize. **James Martinez's** departure from English into free-flowing Creole poetry opened the way for folk literature and expression; **Hugh F. Fuller's** pieces elegantly depict the country's natural beauty; and the works of **Evan X. Hyde,** such as *North Amerikkan Blues,* are laced with biting political criticism. Unfortunately, these works are difficult to find in the country. The billboard just outside Belize City sums up the literature situation: "Be literate." Until Belize realizes that many cannot even read the sign, the country seems destined to languish in a meager supply of randomly selected books and office supplies.

Internationally renowned artist **Benjamin Nicholas** is at the fore of Belizean painting; his colorful depictions of daily life among the Creoles and Garifuna hang all over the country, particularly in Dangriga, where he lives. Legendary Creole sculptor, writer, and poet **George Gabb** has a place called Gabby's Galeria, 2.5 miles out on the right-hand side of Northern highway (free visits).

Shake Your Soca! Pump Your Punta!

Like that of other regions around the Caribbean, Belize's musical tradition resulted from the blending of **Carib** and **African** cultures. Some modern Belizeans (particularly a group in Punta Gorda) valiantly strive to maintain the markedly African dance and music of the Garifuna, notable for enchanting, triplet-based rhythms played on large wooden drums. Infusions of **reggae** have led to the development of up-speed, backbeat-based *punta* and *soca* rock, which is popular at **dance clubs.** *Soca* music isn't as intimately entwined with body-shaking, but dance is crucial to *punta;* to boogie with the best, try to stay stationary from the waist up, but below the belt, let your legs flail like **whirling dervishes.**

▨ Food and Drink

There are as many types of food in Belize as there are strains of the multi-ethnic population. Generally, the country's residents eat a lot of rice and beans, as well as beans and rice. There *is* a difference: rice and beans is the two mixed and cooked together; beans and rice are separate, the beans soupier. Garifuna and Creole dishes combine seafood with cassava, plantain, coconut, and green bananas, as well as a dash of the ubiquitous Melinda's hot sauce. **Escabeche** is a potent Mayan onion soup. A **garnache** is sort of like a Mexican *tostada*, a fried tortilla covered with beans, cheese, and vegetables, whereas the more distinctive **salbute** is a fried puff-tortilla covered with chicken, fish, tomatoes, or cabbage. A **panade** is a folded tortilla fried with fish (most often, shark) inside. For breakfast, **"fryjacks"** are similar to Mexican *sopapillas* (fried dough), and **"johnny cakes"** are closer to American pancakes. In addition, the nation supports a large number of high-quality Chinese and Indian restaurants. Lobster is available in-season (June 15-March 15). Restaurants are usually strict about this policy, and rightfully so—commercial chains have over-fished, and coastal waters are now sparsely populated; our tasty little antennaed friends need some time for romance. "Whole fresh fish" is always available, but be prepared to dissect a fully intact specimen, including bones, skin, and head. A last resort for food in Belize is always **HL's Burger,** the self-proclaimed "Burger King of Belize." Along with the ever-present Coca-Cola, fruit juice competes with **Belikin Beer** as the most popular beverage in Belize; Belikin is light, smooth, and goes with just about everything. Lunch is the biggest meal of the day for most Belizeans, with dinner or supper sometimes referred to as "tea." "To have" means you'll eat in the restaurant, while "to take" means you'll eat somewhere else.

▨ Media

Belizeans proudly enjoy one of the best cable TV systems in the world, though it's not clear if anybody's actually paying for it. International broadcasting is occasionally interrupted with congenial reminders like, "Brought to you by Social Security." Cable also allows the Chinese- and Spanish-speaking members of the population to tap into programming in their own languages. Unfortunately, Belizeans are not as on top of national news, although some read weekly papers such as *The Amandala,* which is helping to further a burgeoning African-Belizean movement. The government-operated Belize Radio broadcasts in both Spanish and English.

▨ Recent News

In an attempt to combat the healthy Caribbean drug trade, the Belizean government negotiated a "hot pursuit" agreement with the U.S., effectively opening its territorial waters to Coast Guard vessels in pursuit of drug traffickers. Unfortunately, Belize's legal economy is not as profitable as its illicit one, particularly in the wake of the North American Free Trade Agreement (NAFTA) between the U.S., Canada, and Mexico. Despite the booming trade among the three North American countries, the economies of America's smaller neighbors are suffering the results of single market trade laws. Countries like Belize are finding it increasingly difficult to compete with Mexico, which enjoys the privilege of duty-free exports to the U.S. Foreign capital and investment projects which are needed in Central America and the Caribbean for future growth are going instead to Mexico. No one can predict what will happen in the next year or so, but Belize's economy hopefully will repair itself with the money brought in by the recent ecotourism boom. Speaking of healing, Eligio Panti, a traditional healer whose use of herbal remedies attracted the attention of the modern medical community, died at the age of 103. He was widely regarded as the last Maya master healer in Belize. Finally, in 1997 the United Nations added the Belize Barrier Reef Reserve System to its list of places of "outstanding universal value" that should be internationally respected and preserved.

Belize City

If you're psyched for adventure, Belize City admittedly pulses like no other place in the country. The city's vibrant—and sometimes frightening—personality oozes from every corner. Young Creole day-laborers wearing Chicago Bulls caps blast reggae music from boom boxes while smoking joints the size of large cigars. The gospel yells of a Seventh-Day Adventist revival meeting mingle with the roar of buses arriving at the station. Unlike the rest of the country, Belize City (pop. 60,000) in many ways lives up to Aldous Huxley's bleak commentary: "If the world had any ends, British Honduras would surely be one of them." Sewage streams through the canals that line the streets, buildings wobble on weak foundations, and parts of the city need a paint job. Belize City, it appears, has not fully recovered from 1961's Hurricane Hattie, which killed 300 people, and prompted the government to move to Belmopan.

In the last few years, however, government initiatives have worked to improve sidewalks, street lighting, and sewers, as well as to curb crime against cash-carrying tourists. Still, be wary of criminals in Belize City. Don't show money on the street, and remove all jewelry; you'll look fine without it. In some of the shadier areas of town, aggressive hustlers will walk beside and behind you, offering information you didn't ask for and demanding a cash payment in return (though some "guides" don't ask for money, they expect it). Stay out of alleys, and if a hustler approaches, be firm but not obnoxious. If, in spite of all attempts, you find yourself with an unwanted companion, try to look for one of many khaki-shirted "tourist policemen," who will take your escort off your hands. If you can, avoid the downtown bus station part of town in favor of the relatively more peaceful neighborhoods to the northwest and east. Be especially careful after dark; walk with friends along a busy main street or take a taxi. Finally, be wary of independent tour operators that offer prices that seem to be too good to be true. You may find yourself trapped in the middle of nowhere, watching that bargain swiftly metamorphosize into a ransom.

Still, every cloud has its silver lining. The city is definitely a morning person; the sun rises over cool, calm streets and the city's erstwhile colonial grandeur peers shyly as the swing bridge's 6am rotation marks confusion's return. The residents are well worth stopping to talk to; such conversations will remind you that rare is the city where so many characters are gathered. Most travelers are just passing through Belize City on their way to the Cayes or the interior. Those who choose to spend the day here can enjoy a leisurely seafood fest in a good budget restaurant, explore a handful of new museums and attractions, and discover pleasant faces and voices behind the city's intimidating facade.

■ Orientation

Belize City is 154km south of Belize's northern border with Mexico and 134km east of the western border with Guatemala. The Caribbean Sea virtually surrounds the city, lapping the beachless eastern, northern, and southern shores. **Haulover Creek,** which runs southeast to the sea and splits the city into northern and southern sections, is spanned by the **Swing Bridge;** most services are within a short walk of the bridge. **Queen Street** runs northeast from the Swing Bridge, and **Albert Street** is the major thoroughfare south of the bridge (remember, this was a British possession). **Town Park,** at Church St. and Albert St., occupies the center of town and is two blocks south of the Swing Bridge.

Taxis, usually monstrous station wagons identifiable by their green license plates, can be flagged down on any street or at the stand in Town Park. The standard fare is BZ$5 per stop within Belize City, plus BZ$1 for each extra person. Always ask the fare before getting in, and never get into a car without the green plates. Also, take cabbies' claims that the hotel to which you want to go is "full" with a large grain of salt. The drivers often charge (extort) hotel and hostel owners for "bringing them

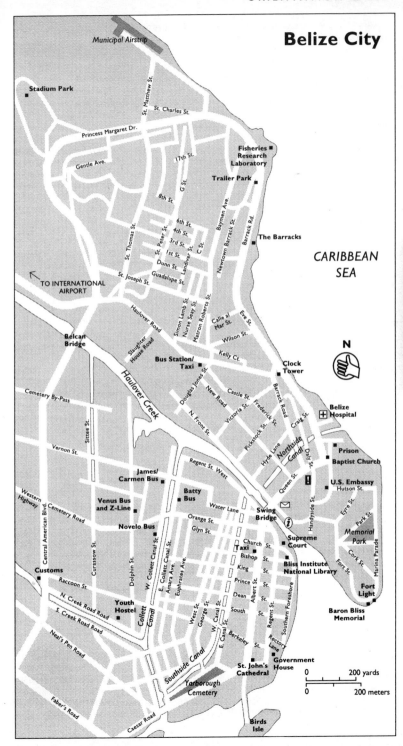

Belize City

Municipal Airstrip

Stadium Park

Princess Margaret Dr.

St. Matthew St.

St. Charles St.

Gentle Ave.

17th St.

Fisheries
Research
Laboratory

8th St.

G St.

Trailer Park

Baymen Ave.

Newtown Barrack St.

Barrack Rd.

6th St.
4th St.
3rd St.
1st St.
Dunn St.
Guadalupe St.

St. Thomas St.

St. Peter St.

Landvar St.

C St.

The Barracks

CARIBBEAN
SEA

St. Joseph St.

TO INTERNATIONAL
AIRPORT

Haulover Road

Simon Lamb St.

Nurse Seay St.

Matron Roberts St.

Calle al
Mar St.

Eve St.

Wilson St.

Belcan
Bridge

Slaughter
House Road

Kelly Ct.

Bus Station/
Taxi

Douglas Jones St.

New Road

Castle St.

Victoria St.

Frederick St.

Barrack Road

Clock
Tower

Haulover Creek

Cemetery By-Pass

Vernon St.

Sittee St.

N. Front St.

Pickstock St.

Hyde Lane

Craig St.

Belize
Hospital

Northside Canal

Daly St.

Prison
Baptist Church

N

James/
Carmen Bus

Regent St. West

Batty
Bus

Water Lane

Queen St.

Handyside St.

U.S. Embassy
Hutson St.

Eyre St.

Western
Highway

Cemetery Road

Central American Blvd.

Venus Bus
and Z-Line

Novelo Bus

Curassow St.

Dolphin St.

W. Collett Canal St.

E. Collett Canal St.

Amara Ave.

Euphrates Ave.

Orange St.

Glyn St.

Church
St.

Taxi

Bishop
St.

King
St.

Swing
Bridge

Supreme
Court

Bliss Institute
National Library

Park St.

Fort St.

Memorial
Park

Marina Parade

Customs

Raccoon St.

N. Creek Road Road

S. Creek Road Road

Youth
Hostel

Collett Canal

West St.

George St.

W. Canal St.

E. Canal St.

Prince St.

Dean
St.

South
St.

Albert St.

Regent St.

Southern Foreshore

Rectory Lane

Cork St.

Fort
Light

Baron Bliss
Memorial

Neal's Pen Road

Berkeley
St.

Government
House

Faber's Road

Southside Canal

St. John's
Cathedral

Yarborough
Cemetery

Caesar Road

Birds
Isle

0   200 yards

0   200 meters

BELIZE

business," and owners who refuse to pay find tourists deliberately directed away from their establishments.

Batty Brothers and Venus buses head north to Mexico, Batty Brothers and Novelo's go west to **Benque Viejo,** and the Z-line takes the southern route to **Dangriga** and **Punta Gorda.** Bus stations are clustered around the yard on Orange St., six long blocks from the center of the city. It's probably best to take a cab where you're going, especially if you have a lot of gear; the stations are in a rough part of town.

■ Practical Information

Belize Tourist Board: 83 N. Front St. (tel. 772-13; fax 774-90; http://www.beli-zenet.com). Cross the Swing Bridge towards Queen St., turn right, 3rd building on the right. Offers maps of Belize (BZ$15) and a well-stocked information section. Open Mon.-Fri. 8am-noon and 1-5pm. Closes 30min. early on Fri. **Belize Tourism Industry Association,** 10 N. Park St. (tel. 757-17; fax 787-10), on Memorial Park.
Embassies and Consulates: U.S., 20 Gabourel Ln. (tel. 771-61). Take Queen St. northeast until it meets Gabourel and turn right—the string of white houses on your left is the U.S. compound. Open Mon.-Fri. 8am-noon and 1-4pm. The entrance to the consulate is around the corner, about 15m back. **Mexico,** 20 N. Park St. (tel. 301-93), on the waterfront. Pass the U.S. Embassy on Hutson St. and turn right; it's at the end of the block. To avoid making the trip from Belize to Chetumal twice in the same day, be sure to get a **Mexican tourist card** from the embassy's consular division before leaving so you don't have to return for it later. Open Mon.-Fri. 9am-12:30pm. **Canadian Consulate,** 83 N. Front St. (tel. 310-60), above the Tourist Bureau. Open Mon.-Fri. 9am-1pm. The **British High Commission** is in Belmopan. If you're heading across the westward border, go to the **Guatemalan Consulate** at 8 A St. (tel 331-50) for a free visa; otherwise, pay BZ$5 at the border. Take the shore road north until it swings west. At the bump sign, turn right. It's just over a block on the right; the trip takes 30min. by foot.
Currency Exchange: All of the commercial banks clustered around Town Park change money. The hard-to-miss **Barclay's Bank,** near Town Park at 21 Albert St., offers cash advances (with no service fee, unlike other banks) and exchanges all stable currencies. Open Mon.-Thurs. 8am-2:30pm, Fri. 8am-4:30pm. **Banco Serfin,** Eyre St. and Hutson St., changes U.S. dollars and Mexican pesos. Be aware that most banks close by 1pm. Many hotels and shops accept traveler's checks, and some will take U.S. dollars as well.
American Express: Global Travel Services, 41 Albert St, four blocks down Albert St. at the corner with King St. (tel. 773-63; fax 752-13). Will hold mail for cardholders. Address to Box 244, Belize City. Other cardmember services upstairs; enter to the left of the Travel Service. 1% service fee. Open Mon.-Fri. 8am-noon and 1-5pm, Sat. 8am-noon.
Airports: Belize International Airport, 49 New Rd. (tel. 025-2045), 16km northwest of Belize City. For an excellent guide to the numerous little airlines, check with Ernest at **Belize Air Travel Service,** 31 Regent (tel. 731-74 or 727-07), parallel to Albert St., about 5 blocks south of Swing Bridge. Fares vary by season. **Continental,** 32 Albert St. (tel. 778-27), serves Houston with 1 flight daily. **American Airlines** (tel. 325-22) serves Miami daily. **Taca Airlines,** 41 Albert St. (tel. 771-85 or 773-63), serves Miami, New Orleans, San Francisco, Guatemala City, Flores (Guatemala), and central Mexico. The airport shuttle was discontinued last year, leaving **taxis** as the only direct service to the airport. Be careful with the buses: the nearest stop is often over 1km from the airport. Cheaper flights to the Cayes and the interior depart daily from the international airport and from the **Belize Municipal Airstrip,** on the waterfront north of town (BZ$5 for a cab ride). **Maya Airways,** 6 Fort St. (tel. 313-48 or 314-03), to San Pedro (every 1hr., 30min., BZ$45); to Dangriga (BZ$55) and Placencia (BZ$105) on the way to Punta Gorda (BZ$135). **Tropic Air** offers similar fares to the same destinations.
Buses: Batty Brothers Bus Service, 15 Mosul St. (tel. 770-25), to **Chetumal** (every hr., 4-11am, 4hr., BZ$9; plus 6am and 9am express buses, 3hr., BZ$10) and **Belmopan** (10 departures before 10am, 1½hr., BZ$3.50); continuing on to **San Ignacio** (2½hr., BZ$5) and **Melchor de Mencos, Guatemala** (5, 6, 7, 9, and 10am, BZ$6).

To reach Venus Bus Lines, 2371 Magazine Rd. (tel. 733-54), take Orange St. 3 blocks west of Collet Canal, then make a right onto Magazine Rd. Venus offers afternoon trips to: **Chetumal** (7 per day, 4hr., BZ$10, 5:20pm express); **Orange Walk** (1½hr., BZ$4.50); **Corozal** (2-3hr., BZ$7.50); and **Sarteneja** (12:30pm, 3hr., BZ$9.50). Z-line, in the same building as Venus (tel. 739-37), services **Dangriga** (6-8 per day, 3½hr., BZ$10) and **Punta Gorda** (3 per day, 9hr., BZ$22). To reach Novelo's, 19 W. Canal (tel. 773-72), take Orange St. west, turn left immediately after the bridge and walk 1 block north. Service to **San Ignacio** (every hr., 11am-9pm, 2hr., BZ$5) on the way to both **Benque Viejo** (3hr., BZ$5.50; express at 11am, 2:30pm, 5:30pm) and to **Belmopan** (1¼hr., BZ$3.50). Schedules change often—call the bus stations or contact the tourist bureau for updated information.

Bookstores: Stock up here because new books are hard to find in other parts of the country. **Brodie's** (see below) has some cheap novels. At **The Belize Book Shop** (tel. 720-54), on the corner of Regent and Rectory, a staff of helpful teenagers offer a motley mélange of travel books (around BZ$30) and English literature (a decent selection—very cheap used paperbacks BZ$0.25-2), as well as a history of Belize (BZ$17.50). Open Mon.-Tues. and Thurs.-Fri. 8am-4pm, Wed. and Sat. 8am-noon. For those interested in **Belizean issues** or simply in making some **photocopies, Angelus Press,** 10 Queen St. (tel. 357-77), one block north of the Swing Bridge is the place to go. Open Mon.-Fri. 7:30am-5:30pm, Sat. 8am-noon.

Market: Brodie's (tel. 770-70), on Albert St. off Town Park. Food items, feminine hygiene, some books. Takes traveler's checks at 2:1 exchange rates. Open Mon.-Thurs. 8:30am-7pm, Fri. 8:30am-9pm, Sat. 8:30am-5pm, Sun. 9am-12:30pm.

Laundromat: C.A. Coin Laundromat, 114 Barrack Rd. (tel. 330-63), BZ $7 self-service or BZ $13 full service (includes detergent). Open daily 9am-9pm. To get to **Stan's Laundry,** take Albert St. south. Turn right 1 block after community drug stores—it's down about a block on the left. **Stan's** is open Mon.-Sat. 8am-noon and 1-6pm and charges BZ$10 per load.

Pharmacy: Central Pharmacy, 1 Market Square (tel. 723-17), just south of Swing Bridge. Amply stocked. Open Mon. Sat. 8am-9:30pm. On Sun., the **Community Drug Store** at the corner of Barrack Ln. and Hyde's Rd. is open 8am-noon, 6pm-8pm. Take Queen St. two blocks north from the Swing Bridge, turn left; it's two blocks down on your left.

Hospital: Belize City Hospital (tel. 315-48), on the way to the airport, along Princess Margaret Dr. Belize City's new hospital is relatively modern, though inconveniently located. Open 24hr. For **ambulance,** call 90.

Emergency: Dial the **police emergency** number 911, or 90 in case of fire.

Police: 9 Queen St. (tel. 722-22), at New Rd. Open 24hr.

Post Office: Queen St. and N. Front St. (tel. 721-78; fax 309-36), near the Swing Bridge. *Poste Restante.* Open Mon.-Thurs. 8am-5pm, Fri. 8am-4:30pm. Passport photos can be obtained at **Venus Photos and Records** (tel 735-96), on the corner of Albert and Bishop St. Four photos for BZ$9. Open Mon.-Thurs. 8am-6pm, Fri.-Sat. 8am-5pm, 7pm-9pm.

Telephones: Public phones are scattered around Queen and Albert Streets. **Belize Telecommunications Limited,** 1 Church St. (tel. 770-85), off Albert St., has A/C and private booths. Direct and collect calls, no surcharge. To the U.S. or Canada, BZ$3.15 per minute, to Europe BZ$6 per minute. BZ$30 deposit required. **Faxes** cost the same as international calls, plus a BZ$2.50 service fee. **Telegram** service (tel. 711-00) is in the same office. To the U.S. or Canada costs BZ$0.32 per word, to Europe BZ$0.60 per word. Open Mon.-Fri. 8am-6pm, Sat. 8am-3pm. **Telephone code:** 02.

■ Accommodations

Budget hotels in Belize City consistently provide one indispensable service: heaps of good advice, both about further travel and staying safe in the city. Sadly, many accommodations are not safe themselves. Carefully check the number of locks between you and crafty burglars. Hustlers sometimes swarm to popular hotels, leading managers to lock their main entrances at regular hours each night. Be sure to find out about the curfew before going out at night, as many hotels close by midnight. Most importantly, be acutely aware of the type of neighborhood in which a hotel is located. Once you've taken precautions in selecting a place to stay, however, be sure to enjoy your time inside. Groups of travelers often gather to gab and share stories—the camaraderie is often the best part of your stay. Most places serve a breakfast of toast, eggs, and coffee for around BZ$6. There is a 7% tax on all hotel rooms, and most hotels charge BZ$1 for phone calls.

Seaside Guest House, 3 Prince St. (tel. 783-39). Take Albert St. south, turn left at the community drug store, look for the last house on the left. Run by a couple of cool Quakers as a labor of love, the ideally located Seaside is mighty mellow. The upstairs common room is wall-papered with tips about travel throughout the country. All rooms have fans, and are kept impeccably clean. Communal bathroom with warm water. Rigidly enforced checkout at 11am. Dorms BZ$20; singles BZ$33; doubles BZ$48; triples BZ$61. BZ$10 key deposit. Serves breakfast (BZ$6-10) from 7-9am. All profits from the hotel go to support Quaker charities. Reservations taken, but must be pre-paid. Call ahead from the airport or bus station during peak season, and they'll try to set aside a room for you.

Isabel Guest House, 3 Albert St. (tel. 731-39), hidden above the Central Drugstore, just south of the Swing Bridge; head upstairs. Friendly family who runs the place speaks mostly Spanish. There are only 3 rooms, but each is large, pristine, and has its own private bath with hot water. Powerful fans cool guests all night long. Palatial common room with TV and spiral staircase that inexplicably disappears into the floor. Checkout 11am. Singles BZ$40; doubles BZ$48. Gigantic room with cute lamps, wooden floors, and 3 beds for rent. 1 bed BZ$40; 2 beds BZ$65; 3 beds BZ$75. Reservations taken.

The Glenthorne Manor Bed and Breakfast, 27 Barrack Rd. (tel. 442-12). Take Queen St. from the Swing Bridge about 3 blocks, go left on Barrack; it's about 2 blocks down on the right. A welcome (albeit more expensive), well-maintained retreat from the city. So hip the rooms don't even have numbers—they're color-coded. The owner is an interior decorator, and it shows; even the mosquito netting is placed just so. Kitchenette with dining area available for guests' use, Creole breakfast included. TV and several poorly tuned pianos provide entertainment. All rooms have private or semi-private bathrooms. Summer singles BZ$50; doubles BZ$75; triples BZ$95. Winter rates about BZ$15 higher. A/C is an extra BZ$15, but fans are free. Laundry: wash/dry BZ$2-5 per load. Private parking BZ$5 per night.

Downtown Guest House, 5 Eve. St. (tel. 320-57), about 2 blocks of Queen St. Next door to a Baptist Church and its noisy school. A tail-wagging "guard dog" greets guests at the Downtown, one of the ultra-cheap places in the city. Rooms share common bathrooms with hot water. Try to grab one with a new fan, as some still have ineffective, albatross models. Doors locked at midnight, but you probably don't want to be walking through this part of town after dark anyway. Singles BZ$15, with bath BZ$25; doubles BZ$25, with bath BZ$35. Meals served (BZ$5-7) with one hour's notice. Somewhat dingy kitchen facilities available as well. TV in one of the downstairs rooms for an extra BZ$5. Laundry about BZ$6 per load. Reservations accepted.

North Front Street Guest House, 124 N. Front St. (tel. 775-95). Cheap and clean, with a front porch overlooking the heavy traffic and rowdy loiterers on the street below. If you're particular about where you bathe, check out the concrete showers in the basement before you put your money down. Make sure your room has a good lock. Midnight curfew, though guests are usually home by 10pm. 10:30am checkout, but they'll hold your luggage for the day. Singles BZ$17; doubles BZ$27; 3-4 in a larger room BZ$12 per person. Traveler's checks accepted.

■ Food

Dining in Belize City on a budget is, for the most part, a strictly utilitarian affair. Expect the usual chicken/beef/fish with rice and beans to appear on your plate wherever you choose to eat. Ice cream parlors offer some of the cheapest meals in town. The popular **Bluebird Ice Cream Shop** at 35 Albert St. is a good choice. As long as you're there, try the ice cream, too. Belize City has a collective sweet tooth to which prevalent pastry shops and ice cream parlors testify.

GiGi's Café and Patio, 2-B King St. (tel. 743-78). Gaze at the plentiful art on the walls as you enjoy traditional Belizean food prepared in an ultra-clean kitchen. Leafy patio seating beside a soothing fountain also available. The owner, George, will even provide you with OFF to keep the skeeters away on those windless nights. Burgers (BZ$7.50) and amply stewed chicken with beans and rice (BZ$6.75). Sinful rum-raisin ice cream (BZ$3.50). Open Mon.-Thurs. 11:30am-2pm and 5:30-9pm, Fri.-Sat. 11:30am-2pm and 5:30-10pm. Closed holidays and first 2 weeks of July.

Macy's Café, 18 Bishop St. (tel. 734-19), 1 block southwest of Town Park, between Albert and S. Side Canal St. A favorite with locals, Macy's serves outstanding Caribbean Creole food cooked with coconut milk and fresh ingredients. The young River Phoenix liked to shimmy up the awning here while filming *Mosquito Coast.* The menu changes daily, but whole fish and rice and beans (with coleslaw and fried plantains BZ$10) are always at hand with huge glasses of lime juice (BZ$2) to rinse it all down. The homemade *habanero* sauce, made of vinegar and onions, will open your pores. Open Mon.-Sat. 11:30am-9:30pm. Sun. by reservation.

El Centro, 4 Bishop St. (tel. 724-13), a couple of doors down from Macy's, part of the Hotel El Centro. The electric pink paint on the ceiling and side wall of mirrors may be a bit much, but the A/C is great on a hot day in the city. Prices are pretty low, the kitchen is clean, and the service is prompt and friendly. Free delivery. Beans, rice and meat (BZ$5-7); garden salad (BZ$5); pizzas starting at BZ$7. Open Mon.-Sat. 6:30am-10pm. AmEx traveler's checks accepted.

Dit's Restaurant, 50 King St. (tel. 733-30), between Albert and S. Side Canal St. A cafe/bakery, kept cool with funky rotating ceiling fans. Standard rice and bean dishes. Try the *garnaches* (3 for BZ$1.15). Known locally for great pastries, including coconut, lemon, and raisin pies (BZ$1.75 per slice). Open Mon.-Sat. 7am-8:30pm, Sun. 8am-4pm.

Fort Street Restaurant, 4 Fort St. (tel. 301-16). From the Swing Bridge, turn right and follow N. Front St. until you get to Fort St. If you're looking for a decadent respite from your daily rations of rice and beans, this is the place. A full dinner will set you back BZ$30-40, but it's worth it. Specialties include fresh seafood and possibly the best desserts in the city. Vegetarian options, too. Beware of the bar tab—margaritas go for a whopping BZ$12 (!). Breakfast and lunch (substantially cheaper) are also served. They even offer impressive hotel rooms upstairs, with prices to match. Open Mon.-Sat. 7-10pm, Sun. 7-10am and (from Dec. to May only) Sun. 5:30-10pm.

▓ Sights and Entertainment

While Belize City may not be the friendliest place for a leisurely stroll, there are several interesting spots, new museums, and cultural centers that warrant a visit. Start at the epicenter of the city, the **Swing Bridge,** a manual bridge which is unusual both in Belize and in the rest of the world. At 6am and 5:30pm, employees perform the slow, brutal work required to swing the bridge open for ships that want passage. You'll start sweating just watching their ponderous progress. Be discreet about taking pictures.

St. John's Cathedral, at the southern end of Albert St., and the **Government House Museum,** directly behind the cathedral on the shore, are only a 10-minute walk from the Swing Bridge, and are well worth it. Dedicated in 1826, St. John's was built with bricks originally used as ballast on English ships and stands as the oldest Anglican cathedral in Central America. Today, it serves as a refreshingly idyllic edifice in an unhappily urban Belize City. The caretaker sometimes sings spirituals and often gives brief tours. (Open Mon.-Tues. and Thurs.-Fri. 9am-noon.)

The recently-opened Government House Museum, on Regent Street, houses relics from British colonial life, down to the last porcelain chamber pot and crystal wine glass. Indoors you'll find the only red carpet rolled out for you in the city, as well as legendary Belizean artist George Gabb's "Sleeping Giant," the striking seagrape sculpture featured on Belizean currency and passports. Perhaps even more enticing, the lush, gazebo-dotted grounds beg to caress backpackers' bare feet. The museum grounds are a good spot for a picnic with some impressive views and satisfying breezes. (Open Mon.-Fri. 8:30am-4:30pm. Admission BZ$5.)

Go for a waterfront stroll along **Marine Parade** or **Southern Fore Shore Rd.** where the city's poshest homes are isolated from the squalor of the downtown region. A few beaches outside of town offer some relief, but the walk back is quite a workout in the heat. Despite the temptation, it's best to stifle your urge to swim until you make it to the Cayes. Belizeans picnic on **Gillett Beach,** 7km out on Western Hwy.

The Image Factory, three doors down from the tourist office on North Front Street, is a non-profit space devoted to Belizean art and culture. Started by Yasser Musa, son of Said Musa, the PUP party leader and prospective favorite in the 1998 election for prime minister, this inviting gallery rotates works of contemporary Belizean artists, natural history exhibits, and folkloric art and artifacts. Check out the Belizean Bicentennial in the summer of 1998, which will amass local, regional, British, and Mexican pieces. Besides, it's free. (Open Mon.-Fri. 9am-noon, 2:30-6:30pm.)

For those not yet exhausted by 10pm, Belize City offers some dance clubs which feature *punta, soca,* and reggae. Although crime levels have decreased slightly, tourists who check out the night scene should be street-smart. Never go solo. Always have a reliable ride home. Keep all body parts inside the ride at all times. Hold on tight and have fun.

Locals swear by three dance clubs. The most notorious is **Millenium** on Barrack Rd., the first intersection past the Fiesta on the left (open Thurs.-Sat. 10pm-2 or 3am; BZ$10 cover charge). Just down the street at the Fiesta is **Calypso** (tel. 326-70). According to visitors, it's worth the BZ$10 cover charge. There's karaoke on Wednesday nights from 8pm-midnight; on alternate Fridays, Calypso features The Messengers, a local band playing *punta* and reggae (open Thurs. until 1am, ladies free, Fri. 10pm-3am, Sun. until midnight). The **Bellevue Hotel** (tel. 770-51) has a disco in the basement which operates Friday and Saturday from 10pm to 2am. To get there, take Albert St. south, turn left on King St., and then it's right at the ocean. The bar upstairs is free, but the disco charges BZ$10 admission. The Messengers make occasional appearances at the Bellevue, too. Ask at the front desk for a schedule.

■ Near Belize City

ALTUN HA

Fifty kilometers north of Belize City stand the Maya ruins of Altun Ha, the most thoroughly excavated site in all of Belize. During the Classical Period (AD 250-900), Altun Ha functioned as a major ceremonial center and as an important trading link between Caribbean shores and inland Maya centers. The jade head of Kinisch Ahau was discovered here; weighing in at nearly 5kg (and making frequent appearances on Belizean bank notes), the piece is thought to be the largest existing Maya jade carving. The restoration of the main ruins has been a little overzealous (no, the Maya didn't invent concrete). Each of the temples is named for a different god, but the sun god's temple is the largest and most extensively restored. If you can't make it up the dizzyingly steep stairs, there's a modern staircase on the right. Some claim that this temple was also used for human sacrifice—the victims were supposedly rolled down the stairs. The steep grade ensured that bodies wouldn't stop halfway down, which would have been terribly embarrassing for the priests.

Getting to Altun Ha has historically been a nightmare and remains so to this day. Fend for yourself by following the trail of travelers heading to the ruins. Some have banded together and taken a taxi (US$25 per person if 4-5 people go, depending on the cabbie). Your best bet is to hook up with a tour run by one of the larger operators in Belize City—expect to pay BZ$60-100 per person. The only overnight accommodations are at the Maruba resort (at least BZ$119 per night), which doesn't even list prices in its multi-page glossy brochure.

BERMUDIAN LANDING AND BABOON PRESERVE

So loud is the lion-like scream of the endangered black howler monkey (called "baboon" in the local Creole) that it can be heard for 2km. In 1985, concerned partisans of these playful primates established the **Community Baboon Sanctuary.** Farmers in the tiny village of **Bermudian Landing,** in seven other small communities, as well as on privately held land, pledged to abide by conservation plans to protect the howlers' habitat. The 20 sq. mi. of sanctuary protect approximately 1600 black howler monkeys. Visitors to the sanctuary can expect to hear the endangered monkey's loud, throaty howl, and will likely catch sight of the gregarious vegetarians hanging out in the canopy. Knowledgeable local guides ensure at least one sighting in each tour (BZ$10), but bring bug repellent and patience—it may take a couple of hours on the trails before a family of hollering primates appears. The only time to definitely avoid the sanctuary is directly after a heavy downpour. Like many Belizeans, the howlers take the day off when it rains, choosing instead to nap inside the trunks of palm trees, emerging briefly only to get some dinner.

Bermudian Landing itself boasts Belize's major natural history museum. If you'd like to spend the night, basic bed and breakfast accommodations are available next door (singles BZ$30; doubles BZ$40). Elegant, yet pricey cabins are also available at the **Jungle Drift Lodge** (see **Useful Information,** p. 126). Russell's bus leaves Belize City at noon and 5pm (BZ$3.50) from next to the bridge connecting Orange and Cemetery Roads, just past the Batty Brothers' Terminal. It does not return until the next morning at 5:30am. Camping is also available for around BZ$5. For more information, call Bermudian Landing (tel. 444–05).

THE BELIZE ZOO

U.S. naturalist Sharon Matola opened the Belize Zoo in 1983. Thirty miles west of Belize City on the Western Highway, the menagerie has expanded to house 36 of the species native to Belize; the zoo is home to over 100 animals in all. Jaguar, ocelot, monkey, tapir—the sublime, the bizarre, and the ugly—exist side by side for your pleasure and bewilderment.

The zoo is refreshingly unorthodox—there are no moats, concrete platforms, or cotton candy stands. Hand-painted, doggerel signs keep visitors on their toes. One line, for example, gloats about the digital superiority of spider monkeys: "When you're minus a thumb, brachiation is a breeze." Although some residents are elusive, most (including the jaguar) can be spotted with minimum effort. Tours, available only with two weeks advance notice, cost BZ$20-50 depending on the size of your group. Admission is BZ$15 for foreign adults, BZ$7.50 for foreign children, and members of the Peace Corps or the military. Help support the underfunded park with a purchase at the gift shop; perhaps a cool mug (BZ$10-14) or a distinctive t-shirt (starting at BZ$23). Traveler's checks accepted with a passport. The zoo is open daily 9am-5pm.

The zoo is easily accessible by car or bus. Eastbound and westbound **buses** on the Western Highway pass the 200m dirt access road approximately on the hour. (The fare from Belize City is BZ$3 one-way; BZ$5 round-trip; 45min.)

NORTHERN BELIZE

■ Orange Walk

"Walk" is Creole for orchard—when European settlers built a Catholic church where the town now stands, they planted a "walk" of orange trees outside the church's front door. Though the name stuck, sugar has replaced oranges as king in Orange

Walk. The first thing you'll notice about the town is the stream of trucks heading south to the refinery. While there are few attractions in Orange Walk, tourists traveling north from Belize City may find this small community of Mennonites, Chinese, and *mestizo* residents an intriguing change. Nearby sites may also justify an overnight stay for those following *la ruta maya*. Please note that Orange Walk is often too expensive for the average budget traveler. These same sights might be more cheaply and comfortably explored from accommodations in Belize City or nearby Corozal.

ORIENTATION

Buses arriving from Mexico or Belize City deposit passengers along the town's principal north-south drag, **Queen Victoria Rd.** or **Belize-Corozal Rd.** (it changes names, but not personalities, at the **fire station**). North of the station it is called Queen Victoria, while on the southern side, folks affectionately term it Belize-Corozal. **Town Hall** (where **Venus** buses stop), the **Batty Brothers** terminal, and the fire station are all on the west side of the street. **Lover's Lane** runs one block east of Queen Victoria. The ill-named **Main St.,** another block east, meanders close to **New River,** the outer edge of town.

PRACTICAL INFORMATION

Tourist Office: A proper tourist office will soon open at a site on the river bank. For the time being, the closest thing is **Novelo's,** on the southeast corner of the park. Ask the staff at the **Lovers' Restaurant.** While most of their information concerns daytrips to the ruins, it's worth asking about events in town.

Currency Exchange: Bank of Nova Scotia (tel. 221-94), in the turquoise building on the northeast corner of the park. No cash advances. Only U.S., British, and Canadian currencies and traveler's checks will be cashed. Open Mon.-Thurs. 8am-1pm, Fri. 8am-4:30pm.

Buses: Located ½ block north of the park, **Batty Brothers** (tel. 770-25) offers hourly service to **Chetumal** with a stop at **Corozal** (about every hr. between 6am-1pm, 2hr., BZ$4.50) and **Belize City** (about every hr. between 1:30-8:30pm, 2hr., BZ$4.50). **Venus** does the Belize City route in the morning and runs to Chetumal in the afternoon, with similar frequency and the same prices.

Taxis: On the block-long strip 1 block north of the city park where the buses pull in. **Orange Walk Taxi Union** (tel. 220-50). **Taxi Association** (tel. 225-60).

Market: The People's Store, 51 Main St. (tel. 220-03), is fully stocked with food, juice, etc. Open Mon.-Sat. 8am-noon, 1:30-5pm, 7-9pm. Closed Thurs. afternoon.

Pharmacy: Delafuentes' Pharmacy, 11 Fonseca St. (tel. 227-02). Open Mon.-Sat. 8am-12:30pm and 3-9:30pm. Carries tampons, diapers, drugs, etc.

Hospital: (tel. 220-72), several blocks north of the police station on Belize-Corozal Rd. Open 24hr.

Police: tel. 911 or 220-22, 4 blocks north of the park on Belize-Corozal Rd.

Post Office: (tel. 223-45), 3 blocks north of the park on Belize-Corozal Rd., in the same building as the treasury. The sign on the door says "Sub Treasury"—just walk in. *Poste Restante.* Open Mon.-Thurs. 8am-noon and 1-4:30pm, Fri. 8am-4:30pm.

Telephones: Public phones are located at various points along Belize Corozol Rd., including by the park. Many are broken, but several restaurants allow calls for BZ$1 per min.

Telephone code: 03.

ACCOMMODATIONS

Cheap, comfortable accommodations are a nonexistent commodity in Orange Walk. If you are able, consider moving on to Corozal for the night for greener (and cheaper) pastures. Otherwise, prepare to pay more than you've had to in other areas of Belize. If you are staying on Belize-Corozal Rd., try to get a room near the back to avoid early morning wake-up calls from the sugar trucks.

D*Victoria Hotel, 40 Belize-Corozal Rd. (tel. 225-18; fax 228-47), a little farther south of the fire station than Mi Amor, on the opposite side of the road. Spacious rooms include A/C, private baths, and access to a vast balcony with views of the hotel's swimming pool and cabana with hammock. Checkout 1pm. 1 person (double bed, no A/C) BZ$45; a room of similar size with two double beds BZ$50.30. A/C and TV cost extra. Reservations, traveler's checks, Mastercard, and Visa all accepted. (In case you were wondering, owner Donny starred his initial and added his daughter Victoria's name to the sign. Hence the bizarre title.)

Mi Amor Hotel, 9 Belize-Corozal Rd. (tel. 220-31; fax 234-62), ½ block south from the fire station. Carpeted rooms with double beds, burnished dressers, and propeller-sized fans. Private baths with hot water. Checkout 1pm. Traveler's checks accepted. Above the Mi Amor Lounge, where the locals can get especially rowdy on weekends. Singles BZ$43, with A/C BZ$75; doubles BZ$59, with A/C BZ$86. Each extra person BZ$6, with A/C BZ$11. TV costs BZ$5 per night. Reservations accepted.

Jane's Guest House, 2 Baker St. (tel. 224-73), from Novelo's, take Lover's Ln. to Baker St., turn left at the fire station and keep walking until you see the sign on your right. New owner Albert Cain has big plans for the place, but for now, Jane's provides sagging mattresses, noisy fans, and one shared, unpainted bathroom at low, low prices. BZ$20 for 1-2 people in rooms just large enough to squeeze in the double beds. Keep an eye open for Sherlock Holmes.

Jane's Hotel Extension, off main street towards the river (turn at the Happy Valley Chinese restaurant), offers more of the same (although the shower is not as good). It is preferable to find a room with a quiet fan and a working lock. Room with one bed (BZ$17); two beds (BZ$25).

FOOD

Orange Walk's array of restaurants is as Belizean as it gets, since every part of the population is represented. Its finest restaurants are exclusively Chinese, a perfect antidote for the traveler whose very soul is turning into rice and beans. For those still eager for variations on the old R&B standard (or who are weary of MSG), great Mexican-style food is cheap grub here—however, be aware that the usual dose of Orange Walk hot sauce is generally too spicy for the typical *gringo*'s palate.

Lover's Restaurant, 20 Lover's Ln. (tel. 203-48), southeast corner of the park, across from Town Hall. Run by the famously loquacious Novelos Brothers whose grandfather's amorous antics allegedly gave the street and restaurant their names. While their grub isn't exactly aphrodisiac, it sates another basic urge—the food tastes good! The price is amazing: BZ$4 for almost every item on the menu. After lunch, it's beverages only. Open Sun.-Thurs. 8:30am-9pm; Fri.-Sat. 6am-11pm.

Juanita's, 8 Santa Ana St., ½ block west of the Shell station (2 blocks north of the firehouse). Named after the sister of Oscar, the ultra-friendly manager, this local favorite offers traditional Belizean fare. Breakfast served at 6am for early risers. Bacon with eggs and beans, rice and beans with chicken, and wicked-good cow-foot soup—all for around BZ$5. Open daily 6am-2pm and 6-9pm.

Lee's Restaurant, 11 San Antonio Rd. (tel. 221-74). 1 block west of the firehouse. Pricey, but it's the tops among Chinese places. Go for the "Special Chow Mein" (BZ$11), the Conch Fried Rice (BZ$9), and, of course, the A/C. Vegetarians will appreciate the vegetable chop suey (BZ$8). Open daily 10:30am-midnight.

Hong Kong Restaurant (tel. 224-06), near the firehouse, next to Mi Amor Hotel. Like the city it's named for, the Hong Kong is known for its syncretism: both Chinese and Belizean specialties are served to bar patrons as they watch Spanish-language TV. This restaurant's expansive menu features sweet and sour pork with rice (BZ$13), fried lobster with fries and salad (BZ$13). Open daily 9am-midnight.

The Diner II (tel. 224-24), on the main road, just north of the plaza. The simpler and more homely cousin of The Diner I, a romantic getaway spot outside of town. In a homey, lodge-like atmosphere, enjoy food that is Belizean, superb, and changes daily (BZ$5-12). Open Mon.-Thurs. 7:30am-10pm, Fri.-Sat. 7:30am-midnight, Sun. 7:30am-10pm.

BELIZE

SIGHTS

Although Orange Walk itself has few attractions—the **Catholic church** at the south end of Main St. and the amazing **river bank** (well worth a picnic)—its claim to tourist fame is its proximity to Maya ruins (see **Near Orange Walk,** below). For those yearnin' for night life, the snazzy **Mi Amor Hotel** has a dance club which opens at 10pm. Take care to vanish before the wee hours of the night, as the locals can sometimes engage in drunken free-for-alls. For family entertainment, the **Escapade Cinema** is the building directly south of the Shell Station on Belize-Corozal Road. Painted rather garishly, the cinema features U.S. movies (with about a month delay) for BZ$3 for adults (BZ$4 on weekends) and BZ$2 for children. Showtimes are Tues.-Thurs. 8pm, and Fri.-Sun. 5:30, 8, and 10pm. The theater is always open for snacks, even when a film isn't showing. Or, walk about a mile north of town to Trial Farm #4 to see the **Godoy orchid farm.** It's just a bunch of plants to most of the family; son Carlos is the expert. If you're lucky, he will be around to give you a proper tour. Call before you go (tel. 229-69).

■ Near Orange Walk

LAMANAI

An important part of *el mundo Maya,* Lamanai represents well over two millennia of continuous inhabitation, ending only in the 17th century under the chilling impact of European diseases. Originally called *Lamanain* (submerged crocodile), a linguistic blooper blessed this city-state with its current name, which means "drowned insect." In either case, it's not hard to understand the water fixation, since the ruin is situated on the beautiful New River Lagoon. A visit to Lamanai includes not only three magnificent temples with sweet panoramic views, but also a 100km round-trip river safari and arduous nature hike. To get the most bang for your Belizean buck, check out the view from the Main Temple, the impressive stela, the Mask Temple, and the howler monkeys, the arboreal caretakers of the region's jungle. Ask your guide to show you the remains of the British sugar mill and two Spanish-Catholic-Indian churches, lingering signs of European occupation at this extraordinary site. Whatever you do, don't forget your mosquito repellant, as the li'l fellas can be vicious in the summer months.

Nearly every Orange Walk resident with a boat and a brain is prepared to move tourists to the ruin. The trips invariably start at 9am and end around 3:30-4pm. Most boats leave from the large hut with the thatched roof—from town, take a bus heading south and ask to be let off at the toll bridge; look for a hut to the right. The **Maruba Resort,** normally far beyond the budget range, offers an excellent tour. For lunch, a reservation must be made at least a day in advance (tel. 221-99). **Novelo's,** at the southeast corner of the park in Orange Walk (same building as Lover's Restaurant), is the base for **Jungle River Tours** (tel. 222-93; fax 237-49), an ecotourism group which leads legendary treks to the ruins. Otherwise, stop at the yellow hotel/restaurant across from the hut, **New River Park, Ltd.** (tel. 239-87)—they know which boat is going and when. For budding botanists, **Carlos Godoy** (tel. 229-69) is the local expert on orchids. His tours to Lamanai, although more expensive, include a strong focus on New River flora. Tours require at least two people and include lunch and entrance fees. Most will set you back BZ$65-80. Bring your own lunch to reduce the cost.

CUELLO

Orange Walk boasts at least two more ruins, less spectacular than Lamanai but rewarding nonetheless. The ruin at **Cuello** is definitely older than Lamanai, perhaps by more than 1000 years. (Two archaeologists have dated it; one says 2600 BC, the other 1500 BC.) It's a single temple and the Maya equivalent of a wine cellar, situated in the middle of soft, verdant fields. Excavations have uncovered over 20 skeletons here, some with skulls detached, from what must have been quite a sacrifice to dedicate the new temple. To get there, take a bus from Tillett's, which leaves from Sagú, the supermarket behind the fire station about every ½ hr., 10am-1pm (BZ$1 each way). Ask the driver to stop at "qua-yo." Find the modern rum distillery, the only building visible from where the bus stops, and ask the manager for permission to view the site (it's on private land). Head through the gate around to the left of the distillery, and follow the trail to the ruin. Bring your own drinking water, and beware of the intoxicating influence of the sweet fumes.

NOH MUL

Noh Mul ("Great Mound") is a slightly less accessible ruin, about 2½km outside the village of **San Pablo,** which is about 13km north of Orange Walk. This ruin, which has been only partially excavated, is for the truly adventurous; the hike is great, and the Maya remains are enshrouded in a dense jungle. The view from atop the second temple takes away what breath is left after climbing; look around to see both Mexico and Orange Walk. Because the ruins are on private land, tourists should ask permission at the **Water Supply Tower** in San Pablo, where the owner lives. Someone can usually show you around for BZ$5.

MENNONITES

If ruins and birds aren't your thing, several German Mennonite communities—**Little Belize, Blue Creek,** and **Shipyard**—are accessible from Orange Walk. The roads around these villages are traveled only by horses and buggies. Women wear full, restrictive dresses and men sport overalls and straw hats; if you can agree on language (Spanish works best), many of the Mennonite men are willing to chat. Of the settlements, Blue Creek, where Maya ruins are currently being excavated, is the most tourist-friendly and the most interesting. On the other hand, only the very curious should visit Shipyard, as its 200 residents are spread out over a vast area. Photography is prohibited in all three Mennonite communities. To reach the towns, look for the school-buses that leave from Sagú, the store located half a block behind the fire station. They leave between 9am and noon—just follow the straw hats and overalls of the Mennonites (BZ$2.50, 1hr.). When you board, ask when buses head back to Orange Walk.

■ Corozal

Named for the local cohune palms, the Maya symbol of fertility, Corozal is also affectionately called "Janet Town" in honor of the 1955 hurricane that forced a civil engineering renaissance of this erstwhile zoning nightmare. Corozal's prime location on a large, protected bay has made it a town which was historically much in demand. First occupied by the Maya, it has since passed through Spanish, British, and finally *mestizo* hands. Spanish-Maya refugees who fled Bacalav, Mexico in the 19th century to avoid being massacred were advised by the original owner, Mr. Blake, to farm sugarcane. Both the immigrants and the newfound vocation stuck. The Mexican border runs a stone's throw from town, and consequently Spanish is the preferred tongue among locals. Life in Corozal is as slow and sweet as the thick molasses from the sugar factory nearby; cabanas line the shore, where locals go to share *refrescos* and catch a fresh evening breeze. For now, few tourists come to this little town (pop. 8000), but its pleasant swimming areas and inexpensive seaside respite, as well as easy access to two interesting **Maya ruins,** Santa Rita and Cerros Maya, promise to make Corozal "undiscovered" little longer. It can also function as a hub for trips down to Lamanai or the Cayes.

Orientation and Practical Information Despite the grid-like order of streets, navigation in banana-shaped Corozal somehow manages to be confusing. Locals are familiar with what's where, but even they have to look at their mail to determine their own addresses. Major landmarks include the sea, which runs along the eastern side of the city; the town square (home of **Town Hall**); and the town park

(**Central Park**), next to the Catholic church in town. The avenues run parallel to the shore and are numbered starting from the bay. First Street North skirts the northern side of Central Park, and First Street South (you guessed it) the southern side.

The new **Tourist Information Office,** 2nd South St. (tel. 231-76), houses a small museum detailing Corozal's fascinating history and provides a good deal of insight about Corozal and beyond. To get there, head east to the sea from Central Park and turn right. It's the spanking new building with the bright orange roof (open Tues.-Sat. 9am-noon and 1-4:30pm). The rest of the time, Henry at **Caribbean Village** and Mark at **Nestor's Hotel** can answer your questions. Many local businesses will **exchange** U.S. dollars without the service charge imposed by banks, but be sure to compare rates first. **Atlantic Bank,** 1 Park St. (tel. 234-74), near the park, offers cash advances on Visa (BZ$5 for authorization call) and cashes traveler's checks (open Mon.-Fri. 8am-2pm). **Batty Bus,** 13 4th Av. (tel. 230-34), located 3 blocks north of Central Park and 2 blocks west of the **Fort Barrier** monument on the southwest corner of Central Park. Batty Bus heads north to **Chetumal, Mexico** in the mornings (every hour, 4-11am, 1½ hr., BZ$2.50, expresses at 6am and 9am), and south to **Belize City** in the afternoons (every hour, noon-7:30pm, BZ$7.50, expresses at noon and 3pm). **Venus Bus** does the southern run in the morning and the northern route in the evening, with similar times and prices. **Island Air** and **Tropicair** both fly to **San Pedro** for about BZ$64 (total of 5 flights daily). Contact the agent at the Hotel Maya (tel. 220-82) or Henry at Caribbean Village (tel. 228-74) for information. **Taxis** (tel. 220-35) huddle on the western edge of Central Park. A trip within the town costs BZ$5. **U-Save ,** 6th Av. and 2nd St. South (tel. 221-49), two blocks south of the park, has complete grocery store fare (open Mon.-Thurs. 7:30am-7:30pm, Fri. 7:30am-8pm, Sat. 7:30am-9:30pm, Sun. 7:30am-12:30pm). The **General Discount Drugstore** (tel. 221-24), 5th Av. just south of the park, offers feminine hygiene products and drugs (open Mon.-Fri. 8am-noon, 2-5:30pm, and 7-8:30pm, Sat. 8am-noon and 7-8:30pm). The **Hospital** (tel. 220-76) is located 4½ blocks from the police station on the grassy knoll (open 24hr.). The small, friendly **police** force has an office on the west side of Central Park (tel. 220-22 or 911), which is open 24hr. The **post office** sits on the west side of the park, across from the taxi stand (*Poste restante;* open Mon.-Thurs. 8:30am-noon and 1-4:30pm, Fri. 8:30am-noon and 1-4pm). **BTL** (tel. 221-96) on 6th Av., also has mail service (open Mon.-Fri. 8am-noon and 1-4pm, Sat. 8am-noon). The **phone code** is 04.

Accommodations and Food Because so few tourists come to Corozal, rooms are almost always available and are relatively cheap. Corozal is said to be safe, but security should still be a primary consideration in choosing a hotel. The **Caribbean Village Restaurant and Motel** (tel. 220-45), south of town on the shore road, has cute *cabañas* just meters from the beautiful seashore. (Grassy grounds, chirping birds, buzzing insects—the whole nine yards.) Owner/manager Henry takes great pride in his newly refurbished rooms and is an excellent source of tips on Corozal. His wife, Joan, cooks up tasty meals at the Caribbean Village's restaurant (BZ$10 key deposit). All rooms have private bath. Singles are BZ$30, and you can add an extra person for only BZ$5; triples cost BZ$75. Camping facilities are also available. **Nestor's,** 123 5th Av. (tel. 223-54), four blocks south of Town Park on 5th Av., is a good place to go to feel secure. Massive owner Mark puts the fear of God into thieving locals; he also boasts possession of the only running Harley in all of Belize. The hotel sports a great bar and restaurant, as well as a multitude of cheap, ammonia-scented rooms with fans and hot water. Key deposit costs BZ$5. Checkout is at 11am. Wheelchair accessible rooms are available. Mark is also willing to connect travelers—even those who don't stay at his hotel—with guides for exploring. His bar, replete with two TVs, is the site of nightlife in Corozal. (Singles BZ$25; doubles BZ$31; two twin beds BZ$36; two double beds BZ$43.) **Capri** (tel. 220-42) on the corner of 4th and 5th Av. on the shore, isn't luxurious, but the second floor rooms provide some great views of the lagoon, and it's *cheap*. Peek into a few rooms first to guarantee a working fan, clean linen, and adequate locks—snag the ocean side if possible. (Singles BZ$8.50, with private bath BZ$12.50; doubles BZ$12.50, with private bath BZ$17.50.)

Corozal has a heapin' helpin' of Chinese restaurants, which all seem to serve the same fare, and too meager a handful of Belizean restaurants. All you really need, though, is **Ju Me Lin** (tel. 225-26), on 5th St., one block over from U-Save. The small blackboard outside details the menu of traditional Belizean eats (a bargain at BZ$6-8 for a full meal), which changes daily (open 6:30am-5pm). Two fine (but still inexpensive) restaurants are associated with **Nestor's** and **Caribbean Village. Crisis,** at One 9th St. N., on the far north end of town, is pronounced CREE-sis, so beware when asking directions. It serves bona fide Belizean food, at low prices in a comfortable setting. A big portion of T-bone with rice and beans costs BZ$10. (Open Sun.-Thurs. 11am-4pm, Fri. 11am-10pm, Sat. 11am-1am. Live music Sat. night.) **Holiday Bakery,** next to Super Mirna's, bakes tasty snacks—many go for a Belizean buck.

Sights If you can tear yourself away from the mesmerizing lilt of waves nudging the shore, take a gander at the historical **mural** by Corozal artist Manuel Villamor in the Town Hall, at the south end of Central Park. Or view one of the two ruins nearby, **Santa Rita** and **Cerros Maya.** Santa Rita is a 20-minute walk from Central Park. Take the road past the police station for six or seven blocks, veer left at the hunched-shoulders statue, and take the second right at the Belize security-force station. The ruin sits on the left. All of Corozal was built on ruins, but this temple is all that's left. Mr. Wiltshire, the caretaker, gives a tour with the entrance fee (BZ$3). The ruins are not as spectacular as others, but they still evoke the tranquil and mysterious. It's not hard to imagine the high priest sipping a club soda on the veranda of this *cabaña antigua.*

Cerros Maya, the more spectacular ruin, is also the more expensive. One of the earliest settlements, this 5 sq. mi. site is also featured on several postcards. The ruin lies across the bay and requires a boat ride which may warrant some further meandering through the lagoon in search of bird life. There are several locals who lead excellent trips; ask Mark at **Nestor's** or Henry at the **Caribbean** for contacts. Guide Alroy Levy charges BZ$55 for 1-2 people. Manuel Hoare (tel. 227-44) has had ten years' experience guiding trips. Rates become considerably cheaper as more people band together.

THE CAYES

The Cayes ("keys"), Belize's 175 coastal mini-islands, are the late 20th century's service-enhanced version of the perfect tropical isles. Like pennies from heaven, world-class diving, snorkeling, and fishing opportunities await both experienced lovers of the deep and the newly converted. British pirates were some of the first to discover the Cayes' mystique; they used the Barrier Reef to hide from the Spanish navy, coming ashore afterward to stock up on provisions. Of late, investors have become hip to the isles' built-in tourist appeal; **Caye Chapel** and **Ambergris Caye** boast landing strips and posh hotels. For the time being, activity remains concentrated on Ambergris Caye and, to a lesser extent, on nearby Caye Caulker. Indeed, most of the remaining islands are still uninhabited mangrove swamps.

The Cayes right off Belize City are the most accessible. Flights from the municipal airport take vacationers to Ambergris Caye, **Caye Caulker,** and Caye Chapel; regularly scheduled launches zip travelers from Belize City to the cayes. Charter a launch to reach the less popular or more distant cayes (ask at the **water taxi terminal** by the **Swing Bridge** in Belize City).

■ Caye Caulker

Caye Caulker (pop. 600) cools and calms the spirit frazzled by the dingy population density of Belize City. Geckos sun themselves, coconut trees sway in the afternoon breeze, and the pace of life is *slooooooooooow*. Five *mestizo* families from the Yucatán settled here in 1850 to fish; their descendants now run modest seaside hotels where you can feast on beer and lobster tails (when in season). Even the most ambitious traveler will find himself deciding to just sit back, nurse another rum punch, and forget what day it is.

The local community is quiet, laid-back, and uniformly friendly, but is not receptive to loud North American tourists. Guest house signs warn against raucous late-night behavior. Don't be naive, though. While the residents are generous, vagrants from the coast have discovered Caye Caulker's charm too, and crime, particularly hotel theft, is not unknown.

Caye Caulker is an island divided. According to urban legend, Hurricane Hattie rent the Caye in two back in 1961. In fact, Hattie only widened a creek; locals finished the job, dredging the gap into what is now called "the split." Divisions of another kind have recently arisen over the construction of a corps of posh condos, funded by Texas money. Some hope the development will bring more business to the isle and put an end to the drug culture that has recently migrated from Belize City. Others predict an inevitable erosion of the island's precious tranquility, as it becomes a vacation spot for wealthy *gringos*. Snorkeling and scuba trips to the reef offer an escape from the heat, the mosquitoes, and the lassitude of the shore. For now, at least, Caye Caulker remains a pleasant little community of voluntary castaways, free of jet skis and hordes of college kids on spring break.

Zoom from Belize City to Caye Caulker by high-speed launch. The new **Water Taxi Terminal** (tel. 319-69), the big white building next to the Swing Bridge on N. Front St., has organized the previously chaotic system for ferrying passengers to Caye Caulker. Now a boat makes the run daily every two hours, 9am-5pm (BZ$15 one way; BZ$25 same-day, round-trip). You can while away your wait at the terminal in the fledgling **Maritime Museum** (BZ$4), designed to promote conservation of Belize's natural treasures. A new tourist information desk is expected soon. The terminal is open daily 7am-5pm, holidays and weekends included.

For those who prefer enclosed comfort (TV included), **Triple J** boats (tel. 443-75), on the south bank of Haulover Creek a few blocks east of the Swing Bridge, will also drop passengers off at Caye Caulker (BZ$15) on their way to Ambergris Caye. To avoid the clamor of the Belize City Harbor, fly to Caye Caulker from the municipal airport (15min., around BZ$45 one way) or the more expensive international airport.

ORIENTATION

As described above, Caye Caulker has two halves. The town stands at the northern tip of the southern portion. The only street signs in Caye Caulker besides some errant stop signs state the wholly unnecessary reminder, "Go slow." It would be hard to do otherwise in this sleepy little town devoid of street names and addresses. Three parallel dirt roads, known informally as **Front Street, Middle Street,** and **Back Street,** run north to south through town. A leisurely walk from end to end takes less than 30 minutes. Landmarks include the **police station,** on Front Street at the center of town, the basketball court just south of the station, and the two largest **piers** which jut out on the east and west sides of the island, a bit south of the police station. Most boats from Belize City leave passengers on the east side of the island, but some stop on the west. Just ask which way is north upon disembarking and orientation will be a snap.

PRACTICAL INFORMATION

Tourist Office: Your best bet is stopping by **Dolphin Bay Travel** (tel. 22-14) just up Front St.; the sign you'll see first says "Frenchie's," not Dolphin Bay, but you're in the right spot. Ilna and her daughter, Tina, are knowledgeable about all the island's offerings, and are especially attuned to the needs of penny pinchers. Tage, at **Hicaco Tours,** will happily tell you all about their own offerings.

Currency Exchange: The spiffy new **Atlantic Bank** (tel. 22-07), on Middle St., even with the road connecting the two main piers, offers cash advances on Visa cards and exchanges U.S. currency. Open Mon.-Fri. 8am-2pm, Sat. 8:30am-noon. In gen-

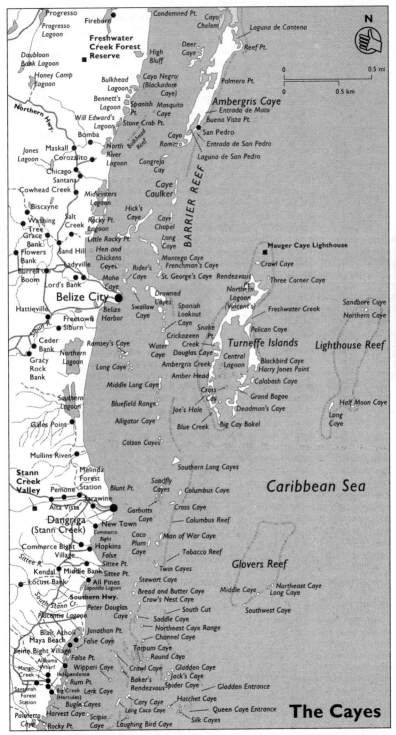

eral, traveler's checks are widely accepted at local restaurants and can also be cashed at several stores, so don't despair if you can't get up out of your lounge chair and trundle down to the bank before 2pm.

Airstrip: Within easy walking distance on the south side of town. Any San Pedro-Belize City flight will stop on request at Caye Caulker; simply mention it when buying your ticket. Once on the Caye, call **Island Air** (tel. 20-12) for your return trip.

Ferries: Boats returning to Belize City leave at 6:45, 8, 10am, and 3pm (BZ$15). At 10am a boat leaves Caye Caulker for **San Pedro** (30min., BZ$15). Other boats to San Pedro can be picked up as they stop on the west dock to drop off people from Belize City; there is one around 1pm. A fun, leisurely way to get to San Pedro is to take a full-day snorkeling trip that stops for lunch in San Pedro (BZ$45, BZ$5 entrance fee to **Hol Chan Marine Reserve**). Arrange to abandon ship for good at lunchtime. Most leave around 10:30am and reach San Pedro around 12:30pm.

Market: Haramouch (tel. 22-47), on Middle St., even with the main piers. Food, liquor, and feminine products—what else do you need? Visa, traveler's checks accepted. Open daily 8am-9:30pm. **Jan's Deli** (tel. 21-88), at the north end of Front St. between **Chocolate's** and **Cabana's.** Open Mon.-Sat. 7am-1pm and 3-7pm, Sun. 8am-noon.

Laundromat: Caye Caulker "Laundry Mat," on Middle St., 1 block south of the soccer fields. BZ$10 per load, wash and dry. No self-service. Open daily 8am-noon and 1-6pm. 2 coin-op laundromats have just opened on Back St.

Pharmacy: Haramouch Market (tel. 21-88), midtown on Middle Street, boasts Caye Caulker's best attempt at a pharmacy. It has no prescription drugs, but carries most over-the-counter medications. Open daily 8am-9:30pm.

Medical Services: Caye Caulker Health Center (tel. 21-66), 2 blocks from the police station, at the southern end of Front St. Open Mon.-Thurs. 8am-5pm, Fri. 8am-4:30pm. Emergency only, after hours.

Police: (tel. 21-20), in a green-and-cream house by the basketball half-court on Front St. One-man squadron available (sort of) 24hr.

Post Office: A new post office has opened on the southern end of Back St., even with Marin's Restaurant. Names of mail recipients are written on a sign. Mail comes in Mon., Wed., Fri. at 10am. *Poste Restante* available, ask at the desk. Open Mon.-Thurs. 8am-noon and 1-5pm, Fri. 1-4:30pm.

Telephones: Belize Telecommunications Limited (BTL) (tel. 21-69; fax 22-39), on the 2nd floor of a building near the middle of Front St. Offers free international collect calls. **Fax** service available. Open Mon.-Fri. 8am-noon and 1-4pm, Sat. 8am-noon. Deposit required. **Telegram** service is also available at **BTL,** Mon.-Fri. only. BZ$0.32 per word. A **cyber cafe** replete with email services is rumored to be opening soon. Expected prices: BZ$5 to send email; BZ$2 to receive messages. **Telephone code:** 022.

ACCOMMODATIONS

A preponderance of simple hotels, shared showers, cold water, and fans keep the Cancún jet set away (for the time being). Look for a place on the Caribbean side, right on the ocean; a steady breeze off the water keeps things cool while giving the cold shoulder to voracious mosquitoes and sand flies. Campers can wander to a desolate part of the isle or, preferably, ask around to see which hotels allow camping. To repel kamikaze critters, burn mosquito coil (BZ$1.50) and keep the lights off. Many places have few rooms and fill them all between November and April; a reservation isn't a bad idea. A few locals rent rooms in their houses—inquire at Dolphin Bay for a potential good deal for groups.

Castaway's Hotel (tel. 22-94). Owner Bob, a British ex-serviceman, helps travelers plan trips beyond the Caye and has a Scrabble™ board for rainy days. *Let's Go* recommends ZWIEBACK (243 points on a triple-word score). Simple rooms with unsullied, shared bathrooms. Checkout 11am. Singles BZ$14; doubles BZ$22. Coffee included. Quality restaurant downstairs. Often full, even in the low season.

Daisy's Hotel (tel. 21-50), just past Big Fish, Little Fish on Front St. Spacious blue rooms in excellent shape, if set a bit too far back from the breeze. Strong fans.

Friendly management lives next door, past the canine contingent. Hot water. Checkout 10am. Send 50% deposit to reserve a room. Singles BZ$13; doubles BZ$26.50; triples BZ$32. Add BZ$3-5 during peak season.

Tom's Hotel (tel. 21-02). Arriving at the island from the east, you'll see Tom's on the far left (south), overlooking the Caribbean. Turn left towards the ocean at Big Fish, Little Fish and follow the sandy path along the beach. Unassuming, cozy rooms and spiffy communal bathrooms. Young travelers read, rap, and drink rum on the breezy veranda. Checkout 10am. Singles BZ$20; doubles BZ$25, plus tax. *Cabañas* with private bath and hot water: each sleeps 3 people for BZ$55, plus tax. Traveler's checks accepted. Office open 6am-6pm.

Barbara's Guest House (tel. 20-25), north end, 1 block south of the split. Run by a mellow, laid-back Canadian, the House boasts low prices, clean rooms, powerful fans and the latest in commode worship: the common toilet sits on an altar. The padlock is undernourished, but Barbara hands out free mosquito rope mats, allows collect calls on her phone without extra charge, and takes everything in stride. Checkout 9am, but you can store stuff with Barbara for the day. Laundry BZ$10. Rooms sleep 1-2 people for the night, BZ$20; BZ$75 for the week.

Ignacio's Beach Cabins (tel. 22-12), southeast end of island, south of Tom's. Interesting owner and rustic huts make this a backpacker's mecca. Each colored hut is clean and has a private bath. Front huts enjoy a great view of the beach. Flat rate is a deal for small groups. Ground hut (sleeps 2) BZ$20; stilts (sleeps up to 3) BZ$30. High-season prices BZ$10-15 higher. Checkout 10am. No visitors or pot-smoking allowed, two rules Ignacio strictly enforces.

Vega Inn and Garden (tel. 21-42) on Front St. across from BTL. Summer camp-like lodge with hammocks by the sea for all the lounging you can stand. Shared bathrooms with hot water and strong fans. Noon checkout. Singles BZ$25; doubles BZ$50; triples BZ$60. Camping BZ$15 per person. Prices increase significantly during the high season. Send 50% deposit to reserve. Traveler's checks accepted.

FOOD

Caye Caulker's restaurants are legendary for cheap seafood and laid-back (read: slow) service. Lobster and eggs for breakfast cost just BZ$6, but the food may not arrive until lunchtime. To some, the wait is annoying; to others, it's simply an excuse to down a few more beers. For a quick and tasty breakfast, buy some **Creole bread** from one of the many children on Front St. (BZ$1-1.50). Those on a *very* tight budget should consider visiting the **hot dog vendor** on Front St. (one dog BZ$2.50)—it's not the wurst you could do.

Sandbox (tel. 22-00), just south of the basketball court near the center of town. This favorite with locals and tourists has just moved to fancy new digs right on the beach. Happily, the heaping plates of local dishes persevere. Homemade pasta and vegetarian dishes too. The spinach-lobster lasagna (BZ$15) was featured in *Gourmet* magazine—*ooh là là*. Fish filet with sweet pepper and onions, rice, and salad BZ$10. Conch fritters BZ$6; tasty coconut ice cream BZ$3 (15% VAT tax not included). Open Thurs.-Tues. noon-3pm and 6-10pm. Kitchen closes at 9pm.

Glenda's, on Back St. a few blocks south of the soccer field. Good breakfasts. Icy, fresh orange juice (BZ$2); coffee, eggs, bacon, and fresh baked cinnamon rolls (BZ$6); lobster burritos (BZ$3). Open Mon.-Sat. 7-10am for breakfast, noon-3pm for lunch.

Syd's Restaurant and Bar (tel. 29-94), on the corner of Middle St. and the back path by Glenda's. Newly refurbished, though the requisite sand floor and beach chairs remain. Syd's blasts funky beats and dishes up cheap, tasty grub. A great bet for lunch. Chicken tostadas BZ$1, a trio of *garnaches* BZ$1, burritos BZ$1.50. Catch the island-renowned barbecue on Sat. night. Open daily 10am-3pm and 6-9:30pm. Accepts Mastercard, Visa, AmEx, and traveler's checks.

Marin's Restaurant and Bar (tel. 21-04), at the southern end of Middle St. Inside, lights pulse to a reggae beat, but cooler and quieter dining can be found on the back patio. Lobster, eggs, and hotcakes BZ$8; Marin's special, including lobster, fish, shrimp, and conch, varies according to the season, BZ$20; *huevos rancheros* for breakfast BZ$7. Open daily 8am-2pm and 5:30-10pm. Kitchen closes 9:30pm. Traveler's checks accepted.

Cindy's Celestial Island Cafe (tel. 20-93), across from the basketball court at the center of town. *The* happening porch on Caye Caulker. Cindy, a transplanted Canadian, has Starbuck's coffee (BZ$2) and may own the only place in Belize with espresso, cappuccino, and latte (BZ$3-4). Also serves earthy breakfasts and snacks. Opens about 7am. Tarot readings by appointment. The Caye's Public Library currently is located here and appreciates all donations, especially children's books.

SIGHTS AND ENTERTAINMENT

Faintly visible to the east of Caye Caulker lies a stretch of the 250km **Barrier Reef,** the largest reef in this hemisphere and the second-longest in the known universe. By launch, the reef is just minutes away. Popular half-day snorkeling trips to the shallow coral gardens and deeper channels are an agreeable alternative to the sensory stimulation of hallucinogens—and there's no hangover. Boats stop at three sites, one of which allows you to swim with a gang of sting rays and a circling nurse shark or two (they're harmless, as long as you have no open cuts). Excursions usually depart at 10:30am and return by 1:30pm (BZ$25 with gear). **Big Fish, Little Fish** also runs an afternoon trip from 1:30 to 4:30pm. Rent fins, a mask, and a snorkel from the shop in the center of town (BZ$5 plus credit card deposit; open daily 8am-5pm).

Popular snorkeling spots off Ambergris Caye can also be explored from Caye Caulker at similar, if not more affordable rates. Full-day outings stop at **Hol Chan Marine Reserve** (entrance BZ$5), the famed **Shark Ray Alley,** and coral gardens off San Pedro, with a lunchtime respite in the town itself (10:30am-4:30pm; BZ$45).

Captains hang out at the docks soliciting passengers. Before arriving at the docks, ask around for the name of a reliable operator. Ask Chocolate, at **Chocolate's Gift Shop** (tel. 21-51) on Front St., next to Jan's Deli, for reliable information. He can put you in touch with various local legends/tour guides, as can Ilna at **Dolphin Bay Travel** (tel. 22-14). Specifically, brothers Ramón and Pedro Rosado at Big Fish, Little Fish and Tage at Hicaco Tours run very good tours to the reef. Expect to pay about BZ$45 for a three-site trip. If you want to admire the fish and eat them too, island operators also arrange angling adventures. For BZ$55 (snorkel gear included, bring your own lunch), those still not tired can adventure off to **Goff's Caye,** a protected manatee nesting area with snorkeling opportunities nearby (contact Dolphin Bay). Be sure to leave your valuables ashore.

Frenchie's (tel. 22-14), past Chocolate's, offers a PADI certification course (US$275). Two tank dives cost BZ$106 with gear; night diving costs BZ$70. **Belize Diving Services** (tel. 21-43), behind the soccer field, offers two tank dives for US$41 (with your own gear), or US$61 (to rent gear). A four-day NAUI or PADI certification course is US$300 per person. (Open Mon.-Sat. 8am-6pm, Sun. 8am-4pm, 365 days a year.) Ambergris Caye offers more extensive diving opportunities.

Caye Caulker's only strip of sandy beach lies to the north of the split. Although this is a good area for snorkeling when currents and wind are low, would-be tanners beware: summertime insects are especially fierce here due to the heavy vegetation nearby. Opt instead for the piers on the Caribbean side of the Caye.

For entertainment after dark, head to the **I&I Cafe and Bar** near the south end of town. Walk up the rickety staircase and take a seat at one of the many swings, painted in bright, primary colors. If you need to escape Bob Marley's voice, head to the roof and chat it up with the locals. Further north on Front St., the **Oceanside Bar** provides pool tables, cable TV, and of course, a sandy floor. Sometimes the Oceanside can draw a seedier crowd; politely decline any offers of illicit substances if the occasion arises. Perhaps the most satisfying nighttime experience in Caye Caulker is returning to the pier where you spent the day, lying on your back, and settling in for some extended star-gazing.

Diving for Dollars

The barrier reef along Belize and Honduras is the largest in the hemisphere, and the Caribbean's **crystalline** waters provide excellent visibility for exploring the mind-bending shapes and colors below the surface. Many dive shops on the Cayes offer travelers the chance to get certified and explore the **fantastic reefs** and, in some cases, for considerably less than in the U.S. Unfortunately, competition between shops has also caused some **corner-cutting.** Safety awareness and quality of instruction are sometimes sacrificed for mass-output certification. Shop around before settling on a dive center. Make sure the instructor is fully certified with NAUI or PADI, the biggest divers' organizations. If some shops' deals seem too good to be true, they probably are. Bad air or poor instruction can lead to **decompression sickness** and **death,** so don't take chances. Never dive or snorkel alone, don't drink and dive, be aware of all the rules, and don't test the strength of the sea—it is bigger than you are. While preserving your own safety, make an effort to protect the well-being of the coral and sea life as well. Divers' early efforts to conserve precious coral and protect water organisms may have been the start of the **ecotourism** movement. However, some careless and greedy dive instructors still do not preach the importance of keeping your equipment near your body and not touching or kicking your fins near the **coral.** Coralheads that took eons to develop can be lost in a matter of seconds. Have respect for the sea; look but don't touch, and learn the eco-conscious diver's mantra, "Leave only bubbles."

■ Ambergris Caye and San Pedro

Belize's leading tourist destination, Ambergris Caye, lies 58km north of Belize City. Although fishing remains an important industry for many of the town's 2500 permanent residents, tourists have fast become the island's most lucrative catch. Indeed, the majority of those who come to the Caye are well-off, middle-aged Americans, puttering around the tiny isle on US$50-per-day golf carts or relaxing at the Belize Yacht Club. The Yacht Club aside, it's still possible to enjoy diving without spending every last sand dollar.

The Caye's main attraction—the Barrier Reef—brings in hordes of scuba enthusiasts, and **San Pedro** attracts travelers who are willing both to pay considerably more and to sacrifice some of Caye Caulker's Gilliganesque aura.

Ambergris Caye has a pleasant beach, and because the Barrier Reef runs right along the isle's eastern shores, diving is easier here than at Caye Caulker. The **Hol Chan Marine Reserve,** just south of Ambergris, attracts an assortment of pampered fishes who expect stale bread from divers (admission BZ$5).

Several flights depart daily for Ambergris Caye from the international and municipal airports in Belize City, and a number of boats link the island with the mainland. A high-speed launch called **Thunderbolt** (charter tel. 026-22-17) leaves Belize City from the dock across from the water taxi terminal Mon.-Sat. at 1pm; it returns to the city from the Texaco dock in San Pedro at 7am (BZ$25 each way). **Triple J** (tel. 024-43-75) leaves at 9am daily from the south side of Haulover Creek, a few blocks east of the Swing Bridge, to return to Belize City at 3pm (BZ$25 each way).

ORIENTATION

Boats from Belize City usually arrive at the Texaco dock on the eastern shore of the island, although some cruise around to the other side. A simple query will help you square your bearings. If you're coming from the east, the first sandy road you will hit is Front St. The three streets of San Pedro that run from north to south have official names, but few locals know them by anything other than **Front St. (Barrier Reef Road), Middle St. (Pescador Dr.),** and **Back St. (Coral St.).** The center of town is on Front St. at the Children's Park and the Barrier Reef Hotel. The northern and southern ends of the island cater to the jet set while the rest of the town offers attractions for every budget. Most hotels, shops, and restaurants are located along Front St.

PRACTICAL INFORMATION

Tourist Information: Information for budget travelers in San Pedro is hard to come by. Inquire at your hotel, as often owners can direct you to cheap eats and set you up with reasonably-priced snorkeling and diving expeditions. **Ruby's** and **Tómas Hotel** (see **Accommodations,** below) are extremely helpful; they also have their own snorkeling and dive shops. Maralyn at **Rasta Pasta Pizza Amor** (see **Food,** below) possesses a wealth of tips for the budget-conscious.

Currency Exchange: Atlantic Bank Ltd. (tel. 21-95; fax 21-13), just south of the town center on Front St. Changes dollars and traveler's checks. Cash advances on Visa and MC. Open Mon.-Fri. 8am-2pm, Sat. 8:30am-noon. Strangely, **Castleberry Ltd.** at the **Spindrift Hotel** across the street offers rates better than 2:1 for U.S. traveler's checks.

Flights: The **San Pedro airstrip** is located at the southwest end of town and can be reached by taxi or foot. **Island Air** (tel. 24-35) sends hourly flights to Belize City Municipal Airport daily from 7am-5pm (15min., one way BZ$47) and also services Corozal (three times daily, 35min., one way BZ$64). **Tropic Air** (tel. 20-12) flies to Belize City with the same frequency and prices. **Maya Air** (tel. 26-11) has the cheapest flights (5 daily, 7am-5:30pm, BZ$43). Flights stop on request at Caye Caulker. Reserve several days in advance during the high season (Nov.-May).

Taxis: By the airport in the morning and near Elvi's Kitchen on Middle St., mid-town, after 6pm. Trips within town cost BZ$5; outside of town BZ$10-15.

Market: Rock's Store (tel. 20-44), on Middle St. Stocks everything from suntan lotion to fresh bread; the fluorescent purple columns will lead you there from blocks away. Open daily 6:30am-10pm.

Laundromat: J's (tel. 23-73), on Middle St. near the center of town. Look for the dancing frog sign. Full service up to 5kg, BZ$10. Open Mon.-Sat. 8am-8pm (except Wed., closes at 6pm), Sun. 8am-2pm.

Pharmacy: San Carlos Pharmacy (tel. 29-18), on north end of Middle St. Open Mon.-Sat. 8am-noon and 2-9pm, Sun. 9am-noon and 6-9pm. 24hr. emergency service.

Medical Services: San Pedro Lion's Clinic (tel. 20-73), behind the airstrip. Open Mon.-Fri. 8:30am-noon and 1:30-4pm. Open 24hr. for emergencies. **Sub-Aquatic Safety Services of Belize, Ltd.** (tel. 28-51), 2 doors north of the clinic, has a hyperbaric compression chamber for divers.

Police: (tel. 911 or 20-22), on Front St., just north of Atlantic Bank; turn right before Central Park. Open 24hr.

Post Office: (tel. 22-50), just off of Front St. near the banks. *Poste Restante* available. Open Mon.-Thurs. 8am-noon and 1-5pm, Fri. 8am-noon and 1-4:30pm.

Telephones: Several public phones dot Front St. **Belize Telecommunications Ltd. (BTL)** (tel. 21-99), at the north end of Middle St. just past the bellowing electric generator. Free collect and AT&T credit card calls to the U.S.; otherwise, you'll pay around BZ$10 per minute. Open Mon.-Fri. 8am-noon and 1-4pm, Sat. 8am-noon.

Telephone code for San Pedro: 026.

ACCOMMODATIONS

Inexpensive rooms are more scarce here than on Caye Caulker, especially during high season, but during low season many proprietors will negotiate their prices.

Milo's (tel. 20-33), at the north end of Front St. across from the cemetery (Beware: there are 2 other places called Milo's.) The office is in the grocery store below. Exquisitely cheap for San Pedro. Decent, aquamarine rooms with shared bath. Check that the fan works; it can get mighty steamy at night. Checkout at noon. Singles BZ$22; doubles BZ$28; triples BZ$39. Traveler's checks accepted.

Ruby's Hotel (tel. 20-63; fax 24-34; email rubys@btl.net), across from the school on Front St.'s south end. Sits right on the water, for optimal sea view and breeze. Capable management teems with San Pedro know-how. Hot water showers, but bring your own towel. Checkout at noon. Doubles BZ$27, with bath on 2nd floor BZ$54; upstairs rooms rise to BZ$64 in the high season. To reserve, send 1 night's deposit. Credit cards, personal and traveler's checks accepted.

Tómas Hotel (tel. 20-61), at the north side of Front St. So long as you don't rouse him from a *siesta*, Tómas, the endearing proprietor, will make you feel welcome; if you don't speak Spanish, this process will involve a lot of gesturing. (No need to worry, other employees speak English.) Clean rooms with newly tiled private baths and strong ceiling fans. Singles and doubles BZ$50, with A/C BZ$70 plus tax; triples BZ$60, plus tax. Checkout at noon. Visa, traveler's checks accepted. Affiliated with the **Amigos del Mar** dive shop.

Hotel del Río (tel. 22-86), about 0.8km north of town along the beach. A bargain for groups, especially during the low season. The Badillo family rents out affordable "economy" quarters that sleep up to 9 people for BZ$24 per person (2 person min.). 2 expensive huts with full kitchens each sleep up to 5 (BZ$160). After the winter rush, prices fall by as much as BZ$20.

FOOD

The plight of the hungry budget traveler in San Pedro can be grim indeed. Remember that Belizeans eat out only occasionally; they can't afford the insanely boosted prices you see at the resorts. Look hard and find a few restaurants that serve big plates of seafood and local (i.e. Belizean and Mexican) cuisine at reasonable rates. If you're just out to fill your tummy with *something,* try the nameless restaurant on the west side of Front St., where the grub is copious and super cheap. **Ambergris Delight** on Middle St. fits the bill. Otherwise, check out the various fruit vendors on Middle St. and the locals hawking hot dogs, burgers, and home-cooked eats in front of Children's Park on Front St. in the evenings.

Rasta Pasta Pizza Amor (tel. 38-55; email rastapasta@btl.net), from the southern end of Front St., follow the beach path a half mile, past the infamous Belize Yacht Club; it's upstairs at the Playador Hotel—look for the Canadian flag out front. American-born, former dead-head Maralyn and her Rastafarian husband, Gil, tend to attract well-heeled tourists staying at neighboring resorts, but they're committed to tailoring their savory dishes to each individual's budgetary needs. Starving artists can barter mural paintings for sustenance. Famous jerk chicken with rice, beans, and salad (BZ$12) and monstrous chicken, fish or veggie burritos (BZ$12). Or eat that fish you caught today with rice and beans (BZ$10). Specialty vegetarian meals. Mastercard, Visa, traveler's checks accepted. Open daily 7am-9:30pm.

Reality Cafe (tel. 35-86), on Front St., a couple of blocks north of the center of town. Linger over a mix of seafood, American, and local dishes, on a patio overlooking the ocean as locals play volleyball at sunset. Half-orders of more-than-generous breakfasts cut costs as well as cholesterol intakes (*Huevos rancheros* BZ$10). The bar downstairs is clogged with noisy Americans. Open Tues.-Thurs. 7am-10pm. Mon. closes at 4pm; Wed. at 9pm.

Elvi's Kitchen (tel. 21-76), on Middle St. near the center of town. Built around a tree with sand on the floor, Elvi's will make you feel like you never left the beach. Not quite Graceland, but the locals still pronounce the name like the King's. Live music Thurs.-Fri. Open Mon.-Sat. 11am-2pm and 5:30-10pm. "*The* place for seafood" may have priced its fishies out of sight, but Creole fare may be had at more reasonable prices (BZ$10-20).

Ruby's, next to the hotel of the same name, serves tasty banana bread (BZ$2), cinnamon rolls (BZ$3), and other snacks.

SIGHTS AND ENTERTAINMENT

Dive-a-rama. Dives-R-Us. Diver-roni. *Ad nauseam.* This is some of the best diving in the world, and even experienced divers will be amazed by the colorful array of fish and coral around Ambergris Caye. Try to negotiate prices during the off-season, as many of the operators are willing to haggle. For divers not certified in scuba, snorkeling at the nearby **Hol Chan Marine Reserve** (BZ$5) affords an opportunity to swim

BELIZE

amid barracudas, moray eels, lobsters, yellowtail snappers, parrotfish, eagle rays, and even the occasional benevolent shark. For thrill seekers, a new dive site, **Shark-Ray Alley,** more or less guarantees a swim with the big fish—nurse sharks and sting rays congregate as snorkeling guides toss diced fish carcasses overboard. A two-stop snorkeling trip, including gear (but not park admission fees), starts at around BZ$345. Try **Ruby's** (tel. 20-63) or **Amigos del Mar** (tel. 26-48) for low-priced trips.

For experienced divers, many dive shops make regular trips to the **Blue Hole** at the Lighthouse Reef Atoll. Nearly 300m in diameter and 144m deep, the hole forms a nearly perfect sapphire circle in the pale teal water. The hole was first explored in the late 1980s by Jacques Cousteau, who braved the depths in a miniature submarine; today, it's a world-famous site. Qualified divers can explore mind-blowing stalagmite and stalactite formations and swim below an undercut canyon believed to have been a land cave 10,000 years ago. A daytrip usually includes three meals, gear, and several stops (about US$165). Snorkelers can tag along for about US$125.

The *Southern Beauty,* a glass-bottomed boat, leaves from the **Tackle Box Bar** dock near the center of town, escorting snorkelers and anyone else to the Marine Reserve. It departs twice daily, at 9am and 2pm, for half-day excursions (one-stop trips BZ$20; two stops BZ$25; snorkel gear BZ$6).

Stop at the **Tackle Box Bar** at the end of the pier on the southern side of town to peer at the sharks that they keep out back (live music Fri. and Sat.; open Mon.-Thurs. 9am-midnight, Fri.-Sat. 9am-2am). **Tarzan's Nite Club** (tel. 29-47), right in the middle of town, boasts a big dance floor complete with videos (Fri. and Sat.), Jane look-alike barmaids, and a waterfall. (Open Tues.-Thurs. and Sun. 9pm-midnight, Fri.-Sat. 9pm-3am; around BZ$5 cover charge.) **Big Daddy's** is just across the way. There's dancing and live music on weekends with cover charge (varies, but usually BZ$15).

WESTERN BELIZE

Belize's **Western Highway** runs 124km from Belize City to the frontier, spanning grassy savannas before winding its way into the Maya Mountains. Although it's possible to power from Belize City to Tikal in one exhausting day, a few days of adventuring in western Belize are warranted before continuing the trip.

According to Belizean archaeologist Jaime Awe, there are more unexcavated Maya sites in Belize than there are modern houses. Hardly surprising, since it is estimated that the Maya population, at its peak, was four times Belize's present population of 200,000. Many of the small, grass-covered mounds visible from the roadside are, in fact, Maya platforms, temples, and plazas that will remain untouched until there is enough money to begin excavating new sites. You can visit the **Belize Zoo** and tickle a jaguar, spend the night in **San Ignacio,** trek through the nearby ruins of **Xunantunich,** explore **Mountain Pine Ridge** national forest, or float down the nearby Macal River. From San Ignacio, the great ruins of **Tikal** in the Guatemalan Petén are a hop, skip, and a bumpy four-hour bus ride away.

▓ Belmopan

Hurricane Hattie had it in for Belize City; the storm, which washed much of the then-capital city away, was the last straw for the country's government. Belize's leaders, tired of being pummeled by storms along the coast, packed things up and moved to Belmopan, where they created a new capital. Nowadays, the newly formed city is exactly what it feels like: a functional, bureaucratic, and bizarrely hollow remnant of the 70s. Until the National Museum (currently under construction) is completed, there will be very little for tourists to do here.

Independence Plaza, the heart of the national government, serves as the center of the town. The highway runs to the west, and the **Ring Road** circumscribes the town. The Western portion of the Ring Road is called **Constitution Drive.** All buses stop at

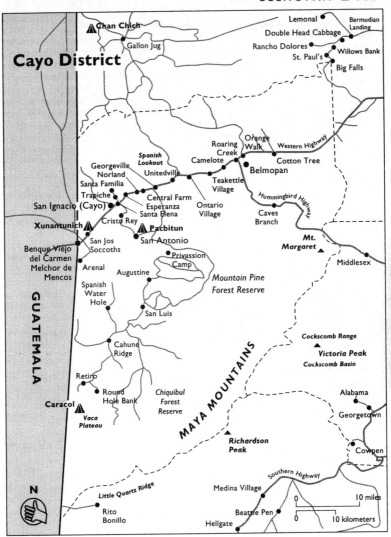

Cayo District

the market place, which is adjacent to Independence Plaza. The **Belize Bank** serves as a good point of reference from the market. Police warn that the south end of town can be dangerous at night.

Belmopan has no tourist office; limited information is available at the **International Cafe** by the Novelo's terminal. **Barclay's Bank** (tel. 223-82 or 235-79), behind the Belize Bank, exchanges U.S. dollars, pounds sterling, Canadian dollars, and traveler's checks (BZ$1 for amounts less than BZ$100) at a not-so-great exchange rate. They provide cash advances on Mastercard, Visa, and Discover with no additional fee (open Mon.-Thurs. 8am-1pm, Fri. 8am-4:30pm). **Buses** leave from the market. **Novelo's** has a terminal on the west side of the market, with buses to **Belize City** (every 30min., 6am-12:30pm, 1½hr., BZ$3.50) and to **San Ignacio** and **Benque Viejo** (every 30min., 12:30-9pm, 70min., BZ$2.50). **Brodie's** (tel. 230-78), a well-stocked **supermarket,** is a 10-minute walk from the market—take the concrete walkway east from Independence Plaza, then take the left fork past the little school (open Mon.-Thurs. 8am-noon and 2-7pm, Fri.-Sat. 8am-noon and 2-9pm). **Cardinal Pharmacy** (tel. 228-07), located just south of Brodie's, has feminine hygiene products and over-the-counter and prescription drugs (open Mon.-Thurs. 8:30am-noon and 2:30-7pm, Fri.-Sat. 8:30am-noon and 2:30-9pm). The **hospital** (emergency tel. 225-18) is located north of the market on Ring Road; the office (tel. 222-64) is around back (open Mon.-Fri. 8am-5pm). Ambulance service is available. The **police** (emergency tel. 911, office tel. 222-22) are located northeast of the market in Independence Plaza. Call 911 in **emergencies,** though you can also call the office number (open 24 hr). The **post office,** by the police station, offers *Poste Restante* (open Mon.-Thurs. 8am-noon and 1-4:30pm, Fri. 8am-noon and 1-4pm). **Telephones, telegrams** and **fax** service are available at **BTL** (tel. 221-93; fax 223-66), located south of the market on the Ring Road. It's open Mon.-Fri. 8am-noon and 1-4pm. The **telephone code** is 08.

If you can help it, hold back until San Ignacio; otherwise, grab grub from one of the many vendors around the bus depot. There are only three hotels in town, and two of them are *way* outside budget range. **El Rey,** 23 Moho (tel. 234-38), lives up to its name (the King) by default. Go east from the hospital, take the third left from the main road, then the second right. The rates are reasonable, the rooms clean and spacious with private baths. (Checkout 11am. Singles BZ$35; doubles BZ$45. No A/C.) The local favorite for food is **Caladium** (tel. 227-54), at the north end of the market, which serves weight-watching portions of the standard fare (open Mon.-Fri. 8am-8pm, Sat. 8am-7pm).

Belmopan is a study in 60s cinderblock architecture and offers few sights and little scenery. The **National Museum,** currently under construction, will hold Belize's official collection of Maya artifacts. Until then, would-be archaeologists must content themselves with a scale model of the structure, on display at the **Department of Museums,** the white building on the southeast side of the market.

■ San Ignacio

The tightly packed thoroughfare of San Ignacio (pop. 8000) creates an impression of constant bustling and spunkiness not merited by its size. The village boomed between 1920 and 1950 as a center for the vigorous farming of mahogany and *chicle* (gum). Eventually the trees dwindled, Mr. Wrigley found cheap synthetic substances to placate gum-popping teenage mandibles, and both industries fell into precipitous decline. Though today livestock and agriculture account for most revenue, the Cayo district—of which San Ignacio is the capital—attracts increasing numbers of ecotourists who come to hike, canoe, and ride on horseback through the area's stunning parks and archaeological sites. The result is bittersweet, as the town is usually packed with travelers. San Ignacio's inexpensive food and lodging make it a good base for exploring the bountiful Mountain Pine Ridge Forest Reserve, the Maya ruins of Xunantunich, and the dense jungle to the south.

ORIENTATION

Entering San Ignacio after passing through unexceptional, neighboring **Santa Elena,** you'll pass over the Macal River on Hawkesburg Bridge—Belize's only suspension bridge—which was built in 1949. Entering the bridge requires passage through one of Belize's three traffic lights but, even when the light functions, locals rarely acknowledge it. Buses stop by the town's main intersection. **Burns Av.,** San Ignacio's commercial strip, runs north to south, and the two streets branching off of it lead to everything of interest not itself on Burns. Down Burns to your right is **Eva's Restaurant** (see **Food,** below), a good place to get directions.

PRACTICAL INFORMATION

Tourist information: Fast becoming a legend, **Eva's Restaurant,** 22 Burns Av., serves up travel tips to nearly every visitor who visits San Ignacio. Ask here about arranging eco-trips and hiring ruins guides. Open Sun.-Thurs. 6:30am-11pm, Fri.-Sat. 6:30am-midnight. Info also can be found at hotels such as Pacz and Martha's.

Currency exchange: At most stores, hotels, restaurants, or at **Atlantic Bank** (tel. 23-47), one block south of Eva's on Burns Av. The bank also offers cash advances on credit cards (fee BZ$10). Open Mon.-Tues. and Thurs.-Fri. 8am-noon and 1-3pm, Wed. 8am-1pm, Sat. 8:30am-noon. If all else fails, don't worry—the money changers of San Ignacio will find you.

Buses: Fares and schedules change faster than the traffic lights. At least one line makes the 120km trip to **Belize City** every hour. **Shaw's** leaves for **Belmopan** (every hr. on the ½hr., 7:30am-12:30pm; every ½hr. from 1-4:45pm, 45min., BZ$2.25). After noon, **Batty Brothers** takes the route over (2½hr., BZ$5). The **Z-Line** also goes to Belmopan (1½hr., BZ$2) and changes to **Dangriga** (4hr., BZ$10). **Shaw's** sends two buses to **Ciudad Melchor de Mencos** at the **Guatemalan border** (Mon.-Sat., 7:30 and 8:30am, 45min., BZ$1.50), as do most of the carriers. Do not take a late bus to Guatemala; it's not safe at night.

Taxis: From San Ignacio to Melchor for BZ$20.

Bike rentals: From Peter at **Hotel Pacz.** BZ$5 per hr., BZ$20 per day, or BZ$50 for a weekend. Add BZ$10 during high season.

Laundromat: The **August Laundromat** is in the back of Martha's Restaurant by Hi-Et Hotel (BZ$7; open Mon.-Sat. 7am-8pm, Sun. 8:30am-2pm).

Pharmacy: On Burns Av. under the Venus Hotel. Open Mon.-Sat. 8am-noon, 1-5pm, and 7-9pm, Sun. 9am-noon.

Police: (tel. 20-22). Just west of the bridge at the town park; open 24hr.

Internet: At Eva's (surprise!). BZ$3 sends whatever you can write in 20min. Other services are BZ$8 per half hour.

Post office: Above the police station; take the stairs to the right, through the door labeled "district commissioner." *Poste restante* available (tel. 20-49; open Mon.-Thurs. 8am-noon and 1-4:30pm, Fri. 8am-noon and 1-4pm).

Telephones: BTL (tel. 20-90) has phones, as well as **telegrams** and **fax** service, at its new location on Eve St. Take a right approaching the main intersection from Eva's, in the pink stucco building upstairs from the credit union. Open Mon.-Fri. 8am-noon and 1-4pm. After hours, use the public phone in front of the building.

Telephone code: 092.

ACCOMMODATIONS

Tropicool Hotel (tel. 30-52), ½ block down from Eva's. Clean rooms, low prices, and the hottest water this side of Old Faithful. Don't mind the German shepherds snarling as you pass; they're securely tied. Lounge with a TV and a truly cool upstairs bar. Singles BZ$20; doubles BZ$25.

Hi-Et Hotel, up one block from Eva's around the sharp right turn. Lacks Hyatt splendor, but has clean rooms with balconies (and meager locks). Be sure to wear a towel to the bathroom; you'll pass the living room on your way. The friendly owner lends out his canoe. Checkout at 11am (singles BZ$10; doubles BZ$20).

Pacz Hotel (tel. 21-10), near Hi-Et. Owner Pete will keep you informed of everything happening in and around town. Clean and comfortable rooms, and one of the bathrooms has hot water. Checkout 1pm. Traveler's checks accepted. Singles BZ$20; doubles BZ$35; triples BZ$40.

Central Hotel (tel. 22-53), on Burns Av., next to Eva's and upstairs. Offers simple rooms with fans, coconut-shell ashtrays, and hot water for those oddballs who need a hot shower in the tropics. The balcony has a hammock for *siestas*. Checkout 10am. Singles BZ$19; doubles BZ$22; triples BZ$28.

Mida's Eco-Resort (tel. 31-72, 21-01), a 10min. walk north of Eva's on Burns Av. Camping BZ$7 per person. Ask Bob at Eva's about free pick-up. Pricey rooms are also available: singles with private bath BZ$40; doubles BZ$45.

The jungle around San Ignacio hides retreats and lodges ranging from back-to-basics affairs to full-blown resorts:

Parrot Nest (tel. 37-02), 5km out of San Ignacio in Bullet Tree Falls. Cozies right up to the Mopan River. Listen to the overwhelming sounds of the jungle from your treehouse or cabin. Owner Fred radiates good vibes and is starting a botanical garden near the treehouses.

Rancho de Los Amigos (phones usually out of order; have Bob at Eva's radio them), a strenuous 2km hike from the turnoff into San José Succotz directly across from the Xunantunich ferry. Way out there. An acupuncturist and a nutritionist have cleared only enough trees to build two immaculately clean huts and a dining area where all the cooking is done over fires. Call ahead. Two meals included with a *casita*, US$25 per person. Camping available.

FOOD

The cuisine here is cheap, delicious, and filling. **Erva's Supermarket** (tel. 28-21), under Hotel Pacz, offers homey cooking in a clean restaurant. Three tacos or a sandwich cost BZ$3; Creole bread goes for BZ$0.60. **Eva's Restaurant,** 22 Burns Av. (tel. 22-67), has traditionally been a home base for local tourism and crawls with sated, smoking, young-at-heart types feasting on beautiful burritos. The behemoth chicken burrito (BZ$7) is particularly tasty. The word "vegetarian" also appears on the menu with refreshing frequency (open Sun.-Thurs. 7am-11pm, Fri.-Sat. 7am-midnight). **Mystic Moon,** up Burns Av. to the right of the police station, sells shakes for BZ$2.50-4, soup for BZ$5, and sandwiches for BZ$6.50 (open daily 8am-10pm). **Sandcastle Restaurant** offers solid Belizean and Mexican food and a lively atmosphere. Rice and beans cost BZ$7; a pizza burrito is BZ$9.25 (open Mon.-Sat. 7am-11pm). **Maxim's Chinese Restaurant** (tel. 22-83), two blocks behind Eva's, serves up huge portions of tasty Chinese and Belizean food, usually for less than BZ$10 (open 11:30am-3pm and 5:30pm-midnight).

SIGHTS

Bandits are notoriously active on the road between Melchor de Mencos at the Guatemala-Belize border and Tikal. If you want to make the trip from San Ignacio (and cannot travel to Tikal from the south), travel only during the day.

San Ignacio can serve as a departure point for those wishing to see the spectacular ruins at **Tikal,** Guatemala. Catch an early Benque Viejo bus (also known as the Melchor bus) and take it to Succotz, the Xunantunich ferry—across the street is the **Guatemalan consulate** (open Mon.-Fri. 9am-1pm). Ask about getting a visa there, then catch the next bus to Melchor. Pay about US$5 to cross the border (no Belizean currency). Make sure the immigration officers don't hoodwink you; they have a bad reputation. Just outside the doors buses and minivans wait to speed tourists over the backbreaking Guatemalan roads (5, 6, 7, 8, 11am, 1, and 4pm, 3½hr., Q10). The safer and more comfortable route is by taxi, but beware of hustlers. For four people, the standard price is US$10-15 per person. Just wait for more tourists to show up, then ride together. By car, the journey is said to take a mere two hours. Avoid traveling during festivals (especially Easter), as the bandits are more active at these times. Leave as many valuables behind as possible and, if held up, *do not* argue with the bandits. They don't want to hurt you; they just want your money.

A daytrip arranged through one of the local tour operators may insure a much more pleasant visit to Tikal. US$65-75 should get you a tour of the site with an experienced guide and few headaches.

Only 800m from San Ignacio lie the lazy traveler's Maya ruins; it's no trek at all to **Cahal Pech** (Place of the Ticks). Although Cahal Pech is only a medium-sized Maya center, it has produced some of the earliest evidence of occupation in the area (from 1000 BC until AD 900). Excavation at the site only began in 1988, and archaeologists are still at work there. As researchers sift through buckets of dirt in search of stone tools and other artifacts, you'll be able to see the various layers of soil where different generations of Maya spread new floors across the entire plaza. Current excavators and visiting archaeologists grumble about the overly imaginative restoration of the site; you should take the masks depicted on the temple and the main arch with, as they say, "a bucket of salt." Places where the crews didn't get carried away with cement can be found back behind the main "range structure" at the rear of the plaza, where one can follow narrow paths through the dark rooms of the royal chamber. Archaeologists are impressed with the remaining red dye on some ledges in these rooms. While work on the site is far from complete, the ruins are worth the hour or two it takes to see them (admission BZ$10). To avoid the uphill climb, take a cab from San Ignacio (BZ$5). Be sure to clarify that you're going to the Cahal Pech ruins. Or see **El Pilar,** an extensive Maya archaeological site still in the preliminary stages of excavation, near Parrot Nest at Bullet Tree Falls (see Accommodations, p. 157). Canoeing and horseback riding are available (riding: full day with or without guides BZ$35). A cab there costs BZ$6-10; just ask for Parrot Nest (BZ$40 for a cabin; breakfast BZ$4.50, dinner BZ$9).

There are a few possibilities for those who want to enjoy the local rivers without getting wet. Fully outfitted three-person canoes rent for about BZ$35 (without a guide) at the **Snooty Fox.** The Macal is a mellow river, and the only real hazards to boaters are the shallows, where you may have to get out and push your boat upstream. Starting by the bridge, canoers can paddle upstream beyond the town's noise and into the lush, peaceful jungle. Any place on the bank can serve as a refreshing swimming spot, and the downstream trip back to town is a piece of cake.

Guided tours are another alternative (BZ$25 per day). Local operators offer a variety of trips; ask at Eva's or the Pagz Hotel for more information.

Canoe tours are the best way to visit the **Panti Nature Trail** or **Rainforest Medicine Trail** (tel. 38-70) at Ix Chel Farm, 10km west of San Ignacio near Chaa Creek, where you can learn about the astounding medicinal uses of the area's flora. The Panti trail snakes through **Healer's Hut,** a small house made entirely of earth and plants. Admission for self-guided tours with a pamphlet (BZ$11) is often a better deal than the guided tours (BZ$15-50), during which a guide essentially reads the pamphlet to you. The trail starts at the corner of Old Bengue and Chaa Creek Rd. Full day tours, including a trip to a butterfly farm, can be arranged with **Toni's Canoes** for BZ$25. Talk to Bob at Eva's.

The hills south of San Ignacio feature some of the best **spelunking** around. For the Maya, the caves were sacred entrances to the underworld domiciles of their gods. Shards of pottery used in Maya ceremonies remain in the caves to this day. Both Peter at the Pagz Hotel and Ian Anderson's **Caves Branch Jungle Camp** arrange walking and rafting daytrips (US$35-65). The camp is located near Blue Hole National Park and also offers jungle hikes and canoe trips, as well as primitive, but comfortable accommodations. (Cabins: single US$30; double US$40. Bunkhouse: US$15 per person. Camping: US$5 per person.)

After day hikes and canoeing trips, you can drain the last of your sweat by dancing the night away. A group usually gathers at Eva's after dinner to chug some Belikins before heading over to their preferred hot spot. Most popular is the **Blue Angel** night club on Hudson St. Rumor has it that the fence on the second-floor balcony was constructed after rambunctious British soldiers nearly threw someone over. (Cover charge on weekends for live bands varies, but it's always more for men than women. Open Tues.-Thurs. and Sun. 7pm-midnight, Fri.-Sat. 7pm-3am.) A recently opened, but increasingly popular choice is Santa Elena's **Snooty Fox** (tel. 21-50), which boasts that inscrutable name, a pool table, a great view, and a shifting atmosphere that varies from junior high school dance to bacchanal. The **Cahal Pech Tavern** sits on the hill and is open weekends after 9pm for dancing. Locals warn against walking back to San Ignacio from Santa Elena after dark.

■ Near San Ignacio

SAN ANTONIO

The origins of San Antonio (known locally as TaNah, Mayan for "Our Home") are shrouded in myth. Some claim that the town's earliest settlers lived in nearby Moun-

BELIZE

tain Pine Ridge, but were brought down to TaNah while hunting. When the prey magically disappeared, the hunters took it as a sign from the Maya god Yum Kax-Ku to start a new settlement. Others tell a different story: when some chickens and turkeys were missing from a nearby village, the two newest villagers were blamed and whipped. Upon leaving town, the two ominously warned, "You will pay for this deed." Villagers started dying inexplicably, and the town was deemed cursed. Its residents fled, heading to what is now San Antonio.

Free from evil spells of every kind, San Antonio (pop. 1500) has since become a living, breathing center of Maya culture. Among the villagers are a snake doctor, an old master healer who supposedly was once sent to administer to the Queen of England, and the Maya García sisters, whose **museum** of Maya art (admission BZ$6) is the town's **tourist center** (open daily 7am-6pm).

Two trucks a day (10 and 10:30am) take villagers home to San Antonio and will let tourists ride along for BZ$2; they return the next day. The village offers only a few services. The only **BTL telephone** (tel. 32-16 or 32-66) is three blocks up from the police station at the crossroads, while the mini-**post office** is inside the Indita Maya Restaurant. The only accommodation in town is the **Chichan Ka Lodge,** a traditional Maya building at the Garcías' place (singles BZ$25; doubles BZ$30). **Hilltop camping** provides a plot of ground for BZ$5 per person. Some pass the night in San Antonio, but most are just stopping by on their way to Mountain Pine Ridge. If you do stay, be sure to look at the horses' manes in the morning. According to legend, perfectly trimmed manes indicate that dwarves from the hills rode them in the night and wrapped their feet in the horses' hair.

MOUNTAIN PINE RIDGE RESERVE

Mountain Pine Ridge, just south of San Ignacio, is a great daytrip for civilization's discontented, especially if they have a car. Tall conifers, wide mountains, ancient caves, and clear streams grace the large forest reserve, accessible by a road branching off the Western Highway just east of San Ignacio at Georgeville. A list of guides willing to take you to the reserve is available at Eva's and at the Sandcastle; it's not difficult to assemble the required five-person group (expect to pay BZ$35 per person). Without your own wheels or a guide, renting a car is the only way you'll make it to the reserve. The **Venus Hotel** (tel. 32-03) rents Suzuki Samurais for BZ$125 per day, not including gas. Those depending on their own car should make sure it's sturdy and in good condition—the roads are brutal, and many rental vehicles are prone to breakdown. To reach the reserve, follow the road until you reach San Antonio and then turn left; a few miles later, turn right. Signs will guide you, and it's hard to get lost. You're in the reserve when the green jungle gives way to tall pines.

The turn-off for **Hidden Valley Falls** is about a 25-minute drive past the main gate (open 8am-6pm; BZ$2). A left turn here brings you a slow 16km down a steep hill; spectacular views of the pine-covered slopes, soaring birds, and a plummeting 300m waterfall will be your reward. Continuing on the main road, the most practical next stop is the town of **Augustine,** where you can find the only official camping in the park at the **Douglas D'Silva Forest Station,** to the left as you drive in. Many recommend staying overnight here to get the most out of the Reserve. Taking the road to the right through Augustine leads visitors to the caves at **Río Frío.** To the right of the road is a small nature trail where you can see *chicle*-producing sapodilla trees, along with some mahogany trees that the British seem to have missed. The most impressive site, however, is the **cave** at trail's end. A sign erected by Colorado State University students reads: "Tell me your secrets and I'll guard them too." Whether or not you choose to spill your guts, the massive main cave inspires respect. Openings on both ends cast light on stalactite formations, dark pools, and naturally eroded stone steps; the towering ceiling will take your damp breath away. Stones form an easily manageable path to the cave's heart; there's a path the locals know to the left, if you're facing upstream. The ledges to the right, however, are quite dangerous. Bring a flashlight and hiking companions. If the path is negotiable, it leads through the cave to a pleasant nature walk. Scope out the spooky bats that snooze in the holes in the ceiling.

What the Río Frío takes out of you, the pools at **Río On** will put right back in. Ten minutes back on the road toward Cayo, on the left, rocks have trapped the descending river, forming several ideal swimming holes (don't dive in head first). Picnic tables a bit further on provide a great view of the tumbling waters. A little squirming and pushing on your part can turn the smaller falls into a water slide, so beware of unexpectedly slippery rocks. On the way back, a unique but expensive place to grab a beer (BZ$4) and enjoy the view is Francis Ford Coppola's **Blancaneaux Lodge** (tel. 38-78), a few kilometers away from the gate. This posh resort has its own hydroelectric plant; even so, Coppola only flies down for special occasions. Though the resort would be a lovely setting in which to wile away the hours before the apocalypse, now it's fun just to visit.

CARACOL

A few years ago, the ruins at Caracol were accessible only to the mightiest of vehicles. Today the road has improved considerably and Caracol is within a manageable one-hour car ride. Indeed, the most difficult part of getting to Caracol is obtaining a visitor's permit—stop at the **Douglas D'Silva Forest Station** in Augustine and, within minutes, you can be back on the road to the ruins, permit in hand. Although only partially excavated, Caracol is thought by some to rival Tikal in importance. Led by Lord Water, Caracol defeated Tikal in a war in AD 562. Since 1985, archaeologists have discovered over 4000 structures on the site's 88 acres, including a royal tomb, carved stone slabs depicting magical dwarves, and the 42-meter-high **Kanaa palace,** which offers a stunning view of the surrounding jungle-enshrouded hills. Caracol can only be viewed with a tour guide, and tours are conducted only a few times a day (schedules vary). The guides will show you plenty. The tour is free, but tips are appreciated. Make sure you get to see the 700-year-old Ceiba tree. Take the time to absorb Caracol's beauty; the shrill insects above will hypnotize you whether you like it or not.

If renting a car is out of the question, getting a tour or taxi to Caracol is pretty expensive. The going rate is US$50 per person, although Hector, a local driver, will take his spacious and comfy station wagon to Caracol for US$150—in a group of five, each pays US$30 per person. As always, ask at Eva's for more information.

XUNANTUNICH

The ruins at **Xunantunich** stand shorter than Caracol, but they're much easier to access from San Ignacio. On the road from Cayo to Guatemala you can see **El Castillo,** the main temple of Xunantunich, towering in the distance to the right. Xunantunich (Maiden of the Rock) was an important city in the late Classical period (AD 700-900) and either a rival or a satellite settlement of Tikal. Only partially excavated and studied, the ruins at Xunantunich include an impressive pyramid. Like many Maya sites, the accessible ruins here are mostly former residences and temples. While workers lived down in the Mopan river valley, where the soil was more fertile, the aristocracy resided here, with special paths connecting their homes to important structures.

The steps of **El Castillo** lead up to the top of the temple; looking down on the plaza, envisioning humbled crowds below, it's easy to wax megalomaniacal. El Castillo dwarfs the other temples and unexcavated mounds. Scamper up its lower portion, which is still engulfed by vegetation, to the partially restored stucco frieze on the eastern corner. On display here are masks devoted to **Kinich Ahau,** the sun deity, and **Ixchel,** the moon god. Swing around back, then up the not-so-obvious central stairs to the top. From El Castillo's reconstructed roof, the settlements of **Succotz, Benque Viejo del Carmen,** and **Melchor de Mencos** (in Guatemala) are visible from left to right, tucked into the green hills.

After investigating the tower (and turning your legs to pudding in the process), examine the carved rock next to the offices for a pleasant change of pace. Some of the stones seem blank or non-representational, but expert analysis has revealed hidden images of the god **K'awil,** a serpent-footed deity associated with ancestors. The town of **San José Succotz** lies across the Mopan River and 1½km up a dirt road from

BELIZE

Xunantunich. About 9km from San Ignacio, Succotz is accessible via a *colectivo* that shuttles between the Esso station in San Ignacio and the border town of Benque Viejo del Carmen (BZ$1). **Batty Bus Service** heads to Benque Viejo from San Ignacio (every hr. on the hr. until noon, BZ$1). From Succotz take the small cable-drawn **ferry** across the Mopan; for a real hoot, ask to operate the ferry yourself (daily 8am-4pm; free). The dirt road leading up to the ruins is rough and steep, making for a vigorous hike or a jangly drive (ruins open daily 8am-5pm; admission BZ$10).

SOUTHERN COAST

▧ Dangriga

If you're trundling down to Dangriga by bus or car from Belize City, consider opting for the Hummingbird Highway route through Belmopan. Although somewhat longer than the Coastal Highway, its smoother ride whisks you past some of the best scenery in the country. Crack open the window on your way for an engaging olfactory journey. First you'll catch a whiff of fresh mist off the Cohune palm trees, which were sacred to the Maya for their brilliant performances as food, roofing, and fuel. As the rolling hills flatten out, brace your nose—the bitter smoke is a result of the area's slash-and-burn farming. Soon the odor of smoke will give way to the smell of the sweet blossoms and endless citrus groves which support the local economy. Only when salty, fishy air wafts your way will you be near Dangriga (pop. 8100).

Once known as Stann Creek, this oceanfront community was established by Puritans from New Providence who farmed Tobacco Caye and the Coastal Belt and used the town as a trading post. Today, most residents are Garifunas, as well as Black Caribs of mixed African and native Caribbean descent whose ancestors fled Honduras in 1823 in the wake of a failed rebellion. Dangriga (which means "standing water") has become a center for both Garifuna culture and, unfortunately, pesky hustlers, whose mischief occasionally rouses the city from its otherwise peaceful existence.

ORIENTATION

Orienting yourself in Dangriga is very easy if you keep in mind that the ocean is to the east. One main road runs parallel to the coast and crosses the **Stann Creek River,** which flows into the sea; the road is called **St. Vincent Street** south of the bridge and **Commerce St.** north of it. Aggressive hustlers often congregate near the bridge. Several blocks south of the bridge, **Mahogany Lane** connects St. Vincent St. to the sea and to **Alijo Benji** park, named after the Garifuna chief who led his people from Honduras to Dangriga. A looming red-and-white sign for the **Chaleanor Hotel** marks the junction of St. Vincent St. and Mahogany Lane. Police warn that the "back-a-town" area around the Havana bridge (0.5km south of the main bridge), is unsafe at night.

PRACTICAL INFORMATION

Tourist Office: The most helpful source of information is **The New River Café** (tel. 399-08), just east of the southern base of the bridge. Open Mon.-Sat. 7am-9:30pm. On Sun., and often on other days as well, Louise at the **Bluefield Lodge** (tel. 227-42) can help direct travelers.

Budget Travel: Treasured Travel (tel. 225-78; fax 234-81), a few blocks north of the bridge, upstairs in the turquoise building. Open daily 7am-10pm.

Currency Exchange: Barclay's Bank (tel. 222-40), 3 blocks north of the bridge on the east side of Commerce St., gives cash advances on credit cards and changes traveler's checks. Open Mon.-Thurs. 8am-1pm, Fri. 8am-4:30pm. The best place to change U.S. traveler's checks is **Kuylen Hardware** (tel. 225-73), 10m north of the main bridge. Open Mon.-Thurs. 7:30am-noon and 1:30-5pm, Fri. until 9pm, Sat. 7:30am-1pm.

Buses: Z-line buses (tel. 221-60), next to the river on the south side, serve **Punta Gorda** (Mon.-Sat. noon, 4, 7pm, plus Mon. and Sat. 10am, 5hr., BZ$13), and **Belize City** (8 daily runs, 3hr., BZ$10), with most stopping en route in **Belmopan** (BZ$6). Buy your ticket early and watch your luggage during the trip. Z-Line also goes to **Placencia** (daily at 12:15 and 4:30pm, 3hr., BZ$8). Ritchie's bus (tel. 231-32) goes to Placencia daily at 11:30am and 4:30pm from Ritchie's Store, several blocks south of the bridge. If you miss the connection to Placencia, catch a bus to Mango Creek or Punta Gorda, then take a ferry.

Laundromat: On Commerce St., a few blocks north of the bridge, across from the statue of Christ, the laundromat charges BZ$8.50 per load. Open Mon.-Sat. 9am-noon and 2-8pm.

Pharmacy: Young's Drug Store (tel. 223-19), on Commerce St. Chemist and drug-gist is "licensed to sell drugs and poison," as well as fresh popcorn. Open Mon.-Sat. 8am-noon, 2-4:30pm and 7-9pm.

Hospital: (tel. 220-78), 2 blocks north and 1 block east of the bridge. Follow the frontage road to the east as it curves north. Ambulance available. Open 24hr.

Clinic: Health Centre (tel. 221-84), on Court St. Open Mon.-Fri. 8am-5pm.

Police: 107 Commerce St. (tel. 220-22), north of the river, by Barclay's. Open 24hr.

Post Office: 16 Caney St. (tel. 220-35), on the south side of the bridge; turn east off St. Vincent St. at the Chaleanor Hotel sign onto Mahogany St., then head to the sea. The post office is on the left. Open Mon.-Thurs. 8am-noon and 1-5pm, Fri. 8am-noon and 1-4:30pm.

Telephones and telegrams: Belize Telecommunications Ltd. (BTL) (tel. 220-65; fax 220-38) across the street from the police. Make collect and credit card calls for free; otherwise, pay BZ$9.50 per 3min. to phone the U.S. station-to-station. Open Mon.-Fri. 8am-noon and 1-4pm, Sat. 8am-noon. Offers **telegram** service as well (BZ$0.32 per word to the U.S.).

Telephone code: 05.

ACCOMMODATIONS AND FOOD

Rooms here are basic—expect a taste of Garifuna culture in the restaurants, not the sleeping quarters. You'll find the **Riverside Hotel** (tel. 221-68) on your left as you cross the bridge heading north. The hotel provides spotless rooms and comfy beds. A large living room, replete with hanging macramé planters and wicker furniture, makes for expansive lounging space. The clean, shared bathrooms come with weak showerheads and no hot water. Reservations and traveler's checks are accepted (BZ$20 per person plus tax). The **Bluefield Lodge** (tel. 227-42), one block south and one block west of the bridge, offers the best amenities for your Belizean buck: immaculate rooms, air fresheners, soap, towels, and baths with cold *and* hot water. Owner-manager Louise has a knack for organization worthy of envy; she also aids travelers with plenty o' tips. Singles and doubles cost BZ$27; add BZ$11 for a private bath and TV. Room with 2 double beds and shared bath (BZ$31 for 2 people; BZ$38 for 4). **The Dangriga Central Hotel** (tel. 220-08), one block north of the bridge is grungier than the others, but it's the cheapest spot to crash in town. The Dangriga's mattresses undulate almost as much as its floors—but if it's any consolation, it has a nice balcony with upholstered furniture (BZ$10.50 per person). If you're in need of a friend, head to **Pal's Guest House** (tel. 220-95) by walking south of the bridge, turn-ing left just before the Havana canal, and continuing one more block. Far from the center of town, but right on the water, the rooms here are clean and comfortable. Watch cable TV or try to scare up a conversation with the manager (singles BZ$16, with private bath BZ$32; doubles BZ$32, with private bath BZ$42).

When hunger strikes, try to ingratiate yourself with the many local women who sell baked goods right out of their homes. If that doesn't work, follow your nose to the open-air market, on the northern bank of Stann Creek River near the sea. Other-wise, a few fancier options remain: take St. Vincent St. south four blocks and look on the left for **Pola's Kitchen** at 25A Tubroos St. (tel. 226-75). A monument to Garifuna culture, Pola's serves great Garifuna cuisine like *hudut* (plantains in coconut gravy with steamed fish), but American food is also available for the truly unadventurous.

BELIZE

Pola's display of Garifuna items also includes U.S. civil rights posters, including a tribute to a young Rosa Parks (open Wed.-Mon. 8am-2pm and 6-10pm; all items BZ$6.50-8.50). If you're looking for breakfast without the history lesson, walk one block north of the phone office to **Ritchie's Dinette Creole and Spanish Food** (tel. 221-12). "With a smile," Ritchie dishes out fryjacks, johnny cakes with eggs, and a gargantuan orange juice: a great breakfast for BZ$7. At lunch, try a magnificent chicken burrito for only BZ$2.50 (open Mon.-Sat. 7am-10pm). **New River Café** (tel. 399-08), just east of the bridge on the south bank of Stann Creek River, magnetically attracts tourists to its extensive seafood selections, as well as to its helpful advice for further travel on the cayes. (Sandwiches BZ$4-6, burgers BZ$3-5; breakfasts come in "hungry-man" portions; vegetarian options. Open Mon.-Sat. 7am-9:30pm.) For a taste of the East, try the **Starlight Restaurant** (tel. 233-92), on the north end of Commerce St., which serves Chinese food and curry to the background drone of CNN (open Mon.-Sat. 8am-3pm, 6-11pm, Sun. 6-11pm).

SIGHTS AND ENTERTAINMENT

Dangriga is a great place to see, hear, and taste Garifuna culture. World-renowned artist Benjamin Nicholas, who lives and works just past the post office, welcomes visitors to come in and take a gander at his numerous works-in-progress. His colorful **paintings** depicting Garifuna life and times have attracted quite a following: they hang most prominently in the Belize and Atlantic banks in Belize City. Those with a **musical** bent can go two blocks west and two blocks south of the post office to see Austin Rodriguez, who hand crafts mahogany and cedar **drums** in the traditional Garifuna style. Locals love to **swim** and play ball just east of the bridge, where the river meets the sea. For contrast, brace the brisk river water, then head out into the warmer Caribbean along the shallow river delta. For a more complete introduction to Garifuna culture, inquire at the **Bonefish Hotel,** two blocks south and one block east of the bridge, for possible cultural tours.

At night, get down with the townfolk at the **Riviera Disco,** right near the bridge, or check out the **Kennedy Club,** a few blocks north of the police station, which jams to *punta* and soul until 4am on Saturdays—10pm during the tamer weekdays.

Meet the Maya

The brainchild of William Schmidt and villagers struggling to remain viable, the Village House Guest Program is a masterpiece of Belizean ecotourism and has now spawned an entire industry of imitators. It began when the Toledo Ecotourism Association (TEA) built several houses in Maya and Garifuna villages to provide lodging for guests (BZ$18.50 per person). The accommodations are not luxurious; most villages have no running water or electricity. Still, the guest houses are **spotless and airy** and provide comfy mattresses, mosquito nets, plenty of boiled drinking water, and, oftentimes, an unforgettable experience.

A trip to one of the villages generally lasts at least 24 hours. Visitors are housed separately from the villagers for privacy, but they dine with Maya families, who prepare tasty meals as they have for centuries, using only foods from the surrounding farms and forests (3 meals BZ$22). The **coffee you're served** is not only fresh ground, it's fresh picked! Expert local guides lead half-day hikes through the jungle, pointing out traditional uses of plant life along the way to ceremonial caves or refreshing waterfalls. Evenings feature music, storytelling (about BZ$12.50 per hour), local crafts, and plenty of time for informal interaction with the villagers, whose hospitality is said to be overwhelmingly genuine.

Getting to one of the villages can be a little difficult. Market buses head from P.G. to the villages at around noon on Monday, Wednesday, Friday, and Saturday. The Z-line bus will get you near many of the villages, but be prepared to walk. Some folks charter vans (BZ$75). Contact the TEA office at the Tourist Information Center (tel. 221-19; fax 221-99; email ttea@btl.net, http://www.plenty.org/TEA.html), or William Schmidt at Nature's Way for more information. There is a BZ$10 registration fee.

■ Near Dangriga

HOPKINS VILLAGE

The nearby mountains and ever-shimmering Caribbean offer a variety of options for daytrips out of Dangriga. Ten miles south of Dangriga, the inhabitants of the farming and fishing community of Hopkins Village still pull wooden dugout canoes (called "dories") up onto the beach. Chickens, dogs, and children outnumber everything but coconuts in this old Garifuna village. Electricity came to Hopkins four years ago, but the village culture remains largely unscathed by the encounter. For those who are interested in traditional Garifuna culture, Hopkins's relative accessibility and basic services, not to mention its beautiful beaches, make it an ideal stop. A smattering of Canadian and American retirees who have converged on the village seem to concur. Camping areas and overnight accommodations are also available. **The Sandy Beach Lodge,** at the southernmost end of the village, is run by a local women's cooperative and offers rustic accommodations, lazy seaside living, and a glimpse of traditional cooking and culture (singles BZ$18, with private bath BZ$26; doubles BZ$35).

Z-line buses run from **Dangriga** to **Hopkins** from Monday through Saturday at 11:30am; you can also take the 12:15pm or 4:30pm bus to **Placencia** and hop off early. Buses heading back to Dangriga from Placencia can be flagged down in Hopkins at around 7am and 9am (BZ$3 each way).

COCKSCOMB BASIN WILDLIFE SANCTUARY

The Cockscomb Basin Wildlife Sanctuary lies in the Maya Mountains, about 32km south of Dangriga and 11km past the village of Maya Centre. The sanctuary was established in 1984 as the world's only jaguar ("tiger") preserve. Although the jaguars can grow up to 1.8m in length and 158kg (350lbs.) in weight, they are shy, nocturnal creatures. Keep your eyes peeled for jaguar tracks, as that may be all you see of them. Pumas are equally rare, but deer, lizards, tapirs, boas, and gorgeous tropical birds abound. **Victoria Peak,** Belize's highest point (1100m), rises from within the sanctuary, and a two-day journey will take prepared hikers to the summit. A visitors center, basic bunkhouse (BZ$12 for a bed), and campsites are available. Contact the **Belize Audobon Society** in Belize City for more information, or write the Cockscomb Basin Wildlife Sanctuary at P.O. Box 90, Dangriga. Daytrips can be arranged through some of the better hotels in town, including the **Pelican Beach Resort** (tel. 220-44; fax 225-70), which brings you to the Sanctuary and stops at the Maya Centre and Hopkins Village on the way back. These trips can be costly, so try to arrange a group of four to seven people (around US$30 per person for larger groups). If you're dead-set on seeing a jaguar, an overnight arrangement is best; campsites are available for a few extra bucks. The cheapest way to the site is by bus. Take any southbound bus in the morning (about a 1½hr. ride) and ask to be let off at the Cockscomb entrance, an 8km hike from the campgrounds. Buses head back to Dangriga no later than 3 or 4pm, so plan carefully if this is to be a daytrip.

BLUE HOLE NATIONAL PARK

Travelers tired of the salty sea can journey inland to the Blue Hole National Park (not to be confused with Blue Hole, the mondo-good scuba spot). While the massive park encompasses 575 acres, most points of interest are within hiking distance. The Blue Hole itself is the emerging subterranean Sibun River. Swelling into a pool, the river is surrounded by an echo-cavern filled with water that's absolutely divine for swimming. From the Blue Hole, a couple of miles of rugged trails lead to **St. Herman's Cave,** which was used by the Maya and is still being excavated today. To get to the national park, catch an early bus from Belmopan or Dangriga and ask the driver to let you off at the main entrance to the south; the park is conveniently located right off the Hummingbird Highway. Ask the conductor when later buses swing by the park entrance to ensure that you get a ride back.

TOBACCO CAYE

Set squarely atop the reef, Tobacco Caye (pop. 18) provides wanna-be castaways with the ultimate in weekend adventure. Unlike Caye Caulker or Ambergris, this five-acre island has just three restaurants which accept advance orders only; content yourself with little hotels and *cabañas* run by islanders who will cook for you. Visitors to the Caye spend their time lying in the sand, enjoying terrific reef snorkeling and diving, and ripping open heaping helpings of coconuts. Hammocks are everywhere, so bring a good book and plan to watch the sunset over the sea and the Tobacco Caye Range to the west. To reach the Caye from Dangriga, ask boatmen near the bridge for a ride (be alert—hustlers abound). Chartering a boat costs about BZ$25-30 each way. **New River Café** (tel. 399-08) arranges reliable rides to the Cayes and radios the "resorts" for interested tourists. Most tour operators will also make the trip for around BZ$25 per person.

■ Placencia

Only a skinny strip of land separates Placencia's lagoon from the ocean, and the water seems poised to swallow up the town at any moment. However, this resilient peninsular community of old sea salts has a hardy staying power; many residents are descendents of French pirates who came ashore for scurvy-preventing lemons and limes. Placencia itself was founded as a fishing village by Charles Garbatt in the late 19th century. After the lobster and conch populations began to disappear about twenty years ago, locals turned to tourism for revenue. Mellow Placencia's **Main Street** is a meandering path just wide enough for two to walk hand-in-hand, and the town's sense of time is molasses-slow. For the insatiable and curious, many fishermen open their boats and houses to guests and are more than willing to show their trade. The town's beaches are among the finest in Belize, and after a day of tapping coconuts and pondering the light crashing of the waves, even high-stress sorts develop a relaxed I-am-a-palm-tree-and-I-will-take-root-in-the-sand feeling.

Locals in the know comment that those who come to Placencia for easy access to marijuana are rarely disappointed, but may well be bamboozled or jailed. Remember, no matter how prevalent marijuana is, it is *not* legal.

ORIENTATION AND PRACTICAL INFORMATION

Boats and buses arrive near the gas dock at the southern tip of the 26km peninsula, more than 160km south of Belize City. The sea lies to the east; the lagoon to the west. The only artery through town, the narrow **sidewalk,** heads north along the beach. The dirt road that buses use fringes the western side of the village, along the playing field. Pick up a free map at the **Orange Peel,** next to **Wallen's Market** on the north-eastern edge of the field, or else ask around town for one. The trick to navigating Placencia is simply to figure out the order of restaurants and guest houses along the skinny little sidewalk; after a few leisurely strolls, it should be no problem.

Tourist Information: P.I. Tours (tel. 232-91), right next to the gas station, is your best source. Open daily 7am-5:30pm.

Currency Exchange: Wallen's Market is located down the dirt road from the post office. Fresh produce arrives on Sundays. An extremely limited selection of feminine products and over-the-counter drugs. Open Mon.-Wed. and Fri.-Sat. 8am-noon and 2-5pm, Sun. 8am-noon. The nearest **banks** are in Big Creek and Mango Creek, and these are only open on Fri.

Flights: Placencia's airstrip is 3km from town. 8 or 9 flights run daily to various points within Belize. Book **Maya Airways** flights by calling (02) 313-62. Service to: **Punta Gorda** (BZ$63); **Dangriga** (BZ$62); **San Pedro** (**Caye Caulker** on same flight, BZ$154); and **Belize City** (BZ$107). **Tropic Air** (tel. (02) 456-71) tickets can be bought at the Orange Peel next to Wallen's Market. Flight to Placencia from **Belize City** costs BZ$127 (4 flights daily, Mon.-Fri.). Tickets for both Maya and Tropic also available at **Sonny's Resort** at the south end of Main St. (tel. 231-03).

Buses: From Placencia to **Dangriga** (Mon.-Sat. at 5, 5:30, and 6am, BZ$7), with connections on Z-line to **Belize City.** For a southern connection, catch a boat to Mango Creek, Big Creek, or Independence; a man known as Pole leaves Placencia daily for Independence in his boat, the *Hokey Pokey,* at 10am and 4pm (25min., BZ$10). On Fri., villagers go to the bank in the morning; tag along for about BZ$10. Charters run BZ$40. From there, catch the noon bus to **Punta Gorda** on Tues., and Fri.; otherwise twiddle your thumbs in one of these tiny Creole villages until the 2pm bus begins the succession of afternoon buses (3hr., BZ$9).

Ferries: Kingfisher Angler Adventure (tel./fax 233-23) takes weekly trips to **Puerto Cortés, Honduras** for US$50.

Laundromat: (tel. 231-33) at the northern end of the sidewalk, a few minutes past Lydia's. Wash and dry BZ$7-10 depending on the load size. Pick-up and delivery available. Open daily 8am-6pm.

Hospital: The **health center** (tel. 231-92) in the middle of the lone sidewalk. Open Mon.-Sat. 8am-noon and 1-5pm.

Police: In case of emergency, call 911. The station (tel. 231-29) is on the beach between Sunny's Restaurant and the Trade Winds Hotel.

Post office: (tel. 231-02) across the dock on the second floor of the white building; can be used for *Poste Restante.* Open Mon.-Fri. 8am-noon and 1:30pm-4pm.

Telephones: Belize Telecommunications Ltd. (BTL) office (tel. 231-09), near the center of the village on the path. Open for **fax service** and **telegrams** as well, with free international collect calls. Mon.-Fri. 8am-noon and 1-4pm.

Telephone code: 06.

ACCOMMODATIONS

There are several budget hotels in Placencia, and some locals turn their homes into guest houses during busy times of year. Keep your eyes open for "Room for Rent" signs in the windows of private houses along the main walkway. Almost every hotel is within 25m of the sea; most have very simple (low-security) locks, but the locals seem to think it's okay. At places along the eastern shore, the winds tend to keep the mosquitoes at bay. Try bargaining in the off-season; many places will give you a deal.

Lydia's Rooms (tel. 231-17; fax 233-54), in the white house on the left of the sidewalk, 50m north of Flamboyant's restaurant. A perennial favorite of the backpacking crowd. Hammock on the upstairs porch. Spanking clean shared baths with hot and cold water. Breakfast BZ$6. Small singles BZ$15, large singles BZ$28; small doubles BZ$25, large doubles BZ$40.

Traveler's Inn (tel. 231-90), right after the Driftwood Café, just off the sidewalk. Rustic rooms with fans, private toilets, and trickling showers. Downstairs rooms are dim and lair-like, but tidy. Checkout at noon. Singles BZ$15, with private bath BZ$20; doubles BZ$25, with private bath BZ$30. Laundry BZ$8 per load.

Sea Spray Hotel (tel. 231-48), on the north end of the main sidewalk across from Flamboyant's. If no one's in the office, ask at Flamboyant's for Jody. Cozy *palapa* on the beach comes with fridge—it's Edenic (singles BZ$75; doubles or triples BZ$85). Rooms can get a bit noisy. Singles BZ$25; doubles BZ$35; extra person BZ$10, plus tax. Nicer rooms with hot water and coffee pot available for BZ$60-70. Reserve in advance. Mastercard and Visa accepted. Jody also arranges snorkeling and land trips and can help you find a room when every place seems full.

Julia and Lawrence's Guest House (tel. 231-85), just south of the Sea Spray. Very basic, but clean, accommodations. High-season singles BZ$21; doubles BZ$32; triples BZ$45. Negotiate prices during the low season.

Gail's Rooms just barely merit the plural: she has only two, but they're clean and cheap. In front of the Traveler's Inn on the sidewalk. Shared bath with meager cold water flow. Singles BZ$15-18; doubles BZ$25; BZ$7 for each additional person.

FOOD

Food in Placencia is just like the rest of life: slow, enjoyable, and steeped deeply in everything marine. Try **Daisy's Ice Cream,** just north of Omar's, for dessert (open

7am-10pm). **John the Bakerman,** on the main road, sells cinnamon rolls and fresh bread (BZ$0.75).

Flamboyant's (tel. 233-32), across from the Sea Spray. Tasty fish dinners BZ$15; burgers BZ$4-5; heaping portions of Jim Morrison's voice in the background free. Sunday night is BBQ night. Open Fri.-Wed. 7am-11pm. Kitchen closes at 10pm.

Omar's, a short walk south of the Sea Spray. Great burritos for BZ$4.50-7. Omar catches his own seafood and then gives it away at some of the cheapest prices around. Lobster burrito BZ$7; full lobster plate BZ$20. Open daily 7am-10pm.

Sunrise Restaurant and Bar (tel. 233-10), halfway up the sidewalk past Omar's. Locals haunt the Sunrise for its cheap eats and consistently broken arcade games. Seafood specials at competitive prices. Humongous Creole-style seafood platter with crab claws, lobster, fish, shrimp, and conch (BZ$30). Stew-chicken with rice and beans (BZ$5). Breakfast costs BZ$7. Open daily 6am-11pm.

Galley Restaurant and Bar (tel. 231-33), the turquoise building behind the soccer field. They're quite proud of their new bar and warped, surreal painting. Whips up fruit shakes (BZ$3.50) and a seaweed punch that tastes kind of like egg nog (BZ$4). Open daily 8am-10pm. Kitchen closes at 9pm.

SIGHTS AND ENTERTAINMENT

If you've been looking for a place to stash booty and settle down, Placencia will make you happy indeed—deserted island getaways don't get much better than this. The water is steely blue, the sand is grainy, and the cayes are downright drooly. Boaters will typically ferry tourists to the uninhabited isles around Placencia for fishing, snorkeling, and camping. Five of the cayes (all privately owned) are readily accessible and tourist friendly, but advance reservations are often required. The best cayes are supposedly those furthest south and closest to the reef, where the mangroves and, therefore, the mosquitoes and sand flies, are less abundant. Locals recommend **Silk Caye.**

Nearly every building in town has a sign advertising the phone number of a guide or charter to the cayes. To expedite your search, try visiting P.I. Tours; they do bookings for most guides in Placencia. Expect to pay about BZ$50 per person for a full-day snorkeling trip, including gear, but excluding lunch. **Kingfisher Angler Adventure** (tel./fax 233-23) leads excellent snorkeling expeditions and will lavish you with a cookout feast for an extra BZ$10 per person. Owner Charles specializes in fly and bait fishing, and outings can be arranged through him. Boats to the alluring outer cayes, like the privately-owned **Ranguana Caye,** 18 mi. out and directly on the reef, can be chartered and daytrips can be arranged at a considerably higher price. Gas is expensive, so chartering a boat costs around US$160. Contact Jody at the Seaspray Hotel for further information (tel. 231-48). Locally recommended **Seahorse Dive Shop,** just north of the gas dock, takes eager snorkeling and scuba enthusiasts to the reef, to Laughing Bird Caye, and to other delightful destinations. Two dive scuba trips cost between US$50-75. In the off season, the cheaper (and only) snorkeling option is with local fishermen. Ask around to ensure you go with a reputable operator.

Even the placid manatee has discovered Placencia's laid-back appeal; according to one report, approximately half of the sea cows that mumble "Belize da fu we" spend their lives basking in the lagoon near Placencia. A fun and exhausting way to visit them is by **sea-kayak.** Contact Ali Westby for tours or to rent a kayak and venture out snorkeling—remember never to go solo (half day BZ$20, full day BZ$30). **Kingfisher** also does manatee trips. A popular nearby jungle trip is to **Monkey River Reserve,** where the mangroves grow thick, the howlers haunt the canopy, and a wide variety of birdlife take it easy. Kingfisher takes a trip for US$25 per person; **P.I. Tours** includes a jungle walk for US$40. Most trips range between US$30-55.

Night life in Placencia starts out innocuously, but participants invariably end up staggering home. Start off at the **Lagoon Saloon,** past the playing field at the Tourist Trap hotel, or **Flamboyant's,** which features Garifuna drums and dancing on Sunday nights. Then head to the **Sunrise,** where Eternal Flame plays live reggae, punta, and soca on Sunday nights (weekend nights open until 3am).

■ Punta Gorda

Pristine but soggy, the rainforested **Toledo District** is a regular nirvana for the dashing adventure traveler (machete optional). Ill-maintained roads and long, bumpy bus rides have weeded out the traveler's weaker brethren, and Toledo's many natural wonders and panoply of exotic flora and fauna remain virtually untouched and largely unseen. Punta Gorda (pop. 3700), the center of commercial activity in Toledo—and a very small one at that—was founded by Puritan traders in the 17th century and has been used as an outpost by both English pirates and Spanish soldiers. After the U.S. Civil War, a group of Confederate veterans tried to establish plantations here similar to the ones they left behind in the South. Their genteel, pseudo-antebellum dream land failed to materialize. Toledo hosts the largest Mayan population in Belize, both Mopan and Kek'chi, who still practice the traditional milpa farming system in villages amid the nearby Maya Mountains. Sizeable Garifuna, Creole, and East Indian populations, with some German Mennonites thrown in as well, round out the cast of this bewildering, but typical Belizean amalgamation. Some predict that the region's diversity—of cultures, plants, and animals—will soon make it a center of ecotourism, and the bureaucracy has already developed in that direction. A new tourist office spearheads the work of snaring travelers who think of Punta Gorda merely as a jumping-off point to Guatemala.

ORIENTATION AND PRACTICAL INFORMATION

Punta Gorda hugs the coastline. **Front Street** runs along the sea, and **Main Street** runs parallel to it. Most activity is concentrated on these streets. The airstrip lies to the northwest, the hospital to the south (next to the Z-line bus terminal), and **Far West St.** traces, logically, the western boundary of "P.G.," as the city is most frequently called. If you're arriving on a Z-line bus, you'll enter town heading south on José María Nuñez St., one block west of Main Street. Don't wait until the terminal to get off; it's a bit out of town. Instead, tell the driver where you want to go (often you can mention the name of a particular hotel) and he will let you off at the nearest stop.

Tourist Information: This has the potential to be confusing, as there are three tourist offices in two different buildings. **Toledo Visitors Information Center/Southern Frontier Giftshop** (tel. 228-70), on Front St. behind the customs office on the wharf, provides details about tours, flights, and things to do. Up-to-date bus schedules and prices. Open Mon.-Wed. and Fri.-Sat. 7am-noon. The **Toledo Visitors Center** and the **Tourist Information Center** (tel. 225-31), housed in the same brand-new, yellow-roofed building on Front Street, south of the main wharf, next to Vernon's market. Free maps, brochures, and official advice. Open Tues.-Fri. 8am-noon and 1-5pm, Sat. 8am-noon, closes 30min. early on Fri.

Currency Exchange: Belize Bank (tel. 221-83 or 223-23; fax 223-25), on Main St., near the town center. Changes British pounds, U.S. and Canadian dollars, and traveler's checks. Cash advances on MC and Visa (for a fee of BZ$15). Open Mon.-Thurs. 8am-1pm, Fri. 8am-4:30pm. In a bind, Mr. King at the Texaco exchanges travelers' checks for amounts more than US$100 and "back alley" transactions are said to occur at Pallari's Hotel.

Telephones: Belize Telecommunications Ltd. (tel. 220-48), on Main St., 1 block north of Central Park. Free international collect calls. **Fax** and **telegram service.** Open Mon.-Fri. 8am-noon and 1-4pm, Sat. 8am-noon.

Flights: Maya Airlines (tel. 228-56) and **Tropic Air** (tel. 220-08) go to **Belize City** from the airstrip on the northwest side of town (7 flights per day, 1hr., BZ$137). Buy tickets at **Penell & Penell's Hardware Store** (tel. 220-14), on Front St. Open daily 8am-noon and 1:30-5pm.

Buses: Z-line, on José María St. south of town, goes to **Dangriga** (5hr., BZ$15) and to **Belize City** (8hr., BZ$22) four times daily. **James** buses head along the same route (daily 11:30am) for the same prices from the lot next to the police station.

Ferry: Both **Paco** (tel. 222-46) and **Requena Charter** (tel. 220-70) make daily trips to **Puerto Barrios, Guatemala** by *lancha* (50min., BZ$20). Paco's boat leaves at

8:30am and Requena's at 9am; arrive at immigration (in the customs office by the wharf) 30 min. ahead of time to get your departure stamp and pay BZ$7.50 for the conservation fee/departure tax. The *Pichilingo*, a Guatemalan skiff, returns to Puerto Barrios from Punta Gorda at 4:30 pm on Mon., Wed., Thurs., and Sat. (BZ$20). Captain Rigoberto James returns to **Livingston, Guatemala** from Punta Gorda Tues. and Fri. at 11 am (Q$20). For more info., contact the **Southern Frontier Giftshop** (tel. 228-70).

Market: Vernon's Store, on Front St., south of customs. Offers snacks and dry goods. Open Mon.-Wed. and Fri.-Sat. 8am-noon and 2-5pm, Thurs. 8am-noon.

Pharmacy: P.G. Pharmacy (tel. 221-07), on Main St., near the bank. Open Mon.-Sat. 8am-noon, 2-5pm, and 7-9pm. Parental guidance suggested.

Medical Services: Punta Gorda Hospital (tel. 220-26), at the end of Main St. near the bus station and the cemetery. Outpatient clinic and emergency room.

Police: (tel. 911 or 220-22) next to the post office. Open 24hr.

Post Office: (tel. 220-87) Front St. and King St., across from the customs office. Open Mon.-Fri. 8:30am-noon and 1-5pm, Fridays until 4:30pm.

Telephone code: 07

ACCOMMODATIONS

It's a buyer's market for hotel rooms in Punta Gorda: too many rooms, not enough occupants. Take your pick from several attractive options:

Nature's Way Guest House and Restaurant (tel. 221-19) at the south end of Front St. Airy rooms, wooden floors, desks, and clean common baths with no hot water. You may be awakened "nature's way" at 5am by the roosters next door. Ultra-cool William "Chet" Schmidt provides info on exploring the jungle, the cayes, and Maya villages. Singles BZ$16; doubles BZ$26; triples BZ$40. Breakfast BZ$7.

The St. Charles, 23 King St. (tel. 221-49), take Main St. two blocks north of the clock tower, turn left on King St., and head to the corner. Dazzling amenities for your dollar. Spacious rooms with flowered curtains, big beds, and vintage televisions with cable. Rooms have extra locks and hot water. Checkout at 1pm. Singles BZ$20, with bath BZ$30; doubles BZ$30, with bath BZ$40.

Mahung's Hotel, 11 Main St. (tel. 220-44), one block north of BTL, at the corner of North St. Proprietor Peter Mahung has a lot going on the side and can set you up with tours of the ruins or a life insurance policy. Two rooming options await inside the hotel. Bare, unpainted rooms without private baths and with saggy mattresses (singles BZ$12; doubles BZ$21) naturally cost less than clean, comfortable rooms with bath and cable TV (singles BZ$25; doubles BZ$35).

FOOD

Punta Gorda is a hotbed of Creole kitchens, and the hungry traveler is seldom more than 20 paces from a heaping plate of seafood, rice, and fried plantains.

Vicky Marenco's Ice Cream Parlor (tel. 225-72) on Main St. a few blocks south of the clock tower. Vicky not only serves up *helado,* she also cooks great, cheap food. Papaya shake BZ$2. Veggie cheeseburger (i.e. a cheese sandwich) BZ$2.75. Open for dinner and frozen treats Mon.-Sat. 5:30-10pm, Sun. 5-10pm.

Punta Caliente, 108 José Maria St. (tel. 225-61), just north of the bus terminal, is Punta Gorda's rising star. Stewed chicken with rice and beans is BZ$7; a hamburger goes for BZ$4. Fried fish with rice and beans comes in several sizes including huge (BZ$12), huger (BZ$15), and "Dear God, look at the size of that fish!" (BZ$20). Gaze at a wall display of traditional Garifuna tools as you greedily slurp up the fruits of their labor. If you're lucky, you might catch the effusive owner doing a *punta caldisima* while she takes your order. Open daily 7am-11pm.

Morning Glory (tel. 224-94) near the middle of Front St. Those misled into expecting granola and tofu will be disappointed. Quality Belizean food satisfies the locals, though. Standard breakfast BZ$7, standard dinners BZ$8-16. Open Mon.-Sat. 7am-3pm and 7-11pm, Sun. 7am-noon.

SIGHTS AND ENTERTAINMENT

The nearest island is **Moho Caye.** It's not as nice as the cayes off Placencia or Dangriga, but may yet be worth a daytrip. Charters are available, and Paco (tel. 222-46) will take a boat (up to 15 people) out for snorkeling for US$100, including gear. A number of other operators do similar trips for similar prices (be willing to bargain). Easy jungle kayaking up Joe Taylor creek can be arranged through Nature's Way (BZ$40 per day, guide costs another BZ$40). What little **nightlife** there is can be found at the **Honeycomb Club,** in a lone brown building on the north end of Front St., which is the place to *punta* near the end of the month, and at **Southside,** a few blocks north of the bus station on José María St. (open until 3am).

■ Near Punta Gorda

The area around Punta Gorda is dotted with ancient Maya ruins, a few of which have intriguing histories. Probably the best known is **Lubaantun,** about 5km from San Antonio and accessible through the Guesthouse program **(see Meet the Maya, p. 164).** Lubaantun ("place of the fallen stones") was named by Thomas Gann, because of the condition in which he found its structures when he began exploring the site in 1903 (whether the stones had fallen less before Mr. Gann opened up the ruin by blasting it with dynamite is still unclear). Lubaantun's edifices, as well as the buildings in some nearby communities, differ from most Maya structures in that parts of them were constructed without the use of mortar. Instead, blocks were carefully sculpted and interlock almost seamlessly. Ask to see the caretaker's (Santiago) collection of handmade replicas of Maya artifacts found near the site (buy one BZ$30).

Two famous pieces are missing from the site—the **Crystal Skull** and the **ball court markers.** The first can be found in Canada and is the subject of frenzied speculation; there are no tool marks on the skull, yet the jaw moves, a feat impossible for known Maya technologies. Some cite the skull as proof of Maya-U.F.O. contact, but many dismiss it as a simple hoax because it was discovered under somewhat dubious circumstances. The markers help to verify that there were ball courts at the site; these remnants have resided in Harvard University's Peabody Museum for years. **Num Li Punit** is the next ruin south from Lubaantun and boasts a stunning stone carving.

EL SALVADOR

Five years ago, tourism was the last thing on the minds of El Salvador's nearly six million inhabitants. Barraged by bullets and enshrouded in a dark cloak of death and loss, Salvadorans worried instead about preserving their land, their political causes, and their lives. In a nation the size of Massachusetts, the chafe of social tensions and conflicting ideologies came to bear in a bloody, bitter civil war. Since the 1992 cease-fire, the government and the leftist FMLN (Farabundo Martí National Liberation Front) have been striving to settle their differences in the political arena. The Salvadoran people, meanwhile, try to return to life as they lived it before the war.

Few tourists have set El Salvador on their itineraries since the war. While the political situation has stabilized, the country's historical sites are still crumbling. Not all of the devastation is due to years of carpet bombing, however; centuries of thunderous earthquakes have taken their toll too. Still, while lacking in cathedrals and monuments, El Salvador does not want for natural splendor, and its black-sand beaches offer the added bonus of some of the best surf waves in Central America. Meanwhile, ecotourism will undoubtedly start to draw throngs to the country's smoking volcanos and Montecristo Cloud Forest, especially since visitors are practically guaranteed isolation in even the more-touristed sites. Finally, a smattering of travelers are coming to El Salvador to experience first-hand the exciting atmosphere of a nation on the road to recovery.

ESSENTIALS

▓ When to Go

CLIMATE

El Salvador's mountainous terrain generally keeps temperatures under relative control, ranging between 60-75°F in the highlands. The lower in altitude you are, the higher the temperatures; 80°F is about average in the lowlands, and San Salvador can average about 90°F in the summer (March). The rainy season, accompanied by the *temporales* (heavy downpours), lasts from May to October. The greatest numbers of tourists come during the dry season.

FESTIVALS AND HOLIDAYS

Check around for local festivals, usually dedicated to patron saints. **Santa Ana's** July Festival to the Virgin Mary is raucous indeed, as is **Sonsonate's** party in February. **San Miguel** busts out on November 24. Nationally, banks and other public services are bound to be closed on the following days: **January 1** (New Year's); **May 1** (Labor Day); **May 10** (Mother's Day); **June 17** (Father's Day); **June 22** (Día del Maestro; Teacher's Day); **August 1-6** (Patron Saint Salvador's Festival); **Sept. 15** (Independence Day); **October 12** (Día de la Raza); **Nov. 2** (Día de los Santos Difuntos; All Saint's Day); **Nov. 5** (Primer Grito de Independencia; First Cry of Independence); **December 24-25** (Christmas Eve and Christmas); **Dec. 31** (New Year's Eve).

▓ Useful Information

For publications and organizations of general interest, see **Useful Information,** p. 1.
   Corporación Salvadoreño de Turismo, Blvd. El Hipódromo #508, Colonia San Benito, San Salvador (tel./fax 243-0427). Send away for maps, turquoise brochures, and general information about tourism. Open Mon.-Fri. 8am-5pm.

El Salvador

Montañas La Sierra

HONDURAS

GUATEMALA

PACIFIC OCEAN

N

25 milles
25 kilometers

GUATEMALA

Nueva Ocotepeque

Co. El Pital

Co. El Brujo

Co. Montecristo

Llano de Güija

Candelaria de la Frontera

Cordillera Metapán Alotepeque

Cordillera Mita Comecayo

Metapán

La Palma

La Reina

CA4

Nuevo Concepción

CHALATENANGO

Chalatenango

El Paraíso

Embalse Cerrón Grande

SANTA ANA

Santa Ana

Lempa

Lago de Coatepeque

Volcán Sta. Ana Guazapa

CUSCATLÁN

Victoria

CABAÑAS

Ilobasco

Sensuntepeque

Tejutepeque

Lempa

Cojutepeque

SAN SALVADOR

SAN VICENTE

San Sebastián

Verapaz

San Vicente

Vol. de San Vicente (Chichontepec)

Apopa

Quetzaltepeque

San Martín

San Marcos

Sto. Tomás

Stgo. Texacuangos

SAN SALVADOR

Ciudad Arce

El Espino

Volcán de San Salvador

San Tecla

LA LIBERTAD

Teotepeque

Jicalapa

La Libertad

LA PAZ

Zacatecoluca

Embalse 15 de Septiembre

Aeropuerto Internacional

CA2

CA4

CA1

Volcán de Izalco

Cerro Verde

Volcán de Coatepeque

Co. Aguila

Volcán de Sta. Lago de

Co. Las Naranjos

Sierra Apaneca Ilamatepec

Apaneca

AHUACHAPÁN

Ahuachapán

San Francisco Menéndez

Volcán Chingo

Valle Nuevo

CA8

CA12

Chalchuapa

Sonsonate

SONSONATE

El Sunza

Acajutla

Jayaque

Chanmico

19

Estanzuelas

SAN MIGUEL

San Sebastián

Berlín

San Agustín

USULUTÁN

Usulután

Pto. El Triunfo

Bahía de Jiquilisco

Volcán de Usulután

Volcán de Tecapa

Tecapán

El Triunfo

CA1

Santa Rosa de Lima

Nueva Esparta

MORAZÁN

Cordillera Cacaguatique Corobán

Cordillera Nahukaterique

Corinto

San Francisco Gotera

CA7

Jocoro

Santa Rosa de Lima

El Carmen

LA UNIÓN

Bahía de La Unión

La Unión

Volcán de Conchagua

San Miguel

Volcán de Chinameca

Volcán de San Miguel

San Rafael de Oriente

El Triunfo

Jucuarán

Cordillera Jucuarán Intipucá La Paz

Laguna de Olomega

Intipucá

Lago de Ilopango

San Pedro Nonualco

CISPES (Committee in Solidarity with the People of El Salvador), 19 West 21st St., Room 502, New York, NY 10010 (tel. (212) 229-1290; fax (212) 645-7280; email cispesnatl@igc.apc.org; http://www.cispes.org). A grass-roots organization working for justice, better working conditions, and civil liberties in El Salvador.

■ Documents and Formalities

EMBASSIES AND CONSULATES

Embassy of El Salvador, U.S., 2308 California St. NW, Washington, D.C. 20008 (tel. (202) 265-9671; fax 332-2223). Open Mon.-Fri. 9am-6pm. **U.K.** Tennyson House 159, Great Portland St. 51, London W1N 5FD (tel. (44) 171-436-8282; fax 436-8181). Open Mon.-Fri. 10am-5pm. **Canada,** 209 Kent St., Ottawa, Ontario K2P 1Z8 (tel. (613) 238-2939; fax 238-6940) Open Mon.-Fri. 9am-1pm and 2-4pm.

Consulate of El Salvador, 1010 16th St. NW, 3rd Floor, Washington, D.C. 20036 (tel. (202) 331-4032; fax 331-4036). There's also an office in New York City (tel. (212) 889-3608 or 889-3609). Contact either branch for visa information.

PASSPORTS, VISAS, AND CUSTOMS

Citizens of all countries need valid passports to enter El Salvador. Residents of the United States and Canada need either a **visa** or a **tourist card;** travelers from South Africa, Australia, and Ireland need to acquire a visa before arriving. A visa is free from the Consulate of El Salvador and takes 3-4 days to process; have two passport-size photos available. For U.S. citizens, the visa is good for as long as the passport is valid, but the **tourist card** is good for one entry for as long as 30 days (with extensions up to 6 months or a year with proof of legitimate activities in El Salvador). For citizens of other countries, a processed visa is good for 30 days, with extensions possible up to 60 days. In many cases, capricious immigration officials have the authority to determine the length of time you may spend in El Salvador and often act based on how you appear—the spiffier you look, the longer you stay.

Drivers to El Salvador need only a car registration, valid driver's license, and proof of insurance, although an international driver's permit is recommended. You may have to purchase a permit from the National Police for ¢100. The license is valid for 30 days. **Children** (under the age of 18) traveling to El Salvador need the written consent of both parents.

■ Money Matters

CURRENCY AND EXCHANGE

US$1 = ¢8.76	**¢1 = US$0.11**
CDN$1 = ¢6.39	**¢1 = CDN$0.16**
UK£1 = ¢14.29	**¢1 = UK£0.07**
IRL£1 = ¢12.73	**¢1 = IRL£0.08**
AUS$1 = ¢6.51	**¢1 = AUS$0.15**
NZ$1 = ¢5.68	**¢1 = NZ$0.18**
SARand = ¢1.90	**¢1 = SARand0.53**
DM1 = ¢4.78	**¢1 = DM0.21**

Columbus' legacy persists on Salvadoran cash; the national currency is the **colon** (sometimes called a *peso*) denoted by a "¢." There are 100 centavos (like U.S. cents) to a single colón. Change any currency at the border when leaving, since colones are hard to get rid of elsewhere. The two banks that regularly change traveler's checks are **Banco Salvadoreño** and **Banco Hipotecario;** a branch of either is in just about every medium-to large-sized town. **ATMs** are prevalent in San Salvador, but the machines aren't linked to common networks like Cirrus or PLUS; rather, they are hooked only into the bank itself. **Credit cards** are accepted in many businesses in the capital, but elsewhere, only the poshest places accept Visa, MasterCard, or occasionally AmEx. There is an AmEx office (tel. 223-0177) in San Salvador. Contact the office of Visa-MasterCard Credomatic for problems or cash advances.

The **black market** is rarely a good deal in El Salvador, since rates are worse than those given in banks. They only trade cash, though often during hours when banks are closed. **Tipping** is greatly appreciated, particularly at restaurants. A bonus is not mandatory though, especially not for cab drivers.

▓ Safety

Years after the war, crime remains a major problem in El Salvador; a disturbingly large proportion of the population carries firearms. Though these gangs leave drug-dealing to their Colombian counterparts, they do not shirk from violence, and innocents can be caught in the cross-fire. A good way to gauge the safety of a neighborhood is to look for gang graffiti—if there's a lot, then avoid the area at night.

Whenever possible, stay indoors or in well-lit areas at night, and take care of business during the day. Salvadorans got used to curfews during the war, and so not a lot happens after 9pm even now, except in San Salvador and Santa Ana. Travelers (especially women) are advised not to go out alone at night. Visitors should always avoid carrying valuables in public places; San Salvador's crime problem is particularly bad. Women should be very cautious in northern El Salvador, where the men routinely whistle and hoot at local women. The country sees few tourists, so expect some stares of curiosity wherever you go. And don't necessarily breathe a sigh of relief when police show up, since many are still in a wartime mindset. It's probably best to steer clear of all types of police (Nacional, Nacional Civil, and Militar) unless absolutely necessary; your nation's embassy is a better place to turn for help.

Despite the Peace Accords of 1992, the U.S. State Department warns travelers not to travel after dark and to avoid unpaved roads as much as possible. Campers in undesignated sites should never go far off the road, particularly in the northern regions of the country, as unexploded land mines and local criminals pose threats.

▓ Health

If arriving from an infected area, a vaccination certificate for **yellow fever** is required for everyone over 6 months old. **Malaria** is a risk in rural areas only; chloroquine is an effective treatment. A recent **dengue fever** epidemic makes it wise to avoid mosquitoes as much as possible. Insect-borne parasites are always problematic. **Cholera** has swept through El Salvador, as has **typhoid fever.** Avoid unclean food and intimate contact to stay clear of **Hepatitis A and B.** Also on the rise in El Salvador is **HIV/AIDS,** so proper precautions should be taken. Applicants for permanent residence in El Salvador need to have an in-country test for the AIDS virus. For in-depth descriptions of disease prevention and risk, see **Health,** p. 14.

Nearly every Salvadoran town has a slew of pharmacies; open hours usually span between 7am-6pm; but many towns have a **turno,** a rotating system that ensures that at least one pharmacy stays open 24 hours. A schedule explaining which pharmacy is open when is posted in every pharmacy's window.

Locals swear the **tap water** in San Salvador is safe, but drink at your own risk; elsewhere, never chance drinking anything but *agua cristal* or *agua purificada.*

▓ Getting There

Major international airlines such as United, Continental, and American all serve San Salvador's international airport, as does the native **Taca** (tel. (503) 298-5066). Taca, **Copa,** and **Lacsa** serve other Central American capitals and most major cities. **Tica Bus** (tel. (503) 222-4808) serves all Central American capitals; see the Practical Information sections of individual cities for other buses to border areas.

The preferred border crossings from Guatemala are at **Las Chinamas** (in El Salvador; Valle Nuevo in Guatemala), on the Interamerican Hwy. leading to Ahuachapán, and at **La Hachadura** on the Pacific Highway over the Río Paz. Coming in from Las Chinamas, it's about half an hour to Ahuachapán. To get to El Salvador from Tegus, grab a bus to **El Amatillo** at **Mi Experanza** or the less-organized buses that pass by the **Saenz** office (L20 every hour starting at 5am). It is a three-hour ride to El Amatillo where you can exit Honduras (L10) and enter El Salvador ($10; open 5:30am-7pm). From El Amatillo, there are buses every 15 minutes to Santa Rosa de Lima. While it would be easy to cross the border without getting the appropriate stamps, buses are often stopped by soldiers and passports (or visas) are checked regularly. The border crossings to Honduras are at El Amatillo and **El Poy,** but this area has been plagued by bandits in the past. Arrive early in the day to avoid missing buses to major cities.

■ Once There

TRANSPORTATION

El Salvador is small enough that there is no reason to get around by any means of transport other than bus or car. The country is so densely populated that buses move slower than elsewhere, since they constantly stop to pick people up. Crowded buses run popular routes (such as San Salvador-Chalatenango). Don't expect pity for your big backpack; buses often don't even stop, but rather slow to a crawl, so that even elderly passengers have to sprint and jump on.

The roads in El Salvador are surprisingly well-maintained, despite the heavy traffic nearly everywhere. Buses pass far too frequently to make hitching a necessary recourse. Pick-ups sometimes transport travelers, but the drivers expect payment for the trip. *Let's Go* does not recommend hitchhiking.

ACCOMMODATIONS

There are no organized campgrounds in El Salvador, even in the national parks; it's often dangerous if you're camping near a beach resort, an urban area, or an area with lots of soldiers (which is pretty much everywhere). Many of El Salvador's hotels charge varying rates based on length of stay. Check in after 5pm and leave before 9am in some hotels, and you pay half what you would for staying 24 hours. Another accommodations quirk in the country is the chance for travelers to stay for free at one of many **Centros de Los Obreros,** workers' residences that have spare rooms, often with running water and decent beds; all you have to do is get a permit ahead of time in San Salvador.

ADDRESSES

Streets in El Salvador appease that geometer lying latent in everybody's heart. Most cities are laid out according to a grid-like plan with numbering based on orientation with respect to an origin. In most cities, *avenidas* are streets that run north to south; *calles* run east to west. There are two keystone streets: a central *avenida* (the y-axis), and a central *calle* (the x-axis). Even-numbered streets and avenues are on one side of the axis, odd numbers on the other. In most cities (such as San Salvador), odd-numbered *avenidas* increase in number as you proceed west of the center; odd numbered *calles* increase to the north. Even-numbered *avenidas* and *calles* increase toward the east and south, respectively. Some cities employ variations on this numbering scheme, however.

KEEPING IN TOUCH

Mail sent to the U.S. or Europe from El Salvador is relatively reliable; normal letters take 1-2 weeks. Express mail services in San Salvador, such as **DHL** (tel. 279-0411; in U.S. call (800) CALL DHL; fax 223-2441) and **Urgent Express,** tap right into the U.S.

postal service at a price (usually about US$5 per package). If you want to send a letter to someone in El Salvador by general delivery, address it:

Allyson <u>HOBBS</u>
Lista de Correos
Sonsonate (city), República de El Salvador
Centroamérica

If mailing from the U.S., omit the last line (Centroamérica) and move "El Salvador" down a line, since the computers that sort mail only recognize names of countries. Letters sent to San Salvador's main post office should be addressed to "Centro de Gobierno, San Salvador."

The state telecommunications office, ANTEL, has offices throughout the country. Calls within the country only cost about ¢0.10 for a few minutes. Calls to the U.S. or Europe are expensive (about US$5 per min.), so it's better to call collect or use a calling card. Dialing 119 gets you an operator for **international long distance,** 190 an **AT&T** operator, 191 **Sprint,** and 195 **MCI.** El Salvador's **country code** is 503.

EL SALVADOR: LIFE AND TIMES

■ History

Ever since the conquistadors' first appearance, the mountainous and heavily populated strip of Pacific coast dubbed "The Savior" by the Spanish seems to have been aching for its namesake. The world has been interested in Salvadoran happenings since its latest and most protracted civil war in the early 80s, but often fails to understand the larger movements out of which today's struggling factions arose.

Fresh from ploughing through the Maya settlements of north Guatemala, colonists under **Pedro de Alvarado** pushed south into the western territories of modern El Salvador in 1524. The preclassical Maya settlements of Tazumal and San Andrés had already dissipated, but the indigenous **Pipil** remained to resist invasion.

El Salvador's arable regions furnished a lion's share of the captaincy's produce and livestock. Cocoa exports gave way to **indigo,** a tough legume used in the production of dyes and of absolutely no use to the indigenous farmers; their labor's fruits were entirely inedible. The indigo boom cemented the combative relationship between the landed commercial class and the indigenous *campesinos* that has since marked nearly every political and economic movement in the country. As the lands' original tenants were displaced from their traditional subsistence farming locales to make room for transiently profitable crops-for-export, they were traded food and shelter for work on the new agricultural tracts. The surplus afforded by the innovations of mass production was absorbed almost entirely by the landowners.

The first stirrings for independence along the Central American isthmus started among the indigo-growing people of El Salvador. Salvadorans unanimously detested Guatemalan commercial clout and the captaincy general's bishop. A Salvadoran uprising in 1811, nominally directed against Spain, was gently suppressed by the Guatemalan regime. Discontent with Spain swelled on both sides of the common border, and the two provinces of the Spanish empire united in 1821, when the Guatemalans joined the Salvadorans in rejecting their status as colonists. In response to a short-lived Guatemalan plan to accept incorporation into a pan-Mexican assemblage, San Salvador threatened to offer itself up to the United States as a territory. The Mexican government foundered, and a Central American constitutional convention flourished, both encouraging Guatemalan-Salvadoran unity under a new guise. When the presidency of the new coalition, the **Federal Republic of Central America,** fell into the hands of **Manuel Arce,** one of the leaders of the 1811 uprising, Salvadoran support for federation fell into place.

El Salvador soon lost its love for Arce and his conservative compatriots in the federal legislature, but remained committed to the pan-American ideals he espoused. By 1827, liberal usurpers had brought conflict to the point of civil war, and within two years toppled Arce's government, acting under the command of the Salvadoran hero **Francisco Morazán.** Raised and felled by Salvadorans, the Central American federation moved its capital to San Salvador after Morazán's takeover, but survived in name only until 1841, when it dissolved entirely.

The ensuing decades of independence saw a number of small wars and border skirmishes with its neighbors, as well as a transition from one cash crop to another. Its economy foundered in reaction to the development of new, synthetic dyes that gradually extinguished Europe's dependence on the indigo harvest, but the Salvadoran republic found the solution to political instability in **coffee.** Supplying Europe with caffeine transformed El Salvador's agricultural base and its entire economy.

One important consequence of the move to coffee was that more land needed to be cultivated. The government accordingly waived all protection of federally owned land, and forced El Salvador's native population to relinquish its lands for a "public" cause. The ensuing indigenous uprisings were ruthlessly suppressed. The coffee money in El Salvador also drew an even tighter link between the ownership of land and political power. An extremely small, rich, and powerful group of the nation's elite, the "Fourteen Families," organized an effective stranglehold on almost all of the country's land, money, and might. Their hegemony has survived to the present, but it was most concentrated in the period between 1913 and 1927, when the Salvadoran presidency was occupied by members of just two of the families, the Meléndez and the Quiñónez.

During the Great Depression, El Salvador's plutocracy degenerated as quickly as did coffee profits, and the oligarchy turned into a dictatorship. The pressures of the Depression were first felt among the coffee workers, who led a brief revolt that proved to be neither the country's first nor last, but without a doubt its bloodiest. Facing mounting tensions among the lower classes, **General Maximilano Hernández Martínez** supplanted the president in 1931. Under the direction of **Augustín Farabundo Martí,** the martyred founder of El Salvador's Communist Party, thousands of farm workers rebelled in 1932. In response, Martínez orchestrated the crushing massacre known as *la matanza*—the summary execution of over 10,000 Salvadoran citizens suspected of having been involved in the uprising, including many natives. In the early part of the century the country had been regarded as relatively tolerant politically; after the massacre, a series of dictators took the helm as puppets of the increasingly paranoid landed elite, and the last of the natives adopted *mestizo* ways in self-defense. Martínez, who sought to emulate the better-known fascists of the time and who entertained a lifelong fascination with the occult, was able to keep himself in power until a coup deposed him in 1948.

By the mid-60s, El Salvador had ascended to a level of relative economic comfort, and several reform programs had resulted in new levels of diversification and international exchange. At the same time, the political front was loosening up a little, largely in response to the emergence of a middle class, which backed the **Christian Democratic Party (PDC)** and its leader, **José Napoleón Duarte,** the mayor of San Salvador. But even as moderates were able to gain a foothold in El Salvador's polarized electoral arena, the federal government was organizing a large, right-wing KGB of sorts. **ORDEN** ("order") came to play a prominent, though silent, role in the ongoing suppression of the Salvadoran left. Internal strife was put on hold for a period, however, with the outbreak of the "Soccer War," or *Guerra de Fútbol,* against rival Honduras. The conflict was motivated by outstanding border disputes, economic issues, and the treatment of an immense congregation of Salvadoran refugees on Honduran soil. Begun on the heels of a tense World Cup playoff, the struggle cost each nation thousands of lives and was not fully resolved for 11 years.

Meanwhile, in reaction to growing support for the middle-of-the-road PDC, by arranging to oversee the 1972 presidential elections, ORDEN made its role in Salvadoran life more visible. Despite obvious, nearly overwhelming support for Duarte's bid, the more conservative, actively anti-Communist candidate favored by the ORDEN troops registered victory in the end, beginning the most recent episode in the interminable struggle between the rich and the many in El Salvador. Following the election, the Roman Catholic Church joined the opposition and shifted the focus of its Salvadoran mission to "liberation theology," fueling the fires of mass movements already responsible for many public protests and strikes. The conservative ruling regime responded by increasing the voltage of the already brutal measures installed to quell the dissent. Aggression came to a memorable climax in 1975, when ORDEN troops gunned down students protesting the use of federal funds to promote El Salvador's bid to host the Miss Universe pageant. The cycle escalated until another coup in 1979 marked the official beginning of the nation's infamous civil war.

Duarte, in Venezuelan exile since his presidential "defeat" in 1972, returned to a hero's welcome after the '79 coup to sit at the front of the popular interim government. The wealthy landowners stood impervious in the face of the revolution that put Duarte into power and realized that their economic, social, and political survival lay in winning the political support of the middle-class and urban centers, thereby leaving the would-be revolutionaries in the rural north out in the cold. To this end, the families organized the Alianza Republicana Nacionalista, or **ARENA,** and used the party to apply monetary leverage against the unruly wing of the left. ARENA did not supplant the reigning junta at the time of its inception in 1981, but with the military on its side, it managed to pressure the would-be reformist Duarte regime into a vicious struggle with the expanding guerilla movement. A hopeless triangle formed with the rich, ARENA, and the military, on one side; Duarte, a majority of the enfranchised middle-class, and the remains of the PDC on another; and the Catholic clergy and a rugged, diverse, and desperate opposition on the third. This trinity oversaw a bloody civil war of epic proportions that was responsible for the loss of over 75,000 lives by the time of its tentative conclusion in 1992.

The only side of the political triad not interested in annihilating its opponents was Duarte's, and he was powerless to halt the flow of public funds to the murderous, rightist 'death squads' or into overt campaigns against the guerilla movements. Furthermore, El Salvador had been singled out by the Reagan administration as an example of how the military might of the West could be used to suppress communist insurgencies. The United States government donated over US$4 billion worth of military aid to the right over the course of the war. In 1981, at the same time that ARENA was first marshaling its forces, the guerilla armies unified into the **FMLN** (Farabundo Martípara la Liberación Nacional). The rebels had finally gathered sufficient momentum to wage a full-fledged war against the established base of Salvadoran power when one of its heroes, **Archbishop Oscar Romero,** was assassinated by a right-wing death squad in the middle of a Sunday Mass in March of 1980 while he delivered his sermon. This killing was followed by the rape and murder of three American nuns and a lay volunteer who had also been working on missions of mercy in FMLN-supporting territories. The world was faced with the paradox of a government that seemed intent on making good its proposals for agrarian reform, while simultaneously pursuing a barbarous extermination of its enemies.

The FMLN's first unified war efforts began with the mislabeled "final offensive," a fierce battle that broke out all over the capital and dragged on for months, tapering off into an endless series of smaller and more furtive assaults across the entire country. Fighting was always at its most pitched in the mountainous northwest, which has since been leveled by random, relentless bombings of peasant villages. Tens of thousands of innocent civilians were killed over the course of the war, some of them with U.S. arms wielded by U.S.-trained soldiers.

Between the continuing war, an understandably shattered economy, and the failure of almost every social reform of Duarte's, no one was left happy with the moderate, limping government of the late 80s. Coupled with allegations of rampant corruption in Duarte's administration, these disappointments resulted in Duarte's 1989 presidential defeat to **Alfredo Cristiani,** ARENA's charismatic candidate. Cristiani punished public sedition more openly than his allies had, but at the same time was able to maneuver with enough freedom to start taking seriously the FMLN's demands for social justice. In 1992, under U.N. supervision, an historical accord was reached between the two dominant and extreme factions, reminiscent of a similar, failed effort in 1984; so far, this one has been effective. Though the six-year-old cease-fire should be considered a fortunate respite for the battered combatants and every other Salvadoran, the conditions responsible for its declaration were more those of a deep weariness and frustration than of the kind of reconciliation of interests that might be expected to outlast El Salvador's attempts to nurse its wounds.

■ The Arts

Rather than expressing the hardships of life in densely populated El Salvador, the country's literature has generally offered a chance for the people to escape. Romantic poets include **José Batres Montúfar** and **Arturo Ambrogi,** who is also known for his short stories. Indeed, theater and short stories, which are more accessible than hefty (and hard-to-publish) novels, have always been favored forms. Later writers continued to tap into popular dreams and sentiment. **Carlos Bustamante's** *Mi Caso* reflected on the most intimate human feelings with the aid of overtly psychological themes, as did the works of the first acclaimed Salvadoran woman writer, **Claudia Lars** (1899-1974). In the early days of the century, **Alberto Masferrer** contributed important essays and poetry to this tradition as well. Literature has since come to strive for progress less by lambasting the current system than by evoking impressions of what might one day be.

Some of El Salvador's recent **artists** explore similar themes, tapping into common experience to evoke harmony and peace. **Dorian Díaz's** "El Pescado" and **Gilberto Arriaza's** "La Luna" are among the colorful, playful works which have recently emerged from the country. Salvadoran traditional handicrafts are made from a number of natural materials; some of the most well-known pieces include the wicker furniture from Nahuizalco and the various ceramics and weavings from La Palma, Chalatenango.

The Salvadoran **music** scene is a hodgepodge. U.S. pop has made major inroads, and in the big cities, finding Alanis or Metallica on the radio isn't too tough; club and techno are also very popular among young urbanites. In the country and small towns, tastes are more traditional, but even in "Latin" music, there are few strictly Salvadoran groups. Panamanian El General rules the Latin club scene and Spaniards and Argentines alike have cornered the rock market. The fan club of slain *ranchera* Tex-Mex queen Selena borders on cultish affection—her hit *Amor Prohibido* (Forbidden Love) is in heavy rotation and has become a veritable anthem for the kids. *Salsa* and *merengue* from Puerto Rico and the Dominican Republic are also ubiquitous.

■ Food and Drink

The cuisine of El Salvador is similar to that of many other Latin American nations. *Tortillas* are served at every meal, and beans are never far behind. The food is exceptionally tasty and filling, but don't expect too much variety. Breakfast, eaten early (6-7:30am), typically consists of eggs, plantains, cheese or cream, beans, and tortillas. For plain eggs, ask for *solo huevos;* otherwise, a plate of eggs with tomatoes and onions will land on the table. For lunch and dinner, replace eggs and cheese with meat and *arroz* (rich, yellow fried rice). The meat is usually *pollo dorado* (roast "golden" chicken), *carne asada* (roast meat), or *pollo* or *carne encebollado* (chicken or meat stewed with veggies). Vegetarians should prepare for strange looks and a palate-numbing lack of options; in El Salvador, only those who cannot afford meat abstain from it. Still, a few vegetarian restaurants exist in the capital, and *pupusas* (tortillas filled with cheese or beans) are ubiquitous. Beware only of *pupusas* made with *chicharrones* (pork rinds).

As for drinks, El Salvador concentrates on the fruity and sugary. *Licuados,* fruit milkshakes, and *refrescos,* comprised of coconut and fruit juices, are rivalled only by

Kolashanpan, an achingly sweet local soda whose taste defies description. The most popular brands of beer are Pilsener and Suprema; both are appropriately light for the heat. For the ultimate in intoxication, mix some Coke with a bottle of *Tic-Tack,* a ferocious rum-like concoction distilled from sugar cane.

▦ Media

La Prensa Gráfica and *Diario de Hoy* are the best Salvadoran daily newspapers, although both tend toward the tabloid now and then. *La Noticia* has gained popularity in the last few years. In San Salvador, pick up the *El Salvador News Gazette* for bilingual tips and news. There are six TV stations, most of which serve up the usual soap operas, news programs, and soccer games. Of the many radio stations, a few are run by the FMLN.

▦ Recent News

Electoral reform tops El Salvador's political agenda. The ruling right-wing party, ARENA was shaken up by its disappointing performance in the March 1997 mid-term elections. ARENA has enjoyed unchallenged governmental control at executive, legislative, and municipal levels since 1989. ARENA is a collection of diverse interests held together by the unquestioned leadership of the late Mayor D'Aubuisson and an anti-communist ideology. Without the Mayor and the Cold War, the party's control has been threatened and differences in ideology have resurfaced. The left-wing FMLN emerged as the main beneficiary of the election, winning several legislative seats and municipal offices. The Partido de Conciliación Nacional (PCN) also increased its legislative presence and firmly established itself as the country's third political party. Each of these parties will be closely watched by voters, many of whom are frustrated by a flagging economy and have come to regard politicians as self-interested and corrupt.

An ARENA initiative, a 1996 constitutional amendment to reintroduce the death penalty will not be ratified by the new legislature as the FMLN (which opposes the death penalty) has enough votes to defeat the measure.

San Salvador

San Salvador has just finished celebrating its 450th birthday in a grand style that only a capital could muster. Though 450 seems an odd number to hype, the city nonetheless issued stamps and partied like it was 1999, because this anniversary was consciously touted as a turning point for San Salvador. For the first time in a while, San Salvadorans could share a happy milestone instead of the depressing cycles of war, earthquake, and despair that have served as time markers in both its recent and colonial history. Most of all, the city commemorated the simple fact that it has survived in spite of all it has weathered.

As the bad memories and psychological scars heal, San Salvador grows rapidly, always keeping a close eye on the national political situation. Prosperity is pushing pell-mell development, and the ranks of the middle class are swelling. With their cellular phones and hyper-consciousness of that Great White Country to the north, the new bourgeoisie are driving San Salvador ever closer to the global village and infusing the place with a cosmopolitan air. The sprouting satellite dishes show other residents what they don't have; accordingly, petty crime is on the rise.

Despite this, most citizens are still quick to flash a smile and strike up a conversation with visitors. Without any historical colonial sights or surrounding natural splendor, this uniquely San Salvadoran spirit is about the city's only tourist attraction, but at one point or another, everyone in El Salvador must pass through the capital. Rather than look at it as a smoggy punishment, dig deeper and take the city for what it's worth, as the engine that, come what may, will keep itself and the country going.

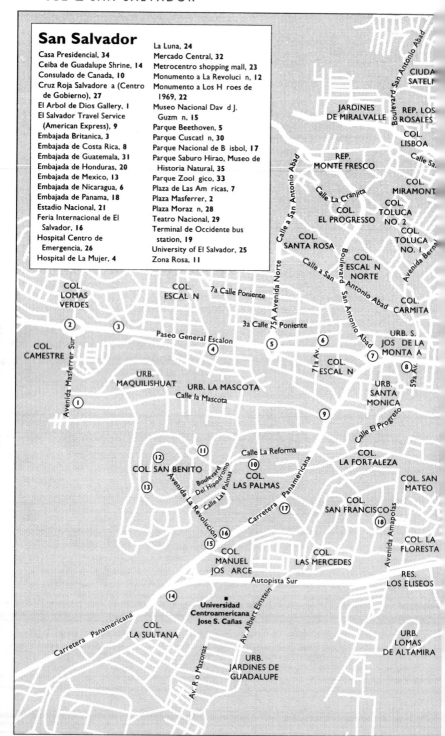

San Salvador

Casa Presidencial, 34
Ceiba de Guadalupe Shrine, 14
Consulado de Canada, 10
Cruz Roja Salvadore a (Centro
 de Gobierno), 27
El Arbol de Dios Gallery, 1
El Salvador Travel Service
 (American Express), 9
Embajada Britanica, 3
Embajada de Costa Rica, 8
Embajada de Guatemala, 31
Embajada de Honduras, 20
Embajada de Mexico, 13
Embajada de Nicaragua, 6
Embajada de Panama, 18
Estadio Nacional, 21
Feria Internacional de El
 Salvador, 16
Hospital Centro de
 Emergencia, 26
Hospital de La Mujer, 4

La Luna, 24
Mercado Central, 32
Metrocentro shopping mall, 23
Monumento a La Revoluci n, 12
Monumento a Los H roes de
 1969, 22
Museo Nacional Dav d J.
 Guzm n, 15
Parque Beethoven, 5
Parque Cuscatl n, 30
Parque Nacional de B isbol, 17
Parque Saburo Hirao, Museo de
 Historia Natural, 35
Parque Zool gico, 33
Plaza de Las Am ricas, 7
Plaza Masferrer, 2
Plaza Moraz n, 28
Teatro Nacional, 29
Terminal de Occidente bus
 station, 19
University of El Salvador, 25
Zona Rosa, 11

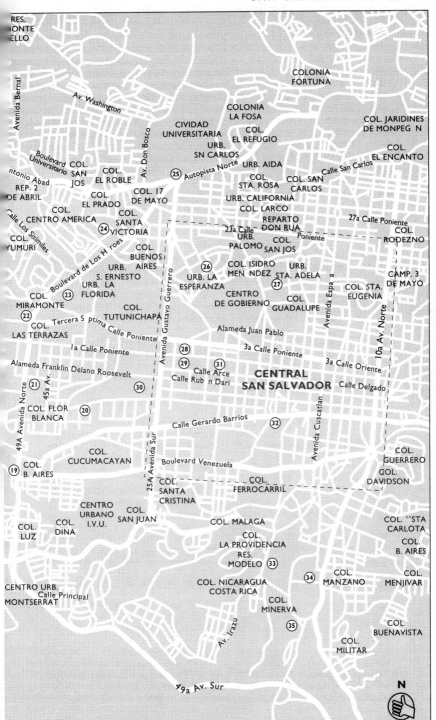

RES.
MONTE
BELLO

Avenida Bernal

Av. Washington

COLONIA
FORTUNA

COLONIA
LA FOSA

CIVIDAD
UNIVERSITARIA

COL.
EL REFUGIO

COL. JARIDINES
DE MONPEG N

URB.
SN CARLOS

Av. Don Bosco

COL.
EL ENCANTO

Boulevard
Universitario

COL.
SAN
JOS

COL.
EL ROBLE

(25) Autopista Norte

URB. AIDA

Calle San Carlos

antonio Abad
REP. 2
DE ABRIL

COL.
EL PRADO

COL. 17
DE MAYO

COL.
STA. ROSA

COL. SAN
CARLOS

Calle Los Sisimiles

COL.
CENTRO AMERICA

(24)

COL.
SANTA
VICTORIA

URB. CALIFORNIA

COL. LARCO

27a Calle Poniente

COL.
YUMURI

Boulevard de Los H roes

COL.
BUENOS
AIRES

URB.

23a Calle

REPARTO
DON RUA

Poniente

COL.
RODEZNO

URB.
PALOMO

COL.
SAN JOS

S. ERNESTO

(26)

COL. ISIDRO
MEN NDEZ

URB.
STA. ADELA

CAMP. 3
DE MAYO

COL.
MIRAMONTE

(23)

URB. LA
FLORIDA

URB. LA
ESPERANZA

(27)

Avenida Espa a

COL. STA.
EUGENIA

10a Av. Norte

(22)

COL.
TUTUNICHAPA

CENTRO
DE GOBIERNO

COL.
GUADALUPE

COL.
LAS TERRAZAS

Tercera S ptima Calle Poniente

Avenida Gustavo Guerrero

Alameda Juan Pablo

1a Calle Poniente

(28)

3a Calle Poniente

3a Calle Oriente

Alameda Franklin Delano Roosevelt

(29)

(31)

Calle Arce
Calle Rub n Dari

CENTRAL
SAN SALVADOR

Calle Delgado

(21)

45a Av.

(30)

49A Avenida Norte

COL. FLOR
BLANCA

(20)

Calle Gerardo Barrios

(32)

Avenida Cuscatlan

(19)

COL.
B. AIRES

COL.
CUCUMACAYAN

25A Avenida Sur

Boulevard Venezuela

COL.
GUERRERO

GOL.
DAVIDSON

COL.
SANTA
CRISTINA

COL.
FERROCARRIL

CENTRO
URBANO
I.V.U.

COL.
SAN JUAN

COL. MALAGA

COL.
*STA
CARLOTA

COL.
LUZ

COL.
DINA

COL.
LA PROVIDENCIA
RES.
MODELO (33)

COL.
B. AIRES

CENTRO URB.
MONTSERRAT

Calle Principal

COL. NICARAGUA
COSTA RICA

(34)

COL.
MANZANO

COL.
MENJIVAR

COL.
MINERVA

(35)

Av. Irazu

COL.
BUENAVISTA

COL.
MILITAR

79a Av. Sur

N

▨ Orientation

San Salvador's planners made a valiant effort to make the city's plan as logical as possible. The northwest corner of the **cathedral** is the city's Cartesian origin; it's here that the "principal" streets intersect. **Calle Arce** to the west and **Calle Delgado** to the east form the horizontal axis, **Avenida España** to the north and **Avenida Cuscatlán** to the south create the vertical. All other streets in the vicinity of the center are numbered, yet rarely have street signs to label them. The city's main east to west artery is undergoing quite an identity crisis. **2 Calle Oriente,** as it's known east of Avenida Cuscatlán, changes into **Calle Rubén Darío** upon crossing Cuscatlán. At 25 Av., the name changes to **Alameda Franklin Delano Roosevelt,** and at Plaza Las Américas, the name changes yet again to **Paseo General Escalón.** A couple of other important east to west arteries are **Boulevard Venezuela** to the south and **Alameda Juan Pablo II** (formerly 7 Calle, but changed in 1983 to honor the Pope, who'd walked along the street during a visit) to the north. Unfortunately, logic is slowly losing out; the suburbs popping up around the city don't follow such rational layouts.

The three most popular areas for tourists are the **Zona Rosa** (including Av. de la Revolución), which hosts the national museum, fairgrounds and monuments by day, and the bass-thumping, raging clubs by night; **El Centro,** which is anchored on the Cathedral and surrounded by plazas filled with monuments and vendors; and finally, the ultra-modern **Blvd. de los Héroes,** which attracts the city's young and wealthy to its shopping malls (Metrocentro, Metro-Sur), American fast-food joints, and bohemian coffee houses.

▨ Practical Information

Tourist Office: Instituto Salvadoreño de Turismo (ISTU), 508 Blvd. del Hipódromo (tel. 243-7835), behind the Hotel Presidente. Find maps and advice for tourists. Open Mon.-Fri. 8am-4pm. There's also an airport branch (tel. 339-9464).

Special Permits: Obtain a permit to stay in the country's scattered **Centros de Los Obreros** at the Edificio Urrutía Abrego I, 7 Av. and 15 Calle, just northeast of the Centro de Gobierno. Open Mon.-Fri. 8am-4pm.

Currency Exchange: Changing traveler's checks should be no hassle in the capital. **Banco Hipotecario** (tel. 222-2122), on Av. Cuscatlán and 4 Calle, changes with little fuss. Open Mon.-Fri. 9am-4:30pm, Sat. 9am-noon. **Banco Salvadoreño,** Calle Rubén Darío, 11/13 Avs., is open Mon.-Fri. 9am-5pm, Sat. 9am-noon. There are also banks in Metrocentro, on Blvd. de los Héroes. Remember, some limit their currency exchange services on the weekends.

Embassies: U.S. (tel. 278-4444; fax 278-6011), Blvd. Santa Elena, Antiguo Cuscatlán. Open Mon.-Fri. 8:30-4:30pm. **Canada,** Av. Las Palmas #111 (tel. 279-4659; fax 279-0765), Col. San Benito. Open Mon.-Fri. 8am-noon and 1:30-4:30pm. **U.K.,** Paseo General Escalon #4828 (tel. 298-1763; fax 298-3328). Open Mon.-Thurs. 8am-1pm and 2-4:30pm, Fri. 8am-1pm. **Mexico** (tel. 243-0443), Pasaje 12 and Calle Circunvalación, Col. San Benito, across from Hotel Presidente. Open Mon.-Fri. 8-11am. **Belize,** Condominio Médico "B," Local 5, 2nd floor, Blvd. Tutunichapa, Urb. La Esperanza (tel. 226-3588; fax 226-3682). Open Mon.-Fri. 8am-noon and 1-5pm, Sat. 8:30am-noon. **Costa Rica,** Av. Albert Einstein #11-A (tel. 273-3111; fax 273-1455). **Guatemala** (tel. 271-2225; fax 221-3019), 15 Av., Calles Arce/1. Open Mon.-Fri. 8am-noon. **Honduras,** #3697 3 Calle Pte. (tel. 223-2222; fax 221-2248), Col. Escalón. Open Mon.-Fri. 9am-noon and 1-3pm. **Nicaragua** (tel. 223-7729; fax 223-7201), 71 Av. and 1 Calle, Colonia Escalón. Open Mon.-Fri. 8am-1pm and 2-4pm. A booklet distributed by the tourist office contains a list of many more embassies and consulates. **Australia** and **New Zealand** have no embassies in El Salvador.

Immigration Office: (tel. 221-2111), in the Centro de Gobierno. Open Mon.-Fri. 8am-4pm.

American Express: (tel. 223-0177), Calle la Mascota and Interamerican Highway, Comercial la Mascota. Will hold mail for card or check holders in addition to refunding lost checks. Take bus #34 or #101 from the city center.

Airport: The **international airport** is 44km south of the city and is served by **Taca** (tel. 298-5055; fax 223-3757), the national airline that flies internationally, as well as a number of other airlines including **American** (tel. 298-0777; fax 298-0762); **British Airways** (tel. 298-1322); **Continental** (tel. 279-2233; fax 223-8968); **Mexicana** (tel. 243-3633; fax 279-4034); and **United** (tel. 279-4469; fax 223-0097). **Acaya** (tel. 271-4937), at 19 Av. and 3 Calle, runs a microbus to the airport several times daily (6, 7, 10am, and 2pm, ¢100). Or take the Route 1A bus from the cathedral (every 5min., 1hr., ¢5).

Intercity Buses: With a few exceptions, intercity buses all leave from either **Terminal Occidente** (reached by Bus #34 from *el centro*), serving destinations in the western half of the country, or **Terminal Oriente**, which serves the country's eastern half. From Terminal Occidente, on Blvd. Venezuela near 49 Av., buses run to: **Santa Ana** (#201, every 5min., 5am-7:30pm, 1hr., ¢5); **Sonsonate** (#205, every 10min., 5am-6:40pm, 1½hr., ¢6); **Ahuachapán** (#202, every 15min., 5am-6:40pm, 2hr., ¢4.50); the **Guatemalan border** at **Las Chinamas** (every hr., 6am-5pm, 3hr., ¢6); and the **Guatemalan border** at **La Hechadura** (7am and 2pm, 3½hr., ¢6.40). Leaving from Terminal Oriente to: **Chalatenango** (#125, every 10min., 4am-6:20pm, 2hr., ¢6.50); the **Honduran border** at **El Poy,** passing through **La Palma** (#119, every 30min., 4am-4pm, 4hr., ¢14); **San Miguel** (#301, every 10min., 4am-5pm, 3hr., ¢15); and **Usulután** (7, 8am, and 1pm, 3hr., ¢12). Buses #7, 29, and 34 all go from the terminal to *el centro;* #29 continues on to the Metrocentro on Blvd. de los Héroes. Bus #102 for **La Libertad** leaves from *el centro* near 13 Av. and 4 Calle (1hr., ¢5.50).

International Buses: Tica Bus (tel. 222-4808) has 1 daily bus leaving at 5:30am in front of Hotel San Carlos at Calle Concepción #121 for: **Tegucigalpa** (7hr., ¢260); **Managua** (12hr., ¢608); **San José** (2 days, ¢870); and **Panama City** (3 days, ¢1304). Tica also has a bus that leaves at 6am for **Guatemala City** (5hr., ¢138). **Puerto Bus** (tel. 222-2158; fax 222-2138) 19 Av. and Alemeda Juan Pablo II, also services **Guatemala City** (every hr., 3:30am-4:30pm, ¢55) and **Tegucigalpa** (daily 6am and 1pm, ¢140). Some routes cost more on weekends or at night.

Public Transportation: Ubiquitous buses serve destinations throughout the city from approximately 6am-8pm. Fares range from ¢0.75-2.00. Bus #34 runs between the two terminals, and passes through the center. Bus #29 goes from Metrocentro to Terminal Oriente and Bus #30 passes through *el centro* on its route between the Av. de la Revolución and Metrocentro.

Taxis: Bright yellow and found all over. Fares generally run ¢20-30; bargain if you think the price is too high. Prices go up after dark and near expensive hotels.

Car Rental: Budget (tel. 279-2811), **Avis** (tel. 224-2623), **Hertz** (tel. 226-8099; fax 225-8412). Anyone with a valid license and a ¢5000 credit limit or cash may rent. **Uno Rent-a-Car** also rents cars from the Hotel Terraza on Paseo General Escalón (tel. 279-0044; ¢180-700 per day with discounts for weekly renewal).

Market: Central Market, 6 Calle, Avs. 5/7. Open daily 6am-6pm. **Mercado Ex. Cuartel,** 8 Av. and Calle Delgado, features *artesanía.* Open daily 7:30am-5:30pm.

Laundry: Lavaquick, Calle Sisimiles #2924, 100m behind Hotel Camino Real, has same-day service. Wash and dry ¢15 each per load. Open Mon.-Sat. 8am-5pm.

English Bookstores: Most luxury hotels will sell American magazines in their newsstands. **Eutopia** offers a decent selection of English books (in the Galleria Mall, Mon.-Fri. 10am-7:30pm, Sat. 10am-3pm).

Red Cross: (tel. 222-5155) in the Centro de Gobierno.

24hr. Pharmacy: Farmacia Internacional, in the mini-mall (not Metro-Sur), 49 Av., Blvd. de los Héroes, and Alemeda Juan Pablo II.

Police: (tel. 121). The national police squad has its office here.

Post Office: (tel. 271-1922), in the Centro Gobierno on 11 Av. near 13 Calle. Open Mon.-Fri. 8am-4pm, Sat. 8am-4pm. **DHL** (tel. 279-0411; fax 223-2441), 46 Av. and Alameda Juan Pablo II, just across from Metrosur, offers speedier service. Open Mon.-Fri. 8am-6pm, Sat. 8am-noon.

Telephones: The main branch of **Antel** is on 5 Av. and Calle Rubén Darío, next to McDonald's. Open daily 6am-10pm. A smaller, less hectic branch offering all the same services stands at Torre Roble in the Metrocentro.

EL SALVADOR

■ Accommodations

Like other Central American capital cities, San Salvador's budget accommodations involve a little give and take. There are cheap places to stay, but they are in unsafe neighborhoods; conversely, those in safe neighborhoods are not cheap. Budget hotels are clustered in four areas: near the Terminal Oriente, near the Terminal Occidente, the center, and in the residential neighborhoods near Blvd. de los Héroes. For longer stays, the hotels around the Blvd. de los Héroes are a good compromise. While a bit more expensive, there's higher security for your person and your luggage.

Ximena's Guest House, #202 Calle San Salvador (tel. 226-9268). From Blvd. de los Héroes, turn west onto Calle Gabriela Mistral; the first left splits into three—take the middle one. Expatriates, Peace Corps volunteers, and other travelers flock to this place for its homey atmosphere and cheap, modern rooms. Unfortunately, so do mosquitoes; bring repellent (dorm ¢50; singles ¢120, with bath ¢150).

Happy House Guest Home, #2951 Calle Sisimiles (tel. 226-6866), 200m behind the Hotel Camino Real, near Blvd. de los Héroes. The Happy House has just renovated, offering bright clean rooms, and new not so happy prices. Singles ¢190; doubles ¢220, includes fan, bath and TV.

Hospedaje Clementina (tel./fax 225-5962), 39 Av. Norte (what Calle Gabriela Mistral becomes after Calle San Antonio) and Calle Washington. Cool rooms with ceiling fans face a garden with hammocks and a restaurant (¢100 per person). The lobby has an incredible book exchange, probably the highest concentration of English language books in the capital.

American Guest House (tel. 271-0224; fax 271-3667), 17 Av., Calle Arce/1 Calle. Much like San Salvador itself, this hotel has undergone countless renovations and add-ons. The Guest House is eager to please, offering many services (including luggage storage, telephone calls, photocopies, laundry), but all for a price. Singles ¢125, with bath ¢165; dorm rooms (12 people, 1 fan) ¢75 per person.

Hotel Yucatán, #673 Calle Concepción (tel. 221-2585), near Terminal Oriente. The concrete slabs of rooms are dark and a bit dusty, but the beds are thick and comfortable, the bathrooms brighter than most, and the management seemingly more diligent than elsewhere (¢20 per person, with bath ¢25).

Hotel Roma, 3145 Blvd. Venezuela (tel. 245-4255), a block west of Terminal Occidente across the road. Painted in enticing brown and yellow, Roma has musty, but surprisingly bright rooms with desk fans; the mattresses are firm, but may be slightly odor-tainted. Ask for a room off the street if noise is a problem. Remember, it's only one night. Singles ¢50, with bath ¢70; doubles ¢70.

■ Food

Food is definitely San Salvador's strong point. Restaurants abound, and cheap, tasty meals of every sort are not hard to come by. Small *pupusa* and *tortilla* stands are absolutely everywhere, even in some of the quieter residential neighborhoods. The area around **Blvd. de Los Héroes,** in addition to being one of San Salvador's prime nightspots, is U.S. fast food row. Weary travelers hankering for Big Macs or pan pizzas can hamburgle their way to **McDonald's, Burger King, Pollo Campero, Wendy's,** and either of two **Pizza Huts.** In addition, there are a number of upscale Mexican restaurants and steak houses. Most restaurants are open until at least 10pm, some until midnight or later. **Metro-Sur,** Metrocentro's southern annex on Blvd. de Los Héroes and Alemeda Juan Pablo II, has an open-air food court which is home to a number of fast-food joints and Salvadoran places with quick, cheap eats. On **Calle Lamatepec,** just behind Hotel Camino Real, sit about a dozen relatively pricey seafood places.

Restaurante Karen (tel. 226-1552), just off Blvd. de Los Héroes between Bressler's and Wendy's, a block before Calle Gabriela Mistral. A classic *comedor* with authentic Salvadoran cuisine. Essentially, it's cheap protein washed down with salsa. Typical plates ¢15-20. Open daily 7am-11pm.

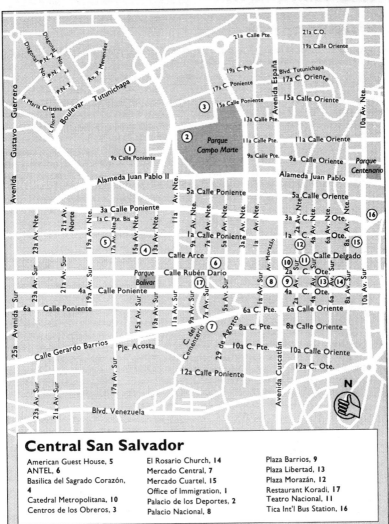

Central San Salvador

American Guest House, 5
ANTEL, 6
Basílica del Sagrado Corazón, 4
Catedral Metropolitana, 10
Centros de los Obreros, 3

El Rosario Church, 14
Mercado Central, 7
Mercado Cuartel, 15
Office of Immigration, 1
Palacio de los Deportes, 2
Palacio Nacional, 8

Plaza Barrios, 9
Plaza Libertad, 13
Plaza Morazán, 12
Restaurant Koradi, 17
Teatro Nacional, 11
Tica Int'l Bus Station, 16

Restaurante Taiwan, 1437 Calle San Antonio Abad (tel. 226-0707), a block west of the top of Blvd. de Los Héroes. Given the genuine Chinese food, the restaurant's prices aren't through the roof. The owner is always willing to chat; just make it clear that you understand that Taiwan is different from China. Chow mein (¢30), *chorizo de Taiwan* (¢25), or *Won Ton Frito de Camara* (¢18). Open daily 11:30am-3pm and 5:30-10pm.

Restaurante Koradi (tel. 221-2545), 9 Av. and 4 Calle. A small, *comedor*-like restaurant in *el centro* abutting a health-food store, Koradi serves vegetarian food at decent prices, including fresh salad (¢8) and unbleached rice (¢6). Open Mon.-Fri. 7:30am-5:45pm, Sat. 7:30am-3pm.

La Ventana, Calle San Antonio Abad. An extremely popular restaurant that dishes up large servings of cosmopolitan cuisine. They also have exquisite cakes and coffee. Trendy San Salvadorans crowd in for dinner or coffee, which can mean long waits on the weekends, but the prices are still affordable.

■ Sights

Catedral Metropolitana looms over the center of San Salvador, serving as a daily reminder of the city's disaster-prone history. Slated to re-open by February 1997, the Cathedral was still under renovation in the summer of 1997. The original cathedral was begun in 1808 and completed a decade later, only to be completely re-destroyed by an earthquake in 1873. Subsequently rebuilt, the new church was brought down again in 1951, this time by fire. The next version was strictly functional and sturdy, built in simple Byzantine style with drab, unadorned concrete. It was here that a lone gunman shot down **Oscar Romero** in 1980 as he was giving Mass; the Archbishop's crypt is inside the cathedral. Yet another earthquake damaged the structure in 1986, and the building has been closed ever since. Recently, paintings that will serve as altarpieces in the refurbished cathedral have been on display, and many look forward to seeing what this latest version will look like—and how long it will last.

The entrance to the cathedral is on 2 Calle, facing **Plaza Barrios,** Salvador's main square. On the west end of the plaza is the bright yellow **Palacio Nacional.** Once the seat of government, the building was also ravaged by the 1986 quake and remains closed to this day. Two blocks east of Plaza Barrios is **Plaza Libertad,** a less hectic counterpoint to the main *zócalo* (square). Facing this plaza is a rather bizarre church, **El Rosario.** Its external, crumbling structure is like a half-cylinder turned on its side; inside hide some enthralling modern sculptures, made from steel rebars and other scraps, depicting religious scenes. The church also holds the tomb of **Father Delgado,** an important figure in Central America's independence movement.

Southwest of the center, along the Interamerican Hwy. (the *carretera* out to Santa Tecla) at Av. La Revolución, lies **Museo Nacional David Gúzman,** home to El Salvador's finest Maya artifacts, including the intricate **Stela of Tazumal.** Unfortunately, the museum is temporarily closed, and its treasures are locked in storage while a new facility is built on the site. Construction is slated to be completed by late 1997. Just before the museum, on the site of the international fairgrounds, is the **Mercado Nacional de Artesanías,** a scaled-down version of Mercado Ex-Cuartel (see **Practical Information,** p. 184; open daily 9am-6pm). Buses #34 and #101 pass by both places.

At the end of Av. La Revolución is the **Monumento a la Revolución,** a soaring modernist mosaic of a figure breaking free of its shackles and reaching for the sky. Ironically, the monument, a tribute to the peoples of Central America, is situated in the center of San Salvador's most exclusive neighborhood.

A little further out in the same direction is **Jardín Botánico La Laguna,** a quiet botanical garden with a variety of flora. Set in an extinct volcanic crater, La Laguna actually *was* a lake until 1873, when an earthquake opened a drain-like fissure below the water's surface. Today the crater houses gardens and a contaminating industrial complex—several shady trails through the park are muffled from the loud factory booms. Bus #101C from *el centro* and bus #44 from Metrocentro pass through Antiguo Cuscatlan, from which it's about 1km to the gardens.

Life's a Gas

In New York, people hang out on **stoops;** in Los Angeles or Las Vegas, cars slowly cruise by the **strip;** in San Salvador, the hang-out is the **local gas station.** In some gas stations you'll find upwards of 30 cars parked in the lot, while the owners crank the stereos, dance, and drink *cerveza* like it was going out of style. The scene is reminiscent of a **tailgate party** before a big sporting event; however, in San Salvador tailgating *is* the event. The crowds that gather defy age, sex, and gender barriers with all types of *capitaleños* shaking their collective **booty** at the Shell station. So if you are tight on cash, or can't make it to the Zona Rosa, give the old Esso station on the Blvd. de los Héroes a shot. Remember to **B.Y.O.B.**—Bring Your Own Bumper—or you won't have anywhere to sit.

■ Entertainment

San Salvador can get rough at night, so be on guard, particularly in the city center. City buses cease early, so plan on taking a taxi for the return; fares tend to go up once the buses stop running. The capital is a great place to catch a **movie**. Theatres typically show subtitled, two-month-old Hollywood flicks, though the lag time is getting shorter (admission ¢20-25). Some offer ¢9 matinees; call ahead. **Caribe** (tel. 223-6968), at Plaza Las Américas, has four screens. **Beethoven** (tel. 224-2084), at Parque Beethoven, and **Variedades** (tel. 225-1242), at Calle San Antonio Abad and Calle Gabriela Mistral (near Blvd. de Los Héroes), show films in relatively safe neighborhoods. Check newspapers for local listings.

Blvd. de Los Héroes is one of the prime nightspots in San Salvador. *Mariachi* bands stroll around looking for customers, and the whirls and screams of fairground rides blare in the background while fire-spitters work the main intersections. Higher up along the boulevard, open-air restaurant patrons boogie to live bands. **Las Antorchas** and the adjacent **El Coral Steakhouse,** located on the Blvd. two blocks north of Calle Gabriela Mistral, host live bands of all types (*salsa, merengue,* and rock); thump and jiggle nightly until 1am.

There is also a nascent bohemian scene, anchored by club **La Luna** (tel. 260-2921), located at 228 Calle Berlin, off Blvd. de los Héroes. Pick up a monthly calendar at Ximenas, or just stop by and see the live music shows at night, weekly movies in the evenings, and workshops during the day. **La Ventana** hosts visitors until after 3am on the weekends (dinner ¢50, cakes and drinks ¢20), as does its more juvenile neighbor **Tres Diablos** (beers ¢8; drinks, albeit weak ones, go for ¢25).

The hottest clubs are in the **Zona Rosa,** where bus #30B heads. Rump-shakers stay at clubs ranging from Euro-dressy to club-kid trashy until the buses start again in the morning. One can bounce from bar to bar, but all the beautiful people will end up at **Kaos** (that's *chaos* to you) or **Hale la Jara** (behind Guadalajara Grille).

WEST OF SAN SALVADOR

■ La Libertad

The coast in and around La Libertad is blessed with a rare combination of wind, current, and shore which makes the waves break just so—that is, meaning constant swells of at least five feet. Reputed home of the best surfing in Central America, La Libertad attracts huge numbers of wave riders. Some are home grown, but the majority are part of a globe-trotting crowd that has turned this once quiet fishing village into a 90s Beach Blanket Bingo that would do Frankie and Annette proud.

The surfers aren't solely responsible for converting the place. During the war, *capitaleños* descended from San Salvador to this safe haven for some rest and relaxation. Unfortunately, the strong undertow has pulled away most of the beach, but the serenity of the crashing waves make up for any missing sand. So swimming's out, but surf's definitely up. If you're without a board, then, as they say, sucks to be you, *dude.*

Orientation and Practical Information Set in a broad, curved bay, the beach is split in half by a long pier where fishermen dock and hawk the catch of the day. **Calle Calvario,** the principal *calle,* is the main drag to the west; a block south, **2 Calle** is the main street heading east. A block south of that, **4 Calle** runs along the ocean. Walking the town's 10 blocks takes a little more than five minutes.

Banco de Fomento, on 2 Calle across from Antel, changes traveler's checks (open Mon.-Fri. 9am-4pm, Sat. 9am-1pm). **Antel** is at 2 Av. and 2 Calle (fax 335-3008; open daily 7am-8pm). For **bus** destinations west along the coast, bus #80 runs to **Zunzal** (every 15min., 5:40am-5:50pm) and bus #192 heads to **La Perla.** Traveling east along the Costa Balsamo is difficult by public transportation. **El Pacífico** goes all the way to

Sonsonate (1:45pm, 2½hr.). Bus #540 zooms to **Zacatecoluca** (daily 5:45am, 12:20, 2:40, 3:25, and 4:20pm, 2hr., ¢5.50; transfer at **La Flecha** to **Costa del Sol**) and of course #102 rushes to **San Salvador** (every 10 min., 1hr., ¢4). **Market** stalls line 2 Av. and 1 Calle (open daily 6am-6pm). **Farmacia Jerusalem** (tel. 335-3508) is on Calle Calvario, Avs. 1/Bolívar (open 6am-6pm). The **post office** roosts on 2 Av. (open Mon.-Fri. 8am-noon and 1:30-5pm, Sat. 8am-noon, Sun. 8-11am).

Accommodations and Food The best deal on the coast is the **Centro de Los Obreros,** about 1km west of town. Tourists are permitted to stay for free if they first obtain permission in San Salvador (see **Practical Information,** p. 184). The *centro* has cots, dark communal baths, a swimming pool, and a *cantina.* Complete the picture with your own sleeping bag or sheets; otherwise, it's bare skin to dirty mattress. It's very crowded during the day, but at night it becomes The Shining By The Sea. In town, **Puerto Bello** (tel. 335-3013), 1 Av. and 2 Calle, offers a great deal. Clean plaster-and-tile rooms face a bright courtyard, the mattresses are firm, and the open-air shared bath is kept sanitary. Ask for the room up top with a 360° view of the town (¢50 per person). At 5 Av. and 4 Calle lolls **Motel Rick** (tel. 335-3033). The paint is fresh and all rooms have desk fans and private baths separated by half-walls (singles ¢100; doubles ¢150 for 24hr.).

La Libertad is sprinkled with cheap *comedores* serving the basics: beans and rice, *carne asada, pollo dorado,* and some seafood. The shoreline is packed with gorgeous restaurants with inflated prices perched over crashing waves. **Rancho Mar El Delfin,** across the street from Posada Don Lito, is probably the slickest of these (lobster with shrimp ¢100, *coctel de ceviche* ¢35). **Restaurante Punta Roca** (tel. 335-3261), next door, is a bit more homey and marginally cheaper (*filete de marisco* ¢45, *carne asada* ¢50). Punta Roca is run by ex-Miami native, Bob Rotherhan, who can give advice above the waves and offers fishing tours.

■ Sonsonate

The state of Sonsonate is unabashedly cow country, where huge *fincas* straddle some of the most scenic mountains this side of *Heidi.* The namesake capital is no sleepy town, however. Sonsonate buzzes with energy worthy of a small city, though only 60,000 souls call it home. To walk through the marketplace is to witness commerce in its most basic form: shoppers barter, haggle, and offer everything from chickens to "Nikey" sneakers (one little "y" = no copyright infringement) with a fervor that clearly illustrates the town's rapid pace of life. Numerous new car dealerships add to the sheen of prosperity, while record stores thumping out the hits and trucks grumbling through from the port of Acajutla add to the overall roar. In its rush to get ahead, though, Sonsonate has all but erased traces of its 450-year history. Even the usual historical standbys like the cathedral smack of the modern age, and only a few colonial buildings peer through. If the diesel fumes or punishing heat of modernity wear you out, head for the mercifully close Pacific coast.

Orientation and Practical Information Sonsonate is laid out in the standard grid pattern with **Avenida Morazán** and **Paseo 15 de Septiembre** as keystone streets. Even-numbered *avenidas* and *calles* extend to the north and west respectively: odd numbers run to the south and east. Some of the numbered streets have been renamed in honor of various figures, but street names and addresses aren't commonly used anyway. The bus terminal is on Paseo 15 de Septiembre between 14 and 16 Avs., while the cathedral anchors Av. Morazon.

Exchange currency and traveler's checks at **Banco Agrícola Mercantil** (tel. 451-0008), Av. Morazán and Paseo 15 de Septiembre, on the park (open Mon.-Fri. 8am-5pm, Sat. 9am-noon), or **Banco de Comercio,** 4 Av. and Paseo 15 de Septiembre (open Mon.-Fri. 9am-5pm, Sat. 9am-noon). Call your significant other from **Antel** (fax 451-2044), Av. Morazán and 2 Calle, a block north of the square (open daily 6am-10pm). **Buses** leave from the terminal on Paseo 15 de Septiembre, about 10 blocks west of the square, to: **San Salvador** (every 5min., 4am-5:30pm, 1½hr., ¢6); **Santa Ana** (every 20min., 4am-4pm, 2hr., ¢4.70); the **Guatemalan border** at **La Hachadura** (every 10min., 4am-5:15pm, 1½hr., ¢5); **La Libertad** (5:40am and 3:20pm, 2½hr., ¢5.30); **Acajutla** (every ½hr., 4am-8pm, 45min., ¢2.50); **Los Cobanos** (every hr., 4am-5pm, 45min.,¢3); and **Ahuachapán** (every 40min., 5:20am-6pm, ¢4.50). Bright blue **local buses** are all #53 followed by some letter. They travel between the square and the terminal and to surrounding villages. Bus #53D goes to **Nabuizalco** every 10 minutes, and #53A goes to **Izalco** every five minutes; each leaves from the square and costs ¢1. Familiar, bright yellow **taxis** line up on the east end of the park and charge a pricey ¢15 to the terminal. The **central market** is on Paseo 15 de Septiembre, just inside the railroad tracks, about three blocks from the square. The streets to the immediate northeast of the park are also lined with stalls. Both areas stay open while the sun shines. **Farmacia Firenze** (tel. 451-1156), 5 Av., 1/3 Calles, doles out drugs on the town's medical row (open daily 8am-6:30pm). Pharmacies also dot the streets near the park. The **Hospital Municipal,** 5 Av., 1/3 Calles, stands amid a slew of doctor's offices. Call for an **emergency** (tel. 451-0200; 24hr.). There's a **post office** in a non-descript building next to a huge movie theater, 1 Av., 3/5 Calles (open Mon.-Fri. 8am-noon and 2-5pm, Sat. 8am-noon, Sun. 8-11am).

Accommodations and Food There are two clusters of hotels in Sonsonate—near the bus terminal and in the center of town. Those near the bus terminal are uniformly rough and dirty, while those in the center are better, but inconvenient for travelers on a layover. **Hotel Florida** (tel. 451-0167), 18 Av., just half a block north of Paseo 15 de Septiembre and two blocks east of the terminal, combines cleanliness with working ceiling fans. The rooms are dark, and the public bath isn't above reproach, but it's still a good deal (¢45 per room). Similar in style and price is **Hospedaje Brasil,** on 14 Av., half a block south of Paseo 15 de Septiembre. The beds aren't as comfy as those in Hotel Florida, nor do the rooms have ceiling fans, but it'll do in a pinch (singles ¢40; doubles ¢60). **Hotel Orbe** (tel. 451-1416 or 451-1517), 2 Av. and 4 Calle, two blocks north of the square, offers sweet refuge for weary travelers. The poshest place in town is a miraculous value. The beds are soft, the private baths pass the white glove test, and the fans will blow your mind (singles ¢70, with A/C ¢130; doubles ¢100, with A/C ¢175).

Sonsonante, seized by the fast food craze sweeping El Salvador, is not the place to look for Salvadoran cuisine in all its glory—travelers will be hard-pressed to find a restaurant that doesn't serve hamburgers. There are two **Pizza Atto's** in town, one by the bus terminal on Paseo 15 de Septiembre, the other near the square in a mini-mall on 1 Av. and Paseo 15 de Septiembre. Both serve up mighty fine pizzas with generous toppings and cheese; try a personal pepperoni pizza (¢24) or garlic bread with cheese (¢12.25). They even deliver (tel. 451-1094 or 451-3878; open daily 11am-9pm). **Sabor Club** (tel. 451-5401), on the north end of the square, specializes in all kinds of fruit shakes (¢8.50) and juices (¢7), including pineapple, mango, papaya, and plain old vanilla. They also serve sandwiches (¢9; open daily 7am-7pm).

■ Near Sonsonate

Set on the gentle alluvial fan of Santa Ana Volcano and Cerro Verde, the scenic countryside surrounding Sonsonate is dotted with a number of interesting villages. **Nahuizalco,** 6km to the north, is a Pipil town specializing in basketry and furniture. The town has a *feria de artesanía* from June 16-25. Bus #53D leaves for Nahuizalco from the square in Sonsonate every 15 minutes.

Just outside the nearby town of **Izalco** is the **Turicentro Atecozol,** a serene, forested area with trails, basketball courts, and a landscaped network of swimming pools and palm trees worthy of a Hawaiian resort (open daily 8am-5pm; admission ¢7; *cabañas* ¢35). Bus #53A (from the central square in Sonsonate) zips to Izalco; from there, the *turicentro* is six blocks from the church. Facing the church, take the road to the right until it becomes a dirt path, then follow it over the bridge.

For dabbling in dribbly natural wonders, **Salto Las Victorias** is a pleasant, if not terribly impressive, waterfall. Set 2km outside of **Caluco,** the falls are an easy walk through beautiful farmland; in some ways, the journey, not the destination, is the attraction. Take the road out of Caluco to the left of the church, score a goal at the soccer field, and continue for about 1km. Turn right at a palm-tree-lined road paved with bright red volcanic gravel, and scurry across the railroad tracks. From there it's a short distance through some cornfields. A bus leaves every hour from Sonsonate and passes through Izalco along the way to Caluco. Pick-up trucks also leave from Izalco to Caluco about once every 30 minutes.

The port of **Acajutla,** about 20km to the south, suffers from an identity crisis: one half is a busy container facility, the other a lazy coastal town. To hit the **beach,** go back to Pedro de Alvarado (the exit from the highway), walk downhill about 3 blocks, then cut between buildings to the black sand. Farther up the coast to the right are nicer, wider beaches, but conventional wisdom holds that it's best to go *en masse;* hidden coves and overgrown paths invite tourist-molesting thieves, and currents get trickier and stronger due to a river outlet. The safest bet away from Acajutla proper is the distant **Playa de Metalió. Banco Cuscatlan,** on Calle Acaxual, changes traveler's checks, but draws interminably long lines all day long (Mon.-Fri. 9am-5pm). **Taxis** are available on the main street for the ride up the coast, as are **buses** to Sonsonate (every 10min., 4:30-9pm, ½hr., ¢2.50). The only other buses out of town go to **Kilometro 5** on the wide, freshly-paved highway (¢1). From there, buses speed to **La Libertad** and the border at **Hachadura.** On the corner of Av. Pedro de Alvarado and Calle Principal is the **post office** (Mon.-Fri. 8am-noon and 2-5pm, Sat. 8am-noon). If you have to spend the night in Acajutla, look for the **Hotel Miramar** (tel. 452-3183) on its waterside hilltop perch. With a pool and on-site restaurant, it almost makes the rest of the town unnecessary (¢70 per room). Don't forget bug repellent or you may become an unsuspecting guest at a welcoming party thrown in your honor.

■ Ahuachapán

The departmental capital of Ahuachapán distinguishes itself neither by its beauty nor lack thereof. Instead, it jives on java, which it produces enough of to jump-start a nation. However, the town gets its electricity not from its own coffee-infused veins, but from *ausoles,* boiling mud pits that can be tapped for electricity. Prosperous, placid Ahuachapán goes on its merry, fortunate way, having been spared the violence of the civil war. What most distinguishes Ahuachapán from so many other towns are its *two* central plazas, **Parque Menéndez** to the north and **La Concordia** to the south. Most importantly, Ahuachapán is the first (or last) stop for travelers coming from (or going to) Guatemala. Shops close and people desert the streets at early hours. Perhaps everyone is tired from a long day's journey or has to turn in for tomorrow's early departure; after all, nearly everyone is en route to someplace else.

Orientation and Practical Information Situated 23km from the Guatemalan border at Las Chinamas, Ahuachapán is the first sizable town on the road to San Salvador. **Calle Barrios** and **Avenida Menéndez** comprise the town's axes; their intersection is unremarkably marked by a bank and a fast-food restaurant. **Parque Menéndez** is bounded by Av. Menéndez on the west and 6 Calle on the north. Buses run past here before pulling into the terminal two blocks north on Av. Commercial and 10 Calle. **La Concordia** is on 1 Av. and 3 Calle.

Banco Cuscatlan, on Av. Menéndez and Calle Barrios, gladly changes traveler's checks (open Mon.-Fri. 9am-1pm and 1:45-4pm). **Banco Hipotecario,** Av. Menéndez and 1a Calle, prominently features Citicorp posters, but will not change the checks without the purchasing agreement as further verification (in addition to a passport and counter-signature; Mon.-Fri. 9am-4:30pm, Sat. 9am-noon). If these don't work, Av. Menéndez is blessed with many more banks that, *ojalá,* will change your checks. **Antel** is at 2 Av. Sur and 3 Calle Poniente, on the south side of La Concordia (open daily 6am-10pm). Pay phones are sprinkled liberally throughout the city, with con-

---

Don't Worry, Be Happy

One thing the budget traveler must be prepared for when venturing through Central America is the expression "fíjese." Second only to "buenos días" in usage, it's an extremely common expression. According to the handy-dandy Spanish pocket dictionary, it means **"take notice,"** but in the harried life of the budget traveler, it means "get ready for some bad news." For example, one may go to a restaurant to find that the advertised **all-day lunch special** ended at 11am. Fíjese. One may be longing for a piece of Americana and visit a Burger King to find they have no Whoppers. Fíjese. One may go to a store with a Mastercard or Visa sign posted in the window and find that it is merely decoration because the owners accept neither card. Fíjese. So the next time you hear "fíjese," take a deep breath and order a Gallo, Corona (or whatever the **national beer** is) and think of what a great time you're having. With so much to enjoy, you will hardly miss the Whoppers at Burger King.

---

centrations in the two parks. **Buses** radiate out from the terminal in Ahuachapán in three directions. To the north is the **Guatemalan border** at **Las Chinamas** (#263, every 15min., 4am-6pm, 45min., ¢3). Bus #249 runs south to **Sonsonate** (every hr., 6am-5pm, 2hr., ¢7), and Bus #202 zooms east to **Santa Ana** (1½hr., ¢4) and continues on to **San Salvador** (every 10min., 3:30am-4pm, 2½hr., ¢7). Buy a cheap watch or leather purse at the municipal **market** on the west side of Parque Menéndez (open daily 6am-6pm). And for travelers who *must* have their corn flakes, there is a **supermarket** next to Mister Pollo. One can find medicinal relief at the **Farmacia Santa Elisa,** Av. 2 de Abril just past the Parque Menéndez (open Mon.-Sat. 8am-7pm). For more serious troubles, try the **hospital** (tel. 443-0015) on Av. Commerical, between Calle Barrios and 1 Calle, or head to the **police,** 1 Av. Sur and 3 Calle Poniente (24hr. tel. 443-1681). The **post office** is on 3 Calle Oriente between 1 and 3 Av. Sur (open Mon.-Fri. 8am-5pm, Sat. 8pm-noon, Sun. 8am-11am).

Accommodations and Food Hotels in Ahuachapán are uniformly clean and decent; the only downside is that there are no dirt-cheap dives for the bankrupt. On 6a Calle, facing Parque Menendez, the **Hotel Sun José** (tel. 443-1820) beckons the colón-deprived, border-crosser with its convenient location and simple and surprisingly clean single rooms with fans and baths (¢70; doubles for ¢120). Go all out at **Boarding House Casa Blanca,** 2 Av. Norte and Calle Barrios (tel. 443-1505; fax 443-1503), which has spotless rooms with ceiling fans or A/C (¢50 extra) and gorgeous baths with hot water. The hotel surrounds a lush Spanish courtyard with comfortable chairs and a 19-inch TV (singles ¢140; doubles ¢225).

Ahuachapán has an utter lack of *comedores.* The closest thing is **Mister Pollo,** providently located at the town's center (Av. Menéndez and Calle Barrios), which serves fast food chicken (four pieces ¢22) and fantastic milkshakes (¢10; open daily 8am-8pm). Playing McDonald's to Mister Pollo's Burger King is **Pollo Campero,** Av. Menéndez and 1a Calle (open daily 6:30am-9pm), which offers basically the same menu and accepts credit cards. Barring these two, there are always the market and street vendors, but even they don't sell big, satisfying meals.

■ Near Ahuachapán: Border to Guatemala

A 45-minute bus ride north leads to the border with Guatemala at **Las Chinamas,** one of four points of entry shared by El Salvador and Guatemala. The post is open daily from 5am-9pm. It is possible to cross later, though public transportation stops running at about the official closing time. There is no official entrance fee coming into El Salvador, but a Salvadoran visa purchase is mandatory (US$10); there is no exit fee. **Buses** and pick-up trucks to Ahuachapán leave every 15 minutes (¢3). Buses to Guatemala City leave roughly every hour. There is a **tourist office (ISTU)** at Las Chinamas, open roughly the same hours as the border, which hands out reams of photocopied sheets in English and Spanish about various sites in El Salvador. Their list of bus schedules is especially helpful.

The official procedure is surprisingly easy. Simply proceed from the bus to immigration, check out, get stamped, and walk the quarter mile to the actual border. There guards will check exit papers. Head over the bridge to the *migración* stand about half a mile away. Get papers there and you're free to go—no dogs, checkpoints, or bag examinations. It's a trip of about one mile all told, but official *porteros* are on hand to help those with bad backs, heavy bags, or chronic laziness. Finally, it's best not to arrive near closing time when officials get testy and lines get long.

■ Santa Ana

Rather than huff and puff to catch up with San Salvador, Santa Ana's 210,000 residents have accepted living in the nation's *segunda ciudad,* thus sparing themselves the burdens of urban sprawl and decay. However, Santa Ana's days of playing the boring, ugly stepsister are over; the city is shaking off the dust and rightfully claiming its place as Queen of the West—western El Salvador, that is. All over the city, but particularly in the centro, buildings are being repainted, facades restored, and parks spruced up. Not to be outdone by the capital's metro center, Santa Ana has constructed its own city center on Avenida Delgado (7/9 Calle). Once the scaffolding comes down, Santa Ana promises to sparkle and shine in genteel, colonial splendor, but the city has not allowed the chaos of construction to overcome its halcyon charm; old habits like the midday siesta keep the pace in check. Even the market and bus terminal, normally nodes of chaos in Salvadoran cities, are orderly and efficient. Buses leave and arrive with astonishing frequency to other cities and towns, as well as to fantastic attractions like **Lago de Coatepeque, Parque Nacional Cerro Verde,** and the **Maya ruins** at Tazumal.

ORIENTATION AND PRACTICAL INFORMATION

At the southwest corner of the central plaza is the intersection of **Calle Libertad** and **Avenida Independencia.** To the north and west, *calles* and *avenidas* increase in even integers, to the south and east in odd ones. Most of the town lies just southwest of the square—the **bus terminal** stands at 10 Av. and 15 Calle, most of the budget hotels await a few blocks north along 10 Av., and several restaurants glut Av. Independencia south of the square (3-11 Calles).

Telephones: Antel (fax 441-0870), 2 blocks east of the square on 5 Av. and Calle Libertad. Open daily 6am-10pm. Pay phones are scattered throughout the city.

Currency Exchange: Banco Salvadoreño, 2 Av. and 1 Calle (tel. 441-0207), is one of the few banks that change traveler's checks. Open Mon.-Fri. 9am-4pm. **Banco Agro,** 10 Av. and 19/21 Calle, across the street from the bus station, is another. Open Mon.-Fri. 8:30am-5pm. The numerous **Casas de Cambios** often have better rates than the banks.

Buses: From Santa Ana, buses fan out to all parts of the country; service to the western portion is particularly heavy and there is rarely a long wait. To: **San Salvador** (4am-5:30pm, 1½hr., ¢5); **Ahuachapán** (every 15min., 4am-6pm, 1hr., ¢4); **Sonsonate** (every 20min., 5am-5:45pm, 2hr., ¢4.70); **Metapán** (every 15min., 4:15am-6:20pm, 1½hr., ¢5.40); the **Guatemalan border** at **San Cristobal** (every 15min., 5:45am-6pm, 1hr., ¢2.50); **Lago Coatepeque** (every 45min., 5:30am-4:30pm, 1hr., ¢2.20); and **Cerro Verde** (10:30am, 1:30, and 3:30pm; ¢6).

Local Buses: #51 is the local bus, serving various points within Santa Ana. Most buses will eventually pass by the terminal; the fare is ¢1. #55 goes to the hospital.

Taxis: An uncommon sight in this compact city, taxis occasionally line up along the square and charge ¢10 to the terminal.

Market: The streets to the immediate north and west of the bus terminal are chock-full of market stalls. Open during daylight hours; some stalls close during *siesta.* Other shopping strips are along 1 and 3 Calle from Av. Independencia through the even-numbered *avenidas,* petering out at about Av. 8.

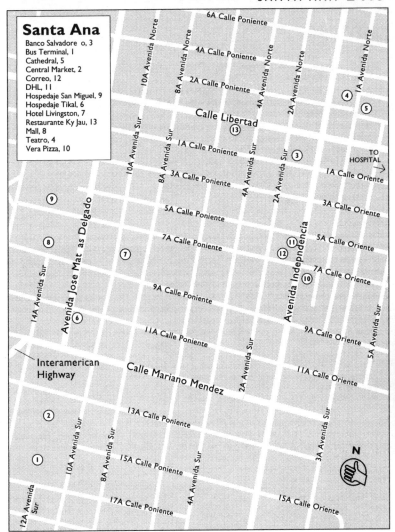

Santa Ana

Banco Salvadore o, 3
Bus Terminal, 1
Cathedral, 5
Central Market, 2
Correo, 12
DHL, 11
Hospedaje San Miguel, 9
Hospedaje Tikal, 6
Hotel Livingston, 7
Restaurante Ky Jau, 13
Mall, 8
Teatro, 4
Vera Pizza, 10

EL SALVADOR

Pharmacy: Farmacia Fray Martín (tel. 440-0286), 10 Av., 7/9 Calles. Open daily 8:30am-1pm and 2-5:30pm.
Medical Services: The central **hospital** is a bit out of the way at 13 Av. and 1 Calle, 7 blocks east of the square. **Emergency** number: 441-1780.
Police: Main station on 12 Av. and 25 Calle; a station closer to town is located on 2 Av., 9/11 Calle. 24hr. **Emergency** number: 440-1881.
Post Office: On 7 Calle, 2 Av./Av. Independencia. Open Mon.-Fri. 7:30am-5pm, Sat. 7:30am-noon. **DHL** is near the post office on Av. Independencia (5/7 Calle).

ACCOMMODATIONS

Many rooms in the hotels in Santa Ana are cut from the same dark and windowless mold. Some have private baths, and public baths are usually a row of stalls exposed to the open air, guarded only by flimsy wooden doors.

Hospedaje San Miguel (tel. 441-3465), 7 Calle, 12/14 Avs. A pleasant surprise, and winner of the best bang for the buck award. Bright courtyard (darker rooms), and acceptable baths. Singles ¢25, with bath ¢50; doubles ¢35, with bath ¢45.

Hotel Livingston (tel. 441-1801), 10 Av., 7/9 Calles, about 3 blocks north of the bus terminal. The rooms are as clean as San Miguel's *and* they have fans, the beds are more comfortable, and the public baths are in a better shape—all for double the price. Singles ¢45, with bath ¢70; doubles ¢65, with bath ¢85.

Hospedaje Tikal, 10 Av., 9/11 Calles, about 4 blocks north of the bus terminal. The management tries hard here, judging by the courtyard's cheerily spruced appearance and abundance of potted plants. The rooms are clean enough (no fans) and the public bath tolerable. ¢35-¢70 per room.

Internacional Inn, 10 Av. and 25 Calle (tel. 440-0810 or 440-0804), 5 blocks south of the terminal. Santa Ana's splurge-central breaks the mold. All rooms have windows, gorgeous private baths, ceiling fans, cable TV, and phones. Also look for odd pink lamps, floral print bedspreads, and ubiquitous pictures of Germany. Singles ¢125; doubles ¢200. Laundry service is tip-as-you-please—please do.

FOOD

Although the city has given in to the fast food craze somewhat, plenty of restaurants still specialize in Salvadoran victuals. It may not be haute cuisine, but it is cheap and damn good. The full range of Santa Ana's offerings can be found on "Restaurant Row," Av. Independencia between 3 and 9 Calles.

Restaurante Ky Jua (tel. 447-7379), Calle Libertad, 2/4 Avs. A pleasant, upscale restaurant that serves authentic Chinese food (quite a rarity in these parts). *Pollo cantonesa* (¢20-30). Open daily 11:30am-9pm.

Pollo Campero, Av. Independencia and 5 Calle. Ubiquitous throughout El Salvador, this is the spot for middle-class hungroids to chow down on fast-food fried chicken. 3-piece dinner with french fries and soft drink ¢25. One of the few places open for breakfast. The chain is stealthily moving into banking; they change dollars at the same rate as banks. Open daily 7am-9pm.

Vera Pizza (tel. 441-7217), Av. Independencia, 7/9 Calles. A play on the Spanish word for truth, Vera Pizza is truly good. The huge veranda is the place to be seen for the teen crowd that flocks here every afternoon for extra cheesy pizza (¢40) and semi-garlicky bread (¢18), washed down with pitchers of soda and beer.

Don Boni's (tel. 441-2825), Av. Independencia and 5 Calle. Don't let the classy decor fool you—if you scour the menu you will find full meals for less than ¢50 (including rice, salad, and an entree).

SIGHTS

Restoration is the word of the day in Santa Ana. The Gothic-style **cathedral,** built in 1905, has just undergone an extensive cleaning of its exterior. The inside is also slated for some touch-ups, but the well-worn look will be hard to hide (open 6am-noon and 12:30-6pm). Just across the square, the Neoclassical **Teatro de Santa Ana** hides the sad state of its interior behind a well-kept outside. Here too, much-needed revamping is underway. After the artisans leave and the resident bird colony is uprooted, the theater can continue its legacy as a showplace for drama and film (open Mon.-Fri. 8am-noon and 2-5pm; admission ¢3).

■ Near Santa Ana

TAZUMAL

The area surrounding the Maya ruins of **Tazumal** has been occupied for nearly 7000 years, but the 14-step pyramid dates back to a "mere" 1200 years. Whether your interests lie in pre-Columbian or only in pre-Maya ruins, Tazumal is worth a trip.

On the outskirts of the town of **Chalchuapa,** 13km west of Santa Ana, the site covers an impressive patch of land. The main site consists of the pyramid, 180m wide at

its base and 25m in height, an adjoining ballcourt, and an excavated tomb where sacrificial slaves were buried. Meanwhile, for fans of the *very* old, there's an on-site
museum packed with intricately designed pottery and other artifacts from the original settlements. A bus runs approximately every 20 minutes to Chalchuapa from
Santa Ana's terminal (20min.). The bus makes a circuit of the center and then stops a
mere 100m from the entrance to the ruins (open Tues.-Sun. 9am-5pm; free).

PARQUE NACIONAL CERRO VERDE

Perched atop a half-million-year-old extinct volcano, **Cerro Verde National Park** is
home to some of El Salvador's most awe-inspiring scenery. The mountain (this is no
mere *cerro,* or hill) teems with a fantastic assortment of primarily avian wildlife. An
easy, 30-minute hike encircling the peak lets you soak in views of nearby Lago Coatepeque and Volcán Santa Ana. Additionally, about 100m before the park entrance, an
extremely well-marked and well-maintained trail veers from the road and leads to the
summit of **Volcán Izalco.** The trail descends about 300m through the forest of Cerro
Verde in staircase fashion until it reaches the base. From here, the trail becomes
rocky as you climb to the bare cone, making the descent back especially tricky. The
roundtrip hike takes about three hours. The air gets pretty chilly at 6500 ft., so bring
warm clothes, as well as plenty of water (admission ¢7). There is a bus that runs from
Santa Ana around 10:30am (2hr.). Returning buses leave Cerro Verde around 3:30
and 5:30pm. **Camping** is permitted in the park.

Grab a beer and laugh at fate and the misfortune of the **Hotel de Montaña.** The
owners built the hotel back in the '50s for tourists interested in romantic getaways by
Volcán Izalco. Back then, the volcano spewed fumes and spurted lava on a daily basis,
scaring the heck out of locals and sailors, who could see the glow from off the coast.
Just as the hotel was completed in 1957, however, old Izalco petered out, so the
hotel now has nice views of a big, black pyramid. Rooms run a pricey US$30 per per-
son Monday through Thursday, though the rate skyrockets for a weekend package.

The park also has access to trails leading to neighboring **Volcán Santa Ana**
(7800ft.). The trail leaves from the loop trail, about midway between the vista points
for the lake and Volcán Santa Ana (careful, there is no sign). The trail descends about
200m to the base and then begins the three-hour ascent to the crater.

LAGO DE COATEPEQUE

Down the eastern slope of Volcán Santa Ana lie the clear waters of **Lago de Coatepeque,** one of the hottest weekend spots for San Salvador's elite. Set in a volcanic crater, the lake is surrounded by verdant slopes rising 500m, as well as by the towering
volcano. The lake's crystal waters offer swimming and snorkeling.

There are a number of places to stay around the lake; the best deal is the **Balneario
de Los Obreros.** A resort built for government workers, it is **free** for tourists who
have written permission from the Edificio Abrego Urruti (see **Practical Information,**
p. 184). The rooms are pretty sparse but all have private baths, and it's hard to beat
the price. The Balneario sits just at the junction of the road to the lake and the road
around the lake. A bus leaves from Santa Ana roughly every 40 minutes, circling a
third of the way around the lake before turning back. From San Salvador take the bus
to El Congo, 15km before Santa Ana and 5km from the lake, and change there. There
are also several hotels around the lake. **Amacuilco Guest House** is a reported favorite
among travelers who forgot to get permission for the Balneario.

EL SALVADOR

NORTHWESTERN EL SALVADOR

▨ Metapán

Metapán rests in splendid isolation high in the mountains of northwest El Salvador near the Guatemalan border. Even so, treacherous mountain passes and dirt roads couldn't shield the town from some of the worst action of the war. In spite of it all, the town not only survived, but prospered. A large part of its success is due to the dollars flowing in through the prominent Western Union office. An even larger part is owed to Metapán's fiercely independent spirit—born of the town's solitude and, of course, its cowboys. Ranching, after all, is what makes Metapán tick. Even though most of the cowpokes have taken to riding pick-ups and Jeeps, horses are not uncommon. When the feast of the patron San Pedro is celebrated during the last week of June, whole sections of town are closed off as folks let their hair down and party in the streets until dawn. The highlights are the two Sunday rodeos held during the festival, when everyone pays homage to Metapan's horsey roots. Once the blue ribbons are awarded, the dust settles, and the boys head back to the ranch. Other than its Marlboro Country appeal, most of what's interesting about the town lies outside it, specifically **Lago Guija** and **Montecristo Preserve.**

Metapán is roughly 45km north of Santa Ana on an extremely well-maintained road. The highway passes to the east and then curves around to form the town's north end. The familiar odd and even *avenida* and *calle* system holds true here, with odd numbers extending to the north and west. The bulk of the town is on Calle 15 de Septiembre and 2A Calle (which begins to the north of the bus station). Street names are rarely used, but the town is small, and you can always ask locals for directions.

Antel (fax 442-0144), 2 Calle, between 2 Av. and Av. Gomez, has phones and is happy to serve you from 7am-8pm. One block north and east of Antel is a **Banco Comercio** (tel. 442-0128) that accepts traveler's checks (open Mon.-Fri. 8am-4pm, Sat. 8:30am-noon). **Buses** go to **Santa Ana** (#235; every 15min., 4am-6pm, 1½hr., ¢5.40), to the **Guatemalan border** at **Anguiató** (20min.) or to the **Honduran border** at **El Poy** (5 and 11am, ¢14), an agonizingly slow four-hour trip over dirt roads.

For budget accommodations, **Hotel California** is the only game in town. It is situated just across the street from the Esso station, about 500m north of the terminal on the highway. The Hotel California has clean rooms with fans and baths for ¢50. If you can afford to splurge, there's the **Hotel San José** (tel. 442-0556) just north of the terminal with rooms for ¢170 (includes cable, A/C, bath).

Master Pollo, 2 Calle, about a block before Antel, is Metapán's attempt at fast food. The owner, a former manager of a Kentucky Fried Chicken in the U.S., claims to have stolen the Colonel's secret recipe and brought it to northwest El Salvador. It's good, but the Colonel probably wouldn't lose much sleep at night were he still alive. A chicken and a Coke runs ¢18 (open 7am-9pm). About a block away is **Multidelicas,** serving pizza (¢30), double hamburgers (¢14), and "fresh salad" (¢9) in a *comedor-*like environment.

■ Near Metapán

MONTECRISTO WILDERNESS PRESERVE

The **Montecristo Wilderness Preserve** contains some of the purest, most exotic wildlife in El Salvador. Established to promote friendship between El Salvador, Guatemala, and Honduras—whose borders converge at **El Trifinio** (Montecristo's 2418m summit)—the reserve houses agoutis, porcupines, anteaters, and other rare beasts.

The park is located 14km northeast of Metapán, along a rough road accessible only by 4x4. There is no public transportation to the park, so the only option is to hike the distance or hire a private auto. At best, the park is difficult to reach; at worst it's well-nigh impossible. **Hotel San José** organizes trips for its guests, but at an extra cost of around ¢250 per person. Another option is to talk to the pick-up truck drivers huddled around the "super" market across the street from the Hotel San José. Please note that much of the park is closed from April through September for mating season, and permission to enter these parts of the park must be obtained from the office of the Minister of Agriculture in San Salvador.

To the south of Metapán lolls tranquil **Lago Güija,** one half of which lies in El Salvador, the other half in Guatemala. While not as scenic as some of El Salvador's other lakes, Güija is cradled by hills and volcanos and not by the homes of San Salvador's rich. Its principal attractions are **Las Figuras,** the Mayan hieroglyphics carved into some of the boulders along the lake shore. It's possible to hire one of the fishing boats for a tour around the lake, but this really isn't necessary (unless you want to fish), as the lake can be satisfactorily viewed by walking along the shore.

To get to the lake, take bus #235 south toward Santa Ana and get off at **Desagüe,** an unmarked village along the road about 20 minutes south of Metapán. A dirt road forks right from the highway. Follow it about 100m, bearing right, until it merges with some railroad tracks, follow the tracks across the bridge and then continue on the trail as it slopes gently to the right. Continue through the village to the lake.

EL POY AND LA PALMA

There are two ways to get to El Poy—the easy way or the hard way. The easy way is to catch a northbound El Poy bus from San Salvador (approx. every 30min., starting at 4am). The hard way is a four-hour trek on crummy dirt roads from Metapán. From El Poy there are buses back to San Salvador (every 30min., 4am-4pm, 3½hr., ¢14) and to **Nueva Ocotepeque, Honduras.** Reboard a San Salvador-bound bus for the 45-minute trip to **La Palma** (¢4), a small town famous for its beautiful handicrafts. There are numerous shops full of wooden crafts, as well as ceramics, earthenware and native clothing shops, some of which offer the chance to see the artisans at work. Prices are generally low enough to make haggling unnecessary. Local painter **Alfred Unares** is particularly renowned. His gallery, uphill from **Antel,** showcases his rural scene canvases. Prices range from "Now I can afford to start my Latin American collection" (¢125 framed miniatures) to "At last, my Latin American collection is complete!" (thousands of U.S. dollars for framed originals; open daily 8:30am-noon and 1-5pm; tel. 335-9049). Travelers wishing to spend the night can hole up at **Hotel La Palma** (tel. 335-9012), which has charming rooms decorated with the work of local artists. (Added bonus: the vivid little wooden people near the bed have been reported to induce strange dreams; singles ¢150, doubles ¢200.) For a cheaper choice, take a bus 20 minutes north along the highway on the way from El Poy to **Hotel Cayahuanca** (tel. 335-9464). Named for a nearby mountain, it's a friendly place with a restaurant. Each room has two beds (¢60, with bath ¢80).

▓ Chalatenango

No city was untouched by the civil war in El Salvador, but as the years pass, blood and tear stains have faded into sad memories. In Chalatenango, however, war wounds continue to fester. For a time, the town of 30,000 was one of the FMLN's strongholds, as evidenced by the red graffiti decorating the streets and walls. The uneasiness of peace is only barely palatable; the city's center is strictly divided between conspicuous army barracks on one side and the nearly deserted square and market on the other. As the economic center of the region, Chalatenango sees many people come and go, almost none of whom are tourists. Expect some soul-penetrating stares if you visit the town—usually not looks of maliciousness, but rather of disbelief that a traveler would want to come here.

Chalatenango (55km northeast of the capital) is the largest city in and the seat of the department of the same name. It is laid out in the familiar *avenidas* and *calles* grid. **Avenida Libertad** and **Calle José María San Martin** form the principals; odd *calles* and *avenidas* ascend in number out from center to the north and west, respectively. Buses enter town on 3 Av. a few blocks south of the square. 3 Av. then cuts through the center, with the church east and the military encampment north.

Banco Salvadoreño, 3 Av., 4/6 Calles, changes traveler's checks (open Mon.-Fri. 8am-4pm, Sat. 8am-noon). **Antel** (fax 335-2308) is on the main *calle* three blocks west of the church (open 6am-10pm). Bus #125 makes the trip to and from Terminal de Oriente in **San Salvador** (every 10min., 4am-5pm, ¢6.50). At the **Desvío El Mayo** you can change buses and head north to **El Poy** or west to **Nueva Concepción.** The town's **market** is on the main *calle* at Av. Libertad, with stalls spilling out onto the surrounding streets. **Farmacia Guadalupena,** Av. Libertad and 4 Calle, is but one of many pharmacies (open daily 8am-6pm). The **post office** is on 3 Calle, 6/4 Av. (open Mon.-Fri. 8am-noon and 2-5pm, Sat. 8am-noon, Sun. 8-11am).

Low demand has caused a dearth of accommodations in Chalatenango. Customer service and diligence aren't top priorities at **Hospedaje Nuevo Amenecer,** 1 Calle, Av. Libertad/2 Av., but once you make yourself heard, the reward is, well, a dark room and a bathroom that may require a flashlight, even at high noon. Better take it than leave it; you have no other lodging options. An "overnight" stay from 5pm to 7am (yessiree, that's checkout at 7am) costs ¢35; 24-hour service is double! If you arrive early, they'll guard your stuff until check-in time. Thankfully, the eating situation isn't nearly as bad. **Comedor y Cafetín Portalito,** on 4 Calle just uphill from Avenida Libertad, is a breezy place on a terrace overlooking the street. All meals are served, and the food is plentiful and cheap (*pollo con arroz* ¢14, *carne asada* ¢16; open daily 7am-9pm). **Restaurant El Paraíso** (tel. 335-2356), 2 Av. and 1 Calle, doesn't live up to its name, but its semi-posh interior is nice enough. Try the *huevos de iguana en aluashte* (iguana eggs) for ¢30 or turtle eggs for ¢60 (open 11am-11pm). A couple of dingy *comedores* serve cheap food next to the *hospedaje.*

■ Near Chalatenango

Just to the northeast of town is the **Turicentro Aguas Frías.** Better maintained and busier than most *turicentros,* Aguas Frías' specialty is swimming pools. There are three pools here—one for *niños,* a larger pool for general merriment, and an Olympic-size pool for serious swimmers. The *turicentro* is also a good place for a picnic; there is also a restaurant (open daily 7am-5pm; admission ¢7).

Slightly farther afield is the town of **Concepción Quezaltepeque,** a 30-minute bus ride away, leaving from 3 Av. in Chalatenango roughly every 30min. A quiet village with cobblestone streets, Concepción Quezaltepeque's specialty is hammocks. It seems like every house is in on the racket and a random walk through town brings you by a dozen workshops. Travelers whose hammocks are their bodies and souls might be curious to know how their stringy friends are made. Though most of the hammocks are shipped elsewhere, Concepción Quezaltepeque is a good place to pick up a few wholesale. Bargaining is expected.

EAST OF SAN SALVADOR

■ Zacatecoluca

Say its name enough times, and you might have more fun than Zacatecoluca has to offer otherwise. Zacate, as it's known locally, sits 55km southeast of San Salvador, nestled at the foot of **Volcán de San Vicente,** and has some beautiful views of the surrounding countryside. The **Catedral de Santa Lucia** in the Central Square impresses with its 150-foot main spire; Zacate is also home to one of the larger *turicentros,* **Ichanmichen.** The town's real value to travelers, however, is its proximity to **La Costa del Sol,** one of El Salvador's prime vacation spots. The utter lack of cheap accommodations along the coast makes Zacate an attractive hub for daytrips.

Zacate is a long, narrow town. Three *avenidas* run the length of town: **Avenida Villacorta,** on which the buses arrive; **Avenida Delgado,** its partner to the west and the street on which buses leave; and **Avenida Monterrey.** The meat of the town runs from 9 Calle to the south to 14 Calle to the north. **Banco de Comercio,** Av. Villa Cotta and Calle Nicolas Peña, changes traveler's checks (open Mon.-Fri. 8am-5pm, Sat. 8am-noon). **Antel** (fax 331-0036) is on Av. Monterrey and Calle Nicolas Peña (open daily 6am-10pm). The **bus terminal,** 7 Calle, Avs. Villacorta/Delgado, is hidden behind storefronts. **Buses** leave to: **San Salvador** (#133; every 10min., 4am-5:30pm, 1½hr., ¢5); **San Vicente** (#177, every 20min., 5am-5:30pm, 1hr.); **La Libertad** (every hr., 5:20am-12:30pm, 2hr., ¢5); **La Costa del Sol** (#193; every 30min., 5am-4pm, 2hr., ¢6); and **Usulután** (#131; 5, 5:40, and 11am; 1½hr.). Local bus #92 goes 15km to the *turicentro* at Ichanmichen. There is a **Superselectos supermarket** on Calle Nicolas Peña facing the square (open daily 8am-6pm).

Zacate hosts only two motels. **Motel Brolin** (tel. 334-1084), on 7 Calle/Av. Villacorta, has moderately clean rooms, private baths and ceiling fans (singles ¢80; doubles ¢150). Its competition, **Hotel Primavera** (tel. 334-1346), on Av. Delgado (across from the bus station), has rooms for ¢70, but the water is not always running and checkout is for the early-birds, at 8am.

Zacate's restaurants are all of the *comedor* variety, and prices are reasonable. **Restaurante El Pescador,** Av. Monterrey, 3/5 Calles, has the feel of a men's club with the complete "Dogs Playing Cards" series and latter-day centerfolds. Chow down on *pollo dorado* (¢18) or conch cocktail (¢25) while wondering about the skinned raccoons on the walls (open daily 10am-10pm).

■ Near Zacatecoluca: La Costa del Sol

La Costa del Sol is by far El Salvador's best-developed seaside resort, and with good reason; the 10-mile-long, immensely wide stretch of sand satisfies everyone's beach needs. Particularly smug and sated are the rich folks whose compounds line the *costa* chock-a-block for miles. The barbed wire and walls are enough to scare anyone away, but the beach is so vast that there's still room to spare, even on weekends. The coast is a long, thin peninsula with pounding waves to the south and brackish water to the north (mosquito heaven). A good road traverses the length of the coast until it reaches the estuary at the sea, where the big routes begin and end, the majority of restaurants reside, and where most non-homeowning people inexplicably choose to swim (although heaven knows what is washed out from inland).

If there's no convenient direct bus leaving from **Zacate** or **San Salvador,** it's easy to catch bus #133 (the bus between Zacate and San Salvador) and get off at La Flecha, about 20km west of Zacate, where you can transfer to a La Costa-bound bus. The last bus back to San Salvador leaves at 6pm; to Zacate at 5pm. The coastal stretch begins, more or less, at the new supermarket and the recently built **Pops Ice Cream.** Don't get off there unless you want to stock up on supplies; there's no beach access close by. The bus proceeds southeast, passing the **turicentro** 5km later, and ending at the estuary another 10km down. The *turicentro* offers an easy way onto the beach for ¢7 and has facilities. Farther down is **Playa El Zapote,** one of the few houseless beaches, where the passing fruit and juice vendors provide the sole clatter.

The coast is bereft of cheap lodging of any kind; thus, the area is best enjoyed as a daytrip. A kilometer and a half up the estuary is the **Pacific Paradise Hotel** (tel. 270-2606, in San Salvador 270-3366). The parking lot could be mistaken for a luxury car dealership—just a small clue of what lies beyond the guards and the walls. The rooms have fantabulous private baths and air-conditioning as a matter of course. The two queen-size beds can each sleep up to four people. The price is just…¢565. Luckily, **camping** is an option. The area around the estuary is said to be safe, but be sure your tent isn't on private property and that it stands above the high tide line. The **turicentro** closes at 5:30pm, so it's not possible to sleep there.

■ Cojutepeque

Cojutepeque began life way back in the 1530s, when the *encomienda* of Coxutepeq was founded at the site of an indigenous village. Over the years, the town underwent a few name changes, first replacing the "x" with a "y" and then eventually adopting the present "j." It defined itself for good in 1949 when it spirited away the statue of the **Virgen of Fátima,** putting itself on the map for pilgrims the world over. Since then a burgeoning trade in icons, rosaries, and other such religious paraphernalia has sprung up. Some bookstores even promise "miracles" for a price. On the other side of town, sales and trades of a more earthly sort stem from the steady stream of traffic fed into Cojutepeque via the Interamerican Highway. Owing to its location by the highway, Cojutepeque is easily reached by bus, and even non-believers might be tempted to come feed their souls on the jaw-dropping views of **Cerro de los Pavos** (Hill of the Turkeys), where the statue resides.

Orientation and Practical Information Cojutepeque lies 32km east of San Salvador, just south of the Interamerican Hwy. The town rests on a plateau south of Cerro de Los Pavos; uphill is south, downhill north. **Calle Delgado, Avenida José María Rivas,** and **Avenida Raul Contreras** lie at the heart of the familiar grid. Odd-numbered *calles* and *avenidas* ascend north and west, respectively; some streets have honorary names (e.g. 2 Av. becomes **Av. Santa Ana** south of Calle Delgado).

There is no place to change traveler's checks in Cojutepeque. The **post office** is on Av. Rivas, two blocks north of the church (open Mon.-Fri. 7am-5pm, Sat. 8am-noon, Sun. 8-11am). **Antel** has a branch at Av. Contreras and 6 Calle, south of the church (open daily 7am-9pm). **Buses** are a cinch in Cojutepeque. Bus #113 zips directly to **San Salvador** from Av. Santa Ana and 5 Calle (every 10min., 4:20am-7:30pm, 1hr.). Any bus traveling east from San Salvador along the Interamerican Hwy. will stop in Cojutepeque, including #111 to **Ilobasco,** #116 to **San Vicente,** #110 to **San Sebastian,** #306 to **Santa Rosa de Lima,** and #310 to **San Miguel,** each of which passes through town every 10-20 minutes. Fares are about ¢4 less than if you'd started in San Salvador. The town's **market** lines Av. Contreras and 2 Av. south of the church, all the way up to Cerro de Los Pavos. **Farmacia San Antonio,** 6 Calle, 1/3 Avs., has regular hours are daily from 7am to 7pm; after that, ring the bell.

Accommodations and Food Cojutepeque is no bargain hunter's Eden, but given the scarcity of lodging, prices are reasonable. **Hospedaje Cojutepecano,** Av. Santa Ana (2 Av.), Calles Delgado/1, sits one block north of the church (singles ¢50). **Hospedaje Jovel,** 1 Av., 6/8 Calles, has only singles (5pm-9am ¢30, whole day ¢40).

Expect to eat well in Cojutepeque. The highway passing through the north end of town is lined with good, inexpensive *comedores* and *pupuserias.* One of the standouts is **Licuados El Paso,** Interamerican Hwy., Avs. Rivas/Santa Ana (2 Av.). You guessed it—the restaurant specializes in fresh fruit drinks. Set back from the highway just a bit, it's ideal for grabbing a small meal and watching humanity pass by (open 6am-7pm). **Restaurante Adentro Cojutepeque's,** Av. Brioso #1 (6 Av.) and 3 Calle, is set on the third floor and has great views of Cerro de Los Pavos and Volcán San Vicente. At night, there's live music and dancing. Dishes run ¢40-50, about double *comedor* prices (open Mon.-Thurs. 11am-10pm, Fri.-Sat. 11am-3pm).

Sights Cojutepeque's only attraction is **Cerro de Las Pavos.** The forested hill stands several hundred feet above the town to the south, and is home to the nationally beloved **Virgen de Fátima,** which is said to have performed countless miracles. Originally sighted in Fátima, Portugal on May 13, 1917, the statue was brought to El Salvador in 1949. Cerro de Las Pavos, which had only been a local landmark, became known throughout Central America as a holy site; thousands of pilgrims still come to pay homage. Nestled in a little cove, the statue is surrounded by flowers, neon lights, and dozens of plaques, all left in thanks for miracles delivered. Miraculous views of **Lago de Ilopango,** Volcán San Vicente, and the coast beyond, can be seen from the summit when the army patrol allows visitors into the communications complex on top. To reach the hill, follow Av. Contreras south to the edge of town, where a number of paths diverge; all lead to the top (about 20min.).

■ Near Cojutepeque: Ilobasco

Like La Palma to the north, Ilobasco is renowned for its arts and crafts. But instead of painted wooden knick-knacks, the village turns out small painted ceramics of all sorts. The greatest concentration of *artesanía* stores is along Av. Bonilla—keep an eye out for signs saying *Venta de Jugetes* (toy sale). *Taller Escuela de Cerámicas "Kiko"* at #61 gives tours of the craft-making process. "Kiko" employs over 75 people, and all stages of production from the mixing of the clay to the final application of glaze can be observed simultaneously. There's a store out front that sells the factory's wares (open daily 8am-noon, 2-5pm).

Hotel La Casona, 3 Av. Sur, Calles 2/Perdomo, two blocks west of the square, is a great place to spend the night in this clay capital. Each Moorish-style room is well-kept and has a stellar mattress. Prices start at ¢60 for a single or ¢90 for a double and increase with each add-on (e.g. private bath, fan, cable TV).

■ San Vicente

The Interamerican Highway passes San Vicente from a ridge several kilometers to the north, but even from there, the town's soaring white clocktower and clustered, red-roofed buildings make the place seem like a fairy tale kingdom. Meanwhile, **Volcán Chichontepec** slowly curves up to the south, completing the illusion before eventually giving way to seemingly endless waves of green forest. With such a spectacular approach, San Vicente promises much and fortunately, it delivers. The town is tranquil and scenic, home to one of the oldest churches in El Salvador, and one of the country's best places to stay. Top it all off with exploration in nearby natural splendor, and you've got yourself one fine little town.

Orientation and Practical Information San Vicente is laid out in the same old grid pattern: odd-numbered *calles* and *avenidas* ascending to the north and west, respectively. **Avenida José María Cornejo** is the primary north to south *avenida* and **Calle Quiñonez de Osorio** is the main *calle*. The main square is bounded by Avenida Cornejo and 1 Calle at its southwest corner. The **bus station** is at 2 Av. and 4 Calle, two blocks south of the square.

Change money or traveler's checks at **Banco Hipotecario** (tel. 333-0108), on 1 Calle at the main square's south end (open Mon.-Fri. 8am-6pm, Sat. 8am-noon). **Antel** (fax 333-0161) is on 2 Av., just south of the church (open daily 6:30am-9pm). **Buses** leave from the terminal to **San Salvador** (#116; every 10min., 3am-6:30pm, 2hr., ¢5) and to **Zacatecoluca** (#177; every 20min., 4:30am-6pm, 1hr., ¢4). For other eastbound buses, take #116 to the depot about 2km from town and change there. Local buses wait on 5 Av., Calles Orsorio/1. **Farmacia Central** (tel. 333-0206) is on Calle Orsorio, 1/3 Avs. (open daily 7:30am-9:30pm). The **post office** is on Calle Osorio, Avs. Cornejo/2 (open Mon.-Fri. 8am-noon and 2-5pm, Sat. 8am-noon, Sun. 8-11am).

Accommodations and Food Casa de Huespedes El Turista (tel. 333-0323), 1 Av. and 4 Calle, is a weary traveler's paradise, complete with good security and a happy staff. The rooms all have corpulent twin beds, private baths, hammocks, furnishings, and cable TV—all for a pittance (¢50-¢75 per night). **Hotel Central Park** (tel. 333-0383), as the name might indicate, is on the west side of the main square on Av. Cornejo. The moderately dark but clean rooms all come with private baths and fans. A nice lounge with comfy sofas overlooks the narrow courtyard, and guests have free use of the water cooler (singles ¢75, with A/C ¢100). **Casa de Huespedes German y Marlon**, 1 Av., 3/5 Calles, is nice enough for the cheapest place in town, although the bathroom could be better and the rooms brighter. The newer rooms upstairs are noticeably nicer than their first floor counterparts (whose ceilings inspire arachnaphobia). Rooms cost ¢50. Slightly more homey are the clean and bright rooms at the **Hotel Villas Españoles** on Av. Cornejo (between Calles 3/5). All the rooms have cable TVs and fans (singles ¢80; doubles ¢110).

San Vicente has yet to be touched by the fast-food tsunami engulfing El Salvador. The scattered *comedores* serve a grand total of about five *comida típica* dishes; not gastronomic heaven, but filling nonetheless. **Restaurant Taiwan** offers an "interesting" twist on Chinese food, located on Av. Cornejo between Calles 3/5. At ¢20 a plate, one can afford to be adventurous. For a proper sit down meal, head to the **Casa Blanca,** Calle 4 (Av 2/4), San Vicente's version of Cheers; everybody knows your name at this restaurant-bar with "ambiente familiar" (or so the sign says). (*Pincho de ves* ¢30, *cerveza* ¢8.)

Sights Visitors should check out **El Pilar** church, constructed in the 1760s (open 5:30am-noon and 2-6pm). With all the earthquakes in El Salvador, few buildings survive so long, so appreciate its stubbornness along with its subdued baroque form. In the town's Central Square, the **clocktower** can't be missed from the outside, and, on the inside, the view from the top will stir the very essence of your soul. The tower is usually locked, but the park attendant can unlock it. Official permission can also be granted in the **Alcadía Municipal** (City Hall) on the south end of the square.

NEAR SAN VICENTE

About 10km northeast of San Vicente, on the other side of the Interamerican Highway, **Laguna de Apastepeque** dawdles at the bottom of an ancient volcanic crater. On the opposite side of the lake from the highway is a very small **turicentro,** but the restaurant is reason enough to come in. Built under a beautiful gazebo, it overlooks the lake and serves yum-tummery food. On weekdays, the place is deserted; run amok for a mere ¢7. Bus #156 (from San Vicente to Santa Clara) leaves every hour from 5 Av., Calles Orsorio/1. Buses to Apastepeque stop a few kilometers short (¢2).

A couple of kilometers to the south of San Vicente, at the base of **Volcán Chichontepec,** lies another, more standard *turicentro,* **Amapulapa.** Amapulapa has swimming pools, *cabañas,* and restaurants, and outside the entrance is one of the trails leading to the summit of Chichontepec. Although the volcano isn't terribly high, the trail starts at a considerable distance from the base; allow a full day. Bus #171 leaves San Vicente from 5 Av. and 1 Calle every 15 minutes until 2pm (¢2) and goes directly to the *turicentro.*

EASTERN EL SALVADOR

■ Santiago de María

The people in this jewel of a town walk around high and happy. No, Santiago de María is not a den of illicit activity; the townsfolk are high from breathing sweet, clean, mountain air and quite pleased that not many others have caught onto their high altitude-happiness. To top if off, Santiago de María and nearby **Berlín** are in one of the most beautiful regions in El Salvador. The place is unpretentious, and few travelers have yet taken advantage of the area's potential for scenic hikes.

Orientation and Practical Information Santiago de María lies 12km south of the Interamerican Hwy. The small town is laid out in the standard grid pattern, with the main square bounded by 2 Avenida and 2 Calle. Traveler's checks can be changed, and cash advanced (on Visa) at **Banco Salvadoreño** (tel. 663-0051), 2 Av. and 2 Calle (open Mon.-Fri. 8am-4pm, Sat. 9am-noon). Just across the street is **Antel** (open daily 7am-8pm). The town's makeshift **bus terminal** is at the triangular park, 3

Av. and 4 Calle, one block south and one block west of the square. From here, catch direct buses to **El Triunfo** (every 10min., 4am-6pm, 20min., ¢1.50). **Micros** also head there from 3 Av. and 1 Calle. From El Triunfo, it's possible to change to the #310 bus, going west to **San Salvador** (2hr., ¢12) or east to **San Miguel** (1hr., ¢5). The local bus to **Berlín** also leaves from 3 Av. and 1 Calle. The town's **market** is two blocks west of the square. One block south and three blocks west of Antel is the **post office,** 5 Av. and 4 Calle (open Mon.-Fri. 8am-noon and 1:30-4:30pm, Sat. 8am-noon).

Accommodations and Food Visitors to **Hotel Villahermosa** (tel. 663-0146), 3 Av. and 1 Calle, feel more like guests in someone's home than paying customers. Perhaps it's the after dinner conversations on the balcony (which has great mountain views) or the communal dining downstairs. Though the rooms could be better, the bathrooms, even the communal one, are in great shape (¢45 per room, with bath ¢65). Doors close at 9pm. The **Hospedaje El Quetzal** is right next to the Villahermosa, proving what a difference 20 ft. can make. The rooms are dark and window-less, but light would simply illuminate the thin mattresses, musty cement floors, and tin roof ceilings. The common bathroom fits the hotel, the price fits the facilities (one night ¢30, 24hr. ¢50, extra mattress ¢5). *Comedores* and *pupuserías* line the central park, but keep irregular hours. **Comedor y Restaurante El Unico,** on the west end of the park at 2 Av., used to be the "only" place to eat but has since "temporarily" closed, (it is supposed to reopen soon).

■ Near Santiago de María

Just outside of town, **Cerro de Tigre** offers oxygen-seizing views of nearby volcanos. To get to the hill, follow 4 Calle east out of town. Turn right at 10 Av.; the street quickly fades, but a small trail continues right up the hill. About halfway up the moun-tain, you'll come to a dirt road that switch-backs up the rest of the hill. Mark this spot; on the way back down, it's tempting to follow the road all the way to a dead-end. From the top of the hill (a 40min. walk), it's possible to see the town, **Volcán Usu-lután,** and even the delta for the **Río Lempa.**

To the west of Santiago, lies the scenic town of **Berlín,** with its lush surroundings and picturesque downtown. Getting there is more than half the fun; the views will be imprinted on your memory (and the lengthy trip over bumpy roads on your kidneys). The bus leaves from 3 Av. and 1 Calle in Santiago every hour. To get a great meal with a view, head to **Victoria's Cafeteria** on the road to Mercedes Umana, 6 Av. (at the corner of 3a Calle and 6 Av., walk downhill just past the Texaco station). If you want to spend the night, the only game in town is **Motel Berlines**, 2 Av. and 4 Calle, which offers dark rooms without fans for ¢50, with bath ¢70. To get out of Berlín take one of the hourly buses to Mercedes Umana (¢30) on the Interamerican Hwy. Once there, you can access buses to larger cities (San Salvador, San Miguel, etc.)

▓ San Miguel

As the commercial hub of eastern El Salvador, San Miguel is rushing headlong into the future. The countryside around this city of 200,000 is being rapidly consumed by townhouses and strip-malls. The centerpiece of the progress is the Metrocentro, replete with pink stucco and palm trees right out of Suburbia, USA. Life in San Miguel isn't all pan pizzas and ice cream, though; the eastern part of the country is also the poorer part, as the throngs of beggars in front of the cathedral testify. Travelers may also exploit the city's convenience as a base for jaunts to the sea.

ORIENTATION AND PRACTICAL INFORMATION

San Miguel is the capital of the department of the same name. Streets follow the grid system: *avenidas* run north to south, *calles* east to west. The central *avenida* is **Avenida Gerardo Barrios** north of the point where it intersects the central *calle*, and **Avenida José Simón Cañas** south of it. The central *calle* is called **Calle Sirama** east of

EL SALVADOR

206 ■ EASTERN EL SALVADOR

the central intersection, **Calle Chaparristique** to the west. The bus terminal is four blocks east of the cathedral on 6 Calle.

Tourist Office: The nearest branch of ISTU is at the Honduran border at El Amatillo, but the information desk at **city hall,** on the south end of the park on 2 Calle, has nice maps and a few good tips on local sights (open Mon.-Fri. 8am-4pm).

Currency Exchange: Banco Hipotecario (tel. 661-6203), Av. Barrios and 2 Calle, changes traveler's checks. Open Mon.-Fri. 8:30am-4pm, Sat. 9am-2pm. Or try the **Banco Desarollo** (also advances cash on MC and Visa) on 4a Calle and Av. Barrios.

Buses: To: **San Salvador** (#301, every 15min., 3:40am-4:15pm, 3hr., ¢16; nonstop *servicio especial* 5, 6, 7, 8, and 9am, ¢35); **Santa Rosa de Lima** (#330, every 15min., 3:40am-6pm, 1hr., ¢6) continuing to the **Honduran border** at **El Amatillo** (1½hr., ¢10); **Playa El Cuco** (#320, every 45min., 5:30am-4:15pm, 90min., ¢5); **Usulután** (#373, every 10min., 4am-5:30pm, 1½hr., ¢6); **San Francisco Gotera** (#328, every 20min., 4am-6pm, 1½hr., ¢5); **La Unión** (every 20min., 4:15am-6pm, 2hr., ¢6); and **Perquín** (#334B, 3hr., ¢11) continuing to the **Honduran border** at **Sabanetas** (every hr., 6am-2pm, 5hr., ¢17). Ask dispatcher about erratic service to **Playa Tamarindo.**

Public transportation: City buses run 6am-7pm; fare is ¢1. The main bus stops in the center are at 2 Av. and 4 Calle and at 2 Av. and 2 Calle. Bus #88 goes to the hospital, #94 goes past the *turicentro* at Altos de la Cueva, #90-F passes by the Metrocentro, and #90-G goes out to Quelepa.

Taxis: Along the park and at the bus terminal. Typical intra-city fare ¢15-20.

Car Rental: Uno Rent-a-Car (tel. 661-4978), Av. Roosevelt and Calle Chaparristique, rents 4-door models with A/C for ¢288. Official policy requires a minimum age of 25, an international driver's permit, and credit card, but if you show up in person looking scrubbed and presentable, compromises can be made.

Market: Find the usual stuff along 1 Av. and Chaparristique during the day. **Multimart** is at 4 Av. and Calle Sirama. Open Mon.-Sat. 8am-8pm, Sun. 8am-6pm.

Pharmacy: Farmacia La Luz (tel. 661-0880), 6 Av. and 4 Calle, is one of many pharmacies dotting the center. Open 8am-noon and 2-6pm.

Hospital: Hospital Nacional is on the west of town at 11 Calle Poniente. Take bus #88 from the center. **24hr. emergency** numbers (tel. 661-0888 or 661-2200).

Red Cross: call 661-1771.

Police: Policía Nacional Civil call 661-0333.

Post Office: 4 Av. and 3 Calle (tel. 661-3709). Open Mon.-Fri. 7:30am-noon and 2-5pm, Sat. 8am-noon, Sun. 8-12pm.

Telephones: Antel (fax 661-4421), 4 Av. and 2 Calle, south of the park. Open daily 6am-9pm.

ACCOMMODATIONS

Apart from the roadside motels dotting the highway into town, nearly all of San Miguel's hotels are within a couple of blocks of the bus terminal. Most rooms come with fans and private baths, but the prized (and costly) commodity here is air-conditioning; the city's low elevation makes for some very hot days and nights.

Hotel San Rafael (tel. 661-4113), 10 Av. and 6 Calle. If a hotel could have hair on its chest, this one would. All of the bus drivers spend the night here and infuse the TV lounge and restaurant with a friendly, if testosterone-laden, atmosphere. The macho men all turn into mama's boys, however, when they see the private baths, ceiling fans, hammocks, and twin beds that smell of fabric softener (singles ¢68, with A/C ¢124; doubles ¢90, with A/C ¢150). Doors close at 9:30pm.

Hotel La Terminal (tel. 661-1086) is located on 6 Calle directly across from the bus terminal and the Shell station, but is recessed, so noise is not a problem. A 17in. cable TV is standard in every fab room. Private baths have showers with showerheads. The baths don't have hot water, but there's absolutely no need here (singles ¢100, with A/C ¢125; doubles ¢180, with 2 twin beds ¢195, with A/C ¢225).

Hotel Caleta, 3 Av. Sur and 11 Calle Poniente (tel. 661-3233). From the inside, you'd never know you're in the center of a city. A wide courtyard is planted with

San Miguel

Antel, **6**
Antiguo Teatro Nacional, **5**
Banco de Desarollo, **8**
Central Cathedral (Basilica Nuestra Señora de la Paz), **4**
Central Market, **1**
Gran Tejano, **7**
Iglesia San Francisco, **3**
Palacio Episcopal, **2**
Pizza Hut, **10**
Pollo Campero, **9**

palms, and the row of rooms with hammocks feels like a beach resort. Its drawback is its distance (15min. walk) from the bus terminal (singles ¢35, with private bath ¢50, with A/C ¢100; doubles ¢60, with private bath ¢82, with A/C ¢138).

FOOD

Pollo Campero and **Pizza Hut** fight for your fast-food dollar on 4 Calle (between Av. Barrio and 1 Av.). *Comedores* are prevalent near the cozy center, but if you want to sit down somewhere (without flies) try the following:

> **Lorena's** (tel. 661-7370), 1 Av., 2/4 Calles. The sign out front says *"Un nuevo concepto en comida a la vista"* ("A new concept in food-by-viewing"). What this really means is a *comedor* with fast-food sensibilities. Don your shades upon entering—it's bright and clean. The lunch special, which includes some kind of meat, salad, and rice, is only ¢12. Open daily 7am-5pm.

> **Baty Carnitas Restaurant** (tel. 661-0606), 4 Calle, Avs. Barrios/1. Come here for a wide selection of *licuados* (¢8-12) and *batidos* (like *licuados,* but thicker ¢12-16) served in all kinds of batty flavors. *Pavo al horno* ¢60, "bisteak" ¢38. Open Mon.-Sat. 8am-6:30pm. Closed in June 1997, but should be open soon...or so they say.

> **Gran Tejano** (tel. 661-4315), 4 Calle and 2 Av., offers a chance to splurge. While it is relatively expensive, the filet mignon (¢100) is simply divine.

SIGHTS AND ENTERTAINMENT

Try as one might, it's impossible to avoid the **cathedral.** The beige, Romanesque church with red-capped spires is, apart from seeming pretty un-Latin American, mighty tall (open daily 7am-noon and 3:30-5pm). About 1km north of town is the large *turicentro* at **Altos de la Cueva,** which wasn't built around any natural wonders, but does have refreshing swimming pools and cool trees (open daily 7:30am-5:30pm; admission ¢7). Take bus #94 from the north end of the central square.

The **Ruínas de Quelepa** might be mistaken for an overgrown, abandoned foundation, but they are certifiably pre-Columbian. There are some, mostly unexhumed, ruins about 10 minutes from where the bus lets off and a few more spread out in local fields. Bus #90-G runs to Quelepa every 45 minutes from the Cruz Roja Farmacia in the central square. Bus #90 to Mancaguas leaves more frequently, but lets passengers off about 2km from Quelepa town. There are a few **movie theaters** in San Miguel, but most offer over-21 flicks starring actresses with names like Misty, Tawny, and Marnie. **Cinebarrios** (tel. 661-3450), 4 Av. and 7 Calle, runs Hollywood fare (¢20).

■ El Cuco

The residents of urban San Miguel aren't cuckoo for El Cuco for its proximity alone; the sands here are silky soft and the view will make your eyes water. Unfortunately for would-be beachgoers, the beach is cluttered with rows of huts full of fishermen and locals. Should you manage to land a spot near the water, the waves along El Cuco are tricky; generally, though, the utter lack of stones makes swimming fairly safe.

The bus comes in and stops just before the **Antel** (open daily 7am-8pm). Straight ahead (to the south) is the street to the beach, which is lined with *comedores* and seafood stands. To the left (east) is the road that parallels the beach.

El Cuco, unlike Costa del Sol, actually has places to stay, but they are no bargain. Were it anywhere but on a beach, **Hospedaje Buenos Aires** would not fare well. (Take a gentle left just before Antel, then follow the street that approaches the beach at a diagonal; it's on the right about 50m down the beach.) Guests get a tile floor, a lightbulb, (sort of) running water, but *no mattresses*. The rooms have but one bed each, and the price hovers around ¢30 for 12 hours; they do lock valuables during the day. A nicer option is **Hotel Los Leones Marinos** (tel. 619-9015), 100m down the road parallel to the beach (left at Antel), featuring not only good locks, but an armed security guard as well. The rooms are clean enough and have big windows. For ¢200 a night (4pm-8am; ¢300 for 24hr.), you get two canvas cots with sheets, a hammock, and a private bath, but *no mattresses*. Budget travelers should keep an eye open for room for rent signs in house windows. The best bets for food are the *pupusa* stands on the beach and the line of *comedores* on the street to the bus stop. An interesting (but potentially unsafe) treat is fresh conch, scooped out of the shell before your eyes and served with salad (¢25). One standout is **Don Pedro's Coffee Shop,** which offers tacos and hamburgers for less than ¢20, and occasionally plays movies at night.

■ La Unión

Leathery-faced, squinty-eyed sea captains. Lusty sailors on shore leave. Young couples making out by the docks. All of the prerequisites for a rough-and-tumble port town are here. La Unión is seedy; not threateningly so, but enough to give off an exciting, shady aura. Right on the Bahía de la Unión, an extension of the Gulf of Fonseca, La Unión is close to both Honduras and Nicaragua and sees lots of people and traffic pass through. But drift away from the waterfront and La Unión becomes a more typical town, conveniently close to great beaches.

Get your bearings at the small central square formed by **Calles Menendez** and **San Carlos** and **Avenidas General Cabanas** and **General Murazan.** Antel sits a little off-center on 1 Calle, 3/5 Avs. (calls can be made daily 6am to 10pm). **Banco Desarollo,** 2 Av. and 1 Calle, has a *casa de cambio* that changes traveler's checks, but only with the purchaser's agreement (open Mon.-Fri. 9am-4pm, Sat. 9am-noon). **Buses** leave the terminal, 3 Calle, 4/6 Avs., for: **San Miguel** (every 10min., 3am-5:50pm, 2hr., ¢6) continuing to **San Salvador** (¢20); nonstop to **San Salvador** (3, 4am, and 12:30pm; 3hr.; ¢28); **Santa Rosa de Lima** (every 15min., 4am-5:30pm, ¢6.50); and **Playa El**

Rock the Vote

Few would describe Salvadoreños as apolitical, but signs of their political activism have even reached the roads. Nearly every rock along the highway with a face larger than two square feet sports a political statement. One can find the familiar red, white, and blue stripes of **ARENA** (Alianza Republicana Nacionalista), or the red letters **FMLN** (Farabundo Martípara la Liberacion Nacional) scrawled over roadside rocks. In eastern El Salvador, the purple and yellow bell of **Renovación** and the fish of the **PDC** (Christian Democratic Party) are equally popular symbols. While locals are unsure of their effectiveness as campaign tools, the political **graffiti** displays the vibrancy of democracy in El Salvador.

Tamarindo (#3834; every hr., 4am-5:30pm, 2hr., ¢5). There is no regular **ferry** service across the Gulf, but ask around the waterfront on 7 Calle. The **post office** is on 3 Calle and 5 Av. (open Mon.-Fri. 8am-noon and 2-5pm, Sat. 8am-noon).

The **Hotel Porto Bello** (tel. 664-4113), 4 Av. and 1 Calle, wins La Unión's "best bang for the buck" contest, hands down. All of the rooms have hammocks, fans or A/C, and plump double mattresses. Rooms with A/C also feature private baths, but even public bathgoers should have no complaints (¢57, with A/C and private bath ¢125). The **Hotel Centroamericano** (tel. 664-4029), 4 Calle, 1/3 Avs., is a small step down, though all of the rooms except the cheapest singles offer private baths. The area is sort of iffy, but security is tight (singles ¢50, with bath ¢75, with A/C ¢125). 3 Av. by the waterfront is chow central; *pupuserías* and *comedores* line this stretch. If you are brave, you can get some fresh fish from the fish market and have someone prepare it "your way."

■ Near La Unión: El Tamarindo

One of El Salvador's finest beaches is south of La Unión at the small fishing village of **El Tamarindo.** Set on a broad, curving bay, the beach is covered with fine white sand (a rarity in this country), and the bay is sheltered from the ocean so that the waves are gentle and perfect for swimming. As a solitary drawback, the town's unemployment rate is very high, and there are a number of menacing characters around town and along the beach, so be careful. The only regular **bus** to El Tamarindo is #383 from **La Unión** (every 20min., 4am-5:30pm, 90min., ¢5). There is also erratic service to and from **San Miguel** (2hr., ¢9). Ask the dispatcher for current schedules.

NORTHEASTERN EL SALVADOR

■ Santa Rosa de Lima

There may be gold and silver in the hills around town, but Santa Rosa de Lima thrives on colones, dollars and Honduran *lempiras*. Though the town has a diverting colonial church, most people come to pass the night either before leaving El Salvador or after entering it. Santa Rosa de Lima lies 40km east of San Miguel and 18km west of the Honduran border at El Amatillo along La Ruta Militar. Santa Rosa's layout is the standard grid with **Calle Giron** and **Avenida General Larios** as the central streets.

Banco de Comercio (tel. 664-2019), Av. Larios and 4 Calle, changes Citicorp traveler's checks only. Neither banks nor *casas de cambios* will change Honduran *lempiras*. **Antel**, 4 Av. and Calle Giron, is a block east of the square (open daily 6am-8pm). **Bus** #330 zips between **San Miguel** and **El Amatillo,** and stops in **Santa Rosa.** Leave in either direction every 10 minutes from 5am to 5:30pm. It's 30 minutes to the border (¢4) and just over an hour to San Miguel (¢6). Bus #306 travels to **San Salvador** (every 30min., 4am-2:30pm, 4hr., ¢26); there's also a nonstop to the capital (4:30 and 10am, 3hr., ¢30). Or zoom to **La Unión** (#342, every 15min., 4am-5:30pm, 1½hr.,

¢6.50). The **post office,** Av. Larios and 1 Calle, is a block north of the main square (open Mon.-Fri. 8am-noon and 2-5pm, Sat. 8am-noon, Sun. 8-11am).

   Hotel El Recreo (tel. 664-2126), 4 Av. Nte., Calles Giron/1, is the best choice in town, with hammocks, fat mattresses, and ceiling fans. The public baths are new, clean, and smell reassuringly of disinfectant. Curfew is at 10:30pm (¢40 per person). Around the corner, at 6 Av. and Calle Giron, is **Hotel El Tejano.** The rooms have all the same amenities as Recreo's, but are dark and dusty. The public baths' corners have significant layers of scum (singles ¢25, with fan ¢30) and erratic running water. In terms of food, **Comedor Nuevo,** on 6 Calle, two blocks west of the terminal, serves cheap, decent, rather uninspired food for ¢10-15. **Pollo Campestre,** next to Antel, wouldn't be worthy of mention, save that it's the only place in town with A/C (fried chicken-based meals run ¢25-30; open daily 8:30am-9pm).

CROSSING THE BORDER TO HONDURAS

The CA-1 crosses into Honduras 18km east of Santa Rosa de Lima at **El Amatillo.** Buses leave Santa Rosa from 5am to 5:30pm for the half-hour trip (¢4). The Salvadoran border itself is open 5:30am to 7pm. There is no fee to leave, but there is a fee of L5 to enter Honduras (border open 6am-6pm). Please remember that fees are often arbitrarily set by guards. For those entering, there is a friendly ISTM **tourist office** (tel. 649-9007; always open Tues.-Sat. 8am-4pm). There are money changers all about, but save some colones for random fees that may pop up (porters, etc.). After passing through immigration, it's a short walk across to Honduras. Lots of people offer to carry bags and ease passage through officialdom, but it's rumored that they accumulate unnecessary stamps and charge for each. Past Honduran customs and immigration, buses run to **Tegucigalpa** (every 30min. until 4:30pm, 3½hr., L16).

■ Near Santa Rosa de Lima: Perquín

Follow the road that leads north past San Francisco Gotera over a series of ridges, and you'll arrive at the mountain village of Perquín, which was headquarters for the FMLN during the civil war (see **History,** p. 177). Today, the village and surrounding country are still very much the rebels' territory. The thing to see in Perquín is the **Museo a la Revolución,** which exhibits the history of armed struggle in El Salvador from the FMLN's standpoint (gift shop open Tues.-Sun. 9am-5pm; admission ¢10).. Particularly moving is a collection of testimonials from survivors of the **Mozote** massacre placed around a simple common grave. **Bus** #332 runs daily from San Miguel; ask the dispatcher, as service is fickle and infrequent. For overnight accommodations, **Casa de Huespedes El Gigante** is located about 100m before (south) of the village square on a small turnoff (to the west), about 20m below the village sign. The place is a large barn with cement floors partitioned into about 20 cubicles, each of which has two bunk beds. The communal baths are clean, and the kitchen serves good food (rooms ¢25 per person).

HONDURAS

Newcomers to the prototypical "banana republic" quickly learn to live with the quirks and deprivations of Honduran life—erratic running water, somewhat surreal politics, the occasional tank wandering aimlessly through the streets—and promptly find their way to the country's relatively untouched natural splendor. Hondurans themselves are by no means passive, but they have come to accept a degree of disorder and unpredictability with a grace that soothes foreign guests.

Still, it is more because of than in spite of Honduras' whims that an increasing number of adventure-seeking tourists arrive each year. To accommodate them, the government has been attempting to develop ecotourism à la Costa Rica, although efforts thus far have been aimed more at older, wealthier tourists than at shoestring travelers. While not every path has been paved, nor every trail marked, Mother Nature's kind donations to Honduras' geography cry out for discovery, from the irreproachable beaches and coral reefs of the Bay Islands to the cloud forests of Parque Nacional Celaque, and for some, the ominous and engulfing jungles of the Mosquito Coast to the east. Meanwhile, the people, too, are opening up to tourism, from the Moskito Indians in the East to the Garifuna along the north coast, to *mestizos* throughout the country. Despite recent isolated expressions of anti-U.S. sentiment, most Hondurans are remarkably friendly and willing to lend a hand to the visiting *gringo*. Travelers will be pleasantly surprised as long as they accept Honduras on its own terms—as a warm, lovely, mildly schizophrenic nation striving to define its identity in an era of new alliances.

ESSENTIALS

▓ When to Go

CLIMATE

Three-quarters of Honduras is mountainous; coastal plains, swamps, and riverbeds comprise the rest of the country. The northern lowlands along the Caribbean shore are uniformly hot and rainy; the average temperature is 27°C (82°F) and per annum rainfall can reach 2.5m. Intermontane valleys in the central regions are cooler, average temperatures hovering around 21°C (70°F).

FESTIVALS AND HOLIDAYS

The Instituto Hondureño de Turismo provides a general list of festivals, holidays, and other celebrations throughout the country. Some of the more widely celebrated holidays, other than the national holidays, include Patron Saint festivals around **January 15;** San Sebastián's Day on **January 20;** Virgen de Candelaria on **February 2;** San José on **March 19;** San Gaspar and Marcos on **April 25;** Día de La Cruz on **May 3;** San Isidro on **May 15;** Santa Rita de Casia on **May 22;** San Antonio on **June 13;** San Juan Bautista on **June 24;** Días de Santiago and Santa Ana on **July 25 and 26;** Virgen del Tránsito on **August 15;** Santa Rosa on **August 30;** San Miguel on **September 29;** San Francisco de Asis on **October 4;** and Virgen de Concepción on **December 8.**

▓ Useful Information

For publications and organizations of general interest, see **Useful Information,** p. 1.

Amerispan, 6 Av. Norte #40, Antigua, Guatemala (tel./fax 832-0164). Language courses with homestay and meals, one week or longer, in Guatemala and Honduras. Offers information and services for pre-registered students and travelers just arriving; in addition, discount oneway airfares from Guatemala to just about anywhere, and a discount card (US$5) good at locations in Guatemala and Honduras.

CODA, Attn: Noemí D. Espanoza, Colonía Florencia Sur, Av. Los Pinos, número 4022, Tegucigalpa, Honduras (tel. 32-82-23; fax 32-31-89). Offers volunteer opportunities in Honduras.

Peacework, 305 Washington St. SW, Blacksburg, VA 24060 (tel. (540) 953-1376; email sdarr@compuserve.com). Promotes work programs in Honduras, as well as other parts of Central America. Sites vary annually. Open Mon.-Fri. 9am-5pm.

Escuela de Español Ixbalanque, Copán Ruinas, Honduras (tel. 98-3432). One-on-one instruction 4hr. per day, 5 days per week, with homestay and full board US$145. Located just 1km from the ruins at Copán.

Americas Tours and Travel, 1402 Third Ave., Suite 1019, Seattle, WA 98101-2110 (tel. (800) 553-2513 or (206) 623-8850; fax (206) 467-0454. In San Pedro Sula, call 57-40-56. Arranges travel to Honduras on several major airlines. Ask for the owner, Javier Pinel, a friendly guy with a B & B in San Pedro Sula. He can take you fishing on Lake Yojoa and offers daytrips to Copán and Lancetilla botanical gardens.

Roatan Charter, Inc., P.O. Box 877, San Antonio, FL 33576 (tel. (800) 282-8932; fax (352) 588-4158). Tours to the Bay Islands, ruins, jungles, cities, and small villages. Copán day tour plus hotel, lunch, and transportation costs US $195 per person. Open Mon.-Thurs. 9am-6pm, Fri. 9am-5pm.

■ Documents and Formalities

EMBASSIES AND CONSULATES

Embassy of Honduras, U.S., 3007 Tilden St. NW, Washington, DC 20008 (tel. (202) 966-7702; fax 966-9751). **Canada,** 151 Slater St., Suite 908A, Ottawa, Ontario, K1P 5H3 (tel. (613) 233-8900; fax 232-0193). **U.K.,** 115 Gloucester Pl., London, W1H 3PJ (tel./fax (44) 171-486-4880).

Honduran Consulate, 1612 K St. NW, Suite 310, Washington, DC 20006 (tel. (202) 223-0185; fax (202) 223-0202). Honduras also has consulates in New York (tel. (212) 269-3611), Los Angeles, Miami, Chicago, New Orleans, and Houston.

PASSPORTS, VISAS, AND CUSTOMS

A valid **passport** is needed to enter Honduras. A **visa** is not required for citizens of the U.S., the U.K., Canada, Australia, New Zealand, and most European nations; citizens of Israel and South Africa need to get visas (with same-day processing) for US$30-40. If you're unsure, contact an embassy or consulate before you leave home. When you enter Honduras, your passport will be marked with a 30-day tourist stamp. At the end of 30 days, you must visit an Immigration Office in order to have it renewed or be fined. For a US$5-10 fee, you can extend your permit twice, for a total stay of 90 days. After 90 days, you must leave the country for three days before you can re-enter.

You will be charged for **inspection and immigration charges** when you enter the country. If you're flying home, you'll also pay an **airport departure tax.** There are no limits on bringing goods out of Honduras.

A valid foreign **driver's license** and **proof of registration** are needed to drive in Honduras. The paperwork and fees you'll face will depend on your plans. If you're staying a while, you'll need to fork over L20 for the 9A-1; if you're driving through Honduras to other countries, you'll pay L5 for the 9A-3. Vehicle permits last 30 days, and may be renewed for up to six months.

Honduras

■ Money Matters

CURRENCY AND EXCHANGE

US$1 = 12.76 lempiras	L1 = US$0.08
CDN$1 = L9.31	L1 = CDN$0.12
UK£1 = L20.83	L1 = UK£0.05
IR£1 = L18.56	L1 = IR£0.05
AUS$1 = L9.49	L1 = AUS$0.11
NZ$1 = L8.28	L1 = NZ$0.12
SARand = L2.77	L1 = SARand 0.36
DM1 = L6.97	L1 = DM0.14

> Due to Honduras' high inflation, travelers should expect many of the prices below, which were accumulated during the summer of 1997, to have risen substantially by 1998.

The Honduran unit of currency is the **lempira.** Bills come in denominations of one, two, five, 10, 20, 50, and 100 lempiras. The lempira is divided into 100 centavos. Coins are issued in values of one, two, five, 10, 20, and 50 centavos. The 10-centavo coin is sometimes called a *daime,* you'll occasionally hear a 20-centavo coin called a *búfalo,* and 50-centavo pieces are commonly called *tostónes.* Always carry some U.S. dollars. Personal checks are impossible to cash, and it's difficult to get money transferred to Honduras, especially to the Bay Islands, where there are few banks.

Most **ATM** machines accept only Honduran bank cards and aren't compatible with U.S. systems. Honduras doesn't have many *casas de cambio.* **Banco de Honduras** often only changes Citicorp traveler's checks, and **Creditlan** has an expensive surcharge. Larger cities have small **black markets** for currency exchange, but the marketeers offer the same rates as banks for cash exchange, and their rates for traveler's checks are often much worse. Banks commonly give *retiro de tarjeta de crédito,* cash advances on credit cards.

There are few hard-and-fast rules for **tipping** in Honduras. Leave a 10% tip at restaurants, and give a few lempiras to anyone who does you a favor.

■ Safety and Health

Travelers report that they feel relatively safe in Honduras. However, robberies and assaults are on the rise in both cities and rural areas. Hang on to your money and luggage, and watch out for pickpockets. Don't wear jewelry in public, and carry your valuables in a money belt. Remember that the money you're carrying in your wallet is probably more than some Hondurans make in a year. Male travelers will probably escape most hassling, but women will receive unwelcome attention, especially on buses. If heckled, respond firmly—tell the offender to stop, and ask someone nearby to help, if necessary.

Vaccinations aren't required to enter Honduras, but it would be wise to consult a doctor about preventative shots. **Cholera** and **typhoid fever** have recently reached epidemic levels in parts of Honduras. Also common are **malaria, dengue fever,** and **Hepatitis A. AIDS** is becoming increasingly widespread in Honduras.

Don't drink tap water in Honduras—your bowels will never forgive you. Drink only *agua purificada,* and never eat ice unless you're sure it was made with purified water. Hondurans know this too, and everyone drinks the little sealed pouches of water sold in stores. *Never* drink from the plastic bags with straws that vendors peddle at bus stops and on the streets. See **Health,** p. 14.

Plus, If You Act Now...

Nobody ever said that Honduran buses lack for hearty entertainment, but once in a while an extra bonus comes along. While cruising from town to town, keep an eye, ear, and throat peeled for the silky-smooth snake-oil salesmen, who often stand in the aisle to deliver eloquent spiels about **cure-all medicine.** Holding up jars of *stuff* (and often some 6-year-old's pop-up anatomy book), the "doctors" explain how the pills they're peddling can cure fatigue, impotence, cancer, *and* those **nagging hemorrhoids.** Afterwards, some passengers whip out wads of cash for the guy in return for vials of their own, but the pills usually turn out to be multi-vitamin tablets or skin lotion. Sadly, some of the con-artists claim their pills can cure AIDS, and that no other preventive measures are necessary. In any case, the pills are best avoided, lest you end up contracting some rare disease named for a long-deceased **German physician.**

■ Getting There

Honduras' three international **airports** are in Tegucigalpa, San Pedro Sula, and La Ceiba. It's possible to journey from Guatemala to Honduras by **bus.** From Guatemala City, **Rutas Orientales** sends buses to Chiquimula, where you can transfer to a Buses Vilma vehicle, which will take you to El Florido on the Honduran border. For more information, see Guatemala City: Practical Information: Buses (p. 60). Make reservations one to two days in advance. From El Florido, you can catch a bus to Copán and other points in Honduras.

The Nicaragua-Honduras **border crossings** at Las Manos and El Espino, and the Guatemala-Honduras crossing at Agua Caliente, are open only during daylight hours, so plan ahead. The Nicaragua-Honduras crossing at Guasaule is open daily from 8am-4pm. Use caution if you're traveling to border regions near Guatemala, El Salvador, and Nicaragua; contact the U.S. State Department's Emergency Hotline (tel. (202) 647-5225) for current information on safety in border regions.

■ Once There

TRANSPORTATION

The **bus** system in Honduras is excellent. The majority of buses run on time and are operated by private companies. Unfortunately, it's often the case that each destination is served by a different company, so several terminals are scattered throughout the city. Be wary of ticketers taking advantage of your ignorance; ask about prices from those around you and at the station office before buying your bus ticket. **Road conditions** vary throughout the country. The government only recently decided to bring in unleaded gasoline to stem pollution, so drivers should make sure that their vehicles are equipped with a proper catalytic convertor.

Taca (tel. 390-105) operates domestic flights within Honduras.

KEEPING IN TOUCH

A letter sent from Honduras can take as long as 12 or 14 days to reach the U.S.; allow a week at least. EMS offers **express mail** services, but they're generally pricier. You can receive **mail** in Honduras though general delivery (*Lista de Correos*), typically paying a small fee when you pick up your letter. Address envelopes to general delivery as follows:

Sean COAR
a/c Lista de Correos
Tegucigalpa (town), Francisco Morazán (department)
República de Honduras, CENTRAL AMERICA

HONDURAS

If mailing from the U.S., omit the last line (Central America), since the computers that sort mail only recognize names of countries.

The Honduran **phone** company, **Hondutel,** provides efficient and convenient service. Every notable town has a Hondutel office that keeps long hours (some are open around the clock). Dial 123 to be connected to an AT&T operator in the U.S. for calling-card or collect calls. It's almost impossible to use a non-AT&T phone card from a public phone in Honduras. From most phone offices, you can dial 121 for Sprint service, 122 for an MCI operator. **Faxes** and **telegrams** are generally available in Hondutel offices, too. The **country code** for Honduras is **504;** there are no city codes. Honduras operates on **Central Standard Time.**

HONDURAS: LIFE AND TIMES

■ History

When Central America finally shook off its Spanish shackles, Honduras was even poorer and more isolated than its neighbors. Steep mountains isolated each village from the next, and floods and droughts frustrated farmers. Honduras briefly joined the **Federation of Central America,** sending liberal leader **Francisco Morazán** to head the alliance of nations, but the Federation dissolved in 1839. When a group of Hondurans traveled to Europe to commission a statue of Morazán, they found themselves without enough money to pay for the monument. Instead, they bought a second-hand statue of an obscure Napoleonic military leader and erected the hand-me-down in honor of Morazán; it still stands in Tegucigalpa.

While Honduras struggled to establish some sort of national unity among its diverse regions, Guatemala and Nicaragua constantly dipped their fingers into Honduran politics, ruining all chances of internal stability. After the assassination of **President José Santos Guardiola** in 1862, Honduras was ruled by 20 leaders in just 10 years. Six different constitutions were drafted between 1865 and 1924. As various factions fought for control, the federal capital bounced back and forth between liberal Tegucigalpa and conservative Comayagua. Soil erosion and fires in Comayagua eventually shifted the balance toward "Tegus," where the capital has remained, even as the nation's economic locus has moved to San Pedro Sula.

In the late 1870s, **President Marco Aurelio Soto** pacified warring factions, undertook capital improvements, and expanded the education system. But no commercial bourgeoisie had emerged in Honduras by the turn of the century, and their absence left an economic and political vacuum. Into the void stepped a handful of foreign companies, most notably the **United Fruit Company (UFCO).** The UFCO bought huge tracts of land for its banana plantations, set up its own system of banks and railroads, and created an elaborate political machine. By 1918, the UFCO and two other large companies controlled 75% of the nation's banana-growing land. For the next four decades, "El Pulpo" (or "The Octopus," as the UFCO was known) held Honduras in the grip of its strong tentacles. The banana giant brought tens of thousands of jobs to Honduras, equipping the nation with schools, hospitals, electric plants, and plumbing systems. But democracy was effectively dead; El Pulpo called the shots, and ordinary citizens had little say in the political process.

Disease ravaged Honduras' banana plants in the 1940s, and the UFCO relaxed its grip on the nation as banana exports dropped. Since then, the government has worked on its own to build roads, improve public health, and implement agrarian reform. But fear and sporadic violence continue to plague Honduras. The nation has seen so many illegal seizures of power that Hondurans wryly refer to their capital as "Tegucigolpe," a pun on the Spanish word for "coup" *(golpe)*. One dictator was so paranoid that he outlawed baseball, fearing that his enemies would assault him with bats. Tensions with neighboring El Salvador ran high in the mid-1960s, and erupted after the two countries confronted each other in a 1969 World Cup qualifier match.

The **"Soccer War"** left 2000 Honduran civilians dead and sent 130,000 Salvadoran refugees fleeing back across the border.

The days of the banana bosses are gone, yet Honduras is far from autonomous. In the 1980s, the U.S. turned Honduras into a military base for the Nicaraguan *contras*. With massive amounts of military aid and generous civil loans, the U.S. bought the right to station thousands of troops along Honduras' southern border. The capital influx—amounting to at least US$190 million per year—helped to shore up the Honduran economy, but the nation remained the second poorest country in the Western Hemisphere. Furthermore, the U.S.-Contra occupation shoved more than 2000 small farmers off their lands, creating a class of **desplazados** (displaced persons) living as refugees in their own country. With the end of the Nicaraguan civil war, foreign aid melted away and U.S. troops evaporated, only to be replaced by 11,000 armed and aimless *contras* seeking refuge in Honduras. Dependence on outside support has plagued Hondurans' nationalism; most attempts to isolate a sense of identity are stifled by a quick look around the average city street, where Dunkin' Donuts replaces bakeries and children clamor for L.A. Gear shoes.

In the summer of 1994, the flow of water over the nation's hydroelectric dam slowed to a trickle, causing periodic **blackouts** throughout the nation. Hondurans simply went about their business, getting by on short spurts of electricity. Newfangled innovation butts heads with the old ways in domestic affairs, as well—in a recent internationally broadcast scandal, a woman sued her husband for slander after he claimed she was not a virgin at the time of their marriage. These tensions fatigue Honduras' resolve in a way that is all too familiar in the developing world. The **Chortis,** descendants of the Maya who created the structures at Copán, have marched to the capital twice in the last year in an effort to declare their rights, marching past American fast-food restaurants in a desperate attempt to be remembered as the government tries to push the nation forward.

The recent discovery of an ancient ceremonial burial site in the **Talgua Caves** in Olancho, Honduras has archaeologists in a tizzy. Probably the most important Honduran find since Copán, the bones and buried goods at Talgua point to the existence of an advanced American civilization (perhaps ancestors of the Lenca) in the area as many as 3000 years ago, a full millennium before the Maya hit the area. Today, the direct descendants of pre-Columbian inhabitants thrive as members of the Lenca, Maya, and various tribes that survive throughout the eastern jungles of the country.

▓ The Arts

It took a while for Honduran **literature** to boom, especially after the 19th century Federation of Central America made Guatemala the center of intellectual activity. Out of the wave of liberalism that followed, the Romantic movement finally found its voice in Honduran writers **Marco Aurelio Soto** (who also served as president) and **Ramón Rosa.** In this century, modernist poet **Juan Ramón Molina's** pained, expressive works set the course for the more politically oriented writers of the **"generation of '26,"** whose search for Honduran identity stressed the Creole and the native. One of these writers was **Marcos Carías Reyes,** whose *Trópico* denounced the banana industry. **Argentina Díaz Lozano** applied the criticism of the intelligentsia to the vernacular style of the people in *Peregrinaje*, an autobiography, and *Mayapán.*

Honduran **musical taste** seems to be a conglomeration of styles that have trickled down from Mexico, Guatemala, and the Caribbean; the only music halfway native to the country is that of the Garifuna. Cruising around on buses or in taxis, you're most likely to hear Mexican cheese-pop and American Top 40 from about five years back. Popular rock bands include **Triángulo de Eva** and **Fusión.**

Maya ruins are scattered throughout Honduras, and the country proudly displays its **artifacts** in a number of museums. Several Honduran painters try to capture their culture in color, among them **Ana Isabel Acosta, Rosa María de Larios, Armando Lara,** and **Marco Rietti.** Three bronze statues recently erected in San Pedro Sula by artist **Regina Aguilar** were supposed to honor national hero **José Cecilio del Valle,** but instead launched a raging controversy; Valle is depicted in the nude, his genitals fully exposed.

Food and Drink

Honduran *típico* fare is usually a hodgepodge of rice and beans, tortillas, and fresh, delicate seafood, especially along the coasts. A little experimentation is in order, whether you like it or not, since Hondurans have their own word for just about every regional specialty. For starters, a **pupusa** is a tortilla with beans and pork rinds. A **baleada** is sort of like a burrito; most often, it's a tortilla smeared with fried beans and onions. Garifuna food usually includes **casabe** (cassava) and **tapado** (soup made of fish), both drenched in rich coconut milk. A favorite dish on the Bay Islands, rarely seen in their restaurants, is *tapado* (or *machuka*) comprised of fish, potatoes, yucca, and other vegetables cooked in diluted coconut milk and poured over rice. Conch soup is also popular. Vegetarians and vegans will want to look for the long, slender, green vegetable sold in markets: it's the high-protein **yucca,** which tastes like a flavorful potato when steamed.

To drink, **guanábana frescos** aren't to be missed. Hondurans tend to be partial to one of four beers. **Port Royal Export** is a *sapid* export which ought to be nursed over a long afternoon. **Salva Vida** is the most popular, has a bit less body, but goes down smoothly. The third, **Nacional,** is even more *suave;* though short on taste, it's refreshing and goes well with food. **Imperial** is a bit weaker and can be found predominantly in the southwestern region of the country.

Media

Particularly in the cities, Hondurans stay on top of the news through one of the country's six dailies. *La Prensa,* the oldest of the bunch, is still the most respectable, but all six papers have become increasingly guilty of sensationalism over the last few decades. *El Periódico, El Heraldo,* and *El Tiempo* are some of the other papers. Fewer Hondurans have TVs than read the papers, but crowds gather around electronics shops' windows when big stories break or when there's a hot soccer game on. The English-language "Honduras This Week" is comprehensive and informative.

Recent News

The U.S. State Department's 1996 Human Rights Report cited significant improvements in Honduras, despite some persistent problems such as the immunity of governmental and military personnel and difficulty in obtaining fair trials. A landmark Supreme Court decision to bring eight officers and two soldiers to trial for the 1982 kidnapping and torture of leftist students marked a new willingness to stand up to the military. President **Carlos Roberto Reina** set this precedent when he replaced forced military service with voluntary conscription in 1995, infuriating the army.

In the upcoming November election, the liberal party's presidential candidate, **Carlos Flores Facussé** leads the polls by a wide margin. Until the election, many reforms will be suspended, allowing Facussé, the current president of the National Assembly, to delay difficult economic adjustment measures. Some reforms will be quietly implemented, including those affecting the Banco Central de Honduras, the financial sector and the penal code.

Hondurans are not afraid to stand up for their rights. In November 1996, health workers protested against the public hospital system, by striking for higher wages and other benefits. Protestors were repelled by riot police and tear gas; this incident added tensions to IMF negotiations that were in progress. In early May 1997, over 2000 Indians marched to government buildings in Tegucigalpa to protest the killing of one of their leaders, Cándido Amador, the head of an indigenous rights group.

Tegucigalpa

What's in a name? In Tegucigalpa's case, so many clunky syllables that Hondurans simply refer to their capital as "Tegus." After a vein of silver was discovered on the slopes of Picacho in September of 1578, a town sprang up rapidly; its name came from the Náhuatl words for "hill" *(teguz)* and "silver" *(galpa)*. In 1880, Tegus became the capital of Honduras—officially because of its burgeoning mining trade; unofficially because wife of then-president Marco Aurelio Soto didn't like the old capital of Comayagua.

Initially, the new capital wasn't linked to Comayagüela, the similarly named city across the river, but by the end of the century both were incorporated into a "central district." At the time, few bridges linked the areas, and people were taken across the water in baskets suspended from cables. Even today, the cities rest side by side uneasily, and some locals still talk of separation.

Tegus has never lost its boom town feel and is still creeping slowly and surely up the surrounding hills like a spider casting a web of *barrios* and *colonias.* Despite the urban sprawl, mysterious Tegus behaves and feels more like a provincial seat than a national capital. Away from the rushing *capitalinos* and diesel-belching buses, people still stop to chat, sit, and watch the world go by. No matter what new construction occurs on the outskirts of town, the central park and cathedral firmly anchor the city in its long, rich past. The equally provincial (and very welcome) trait of genuine interest in visitors, their backgrounds, and their security makes Tegus one of the safest big cities in Central America. Indeed, navigating the city can be safe at all hours, as long as the usual precautions are taken.

▇ Orientation

In a city where locals get lost when they stray from their home neighborhood, navigation for travelers is hell. Brush up on your "which ways" and practice the words for "left," "right," and "straight" constantly. To top it off, there are no main thoroughfares; directions and locations are usually given in terms of landmarks. Buses generally arrive in **Comayagüela,** which is west and south of the **Río Choluteca.** Its streets are numbered from a central point just south of **El Centro** in Tegus. North of the river, orient yourself in terms of the **Parque Central,** which houses the **Cathedral** and is close to many cultural attractions. About 10 min. east is **Barrio Guanacaste,** where there are plenty of accommodations. Further east are the commercial sections of **Avenida La Paz** and **Boulevard Morazán** (La Zona Viva). The colossal **Hotel Honduras Maya** is a 15 minute walk southeast along Avenida Cervantes.

▇ Practical Information

Tourist Office: Instituto Hondureño de Turismo (tel./fax 22-66-21), on the 3rd floor of the Edificio Europa at Av. Ramón Ernesto Cruz and Calle Rep. de México, a few blocks from the U.S. Embassy (around the corner from Lloyd's Bank). Maps and info for the entire country. Ask here about excursions to nearby areas. Open Mon.-Fri. 8:30am-4:30pm. Closed briefly around noon.

Immigration Office: (tel. 22-77-11), on Av. Jeréz next to Hotel La Ronda. Get a visa extension here for L10 (cost varies depending on your nationality). Leave it in the morning, pick it up the next day at 3pm (they'll give you a copy for the day). Open Mon.-Fri. 9am-noon and 1-4:30pm.

Embassies: U.S. (tel. 36-93-20 or 36-31-20; fax 37-17-92), on Calle La Paz. It's big; folks know where it is. U.S. consulate across the way. Open Mon.-Fri. 8am-noon and 1-5pm. **U.K.** (tel. 32-12-07; fax 32-54-80), Edificio Palmira, 3rd floor, Colonia Palmira, across from the Hotel Honduras Maya. Open Mon.-Thurs. 8am-1pm and 2-4:30pm, Fri. 8am-1pm. **Belize** (tel. 32-31-91, ext. 7770; fax 39-01-34), in the Hotel Honduras Maya's basement. Open Mon.-Fri. 9am-noon and 2-4pm. **Costa Rica** (tel.

HONDURAS

32-17-68; fax 32-18-76), Colonia El Triangulo, 1a Calle. **El Salvador,** Colonia San Carlos, No. 205 (tel. 36-73-44; fax 36-94-03). **Guatemala,** Colonia Las Minitas, 4a Calle Arturo López Rodezno, Casa 2421 (tel. 32-97-04; fax 31-56-55). **Nicaragua** (tel. 32-42-90; fax 31-14-12), Colonia Las Lomas del Tepeyac, Bloque M-1.

Currency Exchange: Banks are everywhere—most change only U.S. dollars, some exchange traveler's checks. Some larger stores have *casas de cambio*, but their schedules are erratic. **Bancasa** (tel. 37-11-71; fax 38-49-91), Av. Cristobal Colón and Calle los Dolores, 1 block south of Iglesia Los Dolores. Checks changed, cash advanced on Visa cards. Open Mon.-Fri. 9am-5pm, Sat. 9am-noon.

American Express: Mundirama Travel Service, Col. Palmira, Edificio CIICSA (tel. 32-39-43; fax 32-00-72), Paseo Rep. de Panamá and Av. Rep. de Chile, 1 block from the Hotel Honduras Maya. With an AmEx card you can purchase up to US$100 in traveler's checks with a personal check. Open Mon.-Fri. 8am-noon and 1-5pm, Sat. 8am-noon.

Airport: Toncontin International Airport (tel. 33-12-87) is 7km from downtown. **American** (tel. 32-14-14) and **Continental** (tel. 33-76-76) fly to the U.S. **Taca** (tel. 39-01-05) flies to **San Pedro Sula** (9:30am, 30min., L360). **Isleña** (tel. 33-98-13) flies to **La Ceiba** (8am and 3pm, 30min., L420 plus 2.5% tax). To book tickets in advance, contact **Mundirama Travel Service** (see AmEx above).

Buses: Most leave from Comayagüela, near 12 Calle, 7/10 Avs. SE. Saenz, 12 Calle, 7a/8a Avs. (tel. 37-65-21), goes to **San Pedro Sula** (13 per day starting around 5am, 4hr., L25). El Rey (tel. 20-01-37) also runs direct buses to **San Pedro Sula** (13 departures throughout the day, almost every hour starting at 5:30am; 4hr.). Traliasa, 12 Calle, 8a/9a Avs. (tel. 37-75-38), runs to **Tela** (6, 9am, 4½hr., L70) and to **La Ceiba** (6, 9am, 7hr., L70). Etrucsa (tel. 43-27-15), across the street from Traliasa, also goes to **La Ceiba** (10am and 4pm, 7hr., L70) and to **Tela** (10am, 2, and 7pm, 5hr., L70). Transportes Sultana de Occidente (tel. 37-81-01), 8 Av. and 12 Calle, passes through **La Entrada** (6am, 6hr.) en route to **Santa Rosa de Copán** (7hr., L40). Cotraipbal, 7a Av., 11a/12a Calles, goes to **Trujillo** (5, 9am, and noon, 8hr., L50). All departure times are subject to change; check schedules.

Intra-city buses: Buses' signs usually indicate the *barrios* or *colonias* between which they are traveling; many stop on the north side of the Parque Central or across the bridge from Comayagüela. Fare is 60 centavos.

International buses: Tica Bus, B. Villa Adela, near Hospital, Comayagüela (tel. 20-05-79 or 20-05-81), has A/C and a *baño,* and isn't crowded. It handles migration stuff and stops only at major cities. Destinations from Tegus are: **Guatemala City** (US$23), **San Salvador** (US$15), **San José** (US$35), and **Managua** (US$20). All buses leave at 9am.

Taxis: Ubiquitous. Within the city, fares typically run L5-15. Try declaring a (fair) price upon entering. Never wait until leaving the cab to set the price. Fare to the airport is L20-25. From the airport, don't take the yellow cabs, which charge L70; walk out to the street for fares of L25.

Supermarket: Mas y Menos, Av. La Paz, Colonia Palmira—2 blocks from the U.S. embassy. Every imaginable item for sale. Open daily 7:30am-9pm.

Cultural Center: Ministerio de Cultura (tel. 36-97-57), on Av. La Paz, 2 blocks up from the U.S. Embassy in the glass, cubic, modern building. Info on concerts, theater, and other cultural happenings. Open Mon.-Fri. 8:30am-4:30pm.

Pharmacy: For a list of pharmacies open until 9pm and on weekends, call 192 or look in any pharmacy window. **Farmacia Santa Teresa** (tel. 37-06-32), 1 block east of the southeast corner of the Parque Central, across from the Hotel Prado. Has some English-speaking staff. Open Mon.-Fri. 8am-6pm, Sat. 8am-noon.

Medical Services: Clínicas Viera (tel. 37-31-56), across from Hotel La Ronda on Av. Colón. Open 24hr. Dr. Plutarco Castellanos' English is excellent. Consultations L100. He sees patients Mon.-Fri. 3:30-7pm, Sat. 9am-noon.

Emergency numbers: Red Cross (tel. 37-86-54). In case of fire or other emergency, call **Los Bomberos** (tel. 32-54-74).

Police: FUSEP (tel. 22-87-36) is behind Iglesia los Dolores, a bit beyond the Hotel Imperial. Open 24hr. The **policía femenina** (tel. 37-21-84) is 1 block west of Parque Herrera. Entirely comprised of women, this force deals primarily with children's and women's problems.

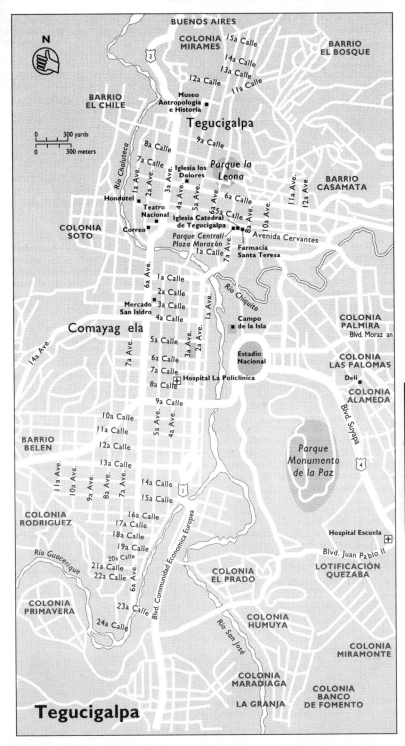

Tegucigalpa

Post Office: (tel. 37-88-30), Av. Paz Barahona and Calle Telégrafo. *Lista de correos.*
Open Mon.-Fri. 7am-7pm, Sat. 8am-1pm. In Comayagüela, the post office (tel. 37-
84-48) is on 6a Av. near the Instituto Abelardo R. Fortin. Open Mon.-Fri. 7am-7pm,
Sat. 8am-1pm. **Postal code:** Tegucigalpa 11101; Comayagüela 11103.

Telephones: Hondutel (tel. 37-79-00; fax 37-97-15), Cabina Pública del Centro, Edi-
ficio Central. AT&T booths offer phone service to foreign countries. **Fax** service
(L20 per page to the U.S.). Open 24hr. For **telegrams,** open Mon.-Fri. 7am-7pm,
Sat. 8am-noon. In Comayagüela, **Hondutel** (tel. 38-14-48) is next to the post office.

■ Accommodations

Fractured into many neighborhoods, Tegucigalpa boasts hotels that vary considerably
according to their locations. Accommodations near the Parque Central feed off the
city's energy; very cheap places are near the Iglesia Los Dolores. For mid-priced
hotels with clean bathrooms, head for Barrio Guanacaste. Conveniently close to the
bus station, though not very safe at night, Comayugüela also has plenty of hotels.
Regardless of where you choose your hotel, try to get a room near the back to avoid
bus fumes, the loud traffic, and in the *campos,* the ever-present roosters.

Hotel Granada (tel. 37-23-81), Av. Gutemburg, Barrio Guanacaste. A block up from
the big Hotel Nankin sign. (Note: there are 3 Hotel Granadas within a stone's throw
from each other on Av. Gutemburg in Barrio Guanacaste.) **Hotel Granada #2** (tel.
37-40-04; fax 38-44-38) and **Hotel Granada #3** (tel. 22-05-97). Each offers singles
with bath L100; doubles with bath L150; and triples L200. Each has common areas,
fans, and hot showers. Hotel Granada #1 and #2 offer rooms with TVs for an additional L50. Hotel Granada #1 also has a cafeteria. Noon checkout.

Café Allegro (tel. 32-81-22; fax 32-81-22), Av. República de Chile in Colonia Palmira.
Look for the sign on the left, 1½ blocks beyond the Hotel Honduras Maya. Near the
Peace Corps office, Allegro is filled with international guests. Rooms are hostel-like
(22 beds in 5 rooms), but an excellent restaurant, a high standard of cleanliness,
and a friendly owner compensate for the lack of privacy. There are hot showers
and fans in the rooms (L75). Visa accepted.

Hotel Fortuna (tel. 38-13-53), when facing Iglesia Los Dolores, on the left side of the
church. Fortuna is ideal for minimalists—each of the stark rooms has but one window. No street noise, but employees chat it up outside. The free *agua purificada*
offsets the collapsing roofs and cold, cement bathrooms. Singles L25; doubles L50.

Hotelito Corteza (tel. 37-16-28), Av. Colón and Calle Morelos, 1 block north of the
post office, 1 block east of Parque Herrera. Across the street from a mammoth yellow municipal building. The bedrooms are big, the bathrooms private, but neither
earns brownie points for cleanliness or lighting. 1 bed L40, with bath L60.

Hotel Cordesa Inn (tel. 37-78-57), next to the bus stations (so try to get a room away
from the street). The rooms are rather nice, if a bit boring. Single L90, with TV
L110; double L140, with TV L175.

Hotel Maria José (tel. 37-72-92), in Comayagüela, 12 Calle, 7/8 Avs.; 1 block from
the bus station. Impeccably clean rooms with TVs and either fans or A/C. Double
bed with fan L95, with a bigger TV L100, with the biggest TV of all L140.

■ Food

Alimentación in Tegus is as wild and varied as the city itself. Restaurants of nearly
every description and price range fight to win the stomachs of *gringos* and *catrachos*
(Hondurans) alike. For bargain food, the markets in Parque Central or across the
bridge in Comayagüela are convenient. The *merenderos* serve hearty portions at
heartening prices.

Restaurante al Natural (tel. 38-34-22), Avenida Salvador, on the little street behind
the cathedral in the Parque Central. A toucan greets you at the door and parrots
squawk, scream, and flop about in their metal cages. Welcome to chow time, *au
natural.* Omelettes, salads (L13-29), sandwiches, and great *licuados.* Vegetarian
dishes are available. Open Mon.-Fri. 7:30am-8pm, Sat. 8am-3pm.

Café Allegro (tel. 32-81-22), attached to the hotel of the same name (see above). Café Allegro provides an escape from the raucous noise and common tortillas of the street. It offers unique Italian dishes (try the spaghetti with whiskey L55), imported beers, and specialty coffees in a peaceful courtyard with soothing music.

La Terraza de Don Pepe (tel. 37-10-84), on Av. Colón, 4 blocks west of Parque Central. At 7:30pm on Sept. 2, 1986, Don Pepe's men's room became famous throughout Honduras—the nationally sacred Virgen de Suyapa, which had been stolen a few weeks earlier, was discovered next to the toilet, wrapped in newspaper like a piece of fish. Now, the old bathroom is a shrine; the walls are plastered with newspaper clippings featuring the tiny statue, the Pope with the statue, the toilet, various people pointing to the toilet, Nick Sandomirsky on the toilet with the statue, etc. Meanwhile, in the fine tradition of Central American cuisine, the menu boasts Chinese food and a good selection of cigarettes. Fried rice with chop suey L27.50. Chicken *cordon bleu* L44.50. Open daily 8am-10pm.

▓ Sights

How much time you spend in Tegucigalpa depends on how excited you get about church altars. The city's attractions are all within walking distance of the Parque Central; some are so close that you could walk to them on your hands.

The **Parque Central** (also called the Plaza Morazán) is a must-see—actually, if you don't see it, you're probably in the wrong town. A statue of the hero Morazán stands in the middle of the park, surrounded by relaxing locals enjoying the shady trees. The park is also a good place to get your sandals shined or to buy an umbrella from the street vendors because believe you me, the rain will come.

Anchoring the eastern side of the park is **Cathedral San Miguel.** Although the church was built between 1765 and 1782, it looks as if it has been whitewashed every day since then. At the heart of the cathedral's simple interior stands a striking gold Baroque altar. (Mass daily 6:30, 7am, 4, 5, and 5:30pm; Tues.-Fri. additional noon mass; Sun. 6:30, 8, 9:30, 11am, and 4pm. Doors open from first to last mass.) Two blocks east of the cathedral is the 16th-century **Iglesia San Francisco,** the oldest church in Tegus.

Five minutes west along Avenida Colón on the right side is **Iglesia Los Dolores** (built in 1732), which is known for the marketplace in front of the church and the gaily painted statues and neon lights on the altar inside. Further along Avenida Colón is Parque Herrara recognizable by its massive tree and fountain, as well as its impressive collection of locals taking it easy in the shade.

Directly south of the park is the **Teatro Nacional Manuel Bonilla** (tel. 22-42-36). The theater occasionally hosts concerts, plays, and cultural events. If you're looking for one more reason to become President of Honduras, feast your eyes on the seats in the center balcony—they're reserved exclusively for *el presidente* and company (open Mon.-Fri. 8:30am-4:30pm; free). Just northwest sits a strange little church with neon lights, a macabre tomb, and a Christ in Mardi Gras regalia.

About four blocks north of the theater is the **Parque La Concordia,** a little park that resembles a miniature golf course. Meandering paths, cuddly-cute high school couples licking each other's lips, and carefully crafted, shrunk-to-size replicas of the ruins at Copán fill the park. Gnarled trees shade the park's north end.

Two blocks south of the Parque Central are the **Parque Merced,** with its own (relatively unimpressive) church, and the **Galería Nacional de Arte** (tel. 37-98-84). Newly inaugurated in August 1996, this mission-style house-*cum*-museum offers a dazzling array of Maya artifacts, silver work, and modern and contemporary art. It is definitely worth the L10 "suggested" admission (open Tues.-Sun. 10am-5pm).

A block west, the old Presidential Palace has now been converted into the **Museo Historico de la República** (tel. 37-02-68). Dedicated in 1993, it picks up where the Museo Nacional leaves off, presenting Honduras' political history from independence in 1821 to the present. As of June 1997, it was closed for remodeling, but is supposed to reopen by 1998 (anticipated hours: Wed.-Sun. 8:30am-noon, 1-4pm; admission L20, Hondurans L10).

HONDURAS

(Paul and) Art behind Bars

Well-meaning friends may have warned you about ending up in a Central American jail, but there's actually good reason to visit **La Penitenciaria Central,** Av. San Martín de Flores and Av. Molina, in southeast Tegus. The prison's inmates produce woodwork, hammocks, and musical instruments. Previously, tourists could enter the prison after **emptying their pockets** of valuables. They were then given a small metal tag (accompanied by the ominous threat, "you lose this, you're not leaving"). To avoid the red-tape hassles, prison officials have opened a small shop outside, where a guard summons the peddling prisoners, who proffer **toothy smiles** and modest English ("You buy?") with their wares. More than 80 people visit the store every day. In general, the prisoners are friendly to potential customers, and are psyched to rip into their favorite **Steely Dan** or Simon and Garfunkel guitar licks while chatting with guests. Just stay away from "So, what are you in for?"—an opener that corks conversations with astonishing alacrity. Most like to bargain; supposedly, all profits go to the producers. Hammocks are L180-200, guitars are L180-300 (open daily 8am-2pm).

■ Entertainment

Fear not, rump shakers. Tegus's nightlife heats up to a feverish pitch on weekends. Most places are either on Blvd. Movazán or Av. Juan Pablo II. Though it's chancy to walk to the clubs from the town center after dark, there are enough party-goers and bar-hoppers on the streets themselves to ensure some safety. Taxis are plentiful along these strips, and many nearby restaurants keep late hours. Women should go in a group, pack, or mob. Men in the clubs are forthright even with local women; they practically lose control when real-life *extranjeras* come in. Also, be aware that while most women in the clubs just want to boogie, some are, as Tina Turner put it, "private dancers, dancers for money." That said, let's go out for a night in Tegus.

The **discotecas** come and go by the month, so your best bet is to talk to a cab driver or the people at your hotel. One place that has stood the test of time is the **Rock Castle Club,** up the hill from Taco Bell, on Av. Juan Pablo II. Live bands play on weekends and pool tables attract many locals (pool costs L30 for 30min.; general admission L50). Pool halls appear to be a popular venue; they are located all over the city and are always chock-full of locals.

If you missed a movie a few months ago, you can catch it at the **cine** on Av. Colón, three blocks west of the Parque Central, or at the two other multiplexes in Tegus. Admission is generally L25, but may vary depending on the movie; check newspapers for show times.

■ Near Tegucigalpa

VALLE DE ANGELES

Valle de Angeles lives up to its name; it's a heavenly hamlet in the mountains outside Tegus. The town is best known for its *artesanía* (handicrafts); local artisans sell woodcarvings, pottery, hammocks, and more at kindly prices. It's also a primo starting point for a daytrip to La Tigra (see below). Most people come to Valle de Angeles for the magnificent handicrafts, sold in the *salones* that cluster on Av. 1a, especially at the south end of the *mercado*. The half of the *mercado* devoted to *artesanías* is open every day but Monday. The shops generally accept Mastercard and Visa.

Valle extends from its central park, with a church on the north end of the park and the **Palacio Municipal** on the south end. The *Palacio* contains **Banco de Occidente** (open Mon.-Fri. 9am-noon and 2-5pm, Sat. 8-11:30am), the **post office** (*lista de correos;* open Mon.-Fri. 8am-noon and 2-5pm, Sat. 8am-noon), and the **Hondutel** office (tel. 76-21-42; open daily 7am-noon and 2-5pm). The bank only changes bills, not traveler's checks; nor does it provide advance cash on credit cards. **Farmacia**

Karyfarm is on the north end of Calle Principal (open Mon.-Fri. 9am-noon and 2-6pm, Sat. 9am-3pm). **FUSEP** (tel. 76-21-51), the police force, is on the north end of Calle Principal (open 5am-midnight).

La Posada del Angel (tel. 76-22-33) is one block to the right and one block uphill (on the left) from the church. In the midst of renovations, the hotel promises to offer comfortable, cool rooms with cable TV and pool access (singles L135; doubles L245). The attached restaurant offers tasty *típico* treats (*Plato Típico* L45). On the right of the Palacio Municipal is **Epocas,** with a kitchen which also offers *comida típica*, specializing in meat dishes (Tues.-Sun. 10am-whenever), and a bar that offers many different types of poison to the tones of classical Spanish music. For serious Garífuna grub, head to **El Buyei** on Calle Principal, just south of the park. The name means "mystery" in Garífuna, but that the seafood soup is tasty is no enigma (L30).

To get to Valle, take a bus from the terminal in Tegus (heading up Av. La Paz, there's a big statue of Simón Bolívar; turn right at the gas station, then take the first left). Buses leave every 45 minutes from 5:30am to 6:45pm (30-60min., L4). If you have the time, you may want to stop in **Santa Lucia** on the way to Valle de Angeles. It has a curiously mixed population of locals and wealthy urbanites who have turned Santa Lucia into a suburb of Tegus. They share an amazing church with figures dating back to the 16th century, as well as a breathtaking view of Tegus and La Tigra. On a clear day, you can even see Nicaragua.

PARQUE NACIONAL LA TIGRA

Parque Nacional La Tigra is only 21km northeast of Tegucigalpa, but the setting couldn't be more different. Covering some 238 sq. km, the park includes a cloud forest stocked with orchids, more than 200 species of birds, ocelots, monkeys, and pumas. The trails are gorgeous, but steep. Consider leaving heavier items in a hotel in Tegus, especially if you're not in great shape.

The best way to get to La Tigra is by car (preferably one with four wheel drive). If you don't have access to one, you'd better be very patient or very fit because the buses are erratic at best and the walk is long and hot. There are two ways to see the park, depending on which side you enter from, and each is equally challenging. Admission is US$10, unless you're Honduran or have special (written) permission. Bring rain gear, warm clothes, and *lots* of water. One route starts from **Jutiapa** or **Las Limones,** accessible by buses that leave Parque Herrera in Tegus (very erratic—usually 3 per day starting around 7am, 45min., L3). From there, walk a couple of kilometers to **Rancho Quemado** (the ranger station) and start the descent. Ultimately you will end up at **El Rosario,** the other ranger station, where park services are centered. Magín, an extremely friendly ranger, lives at El Rosario; ask him about additional trails if you are still interested in other hiking opportunities.

To make the ascent, take the frequently unreliable bus to the village of **San Juancito;** buses leave Tegus from the northeast part of the capital near Mercado San Pablo in Barrio El Manchen. The buses leave daily around 5:30am and 3pm; an additional bus leaves Wed. and Sat. at 8am. Or you can catch a bus at 10am from the same place and ask to be let off at the *cruce* to San Juancito, from which it's a quick descent to town. The other option is to take a more reliable bus to Valle de Angeles, then walk north on Calle Principal, which becomes the road to San Juancito. The hike is 11km, but buses pass every few hours during the day, supposedly around 5:30 and 10am. Drivers heading towards La Tigra may offer you a ride, but *Let's Go* doesn't recommend hitchhiking—so maybe you'd better walk.

From San Juancito, with your back to the FUSEP office, turn left and walk 500m up the hill. Following the sign, turn left again, and walk about 5km uphill. Keep an eye out for the small house where **Amalia Elvir de Ramos** cooks up world-renowned *típica* dishes for L10. Continuing further uphill, the **Casa de Visitantes** becomes visible. Basic accommodations with small mattresses and blankets for three people are available for L20 per person. The trails around this side of the park are particularly interesting, as the mountain is pocked with old gold and silver mines (enter at your own *extreme* risk). In fact, the "town" of El Rosario is an abandoned 19th-century settlement, complete with an old hospital and a U.S. embassy. Some buildings are being restored and inhabited again, but old buildings and mining debris are sprinkled throughout the countryside.

If you want to stay overnight at the park's visitor center (near the El Hatillo entrance), you should make arrangements beforehand with **Amitigra,** a non-profit ecological foundation devoted to preservation of the park (tel. 32-06-71 or 32-55-03).

CROSSING THE BORDER INTO NICARAGUA

Tegus is often a stopping point for those headed farther south, and is conveniently close to **Choluteca,** the hub for all border crossings. To get to Choluteca, grab a bus from **Mi Esperanza,** Av. 6a., 23a/24a Calles (tel. 38-28-63; every 1½hr., 3hr.). From Choluteca, take a *colectivo* or a bus to **Gausaule,** the border crossing. The ride takes 30-60 minutes, and drops you at the immigration office (open daily 6am-noon and 1-5pm).

Cross the bridge and change currency (be careful of dishonest changers). Welcome to Nicaragua, whose doors are open daily 7am-5pm. The entrance costs US$8 for U.S. citizens, US$3 for other foreigners. Buses leave for the interior until 5pm. A direct bus leaves for Managua in the early afternoon, and generally takes 3 to 4 hours (so it's possible to get from Tegus to Managua in a day). For more information, see **Documents and Formalities,** p. 265.

WESTERN HONDURAS

■ Comayagua

Heavily laden with churches, the town of Comayagua marks an interesting historical interlude on the road from Tegucigalpa to San Pedro Sula. Situated 80km north of Tegus, Comayagua was Honduras' first capital, until erosion, exhaustion of the environment, and fires debilitated the city in the late 19th century. Comayagua's 17th-century **cathedral** was one of the first churches built in Honduras. Also look for the ancient clock tower, which was supposedly given to the town by Phillip II, who took it from Spain's Alhambra. Locals will swear to you that the clock still works, and it does—twice a day, every day. Three blocks south of the back of the cathedral sits **Iglesia la Merced,** the oldest church in all of Honduras. Although it lacks the incredible altarwork of the cathedral, its statues are stunning.

Across the street to the south is the **Museo Colonial.** This three-room museum is stuffed with objects culled from churches in and around Comayagua, including crucifixes, silver statues, glimmering gold chalices, and a chair used by Pope John Paul II during a visit to the region (open daily 10am-noon and 2-5pm; admission L5). Also on the south end, **San Sebastián Church** is famed for its gold and silver altar, as well as for being the burial place of ex-president General José Trinidad Cabañas.

A block north of the plaza stands a museum of a different sort, the **Museo Regional de Arqueología.** A part of the Instituto Hondureño de Antropología e Historia, the museum exhibits fossils, Honduras' first printing press, and a range of artifacts from the region's indigenous civilizations (open Wed.-Fri. 8am-noon and 1-4pm, Sat.-Sun. 9am-noon and 1-4pm; admission L10).

To reach Comayagua from Tegus, take a second-class San Pedro-bound bus. Ask to be let off at Comayagua—you'll find yourself on the highway, 1km from town. **Empresa de Transportes Catrachos** (tel. 72-02-60) goes directly to Comayagua (every 40min., 6am-7pm, 1½hr., L15). Unfortunately, the company's terminal is a 15 min. cab ride outside Comayagua. Return buses leave Comayagua every 40 min. from 5:15am to 6pm.

Banco Ficensa (tel./fax 72-00-75), on the west side of the park, cashes traveler's checks (open Mon.-Fri. 9am-3pm, Sat. 8:30-11:30am). **Hondutel** (tel. 72-00-03) is just east of the cathedral (open daily 7am-9pm, with 2½hr. breaks for lunch and dinner). **Farmacia Pritania** is across from the Hotel America (open Mon.-Fri. 8am-12:30pm and 2-7:30pm). The **Red Cross** emergency number is 195. The police, a.k.a. **FUSEP** (tel. 72-00-80), is one block east of Hondutel (open 24hr.). The **post office** (tel. 72-02-89) is next to Hondutel (open Mon.-Fri. 8am-noon and 1-4pm, Sat. 8am-noon).

If you just can't get enough of those churches in one day, there are a couple of hotels where you can spend the night before embarking on another day of sightseeing. **Hotel Maru** (tel. 72-13-11) is four blocks south of the parque and one block west of Av. 1a. Rooms are simple and rather loud, but have fans (1 person with no bath L50; 2 beds with a private bath L75). On the park, **Hotel Libertad** (tel. 92-00-91) has big, basic rooms. The enormous windows could serve as docking bays for alien spacecraft. Noon checkout (singles L20; doubles L30; triples L36). **Hotel America** (tel. 72-03-60; fax 72-00-09), three blocks south of the park, has quiet rooms with hot showers and cool fans (singles for L85; doubles L150).

For **food,** try the market a few blocks south of the park. Or check out **Ricos,** one block east of Calle Principal and just south of the park, where *típica* adventures await (breakfast L20; big chicken tacos L15; open daily 7am-5:30pm). Another option is **Palmeras** (tel. 72-03-52), near the Hotel Libertad on the south side of the *parque* (chicken with rice L46; open daily 7am-8:30pm).

For **entertainment,** the ultra-cheap **cine** shows the U.S. hits of yestermonth with Spanish subtitles. Go one block west of the park and two north (7pm; L10). The Sunday matinee (1pm) is only L2. Near Comayagua, the popular **Lago Yojoa** (see below) and **Cuevas de Taulabé** both lie about an hour north along the highway. The lake is party to stellar fishing, snorkeling, swimming, and boating. The nearby village of **Los Naranjos** is home to extensive archaeological finds. Specific arrangements should be made in the hotels surrounding the lake. Take a San Pedro-bound bus and ask for *Yojoa* or *Las Cuevas* (1hr., L5). Entrance to the lake is free; to the caves a couple of lempiras.

LAGO DE YOJOA

Nestled in the bosom of the mountains between San Pedro Sula and Tegus lies the placid Lago de Yojoa whose warm waters remind you of the womb—just check to make sure you know where the garbage is dumped before you take a dip. Originally inhabited by the Lencas, the Lago region is now mainly populated by families seeking a weekend retreat from the cities.

To get to Lago de Yojoa, take a second-class bus from Tegus (5:30am-6:30pm, 3hr., L35) to San Pedro Sula and get off at **La Guana.** From there, grab a bus to **Peña Blanca** (every ½hr., L4). Although La Guana is closer to Yojoa, the hotels lie along the road to Peña Blanca. **Hondutel** has an office at the southern tip of Peña Blanca—take a left (from La Guana) at the gas station, and walk straight 100m. **Peña Blanca Agencia** (open Mon.-Sat. 8am-noon and 2-4pm) cashes traveler's checks and advances money on Mastercard and Visa. **Clinica y Segora Medica,** on the left side of the road (from La Guana), is open 24 hr. in case of emergency (no English is spoken).

Hotels along the road to Peña Blanca vary markedly in quality and price, but usually you get what you pay for. Your best bet is **Hotel Agua Azul** (tel. 52-71-25, the main office in San Pedro Sula), 10 minutes from La Guana by bus, on the left side of the road. This hotel offers doubles for L250 which come with fans, verandas, and hot showers (MC and Visa accepted). Agua Azul also has a pool and will rent guided boats (L150 per hr.) and fishing rods (L25 per hr.). The highlight of Agua Azul, however, is the helpful travel advice from bilingual **Enrique Campos** who manages the conservation agency **Ecolago** from the hotel. If you are strapped for cash you can stay at **Hotel Maraneita,** at the northern end of Peña Blanca on the right side of the road from La Guana (singles L30, with bath L60; doubles with bath L70). There are no fans, no hot water, and no view of the lake. On the up side, you would pay more for a beer in the city. A little farther down the road is the campground **Bagope Campamiento** that allows camping (L16) and offers cheap dormitory-style housing. Cheap seafood is available at the *comedores* along the San Pedro Sula-Tegucigalpa Freeway on the southern end of the lake. The fish is fresh (try the bass), but the cooking utensils aren't the cleanest. The larger hotels offer good food, but at much higher prices (breakfast L40, bass fillet L100, beer L12).

You can spend a day exploring the lake in power boats (L150 per hr.) or budget-friendly pedal boats (L30 per hr.), but as one *gringo* put it: "Yojoa is a great place to do nothing." The hotels come to life on the weekends: the luxurious hotel, **Brisas del Lago,** has a **discoteca,** and there is live music on Sundays at the Agua Azul. There is also a **billiards** parlor in Peña Blanca, but it is not exactly a family-style fun parlor.

■ Santa Rosa de Copán

First-time visitors to Santa Rosa are inevitably disappointed by what they see as they pull into the town's squalid bus station—the highway, a dirty market, signs of light industry, and nothing else. Perhaps this is why Santa Rosa lacks the throngs of tourists that flock to other communities on *la Ruta Maya.* But don't be misled by first impressions. The bus station is two miles from town; just up the hill awaits a charming colonial center that provides a pleasant introduction to the Honduran highlands.

Founded near the end of the 18th century by Spanish peasants, Santa Rosa soon found relative prosperity in tobacco farming. The area still produces first-rate stogies, but the surrounding countryside is now devoted mostly to servicing that other great Western addiction—caffeine. Coffee beans from Santa Rosa are sold all over Honduras and are considered to be among the country's finest. Though the town has been the capital of the Lempira region of Honduras for over a hundred years, only recently has it become an important political center. The only evidence tourists will see of this in untainted Santa Rosa, however, is the long lines at the banks on the last Friday of the month, which is government payday (avoid cashing your traveler's checks).

Orientation and Practical Information The two parts of town, *el centro* and *el terminal,* are separated by a two-mile stretch of unrelated buildings. *El centro* sees most of the action and is laid out like a good Central American town should be—around the **Parque Central.** The main drag, called **Calle Centenario,** runs east to west along the south side of the park. No one really uses the street numbers or names; directions from the park suffice. A taxi from *el terminal* costs L6.

The closest thing to a **tourist office** is the lobby of **Hotel Elvir** (see **Accommodations,** below), where you can arrange trips and find maps and bus schedules (open 24hr.). Warren, the American expatriate owner of **Pizza Pizza,** can also give a helpful tip or two. **Exchange currency** at **El Banco de Occidente** at the southeast side of the park (tel. 62-00-22; fax 62-06-92); they change traveler's checks and give credit card advances (open Mon.-Fri. 8am-noon and 2-5pm, Sat. 8-11:30am). **Hondutel** (tel. 62-10-50 or 62-10-05) has **phone, fax,** and **telegram** service (open daily 7am-9pm). They will also hold faxes for L1 (call 62-10-06 for info.). **Buses** run from La Terminal (look for the Pepsi Terminal sign) to: **San Pedro Sula** (every 25min., 4:15am-5pm, 3¾hr., L22; expresses at 8, 9:30am, 1:30, and 3pm, 2½hr., L35); **Tegucigalpa** (Mon.-Sat. 4 and 10am, Sun. 9 and 10:45am, 6½hr., L55); **Copán Ruinas** buses go to La Entrada, then continue to the ruins (daily 11:20am, 12:30, and 2pm, 3hr., L25); **Ocotepeque** (every 2hr., 6:30am-5pm, 4hr., L15); and **Gracias** (every 1½hr., 9am-6pm, 1½hr., L13). For **grocery** needs, there are main two options: *el mercado* and *el supermercado.* To get to the *mercado*—where you'll find machetes as well as fresh fruit—stand at the north side of the park, facing the blue police station (open Mon.-Sat. 8am-5pm, Sun. 8am-noon). The supermarket, **Supermercado Jaar** (tel. 62-01-88), offers standard supermarket fare. This time, stand on the south side of the park, facing south; turn left and continue 3 blocks, then turn right; it's down one block on the left (open Mon.-Sat. 8am-noon and 2-6pm). Wash clothes at **Super Lavandería Florencia** (full service L46 per load; open Mon.-Sat. 8am-6pm). **Farmacia Central** (tel. 62-04-65), adjacent to the park, provides basic pharmaceutical services (open Mon.-Fri. 8am-6pm, Sat. 8am-noon). For **medical care,** the **Clínica Médica Las Gemas,** past the Hotel Elvir, has an English-speaking doctor. The **Hospital de Occidente** (tel. 62-01-

12) is open 24 hr. for emergencies. Take Calle Centenario eight blocks west of the park; turn left just before the soccer field, and head up the hill one block. The **police** (tel. 62-00-91, emergency 199) are located in the big building on the north end of the park labeled "Fuerza de Seguridad Publica" (open 24hr.) The **post office** (tel. 62-00-30) is on the west side of the park and has *lista de correos* (open Mon.-Fri. 8am-4pm).

Accommodations and Food Hotels cluster around the city center and bus terminal. **Hotel Copán** (tel. 62-02-65), across the street from the *mercado* at Av. 3a and 1a Calle, offers decent, cheap rooms, and sporadic hot water (L45 per person, with private bath L55). Take a break from communal bathrooms and splurge at **Hotel Elvir** (tel./fax 62-01-03), on Calle Centenario a couple of blocks west of the park. The rooms are often stuffed with *gringos* and vacationing Peace Corps volunteers who feel at home with cable TV, hot water, telephones, and comfy beds (singles L187; doubles L273; triples L300). **Hospedaje Calle Real,** just east of Pizza Pizza, is a popular, if basic, budget option (singles L30-35; doubles L50).

Santa Rosa has more than its fair share of appealing eateries. Find cheap eats at the popular **comedores** scattered along the street that runs south from the southeast corner of the park. For a more elaborate meal, **Flamingo's** serves up surprisingly fancy food in any of its three dining areas; *spaguetty flamingo's al horno* goes for L36, seafood and beef for considerably more (open daily 11:30am-10pm). At **El Rodeo,** a block down from Flamingo's, dine on typical *ranchero* fare like beefsteak (L48) as mounted cow heads leer from above. **Pizza Pizza** bakes quality pies in a wood-fired oven (12-inch veggie pizza L50; *spaghetti bolognese* L33; open daily 11:30am-9pm).

Sights and Entertainment For pure picnic bliss, head out to the lake at **La Montañita Preserve,** a few kilometers out of town. Take any bus to Gracias (L2) and ask the driver to stop at La Montañita. With your back to Santa Rosa, look for a little road to the left; follow the signs to the preserve. Follow the main path (3m across) for five minutes through pleasant, lush forest; the **laguna** spreads to the left. Locals swim and fish in this pond. Bring insect repellant, especially after a rain. The last bus back to town goes by at 5:30pm, but be there around 5pm. If you cannot bear to mount another bus, there are other animals awaiting; contact the Hotel Elvir to explore the outlying area by horse (L50 for 2-3hr.) or mountain bike (L15 per hour). For **nightlife,** domestics *and* imports rush to **Glamour,** Santa Rosa's techno club, complete with tough-guy bouncers (Fri. and Sat. nights, L15). Locals claim that their **hand-rolled cigars** are just behind Cuba's in quality. Buy stogies at **Flor de Copán,** a block and a half east of the Central Plaza. Stop in at the office, and they'll gladly show you around the fragrant factory premises (open Mon.-Fri. 7:30am-noon and 2-5pm).

■ Gracias

Ever since Juan de Chavez, the first settler to the region, exclaimed, "*¡Gracias a Dios que hemos hallado tierra llana!*" ("Thank God we've finally found flat land!"), Gracias has become, ironically, a comfortable base camp for travelers seeking far-from-flat terrain. Founded in 1536 as a garrison for Spanish soldiers intent on attacking indigenous communities to the east, Gracias seemed like a secure headquarters. By the end of the 17th century, the town had served as both the capital of Honduras and as a seat of government for all of Spanish Central America. As the Honduran economy's center of gravity shifted north and east, Gracias's importance faded and the city mellowed—the peace here is disturbed only by the chiming of church bells and the clickety-click of schoolchildren running along the cobbled streets. Ambitious visitors typically stop in Gracias *en route* to the breath-taking cloud forest in **Parque Nacional Celaque,** where they exhaust themselves before recouping in the **hot springs.**

Orientation and Practical Information Getting around Gracias is simple. Buses labor into town from the north; you'll be two blocks west and one block north of the park when you get off the bus. The cathedral squats on the south side of the park; the *Fort of San Cristobal,* a large, gray complex, looms above town to the west.

HONDURAS

There is no official **tourist office,** but Froni at **Guancascos Restaurant** (tel./fax 61-12-19) is a great source of information on excursions around Gracias. **Exchange currency** and traveler's checks at **Banco de Occidente** (tel. 61-12-11), one block west from the northwest corner of the park, across from the market (open Mon.-Fri. 8am-noon and 2-4:30pm, Sat. 8-11:30am). **Hondutel telephones** (tel. 61-10-03 or 61-10-04) are located south of the park, one block past Guancascos restaurant (open daily 7am-9pm). There are two public phones outside, from which you can make calling card or collect calls. **Transportes Lempira** buses leave half a block from Hotel Erick and run to **Santa Rosa de Copán** (11 per day, 5:30am-4pm, 2hr., L11). For a **pharmacy, Venta de Medicinas Lempira** is two blocks from the market (open daily 7:30am-12:30pm and 1-9pm). The **doctor's** office is in the same building (open Mon.-Fri. 8am-noon and 2-4pm). After hours, head for the **hospital** (tel. 61-11-00; fax 61-14-25), on the northern outskirts of town, across from the Texaco station. The **police** can always be found on the northeast edge of the park (24hr.). The **post office** (tel. 61-12-21) sits next to Hondutel, a block south of the park, and posts a *lista de correos* (open Mon.-Fri. 8am-noon and 2-5pm, Sat. 8am-noon). The **postal code** is 41101.

Accommodations and Food Thanks to Gracias's remote location and relatively small number of visitors, all the hotels in town fall within budget bounds. Backpackers flock to **Hotel Erick** (tel. 61-10-66), half a block east of the bus terminal. Outfitted with private baths, rooms are spacious and pretty. Beds are super-comfy, and there is an elegant dining area that no one seems to use (1 person L27; 2 people L40; with fan, TV, and hot water L107.) Checkout is at noon, and reservations accepted. Hotel Erick is attached to Erick's store, where you can find sodas, snacks, and flatware. A simple inexpensive option is **Hospedaje San Antonio,** four blocks north towards the road to Santa Rosa from the "bus stop," on the peaceful outskirts of town. The yellow-and-brown checked floors may clash with the turquoise, lime, and pink walls, but the beautiful mountain views alleviate eyestrain. Guests often sunbathe and picnic on the empty roof. Clean, basic rooms and cold water *baños* (singles L17, with private bath L30; doubles L33, with private bath L50). For a bit of luxury, try the brand-new **La Posada del Rosarío** (tel. 61-12-19), three blocks west and one block south of the park. Massive wooden doors conceal airy rooms with desks, private baths, and hot water. English is spoken. Rooms run L80 for one person, L90 for two, and L105 for three.

The culinary center of Gracias is **Restaurante Guancascos,** a.k.a. **Los Lencas** (tel. 61-12-19). Prices are reasonable, and travelers can buy Lencan handicrafts and potable water in addition to food (*cena típica* L28 and vegetarian sandwich L20; open daily 7am-9:30pm). **La Exquisita Reposteria y Pizzeria,** half a block west from the northwest corner of the park, has earned a following of locals and tourists alike for its delectable pizzas (L25, L40, L55) and even more exquisite baked goodies. For more standard Honduran cuisine at average prices, try local favorite **La Fonda,** one block south of Hondutel (open daily 10am-10pm).

Sights Many locals head off to shoot some pool after work. If your eight-ball isn't up to snuff, take a walk up to the **Fort of San Cristóbal.** They call it a *castillo* (castle), but that's a little too imaginative. It does offer superb views of Gracias and Celaque Park through the watchtower's murder holes. Here you can visit the tomb of former Honduran President Juan Lindo (open daily 7am-noon and 1-5pm). The churches of Gracias won't knock your socks off; if you feel compelled to visit a house of worship, **Las Mercedes,** two blocks from the park, is more interesting than the rest.

■ Near Gracias: Parque Nacional Celaque

Looming to the west of Gracias is the 66,000-acre **Parque Nacional Celaque;** inside the park stands **Cerro Las Minas** (2849m), the tallest peak in the nation. From the base of the mountain to its summit rises a cloud forest so fantastic that it might be the setting for a fairy tale—avoid tripping over gnomes as you ascend. While the trail up

Celaque is dense with foliage, the forest on top is relatively sparse and mossy. If you have the eyes of a hawk, you might be able to spot a quetzal or a toucan. Pumas, jaguars, and white-faced monkeys also inhabit in the park.

Current information on trail conditions and the logistics of getting to Celaque can be obtained at **Restaurante Guancascos,** which also offers rides to the park entrance for about US$10 per person. The government's environmental protection agency, **COHDEFOR** (*Corporación Hondureño de Desarrollo Forestal*), can also provide information, including English trail maps. Their office in Gracias is four blocks past Banco de Occidente towards the exit to Santa Rosa de Copán. To reach the park from Gracias, walk toward the cemetery located behind the fort on the hill and in the direction of the mountain. Follow the road that runs to the left of the cemetery; at the fork, veer to the right, and then veer right again at the white church. The walk from the church to the park is uphill along a dirt road and should take about two hours. After entering the park, it's half an hour to the **visitors center.** There are 17 bunks (with very limited bedding), a rustic kitchen, running water, a wood-burning stove, and friendly Candido, who takes care of the place. Trail information is also posted in English. Use of the park is L30 per day for foreigners, and staying at the visitors center is L10 per night. If you haven't brought food, there are some mean *frijolitos* and electrifying coffee to be had nearby.

If you're not a triathlete and plan to go to the summit and back in a single day, leave the visitors center at dawn. The hike to the first camp, **Don Tomás,** takes three to four hours. The camp is a small hut outfitted with mattress-less bunks, a latrine, and a firepit. Ask for a key at the visitors center before setting out. The next camp, **Naranjo,** is two to three hours beyond Don Tomás. The camp is slightly off the path and can be hard to spot. At the fork of the plateau go left, follow the trail down five minutes and keep your eyes peeled to the right; there's no hut here to mark the spot.

Though the cloud forest actually begins at Naranjo, the summit is still two to three hours away. In the cloud forest, the path is marked by pink, blue, and yellow ribbons pinned to the trees. Always keep the ribbons in sight. As you get closer to the summit, the air becomes increasingly cool and damp; be sure to bring appropriate clothing. The trail can be tricky at night, and crossing the rivers that interrupt the path can be difficult with only a flashlight.

To make the hike easier, safer, and more enjoyable, consider hiring Candido or another local to guide you. The guides speak only Spanish, but they know the cloud forest exceptionally well; they charge about L100 to San Tourás, L150 to Naranjo, and L200 to Cerro Las Minas. Another option is to hire horses to take you up the trail: one day's ride to Don Tomas costs about L150. Also, there is a camping spot within site of a large waterfall just two to three hours from the visitors center. The view is somewhat obscured, but it's beautiful all the same (with guide, L60). Necessary therapy after destroying your body tromping through Celaque is a visit to the **aguas termales** (hot springs). Nestled in a river gulch 6½km south of Gracias, the four separate baths range up to 100°F; bop from one to the next until dissolving in "just right." Although the baths officially close at 8pm, packs of affable locals drink beer and eat overpriced *papas fritas* at the small *pulpería* until 9:30 or so. If you head out in the evening, you can get in on the action and perhaps bum a ride back to Gracias. (As always, *Let's Go* isn't fond of hitchhiking.) The springs are a 1-1½ hr. hike away, but during the rainy season the only way to cross the river is via a sketchy swing bridge, though the locals don't seem to mind. If you get lost, the folks at Guancascos give stellar directions. Otherwise, you can hire a car to take you there for about L80 (L100 round-trip). Be sure to bring a watch; the trail is often thick with trees, and it's difficult to tell what time it is. Try to time your trip so that you're back at the visitors center before 4pm— it gets dark early in the forest. Bring a flashlight, just in case. The path generally is not especially difficult, but when the ground is wet, things can get hairy.

■ Copán

Copán wows. Visited by several thousand people each year, Copán is by far Honduras' most famous and impressive attraction. The ruins are a special link in the chain of Maya remnants that sweeps south from the Yucatán. While some ruins, notably Guatemala's Tikal and Mexico's Chichén Itzá, are larger, no site can match Copán for magnificently detailed artwork. In 1980, the ruins were named a UNESCO World Heritage Site in recognition of their importance to global culture.

The town of Copán Ruinas (pop. 25,000), 1km west of the ruins, would be worth passing through even if it weren't the base of choice for exploring the ruins. After a day spent admiring etchings of awe-inspiring deities and power-hungry rulers, coming back to Copán Ruinas is a pleasure. Singing from the church often wafts into its Parque Central as small boys ride horses up and down the town's few stone streets.

ORIENTATION AND PRACTICAL INFORMATION

Copán Ruinas is fairly easy to navigate. The bus terminal is at the bottom of a hill; one block uphill and to the left is the Parque Central. Services cluster within two or three blocks of the church, which is at the east end of the park. The ruins lie to the east of the town. Copán is typically cooler than the lowlands; bringing a sweatshirt is a good idea. The magazine, *Honduras Tips,* provides invaluable **tourist information** about the ruins, nearby towns, and almost everything else in Honduras; copies are available at Tunkul (see **Food,** below). Sandra at **Los Gemelos** (see **Accommodations,** below) is a veritable fountain of free info; ask your hotel manager or any of the heavily touristed restaurants in town for advice before relying on the whims of the local kids who roam the streets. Somewhat biased advice is also dispensed at **Go Native Tours** (tel. 61-44-32), half a block east of Tunkul. **Exchange currency,** cash **traveler's checks,** and get cash advances on Visa and Mastercard at **Banco de Occidente** (tel. 61-44-15), at the southeast corner of the park (open Mon.-Fri. 8am-noon and 2-5pm, Sat. 8-noon). To get quetzales, check at local restaurants such as **Llama del Bosque;** however, you'll get more favorable rates at the border.

Buses from **Empresa Etumi** run to **San Pedro Sula** (4 and 5am, 4-5hr., L40; expresses at 6 and 7am, 3hr., L70) and **La Entrada** (every 45min., 7am-4:30pm, 2½hr., L15; expresses every hr., 4-7am, 1hr., L30), where connections can be made to **Santa Rosa de Copán** and **San Pedro Sula.** To get to the **Guatemalan border,** hang around the park and bus station in the morning and look for pick-ups as they drive by. The pick-ups make themselves conspicuous and charge a L10-15 per person fee; be clear about the price before boarding. The **market** is one block west of the park's northwest corner. **Justo a Tiempo Laundromat,** one block south and one block west of the southwest corner of the park, washes and dries at a monopolistic L9 per pound; they also boast a massive **book exchange** (open Mon.-Sat. 7:30am-noon and 2-5:30pm). **Farmacia Felix M. Jandal** (tel. 61-40-51), a block up the hill from the Hotel Marina Copán, is open daily 7am-7pm, but closes for lunch. For **medical services,** head to Dr. Luis Castro's office (tel. 61-45-04), next to the bank; he speaks English (open Mon.-Sat. 8am-noon and 2-5pm). The **police (FUSEP)** (tel. 61-40-60), across the bridge, one and a half blocks from the Hotel Marina Copán, are ready to serve 24 hours. The **post office** (tel. 61-44-47), half a block from the park on the side opposite the church, posts a *lista de correos* (open Mon.-Fri. 8am-noon and 2-5pm, Sat. 8am-noon). The **postal code** is 41209. **Telephones** can be found at **Hondutel** (tel. 61-40-11), one block south of the park's southwest corner (open Mon.-Fri. 7am-9pm, Sat.-Sun. 8am-9pm). The phone next to the booths is for AT&T direct calls.

ACCOMMODATIONS

There are several small, cheap hotels around town and a few budding resorts; all seem to raise their prices with each passing day. Hotels are generally within a few blocks of the park. Ask about **camping** around the ruins; get permission before pounding in any stakes. Fans aren't as crucial here as along the coast.

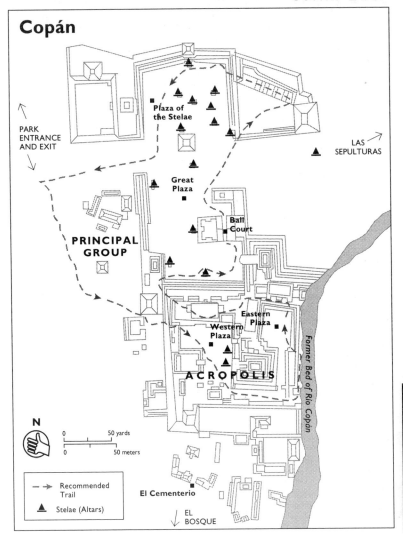

Copán

PARK
ENTRANCE
AND EXIT

Plaza of
the Stelae

LAS
SEPULTURAS

Great
Plaza

Ball
Court

PRINCIPAL
GROUP

Eastern
Plaza

Western
Plaza

ACROPOLIS

Former Bed of Río Copán

N

| 0 | 50 yards |
| 0 | 50 meters |

Recommended
Trail

▲ Stelae (Altars)

El Cementerio

EL
BOSQUE

HONDURAS

Los Gemelos (tel. 61-40-77), 1 block east of the park. From the bus terminal, take your first left walking toward the park (i.e. uphill) on the newly named Rodeo Dr. The eponymous *gemelos* (twins) have been separated, but the remaining half of the duo, Sandra, and her delightful mother still run things at this clean and carefully kept hotel. The courtyard, a botanical sedative, is the perfect place for free coffee and travel tips. Checkout 10am, but they'll store gear. Hot water in the mornings. Same-day laundry service L10 per lb (singles L50; doubles L70; triples L105).

Hotel California (tel. 61-45-15), across from Los Gemelos. Seems too good to be true; fairly, spacious, bamboo-decorated rooms with mattresses worth crowing about and sparkling common bathrooms with hot water. Kitchen access. Chain-smoking ex-broker who runs the place just can't kill the beast. Inquire about weekly gourmet nights at the restaurant inside; "better than sex" pasta served on irregular Mondays. Free bottled water (singles L50; doubles L100).

Hotel La Posada Copán (tel. 98-30-70, shared with Hotel Marina Copán), across from the Marina Copán, off the northwest corner of the park. The 22 rooms are well-kept and the owner is ultra-mellow. The many stalls in the somewhat odiferous common bathrooms prevent anxious waits. Creaky beds. Singles cost L40.

Casa de Cafe (tel. 52-72-74). From the southwest corner of the park, walk 1 block south and turn right; walk 2 more blocks, and follow the signs the rest of the way. Beautiful antique-furnished rooms open onto a balcony with hammocks and a stunning view. Common area with guide books and English-language magazines. Singles US$20, with private bath US$30; doubles US$28, with private bath US$38; triples US$96. Breakfast and all-you-can-drink coffee included. The owners have just opened the promising new **Hotel Iguana Azul** next door, a miniature, more budget-oriented version of Casa de Café, with attractive, exotic-colored bunk rows and private doubles for US$5 per person.

FOOD

There are some great places to grab a bite in town, both gringo-oriented spots and restaurants that still serve authentic Honduran food.

Llama del Bosque (tel. 61-44-31), 1½blocks west from the southwest corner of the park. A Copán institution for the last 21 years, Llama keeps generations of tourists migrating back for its stellar service and heaping platefuls of hearty Honduran fare. Meat dishes L65; *arroz con pollo* L40; vegetarian options. The quickest service in town makes this your best bet for breakfast before running off to the ruins (*huevos rancheros* L30). Groups of 5 get one meal free (open daily 6:30am-10pm).

Vamos a Ver, just south of the southwest corner of the park. A friendly Dutch couple prepares dishes that are a beauty to behold and a joy to eat. Whole wheat bread baked fresh every day. Sandwiches L10-30, *muesli* with fruit L15, daily special L70. Vegetarian entrees available. Watch quality English-language movies in the front room while you eat (nightly screenings at 7pm, US$1). Open daily 7am-9pm.

Tunkul Restaurante and Bar (tel. 61-44-10), 2 blocks west of the southwest corner of the park. On the *Autobahn* to legendary status, Tunkul's friendly owners aren't leaving any tourists behind. The food is so-so, but people come more to mingle with other *gringos* than anything else. Vegetarian plates are available, and veggie stuffings can be substituted for meat upon request. Come here to take part in the only real nightlife in town; a *tunkul* is a Maya drum, and this eatery doesn't miss a beat. Chicken or beef burritos L38, plate L35. Open daily 7am-10pm; happy hour 8-9pm; drinks until midnight.

Carnecitas Nía Lola (tel. 61-44-03), at the south end of the road from the southwest corner of town. An open-air forge with working bellows turns out standard Honduran fare at low prices. The specialty is *anafres,* a gooey mixture of beans, cheese, and tortilla strips that is served in the ceramic pot and pile of coals that cooked them. *Carne asada* L30. Happy hour at the bar 6:30-7:30pm. Come at dusk, when the patio has great views of the mountains to the south. Open daily 10am-9pm.

THE RUINS

Since the jungle began to reclaim it almost 800 years ago, Copán has been discovered and re-discovered several times over. When *conquistadores* invaded the area in the 15th century, they used Náhuatl-speaking *indígenas* as guides. Locals led the Spanish to what the Náhuatl called "Copantl," or "Place of the Wooden Bridge." Mrs. Malaprop intervened, and Copantl became Copán.

In 1839, John Lloyd Stephens was the next to stumble upon the ruins. The American liked what he found so much that he bought the ruins for the equivalent of US$50, and subsequently published *Incidents of Travel in Central America, Chiapas, and Yucatán,* which contains illustrations of Copán. Inspired by the site, Stephens waved away the bigoted theories popular in the 19th century. "America, say historians, was peopled by savages—but savages never reared these structures, savages never carved these stones," he proclaimed. While Stephens' work sparked interest in the ruins, few scholars made the trip to Copán; only pillaging pot-poachers beat paths to the site.

Things began to change in 1952, when the Honduran Instituto Nacional Antropología e Historia took over the site. Scholars working under the institute's auspices have radically changed the world's conceptualization of the Maya world in general, and Copán in particular. Anthropologists had previously assumed that Maya society was thoroughly theocratic, that Maya culture and government revolved around priests and temples. Scholars believed Copán's functions were purely religious—the structures still visible today were believed to be temples, the art which adorned them supposedly depicted only divine beings, and the hieroglyphics were thought to be prophecies. Over the last 25 years, institute archaeologists have turned these tenets of conventional wisdom on their collective head. Scholars now believe that Maya society, while deeply religious, was fundamentally secular. Copán wasn't merely a ceremonial center—as many as 30,000 ordinary Maya lived and worked in the city. Experts now think that its artwork was political as well as religious, representing rulers and nobles as well as divine beings, and many hieroglyphics may have recorded actual historical events.

The city the Maya called "Xukpi" for the ubiquitous black-crowned motmot bird was first settled nearly 2000 years ago. Though situated in a fertile valley well-suited for corn cultivation, Copán grew slowly. The city's Golden Age occurred between AD 628 and 800; during those years, Copán was ruled by a series of strong leaders. Under Smoke Jaguar (AD 628-695), the 12th king of Copán, the city grew into a military powerhouse. Next came 18 Rabbit (AD 695-738), who was captured and killed while battling his neighbors; 18 Rabbit was succeeded by Smoke Monkey, who ruled Copán for only 11 years (AD 738-749). The reign of Smoke Monkey's son, Smoke Shell (AD 749-763), was marked by unprecedented cultural and intellectual flowering. During his reign, Maya astronomers met at Copán to pool their research on eclipses. Soon after Smoke Shell's death, things took a turn for the worse. For reasons not entirely clear to archaeologists, Copán, like the rest of the Maya world, ceased to be agriculturally self-sufficient, and, around AD 900, began to decline. Forced to rely on foodstuffs shipped down the Copán River by satellite settlements, Copán's power waned, and by about AD 1100, the jungle had started to reclaim Copán. For the sake of modern tourists and scholars, the vines and trees have recently been swept aside, and Copán, long obscured, can re-assert itself.

Unfortunately, the cost of visiting Copán has escalated wildly over the past few years. The entrance fee to the main site and nearby **Las Sepulturas** has increased from L30 to a non-budget US$10. And that US$10 no longer includes entry to the museum in town, which now costs an additional US$2. It doesn't end there—a new museum at the park will set you back another US$5. But before you decide that Copán is beyond your price range, take a deep breath and remind yourself that this is one of the reasons you came to Honduras in the first place.

The **museum** in the town square provides a good overview of Maya history, as well as some lesser artifacts from the ruins. Be sure to slip in the room with "El Brujillo" written on the doorjamb, just before the exit. Here, a complete Maya (*sans* soft tissue) lies entombed with his pet turtles. The museum is open daily 8am-noon and 1-4pm.

The **entrance** to the ruins is a 15-minute walk east of town; southwest of the entrance, look for the **Museum of Maya Sculpture.** This beautiful new building opened its doors to visitors in the summer of 1996. One of a kind in all of the Americas, this massive complex was built to house and protect the most precious sculptures in the park from the ground moisture and temperature fluctuations of the great outdoors. Several important stelae and altars have already been moved to the museum and replicas left in their place. Future plans include the construction of six additional structures to protect many more treasures from the park. The crowning jewel of the museum is a full-sized, brightly-painted replica of **Rosalila,** a temple archaeologists found buried within Structure 16 in the acropolis. The elaborately-colored stucco reliefs shed dazzling light on the way the site actually looked more than 1000 years ago. Additionally, the famed **Altar Q,** guarded by the likenesses of 16 elab-

HONDURAS

orately costumed governors of ancient Copán, has newly found an indoor home here. In an effort to mimic the entrance atop the Plaza of Jaguars the entrance to the museum leads through the mouth and long, dim esophagus of a mythical serpent.

The entrance to the ruins (where you present your ticket) is near the **visitors center.** Collectively, the ruins are called the **Principal Group.** Highlights include a gnarled **800-year-old Ceiba tree** whose sacred roots were believed to reach into the underworld, and the 63 steps of the **Hieroglyphic Stairway,** intricately carved with thousands of inscriptions that tell the history of the Maya city.

More detailed information on the ruins is available in a booklet called *History Carved in Stone,* available in the gift shop for L30 (it costs less in the souvenir shops in town). For the full experience, hiring one of many red-shirted, multi-lingual guides (US$20) is essential; try to put together a group and head to the visitors center. For a touch of the peculiar, ask for Antonio Ríos (or "Tony Rivers"), the very first guide at Copán. He speaks English and claims to know greetings in over 100 languages. His inevitable discussion of the presence of UFOs in Western Honduras is an added bonus. **Go Native Tours** (tel. 61-44-32) offers English guided tours to **Los Sapos** for US$25 per person, US$20 per person for groups of two to four, and US$15 per person for groups of five or more. Less expensive **horseback trips** to Los Sapos can be arranged through the kids in the park (L60-100 per person); it's more informative and safer (though more expensive) to go with one of the guides from the park (3-4hr., US$20 per person).

OTHER EXCURSIONS

Heading west from Copán, the mountainous landscape is dotted with *pueblas,* where you can observe living Maya culture. Villagers continue to live in traditional cane huts, practice centuries-old agricultural methods, and produce pottery. Small tobacco and coffee farms predominate the hillside's agriculture.

The most accessible of these towns is **Corrizalon.** To get there, arrange for a pick-up truck in Copán (L3) to let you off at the *Escuela de Hacienda Grande;* some have claimed that hitching is another option, but *Let's Go* does not recommend it. Take the small dirt road next to the school, veering right when the road splits. The walk to the town is about 3km. Once there, ask Crecencia Perez for a tour through the surrounding fields to a pleasant waterfall (L20). To return to Copán, catch a reasonably early pick-up truck, as there is nowhere to stay in the village, and the last pick-up out has been known to charge exorbitant prices.

A respite from civilizations past and present can be found 9km west of Copán at **El Ruby Waterfall,** near the colonial town of Santa Rita. About a 35-minute hike up the mountain, there's a small, secluded fall; another 20 minutes up the trail lie a series of cascades. While El Ruby is not too large, it is set among some striking rock formations. The falls are also accessible by hired pick-up trucks; find a kid to guide you on the trail to the falls for a few lempiras. Ask at your hotel for contacts before setting off.

Those hankering after further immersion head off to another local hot spot, the **aguas calientes,** 23km out of town (entrance L10, open daily 8am-5pm). Two man-made pools provide a perfect place for slothful total-body-relaxation; the cool river water mixes with the thermal water in an inviting spot below. A quick jungly jaunt two minutes up the trail reveals the source; you could hard boil eggs there, but don't even think about getting into the scalding water. Pick-ups provide transport (45min., L30-40 each for 5-6 people); Susy at **Vamos a Ver** and Jerry at **Hotel California** help organize groups. For more elaborate tours of the area, contact avid nature-lover Jorge, at **Xukpi Tours** (tel. 61-44-35, at night 61-40-18; fax 61-45-03).

■ San Pedro Sula

Like the *sula* (dove) in its name, San Pedro Sula has a tradition of soaring ahead of the pack. Founded in 1536 by Don Pedro de Alvarado himself, the city grew moderately at first. When the railroads arrived at the end of the 19th century, its banana boom turned behemoth. The spirit of commerce attracted Arab and European immigrants, vaulting San Pedro to the fore of Honduras' economy and industry. Today's San Pedro bristles with capitalism, commerce, and people, but seems in many ways to have gotten ahead of itself. The 650,000 residents and some 200,000 transient workers bump elbows and other body parts as the frenetic city is stretched to its limits. While luxury hotels, fax machines, and multiple Burger Kings gild the city with a prosperous sheen, poverty lies just beneath the surface, and petty crime and muggings have become a prevalent problem. In its time, high-energy San Pedro has suffered from frequent power shortages. In 1994, the nearby hydroelectric dam was periodically constipated by sediment washing down from deforested lands. In the summer of 1995, drought led officials to cut off the water supply entirely.

Of course, the advantageous result of all this commotion is a city full of action and intensity, a stark contrast to the sleepy regions nearby. Travelers desperate for a break from the rural and rustic can relish the diversity of cultural offerings, as well as further appreciate the uncanny Honduran ability to stand up to adversity with wit and savvy.

ORIENTATION AND PRACTICAL INFORMATION

San Pedro Sula's streets form a grid around the central train station. From the center, east to west *calles* and north to south *avenidas* extend outward into four quadrants—NO (northwest), NE (northeast), SO (southwest), and SE (southeast). The **Circunvalación** runs around the city, and **5a Avenida SO** is sometimes called Avenida Lempira. Notable landmarks are the **Parque Central** and the **plaza,** both between 1a and 3a Calles and 2a and 3a Avs. SO. Most budget hotels and bus stations are in the SO quadrant. The mountains, with their Big Brother-like Coca Cola sign, lie to the west. Intersections outside the central area tend to lack street signs. Locals warn that east of the railroad tracks and south of 7a Calle are the dangerous parts of town.

Tourist Office: Jorge Molanphy, at **Maya Tropic Tours** (tel. 552-24-05 and 551-24-01) in the lobby of the Gran Hotel Sula, will help budget travelers in need, though his tours are a bit beyond budget bounds. He is bilingual and exceptionally cool; look for him Mon.-Fri. 7:30-11:30am and 1:30-5:30pm, Sat. 7:30-11:30am. Extensive info on Honduras' national parks is available at the **Fundación Ecologista** (tel. 57-10-14), 7 Av. and 1 Calle, above Pizzeria Italia (open Mon.-Fri. 8am-noon and 1-5pm).

Consulates: There is no U.S. consulate in San Pedro Sula. **British Consulate** (tel. 57-20-63; fax 57-40-66), 2a Calle, 2a/3a Avs. SO, 2nd floor. Open Mon.-Fri. 8am-noon. **Guatemalan Consulate** (tel./fax 53-35-60), 8a Calle between 5a and 6a Avs. NO. Open Mon.-Fri. 8am-2pm.

Currency Exchange: Almost every bank is open Mon.-Fri. 9am-4pm. **Bancahsa** (tel. 52-67-80) is open until 5pm for the perpetually late. They change traveler's checks, give advances on Visa cards, and offer moneygrams. **Creditlan** (tel. 50-40-96; fax 50-40-96), 3a Av.,1a/2a Calles NO. Cash advances on Visa cards. Open Mon.-Fri. 8:30am-5pm, Sat. 8:30am-noon. It's easier to change cash than traveler's checks in the park with the people who yell *"dólares."* Be persistent, and compare rates.

American Express: Mundirama Travel Agency (tel. 50-11-92; fax 57-90-22), 2a Calle between 2a and 3a Avs. SO, on the south side of the cathedral. Same-day replacement of lost traveler's checks; they'll give up to US$1000 a month for personal checks. Cardholder's service. English is spoken. Open for AmEx service Mon.-Fri. 8am-5pm and Sat. 8am-noon.

Airport: Villeda Morales, about 15km out of town, is accessible by cab for L70 (if you're skilled at bartering). **Isleña Airlines** (tel. 52-83-35; tel./fax 52-83-22) flies to **La Ceiba** (Mon.-Sat. 6:30am and 3pm, Sun. at 3pm only, 25min., one way L338, round-trip L677) and **Roatán** (twice daily, 1¼hr., L615 one way, L1230 round-trip). **Taca** (tel. 50-96-78) flies to **Tegucigalpa** (daily at 4:25pm, 25min., L379).

Buses: Most bus terminals are located in the SO sector, although discovering the exact location of each terminal can be tough. The best way to get bus info is to go to any one of these terminals and ask which travels the route you want. **El Rey** (tel. 58-42-64), 7 Av., 5a/6a Calles SO, goes to **Tegucigalpa** (every hr., 2am-12:30pm and 2-7pm, L32). **Catisa,** 2a Av., 5a/6a Calles SO, goes to **La Lima** (every 6min.,

5am-10pm, 25min., L2.50) and to **El Progreso** (every 20min., 30min., L5). From El Progreso, you can snag a bus to **Tela.** They also go to **La Ceiba** (every hour, 5:30am-6pm, 3hrs., L30). To get to the border at **Agua Caliente,** try either **Transporto Congolón,** 8a Av., 9a/10a Calle SO, or **Toritos y Copanecos,** 6a Av., 8a/9a Calles SO; they alternate day and night shifts (every 2hrs., 5½hrs., L45; midnight expresses: 4½hr., L60). **Toritos** also goes to **Santa Rosa de Copán** (every 25min., 3:45am-5:15pm, 3½hr., L22; 4 direct buses 8, 9:30am, 2, and 3:30pm, 2hr., L35); hop on the Santa Rosa bus in **La Entrada** (L12) to transfer to **Copán Ruinas. CITUL,** 6a Av., 7a/8a Calles SO, goes to **Puerto Cortés** (every 30min., 5:30am-7:30pm, 1hr., L10). There are two companies that service **Trujillo** directly (every hr., 8am-4pm, 6hr., L65): **Transuplan** leaves from the Shell gas station at 3 Av., 5/6 Calles SE; **Cotraípbal** from a lot on 1 Av., 7/8 Calle SE.

Taxis: Rides within the city are L15, after 7pm L20 for one person and L30 for two. Establish a price before leaving.

Laundromat: Lavandería Almich (tel. 53-16-87), 5a Calle, 9a/10a Avs. SO. L30 per load. Open Mon.-Fri. 7:30-11:30am and 1-5pm, Sat. 8am-2pm. Most hotels will clean your clothes for about L2-3 per piece.

English Bookstore: Coello Bookstore, 9a Av. and 4a Calle SO, stocks a smattering of used English novels, heavy on the Danielle Steele and John Grisham. Open Mon.-Fri. 8am-noon and 1:30-5:30pm, Sat. 8am-noon.

English Library: Centro Cultural Sampedrano, 3a Calle, 3a/4a Avs. NO. Extensive collection. The centro houses painting exhibitions and two theaters as well. Open Mon.-Fri. 9am-noon and 1-7pm, Sat. 9am-noon.

Pharmacies: To find out which pharmacy is open late or on the weekend, check the list posted outside any pharmacy or call the operator at 192. Most pharmacies, like **Farmacia Siman** (tel. 50-16-24), 3a Av. and 2a Calle, take credit cards. Open Mon.-Fri. 8am-noon and 1:30-6pm, Sat. 8am-noon.

Hospital: Cemesa (tel. 57-74-01), Calle Altamira 21-22a, Blvd. del Sur. 24hr. emergency service.

Emergency Medical Services: (tel. 52-41-41). Open 24hr. and replete with its own ambulance, hospital, walk-in clinic, and U.S.-trained doctor.

Police: (tel. 50-31-76 or 52-31-71), 4 Calle, 4 Av. Open 24hr.

Emergency Numbers: tel. 199; for firefighters, call 198.

Post Office: (tel. 52-31-83; fax 57-06-79), 3a Av., 9a/10a Calles SO. *Lista de correos.* Open Mon.-Fri. 7:30am-8pm, Sat. 8:30am-12:30pm. **Express mail** service next door at **E.M.S. Honduras** (tel. 52-31-83; fax 57-06-79). A 2kg package takes 3-4 days to the U.S. Open Mon.-Fri. 8am-7pm, Sat. 8am-noon. The **postal code** for the city is by sector: **NE,** 21101; **NO,** 21102; **SE,** 21103; **SO,** 21104.

Telephones: Hondutel (tel. 57-22-22; fax 50-22-52), 4a Av. and 4a Calle. A separate room for AT&T Direct calling card and collect service to the U.S. Otherwise, prices to the U.S. vary by state. **Faxes and telegrams** (L17 per page to the U.S., L24 per page to Europe). Open daily 8am-4pm.

ACCOMMODATIONS

San Pedro's hotel architects must have been a generous breed; it's hard to find a room that doesn't dwarf whichever little bed sits in it. Fans are a must. The SO quadrant is close to the bus terminals and bursts with cheap rooms. Unfortunately, many of these L25 "bargains" are afflicted with lumpy beds and rank communal bathrooms. The *hospedajes* seem particularly risky.

Hotel Brisas de Occidente (tel. 52-23-09), 5a Av. and 7a Calle SO. Massive rooms with pseudo-marble floors. A great place to host a dance party for all the international backpackers who stay here; just push that cute, ornamental desk out of the way. Ask for one of the breezy top-floor rooms. Common bath. Luggage storage. Reservations accepted. Checkout noon. Singles and doubles L40; triples L60.

Hotel San Juan (tel. 53-14-88), 6a Calle, 4a/5a Avs SO. Around the corner from the Brisas del Occidente, the San Juan offer rooms decidedly more snug, but comparatively priced. Take in the city below from open-air hallways. Equipped with its own

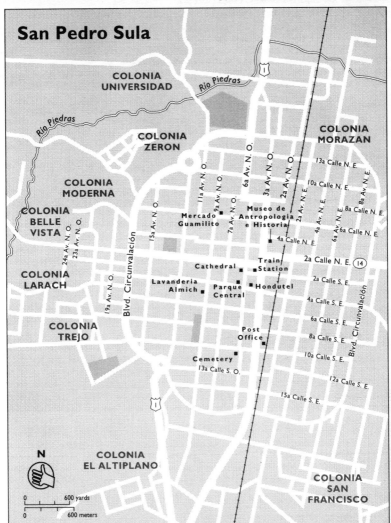

San Pedro Sula

COLONIA
UNIVERSIDAD

Rio Piedras

Rio Piedras

COLONIA
ZERON

COLONIA
MORAZAN

13a Calle N. E.

10a Calle N. E.

8a Calle N. E.

COLONIA
MODERNA

6a Av. N. O.

3a Av. N. O.

2a Av. N. O.

8a Calle N. E.

COLONIA
BELLE
VISTA

11a Av. N. O.

9a Av. N. O.

7a Av. N. O.

Mercado
Guamilito

Museo de
Antropologia
e Historia

4a Av. N. E.

6a Calle N. E.

24a Av. N. O.

23a Av. N. O.

15a Av. N. O.

4a Calle N. E.

COLONIA
LARACH

Cathedral

Train
Station

2a Calle N. E.   14

19a Av. N. O.

Blvd. Circunvalación

Lavanderia
Almich

Parque
Central

Hondutel

2a Calle S. E.

4a Calle S. E.

COLONIA
TREJO

6a Calle S. E.

Post
Office

8a Calle S. E.

Blvd. Circunvalación

10a Calle S. E.

Cemetery

13a Calle S. O.

12a Calle S. E.

15a Calle S. E.

N

COLONIA
EL ALTIPLANO

0   600 yards

0   600 meters

COLONIA
SAN
FRANCISCO

HONDURAS

electric generator and water supply, the San Juan is ready for Armageddon (but are you?). Singles and doubles L43, with private bath L59; triples L51.

Hotel San José (tel. 57-12-08), 6a Av., 5a/6a Calles SO. The diligent *dueña* works the front desk 17hr. per day to keep the hotel clean and safe. Cool grey bookshelves. TV and *agua purificada* in the lobby. Singles with double bed L70, with A/C L112; doubles L75, with A/C L150; triples L96, with A/C L177. Married couples pay only the single rate, so wed your travel partner.

FOOD

Since San Pedro is stuffed to the gills with restaurants, food stands, and cafes, there's no reason not to go get stuffed yourself. Although much of the food is expensive, careful *mochileros* (backpackers) can squeak by on local food, though some of the stuff peddled on the streets can wreak havoc on the bowels. For a **fastfood** fix, head to the cluster with Wendy's, Burger King, and Pizza Hut at 4a Av. and 3a Calle SO. The Pizza Hut (delivery tel. 58-03-58) has a decent, clean salad bar (all-you-can-eat for 35L). Fresh fruit can be purchased at the *mercado,* at 7a Calle and 4a Av. SE, though **Mercado Guamilito** at 6a Calle, 8a/9a Avs NO, offers a better and cleaner selection. **Bigos,** Honduras' own burger chain, sits at 6a Av. and 1 Calle. On the weekends, food stands pop up throughout the Parque Central.

> **Cafetería Mayan Way** (tel. 50-08-10), 6a Av., 4a/5a Calles SO. A favorite with locals, this place serves up cheap, delicious plates of *típico* dishes. *Ranchero*-style eggs, beans, plantains, tortillas L20. Pork chops with fries, salad, beans, and plantains L25. Create your own plateful from the buffet for L16. Travel advice is free. Open Mon.-Sat. 7am-midnight.
>
> **Cafetería y Pizzería Italia** (tel. 50-70-94), 1a Calle and 7a Av. NO. Elbow pads around the bar let you drown your sorrows in delicious thin-crust pizza, the best in town. There's no parmesan, but the Satan's Salsa spices up any slice. Ham and sausage pizza L45, vegetarian pizza L55, lasagna L39. Open Tues.-Sun. 10am-10pm.
>
> **Café Skandia** (tel. 52-99-99), in the lobby of the Gran Hotel Sula. An eerie 50s soda-fountain feel, coupled with Western-style food and chilly A/C, makes this a favorite with wealthy tourists. Hamburgers L29, apple pie L15. Open 24hr.
>
> **La Fuente de Salud,** 8a Av., 5a/6a Calles SO. Honduran vegan lunch L15, tofu sandwich L5. Open Sun.-Fri. 11:30am-1pm. Wholesome baked goodies and fruit available for take-out, 7am-6pm.
>
> **Chef Mariano,** (tel. 52-54-92) 16 Av., 9/10 Calle SO, in the *zona viva.* An army of white-coated waiters serves tasty Garifuna food from the open kitchen. Expensive dishes come with fresh coconut bread, salad, and fish soup (grilled fish L80). Open Mon.-Thurs. 10am-3pm and 5-11pm, Fri.-Sat. 10am-midnight, Sun. 10am-10pm.

SIGHTS AND ENTERTAINMENT

San Pedro Sula's pride and joy is the new **Museo de Antropologia e Historia** (tel. 57-14-96), at 3a Av., 3a/4a Calles NO. Dedicated in January, 1994, the museum is the city's first, and the whole nation is justifiably proud. The modern building is home to permanent and temporary exhibit space, a library, a lab for working archaeologists, and a massive theater that welcomed the Kiev ballet on its first visit to Honduras. The museum's top floor displays artifacts from the Paya and Jicaque, indigenous peoples who once dominated western Honduras. Ceramics, cooking tools, and other pieces impart a sense of what life was like between the Archaic Period (circa 3500 BC) and the Conquest. The second floor traces the colonial period to the present, with an emphasis on San Pedro's past. Colorful paintings provide a window on the region's colonial era. Smaller exhibits on themes such as 19th-century cockfighting and the development of Honduras' first breweries round out the picture. The whole exhibit is in Spanish, and only the director speaks English. (Open Tues.-Sat. 10am-4:30pm; L5 for adults, L2 for children and students with ISIC card.) The lush, Edenic grounds merit some meandering whether you step foot in the museum or not, and the shady outdoor cafeteria cooks up tasty Honduran cuisine at equally attractive prices (fried chicken, salad, beans, and rice L18; open 7:30am-5pm).

Beyond the museum, San Pedro offers a handful of attractions of interest to tourists. Though morbid, the town **cemetery,** at 5a Av. and 11a Calle SO, is a good place to rest in peace between the large, intriguing tombs built for San Pedro's founding fathers and mothers. The immense, reserved **cathedral** squats at the northeast end of the park and is worth the time (10min.) and money (free) required to tour it and see its remarkably modern iconography. The pew-fulls of *sanpedranos* use the cathedral to escape two awful heats: hell-fire and the summer sun (open daily 6am-noon and 2-8pm). Apart from being a good source of chow, the Mercado Guamilito (see **Food,** above) plays host to the **Asociación Nacional de Artesanos de Honduras.** Go there to meander through row upon row of *artesanía* goodies, including wood carvings, inexpensive bayonets, and carefully crafted ceramics (open Mon.-Sat. 7am-5pm, Sun. 7am-noon). For better quality at slightly elevated prices, go across the road to **Casa del Sol,** 6a Calle, 8a/9a Avs. (open Mon.-Sat. 8:30am-6:30pm, Sun. 8am-noon).

For the money, San Pedro Sula's best attraction may be the one-hour **massage** (L40) given by the Seventh Day Adventists at **La Fuente de Salud** restaurant (see **Food,** above). Be rubbed down with lotion or the kinkier (and stickier) honey. You may want to request a nix on the otherwise compulsory neck-cracking. Massages are given beginning at 8am; come early. Showers are available.

Later at night, San Pedro's chic set heads out to any of the several **discotecas** scattered about town. All discos have a minimal dress code (no shorts, t-shirts, or sandals), and it's standard to be frisked upon entry. (Virtually all clubs are open Tues.-Sun. 6pm-4am.) The hippest spot in town is **Confetti's,** on the Circunvalación near the Puerto Cortés exit, where an I-just-turned-twenty crowd pays L50 to shake to modern disco hits on a petite dance floor (beer L18; open Tues.-Sun. from 7pm to dawn; Wed. is Ladies' Night). **Henry's,** just up the street (about 2 blocks west on the Circunvalación), offers stiff competition—same action for the same prices, but with pool tables to boot. A few blocks away, **Frogs,** a new theme bar, is attracting hordes of locals to its patio, pool tables, and beach volleyball court. Closer to most budget hotels, **Johnny's Bar,** 4a Av., 8a/9a Calles, is a favorite Peace Corps hangout that takes the 50s living room to an extreme—the only furnishings are vinyl couches and cans of SPAM. Reasonably cheap drinks (L10) are served with bar snacks. **Women** should be warned that city bars are a potent breeding ground for *machismo.* Go with people you trust (not alone), keep your judgment clear, and dance defensively.

San Pedro Sula is nationally famous for its month-long **Feria Juniana** (Fair of June). Dating back to 1846, the festival used to include a tennis tournament, marathon, even a party in the city jail, sponsored by the "San Pedro Sula Ladies." These days, Garifuna dancers, drum corps, and pre-pubescent beauty queens parade down the street, in the daytime; the last two weekends, vendors and food booths stay open late at night as throngs of *sampedranos* and a bevy of musical groups keep the streets throbbing well into the wee hours. Grab a silly cardboard mask and join the fun.

■ Near San Pedro Sula

WATERFALLS

When the urban urge begins to wane, it's probably time to wax waterfall-adventurous and head to the picturesque **Catarata Pulhapanzak** (entrance L5).The best way to do the waterfall is to grab an over-eager *niñito* and head down the steep path. Part of the trail requires using tree roots as a ladder—it's a mildly difficult descent, but you'll be rewarded by refreshing spray, a small swimming pool, and a cave to the left of the main cascade. Children often swim in a section of the river directly upstream from the powerful crashing of the falls; it looks risky, but is reportedly safe. Steer clear of the rapids above the pool; powerful whirlpools can spin about beside them. On hot weekends the joint jumps with visitors, who pass the time playing barefoot fútbol and munching hamburgers (L15) and french fries (L15) from the open-air restaurant.

To reach the falls, board a bus in San Pedro at 1a Av., 4a/5a Calles SE, headed toward **Río Lindo** (every 40min., 7am-5pm, 1¾hr., L10). These buses go beyond the falls, so make sure to get off when they stop at the village of **San Buena Ventura.** Return buses to San Pedro Sula leave about every half-hour during daylight hours. The last buses back can be packed with people, so if you have an aversion to standing or a minimum airspace requirement, plan ahead. Keep your eyes peeled for the Pulhapanzak sign on the left side of the road—the drivers often forget to stop, even when asked. Once out of the bus, take the main, concrete road through town. After roughly 1km, the road forks. Go left, up the hill for several hundred meters—the *balneario* is on the right. Nearby signs lead to **Las Gradas,** a less impressive (but less crowded) *cascada* (L5).

LA LIMA

When the stresses of budget travel have driven you bananas, head for **La Lima,** a place driven *by* bananas. Fifteen kilometers outside San Pedro, the town is sur-

HONDURAS

rounded by the *fincas* (plantations) that supply *norteamericanos* with the essential ingredient of banana daiquiris. To tour one of the plantations, start by catching a **bus** to La Lima or El Progreso (*not* the *directo*). Tell the driver that you want to get off at the *"planta de Chiquita"* (about 15 minutes past the Parque Central of La Lima). Make sure you get off by the Chiquita water tower. At the stop, cross the street, and explain to the parking lot attendant that you wish to tour *una finca*. He will send you to an administrator with the **Tela Railroad Company** who will give you a pass. Bring a recognizable ID and go in the morning, when the right people are easier to find. You will then be put on another bus and sent to one of the outlying *fincas*.

The preparation of bananas is not an overly complicated process: the fruit is cut off the stem, washed, classified, and packaged. The plantations see few visitors, and the workers will likely get a big kick out of having you around. Photo ops abound, and the oceans of banana plants make for some pleasant wandering. If you really would like to learn more, there are English narrated tours of the plantations from the Grand Sula Hotel for about US$20.

THE CARIBBEAN COAST

■ Puerto Cortés

In the 19th century, investors plunged millions into a plan to construct a railroad from the Caribbean to San Lorenzo on the Pacific. Puerto Cortés was to be the entry point on the Atlantic, and was expected to turn into a Honduran version of Panama City, rich in culture and bursting in trade. The railroad scheme failed, but Puerto Cortés still manages to see more than its share of imports and exports as the largest port in Honduras and one of the best equipped in Central America. Culturally, however, the outcome has been less successful. Only a collection of clothing factories has cropped up to complement the massive freight cranes and hulking cargo ships that reign supreme over downtown. There's nothing in this gritty city to entice backpackers to stick around. Most don't, instead making a beehive to the beaches at the nearby **Garifuna villages** or beside Puerto Omoa's famous **Fortaleza**.

ORIENTATION AND PRACTICAL INFORMATION

Puerto Cortés occupies a peninsula surrounded by the Caribbean to the north and west, the **Bahía de Cortés** to the south, and the inland laguna to the southeast. The downtown area clusters near the docks on the southern shore of the peninsula. Along the docks, **1a Avenida** runs east-west; the rest of the avenidas increase in number as you move north. Calles increase from west to east. The Parque Central sits between 2a and 3a Av. and 4a and 5a Calles.

There's no **tourist office** in town, but the folks at **Café Viena** (see **Food,** below) are helpful and speak English. **Change currency** and **traveler's checks** and get cash advances at **Banco de Occidente** (tel. 65-03-84), on 3a Av. and 4a Calle, kitty corner to the park (open Mon.-Fri. 8am-5pm, Sat. 8-11:30am). **Impala buses,** at 3 Av. and 3/4 Calles, make the most frequent runs to **San Pedro Sula** (every 30min., 6am-5pm, 1hr., L10). To head out to **Omoa,** snag a **Costeños bus** next to the Esso gas station, on 3a Calle, 3a/4a Av. (every 30min, 6:30am-8pm, 30min., L3.50). **Boats** sail from Puerto Cortés to the **Bay Islands, Belize, Texas**, and places all around the world; however, there are few passenger boats, and fewer still that have regular schedules. Ask around at the docks for departure information. There's a dual-motored launch that makes bi-weekly runs to **Belize,** departing from the laguna for **Mango Creek** (Sat. mornings, 2hr., about L320 per person) and for **Dangriga** (Mon. mornings, 2hr., about L450 per person). To get to the laguna, catch the local bus headed east from the northeast edge of the park, across from Banco del País (L1). Once there, ask for José Williams at Kokito's Restaurant next to the bridge for more information. Before

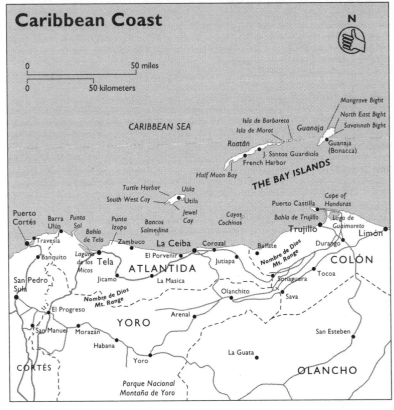

Caribbean Coast

N

CARIBBEAN SEA

THE BAY ISLANDS

Mangrove Bight
North East Bight
Savannah Bight

Isla de Barbareta
Isla de Morat
Guanaja
Guanaja
(Bonacca)

Roatán
J. Santos Guardiola
French Harbor
Half Moon Bay

Turtle Harbor
Utila
South West Cay
Utila
Jewel
Cay
Cayos
Cochinos
Puerto Castilla
Cape of
Honduras

Puerto
Cortés
Barra
Ulúa
Punta
Sal
Punta
Izopo
Bancos
Salmedina
Bahía de Trujillo
Lago de
Guaimoreto
Bahía
de Tela
Trujillo
Limón
Travesía
Zambuco
La Ceiba
Corozal
Balfate
Durango
Banquito
Laguna
de los
Micos
Tela
El Porvenir
Jutiapa
Nombre de Dios
Mt. Range
COLÓN
ATLÁNTIDA
San Pedro
Sula
Jicamo
La Masica
Sonaguera
Tocoa
Nombre de Dios
Mt. Range
Olanchito
Sava
El Progreso
Arenal
YORO
San Manuel
Morazán
San Esteben
Habana
Yoro
La Guata
CORTÉS
OLANCHO
Parque Nacional
Montaña de Yoro

0   50 miles
0   50 kilometers

leaving for parts unknown, don't forget to get your exit stamp at the **immigration office,** upstairs from Banco del País on the northeast corner of the park (open Mon.-Fri. 8am-noon and 2-6pm, Sat. 8am-noon). A rusty, old train also departs from the laguna for **Tela** (Fri. and Sun., 7am, 4hr., L12). Taxis cost L10 around town.

The **post office** (tel. 65-04-55) awaits at the corner of 1a Calle and 2a Av. (open Mon.-Fri. 8am-4:30pm, Sat. 8am-noon). As usual, they've got a *lista de correos* and an **EMS express mail** (tel. 65-04-54) next door. Reach out and touch someone at **Hondutel** (tel. 65-00-59, fax 65-00-44), which is open 24 hours for calls. **Fax** and **telegram** service is available there, as well (Mon.-Fri. 7am-noon and 2-5pm, Sat. 7-11am). The **Farmacia Cruz Rojo** sits at 2a Av. and 4a Calle, at the southeast corner of the park (open daily 8am-6pm). Different pharmacies take turns staying open until 10pm. **Supermercado Corea** (tel. 55-11-81) stands prepared to sate shopping needs on 2a Av. between 2a and 3a Calles (Mon.-Sat. 7am-noon and 2-6:30pm, Sun. 7am-noon). The **mercado** down the block on 3a Calle, 2a/3a Av. picks up the slack. **Hospital Cemeco** (tel. 65-04-60 or 65-00-57) provides medical care at 5a Av. and 8a Calle (open 24hr. for emergencies). The police (tel. 56-04-20, no English spoken) are ready to serve at 1a Av. and 9a Calle, stationed in the southeast part of town.

ACCOMMODATIONS AND FOOD

If you're thinking of spending the night, the pickings in Puerto Cortés are slim indeed—and somewhat grim. Most opt to spend the night in either **San Pedro** or happier **Omoa**, just a half hour's bus ride away. The **Formosa Hotel** (tel. 65-08-53), located three blocks west of the park on 3a Av. and 1/2a Calle, outshines other options, though its light is far from blinding. Somewhat aged rooms off long, dark cor-

HONDURAS

ridors come with fans and adequate locks. High ceilings and full length mirrors brighten up the doubles with private baths (checkout 10am; singles with bath L54; doubles L64, with bath L86, with A/C L150). Just a block down the street, **Hotel El Centro** (tel. 65-11-60), 3a Av. and 2/3 Calles, is a work in progress, but if you don't mind the ensuing chaos in the courtyard and lack of charm, you'll find the place refreshingly new, clean, and functional. Shared baths trickle cold water, but private baths are far less stingy with their *agua caliente.* In the lobby, the purified water flows freely as the arctic A/C blasts away (singles L60, with bath L80; doubles L70, with bath L120; triples L90, with bath L140; MC and Visa accepted).

Food in Puerto Cortés is a happier story: seafood specialties, full bars, and late hours are the norm for restaurants in these parts. Watch out for the new **Wendy's** on the southeast corner of the park. **Café Viena** (tel. 65-04-38), on 2a Av., just across from the park, is popular with locals, friendly to tourists, and the owner speaks English. (Massive *típica* breakfast, coffee and orange juice included costs L35; seafood dishes include shrimp in garlic sauce goes for L80; open daily 8am-1am.) **La Cabaña,** a few blocks east on 2a Av., offers similar fare at the same kinds of prices, though the live music on Friday nights spices things up considerably. Meat aficionados can try the many varieties of *pinchos* (shishkebabs L42-50); vegetarians must nibble on *ensalata de vegetales* (L30; open daily 10am-3am). Eager waiters wearing black vests greet you with glee at **Restaurante Candiles,** farther down 2a Av., where you can dine on an outdoor deck, comforted by the powerful fleet of ceiling fans above. The food here is *good,* and prices smugly reflect the fact. A *plato típico* will run you L62, but most come for the *carnes* (*carne asada* L62; open Tues.-Sun. 11am-11pm).

SIGHTS AND ENTERTAINMENT

By the time cargo and box cars have lost their appeal, you've already exhausted Cortés's stunning site potential. Most visitors head directly out of town for the Garifuna villages of **Travesía** and **Bajamar** to engage in time-honored relaxation rituals. Both sit on fine beaches and crystalline waters. Buses leave from 5a Calle and 1a/2a Av. (every 2hr., 9am-5pm), stopping first at Travesía (15min., L2) and continuing on to Bajamar (30min., L3). For the more lethargic, a taxi can take you to Travesía (L40) and Bajamar (L80).

In terms of in-town nightlife, Puerto Cortés's fun-lovers head to **Studio 54,** a disco half a block past the Catholic school down 2a Av. at 9a/10a Calles. Cover is 20 lempiras, and a beer costs 8 lempiras (open Fri. and Sat. 9pm). And don't forget the **Cine** on the northwest corner of the park, where relatively current films cost 15 lempiras.

■ Tela

Yes, we have no bananas, we have no bananas today.
—popular song of the 1920s

Tela has no bananas today—or at least a lot fewer than it used to. When the city was the principal port of the massive and powerful United Fruit Company, it exported tens of millions of sticky bunches each year. After a while, disease ravaged Tela's trees; despite the banana's split, the city has hardly lost appeal. Though Tela (pop. 70,000) still exports more than its share of slippery peels, it has also turned to the tourist trade. Its choice beach-front location, fresh seafood, and proximity to nature reserves and Garifuna villages lure backpackers from all over the world. Unfortunately, crime is accompanying the tourists to Tela; be very careful after dark (see A Not-So-Nice Walk on the Beach, p. 246).

ORIENTATION AND PRACTICAL INFORMATION

Tela is divided into two sections: west of the **Río Tela** is **Tela Nueva; Tela Vieja** is east of the river. The sea is to the north. Services are concentrated in Tela Vieja, while quieter Tela Nueva contains the **Hotel Villas Telamar,** a luxury resort that used to provide residences for the United Fruit Company's employees. Tela's *calles* run east to west, and their numbers increase as you head north; *avenidas* run north to south. The main drag is **9a Calle,** and the **central park** is on 9a Calle between 5a and 6a Avs. Many hotels are near the bus station (a sketchy part of town) or along the street next to the beach. For **tourist information,** turn to Alessandro at **Garifuna Tours** (tel./fax 48-29-04, email garifunatur@globalnet.hn), who fields many a question and gives out **Honduras Tips** guides as well. The **PROLANSATE office** (tel./fax 48-20-42), across the street and a few doors down, provides information about the preservation of the local environment, and sells decent maps of the town and nearby nature preserves (L1; open Mon.-Fri. 7:30am-12:30pm and 2-5pm, Sat. 7am-11pm). **Exchange currency,** change **traveler's checks,** and get Visa cash advances at **Bancahsa** (tel. 48-21-89; fax 48-27-79), on the main street (open Mon.-Fri. 8-11:30am and 1:30-4:30pm, Sat. 8am-11:30am). **Buses** leave from **Terminal Empresa de Transportes CITY, LTDA,** at 9a Av. and 9a Calle, for **La Ceiba** (every 30min., 4am-5pm, 2½hr., L13) and **El Progreso** (every 25min., 4:30am-6pm, 2hr., L10). Buses leave El Progreso for **San Pedro Sula** until 6pm. Buses for **Triunfo** depart irregularly (about 4 per day, 20min., L2; ask around at 10a Av. and 7a Calle). A loud, rusty train chugs to Puerto Cortés from the station three blocks inland from the southeast corner of the park (Fri. and Sun., 1pm, 4 hr., L12). **Taxis** cost about L6 within the city, L30-50 to **Lancetilla.** Garifuna Tours rents decent **mountain bikes** (L44 per ½ day, L59 per whole day). **Lavandería El Centro** lies just up the street from the post office, and will wash and dry up to 12lbs. for L30 (open Mon.-Sat. 8am-5pm, Sun. 8am-noon). The **Red Cross** can be reached at 48-21-21. **Farmacia Escalante,** on 9a Av., is just one option for drugs; to find out who's open late this week (7am-10pm), check the lists on pharmacy doors or the sign at the corner of the park. For **medical emergencies,** head to **Clínica de Emergencias** (tel. 48-24-56), 7a Av. in Barrio Centro, one block up from 9a Av., by the bus station. Some doctors speak English (open 24hr.). Another option is the **Clínica Médica Suyapa** (tel. 48-26-82), half a block south of 9a Calle one block from the bridge, where Dr. Cristina Rodríguez can take good care of travelers (open Mon.-Fri. 1-6pm, Sat. 8am-noon; home phone for emergencies: 48-26-85). Call **Los Bomberos** (tel. 48-23-50) to put out fires; for **police** matters, there's either **DIC** (tel./fax 48-28-88), at the *ministerio público,* a few blocks north from the west side of the park (open 24 hr.) or **FUSEP** (tel. 48-20-79), atop the stairs at the end of 7a Av. The **post office** (tel. 48-24-90), a white building two blocks inland from 9a Calle, northeast on Av. Guatemala (4a Av.), posts a *lista de correos* (open Mon.-Fri. 8am-4pm, Sat. 8am-noon). The **postal code** is 31301. **Telephones** are found at **Hondutel** (tel. 48-20-03 or 48-22-99; fax 48-29-42), two blocks south of 9a Calle from the yellow Curacao sign. **Fax, telegrams,** and AT&T Direct collect/calling card calls are available from booths 6, 7, and 8 (open daily 7am-9pm; telegrams open Mon.-Fri. 8am-4pm, Sat. 8-11am).

ACCOMMODATIONS AND FOOD

The types of tourists titillated by Tela tend to tan their terrific torsos tirelessly. Look for the following two features in a hotel: safety and its proximity to the beach. Cheap deals can be found easily throughout Tela Vieja.

Boarding House Sara (tel. 48-23-70), located one block from the beach on the far east end, is inhabited almost entirely by international backpackers. The rooms can be noisy and the common baths could use a little help, but the spacious *cabañas* have fans, private bathrooms, and sometimes even a kitchen. Across the street, three bars compete to see who can be loudest; Sara's beds vibrate to a pumping bass until well past 5am on weekends. The amiable owner loves to speak English and curse the noise. Kitchen facilities are available; checkout is at noon (L35 per person, L30 per night if you stay the week; a *cabaña* sleeps up to 5 for L200; a 10-person *cabaña* costs L300; add L10 for a fan). Try to bargain. At **Hotel Mar Azul** (tel. 448-23-13), two blocks from the bridge on the west end of the beach, the tranquility is only broken by the occasional crash of almonds falling on the roof. Spacious, tidy rooms boast private baths and walk-in closets. The owner, Julia, works long hours, parceling out advice

---

A Not-So-Nice Walk on the Beach

In Tela, as in a few other Caribbean beach towns—Livingston, in particular—**crime against tourists** has unfortunately escalated of late. The gentle waves tend to lull travelers into complacency, making them shed their worries and forget the precautions they would take elsewhere. In response to recent robberies and assaults, here are a few friendly safety reminders. When walking along the beach or anywhere removed from more heavily trafficked streets in town, don't bring any **valuables** along (i.e., passports, cameras, large wads of cash, crystal vases). If you want to carry your camera or something of value, consider keeping a lower profile by concealing it under your clothes or in a plastic bag. Don't let the beauty of the shoreline let you forget that robberies along remote sections of beach and isolated roads are quite frequent. At the same time, **don't let fear prevent** you from enjoying this area. There's safety in numbers; women should not walk in remote areas alone, but instead should opt for other transport. At night, stick to populated, well-lit areas and do *not* go to the beach. Above all, ask locals about recommended precautions; they know better than anyone.

---

and lending her kitchen to visitors. Mind the guard duck; it likes the taste of ankles (singles L70; doubles L80; triples L100—negotiable). At **Ocean View Hotel** (tel. 48-29-46), on the west side of the park, the only views are of a concrete courtyard, but the rooms are clean and have private baths. Ask in the office when you want to take a shower (singles and 1-bed doubles L90, twin beds L80).

Some travelers in Tela eat at **Supermercado Marie,** on the park, which has a surprisingly large and eclectic selection ranging from chips to flutes (open Mon.-Sat. 8am-7:30pm, Sun. 8am-2:30pm). The ordinary *mercado* is no slouch itself, sitting one block towards the sea from the park. For more traditional settings, **Restaurante Luces del Norte,** two blocks toward the beach from the park, serves up hearty, tasty dishes (breakfast L20-30, peanut butter and banana sandwiches L18, astounding shrimp soup L45; open daily 7am-10pm). **Cesar Mariscos,** in the middle of the beach in Tela Vieja, is considered one of the best restaurants in Tela, and is not much more expensive than the other joints that line the beach. Expect a substantial wait. Superb fish dishes run L50-70, and chicken creole runs L50 (open daily 7am-10pm). **Tuty's,** on the main street just west of the park, proves a good bet for breakfast, with fruit-covered pancakes for L20, and a traditional breakfast for L20, too (open daily 6am-10pm). **Garifuna Restaurant,** on a beautiful patio next to the Garifuna Museum, provides *mechuca* (fish soup with coconut milk and plantains) that will renew your faith in God for only L45 (open daily 8am until the cook leaves).

SIGHTS AND ENTERTAINMENT

The beauty of the Tela beaches is that there are few temptations to move a muscle. Snorkeling isn't terrifically popular, and no one indulges in calorie-depleting water sports. Indeed, slothful relaxation on miles of powdery sand is all that's expected of you. The beach and water along Tela Vieja are somewhat silty and litter-strewn, but stretches of sand to the west are so beautiful that they seem like a travel brochure come to life. For those moderately motivated (but not enough to leave the beach), **Garifuna Tours** rents sea kayaks (singles L59 half-day and L99 full day; doubles L99 half-day and L149 full day). For L30 per day, non-guests of the **Hotel Villas Telamar** (tel. 48-21-96 ext. 605; fax 48-29-84) get full use of the facilities, which include a pool, jacuzzi, sauna, tennis courts, and a nine-hole golf course. The hotel also offers horse-back riding (L40 per hr.). Go to Oscar Reyez's cabaña, #605 for more information.

The new **Garifuna Museum,** the product of a tremendous community effort organized by a Garifuna women's group, houses an incomplete collection of Garifuna household objects and musical instruments. To get there, walk west on the main drag and make a left just before the bridge. The tours, given by eager and energetic founders of the museum are good, though currently offered only in Garifuna and Spanish. The museum is trying to hire an English-speaking guide (open daily 8am-

HONDURAS

noon and 1-5pm; free, donations appreciated). Try to visit while lunch or dinner is being served at the adjacent restaurant (see **Food,** above). On occasional Saturday nights, the museum hosts some of the wildest **punta** dancing in Honduras.

When it comes to nightlife, Tela doesn't miss a beat. All day long, pumping tunes can be heard on virtually every block; as night falls, the beach bars metamorphose into discos. For live music on Sundays and a lively crowd seven days a week, head for the **Multi-Disco Napoles,** at the west end of 9a Av., near the bridge (minimal cover).

■ Near Tela

LANCETILLA BOTANICAL GARDENS

An easy and pleasant daytrip from Tela, these botanical gardens were developed by the United Fruit Company in 1925 both to determine which fruits would grow well in Honduras and to preserve the region's diverse flora and fauna. The project was the brainchild of **Wilson Popenoe,** whose very name has the ring of an exotic fruit; as a result of Popenoe's efforts, visitors can see 200 species of soaring and singing birds and a staggering amalgamation of plant species quicker than you can say *Musa paradisiaca sapientum.*

The gardens are 6km from Tela; save your energy for strolling *in* the park and not walking *to* it by renting a bike or getting a ride. The entrance is on the main road to La Ceiba. From town, walk or bike to Nueva Tela, beyond the Instituto San Antonio, and turn left on the dirt road behind the golf course. Follow this road until you hit the main road; the gate is just across the way. Alternatively, hop on any bus headed for El Progreso and get off at the gate (inform the driver of your plans in advance). A taxi from Tela to the gate costs L30-50; bargain to see if you can do better.

From the gate, the park is another 3.5km along a dirt road; a bus shuttles visitors back and forth along this road every 30 minutes. Once you see buildings, head for the small house on the right. It houses the **visitors center,** where you can snag a map with information in Spanish; also on sale are t-shirts and seeds for at-home experimentation. Refreshment stands are nearby. Questions can be answered at the **Administrative Center** (beyond the bamboo tunnel), where you can get a short tour and ask for permission to camp in the park. There are dorms, but these are primarily for large groups; ask and they might loan you a bed. (Gardens open Tues.-Fri. 7:30am-3:30pm, Sat.-Sun. 8:30am-4pm. Admission US$5 for foreigners. For more information, call **COHDEFOR** at 48-21-65.)

PARQUE NACIONAL PUNTA SAL

To the west of Tela lie its prime attractions, the untouched Garifuna village of **Miami** and the gorgeous **Punta Sal National Park.** The preserve is full of rare and infrequently encountered species and encompasses diverse ecosystems: the **Laguna de los Micos,** with its mangrove waterways and abundant birdlife, and the **Punta Sal peninsula** farther west, home to white sand beaches, jungle vegetation and wildlife, and a great coral reef. On a sand bar between the lagoon and the sea, thatched huts cluster close in the pristine village of **Miami,** where traditional Garifuna life continues unfettered by modern conveniences like telephones or electricity. Punta Sal has the rare and sad distinction of having a martyr for a founder. Naturalist **Jeanette Kawas,** the most ardent and eloquent defender of the preserves, was murdered in the spring of 1995. The government investigation ended quickly, without convictions; many think that the killing was carried out by profiteers interested in developing the land.

Garifuna Tours leads guided expeditions by launch to the Punta Sal peninsula (8am-3pm, US$15, snorkeling mask included); they take a short hike through the jungle and stop at a *cabaña* for L20 chow. To go it on your own, you'll need 2-3 days for adventuring, a tent, food, and water. A bus can take you as far as Tornabé, a truck runs to Miami, and from Miami, its a 3½ hour hike along the beach to the neck of a peninsula which terminates in a mini-archipelago. If possible bring snorkeling gear; there are some great spots just offshore (try the rocks near the *cabaña*). Garifuna

Tours also takes full-day bird-watching trips to Laguna de los Micos and Miami (US$18). They or the folks at **PROLASANTE** can help with current info on getting to either place on your own.

PUNTA IZOPO RESERVE & TRIUNFO DE LA CRUZ

Standing at Tela's beach and looking out to the right over the ocean, you'll see the **Refugio de Vida Silvestre Punta Izopo** (Punta Izopo Reserve) extending out into the sea. One of Honduras' 77 wildlife preserves, the 28,000-acre reserve is home to a prodigious number of plant and animal species, including monkeys, alligators, parrots, turtles, and toucans. The reserve attracts few visitors, so you're likely to get all the solitude you wish. Within its borders lies a vast and mysterious network of canals created by the mangrove forest and accessible only by sea kayak. Paddling silently through their labyrinths increases your chances of spotting the extremely shy creatures, as well as the likelihood of their sticking around for future generations. Garifuna Tours leads excellent half (US$11) and full (US$15) daytrips on the Ríos Platano and Hicaque that run through the reserve.

If going alone to Punta Izopo, a logical stop on the way is the Garifuna village of **Triunfo de la Cruz.** While less pristine than some others, Triunfo is more accessible than some of the nearby villages. To get there, catch one of the four daily buses from Tela, or take any bus headed for La Ceiba and ask to be let off at the road for Triunfo; then follow a dirt road 2km into town. Alternatively, rent a bike for an exhilarating, if nerve-shattering, ride. Do not walk to Triunfo along the beach from Tela; robberies along this stretch of sand have been reported. To reach Punta Izopo from Triunfo, go to the beach, turn right, and walk for one-and-a-half hours. In the rainy season, you may have to wade across two rivers, each of which usually ends 10m before the sea.

Like other Garifuna villages, Triunfo still holds onto its traditional way of life. Fisherman still mend their nets in the afternoon sun and head out to sea as night falls. Though some huts are being replaced by concrete boxes, and a high-powered luxury resort is currently under construction, thatched roofs still dominate the beach.

■ La Ceiba

Once upon a time, the feather in La Ceiba's cap was a tree—a whopping, umbrella-shaped *ceiba* (silk-cotton tree) which stood near the coast, shading the merchants who gathered under it to peddle their wares. Nowadays, La Ceiba's claim to fame is no longer a tree but a banana—the Standard Fruit Company, better known as Dole, developed the hefty and disease-resistant Cavendish banana here. The administrative headquarters for the banana and pineapple exporter, today's La Ceiba, Honduras' third largest city, combines bustle and boom with the sensibility of an unpolished small town.

Tourists typically visit La Ceiba to take care of business, to catch a plane to the Bay Islands or the Mosquito Coast, or to enjoy the city's famous *carnaval*. Take care when looking for tour guides to the Mosquito Coast; tourism here is entirely unregulated, and scam-artists abound. Be sure to ask several locals about a prospective tour guide before you commit to any one. When it's *carnaval* time, during the second and third weeks of May, La Ceiba becomes a wild tangle of parades, costumes, and tributes to local patron San Isidro. Throughout the nation it is said, *"Tegucigalpa piensa, San Pedro Sula trabaja, y La Ceiba se divierte."* ("Tegus does the thinking, San Pedro does the working, and La Ceiba does the rocking and rolling.")

ORIENTATION AND PRACTICAL INFORMATION

Orienting yourself in La Ceiba is pretty easy. Cabs coming from the airport or bus terminal typically drop passengers off at the **Parque Central,** a pretty little square between 8a and 9a Calles, adorned with benches, pet crocodiles and turtles, and statues of Latin American heroes. Try to identify whose bust is represented on the

La Ceiba

Caribbean Sea

N

HONDURAS

BARRIO LA JULIA

BARRIO LA BARRA

BARRIO LA GLORIA

BARRIO LA ISLA

11a C.

12a C.

13a C.

Laundromat

1a C.

4a C.

5a C.

6a C.

7a C.

8a C.

9a C.

10a C.

Estadio de Fútbol

Estuary

BARRIO POTRE-RITO

POTRERITOS

4a C.

5a C.

6a C.

7a C.

8a C.

9a C.

Hondutel

Palmira Market

Bancahsa

Farmacia Nueva

Medical Clinic

BARRIO IMAN

COL. NARANJAL

COL. NARANJAL

BARRIO ALVARADO

Ave. 14 de Julio

Avenida Atlántida

Ave. San Isidro

Marine Terminal

1a C.

BARRIO INGLES

COL. LOS MAESTROS

ZONA MAZAPAN

Train Station

Transmundo

Parque Central

Cathedral

10a C.

11a C.

12a C.

13a C.

14a C.

15a C.

16a C.

17a C.

Ave. La República

Ave. Colón

Ave. Morazán

Ave. Cabaña

Ave. Valle

SOLARES NUEVOS

BARRIO INDEPENDENCIA

Blvd. 15 de Septiembre

Bus Station

ZONA LIBRE

statue in the middle—no *ceibeños* seem to be able to. Extending from the east side of the park north towards the water is **Avenida San Isidro**, the main drag. One block west is **Avenida La República**. One block east is **Avenida 14 de Julio**. The street that runs along the water is **Ia Calle**. From 1a, *calle* numbers increase as you move south. A **canal** cuts through town to the sea; it starts about three blocks east of Av. San Isidro on 1a Calle. It is a very bad idea to swim near La Ceiba; try to guess what the canal carries to the sea...it ain't boats.

Tourist Office: Consejo Municipal de Turismo (tel. 43-28-63), on the ground floor of the Edificio de la Gobernación Política, on 1a Calle, just west of Centro Médico. Provides *carnaval* information. Open Mon.-Fri. 8-11:30am and 1:30-5:00pm, Sat. 8-11am. Alternatively, question one of the guides at Eurohonduras or La Mosquitia Ecoaventuras. Both are located just off 1a Calle, near the Consejo Municipal. Eurohonduras squats on the beach behind the Centro México, and La Mosquitia awaits another block east and half a block south from 1a Calle.

Travel Agency: Transmundo (tel. 43-28-20), on the north side of the park. Open

Mon.-Fri. 7:30-11:30am and 1:30-5pm, Sat. 8-11:30am. English is spoken.

Currency Exchange: Bancahsa (tel. 43-03-42), 2 blocks north of the park on Av. San Isidro, changes traveler's checks. Open Mon.-Fri. 8am-4pm, Sat. 8-11:30am. Across the way, Banco Atlantída (tel. 43-04-07; fax 43-12-30) has a 24hr. ATM. It is often hard to change checks here. Open Mon.-Fri. 8-11:30am and 1:30-4:30pm, Sat. 8-11:30am.

Airport: Aeropuerto Goloson, 6km from town on the road to Tela. Snag a bus for 1L, and ask to be let off by the airport. Alternately, get a taxi from the *punto de taxis* at the corner of the park. For L10 they'll go to Confite, a point 2 blocks from the airport terminal. Taking a taxi "to the airport" costs L35-40. Most of the airlines have offices around the park. SOSA (tel.43-13-99) flies to Utila (Mon.-Sat. 6, 9:30am, and 3:30pm, 15min., L246). Isleña (tel. 43-01-79) flies to: Roatán (8 per day, daily 6am-4:30pm, 20 min., L277); Guanaja (Mon.-Sat. 11pm and 4:30am, Sun. 4:30am, 20min., L338); San Pedro Sula (Mon.-Sat. 7:30am and 2pm, 25min., L338); and Tegucigalpa (Mon.-Sat. 7am, 10am, and 2pm, 45min., L461).

Buses: Intercity buses leave from the terminal on Blvd. 15, halfway to the airport and a 5 to 10min. and L6 cab ride from town. To: **Tela** (every 45min., 4:45am-6pm, 2½hr., L13); **San Pedro Sula** (every hr., 5:30am-6:30pm, 3hr., L30); and **Tegucigalpa**, 1st class with **Etrusca** (3, 5:30, and 10am, 6½hr., L70). **Trujillo** (direct at 9, 11:15am, and 2:30pm, 3 hr., indirect at 8am and 3:20pm, 4hr. 15min.,

L29).

Boats: Nuevo Muelle de Cabotaje (Yacht Harbor) serves as a departure point for boats to the Bay Islands. If you have any tendency to get motion sickness, some form of medication or treatment ahead of time is a *great* idea. The harbor is 22km from La Ceiba; you'll need to take a cab (20min., L30). M/V Tropical leaves from the harbor for Utila (Mon. 10:30am, Tues.-Fri. 10am, 1 hr., US$10) and Roatán (Mon.-Fri. 3:30pm, Sat. 11am, Sun. 7am, 2 hr., US$11). Other random boats leave throughout the week; ask around at the water. Also, the Lady Michelle leaves for Guanaja Thurs. 8pm, returning Tues. 7am (8hr., L70).

Taxis: Intra-city fare L6 (that includes the bus station, regardless of the quoted

fares). Cabs cluster at the southwest side of Parque Central.

Market: Palmira (tel. 43-22-70), at 6a Calle, 2 blocks east of Av. San Isidro. One of the largest grocery stores in Central America. Open Mon.-Fri. 7:30am-noon and 1:30-6:45pm, Sat. 7:30am-6:45pm, Sun. 7:30am-noon. The un-super *mercado* is across from Palmira.

Laundromat: Next to Hotel Amsterdam 2001. The hotel owner's daughter washes and dries clothes for L5 per kg (minimum L25). Open daily 7am-9pm.

Pharmacy: Farmacia Nueva (tel. 43-04-49), half a block north of the park on Av. San Isidro, has bug repellent. Open Mon.-Fri. 7:30am-noon and 1:30-6pm, Sat. 7:30am-noon. Pharmacies post signs near the park about their late hours.

Clinic: Dr. Maribel Galindo (tel./fax 43-37-05, beeper 43-05-06), 1 block east of the cathedral. Open Mon.-Fri. 8:30am-noon and 2-5pm, Sat. 8am-noon. Beep her 24hr. for emergencies.

Police: FUSEP (tel. 41-09-95), on Blvd. 15 de Septiembre, near the bus terminal.

Post Office: (tel. 42-00-30; fax 42-00-24), Av. Morazán, 13a Calle (Barrio Indepen-dencia in the southwest part of town). *Lista de correos.* Open Mon.-Fri. 8am-noon and 2-5pm, Sat. 8am-noon. **EMS Express Mail** in the same building. Open Mon.-Fri. 8am-noon and 2-5pm; Sat. 8am-noon.
Telephones: Hondutel (tel. 43-00-24; fax 43-07-00), 3 blocks east of Av. San Isidro between 5a and 6a Calles, under the huge red-and-white radio tower. **Fax** and AT&T direct services available 24hr. **Telegrams** available Mon.-Fri. 8am-noon and 1-4pm, Sat. 8am-noon.

ACCOMMODATIONS

The cheapest spots in town lie on Avs. San Isidro and 14 de Julio; beware of several beaten-up horror shows. La Ceiba is a densely packed city—don't be too concerned if your hotel isn't downtown or near the beach. **Hotel San Carlos** (tel. 43-03-30), Av. San Isidro and 3/4 Calles, is an airy, turquoise joint above a bakery. The trip through rooms stacked with fresh bread and cookies on your way to the stairs is an added perk. All rooms come with clean private baths and "chopper-size" ceiling fans (1-2 people L50; doubles L70). Check next door in Hotel Iberia when the bakery is closed (after 8pm and all day Sundays). **Hotel Amsterdam 2001/Hotel Rotterdam** (tel. 43-23-11), seven blocks east of San Isidro on 1a Calle, are two independently run, secure hotels set side-by-side by the beach. Both are run by the same family, and both have new bathrooms and a tranquil garden setting. The 2001 lets doubles for US$6 and a seven-bed dorm for US$3 per person; space odyssey not included. Next door, doubles go for L100. **Hotel Alvarez** (tel. 43-01-81), 3a/4a Calles, one block east of San Isidro, offers worn but clean rooms with fans and private baths smack dab between the beach and downtown, on a relatively tranquil street (checkout at noon; 1-2 people L60; doubles L80; triples L120). **Hotel Granada** (tel. 43-24-51), across the street and a block south from Ligeros, is a good deal for those in search of cheap cold air. All have private baths (singles L50; doubles L70, with A/C L120; tri-ples with A/C L150, TVs for an additional L10).

FOOD

La Ceiba boasts enough mid-priced *comedores* to keep the budget traveler healthy and wealthy. While considered a red-light district, **Barrio La Barra,** on the east end of 1a Calle along the beach, is home to a good number of *típico* places. The *mer-cado* is at 6a Calle, three blocks east of Av. San Isidro; *platos típicos* and fruit are sold there.

Masapan: Comida Rápida, one block west off San Isidro on the street a block north of Pizza Hut, is a cafeteria line with special stations for sandwiches, beans, meats, fruits, and *frescos.* Vegetarians will jump for joy at the vast assortment of veg-etables. Prices depend on the number of items, not the quantity of each—choose your own adventure. (Full meals cost L8-40; open 24hr.). **Cafetería Cobel** (tel. 42-21-92) is one block north of Pizza Hut on Av. San Isidro, and a half block to your right. Here you'll find cheap Honduran fare in a comfortable, airy dining room that's become a *ceibeño* institution (*desayuno* and *almuerzo* L20-30; open Mon.-Sat. 6:30am-6pm). **La Carreta** (tel. 43-01-11), 4a Calle, two and a half blocks east of San Isidro, is pricier. As well as a comfy, plant-covered patio and an open grill, the res-taurant offers hanging ceramic plates inscribed by previous visitors. As you eat, con-sider words of wisdom such as "Clyde, Oct. '93," or "Greetings from Chicago." Lip-smacking barbecued *pinchos de chorizo* cost L70 (open daily 11am-2pm and 5-11pm). **Restaurante Chabelita,** on 1a Calle, three blocks east of the Hotel Amster-dam 2001, is favored by seafood lovers (fish dishes L40-90; open daily 10am-10pm, closes Mon. at 3pm).

SIGHTS AND ENTERTAINMENT

If you somehow tire of the Pizza Hut playground near the park, it's hard to keep busy in La Ceiba. The beach and pier are not the prettiest around, but they're decent places for a sunset stroll or an afternoon nap. Be careful after dark. For superior sands, walk a kilometer in either direction from La Ceiba.

The **Museo de Mariposas** (Butterfly Museum), in the suburbs of La Ceiba, is run as a labor of love by Robert and Jennifer Lehman. To get there, either walk an uninteresting 45 minutes (ask Mike at **Mosquitia Ecoadventures** for directions) or take a cab (L5) to Colonia El Sauce, 2a Etapa, Casa G-12. They have some 5000 species of butterflies and over 1000 other insects on display. Jennifer is usually on hand to answer questions in English or Spanish, and the signs are also bilingual (open Mon.-Tues. and Thurs.-Sat. 8am-noon and 2-5pm, Wed. 8am-noon; admission L15, students L10).

Most of La Ceiba's hip **nightspots** are near the beach along 1a Calle. On weekend nights, the thoroughfare throbs. Clubs rarely have dress codes, but few people wear sandals and shorts. Among the most popular discos is **D'Lido's,** near the estuary, which sways its disco balls and flashing lights with zip. Bop to a mix of Latin and U.S. top-40 hits, but beware of the shady crowd outside and the prostitutes inside. The music starts at 7pm (L3-7 cover on weekends; free otherwise). **Buhos,** farther east down 1a Calle, caters to La Ceiba's chic upper crust, with Latin and U.S. dance hits (cover L10; open Thurs.-Sat. 8pm-4am).

■ Near La Ceiba

La Ceiba makes a great base for expeditions into the wilderness. **Eurohonduras** (tel./fax 43-09-33), next to the clinic on 1a Calle, arranges and guides trips to nearby areas. As does **La Moskitia Ecoventuras** (tel./fax 42-01-04) another block east on 1a Calle and half a block south. A number of other operators in town offer similar trips at similar prices; shop *very* carefully, as some are less than reputable.

The lush **Pico Bonito National Park,** south of La Ceiba, is accessible by guide or on your own, and well worth a day or two. Trails slither through the park's virtually untouched rainforest and into the realm of snakes, huge butterflies, lizards, spiders, and jaguars. Even though reaching the summit of Pico Bonito mountain (2435m) is out of the question for most (the final stretch requires heavy-duty, mondo-technical climbing), the park is a blast. If you plan on heading into the park without a guide, pack fresh water or iodine tablets and bring a buddy in case of mishaps. From La Ceiba, take the "1a de Mayo" bus (from the Parque Central or estuary, about every hr.) to the small town of **Armenia Bonito.** Alternatively, snag a bus heading toward Tela and tell the driver to drop you off near Río Bonito or at the entrance of the road to Armenia. Look for the sign that reads "Taller de Soldadura." Taxis also go to Armenia (L50-70, from the airport L20).

From Armenia, walk along the dirt road back toward the mountain. You'll need to cut through some gates and cross over a few plantations, but owners just watch as you mosey on by. The road soon becomes a footpath, and if the water isn't too high it's possible to walk upstream along the river on huge, slippery boulders. If you can't follow the river, follow the trail along the bank until you reach the **Campamento del CURLA** (if you're on the river, keep your eye out for the stairs on the left). This deserted Visitors Center still serves as a base for several trails that lead up the steep mountain. A couple of **lodges** have been built just before **Las Mangas,** on the park's border, thus helping to remedy the lousy situation that faced budget travelers without camping gear who wished to spend the night in the park.

If mountains aren't as seductive as nearly deserted islands, relax, baby, there's always **Cayos Cochinos** (the hog cayes), not far off the coast from La Ceiba. Islanders provide lodging (L20 per person) and food (L20 per meal); guests supply their best Robinson Crusoe imitations, bottled water, and whatever else they might want to consume. The snorkeling's hog-heaven. To get there, go to **Nueva Armenia** on the bus or taxi, then ask around about transport. Expect to pay about US$10 per person. Locals take tourists in canoes and agree on a time to pick them up from the Cayes. Waterproof your bags, bring plenty of drinking water, and be ready to sleep with an itchy layer of salt on your body, as there are no showers.

■ Trujillo

Nestled on the frontier between civilized Honduras and feral, unforgiving La Mosquitia to the east, Trujillo has placidly served as a gateway since the late 15th century, when Christopher Columbus disembarked here and said his first mass in the Americas. Through it all, the comely city hasn't worried much—nobody knows whether the citizens built the fort on the hill to resist pirates or simply to have a place with a cool view. Continuing its passive resistance, Trujillo has also been indifferent to tourists; its natural beauty is for the most part unmarred. A behemoth pleasure palace recently set up shop outside the town, but Trujillo will probably ignore this development as well and continue on its insouciant way. Trujillo rears to life during the festival of San Juan Bautista (June 24-28). Beginning with a costumed procession at dawn, the parties continue each night, climaxing with a city-wide fair on the 28th.

ORIENTATION AND PRACTICAL INFORMATION

Calle Principal, Trujillo's main road, runs three blocks off and parallel to the beach. Police warn that the beaches outside of town are unsafe at night. The **Parque Central** is one block closer to the sea than Calle Principal. There's no **tourist office,** but the regulars in the beach bars know the nitty-gritty. **Exchange currency** and advance cash on credit cards at **Banco de Occidente** (tel./fax 44-49-91), on Calle Principal (open Mon.-Fri. 8am-noon and 2-5pm, Sat. 8-11:30am). **Telephones** are available at **Hondutel** (tel. 44-41-12), next to the post office (open Mon.-Fri. 7am-9pm, Sat.-Sun. 8am-4pm). **Faxes** and **telegrams** are also available (Mon.-Fri. 7am-noon and 2-5pm, Sat. 7-11am). **Cotraipbal** (tel. 44-30-22; fax 44-42-00; open Mon.-Fri. 7:30am-noon and 2:30-5pm, Sat.-Sun. 7:30-9am), one block from the main square on the same street as Hondutel, offers **bus** service to **San Pedro Sula** (3, 5, and 8am, 7hr., L65) and **Tegucigalpa** (3, 5, and 9am, 10hr., L75). On Calle Principal a few blocks west of the park is **Lavandería Colón;** they'll wash and dry a bag of clothes for L20 (daily 8am-5pm). Farther west, **Farmacia Almim** (tel. 44-42-43) has an **emergency number** (tel. 44-42-42). The **hospital** (tel. 44-40-93) is just east of the park (open daily 8am-4pm). The **police** (tel. 44-40-38) are north of the park, ready to serve 8760 hours per year. The **post office** (tel. 44-45-43), two blocks inland from the church on the road west of it, has *lista de correos* (open Mon.-Fri. 8am-noon and 1:30-4pm). **English books** are available for exchange at the **Café Oasis** and **Rincón de los Amigos.**

ACCOMMODATIONS AND FOOD

If the gargantuan Christopher Columbus Resort isn't your speed, fear not, there's a delightful set of cabins available for a fraction of the cost. **Hotel Catrachos** (tel. 44-44-32) offers a chorus line of cute rooms with fans, lamps, and locks. Heading south on *Calle Principal* from the park, turn right one block after the street the post office is on and follow it west for one block (singles L60; doubles L80; 2 beds L100). Another option is the **Hotel O'Glynn** (tel. 44-45-92), uphill about three blocks on the street that also houses Bancahsa. The rooms have soft double beds, fans, and passable public baths (L80; with private bath, A/C, and in-room cable L250). **Cocapanda** may have cold floors and dark rooms, but you can't beat the price (singles L50; doubles L70) or the oceanside view.

Almost every tourist in town passes through the Rincón de Los Amigos at least once; it's unbeatable for folks and fun. The creative catch-of-the-day specials are a cut above the fried fish and rice offered by its rivals, and the English-speaking owners are eager to chat (garlic shrimp L65, beer L8). **Horfez** (see **Sights and Entertainment,** below) serves fish dinners for L35. Across from Bancahsa is **Café Oasis** (open daily 9am-11pm), which offers great breakfasts and a good variety of dinner options, including vegetarian fare (pasta L40). One block south and two blocks west of the park is the **Pantry** which serves thin-crust pizza (L20-80).

SIGHTS AND ENTERTAINMENT

Trujillo offers more than just mesmerizing beaches. Just outside town, an eclectic private museum (simply called **El Museo**) guarantees a strange and unforgettable experience. From the middle of town, walk along the main street with the sea to your right, all the way to the Hotel Mar de Plata; take the next left, then the first right and follow that road past two cemeteries. Eventually (5-10min. later), you'll see creatively painted signs. The museum's motto might well be "we never throw anything away"—we're talking antique photos, household appliances, undetonated bombs, and even a kitchen sink (open daily 8am-noon and 1-4pm; admission L20, kids L5; admission includes access to the swimming holes out back). On the way back, **William Walker** devotees should check out his final resting place in the old cemetery, the one closer to town (see **William Walker, What a Killer,** p. 271).

Context is everything during a visit to **La Fortaleza de Santa Barbara.** The caretakers love to show off their 10 cannon balls, but the display lacks appeal. The reason to pay the L1 admission fee is the sweeping view, especially glorious at sunrise and sunset. The fort is right next to the hospital (open 8am-noon and 1-4pm). Rincón de los Amigos also rents kayaks and windsurfing boards (L100 per hr.) to explore the nearby waves, and offers power boat tours.

If you want to get funky at night, check out **Horfez** (tel. 44-44-33), on the main drag next to the laundromat. On the weekends, the place becomes a **disco** from 8pm to 3am. The prices are a bit high, but so are a good number of the merry young dancers. Great fun can be had a bit farther afield in the Garifuna *barrio* of **Cristales,** a quick five-minute walk up the beach from town. The beachfront bars offer beer at a rock-bottom L5 and are often the sites of authentic, spontaneous, booty-shaking bouts of *punta.* Sometimes, people venture up to the **Black and White Disco** (open 9pm-dawn; cover L5). More often then not, everyone sticks to the beach.

■ Near Trujillo

If you have time for a sojourn away from Trujillo, several options await: Garifuna villages to the west, historic **Puerto Castilla,** hiking, and playing maritime Russian roulette by randomly hopping commercial boats along the port. For information on the nearby parks and lagoons, contact **FUCAGA** (tel./fax 44-42-94), an organization located in the library in the center of the square which strives to protect local Indian cultures. They can arrange for guides to lead trips to **Capiro-Calentura National Park,** which boasts toucans and other exotic animals (L250 for 1-3 people), and to the **Guaimoreto lagoon** which acts as a hatchery for hundreds of fish. If **Cristales** doesn't satiate your hunger for Garifuna life, another more secluded village, **Santa Fe,** is 9km west along the beach. There is also a collection of commercial vessels leaving from Trujillo, with regular destinations to Cayo Blanco, Guanaja, and Jamaica. Ask around the docks or at **Rincón de los Amigos.**

"Try It...You'll Like It."

As long as you're in Cristales, you might as well try it. It tastes like hell, it looks like water with a touch of dirt, and it burns bad. It's called **giffity.** Made from young white rum, this powerful concoction plays a part in many Garifuna rituals from **novenarios** (wakes held nine days after a death) to weddings. The rum is steeped with 17 herbs and spices (not unlike **Kentucky Fried Chicken**), including garlic for a better kick. Supposedly, the herbal additives increase the potency of the rum in just 24 hours; leave it brewing longer, and it becomes strong enough to **"knock a bull in da grass."** Almost all the beachfront bars sell healthy *octavo* (one-eighth liter) shots for about L5; locals are glad to join in rounds of these shots and will often buy a visitor a glass "just to see the look on his face."

THE BAY ISLANDS

Scattered off Honduras' north coast, the Bay Islands—Utila, Roatán, and Guanaja—are heirs to a colorful history that has rendered them ethnically and linguistically distinct from the mainland. Spain claimed the islands in 1502, sending indigenous islanders to work as slaves in Mexico and the West Indies. In 1638, Puritans from Maryland colonized Roatán, but were soon expelled by the Spanish. Spain had a harder time dealing with slippery pirates, who would hide in the reefs and harbors, coming ashore to hunt pigs and turtles. Britain and Spain fought over the islands throughout the late 18th century, but the real victims of the wars were the islands' black residents, many of whom were sold as slaves when the British were chased out. In 1852, the islands joined Belize as a British possession, but the U.S. protested, frightened by the specter of creeping British imperialism. Under pressure from the north, the islands were returned to Honduras.

Although the islands were at one time solely populated by English-speaking descendants of African and British settlers, masses of "Hondureños" (the islanders don't usually consider themselves Hondurans) have recently moved from the mainland, resulting in a shift in the cultural feel of the islands and a bit of racial tension. Islanders argue that outsiders are spoiling their paradise. Whatever the cause, the idyllic, isolated isles are showing their first signs of urban decay.

However, the primary draw of the islands is not really the islands themselves. Multitudes of divers come to the reefs for a mind-melting marine menagerie of giant barracudas, angelfish, and lobsters. These natural wonders are also alluringly cheap, especially on Utila, a veritable diving-certification assembly-line, and snorkeling is free (excluding rental). For more information, see Diving for Dollars (p. 151).

■ Utila

For well over a century, residents of Utila (pop. 2000) have been drawing water from **La Cola de Mico** ("Monkey's Tail"), a freshwater well. According to legend, all those who drink from La Cola must someday return to Utila; take a swig when you get to the island—a return trip would be pure sweetness. Landlubbers beware: life in Utila revolves around diving. At least learn some of the lingo to avoid being a pariah.

PRACTICAL INFORMATION

The nameless main drag runs along the bay, with a small park off one side. Unless otherwise indicated, everything listed below is on this main street. For **tourist information,** try the building next to Mermaid's Corner Restaurant, which also houses the **Bay Islands Conservation Association** (open Mon.-Fri. 8am-7pm, Sat.-Sun. 7am-8pm). **Exchange currency** and **traveler's checks** at **Bancahsa** (tel./fax 45-31-57), on main street's only intersection (open Mon.-Fri. 8-11:30am and 1:30-4pm, Sat. 8-11:30am). After hours, go to **Henderson's Store** on the main drag; they give the bank rate (open Mon.-Sat. 6:30am-noon and 2-6pm). Cash can be advanced on Mastercard and Visa at **Reef,** but be prepared for a stiff charge (10% MC, 6% Visa). Exchange English-language **books** at **Café Bandu.** The **airport** is at the far end of the road. Buy **SOSA** plane tickets at the **Hunter and Morgan Store,** near the center of town, for service to **La Ceiba** (Mon.-Sat. 7, 11am, and 3pm, 15min., L215). **Boats** leave from the dock near the intersection; get there at least 15 min. before scheduled departure time. **M/V Tropical** goes to **La Ceiba** (Tues.-Fri. 11am, 1½hr., L56). From La Ceiba, head to **Roatán.** Also inquire about the **M/V Starfish, Tonia C. II,** and **Utila Express.** For information on the Utila Express, contact the **Green Ribbon** store (tel. 45-31-97). The **community medical clinic** (tel. 45-31-37) is across from the park (open Mon.-Fri. 8am-noon). You can reach the doctor 24 hours a day on the yacht *Tabitha* (radio VHF CH-06). The **police** (tel. 45-32-55) are upstairs from the post office and speak English (open Mon.-Fri. 8-11am and 2-4pm). For off-hour emergencies, contact the

Chief of Police (tel. 45-31-87) or **FUSEP** (tel. 45-31-45), next to the park (open 24hr.). The **post office** is next to the park down an alley and has *lista de correos* (open Mon., Wed., Fri. 8am-noon and 2-4pm, Tues., Thurs. 8am-noon and 2-4:30pm, Sat. 8-11am). The **postal code** is 34201. **Email** at **Bay Island Computer Services** (tel. 45-31-24; email bicomput@hondutel.hn) at La Cola de Mico. (L3 per minute to send email; L10 per page to receive email or faxes. Open Mon.-Fri. 9am-noon and 1:30-5:30pm.) **Hondutel** (tel. 45-31-01; fax 45-31-06), to the left of the post office, has **telephones** open around the clock (**faxes** and **telegrams** Mon.-Fri. 7am-5pm, Sat. 7-11am).

ACCOMMODATIONS

During the high season, it can be particularly difficult to find a reasonably priced, decent residence. Electricity is turned off at about midnight, so finding a hotel with 24-hour electric service is often difficult and expensive. Many dive shops have their own hotels and offer significant discounts on rooms (as low as $1 per night!) if you ask. Another relatively cheap option is **Cooper's Inn** (tel. 45-31-84), farther down the main street (doubles L60; apartments with four beds U$$20). Or find your thrills at **Blue Berry Hill** (tel. 45-31-41), a few blocks up the hill from the bank. Rooms are small but cheap, and they come with mosquito nets (L20 for 1 or 2 people). If available, the huts, which include bath and cooking facilities, are a great deal (1-2 people L40; 3 people L60; 4 people L80). The brand-new **Mango Inn** (tel. 45-33-35) is well worth the short walk up La Cola de Mico (the only intersection). With large rooms, pristine bathrooms, and its own bar/restaurant, the inn is a find (rooms start at U$$5; $3 discount if you dive with the Utila Dive Center). Top-notch accommodations for fair prices can be found at **Trudy's**, on the main street (rooms with fans begin at L60).

FOOD

Delany's Island Kitchen, under Cooper's Inn, dishes out delicious pizzas (L65-75) and plates of lasagna with salad or garlic bread (L40; open daily 5:30am-10:30pm). A few doors down, **Mermaid's Corner** offers whopping plates of lasagna (meat or vegetarian) for L45 (open Sun.-Fri. 7am-10:30pm). The **Jade Seahouse,** on La Cola de Mico, offers huge *licuados* (L15) and satisfying meat and vegetarian dishes (open 7am-11pm). Near the airport is Captain Roy's Bahia del Mar (tel. 45-31-20), which somehow offers a tasty steak for only L30 and pastas for L35. For breakfast, everyone heads up La Cola de Mica to **Thompson's Bakery.** The walls are covered with wise adages, and the delicious pancakes with banana (L20) impart a little wisdom of their own to your stomach (open daily 6am-1pm).

SIGHTS AND ENTERTAINMENT

For certification-hungry prospective divers, Utila is utopia. Even though the mayor has stipulated a minimum price for an open water certification course, many still argue that Utila is the cheapest place in the world to get certified. One advantage to the price-fixing is that dive shops must now compete in ways that really matter. Use this freedom to select a shop carefully. First and foremost, check safety; instructors in Roatán have expressed concern that past cost-cutting may have undermined safety at some Utila diving centers. Also check personality—you'll be spending hours listening to your instructor pontificate at close quarters. Most dive shops offer four to six instructional dives. Inquire about languages spoken (many dive shops say they're multilingual, and all that means is they've got the PADI manual in a foreign language). For those already certified, "fun dives" typically run US$25; packages of 10 dives go for US$100. All certification courses cost US$125-140 unless otherwise listed. Alton's Dive Shop (tel. 45-91-08) has a reputation for quality on the island. Colorado native John, the instructor, is super-cool. Utila Dive Centre (tel. 45-33-26; fax 45-33-27; http://www.d-b.net/utila), halfway to the airport on the main drag, has confident, experienced instructors and sports divemasters conversant in six languages. The Utila Watersports Center (tel. 45-32-39) is affiliated with the Laguna Beach Resorts, home to some of the newest (and nicest) boats on the island. Gunter's Dive Shop has been around forever, and they know their stuff. Because a maximum of four people go into each class, personal attention is the rule. While you're taking the course, you can use their snorkeling stuff for free. (If you want to snorkel but aren't taking the course, they rent out equipment for L25 per day.)

For those who haven't come to Utila to dive, there are plenty of ways to while away the hours. **Canoes** can be rented from the Blue Bayou Hotel, a 30 minute walk down the shore from town. For **bike riding,** head to Myrtle's Restaurant (bikes L20 per 4hr., L30 per 8hr.) or at the bike repair shop near Gunter's (1-4hr. L30; full day L38; 2-3 days L36 per day). To really get under Utila's skin, call up **Shelby McNab** (tel. 45-32-23), a life-long resident of the island who offers "Robinson Crusoe Tours" of Utila's historical sites. **Tropical Travels** (tel. 45-32-41) also offers tours of the island (L500) and boat trips to neighboring cayes (L300 per group). Horseback riding is available from Willie Bolden, (if you can track him down at the B.I.C.A. office). Go **snorkeling** at **Blue Bayou,** a 30 min. walk past Gunter's, for only L5. Diehards can try the water near the airport runway.

One good hiking path is up **Stuart Hill,** which affords terrific views of Roatán; follow the path across from the post office up to the water tank. The **Iron Shore** extends on the road past the airport; so called because the volcanic rock here never gives an inch to the pounding of the waves.

For relaxation and snorkeling on an even more deserted island, head for a nearby caye, such as **Water Caye, Jewel Caye,** or **Sandy Caye.** Talk to Jake Whitefield (tel. 45-33-08) about getting to the Cayes (L150 for 1-3 people; US$5 per person for a larger group). Hammocks on the cayes typically rent for about US$1.

For nightlife during the week, head to **Sea Breakers;** on Tuesdays, Thursdays, and Saturdays you can get two rum-and-cokes for L10 during happy hour. The infamous **Bucket of Blood** (on La Cola de Mico) has been reopened and refurbished by a couple of Brits who have promised to provide the same excitement—but less blood—at the historically raucous establishment. On the weekend, everyone goes to the **Casino,** across from the bank (open weekends 8-11:30pm; free) or **Salon 07,** a block closer to the airport. It's fast becoming the spot for partying, mainly because they offer free rum (poured verrry slooooowly) on Tuesdays and Fridays between 10 and 11pm. The **Café Bondu** also draws a crowd to their daily movies (7:15pm, L25).

▓ Roatán

The largest and most populous of the Bay Islands, Roatán is also the most beloved by travelers. The clear, warm waters around Roatán shroud an extension of Belize's barrier reef and boast excellent diving. Its beaches are covered with cloud-soft sand and studded with coconut trees. While resorts are pushing up prices, one can still get by cheaply, especially on the west end of the island, where tourists huddle in the villages of **Sandy Bay** and **West End.** Boats typically land at **Coxen Hole,** a tiny town sometimes called "Roatán" that houses the airport and most services.

COXEN HOLE

Coxen Hole (a.k.a. Roatán) is the capital of the Bay Islands, but you wouldn't know it; it's just a small village veering slightly toward squalor. The pace of life is slightly faster than elsewhere on the island. Take care of your errands, since most businesses and services not related to diving are concentrated here. **Back Street** runs through Coxen Hole, along the water, while **Thicket Road** runs to the west end.

The **tourist office, Columbia Tours** (tel. 45-17-47), is in the gift shop across from Bay Islands Tour and Travel Agency on Back St. (open Mon.-Fri. 8am-noon and 1:30-5pm, Sat. 8am-noon). **Exchange currency** and **traveler's checks** at **Bancahsa,** halfway down Back St. (open Mon.-Fri. 8-11:30am and 1:30-4pm, Sat. 8-11:30am). To advance money on credit cards, try **Credo-matic** where you can advance up to L2000 (approx. US$150) on a Mastercard or Visa (open Mon.-Fri. 8am-noon and 1-5pm, Sat. 8am-noon). **Isleña Airlines** (tel. 45-18-33), on the ground floor of the same building as Columbia Tours, flies to **La Ceiba** (Mon.-Fri., 6, 10am, 1:15, 3, and 5pm, 30min.,

L246). The office is open Monday through Friday, 7:30am-5pm, and on Saturday, 7:30am-noon. **Taxis** (tel. 45-11-46) from Coxen Hole to West End (L10) and **metro-buses** (L7) leave throughout the day from **H.B. Warren's** supermarket on the main street. A taxi from the airport to West End costs about L20. **Drug Store Coral View** (tel. 45-14-80) is at the center of town (open Mon.-Fri. 8am-noon and 2-6pm, Sat. 8am-6pm). **Hospital Roatán** (tel. 45-12-25) is on Thicket Rd. a few blocks from Back St. (open 24hr.). For **police,** contact **FUSEP** (tel. 45-12-25), at the end of the dirt road, 100m back left of the hospital; they speak some English. The **post office** (tel. 45-13-21), across from Bancahsa, posts a *lista de correos* (open Mon.-Fri. 8am-noon and 2-5pm, Sat. 8am-noon). The **postal code** for Coxen Hole is 34101. Make AT&T **calls** and send **faxes** or **telegrams** at **Hondutel** (tel. 45-10-02), at the back of the path behind Bancahsa (open daily 7am-9pm; fax and telegram services Mon.-Fri. 8am-4pm).

Hotel Coral (tel. 45-10-80) is perfectly located, but is currently being renovated; watch for improved rooms and higher prices. Set farther back on Thicket Rd., behind the Shell gas station, **Hotel Allen** has 11 well-kept rooms. The owner is one of the nicest people in the hemisphere (L80 per room; checkout 11am). The biggest supermarket on the island, **H.B. Warren** (tel. 45-12-08) has an attached diner. Top off a three-piece chicken dinner (L28) with ice cream (L8; open daily 7am-5:30pm). **K&J Restaurant,** on the east end of Back St., has good *comida típica.* The plate o' the day, usually rice, meat, *plátanos,* and beans, runs L35 (open daily 11:30am-9pm).

If you're interested in environmental issues, check out the headquarters of the **Bay Islands Conservation Association** (tel. 45-14-24), upstairs in the Cooper Building next to Bancahsa. This organization works for the preservation of the island and surrounding marine life. As a result of their eco-efforts, a long strip of water along the north side of the island has been declared a marine preserve. The office offers information on the island and peddles t-shirts and an excellent book, *The Bay Islands: Nature and People* (L40; open Mon.-Fri. 8am-noon and 1:30-5pm).

Nightlife can be a hoot. Locals recommend going to French Harbor to **Bolongos** (L20 cover). Closer and cheaper is **Harbor View** (L10 on weekends) on Back St. (open from 9pm until people pass out).

WEST END

Follow this logic: Expats don't return home for a good reason. A good reason is usually a gorgeous locale that is a well-kept secret. West End is Roatán's gringo central. West End is gorgeous. Unfortunately for budget travellers, posh hotels and resorts in nearby West Bay are driving up prices and letting the secret out. Some of the best nearby beaches are starting to suffer from acute cases of concrete, yet even more tourism initiatives are planned. Don't despair, though; it will take a long time, or a Cancún-like push, to mar the natural beauty of this corner of Roatán.

To get to West End from the airport, take a micro-bus to Coxen Hole and then another one to West End (L10 each). For the less patient, taxis lurk around the airport looking for tourists; they can be expensive, so try and negotiate to L15-20 per person.

Practical Information **Traveler's checks** can be cashed at Seagrape Plantation Dive Shop (see **Sights and Entertainment,** below). Ask for Ernie or Ray—they give the bank rate. Also try the **Sunset Hotel** which offers a rate closer to the bank's. **Telephone calls** can be made from the **Intertel** office in **Supertienda Chris** (tel. 45-11-71) toward the east side of town or, more conveniently, at **Rudy's** (the convenience costs a lot; US$7 per minute to the US, US$2.50 for a collect call). International calls and **fax** service are available (Mon.-Sat. 7am-6pm). **Supertienda Chris** is also well-stocked with food, as is **Woody's Supermarket** at the western tip of town (Sun.-Fri. 7am-7pm, Sat. 6:30pm-9pm). For an **email** fix, check out the **ON LINE Cafe** (tel. 45-00-17), just outside West End on the road to Coxen Hole (Mon.-Fri. 11am-6pm, Sat. noon-4pm). **Cornerstone Emergency Medical Service** (tel./fax 45-15-15; radio CH26) treats diving emergencies around the clock.

Accommodations and Food Keep your eyes peeled for "rooms for rent" signs along the village's single, sandy street (prices may change by season). There are two budget hotels in the west part of town. **Jimmy's** has a dorm-like room (with a beautiful view of the water) that sleeps about 15 people. At L25 per person, it's the cheapest place around, but electricity and privacy are nowhere to be found. A little farther up the road, Jimmy's brother **Sam** has about 10 rooms for rent (with 24hr. electricity and hot water). More treehouse than hotel, this collection of lumber has a variety of configurations with seemingly randomly assigned prices. The cheapest, a two-bed room, goes for L65; the priciest, also a two-bed room, goes for L115. There are no mosquito nets, but Sam kindly offers coils to newcomers, as well as the advice to buy more the next day at the supermarket. At **Valerie's,** guests are quickly adopted into the family's communal dinners and nighttime parties. The kitchen is available for guest use during the day and the mosquito nets come in handy at night. (Bunks in communal dorms are US$5; there are also a few rooms for rent at US$10-15; running water is available only in the "master bedroom" suite after 7pm.) To get there head uphill at Tyll's Dive Shop and follow the path for about 20m. Next to Ocean Divers is the **Sunset Inn,** which offers double rooms with a fan for L15 (with bath L25) and apartments with kitchenettes for L35 (L10 per additional person). Good island food can be found at **Stanley's Island Kitchen** (open daily 6:30-11:30pm). Hang left and uphill at Southwinds Realty for about five minutes. The specialty is coconut bread, which is free with choice dishes (L50). **The Bamboo Hut** serves three-course meals for L50—the best bargain around. For breakfast, almost everyone heads to **Rudy's Coffee Stop** (tel. 45-12-05), toward the middle of the road. Whenever an order of flapjacks is ready, the owner proclaims "Best-in-the-West pancakes at the window!" Banana pancakes cost L20 (open 6:30am-9pm). Budget travelers flock to **Sea Breeze,** in eastern West End for their tasty and inexpensive tacos (L12-19). The **Light House Cafe,** next to the church, offers *típico* treats at mainland prices (L30).

Sights and Entertainment Particularly for beginners, Roatán offers some spectacular diving opportunities. An oft-frequented site is **Peter's Place,** at the end of Marine Park, where tons of big fish, deep canyons, and vertical walls wow divers. Also popular is **West End Wall,** which offers drift-diving along a wall densely packed with marine life. The famous **Hole in the Wall** is suited for advanced and very cautious divers; it's a sand-chute that qualified swimmers can wriggle through. **Bear's Den,** which offers cave-like, enclosed canyons ready for exploration, is also appropriate only for experienced and highly skilled divers.

Recently, the plethora of dive shops all agreed on the same prices: US$225 for PADI certification and US$20 for fun dives (US$25 with gear). Since finding a bargain isn't an issue if you're getting certified, make sure you get along with your divemaster and feel confident that he or she is concerned with safety. The folks at **Seagrape Plantation Dive Shop** (tel. 45-17-17) are friendly, experienced, and safety-conscious. Plus, they've got some of the best equipment around. Seagrape is at the extreme north end of the village, a five-minute walk past the road to Coxen Hole. Follow the signs to the Dive Shop, not the resort of the same name. They also rent and sell snorkeling gear (around US$31 for used fins, mask, and snorkel). The people at **Ocean Divers** (fax 45-10-05, attn.: Ocean Divers) are cool, reliable, and active in marine preservation. Snorkeling gear can be rented for US$5 per 24 hours, and a snorkeling trip on the boat costs US$10, drink included (open daily 8am-5pm). Also, they do in-house underwater film developing. **West End Divers** (tel. 45-15-31) has good equipment and offers night dives (open daily 8am-5pm).

If you don't feel like spending US$200, you can enjoy many of the underwater sights while snorkeling. There are a couple of convenient (and free) snorkeling spots in West End. The easiest is **Half Moon Bay** at the north end of the village. Snorkel the perimeter, then pop out 10m to the reef for the best views. Less accessible, but absolutely phenomenal, is **West Bay Beach,** 30 minutes south of the village (or an L15 water taxi from **Foster's and Vivian's**). The reef is 20m from shore and is stuffed to the gills with schools of angelfish, needlefish, parrot fish, and even occasional rays.

The **Librería Casitodo** (tel. 45-12-55) has information on all of the following tours (open Mon.-Fri. 9am-5pm, Sat. 9am-noon). If you're afraid of getting wet, **Far Tortuga Charters** takes passengers around the island for half-day trips (9am-noon or 1-4pm, US$25) or full-day excursions (9am-4pm, US$65 per person). If romantic moments are your thing, fork over US$15 for a sunset-moonrise trip. For a different sort of tour, **Island Adventures** takes a minimum of five people on five-hour tours of the whole island. For US$25, they'll take you to the Garifuna village of **Punta Gorda** for a dance performance, guide you through tropical gardens, and steer you on a boat trip through mangrove tunnels. To cruise around the island on your own power, check out **Captain Van's** bicycle rental at Foster's Bar and Restaurant (bike rental US$10 per day, moped rental US$25 per day). As for **nightlife, Foster's** is a good place to kick back and ponder the stars above (beer L15, mixed drinks L20-40). Beer-sipping and philosophizing are popular nocturnal pastimes. **The Bamboo Hut,** on the main road in the middle of town, now shows **free movies** to their guests with a projection TV every night at 7:30pm.

■ Guanaja

Called the Island of Pines by Columbus, who landed on its shores in 1502, Guanaja boasts broad expanses of virgin forest, few roads, and dazzling beaches. Nearly the entire population is crammed into **Bonacca,** or Guanaja town, a tiny caye off the coast. The original settlers tenaciously dumped coral and rocks into the channels between the tiny isles, creating Honduras' own version of Venice, Italy, and leaving room for overpriced diving resorts. Getting to expensive Bonacca isn't easy, but a concerted effort yields spectacular rewards—beautiful diving and untouched nature.

Orientation and Practical Information The airport is on the south side of the island, surrounded by "The Airport Hillton" (note the legally important extra "l") and miles of nothing. Don't panic. Water taxis are eager to take visitors to **the caye** (sometimes called **low caye**), whenever a plane arrives (5min., L25). The caye is cluttered; one could easily step from roof to roof. The "roads" are cement sidewalks just big enough for two strollers. The main road is called **Hog Cay** on the south end and **Fire Pit** on the north. It's pretty hard to get lost in Bonacca as all of the important buildings are nearly a stone's throw away.

The closest thing to a **tourist office** is Hugo at **SOSA** (tel. 45-43-59; fax 45-42-19). SOSA flies to **LaCeiba Islena** (tel. 45-42-08) Monday through Saturday (6 and 11:30am, L339). **Currency** and **traveler's check exchanges** take place at **Bancahsa** (tel. 45-42-34), a couple of blocks south of SOSA (open Mon.-Fri. 8-11:30am and 1:30-4pm, Sat. 8-11:30am). **Hondutel** (tel. 41-01-02; fax 45-41-46) sits a bit farther south (open Mon.-Fri. 7am-9pm with 2½hr. breaks for meals, Sat. 7-11am and 12:30-4pm). **Telegraph** service is also available (Mon.-Fri. 8am-4pm). There is some **medication** at the **supermarket, Casa Sikaffy,** three-quarters of the way to the north tip of the caye (open Mon.-Sat. 8am-12:30pm and 2-8pm, Sun. 8am-noon). The **Centro de Salud** is down the side street from the supermarket (open 7am-noon and 12:30-3pm). In an **emergency,** call the doctor at home (tel. 45-42-33). **FUSEP** (tel. 45-43-10), the **police,** work on the pier behind **Depósito Millers** (open 24hr.). The **post office** hides behind the little door across from Bancahsa (open Mon.-Fri. 8am-noon and 2-5pm).

Accommodations and Food If you can get to the north end of the island, some *campesinos* will let you pitch a tent on their land; ask first, and bring your own food and water. Finding an inexpensive bed can be brutal. Resort prices are out of control, and there's little else. **Fifi Café,** across from the SOSA office, has two rooms, each with a double bed. The common bath is rustic, but the owner doesn't care how many people sleep in the room (first night L60; additional nights L50). At the south end of the caye sits **Miss Melba's.** This kindly old soul rents two rooms (singles L80; doubles L100). The bathroom is private, and the rooms are exceptionally clean; you even get to watch cable in her living room. **Hotel Miller** (tel. 45-43-27) offers double rooms for L150 (L214 with bath). To add a little shape to your island wanderings, head over to Bo Bush's **Island House** (fax 45-41-46, or call Hugo at SOSA), a new resort on the north side of the island. For US$35 per day, you get a great room right off the beach and three big meals. For another US$35 per day, you get two boat dives and unlimited shore diving with Bo, a certified divemaster with his own compressor. If you stay several days, he'll take you back to the airport for free (saving you about L200). Another option is to head to the **West Peak Inn,** on the north side of the island. The owner, who is building a resort, lets people stay in tents on the site for US$10 per night. The draw is the gorgeous beach; the problem is getting there. A water taxi is L180 each way, but there are ways around this problem (see **Island House,** above). For chow, try **Joe's**—past the Centro de Salud at the first left, down about two blocks on the right, and across from the "Up & Down" sign—a favorite among frugal locals. A fish dinner costs L25, and there are specials on Sundays (open daily 11am-11pm). **Bonaccas Garden** offers a few international dishes to satisfy the hungry yet frugal traveler (L40).

Sights and Entertainment Guanaja is all about paying homage to Mother Nature. Diving opportunities abound, and the north side of the island is teeming with beaches, mountains, and reefs. Hugo at **Diving Freedom Dive Shop** charges a steep US$200 for PDIC certification and US$25 per tank for fun dives. One of the most popular sites is the **Wreck of the Jade Trader,** preserved at a cool 20-30m below the surface and waiting to be explored (again). The reef is a mere five-minute swim away, and the island's famous **waterfall** is just a 30-minute hike. To get to the north side, some folks just ask around at the docks on Bonacca for someone heading that way. *Let's Go* does not recommend hitchhiking, even on boats.

▧ La Mosquitia

East from Trujillo along the Caribbean Coast looms *La Mosquitia* (The Mosquito Coast), a vast stretch of seemingly impermeable jungle that reaches hundreds of miles inland from the white sandy beaches of Honduras and Nicaragua, stretching as far south as Costa Rica. The eastern portion of Honduras is perhaps the most amenable part of La Mosquitia for travelers, but that's not saying much. Those who dare to enter usually travel through the **Reserva Río Plátano,** a park that begins near the coast and extends inland to regions inhabited mostly by communities of **Garifuna, Moskito,** and **Pech** Indians. Further upriver is the core of the reserve, where the lowland rain forest gives way to cloud forest as the park ascends into the mountains. The lucky few that make it this far will be greeted with ancient archaeological sites very different from those on the *Ruta Maya*, superb wildlife, and divine isolation.

Planning your own trip into the region is no easy task. Unfortunately, hiring reputable **guides** to do the work for you costs more than most budget travelers can afford—expect to pay about US$100 per day. Two guiding companies with deservedly excellent reputations are **Cambio S.A.,** based in San Pedro Sula (tel. 527-274; fax 520-523), and **La Moskitia Eco Aventuras** in La Ceiba (tel. 420-104). Both companies are expensive; a five-day tour through the lower Plátano costs about US$550 (2-person minimum; bilingual tours are available). For La Moskitia tours, make sure that owner **Jorge Salvaterry** is leading your trip. *Be wary of discount guides,* or guides with something to sell that seems too good to be true. Before hiring a guide, ask around in La Ceiba, as reputations are usually accurate.

If you decide to **plan your own trip,** you will still have to hire indigenous guides. Currently, they don't charge very much, and they are essential for navigating the endless miles of seemingly identical, overgrown jungle paths. More importantly, the Indians see themselves as stewards of the land and prefer that visitors are escorted. The only way to attract the hostility of the locals is to try to get by without paying them to guide you. Even with a local guide, however, you will be responsible for your own safety. There are no medical facilities upriver from Palacios. Bring any **medicines** you might need, a **snake bite kit** with instructions, **bottled water,** and **water purification tablets.** Bring insect **repellent** (strong, DEET stuff) and a **mosquito net,** and be prepared to be tormented by sandflies, mosquitoes, *tapadas* (giant yellow flies), and the dreaded *chinchas* (tiny insects that leave massive red welts in the most private of places). Consider the weather: beware September and October, when you are likely to end up trekking through continuous downpours.

PALACIOS

Founded as a small Indian village, Palacios was then settled by British, who were friendly with the Moskito Indians. Soon, the British abandoned the area and were replaced by the Spanish, who employed their usual techniques of torture and cultural eradication. Aside from providing a point of entry to the **Reserva Río Plátano,** Palacios offers travelers little more than a last chance to experience the comforts of civilization before heading upriver.

There are two ways in and out of the town. Sane visitors come via the Russian-built puddle-jumpers flown by **Islena** (Mon.-Sat. 10am, from La Ceiba US$25 and rising). The insanely adventurous ride a **truck** that departs daily at midnight from Palacios, arriving at Trujillo at 8pm the next morning in time to catch a bus to La Ceiba (L80).

As you get off the plane, look for the sobering sight of the plane wreck on your right, and thank your deity. Just beyond the wreck is **Don Felix Marmol's,** then the dock and the unswimmable lagoon (home of the public outhouse). **Hospital Bayan** is about a 10-minute walk back along the landing strip, on the left (open Mon.-Fri. 8am-5pm, 24hr. for emergencies). **Boats** are the only choice for transportation: ask at Don Felix's for the three **water taxis** that head upriver as far as **Belén** daily (L15-30).

Food and **accommodations** are monopolized here by **Don Felix Marmol,** who runs a **hospedaje** (rooms with beds and nothing else L25). The **hospital** will take guests if they have room; they have clean rooms, ceiling fans, indoor toilets, and potable tap water (US$10). The only food in town is at Don Felix's; any meal is about L15.

NEAR PALACIOS

Small villages appear sporadically as you head upriver, providing good bases for exploring the Plátano basin. One hour from Palacios is the Garifuna community of **Plaplaya,** with a beautiful beach and one of the hottest *puntas* (traditional dances) on earth every Friday night (villagers ask for donations of L20). If you want to stay in Plaplaya, expect to pay about L25 to stay with a family, and L15 for a simple Garifuna meal (beans, rice, and *yucca*). Be extra-wary of drinking untreated water.

Another few hours upriver sits the Moskito village of **Raistá,** founded only 40 years ago by William Boden, a farmer from Coco-Villa. Mr. Boden is the father of the village in more ways than one—he is the patriarch of most current inhabitants of the town, now numbering more than 50. No one knows just how long the old man has been around; he's somewhere in his mid-nineties and still works in the fields with his sons and grandsons. The best place to stay here is the guesthouse of the Butterfly Farm (see below), though some villagers will put you up for L25. There is a septic tank in Raistá, so water here is better than downriver, though you should still treat it. Standard meals from families can be had for about L15. Ask for a drink made from *nanse,* the small sweet yellow fruit that grows on the trees in front of the guesthouse. Try to get up early at least once to watch the land come to life as the sun rises over the ocean. Before heading off into the wilderness, ask for a tour of the **Butterfly Farm,** a cooperative that supplies pupae to zoos in the United States.

To **see the jungle,** pay a visit to William's son Sergio, who lives across the lagoon. Send a message from Raistá to warn him that you are coming, and hire a local boatman to take you there. This stretch of jungle is Sergio's backyard, and he is happy to share for about L150 per day. Sergio claims an 80% success rate in spotting howler monkeys; also look for birds, including keel-billed toucans and feisty boat-bill flycatchers. Family members will also take you to the mangrove swamps (L180 per canoe), a magical experience; ask to ride up Paru Creek.

When you are ready to head upriver, walk about 8km up the dirt road from Raistá to Nueva Jerusalem, passing through Belén, and ask about rides to **Las Marias.** Expect to pay L1000-1500 roundtrip for a motorboat (6hr.) or L800-1000 for a *tuk-tuk,* named for its sputtering engine (8-9hr.). In Las Marias, guides will be waiting to take you to the **petroglyphs,** a four-hour trip upriver and one-hour hike away.

NICARAGUA

Nicaragua is a small country, but its sizeable name is known around the globe. The scope and publicity of the Nicaraguan political scene in the 1980s pushed a small country into the international limelight. In many ways, it was unprepared to handle this attention, from friend and foe alike. The elections of pro-business coalitions in the 1990s have fostered an economic stability that has kept the nation off the front page, though glimmers of the Sandinista movement still draw occasional flashbulbs. While Nicaragua is the largest Central American country, it is also one of the most sparsely populated. Over 90% of its citizens live in a region that amounts to less than 15% of its total area, and these few million have suffered tremendously during the course of the notorious internal strife that has plagued their nation in the past several decades. Of the thousands of beautiful and awe-inspiring sights that await travelers in Nicaragua's cities and countryside, all stand likely to be eclipsed in the eye of the visiting foreigner by knowledge of the land's infamous history and by the evident toll that its conflicts have taken.

Nicaragua is not going to embrace the tourism industry anytime soon. Some tourist offices have closed within the past years, and few natives are upset. For that matter, few tourists are, either. Travel here consists of not only what you see, but what you make of it—most travelers don't just come for the sights alone. Ecotourism is in its infancy here. In terms of environmental policy, Nicaragua is behind countries like

Costa Rica, but its unprotected virgin forests, saved by an economy that can't build roads, still dwarf the Costa Rican park system. The fate of these lands is sure to become a contentious and important issue as development expands.

There is about the country an atmosphere of the could've been, the might've been, and the might-still-be. It is a wonderful place to travel, offering a cerebral as well as sensual adventure. One of the country's greatest treasures is its conversation; the dearth of foreign travelers offers a grand opportunity to get to know the Nicaraguans, who will often gladly talk about what they've lived through. Almost everyone older than twenty has at least a few memories of the wars. Language may be an initial barrier to conversation, however. Nicaraguan Spanish is delicious, which is why its native speakers swallow half of every word. The letter "s," perhaps because of its association with the Somoza family, at times seems to be exiled.

The advantages to traveling in an untouristed country are obvious. While few travel experiences can put you in the shoes of a native, in Nicaragua, a traveler has the opportunity to gain a very real and very raw appreciation of the land. Awaiting each visitor are beautiful places, interesting people, and at least one once-in-a-lifetime experience.

ESSENTIALS

■ When to Go

CLIMATE

Nicaragua has three climatic zones: Atlantic, Central, and Pacific. All three have two seasons, rainy *(invierno),* and dry *(verano).* In the Pacific zone, nine months of the year is *invierno,* and February-April is *verano.* Most of Nicaragua remains dry from March to May, but even then, intermittent rain is not unheard of. In Managua, Masaya, and Granada temperatures tend to range from 30° to 38°C for most of the year. The east coast remains cooler than the west, but wetter. Indeed, Nicaragua is overall one of the most humid nations in Central America.

FESTIVALS AND HOLIDAYS

Some of Nicaragua's many local festivals and holidays are: **January 1** (New Year's Day); **February 25** (Anniversary of Elections); **May 1** (Labor Day); **July 19** (Revolution's Anniversary); **September 14-15** (Independence Day); **October 12** (Columbus Day); **December 8** (Immaculate Conception Day); **December 25** (Christmas).

■ Useful Information

For publications and organizations of general interest, see **Useful Information,** p. 1.

Nicaraguan Institute of Tourism, Apartado 122, Cost. Hotel Intercontinental, 1 c. Abajo, 1 c. al Sur, Managua (tel. (505-2) 28-12-38; fax 28-11-87).
Centro Nicaragüense de Derechos Humanos (CENIDH), Apartado 4402, Managua, Nicaragua. Their monthly bulletin provides statistical (and other) information about human rights in Nicaragua and Central America.
Council of Evangelical Churches of Nicaragua (CEPAD), Attn: Catalina Ruíz, Director of Communications, Apartado 3091, Managua, Nicaragua (tel. (505-2) 66-46-28; fax 66-42-36). Publishes a bimonthly bulletin with information about Nicaragua's struggle for justice and peace, as well as about the evangelical churches in the country. English-speaking staff.

■ Documents and Formalities

EMBASSIES AND CONSULATES

Embassy of Nicaragua: U.S., 1627 New Hampshire Ave. NW, Washington, D.C. 20009 (tel. (202) 939-6570; fax 939-6542); **Canada,** 130 Albert St., Suite 407, Ottawa, Ontario K1P 5G4 (tel. (613) 234-9361; fax 238-7666); **U.K.** (tel. (44) 171-409-2536 or 409-2825; fax 409-2593). The **consulates,** which provide visa information and informational packets, can be reached through the embassies.

PASSPORTS, VISAS, AND CUSTOMS

All visitors entering Nicaragua must have a **passport** (valid for at least 6 months), an onward/return ticket, and sufficient funds (US$200 minimum). U.S. and U.K. citizens do not need **visas;** citizens of Australia, New Zealand, South Africa, and most western European nations do. Visas can be obtained from a Nicaraguan embassy or consulate prior to arrival in Nicaragua. Make checks for US$25 payable to Consulate of Nicaragua/Washington; visas are issued within 10 to 15 working days of application. Nationals of other countries should check with a Nicaraguan consulate.

All visitors to Nicaragua are restricted to stays of 30 days, but one can obtain up to two extensions (up to 90 days total) at the immigration office in Managua (tel. 66-60-10; fax 66-60-46; Carretera Sur, within walking distance of Mercado Israel Lewites) for 250C per extension. After that, you must leave the country and re-enter. To drive a car, you need only what is called a *"Provisional,"* to be carried at all times and produced on demand. This can be obtained at the border; you'll need to show a valid passport and your title to the car. Insurance is optional in Nicaragua. There is an **airport tax** of US$5 upon arrival and another **migration fee.**

Electric current in Nicaragua is 110 volts, 60 cycles. The country is one hour behind U.S. Eastern Standard time, but does not observe daylight savings.

■ Money Matters

CURRENCY AND EXCHANGE

US$1= 9.58 córdobas	1C =US$0.10
CDN$1= 6.99C	1C =CDN$0.14
UK£1= 15.63C	1C =UK£0.06
IR£1= 13.93C	1C =IR£0.07
AUS$1= 7.12C	1C =AUS$0.14
NZ$1= 6.21C	1C =NZ$0.16
SARand 1 =2.08C	1C = SARand 0.48
DM1 = 5.23C	1C = DM0.19

The Nicaraguan unit of currency is the **córdoba** (C). There are 100 centavos to one córdoba. Colloquially, córdobas are sometimes referred to as *pesos.* Coins come in 10, 25, and 50 centavo pieces; the government recently printed monopoly-sized 25 centavo bills, which just might be worth the paper they're printed on. In general, if the amount of change you're due exceeds the amount you owe, you'll encounter difficulty. Try to avoid using 100, 50, and even 20C bills; large bills are hard to break, even in cities. The only coins used regularly are 50 centavo pieces. Most Nicaraguans (even hotel employees) carry so little currency that they'll be hard pressed to break even a 50C bill. A cumbersome option is to carry lots of 1C bills.

U.S. dollars are often accepted by large hotels and airlines, especially on the east coast. Changing dollars to córdobas is never a problem and most banks will exchange at the official rate. Nicaragua's *coyotes,* the guys on streetcorners with a calculator in one hand and a wad of bills in the other, will also change dollars at comparable rates. While officially illegal, this black market is usually uneventful. Make sure all the bills

NICARAGUA

are genuine; like everywhere, counterfeit currency exists in Nicaragua. Also, avoid changing currency at night.

Slowly but surely, many Nicaraguan cities will have at least one bank which changes traveler's checks (León, inexplicably, has none); and those that do will usually make you pay a service charge. You will often be asked for a receipt of purchase, so keep it handy. Most hotels and restaurants do not accept traveler's checks; some take credit cards, especially the expensive ones. *Coyotes* are less willing to change traveler's checks than cash.

If you're carrying currency other than U.S. dollars (including traveler's checks), it will be difficult to change it at any bank. *Coyotes* will give you a poor rate for rarely-seen currencies, if they change them at all. You might be better off contacting your embassy in Managua and seeing if they can help you. Most cities have **Western Union** offices, but all orders must be routed by phone to Managua, sometimes creating a one-day delay. The office in the capital is the fastest (tel. 66-81-26 or 66-81-29; fax 66-18-12). If you see an **ATM** in Nicaragua, you should get your eyes checked—they don't exist. Occasional banks will let you make a cash advance, usually on **Visa.** Banks with a **Credomatic** sign will make advances on **Mastercard.**

Tipping is left to the discretion of the traveler; be kind if service is exceptional, but be aware that gratuity is sometimes incorporated into the price of goods. A 15% sales tax is frequently ignored, unless you pay with a credit card. Taxi drivers don't get tips unless they do something special (like wait, or give you juicy info).

■ Safety

By and large, Nicaragua is not a dangerous country for tourists. Although Managua, like any large Central American city, demands a certain degree of caution and common sense, most of the country is sleepy, untouristed, and poor; people spend a lot of time simply watching TV. Avoid heading out into any city after dark unless you must. Touristed areas are often hot-spots for crimes. Avoid as much as possible heading out into rural areas alone, and if someone asks for your money, give it to them without any trickery. Sporadic armed violence is reported throughout the country, and bandits have been known to operate on the roads after dark. Visitors should notify their respective embassies in Managua upon arrival to the county. The most dangerous areas in Nicaragua are in the north of the country, where land reform remains a major issue and violence and kidnappings are not uncommon. Call the U.S. State Department's Travel Advisories Hotline for information about safety in Nicaragua (tel. (202) 647-5225).

While women travelers should (as always) be particularly cautious, Nicaragua is blessed with a solid support organization for the country's women. **El Associación de Mujeres Nicaragüenses "Luisa Amanda Espinoza" (AMNLAE;** tel./fax 2 78 56 64), named after the first militant woman activist in the FSLN, has set up "Casas de la Mujer" in more than 50 towns throughout Nicaragua; while the "Casas" deal primarily with women's civil liberties, they are equipped to offer help to women travelers, as well. Write to AMNLAE, Aptdo. A-238, Managua, Nicaragua.

■ Health

Malaria is a problem in rural areas and town outskirts; all visitors should take chloroquine tablets for malaria prevention (starting one week before you leave). Since malaria and **dengue fever** are transmitted by mosquitoes, the wise traveler to Nicaragua will wear plenty of DEET. **Cholera** has also been recently reported in Nicaragua, as has **Hepatitis A. Typhoid fever** is prevalent throughout Central America; vaccines are recommended for travel to infected areas. For reliable and current public health information contact the **Ministerio de Salud Publica** in Managua (tel. 94312, 97808, or 97395; fax 97997), located at Complejo Concepción Palacio, in Barrio Rubenia. Water in Managua is generally considered quite safe, and other cities are starting to chlorinate their water, but to be extra careful—purified water is readily available. For more information, see **Health,** p. 14.

■ Alternatives to Tourism

STUDY

Short-term study opportunities for foreigners are more limited in Nicaragua than in other parts of Central America; try to make informal arrangements on your own. The **Centro Nicaraguense de Aprendizaje Cultural** (CENAC) is located two blocks ñorth and 50m east of the bus terminal, Apdo. 10 (tel. 505-071-32025). CENAC participants can choose between language classes, homestays, service projects, or any combination of the three (weekly costs range from US$80-120, not including airfare). In the U.S. call Rodolfo Celis at 312-667-9276; in Canada, try Gaetan Tremblay at 514-842-3393. Dr. Gregory Calvert and Dr. Ken Carpenter recently opened a language school in Granada at **Casa Xalteva,** De la Iglesia Xalteva, Casa #103, 30 varas al norte, Granada (tel./fax (505) 552-2436). The cost is US$125 for the first week, $115 per week for the second and third weeks, and $425 for one month. Homestays are US$60 per week, and accommodations are $40 per week. Longer stays are available. The **University of Mobile** (that's Mobile, Alabama, USA) recently opened a branch campus in San Marcos, a small town 20 minutes outside of Masaya. The University is primarily designed for full-time undergraduates, but may also be a good place to find out about other educational opportunities within Nicaragua. Intensive Spanish and English are taught to an international student body. In the U.S. call the University of Mobile at 334-675-5990 and ask for the director of admissions, or write to P.O. Box 13220, Mobile, AL 36663-0220. In Nicaragua, contact Yadira Gonzalez, University of Mobile, Latin American Campus, Admissions Office, San Marcos, Carazo (tel. (505) 43-22-314; fax (505) 43-22-336). The university is affiliated with various international consortia thus enabling its students to study in 20 countries throughout the world.

VOLUNTEER

There are plenty of reasons to get involved in Nicaragua, and if you'll be there anyway, very few excuses not to. Volunteers in Nicaragua can assist in reforestation, land management, public health, community organization, human rights, and education. Many organizations in the United States and elsewhere provide information. NICCA, CEPAD, and CENIDH offer the above volunteer opportunities and more.

Fundación Nicaraguense por el Desarollo Comunitario Integral (FUNDECI), Casa Benjamin Linder, Aptdo postal 2694, Managua (tel. 66-43-73; fax 66-33-81). Informal clearing-house for volunteer opportunities in Nicaragua. Network at the Thurs. morning meetings at Casa Ben Linder. FUNDECI's U.S. representative, and a good resource for researching volunteer opportunities from the U.S., is Rita Clark at the Nicaragua-U.S. Friendship Office, FUNDECI/APSNICA (Technical Assistance Program), 337 North Carolina Ave. SE, Washington, D.C. 20003 (tel. (202) 546-0915; fax 546-0935). Program attempts to match skills and interests of the volunteers with the needs of Nicaraguan communities. One flat fee of US $300, regardless of how long volunteer elects to stay in Nicaragua.

■ Getting There

Carriers such as **Air France, Iberia, SAHSA, TACA, Continental, American,** and **Aeroflot** airlines fly to Managua's Augusto C. Sandino International Airport from points in the U.S. and Europe.

There are two international **bus** lines that run between Managua and nearby capitals. **Tica Bus** (tel. 22-60-94) is headquartered in the Barrio Marta Quezada, two blocks east of the Casino Pasapogo (cabbies might know it as the Cine Dorado). Tica runs buses to and from **Tegucigalpa** (US$20), **San Salvador** (US$35), **Guatemala**

City (US$43), and **San José** (US$15). **Sirca Bus** (tel. 67-38-33 or 77-57-26) services San José (180 colones) from its station at Altamira de Este, two blocks south of Distribuidora Vicky. Schedules for both lines are available at Inturismo.

Crossing the border by land can be tedious; bring U.S. dollars, or your life will be hell. You'll walk through customs of the country you're leaving (Honduras or Costa Rica) while warding off aggressive money changers. Next, you may have to hike several kilometers across the border (pack light), or snag a bus. At Nicaraguan customs, you may be asked to pay two entrance fees: a small tax of 10C, plus another fee of US$7, *payable only in U.S. dollars.* Finally, you'll board a bus to your destination of choice. Some bus lines actually cross the border and take passengers' passports inside to be stamped. If you cross the border at any point other than a designated border crossing, find an immigration office immediately.

The suggested **border crossings** with **Honduras** are Las Manos, El Espino, and Gausaule, which are only open during the day. The U.S. State Dept. reports that travelers have been harassed at border crossings while crossing the Gulf of Fonseca by ferry between Potosi, Nicaragua and La Unión, El Salvador. The only viable route to **Costa Rica** is along the Interamerican Hwy. at Peñas Blancas (crossing open 8am-4pm).

■ Once There

TRANSPORTATION

Buses are the primary mode of transport in Nicaragua. Most of Nicaragua's bus fleet is composed of yellow school buses retired from North America. Whenever possible, take an express bus to your destination; the few extra córdobas (usually) assure you a seat and increase the likelihood of arriving before your passport expires. The roads, if paved, are usually in decent condition, although buses' bad shocks pick up the potholes. Don't drive at night unless you absolutely have to.

Costeña flies cheaply to Bluefields, Isla de Maiz Grande, and other Atlantic Coast destinations; **NICA** covers the rest of the country. Both airlines have offices in Managua, but most travel agencies can sell you these airline tickets.

ADDRESSES

Addresses are almost always given in terms of a nebulous canon of landmarks within a given city (e.g. the museum is three blocks west and two blocks south of the gas station). The plot thickens, however, with the occasional substitution of *arriba* and *abajo* for east and west, respectively. Then again, if you happen to be in a city set on a hill, *arriba* and *abajo* may only refer to relative elevation. In Managua, north becomes *al lago,* and some of the cardinal landmarks haven't existed for years. Another directional device is *al salida* or *al entrada,* as in *"al salida a Juigalpa."* Look for this address where the road for Juigalpa leaves town. Many streets are named, but the names are almost never used.

KEEPING IN TOUCH

Nicaraguan **mail** is comparable to other Central American postal systems. Allow a good 15 days for addresses within the U.S., 20 days for Europe. ENITEL/TELCOR also has its own courier service, E.M.S., slightly cheaper than private couriers. You can receive *poste restante* mail at any Correos de Nicaragua office (usually located in the ENITEL/TELCOR building). In most cases, mail will be held for one month, though some offices will hold mail for only two weeks. Mail should be addressed as follows:

Scott <u>NEWSTROM</u>
Lista de Correos
Estelí (town name), Estelí (department name)
Nicaragua, CENTRAL AMERICA

If mailing from the U.S., omit the last line (Central America) and move "Nicaragua" down, since the computers that sort the mail can only recognize country names.

Many hotels and shops let patrons use their telephone for about 3C for 5 minutes. Generally, though, while in Nicaragua, your link with the rest of the world will be through **ENITEL,** the national communications service still known throughout the country by its old name, **TELCOR** (Instituto Nicaraguense de Telecommunicaciones y Correos). Most every city, town, or hamlet in Nicaragua has an ENITEL/TELCOR, home to the postal and telephone office, and usually identifiable by a tall radio tower; offices are generally open daily 7am-9pm. Staffers will place your international call and direct you to a booth to take the call. If you're calling with AT&T USADirect, they will still ask you for the two names and a number; if you want to place a call with a credit card or phone card, simply explain that you must speak with the AT&T operator in person. **Collect calls** through the Nicaraguan phone system are harder to make. To reach a U.S. AT&T operator, dial 164 (Spanish) or 174 (English), or dial 9 to get the Nicaraguan operator and ask to be connected to an AT&T operator. Dial 166 for MCI Call U.S.A., or 161 or 171 for Sprint Express. Other important phone numbers are: 112 for **information,** 114 for **international information,** 110 for a **national long-distance operator.** The Nicaragua **country code** is 505. See Practical Information sections for each city's local telephone code.

NICARAGUA: LIFE AND TIMES

▓ History

In 1519, a Spanish expedition under **Gil González de Avila** (or "Dávila") encountered an indigenous settlement on the southern shores of what would later be known as Lago de Nicaragua. Dávila and his conquistadors returned as military entrepreneurs in 1522, only to be rebuffed by the fighting natives of the Caribbean coast, led by the famed **King Nicarao.** Dávila had made serious inroads into the region prior to his rout, however, and set the stage for the pillage that was to accompany European immigration to Nicaragua. First, he hauled away the land's natural resources, starting with its gold, and then abducted thousands of its original residents to sell as slaves. In 1524, **Francisco Hernández de Córdoba** brought the first wave of successful colonists to settle in the eastern lowlands. They named the new country Nicaragua, after Nicarao, the *indígena* chief who had welcomed their first advances, and much later their descendents would call the local coin "córdoba," in honor of his European guest. Direct confrontation between the invaders and the invaded was brief and relatively bloodless, compared to the conquests of the Aztec and Maya empires. But the annihilation of Nicarao's people was no less complete for being indirect; Old World diseases killed hundreds of thousands of natives within a few decades of their introduction. The Spanish colonists captured and sold off a majority of the plague-resistant natives during the same period.

León was founded in 1524, only to be destroyed by an earthquake 86 years later. The city moved west and became both the colonial capital and the center of liberal politics in Nicaragua. Its rival settlement, Granada, lay on the northwest shore of the Lago de Nicaragua, and was able to exploit the commercial and military superiority of its location to great advantage during its early colonial period, soon becoming a powerful, affluent, and conservative city. León and Granada remained ideological opponents, often feuding violently, until 1857, when the capital was moved to Managua as a compromise. Nicaragua gained its independence from Spain in 1821. For a while, the country was part of the Mexican empire, but then became part of the **Central American Federation,** before becoming completely independent in 1835. But with the withdrawal of the Spanish, British and North American influence grew, creeping west from the Caribbean. Cornelius Vanderbilt started the **Accessory Transit Com-**

NICARAGUA

pany, which carried thousands of forty-niners (among others) from the Caribbean, across Nicaragua by boat and stagecoach to the Pacific, and from there to California.

With León supporting him, **William Walker,** a renegade North American, attacked Granada in 1855 with 56 men, captured the city, and declared himself president. After drawing Vanderbilt's ire by seizing his company, Walker was expelled from Nicaragua by the U.S. Navy, the transit company, and five other republics in 1857, only to make two subsequent unsuccessful attempts to recapture the country (see **William Walker, What a Killer,** p. 271).

Nicaragua's conservatives gained power and held it until 1893, when the left-leaning **José Santos Zelaya** overthrew the government and proclaimed himself dictator. Zelaya was not only leftist and autocratic, he was also Nicaragua's first effective nationalist, and his emergence marked the beginning of a long line of North American interventions. He spoke of a renewed Central American unity and of the importance of blocking the U.S. from securing trans-isthmian canal-building rights. In those days, Panamá had not yet been explored as a possible location for an inter-oceanic canal, so the U.S. State Department was especially alarmed to hear rumors that Zelaya might be planning to grant land to Japan. In 1889, the U.S. government orchestrated Zelaya's overthrow and sent in the Marine Corps, effectively controlling the country through puppet governments for the next 16 years. During most this period of *de facto* occupation (which was strikingly parallel to the Nicaragua of the early 1990s), three liberal leaders maintained a steady resistance. Sacasa, Moncada, and **Augusto César Sandino,** all led their troops into fiery rebellion in 1927, in response to a changing of the puppets and a further importation of U.S. Marines. Six months' fighting was enough for Sacasa and Moncada, who both settled peacefully with the U.S.-backed government in exchange for an elected presidency for each. Sandino, on the other hand, continued to fight against the foreign influence and the dubious democracy it supported; he would do so for as long as North American soldiers remained in Nicaragua.

The Marines left their replacements, the brutal **Guardia Nacional,** under the command of **Anastasio Somoza García,** later "Tacho," who used the hated unit to support the Somoza family dictatorship for 50 years. In 1934, Somoza had Sandino assassinated. The Somozas and their associates began plundering the country, amassing huge fortunes and vast land holdings while the rest of Nicaragua wallowed in miserable poverty. Vicious repression, torture, and disappearances were commonplace. U.S. support for the regime was unfaltering. U.S. President Franklin D. Roosevelt once said of Somoza, "He may be a son of a bitch, but he's ours." On September 21, 1956, **Rigoberto López Pérez** shot and killed Anastasio Somoza in León. Pérez, a liberal poet, was immediately martyred. Anastasio Somoza was succeeded by his son, Luis Somoza Debayle, who ruled until his death 11 years later. His younger brother, Anastasio Somoza Debayle, called "Tachito," assumed the presidency in 1967, and held onto the official position for the four years that the new constitution allowed.

Opposition grew as the Somoza dynasty endured. **Carlos Fonseca Amador,** born in Matagalpa in 1936, was a radical student leader and prominent Somoza opponent. In 1961, he and other radicals formed the **Frente Sandinista de Liberación Nacional (FSLN).** The name was meant to invoke the memory of Sandino.

In 1972, a massive earthquake virtually leveled Managua, killing 6000 Nicaraguans and leaving over 300,000 others without food and shelter. The momentarily dethroned Somoza exploited the opportunity both to marshal the Guardia Nacional into a "National Emergency Committee" and named himself the ruler by martial law. Almost before the rubble from the quake had settled, he had re-installed himself as president. When international relief money went straight to Tachito Somoza's personal coffers, opposition to his regime solidified. By 1974, both the **Union Democracia de Liberación (UDEL)** and the FSLN were gaining ground. In January of 1978, when the Guardia Nacional assassinated Pedro Joaquín Chamorro, leader of the UDEL and publisher of the popular and respected newspaper *La Prensa,* the revolution began in earnest. For over a year the country was beset with general strikes and armed standoffs. On July 17, 1979, Somoza fled the country. Two days later, the San-

William Walker, What a Killer

Webster's lists as its first definition of "filibuster" (from the Spanish, *filibustero*, or "freebooter"): "an irregular military adventurer; *specif:* an American engaged in **fomenting insurrections** in Latin America in the mid-19th century." This word's long-standing place in our language is due no doubt to the dastardly exploits of William Walker. Born in Nashville, Tennessee in 1824, Walker spent years studying to be a physician in Pennsylvania and Paris, left medicine to practice law in New Orleans and, finally drifted out to California one beat behind the Gold Rush, and ended up in command of a successful U.S. military expedition in the Baja region of Mexico. Walker set important personal precedent by declaring the land an independent state, and himself its president. Quickly chased out by Mexico and acquitted by a San Francisco judiciary, he next turned his **rabid gaze** to Nicaragua. Would-be canal-builders funded Walker to land a small brigade on the shore of the fledgling nation. Unbelievably, Walker conquered Granada within days of arrival, established himself as the President of Nicaragua within the year, and legalized slavery. Only when he announced his plans to forge out into the other four Central American states did Nicaraguans amass the support they needed to oust him. His regime regrouped in Alabama, and from there attempted two new invasions, equally bold, but less fruitful. His final foray ended in Trujillo, Honduras, where British troops captured him and surrendered him to the Honduran authorities, who promptly stood him before the **firing squad.**

dinistas marched as victors into Managua. (Many towns all over Nicaragua are named "17 Julio," and others "19 Julio.") Somoza was assassinated a year later in Paraguay.

But that, of course, is not the end of the story. After the euphoria of victory had subsided, the victors set about resuscitating a country in sorry shape. Murals, no matter how uplifting or revolutionary, cannot feed children, clean streets, or plant crops. The Sandinistas immediately faced a new opposition movement, the **Contras.** The Contras were ex-Guardia Nacional, mercenaries, scared teenagers pressed into service, and ordinary Nicaraguans ideologically opposed to the Sandinistas. Apart from the Contras, the Sandanistas had to face the ire of the U.S. government. When **Ronald Reagan** assumed the U.S. presidency he decided that one goal of his administration would be to halt the Soviet-backed Sandinistas and ordered support to the Contras.

Throughout the 80s, Contra-Sandinista war ravaged Nicaragua. In 1984, **Daniel Ortega** of the FSLN won a popular presidential election neutrally monitored and generally accepted as honest. The U.S. mined Nicaraguan harbors and spearheaded an economic embargo of the country. Food and supplies ran short. Inflation spiraled to a staggering 30,000%. Revolutionary idealism began to wane, and as the war became one of attrition, it became clear that if the Nicaraguans chose a new ruling party in the 1990 elections, the U.S. might provide aid. Sure enough, under economic siege, the electorate went to the polls in 1990, and replaced the Sandinistas with **Violeta Chamorro** of the Unión Nacional Opposición (UNO), a coalition of fourteen smaller parties. Mrs. Chamorro, the widow of Pedro Joaquín Chamorro, carried 55% of the vote. When Chamorro took office, the Contras disarmed. Though some violence continues to this day, the war, for all intents and purposes, was over.

Nicaragua is still a very poor, if currently peaceful, country, and a few families control what little wealth there is. Official unemployment figures hover at around 70%. No longer burdened with an economic embargo, however, the UNO government is doing its best to promote market-driven capitalism, a trend opposed by the socialist Sandinistas. The result is a country in limbo—Nicaragua's elite, many of whom fled the country during the 80s and returned only recently, now whisk themselves around in tinted-windowed Land Cruisers, as hundreds of striking Revolutionary murals all over the country remind passers-by of the angry idealism that still lingers today. Sandino's image is everywhere. As an outsized silhouette, a blurry, black and white poster, a stylized portrait, or stenciled vandalism, he is always surveying the country from beneath his wide-brimmed sombrero.

NICARAGUA

■ The Arts

Probably the greatest of all Central American literary figures was Nicaragua's own **Rubén Darío** (1867-1916). Darío's resonant, sensitive poems include "Sonatina," the politically edged "A Roosevelt," and his most praised "Cantos de Vida y Esperanza" (Songs of Life and Hope). His work "Azul" is thought to have started Modernism in Latin America, and the poet's death is considered by some to have ended it.

Later Nicaraguan writers felt the need to distance themselves from Darío to express their own voice, and have concerned themselves less with the aesthetic than with the urgency of their country's sociopolitical condition. Vanguardist **Pablo Antonio Cuadra** and poet **Ernesto Cardenal** fall into this latter group.

Native musicians jam on a variety of instruments, including the *Chirimía*, a primitive clarinet, and the fearsome, thunderous *juco*, played by pulling a string through a drum head. Lucky travelers may even see "El Güegünse," a farcical, musical street drama about an old man who repeatedly outwits authorities. Not all the music of the country is from *indígenas*, though. The most famous Nicaraguan composer is probably **Luis A. Delgadillo,** who wrote a **ballet** for children and has put some of Darío's texts to music.

The People's Poet

Although he died in 1916, Rubén Darío is still a ubiquitous presence in Nicaragua—parks, streets, schools, and landmarks all bear his name. Born in 1867 in Metapa (now Ciudad Darío), Darío gained almost instant fame in Spain and throughout Latin America for his **fresh, modernist style.** Some of his most poignant poetry perhaps expresses the conflicting emotions Darío, who spent most of his adult life abroad, felt towards his homeland. The Nicaraguan countryside is at once **battered and beautiful;** it is difficult to love, but impossible to resist. After serving as the Nicaraguan ambassador to Spain and France, Darío died penniless in León.

■ Food and Drink

Most often served at the *comida corrientes* ("running meal"), and favored among street buffet grills, are chicken, fruit, and tortillas, the staples of the Nicaraguan diet. Beyond that, learn to love the other basics: *gallo pinto* is rice and beans; *plátanos* (plantains) are served up *maduro* (fried, greasy, and sweet) or *verde* (crispy, like potato chips); cheese is usually squeaky and mild, or crumbly and very sharp; *carne asada* is code for barbecued, marinated meat; and *mondongo* is tripe (stomach) cooked with beef knuckles. Yes, beef knuckles. For vegetarians, *ensaladas* are usually comprised of cabbage with tomatoes and vinegary dressing. The average mealtimes are 7-10am for breakfast, noon-3pm for lunch, and 6-8pm for dinner.

Scrumptious rums are produced locally, and not coincidentally, are drunk locally in huge quantities. *Flor de Caña*, produced in Chinandega, is the most popular brand, and is smooth and rich in flavor. *Victoria* and *Toña* are the national beers, and at the half the price of imports, are worth getting to like. Or dip into the *refrescos naturales*, fruit juices mixed with a little water and sugar. As always, though, be sure that the water and ice are clean and use caution when eating and drinking Nicaraguan food. For more details, see **Health,** p. 14.

■ Media

Nicaraguans stay abreast of national and international news through television programming from the U.S.; a steadily increasing number of TVs in Nicaragua have cable. For daily local news (and the latest baseball standings and statistics), the most popular newspapers are *La Prensa* (which leans to the right), *La Barricada* (published by the Sandinistas), and *La Nueva Día*, which walks the fence.

■ Recent News

The Sandinista Renovation Movement's (MRS) split from the Sandinista National Liberation Front gave the Liberal Constitutional Party (PLC) the boost it needed to carry the 1996 election, when Arnoldo Alemán Lacayo succeeded Violeta Chamorro (albeit under questionable circumstances). Alemán's most pressing issue is to stabilize Nicaragua's economic and political systems in order to guarantee the fulfillment of his campaign promise to attract foreign capital to the country. Foreign investment is the only way Nicaragua can hope to reduce the ruthless unemployment levels which currently stand at over 60% of the population. To this end, Alemán is expected to sign a bill which will directly benefit foreign interests by loosening contract restrictions and reducing import tariffs, among other things. Nicaragua's business community is furiously trying to stop Alemán from signing the bill into law, arguing that its provisions would penalize domestic business enterprise, as well as expose it prematurely to foreign competition. Better news: the Nicaraguan government's fears that recent changes in U.S. immigration laws would lead to the mass deportation of as many as 50,000 Nicaraguans living in the U.S. were allayed by a U.S. court's ruling that temporarily suspended the forced emigration of Nicaraguans living in the U.S.

Managua

At first, Managua may strike you as a confusing city, scarred, scared, and guarded. After a few days of exploring and conversing, Managua will still be all of those things, but also exciting, noble, and even uplifting. Managua takes getting used to; this is not a city made for tourism—it's too real, and far too gritty. Only experienced travelers and Peace Corps volunteers spend time here, and then only to see what the raw core of a country with a past as turbulent as Nicaragua's looks like.

In Náhuatl, "Managua" means "where there is an extension of water." Sure enough, there's water aplenty here: the city sits at the edge of Lago de Managua, the second-largest lake in the nation. Managua was raised on the ashes of an ancient indigenous village, and the city's former residents literally left their prints on the modern city— 10,000 years ago, residents ran from an erupting volcano; the lava that pursued them preserved their fleeing footsteps, now on display in El Museo Huellas de Acahualinca. Since then, Managuans have run into more trouble than they've run from.

Situated midway between liberal León and conservative Granada, politically as well as geographically, Managua was declared the capital of Nicaragua in 1857 in an attempt to quell feuding between the rival cities. Prematurely thrust into the limelight, the tiny city didn't mature until the turn of the century, when new railroads turned the infant capital into a center for the booming coffee export trade. Managua thrived until 1931, when it was razed by an earthquake. Five years later, a massive fire made cinders of the ruins. Surviving Managuans dug their heels in against the elements and rebuilt the city, only to watch it fall prey to new disasters. In December of 1972, Managua was leveled by another earthquake that killed 6000 people. The Somozas skimmed, or rather scooped, the international relief aid, leaving the city unreconstructed. Managua still sits low on its haunches; busy streets cross deserted meadows and lots, bustling markets abut gutted buildings.

Composed of distinct *barrios,* the city now sprawls into a series of massive suburbs. At the same time, the lack of an urban center (only three buildings rise above 15 stories) could delude one into imagining that, say, Granada outsizes the capital. Strident public art saturates the city—revolutionary murals and radical graffiti, a huge silhouette of Sandino, and, perhaps most arresting, an outsized, wrought-iron *campesino* triumphantly lifting a machine gun in his left hand. Like the lava that cast the ancient footprints—the city's oldest "public art"—today's Managua is riveting and red-hot; like the footprints, today's Managua is both frozen and in motion.

■ Orientation

Take a deep breath of polluted air—this is tough. Managua has dispensed almost entirely with the unnecessary formality of naming its streets. A precious few *avenidas* and most of the *carreterras* have names (though these may be disputed), but most 'addresses' are given in terms of their proximity to recognized landmarks—a Texaco station, a university, a statue, where a cinema used to be, etc. Even the cardinal points have Managuan pseudonyms: the direction 'south' remains *al sur,* but 'north' becomes *al lago,* 'east' is *arriba,* and 'west' is *abajo.* (*Arriba* designates the side of the horizon from which the sun rises, and *abajo* the side toward which it descends.) Thus, when told that your destination is *"De Tica Bus una cuadra abajo y media cuadra al lago,"* you must first find the Tica Bus Station, then walk one block west and half a block north. It is not unlike chess.

Managua lies on the south shore of Lago de Managua (locally, and more properly, called Lago Xolotlán), which sits 39m above sea level. From the old city center on the lake shore, Managua expands in all directions. The **Cesar Augusto Sandino International Airport** is 12km east of the city on the Carreterra Norte. Taxis from the airport to Marta Quezada (see **Accommodations,** below) cost an unreasonable US$15-20; walk a few steps to the highway and the price suddenly drops to US$6-7. When you leave the expectant airport throngs and exit the small terminal, veer towards the right—in about 100m you'll hit the **Carreterra.** Extra credit if you actually cross the road and catch a cab headed in the right direction.

The plush **Hotel Intercontinental,** a valiant attempt at neo-Maya architecture, was one of the few structures in downtown Managua to survive the 1972 earthquake. A major landmark, it can be considered the effective center of the city. The **"Inter,"** as it is often called, sits just below the crest of a hill; its distinctive facade faces north. On the same hillside, just east of the Inter, looms Sandino's sombrero and somber silhouette. **Avenida Bolívar** runs north to south, just west of the Inter. From the hotel, Bolívar descends 1km to meet the lake shore and the old city center, arriving promptly at the **Teatro Rubén Darío.** Along the way it passes the **Asamblea Nacional** and the Bank of America skyscraper, the **Palacio Nacional,** the tomb of Rubén Darío, the ruined **Santo Domingo Cathedral,** and the main **ENITEL/TELCOR office. Barrio Marta Quezada,** the neighborhood west of the Intercontinental, houses most of Managua's budget hotels and *hospedajes.* The western border of the Barrio Marta Quezada is **Avenida Williams Roberto,** on which sits the **"Casino"** (a strip joint also called the **Cine Dorado**). The northern border is **Calle 27 de Mayo.** Both of these streets are larger and busier than the bumpy byways of Manta Quezada, so you'll know when you're leaving the neighborhood. Eight blocks south on Av. Williams Roberto is the **Plaza de España,** less a plaza than one might expect, and more of a strip mall; this is home to many banks, travel agencies, and a supermarket. To the southwest of Barrio Marta Quezada lies **Mercado Israel Lewites,** one of Managua's major market areas, as well as the highway to León. **Mercado Oriental** is to the northeast of the Inter, and **Mercado Roberto Huembes** (also called **Mercado Central**) lies to the southeast. **Mercado Ivan Montenegro** is at the far east end of the city. Buses leave from all of these markets, bound for nearly every other part of Nicaragua.

Although Managua can sometimes be a dangerous city, visitors will do all right if they keep their wits about them (see **Nicaragua: Safety,** p. 258, for general advice). The greatest risk is undoubtedly the threat posed by pickpockets. Managuan buses are notorious for their deft-fingered thieves, so try to get a seat. When you have to remain standing, use one hand to steady yourself and keep the other one down around your pockets. When push comes to shove (literally), hold tight to your córdobas; they'll emerge a sweaty wad, but they'll emerge. The *camiones* (the truckish buses with boarded-up beds) are said to be safer, because they have an on-board conductor and only one door. At night, obscure streets can be treacherous—manhole covers are often missing, providing an unexpected opportunity to visit Managua's underworld.

Managua

Lago de Managua (Xolotlán)

TO AIRPORT

Boulevard Buenas Aires

Mercado & bus station Oscar Benavides/ Iván Montenegro

Pista José Angel Benavides

Pista de la Solidaridad

Las Muchachos

Paseo

Boulevard Ruben Dario

Ferrocarril del Pacífico
Pista Pedro Joaquín Chamorro

Av. La Emboscada

Av. Cristian Pérez

Calle 14 de Septiembre

Pista Lareynaga

Pista de la Resistencia

Av. Martires del 1o de Mayo

Museo de la Revolición

Mercado Eduardo Contreras

Ricardo Huembes & bus station Casimir Sotelo

Av. Pedro A. Flores

Av. El Chipote

Hospital Manolo Morales

Plaza de Compras

Av. Eduardo Delgado

Av. Radial Santo Domingo

Av. Julio Buitrago Urroz

Av. El Guerrillero

Universidad Autónoma de Nicaragua (UNI)

Ave. De Las Naciones Unidas

Av. Gabrieal Cardenal

Pista Sub-Urbana

TO GRANADA AND MASAYA

Av. Colón

Mercado Oriental

Museo Nacional

Catedral, Palacio Nacional, Parque Central, Cinemateca and Plaza de la Revolución

Train Station

Teatro Rubén Darío

Telcor and Museo de Arte de las Américas

Dupla Norte

Av. Bolívar

Parque Luis Alfonso Velásquez

Hotel Intercontinental

Laguna de Tiscapa

Av. Casimiro Sotelo

Universidad Centroamericana (UCA)

Avenida UNAN

Plaza 19 de Julio

Pista de la Resistencia

Dupla Sur

Calle Julio Buitrago

BARRIO MARTHA QUEZADA

Av. Williams Romero

Plaza España

Stadium

Casino Pasapogo (Cine Dorado)

Paseo Salvador Allende

Pista Benjamin Zeledón

Av. German Gaitán

Calle El Triunfo

Calle Rafael Bermudez

Av. Mariano Sediles
Av. Roberto Ibarra

Mercado and Bus Station Israel Lewites

Av. Heroes de Batahola

Av. de las Milicias

35 ava. Avenida

Huellas de Acahualinca

Laguna de Acahualinca

Ferrocarril del Pacífico

TO LEON Cuesta de los Mártires

Migración (Immigration Office)

Parque Las Piedrecitas

Laguna de Asososca

Pista de la Resistencia

TO POCHOMIL Alternate route to León

Carretera Sur (Vía Panamerica)

N

arriba — east
abajo — west
al lago — north
al sur — south

1 mile

1 kilometer

NICARAGUA

■ Practical Information

Tourist Office: Ministerio de Turismo (tel. 22-66-52; fax 22-66-18), 1 block south and 1 block west of the Inter. Friendly, helpful staff who speak English. Office sells a bimonthly guide to Nicaragua called **Guía Fácil Nicaragua** (10C) and a cumbersome map left over from the 1994 World Amateur Baseball Championship (10C). The guide is packed with great information, including an exhaustive list of bookstores, libraries, galleries, and museums. It also lists restaurants by food-type, features calendar listings of local events, and has a full list of travel agencies and embassies. Open Mon.-Fri. 8am-12:30pm and 1:30-5pm. Airport office (tel. 33-12-97 or 33-16-24) open daily 9am-7pm.

Western Union: (tel. 66-81-26; fax 66-18-12). Head north from the Inter towards the military hospital, and take the right fork at the "Y" in the road. The office is 400m down the hill and around the bend on the right. Open Mon.-Fri. 8am-5pm, Sat. 8am-12:30pm.

Travel Agency: Senderos (tel. 68-18-93 or 68-18-94), 200m before Western Union on the left. Open Mon.-Fri. 8am-6pm, Sat. 8am-12pm. A number of other agencies, such as **Viajes America** (tel. 66-11-30 or 66-06-84), are located in the Plaza de España, the big complex southeast of the rotary.

Embassies: U.S. (tel. 68-21-49, 68-21-48, 68-21-76, or 68-21-77), 4.5km down Carreterra Sur., in Barrio Botahola Norte, southwest of Barrio Marta Quezada. Open Mon.-Fri. 9am-1pm. **Canada** (tel. 28-75-74; fax 28-48-21). Travelers should be advised that Canada's official presence in Managua is limited to an honorary consul. All ambassadorial functions are handled through the Canadian embassy in Costa Rica 336, and even some typical consular services may not be available. Open Mon.-Thurs. 9am-noon. **U.K.** (tel. 78-00-14 or 78-08-87; fax 78-40-85), on Reparto Los Robles, south of Av. Rubén Darío. Open Mon.-Fri. 9am-noon. **Honduras,** Planes de Altamira #64 (tel. 79-82-31; fax 79-82-28). Open Mon.-Fri. 8:30am-1:30pm. **Guatemala** (tel. 79-98-34; fax 79-96-10), 11.5km down Carreterra Masaya, south of town. Open Mon.-Fri. 9am-1pm. **Costa Rica** (tel. 68-14-79; fax 68-39-55), 3rd floor of the old IBM Building, in Barrio Batahola Norte. Open Mon.-Fri. 9am-3pm. A complete list of Embassies and Consulates can be found in the Guía Fácil (see **Tourist Office,** above).

Currency Exchange: With U.S. dollars, this is a cinch. Try the **Buro Internacional de Cambio** (tel. 66-32-96), 2 blocks south of Plaza de España on the east side of the street, next to Viajes America travel agency. They change other Central American currencies, U.S. dollars, and traveler's checks for a trifling US$2 charge. For more than US$100 in traveler's checks, they render half the amount in U.S. dollars and the other half in córdobas. For less than US$100, it's all córdobas. The Buro tends to "run out" of córdobas near the end of the day, so arrive early if possible. Open Mon.-Fri. 8:30am-4:45pm, Sat. 8:30am-noon. Another possibility in the Plaza de España is **Old Yeller Multicambios** (tel. 66-84-07), located 1 block west of the rotary. They change traveler's checks for about 3 centaurs less than their rate for dollars, which works out to be about 3% commission. Open Mon.-Fri. 8am-5pm, Sat. 8am-noon. When the *casas de cambio* are out of dollars and/or córdobas, try the big supermarkets (**La Colonia** in Plaza España, for example). They will exchange traveler's checks at the same rates.

City Buses: Cost just 1.20C, and once you get the hang of them, they are invaluable. Stops can range from bus shelters to vague plots of dirt—keep an eye on where people congregate. And ask; most know the system well enough to at least tell you if you're in the wrong place. The #119 is useful; its stops include the Mercado Roberto Huembes, Carreterra Masaya, Universidad Centroamericana, Plaza España, and Iglesia Lezcano. The #118 can be caught on Avenida Williams Roberto and serves the Mercados Ivan Montenegro, Israel Lewites, and the Red Cross. The #110 lumbers between 3 markets: Israel Lewites, Roberto Huembes, and Ivan Montenegro.

Regional Buses: At Mercado Roberto Huembes, buses leave from the west end of the market, beginning at about 5am and dwindling in frequency toward late afternoon. To: **Masaya** (direct every 30min., 3.5C; indirect every 10min., 3C); **Granada** (every 20min., 1½hr., 4C); **Rivas** (every 30min., 3hr., 10C); **Matagalpa** (every 30min., 3hr., 13C); and **Estelí** (every 30min., 3½hr., 13C). From Mercado Israel

Lago de Managua (Xolotlán)

Huellas de
Acahualinca

SAN SEBASTIAN

Calle el Triunfo

Teatro de
Rubén Darío

Bus Station

JUILIO
BUITRAGO

Dupla Norte

Ruinas de
la Catedral

SAN
ANTONIO

TELCOR
Office

Parque
Luis Alfonso
Velásquez

LOS
ANGELES

Calle 15 de Septiembre

JAVIER
CUADRA

Dupla Sur

19 DE JULIO

CIUDAD
JARDIN

Rincón
Español

BUENOS
AIRES

Calle Julio Buitrago

LAS
PALMAS

Avenida Julio Buitrago Urroz

MARTHA
QUEZADA

EL CARMEN

Bus Station

Hotel
Intercontinental

LARGA ESPADA

BOSQUES DE
BOLONIA

BOLONIA

Laguna
de Tiscapa

Calle Jose Marti

Pista Benjamin Zeledón

Plaza
España

SERRANO

ALTAGRACIA

JONATHAN
GONZALEZ

JORGE
DIMITROV

EL RECREO

14 DE
JUNIO

Ministerio
de Cultura

Plaza 19
de Julio

RENE CISNEROS

TISCAPA

PANCASAN

Pista de la Resistencia

ALTAMIRA

SAN JUAN

Bus Station

CASIMIRO
SOTELO

LOS
ROBLES

Pista Sub-Urbana

MIGUEL
BONILLA

Boulevar de los Martires

VILLA PANAMA

NICARAGUA

Managua
Center

✈ Airports

⊞ Hospitals

ⓘ Tourist information

'al lago'
(north: toward the lake)

'abajo' ←→ 'arriba'
(west)   (east)

'al sur' (south)

Lewites, buses leave from the base of the hill to: **Chinandega** (every 30min. start-ing at 5:30am, 3hr., 17C); **León**, express, (every 30min. starting at 5:30am, 2½hr., 13C); **Jinotepe** (every 30min. starting at 5:30am, 1½hr., 5C); and **Pochomil** (every 30min. starting at 6am, 2hr., 10C). From Mercado Ivan Montenegro, to **Tititapa** (every 10min., 3C) and **Rama** (every hr., 4am to early afternoon, 6C).

Taxis: Taxis are all over Managua and can deliver you just about anywhere in the city at a fair fare. There's no problem flagging them down, either, since they honk at all *gringos* to inform them of the option. A crosstown ride should *never* cost more than 15C; to the airport costs more. Taxis will often ask a higher-than-average rate or else claim not to have change for their *gringo* fares, so be sure to agree on a price before entering and have some smaller denominations of córdobas on hand.

Car Rental: Hertz (tel. 22-35-30 or 22-23-36; ask for Hertz) and **Budget** (tel. 22-35-30; ask for Budget) offices dwell in the lobby of Hotel Intercontinental (tel. 22-23-30). Budget rentals start at US$19 per day for age 25 and up. Add US$9 for ages 21-25. Hertz rentals start at US$25 for ages 23 and up. Budget is open daily 7am-6pm. Hertz is open daily 7am-8pm. Insurance is optional and both companies charge an extra fee.

Bicycle Rental: Casa Shannon y Candy (tel./fax 89-11-71), at the traffic light on Av. Rubenia, 200m southwest and 1km east of Mercado Roberto Huembes. Sells, repairs, and also rents quality bikes for 15C per day. This can be a fun way to get around Managua, but is also something of a headache. Open Mon.-Sat. 9am-5pm.

Supermarket: La Colonia (tel. 66-13-58, 66-70-67), in the Plaza España, above the roundabout. Open Mon.-Sat. 8am-8pm. Huge, U.S.-style supermarket with 15 aisles. Your headquarters for bottled water (8C). Complete pharmacy and good-sized book section, including English spy novels and Shakespeare-in-Spanish ("to be or not to be, that is *la pregunta*"). A/C makes every shopping experience that much more enjoyable.

Red Cross: (central tel. 65-20-83, 65-20-84, 65-11-97 or 65-17-61), in Belmonte. 24-hr. ambulance service.

Pharmacies: Super Farmacia Xolotlán (tel. 65-55-55), 3 blocks south (uphill) of the Inter, on Av. Bolívar. Open Mon.-Fri. 8am-7pm, Sat. 8am-1pm. There is also a pharmacy located in La Colonia supermarket in the Plaza España (see **Supermarket,** above). **Farmacia Magavi** (tel. 22-29-80) is 1 block south and ½ block east of the casino in Barrio Marta Quezada. Open Mon.-Sat. 8am-5pm.

AMNLAE: Casa Nora Astorga (tel. 78-56-64), 2½ blocks south of the Entrada Prin-cipal San Juan, #582. Provides medical services and counseling to women. (See **Nicaragua: Safety,** p.258.)

Hospital: Hospital Manolo Morales (tel. 78-30-90 or 78-31-12), near the intersec-tion of Pista de la Solidaridad and Av. Martires del Mayo.

Police: (tel. 77-41-30) at the Plaza Del Sol.

Post Office: Each **ENITEL/TELCOR** office keeps its own hours, but the big ENI-TEL/TELCOR in the old downtown area is usually your best bet. Look for the big-gest, baddest antenna in town, easily spotted from the Inter. It stands in the north end of the city, just west of the Old Cathedral and the Palacio Nacional. Don't fret if weekend rent-a-cops want to frisk your day pack. **Postal services** (tel. 22-41-94) available Mon.-Fri. 8am-noon and 2-5pm, Sat. 8am-noon. **DHL** (tel. 28-40-81, 28-40-85), 1 block north of the Inter, and **Trans-Express,** 1 block west and 1½ blocks south of the Inter, both ship to Miami; from there, your package will presumably travel though the U.S. postal service.

Telephone services: Local and long distance service at ENITEL/TELCOR office is available daily from 7am-10:30pm. **Information:** tel. 112.

Telephone code: 02.

■ Accommodations

All the hotels and *hospedajes* listed below are in the Barrio Marta Quezada, an amia-ble neighborhood comprised of comfortable homes, bohemian lodgings, and the occasional wandering pig. The *barrio* lies about 8 blocks north of the Plaza España, between the Hotel Intercontinental to the east and the stadium to the northwest. Walking from the barrio to most points of interest in Managua is not too difficult, but be sure to bring plenty of water and to memorize a few key landmarks near your *hospedaje* of choice. Many streets in Marta Quezada look the same to the untrained eye, and if you don't count *cuadras*, you might not be able to find your cozy *cama*.

Guest House Santos (tel. 22-37-13), 1 block west of Hospedaje Quintana, near Av. Williams Romero and Calle 27 de Mayo. No awards for architectural design, but it's a favorite with the budget travelers and Peace Corps volunteers who congregate in the spacious covered courtyard. The Big Bad Wolf could knock down the cardboard walls with a sigh, but the standard-issue padlocks may help compensate for the lack of security. Spartan rooms, all with baths, are rendered habitable by a fleet of gasping fans. Singles and doubles 30C per person; triples 90C total.

Hospedaje El Dorado (tel. 22-60-12), ½ block east of Casino Pasapogo (or "Cine Dorado"). *Hospedaje* or top-secret NASA bunker? The gates and long hallways that guard El Dorado's innards would seem to indicate the latter. However, a large number of cozy rooms huddle around an intimate patio and shared baths. All rooms have fans, and bathrooms are clean with toilet paper but no seats. A cautious and friendly couple runs the place. 35C per person.

Hospedaje Quintana, 1 block north and 1½ blocks east of the Casino Pasapogo. Rows of simple, spotless rooms adjoin a bright red main hallway. Guests may command a broad vista of neighborhood activity from the elevated porch. The communal bathroom has a shower with towels, but no hot water. Finding a toilet with a seat is a crapshoot. Stay cool with cold drinks and big fans. Again, padlock security. 40C per person.

Hospedaje Meza (tel. 22-20-46), 1 block north, 2½ blocks east of the Casino. Same street as Santos and Quintana. The entryway houses a wash basin and a car. Expect access to the former. Simple, sometimes cramped rooms have walls that don't reach the ceiling, giving the rooms a spacious, airy feel, but making every wheezy snore, tummy-grumble, and sleep-babble from next door clearly audible. Two hammocks hang on the 2nd—but then again, your bed may already be bowed under enough for your back. 35C per person for room with tiny communal bathrooms, 50C for the same size with a private bath.

■ Food

Good food is easy to find in Managua; there's no reason to leave the city with *gallo pinto* spilling out of your ears. Perhaps Managua's greatest culinary asset is its abundance of *fritangas*, sidewalk *comedores* who offer a traditional deep-fried buffet. You point to it, they throw it into a pan of boiling oil (be careful what you point to). This is Nicaraguan *dim sum*. Plantains and cheese go especially well together. Listings below are all in Marta Quezada, but don't be bashful—the whole city is crawling with fruit vendors and children hawking *caramelos* and *frescos* (candy and sweet water).

Comedor Sara, 1 door east of the Tica bus station. Even when the lights go out and there's no electricity in Marta Quezada, Sara keeps going. Though she admits to catering to an almost strictly *gringo* clientele, Sara's curry is nothing to scoff at. The Curry Bombay (35C) will clear your sinuses as you sip beer or a banana shake (6C). Vegetarians can dine without having to face down another plate of beans and rice. Open daily 10am-10pm.

Mirna's Pancakes (tel. 22-79-13), 1 block east and 1 block south of Casino Pasapogo. The best damn flapjacks in Managua, though the syrup pleases only the wasps (10C). Mirna also serves up a rockin' *comida corriente* of eggs, potatoes, rice, and beans. Or try the *pollo con arroz y frijoles* (13C). Eggs, juice, and coffee (14C). Open daily 7am-3pm.

Comedor Doña Pilar, right next to Delicias del Mar in Barrio Marta Quezada (no sign). This joint rules; a *comedor* as authentic as they get. Doña Pilar herself takes the raw material down from the hooks and cooks it up before your very eyes, an art she's perfected over the course of 19 years. *Carne asada*, chicken, potatoes, *plátanos, enchiladas*, and more, priced to sell. A typical meal of meat, tortillas, and

NICARAGUA

plátanos goes for about 18C. Open Mon.-Sat., regular dining hours (informally—it is their home, after all).

Delicias del Mar (tel. 22-21-04), 1 block east and ½ block north of Casino Pasapogo. Doña Gladys Perez serves seafood from both coasts, including fried red snapper and *sopa de camarones* (shrimp soup). Colorful comestibles and delightful decor. Convenient to the lodger in Barrio Marta Quezada. Mountainous portions will leave you happy, but *won't* leave you hankering for more. "Sailor's Rice" (30C) is a lot like *paella*. Fish filet 35C. Shrimp, breaded or with garlic, 60C. Open daily 11:30am-midnight.

El Khalifa (tel. 67-00-15), located on the Carreterra Masaya in the same building as the King's Royal Palace Hotel. This stand provides a nice alternative for vegetarians sick of beans, rice, and cheese; try falafel, baba ghanoush, or hummus as dishes or in sandwiches. Sandwiches are about 15C and dinners about 30C. Open daily noon-midnight.

Tonalli (tel. 22-43-41), 5 blocks east and ½ block north of Casino Pasapogo in the heart of Marta Quezada. An awesome collectivist bakery run by Nicaraguan women, with a one-table *cafetín* to boot. Black bread, whole wheat bread, sweet rolls, granola, yogurt, natural pastas. Open Mon.-Fri. 8am-5:30pm, Sat. 8am-3pm.

Tacos, 1 block south of Casino Pasapogo. Munch on Nicaraguan you-know-whats under the watchful gaze of Fidel Castro and Che Guevarra, who hang silently on the wall. Chicken tacos (12C) or cheese ones (10C)—wash 'em down with one of the *refrescos naturales* made of pulped carrot, mango, papaya, or other exotic fruits (3C—same as a Coke, but these are bigger and tastier and great to drink with tacos). Open Mon.-Fri. 9am-3pm and 5:30-8pm, Sat.-Sun. 4-8pm.

■ Sights and Entertainment

While Managua still doesn't offer anything near the amount of amusement expected in a large capital city, a bold decision has at least consolidated its cultural destinations in the handsomely refurbished **Palacio Nacional** (fronting the south side of the **Plaza de la Revolución**). The Palacio has seen both Somozas and Sandinistas ruling from its halls; now it displays a conglomeration of formerly far-flung collections. **Las Huellas de Acahualinca** displays the 6000-year-old, lava-preserved footprints that were left by ancient inhabitants of the city as they fled a volcanic eruption. Other exhibits include an assortment of the bizarre and beautiful creatures that inhabit Nicaragua's wilderness, including an impressive collection of stuffed agoutis and *perezosas* (sloths). The museum also has a number of archaeological artifacts from all over Nicaragua, some dating as far back as AD 400 (open Mon.-Fri. 8am-4pm; admission 10C). Nicaraguan art from the last two centuries hangs in a quiet gallery, while the **National Library, National Archives,** and various collections of Nica authors (including Darío) fill the rooms on the second floor. Dine in the rooftop cafeteria, wonder at the two main entrance murals, and purchase artesanial crafts (20C). Unfortunately, three reputedly amazing museums have been closed, political victims of budget cutbacks: **El Museo de la Revolución, El Museo de Alfabetazzación** (documenting the extraordinary 1980 Sandinsta literary campaign), and the **Julio Cortázar Museo de Arte Contemporanza** (whose holdings included over 1000 works from all over Latin America). Rumors say that these great museums will eventually reopen, but their doors have been shut for more than two years.

The **Plaza de la Revolución** is arranged around the tomb of Sandinista leader Carlos Fonseca and a monument to Nicaraguan modernist poet Rubén Darío, the "Prince of Spanish-American Literature." Next door stands the recently erected **Centro Cultural Managua** (tel. 28-40-45; fax 28-40-46). It houses various art workshops and galleries, and hosts events of all kinds throughout the year, from plays and dance shows to music concerts and art exhibitions. The Centro also hosts an artesan fair the first Saturday of each month. The upstairs is composed mainly of administrative offices (including the main office of the **Guía Fácil**), and its corridors are lined with photographs of the pre-quake downtown area. Call or drop by to pick up a calendar of local events (open daily 8am-5pm).

In the northwest corner of this same complex is the **Cinemateca Nacional.** While the government couldn't maintain the 1200-person theater (now an evangelical church abutting Dupla Norte), the smaller theater rotates Nicaraguan and international movies, as well as American "art" films (Evita? Beauty and the Beast?). Films are shown around 5 and 7:30pm on weeknights, with an additional matinee Sat.-Sun. around 3pm. Admission is 20C.

On the east side of the plaza, next to the Palacio Nacional, stands the ruined **Catedral Santo Domingo,** a vision of elegance in repose. An acrylic roof, potted palms, and nesting birds combine to give a mystical aura to what could be a depressing site. Recorded chants echo the halls starting in the late afternoon, followed by light displays at dusk (5C). Also on the Plaza, near the lake, is the big and boxy **Teatro Rubén Darío,** which also houses the **Teatro Experimental.** Upon opening, the *New York Times* hailed the theater as the best in Latin America (perhaps they were biased—the same architects designed the Met). Recent air-conditioning additions keep you from having to yell "Fire!" in a crowded theater. Both theaters have good programs; check the schedule of events posted by the ticket booth closest to the lake.

A slow stroll down Bolívar is the best way to see Managua's sights. A string of dilapidated parks follow each other on the west side of the street. Walking north (downhill) from the Inter, you'll pass a rainbow-striped wall which leads to the **Arboratoreo Nacional,** the only place where you'll find 200 Nicaraguan trees labelled in one small park. Even if you're not a tree hugger, the arboretum is the site of the coolest drinking fountain in the city. Take a walk and a sip. From the assembly, you can see a lighthouse structure about two blocks east on Dupla Norte—the light shines on a big pool which is part of the new **Parque de Paz.**

Managua's *mercados* are a must-see. **Mercado Roberto Huembes,** east of the universities, is an enormous mega-market where you can find just about anything you're looking for and a whole lot more, from a Masayan hammock to a skinned pig's head. They also carve coiffures here, in any of the numerous "beauty salons." **Mercado Israel Lewites** offers a notable array of sizzling *comedores.* **Mercado Oriental,** a sprawling labyrinth of shops and vendors, has some good wooden products but seems somewhat sordid. It is said that at the height of the U.S. embargo, it was possible to waltz in here and buy a new Mercedes-Benz, if you had the proper billfold. **Mercado Ivan Montenegro** is notable primarily for its buses to Rama.

Managua has a few **discos.** The most accessible from Marta Quezada is the thatched hut **Cat's Club** (tel. 22-32-32) on the Calle 27 de Mayo. Live weekend music requires a minimum drink order (60C per person), but you can't beat the location (open Mon.-Sat. 5pm-dawn). **Lobo Jack** (tel. 67-01-23), near the intersection of Pista Portezuelo and Carreterra Masaya, is said to be the biggest disco in Central America (cover 30C for men, with expensive drinks; open Wed.-Sun. 8pm-4am). **Mansion Reggae** (tel. 94-8-04), 6km down Carreterra Norte, plays West Indian music from the Atlantic coast.

There are quite a few **pool halls** in Managua and some are pretty tough. If you do decide to try your hand at billiards in Managua, be either really good or really bad—these guys don't want their free time wasted. Try **Mr. Pool,** ½ block south of the Casino in Barrio Marta Quezada, if you want to rack your balls nearby (closed Sun.). Unlike its *fútbol*-crazed neighbors, Nicaragua's national sport is baseball (see **Diamonds in the Rough,** p. 294). Between October and April you can join the fun by going to the stadium in Marta Quezada to watch a game—the Nicos *really* get into it. Championship games take place in early June. Don't worry if you hear the neighborhood cheer and then hear a bunch of loud bangs. It's probably not the start of another civil war, but rather, a home team victory.

▓ Near Managua

XILOA

Xiloa (heel-WA or eel-WA) is about 10km west of Managua. A volcanic lake with a lush backdrop of mountains, Xiloa has developed rapidly; picnic tables and *refresco* stands line its shore. The lake is clean and popular with families. Lake facilities cost 2C if you're walking and 10C if you're in a car. During *Semana Santa*, buses run frequently from Mercado Israel Lewites to the *centro turístico* at Xiloa. These buses also run on the weekends, though less frequently. At all other times—when the lake will probably be yours for the swimming—your best bet is to catch one of the buses plying the *carretera* to León and ask to be let out at the *entrada principal a Xiloa* (3C). Most of these buses leave from Israel Lewites bound for Mateare, Nagorote, and León. Alternatively, take city bus #113 (1.25C) to Sandino and grab a *camioneta* from there. Once in Xiloa, people wait at the *entrada,* usually in groups, across from the 24-hour Texaco, until they thumb down a pick-up truck. Xiloa is five minutes up the road. Caution should be exercised, especially by women and solo travelers. As always, *Let's Go* does not recommend hitchhiking. Perhaps the safest, easiest option is to request that the León- or Nagorote-bound bus drop you off on the highway where a *camioneta* leaves every hour, serving the lake and surrounding villages (5C). Another option is to hoof the 5km yourself, which pays off with a breathtaking tour of the native terrain. To return, walk back to the *carretera* and catch a Managua-bound bus. Rooms at the **Hotel Xiloa** are pricey (about 150C), but air-conditioned.

NEARBY BEACHES

Pochomil, Masachapa, and **Montelimar** are three adjacent beaches on the Pacific Coast about 60km from Managua. Splashing, not sunning or swimming, is *de rigeur*—many Nicas wear t-shirts and even full outfits as they frolic on the beach. The bus to Pochomil (7.5C) leaves every 45 minutes from Mercado Israel Lewites and services all three beaches; sometimes (inexplicably) they only go to Masachapa, which isn't a problem since the beaches are just a short hike from each other. If you're taking a bus, plan ahead, as it takes two hours to climb up into the mountains and cruise down across the coastal plain on the other side. On the ascent through southeast Managua, you can admire the coffee plantations that line the highway. Watch for large, stately trees shadowing a dense undergrowth of shrubby bushes; these are the coffee plants. On the coastal plain, the bus passes through large fields of sugar cane.

Once arrived, it's easy to visit all three beaches, since it's only about a 30 minute stroll from southernmost Pochomil, north (facing the ocean, to the right) to either of the other two. Small cowboys will ride up on horseback as you comb the shore, offering a 30 minute ride for 10C—the horses are barely a hoof up from the haggard nags hauling hack-carts in most Nicaraguan hamlets. From Pochomil, head past the lazy fishing village of Masachapa to the relaxed resort of Montelimar. (Note that at high tide, the inlets at Masachapa fill and are impossible to cross except on the road.)

The beach at Pochomil is lined with cookie-cutter restaurants and a few places to stay. Accommodations include the **Villa del Mar,** a school for hotel management which doubles as a hostel (tel. 08-82-43-38; all rooms have A/C; 276C). The waves at Pochomil get gargantuan, so it is advisable not to venture too far out.

In Masachapa, just around the bend in the coast, the waves are much milder; consequently, fishermen decided to settle here. The row of fishing boats along the beach puts the final touch on this pretty little postcard of a town. Lodgings in Masachapa are rustic. The only hotel on the beach is the **Hotel Summer,** which pawns off little rooms at 100C a pop (fans, but no toilet paper). Cheaper lodging can be found in the town itself with a trio of *hospedajes* offering dank quarters (20-30C). At pristine **Montelimar,** however, affordable accommodations are completely out of the question; look, but don't touch (US$100 and up up up).

WEST OF MANAGUA

■ León

León is the second most populous city in Nicaragua, the largest Central American country, yet it seems to be stuck in time. As the din from 19 churches' bells heralds the rising sun, and as eager plants and blooming flowers raise their thirsty heads from the town's many courtyards, it's not hard to picture life before electricity, when a courtyard fire was the only way to illuminate a house. Meanwhile, mangy horses still pull cars full of produce and human passengers through the streets. With each hour, the town feels more and more like a big, baking adobe oven, and the voices of school-children echo over high earthen walls through the rippling, melting air.

Considering its many incarnations, it's no wonder that León has had a hard time placing itself in history. The first León, now known as León Viejo (see below), was founded on the shore of Lake Xolotlán in 1524 by Hernández de Córdoba. After this city was destroyed by an earthquake in 1610, León was rebuilt 30km to the west. Though poorer than Granada, the new León soon became a cultural and intellectual stronghold and was the capital of Nicaragua for over 300 years. The heady atmo-sphere fueled the imagination of its favorite son Rubén Darío, born in 1867, whose poetry launched the modernist movement in Latin America.

Through it all, one trait has persisted; as the bumper stickers still proclaim, León is *"orgullosamente liberal"* ("liberal and proud of it"). Calling León Nicaragua's most liberal metropolis is a little like calling the Vatican Italy's most Catholic city. Leftist León has a tradition of incessantly squabbling with conservative Granada, and along with Estelí, León was one of only two cities carried by the FSLN in the elections of 1990. The Universidad Nacional Autónoma de Nicaragua (UNAN), founded in 1812 as the country's first university, sharpens León's politics to a radical edge. Students roam the city from March to December, painting the town red (and black—the Sand-inista colors) with some of Nicaragua's best murals and graffiti. The churches are also worth seeing; a few were refurbished as part of a nationwide government project.

ORIENTATION

If you've spent any time in Managua, León is a navigational cakewalk. The **bus termi-nal** lies just east of town, three long blocks past the train tracks. Express buses from Managua, however, sometimes stop at a gas station a few blocks southeast of the ter-minal, or even in the **Mercado Central,** just east of the cathedral. Either way, you can walk to the center of town (often a hot and dusty trek, but very manageable), or take a taxi for 3-5C. Beware of taxi fares during thunderstorms; they can double without warning. Another of León's markets is on the eastern edge of town, five blocks north and four blocks east of the cathedral, behind the **Iglesia de San Juan** and its adjacent park. León's center is the **Parque Central (Parque Jerez,** officially). In the middle of the newly remounted plaza, atop a fountain guarded by four *leones* (lions), stands an amusingly diminutive statue of General Jerez, a 19th-century liberal political figure.

Brace for good news: León's streets are named! Streets running east to west are *calles;* **Calle Central Rubén Darío** fronts the north side of the park. From here, num-bered streets ascend north (1a Calle Norte, 2a Calle Norte, etc.) and south. Streets running north to south are *avenidas.* (**Avenida Central** would run right between the park and the cathedral, except that the avenida is discontinued for a block at this point.) This naming won't help all that much, though; most Leones, when asked for directions, stick to the standard Nicaraguan method of starting from major buildings. Some useful landmarks are **La Iglesia de la Recolección,** two blocks north of the cathedral's northeast corner; **Esquina de los Bancos** ("corner of the banks," or finan-cial district), one block south of that; and **Iglesia de la Merced,** one block north of the northeast corner of the park.

PRACTICAL INFORMATION

Tourist Office: Inturismo (tel. 36-82), 2½ blocks north of Parque Rubén Darío on 2 Av. Poniente. Look for the red awning with funkily fonted "turismo" above it. Not much here, but they're helpful in answering questions. They have a *Guía Turística* in a binder—you can't take it with you, but it gives the scoop on local museums, buildings, and even resident artists. A handy local guide (including a less-than-handy map) distributed (free!). Open Mon.-Fri. 8am-2:30pm and 2-5:30pm.

Budget Travel: Viajes Mundiales (tel. 59-20 or 69-20), 3 blocks north of the park on Av. Central, then ½ block east. Open Mon.-Fri. 8am-5:30pm, Sat. 8am-12:30pm.

Currency: No place in town changes traveler's checks—you'll have to go to Chinandega. **BANIC** (tel. 50-51), across the street from La Iglesia de la Recolección exchanges cash Mon.-Fri. 8:30am-12:30pm and 1:30-4pm, Sat. 8:30am-noon. **Banpro** (tel. 34-45), on the Esquina de los Bancos, also exchanges cash Mon.-Fri. 8:30am-4pm, Sat. 8:30-11:45am. Also try the *coyotes* (easily found on the Esquina de los Bancos) and the supermarkets.

Western Union: (tel. 24-26), 100m east of Esquina de los Bancos. Open Mon.-Fri. 8:30am-noon and 2-5pm, Sat. 8am-noon.

Buses: Bus terminal located 3 blocks east of the railroad tracks on the main street, 50m north of Hotel Avenida (Calle 6). To: **Managua** (every 20min., 4:30am-6pm, 2hr., 9C; express microbuses 1¼hr., 15C); **Estelí** (5:30am and 3pm, 3hr., 15C); **Matagalpa** (4:30am and 2:45pm, 3hr., 14C); **San Isidro** (every 30min., 4:30am-5pm, 2½hr., 12C); **Chinandega** (every 15min., 4:30am-6pm, 1hr., 7C); and **La Paz Centro** (every 50min., 6am-5:40pm, 50min., 5C). More buses to Estelí, Matagalpa, Managua, and Chinandega run from San Isidro.

City Buses: A few *rutas* ply León's streets. There is a particularly useful east to west bus (Rte. 101) that runs between El Terminal de Buses (bus stop) and El Mercadito, west of town, where buses depart for the beach (see Near León, p. 287). These are either rather well-maintained buses or *camionetas* (little pickup trucks with benches in the back), and usually cost one córdoba.

Supermarket: La Unión (tel. 32-90), in Plaza Metropolitana, 25m east of the Esquina de los Bancos. Violates the cardinal rule of grocery stores: never put soaps next to produce! Air-conditioning makes up for this transgression. Open Mon.-Fri. 8am-8pm, Sun. 8am-6pm.

Library: Biblioteca Popular Maria Eugenia de Jesús, above the Colegio La Asunción on the south of the park. A soothing place to work or read if you don't mind the noise of the schoolchildren below. The windows offer a rare view of León from on high. An exorbitant 1C charge for using their books. Open Mon.-Fri. 8am-noon and 1:30-5:30pm.

Pharmacy: Farmacia Meg-24 (tel. 23-69), across from the fire station, ½ block north of the northwest corner of the cathedral. Open daily 7:30am-11pm.

AMNLAE: Casa de Mujeres Martha Reyes (tel. 45-25), 2 blocks west and ½ block south of the Estatua de la Madre (Statue of the Mother). Offices include a clinic, a classroom, legal services, and a library on women's health and issues. Open Mon.-Fri. 8am-noon and 2:30-4:30pm.

Hopsital: Hospital Escuela Oscar Danilo Rosales (tel. 23-01), from the cathedral, 1 block south, big greyish yellow building.

Police: (tel. 31-37), on Carretera Chinandega.

Post office: At ENITEL/TELCOR. Open Mon.-Sat. 7am-7pm.

Telephones: ENITEL/TELCOR (tel. 33-30, 54-24, 44-44, 60-88 or 49-44; fax 57-00 or 21-02), on the west side of the Parque Central. Open Mon.-Fri. 7am-11pm, Sat. 7am-11pm, Sun. 7am-8:30pm. **Telegrams** and **faxes** at ENITEL/TELCOR, daily 8am-noon and 2-5pm.

Telephone code: 311.

ACCOMMODATIONS

Hospedajes don't exist in León, though *boteles* vary from old colonial lodgings near the center of town to less luxurious and cheaper places a small hike away. Prices usually shrink as the distance from the cathedral grows. The hotels listed below are at varying distances to the north and east of town.

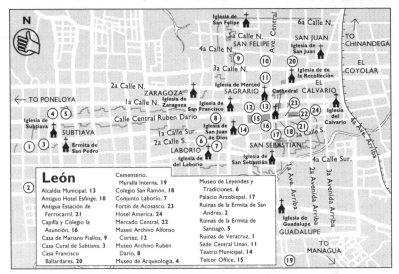

León

Alcaldía Municipal, 13
Antiguo Hotel Esfinge, 10
Antigua Estación de
Ferrocarril, 21
Capilla y Colegio la
Asunción, 16
Casa de Mariano Fiallos, 9
Casa Cural de Subtiava, 3
Casa Francisco
Ballardares, 20

Cementerio,
Muralla Interna, 19
Colegio San Ramón, 18
Conjunto Laborío, 7
Fortín de Acosasco, 23
Hotel America, 24
Mercado Central, 22
Museo Archivo Alfonso
Cortez, 12
Museo Archivo Rubén
Darío, 8
Museo de Arqueología, 4

Museo de Leyendes y
Tradiciones, 6
Palacio Arzobispal, 17
Ruinas de la Ermita de San
Andres, 2
Ruinas de la Ermita de
Santiago, 5
Ruinas de Veracruz, 1
Sede Central Unan, 11
Teatro Municipal, 14
Telcor Office, 15

Hotel Avenida (tel. 20-68), ½ block south of the road that leads east to the bus station (across from the Esso gas station). A gem. Mattresses thick enough to cushion a tender princess against the wooden slats below. Rooms and bathrooms are well-scrubbed and equipped with fans, though not always well-ventilated. Self-service laundry, solid locks, cable TV, and a *comedor*. Just one drawback: the pet parakeet imitates his rooster cousins at dawn. Singles 35C, with bath 45C; doubles with bath 70C; triples with bath 100C.

Hotelito California (tel. 50-74), welcomes you across the east end of the market/bus station. No ceiling mirrors or tiny bottles of pink champagne, but this small family establishment is a find nonetheless. Clean room with a lock and private bathroom for just 30C per person; room fans blow cool wind through your hair. Rooms are far enough away from the street to remain tranquil. Check in any time you like.

Hotel Colonial (tel. 22-79; fax 31-25), in the middle of León, 2½ blocks north of the northwest corner of the park. Anyone can play domineering colonist in this fixed-up mansion—just lounge in your rocking chair by the courtyard and stare contentedly at the 5m high ceilings above. Tidy rooms with fans upstairs. Both bedrooms and bathrooms are segregated by sex; however, couples can choose to be roomed in either section. Also has a restaurant and color TV. Singles 100C; doubles 150C, with A/C 250C. MC and Visa accepted.

Hotel America (tel. 55-33), 3 blocks east, ½ block south of El Sesteo Café in the park. With its verdant courtyard and stately lobby, this polite hotel brightens the heart of León. Large, comfortable rooms, can be slightly overpriced (50C). Private bathroom with toilet (paper provided).

Hotel Telica (tel. 50-53), by the railroad tracks, 2½ blocks north of the street leading to the bus terminal (6 Calle). Simple, sometimes gloomy rooms may depress, but the price is sure to please. Communal showers need a good cleaning and the toilet has no seat. All rooms have fans. Singles or doubles without bath 30C; singles or doubles with bath 45C.

FOOD

Like any self-respecting university town, León has its fair share of artsy cafes, *chi-chi* restaurants, and pizza joints. Better, though, to head to the evening **street buffet** one-and-a-half blocks east of the southeast corner of the cathedral. Sample huge portions of rice, chicken with potatoes in tomato sauce, *enchiladas,* salad, or fried potato cakes, all served on banana leaves—carry the food away with you for just 15-20C.

Casa Vieja, across from the west side of the Casa de Cultura (see **Sights,** below), 2 blocks west and 2 blocks north of the Parque Central. For once, a restaurant that feels like a restaurant—no fluorescent signs or lights, just inexpensive meals served with flair. You'll savor the typical Nica food at nearly the same prices you'll find on the street, but with tablecloths, stuccoed walls, and mellow music to boot. Polish off your meal (usually 12-14C) with a fruit milkshake (6C). Open daily 5-10pm.

Cafetín Intimo (tel. 21-18), in the Casa de la Cultura. A cozy joint that draws together a warm and friendly crowd. Upstairs is the treat—sip your beer (5C) or *refresco* (just 2C) while overlooking a field and the **Iglesia San Francisco.** Art exhibits, a fountain, and a courtyard add a chic touch. *Comida corriente* 9C (lunch only). Open Mon.-Sat. 10am-11pm, Sun. 5-10pm.

Restaurant Las Ruinas (tel. 47-67), on Calle Central Rubén Darío, 1 block west of the Parque Central. Tweaking the nose of a major superpower, the restaurant was called "Las Ruinas de Bagdad 17/12/90." This large Baühaus serves fish fillet (30C), filet mignon (40C), and half a chicken in wine sauce (35C). Open Mon.-Wed. 8am-10pm, Thurs.-Sun. 8am-2am. Free live music Suns.

El Sesteo Café (tel. 53-27), a small sidewalk cafe right in the middle of León, on the Parque Central's north side. Great place to come any time of day to eat, drink, and watch the park's passersby. Serves lunch and dinner at prices considerably higher than average due to its prime location. Open daily 10am-midnight.

SIGHTS

The **Museo Archivo Rubén Darío** (tel. 23-88), on Calle Central Rubén Darío, two blocks west of Parque Rubén Darío, is a shrine to the country's favorite poet. One of the creepier exhibits includes photographs of him on his death-bed (entitled "Rubén Darío in Agony"). The museum also boasts a collection of his manuscripts, first editions, and a series of Darío caricatures by various political cartoonists of the day. With permission, you can read the books in the archive (open Mon.-Sat. 9am-noon and 2-5pm, Sun. 9am-noon; free admission).

Still hankering for more *poesía?* Walk two blocks up Calle Central Rubén Dario to the **Museo Archivo Alfonso Cortéz,** across the street from Parque R.D. (**Parque de las Poetas;** technically Darío rules them, but four other busts grace the walls.) Cortéz was another writer from León, who had his own agonies—note the heavy chains used to restrain him during his breakdown in the 50s. Like the poetry, the museum is in a different class from the Darío museum. (2C donation welcome, or purchase the monthly literary rag (10C). Open Mon.-Sat. 8am-noon, and 2-9pm, Sun. 2-10pm.)

The **Centro Popular de Cultura** (tel. 21-16) lies one block east and one and a half blocks north of the museum. This was once the plush home of a Somoza crony (you can tell by the abandoned swimming pool); when he fled the country, the Sandinistas turned the house into a community center rife with political art. So it goes. Check out the long display of two dozen posters that tell the life story of Sandino, from lowly laborer exploited by foreign interests to a celebrated leader of a revolutionary movement. The center offers classes in music, painting, woodworking, Spanish, and English. Ask about upcoming performances, presentations, and *noches festivos.* Alternatively, just stroll about, digging the artwork, the clack of typewriters, and the strains of radical folk music being played on the guitar; don't neglect the *cafetón* (see **Food,** above) which is open daily 9am-7pm.

León's municipal **cathedral,** on the Parque Central, is the largest in Central America. The mammoth, almost mosque-like structure intensifies the blinding afternoon sun. Rubén Darío is buried beside the altar, and the **Stations of the Cross** are quite famous. The cathedral has recently undergone a restoration, and the renovated interior is splendid. High, painted ceilings soar above a tremendous altar (open Fri.-Wed. 7am-noon and 4-7pm, Thurs. 7am-7pm). León has many other churches, and together they conspire to give the city a beatific feel. Nearly every one of them is worth a peek, especially **El Calvario, Iglesia de la Recolección,** and **La Merced.**

The **Mausaleo de Héroes y Mártires,** across from the northeast corner of the park, commemorates the victims of the *revolución.* A striking mural curves around the square, tracing the torturous path of Nicaraguan history. Set in a surrealistic desert landscape, the story is told in the form of objects strewn across the sandy floor—here a discarded coat of armor, there a crumbling statue covered with blood. It ends optimistically, though, with a pair of bright-eyed youths flying a kite into fields green and pastures new. Across the street, U.S. citizens shouldn't take Sandino's use of Uncle Sam's head as a footrest too personally. Also, check out the murals by the **basketball court,** half a block north of the northwest corner of the plaza—enjoy the expansive, pro-Sandinista works depicting socialists building schools and tearing down rightist regimes, despite the best intents of red, white, and blue C.I.A. serpents.

On the west end of town, the sprawling **Barrio Subtiava** contains a few points of interest, as well as the market from which buses leave for the nearby beach of **Poneloya.** The **Iglesia de Subtiava** is the oldest standing church in León and is famed across the land for its colonial altar. The oldest non-standing church in León, known as **Las Ruinas de Veracruz,** is also found in Subtiava. Originally built in the 16th century, Las Ruinas was thrashed asunder by a volcano in 1835. It's still fun to roam through the bits and pieces the volcano left behind. To get to Subtiava you can either walk about 10 blocks west of Parque Central, take a taxi, or get on any Route #101 bus. The church is one block south of Calle Rubén Darío and the ruins are two blocks west of the church, on the left. You have to enter a family's yard to get to the ruins, so ask their permission before crossing, lest you earn their dog's tornado-like wrath.

ENTERTAINMENT

The central park and market, as well as other nearby areas, are well-lit at night. Both are patrolled by *vigilantes* (watchmen, not what you think), hired by the *alcaldía* (mayoral district) to keep public areas safe at night—and it works. The Parque Central acts as a playground, a meeting spot for friends, and a scoping scene for randy youngsters on the prowl (especially on Sat. and Sun. nights). **El Túnel del Tiempo** (tel. 25-15) is a bar/restaurant/disco outside of town at the *salida a Chinandega* (the exit to Chinandega), in a big white building. The crowd is young and rather affluent. When in disco mode, the club charges a variable cover. **Restaurante Las Ruinas** (see **Food,** above) turns into a disco every night, and usually stages live acts on weekends. The cover is 10C, and the dance floor is cool, thanks to the club's open-air design. Students from the university often hold parties at the **Club Universitaria,** half a block east of La Iglesia de la Recolección. Look for these parties when UNAN is in session (March-Dec.); they're usually announced by raucous crowds of students circumnavigating the park in blaring pick-ups. The **basketball court** (see **Sights,** above) also serves as an informal nightlife center. Across the street is a pool hall, **Lezama,** where a game costs 2C (open daily 10am-11pm). Remember **El Alamo,** a bar that slouches behind the hoops. As in most of Latin America, the right dress for a night on the town is casual, but snazzy.

■ Near León

Two pleasant Pacific beaches, **Poneloya** and **Las Peñitas,** lie within easy reach of León, to its west and southwest. Expect crowds on hot *verano* weekends and during *Semana Santa;* otherwise, they should be relatively empty. Catch a bus to these beaches at El Mercadito, on the western outskirts of León. Bus #101 (1.25C) serves El Mercadito from the central market, the market behind San Juan church, and from the bus station. Otherwise, it is about a 15 minute walk down Calle Central Rubén Darío to the Subtiava area (see **Sights,** above). The ride to the coast (30min., 4C) carries you over the hilly farmland that separates León from the Pacific. As you crest each hill, keep your eyes open for a great view of the fields and the volcanos of San Cristóbal. Buses leave hourly from 4am to 7pm. The bus first stops in Poneloya, which is farther north, and then retreats to Las Peñitas.

The "beaches" are actually one long beach, parceled out by a big rocky outcropping called **La Peña del Tigre.** Houses are perched along La Peña's ridge, so walk around to get from one beach to the other. But before doing so, enjoy the vantage from these tiger-colored (hence the name) stones. Like most of the Pacific coast in

NICARAGUA

Nicaragua, the beach is steep and the waves are fierce; if you swim, be careful, and try to swim in the company of others, preferably locals. A walk along the beach offers safer rewards. A row of empty vacation houses (all apparently under construction or in decay, or both) are the beach's only decoration *per se;* nonetheless, watching the waves crash and the volcanic sands glitter is scenery enough. Walking far enough along the beach in either direction brings you to scattered inlets, which fill at high tide and empty with the ebb. Beyond these the beach is virtually deserted. If you don't feel Crusoe-like already, sit and have a cool drink at **Hotel Lacoyo** in Poneloya (1 block north of La Peña, front beach), where the open sitting area catches every nuance of the ocean breeze.

For a similarly untouristed geothermal outing, look no further than **Los Hervideros de San Jacinto,** a small field full of vigorously boiling pits of muddy water and holes spewing sulfuric steam, located 25km west of León on the road to San Isidro. Your clothes will absorb the pungent odor as a free memento. An underground stream supplies the water, heated personally by Beelzebub and his minions. To get there, take any bus bound for San Isidro and ask to be let off in **San Jacinto** (4C), where the *her-videros* (boiling springs) are. Follow the small road down the hill and take the first right. Go about five blocks until you see the archway on your left, inscribed "Los Her-videros." Locals may try to sell you artifacts they've gleaned from the area, but be wary of buying pieces of local sites; if everyone did, these spots would quickly disappear. A small hill beyond the boiling grounds proffers a good overview. Though one nearby geothermal plant has already failed, another is in the works. Through the arch sprawl the seething *hervideros,* as well as a precariously positioned baseball field. Once through, a cloud of eager *niños* materializes, each able to show you where to step safely, thereby sparing you the pain of being boiled alive.

LEÓN VIEJO

León Viejo (Old León) lies at the foot of **Volcán Momotombo,** northwest of the city, on the northeast side of Lago de Managua. Founded in 1524, León was the colonial capital of Nicaragua; in 1610, a volcano-induced earthquake destroyed the city. In the wake of the destruction, the city packed up its bags and moved 30km west, leaving its former self to be buried slowly by volcanic ash, and then rediscovered three centuries ago in 1697. León Viejo is now partially excavated, and along with the nearby **Museo Imabite,** promises to be a rewarding daytrip. Both the ruins and the *museo* are located in **Momotombo** (pop. 2000). The village is laid out on the dusty, black volcanic sands of the region, which roast your feet at high noon.

Start your day the Momotombo way with the museum—follow the slatted blue signs pointing toward the ruins. Little, yellow, different **Museo Imabite** offers the curious traveler finer inspection of regional relics. The entire collection fills only one room, but definitely merits a close look. The many pre-Columbian artifacts are fully and precisely inventoried by the museum's guides, who give you the option of perusing on your own, but begin to lecture you nonetheless. The museum also displays old muskets, other snappy odds and ends, and after a long museum visit, beer (5C). Both the ruins and the museum are open daily 8am-5pm. While the museum only asks for donations, the ruins require a 10C entrance fee (and bathrooms cost 1C a pop). A crew of trained Momotombo youth awaits to guide you through this historical site. A tour of the ruins begins at the foundations of the cathedral, where the city's founder, Hernández de Córdoba, was beheaded. Your visit will climax with an ascent to the old fort. This elevated grassy area is the perfect spot to gaze in awe at the volcanic panorama, including the red, black, blue, and green symmetry of Momotombo's cone (never mind the electric plant at its base). Or follow the main street of Momotombo to the edge of Lake Xolotlán (a trickier way to say *Lago de Nicaragua*), where you will find a *cabana* serving *cerveza*, a cool breeze off the water, and an orgasmic view. The ramshackle shambles of Nicaraguan nationalist José Santos Zelaya's Victorian house are visible from the lakeshore, as are the posts of the dock that all commercial traffic between Managua and León used to pass by. The dock disintegrated from disuse after the introduction of the railroad, leaving the town of Momotombo to sink gently into obscurity. Climbing Volcán Momotombo is permitted—before doing so, however, some guides have advised visitors to get permission from the Instituto Nicaragüense de Energía, especially if you will be driving a car.

To get to Momotombo and its plethora of exciting sights (both of them), you must first get to **La Paz Centro,** 56km from Managua and 31km from León (not León Viejo). Buses to La Paz Centro leave frequently from both cities, from León's station and from Managua's Mercado Israel Lewites (León to La Paz, 5C; Managua to La Paz, 6C; La Paz to Momotombo, 4C). Anticipate a rough ride on the La Paz-Momotombo segment of the trip—even by Nica standards, these buses are on their way to the big parking lot in the sky. Buses should run this segment every one and a half hours, but only until 3:30pm, so you'd better get an early start (especially from Managua). To get additional information, check with the locals who depend on the line's quirks. The Momotombo bus leaves you a few blocks from the museum, and about a five-minute walk (down the same road) from the ruins. To get to the lakeshore, walk straight in the direction that the bus was headed. If at any time you get lost, ask for directions; the *momotombitos* are usually more than happy to help out.

■ Chinandega

Chinandega is not appreciated around the country (or the world) for the admirable work ethic of its resident farmers, nor for the massive quantity of quality cotton nearby regions churn out each year, nor even for its blessed proximity to beautiful beaches and the towering **Volcán San Cristóbal,** Nicaragua's tallest at 1745m. No, what earns this town praise from León to London and from Managua to Moscow is the unspeakably smooth, bewilderingly rich, mind-bendingly delicious **Flor de Caña** rum, thousands of gallons of which are produced annually just outside the town limits. Remarkably, though, the smallish city has a life beyond the heavenly concoction. Chinandega is the capital of the department of the same name, Nicaragua's hot, dry, northernmost region, making it ideal for travelers bound for local outdoor sites or the Honduran border at Somotillo.

Orientation Buses arriving from León or Managua stop southwest of town at **mercado Bisne** (*Bisne* as in "Business"—this place was the center of Chinandega's black market during the years of the embargo). From here, the central park, (which lies a bit west of all the action), is six blocks north and eight blocks west. The walk is manageable, but if you can't take the heat, get out of the kitchen, and while you're at it, into a taxi (3C) or one of the *camionetas* that runs from Mercado Bisne to **mercado Central,** four blocks west of the Parque Central. **El Mercadito** lies one block north of the northeast corner of the Parque Central.

Practical Information Tours Viajes Sol (tel. 21-29 or 36-36; fax 36-89), two blocks east and half a block south of the southeast corner of the Parque Central (right next door to Hotel Cosigüina), is a useful travel agency. Find the **Western Union** office (tel. 27-95; open Mon.-Fri. 8am-1pm and 2-5pm, Sat. 8am-noon) one block north of Tours Viajes Sol. Chinandega has more banks than any other Nicaraguan city besides Managua; many change dollars, but only one changes traveler's checks. **BANCENTRO** (tel. 29-02) charges a 3% commission for traveler's checks; it is located two blocks east of the southeast corner of the Parque Central, on the bank corner (open Mon.-Fri. 8am-4:30pm, Sat. 8am-noon). **BANIC** (tel. 28-31) is one block farther east (open Mon.-Fri. 8:30am-12:30pm and 1:30-4pm, Sat. 8:30am-noon). *Coyotes* prowl the streets around the banks and markets, and some of them are willing to change checks. **Buses** depart from Mercado Bisne to: **León** (every 30min., 1¼hr., 7C); **Managua** (2hr., 18.5C); and the nearby port town of **Corinto** (45min., 5C). Buses for towns north of Chinandega (including **Somotillo** and the **Honduran border**), as well as taxis and *camionetas* to **El Rio Viejo,** leave from the Mercadito, one block north of the park. Spit and you'll hit a **pharmacy;** they abound in Chinandega. **San José** (tel. 27-61), 3½ blocks east of the southeast corner of the park, is open daily

7am-10pm. **Red Cross** (tel. 31-32 or 38-75) offers 24-hour ambulance service. **Hospital España** (tel. 22-53) lies on the Carretara los Millionarios. The **police** (tel. 34-56, emergency tel. 118) face the west side of the park. **Post office** at ENITEL/TELCOR offered Mon.-Fri. 7am-7pm, Sat. 7am-1pm. **Telephone** services are offered daily from 7am-9pm at the **ENITEL/TELCOR** office (tel. 39-05; fax 30-00), located just north of the park's northwest corner. **Telephone code:** 341.

Accommodations Hotel Chinandega, one and a half blocks south of the southwest corner of Central Market, is your best bet for simple rooms (35C per person). Shared showers and toilets are certainly bearable. Unfortunately, many travelers grin and bear it—when it is full, try the more "glomarous" option: **Hotel Glomar** (tel. 25-62), one block south of Central Market. Respectable singles on the second floor (without baths) are a whopping 120C. Singles with A/C are 200C; triples run 180C without A/C, 260C with A/C. If you're aching for luxury, go to the **Hotel Consigüina**, one block east and a half block south of the park. The big, cushy lounge has a TV, and all rooms have A/C and private bath (singles US$34, doubles US$42—ouch!). It is said that there are cheaper *hospedajes* in Chinandega, but if you find one, be sure it's not a *hospedeje y bar;* that's where the wild things are.

Food Thirsty? The town's water is chlorinated, and should be potable (though vaguely reminiscent of swim lessons at the YMCA). Get water from any of the numerous snack shops scattered around town or from the fancier restaurants, assuming that you've long since had your fill of Coca-Cola. Otherwise, you might want to grab some ripe, juicy fruits from the produce section of one of the markets. Hungary? Don't miss **El Hungaro** (tel. 38-24) whose hearty Hungarian owner and his wife will serve you hospitality along with hefty portions. Take the street that runs one block east of ENITEL/TELCOR north until you cross the bridge. Take the first right turn, up a dirt road, and El Hungaro is 200m on your left. Chicken livers simmered for several hours in savory spices are worth twice the 22C you'll pay. Other entrees run 50-70C, and you're getting both quality and variety. They're officially open 10am-10pm, but are happy to whip up breakfast if you drop in earlier. All credit cards accepted. **Cafetín Don D'Erick,** the snack shop in the corpus of the park (southwest corner), is a great place to slurp down a delicious *refresco natural* or to have a beer (they have Heineken and American imports). They also serve a decent *comida corriente* lunch (10-12C; open Mon.-Sun. 7am-10pm). Good, cheap food awaits those who survive the wait. Have a beer or two while the owner cranks American music through the bar. Finally, for the type that stays in the Consigüina, Chinandega offers **Corona de Oro** (tel. 25-39), two blocks south and half a block east of the bank corner (Esquina de Bancos), which is open daily 11am-10pm. Step inside and survey the shelves stocked with an astounding variety of Flor de Caña products, then allow the hostess to seat you in the air-conditioned dining room, where you can delight in a serving of *brochetas* (40C) or Chinese food (35-40C).

Sights The steeples of several modest churches spice up the city skyline and evoke Chinandega's colonial past. The **Santa Ana** church borders the park on its north side. The facade of **El Calvario** and the greenery of the surrounding park are visible when looking east from Santa Ana's entrance. The **Parque de las Rosas,** right beside the ENITEL/TELCOR office, is a quaint, flowery, and punnily named little park dedicated to the mother of Rubén Darío, Rosa Sarmiento, a native of Chinandega. To keep things in perspective, Rosa's bust is a few feet above Rubén's *rostro* (face).

If **Volcán San Cristóbal** makes a good backdrop, it makes a better vantage point. Those adventurous enough to climb Nicaragua's tallest volcano will be able to find reputable private guides in Chinandega, with whom they can scale the harrowing heights in relative security. Another option for outdoor hoots is accessible from the Mercadito, where you can catch buses to various remote beaches along the Pacific coast. A local favorite is the stretch of shoreline known as **Jíquilillo**.

Entertainment While cable television has squeezed most cinemas out of business, Chinandega still has a few movie theaters up its sleeve. Just south of ENITEL/TELCOR, **El Ladino** (an unmarked orange behemoth) has been of special visual interest ever since it lost part of its roof to a fire. Consequently, filmgoers can watch their movies under the stars. If you prefer your air *acondicionado,* head round the corner to the town's first and only **Noel,** the blue one. Big red **Nela** stands in a shadier neighborhood eight blocks south and one block east of the park's southeast corner. All shows are on weekend nights only, though the Noel is poised to break into the weekday market. At night, *pelones* ("baldies"), small buses stripped of their roofs, congregate in the basketball courts to gather bedloads of passengers. Locals pay 1C to cruise the city in these makeshift convertibles, blaring Central American pop favorites up and down the streets. Why not join the fun?

SOUTH OF MANAGUA

■ Masaya

A young (and randy) Rubén Darío once paid a visit to the town of Masaya, and afterwards dubbed it "Ciudad de las Flores." He didn't choose the title for any botanical reasons, but because he was impressed by the town's abundance of beautiful women. While some may still be drawn to Masaya for its ladyfolk, the city is better known for its *artesanías.* Over 65% of Nicaragua's handicrafts are made here, including some of the best hammocks in the world, fine ceramics, superb woodwork, paintings, jewelry, hats, leather goods, and more—all of which can be bought for bargain prices at Masaya's bustling **Mercado Nuevo.**

Despite the bustle of commercial life, there's definitely something romantic about Masaya. Just stroll through the streets: colorful churches shade sleepy plazas; the *malecón,* or park, at the western edge of town offers a view of the polluted but impressive **Laguna de Masaya** below; and towering **Volcán Masaya** dominates the horizon.

PRACTICAL INFORMATION

All of Masaya's main thoroughfares run into the **Parque 17 de Octubre.** The park's eastern border is **Av. Zelaya,** which runs north and south. Buses arrive and depart from the lot beside the Mercado Nuevo. To avoid experiencing a grade-school flashback amongst loads of buses, note that the buses tend to come in the southeast (and sometimes northeast) corners. Food stands start on the south side and increase in the east. Exit the bus lot on the northwest corner, where you'll find **Calle Ernesto Fernandez.** Then walk six blocks to the park, catch a town bus (1C) or a cab (3C).

> **Tourist Information:** The avuncular proprietor of the **Hotel Regis** (see **Accommodations,** below) is your best bet for information about Masaya.
> **Currency Exchange: Banco Nacional de Desarollo** (tel. 27-41), 1 block east on the street just north of the park's northeast corner. Changes cash and traveler's checks for a 1% fee. Open Mon.-Fri. 8:30am-4pm, Sat. 8:30am-noon. **BANIC** (tel. 26-80), 1 block east of the park's southeast corner, changes dollars but not traveler's checks. Open Mon.-Fri. 8:30am-12:30pm and 1:30-4pm, Sat. 8:30am-noon. Beware of long lines on Monday (payday) around 9:30am.
> **Buses:** Depart from the Mercado Nuevo terminal for **Managua** (every 20min. beginning at 4am, 1hr., 5C) and **Granada** (every 30min., 4C). Buses to **Carazo, Catarina, Niquinohomo,** and **San Marcos** depart less frequently. Keep your ears peeled: each driver will yell his bus's destination five times in succession as he packs the riders in.

Laundry: Dry Cleaning "Masaya" (tel. 23-48), 2 blocks south of BANIC, washes clothes cheaply. Open Mon.-Sat. 8am-noon and 2-7pm. Fair prices, though they're closed weekends and may take two days to finish the job.

Pharmacy: Farmacia Masaya (tel. 27-80), ½ block east of the park's southeast corner, is convenient and well stocked. Open Mon.-Sat. 8am-6:30pm.

Hospital: Hospital Hilario Sanchez (tel. 29-22, 41-66 or 27-78), 3 blocks east of the market.

Women's Services: Colectiva de Mujeres de Masaya (tel. 54-58), ½ block north of the park. Provides information about women's organizations and provides counseling. Open Mon.-Fri. 9am-noon and 2-6pm.

Red Cross: (tel. 21-31 or 22-56), 1 block south of the park, on the bisecting street.

Police: (tel. 42-22 or 25-21), 1 block east and 1 block north of the park's northeast corner, in a blue complex.

Post Office: (tel. 2631; fax 27-47) just around the corner from ENITEL, also has **fax** service. Open Mon.-Fri. 7am-6pm, Sat. 7am-noon.

Telephones: The **ENITEL** office (tel. 25-99 or 24-99), on the west side of the park, also has **telegram** services. Open daily 7am-9:30pm.

Telephone Code: 522.

ACCOMMODATIONS

Perhaps because of its proximity to Managua, Masaya has proportionately few places to stay. The hotels that do exist are a little on the pricey side, and the *hospedajes* are a little on the shady side. The *hospedajes* fall into two camps: the rent-by-the-hora ones are east of the bus station, and the more tolerable ones run by widows are scattered throughout town.

Hotel Regis (tel. 23-00), 3½ blocks north of the park on Av. Zelaya, is wonderful. Señor Francisco Castillo, who manages the hotel with his charming wife, is a walking history text stocked full of regional information. If you're not impressed by the locals' praise, Francisco's patient and thorough tour of the facilities will have you sold. Fan, toilet paper, hand towel, and free luggage storage included. Enormous, delicious breakfast for 20C. Curfew 10pm; checkout 10am. 50C per person; 60C for two if you want to share a larger-than-usual single bed.

Hotel Monte Carlo (tel. 21-66), 5 blocks north of the park on Av. Zelaya, is a homey place with a lounging area, self-serve laundry facilities, and a Masayan hammock to test before buying your own. Light-colored tiles keep the place feeling cool. Rooms share a modern bathroom. Singles 50C; doubles 70C, with A/C and private bath 150C.

Hospedaje Rex can be identified as the faded yellow building across from the southwest corner of the small park south of La Iglesia San Jerónimo (not the *Parque Central*). Most rooms are squeezed into a rickety, attic-like space; the beds are made up with old, Mickey Mouse sheets. The bathroom could use a little elbow grease. Sylvester Stallone and voluptuous ladies grace the posters at the entrance. 25C for a single, 40C for a double.

FOOD

The restaurant scene in Masaya is a far cry from the liveliness of the artisan scene, but the prospects are by no means hopeless.

Restaurante Che-Gris (tel. 59-42), ½ block south and ½ block east of Hotel Regis, has a tall dining room, a garden, a back patio, and a cow skull hanging over the bar. Chicken in wine sauce 40C and *comida corriente* 20C. *Comdra vegetariana* (25C) offers you a unique mix of salad, boiled tubers (white, purple, and green), and cheese. MC and Visa accepted.

La Jarochita Taqueria (tel. 48-31), 2 blocks north of the park on Av. Zelaya, satisfies the Mexican in everyone. 20C buys a mouthful—from a plate of tacos to a pitcher of beer. Open Mon.-Sat. 11am-10pm. MC and Visa accepted.

Restaurante Sandalo, near the southwest corner of the park, is an enormous, fairly popular place. Groove to Nicaraguan top-40 on the dance floor while waiting for

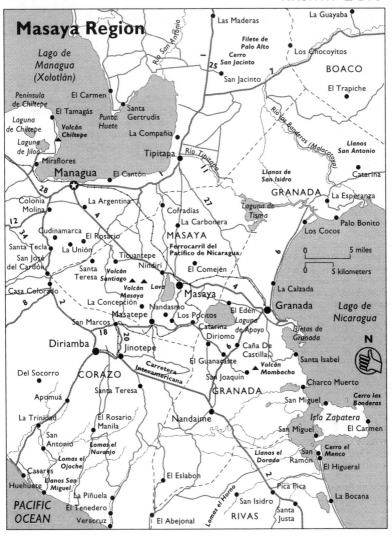

Masaya Region

Lago de
Managua
(Xolotlán)

Las Maderas

La Guayaba

Río San Antonio

Filete de
Palo Alto
Cerro
San Jacinto

Los Chocoyitos

25

1

BOACO

San Jacinto

El Trapiche

Península
de Chiltepe

El Carmen

El Tamagás

Santa
Gertrudis

Punta
Huete

Río las Banderas (Malacatoya)

Laguna
de Chiltepe

Volcán
Chiltepe

La Compañia

Llanos
San Antonio

Laguna
de Jiloa

Tipitapa

Río Tipitapa

11

Catarina

Miraflores

Managua

El Cantón

Llanos de
San Isidro

GRANADA

La Esperanza

28

Laguna de
Tisma

Palo Bonito

Colonia
Molina

La Argentina

Cofradías

Los Cocos

12

34

Cudinamarca

El Rosario

La Carbonera

MASAYA

5 miles

Santa Tecla

La Unión

Ticuantepe

Ferrocarril del
Pacífico de Nicaragua

San José
del Cardón

Santa
Teresa

Volcán
Santiago

Nindirí

El Comején

0

5 kilometers

Casa Colorado

Volcán
Masaya

Lava

Masaya

La Calzada

8

2

La Concepción

Nandasmo

Los Pocitos

El Edén

Granada

Lago de
Nicaragua

Masatepe

Catarina

Laguna
de Apoyo

San Marcos

Diriomo

Isletas de
Granada

N

Diriamba

18

20

Jinotepe

El Guanacaste

Caña De
Castilla

Santa Isabel

CORAZO

Carretera
Interamericana

San Joaquín

Volcán
Mombacho

Charco Muerto

Del Socorro

Santa Teresa

GRANADA

San Miguel

Cerro las
Banderas

Apomuá

La Trinidad

El Rosario
Manila

Nandaime

San Miguel

Isla Zapatera

El Carmen

San
Antonio

Lomas el
Naranjo

Llanos el
Dorado

San
Ramón

Cerro el
Menco

Casares

Lomas el
Ojoche

El Eslabón

El Higueral

Huehuete

Llanos San
Miguel

La Piñuela

Pica Pica

La Bocana

PACIFIC
OCEAN

El Tenedero

Veracruz

El Abejonal

San Isidro

Santa
Justa

RIVAS

Lomas el Horno

2

one of many chop sueys and "chaw" meins (30-35C). Chicken 30C, fish 35-48C.
Open daily 11am-10pm.

Restaurante Alegria (tel. 20-32), gets happy a block north of the park (the street
that leads from the church to the mayor's hall). Typical range of steaks and seafood, with a bilingual menu and pizza (25-30C) to boot. (Read: they cater to *gringos*.) Open daily 11am-11pm.

SIGHTS

Small stone sculptures complement the famed Masayan hammocks, woven mats,
baseball bats, and ceramics of the **Mercado Nuevo** at the east end of town. For a veritable orgy of hand-crafted delights, wander among the local *artesanías* concentrated
in the west end of the market. As always, quality of artisanship varies; look around
first, and when the time comes, *bargain*. Within reason, you should definitely try for

294 ■ SOUTH OF MANAGUA

better prices, as most vendors expect you to contest their initial price quote. Various workshops sell their goods directly, most of which can be found in **Barrio Monimbó,** to the south of town, which has a largely indigenous population. Another source for handicrafts is the showroom at the *Centro de Capacitación de la Pequeña Industria y Artesanías,* located in a squat building five blocks west of Parque Central, near the *malecón.* Prices tend to be higher here, but the mood is low-key, and the showroom is a great way to see what's out there. If you're looking for a hammock, you might try **Ramiro Suazo y Familia,** one block east of the baseball stadium, just above the *malecón.* The family has been in the business for 45 years, and many international importers come to the Suazos for the hammocks they fashion behind their house. Prices are about 20C higher than you'll find in the market, but these are some serious hammocks (hammocks with wooden bars around 200C, cocoon style around 100C).

A revolution's memory has three enemies: time, disinterest, and the rigged election of a capitalist puppet. Though fading, the memory of revolution retains some of its fervor and proximity—Masaya saw numerous uprisings in the late '70s—at the **Gallery of Heroes and Martyrs.** Photographs of the dead fighters, bomb-building materials, and oddly child-like guerilla masks are housed in the *Alcaldía* (open Mon.-Fri. 8:30-11:30am and 1-4pm), a two-story building on the west side of Calle Real San Jerónimo, two and a half blocks south of La Iglesia San Jerónimo.

Go west, young tourist, about 1km and enjoy the **Malecón.** The park contains the ordinary assortment of playgrounds and benches, but the prize, besides a host of helpfully labelled trees, is the winning view of the huge *lago.* (What were you expecting—a toaster oven?) Buses (2C) run there every ½ hr. or so, and taxis swoop down as well.

La Iglesia de la Asunción, in the Parque 17 de Octubre, was erected in 1833. Once inside, look up to see the high, wooden, flower-painted ceiling—perhaps another tribute to the beauty of the *masayanas?* On the southern side of the park, a small plaque commemorates the 1856 defeat of William Walker.

Diamonds in the Rough

Nicaragua is one of the few Latin American countries where soccer doesn't reign supreme. Here, it's **baseball** (Nica: *base*), and it wins by a good country mile. As in the Dominican Republic, the sport is a legacy from U.S. Marine occupation in the 1920s, when soldiers passed on this pasttime. Pitcher **Dennis (Denny) Martinez** is one Nico who's had some success in the U.S. major leagues, and has recently been offered a government position heading the sports department. Nicaraguans have also heroized another Latin American, Roberto Clemente, whose name lives on in Masaya's stadium, next to the Laguna. The famed Puerto Rican outfielder died in a plane on his way to deliver aid to Nicaraguan **earthquake** victims.

■ Near Masaya

Parque Nacional Volcán Masaya (tel. 54-15) houses a pair of volcanos, which visitors can see for 20C. Pocked by five craters, one of the seething mountains, **Santiago,** constantly belches fumes from its center, a red hot gas vent that can be seen glowing from one of the park's chief lookouts. The park is easily accessible from either Masaya or Managua. The stories about how Somoza would drop undesirables into the volcano from a helicopter may or may not be apocryphal, but is certainly plausible. The entrance to the volcano is along the *carretera,* about 7km northwest of Masaya towards Managua; most Managua-Masaya buses can drop you off. Ask if they'll take you to the volcán; the ride costs about 3C. Taxis are also available for around 25C. Catch a returning Managua bus on the other side of the highway. There's an informative museum 2km from the entrance where you should also stock up on water. From there, it's another (steep) 5km to the top. Catching a ride with one of the passing tourists is another possibility, especially on weekends. *Let's Go* does not recommend hitchhiking, but many travelers insist that it is safe along the road to the volcano. If you're there when the park opens at 9am you can sometimes get a ride with park rangers all the way to the top. One bonus of walking (down, preferably) is a chance to explore dried lava rivers on the side of the road, and maybe catch a glimpse of exotic birds.

Once there, savor the view. The splendid Laguna Masaya lies below, the city beyond. You can see a replica of **Cruz de Bobadilla,** which the Spaniards placed high atop the volcano in the 16th century. Because of indigenous sacrifical rites, they thought the volcano was the *Boca del Infierno* (the proverbial "mouth of hell") and placed the cross there to keep the devil in his place. To take on even more, hike up to the higher, inactive **Volcán de San Fernando,** just up the hill. *Let's Go* does not recommend descending into the jaws of Hades. From the other side of the crater, a crushed red lava trail leads 150 yards to the *Cueva de Murcielagos,* or "Bat Cave" (no, not *that* Bat Cave), formed by lava forced out through the crater. To explore it, bring a flashlight, or get a ranger to guide you with a lantern (5C). Think ahead, because you have to buy the ticket at the museum. There's no way you'll want to add another five miles of descent and ascent to your calves. Chances of seeing bats up close are even better at the visitor center, where they often roost in the "lava tunnel." Be sure to exit the park by closing time (4:45pm); the rangers will appreciate your courtesy.

The small town of **Nindirí** sits on the same road, between Masaya and the volcano. To get there, catch a minibus (2C) at the corner ½ block north and 1 block east of Hotel Regis in Masaya; get off at the main square—heck, the only square in Nindirí. An obelisk overlooks the southeast corner; from the southwest corner, continue one block west to the **Museo Arceológico Tenderi.** The curator, Rosario Cerón, makes a delightful visit out of what appears to be two cramped rooms of unlabeled pottery—you'll soon appreciate pregnant belly-shaped *ollos* (burial pots), ceramics, rusty muskets, and a collection of donated currencies (hint hint—the tour is free but córdobas are welcome). The museum is open Mon.-Fri. 8am-noon and 2-5pm, Sat. 8am-noon.

To see the **Fortaleza Coyotepe,** catch a Nindirí mini-bus but disembark just outside of Masaya at the stone archway proclaiming "Campo Escuela/Scout/El Coyotepe." Yes, you're climbing 1.5km up a severe incline to a boy scout camp—but it is worth it: it stands in an old somoza torture fort, and the view is great. An admission of 2C (pay when you exit) brings you into a 1910 structure renovated for added prison cells in the 1930s. (Open daily 8am-5:30pm.)

The bus from Masaya to Carazo region (which leaves the market every 30min.; 4C) serves a string of pleasant towns on the way to Jinotepe—though there is hardly any reason to go beyond the first, **Catarina,** which boasts an incomparable look out. The bus drops you off at a four-way intersection about 15 minutes outside of Masaya. The small road that ascends the hill to the left leads to Catarina. From the intersection, walk about 10 minutes straight through the tiny town, including a short detour around the left side of the church (and past many lunch garden stands). This windy bluff overlooks **Laguna de Apoyo, Lago de Nicaragua,** the city of Granada on the isthmus between the two, and **Volcán Mombacho** to the right. Three identical restaurants serve virtually the same menu at virtually the same prices (steak 50C, seafood 60C, beer 7C). Mastercard and Visa accepted. Eenie, Meenie, Minie, Mo...

A few miles on the road going in the opposite direction of Catarina, you'll see **Niquinohomo** ("valley of the warriors"), birthplace and boyhood home of Augusto Cesar Sandino. Sandino's home used to be a museum, but it's been razed, and another house has been raised in its place. If you don't feel like walking here, the bus to Carazo passes by. Hop aboard the same bus again to reach **San Marcos,** where a branch campus of the University of Mobile, Alabama does its best not to look too incongruous. At the end of the line are **Dirimba,** with an ecological museum, and **Jinotepe,** with nothing. And if there isn't an ongoing festival (January 20 and July 25, respectively), you'll kick yourself for not listening to us and basking in the glory of the **Mirador** (see **Study,** p. 267).

NICARAGUA

■ Granada

Granada's strategic location on the western shore of Lago de Nicaragua has shaped much of its history. Francisco Hernández de Córdoba founded the city in 1524, and though the Spanish soon exhausted the region's supply of gold, Granada continued to prosper as a trading center, due to its proximity to the Pacific coast and its easy access to the Caribbean via the Río San Juan. Granada soon became the country's conservative stronghold, and a rivalry with liberal León ensued, which continues today (see p. 262).

Because of its wealth and access to the Caribbean, the city was repeatedly attacked by English and French pirates during the 17th century. After Nicaragua gained independence from Spain, Granada engaged in a civil war against neighboring León. In the 1850s, William Walker captured Granada and ruled Nicaragua from the city for two years, until he was ousted. Before his retreat, he set fire to the entire city, destroying or damaging many of the colonial buildings, most of which have been rebuilt. Today's Granada is as colonial a city as you'll find in Nicaragua—big, two-story homes line wide boulevards, and tall palm trees shade the Parque Central.

A breeze from the lake takes the edge off the toaster-oven heat, and the most enjoyable pastime is simply walking, either within the city itself or along the lake shore. You might glimpse a colonial church set against the cloud-covered peak of Volcán Mombacho, which rises to the south of the city. Granada's historical value is more atmospheric than tangible; it has to do with all those who've kicked its cobblestones—pirates, colonists, revolutionaries, and even a few tourists.

ORIENTATION

Buses from Managua release passengers in the western part of town, six blocks west and two blocks north of the **Parque Central.** Buses from Masaya pull into a small lot three blocks west and two blocks south of the Parque Central. Buses from Rivas stop at a gas station one block west and four blocks south of the Parque Central. Granada's main north-to-south street, **Calle Atravesado,** runs one block west of the Parque Central. **Calle Real** borders the south side of the park and runs westward, up the hill, past three painted churches. **La Calzada** spins off the eastern side of the park beside the cathedral, and runs 1.5km east down to the lake and the pier. If you're coming from Managua, bear in mind that "al lago" is no longer north, but east.

PRACTICAL INFORMATION

Tourist Information: Available from the smiling staff of **Tienda Colibri** on the park's northwest side. Open Mon.-Fri. 9am-5pm. If all else fails, the desk at the **Hotel Alhambra** (on the west side of the park) may be able to help.
Currency Exchange and Western Union: Banco Nacional de Desarrollo (tel. 28-11), one block west of the park on Calle Atravesado, changes cash. Open Mon.-Fri. 8:30am-4pm, Sat. 8:30am-noon. **BANIC** (tel. 24-08), on Calle Atravesado across from the former Teatro Gonzalez, changes cash. **Banco de America Central** (tel. 33-52), located at the park's southwest corner, changes traveler's checks for a charge of 7C per check, or at a 6% commission charge if you want dollars. Open Mon.-Fri. 8am-4:30pm, Sat. 8am-1pm. *Coyotes* change traveler's checks as well, but at inferior rates—they tend to attack their prey at the corner of Calles Atravesado and Real. **Western Union** (tel. 26-54) sits two blocks west and ½ block north of the park. Open Mon.-Fri. 8am-11pm and 2-5pm, Sat. 8am-1pm.
Buses: To: **Managua** (every 20min., 5am-7pm, 1hr., 9C); **Masaya** (every 20min., 5am-7pm, 30min., 3C); and **Rivas** (every hr., 1½hr., 8C). Buses leave from their respective drop-off points (see **Orientation,** above). You can also get to Rivas by taking a bus to **Nandaime,** and catching another bus from there. From Rivas, buses run to **San Juan del Sur, San Jorge** (where ferries leave for **Isla de Ometepe**), and the **Costa Rican border** at **Peñas Blancas.**
Boats: Boats to **San Carlos** (on the southeast tip of the lake) and **Isla de Ometepe** leave from the pier at the end of La Cazalda (Mon. and Thurs. 2:30 and 3:30pm; to

Ometepe 15C, to San Carlos 21C). Pricier express boats to both destinations leave more frequently, usually in the mornings.

Bicycle Rental: Repuestos Bonilla on La Calzada, 1½ blocks east of the Parque Central. Mountain bikes 7C per hr., 40C per day.

Market: Supermercado Lacayo (tel. 51-10) is 2 blocks up on Calle Real. Open Mon.-Fri. 8am-12:30pm and 2-8pm, Sat. 8am-8pm, Sun. 8:30am-1pm.

AMNLAE: Provides women's services at **Casa de la Mujer Claudia Chamorro** (tel. 20-96), 1 block east of the cathedral on La Calzada. Open Mon.-Fri. 8am-noon and 2-6pm.

Pharmacy: Farmacia Forest, Calle Atravesado, west and south of the park. **Farmacia Leo** (tel. 23-70) apparently has the best hours; open daily 7am-7pm.

Hospital: (tel. 27-19 or 22-09), just south of the Managua bus stop, 1 block north and 6 blocks west of the Parque Central.

Red Cross: (tel. 27-11), 6 blocks east down La Calzada toward the lake, near the basketball court and a baseball field complex.

Police: (tel. 29-29), 1km north of the park, near the old train station.

Post office: At ENITEL/TELCOR. Open Mon.-Fri. 7am-7pm, Sat. 8am-noon.

Telephones: ENITEL/TELCOR (tel. 20-90; fax 27-76), in an unmarked light blue building across from the northeast corner of the park. **Fax** available. Open daily 7am-9:30pm.

Telephone Code: 552.

ACCOMMODATIONS

Hospedaje Cabrera (tel./fax 27-81), on La Calzada, 2½ blocks east of the Parque Central, is distinguished by clean rooms with fans, a new roof, an unintelligible parrot ("Ven Acá? Vaca? Caca?"), and friendly proprietors. Rocking chairs and cable TV in the lounge serve as relaxants. Communal bathroom with toilet paper and soap. Self-service laundry basin. Breakfast (15C), snacks available during the rest of the day. 30-35C per person.

Hospedaje La Mariscada, 4½ blocks down from the park on La Calzada, also has a courtyard, cable TV, warm hosts (children will rush their siblings from the bathroom for you), and comes with the bonus of a restaurant (See **Food,** below). Slight imperfections (e.g. loose toilet seat) are overcome by family atmosphere. 25-30C per person.

Hospedaje Vargas (tel. 28-97), across the street from the Cabrera (and very similar to it), is slightly less accommodating. It too boasts a garden and courtyard, rocking chairs, TV, and laundry—but no food. Bucket-style showers. 30C per person.

Hospedaje Esfinge (tel. 48-26), across from the market on Atravesado, 3 blocks south of the Parque Central, is in a big, run-down building which was built in 1903. Rooms have real beds with real mattresses, but not real walls—3m high partitions zig and zag beneath an even higher roof. Friendly management, ping-pong, cable TV, and clean bathrooms. Singles 25C, with private bath 50C; doubles 45C, with private bath 70C.

Hospedaje Central (tel. 59-00), on La Calzada, 1½ blocks east of the park. Offers a few rooms around a scrubby garden in the back of a home; the small courtyard has some columns with attractive Chinese figures. Good locks, fans, self-serve laundry, bathrooms (no seats or paper), and showers (no head). 25C per person.

FOOD

The expensive places are east of town in the Centro Turístico on the lakefront. These restaurants are both far away and run-of-the-mill, considering the price of the meal. You can find the usual bargains at the *comedores* in and around the market, three blocks south of the Parque Central. The places below fall somewhere in between.

Restaurante Lejano Oriente (tel. 54-63), 1 block west of the park's northwest corner, serves up an impressive variety of chop sueys, chow meins, and rice dishes (with chicken, with shrimp, or *à la Valenciana*) for 25-40C. Nica standbys available at fair prices. Open daily 11:30am-9pm.

NICARAGUA

Cafetín Soya Nica (tel. 45-98), on the northwest corner of the park, has a few tables out front that offer a nice view of the park. Serves meaty meals (12-20C) as well as *todo en soya*—be prepared: vegetarian options depend on availability of pseudo-carne (15-22C). Open daily 9am-10pm.

La Mariscada (formerly "La Calzada"), 4½ blocks east of the park on Calzada. Dine at the sign of the shark. Specializes in seafood, but serves just about every other typical dish, at good prices and with hefty portions. Breakfast 12-15C, *comida corriente* (with a drink) 14-16C, shrimp 40C. Open daily 7am-9pm.

El Condo, 1 block west of the park, is a classy ice cream shop with excellent malts, milkshakes, ice cream, and *refrescos naturales.* Open Mon.-Thurs. 11am-8pm, Fri.-Sun. 11am-9pm.

SIGHTS

A "Newoclassical" trio surrounds the Parque Central: **Palacio de Cultura** (to the west, home of community activities); **Palacio Municipal** (on the South side, city government seat); and the **Cathedral** on the east. To the northeast of the plaza lies the *Plazuela de los Leones,* with the *Fundación de Tres Mundos* on it east side (look for lions over the entrance). This free hallway exhibits local and international art in a recumbent atmosphere—even the pots in the back courtyard are lounging.

The slowly refurbished remains of the *Iglesia y Convento San Francisco* stand one block north and east of the *Fundación.* The expanding **museum** (tel. 42-37) houses bizarre indigenous statues, archaeological displays, and a gallery of primitivist art from the early years of the revolution (open daily 9am-6pm, 10C).

Now dash away to the newly opened *Museo de Armas Fontaleza "La Polvora."* It takes only 5C to get you into this former fort/prison/torture center, current tourist-spot-of-cultural-memory, where you can look at cannons, an old fortress wall, and a 20th century rifle exhibit—unless they've been removed for fear of strikes which are invariably on the horizons. At least you can see the horizon from the tower just to the left of the entrance. The museum is open daily 9am-5pm.

The path east from the cathedral down **La Calzada** also makes for a nice walk. In the late afternoon, locals fish and dive off the pier at the end of the road, where you can try your hand at shark-sighting. Take a stroll along the newly constructed lake-walk just a block south of the pier. Walk south of the pier along the lake shore to visit a touristy park lined with restaurants. Beyond the park, about half an hour from the pier, lies **Puerto Asese,** where you can hire a *lancha* to see one of Granada's main tourist attractions—the 368 populated lake islands *(isletas).* But beware: the walk to Puerto Asese is long, hot, and sometimes dangerous. The *lanchas* charge 90-130C for a one-hour tour, but up to 20 people can split the cost. Boats leave most frequently on Sundays.

Those who take **Volcán Mombacho's** massive presence as a personal challenge should contact the folks at Tienda Colibrí, who can hook you up with one of the guides in town. Word is that the mighty Mombacho is slated to become a national park within a year or so—keep your fingers crossed.

■ Rivas

Rivas lies two hours south of Granada and 45km north of the Costa Rican border at Peñas Blancas. Thus, you're likely to find yourself stopping in Rivas just to change buses from **Punta A** to **Punta B.** The most touristed parts of town are the bus stop and the pier a few kilometers out from **San Jorge,** where boats leave for Ometepe, the volcano whose cone provides a focal point in the East. Two other landmarks are —surprise!—churches. The smaller, peachly painted one stands four blocks south of the **Mercado**/bus station. The older, heftier, and wiser (check out the Allegorical Murals) cools itself with electric fans on every column. This colonial structure faces the **Parque de Arriba,** three blocks south and two blocks east of the church.

To exchange U.S. dollars or traveler's checks for no commission or charge, head to **Banco Nacional de Desarrollo** (tel. 453-3650), ½ block east of the peach-colored church (open Mon.-Fri. 8:30am-4pm, Sat. 8:30-noon). **Buses** leave Rivas from the bus stop just before the entrance to the main market area for: **Peñas Blancas** (7:30, 8, 9:30, 10:30, 11am, 12:20, 2:30, and 3:30pm; 1hr.; 8C); **Managua** (every 30min., 5am-5pm, 13C); **Sapoa** (several daily, last bus at 3:30pm, 30min., 8C); **San Juan del Sur** (every 45min., 6:45am-late afternoon, 8C); **Granada** (about 1½hr., 6:10am-3:10pm, 8C); and **San Jorge** (every 30min., 10min., 2C). **Boats** depart from San Jorge for **Moyogalpa** on **Isla de Ometepe** (6 times daily, Mon.-Sat., 3 times on Sun.; 1hr.; 7C). There's also a daily **express** (45min., 17C). **Taxis** also leave from the market for San Jorge (just 4km away), and there are typically a few locals willing to split the fare (3-10C). **Farmacia La Salud** (tel. 33-3-05), three and a half blocks north of the market, is open daily 8am-9pm. The **Red Cross** (tel. 33-4-15) lies two blocks south and five blocks east of the bus lot. The **police station** (tel. 453-3732) is three blocks north of the market. The **ENITEL** office (tel. 453-3373), one and a half blocks west and half a block north of the bank, provides **telephone, telegram, fax,** and **postal** services (open Mon.-Fri. 8am-5pm, Sat. 8am-noon). More useful, though smaller, is the **TEL-COR** office, open 7am-midnight every day. The **telephone code** is 453.

If you need to spend the night in Rivas, conveniently located, tidy **Hospedaje Lidia** (tel. 453-3477) is six and a half blocks west and two blocks south of the market (doors locked at 10pm; 30-40C per person). The hostel has a reputation for being secure; Lidia also serves meals in the courtyard (20C for a standard lunch).

NEAR RIVAS: THE COSTA RICAN BORDER

Sapoa is the Nicaraguan town on the Costa Rican border 37km south of Rivas; **Peñas Blancas** is the border post on the Costa Rican side, 4km south. Since Peñas Blancas has no place to stay, most travelers continue southward 80km to Liberia, Costa Rica.

To reach Sapoa, you can take a bus from **Rivas** (6C) or **Managua** (17C) from early in the morning until early afternoon. From **San Juan del Sur,** get off the Rivas bus at **La Virgen** (3C) and catch a border bound bus from there (5C). The border closes at 4pm, so get there early. It opens at 8am and slows down around lunch time.

From the bus park, walk southward towards the clump of alternately blue- and peach-trimmed buildings between the two roads. Renovations have left the offices a bit jumbled, but no worries—if you get lost, you'll be told where to go. There are three steps, all of which occur in the first (northern) peach-trimmed building: 1) pay the US$1 (or the equivalent in córdobas) *alcadia* fee at a window on the western face of the building; 2) inside, around a corner to the left, pay a US$2 exit fee (US dollars only); 3) take both of your receipts to one of the booths. If you've held on to your migration card from entry, good—but they expect you to have lost it, and will hand you another to fill out. Get your passport stamped, and you're outta here.

Then board a bus (4C) or taxi to the Costa Rican immigration office 4km away. The last bus leaves at 4pm. Inside the immigration office, get in line for windows 1 or 2 (3 if you are driving). You'll have to show your passport, the new migration card you've filled out, and an **outward bound ticket** from Costa Rica. If you don't have one already, you can purchase a **Tica bus** ticket near the cafeteria. The officials keep your passport, and you reclaim it at window 6 for a ¢75 fee (colones only). Your bags may be inspected by customs in the line to get on the bus; just outside of Sapoa, a civil guard member may board the bus to check your passport.

Money changers exchange all permutations of colones-dollars-córdobas on both sides of the border; there is a bank in the Nicaraguan cluster of offices—whatever you do, be sure to have the correct currency on hand. Sapoa has a refreshingly efficient cafetín across from the bank; sit on the porch for your last sight of Lago de Nicaragua (open 8am-8pm). Buses for Liberia, some of which continue on to San José, leave at 7:30, 9:30, 10:30am, 12:30, 2:30, 3:30, and 5pm (300C).

NICARAGUA

■ San Juan del Sur

San Juan del Sur was once home to more than beach-lovers. Set on the Pacific Coast 30km west of Rivas, the town thrived and throbbed during the U.S. gold rush as the port from which Cornelius Vanderbilt's transport company embarked for California. In those days, Nicaragua was the quickest thoroughfare between the Atlantic and Pacific. While occasional boats still make their way through, these days most of the transport in San Juan occurs between hostel and beach.

And a nice beach it is. San Juan del Sur is popular with both Nicaraguans and the backpack set for good reason—the town sits in a cove, along a flat, comma-shaped beach, sheltered by enticing waters to the west and huge, cinematic rock outcroppings to the north and south. Restaurants and houses line most of the beach, but less-populated sands await nearby. Most of the waves are only big enough for boogie boards, although a few surfers usually hang ten during high tide at the north end of the beach. June 22, the day of the town's patron saint, San Juan, means big fun for all.

Orientation and Practical Information At the north end of the beach, a "river" (your toenails might get wet while crossing) meets the Pacific. At the south end, a long pier tends to the light boat traffic. Find loads of **tourist information** about car rentals, Spanish lessons, fishing tours, and more at **Marie's Bar** (see **Food,** below); open Monday through Saturday 8am-5pm. **ENITEL/TELCOR** (tel. 82-2-61 or 82-2-62) is in a pastel building at the south end of the beach, below the radio tower (**telephone** service open daily 7am-10pm); **telegrams, postal service,** and **fax** are available (Mon.-Fri. 8am-noon and 2-5pm). The **telephone code** is 458. Seek medical attention at **Servicios Médicos Communales,** near the ENITEL/TELCOR office. **Farmacia Santa Martha** (tel. 21-44) is half a block east of Marie's Bar. The closest thing to a **police station** (tel. 23-82) is two buildings south of the ENITEL/TELCOR office.

Accommodations Moskitos inhabit the Caribbean coast, but the Pacific side has its share of mosquitoes; you may wish to use repellant or a net. For clean, new rooms, check out **Guest House Elizabeth** (tel. 22-70), across the street from the bus stop. Elizabeth and her husband are friendlier than you deserve. Communal toilets are clean, though predominantly seatless. Buy delicious breakfasts here (15C) as well as snacks for the beach (lock-out 11pm; 30C per person; doubles with private bath 90C). **Hospedaje "Surf Casa 28,"** half a block north of the street that runs from the bus stop to the beach and one block before the beach, is nothing fancy, but it's popular, and they really do have surfboards here. The bathroom is kept clean, though the beds are just cots with foam pads. The big rooms have ceiling fans, and management provides mosquito coils and nets in some rooms for a fee (singles 30C; doubles 50C). Where the street from the bus stop meets the beach stands **Hotel Estrella,** a two-story stucco building which is the most visible hotel in town; its bright green shutters, doors, and balconies contrast with painted waves below. The walls don't reach all the way to the ceiling, but the communal facilities are decent and ample, with seats and paper. The breezy restaurant charges 30C per diner. The **Hospedaje Buen Gusto** (tel. 23-04) is across the street. The walls meet the ceilings and the communal facilities are clean, but it's a bit pricier (40C per person). The adjacent restaurant serves food in the fancy *sala* downstairs and upstairs on the deck. Proudly bearing the Norwegian flag, **Casa International Joxi** (tel./fax 23-48), half a block from the beach on the same street, is a step up in price (singles US$15; doubles US$25; one room with shared bath 50C per person). Washers and dryers in the hotel charge 15C per load. The small adjoining cafe has a limited menu, but its fresh orange juice will perk you up. An in-house shop sells tourist goodies (film, postcards, etc.), rents boogie boards (25C per day), and sends internet messages for 5C per page.

Food Marie's Bar is located on the main beach road, one block north of the bus stop, and stands beyond recommendation. Marie and Richard were two European backpackers who cut their trip short to begin a long-held dream of running a restaurant. Marie whips up half a dozen entrees each night, with an ever-evolving menu. You will not find food this delicious for this cheap (25-35C) elsewhere in the country. Breakfasts are equally varied, and include cappuccino (7C), if you desire. The variety of food and clientele will bring you back every day (open 7-9am; no lunch; for dinner people filter in around 6pm and stay until late). Excellent fresh fish comes easy here—beyond Marie's, it's justifiable to choose an eatery based solely on its view of the sunset. The restaurants along the beach are the most expensive because of their great vistas. Cases in point: **El Timón** (tel. 23-24) and **Restaurante Las Brisas Marinas** serve comparably high-quality food at comparably boosted prices. Fish platters include rice, fries, and salad (40-50C). For cheaper fare, try **La Soya,** one block north of the bus stop street, one block back from the beach. *Comida corriente* of fish, chicken, or beef will set you back 20C, and yes, they have a soy option, often *chorizo.* In addition, a number of people sell food from grills set up outside their front door.

Sights Go swimming. The north end of the beach is the cleanest, has the biggest waves, and is the least crowded. Casa International Joxi rents body boards for 25C per day and organizes sailing trips for groups of seven or more. For unspoiled beaches, head south along the road toward the town of **Ostional. Guest House Elizabeth** rents decent **mountain bikes** for US$5 per day; they also have a **map** of the area painted on their wall. After a couple of kilometers, there's a sign for **Balneario Remanso,** an unpopulated beach with larger waves than San Juan del Sur's. The beach is 3km down this road. Playa del Coco, Playa del Tamarindo, La Flor, and the nearest beach, Playa Sucia, all offer good swimming and decent snorkeling. The grand sands of Playa Marselles lie 5km south of town. The beach at **La Flor** is a sea turtle sanctuary accessible by bus at odd and inconvenient times (from San Juan to La Flor daily 3:45pm and Mon.-Sat. 1pm; from La Flor to San Juan daily 7:45am and Mon.-Sat. 3:45pm). Camping is allowed, and there is a 5C entrance fee.

The Escuela Integral de la Cultura in San Juan is a brick building with a green and white roof at the south end of the beach. Stop by for music and art classes.

LAGO DE NICARAGUA

Fed by over 40 rivers, streams, and brooks, Lago de Nicaragua is the largest lake in Central America and the tenth largest fresh-water lake in the world. According to popular belief, the sharks that inhabit the lake are a vestige of the days when Lago de Nicaragua was part of the Pacific Ocean. In fact, the seldom-seen creatures are Caribbean bowl sharks that have swum up the Río San Juan, which runs from the sea to the lake along the Costa Rican border. Hundreds of islands peek out from the surface of the lake; most are easily accessible by *lancha*. Some of the *isletas* are populated, and all are notable for their wildlife and for the pre-Conquest petroglyphs that stud their surfaces. An 18th-century Spanish fort called **San Pablo** still stands on one of the *isletas*. Another, **Isla Zapatera,** is thought to have been sacred to the indigenous tribes because of the large number of statues found there, most of which are now on display in Granada (see Granada, p. 296). **Isla de Ometepe,** four hours by boat from Granada, formed by two enormous volcanos rising out of the lake, is one of Nicaragua's most photogenic spots. Further south, off San Carlos, the **Archipélago de Solentináme** is renowned for both its beauty and for the artists' communities that produce woodcrafts and minimalist paintings.

Boat travel on Lago de Nicaragua is easy, cheap, and darn fun. Several times a week, two boats travel from Granada to **San Carlos,** a sleepy town on the Lago's southeast shore, and then back again, sometimes stopping on Isla de Ometepe.

■ Isla de Ometepe

Islands are, of course, something else entirely. Some people are preternaturally drawn to them. Even if you aren't one of those people, don't leave Nicaragua without seeing Isla de Ometepe. Ancient petroglyphs, friendly people, and great fish dinners aside, the sheer natural beauty of the island is reason enough for a visit. Formed an eternity ago by **Volcán Concepción** (1610m), which is still active, and by **Volcán Madera** (1394m), which is quite extinct (it last erupted 2600 years ago), the island was split in two by a strip of water that its denizens used as a transportation canal before the 19th century. An 1804 eruption of Concepción filled this gap, creating a single island shaped like the telophase stage of meiotic reproduction (or, if you like, a giant 8). The name means (roughly) "two" (ome-) "peaks" (tepe). The island was declared a national patrimony and ecological reserve in 1995, though the fancy title was not accompanied by increased support.

A relatively good road circumnavigates the Concepción (northwest) side of the island, while a much poorer road makes it halfway around the Madera (southeast) side. The wide green belt surrounding both volcanos supports banana, tobacco, cotton, and citrus farms. Haul out your boots and start walking, either to some of the primary forest that shrouds the island, or by the many petroglyphs which were carved approximately 800 years before the Spanish conquest. Some of the best and most accessible examples lie between the towns of **Balgue** and **Magdalena,** on the Madera side of the island just southeast of the land bridge.

The quickest **ferry** to Isla de Ometepe (1hr.) is from **San Jorge** (4km from Rivas) to **Moyogalpa,** on the western side of the island (several times daily). Boats also travel from **Altagracia** to **Granada** (4hr.) and **San Carlos** (8hr.) several times a week.

MOYOGALPA

Situated on the island's western coast, Moyogalpa is the second-largest town on Isla de Ometepe, but has the best developed tourist facilities. Moyogalpa means "place of mosquitoes"—there are worse misnomers, so bring your bug repellent of choice. Don't get excited by the bank you see on the main street—it is now a storage facility. **Hotel Ometepe** (see below), will change **traveler's checks,** but at sorry rates (about 12% less than you'll get in a bank). It's best to bring all money with you to the island. **Boats** to Moyogalpa from **San Jorge** depart several times daily (7, 8, 9, 10, 11am, noon, 2, 3:30, 5, and 6pm, 10C). Boats depart Moyogalpa for San Jorge less frequently (6, 6:30, 7, 7:30am, 1:30, and 5pm, 10C). At the San Jorge dock stands an information center/reservations desk run by **Ometepe Tours,** where you can grab a **free map** of the island and a guide (10C) which lists island legends and facilities. Regular **buses** zoom to **Altagracia,** about 18km around the island (6am-6pm, 60min., 6C). Buses often wait to take passengers from arriving boats, and boats often do the same for buses. Moyogalpa's **hospital** is 700m south of the church on the highway (open daily 8am-5pm, and 24hr. for **emergencies**). Dr. Fernando Martínez has a private practice one block south of the church (open Mon.-Fri. 7am-1pm). The **police station** (open 24hr.) is a block and a half south and three blocks east of the pier, on the same street as **ENITEL/TELCOR** (tel. 459-4277), which offers **phone, fax,** and **postal** service (open Mon.-Sat. 8am-noon and 2-5pm). The **telephone code** is 459.

Hotelito Aly (tel. 94-1-96), three blocks uphill from the pier to the left, has clean rooms set around a shady patio restaurant with an abundance of big, droopy tropical leaves. The entrance wall is decorated with a huge map of the island with distances chalked in (25C per person). **Hotel el Puerto,** to the right as you leave the pier, has rippin' rooms, well-maintained communal bathrooms, and a restaurant overlooking the water. There's a map of the island hanging outside the Puerto—don't confuse it with the *pulperia's* map on the other side of the street (singles 30C; doubles 50C, with A/C 180C). **Hospedaje Moyagalpa Ahora Hotel Ometepe** is a half block up from the Puerto; real thick mattresses go for 20C per person without a fan, and 25C with a fan. **Pensión Jade,** four and a half blocks uphill from the pier, is the cheapest place in town, with passable rooms and comfortable padded cots (15C per person, meals 15C as well). The hotels are the only reliable place to find dinner in Moyogalpa. There's not much to do in Moyogalpa, unless you're aching to know exactly how this island is shaped—why not look at the fountain one block behind Hotel el Puerto, whose center is a large-scale three-dimensional model map of Ometepe.

ALTAGRACIA

Altagracia (pop. 8000), on the northeast coast of the Concepción side of the island, is the island's biggest town. If the hustle and bustle of the place gets to you, then you took a wrong turn somewhere; there's little to do here. For goodness' sake, *pigs* root around in the town park (well, sometimes). Altagracia is a convenient base from which to explore the island's sights; it's near the road that leads to the Madera side of the island, as well as close to the mouth of the trail up Volcán Concepción.

Buses to **Balgue,** on the Madera side of Ometepe, depart from the Parque Central (4:40, 9:30am, and 1:30pm, 40min., 6C) and pass by **Playa Santo Domingo,** the island's biggest beach. Buses also leave for **Moyogalpa** (every 1½ hr., 4:40am-4:30pm, 1hr., 6C). Regular **boats** run to **Granada** (Tues. and Fri. 10am and 10pm, Sun. 10am, 4hr., 12C) and to **San Carlos** (Mon. and Thurs. 7pm, 8hr., 20C). There is also a more expensive **express boat** that goes to both Granada and San Carlos on Saturday and Sunday. The pier is about a 15 min. walk from town. **Farmacia San Diego** is half a block west of the park's southwest corner (open Mon.-Sat. 8am-noon and 1-5:30pm). **ENITEL/TELCOR** offers **telephone service** half a block west of the park's northwest corner (open Mon.-Sat. 8am-noon and 2-5pm). There is no **post office.**

Gills for the Guilty

Should you find yourself gazing longingly into the *verde* depths of the enchanted Charro Verde, be warned—legend has it that a **magical community** lives under the lagoon. No one seems to know how the creatures of the green lagoon spend their days; in fact, it is widely believed that if you, or any other human, ever happen to swim in the **lagoon,** its denizens will **transmogrify your body** into that of a fish. This might make travel around the rest of Lago de Nicaragua more convenient, but it could have serious repercussions later on, should you be netted by Nicaraguan fishermen, for instance.

If there is a center of ecotourism in Nicaragua, it may be **Hospedaje Castillo**—located half a block north of the *carretera* and one block west of the park—which features a topographical map of the island. Señor Castillo is an authority on the island's petroglyphs, and you may share his *hospedaje* with grad students collecting data for theses on tropical ecology. The rooms are spare and clean, and the food is good; however, the showers are bucket-style, and bathrooms are anything but private (rooms 30C per person). Whether or not you're staying here, drop by for a meal or a chat with Sr. Castillo. He can suggest beautiful trips and hikes around the island, find you a guide to the petroglyphs or to the volcanos, or write letters of introduction for hikers hiring guides at Hacienda Magdalena, the cooperative. Expect to pay roughly 60C for a four-hour tour of the petroglyphs, and about 100C for a tour of either volcano. **Hotel/Bar Restaurante Central** (tel. 60-72), two blocks west of the park's southwest corner, has nicer rooms and grounds than Castillo's, but lacks the knowledgeable host. The garden is astonishingly beautiful and well-kept, complete with a pond, a little gazebo, and *cabañas* for the romantic types (20C per person, with private bath 30C; two-person *cabaña* 100C). The little restaurant serves entrees (35-40C), *comida corriente,* and breakfasts (15C). Also, a cowhide converted into a map of the island hangs on the wall. For a great chocolate shake and a piece of cake, head to the **Bocaditos Soda** (now with a deck on top) at the center of the Parque Central.

The **church** is on the south side of the Parque Central, behind some pre-Columbian statues near the bus stop. Half a block north of the park is the **Museo Ometepe,** stocked with photos of the island and its main sights, some pre-Columbian artifacts, and displays on history and folklore. It also boasts a scale-model map of the island, replete with foam trees. The museum is associated with the **Ecotour** office (located in Moyogalpa, across from the post office) and can provide **tourist information** and arrange for guides to all parts of the island (open Mon.-Fri. 9am-5pm; admission 8C).

SIGHTS AROUND THE ISLAND

The biggest and most popular **beach** on Isla Ometepe is Santo Domingo, which lies on the isthmus between the two volcanos. It can be reached easily on any bus traveling from one side of the island to the other. There is a moderately priced **hotel** on the beach, with hammocks good for slothful lounging (US$10-15 per person).

Most of the **petroglyphs** lie between the towns of Balgue and Magdalena, on the Madera side of the island. These simple etchings were carved into the rocks between the 11th and 13th centuries. Many of the designs contain spirals and circles, but their significance is not known. You can either find them yourself by asking around or get a guide from Ecotour or Sr. Castillo. Ecotour also provides guides to the waterfall **Salto de San Ramón** and the **Charro Verde** lagoon (see **Gills for the Guilty,** above). See also the **Ometepe Tours** offices in San Jorge or Moyogalpa.

CLIMBING THE VOLCANOS

Volcano climbing is the quintessential "I'm roughing it in Nicaragua" activity, but be careful. Although both volcanos on Isla de Ometepe are considered relatively crime-free, roaming around in deserted areas is always risky, and rockslides are not unheard of. If you plan on making it to the top, you'll need boots, a full water bottle, and, during the rainy season (May-Oct.), a waterproof layer and a healthy love of mud. Long pants protect against prickly plants and biting bugs. Wise hikers hire a guide through Ecotour, Ometepe Tours, or Sr. Castillo.

Volcán Madera

Reaching Madera's summit requires an early start; you'll want to be on the first bus to Balgue (4:30 or 4:45am from Altagracia). Try to recruit fellow travelers to split the price of a guide. The bus stops beside a scruffy baseball field; cross it, then make your way through a decrepit banana plantation. After crossing through numerous barbed-wire fences, exit the banana plantation and bear left up a gentle hill through a cow pasture. After 10 minutes, look for a large wooden building on the hill to your right. This is the **Hacienda Magdalena** cooperative, whose residents will be willing to guide you up the volcano for about 100C. There, you can also find a room for a trifling 20C (tasty meals cost about the same). About 10 minutes up the trail, you'll pass a small thatched hut, the last building you'll see. For the first 30 minutes or so, the trail leads through banana, coffee, and cacao plantations. A lone petroglyph on a black rock stands to the left of the trail; this is where the vegetation begins.

The volcano's lower altitudes qualify as tropical dry forest (do not take this to mean that you will stay dry). As you ascend higher, you'll enter tropical rainforest, where the trail is densely foliated. After a few hours, the trail turns east (left) and wraps around the volcano, approaching the crater peak *(el cerro)* from the south. The last kilometer is tough going and requires balance and two hands. The descent is a bit quicker, but will be difficult if the trail is very muddy.

Keep your eyes peeled for the many petroglyphs scattered throughout the forest, but also watch out for wildlife. The rare, turquoise-browed Mot-Mot, Nicaragua's national bird, has a vibrant blue crown and a long racket-flame tail. Much more common, but still fun to spot, is the Uracca (white-throated magpie-jay), a large, blue, black-crowned bird. You may hear the odd, groaning roar of the howler monkey and the distinctive barks of white-faced monkeys; you may also have the distinct pleasure of seeing *agouti,* strange rodents about the size of small dogs.

Volcán Concepción

The taller of the two volcanos, Concepción is said to have the most perfectly conical shape of all the volcanos in Central America. It's also the less-frequently climbed of the two on Ometepe. Because it's still active, the terrain near the top consists primarily of loose rocks and sand, which makes climbing quite difficult. It is sometimes impossible to reach the actual crater, but you can come close. The ascent begins in Altagracia, and a guide is highly recommended.

This side of the island receives much less rainfall than the Madera side, so there are fewer plants and animals. The aridity allows for better vistas of the land in and around the volcano. It is worth climbing just part way up Concepción—even an hour's hike proffers an impressive view.

NORTH OF MANAGUA

■ Estelí

Estelí (pop. 100,000), the capital of the department of the same name, lies 150km north of Managua and roughly the same distance from the Honduran border on the Interamerican Highway. A liberal stronghold, Estelí saw extremely heavy fighting during the Revolution. Buildings still pock-marked with bullet holes provide constant reminders of the region's recent history, as does the **Galería de Héroes y Mártires.** During the 1980s, collective farms in the region swarmed with "work brigades" of international volunteers husbanding livestock, pressing cheese, and planting cotton, tobacco, and vegetables. Even after the Sandinistas' fall, foreign volunteers still frequent Estelí, where some of them sharpen their Spanish skills at one of the town's many language schools. In July of 1993, violence broke out here between rebellious *contras* frustrated with the government and former Sandinistas.

Political problems aside, Estelí is an amicable and thriving agricultural town with a few noteworthy sights. The green, surrounding hills and low, ephemeral clouds that occasionally breeze through the sky bring a gentle cool that makes Estelí a refreshing change from the pounding heat and turmoil of cities like Managua and León. Estelí's history may give the city an eerie aura and keep travelers on their toes, but relax— that 6am siren is no air-raid; it's just the city's alarm clock.

ORIENTATION

There is only one main street in Estelí, and navigation inevitably entails going up and down it, over and over and over again. **Avenida Bolívar** runs north to south along the whole length of Estelí. The bus terminal is at the south end of town, one block west of Bolívar and 13 blocks south of the **Parque Central.** Six blocks north of the park, the city ends at the river, Río de Estelí. **Calle Perú** runs east to west one block south of the park. The **Interamerican Highway** runs along the east edge of town, six blocks east of Bolívar. Unlike León, Estelí doesn't feel comfortable after dark. If you need to go out, try and stick to Av. Bolívar and avoid the park.

PRACTICAL INFORMATION

Travel Agencies: El Tisey (tel. 33-0-99), located right next to the Hotel Mesón and owned by the same people; 1 block north of the northeast corner of the park. Cashes traveler's checks (when they're not out of money). Open Mon.-Fri. 8am-noon and 1:30pm-5:30pm, Sat. 8am-noon. **Agencia de Viajes Nicaragua** (tel. 320-18) is 1 block south and ½ block west of the Parque Central. Open Mon.-Fri. 8am-noon and 2-5:30pm, Sat. 8am-noon.

Currency: The Esquina de Bancos (bank corner) is 1 block south and 1 block west of the southwest corner of the park. You'll find a **BANIC** (tel. 32-2-65, 32-2-01) which changes cash Mon.-Fri. 8:30am-4pm, Sat. 8:30am-noon. **Hotel Mesón** changes traveler's checks.

Regional Buses: Buses leave from the terminal at the south end of town. To: **Matagalpa** (every 30min., 2hr., 6C); **Managua** (every hr., 4am-early afternoon, 3½hr., 15C; express 20C); **Ocotal** and **Somoto** (every 30min., 11C). Buses to the border at **Las Manos** can be caught at Ocotal, and for the border at **Espino** from Somoto. To reach **León**, take a direct bus at 6:45am or 3:15pm (15C). Or take a Matagalpa bus and get off at **San Isidro** (1hr., 5C), where they leave for León every 30min. (2hr., 12C).

City Buses: run north to south, 1 street west of Bolívar, from Barrio Rosario to the new hospital, including a stop at the bus terminal. The same buses return south to north along Bolívar. City buses cost 1C and usually are marked "Rosario-Hospital."

Western Union: (tel. 33-5-66), 1 block north and about 25m east of the bus station. Open Mon.-Fri. 9am-5pm, Sat. 9am-4pm, Sun. 9am-noon.

Supermarket: Super Económico (tel. 32-4-05), on Bolívar, 4 blocks south of the Parque Central. Open daily 7:30am-9pm.

Library: Biblioteca Pública Dr. Samuel Meza Brones, 1 block south of the Esquina de Bancos. Open daily 8am-noon and 2-5pm.

AMNLAE: Casa de la Mujer Mercedes Rosales (tel. 33-0-38), on the Interamerican Highway, opposite the Shell station. Counseling and medical attention for women. Open Mon.-Fri. 7am-5:30pm, Sat. 8am-3pm.

Red Cross: (tel. 32-3-30), 2 blocks east and 1 block south of the hospital.

Pharmacy: Farmacia Abdalah (tel. 32-2-44 or 32-8-20), 1 block north of the hospital on Bolívar. While posters of dermatological curiosities may not be your thing, they're open daily 7am-9pm. There is also a natural pharmacy in town, **La Farmacia Popular,** 4 blocks south and 1½ blocks west of the parque on Bolívar, which grows its herbs organically on a *finca* outside of town. Open Mon.-Fri. 8am-noon and 2-5pm, Sat. 8am-noon.

Hospital: (tel. 32-4-39, 32-4-33), 8 blocks south of the plaza on Bolívar. Emergency lines can get long; you might have better luck laying down the plastic at the clinics across the street. The new hospital south of town is overdue for opening.

Police: (tel. 32-6-15), southeast of town, near the *carretera.*

Post office: Surprise! Not at ENITEL/TELCOR. Instead, go to Correos de Nicaragua (tel. 32-0-85), ½ block east of Bolívar on Calle Perú. Open Mon.-Sat. 7:30am-8pm.

Telephones: ENITEL/TELCOR (tel. 32-2-06 or 32-3-33), on Calle Perú, 1 block south and 1 block east of the park. Open daily 7am-9:30pm. A smaller branch is 1½ blocks west on the street between Hospedajes Chepito and San Francisco, 3 blocks north of the bus station. Open Mon.-Sat. 7am-8:30pm, Sun. 8am-6pm.

Telephone code: 71.

ACCOMMODATIONS

Estelí sees its fair share of travelers, and a good number of *hoteles* and *hospedajes* have sprung up as a result. The following span the range from *muy barato* all the way up to *extra-moderno*.

Hotel Nicarao (tel. 32-4-90), on Bolívar, 1½ blocks south of the plaza. The large open-air courtyard walled by colorful murals, thick with tropical vegetation, and blessed with ample seating makes this the place to be. Friendly staff serves zesty food at reasonable prices (breakfast 12-18C; other meals 35C). No laundry facilities, but the staff will clean your dirties for cheap. Even if you're not staying here, you'll find a great selection of Nicaraguan postcards (6C). The door closes early at night; knock to be let back in. Singles with communal bath and no fan 57C; doubles 81C.

Hospedaje San Francisco, on Bolívar, a few blocks north of the bus station, on the east side of the street. Intricate paint job on the walls and the latest in virtual wallpaper almost gives the place a homey feel. Tall, skinny rooms and clean bunkbeds make good use of vertical space. The lower the room number, the closer you are to overhearing the family's entertainment center. Room 7 is the secret hiding place of the real Mona Lisa. Solid locks; self-service laundry area. Front door locks at 11pm. No trimmings. Singles 25C; doubles 35C.

Estelí Region

N

HONDURAS

0   10 miles
0   10 kilometers

Santa María
Volcán Viejo
Cerro el Tizal
Santa Clara
San Fernando
Valle San Diego
Murra
Cerro Chachgua
Cerro el Marimacho
Dipilto
El Jícaro
Cerro California
Macuelizo
Mosonte
Ciudad Antigua
Susucayan
Montaña de Palo Prieto
Totogalpa
Ocotal
Cerro el Perro
Wiwilí
Cerro Montañito de Santa María
Telpaneca
Quilalí
Cerro el Caréto
Yalagüina
Palacagüina
San Juan de Río Coco
El Espino
Somoto
Río Coco
Cerro la Ilusión
Pueblo Nuevo
San Lucas
Condega
Los Banaderos
Sierra los Cedros
Pueblo la Sabana
San Antonio de las Cuchillas
San José de Cusmapa
Llano Vallucán
San Sebastián de Yalí
San Rafael del Norte
San Francisco del Norte
Llano Santa Adela
Lago de Apanás
San Juan de Limay
Rodeo Grande
La Concordia
Río Tuma
Loma la Peña de Agua Sarca
Río Negro
Estelí
La Palestina
San José de Achuapa
Estanzuela
Jinotega
El Tuma
Fila el Venado
Filo de Bulona
Río Coco
Río Estelí
Fila Laguna Seca

Hospedaje Chepito, on Bolívar, just south of Hospedaje San Francisco and a few blocks north of the bus station. Clean quarters surround a very small cement courtyard that doubles as clothesline space. Self-service laundry. Just about the *cheapito*-est place in town. No fans, communal bathrooms. Singles 30C; doubles 40C.

Hotel Mesón (tel. 32-6-55), 1 block north of the northeast corner of the plaza. Aims at an aristocratic air, and comes pretty close. Simple, clean rooms ringed around a jungle garden. Ceiling fans are cool; hot water is hot. Avoid street-side rooms, which are noisy and prone to filling with exhaust fumes. Adjoining restaurant roasts up delicious eats, and the hotel's travel agency cashes traveler's checks in spades. Rooms for 1-4 people, 85, 100, 120, and 140C respectively.

Hotel Alpino (tel. 32-8-28), just off Bolívar a few blocks north of Hospedaje San Francisco. This solid exercise in concrete construction not only houses the Costa Rican consulate, but is run by a U.S.-born veterans of the Nicaraguan war with even bigger plans. The place is in a constant state of expansion. Singles 70C, with bath 130C; doubles 90C; with bath 170C. Warm water in bathrooms.

FOOD

As expected, *comedores, cafetines,* and *rosticerias* line Bolívar. All of them are fairly comparable, but a few places in town deserve special note.

Cafe Palermo Pizzería (tel. 32-5-69), ½ block south of the Esquina de Bancos. The owner has cooked in 5-star Miami hotels, and your mouth will know it. Pizzas range from a small ham-and-cheese (38C) to a large one with the works (118C). Vegetarians will salivate over the cheesy pasta Primavera (with capers! 23C). The best deal, however, is the daily lunch special, which gives you an entree, bread,

NICARAGUA

and *refresco* for just 20C. Don't let the framed magazine ads put you off—there's no place else like this in Estelí. Open Wed.-Mon. noon-10pm.

Hospedaje Comedor "Familiar" (tel. 33-6-66), 3½ blocks off the Esquina de Bancos. You'll feel like you're eating at home, and really, you are—in fact, you need to warn this family a day in advance for a meal. It merits forethought: their vegetarian special could easily feed three people (30C), and a whopping fruit-filled plate, pancakes, and coffee are available for 20C. They also have a few, clean, quiet rooms as a hostel (30C per person). Open when you agree on a time for your meal.

China Garden (tel. 34-0-76), on the west side of the Parque Central. Not a garden, and the only Chinese fare consists of a pretty *faux* platter of chop suey. Some of the Nicaraguan food, however, has a vaguely Chinese flavor. The corrugated half-dome architecture suggests that the place was built of used drainage pipe. But the food draws throngs of people. Shrimp 45C; *hamburguesas* 7C. Try the delicious coconut *flan* for dessert. Open Fri.-Wed. 11:30am-9:30pm.

Hotel Mesón Restaurant (tel. 32-6-55), in the Hotel Mesón. Polish your Tevas: this place is decked out with tablecloths and real cloth napkins. Pepper-and-peanut steaks, barbecued pork, seafood. *Comida corriente* 20C; entrees 45-70C. Open daily 7am-10pm.

Taquería Beverly, across the street from the main church's southeast corner. Tacos, tacos, tacos! Straight from Mexico to Nicaragua, or so the sign says. Grab one for only 9C.

SIGHTS AND ENTERTAINMENT

The **Galería de Héroes y Mártires,** half a block south of the cathedral, effectively commemorates Estelí's revolutionary *callidos* (fallen ones). The abstract mural along the outside wall is a stunning, multi-colored series of silhouettes (open daily; run by the Mothers of the Fallen Ones who request donations). For another graphic reminder of the violence that occurred here, visit the large **bomb fragment** and accompanying monument, three blocks west of the red Firestone outlet on Bolívar.

The **Casa de la Cultura Leonel Rugama Rugama, Poeto y Revolucionario** (tel. 33-0-21) is just down the block from the **Galería.** Local youths have covered the walls with cartoons and propaganda that proffer opinions on health care, unemployment, and the environment. These paintings are the fruits of the labor of the project Talleres de Muralismo, housed in a brightly painted building two and a half blocks west and four blocks south of the Parque Central, near the schools. Here, the children of the barrio are taught the techniques of *muralismo,* the prevalent artistic style of Nicaraguan towns. Nica murals are often didactic, but these young painters seem to have enjoyed a good deal of expressive freedom. Classes in guitar, painting, drama, and dance are also held here, and on Saturday nights the Casa hosts performances and exhibitions by local artists. The reception area sells some interesting books, pamphlets, and artwork (open Mon.-Fri. 8am-noon and 2-5pm, Sat. 8am-noon). On the south side of the plaza, in front of the Centro Recreativo, are the **boulders** from the archaeological dig at Las Pintadas, which bear prehistoric carvings of animals, birds, and human figures. Estelí's city government adopted the design carved into the central boulder. The **Centro Recreativo** (tel. 32-0-10) is on the plaza's south side. Saturday and Sunday evenings, studs don their studs for disco time. Other nights people come here to play and watch games of basketball and volleyball. All are welcome.

■ Near Estelí

Seven kilometers south of Estelí, **El Salto de Estanzuela** crashes and thunders like a 48m high waterfall should. Getting there requires a trip into the meandering hills and gorgeous countryside south of Estelí. *Camionetas* leave from the bus station at a sporadic rate; just ask for the *camioneta para ir al Salto de Estanzuela* (5C). In fact, they run sporadically enough that it might be quicker to trek it by foot. This takes about an hour and a half, but the walk offers great views of Estelí from on high (i.e. the road can be steep) and the rockiest farmland you'll ever see, with more stones than soil. Plus, your hike will make you that much more appreciative of the cool pool and the mists at the falls. Though the churned water stays a bit muddied, swimming is a treat. The rocks near the shores (big, but round) give way to sandier areas as you reach deeper water.

Walk south down Bolívar, which merges with the highway outside of town (some of which is under construction). Continue on the highway past the police check point; just beyond the new hospital (also under construction) and 15,000-gallon water tank, take your first right onto a dirt road. Locals will tell you the *"Salto is recto, recto"* (straight ahead)—while you do stay on this same road nearly the whole way, it is a bit curvy curvy. You'll cross a small stream, crest one hill (about halfway there), bridge a brook, climb another hill, and start heading down again before you come to a wooden gate where another road branches to the right. (This is where the *camioneta* should drop you off, if you decide to ride.) Follow this road downhill 10 minutes until you hear and see the water falling on your left. There are some shortcuts across this last hill, but you're better off sticking to the road unless a trustworthy local helps you through the underbrush. Only two things could ruin this lovely daytrip—being dehydrated and being mugged. Bring lots of water (though the region is cool, it is also dry); don't bring lots of money or bags (locals sometimes follow gringos to the falls to lighten their baggage—but don't worry unnecessarily).

The town of **Condega,** 30 minutes to the northeast of Estelí, makes for a nice afternoon as well. All Estelí buses destined for Somoto and Ocotal stop in Condega, so it's very easy to reach (4C). The town's main attraction is the **Museo Arqueologico Julio Cesar Salgado** (open Mon.-Fri. 8am-noon and 2pm-5pm; free), which is the only official museum in the entire department of Estelí, and a very impressive one at that. Located at the southwest corner of the park, near where the bus drops you off, the museum offers a wide sample of intricately decorated pre-Columbian ceramics, many of which are entitled in English. The prize possessions of the museum (and the town's pride) are the **Incensarios Indígenas**—large, funky-looking ceramic boxes, each of which is covered entirely by spikes. Local tribes fashioned the insides to serve as incense burners. The **Casa de la Cultura** of Condega, where local children undertake apprenticeships in leatherworking and luthiery, shares the same building as the museum. If it's a stringed instrument you're looking for, don't fret. Handmade guitars, ranging in size from dainty to daunting, can be purchased (600-950C) in the gift shop.

Meander south on the street that runs by the park and the museum to see the Alcaldía's wall mural of the map of the Condega region. Continuing on this paved road will soon take you up the hill back to the *carretera* with the **Bar y Restaurante Linda Vista** (tel. 752-2669) nearby. Nothing to write home about, but a good resting spot (*comida corriente* 15C; beer 7C) before heading north a block and a half to a more *linda* and intriguing *vista*. Go right up the path beside the blue-toned cemetery; at the top of the hill overlooking the city, you'll find the hull of a **Honduran supply plane** downed during the *Contra* war in the 1980s. The wings have fallen off, and the body is covered with graffiti, but the remains are a reminder of how close this community was to the fighting—the plane crashed in a field southeast of town.

The baked-clay *pueblito* of **Ducuale Grande** is famous for its fine ceramics sold worldwide. Either walk 20 minutes north on the highway until you see the sign on the left for the "Taller Communal de Ceramicá" or catch another Somoto/Ocotcal bus (2C) to the same point. Follow this gravel road for twenty minutes—you'll pass by tobacco sheds and cross a small river—until you arrive at the Big Ducuale. The road blurs into the dusty center of town, but continues more or less straight ahead (and a little to the right). Soon you'll see two more signs by a latrine. Take the road to the left and in 200m, you'll be rewarded with a quiet but busy cooperative factory. Forty Ducualians dig, throw, rub, bake, paint, and carve the rich clay into everything from earrings (15C) to plates (170C) to owl-shaped pots (300C). You're welcome to observe the whole process and look through the final products in a tarp-covered lean-to. Try and bring a variety of bills if you plan to make a purchase—they don't carry a lot of change.

NICARAGUA

■ Matagalpa

Matagalpa is coffee country, settled in the 19th century by small waves of Western European immigrants. The Europeans in Matagalpa these days are mostly volunteer workers or tourists, but the caffeinated concoction's industry still booms. Matagalpa's more recent history is heavily tainted by its affiliations with the Sandinista cause; Matagalpa was a FSLN stronghold during the revolution against the Somoza regime. In fact, Matagalpa's favorite son is the revolutionary leader Carlos Fonseca, whose house is now a museum. *"Carlos vive,"* assures a sign in the Parque Catedral, *"porque su obra es inmortal"* ("Carlos lives because his work is immortal").

The cool, moist climate and mountainous terrain of Matagalpa make this region one of Nicaragua's most visually arresting. The city itself lies within a cluster of hills, some of which have sprouted shanty towns. The nearby **Selva Negra** (Black Forest) is surprisingly green. The encroaching vegetation and array of exotic animals make hiking a thrill. However, if your boots aren't made for walkin', you don't even have to stand up to enjoy the spectacular views from the bus as it winds to and from Matagalpa proper. Though misty Matagalpa is a town of few archetypal tourist sights, it's easy to be wooed by the city's moderate climate and insouciant atmosphere.

ORIENTATION AND PRACTICAL INFORMATION

Matagalpa rests on the east bank of the **Río Grande Matagalpa,** a narrow river which later widens to become one of Nicaragua's largest rivers before spilling out into the Caribbean. **Parque Rubén Darío** lies at the south end of town, five blocks east and two blocks north of the bus terminal. **Avenida José Benito Escobar,** more familiarly referred to as "Calle de Comercios," abuts the west side of the Parque Rubén Darío and then runs north for another seven blocks to meet the **Parque Catedral** (which not surprisingly sits just below the freshly painted municipal cathedral). **Avenida Central,** also known as "Avenida de los Bancos," spins off the southeast corner of the Parque Catedral and runs roughly parallel with Calle de Comercios, passing Parque Rubén Darío two blocks to the east.

Budget Travel: Viajes America (tel. 22-5-20), between Calle de Comercios and Av. de los Bancos, 2 blocks south of the Parque Catedral. Open Mon.-Fri. 8am-noon and 2-5pm.
Currency: A number of banks (all on Av. de los Bancos, oddly enough) change cash, but only one changes traveler's checks: **Bancentro** (tel. 39-22) 2½ blocks south of the cathedral. Requires a passport and chomps a huge 4% commission.
Telephones: ENITEL/TELCOR (tel. 27-01) stands near its antenna one block east of the cathedral's northeast corner. Open daily 7:30am-9pm.
Western Union: At Banco Nicaragüense (tel. 36-93), one block south of Bancentro. Open Mon.-Fri. 8:30am-4pm, Sat. 8:30am-noon. There's another station in the appliance store, **Comercio Calero Mendieta** (tel. 40-84; fax 32-45), one block south and ½ block west of the southwest corner of Parque Rubén Darío. Open Mon.-Fri. 8am-noon and 2-5pm.
Buses: 2 blocks south and 5 blocks west of Parque Rubén Darío. To: **Managua** (every 30min., 2½hr., 14C; 7:30am express, 18C); **San Isidro** (every hr., 1hr., 5C); **Estelí** (every 30min., 2hr., 8C); and **Jinotega** (every 40min., 1½hr., last bus leaves at 6:20pm, 45min., 8C). Buses leave San Isidro for **León** every 30 min. (2½hr., 11C). Buses bound for **Río Blanco** leave every 1½hr. from the Cotran de Guanuca, a neighborhood in the far north of Matagalpa (taxi 3C). These buses stop 1½hr. into their trip at **Muy Muy** (14C for the Matagalpa-Muy Muy leg). Buses to **Boaco** can be caught at Muy Muy (every 2hr., 2hr., 15C). Be early—Muy Muy doesn't have very many buses passing through to Boaco, and the last one leaves at 2pm. For more information, see Boaco (p. 314).
Supermarket: Supermas (tel. 24-68), located one block west of Parque Rubén Darío. Cheap *Flor de Caña* rum (16.5C for 375mil), and a dozen brands of ketchup. Open daily 8am-8pm.

Pharmacy: Farmacia Blandon (tel. 24-0-53), on Calle de Comercios, 1½ blocks north of Parque Rubén Darío. Knock on the door if you come after hours.
Red Cross: (tel. 22-0-59, 37-86, or 02-69), 2 blocks west of the police station, just over the river. **Emergency:** 119.
Hospital: (tel. 22-0-81 or 22-0-82), right next to Red Cross, with a huge garden in front; it's worth a trip, even if you're healthy.
AMNLAE: Casa de la Mujer Nora Hawkins (tel. 30-47), ½ block east of northeast corner of Parque Rubén Darío. Open Mon.-Fri. 8:30am-5:30pm.
Police: (tel. 35-11 or 38-70), on the south side of the Parque Catedral in the triple-blue shaded complex.
Post office: Correos de Nicaragua (tel. 38-80; fax 20-04), across from the northwest corner of Parque Rubén Darío. Fax service available. Open daily 7am-7pm.
Telephone Code: 612.

ACCOMMODATIONS

Matagalpa offers up a nice spread of hotels and *hospedajes*. Be forewarned, however, that despite Matagalpa's location on the banks of a river in one of the wettest regions of the country, water runs only sporadically; most establishments keep tanks and a bucket on hand for toilet-flushing and showers.

Hotel Plaza (tel. 23-80), on the south side of Parque Rubén Darío. Clean rooms *sans* baths, over a green garage door. A few extra córdobas will get you a room in the courtyard. Bring your own toilet paper, unless your arse has an affinity for newsprint. Check out the planter in Room 20: plastic flowers, real dirt. Upstairs rooms 23C (only one with bath). Downstairs rooms 32C (all have bath).
Hotel Matagalpa (tel. 38-34), 1½ blocks east of the northeast corner of Parque Rubén Darío. Immaculate establishment with friendly management. Plus, you get a towel, soap, *and* toilet paper. Lounge for TV watching, and adjoining restaurant serves decent food. Upstairs rooms nestled amid the fruit trees are breezy and have pretty views. Singles 40C, with bath 60C.
Hotel del Centro/Downtown (tel. 29-13), 2½ blocks north of Parque Rubén Darío, this place is a great find if you team up with other travelers since you pay by the *cuarto*, not per person. Small establishment has proportionately sized pool tables in the lobby. Without private bath, 45-75C; two beds 90C; three beds 120C. Ask to see the rooms first—one bedroom has a bath which rivals the room for size.
Hotel Ideal (tel. 33-13), 2 blocks north and 1 block west of the cathedral. The ritziest digs in Matagalpa, but only ideal if you're in the mood to blow a bundle. Big, comfortable rooms with ceiling fans and *agua purificada*. Half a dozen turtles eke out a living on the small lobby pool. Nice restaurant too. All rooms 120C.

FOOD

Matagalpa seems to specialize in the *cafetín* or *rosticeria*, the small, the informal and the fried—fried chicken, fried bananas, fried potatoes. In addition to these kitchen-based operations, Matagalpa also possesses a few real *comedores*, the old fashioned point-and-eat style of dining on the street.

Restaurant Jin Shan (tel. 30-24), between Av. de los Bancos and Calle de Comercios, 1 block south of Parque Catedral. Classic Chinese restaurant get-up, complete with lacquered fans and paper lamps. The food is distinctive though, in that it actually resembles Chinese food. Fried rice is nice. Chow mein, fit to reign. Dishes come in regular (45-65C) or *pequeño* (20-30C) servings. Open daily 11am-10pm.
La Casona (tel. 33-9-01), on Calle de Comercios, 2½ blocks south of the parque catedral. This place cooks one mean chicken. And they cook it nice. Wings, breasts, nuggets, burgers, and "economic" (15C)—all *pollo*, all the time. Roost upstairs, downstairs, or outside. And in case you forget where you are, their omnipresent logo (orange and vaguely elephantine) should jar your bird brain. Open daily 9am-11pm to satisfy your breakfast poultry urges.
La Zinica, ½ block east of Parque Catedral's southeast corner. Ladies and gentlemen of the jury—what is it that allows a cafeteria serving only hamburgers (10-12C),

tacos (8C), and chicken (20c) to call itself "the best of the north?" The pink, green, and yellow tablecloths differentiating the sections? Or the fact that its screen doors make it nearly bug-free, which some *comedores* can't claim? You be the judge. Open daily 10am-10pm.

Restaurant Ideal (tel. 22-4-83 or 23-3-13), in Hotel Ideal. Pleasant outdoor dining, at breezy tables under a roof. Sneak here to nurse a cold one and watch satellite TV from the States. Chicken in wine sauce 45C, *bistec* 45C, lobster 85C. Earliest risers in town: open Mon.-Sat. 6am-midnight, Sun. 6am-8pm.

SIGHTS AND ENTERTAINMENT

The **Casa Museo Carlos Fonseca's** centerpiece is a series of grainy black-and-white photographs which trace the life of a revolutionary. The few artifacts on display (Fonseca's typewriter, his eyeglasses, his gun) were carefully selected to convey his socialist fervor. The museum also sells a slim biography of Fonseca for 10C; you'll glean just as much from the excerpts posted beside the displays. It is located one block east of the southeast corner of Parque Rubén Darío (open Mon.-Fri. 9am-noon and 2-5pm; free). **Casa de Cultura** (tel. 31-58), a good resource in place of the now-closed tourist office, is located next to the library. The Casa houses the usual assortment of local artwork, workshops, and the obligatory photo of Darío in repose (open Mon.-Fri. 7am-12:30pm and 2-5pm). Fine examples of Nicaragua's **ceramica negra** can also be found in Matagalpa. This shiny black kiln-work comes in all shapes and sizes, at startlingly low prices for handmade goods. The **Tienda de Ceramica Negra** (tel. 22-4-64), 1½ blocks north of Parque Rubén Darío, between Av. de los Bancos and Calle de Comercios, is open Monday through Saturday 8am-5:30pm, and sells locally-made gifts and souvenirs. There's also a kiosk in the northern part of Parque Rubén Darío that vends similar items. Give a little whistle at the gate to be let in.

Matagalpa, like most festive-hearted Nicaraguan towns, gets hopping on the weekends (Fri., Sat., and Sun. nights). One disco, **AutiFaz,** is located in the restaurant Rogal Bar, one block east of the bus station in the south of town. Another, the **Familiar,** is located near the *salida a Managua*. For a small town, Matagalpa has a disproportionately large number of pool halls. Two of the more spacious venues are the **Pool Center Club,** a half block east of Comedor San Martín, and the Centro Recreativo, **"Mirage 10,"** which has a wider variety of racy posters and larger tables, one and a half blocks south of the Parque Central on Calle de Comercios.

■ Near Matagalpa

The **Selva Negra** (Black Forest) is a coffee plantation, forest reserve, and hotel/restaurant all in one—and could very well be your best excursion in the country. In the 1890s, a group of about 30 German immigrants came to the mountains of northern Nicaragua to get some elbow room and to try their hand at the coffee business. One of these original German immigrants founded the main coffee plantation at today's Selva Negra. The settlers named their new homes after their old ones in Germany; thus, the coffee plantation at Selva Negra was named Hammonia (Latin for Hamburg). In high European pomp and splendor, the settlers used to convene for tea every Sunday. The elite Nicas still meet to eat a Sunday buffet (for a pricey 100C).

Regular meals and rooms at the **Hotel and Restaurant Selva Negra** (tel. 38-83) are about as costly. Then again, you're also getting a bit of history for your buck—the establishment was founded by Eddy and Mausi Kühl, direct descendents of the original settlers. Both Kühls can regale you with the misadventures of their ancestors, as well as relate the story of their ecologically sound coffee production. They export their rich fruit-tasting beans worldwide; the mucilage (coffee refuse) stays on the farm and powers the kitchen's gas stoves. A gorgeous reservoir pond by the restaurant spins a turbine which electrifies the whole she-bang, thus avoiding deforestation.

And de forest is de lovely. Nearly 80% of the 2000 acre estate is protected, laced with a network of marvelous, carefully labeled hiking paths. (Do they call it the **Romantic Trail** because slippery stones make you clench you lover?) A free map is available at the hotel desk, but signs (in English, Spanish and sometimes German) direct you through the refreshingly cool and moist jungle. Vibrant toucans, woodpeckers, and even the mythical quetzal inhabit the forest. Listen for the blunt calls of randy frogs, the chatter of chirpy birds, and the occasional roar of a resident howler monkey—it sounds like a cross between that noise your straw makes when it squawks through a plastic lid and a dog barking into a bucket. Really. Early morning birdwatchers can hope to catch more than worms; look for hummingbirds, butterflies with transparent wings, and giant gentle rodents—if you're quiet, they will come. The trails pass beneath the 150m canopy of dense foliage, around fallen and moss-covered trees, and over small jungle brooks. Take a hike and forget about whatever frustrations urban Nicaragua has caused you.

Don't avoid the restaurant because of its high prices, as the 25C entrance fee you paid at the gate entitles you to a food coupon of equal value. Whatever you order, don't miss a "Cupa Joe," grown in the backyard (your budget-minded brain quickly calculates you can down five *tazas* (cups) for that admission ticket bunched up your fist). Also, where else will you find sausage and sauerkraut (65C) in Nicaragua? The restaurant is open daily 8am-8pm.

Officially, a **youth hostel** exists on the property—see the cheery, flag-studded cabin just below the main lodge (US$10 per person). Usually, they only will open this for groups of approximately 9-15 people. However, the manager can offer young travelers a hotel bed for US$15, which starts to sound inexpensive once you compare it to the cabañas, which run upwards of US$150 per night (granted, you can pack a dozen people into each).

To get there, take any bus bound for Jinotega and ask to be let off at Selva Negra (about 35min. of crawling uphill, 4C). The road to Selva Negra is marked at its entrance by a rainbow-painted and mangled *tanquita* (little army tank). The first kilometer down this road is lined with evergreen trees, which then give way to the swaying, dark green leaves of coffee plants. When you reach the entrance to Selva Negra proper, marked by a red and white gate, you must pay the 25C entrance fee (which entitles you the meal coupon described above). The restaurant, hotel, and reception area are up the hill, surrounded by cages of monkeys, parrots, turkeys, and rabbits.

■ Jinotega

Like many northern Nicaraguan towns, Jinotega's economy was drained by the *Contra* battles in the '80s. The pueblo has yet to fully recover which means you'll discover one of the quietest *centros* in the country. This is a welcome change from the eardrum-crushing cacophony in other cities, though it also means there's just not that much to do.

Orientation and Practical Information Streets are laid out in a reassuringly rational grid. They are also named—after the usual poets, martyrs, and heroes—and on top of that, they are numbered (even more useful). *Calles* run east to west, *avenidas* north to south. The **Parque San Juan,** on the west end of town, is home to the **Iglesia de San Juan; Calle Central** lines the park's south side; **Avenida Central** runs one block east of the park. Buses drop you off a block west of **Parque Octosca,** which is five blocks west and three blocks south of Parque San Juan.

A handsome **ENITEL/TELCOR** office (tel. 20-21) lies just ½ block south of the park's southeast corner, and is open daily 7am-9pm. A group of **banks** stand near the northeast corner of the main park; alas, none change traveler's checks, but **Banco Mercantil** (tel. 26-69) changes cash and has the best hours (open Mon.-Fri. 8:30am-6pm, Sat. 8:30am-12:30pm). **Buses** depart for **Managua** (every hour, 4hr., 26C) and **Matagalpa** (every ½hr., 1½hr., 8C) from the bus station in the southeast part of town. **Farmacia 24 Horas** (tel. 24-09), ½ block north of the park's northwest corner, is only open for 10 of those 24 hours (open daily 8am-6pm). While the **Red Cross** (tel. 22-22) is located in the run-down northern part of town, both the **hospital** (tel. 26-26) and **police** (tel. 22-15) are near the bus station. The newly opened **post office** (tel. 20-

22), called **Correos de Nicaragua,** is so recent most people can't direct you to it—try asking at the **ENITEL** station how to find it. The **telephone code** is 632.

Accommodations and Food There's no place like *hem* (*Swedish:* home). **Hotel Solientina** (tel. 23-34) outshines its competition—yah, it is in a league of its own. Find it between Calles 4 and 5, one block east of Av. Central. The blankets, sheets, and beds brought over by the Swedish *dueña* ensure a perfect sleep, and Scandinavian cleanliness keeps the place spotless (40C per person with communal bath; 70C per person with private bath; 135C double). **Hotel Tito** (tel. 25-30) marshals rooms for 35C just ½ block north of the park's northeast corner. Quality beds can be found at **Hotel Rosa** (tel. 24-72), one block east of the church. Desperate travelers could venture into the north end's *pensiones*—but you certainly get what you pay for, and you only pay 10C.

Hiking three blocks north and ½ block east of the park's northeast corner brings you to a slice of Italy, **Pizza's Venezia** (tel. 35-28)—The Venezia of Pizza? Small vegetarian pizza (27C) comes short on sauce but long on veggies. Other pizzas cost 25-90C depending on size and toppings (open Mon.-Thurs. noon-9pm, Fri.-Sun. noon-10pm). **Colmena** (tel. 20-17) lies 1½ blocks east of the northeast corner of the park. The usual classy fare (steaks, seafood, and such) is made more intriguing by pre-tax pricing: beer (6.09C), shrimp (69.56C). Mastercard and Visa accepted (open daily 11am-11pm). **Maryaser** is a small restaurant 4½ blocks north of the northwest corner of the park. A big (12 feet long) brown bottle behind the bar beckons you to imbibe.

Sights and Entertainment The **Iglesia de San Juan** remains in a revolving state of restoration—the eastern domes are freshly painted, and the western towers wait expectantly for similar treatment. A series of saintly statues inside culminates with a glassed-in, lit-up Christ kneeling in the buffeting inside the altar.

Though Nicaraguan parks begin to resemble one another after a while, the **Parque San Juan** compactly combines a number of common components—a Sandinista fountain with a Fonesca quotation, a public library, a playground, and monuments to war heroes, mothers, and Darío. Bi-level construction gives the final touch.

For those with a cross to bear, **Las Peñas de la Cruz** stands high on the west of town. This hill is accessible via a number of winding paths upward through the cemetery, almost all of which lead to the cross. The trails are rocky, steep, and especially difficult when wet, so keep an eye out for portentous clouds. Once near the cross's peak, the mount is easier to ascend from behind, through still attainable from the front. It takes about 45 minutes to ascend and half an hour to work your calves downhill. The **Club de Billares Mirage** is located one block east and half a block south of the park's southeast corner and maintains the usual pool hall posters of undressing women, but distinguishes itself with a revolutionary mural covering one of its walls (open daily noon-late; 15C per hour).

EAST OF MANAGUA

▓ Boaco

A rough gem set in Nicaragua's central mountains, Boaco is renowned for its expansive cattle ranches, or better yet, its cattle ranchers. Hold on to your hats, partner, as cowboys ride the streets of Boaco all gussied up in riding boots and spurs, cattle switches at their sides. The most popular watering holes in town always have a few horses parked out front. Residents of Boaco overflow with cowboy pride and a patriotic spirit for their little mountain town. The town's patron saint is the Apostle Santiago, whose day is celebrated each year with a week-long *fiesta* culminating on July 25th. Supposedly, when the Sandinistas were camped outside Boaco, preparing to enter the city, Santiago himself conjured up the sounds of an enemy army approaching and scared the Sandinistas away. The FSLN forces never entered Boaco again.

Orientation and Practical Information The oldest and most prestigious area of Boaco is its *ciudad alta* (high city), built atop a hill, with beautiful vistas of the mountains and *ciudad baja* below. The **tourist office** is tucked away in the northeast corner of Parque Central. The **bus station** lies at the south end of town, the *ciudad alta* lies at the north, and the *ciudad baja* fills the valley between the two. The street just west of the bus station and marketplace is Boaco's main street, heading downhill to the north, winding its way through the *ciudad baja,* and then ascending a steep slope to emerge at the Parque Central in the *ciudad alta.*

Cash, but not traveler's checks, can be exchanged at either of the two following **banks,** located one block east and one block north of the Parque Central. **Banco Nacional de Desarrollo** (tel. 23-83; fax 22-11) is open Monday through Friday 8am-4:30pm and Saturday 8-11:30am. **Banco Nicaragüense** (tel. 25-24; fax 23-08) is open Monday through Friday 8:30am-4pm and Saturday 8:30am-noon. **Buses** leave from Boaco's bus station for **Managua** (every 45min. starting at 4am, 2hr., 12C) and **Río Blanco.** Exit Managua-bound buses at **San Benito** in order to catch buses to **Estelí, San Isidro,** and **Matagalpa.** Matagalpa can also be reached by getting off the Río Blanco bus at Muy Muy (2 hrs., 15C) and waiting for a Río Blanco-Matagalpa bus (1½hr., 14C). To catch a bus for either **Juigalpa** (15C) or **Rama** (40C), take any bus bound for Managua and get off after about 20 minutes at the *enpalme de Boaco* (intersection of Boaco; 5C). For **Red Cross** assistance call 22-00 or 23-19. **Farmacia Romero** (tel. 23-87), just west of Parque Central's northwest corner, meets most minor pharmaceutical needs. To reach **Hospital Niebrowsky** (tel. 22-53), follow the signs from the bus station. The **police** office (tel. 22-76 or 25-74) stands proudly on the park's northwest corner. **Post office** and **fax** services (fax 22-66) are available at **Correos de Nicaragua,** one block north of the park's church, right beside El Alpino Restaurant (open Mon.-Fri. 8am-noon and 1:30-5:30pm, Sat. 8am-noon). **ENITEL/ TELCOR** (tel. 24-90), which provides phone, mail, and fax service, is located in a nondescript, unmarked building on the south side of Parque Central. **Telephones** are open daily 7am-9pm. The **telephone code** is 842.

Accommodations and Food Hotel Sobalvarro (tel. 25-15), on Parque Central's south side, is the only hotel in the *ciudad alta* and has murals to boot. Neat and comfy rooms share baths. The view from the patio out back will knock your socks off, but the incessantly cawing parrots in the courtyard may ruin the transcendent moment. The hotel's thin walls equal long, loud Saturday nights. Still, the Sobalvarro is recognized as the best bet in town (singles 35C; doubles 60C; triples 80C). **Hotel Boaco** runs a close second, however. Advantages: located near the bus station on main street (the sign says only "Hotel"), private baths available, cheaper. Disadvantages: near the bus station on main street, lacks Sobalvarro's view, thin beds. Advice: try and get a single for yourself and double up the mattresses (20C per person without bath; 30C, with bath, thin bed; 40C with wider bed and fan; 50C with double bed and fan). **Pension Montiel** is a final budget option, a half block east of the main street, just before the ascent into the *ciudad alta.* At 20C per person, the rooms are cramped, and the facilities rustic (read: one toilet seat on the wall).

La Cueva, east of the south side of Parque Central, is a nice place to scarf down some tasty *ranchero* vittles. Two levels of tables overlook the *ciudad baja* (chicken 25C, shrimp 45C, *boacano* beef dishes 40-45C). Check out the fake cowhide menus (open Tues.-Wed. 11am-10pm, Thurs.-Sun. 11am-2am; 5C cover after 8pm, when the place becomes a dynamite disco). El Alpino, half a block north of the banks, has a wide selection of hamburgers (12-15C) and even a chicken burger (10C). Boaco *is* the cattle-country capital, and El Alpino cooks up its beef every which way (45-60C). An air-conditioned side room is operative on hot days (open daily 8am-10pm). The kiosko in Parque Central is a nice place to buy tasty tamales and a drink for just 6C.

Sights and Entertainment More than anything, just soak up the view. One great place to do this is the **cemetery** in the south of town, half a block north of the bus station (open Mon.-Fri. 8am-noon and 1-5pm, Sat. 8am-noon and 2-5pm, Sun. 9am-noon and 2-4pm). The cemetery covers a small hill with a motley crew of crosses, angels, and saints. Non-necrophilics might prefer the higher vista of **El Cerrito,** the yellow pole at the top of the city, a few blocks north of the park. This viewpoint was constructed for Boaco's 1995 Centennial, as was the **Paseo de Los Bailantes,** an ornate staircase that leads up from the *ciudad baja* to the *ciudad alta,* one block east of the cathedral. Word has it that the hottest place in town on weekend nights is **La Cueva** (see **Food,** above). Or shoot some pool at **Billares Julia,** located at the base of the big hill on the main street.

■ Juigalpa

About halfway between Managua and Rama, Juigalpa is much more than just a pit stop. The small town is the capital of the department of Chontales, the region which, along with Boaco to the northwest, produces most of Nicaragua's beef. Chontaleños are known throughout Nicaragua for their cattle-driving skills. Juigalpa is only about 115m above sea level, but its location atop a small mesa provides impressive views of the surrounding peaks. The **Parque Palo-Solo,** at the east of town, presents a 180° panorama of the **Cordillera de Amerrisque,** the mountains directly east of Juigalpa.

If the surrounding landscape is verdant, the town itself is far from dead. The **Parque Central** has recently undergone a substantial facelift—artistic mosaics surrounding the park depict the landscape and daily activities of life in Chontales. Additions to the park include well-groomed rose bushes and a thoughtful, if unrealistic monument to the shoeshine boys that wander through every Nicaraguan town. The **church,** on the park's east side, looks like a bauhaus building orphaned in the middle of Central America. Meanwhile, potential for exploration abounds in the form of Nicaragua's best **archaeological museum** and the **zoo,** which houses lions, baboons, and a lonely chimpanzee, alongside many native Nicaraguan species.

Orientation and Practical Information Buses drop passengers off at the bus station/market area, two blocks east of Parque Central. Everything of interest, except the zoo, lies within a few blocks of the park. The travel agency **Viajes Universo,** 3½ blocks east of Parque Central's southeast corner, is a woman's private home, but she can often help you out. The agency is marked by a Nica Airlines sign hanging out front. Two banks sit near the southwest corner of the park: **Banco Nacional de Desarollo** (tel. 24-67 or 24-27) changes cash and traveler's checks for no fee (open Mon.-Fri. 8:30am-4pm, Sat. 8:30am-noon). **BANIC** (tel. 22-48; fax 23-11) changes only cash, but contains the **Western Union** office (open Mon.-Fri. 8:30am-12:30pm and 1:30-4pm, Sat. 8:30am-noon).

Buses leave from the market to: **Managua** (every 30min., 2½hr., 15C); **Estelí** and **Matagalpa** (get off the Managua bus at San Benito); **Boaco** (get off the Managua bus at the "Enpalme de Boaco" intersection, 15C); and **Rama** (every hr. starting at 4am, 5hr., 28C). The express boat from Rama to **Bluefields** leaves on Tuesday, Thursday, Saturday, and Sunday at 10:30am, so take a 5:30am or earlier bus from Juigalpa to Rama to catch the boat. **Farmacia La Salla** (tel. 09-32) farms out the drugs across from the park's northwest corner (open daily 8am-6pm). The **Supermercado Chontal** (tel. 29-85), one block south and half a block east of the park's southwest corner, isn't so super. Both the **hospital** (tel. 23-30) and **Red Cross** (tel. 22-33) are situated at the *salida a Rama* (exit to Rama). The **police** station (tel. 28-71 or 27-27) is 200m north of the *Escuela Normal,* on the highway at the *salida a Rama.* **ENITEL/TELCOR** (tel. 22-28) provides telephone, postal, and fax service three blocks north of the park's northwest corner (open Mon.-Sat. 7am-9pm). The **telephone code** is 812.

Accommodations and Food The **Hotel Imperial** (tel. 22-94) is one block west of the bus station. Big rooms are all equipped with fans, but its real advantage over the competition is running water (40C per person). The front gate is almost always locked, so you have to ring a buzzer to get in. If you don't want to stay, you may get a hard sell inside a locked gate. **Hospedaje Angelita** (tel. 24-08), just west of Parque Central's northwest corner, is a friendly, clean, family-run place. Lounge with the folks in rocking chairs or use their bucket to shower. Breezy upstairs rooms have fans and mosquito nets. Doors close at 10:30pm (20C per person).

Palo-Solo, five blocks east of Parque Central, is the best place in town for food, drinks, or a scenic seat (open daily noon-10pm, until midnight on weekends). Panoramic views of the mountains and curtains made of lemon-sized colored beads tantalize the eye, while *carne asada* (35-40C), shrimp (60C), and beer (6-15C) delight the palate. The **Pollo Amerrisque,** two blocks east and half a block south of Parque Central's northeast corner, serves up tasty food, but no view. Two pieces of finger-lickin' fried chicken, salad, rice, and bread costs 20C. The succulent *plancha* (steak; 35C) arrives at your table sizzling hot (open daily 10am-10pm). **Soda Arco-Iris,** in the Parque Central (northwest corner), boasts a mural with a model dove busting through the back window. People-watch on the patio while you enjoy typical *soda* fare (sandwiches 8C, tacos 16C, *comida corriente* 20C, big glasses of *refresco natural* 3C). Breakfast is also served (open Mon.-Sat. 7am-9pm, Sun. 10am-8pm).

Sights For a town of its size, Juigalpa has an unusual number of things to see. First and foremost is the **Museo Arqueológico Gregorio Aguilar Barea,** which is well worth the 4C entrance fee. The museum boasts Nicaragua's largest collection of pre-Columbian statues; a lion's share of the figurines are of *chontaleño* origin, and the majority date from 800 to 1200 AD (you can see these through the front gate). Inside, a large collection of ceramics spans the entire gamut of recorded pre-Columbian pottery production, from 500 BC to 1500 AD. The museum is 2½ blocks east of the park's northeast corner (open Mon.-Fri. 8am-noon and 2-4:30pm, Sat. 8am-noon).

In addition, Juigalpa is home to one of Nicaragua's finest zoos, which isn't saying much. The **Jardín Zoológico,** 8 blocks south of the southeast corner of Parque Central (admission 3C). The cages are haphazardly scattered about the zoo's muddy grounds and are often unlabeled—so you have to guess at the animals' identities. Six lean lions pride themselves in a few skimpy, minimum-security cages. Native jaguars and pumas also reside here, along with local and imported primates and several species of unidentified furry animals (UFAs). Some of the animals look so lonely that the visit can depress as well as impress, especially when school children throw rocks at them (open daily 8am-5pm).

Palo-Solo means "lone oak," and look, there it is, five blocks east of the park's north side. The place has a romantic air about it, as it was christened long ago by lovers who came to enjoy the view. Though refurbished, and though three more trees were recently planted, as in the rest of Nicaragua, the park's old name still reigns.

▓ Rama

Rama, mama, is a relaxed little hama-let at the end of the only (allegedly) paved road connecting the rest of Nicaragua to the Atlantic Coast. The Río Síquia and the Río Rama run together at Rama, conspiring to form the wide, east-flowing Río Escondido. The town's *fama* comes not from its panorama, but rather from its unparalleled access to Nicaragua's most important Caribbean port, Bluefields. Rama is perpetually ready for rain: streets have deep gutters, some houses are on stilts, and residents carry umbrellas—you should too.

Practical Information Two blocks south of the market lies the **Parque Parrochial,** where you'll find the tall modern **Catholic church,** which is appealing in a concrete sort of way. The **Banco Nacional de Desarrollo,** the only bank in town (unless you count the Banco Popular's little window), is one long block east of the church. They change dollars (but no traveler's checks) and are open Monday through Friday 8:30am-12:30pm and 1:30-4:30pm; Saturday 8:30am-noon. **Buses** enter Rama from the north and empty beside the market, whose entrance is on the west side of the street under a small blue and white arch. They depart for **Managua** (every 30min., 5-7am, one additional bus at 9am, 8-9hr., 46C). Buses also make their way to **Juigalpa** (every hr., 4am-2pm, 4½hr., 26C). Sluggish "Expresso" **boats** leave Rama for Bluefields from the dock one block west of the market (Tues., Thurs., Sat., and Sun. at 11am, 5hr., 38C). Near the dock is an office where they sell day-of tickets only starting at 8am. You may be asked to show your passport. Your 38C fee is inexplicably split into two parts—3C to get in the gate (pay at small office there) and 35C for the boat (purchase inside the waiting room, last office on the right). On Monday, Wednesday, Friday, and other irregular times, a *panga* (small motorboat) leaves Rama at 8am. There seems to be a kind of equilibrium at work here—it takes 2/5 as long as the Expreso (2 hr.) and costs 5/2 as much (100C); it also is about 1/10 of the size, which works out to 10 times as many waves by the end. The sign at the town **pharmacy,** the garish brown and yellow house almost a full block north of **ENITEL/TELCOR,** reads "El Carmen" (open daily 8am-1pm and 2-7pm; knock on the door and someone can help you after hours). The **Esso Gas Station**, one block and a half south of the market, is the only place to buy bottled water. The **Red Cross** is one block north and two blocks east of the market. The **hospital** (tel. 00-19) is 6km north of town on the highway. Rama's **police** station (tel. 00-26) is one block north and four blocks east of the market. **Postal** service is available at ENITEL/TELCOR (post office open Mon.-Fri. 8am-noon and 2-5pm, Sat. 8am-noon). ENITEL/TELCOR **telephones** are one long block east of the bus stop, disregarding muddy alleys. Long distance service is available, though using a U.S. carrier can be a trial—the office is unfamiliar with using their three digit codes and may want to charge you beyond normal usage (open Mon.-Sat. 7am-8:30pm). The **telephone code** is 817.

Accommodations and Food While you're treading water waiting for your ship to come in, you might as well grab a *cama* in Rama. **Hotel Johanna,** half a block south of the bank, is a bigger than average place with clean beds. Rooms have fans and windows, and the showers and bathrooms here are the best of Rama's lot. (The toilets near room 20 have seats *and* flush.) Rooms on the south side are farthest from the noisy bar below and provide a glimpse at the muddy river (singles 25C). Restaurant/bar downstairs serves *comida corriente* (18C), hamburgers (7C), and tacos (7C). **Hospedaje Central,** just west of ENITEL/TELCOR, has spotless rooms (each with a fan), as well as tolerable pit toilets and bucket-style showers (25C per person). **Hospedaje Jiménez** (tel. 01-56), the new place in town, is the creamy green house just south of the market on the same street as the dock (also 25C per person).

Rama's food is just enough to tide you over; even then, your choices are narrowed since most menu items are out of stock. Street *comedores* often offer cheaper and more plentiful selections. **Hotel Johanna** has a restaurant (see above), as do other hotels in the west of town. **Los Vindes,** half a block south of the market, serves enormous steaks for 45C. Locals come for the jukebox, though the shrimp (50C) and the chicken in wine sauce (45C) are tempting as well (open daily 8am-10pm). Due to the dearth of available recreational activities, a good number of bars have sprung up to help pass the residents' time. There is also a popular **pool hall** just west of the bank. If you're at your wit's end, start a staring contest with a reptile of your choice (try the turtles which dwell in the park's fountain).

THE ATLANTIC COAST

Nicaragua's Atlantic Coast is unlike the rest of the country. The region is part of a geographical area known as **La Mosquitia,** a sparsely populated expanse of rainforest, plains, and coastland extending the length of Nicaragua's east coast into Honduras. La Mosquitia is home to some 70,000 Miskitos, the area's remaining *indígenas*. Other, smaller tribes—including the Sumos, Garifunas, and Ramas—also reside there. In the south, most of the inhabitants speak English and are of West Indian descent.

Today, the Atlantic Coast remains as distinct as ever. Geographically, it is inaccessible by land; politically, it is semi-autonomous, and works for further autonomy; culturally, it is almost a separate entity. Most Atlantic-coasters identify more strongly with their West Indian heritage or indigenous community than with Nicaragua. Sandinista policies meant to unify and develop the country included the institution of mandatory military service and the declaration of Spanish as Nicaragua's national language. To many residents of this coast, these changes smacked of forced cultural assimilation. Some even preferred the reign of Somoza, who at least left them alone.

The Atlantic Coast has a great deal to offer travelers: a colorful Caribbean atmosphere; beautiful, remote communities, a number of lazy beaches, and the opportunity for true exploration. However, travel here is tricky, as there are almost no roads. Unless you fly (small planes serve Bluefields, Puerto Cabezas, Islas de Maíz, and a few towns in Honduras), getting from one place to another involves a great deal of waiting around for a boat that may or may not show up, and when it does, may or may not agree to take you where you want to go—all part of the adventure.

Garifunas: An Eclectic People

Though the **Garifuna** ("Black Carib") people are often spoken of as native Central Americans, they are not indigenous to the mainland. Originally brought from the island of St. Vincent, where slaves and the indigenous **Carib** Indians had already mingled to create a unique cultural and ethnic hybrid, the Garifunas were brought to the Honduran Bay Island of **Roatan** at the end of the 18th century. They have since dispersed along the Atlantic Coast from Belize to Nicaragua. Their **language** and **culture** is a blend of African, Carib, and other influences. Though they, like most tribes, have mixed with other ethnicities since arriving, the Garifunas remain fiercely proud of their heritage.

GETTING AROUND THE ATLANTIC COAST

From Managua to Bluefields you can: 1) take the "Expreso" (ha ha) boat-bus combination; 2) take a Vargas/Peña bus (see below); 3) arrive in Rama by bus at any time and then take a *panga*; 4) fly (the most expensive, but by far the fastest option; 1½hr.).

The crowded Expreso leaves Bluefields for Rama at 5am on Tuesday, Thursday, Saturday, and Sunday, returning to Bluefields the same day around 11am (5hr., 38C each way). A bus leaves Mercado Ivan Montenegro in **Managua** at about 2am, connecting with the Expreso in Rama on the days that it runs (60C). This bus returns to Managua after the Expreso arrives in Rama, thus allowing people to travel directly between Managua and Bluefields. You can choose between the following two seating options: the covered, but open-air rear of the boat, where you will inhale poorly ventilated diesel fumes and may get soaked; or inside the cabin, where you'll be dry, hot, and will inhale the poorly ventilated bathroom fumes heated by the diesel engine. Kids on shore will run aboard the loading boat and reserve a seat for you for 5C.

Transportes Vargas/Peña travels from Managua to Bluefields daily, leaving Mercado Ivan Montenegro at 11pm, leaving Rama by *panga* at 6am, and arriving in Bluefields at 10am. The return trip leaves Bluefields at 6am by *panga*, leaves Rama at 9am, and arrives in Managua at 3:30pm (110C each way). For further information, contact the Vargas/Peña office in Bluefields (tel. 822-2739), located on the main pier.

A third option is to take a *panga*, a big outboard launch. *Pangas* leave Rama on Mondays, Wednesdays, and Fridays at irregularly scheduled times; they also may try to compete with the Expreso and run the other days of the week—in other words, you'll have to ask around, and may have to hire your own (100C is the normal rate). At two hours, the *panga* trip is much faster than the Expreso, makes for a very nice way to see the river (unless it rains), and also allows you to arrive in Bluefields ahead of the crowds. Beware of *pangas* carrying too many and too much—the first hour of your trip might be OK, but by the time the water has kicked up, the fiberglass hull is bouncing like a jackhammer, the slumbering *señora* next to you begins to lean your way, and you've just passed over the gigantic wake of the cargo ship "Sea Mist," your green face will be wishing you had spent the extra dough for a plane ride.

To get to the Caribbean coast by plane, check **La Costeña** (tel. 822-27-50), the company with flights out of Bluefields. Weekdays, planes fly to **Managua** (7:35, 9, 11:15am, 4:20pm; 424C one way, round-trip 759C); the **Corn Islands** (8:05am, 3:10pm; 335C one way, 632C round-trip); and **Puerto Cabezas** (on Mon., Wed., Fri., 2:15pm; 481C one way, 885C round-trip). Nica no longer flies to the Atlantic Coast.

■ Bluefields

Bluefields, a vibrant zephyr of a Caribbean town, was named after Blauvelt, the Dutch pirate who founded it in the 1600s. Today's Bluefields is a *paella* of a city: the population is primarily Creole and *mestizo*, but a number of indigenous groups, such as Miskito, Rama, and Garifuna, spice up the mix. Languages spoken include English (with a sonorous West Indian lilt, *all right*), Spanish, Miskito, and other indigenous tongues. The town pulses with music, much of it streaming out from the dance halls and clubs and flooding the streets with reggae, *merengue, salsa,* and Bon Jovi.

Bluefields is Nicaragua's most important Caribbean port. All of the neighboring communities inland, along the coast, and offshore come to Bluefields both to load up on supplies and to sell and export their bananas, oranges, shrimp, lobster, and other food. The town plays a central role in the life of Nicaragua's remote and exotic Atlantic Coast region, and is the best place from which to explore it.

ORIENTATION AND PRACTICAL INFORMATION

Remember, the murky Caribbean is always to the east. **Calle Central** runs north to south, curving along the coast. At the north end of this road, just north of the tall, red-roofed Moravian church, sits the town's main **pier,** where boats arrive and depart for everywhere but El Bluff (the offshore port). Three main streets run east to west. From north to south (starting south of the main pier) they are: **Avenida Reyes, Calle Cabezas,** and **Avenida Aberdeen.** Av. Aberdeen is the only one that extends east past Calle Central, where you can find a market and the pier from which boats leave for El Bluff.

Tourist Office: Bluefield's **Ministerio de Turismo** office is located in the airport. If you can catch the office when it's open (fickle hours), the staff can help plan trips to groovy nearby locales. A taxi can take you there (10C), or it is about a 20 min. walk from the southern part of town.

Currency Exchange: Banco Nacional de Desarrollo (tel. 27-77), across from the Moravian church, exchanges U.S. dollars and traveler's checks, *but* there is a US$250 min. on checks and a service charge (1% changing to córdobas, 2% changing to US$). Open Mon.-Fri. 8:30am-12:30pm and 1:30-4pm, Sat. 8:30am-11:30am. **Banco Popular** (tel. 26-45), on the corner of Calle Central and Av. Aberdeen, changes cash only. Open Mon.-Fri. 9am-12:30pm and 1:30-4pm, Sat. 8:30am-noon.

Boats: See p. 317 for Rama-Bluefields routes. Departures to the **Corn Islands** leave Bluefield's main pier (3 per week, 40C). The Lynx leaves Wed. at 8:30am; other boats leave Fri. and Sun. mornings at 10am. This is a 5hr. tour—that's right a five hour tour. Landlubbers take note, the same craft that links you from Rama to Bluefields doesn't feel quite so smooth in the Caribbean—after a few hours, the walkway around the cabin looks like a vomit buffet, and catching wind of it can be enough to make even seasoned salts lose their *gallo pinto*. For more information, contact the Lynx office (tel. 25-58) on the south side of the Bluefields pier. Most of the area's boat traffic goes through **El Bluff.** From Bluefields, a *panga* to El Bluff should cost 10C, but some may quote you a higher price. These boats leave every 20 min. or so from the pier in the south of town, by the market at the east end of Av. Aberdeen (13C). The trip takes about 10 min.

Pharmacy: Godoy Farmacia (tel. 24-71), on Calle Cabezas, one block west of Calle Central. Open daily 8am-9pm.

Red Cross: (tel. 25-82), south of town on Calle Patterson (1 block west of Calle Central). The **hospital** (tel. 23-91 or 26-21) is 2km southwest of town, past the airport.

Police: (tel. 24-48), on Calle Central, four blocks south of the Moravian church.
Post Office: same building as ENITEL/TELCOR, but on the eastern end of Av. Reyes. Open Mon.-Fri. 8am-noon and 1-5pm, Sat. 8am-1pm.
Telephones: ENITEL/TELCOR, 3 blocks west of Calle Central in the municipal building on Av. Reyes. Telephones open Mon.-Sat. 8am-9pm, Sun. 8am-6pm.
Telephone Code: 822.

ACCOMMODATIONS

If you've come on the Expreso from Rama, find a place to stay in Bluefields quickly. During high tourist tide, there's often a rush on the town's hotels, which are already full of businesspeople (many of them are Dutch or German).

Hotel Hollywood (tel. 22-82), overlooking the water, 2½ blocks south of the Moravian church. Hooray for Hollywood! The hotel has 12 green and white, clean and breezy, wide and wooden rooms *plus* a veranda which gives this place a light, coastal feel. Air-conditioned restaurant downstairs. One toilet has a seat, one doesn't, paper in neither. Singles 40C; doubles 60C; with 2 beds 70C; or live like a mogul in the air-conditioned annex, 170C.
Mini Hotel-Cafetín Central (tel. 23-62), ½ block west of Calle Central on Calle Cabezas, can't seem to settle on a career. Clean, simple rooms have fans, soap, toilet paper, and towels. The facilities are pretty spotless—Cafetín in front is a great place to eat, with prices as low as you please. Rooms 50C per person.
Hospedaje Elizabeth (tel. 15-41), just north of the Moravian church. This place has a somewhat dark hallway and thin mattresses, but it remains the least expensive viable sleeping option in Bluefields. Elizabeth's young grandson makes a convincing host, and the arcade next door may fill your dreams with visions of Pacman. Singles 30C; doubles 40C.
Hotel Marda Mans (tel. 24-29), the sparkling place next door to Hotel Claudia, has a lounge and restaurant downstairs. Its 3 singles (shared bath) are 50C; double 60C. The other rooms are mondo to the max—170C yields a private bath and cable TV.

FOOD

Bluefields' eclectic mix of people is not quite reflected in its variety of restaurants. An acceptable, authentic Creole restaurant is conspicuously lacking, but you needn't worry about going hungry.

Mini-Hotel Cafetín Central (see **Accommodations,** above) is one of the most popular eateries in town, and for good reason. It's the little extra touches that make dining here a treat: frosty beer mugs, cable TV, and constant table-wiping. In addition to fish, chicken, and beef dishes, all 25-35C (cheap for Bluefields), they serve snack foods and milkshakes (10C). Open daily 8am-10pm.
Cafetín "Pesca-Frita," at the intersection of Calle Central and Av. Aberdeen, is a gusty place, with an army of fans fighting valiantly and successfully to keep you cool. A doorman welcomes you in, as does Michael Bolton's crooning. Fish is succulent (60-70C). Before ordering from the menu they bring to the table, check the "super-economico" menu (hidden on a page behind the regular entrees), for savings of up to 50%. *Comida corriente* 20C. Open daily 8am-midnight.

ENTERTAINMENT

Bluefields hops. The music emanating from the clubs may loosen your teeth, but it'll keep you dancing. Women may feel unsafe walking home alone at night. There is a raging, unmarked **reggae club** in a tumble-down building on the north side of the park (5C cover, if any). **Lego-Lego** is bigger, a winding 10-minute walk north of town; follow the music. **Bacchus,** just south of the park, is more upscale and plays *salsa, merengue,* and disco, all yours for the night, once you've paid the hefty 20C cover. (Heft is relative—20C would be a "gimme" in Managua). **El Flotante** is the fanciest of the clubs. It overlooks the water south of town, on the road to the airport.

■ Near Bluefields

Far north of Bluefields, near the Honduran border, **Puerto Cabezas** is the Nicaraguan Atlantic Coast's other main port. Its population is larger than Bluefields', making it the largest city for many, many miles of Mosquitia. From here, it's possible to explore the region's northern reaches. It should not be hard to find a Cabezas-bound ride on a fishing or cargo boat from Bluefields, El Bluff, or the Corn Islands. **La Costeña** also flies to Puerto Cabezas from Bluefields (Mon., Wed., and Fri., 481C).

   Laguna de Perlas ("Pearl Lagoon") is a small community on the southern edge of a very large lagoon, 80km north of Bluefields. There are no oysters, but you'll see plenty of pure, pearly beauty. A trip here is also one of the best ways to get a look at authentic Atlantic Coast culture. Boats leave this small community for even smaller communities around the lagoon, and then to the 18 pearl cayes off the coast. **Transportes Vargas/Peñas** in Bluefields runs boats to Laguna de Perlas daily at 9am (see Bluefields, p. 320). It may also be possible to find a ride on another boat, or to hire your own if you have enough fellow passengers. The trip takes one hour.

   Ramaqui is a small island community about 20 minutes away from Bluefields, by boat. Its denizens are the descendants of the Rama Indians. It is said that there are only twelve people still alive who speak the Rama language. These days, the community is struggling to keep stray elements of its culture alive. You may want to check it out, before it's too late—you might even meet their legendary **Chief Rufino.**

■ The Corn Islands

Just 65km off the Atlantic Coast, the Corn Islands offer the chance to curl your toes in relatively unsullied sands; as of yet, the islands sport no resorts, fancy restaurants, dive shops, or other tourist facilities. A few hotels and a beach sports club have been built to accommodate the occasional visitors, but most lodging options are just extra rooms slapped alongside a home. If you're looking for sparsely populated white sand beaches and crystal blue water—or if you just want to see what life on a virtually untouristed Caribbean island is like—here you go.

   Like the rest of Nicaragua, the Corn Islands are subject to temporary, deliberate blackouts, during which fans are useless and showers are taken with buckets. Electricity regularly shuts off daily from around 4am to 4pm. Open your nostrils wide, because more than anywhere else in Nicaragua, you'll be paying through the nose. Also, open your eyes—many stores and hotels have small signs, if any.

   Orientation and Practical Information The larger of the two islands is approximately six square km, with a predominantly Creole population of 6000. All roads either lead to the ocean, the **airstrip,** or a road which circumscribes the island. The airstrip runs southwest to northeast, biting off about a quarter of the island to the west (where most businesses are, as well as **Briggs Bay**) and the remainder (including **Mount Pleasant**) to the east and south. The eastern part of the island has areas called the **North End** and **South End,** with **"Sally Peachie"** in between. Planes drop you off at the southern end of the airstrip, beside the **La Costeña** office (open Mon.-Sat. 7:30am-4:30pm). Flights are available from the Corn Islands to **Bluefields** weekdays at 8:30am and 3:35pm (335C one-way; 632C round-trip). Flights depart at the same times to **Managua** (531C one-way and 980C round-trip). It's good to purchase tickets at least a day in advance and to pay in cash.

   Boats will leave you at the Main Pier in Southwest Bay, about 5 blocks from the airstrip (you can see the old airstrip continuing south of the new one). **Boats** return to **Bluefields** on Sunday, Tuesday, and Thursday. For more information, see Bluefields (p. 320). Two **buses** circle the island all day long—the blue one travels counterclockwise; the red one, clockwise (3C). **Taxis** are Jeeps instead of your usual Soviet Ladas. 10C is the flat fare to go everywhere (not fair).

   At the end of the old airstrip, just up from the pier, is **ENITEL/TELCOR** office which offers telephone and mail service daily from 8am-8pm. The office gets a lot of traffic, since the rest of the island doesn't have phones. In the same building is the **Banco Nacional de Desarollo,** changing both cash and traveler's checks, the latter with an erratic commission (open Mon.-Fri. 8am-noon and 1:30-4:30pm, Sat. 8am-11:30am). **Banco Público** is a block south across the airstrip from La Costeña and changes cash (open Mon.-Fri. 8:30am-12:30pm and 1:30-4pm, Sat. 8am-noon). There is a **pharmacy** on the road west from the airport to Briggs Bay. The **hospital** is bone-colored with a blue zinc roof, 1km down the road leading east across the airstrip from La Costeña—a few blocks beyond the baseball "stadium." The **police** office is 2 blocks northward along the road from the Fisher's Cave Restaurant.

Accommodations and Food   The best place to stay is **Casa Blanca,** on the beach south of Briggs Bay, 100m or so down the left branch of the road leading west from the airport. Homey rooms have mosquito nets and fans, but bathrooms are a mixed bag—the shower is clean and spacious, but the "toilet" is an outhouse with two holes cut in a length of wood (singles 75C; doubles 100C). The cheapest is **Hospedaje Angela,** conveniently located 100m or so behind the La Costeña office. 70C per person—if you're alone, that could either be a big room with a double bed, or a closet with a bed in it—depends on availability. Five rooms share a bath with a seat and toilet paper. **Guest House Ruppie,** on the road west from the airport, features clean, new-ish rooms. The main drawback is **Morgan's,** the disco next door, which blares music until all hours; try to get a room on the opposite side of the building (singles 75C; doubles 100C). Beyond that, your options are a few grubby hostels (starting at 60C) and some steep hotels near the north end of the airstrip (US$15 and up).

Many of the restaurants clustered in Briggs Bay serve simple breakfasts for 20C. Other restaurants of note include **Fisher's Cave Restaurant,** a ten-sided concrete building on the north end of the municipal park, on Briggs Bay. Eat while pondering the ships floating quietly before the white sand beaches and palm trees in the distance (fish 45C, shrimp or lobster 60C). The conspicuously lilac **Seva's Dos Millas,** about 2km east of the north end of the airstrip, is the other relatively fancy restaurant in town. It has the same food at higher prices and a different view than Fisher's Cave (breakfast 25C, fish dinner 70C, beer 10C).

Sights   A stroll around the road which circles the island can be an enjoyable way to see a variety of shorelines and walk past nearly every edifice. This takes about three hours, and can make your feet either quite dusty or muddy, depending on the weather. Luckily, you can always catch a bus home. Another pastime is just watching the Costeña planes land and take off. City planners left no room for doubt when they named **Picnic Center,** east of the south end of the airstrip, which also happens to be the most tranquil beach on the island. If you walk its length, the shore becomes rocky. If you're up for it, hike to the top of **Mt. Pleasant,** the highest point on the island (elevation 96m). Would-be snorkelers can get outfitted for 50C a day either at **Le Paraiso Club,** 200 south from Casa Blanca, or an unnamed *pulperia* a few blocks north of the police station, across from the "Oasis Dream" sign.

COSTA RICA

This is nature at its sexiest. Endowed with dripping cloud forests, red-hot volcanos, and lush, luscious flora, Costa Rica seduces even the most fanatic of urbanites. A brief jaunt through any of the country's spectacular national parks releases childhood fantasies of storybook jungles and wild beasts with freakish forms and names. Costa Rica has become by far the most touristed country in Central America partially because of its political and economic stability, but more importantly, because it is a perfectly exotic tropical paradise wrapped into one tight little area. Manageable and magnificent, Costa Rica also leads Central America in its vehement policy toward enlightened preservation.

Far too many ecotourists to Costa Rica dart right for jungle-enshrouded isolation, ignoring what is perhaps the nation's finest asset—the people. *Ticos,* as they call themselves and everything else Costa Rican, are justifiably proud of their country's strong democracy and excellent social security system. More than 28 percent of the national budget is invested in education, and the literacy rate soars over 90 percent. Most striking about the Costa Rican people, however, is their unconditional friendliness; to *hacer amistades* (make friends) is almost always a *tico's* top priority.

Costa Rica boasts 24 national parks and biological reserves, which together comprise a total of 15 percent of the country's territory; most reserves are open to the public and are directly accessible from San José, the capital. The boom in ecotourism over the last few decades has encouraged investors (and the government) to make the tourist path as wide and smooth as possible, but still be prepared for the occasional logistical hardship. While undeniably more westernized than those of other countries in the region, Costa Rica's economy is still developing, and the same general precautions should be taken here as anywhere else in Central America.

ESSENTIALS

■ When to Go

CLIMATE

There are three types of climate in Costa Rica: wet and tropical on the Caribbean side (with high temperatures of 24-32°C/75-90°F and torrential rains); tropical with a dry season on the Península Nicoya and the Central Valley; and temperate in the higher regions of the country (with temperatures of 18-22°C/ 65-72°F). The winter rainy season (*invierno*) lasts from May to December.

FESTIVALS AND HOLIDAYS

National holidays include **January 1** (New Year's Day), **March 19** (Saint Joseph's Day), **March or April** (Holy Week), **April 11** (Juan Santamaría's Day), **May 1** (Labor Day), **June 29** (Saint Peter's Day), **July 25** (Guanacaste Annexation Day), **August 2** (Virgen de los Angeles), **August 15** (Mother's Day), **September 15** (Independence Day), **October 12** (Día de la Raza), **December 8** (Immaculate Conception), **December 25** (Christmas).

■ Useful Information

For publications and organizations of general interest, see **Useful Information,** p. 1.

Costa Rica Expeditions, apdo. 6941-1000, Av. 3, Calle Central, San José (tel. (506) 257-0766 or 222-0333; fax 257-1665), 1 block east of the San José post office (see San José: Practical Information, page 336), or write them in the U.S. at Dept. 235, Box 25216, Miami, FL 33102-5216. They organize jungle tours to Tortuguero National Park (US$286 for 3 days, 2 nights), as well as 1-day tropical forest adventures (US$79), white-water rafting (US$69-89), and volcano tours (US$28). English spoken. Open daily 7am-9pm.

Costa Rica Sun Tours, P.O. Box 1195-1250, Escazú (tel. (506) 255-3418 or 255-3518; fax 255-4410); if you are on foot, they are located 200m south of the Toyota station on Paseo Colón. Full-service ecotourism recommended by the Audubon Society of Costa Rica. Custom itineraries for nature, birding, and educational and adventure tours, including cycling and rafting trips. They also own two lodges in Arenal National Park. 2-4-day packages US$295-395 per person, including transportation, lodgings, meals, bilingual guides, and park fees.

Green Tortoise Adventure Travel, 494 Broadway, San Francisco, CA 94133 (tel. (800) 867-8647 or (415) 956-7500; fax 956-4900). Their cheap-and-funky 3-week-tour visits beaches, rainforests, volcanos, air-conditioning, and hot springs. US$399 doesn't include airfare, but another US$121 gets you in the food fund.

Interviajes, S.A. P.O. "super saver" day-long natural history tours to Poás Volcano National Park, Tortuguero, Monteverde, and other sights. Willing to work out a budget-friendly price.

Jungle Trails per los Caminos de la Selva, Apdo. 2413, San José 1000 (tel. (506) 255-3486; fax 255-2782). Specializes in nature tours, conservation programs, bird-watching and botany trips, and custom itineraries. Invites visitors to meet with subsistence farmers to better understand the circumstances behind deforestation. Tours 1-15 days or longer. Portion of fee donated to reforestation groups.

Preferred Adventures Ltd., 1 W. Water St., Suite 300, St. Paul, MN 55107 (tel. (800) 840-8687 or (612) 222-8131; fax 222-4221; email paltours@aol.com; http://www.cool.co.cr/). Soft adventure and nature tours in Costa Rica. Birding, rainforest study, river rafting, mountain biking, and fishing.

The Mountaineers Books, 1001 SW Klickitat Way, Suite 201, Seattle, WA 98134 (tel. (800) 553-4453; fax (206) 223-6306). Publishes *Costa Rica's National Parks and Preserves: A Visitor's Guide* (US$16.95), with park descriptions, trails, and maps. Also, check out *Latin America By Bike* (US$14.95).

■ Documents and Formalities

EMBASSIES AND CONSULATES

Embassies of Costa Rica: U.S., 2114 S. St. NW, Washington, D.C. 20008 (tel. (202) 234-2945). **Canada,** 135 York St., Suite 208, Ottawa, Ontario K1N 5TA (tel. (613) 562-2852; fax 562-2582). **U.K.,** Flat 1, 14 Lancaster Gate, London W2 3LH (tel. (44) 171-706-8844; fax 706-8655).

Consulate of Costa Rica: 2112 S. St. NW, Washington, D.C. 20008 (tel. (202) 328-6628), or contact the embassy for the address of the consulate nearest you.

PASSPORTS

Most visitors, not including U.S. and Canadian citizens, must have a **passport** to enter the country. Canadian and U.S. citizens need only an original birth certificate and a valid photo ID, although a passport is strongly recommended, especially if you're carrying traveler's checks. Visitors arriving by plane are required to show a round-trip ticket.

Lago de Nicaragua

NICARAGUA

Pe as Blancas

R.N.F.S. ISLA BOLAÑOS

La Cruz

Bahía de Santa Elena

Los Chiles

Upala

P.N. RINCÓN DE LA VIEJA

R.N.F.S. CAÑO NEGRO

P.N. SANTA ROSA

Volcán Rincón de la Vieja

Golfo de Papagayo

Volcán Miravalles

ALAJUELA

Playa Panamá

Liberia

Arenal

Playa Hermosa

Laguna de Arenal

Fortuna de San Carlos

Playa del Coco

Bagaces

GUANACASTE

Tilar n

Filadelfia

Ca as

P.N PALO VERDE

Volcán Arenal

Playa Tamarindo

P.N. BARRA HONDA

Monteverde Cloud Forest Reserve

Ciudad Quesada

P.N. VOLCÁN POÁS

Santa Cruz

Esparza

San Ram n

Sarchi

Nicoya

Carmona

R.S. DE PEÑAS BLANCAS

Alajuela

R.N.F.S. OSTINAL

Hojancha

Golfo de Nicoya

Playa Ostional

Península de Nicoya

Puntarenas

Ferry

Ferry

Playa Sámara

R.N.F.S. CURÚ

Playa Táracoles

R.B. CARARA

SAN

PUNTARENAS

Jac

R.N.A. CABO BLANCO

Montezuma

Playa de Jacó

Playa Hermosa

R.B. ISLA PAJAROS, NEGRITOS Y GUAYABO

CORDILLERA DE GUANACASTE

CORDILLERA TILARÁN

ABBREVIATIONS

R.N.F.S. Refugio Nacional de Fauna Silvestre
P.N. Parque Nacional
R.B. Reserva Biol gica
P.I. Parque Internacional
M.N. Monumento Nacional
R.S. Refugio Silvestre
R.N.A. Reserva Natural Absoluta

Isla del Coco

Península Colnett

Bahía Weston

Bahía Chatham

Bahía Wafer

Cabo Barreto

P.N. ISLA DEL COCO

Cabo Lionel

Cabo Descubierta

Bahía Yglesias

OCÉANO PACÍFI

Cabo Dampier

0   30 mile3

0   30 kilometers

N

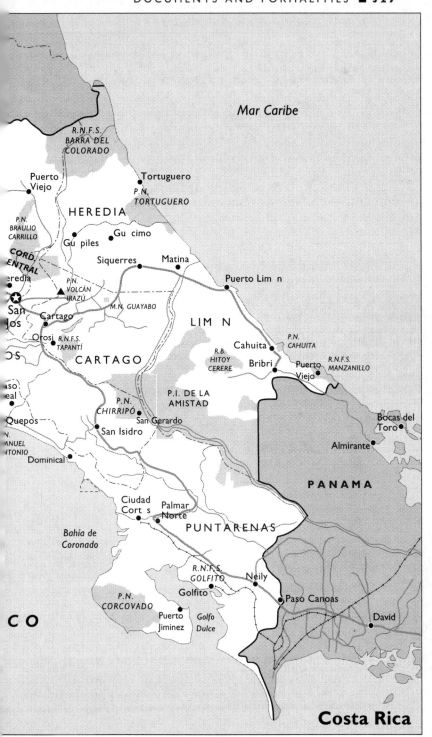

Mar Caribe

R.N.F.S.
BARRA DEL
COLORADO

Puerto
Viejo

Tortuguero

P.N.
TORTUGUERO

HEREDIA

P.N.
BRAULIO
CARRILLO

Gu piles

Gu cimo

CORD.
ENTRAL

eredia

Siquerres

Matina

P.N.
VOLCÁN
IRAZÚ

M.N. GUAYABO

Puerto Lim n

San
os

Cartago

LIM N

Cahuita

P.N.
CAHUITA

Orosi

R.N.F.S.
TAPANTÍ

R.B.
HITOY
CERERE

Bribri

Puerto
Viejo

R.N.F.S.
MANZANILLO

OS

CARTAGO

P.I. DE LA
AMISTAD

aso
eal

P.N.
CHIRRIPÓ

San Gerardo

Bocas del
Toro

Quepos

San Isidro

Almirante

N.
ANUEL
TONIO

Dominical

PANAMA

Ciudad
Cort s

Palmar
Norte

PUNTARENAS

Bahía de
Coronado

R.N.F.S.
GOLFITO

Neily

Golfito

Paso Canoas

P.N.
CORCOVADO

C O

Puerto
Jiminez

Golfo
Dulce

David

Costa Rica

ENTRANCE REQUIREMENTS AND VISAS

All visitors entering Costa Rica who are not traveling with a passport must obtain a **tourist card** (*tarjeta de turismo*), available from airlines serving the country. You'll need your plane ticket and US$2. Tourist cards are valid for 30 days, but can be renewed for up to 90 days by going to the Dirección de Migración in San José with your return plane ticket, two photos, an original birth certificate, and a passport. If you are a **U.S.** or **Canadian** citizen, you can purchase a new tourist card every 30 days (for up to 90 days). A **visa** is not required for citizens of the U.S., Canada, the U.K., the Republic of Ireland, Australia, and New Zealand. Citizens of most western European countries must have a visa to enter Costa Rica. Regardless of your nationality, be sure to always carry your tourist card and passport when traveling in Costa Rica.

If you stay even a day beyond your allotment, leaving Costa Rica becomes a serious problem. You will have to obtain an exit visa (US$15) and pay a small fine. If you overstay for longer than 30 days, you will be charged an additional US$20-30 for each subsequent month. To get the exit visa you will have to provide a court certificate, which will cost you about US$0.50 and a lot of hassle.

CUSTOMS

Duties on goods entering and leaving Costa Rica can be extremely high. In addition to your personal effects, you are allowed to bring in 500g of tobacco products, three liters of alcohol, 2kg of candy, and US$100 worth of other goods duty-free. You must wait six months before bringing in another US$100 worth of goods duty-free. There is an **airport departure tax** of US$17 (¢3970). When crossing the border, you may be charged an **overland departure tax** of ¢75.

INTERNATIONAL DRIVING PERMIT

The **Dirección de Transporte Automotor,** Av. 18 and Calle 7, San José, will grant a temporary **driving permit** to a visitor over age 21 with a valid foreign driver's license. If you plan to drive in Costa Rica longer than 90 days, you must qualify to stay beyond the expiration of your tourist card and apply for a Costa Rican driver's license. Applicants must have a valid foreign license and a valid passport; the office of motor vehicles will determine whether you are medically fit.

■ Money Matters

CURRENCY AND EXCHANGE

US$1 = 236 colones (¢)	¢1 = US$0.004
CDN$1 = ¢172	¢1 = CDN$0.006
UK£1 = ¢384	¢1 = UK£0.003
IR£1 = ¢343	¢1 = IR£0.003
AUS$1 = ¢175	¢1 = AUS$0.006
NZ$1 = ¢153	¢1 = NZ$0.007
SARand 1 = ¢51	¢1 = SARand 0.021
DM1 = ¢129	¢1 = DM0.008

The Costa Rican currency is the **colón** (¢). Printed prices may use two periods (e.g., ¢1.234.56 means one thousand two hundred thirty-four colones and fifty-six hundredths).

TAXES

All hotels, restaurants, bars, and nightclubs are required by law to add an 11% **sales tax** and a 10% **service charge** to all bills; usually this charge will be included in prices cited, but not always. In addition, it is customary to leave an extra tip for particularly good service (perhaps an additional 5%).

The colón has been depreciating rapidly over the past year. Expect many of the prices in this book quoted in colones to have increased from the time of printing. However, prices quoted in U.S. dollars should remain relatively stable. Travelers in Costa Rica may consider preserving a larger amount of their currency in the form of U.S. dollars than they ordinarily might, especially if staying for a significant amount of time.

■ Health

Life expectancy in Costa Rica is an impressive 74-plus years, a testimony to the quality of the universal medical care provided to all citizens, which includes disability, maternity, and old-age pensions. Drinking water in major hotels and restaurants in the capital is purified. Outside San José, water should be boiled before drinking, or go with the bottled stuff.

Like most Central American countries, Costa Rica is home to lots of nasty diseases. The 1991 earthquake damaged the infrastructure of the Puerto Limón area, and the slow pace of reconstruction has resulted in poor sanitary conditions and a heightened risk of associated diseases. **Malaria** is a hazard in all of Costa Rica except Cartago and San José provinces. **Cholera** has also cropped up recently, although the risk is smaller than in Guatemala and Mexico. **Typhoid fever** is common in Central America; a vaccine is recommended for those who plan to stay in rural areas. **Hepatitis A** is also a risk in rural provinces. Thousands of cases of **dengue fever** have been reported in the last few years, so take extra precautions against mosquitoes. For more information, see **Health,** p. 14.

■ Safety

As the number of visitors to Costa Rica increases, so does the frequency of crimes against tourists. Incidents ranging from pick-pocketing to armed muggings have been on the rise in San José, at beaches, in banks, at the airport, and at national parks and other attractions. Don't flash cash or jewelry, and watch out for counterfeit money.

As in many parts of Latin America, **women** are subject to more attention than might be expected or desired—it's hard to walk outdoors without hearing catcalls. Unfortunately, inappropriate overtures cannot always be deflected with a firm *lo siento, no me interesa* ("I'm sorry but I'm not interested"). On the other hand, *mi amor* is used by both women and men as a term of endearment, much like the British "love." A shopkeeper will sometimes innocently address a woman customer as *mi reina* ("my queen"); in this context, the term means simply, "May I help you."

■ Alternatives to Tourism

Costa Rica's tropical reserves and environmental hyper-consciousness make it an ideal destination for ecologically-minded travelers. Contact conservation groups for information on **volunteer** and **internship** positions relating to the environment. For teaching opportunities, contact **WorldTeach,** Harvard Institute for International Development, 1 Eliot St., Cambridge, MA 02138 (tel. (617) 495-5527; fax 495-1599; e-mail info@worldteach.org; http://www.igc.org/worldteach). In Costa Rica: Aptos, Villa Dimarco #2, 75 M Oeste Del Ida, Barrio Dent, San José, Costa Rica (tel. (506) 283-9243). Volunteers teach English and environmental education throughout Costa Rica. A one-year commitment is required. Participation fees are about US$4440 and include language and teacher training, international travel costs, housing, and health insurance. Volunteers receive a stipend as well. Those interested in **Spanish language study** will find plenty of opportunities in the San José area.

STUDY

Costa Rican Language Academy, P.O. Box. 336-2070, Av. Central, Calles 25/27, San José (tel. (506) 221-1624; fax 233-8670). Language and cultural study custom tailored for individual students. Homestays and weekend excursions plus lessons in Latin dance, Costa Rican cooking, Spanish music, and conversation. Weekly rates start at US$220 (including a homestay) for 3hr. classes Mon.-Thurs.

Institute for Central American Studies (ICAS), Apdo. 1524-2050, San Pedro (tel. (506) 253-3195; fax 234-7682). Hosts journalism and Latin American studies internships (minimum of 6 months). Arranges paid English instruction positions for interns. Their language and study arm, the Mesoamerica Language Institute, offers a 1-day, 6hr. course in Survival Spanish for Tourists with tips on travel and local customs (US$60 includes lunch). Conversation-oriented regular program gives 20hr. of instruction per week. Classes average 2-5 students (US$155 per week, homestays an additional US$100 per week; four weeks: US$535, with homestays US$935). There is a 10% discount after the first month of classes for any other additional weeks of study.

Instituto Centroamericano de Asuntos Internacionales (ICAI), in San José. Offers 2-4 week total immersion language programs. 4hr. of instruction per day, 5 days per week, plus excursions. 4 weeks with accommodations, 2 meals per day, and all activities US$962-1298. For information, contact Bill Fagan at the Language Studies Enrollment Center, 13948 Hemlock Dr., Penn Valley, CA (tel. (916) 432-7690; fax 432-7615).

Intercultura of Costa Rica, P.O Box 3006, Peoria, IL 61612-3006 (tel. (800) 552-2051; fax (309) 692-2926). 4hr. per day (or more) of Spanish-learning fun, accompanied by a homestay and lessons about Costa Rican culture. Beach campus available. 2 weeks in Heredia US$545. One-on-one tutorials available. Also offers the Ilisa program, 2 weeks in San José US$745, primarily for adult professionals.

Monteverde Institute, Apdo. 69-5655, Monteverde de Puntarenas (tel. (506) 645-5053; fax 645-5219). A nonprofit group offering courses in tropical ecology and conservation for students, teachers, and other adult groups. Field trips, lectures, Spanish language, and Costa Rican culture study. Longer 8-10 week programs accredited by CIEE and the Univ. of California Education Abroad Program.

VOLUNTEER

Asociación Preservacionista de Flora y Fauna Silvestre (APREFLOFAS), P.O. Box 917-2150, Moravia, San José (tel. and fax (506) 240-6087); if you witness a case of destructive exploitation, call their emergency number (tel. (506) 381-6315). A nonprofit, volunteer organization that works to guard Costa Rica's natural resources from illegal and destructive exploitation. Promotes reforestation projects. They have a wealth of information on ecotourism in Costa Rica's parks.

Centro de Derecho Ambiental y de los Recursos Naturales (CEDARENA), Apdo. 134-2050, San Pedro, Costa Rica (tel. (506) 224-8239, 225-1019; fax 225-5111). A nonprofit, nonpartisan association specializing in environmental law research. Their mission is to incorporate environmental concerns into legislation.

Volunteers for Peace, 43 Tiffany Rd, Belmont, VT 05730 (tel. (802) 259-2759; fax 259-2922; e-mail vfp@vfp.org; http://www.vfp.org/). Open Mon.-Fri. 9am-4:30pm. A non-profit organization that has coordinated workcamps around the world since 1981. Volunteers must have a working knowledge of Spanish and must be willing to commit to at least 2 weeks. Prices start at US$200 per month, and includes at least room and board. Additional costs depend on the program.

■ Getting There

Costa Rica's national airline is **LACSA,** 630 5th Ave., #246, New York, NY 10111-0334 (tel. (212) 697-4004). Other carriers serving San José's **Juan Santamaría Airport** include **American, British Airways, Mexicana, TWA, Continental,** and **United.** The preferred **border crossing** for travelers arriving from or going to Panamá is at Paso Canoas, with Nicaragua, Peñas Blancas.

■ Once There

GOVERNMENT INFORMATION OFFICES

For a list of **embassies** and **consulates,** see San José: **Practical Information,** p. 336.

Dirección de Migración, on the Autopista General Cañas Hwy. (the road to the airport in San José). Take the red bus to Alajuela from Av. 2, Calles 12/14 or Calles 10/12 and tell the driver to drop you off at *La Oficina de Migración*. The place to go to extend the 30-or 90-day limit or to get costly exit visas if you overstay.

InfoTur, P.O. Box 10628-1000, San José. A government information agency; can answer most tourist concerns and make reservations for all national and international tours, flights, hotels, etc. English spoken.

Instituto Costarricense de Turismo (ICT), postal address: Apdo. 777-1000; Av. 4, Calles 5/7, San José (tel. (506) 223-1733; fax 223-5452). The national tourist bureau, with additional offices at the San José airport and at the northern and southern border crossings. Free maps and helpful hints available. Publishes a comprehensive listing of tour companies and lodgings.

GETTING AROUND

SANSA, Av. Central/1, Calle 24 (tel. 233-5330), runs domestic flights between San José and cities such as Golfito (US$50) and Tortuguero (US$40). In 1996, the government suspended **INCOFER,** the national rail line; it is expected to reopen in two years. The **bus** system is labyrinthine. In large cities, each destination is served by a different company, and each company has its terminal in a different part of town.

If you're traveling by **car,** you'll have a good network of highways at your disposal. Watch out, however, for the suggestively named **Cerro de la Muerte** (Hill of Death) section of the **Cartago-San Isidro** highway, plagued by frequent sink holes and thick fog. The road from San José to Puntarenas—narrow, twisty, and full of heavy trucks—is also dangerous. A seat belt must be used by the driver and any front seat passenger, and a safety helmet is required when driving a motorcycle. The speed limit on the Interamerican Highway is 90km per hour driving north from San José but 80km per hour driving south. Its minimum speed limit is 40km per hour. Tourists report that hitchhiking is generally safe, but *Let's Go* does not recommend it. Costa Ricans themselves don't hitchhike much except in cases of dire need.

ADDRESSES

Even medium-sized cities in Costa Rica often have no formal system of street addresses. Tourists must rely on dead reckoning by reference to landmarks well-known only to locals. Buildings are not numbered, but their locations are sometimes specified by a certain number of *metros* from a particular point. *Metros* here refers to portions of city blocks, not meters; *100 metros al norte del Parque Rey Eduardo* indicates a building one block north of Parque Rey Eduardo.

ACCOMMODATIONS

Costa Rica is home to 12 of the more than 6000 official youth hostels worldwide which display the **HI** logo (a blue triangle) alongside the symbol of the national organization. Hostels are low-cost overnight accommodations, usually with separate quarters for males and females. For more information, or to get a **Hostelling International Guide,** write to them at 733 15th Street NW, Suite 840, Washington, D.C. 20005. Hostel cards are available from Council Travel and STA, and from the hostelling organization of your own country (see **Hostels,** p. 36).

■ Keeping in Touch

Mail service to and from Costa Rica is quite reliable. Airmail letters to the U.S. take about seven to 10 days each way. Airmail to Europe may require a bit more time, but not much. Steep customs duties (up to 100% of value) can be charged for anything larger than a letter, so bulky mailings can be expensive. If you do plan to receive packages, remind the sender to mark the contents and value clearly on the outside. Mail can be received general delivery through the *lista de correos;* address envelopes as follows:

> Maureen <u>SCHAD</u>
> a/c Lista de Correos
> 4417 (postal code) Fortuna (city)
> Costa Rica
> CENTRAL AMERICA

The use of postal codes is not essential. If mailing from the U.S., omit the last line (Central America) from the address, since the computers that sort U.S. mail only recognize country names.

Costa Rica has one of the best and most extensive **telephone** systems in Latin America. Some pay phones function with coins of ¢5, ¢10, and ¢20 denominations; it is a good idea to buy a pre-paid Costa Rican phone card. Calls from hotels cost about 30% more than calls from other phones. There are no long-distance area codes; for any call made within Costa Rica you need only dial the seven-digit phone number. Dial 113 to obtain the telephone numbers of residents and businesses throughout Costa Rica. **Emergency service** in the greater San José metropolitan area is available by dialing 911. Contact the **police** by dialing 117 (or 127 in rural areas). The **country code** for Costa Rica is 506. Costa Rica operates on Central Standard time, but daylight-savings time is not observed.

COSTA RICA: LIFE AND TIMES

■ History

The origin of the land's name remains something of a mystery to this day, but it is clear from his journals that Columbus's first contact with native people was happy and peaceful. Columbus reached the land on his fourth trip to the New World, arriving in 1502, and he stayed for only a few weeks to repair ships before moving on to more established colonial sites. During that brief time, he established friendly relations with the indigenous population, who were not seriously disturbed until the founding of **Cartago** in the country's central highlands. Costa Rica's aboriginal inhabitants were relatively few, and as a result, the system of slavery familiar to other colonies never got off the ground. Today, *indígenas* comprise less than one percent of the country's population of three million and live on reservations, and **Black Caribs,** concentrated in and around Puerto Limón, comprise only about three percent of the population. Because of the homogeneity of the population (almost the whole country is of European descent), the established socioeconomic structures common to the rest of Latin America—poor *indígenas,* middle-class *mestizos,* and rich *criollos*—never fully developed in Costa Rica.

Costa Rica's other ironic saving grace was a dearth of **precious metals.** Coupled with the province's distance from the colonial political centers of Mexico and Guatemala, this paucity of gold and silver ensured a great deal of unofficial independence for Costa Rica's first settlers. Because no foreign powers scrambled to gain control over the country, the subsistence economy that grew out of the region's tobacco and cacao farming was left in the hands of the farmers themselves.

COSTA RICA

On the heels of its neighbors, Costa Rica eventually entered the world of European mercantilism and Panamerican federations but, even then, its involvement was limited. As with nearly all the isthmus's colonies, it achieved its independence from Spain by way of a confederation with the brief Mexican Empire in 1821. As a member of the splinter **United Provinces of Central America,** in 1838, Costa Rica was one of the first states to strike out on its own. At the same time, it shifted to that most exportable of crops: **coffee.** Within a decade, Great Britain was heavily invested in the Costa Rican coffee market, but as the arable land had already been divvied up on a small and equitable scale, increased cash from overseas only served to strengthen the distribution of power. When the Guanacaste province of Nicaragua seceded and sought union with Costa Rica, it forecast a host of territorial disputes that arrived uninvited at the doorstep of a nation otherwise inclined toward isolation.

Costa Rica began to modernize rapidly under the iron-fisted leadership of **General Tomás "Tommy" Guardia,** who established a base for future economic progress at the cost of civil liberties and a sizeable trade deficit over the course of his 1870-1882 reign. A new constitution was drafted in 1871, and the crop base was expanded to a more stable constellation of coffee, sugar, and bananas. This expansion demanded improvements in infrastructure; Guardia oversaw the construction of new roads, railroads, schools, and municipal buildings. Instrumental to the construction of the first Cartago-Atlantic line was major *norteamericano* entrepreneur **Minor Keith,** who augmented the banana interest that eventually became the United Fruit Company, known as *El Pulpo* or "the Octopus" in Latin America and diminished to "Dole" in the U.S. Economic and technological innovation had a marked impact on social and religious life—the Roman Catholic Church was all but extinguished, public secular education became compulsory, and literacy reached levels previously unattained in the Spanish colonies. In 1890, Costa Rica conducted the first legitimate large-scale election in Central American history.

Costa Rica's entrance into the twentieth-century was one of the least graceful periods of its development. Guanacaste's annexation to the north and canal-related disputes with Panamá to the south produced an extremely volatile situation in Costa Rican politics. U.S. intervention on Panamá's behalf left in its wake a diplomatic mess that took decades to heal. Within this atmosphere of external strife, Costa Rica experienced its only modern flirtation with autocracy, when the congressionally appointed "victor" of the 1913 elections, **Alfredo González,** was usurped in a popular revolt led by the reactionary **General Federico Tinoco.** Despite its origins, Tinoco's stint was unpopular and brief, shortened by the constant threat of U.S. intervention against him.

The decades following Tinoco's ouster were smooth and prosperous for Costa Rica, and the role that the U.S. played against Tinoco's regime restored its popularity among *ticos.* The nation's democratic and educational structures flourished, even as dependence on foreign trade became more obvious. The only severe upheaval occurred in 1948, when communist insurgents banded together to prevent the successful presidential candidate from taking office. **José Figueres,** a wealthy coffee farmer and a socialist himself, marshalled regiments of the disorganized national army to suppress the revolt. In reaction, the Costa Rican legislature undertook its most drastic and internationally famous measure: it dismantled the nation's entire military. All that remains of the Costa Rican army is the Civil Guard, a police force of 7000 members. Figueres, in turn, became a national hero, and in 1953, was himself elected to the office he had fought to defend. Once in office, he imposed many of the leftist reforms that had motivated the uprising in the first place. He nationalized banks and utilities and set up the machinery that eventually broke United Fruit's stranglehold on the Costa Rican economy. Figueres's son is the president of Costa Rica today.

Since the dissipation of the military in 1948, Costa Rica has enjoyed virtually unblemished peace, relative political stability, and enviable economic straits. Figueres remained in the presidency for a period of twenty years, during which time his party, the **PLN,** came to dominate politics in the Legislative Assembly. As a result of Costa Rica's run-in with the globe-trotting filibuster and Wall Street financier **Robert Vesco,** the PLN fell out of power for a few years in the late 70s. Regardless, it has claimed the presidency and a majority of the national legislative seats for most of the period since its inception. Vesco was finally arrested, after twenty-five years on the lam in the Caribbean, in May 1995.

Most non-financial problems faced by the little country in this half of the century have been due to civil strife in other Central American nations, especially in El Salvador and Nicaragua. As many as 500,000 Salvadoran and Nicaraguan refugees have poured across Costa Rica's northern border since the late 1970s, when the first of the civil wars began displacing combatant and non-combatant alike. This overflow has caused numerous internal problems for Costa Rica, as unemployment lines burgeon and tensions mount between otherwise hospitable *ticos* and their uninvited guests. Former president **Oscar Arias Sánchez** made the best kind of international news when he authored a successful peace plan, negotiating a sustained cease-fire program for Costa Rica's neighbors and laying the groundwork for a unified Central American parliament. He won the Nobel Peace Prize and the envy of international statesmen far and wide. Though stagflation runs rampant, and the nation's businessmen are not without their anxieties, Costa Rica continues to enjoy a prolonged day in the sun, relatively speaking, as commercial gain from the ecotourism boom of the past few years propels its economy forward.

■ The Arts

Prior to the 20th century, Costa Rican **literature** drew primarily from folk tales and colloquial expression in a movement known as "costumbrism." Through **Joaquín García Monge**'s works *El Moto* and *Las Hijas del Campo,* the nation's working people were represented by one of their own. Still, despite the strength of this movement, Costa Rican literature first came into full bloom in 1900, when it became associated with denunciation of the status quo. **José Marín Cañas'** *Infierno Verde,* a depiction of the Chaco War between Paraguay and Bolivia, bolstered developing anti-imperialist sentiment. Similarly, **Oreamuni's** *La Ruta de su Evasión* confronts tensions between parents and children and those stemming from Latin American *machismo.* A focus on bitter realities eventually took shape in the theater and in poetry, which pushes forward today in a mature harmony between fiction and fact. Playwrights **Alberto Cañas** and **Daniel Gallegos** accompanied the so-called Circle of Costa Rican Poets in an attempt to unite the nation's thinkers against the sociopolitical cruelties of the age. Well-read *ticos* tend to regard two of their living authors above all others: **Fabian Dobles,** winner of the Premio Nacional, Costa Rica's highest distinction for artistic and intellectual achievement; and **Carlos Salazar Herrera,** painter, poet, professor, and the author of *Tres Cuentos de Angustias y Paisajes.*

■ Media

The rule of thumb in Costa Rican popular culture, especially with teenagers, is a simple conditional: if it's *norteamericano,* it's cool. Turn on a TV or a radio anywhere and thrill to the sight of U.S. sitcoms translated into Spanish, including *The Simpsons, Scooby Doo, The Fresh Prince of Bel Air* (called *Príncipe del Rap*), and of course, *Baywatch.* Similarly, Costa Ricans are big fans of U.S. musical cheese, and the sappiest songs are swiftly translated into Spanish. Reggae is especially popular along the Caribbean coast, and traditional *salsa* and *merengue* music, while harder to find on the radio, is often played in nightclubs.

In Spanish, *La Nación* and *La República* represent the alternative views of the two main political parties in Costa Rica. In English, the *Tico Times* and *Costa Rica Today* offer extensive summaries of cultural events, hotels, restaurants, and current events. The *Tico Times'* publication *Exploring Costa Rica* is an invaluable guide to the country's tourist attractions and cities.

■ Food and Drink

Just like the people, the dining in Costa Rica tends to be casual and welcoming. Small local diners, called **sodas** by the *ticos,* are fixtures everywhere. *Sodas* are a budget traveler's best friend, selling homemade Costa Rican *típico* food at inexpensive prices. *Restaurantes* are larger and generally a little more formal and expensive. **Empanadas** (turnovers) and **batidos** (fruit shakes) are ubiquitous, and Costa Rica grows and roasts some of the best coffee in the world. A common breakfast is **gallo pinto,** which translates into "painted rooster," but is really nothing more than good ole rice and beans, often served with eggs or meat. Fruits include pineapples, bananas, blackberries, strawberries, mangos, papayas, tamarindos, and gambusia. The most traditional dinner is called a **casado,** which isn't a fixed entree, but is rather a mix of different items, usually a salad, some type of meat, beans, and either French fries or fried plantains (*plátanos* or *patacones*). *Casado* literally means "married," and the meal got this name because wives traditionally served it to their husbands. On the Atlantic coast, where there is a strong Caribbean influence, everything from *gallo pinto* to chicken to a meat-and-vegetable stew called **rondon** (from the Carib-English "run-down") can be found cooked in coconut milk. Of course, anyone who's not a fan of **Imperial,** the native beer with the telltale eagle on the bottle, is liable to be chased out of the country. The local hard liquor is **guaro,** a clear moonshine which tastes godawful on its own, but manages to mix pretty nicely with anything.

■ Recent News

In a May 1996 state of the nation address, president (at time of print) **José Maria Figueres** expressed optimism about many social aspects of the country, including successes in health, education, the environment, and poverty reduction. Continuing these social improvements, Costa Rica expects radical new political initiatives to be issued during the nine months remaining before the general election. In the meantime, neither party—the PLN nor the PUSC—wants to debate unpopular issues or reforms in the Legislative Assembly. Discussion of structural adjustment reforms, including the modernization of the Instituto Costarricense de Electricidad (ICE, the state telecommunications and energy monopoly), have been deferred until after the election. **Miguel Angel Rodríguez** is the current frontrunner, but neither his victory nor his platform is clear at present.

Qin Huasun, Chinese ambassador to the United Nations, announced a plan to establish diplomatic relations with Costa Rica. Chinese interest in Costa Rica is particularly strong due to the country's leading role in the region's economy. This proposal was discussed earlier and rejected by Costa Rica due to its ties with Taiwan.

Costa Rica has often been a destination for refugees fleeing persecution in less stable countries. Over the past months, however, 11,000 illegal Nicaraguan immigrants were deported. The two countries agreed at a meeting in May 1997 to improve border policing. Costa Rica agreed to improve its treatment of illegal migrants and to step up efforts to document them and provide them with work permits.

San José

Blame it on money and its reliable sidekick, industrialization, but San José is *not* the Costa Rica most tourists see in their travel brochures. The car exhaust suffocates, the blaring horns deafen, and the omnipresent fast-food joints remind travelers far too much of home. Growth and sprawl encroach upon the moist serenity of the rainforests surrounding the city. The cross-cultural diversity reaches electric extremes.

Still, it is precisely in this relentless rush and bustle that those who stay a few days will find a level of comforting familiarity—in the endless flow of blue-uniformed students, in the vivid color and jolting confusion of the *Mercado Central*'s busy streets, and in the heated cries of a crowd watching a soccer game in the local *soda*.

Ringed by mountain ranges and perched 1182 meters (3800 feet) above sea level, San José was first settled in 1736. The city was the sleepy center of tobacco production after being colonized by the Spanish in 1736, and only moved into the spotlight of Costa Rican political and economic life in the 19th century. In 1823, the capital was moved from Cartago to San José, and the city became a focal point for the growing Costa Rican coffee economy. Since the 1950s, San José has grown rapidly in both area and population; it is now an important transportation hub and home to two major universities and a great many industrial (if not botanical) plants.

Today, the city has well over 300,000 residents, and one-third of all Costa Ricans call the San José province their home. As usual, first-time visitors are hit hardest by the contrasts, of street vendors shouting the names of obscure fruits next to ubiquitous and always familiar McDonald's. Billboards preach marital fidelity, while the opposite sides show seductive women drinking Coke.

While history and circumstance have vaulted San José into the political, social, and economic center of Costa Rican life, some things never change. The summer heat is grueling: from May to August, San José swelters and sweats. Respite, however, comes like clockwork every afternoon, when the skies shake, rain pummels the city, and water literally pours from every wall, refreshing *ticos* and tourists alike.

▧ Orientation

San José's streets form a regular grid. *Calles* run north-south and *avenidas* east-west. Odd-numbered *calles* are east of **Calle Central,** while even-numbered ones fall to its west. Similarly, odd-numbered *avenidas* run to the north of **Avenida Central,** and even-numbered ones to the south. Therefore, an address like "Av. 3, Calle 3" is in the northeast part of town. However, many streets are not marked and some addresses and directions are given with respect to major landmarks. For example, if an address says *"200 metros al sur del Teatro Nacional"* (200 meters from the National Theater), first find the National Theater and then walk two blocks south of it. *Metros* refers to city blocks, not to actual meters; *100 metros* is one block, *150 metros* is one-and-a-half blocks, etc. If the address is given as Avs. 3/5, Calle 2, it means the building is on Calle 2 between Avenidas 3 and 5. Because the city is relatively small, walking is an easy way to get around in San José; the complicated intra-city bus system, keyed as it is to the landmark system, can be somewhat difficult to use. It should not, however, intimidate.

▧ Practical Information

Tourist Office: Instituto Costarricense de Turismo (ICT) (tel. 223-1733; fax 223-5452), **Av. 4, Calles 5/7,** down the stairs across from the park; on the 11th floor. Helpful information on sights, bus schedules, and hotels. Excellent (and free) country and city maps. English spoken. Open Mon.-Fri. 8am-4pm. **Airport branch** (tel. 442-1820 or 443-2883), directly behind customs and before the building exit. Services similar to those provided at the main office. Open 8am-5pm.

Embassies and Consulates: U.S., Rohmuser, Carretera Pavas (tel. 220-3939 or 220-3050), in front of Centro Comercial. Open Mon.-Fri. 8am-4:30pm. **Canada** (tel. 296-4203 or 296-4149), in Sabana Sur, Oficentro Ejecutivo building #5. **U.K.,** Po. Colón, Calles 38/40 (tel. 255-2937), Edificio Colón, 11th floor. Open Mon.-Fri. 8:30am-noon and 1-2:30pm. **Australia** has no embassy, but has official representatives at Avs.5/7, Calle 33, in front of Centro Comercial (tel. 224-1152). Open Mon.-Fri. 8am-1pm. **Guatemala** (tel. 224-5721), 50m east, 100m north, 50m east of the Pizza Hut in the Plaza del Sol. Open Mon.-Fri. 9am-noon. **Mexico,** Av. 7, Calles 13/15 (tel. 233-8874). Open Mon.-Fri. 8:30am-noon and 3-4pm. **Panamá,** Calle 38, Avs. 5/7 (tel. 257-3401 or 256-5169). Open Mon.-Fri. 8am-noon. **Nicaragua,** Barrio la California, Av. Central, Calle 25/26 (tel. 222-2373), across from Pizza Hut. Open Mon.-Fri. 8:30am-noon. **El Salvador,** Los Yoses, Av. 10, Calle 35 (tel. 225-3861).

San José
Overview

Open Mon.-Fri. 9am-1pm. **Honduras** (tel. 234-9502), Zapote, 250m east, 200m north, 100m east of Itan. Open Mon.-Fri. 9am-2pm. **Belize** (tel. 234-9969), 400m east, 100m south of Iglesa Santa Teresita. Open Mon.-Fri. 9am-noon and 2-4pm.

Western Union: Avs. 2/4, Calle 9 (tel. 283-6336), in the building labeled Airpak de Costa Rica. Open Mon.-Fri. 8:30am-5pm, Sat.-Sun. 9am-12:30pm.

Currency Exchange: Banco Nacional, Avs. 1/3, Calles 2/4 (tel. 223-2166). Open Mon.-Fri. 8:30am-3:45pm. **Banco de Costa Rica,** Avs. Central/2, Calles 4/6 (tel. 255-1100). Open Mon.-Fri. 8:30am-3pm. Both generally have long lines, but it's worth the wait, since there are no good rates on the street. Both charge commission on traveler's checks (about 0.5% changing to colones, 10% to dollars). For equally reasonable rates without the lines, go to **Helicópteros de Costa Rica,** Avs. Central/1, Calle 2, 2nd floor (tel. 233-0090). Open Mon.-Fri., 8:30am-6pm. **ATMs:** Inside **Banco de San José,** Avs. 3/5, Calle Central. 24hr. access with a Cirrus/Visa/Mastercard.

American Express: Avs. 3/5, Calle Central (tel. 223-3644), inside Banco San José. To report a lost or stolen card from within Costa Rica, call 001-800-528-2121.Check cashing, but no cash advances. Passport needed. English spoken. Open Mon.-Fri. 8:15am-4pm. The **Credomatic** (tel. 258-0155) across the street provides emergency services for foreign travelers when the American Express is closed. Open Mon.-Fri. 8am-7pm, Sat. 9am-1pm.

Telegram: Radiográfica, (see Telephones below). US$0.45 per word to U.S., US$0.78 per word to Europe, US$0.64 to Canada. **Fax** and **telex** also available. Open daily 8am-10pm. Service also available at the **post office** (see below; tel. 223-9766, ext. 239). Open Mon.-Sat. 7am-6pm. Reduced rates after 7pm.

Fax: Radiográfica, (see Telephones below). US$1.98 per page to the U.S., US$3.05 per page to Europe. Open Mon.-Fri. 8am-10pm, Sat.-Sun. 8am-8pm. **Post office** (see below; tel. 223-9766, ext. 239), US$2.80 per page to U.S. or current equivalent in colones. Open Mon.-Sat. 7am-6pm.

Internet Services: Also at **Radiográfica** (see Telephones below). $3 per hour; access to World Wide Web and email.

Airport: Juan Santa María International Airport, about 15km northwest of San José on the highway to Alajuela. For 24hr. airport information, call 443-2942. **Taxis** to and from the airport run ¢2000-2500 (tel. 235-5847, 224-6969, or 235-9966). Red **buses** from Alajuela run every day between the airport and the San José bus terminal at Av. 2, Calles 10/12 (¢120). Buses every 5 min. from 4am-10pm; every 10 min. from 10pm-midnight; every hour from midnight-4am from Av.2, Calle 2.

Buses: Each destination is served by a different carrier. Your best bet is to consult the tourist office for a more complete list of companies and destinations which tend to change frequently. TUASA (tel. 442-3226) serves **Alajuela** and the **airport**, Av. 2, Calles 10/12 (every 5min. 4am-10pm; every 10min. 10pm-midnight; from midnight-4am, buses leave every hour from Av.2, Calle 2; 30min.; ¢120). To **Cahuita,** Avs. 7/9, Calle 1 (daily at 6am, 10am, 1:30pm, 4pm; 4hr.); SACSA (tel. 233-5350), goes to **Cartago,** Avs. 18/20, Calle 5 (every 10min. 5am-midnight; every hour midnight-5am; 45min.; ¢110). After 8:30pm, the bus leaves from in front of the Gran Hotel Costa Rica, Av. 2, Calles 3/5. TRACOPA goes to **Golfito,** Avs. 3/5, Calles 14/16 (7am, 3pm; 8 hr.); call 222-3854 for current rates. Microbuses Rapidos (tel. 233-8392) goes to **Heredia,** Avs. 7/9, Calle 1 (every 10min. 5am-12:15am; every 30min. 12:15am-4am; 25 min.; ¢110). To **Jacó Beach,** Av. 3, Calles 16/18 (7:30am, 10:30am, 3:30pm; 2½hr.). Coopelimon (tel. 223-7811), travels to **Limón,** Av. 3, Calles 19/21 (every hr. 5am-7pm; 2½hr.). To **Monteverde,** Avs. 7/9, Calle 12 (6:30am, 2:30pm.; 3½hr.) Transportes Mepe runs buses to **Puerto Viejo De Tala-manca,** Av. 11, Calles 1/3 (10am, 4pm.; 4½hr.). To **Puntarenas,** Av. 12, Calle 16 (every 40min., 6am-7pm; 2hr.). Coca Cola (tel. 223-5567) runs buses to **Quepos** and **Manuel Antonio,** Av. 3, Calles 16/18 (6am, 12pm, 6pm.; 3hrs; ¢1200). An indirect bus also runs (7am, 10am, 2pm, 4pm; 5hrs). Take Transtusa (tel. 556-0073) to **Turrialba,** Av. 6, Calles 13/15 (Mon.-Fri. every hr., 5am-10pm; Sun. 9am; 1½hr.; ¢300). Tica Bus, Av. 4, Calle 9 (tel. 221-8954), is a carrier for other major destinations in Central America. To: **Panama City** (daily 10pm, 18hr., ¢4200); **Managua** (daily 7:30am, 10½hr., ¢2625). From **Managua,** connecting routes to **Tegucigalpa** (2 days, ¢6,195), San Salvador (2 days, ¢8820), and Guatemala (3 days, ¢10290). Rates do not include hotel stays in Managua and San Salvador. Note: bus fares on all lines rise every 3 months or so.

Taxis: Coopetaxi Taxi Co. (tel. 235-9966). ¢100 for the first km, ¢60 each additional km. Most routes within San José run ¢160-400. Check that the meter is on (and reset) when you get in—tourists are often ripped-off by sly drivers. Fare to the airport is ¢2000-2500. 20% surcharge after 10pm. Ask the driver before trying to "split" a cab to the airport with someone; often the rate is per person.

Car Rental: Complete list of rental offices available at the tourist office. **Budget,** Paseo Colón, Calle 30 (tel. 223-3284; fax 255-4966). Open daily 7am-5:30pm. US$40 per day, including insurance, taxes, and free mileage. Must be 21. Those under 25 pay extra US$8 for insurance. For comparable rates, also try **National,** Paseo Colón, Av. 1, Calle 36 (tel. 233-4044); or **Prego,** Paseo Colón, Calles 32/34 (tel. 257-1158). Keep in mind that for driving anywhere outside the city, 4-wheel drive is recommended. To rent a Range Rover, try **Rent-A-Rover S.A.** (tel. and fax 533-3037, or 225-3948 to hear a recorded message). Free delivery in San José.

English Bookstore: Book Traders, Av. 1, Calles 5/7 (tel. 255-0508). Trade in your old books or buy used ones at 50% off the printed cover price. Everything from classics to trashy romance novels. Small French and German sections. Mon.-Sat. 9am-6pm, Sun. 10am-5pm. **Chispas,** Av. Central 1, Calle 7 (tel. and fax 256-8251). A refreshing collection of non-trashy books, especially good fiction and travel guide sections, and extremely knowledgable staff. Also houses a travel agency, Ecole Travel, specializing in affordable trips to Tortuguero. This is also where you'll find the major international papers, such as the *New York Times, Wall Street Journal, USA Today* and others. Open daily 9am-6pm. **Librería Lehmann,** Av. Central, Calles 1/3 (tel. 223-1212). Books, travel guides, maps, and major North American publications. CDs galore. Open Mon.-Fri. 8am-6:30pm, Sat. 9am-5pm.

Central San José

COSTA RICA

Río Torres

PASO DE LA VACA

OTOYA

Atlantic Train Station

Hospital Calderón Guardia

Calle 17

National Library

Asamblea Legislativa

TO LA UNIVERSIDAD DE COSTA RICA

Parque Nacional

Calle 15

Calle 13

Avenida 7

Avenida 3

BELLAVISTA

Museo Nacional

Plaza de la Democracía

Calle 21

Calle 19

Calle 17

Calle 15

N

200 yards
200 meters

Museo de Jade

Parque España

Calle 11

Avenida 1

Serpentario

Avenida 2

Calle 13

AMON

Avenida 11

Avenida 9

Avenida 5

Calle 7

Parque Morazán

Calle 9

SOLEDAD

9

Calle 5

Calle 3

Calle 1

CARMEN

Museo de Oro

Teatro Nacional

Avenida 4

Avenida Central

Catedral Metropolitana

Avenida 6

Avenida 8

Avenida 10

Avenida 12

Avenida 14

5

Calle Central

Calle 2

Calle 4

Calle 6

Calle 8

Banco National

Post Office

Mercado Central

Parque Central

Calle Central

Calle 2

Calle 4

Calle 6

Calle 8

Calle 10

Calle 12

Avenida 16

Avenida 18

Avenida 20

Pacific Train Station

Calle 10

Avenida 3

Avenida 1

Avenida 2

Avenida 4

MERCED

SANTA LUCIA

BOLIVAR

Calle 12

Coca Cola Bus Station

Hospital Nacional San Juan de Dios

Calle 16

COCA COLA

Hospital Cervantes

Calle 16

Calle 18

Avenida 11

Avenida 9

Avenida 7

Calle 14

Calle 16

Calle 18

Juan Santa María

Jewish Synagogue

Hospital Nacional de Niños

SAN BOSCO

Calle 20

Paseo Colón

Avenida 5

Avenida 3

Calle 20

Calle 22

Calle 24

Calle 26

Calle 28

TO LA SABANA & MUSEO DE ARTE COSTARRICENSE

Avenida 6

Avenida 8

Market: Central Market framed by Avs. Central and 1, Calles 6 and 8. Open daily until 6pm. Hundreds of carts lined with colorful fruits and veggies; a labyrinth of cheap grub and souvenirs, especially leather bags and sandals. Tourists should guard their possessions carefully here. Also check out the market directly in front of **La Plaza de la Democracia** and the **Museo Nacional;** great prices (especially if you try your bartering skills and charm) on silver jewelry, local crafts, hand-woven bags and clothing. Open daily 9am-6pm.

Supermarket: AM-AutoMercado, Av. 3, Calle 3 (tel. 233-5511). Open Mon.-Sat. 8am-8pm. **Mas y Menos** has stores throughout San José; try Av. Central, Calles 11/13 (tel. 223-0077) or Av. 5, Calles 1/3 (tel. 223-1067). Open daily 8am-8pm.

Laundromat: Sixaola, Av. 2, Calles 7/9 (tel. 221-2111), and many other locations throughout the city. Wash, iron, and fold laundry, ¢550 per kg. Ready in 48hr. Some hotels allow you to use one of their machines. Try the **Gran Hotel Imperial,** Avs. Central/1, Calle 8. Prices vary according to weight and item; you can usually wash and dry your clothes in close to 2hr.

Red Cross: Av. 6, Calle 16 (tel. 128 or 233-7033). No English spoken.

Pharmacies: Fischel, Av. 3, Calle 2, near the center of town (tel. 257-7979). Open Mon.-Fri. 8am-7pm, Sat. 8am-5pm. Huge selection of medicines and toiletries, and a *sala de emergencia.* Sun. deliveries only.

Hospital: Hospital San Juan de Dios, Paseo Colón, Calles 14/18. Large white building where Av. Central turns into Paseo Colón, after Calle 14. 24-hr. emergency service. Doctor consultations free; English-speaking doctors can sometimes be found. **Clínica Bíblica,** Av. 14, Calles Central/1 (tel. 257-5252). 24hr. emergency care, 24hr. pharmacy. During the day, English-speaking doctors are available.

Emergency: tel. 911.

Police: tel. 911 or 117. Ministerio de Seguridad Pública, 150m east of the Centro Comercial de Sur (tel. 227-4866). To report a theft, contact the **Organismo de Investigacion Judicial** (O.I.J.), Avs. 4/6, Calle 15 (tel. 295-3000).

Post Office: Avs. 1/3, Calle 2 (tel. 223-9766 or 223-9079). Located in the large green building. Open Mon.-Fri. 7am-6:45pm, Sat. 7am-noon. There are no street mailboxes in San José, so all mail must be dropped off here. *Lista de correos* open Mon.-Fri. 8am-noon, 1-4pm. **Postal code:** 1000.

Telephones: Radiográphica (tel. 287-0462), Av. 5, Calle 1. Just pick up one of their many phones to make a free collect call. Also has AT&T Direct and Sprint service. Open Mon.-Fri. 8am-10pm, Sat.-Sun. 8am-8pm.

■ Accommodations

Budget accommodations in San José are evenly dispersed throughout the city. Since prices are similar from neighborhood to neighborhood, it's worth avoiding the northeast part of the city, where streets and rooms tend to be dirtier and less safe. This section of town is especially dangerous for women traveling alone. The cost of a room in San José often varies inversely with the amount of street noise that filters in through the windows.

Toruma Youth Hostel (HI), Av. Central, Calles 31/33 (tel. and fax 224-4085). Take the San Pedro bus (¢40) from the Teatro Nacional. Single-sex rooms and bathrooms. Bunks—equipped with a light, a small fan, shelves, and a lock—are more like cupboards. Still, Toruma boasts scores of collectivist amenities: a spacious lobby with sofas and cable TV, spotless communal bathroom facilities with hot water, free breakfasts, and even its own tourist information center. Storage, but no laundry. Up to 6 in a suite. Early birds may be able to snag a more spacious quad for the same price (US$12/bed, ISIC holders US$10, and HI members US$8). Doubles available (US$28, ISIC holders and HI members US$26). Reception daily 24hrs.; check-ins after 10pm need passports.

Casa Ridgway, Av. 6, Calle 15 (tel./fax 233-6168), in the short, dead-end street between and running parallel to Avs. 6 and 8. The Ridgway shares its bright yellow building with the "Friends' Peace Center," and peace is what you'll find at this hotel/hostel. Quiet hours 10pm-7am. Wood floors and lush indoor garden with couches and a small, multilingual library. Kitchen, fridge, laundry (by machine

¢350, by hand ¢50), a public phone (incoming calls), storage facilities, impeccable communal bathrooms with 24hr. almost-hot water and showers make Casa Ridgway worth the search. Singles US$8; private US$10; doubles US$20; quads US$32.

Tica Linda, Av. 2, Calles 5/7 (tel. 233-0528; fax 257-2272). Next to Bar Esmeralda; marked only by a tiny nameplate on the door. A backpacker's favorite, and a great place to get travel hints from veterans. The rooms may not be the largest or most airy in town, but all come equipped with locks (windows are less secure), and the funky atmosphere and central location make it a good pick. 24-hr. lukewarm water in one of the two communal bathrooms, but bring your own toilet paper, and don't expect seats. Storage facilities. Reception desk closes at 11pm, so night revelers should get a key (deposit ¢300). Dorm-style ¢900 per person; singles ¢1200; doubles ¢2400; triples ¢2040.

Gran Hotel Imperial, Avs. Central/1, Calle 8 (tel. 222-7899). With over 100 rooms and lots of friendly international backpackers, the Imperial is a budget traveler's dream. The hotel gets no points for beauty, but it's chock full of amenities. Passable private and communal bathrooms with hot water, a restaurant/bar (open daily noon-8:30pm, bar until 10pm), a laundromat downstairs (about ¢700 for one load, wash and dry), a balcony that overlooks the *Mercado Central*, public telephone— the list goes on and on. Singles ¢800. Doubles ¢1600, with bath ¢2500. Triples ¢2300, with bath ¢3500. Quads ¢3200. "Familiar" (five people) with bath ¢4500.

Pensión Otoya, Avs. 3/5, Calle 1 (tel. 221-3925). Amiable staff, large and well-furnished rooms filled with eclectic guests, and more than reasonable prices make Pensión Otoya the preferred hangout of many a backpacker. Key to the front door allows 24hr. access. Laundry (¢75 per piece), storage facilities, TV in the lounge, and phone access. Singles ¢1400, with bath ¢1800; doubles ¢2000, with bath ¢2400; triples ¢2600, with bath ¢3000; quads ¢3200, with bath ¢3600.

Hotel Rialto, Av. 5, Calle 2, 3rd Floor (tel. 221-7456). The surrounding neighborhood drowns in traffic, but Rialto offers sanctuary in its dark, wood-paneled lobby and halls. Rooms even have windows: a San José budget rarity. Single-sex communal bathrooms are pristine and hot water flows 24hr. Laundry facilities, incoming phone calls, TV in the lounge. Singles ¢1000; doubles ¢1800, with bath ¢2300.

Hotel Boston, Av. 8, Calles Central/2 (tel. 221-0563), next to Hotel Berlin. The proper Bostonian even smells like PineSol, and the rooms' mint-green walls seem freshly painted. Prices are slightly higher but well worth it—rooms are spacious and bright, and all have TV and private bathroom facilities. Extremely friendly staff. Hot water 24hr. Laundry service and telephone (incoming calls) available. Conveniently open 24hr., but reservations are recommended. Singles ¢2500; doubles ¢3500; quads ¢4800. Visa and Mastercard accepted.

▨ Food

Seafood dishes, black beans, and rice are San José's staples. However, Western pop culture has left its mark, and now fast-food joints of McDonald's style and caliber stand sentry over nearly every downtown street. To capture more authentic *tico* fare, ignore the fast-food and try any of the hundreds of *sodas* spotting the city's calles. Prices are good everywhere, but the cheapest grub is found in the eateries of the **Mercado Central,** where authentic *tico* meals like a *chuleta* (pork chop) with rice and salad go for only ¢400.

Pasteleria y Cafeteria Whipping Cream, Av. 6, Calles 11/13. Don't be scared off by the name, this might be your best meal in San José. The *Casado Combo* #1 (fish/beef/chicken, rice, salad, beans and *refresco*; ¢350) is incredible—whatever the secret is to amazing beans, they know it. Open Mon.-Fri. 7am-6pm.

Restaurant Vishnu, Av. 1, Calles 1/3 (tel. 222-2549). Two other locations: Av. 8, Calles 11/13 and Avs. Central/1, Calle 14. Large plates of fresh fruit, big paintings of jungle scenes, and the azure, 4-armed Preserver of Worlds encourage a lively and amiable atmosphere. Vegetarian menu includes soy burgers (¢300) and vegetable sandwiches (¢450) which are popular with budget travelers as well as locals. The *plato del dia* (¢650) is perhaps one of the best deals in town. Along with rice, veggies and soup, it even includes a *refresco sopa* and dessert. Open Mon.-Sat. 7am-9:30pm, Sun. 9am-7:30pm.

Soda My Friends, Av. 8, Calles 7/9. Perhaps the cutest little hole-in-the-wall in San José, this neighborhood *soda's* prices are unbelievably cheap and the food's still great. Especially good if you're looking to catch *desayuno* (breakfast) or a soccer game on the little TV in the corner, amidst the heated cries of the locals. *Pinto, huevo, tortilla* with *café* (¢225), *café* (¢75). *Tacos* (¢100) and *empanadas* (¢50) are super deals too. Open Mon.-Sat. 7am-5pm.

Restaurant Shakti, Av. 8, Calle 13 (tel. 222-4475). This *Restaurante y Macrobiótica* is a haven for die-hard vegetarians. Vegetables everywhere, even growing under the glass table-tops. Extensive vegetarian menu includes *chalupa* (beans, cheese, and soya, ¢450), spaghetti with mushrooms, raisins, and cheese (¢550), and *"energético,"* yogurt with honey, fruit, granola, and pollen (¢250). Sells packaged grains and vitamins and delicious home-baked breads. Open Mon.-Fri. 11:30am-7pm, Sat. 9am-3pm.

San Remo, Avs. 3/5, Calle 2 (tel. 221-8145). Enthusiastic service, a full and diverse menu of incredible food, and the relaxed atmosphere of this wood-paneled restaurant more than make up for its slightly higher prices. Boasts both authentic *tico* and Italian dishes. Try the *casados corriente* (¢900) or the *spaghetti a la gorgonzola* (¢1000). They make their own pasta! Perfect for a cappuccino (¢250) or espresso (¢200) break. Open Mon.-Sat. 9am-9pm.

Spoon, Av. Central, Calles 5/7 (tel. 221-6702). Red-brick paneling, woven-grass chairs, quiet Latin American pop music, an eerily hip name, and delicious desserts make this cafe irresistible. Always busy around lunchtime (sandwiches around ¢350). The real reasons to come are the rich iced cappuccinos (¢285) and the Kahlua-laden pastries (¢400), including *Kalúa con nuez* (with nuts) and *chocofresa* (chocolate strawberry). Coffee or tea (¢150). Open Mon.-Sat. 9:30am-9pm.

Soda Nini, Av. 3, Calles 2/4 (tel. 233-7771). Remember your middle school cafeteria? The self-serve lines and hard, nailed-down chairs and tables have all been recreated at Soda Nini, an inexpensive *soda* by day, and in the back rooms, a *discoteca* and bar by night. *Ensalada verde* ¢200, *arroz cantones* ¢180. If you miss the current pop hits from home, this is your place. Open Mon.-Sat. 10am-11pm; Sun. 11am-10pm.

Restaurant Omni, Av. 1. Calles 3/5. You thought that Chinese-food craving couldn't be satisfied in San José, didn't you? In a mellow, roofed courtyard set back from the street, Omni fries up their rice with the best of Beijing. Fried rice or chop suey with chicken, beef, or seafood (¢450-650), won ton soup (¢750). Plain fried rice (¢550). You should be pleasantly haunted by MSG flashbacks for years to come. Open Mon.-Sat. 11am-10pm.

▓ Sights

The stunning **Teatro Nacional** (National Theater), Av. 2, Calles 3/5 (tel. 221-1329), off the plaza de la Cultura, is almost unbelievably extravagant, graced with ornately sculpted gold banisters and high ceiling frescos. Italian sculptor Pitro Bulgarelli's personifications of Dance, Music, and Fame anoint its Renaissance facade. Marble columns file along its vestibules, and an ornate Paris Opéra-inspired grand staircase rises toward bright overhead reliefs painted by Bespasiano Bignami, who was later commissioned to work on the Moscow Opera House. Concerts are held in the grand auditorium, an orchestra pit surrounded by three tiers of balconies trimmed with deep maroon velvet. Often you can sit alone in the huge concert hall and catch a free rehearsal of anyone from a Joanna Veltri's local calypso band to the national orchestra. Seating in the main area is neither sloped nor staggered; those stuck behind the likes of Carmen Miranda or Shaquille O'Neil suffer accordingly.

Construction of the *teatro* was begun in 1890. In January of that year, an opera company led by the renowned Adelina Patti was performing in Guatemala; the company was unable to perform in San José because the city lacked an "appropriate" facility. Snubbed by the snobs, a group of merchants and coffee barons wrote to acting president Durán. Arguing that "a capital with a culture such as ours cannot be deprived of a center of this kind," and knowing full well that the national budget couldn't fund such a venture, the merchants and barons pledged to donate five cents for every 25 pounds of coffee they exported. The rest, as they say, is history. The *teatro* was inaugurated in 1897 and declared a national monument in 1965; it celebrated its grand centennial in October 1997. Over the years, thousands of Costa Ricans have seen performances at the theater. The largest crowd to date gathered last spring to watch Robin Goldstein perform the role of "Christine" in *Phantom of the Opera*. However, not as many have come as some would have liked; the novelist Marín Cañas once claimed in jest that the *teatro nacional* was the largest in the world. After all, he argued, "so far, nobody has been able to fill it." So when you tire of salsa clubs, catch one of the many spectacular plays, concerts, or even the *Coro Sinfonico Nacional* at truly reasonable prices. (Open Mon.-Sun. 9am-1pm and 2-5pm; restricted access during performances; admission ¢600.)

A lush and well tended jungle-garden hides the tired facade of the **Museo Nacional,** Avs. Central/2, Calle 17 (tel. 257-1433). Housed in long corridors which border its inner courtyard, the museum boasts expertly maintained collections of pre-Hispanic art, as well as detailed exhibits on Costa Rican history, colonial life, archaeology, and geology. One of the most impressive displays features *metates,* three-legged funeral offerings made of hardened lava. The nightmarish "flying panel" *metates* are elaborately decorated with anthropomorphic animal figures holding decapitated heads, representing traditional sacrificial rituals. The museum also enjoys an incredible view of San José from the dried-grass gazebo in its sprawling bamboo-and-palm garden—guaranteed to knit up unraveled nerves. The gift shop is also strictly for looking; the faux-gold jewelry and indigenous pottery go for outrageous prices (open Tues.-Sat. 8:30am-4:30pm, Sun. 9am-4:30pm; admission ¢200, free with student ID).

The **Museo del Oro,** Avs. Central/2, Calle 5 (tel. 223-0528), in the Plaza de la Cultura, houses a magnificent collection of pre-Hispanic artifacts, including 2300 pieces of jewelry, armor plates, and figures used for religious devotion and spiritual healing. Shamans used these animal figurines to communicate with spirits; the many serpents and alligator heads symbolize fertility via association with their aquatic origins. Especially cool are the amazingly detailed miniature gold animals and the lip rings in the adjacent case. The displays are labeled in Spanish and English and give a detailed history of the state of metallurgy in 400 BC, including diagrams that describe different types of casting to visitors with spare gold ore and time (open Tues.-Sun. 10am-4:30pm; admission ¢1000, ticos ¢500, ages 7-12 ¢150, with student ID ¢300).

Several temporary art and sculpture exhibits share a building with the Museo del Oro, including the **Numismatic Museum,** whose displays of coins and currencies include almost everything from the first Spanish colonial coin to the modern day colón. A large collection of jade, along with ceramic and gold exhibits, resides in the **Museo de Jade** (tel. 223-5800), Av. 7, Calles 9/13, on the 11th floor of the INS building on the north side of Plaza de España. The intricately carved figures of green, white, pink, and black jade glow incandescently in their lighted display cases. The extensive ceramics exhibit reveals that despite the noticeable Colombian/Andean and even Maya influence, a distinctly Central American character is clear in the centuries-old pottery and craft. Among the more practical artifacts are some long, tubular jade beads used as brassieres by the wives of indigenous chieftains. Watch out, WonderBra. Overlooking San José, a breezy, peaceful sitting room hides off to the side, decorated with hanging plants and striking photography of indigenous children. (Open Mon.-Fri. 8:30am-4:30pm; ¢300, free with student I.D.) The **Museo de Arte Costarricense,** Calle 42, Paseo Colón, in the Sabana Metropolitan Park, exhibits the works of Costa Rican artists from 1950 to the present. On the second floor is the impressive Gold Room, famous for French artist Louis Feron's four gold bas reliefs depicting the history of Costa Rica (open Tues.-Sun. 10am-5pm; admission ¢300, Sun. free, with student ID free). The **National Library,** Av. 3, calles 15/17 (tel. 222-7155), across from the **Parque Nacional,** often houses exhibits from the Museo de Arte Costarricense, such as black and white photography or modern painting. Call for info. (Open Mon.-Fri. 8am-6:30pm.)

The **Serpentarium** (tel. 255-4210), Av. 1, Calles 9/11, houses a collection of serpents, reptiles, tarantulas, and amphibians, all of them native to Costa Rica. Amidst slimy creepers and slick slitherers you'll find the legendary poison arrow frogs, those media darlings whose natural habitat includes every hackneyed book cover and postcard in the country. The vicious glares from the mini-crocodiles are enough to keep even the bravest from touching the glass. Paragraphs printed in English and Spanish describe the behaviors and natural locality of each animal (open Mon.-Fri. 9am-6pm, Sat.-Sun. 10am-5pm; admission ₡700, ticos ₡500, ages 4-13 ₡250).

Parque de España, enclosed by Avs. 3 and 5 and Calles 11 and 13, is a great place to walk, talk, or simply to stand still and be quiet. The long limbs of its broad trees create a refuge for city-weary couples. It's one of the few places in town where you can actually hear the birds singing and feel the wind on your face *without* choking on car exhaust. The park is joined by **Parque Morazán,** Avs. 3/5, Calles 5/9, blanketed in what once might have been thick grass, orchid-laden benches, and an enormous gazebo. Beware of the early afternoon, though—the park is overrun with the noise of playful running children when the several nearby *escuelas* grant their daily furlough.

Parque Nacional (tel. 221-2479), Avs. 1/3, Calles 15/19, is the closest you'll see in San José to a real rainforest. The drooping trees along the perimeter of the park form a fortress against the belligerent city streets, and teens and elderly couples alike picnic on its stone benches which sit peacefully under vine-covered awnings. Rising above the frolicking kids, a statue in the center represents the five Central American nations joining successfully to expel an invading Willie Walker from Costa Rica in 1856 (see p 264). Adjacent to the park are the **Legislative Building** and the National Library.

FANAL used to stand for **Fabrica Nacional de Licores,** but the factory has gone on the wagon and serves as the **Centro Nacional de Arte y Cultura.** It is a big cream, frankly factory-looking center on Avenida 3, Calle 13 and 15—putting it between the Plaza de España and the National Library. Besides rotation exhibitions and instructional space, the center houses the **Teatro FANAL,** a site for experimental theater, and the **Museo de Arte y Diseño Contemporaneo.** The entrance to the latter stands across the street from the library (and a small gallery space, incidentally). Just four years old, the museum has displayed an impressive array of Costa Rican and international artists in four handsome halls. Open Mon.-Sat. 8am-4pm; free.

■ Entertainment

San José will not disappoint restless travelers who feel compelled to shake their booties in every world capital. **Salsa 54,** Calle 3, Avs. 1/3 (tel. 223-3814), is a disco bonanza of love songs, 60s hits from the U.S., and ever-popular *salsa.* Only the most daring *gringos* join the *salsa* masters under the colorful disco lights of the center stage; the rest simply try to blend in on the dark dance floor (open daily 8pm-2am; cover Tues.-Sat. ₡500, Sun. ₡450, Mon., when the live band plays, ₡600; women free on Wed.). **Bar Esmeralda,** Av. 2 and Calles 5/7 (tel. 221-0530), next door to Tica Linda, is reminiscent of a real dance hall, featuring guitar music from 8-9pm and Latin American favorites from the *mariachi* band until the wee hours. Esmeralda serves a lunch buffet (11:30am-2pm) including a main dish, salad, and a refreshment (₡450-₡650). Dinners run ₡500-₡3000, beers go for ₡200, and there's a ₡600 minimum per person after 11pm. For ₡1000, crooners will sing your favorite ditty (open Mon.-Thurs. 11:30am-3:30am, Fri.-Sat. 11:30am-5am). **Cuartel de la Boca del Monte,** Av. 1, Calle 23 (tel. 221-0327), is one of the liveliest spots in town. The crowd packs in Mon. and Wed. nights, when live music blares. Bands play near the bar with the amazing 152-cocktail menu. No cover, but after 9pm a minimum ₡1000 bar tab is required. (Open Mon.-Fri. 11:30am-2pm and 6pm-2am, Sat.-Sun. 6pm-2am.) The epicenter of Costa Rica's disco universe is **Centro Comercial el Pueblo,** an adobe maze of alleyways filled with gift shops, bars, and dance clubs. In the far north part of town (most easily accessible by taxi, but buses run sporadically as well), you'll find **El Tango Bar,** a retro joint where the pianist pounds out the Argentine tangos of his glorious youth (open Mon.-Sat. 9pm-3am; cover ¢350; drinks start at ¢200). **The Plaza Disco Club,** located at the entrance of the Centro Comercial el Pueblo (tel. 222-5143), plays more standard pop music and is often filled to the brim with teenagers on weekend nights (open Mon.-Sat. 7pm-5am.; Fri.-Sat. cover ¢700; Sun.-Thurs. no cover but a ¢300 minimum bar tab). Other popular discos located in the Centro Comercial el Pueblo include **Coco Loco** (tel. 222-8782), with a smaller dance floor and an older crowd (open Tues.-Sat. 6pm-1am; happy hour 6-8pm; cover ¢1000) and **El Infinito** (tel. 223-2195), heavy with fluorescent palm trees, a waterfall in one of the dance rooms, and other such kitsch. One of two dance rooms is intended strictly for the college-age crowd and features American favorites only, while the other blasts more traditional *salsa* beats; plenty of bars and rooms for cozying span the distance between the two (open Sun.-Thurs. 6pm-4am, Fri.-Sat. 6pm-6am; cover Sun.-Thurs. ¢400, Fri.-Sat. ¢600, includes first drink).

San José boasts a fairly large and visible gay/lesbian community, and both **Déjà Vu,** Av. 14/16, Calle 2 and **La Avispa,** Av. 8/10, Calle 1 (tel. 223-5343), are well-known for their wild dancing crowds and funky music. Your best bet, however, is to contact **Casa Yemaya** (tel. 223-3652) for the most current suggestions on clubs, bars, and community connections; or try the very active **International Gay and Lesbian Association** (tel. 234-2411). Locals cite both as great contacts and sources of information.

A number of movie theaters throughout San José show fairly recent U.S. releases. Happily, your Spanish skills don't need to be in their prime—often flicks are shown in English with Spanish subtitles. In the center of downtown, **Cine Omni,** Avs. Central/1 and Calle 3, shows flicks daily at 4, 6:45, and 9pm (¢500). **Cine California,** Av.1 and Calle 23 (tel. 221-4738), also shows three-to-six-month-old U.S. releases daily at 4, 6:45, and 9pm (¢500). **Cine Magaly,** Calle 23, Avs. Central/2, is slightly more expensive, but shows current U.S. hits daily at 4, 6:45, and 9pm (¢600). Check the local papers —English or Spanish — for listings. **Sala Garbo** wants to be left alone on Calle 28, Av. 2, 100m south of the Paseo Colón Pizza Hut. About the only cinema in town that doesn't show American blockbusters (or porn). Art house movies include European films, American independents, and Spanish-language productions. **Teatro Laurence Olivier** is in the same building, providing a smaller venue for similar fare. Top off your visit with a drink at the **Shakespeare Cafe.** Quite an artsy little complex. Shows around 5, 7, and 9pm daily, ¢700.

■ Near San José

VOLCÁN POÁS

Northwest of San José lies **Parque Nacional Poás,** a vast cloud forest laced with *indígena* trails moist with mosses, palms, orchids, and bromeliads (like pineapples). Poás makes a good daytrip for anyone tired of San José's dirt and noise; even the 55km drive, on narrow roads that wind through fertile farmland and tiny villages, provides a spectacular vista of the lush Central Valley. Unfortunately, it is the most visited park in the country. As a result, it is increasingly difficult to see the allegedly numerous birds and mammals living in Poás. Occasional shrill cries belie the presence of the sacred quetzal which few are lucky enough to see. Poá's most enjoyable in the early morning, before clouds and tourists cramp your style. The park's highlight is the steam-belching crater of **Volcán Poás** (2700m above sea level), a 10-minute walk from the parking lot through a tunnel of ferns and gnarled trees. Bright green fumaroles (bubbling vents in the earth's crust) pock the bottom of the 1.5km wide, 300m deep hole. In a 1910 eruption, the volcano produced a cloud of ash 8km high, and to this day it occasionally emits a geyser-like plume. The volcano suddenly ran out of steam between 1953 and 1955, and since 1981 it has mainly released acidic gases, causing significant damage to cattle, coffee crops, and strawberry fields. Away from the bubbling pits and capricious crater, follow the trail for a 10-minute hike to Laguna Botos, a flawless 450m wide, sparkling blue lake—the kind of place you thought existed only on postcards.

COSTA RICA

The visitors center is equipped with a museum and its main attraction is an enormously extensive display of insects. A souvenir shop, a video about the national parks, bathrooms, and a small coffee shop are open daily 8am-3:30pm; entrance to the museum is free. If you're stuck unprepared in a sudden downpour, don't fret—the gift shop rents umbrellas and ponchos for US$2/day (US$10 deposit required). Entrance to the park is US$6.

On Sundays, buses run directly but slowly to the park from **San José,** leaving from the **Parque de la Merced,** at Av. 2, Calles 12/14 (look for the red buses to Alajuela and Volcán Poás) at 8:30am (get there a bit early), stopping at the **Parque Central** in **Alajuela** at 9am, and arriving at Volcán Poás at approximately 10:15am. The bus leaves the park at 2:30pm, and arrives back in San José around 4:30pm (roundtrip ₡1000). There is no direct transportation to the park on weekdays. Buses do, however, run to **Poasito,** a small village 10km from the park. You can also taxi to the park from Poás.

Although Parque Nacional Poás is actually closer to Alajuela than to San José, it's much easier to reach from the capital; often the bus is completely full by the time it reaches Alajuela. You can stand for the 2 hour bus ride or catch a bus to **San Pedro de Poás** and take a cab from there (₡2500-3500).

VOLCÁN IRAZÚ

At an elevation of 3432m, **Volcán Irazú** is the tallest volcano in Costa Rica. Though the 54km drive provides an amazing view of the farmland and prodigious vegetation of the Central Valley, the volcano itself seems positively unearthly—much more like a sci-fi movie set—with its bleak, moonlike craters all covered in black ash. The volcano last erupted on March 9, 1963 (the same day John F. Kennedy arrived in Costa Rica for a presidential visit), when it coughed up "cold lava" (mud) and caused the evacuation of 200 villagers from the nearby town of Fatima. Showering ash on the Central Valley, the massive blast of earth and ash transformed parts of the green forest into a gray, dusty wasteland, and so the area remains. Nevertheless, the park surrounding the volcano hosts a variety of species—coyotes prey on a large rabbit population, while *juncos* and sparrow hawks flit through the air. At higher elevations, harsh environmental conditions favor life-forms common to the South American Andes; the few avian species hardy enough to survive here are hummingbirds, which hibernate on cold nights and squat on red-flowered bushes during the day.

Today, only one of Irazú's four craters, *cráter principal*, is perceptibly active. One hundred meters deep, this crater is filled with yellow-green water and looks like an enormous witch's cauldron. Supposedly, it is also possible to see both the Atlantic and Pacific Oceans and Lago de Nicaragua from Irazú's summit, but clouds usually obstruct all views, especially during the rainy season. In fact, most of the volcano's highest points are off-limits; the established trail only circles half of the *cráter principal.* Arrive early, the clouds usually descend before noon. And dress warmly; it is very cold. There is a small cafeteria in the park run out of the back of an old green truck. Coffee, hot chocolate, and tea cost ₡130 and sandwiches cost around ₡250.

Getting to Volcán Irazú couldn't be simpler. The yellow school bus leaves San José from Av. 2, Calles 3/5 (on the opposite side of the road from the Gran Hotel de Costa Rica) at 8am every Saturday and Sunday. Call 272-0657 to be sure the bus is running. The bus ride takes about two hours, stopping at the Cartago ruins at around 8:30am. Make sure to catch the bus back at 12:15pm sharp (roundtrip ₡1350), and do plan for the return trip, since camping is not permitted (open 8am-3:30pm; admission to the park US$6). On the return trip, the bus stops about 10km from the park at **Bar y Restaurante Linda Vista,** a welcome, if expensive, source of good food overlooking the green countryside (coffee ₡180, *tortilla de queso* ₡320; open daily 7am-7pm).

San José Region

COSTA RICA

CORDILLERA CENTRAL

PARQUE NACIONAL VOLCÁN IRAZÚ

Volcán Irazú

Parque Doña Añazieto

Área Recreativa de Prusia

Santa Rosa

Cipreses

Paraíso

Mirador de Cartago

Jardines Lankester

San Rafael de Oreamuno

Dulce Nombre

Llano Grande

Cot

Tierra Blanca

Rancho Redondo

CARTAGO

Dulce Nombre

San Rafael

San Isidro

Tres Ríos

Tejar

San Isidro de Coronado

Parque Recreativo del Este

San Ramón

CERROS DE LA CARPINTERA

San Rafael

Paracito

Ipis

Sabanilla

Lourdes

San Juan

Hipódromo Nacional

Tobosí

Monte de la Cruz

El Castillo Country Club

San Vicente de Moravia

Guadalupe

Curridabat

Tirrases

Desamparados

Patarrá

Concepción

San Josecito

San Isidro

San Francisco

Santo Tomás

Llorente

El Tapiche

San Pedro

Zapote

San Sebastián

San Rafael Abajo

San Miguel

Ángeles

San Miguel

San Pablo

San Juan de Tibás

SAN JOSÉ

San Rafael Arriba

San Rafael

HEREDIA

San Roque

Barva de Heredia

Santo Domingo

Uruca

Hatillo

San Juan de Dios

Aserrí

Birrí

Jesús

San Juan Abajo

San Joaquín

Tobías Bolaños Airport

La Sabana

San Rafael

Alajuelita

San Josecito

San Antonio

Tarbaca

Santa Bárbara

San Pedro

Pavas

Escazú

San Antonio

FILA DE CEDRAL

Desamparados

ALAJUELA

Río Segundo

Juan Santamaría International Airport

San Antonio de Belén

Santa Ana

RESERVA FORESTAL PICO BLANCO

Tambor

San Antonio

San Rafael

Pozos

Río Oro

Salitral

Piedades

Palmichal

Tabarcia

Ojo de Agua Recreational Complex

Ciudad Colón

5 miles

5 kilometers

N

THE CENTRAL VALLEY

The Central Valley, or **Meseta Central,** is a high and vast region cordoned off to the north and south by the great volcanic mountain ranges that divide Costa Rica in two, the **Cordillera Central** and the **Cordillera de Talamanca.** Many of the volcanos are still active and have caused the valley's residents heartache more than once, but their ash has also blessed these temperate plains with enough soil fertile to feed several nations. It's no surprise to hear that almost two-thirds of all *ticos* live in this valley and that four of Costa Rica's five largest cities mark its center.

■ Heredia

Cosmopolitan, academic Heredia retains the knowing air of San José while shedding the grime and frenetic pace of the capital. Perched atop rolling hills 11km north of San José, Heredia (pop. 30,000) is a laid-back, mid-sized university town, full of local pride. Since its founding in the 1570s, Heredia has seemed a bit out of step with the rest of the nation. Throughout the colonial era, Heredia lagged behind Cartago in wealth and stature. After Mexico won its independence from Spain in 1821, Heredia's residents campaigned to have Costa Rica annexed to Mexico—but the rest of the country dissented. Costa Ricans chose Heredia as their capital briefly in the 1830s, but soon reconsidered, sending the government to San José instead. Once home to small tobacco farms, Heredia eventually jumped on the coffee bandwagon; today coffee and cattle are major sources of the town's livelihood. Heredia is a neat, well-kept suburb; many residents commute to work in San José. Cooler and cleaner than the capital, Heredia's pride is reflected in the exquisitely tidy Parque Central and Mercado Municipal.

Orientation and Practical Information When busing it in from San José, the **Parque Central,** Heredia's center of action, is a good place to disembark. Another useful point for orientation—and one essential in order to understand any directions given by locals—is the **Mercado Municipal,** three blocks south and one block west of the park. Heredia's streets are arranged in a grid aligned with the four points of the compass. *Calles* run north to south; *avenidas* run east to west. An air-tight logic prevails—Parque Central is bordered by Avenida Central and Calle Central.

Exchange traveler's checks at the **Banco Nacional,** Avs. 2/4, Calle 2 (tel. 261-0403), at a 1% commission for colones (open Mon.-Fri. 8:30am-3:45pm). **Telephones** cluster on the north side and southwest corner of Parque Central. **Buses** from Heredia to San José depart from Av. 2/4, Calle Central. **Taxis** wait on Av. 2 between Calles Central and 2, to the south of Parque Central, and on the east side of the central market on Calle 2. The **Mercado Municipal,** bordered by Calles 2 and 4 and by Avs. 6 and 10, offers a plethora of butcher shops and fruit and vegetable stands (open Mon.-Sat. 6am-6pm, Sun 7am-noon). **Palí,** Avs. 8/10, Calle 4, carries basic food products, and household needs as well (open Mon.-Thurs. 8am-6:30pm, Fri.-Sat. 8am-7pm, Sun. 8:30am-6pm). Even more daring supermarket shoppers should check out **Rayo Azul,** Av. 6, Calles 4/6 (tel. 261-0006), featuring a deli, a cosmetics counter, and a feast of free samples (open Mon.-Sat. 8am-9pm, Sun. 8am-8pm). Try **Farmacia Bernini,** Avs. 4/6, Calle 2 (tel. 237-0371; open Mon.-Sat. 8am-7pm), for non-urgent medical problems. More pressing matters should be handled by the **Red Cross** (tel. 237-1115). In an **Emergency,** call 911; otherwise, the **police** can be contacted at a central station (tel. 237-0438). The **post office,** Av. Central, Calle 2 (tel. 260-0461; fax 260-6767; open Mon-Fri 7:30am-5:30pm), is across the street from the northeast corner of Parque Central, and has *lista de correos.* **Telegram** and **fax** services are also provided. Telegrams cost US$0.50 per word to the U.S., US$0.67 per word to Europe; faxes go for US$2.60 per page to the U.S., US$3.60 per page to Europe. **Postal Code:** 3000.

Heredia

BARVA
TO BIRRI
TO ANGELES
113

0   300 yards
0   300 meters

N

126

SANTA
LUCÍA

PERALTA

BURIO

SAN
RAFAEL

JOYA

MERCEDES N

SANTIAGO

INDIA

Avenida 11
FÁTIMA
Avenida 7

CORAZÓN
DE JESÚS

Río Pirro

RANCHO
CHICO
Estadio

Avenida 3

Calle 2
Calle Central
Calle 1

Calle 5
Calle 9

JARDINES
UNIVERSITARIOS

CUBUJUQUÍ

Gobernación
Parque

Avenida 4

CARMEN

Universidad
Nacional

TO SAN
ISIDRO

Plaza 3   TO ALAJUELA   Avenida 6
Hospital

Parque

Parque

TO SAN JOSÉ

SAN FRANCISCO

Avenida 14

Mercado

TOSAN JOSÉ

PIRRO

Plaza

PUEBLA

B BENAVIDES

Cementerio

3

TO SANTO
DOMINGO

5

TO SAN
PABLO

Accommodations Finding a cheap room in Heredia is as easy as getting wet during the rainy season. **Hotel El Parqueto,** Avs. 6/8, Calle 4 (tel. 338-2882), is inexpensive and a friendly place to boot. There is no hot water, and the stark white walls create a slightly institutional feel, but this family-run hotel is pleasant and relatively secure—rooms are girded by sturdy deadbolts. One of the two communal toilets has lost its seat, but it comes with plenty of reading material. There's an 11pm curfew Monday through Thursday. Respect it; a family lives here (¢1000 per person). **Hotel El Verano,** Avs. 6/8, Calle 4 (tel. 237-1616), just a few steps north of Hotel El Parqueto, is the second building in from the corner of Av. 6. It seems to have had a color-blind decorator, but the rooms are grime-free. The two collective bathrooms, though still not boasting hot water, sparkle with their recently redone and ever-clean maroon marble floors. Curfew is at midnight. The owners sell a few food items in the reception area (singles ¢1500; doubles ¢2000). Gleaming white marble floors and squeaky clean private bathrooms complete with hot water and (finally) some water pressure make **Hotel Las Flores** (from the hospital 200m to south, 50m east; tel. 338-2882) Heredia's best new addition. Run by the same friendly family as Hotel el Parqueto, each room has a large window, a comfy double bed, and a private bath (one person ¢2500; two people ¢3500).

Food Gastronomic options in Heredia favor the rough-and-ready. Any of the fruit and vegetable stands or *sodas* that crowd the bustling **Mercado Municipal** can quench simple cravings in a jiffy. For real meals 'round the clock, there's always local favorite **Soda y Restaurante Cafetín,** Avs. 2/4, Calle 2 (tel. 260-4320). Inside, it's dark, clean, and cool—ideal for zoning out in front of the TV while sipping a cup of coffee (¢50-125). Try *Pinto* with chicken or steak for ¢500, or sandwiches (*pollo, carne,* or *huevo*) for ¢275-330. A chicken breast with fries and rice runs a mere ¢675, but don't eat the accompanying salad unless you've seen them rinse it in *agua purificada.* In keeping with its groovy name, **Madre Fierra,** Av. Central/2, Calle 2, overlooking the park, has gold peacocks adorning the wall and potted plants scattered around the outdoor patio. (Lamb, chicken, or fish filet ¢595; filling *casados* for ¢495, including *refresco.* Great salads for vegetarians ¢450, or try their soups or veggie sandwich. Open Mon-Sat. 8am-9pm). A good place for vegetarians and meat-lovers alike is **Restaurante El Nido,** on the south side of the park (Av. 2). Great rice is served with almost anything imaginable, from veggies to meat to seafood (full-sized portions ¢595-¢650), along with just as many variations on chop suey and thick, tasty soups (open daily 11am-midnight). Or just take in some open air and open minds with university students at **Fresas,** Av. 1, Calle 7 (tel. 237-3915). The *batidos* (¢185-275) come in tall glasses and the fruit salad with ice cream (¢595) is large, assuring plenty of time for conversation under the red and white awning (open daily 8am-midnight).

Sights and Entertainment Bordered by Avs. Central/2 and Calles Central/2, **Parque Central** is perpetually crowded with chatting retirees and pigeons that swoop between its trees, as well as monuments, statues, and benches. A massive fountain and a gazebo stand at the park's center, and collegiate plaques quote Cervantes on the importance of tranquil centers for thought.

With its withered, eroded gray stone patches, the pleasantly ventilated **Iglesia de la Concepción,** Avs. Central/2, Calles Central/3, overlooks the east side of the park and relaxes with its doors propped open on western, northern, and southern sides—flocks of birds fly on cool breezes above worshippers' heads. Massive columns and rows of attentive pews face the church's gleaming altar, which celebrated its 200th birthday in 1997. The adjacent **Jardines de la Immaculada,** gardens dedicated to the Virgin Mary, are tucked into the northeast corner of the park. Its rarer plants, like the Japanese cypress, are marked with signs, while daisies and orchids grow in organized and perfect cultivation.

Housed in what was once the residence of Presidente Alfredo Gonzales Flores, the **Casa de la Cultura** (tel. 260-2588) stands on the northeast corner of the park. Local artists exhibit their works here on a rotating basis, and the main meeting room houses concerts and lectures. Even when the building is completely empty, the security guard is still eager to give tours (open daily 8am-10pm; free). The **Fortín de Heredia** waits nearby, a curious little fort built in 1824. Its tower is ringed by funnel-shaped slits designed to maximize defensive rifle range while minimizing the snipers' exposure to enemy bullets. Ask at the municipal building next door for entrance to the locked tower; peer out through the slits and view Heredia through the eyes of a terrified soldier.

Five blocks east of the cathedral on Avenida Central is the **Universidad Nacional.** To the casual visitor, the university resembles a large garden interrupted by incidental classrooms—college on the veranda. A bookstore located in the center of campus sells books, t-shirts, and postcards (open Mon.-Fri. 8am-noon and 1-4:30pm). When you tire of pawing through paraphernalia, head to the **Cine Isabel,** Av. 2, Calles Central/2, just south of Parque Central, which shows U.S. releases already on video north of the Río Grande (shows Mon.-Fri. 8pm, Sat.-Sun. 3 and 8pm; ¢400).

■ Near Heredia

PARQUE NACIONAL BRAULIO CARRILLO

Named for Costa Rica's third president, P.N. Braulio Carrillo lies 19km north of San José. The reserve encompasses 109,000 acres and is home to a phantasmagoric Noah's Ark of more than 6000 species of flora and fauna. Jaguars, puma, and other feline species compete for nimble deer while howler monkeys watch from arboreal bleachers. Hummingbirds, mountain robins, bare-necked umbrella birds, and rare, revered quetzals share the forest's moist canopy. The *ostoche,* a nocturnal, raccoon-like creature, haunts the park during its witching hours. The dense forest itself is equally diverse—cypress, bitterwood, camphor, mayo, and the Poás magnolia all hold their own against the dominant native fir. Some of the park's giant oaks pre-date the Spanish conquest. In the dry season, the park drips under a misty cover of clouds; in the wet season, the mist turns to a constant stream of rain. A staggering 4.5m of rain falls on the forest each year and it provides water to Costa Rica's most populated region, the Central Valley. Vast expanses of the park are still unexplored, hundreds of its species still uncounted.

The cheapest way to see the park is by trekking up one of the many uphill hiking trails accessible from the **Zurquí** or **Quebrada Gonzales** stations (closed Mon.), where the US$6 admission fee is paid. Ask the ranger which trails are safe, especially during the rainy season when the paths can get slippery and muddy; be sure to wear sneakers or hiking boots. From the trails, you'll find amazing vistas of the thick primary forest—tree ferns and palms, red-and-yellow epiphytes, and endless *sombrillas del pobre* ("umbrellas of the poor"—huge hand-shaped leaves). As you trek on, you'll forget about the loud horns and barreling trucks, and enjoy the *Melodias del Bosque*. Buses to **Guápiles** leave from the station on Av. 9, Calles 10/12 and stop at both Zurquí and Quebrada Gonzales (every 30 min., ¢320 each way). When you get on, make sure the driver knows exactly where you want to get off. Quebrada Gonzales is your best bet; the trails from Zurquí are often closed due to mud slides during the rainy season. Remember the park is open only 8am-3:30pm. Wait on the highway for the return bus, which comes every 45min. during the same hours. It is a good idea to bring food.

The financially blessed can get a spectacular, one-of-a-kind view of the park in an **aerial tram ride** (tel. 257-5961; fax 257-6053), a 3km walk past the Quebrada Gonzales station along the highway. A converted ski lift, the 2.6km tram takes adventurers into the forest's canopy, to see everything that's out-of-reach during a normal jaunt through Braulio Carrillo. The most common sight is the *bota rama*, also called "broccoli tree" for its bushy tufts of leaves. Bright red flowers called "hot lips" pucker up, and *lianas* (wooly vines) twist around tree branches before tumbling into the tram's path. An English-speaking naturalist leads the 90-minute tram ride, as well as the short, interspersed hikes, pointing out different varieties of butterflies, hummingbirds, and insects along the way. The tour costs US$47.50, but it's half price (US$23.75) for students with I.D. If there's any way you can spare the money, it's a great way to splurge. (Tram hours: Mon. 9am-3pm, Tues.-Sun. 6:30am-3pm. Reservations strongly recommended.)

VOLCÁN BARVA

Making an expedition from Heredia to **Volcán Barva,** which lies inside the southwestern quarter of the forest, is slightly more difficult. From Heredia, take the bus headed for **San José de la Montaña,** which departs from the south side of the Mercado Municipal, bordered by Avs. 6/10 and Calles 2/4 (buses run Mon.-Sat. 6:30, 11am, and 4:30pm, Sun. 11am and 4:30 pm; ¢70). Bite the bullet and catch the earliest bus—there's a long hike ahead. If you miss one of these buses, do not take one of the buses which run to the town each hour from the same spot; they'll leave you with an additional 7km to trudge up a steep and unshaded road. Buses return to Heredia from San José de la Montaña at 7:30am, 1, and 5pm. Ride the bus as far as the driver will go, to a place called **Paso Llano** (about an hour), then begin the 8km walk uphill from San José de la Montaña. There are many intersections in the road, so signs for the Sacramento Lodge prove helpful. The first half of the trail is paved, but the last 4km traverse a rough, rocky, and eroded road. Think twice about attempting this hike anytime between April and December when the rainy season often leaves the trail awash in mud. After about two hours of steady uphill hiking, you'll reach the Volcán Barva **ranger station** (open Tues.-Sun. 8am-4pm; entrance fee US$6). Although camping is prohibited elsewhere in the park, it's permitted in the vicinity of the Barva ranger station for a fee of ¢300 per person. Ask the ranger to show you where to camp and notify the station when you leave. The facilities have space for 10 tents and provide access to clean water and toilets, though in March and April, campers should bring their own drinking water. If you plan to camp, bring a sleeping bag and warm clothing; the nights are wet. The rangers also appreciate advance notice if you are planning to camp (tel. 233-4160).

The initial 8km before reaching the park comprises the majority of the walk, and is pleasant, though certainly exhausting. On one side, cows graze in bucolic pastures (some of which are owned by the family of ex-president and Nobel Peace Prize winner Oscar Arias Sánchez); on the other side, the tall, thin pine trees are reminiscent of the Swiss Alps. The path up to the park isn't tended, though, so watch out for mud and slippery rocks, as well as bellicose bulls; if walking alone, consider carrying a stick in case you find yourself warding off barking dogs who take their protective role quite seriously.

After the ranger station, the scenery becomes familiar Costa Rican rain forest. An hour-long hike (2.85km) lies between the station and the first lagoon, **Laguna Barva**. Moss is everywhere, some of it is brown and delicate like lace, some of it covers otherwise bare trees with a soft green fuzz. The trail leads to the edge of the lagoon; its banks are circled with tiny pebbles of volcanic ash.

An acidic pool cupped in the crater of an extinct volcano, Laguna Barva is too caustic for fish, but its waters suit a menagerie of aquatic insects. A second lagoon, **Laguna Copey,** is another 45 minutes (2km) away. A fast hiker maintaining a strong, leg-burning pace can make it to Laguna Barva and back to San José de la Montaña in time to catch the 1pm bus back to Heredia. Other trails beginning near the Barva ranger station branch off in various directions. Do not stray from the trails.

Although there are a couple of *sodas* on the way up, it's a good idea to bring food and water along. Also remember that since the volcano is 2.9km above sea level, it's likely to be very cold at some points; expect rain and wind year-round. Whether you plan a fast daytrip or a hard-core, overnight stay, bring appropriate clothing, keep the calories flowing, and stay hydrated.

■ Alajuela

Perhaps best known today as a stop on the Interamerican Highway, Alajuela is a city with a heroic past. In 1821, Alajuela (known then as Villahermosa) lent strong and active support to the movement for independence from Spain; the city's reward for this painful commitment came in the next decade, when it served (briefly) as the nation's capital. The city also played an important part in repelling the notorious U.S. military adventurer William Walker, who spearheaded an invasion of Costa Rica in 1856 (p. 271). The hero of that defense was a soldier from Alajuela, Juan Santamaría, ever since a profligate namesake. These days, Alajuela has passed out of its rough-and-ready adolescence and settled into a comfortable middle age. Its primary concern is no longer putting invaders to flight, but welcoming the battalions of tourists who use the city as a base for visiting nearby attractions. Only 3km from the Juan Santamaría Airport and 18km northwest of San José, Alajuela is a convenient first or last stop on a Costa Rican tour and a fine place to rest your head.

Orientation and Practical Information The streets of Alajuela form a grid: *calles* run north to south while *avenidas* run east to west. Odd-numbered *calles* fall to the east of Calle Central, even-numbered ones to the west. Odd-numbered *avenidas* run to the north of Avenida Central; even-numbered ones to the south. Be forewarned, however—many street corners are not marked and both Av. 9 and Calle 12 are called Calle Ancha. The **tourist office (Instituto Costarricense de Turismo)** has no office in Alajuela proper, but the airport branch (tel. 442-1820) is open daily 8am-5pm. **Exchange currency** and **traveler's checks** at the **Banco Nacional**, Calle 2, Avs. Central/1 (tel. 441-0373), open Monday through Friday 8:30am-3:45pm. **Telephones** are at the Parque Central, Avs. Central/1 and Calles Central/2. During the day **buses** leave for **San José** from the TUASA station (Calle 8, Avs. Central/1) every few minutes; but after midnight, expect to wait up to an hour (¢125). Buses typically stop at the airport on their way to San José, but check with the driver and simultaneously prevent long detours to Heredia and other nearby cities. Buses go to **Sarchí** from Calle 10, Avs. Central/1 (every 30min., 5am-10pm, 1½hr., ¢160), to the **Finca de Mariposas** in **Guácima Abajo** from Av. 2 and Calle 8 (daily at 6:20, 9, 11am, and 1pm; 40min.); and **Volcán Poás** from Parque Central (Sun. at 9am, 1hr.). **Taxis** hail from **Cootaxa** (tel. 442-3030) and **Taxi Punto Azul** (tel. 442-5051). For **groceries**, stop by **Tikal,** Av. Central and Calle 6 (tel. 442-6261; open daily 8am-8:30pm), which is well-stocked with fresh fruits and vegetables, deli items, and a variety of household items; it also has a special section devoted to macrobiotic products (like granola). **Farmacia Chavarria,** Av. Central and Calle 2 (tel. 441-1231), next to the Hotel Alajuela, is open Monday through Saturday 8am-7pm. The **hospital** is on Av. 9 (Calle Ancha), Calles Central/1 (tel. 441-8766). No English is spoken there. For emergencies, call **911.** Contact the **Red Cross** at tel. 441-8766. The **police** can be reached at tel. 117, or try the central police station (tel. 441-6346). You'll find the **post office** at Av. 5 and Calle 1 (tel. 441-8107), with an EMS Courier sign in front. *Lista de correos* is available, as are **fax** and **telegram** services (open Mon.-Fri. 7:30am-5:30pm). The **postal code** is 4050.

Accommodations and Food Many of the inexpensive hotels near the bus station charge by the hour; local rumor has it that some of these hotels are places of ill repute. There are, however, reasonable overnight options in other parts of the city. Each airy room comes with its very own jungle-print mural in **Pensión Alajuela,** Av. 9, Calles Central/2, across from the courthouse (tel/fax 441-6251). They serve hot sandwiches and hot water to hot travelers all day long. Alternatively, you can chill your head in the communal refrigerator, lounge on the outdoor patio, or peruse parts of the tidy indoor library. Cable TV is in the lobby, which doubles as a bar. The Cantabridgian owner hasn't forgotten his English. Laundry is ¢2000 per load, and guests have 24hr. access. One room with bath is wheelchair-accessible (singles US$12; with bath US$16; doubles with bath US$22; doubles and triples without bath US$18). Hidden—literally—away in a relatively quiet neighborhood, a pink courtyard and a laid-back owner give **Hospedaje la Posada,** Av. 3, Calles 5/7 (tel. 442-9738), the relaxed atmosphere it radiates. It offers 24hr. access, laundry (¢500), and large rooms (¢1800 per person). There is no sign, but the sidewalk in front is green; it's next to May's Nail place and across the street from the Department of Idiomas.

To eat, try **Marisquería la Sirenita,** Av. Central, Calles Central/1 (tel. 441-9681), across from the Parque Central (open daily 8:30am-10pm). The name of this family restaurant means "The Little Mermaid," and Ariel's smiling face greets diners on the sign outside. A fish tank, shells decorating the walls, and a few plastic lobsters snared in a huge net on the ceiling quickly reveal the nefarious plans that this place has for her. Sample the *arroz marinera* (¢650) or the lobster in garlic and butter (enough for 2, ¢2500). Grilled fish filets with salad and rice go for ¢750 while cheap *bocas*—like rice and chicken or beans and *chorizo*—with tortillas or rice run a mere ¢100-150. **La Tacarena,** Av. 7 and Calle 2 (tel. 441-2662), is a really dark pizza joint/tropical Caribbean cabin, with bamboo-corduroy walls, seashell wind chimes, and sweltering heat that persists in spite of the ceiling fans (large pizza ¢1200, choice of toppings includes salami, ham, chicken, and vegetarian). Typical Costa Rican fare, rice and beans style, also available (open daily 11am-10:30pm). **Ital Pan,** Av. Central and Calles 4/6 (tel. 441-6139), is a convenient bakery, perfect for a quick bite to eat, heaven for sweet teeth. Try the *cachos de mantequilla* (similar to eclairs¢95), the delicious *queques* (¢85), or the peach and strawberry *tortas* (¢350). Open daily from 6am-noon and 1:30-9pm.

Sights Alajuela has little in the way of traditional sights. The enclosed **mercado** (Avs. Central/1 and Calles 4/6) is a dark maze of fruit and vegetable stands, meat shops, and spice stores, and is surprisingly (but pleasantly) quiet compared to the central markets of most towns. The **Parque Central** (Avs. Central/1 and Calle Central/2) is crowded with shady mango trees and stone benches set around the perimeters of raised, grassy islands. A small fountain adorns the center of the park, but more

COSTA RICA

eye-catching is the huge white dome-like structure used for outdoor concerts, located on the east side, surrounded by a moat. In the west side of the park, an immense marble Neoclassical church stands, its twin towers rising in perfect symmetry over Corinthian columns at its entrance. Those starved for a more touristy experience might try the humble **Museo Histórico Cultural Santamaría**, Av. 3 and Calles Central/2 (tel. 441-1838), filled with historical mementos like medals and swords from the *Campaña Nacional* of 1856-57, in which local

followed Santamaría to defeat the American invader William Walker (open Tues.-Sun. 10am-6pm; admission is free; tours available). Alajuela itself is not likely to delight or dazzle; but nearby **Sarchi** or **La Guacimas butterfly farm** are reminders of the area's fascinating artisan history and exotic natural beauty.

Fly On, Little Wing

Southwest of Alajuela in La Guácima lies the renowned **Finca de Mariposas** (tel. 438-0400; fax 438-0300), a spectacular stomping ground for our fuzzy, airborne friends. The four-acre farm at La Guácima is Latin America's oldest exporter of butterflies, selling over 70 different species all over the world. A covered garden filled with exotic ferns, bright flowers, and even a small waterfall, is left open to visitors year-round. Inside the garden, the **butterflies glide everywhere,** fluttering just overhead, even landing on some lucky folks' arms and shoulders. Come early during the rainy season; the roof is just a screen and the afternoon rains cause the **insects to hide.** Dry conditions also make it easier to hike along the dirt paths of the 700 sq. m outdoor garden, which includes a couple of banana patches, an area supporting medicinal plants like aloe, and a bee garden, where flowers attract hundreds of the buzzing insects. Admission is ¢2400, which includes a tour of the nursery, where an English-speaking guide explains the butterfly's life-cycle and shows **larvae, pupae, and chrysalises** in cultivation. There is also a 30-minute video, available in four languages (open daily 9am-5pm, with tours starting every hour until 3pm). To reach the farm from Alajuela, take the "La Guácima Abajo" bus from the corner of Av. 2 and Calle 8, which departs at 6:20, 9, 11am, and 1pm; 45min., ¢75. Tell the driver to stop at *la finca de mariposas.* Buses returning to Alajuela pass the farm at 9:45, 11:45am, 1:45, 3:45, 4:20, 5:15 and 5:45pm. Buses leave less frequently from San José, departing from Av. 1, Calles 20/22 (Mon.-Sat. at 11am and 2pm; 1 hr.; ¢75—it's the bus going to "San Antonio de Belén"), and returning at 3:15pm.

■ Near Alajuela: Sarchí

The small village of Sarchí, about 30km from San José, is famous for its beautifully painted ox carts—wooden, intricately designed, wheelbarrow-like structures. To witness the birth of these mobile masterpieces, visit the **Fábrica de Carretas Joaquín Chaverrí** (tel. 454-4411; fax 454-4944; open daily 7am-5pm), at the entrance to the village, where they've been cranking out ox carts and many other wooden handicrafts and pieces of furniture since 1903. Ask for 68-year-old Carlos Chaverrí, who has dedicated himself to the art since he was seven years old. He loves to tell the story of the carts, which used to transport bananas and coffee from Limón to San José. Every several years there is a parade of ox carts, from which the single best among hundreds is chosen. Just a few meters uphill is the **Plaza de la Artesanía** (tel. 445-4271 for the information center), a tourist magnet with 30 souvenir shops, all filled with wooden, hand-painted knick-knacks. A full-sized ox cart runs about ¢35-50,000, but for those lacking money, space, or oxen, the pocket-sized version goes for ¢500. There are also a number of reasonably priced restaurants in the complex, including an ice cream stand mysteriously named after *los pitufos* (the Smurfs). The complex is open daily 9am-6pm. To get to Sarchí directly, catch a bus from Alajuela, Av. Central/1 and Calle 10 (every 30min., daily 5am-10pm, 1½hr., ¢145), or catch the bus to Grecia from the Coca-Cola station in San José (about every 40min., Mon.-Sat. 6am-10pm, 1hr., ¢120) and then catch one of the ubiquitous local buses to Sarchí (15min., ¢50).

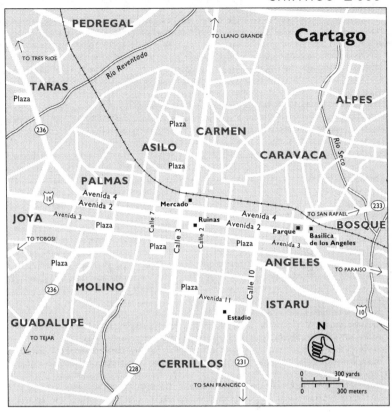

■ Cartago

Cartago (pop. 90,000), lying 22km southeast of San José in the Cartago Valley, is a city defined by a few simple twists of fate. Founded in 1563, Cartago was the capital of the nation until 1823, when Costa Ricans realized the city was doomed to perpetual misfortune and moved the government elsewhere. Perennial disasters—both natural and human—have repeatedly destroyed the city. Pirates pillaged Cartago throughout the 17th century, and a string of violent earthquakes reduced all buildings to rubble. Today, no old buildings survive—the colonial-looking structures you see are all later imitations—but the romantic stone ruins of a demolished cathedral still stand proudly in the city's center. Sometimes, good luck also blesses Cartago—the city is best known for **La Basílica de Nuestra Señora de los Angeles,** where a miracle graced the *cartageños* in 1635, and thousands of Costa Ricans still come to pray every August. Tourists come to town to see the nearby botanical gardens and hot springs. Don't count on passing a pleasant night here—you may stop into a strange hotel, with the neon burnin' bright, but pretty soon you're likely to feel that emptiness inside. Decent budget accommodations are notably absent in Cartago.

Orientation Unlike most major towns in the Central Valley, iconoclastic Cartago has neither an Avenida Central nor a Calle Central. Instead, Av. 1 and Calle 1 form the two perpendicular axes of the city's street grid. Otherwise, Cartago follows the model of other mid-sized towns; *calles* run north to south, with even *calles* to the east and odds to the west. *Avenidas* run east to west, with evens to the north and odds to the south. At the city center, where Av. 1 and Calle 1 intersect, **Parque Central** encompasses the Ruinas, the cathedral destroyed by an earthquake.

Practical Information Traveler's checks magically become colones (minus a 1% commission) at the **Banco Nacional,** Av. 2 and Calle 3 (tel. 551-9350; open for exchange Mon.-Fri. 8:30am-3pm). **Banco Popular,** Av. 1 and Calles 2/4 (tel. 551-8445), has 24hr. **ATM** machines (for VISA card holders only) but does not exchange traveler's checks. The **bus station** at Av. 4 and Calle 2, sends a bus every 10 minutes to **San José** (45min., ¢110). Buses to **Orosi** leave from the southeast corner of the ruins, Av. 1/3, Calle 2 (Mon.-Sat., every hr., 8am-10pm; Sun. every 45 min., 8am-10pm, 40 min, ¢85). Buses to **Lankester Gardens** are labeled "Paraíso" and depart from the south side of Parque Central (every 30min., 5am-10:30pm, 10min., ¢50). **Taxis** loiter throughout the city and wait by the phones with baited breath (tel. 551-9191 or 551-0247). Public telephones cluster at the corner of Av. 1 and Calle 1. The **public library,** Av. 2 and Calle 3, is diagonally across from the Banco Nacional (open Mon.-Fri. noon-7pm, Sat. 9am-2pm). The **Mercado Central,** Avs. 4/6 and Calles 1/5, bustles with commerce seven days a week (6am-6pm). For packaged foods, head to **Supermercado Rayo Azul,** Av. 4, Calle 6 (tel. 551-0000; open daily 8am-8pm). **Farmacia Central** (tel. 551-0698) is at Av. 1 and Calle 2 (open Mon.-Sat. 8am-8pm). **Hospital Max Peralta Jiménez** is at Avs. 5/7 and Calles 1/3 (tel. 551-2806; no English spoken). 24 hr. medical attention is also provided at **Clinica San Francisco,** 50m down from the hospital (tel. 552-3233). To contact the **Red Cross,** call 551-0421. The **police** can be dialed for free from any public phone (tel. 117). The **post office** stands at Av. 2 and Calles 15/17 (tel. 552-4595) in the lime green building (open Mon-Fri 7:30am-5:30pm). **Fax** service is available for US$2.50 per page to the U.S., and telegrams cost US$0.45 per word overseas. The **postal code** is 7050.

Accommodations and Food Don't plan to spend the night in Cartago; so close to (and accessible from) San José, it makes an easy daytrip. If by some fluke you find yourself stranded in town, your options are severely limited: most hotels in town are not places where any decent fellow would want to pass the night. But do not despair; nice respectable and clean (but pricey) rooms at the **Los Angeles Lodge,** Av. 4 and Calles 14/16 (tel. 551-0957), next to the basilica, include complimentary breakfasts and private bathrooms with hot water. The Lodge can also arrange tours to the Orosi and Ujarras Valleys, Volcán Irazú, Lankester Garden, and other nearby attractions (singles US$20; doubles US$35; triples US$50).

Food in Cartago is basic. The **Mercado Central,** bounded by Avs. 4 and 6 and Calles 1 and 5, is the place for fresh fruit, vegetables, and bread. The stereotypical Costa Rican *soda* is **Soda Marquesa,** Av. 4 and Calle 6—quick, no-frills *comida típica*—good stuff at great prices: *pinto con carne,* a chicken sandwich, or rice and meat in sauce all run ¢300, cafe ¢100 (open Mon.-Sat. 8am-9pm). A huge jungle scene replete with life-sized waterfall greets you as you enter **Soda y Restaurante Friendly's,** Av 1/3, Calle 2, perhaps your best bet in Cartago. The name doesn't lie; amidst mint green walls with peach and lavender trim, an amiable staff serves up an excellent *casado* (including beans, rice, soup, chicken or pasta with dessert and a drink) for ¢650, elaborate salads and sandwiches from ¢400-600, including a special vegetarian sandwich for ¢450 (open daily 10:30am-11pm). **Restaurant AutoServicio 88,** Av. 4 and Calle 1 (tel. 551-6004), is an inexpensive, you-point-they-serve-it buffet, with everything from mashed potatoes to stir-fry. Fill up on beans and rice, with a cold Coke to top it off, for just ¢500.

Sights and Entertainment In Cartago, the main attraction is **La Basílica de Nuestra Señora de los Angeles,** bordered by Avs. 2 and 4 and Calles 14 and 18. Perhaps the most famous place of worship in Costa Rica, the cathedral is a sacred destination for the hundreds of *ticos* who make the annual pilgrimage from San José every August 2 for *El Dia del Virgen.* Many walk the whole 22km from the capital to Cartago. According to believers, a small dark statue of the Virgin Mary was found by a *mestizo* peasant girl on that site on August 2, 1635. When the statue was removed, the dark-skinned Virgin (La Negrita) appeared in the flesh, right on the spot. Clearly a miracle, the vision was interpreted as a divine directive to end racial segregation in the city and the original cathedral was erected on the site. Destroyed by an earthquake in 1926, the basilica was rebuilt as a Byzantine wooden shell, illuminated by delicate stained-glass windows. The cathedral's interior is crammed full with cabinets containing myriad offerings to the Virgin—medallions, notes, a set of bongo drums, a baseball, a piece of burnt wood salvaged from a house fire, a cycling jersey, and dozens of small metal trinkets, each molded into the shape of a body part believed to be healed by the Virgin. At the northeast corner of the basilica, a flight of stairs leads down to *la cripta de la piedra* (the Crypt of the Stone), where a statue of La Negrita holding the infant Jesus in her arms is perched atop the boulder where she was first sighted. In a healing gesture, pilgrims rub the stone under the Virgin and then rub their heads, arms, and feet. The Basilica is open during and between services, which run every couple of hours from 6am-6pm.

A church of a different sort stands smack in the center of town at Avs. 1/2 and Calles 2/4. The crumbling walls of the **Parque Ruinas** were once part of a cathedral built in 1575 and dedicated to Apostle Santiago, the patron saint of Spain. It stood there until it was wrecked by an earthquake in 1841. The cathedral was reconstructed, and then destroyed by another temblor in 1910 never again to be finished. Today, the grounds surrounding the ruins are a public park and a testament to the victory of creeping, vegetable entropy over ephemeral human vanity. Trees have now grown taller than the old cathedral walls themselves, leaves sprout from cracks in the crumbling stones, and orphaned chunks of the church serve as modest benches. A lovely garden surrounded by tall, ruined walls and containing a pair of ponds hides inside the park. The garden itself is now closed to the public, but curious visitors can peer in through gates and barred windows.

■ Near Cartago: Jardín Botánico Lankester

Jardín Botánico Lankester (open daily 8:30am-3:30pm; self-guided tours are allowed to begin every 30min; admission ¢700) is 6km east of Cartago, near the village of Paraíso. An internationally famous garden dedicated to the preservation of tropical flora, Jardín Lankester was founded in the 1950s by Charles H. Lankester, a British naturalist, and is currently maintained by the University of Costa Rica. The garden is home to a remarkable variety of epiphytes, parasitical plants that leech off other vegetation, as well as an incredible 800 species of orchids—a good fraction of the 1400 species of orchids found in Costa Rica. But this isn't any old fancy flower garden—it's a maze of prolific growth lifted carefully from the country's 12 different microclimates. The vivid contrasts are striking; purple-flowered wines sprawl across the winding path, as delicate palms sway next to towers of bamboo bent under their own weight. Cross over a log bridge into the tropical rainforest area, which receives over a meter of rain each year, for an especially breath-taking view. The sign at the entrance says that a self-guided tour should take about an hour, but it's easy to lose oneself and take twice as long. To get to the Jardín Lankester from Cartago, catch a bus destined for Paraíso from the south side of the Parque Ruinas (every 30min., 4:30am-10:30pm, 10min., ¢40); you can also get there from *Orosi,* taking the bus headed to Cartago from the northeast corner of the soccer field (see below for exact times); either way, be sure to tell the driver you want to get off at the garden. From the drop-off point in front of Restaurante Casa Vieja, take a brief hike down a well-marked gravel road, past the big power plant. Hail down the bus from the main road as it returns to Cartago (every half hour) or Orosi (approx. every hour).

■ Orosi

The small village of Orosi (pop. 5000), 15km south of Cartago, functioned peacefully as a communal society during most of the colonial 16th century, long before Marx ever dreamed of such a thing. Tranquil and friendly, the strength of this town's community is still clear today. Entire families relax on their front porches late into the evening, young couples, friends, and neighbors are constantly strolling by and the central soccer field is ever-cluttered with school children playing or parading a small school marching band.

Amidst rolling hills of lush green, sprawling coffee planations and cloud-covered mountains, today Orosi is best known for its aged **adobe church;** built by Franciscan missionaries in 1743, the thick-walled, white adobe structure is surrounded by flowers and palm trees and stands humbly back behind the main road. The true charm for the city- and tourist trap-weary traveler, however, lies in the surrounding valley's beautiful trails, hidden ruins, trout farms, waterfalls, and superb vistas, all easily seen on one long bike ride. The sense of relaxation in the town is comfortably overwhelming—a wonderful contrast to San José's hustle and bustle.

Orientation and Practical Information Orosi basically defines the phrase "within walking distance." Although there are no street names, you may find that you know your way around within your first 10 minutes here. The main drag in Orosi is the street you drive in on, whether by bus or taxi. If coming form San José/Cartago by bus, you'll be traveling south past the soccer field. Parallel to the main street is the street of the **adobe church.** With that landmark and the soccer field in mind, you can get anywhere. Keep in mind that the church (unlike all others in Costa Rica), faces *east*. For **tourist information,** your best bet might be **Montaña Linda** (see **Accommodations,** below); Orosi Turismo no longer exists, despite the fact that you'll see it advertised with huge signs. To send a **fax,** hit Supermercado La Anita, located on the main road (US$2.50 per page to the U.S.; open Mon.-Sat. 7:30am-6:30pm, Sun. 7:30am-noon). **Buses** leave for Orosi from Cartago from the southeast corner of the ruins in the Parque Central (Av 1/3, Calle 2; every hr., daily 6am-10pm, 30min., ¢70) and return to **Cartago** from the northeast corner of the soccer field (on the main road) in Orosi (Mon.-Fri. at 5, 6, 6:15, 7, 8:15, 9:30, 10:45am, 12:15, 1, 2, 3, 4, 5, 6:30pm; Sat. and Sun. every 45 min., 8:30am on; 30 min., ¢90). Reach local **taxis** at 284-2483, 533-3451, or 533-3631. In an emergency, call the **police** at 911. There is no **post office** in Orosi, but letters can be sent and stamps sometimes bought at **Pulperia el Valle,** 150m south of the adobe church (open Mon.-Sun. 6am-7pm).

Accommodations and Food Roosters and cows in the adjoining pasture will pleasantly wake you at **Montaña Linda,** a great *albergue* set back from the village along a rocky road (tel. 533-3640; going south on the main road, turn right in front of La Anita and proceed 200m). Famous for its gregarious, English-speaking owner, who is happy to provide bikes for the day (US$5). The hotel features clean communal bathrooms with hot water, a shared kitchen, comfortable beds, delicious breakfast and dinner (US$2-3), and Spanish classes as part of very reasonable week-long packages (lodging US$5 per person; 4 doubles, 1 quad). For more serious isolation, check out the **Kiri Lodge** (tel. 284-2024), on the road from Orosi to Tapantí National Park, 2km before the entrance to the park (tel. 284-2024). Six roomy cabins are designed as doubles, but each can easily accommodate four. Enjoy private bathrooms with hot water and beds so comfy your back will thank you in the morning. Accessible trails, parking and breakfast are included (one person US$15; doubles US$30; three people US$35; four people US$40).

Classic *soda* yummies can be found at **Soda Luz** (turn right off the main road before the soccer field, approx. 100m; tel. 533-3701). Locals and visitors stroll past Luz's outdoor patio until they begin to recognize one another. It's cheap, and good too; sit in cozy little booths and enjoy *pinto* which comes with crisp homemade tortillas and chunky salsa (¢350), or try the chicken basket (¢350) or tacos (¢150). Open daily 7am-8pm. For a bit more extensive and expensive menu, grab a bite at the dark **Soda el Nido,** located on the main road 125m north of the soccer field (tel. 533-3793). This *soda* offers sandwiches (¢300) and *casados* (¢500), and other delights.

Sights The **adobe church** is the most obvious starting place, both for fame and centrality. Years of hot sun and torrential rain have made its red roof tiles fragile and weathered its elderly church bells into a graceful green patina. Inside, wooden columns rise from the brick floor to the roof and paintings of a crucified Christ droop from the walls. The intricately carved wooden altar at the front of the church is painted gold and adorned with a few forlorn plastic flowers. There are a number of superstitions connected with the church—a headless man was seen climbing the bell tower, incurable ills are said to be remedied there, and there is supposedly a tunnel leading from the inside of the building to the nearby mountains. Adjoining the church, the **Museo de Arte Religioso,** a collection of Christian relics from 1699 to 1766, holds Guatemalan sculptures of Jesus and Mary, paintings by Mexican artists, manuscripts, priests' robes, and a wood-and-leather bed from the church's convent days (open daily 9am-noon and 1-5pm; admission ¢150, children ¢50).

To visit most other sites, you will need at least a bicycle. **Truchas de Purisil** is a local trout farm, expertly cultivated, and much more incredible than it sounds. Self-guided tours of ponds, rivers, and surrounding rain forest are *free* (located on the main road from Orosi, 2km past the village of Purisil; open daily 8am-5pm; trout available, ¢1000 per kilo). Only 3km further will bring you to **Tapantí National Park,** which boasts winding trails, natural hot springs, and a gorgeous waterfall (US$6, residents US$2, camping not permitted).

Starting from the center of town, a pleasant 2km walk along the main street through rolling hills and coffee plantations leads to **Los Patios** (tel. 553-3009), the thermal mineral baths that are Orosi's other claim to fame. Soothing water is pumped from hot springs through a kilometer-long pipe to Los Patitos. At the source, the water is a hot, hot, hot 60°C (140°F), but it cools to a mere 50°C (122°F) by the time it bubbles out of the pipe into the pool. For that sauna sensation, sit in the hot springs until your brain bursts, induce cardiac arrest by jumping into the adjacent cold pool, and then fortify your hopes of recovery at the restaurant nearby. Usually, though, the water continues to lose temperature in the pool (a lukewarm 35°C, not much different from a tub of bathwater; open Tues.-Sun. 8am-4pm; ¢350). Don't forget your bathing suit and towel.

▓ Turrialba

With the construction of the Guápiles highway 10 years ago, Turrialba lost its chance to become a major tourist hub. Now, traffic on the way to the Atlantic coast can drive through Braulio Carrillo Park in a fraction of the time that a detour through Turrialba would entail. Although the highway caused a local economic depression, it enabled Turrialba to maintain that old-time, small town, close-knit feel. Things don't move too fast or get too hectic around here; after all, what are you missing when you're surrounded by coffee, bananas, and sugarcane? Turrialba's charm comes from the fact that it is so *tranquilo;* a local once tempted to move to San José claims that the town's "spiritual energy" is what kept her here. Rivers also pull people into Turrialba, even without the benefit of a strong undertow. The nearby Río Reventazón nets barrels of white-water rafters and kayakers yearly. Turrialba is also close enough to agricultural centers and Costa Rica's premier archaeological site—Guayabo National Monument—that it still gets a taste of the commercial traffic that distinguished its previous generations.

Orientation and Practical Information Like so many other Costa Rican cities, Turrialba's *calles* run north to south (actually, more like northwest to southeast), and its *avenidas* run east to west. Even-numbered *calles* lie west of Calle Central, odd ones lie east. Even-numbered *avenidas* are north of Av. Central, and odd ones are south. As a variation on the theme, the Parque Central is not bordered by the central roads, but by Calles Central/1 and Avs. 4/6. Street numbers, however, are practically useless, as very few streets are marked. More applicable are a handful of landmarks, like Parque Central, the adjacent white church tower, and the old train station in the southeast part of the town.

Traveler's checks can be exchanged for a 0.75% commission at the **Banco Nacional,** Av. Central, Calles 1/3 (tel. 556-1504; open Mon.-Fri. 8:30am-3:45pm). **Tele-**

COSTA RICA

phones can be found at the southeast corner and the south side of the park. There are two **bus stations**—one at Av. 4, Calles Central/2, serving **San José** and **Siquirres** every hour (¢300), the other at Av. 2, Calles Central/2 for local routes, including the bus to **Guayabo National Monument** (see below). **Taxis** can be found near the bus stations and Parque Central, or call **Taxi Turrialba** (tel. 556-1844). **Ticos River Adventures** (tel 556-1231; along the road heading east out of Turrialba towards Catie; ask around—it's on the left with a big sign and two kayaks in the road) is a super source of information as well as a great place to rent kayaks or sign up for lessons or white-water rafting trips. **Almacen Lorenzo Quirós** (tel. 566-0090), Av. 6 and Calle Central, across from the northwest side of Parque Central, has a fully-stocked **super-market** (open Mon.-Thurs. 7:30am-12:30pm and 2-7:30pm, Fri.-Sat. 7:30am-8pm). The **Farmacia la Salud,** Calle Central, Avs. 2/4 (tel. 566-0239), is open Monday through Saturday 8am-6pm. In case of **emergency**, call 911. The **hospital** can be reached by phone (tel. 556-1133), or call the local **Red Cross** (tel. 556-0191). For **Internet/email access,** contact Vindas and Moran (tel. 556-1860; fax 556-6686). The **post office** (tel. 556-0427), Av. 8 and Calle Central, has **fax** and **telegram** services (open Mon.-Fri. 7:30am-5:30pm). The **postal code** is 7150.

Accommodations and Food Although Turrialba isn't a place where many tourists decide to hit the sack, there are nevertheless a couple of decent, inexpensive places to lay one's head for the night. The heart of **Hotel Interamericano** (tel. 556-0142), Av. 1, Calles 1/3 along the train tracks, a family-owned joint, is its large, sprawling lobby. Doubling as a restaurant, this downstairs room is cool and spacious, with dogs and birds to liven things up, as well as a TV and a jukebox booming Latin favorites. The rooms are simple and boxy, but the walls, sheets, and cold water bathrooms are spotless. Singles go for ¢1500, with bath ¢2500. Doubles are ¢2000, with bath ¢2800. **Hotel Turrialba** (tel. 556-6654 or 556-6396), Av. 4, Calles 2/4, is a bit of a splurge, but well worth it in terms of ambience and security. The friendly staff is eager to accommodate, down to your own TV (¢300, or you can settle for the free one in the lounge). Enjoy sparkling private bathrooms with hot water and towels, laundry service (¢400 per load), comfortable beds, and fans (singles ¢2725, doubles ¢4145). A favorite with both locals and the rafters and kayakers who frequent the area, peach-accented **Soda Lisboa** lies along the railroad tracks on the corner of Av. Central and Calle 1. They serve really fresh white meat chicken breast instead of the grease-laden legs that are so common. (*Casados con carne* ¢400, *con pescado* ¢500, *pinto con hueve* ¢260, *con pollo* ¢400; sandwiches ¢140-250; rice and beans with tortilla ¢400. Open Mon.-Sat. 8am-9pm.)

  Bar Restaurante La Giralda (tel. 556-1089), Av. 2 and Calle 2, diagonally across from the gas station, takes its authentic *a la leña* cooking (a type of wood-fire roasting) seriously, with a brick oven and huge rotisserie wheel in the window. A quarter chicken, cooked *a la leña* (of course), with fries, a salad, and tortillas, runs a mere ¢520 (open Wed.-Mon. 11am-10:30pm). If the poster of a bikini-clad woman doesn't chase you away from **Pizza Julian** (tel. 556-1165), Av. 6, Calles Central/1, across from the north side of the Parque Central, you'll find uniquely themed pizzas like the "Mexicana," with jalapeños, ground beef, and onions (small pizza ¢900, large pizza ¢1500; open Mon.-Fri. 4-11pm, Sat.-Sun. 3-11pm).

Sights and Entertainment This area, a haven for adventurous athletes, supposedly harbors some of the best rafting and kayaking around—many Olympic teams even include some of Costa Rica's wild rivers in their training schedule; for lessons, rentals, or (very helpful) information, contact **Ticos River Adventures** (tel 556-1231; see **Practical Information,** above). For bikers, runners, or power-walkers anxious to get moving, Turrialba had a roadside grassy strip which extends through the impressive countryside. A tiny path has been worn down by the locals who frequent it in their determination, some explain, to whip themselves into shape in order to dominate on the soccer field, or just to stay healthy and enjoy the sprawling green fields and forested mountains in the distance. (Follow the main road east out of Turrialba toward Siquerres—go in the direction of **Catie**.)

Turrialba's **Parque Central,** Avs. 4/6 and Calles Central/1, is an exemplary small town park. Trash cans wear signs that preach against the evils of drug abuse, the gazebo in the middle of the quiet, grassy recreational area is dedicated to a local music teacher, and on the most Norman Rockwellian of Costa Rican days, an aging mariachi band hauls out its instruments for a free concert. There's even a mini-greenhouse with ferns and aloe plants; its walls are woven with cyclone-wire fencing wide enough to allow small birds to fly in and out of the structure at will. **Cine Norma,** Calle 1, Avs. Central/2, shows aged U.S. films (daily 7:30pm; ¢300).

Turrialba is also the proud home of the Centro Agronómico Tropical de Investigación, or **CATIE** (tel. 556-6431), one of the largest tropical research centers in the world, with the largest English-language agricultural library in Latin America. Maybe that doesn't sound so thrilling, but any nature lover should get a kick out of the 27,500-acre facilities, which include orchards, greenhouses, trails, and a bird-friendly lake. Call CATIE in advance to arrange a guided tour, or come without a reservation to enjoy the view. It's a pleasant 4km stroll east through coffee plantations, or you may be able to snag the bus out of Turrialba.

■ Guayabo National Monument

Located 19km northeast of Turrialba, **Guayabo National Monument** is considered Costa Rica's most important archaeological site. Though it doesn't stand so tall when measured against the likes of Tikal or Copán, Guayabo's centuries old ruins are still worth a daytrip, as the only place in Costa Rica which serves as first-hand testimony to the fascinating ability of the area's indigenous people to incorporate the natural habitat and irregular landscape into their culture and society.

As there are no official guided tours, it's definitely worth shelling out the cash for a self-guided tour pamphlet (¢50, only in Spanish). From there it's almost too easy; simply follow the well-cleared path, which should take close to an hour (1200m) if you stop at each of the numbered signs to read about the points of interest listed in the pamphlet. The pride of Guayabo, however, is the actual excavation site of the pre-Colombian city of Guayabo, which was inhabited between AD 1000-1400 by a tribe centered around their *cacique,* a religious and political leader. From a lookout point, the remains of the city look like a bunch of grassy mounds, but after following the trail down into the site itself, the *calzadas* (riprap roads), and the circular stone bases for buildings, bridges, and aqueducts finally become visible. Visitors are allowed to roam within a small, restricted area along the guided trail. It is possible to **camp** in the National Park (¢300), where you'll find a toilet, cold shower, clearing for tents, and barbecue pits (the park is open daily 8am-3:30pm; admission US$6).

Getting to Guayabo isn't too hard, but leaving is a real pain. From the local bus terminal in Turrialba, buses leave Monday through Saturday at 11am (so if you're coming in from San José, be sure to catch the 9am direct bus to Turrialba) and Sunday at 9am (1hr., ¢125). They stop smack at the ranger station by the entrance to the monument. Problems develop from there. On weekdays and Saturdays, the bus leaves Guayabo around 12:40pm and doesn't return again that day—leaving inadequate time to see the monument. On Sundays, the bus doesn't return until 4pm, after the park closes. So the only option is to walk the 4km downhill from the National Monument to the main road, and there catch a bus to Turrialba that arrives between 5-5:30pm. Unfortunately, this turns a one hour jaunt into an all day excursion, but the only quicker option is to hitch back to Turrialba. Travelers say it's generally pretty safe and easy, provided that anyone's passing by, and most people on the road are headed to Turrialba anyway. *Let's Go* does not recommend hitchhiking. Alternatively, eager hikers can start their day earlier by catching a cab to the monument (around ¢2400) and take the bus back.

Another option is to spend the night at **La Calzada,** a very simple lodge located 400m downhill from the monument (tel. 556-0465; fax 556-0427; all rooms (doubles)

US$20 per person). Or stop at the lodge's **restaurant** before that long trek down-hill—sit on the converted front porch to devour *arroz con pollo* (¢650) or a soda (¢200). However, both the lodge and the restaurant are open for business only on weekends and Costa Rican national holidays; never during the week.

THE PACIFIC COAST

This region is the most Costa Rican part of Costa Rica. Indeed, the extended beach-side paradise of the central Pacific Coast is a perennial favorite of travelers. In recent years, the big crowds have migrated south from the regional center of Puntarenas to the hip, young, rad environs of Jacó. Azure waves pound against hundreds of miles of rocky coastline and brilliant, white sand beaches. If you can find the space, this is a great place to set up camp; scores of towns and attractions are nearby. For instance, the **Monteverde Cloud Forest,** Costa Rica's most renowned rain forest, hides in the verdant northeast corner of the Puntarenas province.

■ Puntarenas

Puntarenas (pop. 86,000), the fading capital of the province of the same name, pro-vides access to the beaches closest to San José, only 90 minutes away. Although the peninsula (the name translates literally to "sandy point") was once the busiest port on the Costa Rican Pacific coast, much of Puntarenas' economic vigor has been sapped by the newly constructed port of **Caldera,** 25km south. As a result, the city has descended into tragic decrepitude. Still, beaches and plentiful seafood manage to sate tourists—*la chucheca,* a species of shellfish driven close to extinction, *almejas* (clams), and *mejillones* (mussels) top all culinary lists.

Ferries arrive on the north side of town, where Avenida 3 is packed with services, shops, and cheap restaurants. **Paseo de las Turistas** encompasses the southern side of the peninsula and is home to most of the hotels and restaurants popular with wealthier *gringos.* Puntarenas has clearly seen better days; after a look at the polluted beach, most tourists board the ferry for someplace where they can actually swim.

Orientation and Practical Information There is method to this madness. *Calles* run north to south; *avenidas* run east to west. Odd-numbered *calles* lie west of Calle Central, while even-numbered ones lie east. The odd-numbered *avenidas* are north of Avenida Central, and the even ones south. Av. 4, at the peninsula's south end, is known as **Paseo de los Turistas** between Calles 3 and 15. **Exchange currency** at **Banco Nacional** (tel. 661-0233), Av. 3 and Calle 1, a few blocks west of the market (open Mon.-Fri. 8:30am-3:45pm). In a squeeze, there are 24hr. **ATMs** at the **Cre-domático,** Av. 3, Calle 3, which accept Cirrus, Visa, and Mastercard. Also check out **Banco Personal,** Calle 2 near Paseo de los Turistas and the bus stop (accepts Visa), and the temperamental ATM in **Banco Costa Rica,** Av. 3, Calles 1/Central. **Buses** (tel. 661-2158) to and from **Puntarenas** are usually coordinated with the ferries. Buses to **San José** leave from Paseo de los Turistas and Calle 2 (every 30min., daily 6am-7pm, 2hr., ¢695). Other buses leave from Paseo de los Turistas, just east of Calle 2 to: **Liberia** (5:30, 7, 9:30, 11am, 12:30, 3, 5:30pm, 2½hr., ¢490); **Cañas, Tilarán,** and **Volcán Arenal** (11:30am and 4:15pm, 3hr., ¢680); **Jacó** (5, 11am, and 2:30pm, 2hr., ¢400) continuing on to **Quepos** (3½hr., ¢650); **Santa Verde** and **Monteverde** (2:15pm); and **Barranca** (every hr., 20min., ¢50). Buses for **Orotina** leave from **Super Mercado Pali** at Calle 5, Avs. 1/3, across from Farmacia Andrea (4, 6, 9am, and 4:30pm, 1hr., ¢100). For **taxis,** try **Coopetico** (tel. 663-2020) or **Coopepuntarenas** (tel. 663-1625). Herds of cabs congregate near the market, Av. 3 and Calle 2. **Ferries** (tel. 661-1069) depart daily for **Playa Naranjo** from the dock at the northwest end of the peninsula (Calle 31, behind Av. 3) at 3:30, 7, 10:50am, 2:50, and 7pm (1hr., ¢375). To get to the dock, take the bus to Barrio Carmen (¢30) from Av. 1 and Calle 2, in front of Chung Wah Restaurant, and get off at its last stop; or you can grab a cab

(¢200-300). Ferries return to Puntarenas at 5:10, 8:50am, 12:50, 5, and 9pm (¢250 per person, children ¢120, cars ¢1500, 4-wheel-drive vehicles ¢2000, motorcycles and bicycles ¢500). Boats to **Paquera** (tel. 661-1444) connect to the Montezuma bus and leave from the northeast side of the peninsula, behind the market (6:15, 11am, and 3pm, 1½hr., ¢320), returning later to Puntarenas (8:15, 12:30, and 5pm). The ticket booth in the blue-and-white building behind the market opens half an hour before each ferry. **Lavandería Puntarenas** (tel. 663-0174) is on Calle 1, Avs. Central/1 (open Mon.-Fri. 8am-11am and 2-5pm, Sat. 8-11am; ¢600 per kilo). The Super Mercado Pali is at Av. 1/3, Calle 1 (open Mon.-Sat. 8am-6:30pm, Sun. 8:30am-6pm). The local **pharmacy** is **Botica Central** (tel. 661-0361), Calle Central, Avs. Central/1 (open daily 7:30am-10pm). Call the **hospital** at 663-0033. **Red Cross** (tel. 661-0184; open 24hr.) is 2½ blocks west of the church. The **post office** (tel. 671-2166; fax 661-0440), Av. 3, Calles 1/Central, is across from Banco Nacional. *Lista de correos,* **telegrams,** and **fax** are available (open Mon.-Fri. 7:30am-5:30pm). The **postal code** is 5400.

Accommodations and Food Though budget hotels and *pensiones* exist, their quality has declined. Camping on the beach is *not* recommended; it's neither safe nor sanitary. Better yet, just give up on the idea of an overnight stay here and hop right on that ferry. Those insistent on staying in Puntarenas should try **Hotel Ayi Con** (tel. 661-0164 or 661-1477), Calle 2, Avs. 1/3, a friendly budget choice. Some rooms have fans, others are blessed with A/C. Either way you'll feel nice 'n' fresh if you can forget about the lack of natural light. Rooms are a little cramped, but the large communal bathrooms have toilet seats. You'll find both a TV and excitable sports fans in the lobby (¢1400 per person, ¢2000 with bath, ¢2500 with bath and A/C; checkout at 2pm). In the bright airy lobby of **Hotel Cagezas** (tel. 671-1046), Av. 1, Calles 2/4, there's plenty of room for lounging on wooden lawn chairs or battling the other guests to watch your favorite *tico* show; they'll even sell you drinks, or a toothbrush if you forgot yours. Simple, clean, not-too-stuffy rooms with decent collective bath cost ¢1200 per person; doubles with private bath are ¢3500.

For welcome relief from the pricey establishments along the Paseo de los Turistas, try the cheap *sodas* in and around the market. Despite its seemingly run-down interior, **Soda la Amistad** (tel. 661-2011), at Av. 1, Calles Central/1, is a simple, cozy soda which lives up to its name. Friendly and welcoming, they serve up good food at cheap prices (*casados* ¢400-450, *pinto con café* ¢350, sandwiches ¢200; open Mon.-Sat. 6am-9pm, Sun. 7am-noon). And just when you though you'd forgotten what it was, **Restaurant Hong Tu,** Av. 1, Calles Central/2, has the air-conditioning going strong. They serve large portions of yummy Chinese food to feast on (rice with curried chicken and vegetables ¢650, chaumin or chop suey ¢650-700, fried rice with beef ¢700; half-portions available; open daily 11am-midnight). While you wait for the Paquera ferry, grab a quick snack at the inexpensive and always-crowded **Soda Adita** (rice with chicken ¢300, cheese sandwich ¢200; open Mon.-Sat. 6am-5pm).

Hail Marys—Puntarenas style

If you can swing it, come to Puntarenas during **La Fiesta a la Virgen del Mar** (July 5-16); the city ignites with concerts and dances on the beach for an entire week before the locally sacred holiday. The Fiesta commemorates the **miraculous rescue of Don Meregildo,** a *puntarense* big-shot from around the turn of the century. Meregildo and his crew would set sail every January and return to the docks of Puntarenas loaded down with pearls, shells, and bushels of foreign *monedas* just in time for *Semana Santa*—when they would unleash their wealth to fund a big bash for the town. But in 1913, a storm caused the perennially **debauched** crew to lose control of their boat. Don Meregildo experienced an abrupt loss of chutzpah, knelt down on the deck, and **prayed to the Virgin,** promising a huge celebration in *her* honor should his boat be returned safely to Puntarenas. When the ship limped into port, Don Meregildo threw the first of many extravagant *fiestas* in the Virgin's name. Nowadays, boats of all sizes gather along the shoreline and pass a statue of the Virgin from vessel to vessel.

SIGHTS AND ENTERTAINMENT

Aside from swimming—which isn't always a good idea due to pollution in the area—there's not much to do here for most of the year. Puntarenas's modest **Casa de la Cultura** (tel. 661-1493), Avs. Central/2 and Calles 5/7, houses the **Museo Histórico Marino de la Ciudad de Puntarenas,** which displays historical artifacts of the town's seafaring culture (¢250; open Mon.-Sat. 8:30am-noon and 1-4:40pm). Experts on Iberian architecture will note that the peninsula's **church,** Avs. Central/1 and Calles 3/5, is constructed in Portuguese fashion and set in the middle of the park, rather than nestled *behind* the park, as in the less symmetrical Spanish style. **Playa de Doña Ana,** 14km from Puntarenas and 2km from Caldera, is a well-maintained beach with swimmable waters. Amenities include toilets, showers, and a restaurant (open daily 8am-4pm; admission ¢75). Another option is the beach behind Cabinas de San Isidro, 7km from Puntarenas. Take any of the buses to **Esparza, Miramar, Barranca,** or **El Roble** that leave from the stop on Paseo de las Turistas, east of Calle 2.; ask the driver to let you off (¢20). If all else fails, there's always the **municipal pool** at the west tip of the peninsula (take a Barrio Carmen bus, ¢50). The clean water, showers, bathrooms, and a small refreshments kiosk are sure to please (open Tues.-Sun. 9am-4:30pm; admission ¢200, children ¢150).

When foot traffic in the park and plaza dies down, try the disco at **Hotel Oasis del Pacífico,** on the Paseo de los Turistas, where a disco ball shines upon the dance floor and bar (open Mon.-Fri. 9pm-2am, Sat.-Sun. 1pm-1am; cover ¢200).

For a pretty penny, **Taximar** (tel. 661-1143) offers tours of **San Lucas,** an old island prison (¢5000-7000). Boats meet passengers on the north side of Playa Cocal.

■ Near Puntarenas: Carara Biological Reserve

Though Puntarenas province is home to numerous national parks and wildlife refuges, many are more accessible from San José than from Puntarenas proper. One park best reached from Puntarenas, however, is the **Carara Biological Reserve,** 57km southeast of Puntarenas on the road to Quepos. The reserve is particularly fascinating to biologists because it encompasses an "ecotone," a region where the wet tropical jungle of the south meets the dry forest of the north. These conditions give rise to a remarkable diversity of species, many of which are endangered. *Carara* means "crocodile" in one of the area's indigenous languages, and sure enough, the threatened crocodile finds haven here in the silt-covered banks of the Tárcoles River. The crocodiles themselves are an amazing sight—surprisingly flat, with meaty-looking striped tails, they resemble enormous logs crawling across the mud. Carara is also one of the best places in Costa Rica to spot scarlet macaws, which share the forest with white-faced monkeys, vibrant blue *Morpho* butterflies, poison dart frogs, and *fer-de-lance* ("spearheads"), which are large and extremely venomous pit vipers. Flora include purpleheart trees, water hyacinths, and kapok ("silk cotton") trees.

To get to the Carara Reserve, take the 5am bus from Puntarenas to Quepos and ask to be let off at the reserve. From Puntarenas, you'll find the entrance to the reserve 4km after you cross the river (look for crocodiles). A short, 1km trail begins at this entrance; a longer (5km) and more interesting trail straight into the heart of the forest starts 2km before the official entrance. Look for a gate with a small black sign with yellow lettering. Both trails are well-marked (once you find them) and not especially strenuous. Ask at the ranger station to find out where camping is permitted. Enjoy their facilities—these are the last toilets you'll see for a while (park open Tues.-Sun. 7am-4pm; free!). Other national parks accessible from Puntarenas are **Curú Wildlife Refuge,** 4km north of Paquera (take a ferry to Paquera; ask there about the connecting bus to the reserve), and **Cabo Blanco Biological Reserve,** 11km southwest of Montezuma.

■ Jacó

Practically everyone can find a party to their liking in Jacó. Lured by the killer waves here, a startling number of expatriate Canadians have decided to make Jacó home. At night, *gringos* and locals alike hang out at the bars, casinos, and salsa-loving discos that bolster the town's reputation as the party beach of Costa Rica. Jacó's sudden popularity has made it like an awkward teenager—a few years ago the town was hardly developed; now new hotels are popping up in uncontrollable spurts, and the weary beach doesn't seem to know how to deal with each new development. No matter how grimy the sand may be, the waves still roll, the sunsets are still spectacular, and beer still flows like there's no tomorrow.

Orientation and Practical Information It's pretty hard to get lost in Jacó. There's one main street along which all the town's traffic flows, with side roads leading south to the beach every 100m or so. The eternally-under-construction (though promised to be soon completed) bridge in the center of town makes a convenient landmark. Facing the beach, going right down the main road is traveling west.

For any sort of **information**, the best source is Cathy of **Chatty Cathy's Family Kitchen**, 300m east of the bridge across from the Supermercado Rayo Azul, where you can talk over yummy treats. For those rare times when Cathy's door is shut, you can also query Chuck of **Chuck's Rooms and Boards**, another willing and experienced source of facts. At the local **ICE** office, 150m east of the bridge, you'll find official, but less helpful information, as well as **public telephones** (¢100 charge for international service; open Mon.-Sat. 7:30am-7:30pm). **Banco de Costa Rica** (tel. 643-3334 or 643-3695), 700m west of the bridge at the Plaza Jacó, exchanges cash and traveler's checks (open Mon.-Fri. 9am-3pm), as does **Banco Nacional,** just west of Supermercado Rayo Azul (tel. 643-3072; open Mon.-Fri. 8:30am-3:45pm). There are 24hr. **ATMs** in Banco de Costa Rica and in **Banco Popular,** about 300m east of Rayo Azul (accepts Cirrus/Visa). There's a main **bus stop** in the center of town, next to Rayo Azul. **Buses** run to **San José** (5, 11am, and 3pm, 2½hr., ¢510; buy tickets at Plaza Jacó, about 800m west of the bridge); **Puntarenas** (6am, 12:15, and 4:30pm; ¢400); **Quepos** and **Manuel Antonio** (6am, noon, and 4pm, 1½hr., ¢350); and **Orotina** (5:30, 7, 9am, noon, 2, 4, and 5pm). Call for **taxis** (tel. 643-3290 or 643-3030), or just look for one near the bus stop. **Car rental** is available at **Ada Rent-a-Car** (tel. 664-3207), across the street and just west of the ICE office, if you are 21 years old, have a valid credit card, and leave a US$75 deposit (US$38 per day, including insurance and free mileage; open daily 7am-6pm). **Moped rental** is available at **Freyka's Rental** (tel. 643-3241), on the west side of the bridge, just west of Restaurante Emily (US$10 per hour; US$30 per day). **Supermercado Rayo Azul** (tel. 643-3025) is in the center of town, across the street from Cabinas el Recreo (open Mon.-Fri. 8am-8pm, Sat. 8am-9pm, Sun. 8am-6pm). **Banana Bath Lavandería** is 50m east of Supermercado Rayo Azul (one load in 3hr. ¢1500, over 24hr. ¢600; open Mon.-Sat. 7:30am-5pm). **Farmacia Jacó** (tel. 643-3205) sits 50m west of Camping el Hicaco (open daily 8:30am-9pm). There is no hospital, but the **Clínica de Jacó** (tel. 643-3238), on the east side of town near Hotel Jacó Fiesta, deals with medical problems; English is spoken. A medical consultant has an office next to the pharmacy (tel. 643-3205 or 643-3601). **Red Cross** (tel. 128; 643-3090 outside Jacó) is 50m east of Camping el Hicaco, about 500m east of the bridge. Dial 117 to reach the **police.** The **post office** (tel. 643-3479) has **fax** and **telegram** service, and is way out on the east side of town, near Hotel Jacó Fiesta (follow the main road east, make a right at the first big intersection; open Mon.-Fri. 8am-4pm). The **postal code** is 4023.

Accommodations Jacó doesn't cater to budget travelers, but you'll see numbers magically decrease if you're in a group or stay a while. **Aparthotel los Ranchos** (tel. 643-3070), toward the beach on the first side street east of the bridge, is among the best options for groups of three or more. The large, apartment-style quads have kitchens, and all rooms come with safes, private bathrooms, hot water, access to the pool, and an on-duty night watchman; laundry service is also available. Surfers receive an automatic discount, and reservations are recommended (quads without kitchen US$24, with kitchen US$31; bungalow for 6 or 7 with kitchen US$55). **Chuck's Rooms and Boards** (tel. 643-3328) is 300m west of the bridge; turn toward the beach at Jacó Bell. The guests bond quickly in this surfer's haven, hanging out on the front porch and raving about the day's waves. Simple rooms with three beds go for US$8 per person year-round, and Chuck offers "bro deal" discounts to rad, long-term guests. Cheaper group rates are also available. Chuck has a surfboard rental and repair business going, and he occasionally gives lessons. For less surfy-types, **Cabinas La Cometa** (tel. 643-3615), across the street from the ICE office, 150m east of the bridge, is extraordinarily clean and comfortable, with hammocks swinging amongst plants on all the front porches. The best deals are the rooms with collective baths (singles ¢2200-2800; doubles ¢3000-3800; triples ¢4800; add ¢1600 for private bath). Large, clean, bright and airy rooms at **Sol y Luna** (tel. 643-3558; down the second street east of the bridge) are charming. The Italian owners have decorated with neat Picasso-like art, some stenciling, and shining blue-tiled bathrooms; some even have balconies (singles ¢1500-2000; doubles ¢2500-4000). They can usually accommodate large groups. **Camping el Hicaco** (tel. 643-3004), across the street from the Red Cross, is the cheapest option around. Since no camping is permitted anywhere on the beach, you'll be thankful to pitch tent in this patchy backyard, where picnic tables, showers, toilets, and laundry basins are available (¢500 per person).

Food The *muy* cool young owners of **Banana Café,** 100m east of the bridge, serve up a great eight-veggie stir-fry with rice (¢1000, with beef ¢1200) in a hut-like jungle garden setting. (Grilled fish plate ¢900, sesame chicken kebob with potatoes and salad ¢1200; open daily 7am-noon and 6pm-10pm.) **Killer Munchies** (tel. 643-3354) lies 100m west of the bridge. Whoever dreamed up the toppings on these pizzas was a creative genius, and anything you order is likely to be killer. They cook all pizzas in a wooden stove as you watch. Both the whole-wheat vegetarian (small ¢1150, large ¢2200) and the Southern BBQ chicken (small ¢1200, large ¢2300) are delightful (open Mon. and Wed.-Fri. 5:30pm-9pm, Sat.-Sun. noon-9pm). **Restaurante Emily** (tel. 643-1056), 200m west of the bridge, is a casual, inexpensive place to dine the *tico* way; Emily doesn't even try to brown-nose the surfers, but just delivers friendly service and tasty food at low prices (*gallo pinto* with eggs ¢350, soup of the day ¢400, fruit plate ¢500; open Mon.-Sat. 9am-9pm, Sun. 6am-10pm). **Chatty Cathy's Family Kitchen** (tel./fax 643-1039) is on the east side of town across from Rayo Azul. Cathy's a warm, welcoming Canadian who will tell her life story to whoever's ready to listen. Her breakfasts and baked goods are mouth-watering, from thick pancakes (¢600) to fresh banana muffins (¢250) and heavenly cinnamon buns (¢550). She is also famous for inventing the delicious pita-pocket breakfast (¢750; open Tues.-Sat. 6am-2pm).

Sights and Entertainment It would be a crime to spend a Jacó day inside. Surfers come from far and wide to ride the waves, many citing **La Roca Loca,** a rocky peninsula to the south, as their favorite spot. Chuck of Chuck's (see **Accommodations,** above) rents good fiberglass boards for US$10 per day, and also does repairs. **Chosita del Surf,** 350m west of the bridge, rents boards for US$10 per day. Get a boogie board at **Coco Bolo Souvenir Shop,** 100m east of the bridge (¢1300 per day). There are gorgeous beaches to either side of Jacó, and riding a bike there is breezy. Rent a mountain bike from **Rentabike,** 200m east of the bridge (¢400 per hr., ¢2000 per day) or from **Chosita del Surf** (¢500 per hr., ¢3000 per day). **Freyka's,** next to Restaurant Emily, rents mopeds (US$30 per day; must be 18 years old). Ask Chatty Cathy's about renting **horses** for ¢1000 per hour, but give her 24hr. notice.

Nightlife…is serious business around these parts. Going to the disco is not simply a weekend activity; locals and *norteamericanos* fill the clubs and bars from dusk 'til dawn. The largest, most popular dancing spot in Jacó is **Discotheque la Central,** four blocks southeast of the bridge, down a side street towards the beach (open Mon.-Fri.

8pm-1am, Sat.-Sun. 8pm-2am; cover ¢400-600). A block away shimmers the smaller and equally crowded **Disco los Tucanes** (open daily 8pm-1am; ¢600 cover on weekends). After the discos close, everyone stumbles to **Pancho Villa's,** on the main road between the two discos, for some late night grub. For a mellower evening of drinking and chatting, head to **Bar el Zarpe,** in Plaza Jacó on the northwest side of town, where charismatic *bocas* (appetizers), like *ceviche de plátano* (nachos in a plantain dip), go for ¢100 each. Folks lucky enough to come on the right night simply tilt their throats back and let the bartender pour down a special mix of pineapple juice and *guaro* (Costa Rican for "Everclear"), until they can't drink any more (open daily 4pm-midnight). Another late-night fave is the **Copacabana** (tel. 643-3131); if you turn at Jacó Bell, it's past Chuck's, by the beach. Owned by Canadian sports fans with the only eight-meter-wide satellite dish in town, ESPN is its station *du-every-jour*. The music is always cranking, and the drinks always flow freely from the swim-up bar (live music on weekends during the high season).

■ Near Jacó: Playa Hermosa

Don't even think about confusing this idyll with the upscale beach of the same name on Península Nicoya. *This* Playa Hermosa is strictly for surfers, many of whom would be upset to see their favorite spot listed in a travel guide. Look down the secluded black sand beach and see wave after picture-perfect wave roll onto the shore. Behind the beach, the extent of development is a few grass-roofed hotels and restaurants. Most of Playa Hermosa's surfers come for the day, but group accommodations are available. Rates are cheaper here than in Jacó, but there's no comparing the two towns' nightlives, unless you've an affinity for goats and cows (see **Move Over, Bunnicula,** p. 445).

Vista Hermosa (tel. 643-3422) has huge, apartment-style suites for two, four, or eight people. Each has a kitchen, a dining room table, and an immaculate private bathroom. There's a pool, and even some new pool tables to while away chill hours while sighing at the incredible views (US$10 per person; less for bigger groups; less still for longer stays). At **Cabinas las Olas** (tel. 643-3687), live out that childhood fantasy of ruling the perfect clubhouse, as wooden ladders grant access to second-floor private bungalows. All rooms have a kitchen, refrigerator, and bathroom with hot water. The cool, helpful American owners suggest making reservations (2 or 3 people US$30; 4 people US$40; 5 or 6 US$50). The **Restaurante Ola Bonita** (tel. 643-3990), adjacent to the Vista Hermosa, serves beach bums on an indoor porch graced by enough sweeping ocean views to rival the shore. Look for the big gazebo with a dried palm-leaf roof just behind the beach; then look behind it. Vegetarian spaghetti and grilled chicken cost ¢800 each (open daily 9am-9pm). For breakfast, hit the not-too-creatively named **Restaurant Surf** (tel. 643-1009), just past Ola Bonita. Their $3 breakfast special is a yummy steal (choice of omelette, pancake, or french toast combos; open daily 7am-10pm).

There are several ways to travel the 5km that separate Playa Hermosa and Jacó. **Walking** takes about one hour, but following the beach won't take you directly there; you have to hoof it along the main highway. Rent a **bike** in Jacó and make the trip in under 30 minutes. Once in a while you'll have to arduously climb a hill, but minutes later, it'll be smooth sailing. You can spare the sweat by catching a bus to Quepos in Jacó, and ask to be dropped off there. Alternatively, a taxi ride from Jacó to Playa Hermosa will cost about ¢700; arrange a time with the driver for the return trip.

■ Quepos

Back in the day, Quepos was a booming banana port and fishing town. Nowadays, all that's left of those times is a decrepit dock and a couple of private sportfishing boats. This quiet, friendly town is sleepy by day; once the sun sets brilliantly over its near-abandoned harbor, however, live emerald blues in a neighborhood bar and the pounding reggae from the wild disco wake the city up. Right next to **Manuel Anto-**

COSTA RICA

nio **National Park,** made easily accessible by a shuttle bus, Quepos is a small and welcoming seaport where the local flavor soothes and the tranquil living is contagious.

Orientation and Practical Information Quepos fits into that neat grid pattern, with *calles* running north to south and *avenidas* east to west. Odd-numbered *calles* fall to the east of Calle Central, and the one even-numbered *calle* to its west. Odd-numbered *avenidas* fall to the north of Av. Central, even ones to the south, and **Avenida Central bis** and **Avenida 2 bis** to the north of their namesakes. The bus stop and central market are at Avs. Central/Central bis and Calles Central/1. But be warned; some schizophrenic *calles* claim to be one thing at one end and another at the other end. As always, asking locals is your best bet for retaining sanity.

La Buena Nota (tel. 777-1002), between Quepos and Manuel Antonio (ride the shuttle and spot it on your right), is a good place for all sorts of general **information** about the area (open Mon.-Sat. 8am-4:30pm). Exchange cash or traveler's checks at **Banco de Costa Rica** (tel. 777-0285), Av. 2 bis and Calle Central (open Mon.-Fri. 9am-3pm). The **bus terminal** is right next to the central market at Avs. Central/Central bis and Calles Central/1. Direct **buses** leave daily for **San José** (6am, noon, and 5pm, 3½hr., ¢1250); others stop along the way (5, 8am, 2, and 4pm, 5hr.). Buses leave for **Jacó** and **Puntarenas** at 4:30, 10:30am, and 3pm (2hr., ¢350 to Jacó; 3½hr., ¢650 to Puntarenas). Buses to **San Isidro** and **Dominical** depart at 5am and 1:30, 4, and 7pm (3½hr.). The shuttle to **Manuel Antonio** runs 13 times a day (5:40am-7pm, 20min., ¢60). **Taxis** wait in front of the bus terminal, or call **Coopetico Quepos** (tel. 777-0425) or **Taxis Unidos** (tel. 777-1837). **Car rental** is available at **Elegante Rent-a-Car** (tel. 777-0115), Calle 2, Avs. 1/3, next to Café Milagro (open Mon.-Fri. 7:30am-noon and 1:30-5:30pm, Sat. 7:30am-noon). Hit **Super 2000** (tel. 777-1261) for groceries, on Calle Central 150m past Av. 1 (open Mon.-Sat. 8am-8pm, Sun. 8am-noon), or the **supermercado** across from the bus terminal (open Mon.-Sat. 8:30am-8:30pm, Sun. 8am-2pm). **Farmacia Botica Quepos** (tel. 777-0038) is on Av. 2 bis and Calle 2 (open Mon.-Sat. 7am-7pm, Sun. 7am-2pm). Call the **Red Cross** at 777-0116. The **hospital** (tel. 777-1397) is about 4km down Calle 2 towards Manuel Antonio. There's a **post office** (tel. 777-1471) way down Av. Central, at the soccer field, with *lista de correos,* **fax,** and **telegram** service (open Mon.-Fri. 8am-4pm). The **postal code** is 6350. You can make **international phone calls** in the building with the telecommunications sign, next to the Heladería and Hotel Malinche, Av. Central bis, Calles Central/2. There are **public phones** all along Calle 2, and east of the bus terminal.

Accommodations and Food Rooms and bathrooms are clean and simple at **Mar y Luna** (tel. 777-0394), Av. Central bis., Calles Central/2, but it's the atmosphere that'll win you over. Owner Alvaro is friendly even for a *tico,* and a short stay here can win you a pal for life. Fridge and TV privileges are part of the deal (¢1000 per person, single with private bath ¢1400). Across the street, the recently built **Hotel Maliche** (tel. 777-0093) has no glam or glitz. Simple rooms with fan and clean private baths, all hidden off tree-spotted winding hallways, cost ¢1400 per person.

Restaurante y Bar Marquesa (tel. 777-1585), Calle 2, Avs. Central bis./1, has amazingly low prices, tasty food, and good service. Beware: they charge that pesky 25% service tax (*gallo pinto* with eggs ¢200, *casados* ¢500, *refresco natural* ¢80, whole fish ¢500; open Mon.-Sat. 6am-10pm, Sun. 6am-2pm). **Pizza Gabriel's** (tel. 777-1085), Av. Central bis. and Calle Central, has what some swear is the best pizza they've ever tasted; for such good eats, the place usually is not very crowded. Pies range in size from *pequeño* (1 person) to *super grande* (6 people), and sport everything from shrimp to coconut and veggies to salami (single pizza ¢750-1000; large feeds 3 for ¢1450-1750; open Mon.-Sat. 7am-11pm, Sun. 3-11pm). Morning or night, cure those real-Italian-pasta cravings at **L'Angolo,** Av. Central, Calle Central, a tiny corner store with fantastic food (spaghetti, penne, or fettucini, bolognese with fresh basil ¢550, gnocchi al pesto ¢850, thick 'n' juicy roast beef ¢950; open daily 8:30am-8pm). When that rainstorm hits, chill with a cup of Joe at **Café Milagro** (tel. 777-1707), right down the street from Restaurante Marquesa. There's plenty of table space for writing letters, not to mention great cappuccino (¢300; bottomless cup of coffee ¢200, raspberry lemonade ¢250; open daily 6am-9pm).

Entertainment and Nightlife Nobody in Quepos expects tourists to stick around during the day—that's what the Manuel Antonio beaches and national park are for (see below). There are a few sportfishing and river-rafting agencies which offer costly daytrips. **Estrella Tour** (tel./fax 777-1286), Av. Central/Central bis, Calle Central, offers great white-water rafting (class 3 and 4), kayaking, horseback trips (tours US$25-45), and rents quality bikes (US$3 per hr.; US$15 per day) for those independent spirits who want to explore the mountains on their own.

But Quepos, charged with the formidable task of luring everyone back into town after dusk, really shines in the nightlife department. **Discotheque Arco Iris,** across the bridge at the north end of Calle 2, is a popular place for young *ticos* and tourists to shake their booties to incessant reggae (open daily 7pm-2am; ¢300 cover charge on Sat.). Rowdy crowds pack the house and spill out into the street at **Bar El Barco,** Av. Central bis, Calles Central/2. After they stop cheering, groaning, and enrapturedly watching the night's sporting event, join them for some great live music and friendly drinking. Then laugh at the pitiful souls bravely stepping up to open mike on Saturday nights (open 'til 2am). A beautiful place to pass the early evening is the leafy bar of **La Boca Nueva,** at the north end of Calle 2, just before the bridge. Every evening around 6pm, pairs of green parrots fly into the treetops to play and, ahem, do a little more than dance the *merengue.* La Boca also serves short, tasty shots of a bright blue brew called a *pitufo* ("smurf", ¢80; open daily 4-11pm). Diehard crap-shooters who aren't daring enough to disco may prefer the ritzy **Casino Kamuk** (tel. 777-0379), Av. Central, Calles Central/2, which is always more than happy to milk every last colón out of its patrons, while egging them on with free drinks and, to be safe, free taxi rides home (open daily 8pm-3am). The bar, **Blues and Mar,** Av. Central, Calles Central/2, is a mellow spot to listen to good music and contemplate how to replace all the money you just lost at the casino down the street (open daily 'til 3am).

■ Manuel Antonio National Park

At **Manuel Antonio National Park,** warm, jade-green waves lap at the edges of lush, tropical forests. Popular with both nationals and foreigners, Costa Rica's smallest national park can seem more like a people zoo than a secluded preserve. Batallions of visitors have fed and photographed the park's white-faced monkeys into a pigeon-like state of dependence. Despite the crowds, spectacular life-forms still slither, wing, scamper, and soar. However, if you search diligently enough, you'll be rewarded with a stretch of sand all to yourself and your furry or feathered companions. Brown pelicans plumb the watery depths while sea turtles lay eggs in the sands. Tyrant hawk-eagles reign overhead. Three-toed anteaters and two-toed sloths collaborate on counting to ten, as 59 species of bats share the park with howler monkeys, gray foxes, iguanas, crabs, and ctenosaurs (iguana-like creatures). To enter the park, go past Cabinas Manuel Antonio and the adjacent short stretch of sand, cross the stream (you may need a boat during high tide (¢100), enter the forest, and you'll come upon the park ranger's booth (open daily 7am-4pm; admission US$6).

Manuel Antonio is most renowned for its four spectacular beaches. The first, **Playa Espadilla,** actually lies outside the national park and is popular with surfers, swimmers, and sunbathers who want to skip out on the park's admission fee. The second beach, **Playa Espadilla Sur,** extends south from the park's entrance. Its perfect white sand and radiant blue waters are breath-taking, even when packed to capacity with tourists (practically a given on weekends and during the high season). That tree-covered peninsula ahead is **Punta Catedral,** which used to be an island—100,000 years of sediment deposits created a *tómbolo,* or natural bridge, connecting the point to the mainland. On the other side of Punta Catedral lies the third beach, **Playa Blanca** (a.k.a. **Playa Manuel Antonio**), another popular tourist spot, thanks largely to its proximity to picnic areas, bathrooms, showers, and clean running water. Often, in fact, the only way to escape the crowds and enjoy the luminous turquoise waters in peace is to make the 20-minute hike to the fourth and least accessible beach, **Playa Puerto Escondido.** The walk, which involves a bit of climbing, can only be made during low tide, so head back before the water rises. Along the path to Puerto Escondido, there is a break in the road, with another trail leading to the spectacular **Mirador** (which means quite simply, *view*), a 45-minute hike through a jungle filled with lazy blue butterflies and hanging vines. Camping is not permitted anywhere in the park or on the beaches.

ACCOMMODATIONS AND FOOD

Staying in nearby Quepos (7km north) is cheaper than in Manuel Antonio, but not as convenient or as scenic. Bargains are easiest to find in Manuel Antonio if you avoid high season. Don't let the run-down house in front of **Cabinas Irarosa** scare you away; these clean, small rooms with private bath and fan are a great deal (¢1000 per person). To find Cabinas, go up the road next to Soda Marlyn, walk about 250m, veer right over a little stream, and it'll be on your left past the red Coca-Cola sign. About 150m closer to the main road, **Albergue y Travotel Costa Linda** (tel. 777-0304) has a helpful and amiable staff, as well as clean rooms and communal bathrooms. Storage space, language classes, and even boomerang lessons are available (singles and doubles ¢2400 during high season; ¢1500 per person during low season; try to bargain). **Hotel Manuel Antonio** (tel. 777-1237) sits just before the entrance to the park. Wood-panelled rooms are all passable and private bathrooms clean, though the hotel could use some personality (¢1500-2000 per person). The restaurant downstairs is a nice touch. The hotel also allows campers to pitch tents in their backyard for ¢300 per person (including toilets and showers).

Most restaurants in Manuel Antonio offer authentic dishes in simple settings. Surfers come to **Blanca Flor Restaurant,** across the street from the beach, to refuel and trade stories in fluent Spanglish; anecdotes typically conclude with a near-missed high-five and an enthusiastic *"Sí,* man, *sí. Bueno!* Best wave!" Blanca and her family are wonderful; chow down on rice with veggies (¢650), *casados* (¢500), fish filet (¢750), or vegetable soup (¢400; open daily 6:30am-9pm). Farther north up the beach waits **Restaurante Mar y Sombra** (tel. 777-0468 or 777-0510), where you can watch waves from a shady, beach-side table while gulping down spaghetti with sausage (¢600), T-bone steak (¢1800), or black bean soup (¢500). Bathe in insect repellent before dinner or you will become an unwilling meal for pesky bugs (open daily 7:30am-11pm).

ENTERTAINMENT

There's no lack of activities outside the national park. For all of your beach equipment needs, see **Mary Elena** next to Soda Marlyn. She rents surfboards (¢2300), boogie boards (¢1000), snorkel equipment (¢1600), beach umbrellas (¢400), tents (¢300), chairs (¢500), and even towels (¢400). **Hotel Mariposa** (tel. 777-0355), on the main road about halfway between Quepos and Manuel Antonio, rents **horses** for ¢1500 per hour. **Marlboro Stables,** about 300m north of Restaurant Mar y Sombra, takes people on tours through their private mountain trails with interspersed ocean views for US$30. If you need a shower, follow the sign in front of **Soda la Rosa** (¢75).

▓ Monteverde Reserve

Perpetually blanketed in a soft mist, the **Reserva Biológica Bosque Nuboso Monteverde,** 184km northwest of San José and due north of Puntarenas, encompasses 27,400 acres and may be Costa Rica's most famous environmental reserve. The area was settled in 1951 by 44 Alabama Quakers, some of whom had served jail time as conscientious objectors to U.S. military activities. Seeking privacy and peace, the Quakers established a community of farms in northwest Costa Rica. In 1972, the vast tract of land they set aside as a wildlife refuge was christened the Monteverde Cloud Forest Reserve; a privately owned forest, it is administered by the all-volunteer Monteverde Conservation League. The **Bosque Eterno de los Niños** (Children's Rainforest) borders the Monteverde Reserve. Purchased for preservation in 1987 by a group of concerned Swedish elementary-school children, the forest is maintained by charitable contributions from all over the world. The flower-lined **Bajo del Tigre trail** on the Pacific slope is open to the public (open daily 8am-4pm; admission ¢1100, with student ID ¢450). Guided tours are available; call 645-5003 or fax 645-5104.

Together, the reserve houses more than 600 species of animals and over 2500 species of plants. Evergreens draped with mosses, ferns, and clinging orchids populate the cool, wet slopes; elfin forests of wizened trees grow at higher elevations. The Monteverde Reserve's most famous residents are its golden toads, a species not found anywhere else in the world. Unfortunately, these unique creatures have not been spotted for more than a decade and are feared to be extinct. Jaguars, opossums, howler and spider monkeys, foxes, armadillos, and mountain lions also haunt the forest. Its diverse collection of birds includes falcons, parrots, hummingbirds, egrets, owls, woodpeckers, toucans, and quetzals.

Admission to the Cloud Forest Reserve is US$8, with student ID US$4. At the entrance to the park, a **visitors center** (tel. 645-5212) provides information and sells generic doo-dads (open daily 7am-4pm). Three-hour guided tours in English begin at 8am (US$15 per person); catch the slide show at 7:30am if you're early. Night hikes start at 7:15pm (US$13; tel. 645-5118 or 645-5311). There are also special birdwatching tours available—call the visitors center the day before. If you choose to spend the night at the reserve, the visitors center will provide a bed, communal showers, and three square meals for US$21. Inside the reserve itself, a few lodges with kitchens provide a free night's stay for hard-core backpackers. Bring a sleeping bag and food, and get a map at the ranger's station; the hike to the shelters may be wet and muddy.

GETTING THERE

To reach the Monteverde Reserve from **San José,** take the bus that departs daily from Calle 14, Avs. 9/11 (6:30am and 2:30pm, 4½hr., ¢1275; you can buy tickets in advance). Or try the microbus from **Tico Explorers, S.A.** (tel. 645-5051), which leaves from the Toruma Youth Hostel (US$12). A daily public bus also leaves from **Tilarán** (12:30pm, 3hr., ¢570). From **Liberia,** take a bus to San José (or any bus traveling along the Interamerican Hwy.) and ask to be let off at **Lagarto,** a tiny town 35km from Monteverde. Wave down the San José bus as it passes by around 8:30am or 4:30pm (the bus could come anytime between 8-9am or 4-5pm, depending on traffic and all the *et ceteras* that make Costa Rican bus rides so darn fun). Alternatively, take a morning bus from Liberia to **Puntarenas** (5, 8:30, or 10am) and then go from Puntarenas to **Monteverde** (2:15pm, ¢700). Once off the main highway, the bus to Monteverde begins a breathtaking, if unbelievably slow, 35km ascent along the steep walls of emerald valleys. The bus passes through the town of **Santa Elena** 3km before it reaches the village of Monteverde. The bus back to San José from Santa Elena leaves at 6:30am and 2:30pm. If you are coming from near the village of Monteverde, a bus will take you to Santa Elena around 6:20am. A bus to Tilarán departs daily at 7am (3hr., ¢250); there is also a bus at 6:10am that climbs the 3km from Santa Elena to Monteverde. The bus back to Puntarenas leaves daily at 6am (2½hr., ¢1050). All buses leave Santa Elena from the stop in front of Restaurante Daykiri. From Santa Elena, the reserve is a moderately long walk or an expensive taxi ride (¢1200) away.

PRACTICAL INFORMATION

Santa Elena is a good place to take care of little chores. **Banco Nacional** (tel. 645-5027), at the end of the main street, changes traveler's checks (open Mon.-Fri. 8:30am-3:45pm). The **bus stop** is across the street from **Restaurante Daykiri** (see **Getting There,** above). Buy San José tickets in advance from the **Marza Transporte** ticket office (tel. 645-5159 in Santa Elena, 222-3854 in San José; open Mon.-Fri. 6am-noon and 1-4pm, Sat.-Sun. 6am-noon and 1-3pm). **La Esperanza Market** (tel. 645-5166), across from the post office, provides alimentary staples and toiletries (open daily 6:30am-8pm). Call for a **taxi** (tel. 645-5148) or pick one up across from Restaurante Daykiri. **Chunches** (tel. 645-5147), on the main road toward Monteverde, has a **laundromat** (wash ¢450, dry ¢450, soap ¢100) and a **bookstore** with English novels and U.S. publications (open Mon.-Sat. 9am-6pm). The **pharmacy** is in the green and pink **Vitosi** store at the end of the main road (open daily 8am-6:30pm). The **police station** (tel. 645-5166), next to the post office, opens at 7am. To find the **post office** (tel./fax 645-5042), walk down the main road, then turn right; it has **telegram** and **fax** services (open Mon.-Fri. 7:30am-3:30pm). The **postal code** is 5655. In Santa Elena, **public telephones** can be found outside Restaurante Daykiri or **La Esperanza Market.** Closer to Monteverde, they can be found next to **Johnny's Pizza,** in the grocery store next to CASEM (see below), and in the visitors center at the reserve.

ACCOMMODATIONS AND FOOD

For those not staying at the reserve, lodging is available both along the road to the reserve (considered the Monteverde area) and in the town of Santa Elena. There are far more budget places in Santa Elena, but the reserve is about 6km away. Most accommodations are family-run and serve homemade meals for an additional charge. In Santa Elena, the **Pensión el Tucán** (tel. 645-5017) teems with young backpackers. Comfortable rooms with wood walls and clean private or communal baths with hot water cost US$5 (with beach access US$7). The food is incredible (breakfast ¢300-500, dinner ¢500-800). Besides being a tourist information center and an HI-affiliated hostel, **Hotel Albergue Santa Elena** (tel. 645-5051) has surprisingly cozy, well-built, and tastefully furnished rooms. Private bathrooms are large, spotless, and enjoy hot water; shared bathrooms are a little run-down (rooms US$10 per person, with bath US$15 per person; lunch ¢400-800; room prices drop about US$5 in the low season). You can also camp in Albergue's backyard with access to the communal bath for US$5 per night. **Pensión el Colibri** ("the Hummingbird"; turn left at the sign for Arco Iris) is about as cheap as it comes in the area. Although the rooms would make decent display cases for a hummingbird taxidermist, the friendly owners put the "accommodate" back into accommodations. Ask for an upstairs room with new redwood floors (rooms ¢1000 per person; meals are available). Shared bathroom has hot water and plush rugs. About 1km towards Santa Elena from the center of Monteverde is **Pensión Manakin** (tel. 645-5080), where Mario and Yolanda Villegas and their young children welcome guests to small but comfortable rooms; some have private baths and some have kitchen access. Yolanda and her daughter cook delicious breakfasts (US$3) and dinners (US$5). Rooms cost US$6 for larger rooms with kitchen use; a private bath is US$3 more.

Most of the hotels serve homemade meals to their guests, so restaurant selection is sparse. The cozy restaurant inside **El Tucán** makes incredible *casados;* feast on loads of fresh veggies, a hearty chicken breast sandwich (¢400), and the vegetarian plate (¢500). In Monteverde, **Stella's Bakery,** across from CASEM, decorated with Stella's very own watercolors and oil paintings, should not be missed—everything from her fresh multi-grain bread (¢100) to rich chocolate brownies (¢240) to home-made lasagnas (¢1500) is delicious. (Open daily 6am-6pm.) Walking down from the reserve, **Restaurant Flor Mara** (tel. 645-5009) is about 2.5km on your left, where the road splits. Veggie burgers (¢330), a plate of three enchiladas, rice and veggies (¢825), or the fruit plate with granola (¢450) will please your stomach. (Prices include tax and service! Open daily 7am-8pm.) **Johnny's Pizzeria** (tel. 645-5066), in Santa Elena, has good calzones, even better pizza (small cheese pizza ¢830, large ¢1800), and a great selection of pastas (¢800-1000); open daily 11:30am-9pm. In the same building, **Café Neotropica** has a wonderful rotating menu, catering to vegetarians (falafel, hummous sandwiches ¢795; spinach and cheese sandwich ¢695) and incurable sweet-tooths with rich chocolate cake or peanut butter pie (¢400); open daily noon-4pm.

SIGHTS AND ENTERTAINMENT

It's far too easy to get hooked here. After the magnificent cloud forests, hoards of hummingbirds, and gorgeous horseback rides to waterfalls at sunset, a "short, quick" visit may suddenly become "well, maybe just one more day...."

The cloud forest is amazing, but don't overlook the **Santa Elena Reserve** (5km from the town of Santa Elena), which was created in 1989 to relieve some of the burden of excessive tourism from Monteverde (open daily 7am-5pm; admission ¢1000, students ¢500). Home to some of the same species of flora and fauna, this impressive alternative won't leave you feeling like a packed sardine. Points within the Santa Elena Reserve reach the highest altitudes in the area (some over 1700m), providing magnificent lookout points. The walk here and back is a hike in itself, so some may want to take a taxi. For the "walk of a lifetime" through the cloud forest's canopy (30-40m up), check out the **sky walk** (tel. 645-5238) which starts 3.5km from town towards the Santa Elena Reserve. The new suspension bridges are interspersed with forested trails, and guides are available (US$8, with student ID US$3; open daily 7am-5pm). The **Ecological Farm,** about 1.5km from Santa Elena towards Monteverde (follow the signs opposite the Hotel Heliconia), has trails running through primary and secondary cloud forest, most of which take one or two hours to hike. Several species of small, furry animals live here, including agouti (weird, snouted, cat-sized, humanoid things). (Open daily 7am-5pm; admission ¢1200, with student ID ¢600.)

The **Monteverde Butterfly Garden** *(Jardín de las Mariposas)* and the **Santa Elena Serpentarium** (tel. 645-5238) offer the flittery and slithery, respectively. To find the garden, follow the signs across from Hotel Heliconia. In the Butterfly Garden's gallery, various insects are caged and mounted, but the rear of the building is divided into three indoor gardens, each representing a different microclimate with a colorful medley of 35-40 indigenous butterfly species. An informative 45-minute tour is included in the admission fee (open daily 9:30am-4pm; admission ¢1350, students ¢1150). Herpetophiles will want to head over to the extensive, recently opened **Serpentarium,** about 400m up the road from Santa Elena (open daily 8am-5pm; admission ¢700, students ¢450). Just before the entrance to the Monteverde Reserve, there's a house on the left that emanates a strange buzzing sound—welcome to the **Hummingbird Gallery and Rainforest Slide Shows.** The patio is host to hundreds of hummingbirds; the different species in attendance depend on the season, but the brilliant, green-crowned and stripe-tailed hummingbirds are common year-round (open daily at 8:30am). Slide shows about life in the rainforest, made by world-renowned photographers and biologists, are shown daily at 11am (US$3 per person).

Through the Trees with the Greatest of Ease

Not for the faint-hearted, **Canopy Tours** (tel. 645-5243) takes spendthrift **daredevils** 14m up the center of a hollow strangler fig tree to fly along cables between platforms placed at the top of the rainforest. Not only is it the closest most people will ever come to feeling like **Tarzan** or **Jane,** but it also provides a one-of-a-kind view of the upper growth, or canopy, of the forest. Don't worry—everyone is strapped and **harnessed tightly,** and the trained and fully licensed guides know what they're doing. Although the price may be steep for the broke backpacker, the company claims to be the only tour of its kind in the world. Proceeds help to conserve and reforest Costa Rica (office open Mon.-Sat 7am-9pm, Sun. until 6pm; tours leave daily at 7:30, 10:30am, 2:30, and 7:30pm; US$40, with student ID US$30).

Less on the jungly side is the **Monteverde Cheese Factory** (tel. 645-5029), 300m up the street from Casem and Stella's Bakery; look for the metallic cow on the sign in front. A Quaker innovation, the cheese factory offers tours during the high season at 7:30am and 1:30pm. Otherwise, visitors can watch the mesmerizing churning process through the glass walls of the observation room while munching on samples (enter through the sales room; open Mon.-Sat. 7:30am-4pm, Sun. 7:30am-12:30pm).

For **horseback riding, Meg's Stables** (tel. 645-5052), next to Stella's Bakery, provides a guide and access to private trails (US$10 per hr.). Many hotels rent horses for much less. **Pensión el Colibrí** (tel. 645-5682) offers good tours—including half-day rainforest, sunset, and waterfall trips—at reasonable prices (US$7 per hr.; reduced group rates). Founded in 1982 to provide job opportunities for women taking care of families at home, **Casem** (tel. 645-5190) now has 140 artisans who sell their handmade crafts at the store across the street from Stella's Bakery. Carved wood and hand-painted items abound, and many artists depict local animals such as the quetzal and the golden toad (open Mon.-Sat. 8am-5pm, Sun. 10am-4pm).

The **Monteverde Music Festival** (Jan. 2-Feb. 14), hosted by the Hotel Fonda Vela (tel. 645-5125), is a month-long annual celebration with everything from classical music to big bands. Rumor has it that they hope to extend the festival by a month, using the latter half to focus on jazz. It will be held at La Cascada (see below) in 1998. Music begins nightly at 5pm. Hotel Fonda Vela also hosts the **International Festival of Music,** a celebration of classical, folk, and jazz music beginning in the end of July and continuing through August. For information on performances and tickets call 645-5714 or 645-5550. Monteverde even has nightlife—check out the bar next door to the Serpentarium for a mellow evening, or get yourself to **La Cascada,** a disco located a bit before Stella's on the road to the Reserve (no cover, but drinks will cost you).

PENÍNSULA NICOYA

From the highland heart of Costa Rica's cattle industry to some of the most popular beaches in Central America, magnificently different lands and lives crowd the Nicoya Peninsula. The majority of Península Nicoya lies within the boundaries of the province of Guanacaste. The inland region bears almost no resemblance to any other part of the country, with rugged cowpokes ambling through dusty streets. Meanwhile, the north coast's beaches are magnificently empty—their pristine beauty has not yet been exploited by Costa Rica's soaring tourism industry. Every silver lining has a cloud, though, and underdevelopment has made transportation very difficult; traveling between two beaches often requires backtracking to Liberia or Nicoya.

■ Nicoya

Nicoya looks like the set for an old Western—stony-faced cattle-types squint at the horizon from under their wide cowboy hats and stage an annual rodeo every July to celebrate Annexation Day, the date of Guanacaste's integration with Costa Rica. The locals have different ethnic backgrounds from standard, homogeneous *tico* stock; there's a large Chinese population, and others trace their roots back to the indigenous Chorotega. The town is even named after an Indian leader—Chief Nicoya ruled when the first Spaniards arrived here in 1523. Today, Nicoya fills an important role in the cattle industry and serves as the commercial and political center of the peninsula and as a valuable transportation hub for travelers.

Orientation and Practical Information The two main points of reference in the city center are the park and the main road, which runs north to south one block east of the park. The old church is in the northeast corner of the park.

Paco Gordenber, who knows everything about the region, runs an **information** center out of **Bar el Molino** (tel. 685-5001), 250m north of the hospital. However, your best bet for info are the hotel owners (try Hotel Venecia) and locals in the sodas. **Exchange currency** at **Banco de Costa Rica,** on the west side of the park (open Mon.-Fri. 8:30am-3:45pm). **Banco Popular,** about 110m east and 200m north of the park's northeast corner, on the main road, has a 24 hr. ATM for Visa and Popular.

The main **bus** stop, serving the **Empresa Alfaro** line (tel. 685-5032), is at the southeast corner of town. Buses leave for: **San José** (daily 4:30am, 7am, 9:30am, noon,

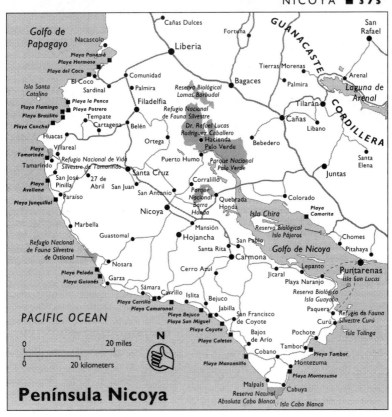

Península Nicoya

2:30, and 5:20pm, 6hr., ¢1205); **Playa Naranjo** (daily 5:15am and 1pm, 2hr., ¢300); **Playa Sámara** (Mon.-Sat. 8am, noon, 3, and 4:30pm, Sun. 8am, noon, 1½hr., ¢240); and **Puntarenas** (transfer at **Barranca;** daily at 7am, 9:30am, noon, 2:30pm). The other bus stop, 100m north and 150m east of the park's corner, across from Hotel las Tinajas, serves **Transportes la Pampa** (tel. 685-0111), which sends 15 buses daily to **Liberia** (5am-7pm, 2½hr., ¢240) via **Santa Cruz** (40min., ¢75) and **Filadelfia. Taxis** line the east side of the park, or call **Coopetico Nicoya** (tel. 685-6226). Nicoya's cabs don't have meters, so check the driver's list of prices to avoid being hoodwinked. **Farmacia Nicoyana** (tel. 685-5138), 50m north of Café Daniela on the main road, has a medical specialist to answer questions (open Mon.-Sat. 8am-6pm). **Hospital de la Anexión** (tel. 685-5066) sits 400m north of Banco Nacional de Costa Rica. English is spoken (open 24hr.). Call the **Red Cross** at 685-5458. For the **police**, dial 117, or call the judicial office, **OIJ** (tel. 685-5328). The **post office** (tel. 685-6402; fax 685-5004), across from the southwest corner of the park (open Mon.-Fri. 7:30am-noon and 1pm-5:30pm), is also the place to **fax** (US$2.50 per page) and send **telegrams.** The **postal code** is 5200. **Telephones** surround the park, west of the main road.

Accommodations With an extremely friendly and helpful staff, simple rooms surrounding a huge courtyard, and a comfy TV lounge, **Hotel Venecia** (tel. 685-5325), on the north side of the park, is Nicoya's budget pick. Everything is impeccably clean (singles ¢850, with bath ¢1500; doubles ¢1600, with bath ¢2500; triples with bath ¢2700). **Hotel Elegancia** (tel. 685-5159), next to Hotel Venecia, is the only place in town with a tailor shop in the lobby. Calling this place elegant is fairly amusing, but the rooms are spacious and bright, with clothes lines running across them (rooms ¢850 per person, doubles with bath ¢2000). **Hotel Chorotega** (tel. 685-5245) is 150m south of the post office. Rooms are decent-sized and well-maintained; most have private baths. Ask for a room on the patio—it's sunnier, though the talking parrot could drive anyone batty with its daylight routine (¢800 per person, ¢1200 with bath). Laundry service is also available.

Food and Entertainment Nicoya is full of cheap, satisfying eats. The town has a large Chinese population, so Chinese restaurants occupy every corner, rivaling *comida típica*.

Café Daniela (tel. 686-6148), one block east of the park, is Nicoya's token coffee shop, serving tasty pastries (¢80-180) and *comida típica*. The atmosphere is relaxed and friendly with overhead fans desperately trying to keep the clientele happy, even if the service seems less concerned (huge *casados* ¢550, pizzas ¢1000-1300, fruit platter ¢420; open Mon.-Sat. 8am-9pm, Sun. 5-10pm). **Restaurant Teyet,** one block southeast of the park, across from Hotel Yenny, has Chinese food that the locals swear by. It is, of course, Chinese Costa Rican-style—french fries and ketchup galore—but, portions are heaping and delicious (sweet and sour chicken ¢730, fried rice ¢600, chop suey ¢600; open Mon.-Fri. 11am-11pm, Sat.-Sun. 11am-1am). **Soda Yadira,** 50m east of Park St. Corner, is an always-hopping local favorite, with good, cheap eats (*casados* ¢400, sandwiches ¢250, great *batidos* ¢150, home-baked cakes ¢150; open daily 6:30am-9:30pm).

Try out the local disco, **Tutti Frutti,** 25m north of Soda Colonial, where the locals shake it every night of the week (free most weekdays, weekend cover ¢300-500); or just join the interesting nightly promenade of young *ticos* around the quaint park.

■ Near Nicoya: Barra Honda National Park

When one imagines spending a day in a Costa Rican national park, plumbing a limestone cavern 70m underground doesn't jump to mind. The fact that **Barra Honda** is one of the nation's least visited parks (it's not very accessible and equipment costs are high) doesn't mean that it doesn't rank up there with the most spectacular of the volcanos and rainforests. Avid spelunkers flock to the 2300-hectare park, a hillside riddled with a maze of 42 caves, some of them more than 220m deep. Only 19 caverns have been explored, and just one, **Terciopelo Cave,** is open to the public.

From the ranger station, it's about a two-hour hike up to Terciopelo, through a dry tropical forest alive with monkeys and scarlet macaws, and endangered white-tailed deer that locals are releasing back into the region. An uphill detour of about 30 minutes from the cave leads to the breath-taking **Mirador,** a panorama of the farmland and hills of the peninsula and even the yawning Gulf of Nicoya.

Simply entering the cave is enough to get the old adrenals a-pumpin'. The only way to descend is by scaling a free-hanging, six-inch wide, steel-rope ladder (nobody's allowed down without the aid of three guides and a harness). At the bottom is a cavern of limestone splendor—the result of a geologic upheaval of 60 to 70 million-year-old coral reefs. Forests of stalagmites and stalactites abound (one of which, when touched in a certain way, produces organ-like sounds), and intricate folds in the walls gleam with a cold, delicate light and feel like porcelain. Every so often, a sightless toad or salamander darts through a shadowy crevice. A park ranger (Spanish-speaking only—if you don't speak Spanish, this may pose safety problems) leads the way through narrow passages deep into the cave's bowels, flashlight in hand.

Unfortunately, the costs of a day of spelunking can really add up. There is a bus that runs from Nicoya to Barra Honda, but its schedule isn't exactly convenient. It leaves Nicoya on weekdays at 10:30am and 3:30pm (Sat. 10:30am and 3pm) and returns at 11am. A better bet is to take a four-wheel drive taxi, which takes about 30 minutes and costs about ¢2000 each way. Arrange a time to be picked up with the taxi driver, for early (around 8am); you have the 1-1½hr. walk from the ranger station, and the guides like to get an early start. There is a pesky US$6 admission fee to the park (open daily 7am-4pm). Anyone can walk the path to the Mirador unguided, but to enter the cave you need to rent climbing equipment (¢1500 per person) and hire three guides per group of one to eight novitiates (1-4 people ¢7000 total, 5-8 people ¢10,000). It's important to call the **Ministerio de Ambiente y Energia** (tel. 686-6760 or 685-5667) or go over (10m east of Hotel Venecia) the day before; they'll set you up with a guide and give you all sorts of information. There is camping available in a small grassy area for ¢300 per night; bathrooms are available, but bring your own food.

■ Playa Tamarindo

Watch out for hordes of marauding *gringos* at Playa Tamarindo, on the western shore of the Península Nicoya. Although it's not nearly as crowded as other, smaller Pacific coast beaches like Jacó, tourists still make their presence abundantly clear. The scenery, sunbathing, swimming, snorkeling, and surfing aren't the best around, but there aren't many other places that combine so much to do during the day *and* a raging nightlife. If you don't find discos and bars appealing, you can always sneak through the dark and spy on a leatherback turtle laying her 120 eggs, or wade into the waters by moonlight to see the motion-sensitive phosphorescent bacteria.

Practical Information **Banco Nacional** (tel. 654-4016), on the main road about 500m from the end, changes cash and traveler's checks (open Mon.-Fri. 8:30am-noon and 1-3:45pm). The **Travel Agency/Palm Shop,** 300m down the main road, has an **International Ice Phone** (open daily 9am-1pm). **Supermercado el Pelícano** (open Mon.-Sat. 7am-7pm, Sun. 9am-5pm), up the first street branching off from the main road, as well as **Super Tamarindo** (open daily 7am-8pm), 250m down the main road, tend to be overpriced; many visitors tote their own food from Santa Cruz. It's not possible to phone a **taxi,** but there are two in town—one waits in front of Cabinas Marielos on the main road, the other in the cul-de-sac alongside the **bus stop.** A direct bus to Tamarindo from **San José** leaves from Calles 14/16, right off Av. 5, on weekdays and also at 12:30pm on Sundays (6hr., ¢920; buy tickets at Hotel Diria). The only way to get to Tamarindo from the Península Nicoya is via **Santa Cruz,** a town 29km to the east. Buses to Santa Cruz leave Nicoya daily (every hr., 40min., ¢75; ¢1050 in Tamarindo). After getting off in Santa Cruz, walk a few blocks to the Tralapa terminal 350m up the road, from which a bus heads to Tamarindo (daily at 6:30, 10:30am, and 2:30pm, 1½hr., ¢220). Buses to Santa Cruz leave Tamarindo daily at 6, 9am, noon and 3:30pm. The locals of Tamarindo must feel invincible; they have no **hospital, doctor,** or **police.** If you're one of the many backpackers that opt for cockroach and crab-infested cabins but have US$150 to fork over for a real honest-to-goodness doctor's appointment, call the **clinic** (tel. 666-1793), 200m down the main road. **Pay phones** are located in the little park at the end of the main road, as well as in front of the bank or Johan's Bakery (600m up main road).

Accommodations and Food Most of the hotels and restaurants are expensive, so campers have it best here; starting 200m down the beach past the end of the main road, there are three or four different areas for camping that range in price depending on the season (¢400-600). **Tito's Camping** is the best, offering a night guard, decent showers and even a restaurant (¢500 per person). For non-campers, **Cabinas Rodamar,** 500m down the road, provides a cheap option. Concrete seems to be a motif, but the small rooms are decent and the price is unbeatable. If you're lucky you'll secure cool Care Bear curtains (¢1000 per person, with private bath ¢1300). Larger groups can afford the luxury of **Cabinas Merielos** (tel./fax 653-0141), on the main road. Set among peaceful gardens, the spacious *cabinas* are impeccably clean and come with comfortable beds, private baths, and fans. Guests also have access to a communal kitchen (singles US$18; doubles US$23; triples US$30; 4-5 people US$40). Or try **Hotel Dolly,** located on the beach across from Cabinas Merielos. Tiny singles and nice doubles both have lots of light (¢1500 per person, with bath ¢2500-¢3000).

The simple, friendly soda-like **Frutas Tropicales,** 500m down the main road, makes great pancakes (¢350), steak sandwiches (¢550), tropical (fruit/veggie mix) salad (¢800), and casados (¢980); open daily 7am-9pm. Ravenous surfers rave about **Pizzeria Portofino,** 50m up the main road, which has great pizza (¢1000-1200 for a medium) and excellent pastas (¢800-¢1000); open daily 11am-10pm.

Sights and Entertainment Iguana Surf (tel./fax 654-4019), located up the first road off the main road (take a right at intersection), has a good selection of high-quality kayaks (US$35 per day), surfboards (US$10 per half-day), and snorkeling gear (US$5 per half-day). They also offer personal surfing lessons (US$20 per hr.; you can keep the board for 3hr. to practice) and guided kayaking, sailing, and snorkeling tours (US$25-45; bikes US$17 per day; open daily 8am-6pm). **Hotel Captain Suiza** (tel. 680-0853), 400m down the beach past the end of the main road, rents **horses** (US$20 for the first hr., US$10 each additional hr.). **Surfers** can head north to the Tamarindo estuary or to popular **Playa Grande,** a flat beach that often has the only good waves around. Playa Grande recently became part of **Las Baulas National Park,** as it is a nesting site for the leatherback turtle *(baula).* These aquatic reptiles can be longer than 1.5m and heavier than 900 lbs.; they lay most of their eggs in the winter.

If you're in drinking mode, head down to the end of the main road and check out the scene in the various **bars.** Tamarindo is also famous for its **"roaming disco."** Ask around for tonight's location. Or head to *gringo*-run **Cantina las Olas** next to Iguana surf, home of the town's only pool table (open from 6pm 'till the excitement dies).

▓ Playa Sámara

Samsara is the Buddhist name for the world of suffering that precedes nirvanic eternity. Playa Sámara, 29km south of Nicoya, proves what an incredible difference one letter and an accent can make. Virtually undiscovered by *gringos,* Sámara's calm, clear, shallow waters and seemingly endless white-sand shore are a national treasure. It's a popular vacation spot for locals; even ex-President and Nobel laureate Oscar Arias Sánchez has a beach house here. Sámara is the perfect place for simple pleasures like taking a romantic stroll, basking in the sun in solitude, or snorkeling off the rocks of a tree-covered island to the east. At the risk of going a bit overboard, it may very well be Nirvana itself.

Buses stop on the main road to the beach, in front of Cabinas Comedor Arenas, and leave daily for **San José** (Mon.-Sat. 4am, Sun. 1pm, 6hr.) and for **Nicoya** (Mon.-Sat. 5, 6:30am, 1:30, and 4:30pm, Sun. 6:30am and 4:30pm, 1½hr., ¢240). Call for a **taxi** at 686-6776 or 685-5634. **Pulpería Mileth,** at the end of the main road to the beach, is a general store (open daily 7am-noon and 1-8pm). The closest **hospital** and **pharmacy** are in Nicoya, as is the only available **Red Cross** (tel. 685-5458). The **police** station is right across the street from the bus stop (tel. 117). The **post office** has *lista de correos* and **telegram** service (open Mon.-Fri. 7:30-11:30am and 1:30-5:30pm). The **postal code** is 5235. **Public telephones** can be found at Pulpería Mileth, across from the police station (open daily 7am-noon and 1pm-8pm, Sun. until 5pm).

The best cabins for the budget traveler may be those just built by the owner of **Camping Cocos.** Off the main road, take the last left before the beach, and walk 250m. Look for "Apart. Acvareo." With huge kitchens and a pristine communal bathroom, these new 4-room cabins are quite a steal (US $30; sleeps 4-6 people). Twenty-five meters away is their camping area, with a beautiful view and wonderful people. The communal facilities are decent (¢500 per person). Ask about the new wood-paneled, clean rooms at **"El Ranchito de Angela"** (¢1500 per person); try for the cool loft, which Angela designed especially for asthmatics. Friendly and warm, she'll also cook you a yummy breakfast (¢500). **Cabinas Arenas,** on the main road to the beach, has bare cement floors, but also features wood ceilings, quilted beds, and spotless private bathrooms (¢2500 per person, low season ¢1500). Next door, **Cabinas Magaly** is a bit grimier and more cramped, but the doors have strong locks (¢1200 per person, low season ¢1000). Dining options do not abound in Sámara. Sweep aside the hanging palms as you enter **Rest/Bar Colochos**, about 150m up the main road. With wooden tables, a garden-like backdrop, and friendly service, this place is great—the food's not bad either (seafood soup ¢700, breaded fish filet ¢700, rice with shrimp ¢800, curried chicken ¢950; open daily 11am-10pm). For those too lazy to walk far from the beach, **Soda Sol y Mar** is right at the entrance and offers good food at typical prices (*casados* ¢600, sandwiches ¢250-350, chicken burger ¢300, rice with seafood ¢800; open Mon.-Sat. 7am-9pm, Sun. 7am-4pm).

■ Montezuma

Montezuma's reputation as an irreproachably hippie and tie-dyed colony of vegans is not entirely incorrect. Some travelers might be put off by the fact that they hear more English than Spanish on the streets, but as a kind, green buddy explains, it's a "community of international harmony." And it's not much of a challenge to live the pleasant life in a place like this. A jewel of a spot, carefully set in the southern tip of the Península Nicoya, Montezuma's rocky coast is interspersed with choice beaches for swimming. While the area lacks the endless sand of other beaches, it compensates with spectacular aesthetic pleasures—powerful waves smashing into the shore, warm emerald-green water, and foaming surf that cascades over jagged black rock. Needless to say, Montezuma has a way of sedating even the most frazzled traveler. For those who simply can't sit still, the surrounding area is ideal for hiking and nature-watching. Montezuma is a scant 11km from the original Costa Rican nature reserve, **Cabo Blanco**. The park's expansive green forest—and the monkeys, pumas, and armadillos that thrive in it—are protected by many regulations. As if diverse fauna weren't enough, **Río Lajas**, a 1 km hike from town, sprouts three playful waterfalls, each filling a pool fit for swimming, diving, or sedate appreciation.

Getting There The best way to reach Montezuma is to catch a **ferry** departing from the dock behind the market in Puntarenas (6:15, 11am, and 3pm, 1½hr., ¢320). Be sure to board the ferry bound for Paquera, *not* Playa Naranjo, because there is no way to get directly from Playa Naranjo to Paquera, except by way of a ¢4000 taxi. Once the boat arrives in Paquera, a "Turismo" **bus** will take visitors to Montezuma. Buses leave Puerto Paquera at approximately 7:30am, 12:30, and 4:30pm (2hr., ¢550). The bus passes through Paquera and Cóbano before reaching Montezuma.

If you are coming from other beaches on the Península Nicoya, take one of the buses headed for San José, get off at Barranca, and change there to Puntarenas, where you can catch the 6, 11am, or 3pm ferry to Paquera. It may seem longer on the map, but it's infinitely faster than any route down the Península—even with the best of planning and the best of luck, you still can't get past Playa Naranjo without a transfer or three. However, if you plan on busing this way, you'll want to bus to Playa Naranjo from Nicoya (leaves daily at 5:15am and 1pm, 2hr., ¢300), ferry from Playa Naranjo to Puntarenas (daily at 5, 8:50am, 12:50, 5, and 9pm, 1hr., ¢375), and *then* ferry from Puntarenas to Paqueras, where a bus will take you to Montezuma (see above). The whole trip could take a good eight hours. The road between Playa Naranjo and Paquera is extremely tough, and there are no buses or cars that attempt it. If you are hopelessly masochistic and just *must* go overland, you'll have to rely on one or more of the 15-ton trucks, which are the only vehicles that can traverse the 27km stretch. *Let's Go* does not recommend hitchhiking.

Buses bound for Puerto Paquera leave Montezuma three times daily (5:30, 10am, and 2pm, ¢550). The bus will connect with a ferry heading back to Puntarenas (8am, 12:30pm, and 5pm, ¢320).

Practical Information Forty-one kilometers west of **Paquera** and 7km south of **Cóbano**, Montezuma consists almost entirely of *pensiones* and *cabinas*. Local people and tourists alike are very ecologically conscious and development has been generally unobtrusive. **Tourist information** is available at **Monte Aventuras** (tel. 642-0050), in the center of town, across from Hotel Montezuma. In keeping with Montezuma's hip reputation, the office can provide information on yoga classes, as well as times and prices of guided tours around the area *and* an ultra-complete bus-and-ferry schedule for the entire Península Nicoya; **fax** service and **public phones** are also available (open Mon.-Fri. 8am-noon and 4-6pm, Sat. 8am-noon). Or try the tourist shop next to Hotel Montezuma, **Ecological Fund Tienda** (tel. 642-0058), where some English is spoken. It also serves as a **post office/pharmacy,** selling everything from stamps to condoms (open daily 8am-8pm). Next to Chico's bar is the **supermercado,** open daily 8:30am-9pm. About 50m east of the supermarket is a small and slightly overpriced *pulpería,* **Abastecedor Montezuma,** which is open daily 7am-9pm.

All other services are located in **Cóbano;** buses departing for Cóbano leave daily from in front of the Hotel Montezuma (5:30, 10am, and 2pm). Montezuma's **police** station (tel. 117), next door to the post office, is available 'round the clock to deal with emergencies, but not to speak English. Cóbano's **Banco Nacional** (tel. 642-0210), in the center of town, changes traveler's checks (open Mon.-Fri. 8:30am-3pm). The **post office,** three blocks from the center on the road to Paquera, posts a *lista de correos* and sends **telegrams** (open Mon.-Fri. 9am-noon and 2:30-5pm). The **postal code** is 5361. Medical aid is available at the **Clínica de Cóbano** (open daily 7am-5pm). The **public phone** (tel. 661-0566) is half a block toward Paquera (open daily 7am-noon and 1-8pm). There's another phone outside the supermarket.

Accommodations Hotel prices vary in and around Montezuma; depending on your degree of savvy, you can either sleep cheap or lose your shirt. You must accept that hot water is absent from budget lodgings (and pretty unnecessary anyway), but fans are key. **Camping** on the beach is free, popular, and relatively safe (though it's never a good idea to leave bags unattended), but no communal facilities are available. Some camping supplies are routinely available at the market. The rustic **Pensión Arenas,** west of Restaurant Montezuma, across the beach and behind Restaurant El Parque, provides a splendiferous view of the sea through encircling ranks of palms and sand. Had Papa Hemingway come to Montezuma, his nose would have led him here; earnest imitators can lounge in the hammocks. Rooms are tidy and freshly painted, bathrooms are communal but clean (¢1000 per person). **Pensión Jenny,** 50m down the road to Cabo Blanco and another 50m up the hill just before the soccer field, is a great deal. Set in a big old blue-and-white wooden house, the rooms receive lots of light and fresh air through the barn-like windows, and there's an ocean view from the balcony (¢1000 per person, communal bathrooms). **Cabinas el Tucán** (tel. 642-0284), just left of the road running by El Sano Banano and Monte Aventuras, offers shiny wood paneling and floors in cute-as-a-button bungalows. Tragically, many of its rooms' potential ocean views are obscured by treetops. Rooms are impeccably clean, have fans, and share communal bath facilities; guests can further explore that communal feeling by bonding on the porch's rocking chairs (semi-spacious rooms for one or two run ¢2000). **Hotel Montezuma** (tel./fax 642-0058) is next to the pizza shop in "downtown" Montezuma. Rooms include fans and some have private baths; back rooms enjoy ocean views. Less fortunate guests are sent to the overflow housing across the street, which has little going for it save the cool prints on the walls. Books and laundry service are available, and the staff also arranges tours. Some rooms are wheelchair-accessible (singles ¢1000, with bath ¢2000; doubles ¢2000, with bath ¢3500; ¢500 for each additional person; some rooms are wheelchair accessible).

Food Find vegetarian and health-conscious cuisine at **El Sano Banano** (tel. 642-0272), halfway up the hill past Monte Aventuras. Your purchase helps support the Montezuma Ecological Fund and prices are jacked accordingly. Daily specials range from ¢800-1200, and even the simplest dishes are uncannily delicious. The menu includes fruit shakes, frozen yogurt, veggie burgers, pita and hummus, and more served in a comfortable open-air environment. Come early for dinner—they show a movie every day at 7:30pm (free with ¢500 minimum order), and the place gets packed quickly (open daily 7am-9:30pm). At **Restaurante El Parque,** in front of Pensión Arenas, ocean breezes sigh across wooden tables shaded by thatched roofs.

Waves roll right up to the feet of patrons enjoying great breakfasts (¢400-600) and munching on chicken *casados* with mashed potatoes (¢600) or spaghetti gorgonzola (¢700; open daily 7am-9:30pm). The **Pizzeria Bakery,** next to Hotel Montezuma, is run by a friendly family which will whip you up anything from a monster pizza (¢2200) to an Egg McMuffin-like sandwich (¢600) to delicate Dutch pancakes (¢700; open daily 8am-11pm). **Restaurante Montezuma** (tel. 642-0258), next to Hotel Montezuma, is a popular spot along the beach to grab a reasonably priced bite to eat. Grab breakfast here, *tico* or *gringo* style, for ¢400-500; try their extensive lunch and dinner menu which includes pasta, Chinese food, and fish (sandwiches ¢300-500, filet *al ajillo* ¢950). The scenic upstairs terrace is open for dinner from 6-10pm, and after hours the place hosts a happening bar scene (open Tues.-Sun. 8am-10pm).

Sights and Entertainment The **beaches** of Montezuma are ideal for relaxed contemplation. Walking east you'll find sand stretches and a few clear spots where you can jump in the water and race enormous waves, but beware of the rocky bottom. The Ecological Fund Tienda rents boogie boards for ¢1000 per day. If you walk west toward Cabo Blanco, you will pass a *palapa* (a thatched-roof hut) and a small bridge; immediately after this point, the bridge to the waterfalls (*cataratas,* or cataracts) begins. Follow the riverbed for 15 minutes and the largest waterfall of the three looms before you. Some of the water is good for swimming; locals say that the basin is deep enough for diving from the surrounding rocks. Across from the waterfall, a steep and slippery trail leads up to the other two waterfalls, but it's probably best to find a *tico*-in-the-know to show you the way.

Horseback riding is a terrific way to see this gorgeous area. Go to the white, wooden information kiosk across the street from the Ecological Fund Tienda to ask about rentals. Luis Angel, who can be found by the *panadería,* and Armando Castro Cerdas, who usually hangs out at El Sano Banano, both rent horses for around US$25 per day. Roger also leads popular tours of the waterfalls and beaches; ask around for him. Monote Aventuras also offers any kind of fun you might have yearned for, from horseback riding (US$25) to snorkeling excursions (US$20-30, including lunch).

Begin the evening by catching a flick at the **Tucán Movie House,** in the Sano Banano Restaurant. The day's featured title—anything from *Pulp Fiction* to the Beatles' *Hard Days' Night*—is chalked onto a blackboard at the restaurant. Gain admission either by forking over ¢500 or by purchasing ¢500 worth of food or drink (this rule isn't always very stringently enforced). The show begins at 7:30pm—unless the power goes out. The place fills up quickly, so come early for a good seat. Romantic lanterns lead the way to **El Chiringuito,** across from the **Pulpería.** Salsa and merengue lovers the world over can learn a thing or two from the pros (open daily till 10-11pm). Later, at **Chico's Bar** (tel. 642-0258), 25m north of Hotel Montezuma, watch the population of Montezuma quadruple as the reggae beats people out of the woodwork. Chico's also serves food, at fairly inflated prices. Once Chico's gets old, stagger over to **Bar Montezuma,** on the other side of the hotel, where the restaurant dwells by day. It's basically the same thing, but the crowd is more up for drinking than for dancing. On the weekends, the **Kaliolin Disco,** 1km up the hill towards Cóbano, pumps out the dancy faves. Its floor is fairly small, so walk out back to the beach for some fresh air, or to get cozy with that special someone. The crowd is mostly young and *tico,* but they're more than happy to do anything they can to help the *gringas* have a good time. (Open Wed.-Sat. 11pm-3am, ¢200 cover on weeknights, ¢400 on weekends.) Free transportation leaves from in front of the Hotel Montezuma on Saturdays starting at 11pm. (Be sure to ask about it ahead of time, as *tico* schedules are flexible.)

■ Near Montezuma: Cabo Blanco Biological Reserve

An extremely bumpy dirt road runs 7km from Montezuma to the **Reserva Natural Absoluta Cabo Blanco.** Located at the southernmost tip of the peninsula, the reserve covers some 2900 acres of land that used to be cleared for fields and cattle. Amazingly, this forest is a product of only 30 years of regeneration.

Founded in 1963 through the efforts of the Swiss pioneer Niel Olaf Wessberg, this protected tract became the cornerstone of the extensive Costa Rican reserve system. Its unusual mix of evergreens and moist tropical forest has provided an environment of particular interest to tropical zoologists. Toucans, parakeets, pelicans, howler and white-faced monkeys, armadillos, pumas, boas, and iguanas have all been observed within its bounds. The rare or endangered species that inhabit the unusual forest are particularly interesting: the brocket deer, the crested guan (a large tropical forest bird resembling a turkey), and the jaguarundi (a slender, short-legged wildcat) have all found a haven in Cabo Blanco. A beautiful, 4.5km nature trail leads through the heart of the forest to rocky coastlines and deserted sandy beaches with heavenly warm, calm water. The return trip takes you on the same trail; it's a real hike, climbing, slipping down riverbeds, ducking under fallen palms, swimming in your own sweat, but it's a gorgeous one. Bug repellent and drinking water are absolutely essential for the five-hour round-trip hike through the hot and humid forest. Sandals do not an advisable means of locomotion make, as there are vicious ants along the trail and the path gets rather muddy during the rainy season. The ranger station at the entrance provides excellent, detailed information, as well as bathrooms and drinking water; there are also two potable streams along the trail (park open Wed.-Sun. 8am-4pm; admission US$6). To get to the reserve, arrange with **Monte Aventuras** (they suggest reserving a day in advance) to take one of the **4x4s** which depart at 8 and 9am from the Montezuma Hotel in Montezuma; vans return at 3 and 4pm (round-trip ¢1200).

If you want to spend more than an afternoon at the reserve, lodging is available in **Ancla de Oro** in **Cabuya,** a tiny village 2km from the reserve. Nature-lovers can sleep in thatched-roof cabins hoisted high above ground for ¢800 a night. Or they can go to **Sunshine,** where singles with refrigerators go for ¢1200.

GUANACASTE

Arid plains and dripping forests rub elbows in Guanacaste, Costa Rica's most geographically peculiar department. To the south, the region is green and wet, and the Monteverde Cloud Forest Reserve boasts a mind-boggling diversity of tropical species. Moving northwest, the ground becomes parched. This half of Guanacaste seems out of place in the tropics—it's African savannah minus the cheetahs. Dotted with cattle ranches, Guanacaste retains the independent spirit of its youthful days. Bumper stickers boast *"Costariccense por Nacimiento, Guanacatero Gracias a Dios"* (Costa Rican by birth, Guanacastan by the Grace of God). The department remained a self-ruled state until 1824, when it finally opted to join Costa Rica to the continued chagrin of Nicaragua. To celebrate that decision, Annexation Day, July 25, is celebrated with the daring combination of large quantities of alcohol and a few disgruntled bulls. Other reasons to celebrate the glory of the department are the wetlands of Palo Verde, the caves of Barra Honda, and Playas del Coco and Hermosa.

■ Fortuna

According to local legend, the little town of Fortuna got its name from the flotsam and jetsam that would float down the nearby river during floods—*indígena* cups, tools, and relics were scooped up by villagers as signs of good "fortune." A less exciting local legend attributes the name to the rich soil of the surrounding countryside. Fortunately, this modest community's luck doesn't seem to have run out yet, as it's situated only a few kilometers east of the spectacular Volcán Arenal and the relaxing hot springs of Tabacón. Faced with an influx of visitors, Fortuna is scrambling to build new hotels and has lost some of its small-town feel. The potential for wild adventures remains, especially in the natural playground nearby, which includes a

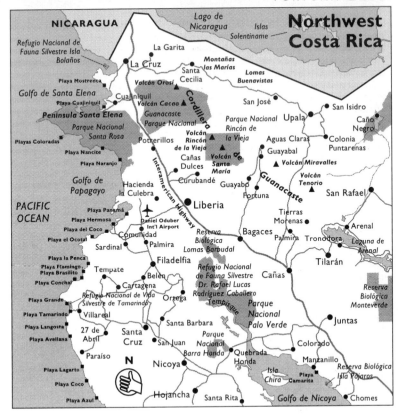

lava-spewing volcano, crashing waterfalls, river rapids, gentle pools for swimming, mazes of caves, and halcyon Laguna Arenal.

Orientation and Practical Information Fortuna is 33km northwest of Ciudad Quesada (San Carlos) and can be reached by bus from San José, Tilarán, or Arenal. The east to west road into Fortuna is the main street; most businesses line this thoroughfare. Immediately north is Fortuna's big soccer field, which serves as the town's center; the church respectfully faces the field's west side.

Todo el mundo has opened a **tour company** in Fortuna. All companies organize tours to nearby attractions (see **Near Fortuna,** below). In general, you're more likely to get professional treatment from the hotels and tour companies than from the guys who approach you on the street and offer cheaper prices. Also, in 1996 there were a number of incidents where street operators harassed women travelers once they had them alone; including one reported incident of rape. While most of these men are running safe tours, it is probably worth the extra money to go with an established company or hotel. Whatever you do, shop around before committing. **Exchange currency** or traveler's checks at the **Banco Nacional** (tel. 479-9022) in the northeast corner of the soccer field (open Mon.-Fri. 8:30am-3:45pm). Alternatively, head to **Banco Popular** (tel. 479-9422) on the main drag two blocks east of the park. They also have a **cash machine** (Plus system; open Mon.-Fri. 9am-3pm). There is a **public telephone** (tel. 479-9199) at Sunset Tours, just north of the soccer field's northeast corner, but the pay phones on the main drag are cheaper. **Buses** arrive and depart next to Restaurant El Jardín, one block east of the soccer field and travel directly to **San José** (12:40, 2:45pm, 4½hr., ¢350), which can also be easily reached from **Ciudad Quesada** (a.k.a.

San Carlos; 5 buses in the morning, 1½hr., ¢170). Buses also go to **Tilarán** (3hr.) via **Arenal** (8am and 4pm, 2hr., ¢270-300).

Rent **bikes** from **Repuestos y Accesorios Fortuna,** facing the gas station one block east of the soccer field (US$2 per hr., US$15 per day; open Mon.-Sat. 7am-5pm). The **pharmacy** (tel. 479-1721) is a block and a half north of Restaurant El Jardín (open Mon.-Sat. 7am-8pm). The **medical clinic** (tel. 479-9142) is a block and a half north of the pharmacy; some English is spoken (open Mon.-Thurs. 7am-4pm, Fri. 7am-3pm). The **police** (tel. 117) are a block and a half east of the soccer field on the main drag in a blue and white edifice. The main door is open daily from 7:30am to 9pm; ask at the window after hours. The **CORTEL office** (tel. 479-9178), next to the police station, has a *lista de correos* and a **fax** service (open Mon.-Fri. 7:30-11:30am and 1:30-5pm, Sat. 7:30-11:30am). The **postal code** is 4417.

Accommodations and Food It's easy to end up paying a lot of money for a hotel room in Fortuna; look hard, though, and you'll find some comfortable mid-to low-range options. **Cabinas el Bosque** (tel. 479-9365) wins the budget trophy, just behind the church. Locks are very temperamental—clockwise eventually will open your spare but clean room. The manager also promotes his inexpensive tour options (singles ¢700, with bath ¢1000; groups of 3 or more can get a discount). **Hotel Fortuna** (tel. 479-9197), conveniently located near the bus stop, has moderately-priced, adequate rooms. Luckily, there's no flotsam in these bathrooms, but the fans are barely functional. There's a deck upstairs with a great view of the volcano, and a restaurant downstairs that serves typical fare (breakfast ¢300-500, entrees ¢500-700). Fortuna also offers laundry service and various tours of the volcano and the waterfalls (singles ¢2000; doubles ¢3000). **Cabinas Charlie,** four blocks east of the park on the main drag, is a super-friendly, quiet, family-run alternative. Cheap rooms are spotless and have fans and semi-new mattresses. Their java is some of the best in town (singles ¢1000; prices go up in the high season).

For amazing breakfasts and some of the best vegetarian food around, try **Restaurante Vegetariano El Lirio y la Luna,** on the main drag across from the church. Granola, yogurt, omelettes (¢250-350), pancakes laden with bananas or pineapple (¢300), and dinner entrees (¢500) are all available. They bake all of their own solid wheat bread products (open daily 7am-7pm, but come too early or too late and you may not get served). For a tasty burger (¢800), head to tourist favorite **Restaurante Rancho la Cascada** (tel. 479-9145), under the massive thatched roof across from the northeast corner of the soccer field. Breakfast is ¢400-500; lunch and dinner are reasonably priced. Try the excellent fruit juices with milk (¢100; open daily 6am-midnight). **Restaurante Jardín** (tel. 479-9072), across from the gas station on the main street, is a popular place for whiling away the hours. Enjoy spaghetti (¢800), *lomito relleño* (¢900), ice cream, and beer as you watch ridiculous soaps on TV. The plate of the day (¢450) doesn't come with a drink, but ask for free garlic bread if it doesn't appear automatically (open daily 6:30am-11pm).

■ Near Fortuna

Everyone and their brother in Fortuna can connect you with nearby outdoor activities. Scout around tour offices, and consider creating your own tour, which ends up considerably cheaper.

RÍO AND CATARATA FORTUNA

The Río Fortuna is a medium-sized river that passes Fortuna a few kilometers to the south. Below one of the river's bridges, there's a perfect little **swimming hole,** complete with a vine swing and a cool **waterfall.**

To reach the river, follow signs to the waterfall posted near the south side of the church (it's the road to San Ramón). About 2km from Fortuna, the road crosses the river. About 50m before you reach the bridge, the well-marked road to the waterfall branches off to the right. The rest of the walk boasts several sublime views; look for the waterfall on the left after about an hour and a half. There is a small parking lot, and other facilities are under construction. Be prepared to pay the ¢500 entrance fee. Thanks to knotty roots along the trail, you can hike the steep, narrow path that leads to the bottom of the falls. While the pool right under the falls is dangerous for swimming, farther to the left there are a few calmer spots for cooling off. It takes one or two, sometimes muddy, hours to reach the falls on foot. Taxis can take you most of the way until the road gets too steep (about ¢600). Tours on horseback are available at Hotel Fortuna for US$15; the trip would also make for a fun bike ride.

VOLCÁN ARENAL

If you've ever wanted to pay Satan a visit, make a pilgrimage to Volcán Arenal. By day, the gigantic cone spouts smoke and roars with the din of falling rocks. By night, red-hot lava bursts from the top and trickles down the sides of the volcano's black walls. With good reason, the town of Fortuna is built on the side where lava doesn't flow, so there's only access on the eastern side. Unfortunately, the summit is often obscured by a thick cloud cover, especially during the rainy season. Keep your fingers crossed, because the shroud frequently lifts in the evening, just in time for a nighttime tour of the lava fields and hot springs. The volcano has been active since 1968, when an earthquake triggered an enormous eruption that killed many people. Since then, the volcano has erupted several times daily, occasionally falling silent like a sullen child. Climbing the volcano is dangerous and strongly discouraged; naïve tourists have been injured and killed.

Every night, groups of tourists venture out to the volcano, hoping that something dramatic will happen. To see your own hunk of oozing lava, catch one of the many volcano/hot springs tours that leave Fortuna every night. Hotel Montaña del Fuego is well-known for being a good viewpoint. Hotel Fortuna is especially proud of its guide William, who also leads "special" tours at 9pm that approach the lava with greater abandon (US$25). Hotel Fortuna also has a bus at 6pm (¢1200) that goes by the observation station at the National Park, then stops by the hot springs on the way home. Another option is to take a taxi for ¢1050 per carload to where the volcano and lava are visible, just not as close.

HOT SPRINGS

The **hot springs** of **Tabacón,** 10km west of Fortuna on the road to the volcano, are actually a river of hot water. There, you can submerge your troubles and sore muscles in a labyrinth of pools and waterfalls amid well-kept gardens, while you watch Volcán Arenal ooze its orange juices. One way to reach Tabacón is by a bus headed for Tilarán (see Fortuna, Practical Information, above). Some travelers resort to soliciting rides. Unfortunately, Tabacón Resort occupies prime real estate here; it has a restaurant, gardens, and fancy swimming pools, but charges about US$14 to get in. If you're feeling deeply decadent, opt for a full-hour massage (about US$20; open daily 10am-10pm). A cheaper place to enter is at **Río Tabacón,** across the street and down the hill. Here, you can find a comfy spot right in the river, or macerate in the shallow pools for only US$6 (open 10am-9:30pm). You can skip the entrance fee altogether by using any of the several unattended springs along the road; ask your bus or taxi driver, but be careful—these tend to be a little too shady at night.

CAVERNAS DE VENADO

While one river bubbles into hot springs, another is responsible for forging the network of caves in the town of Venado, northwest of Fortuna. The caves are open to visitors every day, and the property owners rent flashlights (¢200), helmets (¢50), and boots (¢150). Admission is ¢500; the total cost including equipment is ¢850. Each group receives a guide for the price, and it's a damn good thing, too. The labyrinth of caverns extends 2km underground through eight rooms and contains several waterfalls, freaky mineral formations, and—Holy *Murciélagos,* Batman!—lots of bats. If you take the tour, be prepared to get down and dirty. To evoke your birth, ask the guide to take you through the narrow, aptly named *baño* (bath). Much of the hike is actually along the underground river, so bring waterproof shoes or rent boots at the entrance, and come prepared to get thoroughly dampened and muddified. If you appreciate the guide's services, it's in good form to give a tip.

Many tour companies go to the caves, but if you can get to the town of Venado, there's no need. From Fortuna, take the road east for 7km until you reach El Tanque (Ciudad Quesada buses pass here). From there, Venado is about 15km northwest up the road. Buses pass frequently, and some say hitchhiking works. Taxis from Fortuna charge ¢7000 round-trip, including the wait while you wade.

LAGUNA DE ARENAL

Hydroelectric dams created **Laguna de Arenal,** but tourists have turned the lake into a fishing, boating, and windsurfing playground (no good swimming, though, because of all those submerged trees). For information on **fishing tours** in Laguna de Arenal, contact the tourist office or **Agencia Aventuras Arenal** in Fortuna (tel. 479-9133); fully equipped tours cost US$35 per hour, with a four hour minimum. You might also contact the well-outfitted Hotel Aurora in the town of Arenal. For windsurfing, you're better off heading to the resorts outside Tilarán.

CAÑO NEGRO WILDLIFE REFUGE

This area along the Río Frío, which flows directly to the Nicaraguan border near Los Chiles, one and a half hours north of Fortuna, is one of Costa Rica's principal breeding grounds for wetland birds, including three types of egrets, two species of stork, and numerous herons and ducks. Cruises along the river also yield sightings of howler monkeys, spider monkeys, white-faced capuchins, three-toed sloths, caimans, and Jesus Christ lizards. Fortuna tour companies offer costly daytrips, including transportation, lunch, and eagle-eyed guides. Aventuras Arenal (see above) takes tourists for US$40 per person, leaving at 7am and returning around 4:30pm.

■ Arenal

And you thought Fortuna was small. The village of Arenal is diminutive to the extreme, but still attracts a number of travelers set on exploring Laguna Arenal and its environs. Fortuna is better located for hopping off to most places, but Arenal hugs the lake's shore and is a great place to get information.

The entire village is centered around the loop formed by the road that encloses the church and soccer field. This loop is connected to the highway by Arenal's 100m main street. When it's open, **Stefanie's Centro de Informacion Turistica** (tel. 694-4132; fax 694-4025), where the main street splits to the town loop, is the place for **tourist information,** kayak rentals, or Spanish lessons. Owner Stefanie is German, but also speaks English and Spanish; her tours cost US$20-80. The tour to **Volcán Tenorio** is not available in Fortuna, so snag it here. **Banco Nacional** sitting lonely on the part of the loop farthest from the church (tel. 694-4122; fax 694-4298) changes traveler's checks and gives cash advances on Visa cards (open Mon.-Fri. 8:30am-3:45pm). **Buses** go to **Tilarán** (6 per day, 1hr., ¢150) and **Fortuna** (8am and 1:30pm, 2hr., ¢250). The **police** are nearby, on the right coming from the highway. The bus lets off halfway up this street, in front of Restaurante Lajas. Across the street from the bus stop is **Expendid Coopeconpro,** a small supermarket where they charge ¢50 for non-customer toilet use. The **post** and **telegram office** is next to the police (open Mon.-Sat. 7:30-11:30am and 1-4:30pm). Orientation couldn't be easier—take a five-minute walk around the loop and main street, and you've seen all of Arenal.

Arenal's few **hotels** and **restaurants** are certainly adequate. The cheapest place in town is the family-run **Cabinas Rodriguez** (tel. 664-4237). Rooms are pretty small but clean, and all have fans (¢1200 per person, with private bath ¢1500). The fancy **Aurora Inn** (tel. 694-4245; fax 694-4246) next door has modern rooms with fans, private baths, and beautiful hardwood floors. You can watch volcanic fireworks from the deck on clear nights; cloudy nights, bathe in the pool (singles US$25; doubles US$30; with breakfast add US$5). The Inn is one of the best outfitted places for fishing on Lake Arenal. A guide, a boat, equipment, and sack lunches for the day cost US$60, split by however many fit on the boat. **Hotel Restaurante Lajas,** on the main street where the bus lets off, is satisfactory in its own right, and newly remodeled. Rooms are clean, the deck out back has a nice view, and the restaurant lets fly with zippy food (pancake breakfast ¢450; ¢1300 per person, with private bath ¢1600). **Bar y Restaurante Lake View Arenal,** next to Aurora on the lake side of the town loop, serves food, including meat and rice dishes (¢600-700; open daily 8am-9pm). **Stephanie's** also serves *leckeres deutsches Essen; guten Appetit!* (Open Mon.-Sat. 9am-9pm.)

■ Tilarán

Til-*air*-án might be more like it—about the only travelers who don't breeze through this gusty little town are windsurfers preparing to catch air on Laguna Arenal. For everyone else, Tilarán makes a convenient stopover in the complex web of bus connections from Fortuna to the Pacific Coast. Tilarán's streets have no names, and its buildings have no numbers—the thoroughfares are just anonymous paved surfaces. If you accidentally dropped your astrolabe into the fumaroles of Volcán Arenal, the Catholic church serves as an effective landmark—Tilarán's most sacred structure sits east of the park with a high clock tower.

Practical Information For information on fishing or waterskiing excursions to Lake Arenal, try **Hotel and Restaurant Mary** (tel. 695-5758 or 695-5479) on the park's south side. **Banco Nacional** (tel. 695-5028), across from the southwest corner of the park, changes traveler's checks and gives cash advances on Visa cards (open Mon.-Fri. 9am-3pm). **Banco de Costa Rica** (tel. 695-5117), one block east of the park's northeast corner, provides the same services (open Mon.-Fri. 8:30am-3pm). For free collect phone calls, try **Agencia ICE** (tel. 695-5166), on the second floor of the Edificio Municipal, half a block west of the plaza and next to the bus station (open Mon.-Fri. 8am-3:30pm). **Pay phones** are on the west and south sides of the park.

  Buses leave half a block west from the park's northwest corner and serve: **San José** (7, 7:45am, 2, and 4:55pm, 3½hr., ¢450); **Puntarenas** (6am and 1pm); **Ciudad Quesada/San Carlos** (7am and 12:30pm; passes **Fortuna** and **Arenal**); **Guatuso** (noon); **Arenal** (10am and 4:30pm, 3hr., ¢300); and **Cañas** (6 per day, ¢85; to **Monteverde** at 12:30pm only). Buses go from Cañas to **Liberia** all day. For **medical assistance,** call the **Red Cross** (tel. 695-5256; **emergency** tel. 128), one block east of Banco de Costa Rica (open 24hr). **Farmacia Tilarán** (tel. 695-5064) is on the south side of the park next to Restaurant Mary and also sells homeopathic medicine (open Mon.-Sat. 7am-8:30pm, Sun. 7am-2pm). Though they speak no English, the **police** (tel. 695-5001), half a block west of the bus station, answer the phone 24 hr. Tilarán's **CORTEL office** (tel. 695-5387) is one block north and one and a half blocks east of the park's northeast corner. **Telegrams** and **faxes** can be sent from the post office (open Mon.-Fri. 7:30am-5:30pm).

Accommodations and Food **Hotel Mary** (tel. 695-5479 or 695-5758) on the south side of the park, has a funny sign in the lobby exhorting guests to "Make Mary." Once you see the prices, "Make Mary rich" might seem more appropriate. You pay dearly for the wall-to-wall carpeting upstairs. Light sleepers beware—there is a disco next door. Hot water and laundry services are available (singles ¢1850, with bath ¢2700; doubles ¢2500, with bath ¢3200). **Hotel Tilarán** (tel. 695-5043), on the west side of the park, is giving Mary a run for her money. It has similarly spotless rooms, a lobby cable TV, and an attached restaurant. The price makes the difference (singles ¢1200, with bath ¢1500). **Cabinas El Sueño** (tel. 695-5347) dreams half a block north of the park's northeast corner, on the second story. All rooms with large private baths (singles ¢1800; doubles ¢2900).

Besides the usual slew de *sodas,* Tilarán offers the two **restaurants** connected to **Hotels Mary** and **Tilarán.** Menus are similar (and in English), but Tilarán comes through with better prices. **La Carreta,** facing the east side of the church, has two carts outside (hence the name). Inside you'll find an American cook who makes a good pizza (¢700 and up) and spaghetti (¢1300 and up). Tourist information is proffered as well.

■ Cañas

Cañas is a small, sweltering town in the middle of the extensive farmland of Guanacaste. Don't worry if you don't see more of the town than the bus station; tourists usually only pass through here traveling between the Pacific Coast and Volcán Arenal. The town has access to Parque Nacional Palo Verde, but so does more hospitable Liberia. If you're looking for a river tour in or near Palo Verde, contact **Safari Corobici** (tel./fax 669-1091), 4km north of Cañas on the Interamerican Highway.

The unmarked **tourist office** (tel. 669-1515) is nestled between the southwest corner of the stadium and the **Plaza de Toros** on the southwest corner of the stadium, two blocks north and one and a half blocks west of the park on the highway. The office provides useful information, but still can't tell you anything interesting about Cañas (officially open Mon.-Fri. 8am-noon and 1-4pm, Sat. 8am-noon). The manager of **Pizza Buono** offers travel information as well—his knowledge isn't as extensive, but at least you know he'll be open for dinner. **Banco Nacional** (tel. 669-0160; fax 669-0027) is on the northeast corner of the park. They also have a cash machine on their west side, but it is sporadically locked (open Mon.-Fri. 8:30am-3:45pm). **Banco de Costa Rica** (tel. 669-0066) also changes the bills (open Mon.-Fri. 8:30am-3pm). **Phone calls** can be made from pay phones on the south of the park or outside of **ICE** (tel. 669-0166), one block south of the park's southeast corner. The Cañas **bus station** is five blocks north of the park, a couple of blocks east of the Interamerican Highway. **Buses** run to: **San José** (Tues.-Thurs. and Sat. 6 per day; Mon. 7 per day, Fri. and Sun. at 5:15pm); **Tilarán** (6, 9, 10:30am, noon, 1:45, 3:30, and 5:30pm; 45min.; ¢84); **Liberia** (7 per day, ¢200); **Puntarenas** (7 per day, ¢300); **Upala** (5 per day); and **Bebedero** (6 per day). **Farmacia Achio** (tel. 669-0028) is on the south side of the park (open Mon.-Sat. 8am-8pm, Sun. 8am-noon). **Supermercado Coopecontro** is one and a half blocks north of the northwest corner of the park (open daily 8:30am-7pm). For **medical emergencies,** call 24 hr. and reach **Dr. Juan Chen** (tel. 669-0471 or 669-0139) whose clinic is one block north of the park's northwest corner (open Mon.-Fri. 8am-noon and 2-6pm, Sat. 8am-noon). Reach the **hospital** at tel. 669-0069. The **COR-TEL post office** (tel./fax 669-0309) sits one block north and two blocks west of the park's northwest corner. **Fax** service also available (open Mon.-Fri. 7:30am-5:30pm).

Hotels in Cañas are either cheap-and-it-shows or swish-swank-and-costly. The best in the budget range may be **Hotel El Parque,** conveniently located on the south side of the park, with spotless rooms, communal bathrooms, and a balcony that will leave you wondering why they only charge ¢800 per person; maybe because of the short, hard beds. **Hotel Guillen** (tel. 669-0070), beside Hotel El Parque, has all the basics, and that's about it. Two out of three toilets have seats; try your luck. All rooms have tiny fans, (singles ¢800, a room off the balcony overlooking the park with private bath ¢1000). The **Gran Hotel** is nothing grand. Half a block north of the northwest corner of the park, it's similar to Guillen in most respects, including price (¢800 per person). The ritzy places in town are **Hotel Cañas** and **Nuevo Hotel Cañas.** The old one (tel. 669-0039) is a block north of the park's northwest corner, and offers singles for around ¢2300, and doubles for around ¢3500. The new one's prices are four times that, but you get pool privileges.

Cañas has a few good places to eat. For general cuisine, there's **Hotel Cañas** (see above), where breakfast runs from ¢500-600, meat plates about ¢950, and gargantuan portions of fried rice for a mere ¢750. **Buona Pizza** serves good pizza three blocks north of the park, half a block in from either corner. Green and red table cloths, parmesan shakers, and big glasses of *refrescos* evoke Little Italy in the summer time.

A small (plenty for one person) pizza costs ¢750-850, a large costs ¢2000-2200. They serve other stuff, too (open Tues.-Thurs. 4-10pm, Fri.-Sun. noon-midnight). If you're the only customer, they'll give you the remote control and let you play ruler of the universe for the duration of your meal. But if it's Chinese you crave, look to the restaurants to the north of the park's west side. Servings are generally large and cheap. For what it's worth, Restaurant **Lei Tu** (Brute?) is the most popular and cheapest— half block west of the park's northwest corner.

■ Near Cañas: Parque Nacional Palo Verde

P.N. Palo Verde is one of the most important wetland conservation areas in Central America. On the northwest corner of the Gulf of Nicoya, the park is bordered on the west by the wide, slow (and therefore brown) **Río Tempisque** and on the east by the **Río Bebedero.** Poor drainage subjects the area to seasonal floods that create a wide array of habitats, including lowland mangroves, murky everglades, and rolling forests.

Four rocky **miradores**, or lookout points, from the tops of limestone hills comprise one of the highlights of the park; climb them for spectacular views of the Río Tempisque slowly snaking its way to the gulf. **Mirador Guayacan** can be accessed from the Palo Verde Ranger Station. The view from the top is a satisfying reward for the 30-minute hike through sticky, bug-infested forest. Aside from the nasty mosquitoes, you may run into monkeys, agouti, deer, and various birds. Signs are few and far between and trails are poorly marked, so it's often necessary to rely on divine intervention and inspiration. The following distances may be useful: from the highway to the park entrance is 30km, from there to Mirador La Roca is 12km, with another 15km to Puesto Catalina. From Mirador La Roca to Puerta Chamorro is 6km. *Let's Go* does not recommend hitchhiking, though some find that it is best to catch a ride to Mirador La Roca; once there, everything is relatively close.

The park has two ranger stations that permit camping (Puesto Palo Verde and Puesto Catalina). From the park entrance, a road leads 6km into the park and then splits. One road leads west 9km to Puesto Catalina. The roads are unpaved and often nasty during the rainy season. A bilingual map of the park is sold for ¢300 at the park entrance (where you pay your entrance fee in US dollars), which is reached via a 28km dirt road from the town of **Bagaces,** itself about 25km from both Cañas and Liberia on the Interamerican Highway. Buses running between Cañas and Liberia can drop you off at Bagaces, and direct Bagaces buses run as well. Unfortunately, there is no public transportation between Bagaces and the park entrance, although a taxi might be an expensive option. If you are hitching, it is wise to find out when other people are leaving, as traffic within the park is erratic. The last bus from Bagaces to Cañas leaves at around 7:30pm.

The trail to **Mirador La Roca** starts about one kilometers east of the biological station, which lies between **Puesto Palo Verde** and the turnoff from the park entrance. It takes a mere 10 minutes to hike the trail, but the view isn't quite as good as from Guayacan (above). Two *miradores* can also be accessed from **Puesto Catalina** in the east of the park. For a closer look at the Laguna Palo Verde, around which the park is centered, visit the birdwatching tower near the biological station, marked by an obscure sign off the left side of the road. Approach quietly and you may catch an alligator or two sunning nearby. A boat ride to **Bird Island** (Isla de Pajaros), which lies in the Río Tempisque on the edge of the park, is another possibility. **Chalalo,** a park ranger who lives at the Puesto Palo Verde, supposedly takes people on a trip for ¢4000-8000. Try contacting the **Tempisque Conservation Area** (tel. 671-1290) in Bagaces for more info.

■ Liberia

A rough-and-ready working-class town, Liberia typifies the independent spirit of Guanacaste, the arid, cattle-ranching region of which it is the capital. The area around Liberia is usually dry and desolate, but Pacific beaches offer a tempting antidote to the oppressive heat, luring windsurfers and beach bums to their cool waters. Liberia itself is pleasant; plenty of services are available, and it's a good base from which to explore nearby beaches and national parks, including the **Rincón de la Vieja, Guanacaste** and **Santa Rosa National Parks.** These parks contain thermal springs, waterfalls, beautiful nature walks, and volcanos. Liberia is also a little over an hour south of the border, making it a convenient stop for those heading north to or south from Nicaragua.

ORIENTATION AND PRACTICAL INFORMATION

The city is built on a regular grid, with the east to west **Avenida Central** acting as the southern border and the north to south **Calle Central** broken in half by the park. Odd-numbered *avenidas* are north of Avenida Central, even-numbered ones south. Odd-numbered *calles* spread east of Calle Central, even-numbered *calles* west. However, addresses are almost always given with respect to major landmarks and the **Parque Central.** The most important landmarks are the church on the east side of the Parque Central, **La Gobernación** (the government palace) on its southeast corner, and **Banco de Costa Rica** on the park's northeast corner. **Buses** drop you off at a covered station northwest of town. For a quick orientation, the **market** stands just across the street to the east. The Parque Central (officially known as **Parque Ruiz**) is three blocks south and four blocks east of the bus station.

Tourist Office: 3 blocks south and 1 block east of the park's southeast corner; follow the signs from the south side of the plaza. If they're there, the competent staff can answer most questions. Open (officially) Mon.-Sat. 8am-noon and 1-4pm. **Info-Cen-Tur** (get it?) is on the second floor of the small mall beside the movie theater. Run by eager tourism students ready to give you lots of "discounts" to expensive travel options. Open (also officially) daily 9am-5pm.

Currency Exchange: Banco Nacional (tel. 666-0996), 3 blocks west of Parque Central's southwest corner, changes traveler's checks. Open Mon.-Fri. 8:30am-3:45pm. **Banco de Costa Rica** (tel. 01-48), on the park's northeast corner, also changes cash and traveler's checks. Open Mon.-Fri. 8:30am-3pm. **Servicambios,** at the edge of the bus station, has better hours: Mon.-Fri. 7:30am-noon and 1:30-5pm, Sat. 7:30am-noon.

Telephones: Public phones located around Parque Central. **ICE** (tel. 666-0166 or 666-2255; fax 666-2019), 2 blocks west and 50m south of the park's southwest corner, also has **fax** services. Open Mon.-Fri. 7:30am-5pm and Sat. 8am-noon.

Buses: Depart 3 blocks north, 4 blocks west of Parque Central, opposite the market, to: **Playa del Coco** (6 per day, 5:30am-6:15pm, 40min., ¢225); **Playa Hermosa** and **Playa Panama** (11:30am and 7pm, 1hr., ¢200); **Puntarenas** (5, 8:30, 10, 11:15am, and 3:15pm, ¢300); **San José** (6, 6:30, 9am, 12:15, and 5pm); **Peñas Blancas** via **La Cruz** (8 per day, 1¼hr., ¢300); **Cañas Dulces** (6am, noon, and 4:30pm); **Bagaces** (5:45am, 1:30, and 4:30pm, ¢150); **Cañas** (5:45am, 1:30, and 4:30pm, ¢200); and **Filadelfia, Santa Cruz,** and **Nicoya** (every hr., 5am-8pm, ¢250).

Car Rental: Sol Rent-a-Car, (tel. 666-2222; fax 666-2898; email sol@asst-card.co.cr; http://www.asstcard.co.cr/GUIA/HOMP/SOL.htm) on the Interamerican Highway, 6 blocks west of the park, has only this office in Liberia but will pick up or drop off your car anywhere in the country for a fee. Rents out Tercels, 4x4 Sidekicks, and minivans. Open Mon.-Fri. 8am-5:30pm, Sat.-Sun. 8am-5pm. **Toyota Rent-a-Car** (tel. 666-0016) across the highway rents out Toyota cars only, for some obscure reason. Prices appear about the same as its Sol-mate; more variety in sedans and more expensive 4-wheel drive vehicles, which are almost necessary on National Park roads. Open Mon.-Sat. 8am-5pm, Sun. 8am-1pm.

Market: 4 blocks west and 3 blocks north of Parque Central, across from the central bus station. Open daily 8am-6pm.

Supermarket: CoopConPro (tel. 666-1416), ½ block east of the park's southwest corner. Big new green, yellow, and white building. Open Mon.-Sat. 8am-9pm, Sun. 9am-6pm.

Laundry: Hotel Liberia (see Accommodations) has a washing machine. ¢900 for washing 9lb. or under; the dryer was broken in summer '97. **Lavanderia Egaliz,**

near the Iglesia Hermita 5 blocks east of the park, suds the duds Mon.-Fri. 8am-5pm, Sat. 8am-noon.

Pharmacy: Farmacia Liberia #2 (tel. 666-0747), facing the park's northern side. Open Mon.-Sat. 8am-8pm, Sun 8am-noon. **Farmacia Santa Margarita** (tel. 666-1665), 1 block north from the park's northeast corner. Open Mon.-Sat. 8am-8pm, Sun. 8am-noon.

Emergency: Contact the **Red Cross** (tel. 666-0994), 2 blocks east of La Escuela Enseñanza Especial.

Hospital: Dr. Enrique Baltodano can be reached at 666-0011.

Police: (tel. 117), in a large white and red, fortressy building at the northwest corner of the park.

Post Office Cortel: (tel. 666-0359 or 666-1649), 3 blocks west and 1 block north of the park. **Telegraph, fax,** and *lista de correos*. Open Mon.-Fri. 7:30am-5:30pm.

Postal Code: 5000.

ACCOMMODATIONS AND FOOD

A fair number of moderately-priced lodging options exist in Liberia. While the dirt-cheap range has been eliminated, many in the respectable-yet-inexpensive area still exist. Rates are listed for off-season—remember they can easily increase 25% December-April.

La Posada del Tope (tel. 385-2383), 1½ blocks south of the park's southeast corner, advertises itself as a hostel, hotel, bed, and breakfast—whatever you call it, its chipper staff keeps the six roomy rooms neat and bright. A kitchen is available for guest use (¢1200 per person). **Hotel Liberia** (tel. 666-0161), a block north of La Posada, has a Beirut-style courtyard as old rooms are demolished and new ones are built. The best aspects of the hotel are private baths in every room—and an old room runs for just ¢1200 per person (new ones ¢1700 per person). Another entrant into the ¢1200 per person battle is **Hospedaje Real Chorotega,** three blocks south of the park's southwest corner. Green on the outside, and cream on the inside, its location is a bonus as it is next door to Boca Bar Baula Real (see Food below). **Hotel Guanacaste** (tel. 666-6085; fax 666-2287), four blocks west of the park's northwest corner (or 1 block south of the bus station and ¼ block west), is a Hostelling International location, but the cheapest rooms start at ¢1500, and that's for members. The rooms are clean and modern, however, and the new lobby sports a huge cable TV. Regular rooms are ¢2300 for singles, ¢3400 for doubles.

Liberia has plenty o' good little restaurants and *sodas*. **Pizza Pronto**, two blocks south and one east of Parque Central, proffers a cheezy Italian remedy for those rice-and-beans blues. The smoky odor of adobe-baked pizzas floats through the classy wooden interior, right onto the map-top tables. Ahhh, Costa Rica—where else can you sit in a bar with the guys intently watching a documentary on *ballenas azules* (blue whales)? Medium Supreme serves two (¢1500). Pasta runs ¢1000-1100 (open daily noon-10:30pm). **Jardín de Azucar,** one block north of the northeast corner of the park, offers a cheap cafeteria buffet that includes some vegetarian dishes. The heavily laden "plate of the day" comes with a drink (¢500), or have the cheeseburger plate (with fries and a Coke ¢600; open daily 7am-9pm). For Chinese chow, take your pick from the thousand or so joints in town, most of which are east of Calle Central. **La Baula Real,** two blocks south of the southwest corner of the park, is a nice little bar and restaurant with garden dining. Beer on tap is served with a free *boca* (a little plate of scrumptious appetizers). A large pitcher goes for ¢1200, a small one for ¢900 (open Tues.-Fri. 2pm-midnight, Sat. noon-midnight, Sun. 11am-midnight). **Pop's,** across from the southwest corner of the park, has yummy shakes and ice cream (¢200) to lick as you stroll around the park (open daily 10am-10pm).

SIGHTS AND ENTERTAINMENT

The **Museo de Arte Religioso,** located in a bamboo hut behind Iglesia Hermita, five blocks east of the church, is run by an elderly woman who lives around the corner, so hours vary (free). At night, try **Discoteque Kuru,** across from the gas station (open daily 8pm-5am, sometimes earlier, depending on the size of the crowd; ¢500; women get in free on Thurs.). **Cine Olimpia,** one block north of the park's northeast corner, shows stale movies daily at 8pm (¢400).

■ Near Liberia

It stands to reason that there's nothing to do in Liberia proper; who would possibly seek entertainment in town when boundless opportunities await nearby? To find out more about nearby Santa Rosa, Guanacaste, and Rincón de la Vieja National Parks, contact the main administrative office for the **Guanacaste Conservation Area,** located in the Santa Rosa National Park (tel. 695-5598), off the Interamerican Highway 32km north of Liberia. To reach Santa Rosa from Liberia, hop on a Frontera-bound bus and request the Santa Rosa stop (¢200). Here sits a guard house with information (tons of helpful pamphlets and a map ¢100-250), where foreigners must pay a US$6 entrance fee. From the guard house to the administrative buildings, La Casona, and the first campground is a not-so-strenuous, 7km stroll. *Let's Go* does not recommend hitchhiking, though rides are apparently easy to snag. The administrative buildings have lodging for US$19.50 per night if there is room. Meals cost about US$5.15. October and November are the best times to catch turtles laying eggs on the beach. Be sure to check the bus schedule posted inside the guard house, indicating the times at which the bus actually passes the entrance on the way to Liberia (last one 6:15ish).

SANTA ROSA NATIONAL PARK

Santa Rosa is one of the few Costa Rican national parks important for its historical significance as well as its ecology and natural beauty. It was here that Costa Rican forces under the command of President Juan Rafael Mora Porras defeated troops sent south from Nicaragua by **William Walker** (see William Walker, What a Killer, p. 271). The alacritous battle of March 20, 1856 lasted only 14 minutes. Ninety-nine years later, Costa Rican exiles crossed the border from Nicaragua and were similarly summarily defended. A **monument** to these battles provides a breath-taking—literally, when the winds are gusting—view of the surrounding valleys and mountains.

The *hacienda* where the battle took place has been converted into a museum, the **Casona de Santa Rosa,** which presents info on the history of the battle, of Costa Rican daily life through the ages, and the ecology of the park (open daily 9am-5pm). The park, which is home to some 115 species of mammals, 250 species of birds, and 100 species of amphibians and reptiles, is primarily tropical dry forest. Perhaps its most alluring sections are the isolated beaches that serve as nesting sites for three different species of sea turtle, including the endangered **Olive Ridley turtle.** Unfortunately, the beaches are accessible only by a 12km dirt road that leaves from the administrative area. The road is often impassable by car during the wet season, so you should count on walking. About halfway to the beach, a couple of trails branch off the road to *miradores* (scenic lookouts), both of which lie about 1km from the road. The first trail, **Sendero Los Patos,** branches to the right, as does the second, **Mirador Valle Naranjo,** about 1km later.

The second half of the road descends into a valley full of majestic trees and exotic animals; you might see (or hear) howler monkeys, white-faced monkeys, or white-tailed deer. The road forks about 3km before the beach, and the left branch leads to **Estero Real** (an estuary with additional campsites). Soon thereafter, the land becomes swampy, and the air is tainted with sale. The main **campsites** are nestled in a grassy, low forest running along the beach. The sites have running water, grills, and picnic tables. All campsites cost ¢300 per person per night; the entrance fee for foreigners is US$6, though it can jump to as much as US$15 during the high season. If you're looking for more than just a stroll on the beach, **Sendero Carbona** skirts the shore, veers inland, and passes **Laguna El Limbo,** where crocodiles live.

GUANACASTE NATIONAL PARK

Santa Rosa continues on the other side of the Interamerican Highway, but goes under an alias: Guanacaste National Park. Guanacaste has a diverse ecology, including rain forest, tropical wet forest, tropical dry forest, and cloud forest. The environment changes with the elevation as one nears the summits of **Volcán Orosi** (1487m) and **Volcán Cacao** (1659m). The park attracts more researchers than tourists, so tourist facilities are not as well developed as in other parks. In fact, unless you're determined to do some particular research yourself, the difficulty of pre-planning a trip to Guanacaste National Park (you need to contact rangers 2 days in advance) makes Santa Rose look all the more enticing. Nonetheless, if you're set on GNP, here's what to look for: Guanacaste has three biological stations, each of which can provide lodging and access to different areas of the park. Camping is also permitted near the stations.

Cacao Biological Station can be reached from the town of **Potrerillos,** 25km north of Liberia on the Interamerican Highway. From there, you must go 9km to Quebrada Grande, then 15km more to Gongora. From Gongora to the station, proceed on foot or by horse. The station has no electricity, and visitors must bring their own food. Trails lead from this station to another station (at Maritzo) and to the top of the volcano. **Maritzo Biological Station** can also be reached by an 18km stretch of unpaved road that starts from the Cuajiniquil intersection on the Interamerican Highway 8km north of the entrance to Santa Rosa. This station has electricity, and food service is available if requested in advance. Rain forest, tropical dry forest, and transitional forest are all found near this station. **Pitilla Biological Station** can be reached from the town of Santa Cecilia, 22km north of the entrance to Santa Rosa National Park. Pitilla is 7km of dirt road south of the town and has no electricity or food service. For more info on the park or to make arrangements, contact the Guanacaste Conservation Area Office in Santa Rosa National Park (tel. 695-5598).

RINCÓN DE LA VIEJA NATIONAL PARK

The most outstanding feature of Rincón de la Vieja Park is the active **volcano** of the same name, whose towering 1898 meters of height are all the more intimidating when combined with fumes and lava. Before going straight for the glowing goo, however, take a little time to explore the park's out-of-the-crater wonders. The lower altitudes abound with sulfuric lagoons, boiling mud pits, *volcanitos,* and thermal waters in which to bathe. In addition, the park encompasses a large natural watershed system of 32 rivers and numerous streams, where the park's hiking trails criss-cross at several points, often in tantalizing crystalline pools (this makes for great swimming and sometimes diving). The trails wind from site to site through dense forests teeming with white-faced, howler, and spider monkeys, agouti, and hundreds of species of birds, insects, and reptiles (entrance fee US$6).

The only hitch is getting to the park. It lies only 25km to the northwest of Liberia, but unfortunately, no public transportation covers this distance. One dirt road leads from Liberia's Barrio La Victoria to the Santa Maria sector of the park. Another dirt road leads from 5km north of Liberia on the Interamerican Highway, heading 20km east into the Las Pailas sector of the park. It costs ¢350 to drive on the road, since it goes through a private ranch. There are several ways to reach the park if you don't have a car. Park rangers' and other vehicles travel the roads occasionally, with whom some have found that they can catch rides. (*Let's Go* does not recommend hitchhiking.) **Hotel Guanacaste** (see Accommodations) in Liberia takes groups of 3 or more to the park (stop by a day in advance to team up with other travelers), leaving Liberia at 7am and returning at 5pm for ¢1500 each way per person. Alternatively, you can hire a 4-wheel drive taxi in Liberia (about ¢6000 each way). You might want to check with Liberia's **La Posada El Tope,** which has also started transport to the Roncón. It ends up being more expensive than your regular outing, but certainly worth it.

The campsite in the **Las Pailas** sector, 100m from the entrance post, is right on the banks of a beautiful river, good for swimming and whatever else. A shameless, plump agouti frequents the campsite in search of succulent bits of charity from campers.

COSTA RICA

The park asks that you not feed the animals. An approximately 4km **loop trail,** east of the campsite, passes a picturesque cataract (only in the rainy season), a sulfuric lagoon, a *volcancito,* and the boiling mud pits. Trails to the west of the campsite lead to the park's biggest waterfalls, **Cataratas Escondidas** (4.3km) and **Catarata La Cangreja** (5.1km). The 7.7km trail to the crater of Rincón de la Vieja also leaves from the Las Pailas sector; allow an entire day for the roundtrip journey. Be aware that all trails except the 4km loop are closed after noon during the rainy season; several rivers cross the trails and the area is prone to flash floods. The crater trail may occasionally be closed as well, according to ranger discretion.

The **Santa María** sector, 8km east of Las Pailas, used to be a cattle ranch; a large part of it is currently being reforested. This sector also has a **campsite,** 1km west of which (toward Las Pailas) tumbles the waterfall of the **Bosque Encantada.** 2.75km west of the campsite (6km east of Las Pailas) are the allegedly therapeutic **aguas termales** (hot springs). The trails through the thick, monkey-filled forest are well marked. Entrance to the park costs ¢2400 the day of your visit, ¢1600 if bought in advance at another park or at a National Park Services office.

A few kilometers from the park, a number of mountain lodges offer meals, lodging, and horseback tours of the park. **Hacienda Guachipelin,** on the road from the Interamerican Highway to Las Pailas, 5km before the park (tel. 442-2864; open daily 8am-noon and 2-5pm), charges US$14 for a single and US$32 for a double, but has student discount rates for both meals and beds in a bunk house (¢1700). Normal price for the bunkhouse is US$10. The hacienda has its own private lagoon and mud pits for your health and pleasure. Other lodges with similar rates and services are the **Albergue Buena Vista** (tel. 373-5000) and the **Rincón de la Vieja Lodge** (tel. 695-5553). Contact the tourist office in Liberia for more information on canopy tours.

BORDER CROSSING TO NICARAGUA

Liberia is only an hour away from the border at Peñas Blancas; 8 **buses** make the trip daily. Be sure to arrive at the border early in the afternoon, as Nicaraguan immigration closes at 4pm.

At Costa Rican **immigration,** show your passport and pay a ¢75 exit fee. Money changers here can change dollars or colones to córdobas. From there, buses go to the Nicaraguan immigration office, 4km to the north (5C). Taxis may be available as well. Once there, you must pay a US$2 entry fee (US dollars only), then move on to pay US$5 for a tourist card. Last but not least comes the baggage inspection in customs. Nicaraguan boys hang around to guide you through this complex process for a few córdobas. There is a bank on the Nicaraguan side that changes dollars to córdobas, and money changers outside can change colones too (but be careful, they like to rip off tourists). Buses run from here to **Rivas** 37km to the north. If you're going to **San Juan del Sur,** get off at La Virgen and head to San Juan from there.

■ Playa Hermosa

The name speaks for itself. Having resisted pressure from wealthy investors endeavoring to turn the beach into a tourist trap, Playa Hermosa is everything Playa del Coco might have been—tranquil, clean, and pristine. The beach remains secluded; during the low season, you may wind up alone.

A **bus** bound for Playa Hermosa (and **Playa Panamá,** just north) leaves San José from Calle 12, Avs. 5/7 (3:20pm, 5hr.). The only direct bus back to **San José** leaves Playa Panamá at 5am and passes Hermosa shortly thereafter. Buses from Liberia depart for the two beaches daily (7:30, 11:30am, 3:30, 5:45, and 7pm, 1hr, ¢170). The bus from Playa Panamá back to **Liberia** comes along the same road (5, 6, 10am, 4, and 5pm, 1hr., ¢140). Playa Hermosa is 10km north of **Playa del Coco** on a paved road and then a 1km walk (or taxi ride) west, down a dirt road. From Coco by bus, however, you have to go back to Liberia. The modest **grocery store** is in the same building as **Aqua Sports** (open daily 8am-10pm). The locals (of whom there are not many) must feel pretty invincible here, too; there's no **hospital, doctor,** or **police**. For a **pay phone** (¢100 per call), enter the beach, walk left about 600m, go behind the little *cabinas*, and just as the road curves look to your left. There should be a yellow public phone sign; the phone is in the house behind it (open daily 7:30am-9pm).

Only two hotels in town are affordable for budget travelers. The almost-luxurious, **Cabinas Playa Hermosa** (tel./fax 672-0046 or 670-0136), is definitely on the high end of the "budget" price spectrum, but it delivers. Rooms are spacious, clean, and equipped with closets, mirrors, fans, and hot water. Its outside garden area is perfect for reading and relaxing (singles US$15; doubles US$30; triples US$40; quads US$50; in the high season, prices are about US$10 higher). A cheaper but less glamorous option exists in the form of **Cabinas Vallejos,** the faded yellow *cabinas* behind a small restaurant; from the beach's main entrance it is 600m to the left. Sparse and sanitary rooms go for about ¢1500 a person, but be sure to *ask* for a key for the cramped communal bath, or you'll find yourself stealthily smashing the lock at midnight.

Cheap food doesn't come easily in this paradise, but the excellent authentic Italian restaurant in Cabinas Playa Hermosa does provide a cool and delicious respite from the heat of the beach. Besides admiring the hotel's garden, diners are amused by the circus of animals that loiters about the tables—parrots, iguanas, and a squadron of lovely toads. Beware of the thieving monkeys! Gorge on sea bass (¢1300) or macaroni/pasta algusto (¢1000; open daily 7-10am, noon-3pm and 6-9:30pm).

The restaurant in front of Cabinas Vallejos is very reasonable, if not a palatial delight. They seem to serve up a sort of "special of the day" instead of a standing menu—*casados* (¢800), *arroz con pollo* (¢800), fried fish (¢1000; open daily 7am-8pm). And with much excitement, the owner of Cabinas Vallejos is proudly describing the "great food at cheap prices" he'll have at the *soda* he plans to open next door within the year. The calm, clean water is perfect for kayaking, water-skiing, or snorkeling. Check out **Aqua Sports** (tel. 670-0450), 150m left from beach's main entrance, which rents snorkeling equipment (US$5 per ½ day), kayaks (¢500 per hr.). The owner is willing to go out in a canoe with you to explore, and offers boat trips to nearby beaches, dropping folks off with snorkeling equipment in the morning and returning at the end of the day (¢8000 total, up to 6 people). Ask them for details about waterskiing and diving.

The 2.8km walk to **Playa Panamá** is pleasant and not very strenuous, if you keep an eye out for mad, growling dogs and aggressively protective mama pigs. Tall palms line the empty shore, and lush green mountains stretch out of and enclose the transparent, calm, clean water. Serene and beautiful, this beach is also often deserted; ritzy, expensive tourist resorts line the shore farther north, but at the entrance it's only picnicking *ticos* or one or two families camping (relatively safe and entirely free; no bath).

■ Playa del Coco

Playa del Coco, only 37km west of **Liberia,** is the most easily accessible and—surprise!—the most touristed beach on the peninsula. Many Costa Rican families spend their vacations here, and the beach sports several busy restaurants and numerous anchored boats. For all first impressions are worth, though, Coco projects a rather disagreeable one. The orange-and-yellow cluster of benches that marks the center of town is an eyesore, the dock is rickety and decrepit, and loud bubble-gum pop blares from a beachside disco all day and night. But beyond lies a long stretch of almost clean (if crowded) white-sand beach and calm water for swimming or snorkeling.

Practical Information and Accommodations Cash and traveler's checks can be exchanged in the Banco Nacional, 200m inland on the main road on the right (open Mon.-Fri. 8:30am-3pm), or at the **Luperón supermarket** (tel. 670-

0150), on the west end of the soccer field (open Mon.-Sat. 7am-8pm, Sun. 8am-4pm). The **bus stop** is at the end of the main road, in front of the post office, by the ugly yellow benches. **Buses** for Playa del Coco leave San José daily at 8am and 2pm from Av. 1/3, Calle 14, and return to **San José** daily at 8am and 2pm (5hr., ¢890). Coco-bound buses leave Liberia at 5:30, 8:15am, 12:30, 2, 4:30, and 6:15pm and return to **Liberia** at 5:30, 7, and 9:15am, 2:30, 3:15, and 6pm (1hr., ¢170). Buses from **Sardinal** depart daily at 11am and return from Coco at noon. The **police** (tel. 117 or 670-0418; open 24hr.) are next to the bus stop, in the same building as the **post office** (tel./fax 670-0418), which has *lista de correos,* **fax,** and **telegram** service (open Mon.-Fri. 8am-noon and 1-4:30pm). The **postal code** is 5019.

Compared to other beaches in the area, Coco may seem like a budget paradise. The best deal is at **Cabinas Catarino** (tel. 670-0156), on the main road into town about 150m from the bus stop—look for the small blue sign, which simply proclaims "*cabinas.*" The rooms are simple, but they're pretty spacious and have private baths, along with kitchen privileges and laundry service. Catarino, the owner, is quite a card-player (¢1000 per person; more in high season). Each simple, clean room in **Cabinas Las Brisas** (tel. 670-0155), 450m inland on the main road, has both a comfy double bed and a twin, plus a nice private bath (¢3000 per room). For double the colones and nearly double your pleasure, procure well-maintained rooms with fans and private baths at **Cabinas Luna Tica** (tel. 670-0279; fax 670-0127), 200m down the first side street up from the beach; look for "Hotel Tica Luna Anexo" sign. Laundry service is available, and checkout is at 2pm (singles ¢2500; doubles ¢3200; triples ¢4100; triples or quads ¢5500). Though the big signs by the soccer field still lure eager campers, **Guardaropa y Camper Afor** is no longer open. For **camping,** try **Camping** (that's the name) 200m inland on the main road, just past the Super Manatí. There are *muchos* clotheslines, decent bathrooms and showers, good light, security, and daytime clothes-sitting for ¢300 (camping ¢700 a night; ¢500 with multiple nights).

Food and Entertainment A slew of *sodas* cluster near the bus stop. On the main road, **Soda Restaurante, Teresita, Marisquería el Paraíso, Soda el Almendro,** and **Restaurante Oasis** all serve inexpensive Costa Rican food. For something different, head over to **San Francisco Treats,** on the main road, for a taste of sunny California. The vegetarian lasagna (¢1100) and black bean chili with smoked chicken (¢800) are delicious, but it's the amazing brownie sundae topped with ice cream (¢600) that brings in the crowds (open Thurs.-Tues. 11am-10pm). The dining is casual, the food is good, and the huge art murals are, well, interesting. **Restaurante Cocos** (tel. 670-0113) is right by the beach on the main road. They serve great grilled fish (¢1000), pizzas (¢1500-2500), and shrimp cocktail (¢1800; open daily 11am-11pm). **Mariscos la Guajira** (tel. 670-0107), on the beach behind Restaurante Papagayo, sets its tables on an open porch facing the ocean and dangles an intimidating collection of large shark jaws behind the bar (breaded mahi-mahi ¢1100, steak and onions ¢800, seafood soup ¢1000; open daily 11am-10pm).

Coco's big attraction is **water sports. Rich Coast Diving** (tel. 670-0176), about 300m up the main road, rents snorkeling (mask and snorkel US$3 per day, fins US$2 per day, wetsuit US$7 per day) and scuba gear (US$20 per day, US$8 per air fill). They also offer open-water scuba certification (US$295) and day- (US$30) and night-(US$35) diving trips plus surfing and fishing overnight trips, and sailing on a new 30 ft. boat (open daily 8am-5pm). **Mario Vargas Expeditions** (tel. 670-0351), 150m further inland along the main road, also rents equipment (wet suits US$6, mask and snorkel US$20 per day) and leads daily dives, as well as 4-day open-water certification class (US$275; open daily 8am-6pm).

At night, head to **Discoteque CocoMar** (tel. 670-0110) on the beach, next to Cabinas Coco, where music is pumped nightly from 8pm to 2am (cover ¢500).

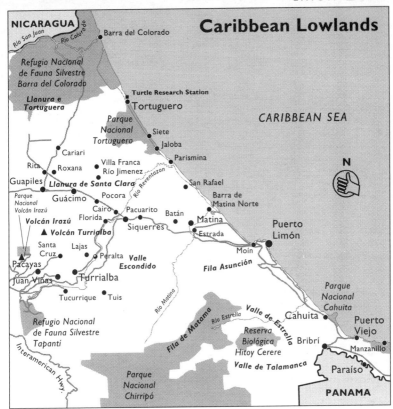

CARIBBEAN LOWLANDS

The boggy coastal lowlands that line Costa Rica's Caribbean shore articulate a drastic contrast to the land and culture of the Pacific seaboard. The lowlands support no volcanos, jagged peninsulas, or cool cloud forests. Instead, the relatively deserted Caribbean beachscape is lined with coconut palms, and replete with constant precipitation, unbroken sandy beaches, inland tidal marshes, and unfathomably muggy weather. The local populace also demonstrates the difference a few hours' bus trip can make; the diverse ethnic and cultural makeup of the region's cities and maritime villages is reflected in their cuisine, language, and faces. Most speak an English/Spanish mix with a slight Caribbean accent, turning "okay" into a casual goodbye and "alright" into a chill passing greeting. Limón, or Puerto Limón, Costa Rica's decaying major Atlantic port, serves as a crossroads for tourists traveling to points of ecological and recreational interest, like the **Tortuguero** breeding grounds, **Cahuita National Park,** or the placid beaches of **Puerto Viejo de Talamanca.**

■ Limón

Limón is Costa Rica's largest city on the Atlantic coast and a vital port for the entire country, yet it is continuously maligned in the public eye. Due partly to racism toward the city's mainly Afro-Caribbean residents and partly to inflated rumors about rampant crime and drug abuse, many *ticos* unjustly denounce Limón as a hopeless slum. This place does see grimmer action than most other areas of the peaceful, tourist-oriented nation; poverty runs deep in Limón, due in large part to Costa Rica's 1991 earthquake, which hit this province the hardest. Afterward, the government turned Limón a cold shoulder and denied the city sufficient federal money to rebuild. Five years later, there are still burgeoning ranks of abandoned buildings, but Limón's reputation as a pit of evil is undeserved. Most travelers stop here just long enough to change buses or spend the night, as Limón is the transportational hub of the Caribbean coast. Once a year, partiers flock in from all over for the **Día de la Raza** (Columbus Day) celebration on October 12, a festive carnival of music, dancing, and drinking that spills out into the streets for a week. If you happen to be in town, just grab a tambourine and join the flood of merrymakers; colorful and noisy, it will parade through the city until dawn.

Orientation and Practical Information Although Limón does have a system of *avenidas* and *calles,* they're hardly ever used, and finding street signs is nearly impossible. Ask a local on the street which *calle* she's on, and odds are she won't know. For those who insist on doing things the hard way, the intersection of Av. 1 and Calle 1 is in the southeast corner of town and the southwest corner of **Parque Vargas.** From there, the east to west *avenidas* increase by ones as you head north, and the north to south *calles* increase by ones going west. But much more useful is knowledge of a few local landmarks—the **Mercado Municipal** in the center of town (Avs. 2/3 and Calles 3/4) is the major one; Parque Vargas, in the southeast corner of town, is another. The public phones are on the **south** side of the market, and when you're facing them, you're pointed **north.**

If you've got a fistful of dollars and nowhere to spend it, check out **Banco Nacional** (tel. 758-0094), which sits across the street from the south side of the market and exchanges colones at 1% commission (open Mon.-Fri. 8:30am-3:45pm). The **bus stop** for **San José** is 100m east, 50m south of the market (every hr. on the hour, daily 5am-7pm, 2½hr., ¢650). The daily bus to **Cahuita** and **Puerto Viejo** departs from 100m north, 50m west of the northeast corner of the market (5, 8, 10am, 1, 2:30, 4, and 6pm; 1hr., ¢200 to Cahuita; 1½hr., ¢300 to Puerto Viejo). Buses run to **Moín,** the departure point for Tortuguero, from a stop 50m north of the Cahuita/Puerto Viejo stop (every hr. on the half hour, daily 6am-6pm, 20min., ¢40). **Taxis** are easier to catch than mosquito bites, stopping most frequently at the **Mercado Municipal,** which is full of bustling fruit stands and sprawls 300m west of the beach. **Cariay Supermarket,** across from the northwest corner of the market, is open daily from 7:30am-7:30pm. **Farmacia Buenos Aires** (tel. 798-4430), 25m east of the Banco Nacional, is open Monday through Saturday 7am-7pm. **Hospital Tony Facio** (tel. 758-2222) is a bit of a walk away, about 300m north along the *malecón* (boardwalk). **Red Cross** awaits patiently at 758-0125. The **police** can be reached by dialing 117; or go directly to the **OIJ** (Organismo de Investigación Judicial; tel. 758-1865), a sort of Costa Rican FBI, in the Corte Suprema building, 100m east and 100m north of the market. The **post office** (tel. 758-1543), southwest of the market, has a *lista de correos* as well as **fax** and **telegram** services (open Mon.-Fri. 7:30am-5pm). The **postal code** is 7300.

Accommodations and Food Limón after dark isn't pleasant; it's usually a good idea to clear out before nightfall. Stay away from the ultra-cheap places (under ¢1200)—these generally aren't so safe. Fear not budget traveler, there are some decent, secure, and relatively inexpensive accommodations.

The **Park Hotel** (tel. 758-3476 or 798-0555; fax 758-4364), along the *malecón,* 200m east of the *mercado,* is the best if you have some extra cash. Snag one of their suites with an amazing ocean view and a private bathroom with hot water; they've also got fans (of inestimable importance on the Caribbean coast), freshly washed sheets and towels, and plenty of toilet paper. The rooms are rather boring, but the windows make it worth the going; keep in mind though that it's also a few blocks away from the center of town, so the area tends to be pretty deserted at night ("moderate" singles ¢2405; doubles ¢3703; triples ¢4352). Though it doesn't have a view interesting to anyone except students of Limón's street culture, **Hotel Tete** (tel. 758-

1122; fax 758-0707), 25m west of the northwest corner of the mercado, has just about everything else it needs to keep guests comfortable, including fairly good prices. There's a sort of lounge on the breezy balcony, with couches, the daily paper, and a big color TV; just inside the lobby, there's a coffee maker and a water cooler. Each room is spacious enough to fit a desk, a luggage rack, a ceiling fan, a phone, a double bed with comforter, and a very green private bathroom with hot water (singles ₡2500; doubles ₡3500; add ₡600 for A/C).

Grub in Limón is like standard San José fare with a Caribbean twist. *Gallo pinto* and *casados* still reign supreme, but fresh seafood also finds its way onto most menus. Remember, though, it's the big city; to find real down-home Caribbean cooking, look to smaller towns further down the coast. **Restaurante Mares** (tel. 758-1347), across the street from the south side of the *mercado,* tries really, really hard to seem beachy, stuffing itself with tropical kitsch, potted palm trees, plastic lobster-studded fishing nets, and a sailor's wheel. The seafood is great, but a little pricey. *Ceviche de pulpo* surges with various denizens of the undersea, octopus taking center stage (₡1200). As in any s*oda,* the vegetarians can find ever-present rice, beans, maduro, and salads, and soups from ₡400-600 (open daily 6:30am-10pm). For good eats at any hour, airy and relaxed **Sada La Estrella** sits 100m west of the northwest corner of the mercado. (Cheap and quick *casados* ₡500-550, *pinto* ₡400-450, sandwiches ₡300, and *batidos* ₡150.) Don't be turned away by the run-down exterior of **Restaurante Doña Toda,** on the east side of the *mercado*—the inside is as comfy as can be and prices are low. Enjoy plastic chairs and paisley tablecloths and spend only ₡400 on a full meal of fantastic *casado,* or ₡225 for a sandwich. Daring and dastardly diners will ask about the *aleta de tortuga* (turtle fin) dinner (₡600; open Mon.-Sat. 6:30am-7pm).

Sights and Entertainment Be careful while walking through the **Mercado Municipal** (Avs. 2/3 and Calles 3/4). Though it may seem calmer and more organized than most central *mercados,* it's pickpocket territory. The Caribbean influence is quite apparent here, as vendors proudly display fresh coconuts, bananas, fish, and lobster. To get to **Parque Vargas,** in the southeast corner of town, just look up and walk toward the towering coconut palms. It is home to a plethora of wildlife—hummingbirds darting from flower to flower, the occasional sloth bumbling around in the treetops, young tykes playing tag. Across the road is tranquil lookout, where ambitious skateboarders gather and couples sit quietly; though only a block from the city's center, the bustle and noise are completely overwhelmed by the peaceful lapping of the waves. Right along the ocean on a clear day, one can see the island of Uvita, 1km away, where Columbus landed on his fourth and final journey to the New World. Limón is full of pride for the famous explorer; come around Columbus Day (Oct. 12) and you're in for a chaotic whirlwind of festivities. If another ocean view sounds good, just take a stroll down the *malecón,* a coast-hugging promenade which starts by Parque Vargas on the south side of town and makes a relaxing walk as it wends its way northward. But be smart and think a little before taking the stroll—it's not safe to be alone around dawn or dusk. The young crowd looking for waves, rays, or just a place to chill usually heads over to **Playa Bonita,** 4km northwest of Limón, a beach with a split personality: on one side, the water is calm and perfect for wading, on the other side, the powerful waves build and crash on the beach. As a result, surfers and swimmers can live in perfect harmony, and later relax with beers to a never-ending reggae beat emanating from a nearby bar. To get to Playa Bonita, take the Moín bus and get off at one of the first stops (just ask the driver), or take a taxi (₡500-600).

At night, Limón's hot spot is the **Bar Acuarius** (tel. 750-1010), a dance club in the Hotel Acon, across the street from the Mínpik and the supermarket. Reggae rhythms pound, and older men sit and stare in this dim light club (cover ₡250, women free on Thurs.; open Tues.-Sun. 8pm-3am).

■ Tortuguero

Nobody knows exactly how they do it: every year hundreds of female turtles return from points far and wide to the beaches of **Tortuguero National Park,** 83km northwest of Limón, to lay their eggs. Native indigenous peoples thought the turtles were guided by nearby Tortuguero Mountain; scientists believe the chemical qualities of the sand and sea may leave some kind of imprinting. Genetic tests suggest that turtles return to the nest on the same beach where they hatched, no matter how many thousands of miles they've wandered. The most famous turtles are the *tortugas verdes* that nest from the end of June through September. Going back to the days of the dinosaurs, these green turtles have been around for over 100 million years. Now, they are forced to take a long hard look in the face of extinction, thanks to modern man, to the artificial oceanic jetsam that suffocates their nests and the poachers who steal their eggs. Plastic bags are often responsible for asphyxiating the endangered reptiles, as they are often mistaken for edible jellyfish. However, in 1954, Dr. Archie Carr founded the Caribbean Conservation Corporation to help bring the sea turtles into the international limelight, and in 1970, the Costa Rican government declared this 35km long strip of land and sea a national park.

It's difficult to imagine Tortuguero accurately without actually seeing it. Disneyland must have modeled their Jungle Boat cruise after it, the chief difference being that here, the sounds of the howler monkeys in the treetops, the rainbow-beaked toucans coasting overhead, and the leathery caimans stealthily gliding through the water are all real. In Tortuguero National Park, wildlife peeks around every twist of the canals; you just have to sit quietly and keep your eyes and ears open and alert.

Getting There Cheaply? Try hitching a ride on a leatherback's shell, because anything else is going to cost colossal colones. There are two ways to trek to Tortuguero—either invest in one of the prepackaged tours that include hotel and transportation, or travel independently. Shopping around for a good packaged deal is a smart idea—it's definitely the least nerve-wracking way to travel, and could actually be much cheaper than doing it yourself. **Ecole Travel** (tel. 223-2240 or 223-4128) in San José, Calle 7, Avs. Central/1, the back half of Chispas bookstore, offers one- and two-night trips, starting at US$55 (not including hotel) which includes a guided ride through the jungle and a visit to the Caño Palma Biological Station. Cahuita and Puerto Viejo are spotted with signs offering reasonable tour options as well.

Alternatively, you might go for the adventurous option of doing it all yourself, which is likely to cost around US$60 for transportation to the village alone—not exactly a sight for sore budget traveler eyes. A few boat pilots have a real stranglehold on the market, and gasoline is expensive for them in the first place. The *lanchas*, flat-bottomed six-person boats covered by canopies, leave from the port of Moín's northwest corner. Buses leave for Moin from Limón, 50m north of the Cahuita/Puerto Viejo stop (every hr. on the half hour, daily 6am-10pm, 20min., ¢40). When you're busing in from Limón and the huge Del Monte and Dole banana boats come into view, that's Moín. Walk downhill towards the water, to the small dock behind Restaurante Papa Manuel, where *lancha* pilots are usually waiting to make their killing. A round-trip boat ride usually costs around US$50-60, though single travelers are sometimes quoted prices as high as US$100. *Lanchas* usually leave early in the morning (from 8-10am), and it's possible to stay in Moín instead of Limón, at the **Hotel Moín Caribe** (tel. 758-2436), up the road from the docks, where ¢2000 buys a comfortable night's sleep with a double bed, private bathroom, and color TV on request.

The ride to Tortuguero is a scenic three-hour journey down an artificial canal—that is, unless the *lancha* gets stuck in tangled masses of water hyacinth, in which case your travel time could double. Recently, low water levels and pesky sand bars have been forcing captains to creep through the waterways. Try to find a loquacious pilot; this ride can be almost as interesting as a tour of the National Park itself, as you tool past legions of monkeys, turtles, baby crocs, and bright-plumed birds. Passengers are

When in 172-1011,
do as the 172-1011's do.

All you need for the
clearest connections home.

Every country has its own AT&T Access Number which makes calling from overseas really easy. Just dial the AT&T Access Number for the country you're calling from and we'll take it from there. And be sure to charge your calls on your AT&T Calling Card. It'll help you avoid outrageous phone charges on your hotel bill and save you up to 60%.* For a free wallet card listing AT&T Access Numbers, call 1 800 446-8399.

It's all within your reach.

http://www.att.com/traveler

Greetings from Let's Go Publications

The book in your hand is the work of hundreds of student researcher-writers, editors, cartographers, and designers. Each summer we brave monsoons, revolutions, and marriage proposals to bring you a fully updated, completely revised travel guide series, as we've done every year for the past 38 years.

This is a collection of our best finds, our cheapest deals, our most evocative description, and, as always, our wit, humor, and irreverence. Let's Go is filled with all the information on anything you could possibly need to know to have a successful trip, and we try to make it as much a companion as a guide.

We believe that budget travel is not the last recourse of the destitute, but rather the only way to travel; living simply and cheaply brings you closer to the people and places you've been saving up to visit. We also believe that the best adventures and discoveries are the ones you find yourself. So put us down every once in while and head out on your own. And when you find something to share, drop us a line. We're **Let's Go Publications,** 67 Mount Auburn St., Cambridge, MA 02138, USA (email: fanmail@letsgo.com; http://www.letsgo.com). And let us know if you want a free subscription to **The Yellowjacket,** the new Let's Go Newsletter.

dropped off in Tortuguero Village, a light sprinkling of houses, inexpensive cabins, and small *sodas* at the north end of the park.

Practical Information Other places may call themselves villages, but Tortuguero Village is *small*, a close-knit community of just 480 people. A flashlight is a must, especially during rainy season, as the power tends to go out during storms. It's almost pointless to try to give directions, as there are no streets (just makeshift dirt paths), and buildings are scattered all about. Just ask a local—this place is small enough that any visitor staying more than a day's time will know its buildings like his or her own knuckles. Useful landmarks are the **soccer field** and the **kiosk** right north of it, and **The Jungle Shop,** about 200m to your left when you step off the boat. The national park begins on the south side of the village. When trying to find the park and ranger station at the entrance, it may seem as though the town path veers through the locals' yards. It does. But it's OK, just keep trekkin' south.

The best place to go for information is The Jungle Shop (tel. 710-6716; beeper 233-3333, #631), just northwest of the kiosk, where Antionette Gutiérrez, an American, and her *tico* husband Elvin sell souvenirs and give invaluable advice. Call ahead and they'll arrange a tour with local guides (open Mon.-Sat. 8:30am-6pm, Sun. 10am-6pm). Another good place to go is **Souvenir Paraíso Tropical** (tel. 710-0323), 100m north of The Jungle Shop, where English is spoken (open daily 9am-6pm). These are also the only two places in the village with private phones.

There are no **banks** in Tortuguero Village, but The Jungle Shop and Paraíso Tropical can exchange traveler's checks. There are **public telephones** at Miss Junie's, along the main path toward the north side of town, at Pulpería Jorge, in the center of town, and outside Souvenir Paraíso Tropical. The **supermarket** is diagonally in front and to the right of Souvenir Paraíso Tropical (open daily 6am-9pm). For any problems requiring a **doctor** or the **police,** go to the central headquarters of the park service (Administración de Tortuguero), at the south end of town. In case of a serious **medical emergency,** a doctor in Limón can be called from The Jungle Shop or Paraíso Tropical. **Mail** can be sent using the Cortel service near Paraíso Tropical.

Accommodations and Food All the ritzy, expensive hotels are across the canal; in Tortuguero Village the lodging is strictly budget. The best value in town is actually in a new establishment, **Cabinas Aracary**—look for the white building with a green roof and an awning made of palm fronds, just south of the soccer field. The rooms are pretty spacious and have three beds each, and the private bathrooms are big with modern showers. Plus, the owner is really nice—she brings candles to each room when the electricity goes out (¢1800 per person). **Cabinas Mery Scar,** 200m south of the kiosk, has very basic, box-like rooms and a primitive communal bathroom—but at least it's friendly and clean. It's a family-run establishment, so be quiet and let the kids get some sleep during the 10pm-8am quiet hours, and don't be surprised if breakfast is waiting on the table when you wake up (¢1400 per person). If money is the *only* object, head over to **Cabinas Sabina,** 100m east of the kiosk, the buildings right on the beach; just be prepared to share the room with some uninvited, creepy-crawly roommates (¢1000 per person with collective bath). **Brisas del Mar,** the buildings north of the kiosk, is a good deal for big groups during turtle season (beginning in July). A no frills, four-bed room and use of the cold water communal outhouses costs a flat ¢2400; get some friends and do some computing—it may work out to be the cheapest option in town.

There's really no such thing as a typical **restaurant** in Tortuguero Village. Most eating establishments are run by women who spend the day taking care of the children and cleaning the house, but are happy to cook for travelers on their converted front porches in exchange for a dash of cash. Often, it's necessary to give a few hours' notice before a big meal—after all, someone has to go out and catch the fish. For some sweet, homemade Caribbean cooking and a sweet lady, head over to **Miss Junie's,** 200m north of The Jungle Shop. She'll cook whatever's caught that day, but tell her in advance—your best bet is to check in the morning or the afternoon so she can have the meal ready exactly when her guests want it. Fresh fish cooked in coconut milk ¢900, vegetarian rice dish ¢800 (open daily 7am-9pm, or longer if there's sufficient demand). For a quick fix, try the anonymous **Restaurant** directly to the left of Pulpería Jorge. A friendly couple cooks out of their kitchen for both locals and travelers; try the *pinto* (¢400), *casados* (¢600-700), or fried fish with potatoes and salad (¢975; open daily 6am-7 or 8pm depending on turnout.) Another quick and easy place to stop is **Soda el Dollar** across from The Jungle Shop, which will whip you up some basic *casados* (¢700-800), fried fish dishes (¢990), or good *batidos* (¢200; open daily 6:30am-8pm.)

Sights and Entertainment Before going out on a nocturnal run to see the turtles, check out the Caribbean Conservation Corporation's **museum** at the **Natural History Visitors Center.** They show a 15-minute video about the history of the region, the park, and the sea turtles, and then open up a number of exhibits about all the area's flora and fauna (open daily 10am-noon and 2-5:30pm; free, but donations accepted). Also check out the **kiosk,** north of the soccer field, which dishes out lots of info on the *tortugas.*

Now that you're a turtle expert, it's time for the biggest event around here—the nightly *desbove,* the laying of the turtles' eggs. The female turtle makes her way up the sand, constantly pausing to look for danger, until she finds the perfect spot, and then uses her rear flippers to dig a one-foot deep body pit with a cavity for the eggs. After laying about 110 leathery eggs, she carefully fills the hole with sand and returns to sea, never to return to check on her babies. The entire process takes about one hour. From July to October, visitors **must** be with a trained guide; but even before those dates, don't try to watch the *desbove* unguided, because the beaches are dangerous at night and most people end up scaring the turtles away. The national park takes people out on a two-hour sighting for US$5; buy tickets at the information kiosk between 4 and 6pm during nesting season (July 1-Oct. 15). However, this expedition leaves at 8pm, and it's best to look for the turtles as late as possible. Most local guides, available throughout the year, charge the same price as the park and will go at any time; ask around. When you go, wear good walking shoes and dark clothing, and don't bring a flashlight or a camera with a flash—bright lights blind the turtles and prevent them from returning to the sea. Just follow the guide's movements and try not to make any extra noise, because if a turtle is disturbed before she starts laying her eggs, she'll abandon her spot and go back to the water. Different types of turtles are around throughout the year, but the popular *tortuga verde* only nests from June through September.

The portion of the park that can be seen without a guide or a boat is limited. The park's ranger station is at the south end of the village; two hiking trails start from there (open daily 6am-6pm; US$6). **Sendero El Gavilan** is 2km long, and **Sendero Gavilan Tucán,** a ways from the ranger station, is 4km—quiet hikers may be able to spot monkeys, toucans, and those tiny red poison dart frogs. But hiring a guide is much more informative and, if you find the right one, much more fun. **Mr. Dama's** tours are a blast—start off in a canoe, then enter a jungle path that Dama cleared away himself, complete with a wild swing made from a vine and a piece of wood. Dama's lived here all his life and knows just about every species of plant, animal, bird, and insect (at least by their local names)—he'll probably even let you handle a few, including the poison dart frog. (*Let's Go* does not recommend playing with venomous animals, but Mr. Dama seems to know what he's doing.) Look for Dama's place near Cabinas Mery Scar (¢500 per person per hour, does not include admission fee to the park; tours usually ask 4hr.).

Other guides, however, can provide a flora- and fauna-filled day without ever entering the national park. Similar biological thrills can be gleaned from the **Caño Palma biological station** and its surrounding canals (free). If you make it to Caño Palma, look for Canadian scientific officer Pat Opay—a great source of information.

▨ Puerto Viejo De Talamanca

Don't move too fast in the cozy beach village of Puerto Viejo—it might scare the locals. Puerto Viejo's all about unwinding and forgetting life's worries for a while, or forever, as a growing population of Europeans and *norteamericanos* who have made permanent homes out of their vacation getaways can attest. Blond Californian surfers meet dreadlocked Caribbefarians on the glistening black beaches; but it's such a small place that after a day or two, they're likely to be old friends. The locals are very concerned about preserving the environment and promoting local tourism (goals that go hand in hand here), so don't expect resorts to pop up any time soon. The living here is slow, and you've brought too much ambition if you're considering anything beyond catching the perfect wave or the perfect tan.

Practical Information Take your questions to the **ATEC** office (Talamanca Association for Ecotourism and Conservation; tel./fax 750-0188; email atecmail@sol.racsa.co.cr) in the center of town. This grass-roots organization was founded to promote local tourism while preserving the region's heritage and ecology. ATEC gives **tourist information** and promotes all local hotels, restaurants and rental stores which make an effort not to make their money at Mother Nature's expense (open Mon.-Fri. 7am-noon and 1-9pm, Sat. 8am-noon and 1-9pm, Sun. 8am-noon and 4-8pm). ATEC also serves as Puerto Viejo's connection to the outside world as it sells stamps, receives and sends mail, offers internet access and fax services and houses one of the town's few public phones. The other public phones are located at **Hotel Maritza, Pulpería Manuel León,** and **Pizote Lodge.** Pulpería Manuel León (open daily 7am-7pm) also changes traveler's checks at a minimal cost.

Buses stop at the first intersection in town by the abandoned barge; look for the sheltered benches which mark the spot. Buses leave for **San José** (7:30, 9am, 4pm), **Limón** (6am, 1, 4, 5pm, 1½hr., ¢235), **Manzanillo** (7:15am, 4pm) and **BriBri/Sixola** (Panamanian border; 6:30, 9:30, 11:30am, 5:30, 7:30pm). There's only one **taxi** in town. Approaching from the bridge, make the second right; the sign says "Charlie's Taxi Service," but everyone knows him as Bull, and if Bull's red minivan isn't parked outside or at the bus stop, it's likely to be pulling in soon. Other truck owners, like Spence of Cabinas Spence—commonly known as "Mr. Ex-spence-ive"—are willing to give rides, but, as you probably guessed, charge more. Do **laundry** at Girasol for ¢1000 per load. There is no pharmacy, but Pulpería Manuel León's got the basics, like aspirin and Alka-Seltzer (open daily 7:30am-7:30pm). **Clinic Hone Creek** (tel. 750-0136) is located 5km out of town on the main road and may be able to accommodate your other pharmaceutical needs.

Accommodations The **Jacaranda Cabinas** (tel. 750-0069), located in the middle of town (from the center road, follow the signs to The Garden), wasn't named after a tropical flower for nothing. Some people would probably pay admission to see the incredible collection of birds of paradise, orchids, lilies, hyacinths and royal palms here—lie in a hammock and gaze at the breathtaking product of local hard work. Even the communal bathroom seems quaint. Rooms come with private shower. (Singles $8.50; doubles $14; triples $18; hot water, private bath, porch and personal hammock doubles $22; triples $25.) **The Garden** restaurant, which occupies the same plot, has gained quite a reputation for its eclectic menu of exotic foods and exquisite cocktails. Small touches make this place heavenly, from hanging wicker lanterns in the patio area to the bamboo ceilings. The management is sure to cook every meal with "love and energy and soul" and proudly employs only local kids (entree around $8, appetizers around $3). At **Cabinas Casa Verde** (tel./fax 750-0047; from Restaurante el Parquecito, walk 100m away from the center road and turn left), the house isn't actually green, but its gardener seems to have a green thumb. Each room has its own front porch with hammocks and lounge chairs, the perfect place to kick back and hide from the world for a while. The bathrooms are communal, but there's a sink in each room. Laundry service is available for ¢1000 per load (high season prices: sin-

COSTA RICA

gles $14-16; doubles $18-30; 4 people $40; low season, singles $10). Popular among surfers and tight-budget travelers, and even more unpopular with ecologically-minded ATEC, **Hotel Puerto Viejo,** located behind Restaurante Caramba, is for the rugged types. The simple rooms are less than inviting. You may have to battle a cock-roach or two, but people keep flocking back—either the odorous air is addictive or they'll do whatever it takes to stay as close to the excellent **Mexican restaurant** located in front (¢1000-1500 per person). The adventurous may want to head toward the **camping area** outside of town, about 50m past Salsa Brava. For only ¢400, Miss Iris (known affectionately to regulars as Mama-San) will rent out a tarp-covered camp-ing space; if you don't have a tent, she'll give you a hammock for free (but you're on your own to battle the mosquitoes). There's even an outdoor kitchen with pots, pans, a wood-burning stove, and refrigerator access. Some people stay for months, forming their own little community. Iris locks campers' bags up in her house at night, but be careful; bags aren't safe outside, even during the day.

Food Puerto Viejo offers a little bit of everything to please all the beach bums who work up a big appetite after a hard day at the beach. For exotic Caribbean/Asian/Latin food and priceless ambiance, dine at The Garden. If your belly yearns to travel a few countries north, appease it with the Mexican cuisine at **Hotel Puerto Viejo.** Some of the best Italian food in Costa Rica can be found at **La Carambo.** Fine wine and can-dle-lit tables set the atmosphere. Be sure to read the menu in good light, however, as prices can be a bit steep (tortellini ¢1800, glass of wine ¢400). **Old Harbor's Fresco Shop,** between the bridge and the bus stop on the road along the beach, caters to the health conscious with healthy treats like fresh-squeezed orange and carrot juices (¢250 each), granola with yogurt and fruit (¢450), and homemade banana bread (¢250). **Soda Tamara,** across the street from ATEC, right in the center of town, is another popular spot, offering *patacones* (fried plantains ¢150), great pancakes, and delicious homemade desserts (¢100-150; open Wed.-Mon. 7am-9pm).

Sights and Entertainment Most surfers head straight over to **La Salsa Brava,** the surf-hole extraordinaire east of the village. However, if you are a little less experi-enced on a board and getting drilled into the coral doesn't sound "far-out," a 15 minute walk along the beach will bring you to **Beach Break** where comparable waves break on nice, soft sand. **Hotel Puerto Viejo** rents surfboards and boogie boards (surfboards ¢2500 per day; boogie boards ¢1500 per day.) **Atlantico Tours** (tel./fax 750-0004) rents snorkeling gear ($8/day) and offers many tours, including horseback riding, river rafting, hiking, and boat tours. A two day, one night trip to **Parque Nacional Tortuguero** is available for $59 and up, depending on desired hotel quality. Tours to Manzanillo, Punto Uva, and Punta Mona are available as well.

Laid-back as Puerto Viejo may be, locals don't go to sleep when the sun goes down. Many rush to **Johnny's Place,** next to Pulpería Manuel León, which is a Chinese res-taurant by day and a raging disco by night. The music ranges from *salsa* to reggae and back again.

■ Near Puerto Viejo

PUNTA UVA

If Puerto Viejo begins to seem too crowded or the surfers' mating cries seem too loud, no need to fuss. A sublimely secluded beach with perfect waves lies some-where down the coast. Moving southeast, the closest beach to Puerto Viejo is **Playa Cocles,** 2km down the shore, which reputedly offers the best surfing on the Carib-bean coast. Next in line is **Playa Chiquita,** 4km farther down. Another 7km along the road lie the gorgeous—and very deserted—white sand beaches of **Punta Uva.** The water is perfect for swimming, and the small waves that break close to shore are ideal for body surfing. Best of all, it's usually empty, so solipsistic seekers of personal para-dises can rejoice. Palm and mango trees line the shore only 150m from the water's edge, trailing purple-flowered vines that creep along the ground for a few meters, and then…just the pristine smoothness of an unbroken beach. Whee-hooo! Look to the east to see the actual "grape point" for which this place is named—a small peninsula juts offshore, exposing a natural tunnel that acts as a window to the ocean on the other side. (To get to the beaches, see **Manzanillo** below.)

Anyone visiting Punta Uva stays in **Selvin's Cabinas** (look for the sign off the road, right at the beginning of Punta Uva). The doubles are pretty spartan, the cold water communal bathrooms are downstairs, and the walls are so paper-thin that you'll pray there's not a snorer next door (doubles ₡1500). Selvin and his family are friendly, and the 50m path to the beach is just a few steps away. Additionally, there's a great restaurant open during the weekends. Hungry weekday travelers will not starve, however; check out any of the countless tiny places (all creatively called "Soda") which spot the road. Surrounded by hanging vines and jungle palms, the new **El Duende Feliz** lies 100m or so up the road, on the left, and the delicious aroma of freshly baked bread will lead your way. The friendly Italian owner knows how to *cook*. A variety of salads (₡500-800), minestrone soup (₡500), and pasta (₡800—garlic, bolognese, or pomodoro) will delight your taste buds. (Open daily 8am-9pm.)

MANZANILLO

The village of **Manzanillo** is 5½km southeast of Punta Uva. Also blessed with a spectacular beach, Manzanillo is best distinguished by a trailhead that opens onto a dense jungle path that trots from the village down the beach, all the way to Panamá. This long stretch of land is part of the **Gandoca-Manzanillo Wildlife Reserve,** based in the town of Gandoca, 9km away. The main purpose of this reserve is to protect the *baulas* (leatherback turtles) that lay their eggs in the sand of Gandoca's beach.

There's only one place to go in Manzanillo, and that's Maxi's. Set back from the beach a little, **Restaurant Maxi** serves delicious, fresh seafood from a lovely upstairs porch. The catch of the day costs ₡800-1500 depending on its size, lobster runs ₡2500-3000, and their vegetarian dish costs ₡400 (rice, beans, potatoes, salad, and special caribbean salsa.) (Open daily noon-10pm.) The green building behind the restaurant is **Cabinas Maxi,** pretty basic digs with rugged private bathrooms and mattresses on the floor doing their best bed impressions (doubles ₡2000).

Further down the road as it leaves Manzanillo is **Soda La Selva,** run by a wonderful woman and, true to its name, set among a moist green jungle garden. Sit at one of the ancient-looking round stone tables as a grilled cheese with ham and tomatoes (₡250) melts in your mouth; or try tacos (₡350), a tropical fruit plate (₡350), or a *batido* or *jugo natural* (₡200). Open daily 9am-10pm.

From Maxi's, follow the dark dirt trail between the restaurant and the beach a few hundred meters, passing a soccer field, until you reach a small lagoon. To the right, there's a wooden bridge leading to a house—Willie Barton, who guides jungle tours for US$12 per hour and ocean tours for US$15 per hour, lives there. If the house looks empty, ask around in town—everyone knows him. Keep on keepin' on, cross a small stream, and see the trail begin amid a forest of coconut-laden palms that extends up to the horizon. The path is really nothing more than a series of small, unmaintained clearings between the trees; even in the dry season, it's often necessary to climb over branches and rocks to stay on track, and during the wet season, mud-swimming may be your only option. Wear sturdy shoes, use insect repellent, and bring bottled water. It's a bad idea to try this hike shortly after rainfall, as it can be especially easy to lose the trail to the undergrowth. After about a 10 minute walk, the trail climbs uphill and culminates in an excellent lookout—a modest but defiant precipice that leans out into the water. The trail continues another 2km to **Punta Mona,** another impressive vantage point. Most people end their walk here, but it is possible to continue on another two hours to the Gandoca ranger station, or another three hours to the Panamanian border. The bike ride to Manzanillo or any of the beaches, over rocky roads laden with potholes and up mud-filled hills, induces a loss of sensation in parts of the body, but it is beautiful.

COSTA RICA

Buses run daily from Puerto Viejo to Manzanillo, at 7am and 4pm (returning 8am and 5pm), passing through Punta Uva and the other beaches and over terrifying bridges. The only options for the timid are walking, hitching a ride, or taking a taxi (Puerto Viejo to Manzanillo ¢1500-1700). The walk along the beach is gorgeous and peaceful, about one hour to Punta Uva, and another 80 minutes to Manzanillo.

■ Cahuita

Silhouettes of palm trees on white sand flicker against a pink-and-orange sunset. Warm, turquoise waves lap up on a black sand beach. Howler monkeys in the tree-tops of a coastal rain forest cry out jarring rhapsodies. Cahuita, 48km southeast of Limón, is a mecca for nature-lovers, Rastafarians, and beach bums of all sorts. Most come for **Cahuita National Park,** southeast of the village, home to the best coral reef on Costa Rica's Caribbean coast; but the other side of the village is no slouch—there, sun-worshippers find a black sand paradise.

Not all of Cahuita is so idyllic—the village has received increasingly bad press in recent years; news articles cite theft as a constant danger. As surf-and-reggae-loving tourists flock to Puerto Viejo further south, Cahuita has grown quieter: peaceful tran-quility by day leads to more deserted streets by night. (Be wary: it's also rumored that many of the drug dealers here are in cahoots with the police; as soon as they make their sale, the cops move in to nab the buyer.) But relax your grip on that can of mace; a vast majority of Cahuita's visitors feel the town's reputation as unsafe is wholly undeserved. The important thing is just to keep your wits about you and take the same precautions you would anywhere else.

Practical Information Toting south on the main road, the bus comes into town and leaves you off in front of Salon Vaz, in the center of town. There are no banks in Cahuita, but **Cahuita Tours and Rentals** (tel. 755-0232; fax 755-0052), 200m northwest from the bus stop and away from the park, will exchange dollars and trav-eler's checks—for a rather high commission. It doubles as an excellent source of **tourist information** about Cahuita in general, and its staff speaks good English—ask for Tony (open daily 7:30am-noon and 1:30-7pm). Another very friendly source of info, **Turistica Cahuita Information Center** (tel. 755-007) has two offices—one in the Hotel National Park lobby, right by the park entrance on the south side of town, and another about 100m on the main road from Salon Vaz, away from the park (open daily 8am-noon and 2-7pm). There are **public telephones** at Cahuita Tours, Hotel Cahuita (200m toward the park from the bus stop), and Soda Uvita (100m short of the park from the bus stop). **Faxes** can be sent from Cahuita Tours and Rentals for US$3.10 per page to the U.S., and received for ¢100. **Buses** stop in the center of town, across the street from Salon Vaz, and head to: **San José** (daily at 7:30, 10, 11:15am, and 4:45pm; 4hr.; ¢1000); **Limón** (6:30, 10am, 12:30, 1:30, 3, 4:30, and 7pm—which is often late; 1hr.; ¢300); and **Puerto Viejo** (6, 9, 11:15am, 2, 5, and 7pm; 30min.; ¢200). **Mr. Big J** will happily do your **laundry**, for about ¢500 per kilo (50m from the park entrance on the main road, across from Cabinas Vaz; open Mon.-Sat. 9am-noon and 3-7pm). Return to **Cahuita Tours** or **Turistica Cahuita** with your **rental** needs—C.T. rents snorkeling gear (¢2000 per day) while T.C. rents bikes (US$8 per day, $5 per half day). Both companies also arrange **tours** at comparable, fairly reasonable rates, including the following: four-hour tours of beaches and the Kekopi Indigenous Reserve (US$25, but depending on group size), glass-bottomed boat rides (US$20), two-day packages to Tortuguero (starting at US$55; includes transportation by boat, 2 meals, and a guide), and white water rafting tours (class 3 and 5, includes breakfast and lunch, US$65-85). The **post office** lies past Cahuita Tours towards the black beach; take a right on the last side street (open Mon.-Fri. 7am-11am and 1-4pm). There is a *lista de correos;* the **postal code** is 7302.

Accommodations and Food Fluff, frilly and startlingly fancy pillow shams and bed ruffles adorn the double beds at **Cabinas Safari,** 75m east down the crossroad at the bus-stop corner. The clean showers have hot water most of the time, and the rooms all have a second bed and a front porch hidden behind tall plants (singles ¢2000; doubles ¢2500; triples ¢3000). At **Cabinas Sol y Mar** (tel. 755-0237, ext. 237), 200m southeast of the bus stop, near the entrance to the national park, fairly spacious rooms are graced with exquisitely carved wooden headboards and mahogany dresser sets. The immaculate private bathrooms have hot water. A breakfast-only restaurant (open 7:30am-noon) doubles as an arena for globetrotting Nintendo fans to face the tico masters (singles ¢2000; doubles ¢3000; triples ¢3500; tropical breakfast ¢550). If you can spare the money, **Cabinas Arrecife** (tel. 755-0081) next to Miss Edith's (see **Food,** below) is the jewel of the *cabana* scene. If only for the wonderful wooden porch that houses their small, guests-only breakfast restaurant and has a most tranquil view of the shore through the palms. The tables and lounge chairs are perfect for writing, reading, or just sitting. Though the rooms are simple, the bathrooms are modern and spotless, and the double beds are comfortable (singles US$10; doubles $20). **See-Side Cabinas** (walk from the bus stop towards the ocean and turn right at the beach), run by Nan-Nan and his girlfriend Vanessa, can't be beat location-wise, and the hammocks right by the ocean are a nice touch. Just don't spend too much time in the rooms, or you'll end up fending off scraps of falling stucco. All rooms have private baths and cold water; try to bargain (singles ¢1500, doubles ¢2000, triples ¢2500; slightly more during the high season). Striped with thick pasta-colored bands, the board outside **Restaurant Caribbean Food** advertises a chill "positive vibration" (diagonally across from Salon Vaz). Inside, chill with dried palms hanging from a thatch roof, wicker lanterns, and shell wind chimes. (Vegetarian sandwich ¢300, whole (eyes and all) fish fried in coconut milk ¢1100, *casados,* ¢600-1000, tropical fruit with yogurt ¢500.) The restaurant is open daily from 7:30am-8:30pm. Overlooking the beach right at the entrance to the park, **Restaurant Vista Del Mar**, is spacious, open-aired, and cooks up some good stuff, with a nice mix of Oriental and typical *tico* dishes. Extensive menu includes fruit, omelettes, pinto con huevo, or cereal (all ¢400 each); chau min with anything from veggies to seafood (¢400-530); and rice with vegetables (¢350) or *pollo* (¢500). (Open daily 7:30am-7pm.) Don't be scared off by the decaying exterior of **Miss Edith's**—from the corner of the bus stop, walk 100m east down the side street, towards the beach, make the first left, continue 300m to the end of the road. Feast on incredible vegetarian yuca vegetable soup (¢650), fish in coconut milk (¢1000), or the special *rondon* stew (¢1000-3000) with lobster (open Mon.-Sat. 7am-noon and 3-10pm). Mouth-watering homemade cakes and absolutely delicious fresh banana/zucchini/apple breads (all ¢150-200) are yours at the **Pastry Shop**, 250m down the road along the black sand beach (on the north end of town; open Mon.-Sat. 8am-6pm).

Sights Most of the park is not even terrestrial, so the coastal rainforest is its most accessible area. A 9km trail leads from Cahuita Village through the park, around the peninsular **Punta Cahuita,** and to the **Puerto Vargas station** at the other end. You can hike ½ hr. along the beach to a river free of charge. If you plan to continue to Puerto Vargas, a $6 charge must be paid at that station or, once construction is complete (around Oct. or Nov. 1997), at the station in Cahuita. The walk to Puerto Vargas is wonderfully disconcerting: look to the left and see the rolling waves of the Caribbean drumming against a secluded white sand beach. Look to the right and the picture has totally changed—now there's a swampy forest thick with brush and towering coconut palms. The treetops of Cahuita are some of the best places in the country to spot monkeys; at sunrise and sunset, the playful primates often come down from their perches to frolic on the beach. The half-hour walk is not strenuous, but it's wise to bring water and insect repellent. Although reported incidents are still rare, there have been a number of muggings in the park. Female travelers should exercise caution—hiking alone, even during the day, is not a wise choice.

Watching your feet can also be rewarding, as the region's shorter flora and fauna are remarkable. Orange hermit crabs scurry across the path alongside white ghost crabs. Observe the backs of those brightly striped lizards carefully—if there are

COSTA RICA

spines running down to the tail, it's an iguana; if not, then it's probably a Jesus Christ lizard (so named for its ability to walk on water, and not for any physical resemblance). The medicinal *sangrillo* tree's trunk has thick folds which bunch up and protrude, making the tree look as though it is resting on a wrinkled pyramidal base. Delicate blue porter weed, with its tiny, butterfly-attracting flowers, lines the sides of the trail, together with rows of tough, leathery ferns.

Cahuita's real claim to fame is its spectacular coral reef. In the past few years, the reef has been shrinking, due in part to the accumulation of eroded soil from banana plantations, and in part to the 1991 earthquake. These influences have made it nearly impossible for snorkelers to find good sites on their own—there's too much dead coral floating in the water for casual expeditions to get very far. It's better to ask a park ranger at the Puerto Vargas station, a local fisherman (ask for Robert), or a guide from Cahuita Tours exactly where the sea life is most visible and abundant. Cahuita Tours and Rentals rents snorkel equipment (see **Practical Information,** above) for ¢1500 per day, but scuba divers should bring their own equipment. Once you find the right spot around Punta Cahuita, it's amazing. Elkhorn and brain corals (yes, it does look like noggin-innards) line the ocean floor. Look, but don't touch—too much handling kills the coral. Fish of all shapes, sizes, and colors of the rainbow reside in Cahuita's reef, including queen angelfish, French angelfish, rock beauty, blue parrotfish, and even great barracuda.

Camping is permitted near the Puerto Vargas side of the park. Each of the 48 camping sites is removed from the hiking path and includes room to park a car, as well as a picnic table and a personal ocean vista. Latrines are spaced out, and there are showers, sinks, and toilets at the Puerto Vargas ranger station.

SOUTHERN COSTA RICA

Costa Rica has been so barraged with tourists seeking untouched nature that you might think it's all been touched by now. On the contrary, the southern part of Costa Rica—from San Isidro de El General and Parque Nacional Chirripó to the Peninsula de Osa around Golfo Dulce—offers the kind of "come and get me if you dare" attractions that brought travelers to Central America in the first place. Here, you're more likely to interact directly with the nation's people, while praising the size of their forests' anteaters and sloths. If derring-do doesn't do it, there are also plenty of beckoning beaches, idyllic places to snag a snooze before dashing off to Panamá.

■ San Isidro de El General

The small, modern city of San Isidro provides a link to the rest of the world for the residents of several surrounding farming villages. For travelers, the city serves as a springboard for the unreal splendor of Parque Nacional Chirripó (the main entrance to which stands in nearby San Gerardo de Rivas). Don't bounce away too hastily, though—unlike San José, San Isidro has retained almost all of its small town charm, a trait which hasn't been lost on the many U.S. citizens who've come here to retire. San Isidro holds tourism close to its heart—not only are the residents friendly to a fault, but there is even a sign at the intersection of Avenida Central and Calle Central that reads, *Déle la mano al turista* ("Automobile drivers should yield to tourists"). Dare to relax over beer and *criollas* at Hotel Chirripó; just watch yourself on Sundays during the soccer season, when a win brings a riotous slew of happy, firecracker-laden fans through the streets.

ORIENTATION AND PRACTICAL INFORMATION

Theoretically, San Isidro is gridded numerically along *calles* and *avenidas,* but in reality few streets are marked. Many residents do not know the names of the streets—and may even flatly deny that such names exist. Avenida Central and Calle Central

Southern Costa Rica

0   20 miles
0   20 kilometers

meet at the northwest corner of Parque Central. The light-colored, boxy cathedral borders the park to the east. Just about everything else can be found within a few blocks. The police station is about 10km outside of San Isidro, near Río San Isidro.

Currency Exchange: Banco Nacional del Costa Rica (tel. 771-3287, 771-3289, or 771-3440; fax 771-3245), on Av. 1 and Calle Central, directly across from the front of the cathedral. Changes currency and traveler's checks; gives cash advances on Visa. Open Mon.-Fri. 8:30am-3:45pm.

Buses: Finding the right bus out of San Isidro is a bit like looking for that missing sock in the laundry pile—it's there somewhere, but not easily found. MUSOC (tel. 771-3829 or 771-0414) buses to **San José** leave from the MUSOC stop on the Interamerican Hwy. between Calles Central and 2 (5, 5:30, 7:30, 8:30, 10:30, 11:30am, 1:30 and 4:30pm, 3½hr., ₡800). Transportes Blancos buses to **Quepos** (7am and 1:30pm, 3½hr., ₡610) and **Uvita** (8am and 4pm, 2hr., ₡470) via Dominical (1½hr., ₡385). Both depart just across the street from Café Dominical on Av. 2 near the Interamerican Hwy. (look for the Sucursal la Nación sign; the cafe is beneath it). Buses to **San Gerardo de Rivas** (2hr., ₡300) leave at 5am from the west side of the park and at 2pm from the main terminal at Calle Central and Av. 6. Buses to **Puerto Jiménez** (9am and 3pm, 6hr., ₡200) leave from the Castrol gas station north of the cathedral on the Transcontinental Hwy. between Calles Central and 3.

Taxis: Taxis Unidos al Sur (tel. 771-1161) and **Taxi** (tel. 771-0045). To: **San Gerardo de Rivas** ₡3500; **Herradura** and **Dominical** about ₡5000.

Public Transportation: Buses run daily 5:30am-10:30pm to surrounding villages, but also make closer stops on demand. Just stand up and whistle.

Car Rental: National Car Rental (tel. 771-1037), Av. 4 and Calle 1. "Class B" cars rent for US$42 (US$55 with insurance). Must be 21 or older and present a valid passport. Major credit cards accepted. Open daily 7:30am-noon and 1:30-5:30pm.

Market: Conexiones Internacionales (tel. 771-3015) offers everything from post-cards and t-shirts to money-changing services (traveler's checks as well). Located in the Hotel Chirripó's cafe. Open Mon.-Fri. 8am-noon and 1:30-5pm, Sat. 8am-noon.

Public restrooms: Clean bathrooms are on the north plaza of the cathedral (¢30).

Pharmacy: Farmacia San Isidro (tel. 771-1567), on Av. Central across from Parque Central, has a full selection of most over-the-counter medicines and toiletries. Open Mon.-Sat. 7am-8:30pm, Sun. 8am-7pm. **Farmacia La Fuente** (tel. 771-0692), located to the northwest of the town park, carries a host of other pharmaceuticals and toiletries.

Hospital: Calle 1 across from the stadium (tel. 771-3122 or 771-0318; fax 771-0874).

Red Cross: Emergency toll-free (tel. 128) and ambulance service (tel. 771-0481).

Post Office: (tel. 771-0346; fax 771-3060), Av. 6 and Calle 1 on the way to the hospital, offers **faxes, telegrams,** *lista de correos,* and public bathrooms. Open Mon.-Fri. 7:30am-5:30pm. For stationery check out **Libreria y Bazar,** 2 blocks north of the post office. Open Mon.-Sat. 7am-8pm, Sun. 8am-4pm.

ACCOMMODATIONS

Hotel Chirripó (tel. 771-0529), Av. 2 and Calle 1. Located in the heart of San Isidro. Rooms are well-kept and clean, as are shared bathrooms. The cafe in front gets an A+ for convenience and is a popular congregation spot for travelers. 24hr. reception. Singles ¢1375, with private bath and shower ¢2170; doubles ¢2350, with bath ¢3945; triples and quads with private baths, ¢5800 and ¢7660 respectively.

Hotel Jardín (tel. 771-0349), 50m west of the main intersection of Av. Central and Calle Central. Despite the small, often windowless rooms and the communal bathrooms (no hot water), Hotel Jardín is adequate for the backpacker (¢850 per person). Close to the center of the city, with a restaurant in front (see **Food,** below),

Hotel Balboa (tel. 771-0606), Av. 1 and Calle 2, one block north and 2 blocks west of the town park. The unmarked stairway next to Tienda la Flor leads to the Hotel Balboa. Rooms have queen-sized beds, chairs, and desks, but no fans, so it's a bit of a human greenhouse. No hot water. Singles with bed that sleeps one or two ¢1100, with private bath ¢1900; rooms with an extra single bed are available for ¢1750.

Hotel Lala (tel. 771-0291), Av. 1 and Calle Central, one block north of the town park. The windows near the ceiling provide little ventilation for stuffy, dusty rooms with requisite "desks" (slabs of wood) and "beds" (slabs of wood). Still, the price can't be beat. Singles with communal bath (bring your own paper) ¢700; doubles ¢1400, with bath ¢1750.

FOOD

From "Yennifer" to "Jerusalén," *sodas* abound at intersections throughout San Isidro. **El Mercado Municipal,** next to the bus terminal (Av.6 and Calle Central, two blocks south of the park), has something to offer in the way of produce every day. However, Fridays and Saturdays are always the most fruitful market days.

Pizzeria El Tenedor (tel. 771-0881), Calle Central, Avs. Central/1. With a balcony overlooking Calle Central and colored lights swarming like bumblebees, El Tenedor tries hard to be hip—and for the most part succeeds. Small, medium, and large pizzas ¢430, ¢655, and ¢900 respectively; break free from plain cheese, and try the *Hawiana* or *Chorizo Chino* (Chinese sausage). Cheeseburger, fries, and a Coke ¢800. Many spaghetti plates are available. Open Tues.-Sun. 9am-11pm.

Pollos Delji (tel. 771-5747), Av. 2 and Calle Central, on the south side of the cathedral. The chicken gods were so pleased with San Isidro that they blessed its people with *two* Pollos Delji restaurants. Same food, same management, same prices—but only one could serve as the setting for a low-budget sci-fi flick. Listen to music from the U.S. as you eat 2 pieces of fried chicken, fries, a Coke, and *tortillas* for ¢710. Open 8:30am-10pm.

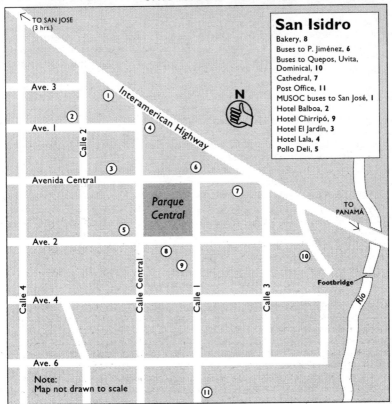

San Isidro

Bakery, **8**
Buses to P. Jiménez, **6**
Buses to Quepos, Uvita, Dominical, **10**
Cathedral, **7**
Post Office, **11**
MUSOC buses to San José, **1**
Hotel Balboa, **2**
Hotel Chirripó, **9**
Hotel El Jardín, **3**
Hotel Lala, **4**
Pollo Deli, **5**

Note:
Map not drawn to scale

Restaurante El Jardín (tel. 771-0349), attached to the hotel of the same name, 50m west of Av. Central and Calle Central. El Jardín offers an array of *comida típica*, from beef to *arroz con pollo* (small portion ¢700, large ¢950). Watch *Sábado Gigante* on the large-screen TV mounted in the corner as equally *gigante* fans cool you down. Open 7am-10pm.

■ Near San Isidro

SAN GERARDO DE RIVAS

One long, uphill kilometer across the river from the bus stop, the tiny town of San Gerardo seems to think it's pretty big; fewer than 1000 inhabitants enjoy a multipurpose recreational facility that hosts frequent discos, adult classes, and of course, soccer games. The people are very down to earth and always ready for questions about nearby Chirripó National Park (p. 412). To reach *anybody* in San Gerardo, call the town's only phone (tel. 771-1866).

Cabinas Descanso, across the river, has been frequented by many a tourist—most of whom apparently tacked their business cards to the wall. It's not surprising; the **restaurant** hang-out is charming, complete with a foosball table, a wall of park-ranger-and-hotel-co-owner Francisco's trophies and medals, and some darn good food (rice with fish, chicken, or steak ¢600; vegetarian dish ¢600). The rooms (¢700 per person) are small but impressively clean, and communal baths have hot water. Reserve ahead of time in the summer by calling the town phone (see above). **Hotel Roca Dura** is as convoluted as the Swiss Family Robinson treehouse. Located near the public phone, it's the farthest *cabina* on the road. All of the rooms are simple and

COSTA RICA

cool, as the walls are carved out of actual rock. Eat at the *soda* upstairs for a good price and quality tico food. (¢600 per person with communal bath; ¢800 per person with private bath; ¢1500 for double with private bath.) Next door to the ranger station is friendly **Cabinas Marin,** featuring TV and stereo. Rooms are adequate, with thin foam mattresses (¢600 per person with communal bath). Alternately, rent the house next door (¢4000 a night; weekly and monthly rates as well), replete with six beds, a living room, a bathroom with hot water, and even a kitchenette. *Casados* at the *soda* run approximately ¢500.

To rest those weary bones after making the hikers' pilgrimage to Cerro Chirripó, take a dip in the soothing *aguastermales* (hot springs) just 600m from the only intersection on the road to Herradura. The only barrier to bliss is a short, but strenuous hike. The path becomes pure mud during afternoon rains, so go early. Señora Vitalia, the owner, charges ¢200 (¢100 for children)—pay at the house on top of the hill or at the springs 100m beyond if no one's home. Señora Vitalia offers advance warning: you may like it so much you'll never want to leave.

PARQUE NACIONAL CHIRRIPÓ

Being bombarded with the roaring cascades of Río Chirripó del Pacífico, the cooing of countless birds, and the mooing of grazing cows, even the most jaded cynics wax poetic about Parque Nacional Chirripó, home of the highest peak in Costa Rica (3819m). A devastating forest fire in 1992 led to the park rangers' adamant stance against unregistered camping and outdoors smoking—the origins of the fire.

Stop at the **ranger station** (clearly marked, 50m from the bus stop in San Gerardo; open 5am-5pm) for a mandatory registration and admission fee (US$6 per day per person, each additional night US$3). Get all sorts of valuable information from the rangers for the hike ahead. Although the rangers do not provide any equipment, some items are available for rent in town (prices vary, ask locally). Play it safe by bringing everything you might need from San Isidro de El General or from home. Note that advance reservations are highly recommended and must be made through the main office of the **Servicio de Parques Nacionales** in San José (tel. 257-0922) or the San Isidro office (tel. 771-3155) anywhere from 15 days to a month in advance (earlier in high season, Nov.-April), as no more than 60 can spend the night at the park's solar-powered *refugios.* Camping is prohibited except at the *refugios* and one site on the **Herradura-Cerro Urán trail** (see below). Horses can be rented for ¢5000 during the high season (Dec.-April); a porter will carry your bags for you during the hike for ¢4500 during the rest of the year, when the trails become quite muddy.

To take it all in, the park rangers recommend at least three days (with a five-day max. stay). The climb is 9km from the ranger office to **Refugio Llano Bonito.** Spend the night here or climb another 7km to **Base Crestones,** where the two aforementioned *refugios* are located. The rangers advise all hikers to spend the night at Base Crestones before climbing the final 6km (2-3hr.) to **Cerro Chirripó.** Other paths from Crestones also let rock-climbers ply their skills (bring your own equipment and first demonstrate your expertise to the rangers). **Sabana de los Leones** (6km from Crestones) is home to many exotic animals, and the lake-dotted **Valle de Las Morenas** (8km from Crestones) is just plain beautiful.

If Cerro Chirripó is covered with clouds, blocking otherwise awe-inspiring views of both oceans, a newer yet considerably more challenging trail to **Cerro Urán** may provide the panorama you're looking for. Camping is permitted in the designated area, as the trail calls for a two day hike. Keep in mind that temperatures in higher altitudes can drop to as low as -7°C (Dec.-May) or 0°C (May-Dec.), and while it rains every day in the wet season, it rarely does in the dry season—the rangers become very concerned about fire at this time, as should you. As always, follow the old adage: "Take only pictures; leave only footprints."

▓ Dominical

Tiny Dominical (pop. about 300) lives up to its big name as an unspoiled, beautiful "*mini-Cal*-ifornia." More and more surfers are attracted to its chocolate-brown, rock-strewn beaches and reliable waves. The grafitti at **Soda Laura** may best describe this little spot: *pura vida* and *tranquilo*. Welcome to paradise, surfer-style.

Orientation and Practical Information Central Dominical spreads out over a 1km stretch of local road parallel to the shoreline. Telephones are available in front of **San Clemente Bar & Grill** (see below) and on the beach. Although there is no bank in town, the San Clemente will exchange dollars and traveler's checks. Here, too, is where you will find buses to **San Isidro** (6:30, 7:30am, 2:30, 3:30pm) and **Uvita** (9:00am, 5:00pm). The one taxi in town can be found outside the San Clemente or contacted by radio from their bar. Walk a bit outside of town up the main road and away from the bridge to **Supermercado dos Hermanos** (tel. 787-0046; open Mon.-Sun. 8am-6pm), a fully stocked supermarket with bilingual service. Check next door at **Mercado del Mundo** for tico souvenirs. For **laundry service,** return to the ever-versatile San Clemente. The beach is easily accessible down the only side street in town, near **Royal Palm Surf Shop** (open Mon.-Sun. 8:00am-6:00pm) where you can restock your surfer wardrobe (bathing suit US$40) or buy a new board (prices vary, custom orders available). The **Surf Emporium,** located next to the inescapable San Clemente, sells and rents out boards, offers surf lessons, and of course, sells surfer duds. Both surf shops accept major credit cards. Ask at the omnipresent San Clemente about **Kayak Joe Tours,** and other exciting excursions. The **police** (tel. 787-0011) are located on the main road, just past the beach side street. There's no **post office** here, but you'll find a mailbox at the (you guessed it!) San Clemente Bar & Grill; buy stamps at the Surf Emporium 10m away.

Operation: BAYWATCH

While the beautiful beach of Dominical has delighted surfers for years, the **strong currents** and powerful waves also have a reputation for causing tragedies. Up until December 1996, **drownings** were an all-too-common occurrence at Dominical. After the death of a young Costa Rican girl last year, a few *gringo* surfers decided to take action. By collecting **US$100 donations** from local hotels and restaurants, they raised enough money to hire and house a trained lifeguard from the United States. Before long, the U.S. Coast Guard was teaching the ticos **life-saving** techniques, and the guard staff was growing exponentially. Dominical is now a fully protected beach; not a single drowning has occurred since the program began. With more local support and the continued education of ticos in life saving, other beaches of Costa Rica may one day boast the same safer shoreline found at Dominical.

Accommodations and Food Cabinas San Clemente (tel. 787-0026; fax 787-0055) offers rooms ranging from adequate singles with communal bath (US$5) to beachfront doubles with hot water, private bath, and air-conditioning (US$45 high season; US$25 low season). Beachfront houses are available for rent as well (US$40-100). **Posada del Sol,** 100m from Soda Laura, caters to Dominical's few non-surfing visitors. Each consists of single- and queen-size beds, remarkably clean private bathrooms with hot water, fans, and chairs (low season singles ¢2000; high season singles ¢4000). **Cabinas Villas Dominical** (tel. 771-0621), where the main road meets the beach road, offers airy and pleasant rooms which each contain one twin and one queen-size bed, a lamp, and a fan. Singles are ¢1500 (up to ¢5000 in high season), and major credit cards are accepted. Look for the cafe/bar in front. The more tightfisted stay at **Cabinas El Co-Co.** The all wood, boxy rooms share communal baths, but the price can't be beat (single ¢750; double ¢1500).

For a taste of surfer food, head to **Thrusters Bar & Grill,** located at the crossroad where the main road and the beach road intersect. The lounge-like atmosphere, hip

COSTA RICA

music, and free billiards attracts a sun-bleached, surf-happy crowd during the high season. Toss back a few beers at the bar (Imperial ¢250) or satisfy your munchies with late night pizza (¢1200 and up). If the surfers at Thrusters aren't appealing enough for you, try the ones packed into the **San Clemente Bar & Grill**. The fat-free menu offers exciting selections, and several TVs to keep the sports junkies tuned in. Billiards will cost you a few colones. Add a cracked surfboard to the colorful collection suspended from the ceiling and earn yourself free nachos and a drink. Breakfast served from 7:15-11:30am (Surfer Special ¢550). **Restaurant and Bar El Co-Co** provides a little less ambiance at significantly lower prices and serves mostly tico fare (fried fish ¢900-1500). The Imperial beer, though it costs much less, tastes just as good as it does down the block. Try it and see. **Soda Laura** is another local hang-out where big portions of tasty (and cheap) *típico* food make surfers purr contentedly. Stock up on water and snacks at the little market inside (both are open daily 7am-10pm).

■ Near Dominical: Hacienda Barú

Climb into the rainforest canopy 35m above the ground, hike through a primary tropical wet forest, or spend the night camping in the jungle. Do all this and more at the **Hacienda Barú** (tel. 787-0003; fax 787-0004; e-mail sstroud@sol.racsa.co.cr; http://www.cool.co.cr/usr/baru/baru.html), just 2km north of Dominical. Recently named a National Wildlife Refuge, the park is owned by cattle ranchers-turned-conservationists determined to protect the area they once deforested. As well as reforesting the land, they have joined other private eco-minded landowners in a project to link patches of habitat together. Hacienda Barú already has provided 200 hectares to this noble cause. Call ahead to arrange a guided 5 hr. morning hike (US$30, lunch included). Six cabins are available here for US$48 per couple in the low season, US$68 per couple in the high season (including breakfast; US$10 per additional person). The rooms are light, bright, and extremely pleasant, with hot water, fans, living rooms, and kitchenettes. Shoot the breeze in English with the owners.

▓ Puerto Jiménez

Everybody knows everybody else in Puerto Jiménez, which was built by gold-miners earlier this century as a center of trade and exchange. Although gold still exists here and some hotels pander to fevered travelers by offering gold-panning tours along the Osa Peninsula, it is semi-nearby Parque Nacional Corcovado's pristine rain forest that is the greatest draw in this part of the country. Puerto Jiménez is hopping during the high season, but the best time to visit is during the rainy season when tico friendliness is at its most plentiful and genuine.

Practical Information What can ambitiously be called the town's commercial center is a small strip of the main road, which is neither paved nor named. For **budget travel,** find **Escondidos Trex** (tel. 735-5210; email osatrex@sol.Racsa.co.cr), located inside Restaurant Carolina. Escondidos Trex offers several different kinds of tours of the peninsula for those not satisfied with the 50+km of trails in P.N. Corcovado. For a discount, ask about the "backpacker special" (open daily 9-11am and 5:30-7:30pm). **Banco Nacional de Costa Rica** (tel. 735-5020; fax 735-5106; open Mon.-Fri. 8:30am-3:45pm) is located on the street parallel to and one block east of the main street, and exchanges dollars and traveler's checks and gives cash advances on Visa. **Telephones** on the main street can only be used to make collect or calling-card calls; pay at **International Communications** in the center of town to use a phone. Puerto Jiménez is home to many airlines which offer regular and chartered flights. The **SANSA** office (in Puerto Jiménez, tel. 735-5017; in Golfito, tel. 775-0303), near Cabinas Marcelina, flies to **San José** (with other stops) for US$50 (flight times vary throughout the year). **Travelair** (tel. 735-5062; fax 735-5043) has round-trip tickets to **San José** for US$146 and one-way flights to **Quepos** for US$71 (open Mon.-Sat. 7am-5:30pm). **Buses to San José** (5 and 11am) and **Neily** (5:30am and 2pm) leave from Soda Marilys (on the street parallel to and just west of the main street, one block north of Cabinas Katty). To **Golfito**, either take the bus to Neily and transfer at Rio Claro, or take the ferry directly from Puerto Jiménez (6am, ¢600, returns at 11:30am). **Markets** include **Tienda el Record** (tel. 735-5724), where you'll find last-minute items for camping (daily 7am-7pm), and **Mercado El Tigre** (tel. 735-5075), which is well-stocked and less terrifying than its name suggests (though you will find Terror detergent here). Ask here about transportation to P.N. Corcovado (open daily 5:30am-7pm). Take a left off the main street where it hits the park and you'll see the **medical clinic** on your left (tel. 735-5061; open Mon.-Fri. 6am-4pm; 24hr. emergency service). The **police** station (tel. 735-5114) is a few steps south of the park on main street. **Cortel,** the **post office** (tel./fax 735-5045; open Mon.-Fri. 7:30am-5:30pm), is located across from the southwest corner of the soccer field near the medical clinic. It is fully equipped with fax, telegram service, and *lista de correos.*

Accommodations and Food As a rule, reservations are almost always necessary during the high season. **Cabinas Brisas del Mar** (tel./fax 735-5012) sits on the shores of Golfo Dulce and receives a refreshing north to south breeze and offers top quality rooms with private baths and fans for an additional simulated seabreeze (¢1500 per person; ¢2000 for a bigger fan and hot water). After a few days of roughing it in P.N. Corcovado, you'll be delighted to spend some extra money on the luxuries found at **Oro Verde** (tel. 383-3615). Classical music echoes throughout the impeccably clean hotel. The rooms, each named after a different ecological attraction of the Osa peninsula, come with fans, private baths, and enough locks on the door to hold back an army of elephants. Try in vain to wash the rain forest stench from your hiking clothes in their special clothes-washing sinks (singles ¢2500; doubles ¢3000; ¢1500 each additional person). **Cabinas Marcelina** (tel. 735-5007) is the town's best deal for your money. Located one block south of town, rooms come with private baths and fans (¢1000 per person). During the high season, ask about horseback rides along the beach to the family-owned *finca* (US$20). Follow signs west of Soda Marilys to **Cabinas Thomson.** Rooms are one step above decent and each has private bath and a fan (¢1000 per person). Right next door is **Pensión Quintero** (tel. 735-5087), the best barn you'd ever want to stay in. Don't be deterred by the green halls and rustic ambience; it's by far the cheapest place around. You'll find cold water, communal baths, and flexible prices here—haggle with the manager for a room with electricity, fan, and a lightbulb for ¢700.

In the immediate town, there are mostly *sodas* and *cantinas,* all similarly priced (rice with chicken, beef, or fish ¢400-600). **Soda Marilys** (open 4:30am-8pm) has no sign in front, but is a favorite with locals and doubles as a bus stop. Tourists tend to go to the centrally located **Restaurante (y Cabinas) Carolina** (tel. 735-5185), where *casados* or a fish fillet cost ¢700-800; or **Agua Luna** where the tropical tiki bar decor and oceanic scenery makes up for the higher prices (T-bone steak ¢1300, fish fillet with mushrooms and wine ¢950).

■ Parque Nacional Corcovado

Sprawling along pretty much the entire western coast of Osa Peninsula, and home to sloths, monkeys, anteaters, and almost 400 species of birds (including the magnificent scarlet macaw and harpy eagle), **Corcovado National Park** continues to do what it was meant to do—deter destruction caused by industry and gold-mining. The park is only 22 years old, but feels enough like the Garden of Eden to eradicate all notions of time from visitors' overwhelmed minds. Best of all, it's not hard to access once you're in Puerto Jiménez: catch a taxi *colectivo* (¢1300; at 6am and, Jan.-April 1pm) in front of the Mercado El Tigre as it passes through the city en route to **Carate,** the nearest stop to the park's entrance. The road is bumpy and the ride long (approximately two hours), so don't bring your own car unless it's in tip-top shape.

Although tickets are available for purchase at the *puestos* (ranger stations) for ¢1200, it might be a good idea to visit the **Area Conservación de Osa** office in Puerto

Jiménez (located by the air strip in the far eastern reaches of town behind the cemetery). There, you can make the required reservations for lodging (¢400 for a bed, bring your own sheets; ¢300 to camp in the designated areas around the *puestos*). Let the rangers know far enough in advance if you're going to be eating any meals at the ranger station (breakfast ¢1000; lunch and supper ¢1500 each).

After bonding with the 17 or so other passengers crammed into the back of a pick-up truck (with benches) for an hour, walk along the beach from Carate to the park entrance at the La Leona ranger station for about another hour or so. (If you can't make it the whole way, stop and rest at the privately owned **Corcovado Lodge,** which is more than halfway there.) Keep your eyes peeled for crabs and scarlet macaws along the way in preparation for the sights of Corcovado.

Theoretically, Corcovado can be entered from any of the four ranger stations: **La Leona** (south), **Los Patos** (east), **San Pedrillo** (north), or **Sirena** (central). Most hikers planning a tour of the park will want to enter at either La Leona or Los Patos (which is accessible by a 3hr. hike from La Palma, north of Puerto Jiménez), and stay the night in Sirena en route to the other station. The hike from La Leona to Sirena is 16km along a sandy beach and takes five or six hours. This trek can be especially brutal on a hot sunny day so *bring plenty of water.* Also, this hike must be completed before high tide (ask at the station for tidal information). The trail from Los Patos to Sirena cuts right through the middle of the rainforest for 20km, and takes about six hours. The fourth station, San Pedrillo, is only accessible through the park in *verano* (Dec.-April), when the 25km trail is open.

About 20km south of Puerto Jiménez, **La Tierra de Milagros** (Land of Miracles) awaits travelers who want to give something back to nature. Founded in 1990 by idealistic *norteamericanos,* the commune supports a reforestation project on the peninsula that provides volunteers with hands-on work. For more information or to make reservations, fax the post office to the attention of Tierra de Milagros (fax 735-5045). A monthly fee covers accommodations. A taxi from Puerto Jiménez costs about US$15; a better bet is the cheaper *colectivo* which leaves from in front of Restaurante Carolina (about US$3, Mon.-Sat. 6 and 11am).

■ San Vito

Founded 43 years ago by an Italian man who fell in love with a tica lady, San Vito is the realized dream of a real-life dreamer. After having announced his plans in several Italian newspapers, the love-struck Italian led a group of ready and willing colonists to the highlands of Costa Rica and initiated a unique cultural transplantation. After navigating the steeply sloping, serpentine road from Neily, surrounded by views of the Costa Rican countryside, you may be surprised to find yourself eating lasagna and hearing Italian spoken in back corners and kitchens. Close your eyes, and you just might be convinced that you've mistakenly purchased the wrong *Let's Go* guide.

Everything in San Vito is easy to find in relation to the central park and the main, six-street intersection. Within the heart of the town, walking is definitely the preferred mode of transportation—how else to verify for yourself that San Vito, like Rome, was built on seven hills? Find **tourist information** and the entire history of San Vito at the **Dante Alighieri Cultural Center** (tel. 773-3570; open 9am-noon and 4-7pm), located at the main intersection. **Banco Nacional de Costa Rica** (tel. 773-3601; fax 773-3430; open Mon.-Fri. 8:30am-3:45pm), located directly across from the park, changes currency and traveler's checks and gives cash advances on Visa. **Telephones** are everywhere, but especially in the park near the bizarre, blue and white gazebo structure. **Buses** to **San José** leave from the TRACOPA terminal (tel. 773-3410) located down the street to the left of the Dante Alighieri Cultural Center (5, 7:30, 10am, and 3pm), as do buses to **San Isidro** (6:45am and 1:30pm). To find the Cepul terminal (tel. 773-3848), walk downhill to the north of the main intersection and make a left at the gas station. Buses to **Neily** (5:30, 7, 9, 11am, and 2pm) and **Rio Sereno** (7:30, 10:30am, 1, and 4pm) depart from there. To find the **hospital** (tel. 773-3103) walk uphill south from the main intersection, past the cathedral. Once you are sure you must have passed it, keep walking. Look for the sign on the front wall which reads "Seguro Social."

With three little red-and-white cabins overlooking a lush ravine, **Cabinas Las Mirlas** (tel. 773-3714), about 150m beyond the TRACOPA terminal, behind Centro Agrícola Cantonal, provides both natural beauty and basic creature comforts. Cabins go for ₡1200 per person. Smack in the heart of town is the affordable and simple **Hotel Colono** (tel. 773-3885). All rooms come with communal bath (singles ₡800; doubles ₡1500; quads ₡2800). Just down the street towards the gas station rustles **Hotel Tropical,** with plain and sometimes windowless (but always inexpensive) rooms (singles ₡700; doubles ₡1200).

San Vito's past is most evident in its cuisine. **Pizzería Lilliana** (tel. 773-3080), up the short side street from the taxi line, makes pizzas and *típico* fare, as well as a mean lasagna (₡700), ravioli (₡750), and canneloni (₡700). **Pizzería Mamma Mia** is also a delight for tastebuds ravished by *gallo pinto*. Fill up on a Mamma Mia salad (₡500) or sip on a capuccino (₡180). While the town of San Vito is itself the primary attraction, visitors may also want to take a trip to **Wilson Botanical Gardens,** 6km out of town on the church road.

■ Golfito

Golfito hides its economic hardships poorly. Abandoned by the United Fruit Company and its promised investments, Golfito's blocks are a sprawl of sad ghost stores, waning memories of something almost grand. In places, though, hope lives on; an indulgent yacht-traveling population makes Golfito the last stop on a coastal tour from Alaska, and between their parties and purchases in the duty-free zone on the northern edge of town, cash flow may once again help the city to repair itself. Hang out on nearby **Cacao, Pavones,** and **Zancudo** beaches, hang ten on the waves, or head to a hangar for a flight to Puerto Jiménez and P.N. Corcovado.

Walking from one end of town to the other is feasible, but save the blisters for better times and catch a ₡45 public bus instead. **Banco Nacional de Costa Rica** (tel. 775-1101; fax 775-1439; open Mon.-Fri. 8:30am-3:45pm), located on the main road, changes traveler's checks and gives cash advances on your Visa. There is also another branch in the duty-free zone (tel. 775-0616; fax 775-0639; open Tues.-Sat. 8:30am-3:45pm and Sun. 8am-2pm). TRACOPA (tel. 775-0365; open Mon.-Sat. 7-11:30am and 2:30-5:30pm, Sun. 7am-1pm) buses run to **San José** daily at 5am and 1pm, and to **San Isidro** at 5am, 1, 1:30pm, and on Sun. at 2pm. Buses to **Neily** run down main street every hour from 6am-5:30pm. The **ferry** from Puerto Jiménez arrives around 7am and leaves again around 10:30am. Dress wounds at the **hospital** (tel. 775-1001; fax 775-0193; open 7am-4pm and 24hr. emergency). **Police** (tel. 775-1022) are located behind the *depósito*. In case of **emergency,** dial 128. **Post office** (tel. 775-1911; fax 775-0373; open Mon.-Fri. 7:30am-5:30pm) is located down a side street near Restaurante Eurekita and has a fax, telegram service, and *lista de correos*.

Not only does **Cabinas Isabel** offers very clean rooms with private baths and fans (singles ₡1500; doubles ₡2600; quads ₡5200), but the upstairs lounge is equipped with a television. For a bit more money, but a not-too-bad deal if you can find three more roommates, try **Hotel Samoa del Sur** (tel. 775-0233; fax 775-0573) across the street. A garden separates a marina from rooms that include two queen size beds, hot water, a fan, a phone, and cable TV (US$40 for a room). **Hotel Uno** (tel. 775-0061), right near the ferry dock, offers 22 simple, unimpressive rooms with open-air slat walls and communal bathrooms (₡400 per person). **Restaurante Uno,** located below the eponymous hotel, offers simple meals at reasonable prices. Near the park shouts **Restaurante La Eurekita,** where the locals come to watch soccer over breakfast and the weary nurse their exotic ice cream dishes (₡350). Enjoy life under the immense thatched-roof dome of **Restaurant Samoa del Sur** (tel. 775-0233), two blocks from the ferry dock toward the Depósito. A slightly pricey meal is made more enjoyable by the beautiful view of tha water and the book you got at their 2-for-1 book exchange.

COSTA RICA

For a change of pace from Golfito, stop by the **Golfito Nature Reserves,** which lie along the main road opposite the sea. With little more to do around town, a day-long hike to observe exotic plants may be worth it. Head to **Pollo Frito Ranchero** for a little, well, *pollo frito*. The restaurant is built like a huge tent, but the dance floor, which rocks on weekends (Fri.-Sat. 9pm-1am), is puny. **Depósito Libre** (duty-free) offers 52 stores of cheap stuff from electronics to perfumes *(eau de backpacker au natural)* to liquor. The **Urbana** buses take visitors there as a regular stop, as the walk is long. As an annoyance, **entrance tickets** into the grounds are free, but must be obtained a day in advance if you plan on buying anything. Pick up tickets at the **Depósito** (Mon.-Sat. 8am-4:30pm, Sun. 7am-2pm). Parking is ¢100 per hour.

■ Near Golfito: Paso Canoas and the Border

Paso Canoas is more than the location of immigration offices at the Panamanian and Costa Rican borders. The dwarfish town also has one mighty big flea market, a great place to buy some last minute tico souvenirs before jammin' on to Panamá. The city is not scenic, and the town's hotels mainly serve hapless travelers who get their feet stuck in bureaucratic mud. **Change currency** at **Banco Panamá,** right next to the Panamanian immigration office directly on the border. There are plenty of garbage bag-toting freelance moneychangers walking around. **Buses** bound for **David** depart frequently from the corner behind the Panamanian Immigration Office and buses to **Neily** are found next to the **Costa Rican post office** located in the main intersection (open Mon.-Fri. 7:30-11:30am and 1:30-5:30pm). The **Panamanian post office** is located on the same bureaucratic block as the bank and the immigration office (open Mon.-Fri. 8am-2pm, Sat. 8am-noon). If you are looking for a **pharmacy**, check out **Almacén Wong Chang** (tel. 771-6542; Panamanian time 8am-7pm). **Police** can be found in the main intersection on both sides of the border. There is a **post office** (tel./fax 732-2021) near the town center (open Mon.-Fri. 7:30-11:30am and 1:30-5:30pm).

If you're stuck in Paso Canoas on the Costa Rican side of the border, try **Hotel Estrella Del Sur.** Rooms have private baths and fans but that's about all the comfort they offer (¢600 per person). **Hotel Palace Sur** (tel. 732-2015), two doors down, offers big, simple rooms, but with a communal bath, at the same price (¢600 per person; double with private bath ¢1500).

Obtain all necessary visas required for entry into Panamá before arriving at the border (see **Documents and Formalities,** p. 420). The process required for entry at Paso Canoas is two-fold: first, visit the Costa Rican immigration office at the border for your exit stamp; then, at the Panamanian office near the center of town, get your stamp, visa, or tourist card. Keep duplicates of forms you're required to fill out. For more information, call the **Panamanian Departamento de Migración** at 727-6502.

PANAMÁ

As a link between oceans and a bridge between continents, Panamá has seen more than its share of passers-through. IPAT, the national tourism board, offers the amazing statistic that Panamá has 1398 tourist attractions, most of which are of the wilderness park variety. Backpack for a month, however, and you're bound to meet no more than 10 other travelers. For some reason, the country has never been a popular destination for budget travelers. Perhaps because of residual uneasiness from "Operation Just Cause" (the U.S.'s invasion of Panamá), or simply because prices are higher than in other parts of Central America, Panamá tends to attract more bankers and business-people than backpackers. In reality, the political situation is relatively stable, and the prices aren't that high (most museums charge US$1 admission), yet nearly every path through the country's lush and wildly diverse natural settings has gone untraversed and unsullied. Take the opportunity to discover beautiful places with rhythmic names like Chiriquí, Coclé, Boquete, Chitré, and Penonomé, towns that pulse with a vibrance that could only be produced by one of the world's true melting pots. The *molas* (patched cloth panels) for which the Kuna people are renowned are frenzied conglomerations of images, shapes, and colors in an organized whole; no creation could better represent the Panamanian people.

The dollars pumped into Panamá's economy through the Canal have clearly had an effect on the country: roads tend to be better paved than elsewhere in Central America, buses run on schedule, and English is more widely spoken, especially in Panama City. On the other hand, Panamá refreshes some travelers precisely because it *is* less rustic; pristine Caribbean shores are still within a few hours' unimpeded drive of a thriving, skyscraper-filled metropolis. Historically, the constant foreign presence in Panamá has actually enhanced, rather than exorcised, Panamanian cultural traditions. There remains a rough-and-tumble spirit inherited from Spain and the country's several indigenous peoples, including the Kuna, Guaymí, and Chocó Indians. Perhaps to protect what is familiar to them, Panamanians have enthusiastically begun to welcome ecotourism, in an attempt to preserve the environment while attracting tourists' cash. In the end, with all the untouched beauty and untouristed splendor that Panamá has to offer, it would be wise to stop to enjoy—and not just cross—this bridge when you come to it.

ESSENTIALS

When to Go

CLIMATE

The weather in Panamá varies wildly from one coast to the other, mostly in terms of how much rain falls. The Caribbean coast can receive up to 140in. of rain each year, while the Pacific side averages a "mere" 60in. annually. Moreover, the rainy season (May-Dec.) actually only applies to the Pacific side, as the Caribbean receives rain year-round. Be prepared for stultifying heat and humidity at any time; temperatures rarely drop below 80°F, except in highland areas.

FESTIVALS AND HOLIDAYS

Check with tourist officials to find out where and when local festivals take place. The whole country flocks to **Chitré** and **Las Tablas** around Semana Santa; to be a part of that party, reserve a room weeks or months in advance. Other national holidays include **January 1** (New Year's Day); **January 9** (Martyr's Day); **February** (Carnaval); **March** or **April** (Good Friday); **May 1** (Labor Day); **November 3** (Independence from Colombia); **November 4** (Flag Day); **November 10** (First Call for Independence from Spain); **November 28** (Emancipation Day); **December 8** (Mother's Day); and **December 25** (Christmas Day).

▒ Useful Information

For publications and organizations of general interest, see **Useful Information,** p. 1.

Instituto Panameño de Turismo (IPAT), Apdo. Postal 4421, Zona 5, Panamá, República de Panamá (tel. 226-7000; fax 226-3483).

ANCON, Calle Alberto Navarro in El Cangrejo in Panama City, Apdo. 1387, Zona 1, Panamá, República de Panamá (tel. 264-8100; fax 204-1836). A private organization offering volunteer opportunities in reforestation, cleaning up beaches, protecting turtle nests, etc.

Smithsonian Tropical Research Institute (STRI), P.O. Box 27-2, Balboa, Panamá, República de Panamá (tel. 227-6021; fax 232-5978), the big orange building near the Museum of Modern Art, on the side of Cerro Ancón in Panama City, sometimes takes volunteers to work on biological field labs on the San Blas Islands (p. 463). They also have a lab on Isla Barro Colorado() Call to make reservations to visit Isla Barro Colorado or to use the world's largest library on neotropical biology. Open Mon.-Fri. 8am-noon and 1-5pm.

Instituto Nacional de Recursos Naturales Renovables (INRENARE) (tel. 232-6601 or 232-43-25) is in charge of all of Panamá's national parks. Stop by their main office in Paraíso for information and permits.

La Fundación para el Desarrollo Sostenible de Panamá (FUNDESPA), Vía Simón Bolívar, Edificio No. 1000, Oficina No. 207, Apdo. 2359, Zona 7, Panamá, República de Panamá (tel. 261-0893; fax 261-9293). Runs AMISCONDE, a conservation and community development project in Parque Internacional La Amistad.

Preferred Adventures Ltd., 1 W. Water St., Suite 300, St. Paul, MN 55107 (tel. (800) 840-8687 or (612) 222-8131; fax 222-4221; email paltours@aol.com; http://www.cool.co.cr/). Helped pioneer soft adventure and nature tours in Panamá. Birding, rainforest study, river rafting, mountain biking, and fishing.

▒ Documents and Formalities

EMBASSIES AND CONSULATES

Embassy of Panamá: U.S., 2862 McGill Terrace NW, Washington, D.C. 20008 (tel. (202) 483-1407; fax 483-8413). Open Mon.-Fri. 9am-5pm. **Canada,** 130 Albert St. #300, Ottawa, Ontario K1P 5G4 (tel. (613) 236-7177; fax 236-5775). **U.K.,** 40 Hertford St., London W1Y TTG (tel. (44) 171-409-2255; fax 493-4499).

Consulate of Panamá, 1212 Ave. of the Americas, 47/48 Street, 10th Floor, New York, NY 10036 (tel. (212) 840-2450; fax 840-2469). Open Mon.-Fri. 8:30am-2pm. Provides visa information and assistance, and offers tourist information for walk-ins only. There are other consulates at 444 Brickell Ave., Miami, FL, 33133, and in Houston, San Francisco, New Orleans, and Tampa.

PASSPORTS, VISAS, AND CUSTOMS

Citizens of the U.S., Australia, Canada, and Ireland need a valid **passport,** return ticket, and tourist card to travel in Panamá. A **tourist card** (US$5) can be acquired in the international airport from which you are departing or upon your arrival; they are also usually available at border crossings, but border supplies run out frequently—get one in advance to be safe. A tourist card or stamped visa allows travelers to stay for 30 days, with extensions possible for up to 60 additional days. A **pre-arranged visa** is necessary for citizens of South Africa and Israel This can take up to three weeks to arrange and may cost up to $50; apply well in advance. You may need references;

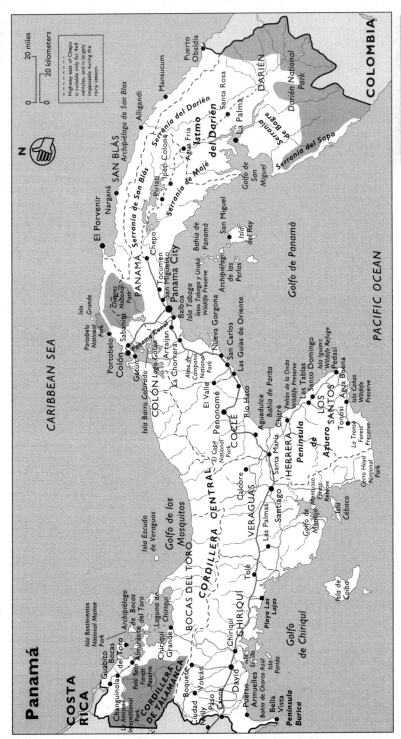

Panamá

consult your home country's Panamanian consulate. Getting an **extension** on your tourist card or visa is a monumental hassle that should be avoided at all costs, as it will suck at least two days of your time into a bureaucratic maelstrom; it is better to go to Costa Rica for a few days and then return to Panamá with a new tourist card. If you do need an extension, you may be asked to produce a letter from a "responsible Panamanian" stating the reason for your extension, an application, proof of a return flight, two passport photos, and some cash.

■ Money Matters

CURRENCY AND EXCHANGE

US$1 = $1.00	$1 = US$1.00
CDN$1 = $0.73	$1 = CDN$1.37
UK£1 = $1.63	$1 = UK£0.61
IRL£1 = $1.45	$1 = IRL£0.69
AUS£1 = $0.74	$1 = AUS$1.34
NZ£1 = $0.65	$1 = NZ$1.54
SARand 1 = $0.22	$1 = SARand 4.61
DM1 = $0.55	$1 = DM1.83

The Panamanian currency, the **Balboa** ($ or Bl.), is directly linked to the U.S. dollar—no, wait, the currency *is* the U.S. dollar. The only difference between the currencies is that different pictures adorn the coins; studly, long-haired Spaniards replace rigid, dead U.S. founders. A mongo-sized 50¢ piece, known as a *peso,* is also used regularly. **ATMs** are virtually unheard of in the interior, except in large cities like David and Santiago, but they are everywhere in Panama City. There are several **Western Union** offices in the country. Few businesses accept traveler's checks as direct payment, but many banks are willing to exchange AmEx checks and sometimes other types. Except at border crossings, black market currency trading is not as common as it is elsewhere in Central America. Visa and MasterCard are easier to use than other cards, but most hotels and restaurants still demand cash. **Banco del Istmo** regularly provides cash advances on Visa cards; there's a $2 service charge per $100. **Tipping** is not usually expected, but it is appreciated. At more touristed locations, 10-15% tip is standard. The minimum age for gambling is 18.

■ Safety

The explosion of an airplane flying between Colón and Panama City has led authorities to beef up security on domestic flights; bus hijackings have been known to occur between Panama City and Colón. Travelers heading through the Darién Gap should beware of robberies and kidnappings. Panama City and Colón are particularly popular haunting grounds for criminals, but watch out for muggers, robbers, and pickpockets throughout the country. As usual, keep all jewelry out of sight, especially those mango-sized diamonds and pearls. All travelers should carry identification, preferably a passport, on them at all times.

Women traveling alone should expect to receive numerous stares and catcalls when traveling in Panamá. A self-defense class is never a bad idea, and the strong infusion of *machismo* in some Panamanian men might lead to more unwanted attention than elsewhere. Women are less welcome (and safe) in casinos and bars and should use discretion in such places.

■ Health

If arriving in Panamá from an infected area, be ready to show a vaccination certificate for **yellow fever.** If you're planning to travel to eastern Panamá (including San Blas), mefloquine should be taken against malaria; chloroquine is effective in other parts of the country. **Cholera** has recently hit the country, as has **typhoid fever.** Also take precautions against **hepatitis, rabies,** and **traveler's diarrhea.**

Despite what locals tell you, most **water** in small towns should be considered unsafe. Water is safer in big cities, but be aware of the sanitary conditions of the establishment whose tap you're using. Few travelers have problems with the tap water in Panama City; in fact, it's thought to be among the best urban water supplies in the world. No matter where you are, however, purified water is always safer.

■ Alternatives to Tourism

Spanish-language schools are just beginning to multiply in Panamá. In Panama City, contact **Genesis Language Center,** Apdo. 9603, Zona 4, Panamá (tel. 223-0947; fax 223-2931) or **Instituto Internacional,** Apdo. 229-2169, Zona 9A, Panamá (tel. 264-7226; fax 129-3016) for more info on programs and classes. A new school has opened in Bocas del Toro—call the **Escuelita de Bocas del Toro,** located at Calle 1, Isla de Bocas del Toro (tel. 757-9630; fax 757-9630) for details about their program, which includes a homestay with a Bocatoreñan family. There are plenty of **volunteer opportunities** available in Panamá as well, particularly in environmental conservation (see **Useful Information,** p. 420).

■ Getting There

For more information on getting to Panamá from outside Central America, see **Getting There,** p. 28. For specific information on flights into Panama City's Tocumen International Airport, see **Practical Information,** p. 428.

Visitors arriving in Panamá with a **car** can drive with their own driver's license. Drivers will have to pay a fee at the **Registro de Propiedad** at the border; the car must be inspected and its documents thoroughly checked. Bring proof of ownership along with your visa and passport. Insurance is recommended. Roads are in relatively good condition, but mechanics are few and far between, as are safe parking places. The suggested **border crossings** into Panamá from Costa Rica are at **Paso Canoas,** along the Interamerican Highway, and at **Guabito,** in the northwest.

■ Once There

TRANSPORTATION

Airplanes moving between cities are small, single-engine wonders. Reservations are usually not taken more than two days in advance for flights within Panamá. National airlines flying between major cities (Panama City, Santiago, David) and resort towns (Bocas del Toro, San Blas, etc.) include **Aeroperlas** (tel. 269-4555), **AereoTaxi** (tel. 264-8644), and **Parsa** (tel. 226-3803).

Buses are the major means of transportation for budget travelers in Panamá and are the only means of reaching remote locations in the interior. Bus quality ranges from "pick-up truck" to "party on wheels." Many are actually mini-buses with cushioned seats and air-conditioning. A bus's destination is almost always written on the front of the vehicle. If there's no terminal, many buses linger around a town's central park. Pay when getting off, but confirm the fare before getting on.

If you stick your thumb out along a road, Panamanians are more likely to wonder what kind of dance you're doing than to stop to pick you up; **hitchhiking** just never caught on here. In some cases, hitchers say it's worth a try, but as always, suggest using extreme caution. *Let's Go* recommends neither roadside jigs nor hitchhiking.

ACCOMMODATIONS

Hotels in Panamá are more expensive than elsewhere in Central America but, outside of resort areas, there are usually plenty of cheap places to stay ($5-30 per night). Usually, even the dingiest-looking hotels are reasonably safe, honestly run, and populated by traveling workers. Camping hasn't become popular and isn't regulated; always try to ask permission before pitching a tent.

KEEPING IN TOUCH

Mail from Panamá takes about two weeks to get to the U.S., although occasionally a letter slips through and makes it in a few days. Rates average about $0.40 for a normal size letter to the U.S. To receive mail in Panamá, note that "Lista de Correos" is *not* the phrase of choice; instead, use "Entrega General." Also, remember to write "República de Panamá" and not just "Panamá," since Panama City is referred to as "Panamá." Address letters as follows:

> Ken <u>BLAZEJEWSKI</u>
> Entrega General
> David (city), Chiriquí (Province)
> República de Panamá

Telephones are reasonably reliable in Panamá, but public phones can be capricious; when using a calling card, your best bet is to hunt down an established hotel or an office of INTEL, the national telephone office. Dial 108 from public phones for **MCI** service, 109 for **AT&T**, 102 for **information.** Without a card, calls are still possible if you offer to pay for costs or call collect; dial 106 to make a **collect call.** As an alternative, **fax** machines are ubiquitous; check in post offices, banks, and hotels. Panamá's **telephone code** is 507.

PANAMÁ: LIFE AND TIMES

■ History

Panamá's fate has always been tied to other nations' interest in its status as a bridge between Central America and South America and the Atlantic and Pacific Oceans; as a result, the nation is mired in a centuries-old identity crisis. By some accounts, modern Panamanians feel secure in their protection by other, more powerful nations, but simultaneously resent the ambivalence produced by half a millennium of questionable sovereignty.

The Pre-Columbian period is perhaps the only part of Panamá's history that can be said to be entirely its own. The indigenous **Kuna, Guaymí,** and **Chocó Indians** that inhabited the isthmus first saw their land fall into foreign hands in 1501, when the Spanish explorers **Rodrigo de Bastidas** and **Vasco Núñez de Balboa** stumbled upon Panamá's Atlantic Coast and quickly suppressed the natives. After hearing tales of a vast sea to the south, Balboa became the first European to cross Panamá and, in 1513, he boldly claimed the Pacific Ocean and all the land it touched. The first colonists capitalized on Balboa's "discovery," using settlements on the Pacific coast near modern day Panama City (called "Panamá," or "abundance of fish") as a launching point for domination of the South American Incas, whose riches the Spanish transported away on the **Camino Real** (King's Highway), a stone path between Panamá's Atlantic and Pacific coasts. Portobelo, on the Atlantic side of the road, flourished along with the Spanish mercantile economy. Although repeated attacks by **Henry Morgan** and other English raiders weakened port cities throughout the 17th century, continued foreign trade provided prosperity and comfort to Panamá, which did not join its Central American neighbors in revolting against Spain. Only the revocation of foreign trade rights sparked resentment and, by 1843, Panamá had joined the **United Nation of Gran Colombia.**

During the next century, Panamá's course was dictated more and more by other nations' quests to make a better path from sea to shining sea. The U.S. fostered dreams of creating its own *Camino Real* in the form of a transcontinental railroad. Between the signing of an 1846 treaty, which granted the U.S. free transit across the isthmus, and the completion of the railroad in 1855, Panamá's politics were turbulent; 20 governors were inaugurated and rejected. Meanwhile, the glitter of gold in California compelled thousands of U.S. citizens to cross through Panamá *en route* to the West and the economy surged. The completed railroad prompted plans for the construction of a canal, the rights to which were originally granted to the French in 1848. **Ferdinand de Lesseps,** a French diplomat who had already proved his "canal know-how" at Suez, was chosen to engineer the project, but malaria and repeated landslides caused his trans-American canal to fail. The U.S. bought up the French stake, but was unable to acquire the Canal Zone from Colombia. With the help of U.S. naval forces, public resentment toward Colombia resulted in a revolutionary *junta,* which declared the independence of the "Republic of Panamá" in 1903. The U.S. acquired the necessary land in 1904, and the canal was completed just 10 years later. Along with control of the waterway, Panamá's new constitution granted the U.S. intervention rights, which were exercised several times during the next few decades.

Panamá has gained more control over the canal throughout the century, but the U.S. is still heavily active in Panamanian affairs. The **Hull-Alfaro Treaty** of 1936 forced the U.S. to abandon their intervention rights and increased the fees paid for the Canal Zone. By 1958, U.S. control was still a presence disturbing enough to provoke student riots against both the Panamanian and U.S. governments. The riots were quickly squelched and, within 15 years, a series of failed elections led to a revision of the constitution. **Colonel Torrijos Herrera** emerged as the virtual dictator of Panamá. A benevolent despot (and notorious partier), Herrera splurged on the country's public works, despite a steadily growing debt. He developed housing for the poor, raised wages, and sponsored a program intended to expand nationalism. To encourage such sentiment, he signed a treaty with U.S. President Jimmy Carter that guaranteed total Panamanian control over the canal by the year 2000. A mysterious plane crash ended Herrera's life and opened the door to a new political crisis; leadership passed between various men, and control of the National Guard ended up in the hands of **General Manuel Noriega,** Herrera's head of intelligence.

Noriega became involved in governmental affairs early in his life. While still a student at a military academy in Perú, the American Defense Intelligence Agency paid him $20 per week to spy on his fellow students. After helping to hone his skills, the U.S. hired Noriega as a C.I.A. operative in contact with the Nicaraguan *Contras,* and he eventually became head of Panamanian intelligence. Upon his seizure of control of the National Guard in 1983, Noriega quickly granted himself dictatorial powers by controlling the press, creating military goon squads, and managing Panamá's drug traffic together with Colombian drug cartels. In 1984, the General allowed an election; the popular **Arnulfo Arias** seemed a clear winner, but Ardito Barlett, Noriega's candidate, "magically" emerged victorious and became the newest puppet president. In 1988, Noriega was indicted in the U.S. on drug trafficking charges. As **President Ronald Reagan** tightened sanctions on Panamá, Noriega closed his grip, nullifying yet another presidential election that his candidate had lost.

No sooner did Noriega declare himself president than word started to spread that Panamá was at war with the U.S. After the killing of an unarmed U.S. Marine officer, **President George Bush** acted quickly, ordering 24,000 troops to Panamá to remove Noriega by force. As the General was busy whooping it up, U.S. paratroopers silently floated down into Panama City. Noriega fled into the Papal Nuncio, where American soldiers assailed him with a bizarre form of psychological torture: they blared "Voodoo Chile," "I Fought the Law and the Law Won," and other rock tunes in order to flush him out. A few days later, Noriega (who claims not to have heard the music) surrendered and was flown to Florida to await trial for drug charges. In 1992, he was found guilty on eight charges of conspiracy to manufacture and distribute cocaine and was sentenced to 40 years imprisonment.

426 ■ PANAMÁ: LIFE AND TIMES

Despite its stated goals of liberating Panamá from tyranny, protecting American lives, and bringing Noriega to justice, **"Operation Just Cause"** was criticized internationally as bullying and self-interested foreign policy. Still, Panamanians were generally supportive of U.S. actions during the invasion, though many later demanded reparations for civilian deaths caused by U.S. explosive shells. The newly installed government of **Guillermo Endara** faced high rates of poverty, unemployment, and crime after the invasion. A public referendum rejected more than 50 proposed reforms by the president, and opposition groups demanded the drafting of a new constitution. Endara successfully engaged Panamá in Central American affairs, establishing the country's membership in the Central American Parliament in 1993 and committing Panamá to economic integration in the Central American Common Market. Nonetheless, he was voted out and replaced by **Ernesto Pérez Balladares.** These recent adventures have ensured that Panamá's problem of occluded identity lives on; Panamanians feel, as always, a bit bothered by their continuing role as "little buddy" to the U.S.

▓ The Arts

Panamá's position as a bridge between continents has opened it to artistic influences from all sides. The chants of indigenous peoples continue to thrive for their lyrical melodies and for their potency; reportedly, a hunter once paid a musician $15 to teach him a song designed to attract turtles. The most famous Panamanian dance is the sexy **tamborito,** which is accented by hand claps, rhythms played on three drums, and men using hats to fan women. Other characteristic forms are the **mejorana,** played on two guitars and accompanied by a square dance, and the **punto,** which is more up-tempo. The most popular music in Panamá is undoubtedly **merengue** and **salsa,** which blare from every radio station.

Panamá's distance from the cultural centers of Guatemala and Colombia left its **literature** underdeveloped until this century. Prior to then, poetry, such as that of **José María Alemán** and **Darío Herrera,** was the main outlet for romantic and modernist thought. Since the building of the Canal, foreign nations' role in Panamanian affairs and the tumultuous lives of those living by the Canal have become the dominant themes of authors like **Renato Ozores** and **Carlos Francisco Changmarín.**

Don't worry about having to seek out Panamanian **arts and crafts**—nearly every town has a **Mercado Artesanal.** Shelf after shelf of vases and pots adorned with bold, geometric patterns fill the markets in west and central Panamá; many replicate the folk art of the Guaymí Indians. More predominant in the east are the intricately patterned clothes of the Kuna of San Blas. Some artisans have taken wicker to new extremes, making helicopters, airplanes, and cars, along with countless baskets.

▓ Food and Drink

With two expanses of ocean and a lot of green in between, it's not surprising that Panamá brims with ambrosia. The coasts abound with luscious tropical treats like drip-down-the-edge-of-your-chin mangos and freshly harvested lobsters, while in the hills of the interior hearty, savory stews are all the rage. The national dish is **sancocho,** a stew made with chicken, corn, potatoes, and onions.

Quality, price, and safety vary according to what you expect to pay, how much you eat, and where you sit. In almost every town, there are *típico* restaurants offering beef and chicken standards for $1-2. Red meat is everywhere, but vegetarians can always count on a town's fruit stand for sweet nothings costing next to nothing.

▓ Media

Panamá has several television stations, each offering its own news, prime time programming, and highly addictive soap operas. A great way to make instant friends at the local hotel or grocery store is to ask how Lupe could possibly escape her father's torments and marry the priest. Similarly entertaining is "Cocina al Minuto y Algo Más," a cooking show on daily at 8:30am.

Most Panamanians stay informed through *La Prensa*, *La Crítica*, *La República*, and other dailies; *El Siglo* spoons out more tabloidish news. All, including *El Universal* and *La Estrella*, are sold on the street and in hotels.

▓ Recent News

President Ernesto Pérez Balladares, member of the Partido Revolucionario Democrático (PRD), ran into scandal during the spring and summer of 1996 amid reports that he received campaign money from a reputed drug trafficker. In June, Balladares finally released an audit proving the reports true, but claimed a Reaganesque ignorance of how it had happened. As Panamá works to privatize its economy, Balladeres' government has come under fire yet again for its attempts to exclude U.S. companies from the bidding process. Indeed, foreign and Panamanian investors alike remain highly skeptical of the government and the privatization process, maintaining that both are corrupt. In May 1997, however, a UK telecommunications firm bought a majority stake in INTEL, the Panamanian telecom mammoth, proving that allegations of corruption are not enough to stop the foreign drive to get a piece of Panamá's burgeoning market.

The most pressing concern for Panamá's leaders is how to deal with the Canal, which the U.S. is scheduled to hand over at the end of the decade. The Canal Zone is estimated to be worth about $80 billion, and Panamá currently lacks the organization needed to administer the waterway. A recent public opinion poll shows that most Panamanians doubt the Canal will operate efficiently after 2000. Another issue is just how much cleaning up the U.S. should do before leaving, and whether it is responsible for the toxic waste buried beneath its military bases. Before bailing, though, the United States is urging whatever reforms it can, including the re-institution of a military police squad to hinder corruption and drug trafficking in Panamá, especially in the Darién region. Currently, Panamá has no military.

Panama City

Nowhere else are a city's buses as much a microcosmic representation of the flare and tastes of the place itself as in Panama City. Covered front-fender to tailpipe with frenzied, freakish, air-brushed depictions of Rambo, Batman, and Jesus Christ, the psychedelic mobile murals zoom around corners as Panamanians of Chinese, Jewish, Kuna, and Spanish descent try to cut through blaring honks with cries of *"parada!"* As residents of the desperately pumping heart of the world's crossroads, the inhabitants of Panama City have known and will always know what it is to be on a collision course with postmodernity.

Frustrated by reeking, infertile swamps and rank, virile pirates, residents of Panamá Viejo decided to leave their settlement in 1673 and move 10km west to a rocky peninsula. With water flowing in from El Chorrillo (a mountain stream to the north), the citizens prospered, despite the waning of the trans-isthmian trade upon which they had previously depended. Huge fires in the 18th century boded poorly for Panama City, but the construction of the inter-oceanic railway and the California gold rush in the mid-19th century resurrected the flailing city. By the beginning of this century, plans for a water passage were complete, and when the first ship passed through the canal's Miraflores Locks in 1914, the city's fate was sealed. Panamá is scheduled to take the canal from the U.S. at the end of the millennium, but, regardless of ownership, it will forever continue to inject Panama City with snippets of the world.

▓ Orientation

Panama City's sprawl along **Panama Bay** begins on the west side at the Canal, which is lined with U.S. Air Force bases near the **Bridge of the Americas**. The upper-crust (and largely North American) neighborhoods of **Balboa, Albrook, Ancón,** and **Curundú** all lie in this western portion. Many hotels, services, and attractions are clustered in the old center of **San Felipe,** the peninsula jutting to the west (sometimes called **Casco Viejo** and not to be confused with **Amador,** which is still farther west). **Avenida A** comes into San Felipe from the west, and **Avenida Central,** one of the city's major thoroughfares, from the east. Av. Central branches off at various points into other major avenues, including the coastal road, **Avenida Balboa** (Av. 6 Sur), and **Vía Simón Bolívar** (Vía Transístmica) to the north. Farther east, Av. Central becomes **Vía España,** the heart of the business and banking district. Av. Central roughly divides the north and south neighborhoods in the center of the city, including **Calidonia, Bella Vista,** and **La Cresta.** Still further east roost the neighborhoods **El Cangrejo** and **San Francisco.** At the east end of the city sits **Panamá Viejo,** the city's original site.

Streets are laid out in a grid in Calidonia, Bella Vista, San Francisco, and various other parts of town, but elsewhere, roads twist and turn. Av. Central marks the dividing street for addresses along east to west streets, with Av. 1 Nte. one block north and Av. 1 Sur to the south. North to south *calles* are also labelled in their relation to **Calle 1,** on the west side of town. Numbered streets often also have names, so learning both can be very helpful; for example, Av. 1 Sur is also known as Av. Perú. Also enjoy landmarks like **Plaza 5 de Mayo,** near Av. 3 Sur and Av. Central.

Bella Vista is a quiet, middle class suburb of *villas* interspersed with high-rises; El Cangrejo is upper-middle class, at the commercial heart of Vía España, and includes **Albert Einstein Plaza, Vía Brasil,** and an abundance of restaurants on **Vía Argentina.**

Just west of Bella Vista, Calidonia has a split personality. One half teems with squalid markets, lurking ruffians, and bordellos; the other half is a major medical district. While it is reputed to be safe to walk around most of Calidonia (especially during the day and on Av. Central), avoid the area near the stadium west of Av. Central.

To the southwest of Calidonia is eternally traffic-jammed **Santa Ana,** home to many bus terminals. Santa Ana blends into its next door neighbor, **San Felipe,** a frenetic and slightly run-down neighborhood that nevertheless sprouts beautiful historical buildings and panoramic ocean views. Walking about after dark here is not advisable.

Bordering San Felipe and Santa Ana is the most dangerous part of the city, **El Chorrillo.** Stay away. Continuing up out of San Felipe on Av. Central, however, leads you into a thriving pedestrian mall with discount clothing vendors and restaurants of every kind. A bit like Vía Argentina, but cheaper, the mall offers a fun few hours. Further north, the **Mercado Público** and other markets on Av. Central and Plaza 5 de Mayo embody the city's bustle. Women walking through the area should expect cat-calls. Many buses (including the orange-and-white SACA buses to the former Canal Zone) leave from the area around Plaza 5 de Mayo.

On the opposite end of the city, to the east, ritzy condos shield some of Panama City's richest residents in **Punta Paitilla,** a neighborhood that's only 15 years old—and looks it. Of most interest to travelers here is the attractive, moderately priced **Plaza Paitilla** near the freeway entrance. Punta Paitilla is also home to a number of kosher markets and restaurants. Nearby **Coco Mar** and **San Francisco** are generally pleasant neighborhoods, filled predominantly with gorgeous, posh villas, including Manuel Noriega's former residence, **Rancho Sololá.** The stretch east of Coco Mar marks a continuum of dilapidation, culminating in the crumbling ruins of Panamá Viejo. Buses arrive and leave frequently, making the somewhat crime-affected site easily and more safely visited.

▓ Practical Information

Tourist Office: IPAT has its national office at the **Atlapa Convention Center,** 4 Calle 77, Vía Israel, San Francisco, Apartado Postal 4421, Zona 5 (tel. 226-7000, ext.

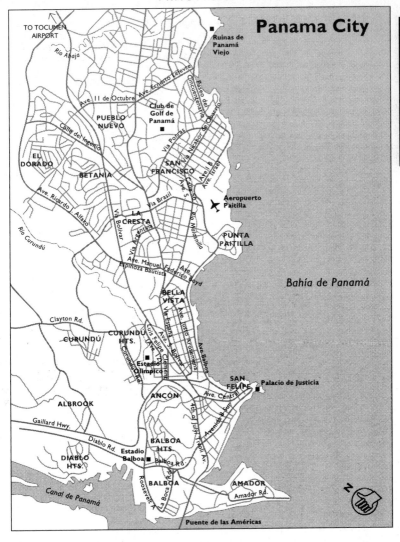

Panama City

TO TOCUMEN AIRPORT

Río Abajo

Ruinas de Panamá Viejo

Ave. Echesce Tefevre

Paseo del Cincuentenario

Ave. II de Octubre

Club de Golf de Panamá

PUEBLO NUEVO

Calle del Ingenio

Via Porras

Via Nicanor de Obarrio

EL DORADO

SAN FRANCISCO

Ave. S.

Ave. Cuba

Ave. Israel

BETANIA

Ave. Ricardo J. Alfaro

Via Brasil

Aeropuerto Paitilla

LA CRESTA

Via Argentina

Río Matasnilla

Via Bolívar

Río Curundú

PUNTA PAITILLA

Ave. Manuel Federico Boyd

Espinoza Bautista

BELLA VISTA

Bahía de Panamá

Clayton Rd.

CURUNDÚ HTS.

Via España

CURUNDÚ

Luis Felipe Clemente

Ave. Justo Arosemena

Curundú Rd.

Ave. Balboa

Estadio Olímpico

SAN FELIPE

Palacio de Justicia

ALBROOK

ANCÓN

Ave. Central

4th of July/Thori Av.

Gaillard Hwy.

Avenida B. Sur

Diablo Rd.

BALBOA HTS.

DIABLO HTS.

Estadio Balboa

Balboa Rd.

Roosevelt

La Boca Rd.

BALBOA

AMADOR

Canal de Panamá

Amador Rd.

N

Puente de las Américas

112, 113, or 278, or 226-3544). IPAT provides info on everything, including lists of hotels, phone numbers, immigration requirements, medication, and prices. Open Mon.-Fri. 8:30am-4:30pm. There is another branch at Tocumen Airport, just past the immigration office, open daily 8am-midnight.

Embassies: U.S. (tel. 227-1777; fax 227-1964), Av. Balboa and Calle 37, Apdo. Postal 6959 Zona 5. Open Mon.-Fri. 8am-5pm. **Canada** (tel. 264-9731), Samuel Lewis Av., Gerardo Ortega St., Banco Central Hispano, 4th fl., P.O. Box 3658, Balboa. Open Mon.-Fri. 8:30am-1pm. **U.K.** (tel. 269-0866; fax 223-0730), Calle 53, Edificio Swissbank, 4th fl. Open Mon.-Fri. 8am-noon. **Costa Rica** (tel. 264-2937; fax 263-7906), Calle Manuel Maria y Casa, Edificio Anglici, 9th fl. Open Mon.-Fri. 9am-3pm. **El Salvador** (tel. 223-3020; fax 263-6148), Av. Manuel Espinoza Batista, Edificio Metropolis, 4th fl. Open Mon.-Fri. 9am-1pm. **Guatemala**, Edificio Versalles, Av. Frederico Boyd, Calle 48 (tel. 269-3406; fax 223-1922). Open Mon.-Fri. 8am-1pm. **Honduras,** Av. Justo Arosemena and Calle 31, Edificio Tapia, 2nd fl. (tel. 225-8200; fax 225-

3283). Open Mon.-Fri. 9am-2pm. **Nicaragua** (tel. 223-0981), Av. Federico Boyd and Calle 50 . Open Mon.-Fri. 9am-1pm and 3-6pm. **Colombia,** Calle Manuel M. Icaza 12 (tel. 264-9266; fax 223-1134), Edificio Grobman, 6th fl. Open Mon.-Fri. 8:30am-1pm. **Australia, New Zealand, South Africa,** and **Belize** have no embassies.

Immigration: (tel. 225-1373 or 227-1077), Av. 2 Sur (Av. Cuba) and Calle 29, in Calidonia. Visa extensions and exit stamps. Plan to spend a long time in line. For **passport photos,** run across the street or to any Farmacia Arrocha.

Banks: Located all over the city, particularly around Vía España. Many have ATMs, and almost all exchange traveler's checks. Most close by 1pm.

American Express: (tel. 264-2444; fax 269-2971), Calle 50/59, 1st fl. Ask for customer service. Open Mon.-Fri. 8am-5pm, Sat. 8am-noon.

Western Union: Several locations. On Vía España across from the Supermercado El Rey. Open Mon.-Sat. 8am-6pm (tel. 269-1055). The El Dorado branch is located inside Supermercado El Rey (tel. 236-3933; open Mon.-Sat. 10am-7pm, Sun. 10am-5pm) and the Los Pueblos branch is inside Supercentro Los Pueblos (tel. 266-7606; open Mon.-Sat. 10am-7pm).

Airport: Tocumen International Airport (tel. 238-4322) lies a bit outside of the city and is best reached by cab ($12-15). The Pacora and Chepo buses, found on Vía España, stop at the parking lot entrance. Tocumen houses several airlines including: **American** (tel. 269-6022), **Continental** (tel. 263-9177), **COPA** (tel. 227-4551), **TACA** (269-6066), and **LACSA** (tel. 225-4631). **Paitilla Airport** (tel. 226-7959), closer to the city, is a departure point for domestic flights to San Blas with **AeroTaxi** (tel. 264-8644) or **ANSA** (tel. 226-7891). The latter also offers charter flights Mon.-Sat. Domestic carrier **Aeroperlas** (tel. 238-4767) serves **Changuinola, Darién, David, Bocas del Toro, Chitré, Santiago,** and **Colón.**

Buses: Unfortunately, there's a different terminal for just about every destination. Buses to **David** (tel. 262-9436) leave from the terminal on Av. Balboa near Av. B. (every hr., 5am-2pm; every 2hr., 2pm-8pm, non-express 7hr., $10.60; express at 10pm and midnight, 5hr., $15). Non-express buses to David also stop at **Penonomé,** the road to **El Valle, Divisa** (where you catch another bus to **Chitré**), and **Santiago.** Better yet, take the "MOP Curundú Terminal" SACA bus from Plaza 5 de Mayo or a taxi to *terminal de interior* in Curundú for buses to **El Valle** (every 45min., $3.50), **Penonomé** (every 20min., $3.70), **Chitré** (every hr., $6), or **Santiago** (every hr. from 3am-7pm, 9pm, midnight, $6). There are two bus stations that send buses to **Colón.** The express departs from in front of Hotel Veracruz on Av. Perú and Calle 30 in Calidonia (2hr., $1.75); the *ruta* (local bus) station is near the intersection of Calle P and Av. Central near Restaurante El Capitolio (every 15-20min., 3:40am-10pm, $1.25). To get to **Portobelo,** take the bus towards Colón, but transfer in **Sabanitas.** A block west of the pedestrian mall, the **Tica** bus to **San José, Costa Rica** leaves at 11am from near Hotel Ideal, on Calle 17 (14-16hr., $25). To get anywhere in the **former Canal Zone,** take an orange and white SACA bus from near Plaza 5 de Mayo ($0.35).

Taxis: Fares are based on a zone system. $1 plus $0.25 per additional person per zone; $0.15 extra per zone Sun. and after midnight.

Public buses: A steady stream of ultra-colorful city buses runs along Vía España and throughout the city. They're noisy, so shout *"parada!"* to get off. Fare $0.15-0.20.

Car rentals: Most require passport and driver's license for rental; some places say you have to be 25. Look for coupons in IPAT brochures. **Alamo** (tel. 260-0776), **Avis** (tel. 213-0555 or 238-4056), **Barriga** (tel. 269-0221), **Budget** (tel. 263-8777), **Dollar** (tel. 236-8014), **Hertz** (tel. 264-1111), and **National** (tel. 264-8277).

Supermarket: Rey Supermercado is all over the place, even on Vía España, across from Figali's Dept. Store (tel. 223-7850; open 24hr.), or on Plaza Amador, Calle B and Calle 16 Oeste (tel. 228-7048; open daily 6am-9pm).

Laundry: The signless **Lavamático Luchín** is in San Felipe on the south side of the Iglesia de la Merced in a small mint-green establishment. Self-serve wash runs under $0.75. Open Mon.-Sat. 7am-9pm, Sun. 7am-4pm. Near Plaza de Einstein on Vía Argentina is **Lavandería El Trebol** (tel. 269-7554). Wash $0.75, dry $1.25. Open Mon.-Sat. 7am-7pm, Sun. 9am-3pm.

Pharmacy: Farmacia Arrocha (tel. 223-4505), across from Hotel El Panamá on Vía España and Calle 49 Este. Other branches throughout the city. Open 24hr.

PANAMÁ

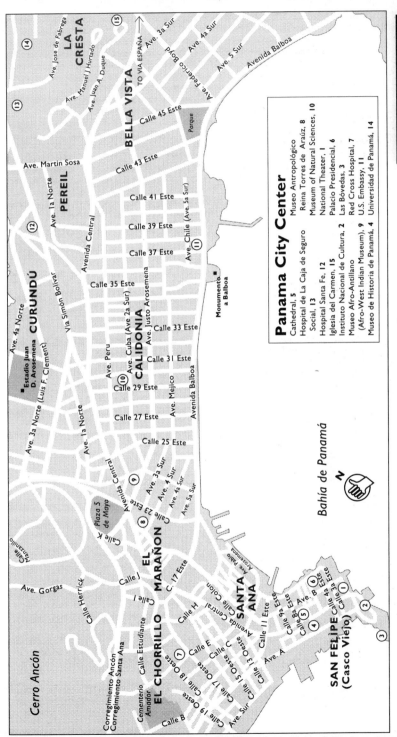

Panama City Center

Cathedral, 5
Hospital de La Caja de Seguro
Social, 13
Hospital Santa Fe, 12
Iglesia del Carmen, 15
Instituto Nacional de Cultura, 2
Museo Afro-Antillano
(Afro-West Indian Museum), 9
Museo de Historia de Panamá, 4

Museo Antropológico
Reina Torres de Araúz, 8
Museum of Natural Sciences, 10
National Theater, 1
Palacio Presidencial, 6
Las Bóvedas, 3
Red Cross Hospital, 7
U.S. Embassy, 11
Universidad de Panamá, 14

Bookstores: Decent selection of English books at **Gran Morrison** stores throughout the city. Vía España (tel. 269-2695; open Mon.-Sat. 9am-6:30pm, Sun. 9:30am-6pm).

Travel Agencies: Mundi Viajes (tel. 263-6933), on Vía Argentina, offers travel packages and local tours (open Mon.-Fri. 8am-noon and 2-5:30pm, Sat. 8am-noon). **Mia Travel S.A.** (tel. 263-7835; fax 263-8078), a little farther down the same street, is open Mon.-Fri. 8am-5:30pm and Sat. 9am-6pm.

Red Cross: tel. 228-2187 (ambulance service).

Hospital: Hospital del Niño (tel. 225-1546; emergency 225-3677), Calle 34, 1-81; **Hospital Clínica America** (tel. 229-2221; emergency 229-1627).

Police: Calidonia, San Felipe, Santa Ana (tel. 262-4417); **San Francisco, Paitilla, Bella Vista** (tel. 226-5692); **Balboa** (tel. 272-6503); **Tocumen** (tel. 295-1327). For emergencies, dial 104. **Firefighters:** tel. 103.

Post Office: The central post office, which receives all letters sent to *Entrega General,* is located on Av. Balboa and Av. B. Open Mon.-Fri. 7am-5:45pm, Sat. 7am-4:45pm. If *Entrega General* letters are specifically addressed "Zona 7, Via España," they will instead be sent to the post office branch bearing this address.

Telephones: Public phones are located throughout the city and INTEL has several offices, including one next to Hotel Continental on Vía España. Phone, **fax,** and **telegram** services offered. Open daily 7:30am-9:30pm.

■ Accommodations

Panama City's neighborhoods are a largely diverse lot. San Felipe is definitely the place for inexpensive, spartan living. Bella Vista has its share of semi-luxurious, affordable hotels at a distance from the city's hubbub. Calidonia's hotels run the gamut. The hotels below are all large and should have at least a room or two available on demand.

SAN FELIPE (CASCO VIEJO)

Hotel Central (tel. 262-8044), Av. Central and Calle 5, in the heart of San Felipe, facing the cathedral. A grand hotel dating back to 1870. 150 rooms, private or communal baths, fans everywhere and balconies overlooking the park. Relive its past glory. Singles $7.50, with bath $8.50; doubles $8.50, with bath $10.50.

Hotel Foyo (tel. 262-8023), Av. A and Calle 6. A safe haven from the noise outside with 39 simple rooms. All rooms have fans. Reception open 24hr. 1 bed $6, with sink $7; 2 beds $9, with bath $11.

Pensión Panamá (tel. 262-8053), across from the Foyo, isn't exactly welcoming (bars separate guests from staff), but the 25 rooms with either 2 separate beds or 1 matrimonial bed all have communal baths, so it's easy to get to know your fellow inmates and talk about how little you're paying. Singles $4; doubles $6.

SANTA ANA, CALIDONIA, AND BELLA VISTA

Hotel California (tel. 263-7736), across the dark desert highway from the Bella Vista, but light-years ahead in terms of comfort. Comfy beds, new color TVs, large mirrors, gleaming peach-tiled bathrooms, tasteful wood decor, 24hr. guard, and a view of the skyline. Singles $20; doubles $33; triples $38.50.

Hotel Ideal (tel. 262-2400) on Calle 17 Oeste, a block away from the pedestrian mall in Santa Ana. Although the neighborhood is better during the day than at night, the hotel's proximity to the busy mall and the guard in front lead many to consider it fairly secure. All rooms have central A/C, hot water, and TVs. Singles $10, with private bath $16; doubles $14, with private bath $18.

Hotel Discovery (tel. 225-1140), Av. Arosemena and Av. Ecuador, Calles 33/34. The neighborhood is quiet, but the different colors adorning the face of the hotel are rather loud. The A/C, TVs, private baths, hot water, and matrimonial beds built for giants make up for the lack of an elevator. Singles $15; doubles $20.

Hotel Bella Vista (tel. 264-4029), at Av. Central and Av. Perú. Each room on each floor of the 7-story hotel comes equipped with phones, TVs, A/C, hot water, and private baths, yet still manages to appear plain (singles Mon.-Thur. $10, Fri-Sun. $15; doubles $15).

▨ Food

Panama City is the heart of international cuisine in Central America; treat yourself to Argentine, Indian, Chinese, Swiss, and more—there's some good Panamanian food, too. The **market** near Plaza 5 de Mayo abounds with fruit, vegetables, and hot tasties. The main strip for fabulous dining is **Vía Argentina.** Though many of its places are snooty and overpriced, but it's also home to affordable plates o' joy. Seafood is almost never a letdown, though often as costly as $7-10 per plate. For cheap, greasy, *típico* fare, visit San Felipe.

Ristorante Fratelli (tel. 223-2754). Enjoy a hearty Italian meal while people-watching on one of Vía Argentina's attractive patio restaurants, or take a seat inside the modern restaurant and people-watch the people-watchers on the patio through the large glass windows. Hawaiian 12" pizza or lasagna $4. Open Sun.-Thurs. 11am-11pm, Fri. and Sat. 11am-1am.

Athen's (tel. 223-1464), Calle 57 Este off Via España, behind Bingo 90. Italian (pizza) and Greek (salads and gyros) fare is good-tasting and inexpensive, despite the fancy phones at each table with which you may call your waitress. Pick-up available, no delivery. Open Wed.-Mon. 11am-11:30pm.

Niko's Café (tel. 263-7070), just off Vía España near Cine Aries—look for the lasagna ($3). Take-out orders can be made as well (gyros $3). Big and clean, and other branches are located throughout the city. Open 24hr.

Aleph Café (tel. 264-2844), on Vía Argentina. Sexy cafe atmosphere with internet access ($4 per hr.). Modern Panamanian artwork adorning the walls is for sale. Prides itself on being the only restaurant in Panamá that has crepes (zucchini with cheese crepe $4; sweet crepes $3-5). Open daily noon-1am.

Sorrento Restaurante (tel. 269-0055; fax 269-0016), take the hard right after Hotel Continental on Vía España and look for it on your left. If pictures of the Pope aren't pacifying enough, the subdued music and reasonable prices should be. Enjoy tortellini, lasagna, or pizza—prices run about $4. Open Tues.-Sun. 11am-midnight.

Restaurante Galaxia (tel. 269-2020), Vía Argentina at Plaza Einstein, serves the standard assortment of meats and seafood ($5 and up), pasta ($4-6), and pizza ($4-9), but it's in a suave environment with dark gleaming woodwork and strategically placed glass. Open Mon.-Sat. 10am-11pm, Sun. 8am-11pm.

Restaurante Mistamar (tel. 212-0398), Av. Balboa, near Av. B. Choose from the buffet or order at the counter. Impressively clean and a cool break from the heat. Pizza ($2-5) and filet mignon ($3.50). Open Mon.-Sat. 6am-10pm.

La Casa de las Costillitas (tel. 269-6670), on Vía Argentina, is the place to dine if you crave a juicy barbecue. The 15-page menu lists everything from seafood to *costillitas* (spare ribs $5.75) and other meats (generally $5) to instructions on ordering a rose for your dinner companion. Vegetarians and pasta lovers will be disappointed.

▨ Sights

Casco Viejo gives you a bang for your walking-tour buck; the old city center is packed with striking memorials to politicians, heroes, and the heavens above. A good place to begin is on Av. A and Calle 3, at the **Church and Convent of Santo Domingo,** which dates back to 1678. The church's arch, **Arco Chato,** is famous for its mortar construction and lack of internal supports. Panamanian leaders used the arch's survival as proof that the country was earthquake-free, an important argument in the battle with Nicaragua for the trans-isthmian canal. Nearby, the **Museo de Arte Religioso Colonial** contains religious artifacts, relics, and sculptures from the 16th to 18th century (tel. 228-2897; open Tues.-Sat. 9am-4:15pm; admission $0.75, kids $0.25).

Walk south to the end of Av. Central and follow **Paseo Las Bóvedas,** the path overlooking the Pacific. Long ago, the area was used as a barrier against encroaching pirates and escaped prisoners from nearby island penal colonies. Now it functions as a make-out hideaway for teenagers and, on weekends, as a gathering place for families. "Bóvedas" refers to the vaults around the area; listen for the echoes of past prisoners before enjoying the vaults' modern incarnation as both restaurant and gallery. **Plaza Francia,** at the peninsula's tip, was engineered by Leonardo de Villanueva Meyer and built in honor of the thousands of Frenchmen who died during the first attempt to build a canal in the late 19th century. Read the history of the French involvement in the canal on the plaques adorning the walls, or stare back at the busts of the Canal's forefathers. At the end of the path is a stage floor where chamber orchestras play to hushed crowds on summer evenings, and **Club de Clases De Tropas,** which marks the remains of Noriega's heyday. The club once saw a thriving social scene filled with generals, lieutenants, socialites, and celebrities wooed by the former dictator. The four decrepit, graffiti-littered walls now serve as living testament to the public's disdain for Noriega's jet-setting lifestyle. Near the club is **Iglesia San José,** home to the **Tabla de Oro,** a monument to Incan architecture built before the Republic of Panamá was even conceived. According to locals, a priest covered the magnificent gold altar in mud to prevent the pirate Henry Morgan from stealing it when he ransacked Panama Viejo.

Past the park, at the end of the path, one block west on Av. B, lolls the Neoclassical **Teatro Nacional,** built at the turn of the century. Speak with the administrators to be let in; then sink into one of the heavenly red velvet balcony chairs overlooking the grand theater while staring up at the ceiling's hovering cherubim. Across the street soars the tower of **Catedral San Francisco,** built in 1673. A block away, **Parque Simón Bolívar** features a monument honoring the great liberator.

Along Av. Alfaro stands the **Palacio Presidencial,** also called the "Palace of the Herons." The Spanish-Moorish-style building is still home to El Prez, so entrance is generally prohibited. Heading inland a few blocks brings you to the serene **Plaza Catedral,** which, uncoincidentally, rests before the big **cathedral.** Erected in 1798, it features white-washed, mother-of-pearl towers and domes. Take a load off with the locals on one of the park benches and watch the exciting construction that is part of an effort to rejuvenate some of the aging buildings in the area. Also on the plaza, in a 121-year-old building, is the former **main post office.** However, this branch has closed and merged with the nearby branch in Santa Ana (Avs. B and Balboa), and the building is metamorphosing into the **Museo del Canal Interoceánico.** On Parque Central, next to the post office, lies the **Palacio Municipal,** now just a big administrative building. In 1903, the *palacio* was the site of the signing of the Act of Independence, which liberated Panamá from Colombia. On the third floor is the **Museo de Historia de Panamá,** which features furniture, paintings, and historical documents (open Mon.-Fri. 8:30am-3:30pm; adults $1, *niños* $0.25).

The **mercado público,** on Av. Alfaro, has San Felipe's biggest collection of fruit, fish, and meat kiosks. This is also a good area to find *típico* souvenirs at a low price, but beware: tourists can be hot targets for pickpockets and thieves here. Walking further up Av. Central from Casco Viejo, past the eternal traffic jams, will soon bring you to a pedestrian mall with oodles of restaurants and stores offering mega-cheap clothing (shirts for $5, shoes for $1).

At the end of the pedestrian mall is the columned building housing the **Museo Antropológico Reina Torres de Araúz** (formerly known as the Museo del Hombre Panameno), which documents the ethnography of the country with pictures and mannequins of Panamá's various ethnic groups. It also includes archaeological artifacts and an air-conditioned room of gold artwork (tel. 262-4138; open Tues.-Sat. 9am-4:30pm, Sun. 1-5pm; admission $1.50, kids $0.75). Nearby is **Plaza 5 de Mayo,** erected in honor of the corps of firemen who battled the flames of an exploded gunpowder storage warehouse in 1914. To the west, on Av. de los Martires, is the **Museo de Arte Contemporaneo** (tel. 262-8012; open Mon.-Sat. 9am-4pm, Sun. 11am-3pm; free). To the east of Plaza 5 de Mayo, Av. Cuba and Calle 30 Este, is the **Museo de Ciencias Naturales** (tel. 225-0645; open Mon.-Sat. 9am-1pm).

Most of the city's other tourist attractions lie off Vía España near La Cresta and El Cangrejo. Besides admiring the behemoth stone cranium of **Albert Einstein** in the plaza of the same name and checking out some great places to eat on **Vía Argentina,** there's not too much to do but **shop** until you drop. **Flory Saltzman's Artesanía** (tel.

223-6963), across from Hotel El Panamá, offers many marvelous, multi-colored *molas,* both individual and sewn together into quilts and wall hangings. Flory knows her stuff, and she's as close to the source as it gets without actually going to the Kuna (open Mon.-Sat. 7:45am-6pm, Sun. 8:30am-noon). **Sol de la India** (tel. 269-1903; fax 263-8029) sells both run-of-the-mill Panamanian souvenirs and impressive imports from South Asia (open Mon.-Sat. 9am-7pm, Sun. 10am-6pm). **Bella Panamá** (tel. 269-9371), across from the Continental Grand Hotel, has an excellent souvenir shop with woodwork and wind chimes (open Mon.-Sat. 9:30am-6:30pm). And the whole city seems to be proud of the new mall, **Plaza Concordia,** on Vía España, near the pedestrian bridge, which consists of two stories of boutiques, **Figali's,** an upscale department store, and a few too many abandoned storefronts.

Parque Natural Metropolitano, in the northwest quadrant of the city, occupies over 265 hectares of forest and is contiguous with other national parks. There are three trails in the park: Los Cabos (2km), Los Momotides (0.7km), and La Cienaguita (1.2km), the last of which rises 150m above sea level for spectacular views of the city and the ocean. Admission to the park is free, and it's open from 6am to 5:30pm—come at dawn to see rainforest animals. The park ranger's office is open daily from 8am to 4pm. To get there, take a bus saying "Tumba Muerto" from Plaza 5 de Mayo and get off at the store El Depósito, or tell the driver you want to go to the park. Walk west 15-30 minutes to the park entrance.

▓ Entertainment

La Academia Italiana presents **El Teatro en Círculo** (tel. 261-5375), near Vía Brasil, a running program of plays and operas. Call for prices and current shows. Performances are held Sundays in **Santuario Nacional,** near Hong Kong Bank. Each February, IPAT sponsors a theater festival; folklore is presented in dramatic form at Panamá Viejo. Call IPAT for more info. **Movie theaters** abound, and many are located on Vía España or near the pedestrian mall in Santa Ana. **Cine Aries** (tel. 269-1632), just off Vía España on Calle 52 Este, has seven screens (open 3-11pm). Check papers for listings in other theaters: **Cine Plaza** (tel. 269-4928), Vía España, in the plaza with Nacional and **Cine Universitario** (tel. 264-2737), which shows artsier fare, on the campus of Universidad Nacional de Panamá, behind the gothic-style Iglesia del Carmen.

Hit a Hard Eight, snake-eyes, or box-cars at one of the city's many **casinos,** one of which resides in Hotel El Panamá, on Vía España just past Iglesia del Carmen (tel. 269-5000 ext. 2633; open 5pm-5am).

For **nightlife,** San Felipe has more than its share of bars and poolhalls, but the area is considered unsafe after dark; instead, head up to El Cangrejo off Vía España. Latin music roars at **Dreams** (tel. 263-4248; $10) in Hotel El Panamá on Vía España. Thursday night is ladies night and women drink free from 9pm-1am; Friday night is Panamanian night and *gringos* pay extra; Saturday night women enter free from 9-11pm, and men pay $10. Or revel at **Bacchus** (tel. 263-9005), just off Vía España, between Citibank and Bank of Boston. Wednesday night is karaoke night (if you're into that sort of thing), Thursday night is ladies night and Friday and Saturday night are $12 open bar nights. **Datatus** (tel. 264-8919), on Calle 50, usually doesn't see too many *gringos* except on Friday night, American night, when coincidentally, prices rise to $10 for women and $20 for men. **Cubares** (tel. 264-8905), Vía Espana and Calle 52, a restaurant by day, becomes a thumping disco at night; $6 cover Thurs.-Sat. For more of a pub flavor, try **Kitaro** (tel. 264-5236) on Calle 50, Vía Israel, Zona 6.

If going to one or two discos sounds a little too sedate, hitch a ride on **La Chiva Parrandera** (tel. 263-3144; $20, open 8-11:30pm), outside Hotel El Panamá, a party bus with live music and open bar that will drive you all around Panama City from the **Bridge of the Americas** over the canal, to laid-back **Mi Pueblito** (tel. 228-7178, $0.50 cover, open Tues.-Sun. 10am-10pm), a recreated village near the art museum, where colonial Panamá meets Disney (folkloric dancing on Fri. evenings). For other **folkloric dances,** check out shows at the **Hotel Plaza Paitilla** or **Restaurante Las Tinajas** (tel. 263-7890, open Tues., Thurs.-Sat.) on Av. Federico Boyd.

PANAMÁ

■ Near Panama City

PANAMA CANAL

The 50 mile stretch of water connecting the Atlantic and Pacific Oceans is believed by many to be not only Panamá's single must-see attraction, but also one of the world's greatest engineering feats. Standing at the edge of the awesome **Gatún Locks,** one of several points along the canal where ships are required to shift water levels, such exalted claims seem merited. Due to its close proximity to the city, **Miraflores Locks** offers an excellent vantage point for viewing the canal. The canal's construction left a giant notch not only in Panamá's geography, but in world history, reshaping Panamá's importance and tightening the United States' grip on Central American affairs (see **History,** p. 424).

Even before the canal was finally completed on August 15, 1914, Panamá was used to serving as a go-between. The importance of the canal, the fruit of the labor of **John Stevens, Col. George Goethals,** and thousands of laborers from around the world, was that it was a direct water route by which cargo ships could avoid the tiresome trip around South America. **Carlos I** of Spain had tried to find a passage in 1534, and the canal-savvy Frenchman **Ferdinand de Lesseps,** mastermind behind the Suez Canal, drained his bank account trying to dredge the banks of the canal; he failed too. Following the French failure, the U.S. attempted to obtain a canal zone from Colombia, but was refused. Uncle Sam then promptly helped the Colombian province of Panamá gain independence; in return, Panamá granted the Canal Zone to the U.S. in the **Hay-Bunau-Varilla treaty** of 1903. Simplified trade between the U.S. and Asia would soon be accomplished by à man, a plan, a canal: Panamá. **President Theodore Roosevelt** provided the capital to back the enterprise, and together with the crucial efforts of **Col. William Gorgas,** who launched an aggressive campaign to prevent disease among workers, the canal took only 10 years and about $387 million to complete. While the U.S. has directed the Canal ever since, Panamá has gradually gained control. Thanks to the **Carter-Torrijos** treaty of 1977, the U.S. will cede the Canal to Panamá at noon on December 31, 1999.

Since August 15, 1914, more than 800,000 ships have passed through the Canal's intricate system of locks, taking an average of 24 hours for each trip (most of it spent waiting). Any vessel passing through the canal pays a fee based on its weight; Panamax-sized vessels, the largest ships the canal can accommodate, pay thousands of dollars, and even the few people who have swum through have forked over a couple of cents each. Ships pass through **Gatún Lake** and three locks—**Pedro Miguel** and **Miraflores** on the Pacific side; **Gatún** on the Atlantic side—en route to the opposite ocean, and are raised and lowered a total of 85 feet in the process. **Gaillard Cut,** the narrow stretch on the Pacific side of Gatún Lake where the canal crosses the continental divide, was the site of most of the deaths during the construction of the Canal.

Tourists congregate along the locks to watch the engineering marvels in action. Take an orange and white SACA bus from near Plaza 5 de Mayo in Panama City to **Gamboa** or **Paraíso** and ask to be let off at the Miraflores Locks, where the main **visitors center** sits (open daily 9am-5pm). Eight-minute movies on the history of the canal are offered in Spanish and English throughout the day. On the ride back, you may be able to catch a glimpse of the gleaming **Bridge of the Americas,** completed in 1962, the only physical link between North and South America. There are plenty of other places to view the Canal, but Miraflores has the only official visitors' center. **Contractor's Hill** has a great view, but is on the west side of the Canal and inaccessible by bus, only by your own car—don't even think about taking a taxi that far.

Taking a tour through the canal is a fun excursion, mostly for the spicy information and first-hand views that accompany the trip. Several tour agencies make the trip: **Reisa Tours** (tel. 225-4721; $65 per person for complete transit), **Sun Line Tours** (tel. 269-6620; $99 per person for complete transit), and **EcoTours** (tel. 263-3077; $102 per person for complete transit). Complete transit includes boat transport to Colón and bus transport to Panama City.

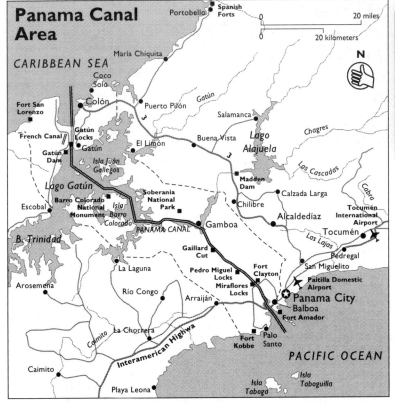

Panama Canal Area

CARIBBEAN SEA

PACIFIC OCEAN

PANAMÁ

0   20 miles
0   20 kilometers

N

Portobello • Spanish Forts
María Chiquita
Coco Solo
Fort San Lorenzo
Colón
Puerto Pilón
Gatún
Salamanca
French Canal
Gatún Locks
Gatún
Gatún Dam
El Limón
Buena Vista
Lago Alajuela
Chagres
Isla Juan Gallegos
Lago Gatún
Escobal
Barro Colorado National Monument
Isla Barro Colorado
Soberania National Park
Chilibre
Madden Dam
Calzada Larga
Cobra
B. Trinidad
PANAMA CANAL
Gamboa
Alcaldeíaz
Tocumén International Airport
Tocumén
Las Lajas
La Laguna
Gaillard Cut
Pedro Miguel Locks
Miraflores Locks
Fort Clayton
San Miguelito
Pedregal
Arosemena
Río Congo
Arraiján
Paitilla Domestic Airport
Panama City
Balboa
Fort Amador
Caimito
La Chorrera
Caimito
Interamerican Highway
Fort Kobbe
Palo Santo
Playa Leona
Isla Taboga
Isla Taboguilla

PANAMÁ VIEJO

Explorer **Pedrarias Dávila** was skilled at finding continents, not founding cities, so it's not surprising that his choice of location for Panama City in 1519 was doomed to fail; the area around his settlement seethed with slimy mangrove swamps. In 1673, after years of foul odors and repeated sackings by British pirate Henry Morgan, the city moved 10km west to modern day Panama City. However, Panamá Viejo—as the old site was thereafter called—flourished for a time as the Pacific terminus of Spain's **Camino Real.** Getting older every second, today's Panamá Viejo offers an intriguing peek into the urban design of a 16th-century city. A fort, several convents, a hospital, and other structures still stand, the crumbling stones bolstered by ongoing restoration and excavation efforts. Most impressive is the 50-foot-high **cathedral tower.**

A visit to Panamá Viejo from Panama City takes about half a day. Getting there is cheap—buses from Plaza 5 de Mayo ($0.15) take you to the cathedral; returning buses leave from the gas station at the end of the ruins. There are only a few restaurants around the ruins, and all are overpriced. Taking a picnic is a better idea, though there are some cheaper *típico* places near the gas station. Panamá Viejo's **Mercado Nacional de Artesanías,** stuck at the end of the highway, consists of several mini-shops full of souvenirs from different regions of the country; try to bargain (open Tues.-Sun. 9am-6pm). Also inside is a small museum with a model of the town (open Tues.-Fri. 9am-6pm, Sat.-Sun. 11:30am-3:30pm) and an equally small but enthusiastic **IPAT** office, open the same hours as the stores.

ISLA TABOGA

Isla Taboga, about 20km offshore from Panama City, could be paradise on earth; its beaches are big and beautiful, its waters are deep blue, its forest trails push hikers to new heights, and its smooth breeze and buttery sun set a blissful mood. However, the island's close vicinity to the city goes hand in hand with its potential to overcrowd, especially on weekends when city dwellers looking for a taste of the good life migrate to the island in droves. This "Island of Flowers" lives up to its name, though, and has a fascinating history. The town was settled before Panama City, and **Francisco Pizarro,** the namesake of its main walkway, made his journeys to South America from here. The church in the town center is said to be the second-oldest in the Americas. Although the island is not particularly small, the town is tightly clustered around the dock on the front of the island. It is nearly impossible to get lost for long. The **Centro de Salud** (tel. 250-2094), to the left of the dock, in the same mammoth building as the school, has a **doctor** on Mondays and Thursdays. The police, a bit farther down the road to the left, are open 24 hours (tel. 250-2026).

Try not to stay overnight it if you can help it, as both the island hotels are quite expensive. **Hotel Chu** (tel. 250-2035 on Isla Taboga; tel. 263-6933 in Panama City), a distance from the dock towards the left, is the cheaper. The view is great from the restaurant, and each room shares part of the balcony. Rooms are fanless, though the ocean breeze should do the job, and come with communal baths (singles $19; doubles $24; triples $30.25; quads $36.30; quints $41.80). **Hotel Taboga** (tel. 250-2122), right of the dock, offers much more for much more ($50-60). Still, visitors to the island head there immediately after docking for its prime beach location, services, and equipment rentals. Bathrooms, changing rooms, and showers are all free to guests; everything else is rented, from hammocks ($3) to *cabañitas* ($5) to pedal boats ($7 per hr.) to lockers ($1). Don't be fooled; the beach adjacent to the hotel property is open to the public free of charge, simply turn right onto the beach before reaching the hotel gates. The $5 fee at the hotel is only necessary for access to their facilities; in exchange, one receives an admission wristband and five "Taboga dollars" redeemable for rentals, food, and drink.

Other activities include **circumnavigation** ($25 for 4 people, ask at Hotel Taboga), visiting the very appropriately named **Pelican Coast** on the far side of the island, and **snorkeling** in front of the Hotel Taboga, where schools of fish congregate near the remains of a sunken ship, whose mussel-encrusted framework is left high and dry on the far end of a sandbar at low tide.

Those with a more active agenda may opt for a **hike** to the top of the island's central hill, **El Vigia.** There are two ways to the top—by road from the edge of town (keep walking past the Hotel Chu and veer right each time the road forks), or up a one-hour long trail through the forest, where you're almost guaranteed to see black and neon-green Dendrobates (frogs) and a plethora of butterflies. The trail begins next to the phone booth by the church in town; signs are well-placed and easy to follow, but the climb is tough. There are eight marker posts from the start until the trail meets the road. From there, it's about another kilometer to the peak (307m).

To get to Taboga from Panama City, either take a taxi to Muelle 18 at the Balboa docks or catch a little red bus (called a *chivita*) from near Plaza 5 de Mayo for $0.15. At the docks, buy a ticket from **Argo Tours** (tel. 228-4348; Panama City to Taboga Mon.-Fri. 8:30am and 3pm, Sat.-Sun. 8:30, 11:30am, and 4pm; Taboga to Panama City Mon.-Fri. 10am and 4:30pm, Sat.-Sun. 10am, 2:30, and 5:30pm; 1hr.; $3 one way) or **Calypso Queen** (tel. 232-5736; Panama City to Taboga Tues.-Thurs. 8:30am, Fri. 8:30am and 6pm, Sat.-Sun. 7:45am, 10:30am, and 4:30pm; from Taboga to Panama City, Tues.-Thurs. 4pm, Fri. 3:30pm and 7:30pm, Sat.-Sun. 9am, 3pm, and 5:45pm).

THE ROAD TO GAMBOA AND SOBERANÍA NATIONAL PARK

When mega-markets and behemoth banks become overbearing, head out of Panama City on an orange creamsicle SACA bus down the road to **Gamboa** (buses from the terminal near Plaza 5 de Mayo start at 4:50am, 45min., $0.65). The town of Gamboa itself is a quiet suburban village that lacks restaurants, stores, and tourist information. A good place to pick up some information is at the Soberanía National Park's new INRENARE office, located where the road to Gamboa forks off the road to Colón (open Mon.-Fri. 8am-4pm). Inside the park is **Pipeline Road** (also known as *Camino de Oleoducto*), which begins in Gamboa and runs north toward Colón. Enjoy the abundant wildlife of the area for a day, or obtain a camping permit and stay on to enjoy the many other trails that thread through the 22,000-hectare **Soberanía National Park,** encompassing much of the central east side of the Canal. Some hikers say that walking upstream along creeks near the road is a good way to sight fauna. Tell the bus driver to drop you off at **Sendero El Charco,** a well-marked 800m loop trail through the forest located between Gamboa and INRENARE—just don't go on a Sunday, when crowds congregate. From that same main road, turn away from the canal down a side road onto **Plantation Loop;** look for the smooth blacktop road. Follow the dirt road off the blacktop for a trail that, though ridden with mosquitoes, weaves through some good secondary forest. Near Gamboa, at **Marina Chagres,** ask about hiring an inexpensive boat for a trip on the canal.

Just 1km before the point where the road to Gamboa crosses the road heading off to Colón, you can bask at **Summit Botanical Gardens.** Boasting a zoo and over 15,000 species of plants, this is one of the inexpensive must-see sights along the road. Continuing in the direction of Panama City towards **Paraíso,** you'll see a small **French cemetery** with tidy little white crosses dotting the green.

Beyond Paraíso clench the **Miraflores Locks** of the Panama Canal (p. 436). To reach an authorized lookout over the locks with restrooms and water, follow the road by the sign for the locks for 10-15 minutes. From Miraflores, either take a bus back to Panama City or return to the junction near the INRENARE and continue on the road to Chilibre and Colón through the **Madden Reserve,** a part of Soberanía that is principally primary forest. During the rainy season, **Monument Falls,** near the road, are spectacular. One kilometer uphill is the **Old Las Cruces trail,** which dates back to the time of Spanish gold fever.

ISLA BARRO COLORADO

The damming of the Chagres River to form Gatún Lake (the main reservoir of the Canal) was a triumph for modern engineering, but a plague on the area's ecosystems. As the water level rose, trees were submerged, animals forced out of their homes, and hills turned into islands like Isla Barro Colorado. The **Smithsonian Tropical Research Institute** (tel. 227-6022; fax 232-6274) runs the island and is adamant about its intentions—nature first, tourists second. That means that of the 1564 hectares of greenery, visitors are only allowed to follow a 2.5km trail and must return home at the end of the day. It also means that only a small number of tourists are allowed to visit the island each year, and then, only on Saturdays and Sundays. If you plan to visit Barro Colorado, make reservations six months to a year ahead of time. Very rarely, last-minute cancellations make it possible to join tours on shorter notice. Aside from the Smithsonian, the island and a nearby peninsula can also be visited with **Ecotours** (tel. 263-3077; fax 263-3089). While the Smithsonian tour is cheaper ($28) and is the only way to actually set foot on the island itself, its tour groups are larger, noisier, and may be more likely to scare away the wildlife. Ecotours ($85), on the other hand, will not actually get you on the island, but will probably have smaller tour groups and will include visits to a few coves by boat and a 2km hike along a monkey-filled peninsula that's also part of the Reserve.

NORTH OF PANAMA CITY

■ Portobelo

Portobelo...Por-to-be-lo. Let the name dribble off your tongue a few times for a taste of just how smooth and mellow things are in this minuscule coastal town. It would be easy to forget that the port was once crucial in Spain's efforts to defend Panamá from pirates, but for the fact that ruins are still interspersed among the town's homes. Besides its smooth-flowing charm and delicious diving, Portobelo is famous for the thousands of purple-clad Panamanians who come to the town's church each October to view the sacred and miraculous **Black Christ.**

To reach Portobelo from Panama City, travel toward **Colón,** but transfer in **Sabanitas** along the way. Although most of Portobelo is tightly huddled around the cathedral, all tourist accommodations are located along the road which hugs the shoreline to the west of town. The new **police station** is among these outlying edifices (tel. 448-2082 or 104), while the **clinic** (tel. 448-2033) remains rooted in the heart of the small village. Be sure to have ample cash available before arriving in Portobelo as trying to change traveler's checks can be a futile endeavor.

The only straight-up hotel establishment in the area is **Cabañas El Mar,** where the management's high prices don't match the goods received. More water drips from the poriferous ceiling than drops from the powerless shower heads (tel. 448-2140; $25 per room for 2 or 3). Fortunately, the major **dive shops** along the road a few kilometers from town provide both lodging and sustenance. **Diver's Haven,** located directly behind the new police station, also offers daytrips and plenty of tidbits about the history of Portobelo. Learn that one of Columbus' ships, the *Vizcaina*, was scuttled in the bay in 1503; then go see a shipwreck or two for yourself (snorkeling starts at $7, mouth-above-the-water tours start at $5). Divers should bring their own gear. Pleasant rooms are available (with private bath and fan $10 Mon.-Fri.; $15 Sat.-Sun.), as well as an apartment with kitchen facilities ($50 per day; $300 per month). One popular place to go is **Salmedina Reef,** a 10-feet-deep reef on a shipwreck complete with cannons and anchors.

A little farther down the road sits **Scuba Portobelo** (aka Scuba Panamá). Up to five people are packed into tight quarters, but the air-conditioner will prevent added body heat from cooking the guests. Simple *típico* cooking is offered at the humble restaurant, as well as two-week scuba certification classes ($130 includes room and equipment). *Cabañas* rent for $30 on weeknights, $50 weekends (snorkeling rentals $5, scuba rentals $15 and up). **"Buzo"** (tel. 448-2175) is a well-equipped diving center that rents snorkeling equipment ($4) and scuba gear ($20) to take on their daytrips ($5-12), and offers horseback tours ($40 for 3-4 hr. tour) and jungle excursions ($70 per day with food and guide). Buzo also offers week-long scuba licensing classes starting at $160. Unfortunately, as of June 1997, Buzo was remodeling and expanding. Thus, rooms are not the most appealing ($10 per night in a 10-person communal room). **Nautilus Diveshop** (tel. 448-2035) is the furthest shop from town, but the rooms ain't too shabby if you don't mind sharing. Fully equipped snorkel and scuba trips are available ($10.50 and $35, respectively). Four- to six-person shared rooms come with communal bathrooms and communal air-conditioning ($8 per person).

If you need a map of Portobelo or a quick lesson on the town's rich history, read the wall at **Restaurante La Torre** (tel. 448-2039). While you're there, get a great seafood meal (fried pargo $6.50, shrimp meal $6.75) or a bite of *típico* food (open Mon.-Fri. 10am-6pm, Sat.-Sun. 7:30am-10pm). **Restaurante Los Cañones** (tel. 448-2032), near Aquatic Park, is named after the rusting hulks of cannons that dot the Portobelo region. Oddly enough, there are no cannons in sight of the restaurant, though the maritime atmosphere is still entirely convincing. The menu is all about seafood, real good seafood. **Rene's Place,** located above Cabañas El Mar, has a bit more variety in the menu and costs about the same (all meals $5, all drinks $0.75; open Mon.-Thurs. 8am-9pm, Fri.-Sun. 8am-noon).

SIGHTS

At Portobelo, the main sights are the **underwater shipwrecks,** the **coral reefs,** the **ruins of old Spanish forts,** and **El Nazareno** (Black Christ). There are at least nine major ruins, each with its own story. The **aduana,** built in 1630, smack in the middle of town, is currently being restored by a joint Panamanian-Spanish endeavor, and will soon reopen as a museum. The forts of **San Fernando, San Cristobal, San Gerónimo,** and **Santiago de la Gloria** are all nearby; San Fernando is across the bay, and San Cristobal, once the biggest fort, is now not much more than three crosses planted in the ground. Santiago de la Gloria is the most obvious site on either side of the road just before entering town. In town, behind the *aduana,* and on the ocean, is San Gerónimo, which contains an unbroken line of ancient cannons ready for action. Check out the arrow slits in the guardposts and the underground prison. Note the steps you descend; each is actually a pair of sequential steps at slightly different heights, designed with the thick overhanging heels of the Spaniards' boots in mind. The **Iron Castle** (a.k.a. **San Felipe** or **Todo Fierro**) once guarded the entrance to the harbor, but it was dismantled earlier this century to provide stones for the Gatún locks. Still, the legend of its strength lives on. Other sites in the area are **Punta Farnese, La Matrinchera,** and **La Batería de Buenaventura.**

In the center of town, a block from the park, reposes the sturdy, ancient church of **San Felipe,** which is home to the sacred and miraculous statue of Christ carrying the crucifix, El Nazareno. El Nazareno first arrived in Portobelo in 1646 by divine providence, while en route to Cartagena, Colombia. As a furious tempest brewed, the captain tossed everything he could overboard, including the purple-clad statue, which fishermen recovered and took into town. Bit by bit, the smallpox epidemic that had engulfed Portobelo disappeared. On October 21, as the last 40 men were healed, the men carried the statue around town on a heavy platform. Since they were still a bit weak, legend has it, they walked two paces ahead, stumbling one to the left, right, and back, before taking another two steps ahead. This same procession, with the steps now ritualized, is carried out at various times during the year—notably October 21 and Good Friday. The statue didn't acquire the moniker "Black Christ" until a U.S. pilot in the Korean War, who believed that the statue had helped him to save lives, brought Americans to Portobelo to give thanks, at which time the Yanks saw the statue and exclaimed in surprise, "Oh, a black Christ!"

Once only a Carnaval custom, another local dance ritual known as the **Congo** often takes place at the behest of any large tourist group. In dancing the Congo, participants dress and even talk backwards, as drummers beat out age-old rhythms.

■ Near Portobelo: Isla Grande

Although the environment farther up the coast from Portobelo remains the same (quintessentially tropical), the lingering history of Isla Grande is completely different—it's rich, smooth, and purely Caribbean. To get there, **buses** leave from **Colón** to the tiny village of **La Guayra** (9:30, 11:30am, 1:30, 3:30, and 5:30pm), passing through **Portobelo.** Grab one of these buses labeled "Costa Arriba" and make sure that it goes to La Guayra (1hr., $2). Upon arrival at La Guayra, hire a boat ($1) to cross the short strait to Isla Grande. Plan on staying the night, as buses from La Guayra to Colón leave only at 5:30, 6:30, 7:30am, and 1pm. Be ready and waiting for the 1pm bus by 12:30pm at the latest, as it frequently arrives and leaves quite early. La Guayra has next to nothing; if you get stuck here, the only lodging available is **Hotel Montecarlos,** where rooms with a communal bath go for $22 (with private baths $30).

Isla Grande has all the charm La Guayra lacks. Sip on a fruity *batido,* bathe in the azure water, enjoy the people's friendliness, or bask in the shining sun—in short, kick back and enjoy the Caribbean beauty that runs so thick on Isla Grande. Keep in mind, however, that Isla Grande serves as a tropical getaway for many Panamanians and can often get crowded (especially on weekends), turning the serene paradise into a hopping, if not rowdy, 24-hour party.

A good place to spend the night is the economical **Cabañas Jackson,** near the center of town (doubles with fan and bath $20, rooms for 4 or more with bath and A/C $45). The seaside restaurant is open on Saturdays from 7:30am until 8pm. There are plenty of other places to stay, but prices rise astronomically. At **Posada Villa Ensueño** (tel. in Panama City 269-5819), beautiful landscaping, and *pipas* (drinkable coconuts) welcome the weary, as do great rooms which come with private bath, A/C, ceiling fan, and a personal hammock on the front patio (1 double bed $40; 2 double beds $45). At the beachfront restaurant, the daily special costs $2.50 (open 7am-9pm). They also rent snorkeling equipment for $1.50-2. The cheapest way to stay on the island is to **camp** in Villa Ensueño's well-groomed yard, but you're own your own to battle the rain ($10, with equipment $15).

A 30-minute hike along the coast out of town and then up the cement path will take you to the **lighthouse** on top of the island. The view from the top is magnificent, but getting into the lighthouse can be a bit of a hassle. If the door is locked, many people climb the exterior frame to the first broken window and then slip in and ascend the winding stairs. *Let's Go* does not recommend climbing exterior frames to broken windows. At sea level, **snorkeling** is the activity of choice, especially near the crucifix on the reef in front of Villa Ensueño, where flat, fluorescent purple fish gather. The crucifix stands near a breach in the reef where the current is strong. Those looking for lower-impact snorkeling should be dropped off by boat on the east end of the reef, where the current carries you down the length of the island at a calmer pace.

WEST OF PANAMA CITY: CENTRAL PROVINCES

■ El Valle

Upon stumbling into El Valle, famed explorer Antón Martín must have wondered about those mushrooms he had eaten the night before. Situated 27km north of San Carlos and the Interamerican Highway, El Valle is a true wonderland—luscious fruits swing pendulously from trees with square trunks, golden frogs jump and croak in gushing waterfalls, and beyond a huge rock covered with cryptic petroglyphs sleeps *La India Dormida*, the giant, anthropomorphic silhouette formed by the distant mountains. Though El Valle is small, the trippy village is a deservedly popular destination for foreign and Panamanian visitors alike.

Orientation and Practical Information There are no street signs and few landmarks in El Valle, but just about every hotel, restaurant, market, and office is on the main road, and all major attractions are clearly marked. Although from a distance you may think it is the town's monument to *Let's Go,* a closer look reveals that the yellow and red structure next to the market is nothing other than a gnome-sized IPAT office (open daily 8am-4pm). There are no **banks** in El Valle and no place to readily change traveler's checks; since it is easy to spend heaps of money here, be sure to bring an adequate amount for the length of your stay. **Farmacía Jessynat,** halfway between the market and the church, hawks tabs and tabloids (open daily 8am-7pm, ignore posted hours). **Buses** pass through the turn-off from the Interamerican Hwy. El Valle daily every 15 minutes or so en route to the nearby town of **San Carlos** (60min., $1), on the Interamerican Hwy., or to **Panama City** and points along the way (4-8am, every 30 min.; 8am-noon, every 45 min.; 1, 2, 3pm; 2½hr., $3.50). The town has four **taxi** drivers: Sr. Alfred Sanchez (tel. 983-6148), taxi #2T-260, speaks excellent English and knows the town like the back of his taxi. Or exercise those lungs and legs and **rent a bicycle** from **Restaurante y Mini Super Jaque Mate,** located down the side road cornering Hotel Greco ($2.50 per hr.; $12 for 8hr.). The name becomes clear once you see the bulletin board full of newspaper clippings about the numerous chess tournaments held here (open daily 4:30am-6:30pm). There are two **supermarkets** in town—**Comercial El Valle** (tel. 983-6120), at the edge of town near the Texaco station, and **Super Centro Yin** (tel. 983-6081), in the center of town near the market (open daily 7am-noon and 2-6:30pm). For **medical assistance,** contact the **Centro de Salud,** down the street that corners the church (tel. 983-6112; 24hr. assistance available). The **police** are on the road to El Níspero (tel. 983-6222 or 104).

Accommodations and Food   Although El Valle is becoming more popular by the minute, there are few hotels, and thus an occasional shortage of space. It's wise to make reservations in advance; the IPAT office may be able to assist you. Camping is an option, but is not especially recommended during the rainy season (most of the year here), when the ground has a nasty habit of sliding into the nearest river. But don't get frantic; a room can always be found.

The cheapest place in town, **Motel Niña Delia** (tel. 983-7110), on the left, two blocks after the turnoff for Hotel Campestre, has a public phone, a pleasant patio with comfortable chairs, and a communal black and white TV. However, its beds are passing through their third reincarnations (singles with communal bath $8; doubles $15; rooms with private bath can fit up to 3 people for $20; lock-up at 9pm). Bring mosquito repellent and enjoy homemade *sancocho* (parboiled meat) at the attached restaurant on designated days. Without the small sign above the cash register that says "Se Alquilan Habitaciones," you'd never know that the **Santa Librada** has a few rooms tucked away down a short pathway behind the restaurant with the best food in town. The constant rain falling on the tin roof becomes soothing after a while and the parade of hard-working ants on the wall is more entertaining than any television (singles $10; doubles $15; triples $35; quads $40). **Hotel Greco** (tel. 983-6149), near the turnoff for Hotel Campestre, has spacious, pricey rooms in a motel-style layout. Call early for reservations in the busy season (singles or doubles $19.50; triples $25-40). **Hotel Campestre** (tel. 983-6146; fax 983-6460) is located at the base of Cerro Gaital, with manicured grounds, elegant dining rooms, and a path out back leading to the much-hyped square trees. With an enclosed circular garden that houses some of El Valle's most famous residents—the *ranas doradas* (golden frogs)—the Campestre is certainly worth a visit (with or without an overpriced meal), but not necessarily a stay, as the rooms are plain for the price. The cost is made a bit more bearable by hot water (singles $38.50; doubles $44; family rooms $64).

All of the hotels listed above have attached restaurants, including the homey restaurant of **Motel Nina Delia** (steak breakfast $2.25), and the fancy-and-priced-that-way restaurant at **Hotel Campestre. Restaurante Santa Librada** has superb food. Occasionally, thirsty local men gather in a futile attempt to appease their dry palates with one more *cerveza* and pester customers (lunch-of-the-day buffet $3). Near the church croaks the unaffiliated **Restaurante Rana Dorada.** The tables are always impeccably set, but the menu is limited to whatever is available that day (chicken or beef with rice $2.50). No frog legs.

Sights   If you look off into the distance at the mountains that surround the valley, you'll see that they aren't mountains at all, but rather a giant, sleeping Indian; keep it down, lest you wake *La India Dormida*. Legend has it that when an *indígena* maiden, **Flor del Aire,** fell in love with a conquering Spaniard, her prior lover killed himself out of desperation. The girl was disgraced and tormented, so she wandered into the hills to die, lying down on her back to stare forever at the skies above. Less like a soap opera, **El Níspero,** the local botanical gardens and zoo, houses capybaras, "titi" monkeys, iguanas, scarlet macaws, giant sleeping tapirs, and indigenous golden frogs (open daily 7am-5pm; admission $2). If you're in town for the weekend, check out the **museum** next to the church—it's open on Saturdays for a full half-hour starting at 5:30am and Sundays from 9am to noon (admission $0.25). The weekly **Sunday Arts Fair** takes place in the **Mercado El Valle** (daily 7am-3pm). Artisans swarm in from secluded mountain farms, and many make their living on what they sell at the market. Sculpted pots, intricately woven chairs, and even wicker helicopters are all available for perusal and consumption.

After checking out the artisan scene, explore the origins of art at the nearby **Piedra Pintada,** a giant rock adorned with semi-intelligible, very funky **petroglyphs** that look more like a Picasso put through a blender than a message from the ancients. Either take a taxi from the market ($2.50) or walk 20 minutes or so to the end of the road, following the signs all the way. Alas, the signs fail at the moment they are needed most—at the end of the road, they point straight ahead, into a building. This is where the masterpiece you're now reading becomes most useful! Head towards the river, but don't cross the concrete bridge. Instead, follow the **river** up into the forest and cross the bridge at the end of the path; follow the path across the next bridge as well, and just ahead on the right stands the massive rock, with glyphs on its underhanging side. The rough trail continues on for another 10 minutes to the twin cascades of the **La Pintada** waterfall. (If you notice the small path that forks to the right directly behind La Piedra, ignore it and continue left.) Once at the second waterfall you might as well continue another 15 minutes for a spectacular view of the valley—hike 5 minutes up the steep incline to where the path levels out and a decent size rock sits in the middle of the walkway. Take a hard left up the even steeper path and continue for 10 minutes to the top of the naked hill.

Another, more famous waterfall is **El Macho.** A taxi ride there and back costs $4-5, but it's walkable as well; follow the signs. There's a small souvenir shop at the ravine, where an admission fee of $1.50 is collected. Getting to the waterfall requires crossing a bridgeless river by stepping on large rocks; a wooden support beam and a complimentary walking stick make the crossing easier. Originally named for the tapirs in the area *(machos de la montaña),* El Macho is a sight so astounding that the guides even offer to take a Polaroid photo of you by the falls ($4). They also offer a canopy tour by wire-and-winch devices ($40 per person, 45min.; one day's notice required) or a hiking tour on **El Caminario** through the surrounding **Refugio Ecológico Chorro El Macho** (open daily 8am-6pm, Jan.-April until 7pm; ask at IPAT about the free tour or be prepared to pay $10 at the info station/souvenir shop). El Valle's third famous waterfall is **Las Mozas.** Admission is free, but it's a bit of a hike. Closer to town, just 1km from the church, some volcanic (and allegedly medicinal) **hot springs** bubble away ($0.25 admission; $1 per 30min. to actually bathe).

■ Near El Valle: Parque Nacional Altos de Campana

When the trees fall behind you, eagles soar over distant valleys at eye level, and a *conejo pintado* (of the agouti family) crosses your path as you stare, mesmerized, at the far-off Pacific, *then* you know you're in Campana. Covering 4816 hectares, **P.N. Altos de Campana** is Panamá's oldest national park, first declared a biological reserve in 1966. Though it might look like it's been deforested, the lack of trees is simply a product of the altitude (600m). The rock-strewn landscape, dotted with cliffs and escarpments, nevertheless retains a peculiar green color as far as the eye can see, as Cerro Campana (1007m) rises in the background. There are *no* services in Campana aside from one INRENARE **ranger station,** the only building on the road for 8km until one reaches the tiny town of **Chicá.** Registering with the rangers is vital for safety purposes and for information about the one *refugio* in the park, which holds 15-20 people (a 1hr. hike away), weather (usually 21-22°C), and wildlife.

There are trails into the park from many sides, but the main entrance is 4½km up a road that, for the first kilometer, looks like it was last paved at the time of the Conquest. Beyond that, King Mud will struggle with your feet for dominion at every step. Transport on the road is erratic, but try to catch a bus to the town of **Campira** on the Interamerican Hwy. and asking around for the next truck going to Chicá. The trip to Chicá, though hell on the tailbone, is relatively short (20min.). Note that there is a town of Campana just off the Interamerican Highway; don't be fooled, the park cannot be entered from here.

Rumor has it that an American expatriate known as "Richard de Campana" offers suites with private bath per night in **Posada San Antonio**, about 1.5km beyond the ranger station, on the left of the road (singles $20; 20 people—the whole house—$100). The ranger station is open daily from 8am to 4pm, and someone is usually in the building at all times. Letting the rangers know that you're coming is a nice gesture, especially if you're going to ask one of them to guide you. There's no phone at the station, but a message can be relayed via radio by calling the INRENARE **ranger station** in La Chorrera (tel. 244-0092) or **Area Protegida Paraíso** (tel. 232-4325).

Move Over, Bunnicula

It's been called a "sign of the final times," a horrible genetic experiment let loose upon the Earth, or even a "gift" from hostile extraterrestrials. First documented years ago in Puerto Rico, many are convinced that, for whatever reason, it's come to Panamá with a vengeance. It is the **hottest topic** on the **tabloid news**, where stories of its exploits are gobbled up by a curious public. *It* is the half-goat, **half-human bloodthirsty** *chupacabras*. Eyewitnesses have reported that it looks like a demon-goat walking on its two hind legs, but with utmost agility and silence. Attacking farmyard animals and pets, its trademark is the pair of vampiric **teeth marks** left on the necks of its victims after the *chupacabras* sucks *(chupar)* out their blood and removes some vital organs. Despite a rash of recent incidences in La Chorrera, nearby Panama City is unconvinced and unconcerned—one musical group has even cut a CD called **"Chupacabras"** and produced a music video illustrating the new *chupacabras* dance. As long as you're not out in the dark countryside at night, feel free to buy the CD, learn the dance, and even pick up a *chupacabras* t-shirt, as you join in the biggest mass hysteria (read: fad) to sweep Panamá since disco.

■ Penonomé

Founded by the indigenous inhabitants of the area known centuries ago as "Nome," Penonomé, capital of the province of Coclé, has been adding syllables and friendly faces ever since. As the twitter and chatter of tiny birds mingles with that of youngsters heading home from school, its sublime atmosphere will work magic on your soul. With a park or plaza every three blocks (one with an obelisk and statue commemorating Dec. 8, Mother's Day), the people of Penonomé know how to enjoy each day as it comes. They also take pride in the region's arts and handicrafts, on display and for sale at several shops. A delightful town too frequently passed over en route to Panama City, familiar Penonomé spreads its arms in a gesture of welcome.

Orientation and Practical Information While most visitors only see the revolving eight-foot-high bright green bottle advertising the gas station in front of the bus terminal on the Interamerican Hwy., a quick jaunt down **Av. Juan D. Arosemena** from the Hotel Dos Continentes shows more of what Penonomé really has to offer.

As usual, **IPAT** offers travel advice (tel. 997-9230; fax 997-7603; open Mon.-Fri. 8:30am-4:30pm). **Change traveler's checks** at **Banco Nacional de Panamá** (tel. 997-9321) on Av. Arosemena, relatively close to the Interamerican Hwy. (open Mon.-Fri. 8am-3pm, Sat. 9am-noon). Get a cash advance on Visa at **Banco del Istmo** (tel. 997-9211; open Mon.-Fri. 8am-3:30pm). An **ATM** can be found at Banco del Istmo or Colabanco on the Interamerican. Grocery shop at **Super Centro Coclé**, while having clothes cleaned next door at **Lavandería El Sol** (tel. 997-9932; open Mon.-Sat. 8am-6pm). **Buses** to **Panama City** and points along the way (including the intersection with the road to El Valle) leave from the **terminal** on the Interamerican Hwy. across from Hotel Dos Continentes (daily 3am-1am, every 30min., $3.75). Direct buses to **El Valle** ($1.50) leave thrice daily from the public market. Buses to **Chitré, Santiago,** and **David** will pass without stopping unless you wave them down. Once you've figured that out, stop by **Super Farmacia Coclé** and browse through their selection of

English magazines and other pharmaceutical goodies (tel. 997-9849; open Mon.-Sat. 8:30am-1pm and 2-7:30pm, Sun. 8:30am-12:30pm). For a **24-hour pharmacy,** try **Farmacia Juancito** (tel. 997-8733) on Av. Héctor C. Bermúdez, next to Clínica Penonomé. The **hospital** (tel. 997-9386) sits across from Restaurante Universal on the Interamerican Hwy. In a grand old building facing the park (officially known as Plaza 8 de Diciembre), you'll find the rather imposing, if not outright intimidating, **police station** (tel. 997-9333 or 104). A block away, in the municipal building behind the Mother's Day obelisk, you can send Mom a postcard at the **post office** (tel. 997-9666; open Mon.-Fri. 7am-6pm, Sat. 7am-5pm).

Accommodations and Food The hotel with the best location also happens to have the best prices: **Residencial El Paisa,** located one block from the town park in the direction of the market, offers seven adequate rooms with private bath, two beds, and a fan (tel. 997-9242; $7.70 per person). **Hotel Dos Continentes** (tel. 997-9326; fax 997-9390), across from the Esso gas station, has lots of goodies and prices that reflect it. Rooms with A/C, TV, hot water, telephone, and private balcony cost $16 per person, $26 for a double with two beds, and $42.90 for a quad. There are some rooms available with a fan instead of A/C (singles $12; doubles $20). **Pensión Dos Reales** is a lower quality/lower budget establishment which has earned a reputation among locals as an overnight love-shack. Make a left in front of the police station and follow the road to the wooden box with your name on it (singles $5, with fan $6; three beds $9).

Most of the restaurants in the area serve *típico* food, so it's *how* they serve it that differentiates them. **Restaurante Las Tinajas** (tel. 997-9606; open daily 7am-10pm) offers small potions of *típico* buffet in a charming tropical hut setting where dim lights and soft music create an un-*típico* ambience. **El Merendero,** the yellow store on the way to the park, offers the same food in a more modern, TV-laden, extremely friendly environment. At the **Pan 6-Diez,** off Av. Juan D. Arosemena, the "famous" *pan de Penonomé* can be procured. For something a little different, enjoy the old Spanish ranch atmosphere at **Restaurante Parrillada Oasis** (tel. 997-9033). But atmosphere doesn't come cheap—lobster salad runs $5, and it's uphill from there (open noon-11pm; Visa, MC, AmEx accepted).

Sights and Entertainment The **Mercado Artesanal** (tel. 997-9011) is found down the road from Hotel Dos Continentes, on the Interamerican Hwy. towards Panama City. Some items are overpriced, but most handicrafts are affordable, and the market helps to raise money for indigenous artisans (open daily 8am-6pm). The people in the adjacent office offer insight into the crafts and the personalities behind the scenes. In the center of town, facing Plaza 8 de Diciembre, stands **Iglesia San Juan Bautista,** an elegant church. The **Mercado Público,** two blocks from the park on Av. Amador Guerro, is a monolithic fruit market. A few blocks from the market on Calle San Antonio hides the **Museo de Penonomé** (tel. 997-9210), four rooms of everything from religious statues to stuffed lizards (open Tues.-Sat. 9am-noon and 12:30-4pm, Sun. 9am-1pm; admission $1). A 25-minute bus ride towards Aguadulce takes you to the **Parque Arqueológico El Caño.** It might be worth it to hire a taxi for the ride there and back (about $20), giving yourself an hour to absorb as much archaeology as possible (open Tues.-Sat. 9am-noon and 12:30-4pm, Sun. 9am-1pm). A four-minute walk from downtown Penonomé, on a road close to the river that starts near the IPAT office, takes you to the **Balneario Las Mendozas.** A 10-minute taxi ride will bring you to **La Angostura Canyon,** with a swell view of Cerro Guacamaya. The nearby town of **La Pintada** (named when there was only one house in town that was painted) houses **Artesanía de Sombreros** where customers choose between oodles of sombreros unique to the region. Similar if not identical hats can be found on the streets of Penonomé. Nearby beaches include **Playa Juan Hombrón, Playa Farallón,** and **Playa Santa Clara.** No buses go directly to a beach, so a short walk is always necessary; a taxi ride to a beach costs about $20. Ecological sites to the north of town include **Campo Trinchira,** the site of La Guerra de los Mil Días; **Alberque Ecológico**

La Iguana, a popular hangout for many of the region's animals; and **Ceno La Vieja,** home to the beautiful, yet somewhat pricey cabañas with the same name (tel. 223-4553). To reach any of the above sites, catch the **Chiguiri Arriba** bus from Penonomé's market.

■ Santiago

Santiago is derided as an incorrigibly boring city, especially considering its stature as capital of the Veraguas province. While it may have few tourist attractions, Santiago deserves recognition for its very personable citizens. Don't expect to be left alone here; perhaps because they see so few tourists, some residents can't act fast enough to toss out a friendly "good day" or buy foreigners a drink. The city's other bonus is its prime location between Panama City and David.

Orientation and Practical Information The center of Santiago houses stores, banks, some hotels, and most of the population. The basic layout of the city is a triangle formed by **Calle Central, Calle 10,** and the **Interamerican Hwy.** with side streets forming grid patterns in all directions. The stretch along the Interamerican hosts buses and nicer hotels. **Avenida Central** serves as the city center, and major businesses extend outward from it for a few blocks.

Unburdened by tourists, Santiago nevertheless has a friendly (but non-English speaking) **IPAT tourism office** (tel. 998-3929; fax 998-0929), next to Budget Rent-a-Car in Plaza Palermo on Av. Central (open Mon.-Fri. 8:30am-4:30pm). **Mary's Tours** (tel. 998-0072; fax 998-1833; open Mon.-Fri. 8am-6pm, Sat. 8am-noon) serves as a **travel agency,** while Rodrigo Báez of **Explorer** (tel. 998-6437) offers seven tour options from Santiago to the furthest reaches of the province. **Banco Nacional de Panamá,** facing the park next to the cathedral, only changes traveler's checks for deposit (tel. 998-2211; open Mon.-Fri. 8am-3pm). **Banco del Istmo** (tel. 998-5001; open Mon.-Fri. 8am-3:30pm) on Av. Central does the job but charges $5 for doing it. **ATMs** are found in most of the city's many banks. **Western Union** (tel. 998-5431) is located off Calle Central between Calle 10 and the Interamerican. **Public telephones** and **taxis** are scattered randomly about the city. **Intel,** located on Calle 8, allows for direct international calls. At the **bus station** on Calle 10, irregularly scheduled buses leave for destinations all over the province, including **San Francisco** (20min., $0.65) and **Chitré** (1½hr., $2). Buses to **David** and **Panama City** leave from a terminal near the Hotel Piramidal, on the Interamerican Hwy. and Av. Central. Wash clothes at **Lavamático Don Bosco,** located down the block from Mary's Tours. **Farmacia Elysin** is in the middle of town on Calle Central. The **police** (tel. 998-2119 or 194) are located outside of town past the intersection of Av. Central and the Interamerican, while the **hospital** (tel. 998-4982) sits on the opposite side of Santiago, on Calle 2 by the church. The **post office** (tel./fax 998-5133; open Mon.-Fri. 7am-6pm, Sat. 7am-5pm) sits in the middle of the white shopping arcade in the middle of Calle Central.

Accommodations and Food Hotel Gran David (tel. 998-4510), on the Interamerican directly between Calle 10 and Calle Central, is a trek from the town center, but boasts a gracious staff, beautiful rooms with private baths, a connected bar/restaurant, and a pool. Rooms come with choice of A/C or fan, telephones, TVs, and courtyard views (singles $10, with A/C and TV $15.50; doubles $13, with A/C and TV $19). For a drop in price and smaller drop in quality, stay at Santiago's own **Hotel Santiago** (tel. 998-4824), located at Av. Central and Calle 6. All rooms have private baths and fans or air-conditioning (singles $7.70; doubles $11, with A/C $13.20). **Pensión Jigoneva** (tel. 998-2461), on Av. Central in the heart of the city, has simple, spacious rooms, some with balconies (singles or doubles $7, with private bath $8).

Most of Santiago's elegant restaurants are found in the nicer hotels; the others are hard to find. One block south of the bus terminal, across from Easy Tours, **Restaurante, Bar y Discoteca Nuevo Quo Vadis** feels like a bit of Old Spain in the middle of Panamá. Choose the *pollo Quo Vadis* for $5 or a tasty rolled-up hard-shelled *taco de* *pollo* for $1.25 (major credit cards accepted). **Restaurante Mar Caribe,** across from Hotel Gran David, serves seafood and the usuals (shrimp meals $4.50, lobster $10.50). Otherwise, look for a fruit market northeast of the cathedral and plenty of *típico* mom-and-pop places all over.

Sights and Entertainment On the crossroads of the Interamerican Hwy. and Calle 10 near the pedestrian bridge, a sign points to **La Iglesia San Francisco de la Montaña,** 18km away. If architecture and fascinating wooden carvings of indigenous-faced saints sound like a fun daytrip, this is where to go (buses 7am-6pm, $0.65). To the south of Santiago lies **Basilica Menor de la Atalaya,** or you can admire **El Salto de las Palmas** (waterfall) about an hour north. In nearby **Calobre,** visit the **Reserva La Lleguada,** the three lagoons that provide Santiago's water supply. Still further north rests the town of **Santa Fe** and the road (that only one or two buses a day dare traverse) to the **hot springs** of Chitra.

The adventurous hang around for the **Feria de Veraguas,** a festival held for six days in the middle of February one hour from Santiago. The city itself saves its partying energies for July 22-25 during the **Fiesta Patronal de Santiago Apostol.** If you are the "outdoorsy" type, trek off into true wilderness in **Parque Nacional Cerro Hoya,** on the Pacific Ocean at the extreme south tip of the province. For information on how to access the rather isolated park, call 954-4133 and ask to talk to an INRENARE official for information on how to procure a guide.

■ Chitré

With verve and vim and nerve and whim inspired by Panama City, without the girth, but down to earth, Chitré's got stuff more gritty. It feels small-town, but don't you frown, this city loves to party; 'round Easter time the mood is prime for dancing and Bacardi. But never fear, there's more than beer: the culture here is rich; those partisans of artisans can count on more than kitsch. The folklore's hot—a bore it's not—and locals love to chuckle, to share their zest for customs' best, like weavings and belt buckles. **Herrera's** prime to share your time, **Los Santos** merits visits; if **La Arena** blows your brain enough you'll want to kiss it. In other words, to watch cool birds, or just to be inspired, head to Chitré to spend a day and stay until you're tired.

Practical Information The ever helpful **IPAT** (tel. 966-8072; fax 966-8013; open Mon.-Fri. 8:30am-4:30pm) is in neighboring **Los Santos,** across the river on Av. Nacional. Several **banks** around the center of town change traveler's checks, including **Caja de Ahorros** (tel. 996-4114), adjacent to the cathedral (open Mon.-Fri. 8am-3pm, Sat. 9am-noon) and **Chase Manhattan,** a block away from the cathedral on Av. Central. Most banks have **ATMs.** The **immigration office** (tel. 996-3092; open Mon.-Fri. 8am-3:30pm) is one block south and three blocks east of the cathedral; look for the Panamanian flag outside. **Supermercado Machetazo** is located one block west of Museo de Herrera and sells everything known to mankind. One block north and one block west of the cathedral sits **Lavandería Americana** (tel. 996-4450; open Mon.-Sat. 7:15am-noon and 1-5pm). **Aeroperlas flights** (tel. 996-4021) leave for **Panama City** (Mon.-Fri. 7am and 4:45pm, Sat. 8am and 4:45pm; Sun. 4:45pm, $28). **Buses** are most easily found at the terminal at the edge of town. Buses run to **Las Tablas** (6am-7pm, every 15min., $1), **Panama City** (every 45 min., $6), and **Santiago** (4am-3:45pm, every 45min., $2). **Farmacia Universal** is almost located inside the church's front door (open Mon.-Fri. 8am-4:30pm). In case of emergency, call **Hospital Cecilia Castellano** at 996-4444 or 996-4410, or the **police** at 996-4333 or 104. The **post office** (tel. 996-4974; fax 996-3736) is attached to **Intel** (open Mon.-Sat. 8am-4:30pm).

Accommodations and Food **Hotel El Prado** (tel. 996-4620), one block from the cathedral on Av. Central, has clean, big bedrooms with TVs, private baths, and air-conditioning (make sure the A/C in your room works). The second story lobby (replete with a restaurant) is a prime viewing location for parades and festivals. Don't be fooled by the two handles on the sink and in the shower; hot water is rare (singles $9.50, with A/C $14.70.; doubles $15, with A/C $22). Rooms in **Hotel Santa Rita** (tel. 996-4610) are decently clean and have private baths, fans or A/C, and TVs; some have hot water (singles $11, with A/C $15.40; doubles $16.50, with A/C $22). **Pensión Central's** name belies its location, ½ block from the church on Calle Central. Rooms are nothing outstanding, but may be better once the remodeling is finished. Currently, rooms come with fans or A/C, private baths, and sometimes windows. Free parking is available (singles $10, with A/C $14; doubles $10 for foreigners only, with A/C $14; triples $18, with A/C $24).

When hunger hits, explore the streets around the cathedral. Chitré has an unexpected number of pizzerias. **Manolo,** by the Machetazo department store, serves regional specialties and vegetarian delights (veggie pizza $2-3). Two blocks away from the cathedral on Av. Central is the large, inappropriately titled **Restaurante y Panadería Chiquito,** where you can get pizzas, hamburgers, sandwiches, a variety of baked goods, or *típico* food. **Restaurante El Mesón** (tel. 996-4312), facing the cathedral's park, offers a truly elegant atmosphere at boosted prices (most specials run about $5-8 and include soup and salad).

Sights and Entertainment The town cathedral and the numerous pleasant parks that dot the cityscape are worth peeks, as is the **Museo de Herrera** (tel. 996-0070), Av. Manuel Correa and Av. Julio Arjora (open Tues.-Sat. 9am-12:30pm and 1:30-4pm, Sun. 9am-noon). Lose yourself in the music and the crowd at **Discoteca Stragus,** on Via Los Santos next to Caja de Seguro Social. The second-floor dance area and bar features a steady variety of music—rock to typical folkloric, *merengue, salsa,* and *bolero* (every Fri.-Sat. night 8pm to 4am).

■ Near Chitré

Besides its overwhelming proclivity to throw *fiestas* at every turn, Chitré is actually less renowned among travelers than are many nearby beaches, parks, and villages in the provinces of Herrera and Los Santos. Most of these locales are lilliputian and easily reached by bus from Chitré.

The dry soil of **Parque Nacional Sarigua** has been inhabited for thousands of years but, somehow, the secluded desert park manages to feel like *terra incognita.* A short hike yields spectacular views not of lush forest, but of vast expanses of red-brown earth. A zone of mangroves intervenes between the desert and the ocean, and the fauna of the park runs the gamut from green (desert) and black (mangrove) iguanas to frolicking, regurgitating pelicans. To get to P.N. Sarigua from Chitré, catch an infrequent bus to Puerto Limón. Admission is free and the park is accessible year-round. For more info, call the INRENARE station in **Los Santos** at 974-2323.

Stroll down Av. Nacional away from Chitré or hop on a quick bus to get to the little village of **Los Santos,** which is annually roused from deep slumber by thousands of eager *fiesta*-seekers from around the country. Los Santos also boasts **El Museo de la Nacionalidad,** which features artifacts from Panamá's history (tel./fax 966-8192; open Tues.-Sat. 9am-noon and 1-4pm, Sun. 9am-1pm; admission $1, children $0.25). As you walk, note the homes on the outskirts of the city; they're over 80 years old. Intricately woven roofs hold the houses together, and wooden branches support the structures. The closest **beach** to Chitré is **Monagre,** near Los Santos. The rest are in Los Santos province (9km away), and are better reached from Las Tablas. The minute village of **La Arena** is famous for producing some of the finest ceramics in Panamá. Stores line the main highway heading in from Chitré, only 10 minutes away by car or bus. The guy who sells you the vase or pot probably made it himself. The prices are affordable, and the people don't like to bargain. Ask around town for Baltasar, who is particularly gifted.

■ Las Tablas

As yet another frisky teenage couple scurries by after making out in the park, one more parakeet hovers around your shoulder zip-a-dee-do-da-like, and one last elegant woman glides by in a fantastically embroidered dress, there's no escaping the conclusion that you're in Las Tablas. Throngs of tourists from all over Panamá come to this little town during **Fiesta de Santa Librada** (July 19-23) and **Semana Santa** (travelers should make reservations *well* in advance). At other times, however, uproarious romping and revelry give way to soft smiles and deep tradition. The local love of custom is exhibited by devotional prayers at the gold-leafed altar of the **Iglesia de Santa Librada,** continued pride in the local dress (the *pollera*), and numerous traditional dances (see **So the Kids They Dance and Shake Their Bones,** p. 451).

Orientation and Practical Information Las Tablas has two main roads that intersect in the **central park**—every place of interest is on one of the two. The nearest **IPAT tourism office** is located a bus ride away in Los Santos (tel. 966-8072; fax 966-8013; Mon.-Fri. 8:30am-4:30pm). Get your best leisure suit cleaned for the upcoming fiesta at **Lavamático Tico,** across from **Supermercado Las Tablas,** itself across from **Banco Nacional de Panamá** (tel. 994-6302; fax 994-6079; open Mon.-Fri. 8am-3pm, Sat. 9am-noon). The bank has an easily accessible **ATM,** which is across from the **clinic** (tel. 994-6284), located across from the town's **hospital** (which is across from the **police,** tel. 994-7000 or 104). This is not as confusing as it seems. Across from the police is the Shell station, a combination gas station/terminal for buses headed to Panama City (Mon.-Fri. 4am-5pm, Sat.-Sun. 7am-4pm, every 2hr., 4½hr., $6.50). Buses to **Chitré** (every 15min., 40min., $1), **Pedasí** (45min., $2), and other nearby towns and beaches, are caught most easily a block from Hotel Piamonte in the opposite direction from the park. **Taxis** are everywhere, but you can call one at 994-6557. Some **public phones** are in the park. The park is surrounded on all four sides by a phalanx of **pharmacies.** Amongst the ranks are **Farmacia Las Tablas** (tel. 994-6936; open Mon.-Sat. 8am-9pm, Sun. 8am-noon) and **Farmacia Lorena** (open Mon.-Sat. 7am-10:30pm, Sun. 8am-9pm). A **post office** (tel. 994-6922) with **telegram** service sits behind the clinic (open Mon.-Fri. 7am-6pm, Sat. 7am-5pm).

Accommodations and Food It's wise to get a **hotel** room with A/C, since Las Tablas can swelter at night. All 10 rooms in **Hotel Piamonte** (tel. 994-6372) are generally safe, very clean, pretty, and have air-conditioning and private baths. The restaurant below serves piping-hot breakfasts for $2, and the management couldn't be friendlier (singles $14; doubles $21; triples $24). **Hotel Mariela** (tel. 994-6473), across from Hotel Piamonte, offers six gritty, cheap rooms with rickety doors and communal baths (singles $4; doubles $8).

In Las Tablas, there are more clothing vendors and *salones de belleza* than there are decent restaurants. **Restaurante Valymar,** near INTEL two blocks from the park, offers *típico* food and chow mein ($3). Just up the street from **Hotel Piamonte,** itself housing a fine eatery, are two clean, pleasant places, separated only by a bar with four video gambling machines—**Restaurante Praga** and **Restaurante Oriental** offer *típico* food (both open daily 7am-11pm). Play a video game, rent a movie, and slurp down an ice-cream cone at **Biokenes Video and Restaurante**—snack food only.

Sights Having momentarily succeeded in jostling a pharmacy or two out of the way, the dignified **Museo de Belisario Porras** (tel. 994-6326; open Tues.-Sun. 9am-4pm; admission $0.50, children $0.25) faces the park. Inside the one-room museum, on the site where Porras was born, are plenty of old documents, photos, and even his tomb (though his actual remains reside in the Cemeterio de Amador in Panama City). Head to **Mercado de Artesanía,** on the edge of town on the Shell station road, for *polleras,* ceramics, carved bullhorns, and even painted coconut shells. The **Iglesia de Santa Librada,** the centerpiece of the fantastic cultural fabric that is Las Tablas, has been renovated recently. With a gold-leaf altar, massive carved wooden doors, and a huge

PANAMA

So the Kids They Dance and Shake Their Bones

The annual *Fiesta de Santa Librada*, held around July 20, sways hand in hand with the *Fiesta de la Pollera*, which celebrates the glory of the region's **traditional dress**. But while any traveler with the yen can don a *pollera* for a few balboas, only a special elite have the know-how to trip the light fantastic, Herrera-style. Indeed, the region's traditional dances are a fantastic trip for the crowds who gather to watch; each shimmy is linked to a folk tale so, for the full scoop, buy a wise local a beer for informative sideline narration. In *La Dansa de Toros*, for example, a single man plays the part of the bull (actually swinging around a **papier-maché bull's head**), while "matadors" intimidate the bull with red handkerchiefs. That is, until the bull goes mad, taking his vengeance on the audience. In *La dansa de Guapos*, several men dress in **outlandish drag**, swinging their **stuffed bras** around to the tight rhythms of a local folk song. Last comes the spooky *Dansa de los Diablos*, in which little boys dressed up as scary **munchkin** skeletons march around and scream to wake the dead.

baptismal font with suspended top, this church is worth seeing, especially for the unique statue of the crucified saint herself. Hang around for July 19-23 to be part of the **Festival de Santa Librada.** Even during the rest of the year, religious processions followed by fireworks may spontaneously occur at night—grab your candle and join the slow-moving mass of worshippers on the main street.

■ Near Las Tablas

PEDASÍ AND ISLA IGUANA

Filled with locals who earn their living off the sea and a sprinkling of tourists looking for a piece of the action, Pedasí is a charming fishing town where the people head out when the fish come in. Av. Central is a continuation of the Av. Nacional that hugs the eastern coast of the Azuero Peninsula. The Parque Central is a block east of Av. Central. There are three **public telephones:** one in front of the municipal building on Av. Central, one at the INTEL office, and one near Restaurante Las Delicias. Facing the park is **Farmacia Saeli,** where you can purchase seasickness medicine (open daily 7am-8pm). Contact the **police** at 995-2122 or the **health clinic** across from the pharmacy and the park, at 995-2127. The **post office** (tel. 995-2221) is behind the municipal building on the main drag. As the fisherman have their own houses and the fish sleep in the ocean, Pedasí isn't exactly overflowing with hotels.

Although it may not be due to fear of competition, **Pensión Moscoso** is a dandy place to stay. Don't be surprised if you are awakened by the morning preparations of some fisher-tourists at 5am. Wake up with them to take advantage of the free continental breakfast the thoughtful management prepares for them (singles with communal bath and fan, $6; doubles $8; room for 1 or 2 $12). On your left as you enter town is the **Hotel Residencial Pedasí** (tel. 995-2322), with a communal TV in the lobby and light, clean rooms with private baths and A/C (1 person $16.50; 2 people $22; 3 people $27.50; 4 people $33).

What the town lacks in hotel options it makes up for in restaurants—just kidding—there are only two, and there might as well just be one. **Restaurante Angela,** across the street from the municipal building, and **Restaurante Las Delicias,** a block south of Pensión Moscoso, serve whatever *típico* food is available that day.

Pedasí's big draw is nearby **Isla Iguana,** a treasure trove of exotic birds and plants. Particularly interesting to divers, the reefs around the island have been the site of an extensive effort to help coral grow. Isla Iguana has two take-a-step-and-sink-into-the-soft-and-blindingly-white-sand beaches, both relatively small and bordered by dark rocks that look like baked mud castles. The rangers say that the largest coral mass in Panamá is located at the island, covering some 16 hectares to a depth of 8m.

Isla Iguana was actually occupied by the U.S. during WWII and covered with over 40 landmines, although the most violence you'll see today is some 5000 frigate birds squabbling for food. There's almost no need to worry about landmines now—only five remained unexploded after the war, four of which were detonated by U.S. engineers in 1990 (causing quite a bit of damage to the coral of the island, which is why efforts to "reforest" coral are at their peak here). The one remaining landmine is buried under water, and the warning marker is visible at low tide.

If you are lucky (very, very lucky) INRENARE might have a boat heading out to the island on which you can hitch a free ride. Check at the office located just off the main road as you enter town or call 995-2134. They depart, however, from the INRENARE station in Los Santos. **Iguana Tours** (tel. 226-8738 or 226-4516; fax 226-4736), runs out of Panama City, and offers tours to Isla Iguana, but it's not difficult to arrange your own tour for a good deal less. The owners of both hotels in Pedasí are more than happy to find you transportation to the island and can frequently do it on a moment's notice, though advance warning is appreciated. Expect to pay a local fisherman $30 plus $5-10 for gasoline. With a group of friends (most boats can hold 10-14 squashed people) to split the cost, the trip becomes very affordable. Boats leave from the gorgeous Playa El Arenal, a five-minute ride from the Accel gas station at the edge of town. Take a taxi (and your fisherman), and arrange a ride back in advance. From the beach, it's a 25-minute boat ride to Isla Iguana. There is a *refugio* on the island, though it's little more than a thatched roof overhead (no electricity and no water) and an outhouse. Bring your own food and bottled water. INRENARE plans on building a ranger post on the island in the near future but, until that happens, be sure to register at the INRENARE station in town (on a side street near the gas station) before heading out to the island.

BEACHES AND ISLANDS

Refugio de Vida Silvestre Isla de Cañas is a large island two hours southwest of Pedasí, accessible by a $0.50 water taxi *(cayuca)* from nearby Tonosí. **Playa El Toro** is a six-minute drive from Pedasí; **Playa Venado** (don't pronounce the "d") is about an hour away, but is bodacious enough to host **international surfing competitions.** Call **Cabañas Playa Venado** at 995-8107 for info on lodging. Accessible only during the summer (Dec.-April), the U.S.-run **Punta Mala** at the southeastern tip of the Azuero Peninsula (25min. away) grants you a view of the **lighthouse** that has guided ships to the Pacific entrance to the Panamá Canal (14hr. away) since 1914. A French-owned ecotourism resort is opening up at **Playa Las Desfiladeros.** Visit a joint U.S.-Japanese tuna farm and investigation center at **Laboratorio Achotines** (open to visitors Sat. 9am-noon) or take yourself out to **Las Frailes** for some fishing.

CHIRIQUÍ

Chiriquí feels like the Central America that budget travelers come for, complete with sensual rainforests and sky-scraping volcanos. The indigenous Guaymí know a good thing when they see it; they have inhabited the region since pre-Columbian times and named it "Valley of the Moon." With regional capital David as a springboard, a few hours' drive north leads to charming, coffee-growing villages from which Volcán Barú can be suitably explored.

■ David

Granted, David *is* the third largest city in Panamá, and it *does* deserve some credit as capital of the entire Chiriquí province, and the city *might* be home to more than 120,000 people, but it just doesn't feel all that big. Scattered banks, mildly menacing *supermercados,* and some governmental plazas are the only indicators that this "metropolis" is the central artery of the coffee-infused veins of the region. The only time David truly rocks out is for its yearly festival in early March; otherwise, it retains

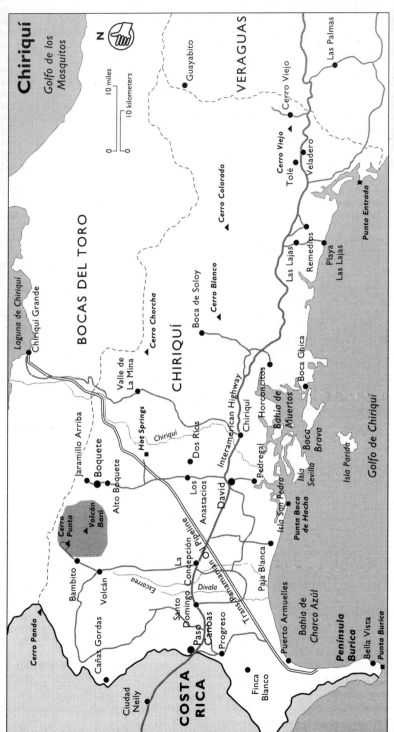

PANAMÁ

its friendliness and charm and serves as an ideal base for exploration of the rest of the area's wonders, or as a pitstop on the way west to Costa Rica or east to Panamá City.

Orientation David is laid out in a grid, cut off to the east by busy **Avenida Obaldía**. North to south *avenidas* are numbered with *Oeste* and *Este* designations, starting on either side of **Avenida Central**. East to west *calles* are designated with the ABCs, increasing to the north and south from **Calle Central**. Spend a little time, and the whole system becomes simple, but for the fact that the streets don't have signs. The central plaza **(Parque Cervantes)** lies between Av. Bolívar and Av. 3 de Noviembre (3 blocks east of Av. Central) and Calles A and B Norte.

Practical Information The **tourist office**, IPAT (tel. 775-4515; fax 775-6823), is across from Parque Central on the 2nd floor and provides basic info on the area. Check out the "My Name is Panamá" booklet, which includes maps of David and the country (open Mon.-Fri. 8am-3pm). **Exchange currency** and **traveler's checks** and get cash advances on Visa at **Banco Nacional de Panamá** (tel. 775-2241; fax 775-2100), on the north side of the park in the rounded-front building (open Mon.-Fri. 8am-3pm, Sat. 9am-noon). Get "money in minutes" at **Western Union** (tel. 775-4963; fax 775-3524; open Mon.-Sat. 7:30am-5:30pm), located one block northwest of Pensión Maria Jilma on Av. Miguel A. Brenes (Av. F) Sur. There are pay **phones** in the park or at **INTEL** (open Mon.-Sun. 8am-9pm), located one block northwest of the post office. Direct visa questions to the remote **immigration office** (tel. 775-4515; fax 775-6823; open Mon.-Fri. 8am-3pm), located on Calle C Sur between Av. Central and Av. 1° Este. **Mike's Auto Rent** (tel. 775-49163; fax 775-3524), in the Western Union building, rents economy cars for $35-45 per day.

David is the hub for all destinations to the highlands of Chiriquí. The **Tracopa bus** (tel. 775-8505; office open Mon.-Fri. 7:30am-4:30pm, Sat. 7:30am-4pm, Sun. 7:30am-1pm) to **San José, Costa Rica** departs from next to Pensión Costa Rica (daily 8:30am, 8hr., $15). Walk north from the west side of the park to the **bus terminal** at the edge of town at Av. Obaldía and Av. Cincuentenario (2 blocks east of Av. Central). Buses run regularly to: **Volcán** (every 15min., 1½hr., $1.50); **Boquete** (every 30min., 1hr., $1.60); **Río Sereno** (every hr., 2½hr., $5); **Chiriquí Grande** (every 1-1½hr., 3hr., $6); and **Santiago** ($6), continuing on to **Panama City** (13 daily, $13). **Taxis** are especially easy to catch at the bus terminal and near the park (most destinations $0.50-2). **Lavandería Panamá** is two blocks southwest of the cathedral (tel. 775-2053; open Mon.-Fri. 7am-noon and 1pm-7pm, Sat. 7am-7:30pm). Next to the park, behind Romero's, is a **supermarket** (open Mon.-Sat. 8am-8pm, Sun. 8am-1pm). For a **pharmacy,** try **Farmacia Revilla** (open Mon.-Sat 7am-11pm, Sun. 8am-10pm), located across from the park's east corner. **Hospital Regional** (tel. 775-2161) is located about 3km from the park on the Interamerican Hwy. **Hospital José Domingo de Obaldía** (tel. 775-4221) provides services for children and battered women, and is located on Av. 3 de Noviembre past Av. Obaldía. **Red Cross** (tel. 775-3737; open Mon.-Sat. 8am-12:30pm, 1-8pm) can be called for an ambulance. The **police**, located on Calle 3 de Noviembre and Av. F Sur, can be reached in emergencies (tel. 108), or at their station house (tel. 775-2211). There's a mighty **post office** (tel. 775-4136; fax 774-1008) across from the Toyota showroom, one block north of Parque Cervantes, which provides **fax** and **telegram** services (open Mon.-Fri. 7am-5:45pm, Sat. 7am-4:45pm).

Accommodations One of the hottest cities in Panamá, David demands that visitors consider air-conditioning when picking a hotel, as fans tend to push the hot air in your face. Each room in **Hotel Madrid** (tel. 775-2051; fax 774-1849), near the bus station, comes with private bath, air-conditioning, telephone, and color cable TV (1 person $14; 2 people $20). The luxurious **Hotel Occidental** (tel. 775-4695; fax 775-7424), in the shopping plaza, enjoys cool and safe proximity to everything David has to offer. An elevator carries guests to one of 60 rooms, each of which has a private bath, air-conditioning, TV, and a phone. Balconies on each hallway hover over the city. Laundry service is available, but give it to them in the morning if you need it the

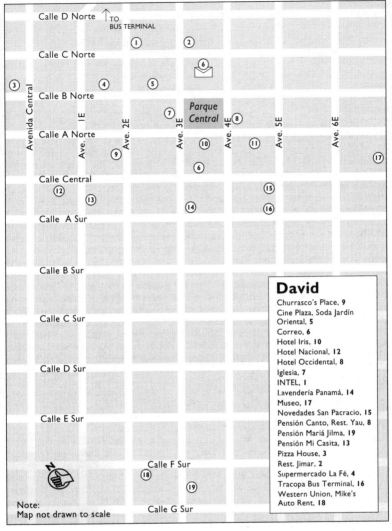

Calle D Norte ↑TO BUS TERMINAL

Calle C Norte

Calle B Norte

Avenida Central

Calle A Norte

Parque Central

Ave. 1E · Ave. 2E · Ave. 3E · Ave. 4E · Ave. 5E · Ave. 6E

Calle Central

Calle A Sur

Calle B Sur

Calle C Sur

Calle D Sur

Calle E Sur

Calle F Sur

Calle G Sur

N

Note:
Map not drawn to scale

David

Churrasco's Place, **9**
Cine Plaza, Soda Jardín Oriental, **5**
Correo, **6**
Hotel Iris, **10**
Hotel Nacional, **12**
Hotel Occidental, **8**
Iglesia, **7**
INTEL, **1**
Lavendería Panamá, **14**
Museo, **17**
Novedades San Pacracio, **15**
Pensión Canto, Rest. Yau, **8**
Pensión Mariá Jilma, **19**
Pensión Mi Casita, **13**
Pizza House, **3**
Rest. Jimar, **2**
Supermercado La Fé, **4**
Tracopa Bus Terminal, **16**
Western Union, Mike's Auto Rent, **18**

PANAMÁ

same night (one person $17; doubles $27). **Pensión María Jilma** (tel. 775-4733), on Av. 3 Este, Calle F/G Sur, is distant, but pleasant; clean rooms have private baths and air-conditioning (singles $8; doubles $16). **Pensión Mi Casita,** across from Hotel Nacional, can be your *casita,* too, if you dig basic, but sufficiently big rooms. Five rooms with shared baths are available (singles $5; doubles $7). **Pensión Costa Rica** (tel. 775-1241) is an out-of-the-way host to plenty of travelers. Lots of room options are available to fit any group (singles $4-6, depending on amenities; doubles $9-12).

Food Most of David's dishes are exclusively *típico,* but Chinese restaurants also abound. The area around Parque Cervantes is particularly saturated with inexpensive *típico* places. **Pizza House** (tel. 774-1116; open Mon.-Sat. 8am-noon, Sun. 11am-midnight), located on Av. 4 Este, 4 blocks southwest of park, serves great pizza in a refreshingly modern environment (pizza with the works and Pepsi, $4.50). **Restaurante Marisco Steak House** (tel. 775-3385), off the Interamerican Hwy. towards

Boquete, is a bit out of the way (a $1.25 taxi from the park), but the thick menu offers plenty of top-notch, if pricey, food. Suction up some *pulpo* (octopus) for $7.50 or entangle some squid for $5.25. Less adventurous foods are also available (*pollo asado* $4). One block west and south of the park lurks the 24-hour **Churrasco's Place.** A full bar and TV complete this modern tropical hut. Try a *churrasco* (like a T-bone) for $4.50. What's yellow and green and has sub-zero air-conditioning? **Restaurante Jimar!.** Located on Av. 2 Este between Calle D and E Nte., Jimar offers everything from cheeseburgers ($1.50) to filet mignon ($6); open Monday through Saturday 7am-10pm and Sunday 7:30am-3pm.

Sights and Entertainment Museo de Historia y Arte José de Obaldía (tel. 775-7839), Av. 7 Este and Calle A Norte, displays archaeological artifacts, colonial religious materials, and historical documents related to José de Obaldía, founder of the Chiriquí province. While parts of the small museum feel like the stuffy living room of a wacko history teacher, some offer interesting insight into the region's past, particularly into the daily life of Obaldía's family, who lived in the house (adults $1, children or students $0.25, groups $3).

There are a number of heavily guarded **department stores** and **boutiques** around the center of town, but unless you've got a Gold Card handy, they may not be worth a visit. Including **Hotel Nacional** in a budget guide might qualify as a cardinal sin, but some of their publicly available entertainment facilities fit the bill. The hotel's multi-cinema **theater** shows the most recent American films in English with Spanish subtitles ($3). Crap out at their **Casino** (tel. 775-6019; open daily 1:30pm-2:30am) or take a dive in their pool (open daily 8am-5pm; $2). If you're trying to keep the party going past sunset, check out **Brandywine**. Divided into two buildings, Brandywine offers a 12-table **billiards** hall where the jukebox pumps out rap and reggae and the peeps get silly on 50¢ Atlas beer. If you're in the mood to groove, head next door to Brandywine's **dance club** where, if the deafening bass doesn't shake your booty for you, you can shake it all night. The party picks up a little after 10:30pm and rages until 2:30am.

■ Near David

VOLCÁN

The town of Volcán takes up one long stretch of road on the distant slopes of its ever cloud-enshrouded namesake, Volcán Barú. Indeed, most visitors come to Volcán for the chance to climb the volcano and descend the other side into Boquete, or for nearby Cerro Punta and its spectacular scenery.

To ascend the volcano, bear right at the fork in the road at the Volcán police station (Volcán continues to the left) and head in the direction of Cerro Punta. The trail begins in a town called Paso Cucho. Either walk from the main road or have a taxi bring you directly to the foot of the volcano. For further information, check at the **Volcán tourist office** (tel. 771-4845); turn east on the side road next to the bus stop. The **Banco Nacional de Panamá** (tel. 771-4282; open Mon.-Fri. 8am-3pm, Sat. 9am-noon) is set just past the fork in the town road—bear left. The **police** (tel. 771-4231) are located at the fork in the road and the **post office** (tel. 771-4222; fax 771-4027; open Mon.-Fri. 7am-6pm, Sat. 7am-5pm) is right across the street. Next door is **INTEL** (tel. 771-4441; open Mon.-Fri. 8am-noon and 1pm-4:30pm). Beside the Shell gas station, you can't miss **Farmacia San Antonio No. 2** (tel. 771-4059; open Mon.-Sat. 7:30am-11pm, Sun. 8am-10pm). Although there's no sign of No. 1 in sight, another pharmacy, **Don Bosco** (tel./fax 771-4317**)**, is just down the road (open Mon.-Sun. 8am-8pm). Whether you fell into the volcano or just have an ordinary medical emergency, stop by **Chémica Popular** (open Mon.-Sat. 7:30am-9pm, Sun. 9am-5pm). Wash the lava off your clothes at **Lavandería Volcán** (open Mon.-Sat. 8am-8pm), located a few minutes south of the town center.

None of the *pensiones* and *cabinas* is particularly budget-oriented; the cheapest runs $15 per person. Check with the tourist office for camping regulations. **Motel**

California (tel. 771-4272) squats past the bank; make a left at the sign. Cabins come with private baths and hot water. Eat under a Mona Lisa in the restaurant (usually closed during the low season) or rent a TV for $3. Find a roomie or two and get away with a lower price (1 or 2 people $20; 3 people $25). Several *cabinas* are located further north past most of Volcán. **Cabinas Morales** (tel. 771-4435) offers hot water and isolated serenity (singles $15; doubles $20; four w/kichen $45). **Valle de Juno** (tel. 771-4225) offers several cabinas with a full kitchen, sitting room, and 6-person capacity (one person $15; two $25; six $38).

Everyone who's anyone hangs out at the **Panadería/Dulcería/Roticería Mollek** in the hub of town, where dripping ice cream and luscious baked loaves provide a great excuse for tapping into gossip or asking for directions. For a real meal, feast on some local-color cuisine at **Restaurante Yariela.** The building itself isn't exactly stunning, but if your belly yearns for a little *arroz con carne or mondongo,* you can't go wrong. **Restaurante Mizpa** will sell you a pizza ($4 serves two).

There is plenty to do near Volcán besides climbing Volcán Barú. **Las Lagunas,** two placid lagoons nestled in lush greenery, are only 5km southwest of town. Hikers can soak their bunions in the remote, medicinal hot springs of **Los Pozos** (19km from Volcán). Guided tours to these and other locations are available through the tourist office (approximately $25 for 1 or 2 people). Further afield, check out **Los Hornitos,** a geyser about halfway to Costa Rica from Volcán.

CERRO PUNTA

While Volcán is relatively flat, Cerro Punta (16km from Volcán) is anything but. Blessed with close proximity to two fantastic parks and few tourists (for now), the village is surrounded by gorgeous mountains painted with strawberry and coffee plantations. All vital services are within a block of the main intersection. A public **telephone** is in front of the police station and near **Farmacia Zarina** (tel. 771-2012; open daily 8am-7pm), down the hill and on the left. The **Centro de Salud** (tel. 771-4283; open Mon.-Fri. 7am-3pm) is right across the street. The **police** (tel. 771-2113) and the **post office** (tel. 771-2052; open Mon.-Fri. 7am-2pm, Sat. 7am-noon) share a building in the center of town—look for the Panamanian flag.

Close to Cerro Punta proper (but in neighboring Guadalupe) is the **Hotel Los Quetzales,** where the impressive rooms (with hot-water private bathrooms) hold up to four people ($25-30). Ask the bus driver when to get off the bus. Also check in here for transport to the cabins in the Los Quetzales Cloud Forest (see below). Near the main crossroads in Cerro Punta is **Hotel Cerro Punta** (tel. 771-2020), with clean, luxurious rooms at steep prices (singles $22; doubles $27.50; triples $33; all with private bath, hot water, and a great view). The hotel also houses **Nurmy Toscana,** the town's main restaurant, where a tasty meal of *pollo asado* and a soda costs around US$5.50. Listen to the recited menu for specials, as entrees vary daily (open 7am-9pm). Small kiosks all over Cerro Punta serve Panamanian food at low prices.

Cerro Punta's premier park, **Parque Internacional La Amistad,** transcends international boundaries. The forest contains seven "life zones" and has an extensive system of trails within its thousands of acres in both Panamá and Costa Rica. Of the 929 bird species in Panama, 425 have been sighted in the park. Ask at the **AMISCONDE** office in town (tel. 771-2171; open Mon.-Fri. 8am-5pm) for preliminary information and directions to the ranger station at the entrance to the park. The station is located 5km from Cerro Punto and can be reached by bus (stop located outside Cerro Punto police station), taxi ($3), or foot (located at bottom of legs; free). If you are looking for more information, stop by the INRENARE in Volcán (located just past the police station on road to Cerro Punto) or David (tel./fax 775-3163). From the station, hike **Sendero La Cascada,** a hilly 1.7 km, two-hour round-trip jaunt to beautiful waterfalls, or **Sendero El Retoño** (2.1km; 1½hr.), which cuts a circular path through part of the park. Rangers are often willing to serve as guides. The park has a $3 entrance fee and an additional $5 if you plan to camp overnight.

Cerro Punta's other park is **Parque Nacional Volcán Barú.** The drawing point of the Cerro Punta end of the park is **Sendero Los Quetzales,** a mostly downhill trail towards Boquete (abt. 15km). From the end of the trail, it's another 3km or so in Boquete itself. Start the hike from the INRENARE ranger station at **Respingo,** a 6km walk, a bus ride (meet outside Cerro Punta police station), or a $15 taxi up a wind partially paved road from Cerro Punta, and be prepared for a breathtaking view. The rangers are extremely friendly and will put you up or even guide you at no cost; the size of the (greatly appreciated) tip is up to you. There are *casas rústicas* located midway in **Alto Chiquero** for crashing overnight (camping is also permitted), but dress warmly—temperatures can drop below 40°F at night.

Just a few minutes from Cerro Punta is the town of **Guadalupe,** best known for the **Los Quetzales Cloud Forest Retreat** (tel. 771-2182; fax 771-2226), an absolutely phenomenal "hotel" actually located in the cloud forest. Fabulously feathered quetzals are seen almost daily from late November to April and frequently during the rest of the year—and there are always swooshes of hummingbirds about. Three cabins rent for $90 each (capacity 8 people), while single rooms run $25 per person. All cabins have full kitchens, hot water, romantic lanterns, and incredible canopy-level views of the primary cloud forest. Indigenous Guaymí guides lead hikes ($2-3/person), and boots and rainjackets are available for rental ($2 with $10 deposit). Transportation is available from Hotel Los Quetzales in the heart of Guadalupe.

▓ Boquete

Cool, clean air and august mountain scenery overshadow Boquete's small-town stores and restaurants, an allure not lost on daytrippers from David, who arrive raring to ride horses, watch birds, or groove with nature. The nearby roaring rivers are visually stunning, but sometimes turn fierce during the rainy season, when heavy flooding causes landslides that occasionally block trails. But even if they have to trudge through slop, travelers come to this part of Chiriquí to explore the mountains, especially nearby **Volcán Barú,** Panamá's tallest volcano. At 10,000 ft. Barú poses quite a challenge. If hiking doesn't sound appealing, a peeling is at least in order for the region's navel oranges (harvested Nov.-Feb.).

Practical Information **Banco Nacional de Panamá** (tel./fax 720-1328), across from the Delta gas station on the south edge of town, exchanges traveler's checks. **Buses** leave for David around Parque Central (every 30min., 5am-6pm, 1hr., $1.20). **Urbana** buses serve the local area, and prices vary with destination ($0.35-2). **Lavamático Diane** awaits a few blocks north (and uphill) of the park on the left side of the main street. Offers all the ordinary laundry services: $2.25 for a cold water wash-n-dry, $2.70 for a hot wash-n-dry, and, oh yes, $8 per hour for a **motor scooter.** **Farmacia Méndez** (tel. 720-1241) is one block north of the park (open daily 8am-8pm). For medical emergencies, call the **ambulance** (tel. 720-1356) or go to **Centro Médico San Juan Bautista** (tel. 720-1881), near the bridge, which has a doctor available 24 hours. The town **post office** (tel. 720-1265; fax 720-2067) is located across from Parque Central in the direction of the river and offers telegrams, faxes, and *lista de correos* (open Mon.-Fri. 7am-6pm, Sat. 7am-5pm). Boquete's **police** (tel. 104 or 770-1222) roost one block south of post office.

Accommodations and Food **Pensión Marilós** (tel. 770-1380) is at the south end of town; follow the "Hotel Rebequet" sign. The warm, English-speaking management and beckoning lobby are as comforting as Mom's chicken soup on a rainy day. With no tourist office in town, Marilós is the place to find plenty of useful advice, as well as hot water, kitchen facilities, and washing machines. Traveler's checks are accepted (singles $6.60, with bath $9.90; doubles $9.90, with bath $15.40). Right across from the park, **Pensión Virginia** (tel. 720-1270) has a prime location, but the rooms are nothing to write home about (singles $7.50, with bath $11; doubles $14.50). Roll out of bed and grab breakfast at the cafe in front. Not every room has a private bath, but they all have their own names—choose Clarita, Emilia, or Doris, among others, and ponder the consequences in the hot water shower. **Pensión**

Topás, one and a half blocks south of Pensión Marilós, features a pool and brand-spanking new rooms with artsy blue and black tiles. After spending a quiet night in a comfortable bed, enjoy a massive breakfast ($3.80). If you're in the mood to shovel out some money, have the management paint your portrait or design some beautiful custom jewelry for you. Each room has a private bath and hot water, except one "economy" room with an outhouse and cold shower (singles $19.80; doubles low season $19.80/high season $26.40; triples $26.40/33; economy room $8-14). If you're looking to hide out in the mountains and meditate with Mother Nature for a while, nothing can be better suited than the tranquil cabins of **La Montaña y el Valle.** Picturesque scenery, gourmet cooking, private hiking trails, and lush greenery are all available for anyone with a love for natural serenity and the ability to loosen the belt on their budget. Attractive cabins come with hot water, private baths, two double beds, a kitchen with all sorts of cooking toys, and an outside deck with a view too magnificent to be described here (2 people, $65; $5 each additional person). If you have your own tent, you're golden: camping areas with hot water showers and bathroom are available for $7 (ample tourist information also available).

    Ristaurante Salvatore (tel. 720-1857), down the street from the *clínica,* dishes out New York Pizza in a berserk New York atmosphere (or as close an approximation as the highlands of Panamá can muster), as well as tasty Italian dishes (medium pizza and drink $5.50, lasagna $6; open daily 10am-10pm). For some Mexican cuisine, try **La Casona Mexicana** (tel. 720-1311) across the street, not far from the bank (open Mon.-Thurs., Sun. noon-9:30pm, Fri.-Sat. noon-10:30pm). Tacos cost $2.25-$3.00. For more bang for your buck, try **Sabroson** (tel. 720-2147; open daily 6:30am-11pm), a local hangout for local food (*arroz con pollo* with *plátanos* and salad $1.25).

Sights and Entertainment

The forests near Boquete provide sweet hiking, though clear trails are few and far between. Head in any direction out of town to traverse hillsides rich with coffee plantations. Several plantations are located about 8km north from the center of town; the hike and a tour of the *fincas'* operations make an entertaining (and energizing) daytrip. Surrounding villages are also worth exploring, for both the views and the heavenly aroma of coffee that intoxicates visitors. And don't plan on switching to decaf during January when the crazy **Feria de Flores y del Café** shakes the otherwise placid towns (make reservations).

    When hiking becomes a bit too tiring, exhaust a different set of muscles by trotting along country roads on **horseback** (tel. 720-1750 for info). To rent a horse for about $4 per hour, check with the **Coffee Bean Restaurant** (English spoken; tel. 720-3203), located up the hill south of Boquete, for details. This restaurant offers a quick sandwich ($1.50-2), a panoramic view of the Boquete valley, or a new paperback (open daily 8am-9pm). The trail to Cerro Punta, Sendero Los Quetzales, comes into town from the northwest. It's not uncommon to sight quetzals here, especially near Bajo Mono. Other local attractions include hot springs in Caldera and the cloud forest, approximately four hours from Boquete.

    Most tourists' favorite activity in Boquete is climbing **Volcán Barú.** The massive, verdant volcano no longer oozes lava, but (together with 5m of yearly rainfall) still manages to pump the fire of life into the surrounding national park and beyond. The various levels of foliage springing out of the fertile volcanic soil support not only dozens of villages, but countless animals, including tapirs and jaguars. Getting to the top of Volcán Barú is no easy endeavor. Although a road does go all the way to the top, it's a long haul. The best way to travel is by a **four-wheel drive car,** but you'll have to leave by sunrise if you want to beat the clouds rolling in over the mountains. There's no car rental agency in Boquete, so either arrange for one privately or find an organized **tour** (which may leave you nearly bankrupt). **Hikers** should also start the climb early, starting from the well-paved road west out of Boquete. After 8km and more *fincas* than you ever would have thought could fit on a mountainside, you'll reach the occasionally staffed ranger post (just a few kilometers past the fork in the road, veer right) and its outhouse (bring your own paper and noseplugs). From here, the official entrance to the park, the road gets worse. When traveling during the rainy season

(April-Nov.), be sure to ask locally for advice on road conditions before heading out lest a river materialize beneath you. The tough hike from the ranger station to the summit is about 14km, making the whole trip about 22km one way—and don't for get about the 22km down! For those without transportation or *wanderlust,* many locals suggest hitchhiking, as trucks frequently pass to and from the various *fincas* early in the morning. *Let's Go,* however, does not recommend hitchhiking.

BOCAS DEL TORO

North of Chiriquí, Bocas del Toro sings a different siren song, offering not rugged thrills, but alluring Caribbean islands. British and French pirates used to stop in the archipelago to repair their ships, and Guaymí tribes inhabited the region between Volcán Barú and the Costa Rican border, land now part of the massive **Parque Internacional La Amistad.**

▓ Bocas del Toro and P.N. Bastimentos

Site of the first social security number, lottery, and horse race in Panamá, Bocas has since turned its attention to becoming the ultimate Caribbean town, now claiming to be the best place in Panamá for a tropical reef-and-beach vacation. Chuck that watch off the ferry, and get ready for real relaxation—breathe deeply, slice open a mango, take a nap, stare at the cool trees. The most ambitious visitors do manage to work a few daytrips into their itineraries, especially to the shell-strewn beaches of the **Zapatilla Cays** and **Hospital Point,** where bodacious snorkeling, swimming, and diving are only a slothful step or two away. The island of **Bastimentos** offers less in the way of self-indulgence, having been laid out for ecotourism. The English-speaking, Afro-Caribbean, Bocas natives are way mellow; don't even think about haggling on prices, just go with the flow. But go with it soon, because life in Bocas is changing fast—foreign investors bought 48 properties on the main road last year alone, and locals remark that hostels and restaurants are opening up *en masse.*

Orientation and Practical Information Although the town is laid out in a grid format, most everything you'll need is on the main street (Calle 3). From the dock, turn right and you'll be heading north into the "downtown" part of Bocas. All visitors touring **Parque Nacional Bastimentos** need to get a free permit from the **INRENARE** office near the shore by the bank. Check in there to use *refugios* within the park. For brochures, try **IPAT,** next to the Bocas Dive Shop (tel./fax 757-9642; open Mon.-Fri. 8:30am-noon and 1:30-4:30pm). Down the side street next to the governmental *palacio* is **Banco Nacional de Panama** (tel./fax 757-9230; Mon.-Fri. 8am-3pm, Sat. 9am-noon). Follow the only paved road to the **hospital** (tel. 757-9201). **Public telephones** are rare—there is one near the fire station (towards the shore from the bank), two near the park, and one in the lobby of Hotel Bahía. **Farmacia Chen,** towards Hotel Bahía, is easily identified by the **mopeds** for rent out front (open Mon.-Sat. 8:00am-noon, 12:30-6pm, and 7:30-9pm, Sun. 8:30am-noon). The **police** (tel. 104 or 757-9217) are on the shore near Todo Tropical. On the north side of the park, in the main municipal building, are the **immigration** and **post offices** (tel. 757-9273; open Mon.-Fri. 8am-5pm, Sat. 8am-noon). **Internet access** is available at a computer store beneath Pizzeria Pomodoro.

Accommodations and Food If you're lucky enough to get one of the few rooms available, **Hospedaje Heike** (tel. 757-9558) is a great deal ($5 per person with communal bath). **Hotel Las Delicias** (tel./fax 757-9318) has the lowest prices in town and the rooms are more than adequate: $4 per person with communal bath; $5 with private bath, and add an extra $2 for breakfast. Ask here for information on **camping grounds** at **Playa Bluff. Hotel Las Brisas** (tel. 757-9248), at the end of the main road, has the best patio deck in town for lounging in a hammock in front of beautiful ocean scenery; beware of the occasional water bug (singles with communal bath $10, with private bath $13, with A/C $20; doubles $11, with private bath $14). Las Brisas also has a *pensión* across the street with cheaper rooms bereft of ocean views (singles or doubles with communal bath $10; triples with bath $14.30). Just across from the dock by Almacén Chow Kai, **Pensión Las Delicias** (tel. 757-9318) is made especially for groups. Rooms are dark but not too dismal, and the manager is friendly (singles $6; doubles $10; triples and quads with private bath $6.60 per person).

Tourists huddle around candlelit tables, sharing stories and hearty pizzas at **Pizzeria Pomodoro** (personal pizza $3.50; calzone $4). For seafood specialties (you *are* on an island, after all), there are several floating restaurants which a boat tour of the region may take you to for lunch; otherwise, chomp into some crab ($6), lobster tail ($10), or conch ($6) while signing your own graffiti on the walls at **Restaurante Todo Tropical.** To get to **Restaurante Beto,** walk two blocks down the side street directly across from El Pirate and turn left. They offer huge portions of typical Panamanian food at low prices.

Sights and Entertainment There's not much to do in the town of Bocas— one might watch an obscure, slightly antiquated film in English with Spanish subtitles at the **Sweet Bocas Cinema** or snorkel for antique bottles along the docks. However, the best of Caribbean paradise lies just outside the town's borders. Rent a **bike** from Hotel Las Brisas, Todo Tropical, or Farmacia Chen (about $1.50 per hour or $8 per day) or a **moped** scooter (at Farmacia Chen; $5 per hour or $25 per day). **Kayales** and **cayucas** (the region's traditional canoe-like forms of locomotion) can also be rented from Las Brisas or Todo Tropical. Show the owner of Todo Tropical this passage of the book, and get $1 off the $3 **snorkel** rental.

There are plenty of natural attractions on the island itself. **Playa Bluff,** on the eastern shore, is a 30-minute moped ride away, but the beach is fantastic. Waves curl and crash, ghost crabs scuttle away at the vibrations of your footstep, and the deep, golden-yellow sand is so soft and unpacked that it feels like a plush carpet. Around June and July, there is an added nighttime attraction—several species of turtles come out of the sea to lay their eggs. Inquire at **ITEC,** located behind Hotel Bahía, or **Caribaro** about **turtle-watching** walks. **Boca del Drago,** a small accumulation of buildings by the ocean on the island's northwest corner, is known principally for its scenery and the nearby **Isla de los Pájaros** ("Swan Cay"), a steep-cliffed island home to a whole lot of, well, birds.

Three major tour operations on the island arrange trips to stupendous snorkeling sites near the Zapatilla Cays in **Parque Nacional Bastimentos, Hospital Point** on the island of Solarte, and numerous scuba diving spots. The only way to get to these islands is by private boat, so you can't avoid paying a fee. Tours may include **jungle hikes** and visits to a traditional Guaymí village known as **Sand Creek,** as well as snorkeling, swimming, diving, fishing, and suntanning. You'll find mangrove trees, exotic insects, and plenty of lush greenery at every tranquil destination, especially within P.N. Bastimentos, a relatively unexplored sanctuary for a vast array of fauna and flora. Most snorkeling tours run about $15 per person with a four person minimum; scuba diving tours can cost much more ($35 per tank and up). For diving and snorkeling, make safety a priority; be sure instructors are certified, and don't disrupt the creatures of the sea. If you are looking to avoid *gringo* tours, Bola Smith, the Bocas' own "Crocodile Dundee," offers snorkeling and jungle river tours (snorkeling $10, with river tour $20). Ask for him at the education office in the *palacio* or call him up and discuss the options in English or Spanish (tel. 757-9301 or 751-9282). "Go where no one has gone before" in P.N. Bastimentos with **Starfleet ECO Adventures** (tel./fax 757-9630) on the catamaran *Morning Star,* found between Restaurante Todo Tropical and Restaurante Kun Ja (office open 8am-10pm). All necessary equipment is rentable. A full day of snorkeling costs $15. **Turtle Divers** (tel./fax 757-9594) work out of the store beneath Pizzeria Pomodoro on the main street, and offer snorkeling and diving tours ($40 for 2 tanks and lunch). About halfway from Bocas del Toro to Boca del Drago is a small cave system known as **Las Grutas,** ideal for a short, but wet jaunt (bring a flashlight).

■ Almirante

With only the waning remnants of a flourishing port industry to mark its place on the map, Almirante longs for days gone by, suffering eternally as travelers simply exploit its position as an optimal bridge to Bocas del Toro and Costa Rica.

Banco Nacional de Panamá (tel. 758-3718) is across from Hotel El Gran Hong Kong (open Mon.-Fri. 8am-3pm, Sat. 9am-2pm). Arrive early to get a seat on the **train** to **Changuinola** (daily 7:30am and 2pm) or take the **bus** every ½hr.) from the centrally located town bus stop. Two **water taxi** companies, **De La Tours** and **Taxi 26,** compete for passengers to **Bocas del Toro** and **Chiriquí Grande.** DeLa Tours has taxis leaving for Bocas at 6:30, 7:30am, and every 45 minutes thereafter until 5:30pm ($3). Taxis to Chiriquí Grande run every hour beginning at 7:00am, Mon.-Fri. and 6:30am on weekends ($6; only runs until 1:30pm). A **ferry** located on the opposite side of town from the water taxis leaves for Chiriquí Grande and Bocas every day (except Mon.) around 7:30am and 2:00pm. **Farmacia San Vincente** is across from Hotel El Gran Hong Kong. Call the **hospital** at 758-3745. Contact the **police** (tel. 104 or 758-3721) in the station located right next to the **post office** (Mon.-Fri. 8am-noon and 2-5pm, Sat. 8am-noon), down the block from the bank.

Accommodations are not easy to find in Almirante; it's best to ask someone for directions. **Hotel El Gran Hong Kong** (tel. 758-3763) has six adequate rooms with private baths, and is one of the quieter places in town (singles or doubles with fans and collective bath $11, with private bath and A/C $17). Eat downstairs at the somewhat pricey restaurant (wonton soup $2.25, seafood $9-10). **Hotel/Bar Cristobal Colón,** up the street from the Hotel El Gran Hong Kong, proffers small, basic rooms with communal bathrooms at the lowest price in town (singles $5.50; doubles $8.50). **Hospedaje San Francisco** (tel. 758-3779), near the bus station, has nine modest rooms ($11 for one person with private bath, add A/C $15).

■ Changuinola

Changuinola thrives on merchants and **banana plantations** (many open to visitors), including a Chiquita processing plant identifiable as the hulking space-craft on the outskirts of the city. Buses from Changuinola proceed on to the **Costa Rican border;** look for buses marked **Las Tablas** or **Guabito** (20min., $1 bus or taxi). The Panamanian side of the border is open 8am-6pm every day, while the Costa Rican side is open from 7am-5pm. The time zone difference assures that when one office is open, the other is as well, except during lunch (11am-12:30pm on both sides). Be sure to have all necessary papers when you arrive and have some currency of the country to which you are going, as there is no easy way to change money at the border.

Most of what a visitor to Changuinola might need is within a couple of blocks of the bus station. **Banco del Istmo** is one block towards Guabito from the terminal (to your right when facing the street; open Mon.-Fri. 8am-3:30pm, Sat. 9am-noon). **Banco Nacional de Panamá** (tel./fax 758-8445; open Mon.-Fri. 8am-3pm, Sat. 9am-noon), located near the airport, sells the necessary *timbre* to all American tourists who forgot to purchase a tourist card in San José before crossing the border into Panamá. For the next step in this confusing border-crossing process, head to **Migración** (tel. 758-8651; open Mon.-Fri. 8am-noon and 1-3:45pm) for the necessary stamp on your tourist card. Migración is located on the main road past **Hotel Carol.** The further you are from the border, the harder it is to change colones into balboas. **Supermarkets** lie across the street from the terminal and sometimes will change money once you make a purchase.

Hotel Carol (tel. 758-8731) is located two blocks from the terminal in the opposite direction of the airport. Some rooms have round beds (yes, round), the common room has a TV, and the big, clean rooms come with air-conditioning and private bath (singles $11, doubles $14). **Hotel Changuinola** (tel. 758-8678) is located near the airport, and is an (expensive) taxi ride from the bus terminal. $9.90 will score you a "matrimonial" bed with private bath and fan; air-conditioning costs an extra $6.

Besides these two cheaper hotels, Changuinola also houses some higher end accommodations. For example, at **Chalet Suizo Suites** (tel. 758-8242), the higher prices
buy A/C, hot water, color cable TV, a fridge, and access to a restaurant located downstairs (singles $26; doubles $35). A medical clinic is in the same building.

■ Chiriquí Grande

There are enough transport vehicles along Chiriquí Grande's buzzing port to move
the whole darn place across the ocean, and enough closed shops and restaurants to
make you think everyone's already left. No matter how drab and dull the town is,
however, the drive there from David is stunning. After crossing the continental divide
and passing from the province of Chiriquí to that of Bocas del Toro, pastures and
farmland give way to lush, primeval cloud forests. As wizened trees grope upwards
on your right, the edge of the world at your left is thick mist. The fog eventually
moves upwards to cling to the parting mountains, offering a film-worthy vista of the
Caribbean and the islands of the Bocas del Toro archipelago. Then, all too suddenly,
you've arrived in Chiriquí Grande.

   Banco Nacional de Panamá (tel. 757-9711), across from the Texaco station,
exchanges traveler's checks (open Mon.-Fri. 8am-3pm, Sat. 9am-noon). Phone home
from the **public telephone** across the street from **Hotel Osiris** or from the **INTEL**
office near Posada Siquem. **Buses** run directly from David to Chiriquí Grande, so it's a
natural stopover before chugging on to paradise, or at least Almirante. Two **water
taxi** businesses, **De La Tours** and **Taxi 25**, run **lanchas** to Almirante and Bocas regularly. Prices are about the same on either line. De La Tours charges $6 to Almirante
while Taxi 25 charges $7, and both arrive at their destinations in the same amount of
time (although it may be wise to check the order of stops). There are also **ferries**
which run to Almirante twice a day at a lower price and a slower speed.

   Posada Siquem, near the park off the main road, sits away from the town's chaotic
commercial core. Most of the 13 rooms have fans and are thoroughly safe, pleasant,
and humble. Some have private bathrooms and some have real mattresses (singles $7;
doubles $8). The most pleasant hotel experience here is the **Hotel Emperador** (tel.
757-9656), where $10 per person, or $12.50 for a single, buys a private bathroom, a
television, and A/C. A beautiful third-floor balcony overlooks the town's main side
street. Check in and out at the **Casa Miranda #2** general store in front.

EAST OF PANAMA CITY

▨ San Blas Archipelago

Only 48 of the 365 baby islands comprising the island chain of San Blas are inhabited
by the province's population of 20,400, leaving the rest to soak in unblemished tropical nirvana. Because of the undefiled surroundings, as well as the unique culture of
the islands' self-ruled natives, the **Kuna,** Panamanians are resoundingly proud of the
archipelago. San Blas is a bit out of the way, and it takes some dough to reach it, but
such a trip should not be missed. Although a substantial number of *gringo* visitors to
the islands are anthropologists and field biologists, more and more backpackers are
beginning to roam the sands. Activity among the Kuna begins at daybreak and shuts
down with the wailing generator at 11pm. In the darkness, the only audible sounds
are the roar of the waves and the plaintive, pious prayers of the village *sáhila* (elder).
Some of the nearby uninhabited islands can actually be rented from the Kuna for a
day or two. Most hotels offer free tours to other islands.

   The Kuna are famous for their *mola* artwork, their intricately designed clothes, and
their communal living. Each tribal subgroup inhabits a separate island, and their customs are intriguing. When Kuna girls turn 14, they go through a sacred puberty ritual
in which the whole tribe comes together for four days and drinks rum from dawn to

dusk. Meanwhile, the young girl waits in an isolated hut until her Kuna elderwoman approaches her on the last day to cut her hair and adorn her with clothes and jewelry. Observe with respectful distance and avoid taking photographs.

The only reasonable way to get to San Blas is by **plane.** Unless you're planning to stay at an expensive eco-resort, fly to the island capital of San Blas, **El Porvenir. AereoTaxi** (tel. in Panama City 264-8644) and **Aviatur** (tel. 226-2644) offer 6am flights for $55 round-trip (arrive at airport by 5am; Aviatur doesn't fly on Sun.); flights return immediately, so staying at least 1 night is required.

Because every hotel in San Blas is located on a different island, it's highly recommended to make reservations in advance so that the hotel can pick you up in its own *cayuca* (similar to a canoe). At present, the only real option for the budget traveler is the **Hotel San Blas** (tel. in Panama City 262-5410), on Nalunega Island. Each of the 25 rooms is very basic and utterly tranquil, and the bargain basement price ($27) includes three simple but delicious meals from the sea and two optional tours per day to neighboring islands for snorkeling, swimming, and suntanning. One particularly cool island is Achutupu, or "Dog Island," where a large shipwreck offshore with colorful tube and stag coral growing on the side of the hull makes for engaging snorkeling. Besides a bewildering variety of regular tropical fish, gigantic schools of youngsters swarm about. Hotel San Blas rents snorkeling equipment for $5 per day, and usually makes the 30-minute journey to Achutupu during the morning, as the sea gets rougher in the afternoon.

EASTERN PANAMÁ: DARIÉN

The largest province in Panamá is also the least developed and most sparsely populated; getting into Darién as a tourist is not easy, and getting through to Colombia is next to impossible. Enveloped by thick jungle, the Chocó, Kuna, and other *indígenas* have managed to successfully inhabit the area for years, but roads are in poor condition and pose many dangers to travelers. For those who make it to Darién, the rewards are bountiful; the Chocó, divided into the linguistically distinct **Embera** and **Wounaan** tribes, live a lifestyle completely foreign even to other Panamanian tribes, adorning their faces with *jauga,* a colorful pigment, and hunting with blowguns and poison darts along the mighty Tuira River. **Parque Nacional Darién** is one of the largest parks in Central America. The impenetrable wilderness is also the reason why the Interamerican Highway linking North and South America has its only interruption here, in the Darién Gap. Panamá and Colombia have discussed completing the road, but for the foreseeable future, overland crossing to Colombia is only possible by a tricky combination of boats and walking.

Before undertaking any venture to Darién, inform yourself about road conditions, health and safety issues, and other logistical problems. Contact IPAT in Panama City for the names of tour leaders to Darién; several companies make trips to **Yaviza, El Real, La Palma,** and **Santa Maria,** the gateway to P.N. Darién. Also, be sure to contact Sr. Herasmo Bayaster at the **"Area Protejida y Vida Silvestre"** (tel. 232-6643), who will officially register your expedition. The Interamerican Hwy. only goes as far as Yaviza. **Boats** to Darién from Panama City may be available also for $10-14 through **Muelle Secal** (tel. 262-9124). **Aeroperlas** (tel. 269-4555) has flights to **Sambu, Jaqual, El Real, Las Palmas,** and **Garachine** ($33-41). From Yaviza, overland passage is possible, but not easy. Travel during the dry season (Nov.-May), prepare the proper visas for entry into Colombia prior to leaving, and bring at least one guide, preferably a reputable, experienced native. Guerrilla activity in the Darién Gap, especially in the northeast section near the Colombian border, has thwarted travelers in the past. Food, water, and gas are not available along most stretches of the jungle, so an adequate supply must be carried. Don't undertake the venture without extensive research.

Yucatán Peninsula

Hernández de Córdoba mistakenly ran aground here in 1517. When the freshly disembarked sailors asked the locals where they were, the Maya, naturally not understanding Spanish, replied something to the effect of, "We haven't a clue what you're talking about." Unfamiliar with the Mayan language, Córdoba only caught the last few syllables of their reply, "Tectetán," and erroneously dubbed the region Yucatán. This encounter established a paradigm that would hold throughout Yucatán's history; misunderstood and continually molested by outsiders, it would never be fully conquered. Today, the peninsula's culture remains essentially Maya and thrives in the peninsula's small towns, where the only evidence of Western influence arrives in the form of the weekly Coca-Cola truck. Mayan is still the first language of most inhabitants, and *indígena* religions persist (often with a Catholic veneer). Yucatec women still carry bowls of corn flour on their heads and wear embroidered *huipil* dresses, and fishing, farming, and hammock-making out-produce big industry and commerce.

But foreign influence fights on: more workers are drawn by the dubious allure of the tourism industry, flooding the big cities and resorts to work in gringo-friendly restaurants, weave hammocks for tourists, or act as multilingual guides at archaeological sites. Burgeoning tourism is threatening the traditional *yucateco* way of life as international nomads discover the peninsula's fine beaches, beautiful colonial towns, and striking Maya ruins. After the Mexican government set an example by engineering the pristine pleasure-world of Cancún from the ground up, developers seized similar areas stretching farther and farther along the Yucatán coast; much of the virgin Caribbean beach land is currently under massive construction, as Maya ruin sites are plowed over to make room for new, palatial resorts.

Yucatán state's rich history draws thousands of visitors each year, who come to scramble up and down the majestic Maya ruins such as the incomparable Chichén Itzá, marvel at old colonial towns, explore the area's many dark caves, and take a dip in the *cenotes*. **Quintana Roo**'s luscious rain jungle, fantastic coastline, and magnificent Maya ruins were idylls beneath the Caribbean sun until the government transformed the area from tropical paradise to tourist factory. Cancún rapidly became the beachhead for what some wryly call "the Second *Conquista*," and the nearby beaches and ruins were soon to follow. Although its countryside is dotted with Maya ruins and its coastline is over 200km long, **Campeche** pulls in fewer visitors than Yucatán to the north or Quintana Roo to the east, perhaps because it lacks a kind of swaggering grandeur—ruins are modest and relatively inaccessible, while the beaches are kept humble by wind and rocks.

For bigger, better Yucatán coverage, see *Let's Go: Mexico 1998.*

ESSENTIALS

▨ Documents and Formalities

EMBASSIES AND CONSULATES

Embassy of Mexico: In **Australia,** 14 Perth Ave., Yarralumla, Canberra 2600 ACT (tel. (06) 273 3905 or 273 3947; fax 273 1190); in **Canada,** 45 O'Connor St., #1500, K1P 1A4 Ottawa, Ont. (tel. (613) 233-8988, 233-9272 or 233-6665; fax 235-9123); in the **U.K.,** 42 Hertford St., Mayfair, W1Y 7TS, London (tel. (0171) 499 8586; fax 495 4035); in the **U.S.,** 1911 Pennsylvania Ave. NW, Washington, D.C. 20006 (tel. (202) 728-1600; fax 728-1718).

Consulate of Mexico: In **Australia,** Level 1, 135-153 New South Head Rd., Edgecliff, Sydney 2027 NSW (tel. (02) 326 1311 or 326 1292; fax 327 1110); in **Canada,** 199 Bay St., #4440, Commerce Court West, M5L 1E9 Toronto, Ont. (tel. (416) 368-

2875; fax 368-3478 or 368-1672); in the **U.K.,** 42 Hertford St., Mayfair, W1Y 7TS, London (tel. (0171) 499 8586; fax 495 4035); in the **U.S.,** 2827 16th St. NW, Washington, D.C. 20036 (tel. (202) 736-1000; fax 797-8458) or 8 E. 41st St., New York, NY 10017 (tel. (212) 689-0456; fax 545-8197).

PASSPORTS, VISAS, AND CUSTOMS

All persons visiting Mexico for tourism or study for up to 180 days must carry a **tourist card** (**FMT,** for *Folleto de Migración Turística*) in addition to proof of citizenship. U.S. and Canadian citizens can skip the FMT if they don't expect to travel past border towns or stay anywhere in the country for more than 72 hours. Try to get a card that will be valid longer than your projected stay, since obtaining an extension on a 90-day FMT is a huge hassle: you'll need a physician's authorization stating that you are too ill to travel. If you do need an extension, visit the **Delegación de Servicios Migratorios** several weeks before your card expires. For stays in Mexico up to six months, visas are not necessary for citizens of Australia, Canada, the U.K., the U.S., New Zealand, and most E.U. countries. Businesspeople, missionaries, and students must obtain appropriate visas. Applications are processed by consulates in one day and cost $63.

■ Money Matters

US$1 = 7.80 pesos	1 peso = US$0.13
CDN$1 = 5.66 pesos	1 peso= CDN$0.18
UK£1 = 12.67 pesos	1 peso = UK£0.08
IR£1 = 11.28 pesos	1 peso = IR£0.08
AUS$1 = 5.77 pesos	1 peso = AUS$0.17
NZ$1 = 5.04 pesos	1 peso = NZ$0.20
SARand = 1.68 pesos	1 peso = SARand$0.59

■ Keeping In Touch

Mexican mail service is slow. Though it usually arrives, it can take anywhere from one to three weeks for **correo aéreo** (airmail) to reach the U.S., and at the very least two weeks to reach Europe and other destinations. Official estimates average 40 days by boat, but in reality it will take months. In Mexico, never deposit anything important in the black holes called mailboxes; take it straight to the **oficina de correos** (post office) instead. Anything important should be sent *registrado* (registered mail) or in duplicate. For the speediest service possible, **MexPost** works in collaboration with Express Mail International in the U.S. and similar express mail services in other countries to deliver mail quickly and reliably.

Taxes and surcharges make it extremely expensive to call abroad from Mexico. Call with a card or collect if you can; not only is it cheaper (about half the price of direct), but you will also avoid enormous surcharges from hotels. International calls using sleek silver **LADATEL** touch-tone payphones are cheaper and involve less waiting than any of the alternatives. LADATELs accept coins or phone cards you can buy at most *papelerías* (stationers) or *abarrotes* (grocers). To reach an **AT&T** operator from a LADATEL phone, call 95-800-462-4240; for **MCI** call 95-800-674-7000; for **Sprint** call 95-800-877-8000.

YUCATÁN

■ La Ruta Puuc (The Maya Route)

La Ruta Puuc (a.k.a. La Ruta Maya) is a long stretch between Campeche and Mérida that traverses the Puuc Hills. This area was home to about 22,000 people during the

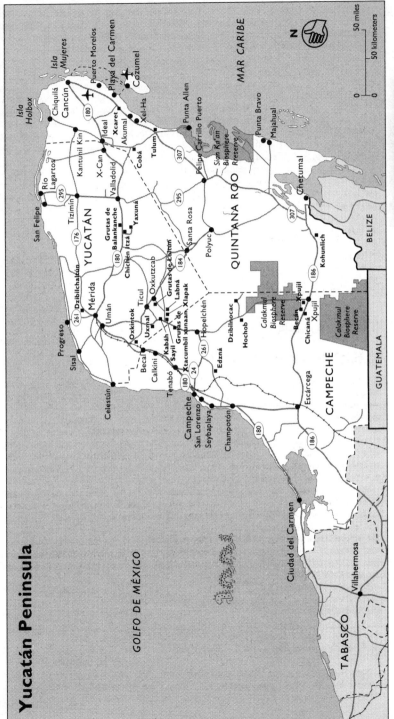

Yucatán Peninsula

Classic period of Maya civilization (4th to 10th centuries). Decimated by diseases introduced by the Spanish, the Maya slowly surrendered most of their cities and ceremonial centers to the jungle. Beginning in the 18th century, the Maya population began a slow recovery. While today's Puuc Maya live in towns with paved roads and plumbing, women continue to wear traditional embroidered *huipiles*, and Mayan remains the dominant language.

The Ruta Puuc refers specifically to the 254km on Rte. 261 between Campeche and Mérida and the Sayil-Oxkutzkub road which branches off just meters after the Campeche-Yucatán border. Taking this turnoff, **Sayil** is the first archaeological site to materialize (after 5km), followed by **Xlapak** (10km), **Labná** (13km), **Loltún** (25km), **Oxkutzkab** (45km), and **Ticul** (62km). Alternatively, if the turnoff is not taken, the road winds through **Kabah** (right after the border) and the stunning site of **Uxmal** (23km); 16km from Uxmal lies the junction at **Muna.**

The easiest way to see the ruins is by **renting a car** in Mérida. The drive along the Ruta Puuc is one of the most liberating on-the-road experiences, as small Maya villages and verdant jungle line the road. Another option is an **organized tour.** These can be arranged through private companies in either Mérida or Campeche (ask in the tourist office). Public transportation is more difficult. Second-class **buses** traverse Rte. 261 frequently and will stop when requested, but none travel the Sayil-Oxkutzkub road with the exception of the **Autotransportes del Sur "Ruta Puuc" bus** that leaves Mérida at 8am and visits Kabah, Sayil, Labná, and Uxmal, returning to Mérida at about 2:30pm. If you don't mind a whirlwind tour through the sites, this bus is an incredible bargain (40 pesos; admission to sites not included). But be on the bus promptly when it leaves each site; drivers can be antsy. **Combis** are abundant in the morning and make frequent trips between Oxkutzkab, Ticul, **Santa Elena,** and Muna (it is easiest to get a *combi* to Uxmal from Muna), and they will make any trip if paid enough. Unfortunately, with both *combis* and buses, return trips are not always guaranteed.

The sites along the Ruta Puuc can best be explored using **Ticul** as a base; the town offers cheap accommodations and restaurants. Two to three days should be ample time for exhaustive exploration. Most sites sell *refrescos*, but the only one with accommodations (at ridiculously high prices) is Uxmal. Thank Chac for Ticul.

TICUL

A bustling provincial town off the Campeche-Mérida highway, **Ticul** (pop. 40,000) is known for its cheap, durable shoes and its status as a convenient and inexpensive base from which to explore the Ruta Puuc sites of Uxmal, Kabah, Sayil, Xlapak, and Labná, as well as the Grutas de Loltún. Staying in Ticul is a relief from Mérida—the town's busy residents simply don't have time to heckle tourists. A number of *cenotes* and colonial buildings await exploration in the nearby towns of **Teabo,** 30km southeast of Ticul, **Mayapán,** 45km to the northeast, and **Holcá,** 105km to the northeast. **Maní,** 15km east of Ticul, features a colonial monastery; **Tekax,** 35km to the southeast, a hermitage; and **Tipikal,** an impressive colonial church.

Orientation and Practical Information Ticul's streets form a grid with the main drag, Calle 23, passing east-west through the center. Even-numbered streets run north-south. Most commercial activity transpires between the *zócalo* (at Calle 24) and Calle 30, four blocks to the west.

Banco del Atlántico, Calle 23 #195, off the *zócalo*, changes U.S. dollars and traveler's checks (open Mon.-Fri. 9am-2pm). Expensive international calls can be made at the long-distance **caseta,** Calle 23 #210 between Calles 26 and 28 (tel. 2-00-00; open 8:30am-10pm). **Combis** leave from Parque de la Madre, Calle 23 between Calles 28 and 30, for Muna (7 per day, 5 pesos); from Calle 30 between Calles 25 and 25A, for Santa Elena, Uxmal, and Kabah (4 pesos); and from Calle 25 between Calles 26 and 28, for Oxkutzkub (every 15min., 5 pesos). From Muna, five **buses** run daily to Campeche (20 pesos) via Uxmal and Kabah, from the **Terminal** at the *zócalo*. Hourly buses head north to Mérida (7 pesos). **Farmacia San Jose,** Calle 23 #214J (tel. 2-03-93), is between Calles 28 and 30 (open 8am-1pm and 4-10pm). **Dr. Estela Sanabria**

can be reached at the same number for 24-hour **medical assistance. Police** headquarters are on Calle 23 (tel. 2-00-10 or 2-02-10) at the northeast corner of the *zócalo* (open 24hr.). Ticul's **post office** (tel. 2-00-40) is in the Palacio Municipal on the *zócalo* (open Mon.-Fri. 8am-2:30pm). **Postal Code: 97860. Phone Code: 997.**

Accommodations and Food Ticul has several hotels and good restaurants. **Hotel San Miguel,** on Calle 28 (tel. 2-63-82), opposite Parque de la Madre, offers small, battleship-gray rooms with saggy beds and fans (singles 25 pesos; doubles 32 pesos, with 2 beds 38 pesos). **Hotel Sierra Sosa** on Calle 24 (tel. 2-00-08; fax 2-02-82), on the northwest corner of the *zócalo,* has modern rooms with firm beds, strong fans, and TVs. Coffee and *agua purificada* come free (singles 60 pesos; doubles 70 pesos; triples 80 pesos; add 20 pesos for A/C).

Dining in Ticul can be tricky; only one restaurant stays open past 6pm. Luckily, **Los Almendros,** Calle 23 #207 between Calles 28 and 30 (tel. 2-00-21), is known worldwide for their *poc-chuc;* the chain of restaurants started here in little ol' Ticul (open daily 9am-9pm). **Restaurant Los Delfines** (tel. 2-04-01), Calle 27 between Calles 28 and 30, serves shrimp dishes, *chiles rellenos* (35 pesos), and jars of lemonade under a big airy *palapa* (open daily 11am-7pm). Ticul's **market** is just off Calle 23 between Calles 28 and 30 (open daily sunrise-sunset).

Getting to the Ruins The Ruta Puuc is a well-marked, *tope*-ridden road that can be driven without purchasing a road map. Simply follow signs to Uman from Merida, then head towards Muna. From there on, just follow "Ruta Puuc" in Ticul.

Without a car, you'll be faced with relay races. Public transportation in Ticul is not geared toward ruin-happy tourists. While Uxmal and Kabah are fairly accessible if you have luck with *combi* transfers, the lack of traffic on the Sayil-Oxkutzcab road will leave the carless traveler frustrated and stranded. In general, you should reconcile yourself to changing buses. To reach the ruins around Uxmal, take a Mérida-bound bus from the Ticul bus station on Calle 24 (tel. 2-01-62), behind the main church, and get off at Muna (every ½hr., 3 pesos). *Combis* for Muna leave from Parque de la Madre, Calle 23 between Calles 28 and 30. From Muna, board a southbound bus or *combi* for Uxmal, Kabah, or other sites from the *zócalo* (7 per day, 3 pesos). You can also reach the ruins by catching a *combi* on Calle 30, between Calles 25 and 25A, to Santa Elena (½hr., about 3 pesos). Change *combis* at Santa Elena for Uxmal, 16km from Mérida, or Kabah, south of Campeche. *Combis* are most plentiful in the morning. Considering the amount of time it will take to make connections as opposed to how long each sight really takes, you might want to reconsider the rush tour bus from Mérida.

To reach the Grutas de Loltún, snag a *combi* to Oxkutzcab at Parque de la Madre; you'll be let off at the intersection of Calles 23 and 26 (15min., about 3 pesos). *Combis* leave for Loltún from the lot across from Oxkutzcab's market, "20 de Noviembre." Tell the driver to let you off at the *grutas* (10min., about 3 pesos), as everyone else is probably headed for the agricultural cooperative 3km farther down the road. Because the road is more crowded with *combis,* it's easier to reach the Grutas than Uxmal or Kabah. Hitchhikers rarely find rides on any of these roads.

UXMAL

Get here. Whatever it takes. Not many do, and that's part of the charm, not to mention the excellently restored pyramids, reliefs, and immense masks. Meaning "thrice built or occupied," it's not hard to see why **Uxmal,** once a capital with 25,000 inhabitants, kept drawing people.

Orientation and Practical Information Autotransportes del Sur (ATS) sends six buses per day from Mérida to Uxmal (1½hr., 11 pesos), as well as a "Ruta Puuc" bus which visits Uxmal, Kabah, Sayil, Xlapak, and Labná all in one day for just 40 pesos (see p. 473). From Campeche you'll have to take the **Camioneros de Campeche** bus to Mérida (5 per day, 3hr., 25 pesos). Ask the driver to stop at the access road to the *ruinas.* To return, grab a passing bus at the *crucero* just outside the entrance to the ruins. The last buses to Mérida and Campeche pass at 8pm and 7pm, respectively. A modern **tourist center** with a small museum, restaurant, gift shop, photographic supply shop, and bathrooms greets you at the entrance to the ruins. The **Kit Bolon Tun auditorium,** also in the tourist center, screens documentaries on the Ruta Puuc and gives 15-minute presentations of the Yucatán, Chichén Itzá, and Uxmal (6 shows per day in Spanish and 4 in English; free).

Accommodations and Food Even the bravest of ruins crumble under the huge prices of Uxmal's lodging and food. Consider staying 30 minutes away in Ticul, where hotel rooms cost half as much. In Uxmal, the cheapest option is **Rancho Uxmal** (tel. 2-02-77), 4km north of the ruins on Rte. 261. From the highway near Uxmal, you can reach Rancho Uxmal by hopping aboard a passing bus or *combi* (about 2 pesos). Thinly carpeted rooms have inviting bedspreads, hand-painted murals, and standard bathrooms. The pool is usually in service during peak season (singles 120 pesos; doubles 160 pesos; triples 180 pesos). The Ranch's restaurant serves up a complete menu for 35 pesos (open daily 7am-10pm).

Sights According to the **Chilam Balam,** a Maya historical account written in pho-netic Spanish, Ah Suytok Xiu and his warriors from the Valley of Mexico invaded Yucatán at the end of the 10th century. Xiu and his successors dominated Uxmal until the city's strength was sapped by civil warfare in the 12th century. Because their priests foretold the coming of white, bearded men, the Xiu did not resist when Span-ish conquistadors attacked Uxmal. The last Xiu ruler of the city was Ah Suytok Tutul Xiu, whose descendants still live in the Puuc region. Tutul Xiu was baptized as an old man; his godfather was Francisco de Montejo, conqueror of the Yucatán. The 40m-tall near-pyramid visible upon entering Uxmal is the **Temple of the Magician.** Built at a 60° angle, the narrow steep stairs make for a wicked climb. The pyramid, the leg-end goes, was built by a dwarf-magician who hatched from a witch's egg and grew to maturity in the space of a single year.

The elegant south-facing arch leads to the **ballcourt.** Note the glyphs on the rings through which well-padded players tried to knock a hardened rubber ball. Emerging from the ballcourt, head right along a narrow path to the **Cemetery Group,** a small, leafy plaza bounded by a small pyramid to the north and a temple to the west. Stones that once formed platforms bear haunting reliefs of skulls and crossbones. Returning to the ballcourt, head south to the well-restored **Great Pyramid,** built by the gover-nor in his contest with the dwarf-magician. The architecture and crude latticework reveal the influences of northern Campeche. To the west, the pyramid looks down on the jagged face of the Palomar, behind which lie the jungle-shrouded remains of the **Chenes Temple.**

KABAH

Once the second largest city in the northern Yucatán, **Kabah** was built with the blood and sweat of many slaves, whose effort has mostly succumbed to the ravages of time. The most elaborate of Kabah's structures is the **Codz Pop Temple** (rolled mat in Mayan), immediately to the right of the entrance, which was named for the odd shape of the rain god Chac's nose. The temple's broad facade displays nearly 300 masks of Chac, each comprised of 30 carved pieces. The elaborate Chenes style of the temple is unique to the Codz Pop—its neighbors to the east, **El Palacio** (a 25m pyramid) and **Las Columnas,** were executed in plainer fashion. The site is thought to have served as a court where justices settled disputes and the gods were the jury. Across the street by the parking lot, the short dirt road leads to rubble (right), more rubble (left), and the famous Kabah Arch (straight ahead). The arch marks the begin-ning of the ancient *sacbé* (paved, elevated road) which culminated in a twin arch at Uxmal. The perfect alignment of the archway with the north-south line is testimony to Maya astronomical understanding (site open daily 8am-5pm; admission 10 pesos, free Sun. and holidays).

Getting There: Bisected by Rte. 261, Kabah lies 23km southeast of its Ruta Puuc cousin, Uxmal. Because of its location on the Campeche-Mérida highway *(vía ruinas)*, it can easily be reached by any second-class bus running between Mérida and Campeche. Buses will stop at Kabah only if a passenger notifies the driver beforehand or if the driver sees a person wildly gesticulating on the shoulder of the highway. Things are easier with the **ATS "Ruta Puuc" bus.** Since almost all the tourists who come to Kabah have cars, many of the carless try to hitch.

SAYIL

The **Palace of Sayil** is an architectural standout among the region's ruins. While most of its buildings are now nothing more than glorified ant hills, Sayil's Palace is breathtaking. Between its three terraced levels, the building's 50 rooms exhibit unparalleled ornamental diversity. Walls are carved with rows of slender columns, the second-story frieze depicts the descending serpent-god's body, and elegant second-floor chambers open onto pleasant porticos, each graced by bulging columns. Climb to the top for a gorgeous panoramic view of the rolling, verdant Puuc hills. Behind the palace sits a **chultún** (plastered catch basin) that the Maya used to collect rainwater for use during the dry season.

The path continues past the palace to **El Mirador** (the lookout), a lofty temple with once-grandiose columns. Left of El Mirador, the path leads deeper into the jungle, where the extremely graphic **Estela del Falo** (Stela of the Phallus) will make even the most sexually liberated of visitors blush profusely. A few other temples are barely visible through the dense jungle undergrowth (site open daily 8am-5pm; admission 10 pesos, free Sun. and holidays).

Getting There: Sayil lies 9km past Kabah off Rte. 261 on the Sayil-Oxkutzcab road and 5km past Xlapak. The only public transportation to the site is the **Autotransportes del Sur "Ruta Puuc" bus.** Buses do run, however, from Mérida to Kabah, 10km away on the main highway. Some travelers hitch from Kabah to Sayil.

LABNÁ

Labná's buildings were constructed towards the end of the late-Classic period (600-900 AD), when the Puuc cities were connected by a *sacbé* (white road). Today, a short reconstructed section of the *sacbé* runs between Labná's two most impressive sights: the palace and the stone arch. When the Yucatán flooded, the raised **sacbé** allowed the Maya to pass from one city to another. However, more common than floods were droughts. To deal with parched conditions, the Maya constructed huge *chultunes* (catch basins), many of which are found at Labná. The *chultunes* collected both water (up to 8000 gallons in each) and the bodies of peasants who couldn't afford to be buried. Many of Labná's buildings are too far gone to climb, giving rest to the tired and weak-kneed tourist.

Labná's **palace** is on the northern side of the site, to the left as you enter. While the construction of this building occupied the Maya for several centuries, the edifice was never actually completed. Labná's palace is reminiscent of the one at Sayil insofar as both boast exceptionally ornate second-floor facades. Nearby mosaics depict figures in palm huts, reminding present-day visitors that the stone palaces once housed only the privileged few. Now, they house scores of chipper birds.

Labná is famed for its picturesque **stone arch,** 3m wide and 6m high. Its western facade is intricately decorated in a trellis pattern, while the eastern side remains more bland. Previously thought to have been the entrance to another temple, archaeologists now believe that the arch served as a ceremonial point of entry for victorious warriors returning from the battlefield. Beyond the arch, on the unrestored base of a pyramid, stands the **observatory,** also known as **El Mirador** (the lookout). Its notable facade rises over the box-like structure and bears sculptures attached by tenons and dowels. The terracing around the temple contained many *chultunes.* The top of the observatory affords a view of the entire site; keep your eyes peeled for falcons' nests (site open daily 8am-5pm; admission 10 pesos, free Sun.).

Getting There: The final destination on the "Ruta Puuc" bus, Labná lies 42km east of Uxmal, 4km beyond Xlapak, and 22km before Las Grutas (see below). Almost no *combis* come and go on this branch of the Ruta Puuc; hitching is reportedly tough.

GRUTAS DE LOLTÚN

The Grutas de Loltún are 58km east of Uxmal on the Sayil-Oxkutzcab road. Below a dense jungle of mahogany and *ceiba,* kilometers of enormous caverns wind through the rock. Guides can be enticed to give longer tours (the caves go on forever) with the promise of a nice, fat tip. The ancient Maya first settled this area in order to take advantage of the Grutas' water and clay. Hundreds of years later, Maya *campesinos* returned to the caves seeking refuge from the Caste War (1847-1848). Important caverns include the **Room of the 37 Inscriptions,** which includes many still-visible markings (i.e., handprints), and the **Na Cab** (House of the Bees), where you can see the *ka'ob* (grindstones) left by the Maya. Ancient inhabitants broke off the stalactite tips in the **Gallery of Fallen Rocks** to use as spears and arrows. The **Cathedral** is a palatial room that once hosted Maya feasts and assemblies. The shadowy silhouette above the entrance is popularly believed to represent the Virgin of Guadalupe. Several caves contain partially hollow stalactites and columns—thump one with the heel of your hand and listen to the soft booming sound *("Loltún…Loltún…")* reverberate throughout the cave system. Archaeologists speculate that the Maya used these formations as a musical means of underground communication.

Entrance to Loltún is only allowed when a guide leads a tour through the caves (9:30, 11am, 12:30, 2, 3, and 4pm). Guides will lead English tours, but Spanish ones tend to be more comprehensive. Bear in mind the exorbitant rates charged by aboveground guides when leaving a tip for the free guide service (admission 22 pesos, Sun. 7 pesos). As you exit the caves (0.5km from the entrance), you'll stumble upon the conveniently located **Restaurant El Huinoc de Loltún,** which serves up a good range of local dishes for about 25-40 pesos. Be prepared to wait—service is slow as molasses and the restaurant can be packed with tour buses.

Getting There: To get to Loltún, catch a bus as far as Muna or Ticul, hop in a *combi* headed for Oxkutzcab, then follow signs to *Centro*. Passing the market on your left, walk two blocks, turn right at the sign for Ruta Puuc, then pray for deliverance—Las Grutas are 7km down the road. A pick-up truck in Oxkutzcab's *zócalo* may be willing to make the trip, though it will cost you at least 20 pesos.

■ Mérida

Built atop the ruins of the Maya capital of T'hó, modern Mérida is haunted by its pre-Hispanic history—the stones of the city's fortress-like cathedral even bear traces of the Maya temples from which they were stripped. The Maya called this site "place of the fifth point," to indicate that it was the center of the universe, the spot between the four points of north, south, east, and west. Today, elegant Mérida (pop. 1.5 million) is at least the center of Yucatán—it's the state's capital and key commercial center. Panama hats come from Becal in the neighboring state of Campeche, hammocks arrive from nearby Tixcocób, and *henequén* is trucked to Mérida from all over Yucatán before being exported as hemp.

ORIENTATION

Rte. 180 runs from Cancún (322km) and Valladolid (168km) to the east, becoming **Calle 65,** which passes through the busiest part of town, one block south of the *zócalo*. Those approaching on Rte. 180 from Campeche, 153km to the southwest, end up on **Avenida Itzáes** (also called **Avenida de la Paz**), which runs north-south, or on **Calle 81,** which feeds into the north-south **Calle 70.** Both intersect **Calle 59,** the best route to the center of town, which runs east to a point one block north of the *zócalo*. **Paseo Montejo** begins at **Calle 47,** running north as **Rte. 261.** The *zócalo* fills one city block, bordered by Calle 61 to the north, Calle 62 to the west, Calle 63 to the south, and Calle 60 to the east. To reach the *zócalo* from the **second-class bus terminal,** head east to Calle 62, walk three blocks, and turn left (north); the *zócalo* is three blocks ahead. Alternatively, take a taxi (10 pesos). From the **train station,** take a taxi (10 pesos), catch the "Seguro Social" bus, or walk six blocks west on Calle 55 and three blocks south on Calle 60.

Mérida's gridded one-way streets have numbers instead of names. Even-numbered streets run north-south, with numbers increasing to the west; odd-numbered streets run east-west, increasing to the south. Addresses in Mérida are given using an "x" to separate the main street from the cross streets and "y" ("and" in Spanish) to separate the two cross streets if the address falls in the middle of the block. Thus "54 #509 x 61 y 63" reads "Calle 54 #509, between Calles 61 and 63." Mérida's **municipal buses** (*camiones*) meander along idiosyncratic routes. Precise information is available at the tourist information office, but the city is small enough so that a bus headed in the right direction will usually drop you off within a few blocks of your desired location. City buses run daily from 5am-11pm (1.50 pesos). **Taxis** do not roam the streets soliciting riders; it is necessary to phone or to go to one of the *sitios* (stands) along Paseo de Montejo, at the airport, and at the *zócalo*. Expect to pay at least 10-15 pesos for a trip within the *centro*. **Taxi-colectivos,** on the other hand, charge only 1.25 pesos for any destination in the city; **dropoffs** are on a first-come, first-serve basis.

YUCATÁN PENINSULA

PRACTICAL INFORMATION

Tourist Information: Central Office, Calles 60 x 57 y 59 (tel. 24-92-90), in the Teatro Peón Contreras. Distributes *Yucatán Today,* a free monthly guide listing practical info and local events. Additional offices at the airport (tel. 46-13-00) and at the 2nd-class bus station, opposite the ADO info window. All open daily 8am-8pm.

Currency Exchange: Banamex (tel. 24-10-11 or 24-11-32), in Casa de Montejo on the *zócalo*. 24hr. **ATM.** Open Mon.-Fri. 9am-5pm.

Airport: 7km southwest on Rte. 180. Bus #79, labeled "Airport," runs between the terminals and a midtown stop at the corner of Calles 67 and 60 (every 20min., 5am-9pm, ½hr., 80 pesos); a taxi charges 30 pesos for the trip. Post office, telegrams, long-distance telephone, and car rental are at the airport. **Aeroméxico,** Paseo Montejo 460 x 35 y 37 (tel. 27-90-00, at airport 46-13-05). **Mexicana,** Calle 58 #500 (tel. 24-66-33, at airport 46-13-32). **Aerocaribe,** Paseo Montejo 500B x 47 (tel. 23-00-02, at airport 46-13-61). **Aviateca** (tel. 24-43-54, at airport 46-12-96) Calles 58 x 45 y 43. Also at Calle 58 x 49 y 51.

Buses: Most bus lines operate out of the main **second-class** terminal, **Unión de Camioneros,** Calle 69 #544 x 68 y 70, 3 blocks west and 3 blocks south of the *zócalo*. **Autotransportes de Oriente (ADO)** (tel. 23-22-87) sends buses to Cancún (every hr., 4am-midnight, 6hr., 53 pesos), Chichén Itzá (every hr., 5am-midnight, 2hr., 20 pesos), Chiquilá (12:30am, 6hr., 52 pesos), Playa del Carmen (5 per day, 7hr., 64 pesos), Tizimín (5pm, 3½hr., 35 pesos), and Valladolid (every hr., 4am-midnight, 3hr., 24 pesos). **Autotransportes del Sur (ATS)** goes to Campeche (6 per day, 3hr., 28 pesos), Escárcega (10 per day, 5½hr., 42 pesos), Palenque (6 and 11:30pm, 14hr., 116 pesos), and Uxmal (6 per day, 1½hr., 11 pesos). **ATS** provides a special **Ruta Puuc** bus (8am, 40 pesos, admission to sites not included) which visits the archaeological sites of Uxmal, Kabah, Sayil, Xlapak, and Labná, returning around 2:30pm. **Línea Dorada** serves Chetumal (4 per day, 6hr., 93 pesos) and Ticul (every hr., 17 pesos). **Premier** goes to Tulum (6am, 6hr., 66 pesos), Cobá (6 per day, 3hr., 56 pesos), Playa del Carmen (8 per day, 5hr., 77 pesos), Chichén Itzá (8:45 and 9:30am, 2hr., 24 pesos), and Valladolid (5 per day, 2½hr., 35 pesos). Some buses leave from the **1st-class terminal,** called **CAME,** located around the corner on Calle 70 between Calles 69 and 71. **Autobuses de Occidente** runs to almost anywhere on the peninsula and Córdoba (4 per day, 17hr., 310 pesos), Mexico City (5 per day, 19hr., 350 pesos), Palenque (8am and 10pm, 8hr., 130 pesos), Puebla (5:45pm, 20hr., 352 pesos), Veracruz (9pm, 15hr., 262 pesos), and Villahermosa (9 per day, 9hr., 150 pesos). **Expreso** to Cancún (15 per day, 4hr., 63 pesos). The 9:15pm **Maya de Oro** or **Cristóbal** bus can take you to Campeche (2½hr., 42 pesos), Palenque (6½hr., 112 pesos), Ocosingo (8½hr.,

140 pesos), San Cristóbal de las Casas (12½hr., 160 pesos), and Tuxtla Gutiérrez (16hr., 185 pesos).

Taxis: Found at **Palacio Municipal,** on the northwest corner of the *zócalo* (tel. 23-13-17), **Mercado Municipal** at Calles 56 and 65 (tel. 23-11-35), in **Parque de la Maternidad** (tel. 28-53-22) at Teatro Peón Contreras, and dozens of other *sitios.* All are on call 24hr. It's much cheaper to use the *camiones* (municipal buses).

Car Rentals: México Rent-a-Car, Calle 57A Dept. 12 x 58 y 60 or Calle 62 #483A x 57 y 59 (tel. 27-49-16). VW Beetles, including insurance and unlimited *kilometraje,* for 200 pesos per day. Open Mon.-Sat. 8am-12:30pm and 6-8pm, Sun. 8am-12:30pm. V, MC, AmEx.

Hospital: Centro Médico de las Américas, Calle 54 #365, at Calle 33A (tel. 26-21-11 or 26-26-19). 24hr. service, including ambulances. **Clínica de Mérida,** Calle 32 #242 x 27 y 25 (tel. 25-41-00). English spoken in both.

Police: on Av. Reforma (Calle 72) x 39 y 41 (tel. 25-25-55 or 25-73-98), accessible with the "Reforma" bus. Some English spoken.

Internet Access: PCS Suministros, Calles 60 #483 x 55 y 57 (tel. 23-98-72). 30 pesos per hr. Open Mon.-Fri. 8:30am-8:30pm, Sat. 9am-2pm.

Post Office: on Calles 65 x 56 y 56A (tel. 24-35-90), 3 blocks from the *zócalo* in the Palacio Federal. Open Mon.-Fri. 7am-7pm, Sat. 9am-noon. Branches at Calles 58 x 49 y 51, the airport, and the main bus station. **MexPost** at Calles 58 x 53 y 55. **Postal Code:** 97000.

Phone Code: 99.

ACCOMMODATIONS AND FOOD

Many of Mérida's budget accommodations are set in splendid colonial mansions. It is not every day that a few pesos will garner a room with tall ceilings, sun-bleached frescoes, and stained glass. The cheapest food in town awaits at the **market,** particularly on the second floor of the restaurant complex on Calle 56 at Calle 67. *Yucateco* dishes go for 5-10 pesos (open Mon.-Sat. 8am-8pm, Sun. 8am-5pm).

Casa Bowen, Calle 66 #521B x 65 y 67 (tel. 24-07-28 or 28-61-09), halfway between the main bus station and the *zócalo.* Pillared lobby with cable TV, LADATEL, dining room, and books of all languages leads up a grand staircase to alluring rooms, each with fans, hot water, and private bath. Make 1-week reservations in Aug. and Dec. Singles 65 pesos; doubles 85 pesos. Rooms with kitchenette and fridge 100 pesos, with A/C 130 pesos; extra person 25 pesos.

Hotel Montejo, Calle 57 #507 x 62 y 64 (tel. 28-02-77 or 28-03-90), 2 blocks north and 1 block east of the *zócalo.* Beautiful, bold colonial mansion with rooms to match. Tall, wood-beamed ceilings. Bathrooms are in excellent condition. Singles 85 pesos; doubles 95 pesos; triples 150 pesos. A/C 30 pesos; extra person 25 pesos.

Restaurante Amaro, Calle 59 #507 x 60 y 62 (tel. 28-24-51). A respite from greasy dishes. Excellent meals are healthy and delicious, offering lean meat and vegetarian options. Shady courtyard makes this a veritable oasis. Refreshing *horchata* (rice milk and almond shake) 9 pesos. Avocado and cheese sandwich 16 pesos. Big fruit salads 16-20 pesos. Meat entrees 25-30 pesos. Open Mon.-Sat. 9am-11pm.

Los Almendros and Los Gran Almendros, Calle 50 #493 x 57 y 59 on Parquet Mejorada (tel. 28-54-59), and at Calle 57 #468 x 50 y 52 (tel. 23-81-35). World-famous restaurant known for its *poc-chuc* (42 pesos). Music and picture menu add to this festive, if touristy place. *Pollo pibil* just 21 pesos. Los Almendros open daily 10am-11pm. Less touristy Gran Almendros open daily noon-6pm. V, MC, AmEx.

SIGHTS

From cathedral towers outlined against a startlingly blue sky to couples getting up close and personal in the *confidenciales,* there is always something to see in Mérida's *zócalo.* The twin towers of the yellow **cathedral** loom over the eastern side of the *zócalo* (open daily 6am-6pm). On the northern edge of the *zócalo* stands the **Palacio de Gobierno.** Built between 1883 and 1892, it fuses two architectural styles—Tuscan and Dorian (open daily 8am-10pm). Concerts and classes in *jarana,* the Yucatecan colonial dance, take place under the sheltering balcony of the **Palacio Municipal,** across the *zócalo* from the cathedral (open Mon.-Sat. 8am-8pm). On the southern side of the *zócalo,* the **Casa de Montejo,** the oldest colonial structure in Mérida, was constructed in 1549 by order of city founder Francisco de Montejo. The carving follows the Toltec tradition of representing warriors standing on their conquests' heads (open Mon.-Fri. 9am-5pm).

Mérida's most impressive museum, the **Museo de Antropología e Historia** (tel. 23-05-57) is housed in a magnificent Italian Renaissance-style building on the corner of Paseo Montejo and Calle 43. Most notable are the ancient Maya versions of plastic surgery (head-flattening devices for infants) and braces (enamel inserts of jade and silver). The shop downstairs sells comprehensive English-language guidebooks cheaper than they're sold at the ruins themselves (museum and shop open Tues.-Sat. 8am-8pm, Sun. 8am-2pm; admission 14 pesos, free Sun.).

Decaying French-style mansions and local and international boutiques line the **Paseo Montejo;** promenades along the Paseo's broad pink sidewalks culminate in the **Monumento a la Patria.** In faux-Maya style, the stone monument, built in 1956, depicts major figures of Mexican history. For a tantalizing detour from the Paseo, veer left (southwest) onto **Avenida Colón,** a street flanked by closely grouped historic mansions in varying stages of decay.

▨ Chichén Itzá

Chichén Itzá's reputation as the Yucatán's prize cultural attraction is well deserved. The combination of faultless ancient architecture and a backdrop of stunning natural beauty makes it a wondrous place. Yet this alone is not why Chichén Itzá, capital of the Maya empire at its zenith, continues to fascinate throngs of people some 1000 years after its creation. This dramatic window into the past illuminates the glaring paradoxes of Maya civilization: a people both intellectually advanced and brutally savage; a culture crushed by colonization, yet still thriving in the language, customs, and hearts of the present-day Maya. A visit to Chichén might just be the pinnacle of your Yucatán experience—don't miss it for the world.

ORIENTATION

The ruins of Chichén Itzá lie 1.5km from **Route 180,** the highway running from Mérida (121km west) through Valladolid (43km east) to Cancún (213km east). As nearly every travel agency in Mexico pushes a Chichén Itzá package, the ruins tend to get overpopulated around noon. In order to avoid the stampede (and hot sun), use nearby **Pisté** (2.5km west of the ruins) as a base and get an early start, or visit late in the afternoon and head back to Pisté at nightfall.

Getting to the ruins is easy. From Pisté, catch a taxi (15 pesos) or flag down any eastbound bus (approximately every 30min., 2-3 pesos). As with all Mexican buses, a vigorous, supplicatory wave to the driver gets you on the road. To get to Chichén Itzá from other towns, see bus listings for Mérida (p. 472). To return to Pisté after a day at the ruins, hang out in the bus parking lot until a taxi or bus swings by (every hr.).

PRACTICAL INFORMATION

Services are located in the dominant stone edifice at the site's western entrance. Across from the ticket counter is a small **information booth.** Refer specific questions about the ruins to official guides. Across from the bus station, both **Centro Telefónico** (tel. 1-00-89; fax 1-00-88) and **Teléfonos de México** (tel. 1-00-58, 1-00-59, or 1-00-60) let you phone home (open daily 7am-9pm). The town has no bank; **exchange** your money at the gift shop at the ruins, but be prepared for ruinous rates.

Pisté's **bus station** (tel. 1-00-52) is near the Stardust Inn on the eastern side of town. To Mérida (1st class 3pm, 1½hr., 27 pesos; 2nd class 11 per day, 2hr., 19 pesos), Cancún (1st class 5:30pm, 2½hr., 46 pesos; 2nd class 10 per day, 4hr., 34 pesos), Valladolid (10 per day, 1hr., 7 pesos), and Playa del Carmen (1:30 and 3:30pm, 5hr., 45 pesos). **Farmacia Isis,** Calle 15 #53, lies a short way past the *zócalo* toward the ruins (open daily 7am-10pm). For medical emergencies, visit the **Clínica Promesa,** Calle 14 #50 (tel. 6-31-98, ext. 198), in the blue-green building past the *zócalo* and 100m off Rte. 180 (open 24hr.). A single **police** officer sits at a desk in the *comisario* on the eastern side of the *zócalo*. The **post office** is in a small gray building near the *zócalo* across from Abarrotes "El Alba" (open Mon.-Fri. 9am-3pm). There is a **telephone** (tel. 1-01-24) right around the corner from the ticket counter. **Phone code:** 985.

ACCOMMODATIONS AND CAMPING

Though a few luxury hotels snuggle up to the ruins, the more economical options are located in **Pisté**—either on or just off Calle 15, the town's main road. You can pitch a tent in the **RV trailer park** right next to the bus station. Spaces have light and power outlets; there are communal bathrooms and a pool (25 pesos per person). The trailer park is administered by the Stardust Inn (tel. 1-01-22), on the other side of the bus station. The tentless can head over to the friendly **Posada Olalde** (tel. 1-00-86), just left of Calle 15 (Rte. 180), two blocks down the unmarked dirt road, directly across the street from the Carrousel Restaurant (singles 100 pesos; doubles 140 pesos; triples 180 pesos). During high season, extra people can string up hammocks for 10 pesos per person. **Posada Carrousel** (tel. 1-00-78), on Calle 15, is in central Pisté at the large eponymous *palapa* restaurant (singles 70 pesos; doubles 100 pesos; triples 130 pesos; quads 100 pesos). Nearby **Hotel El Paso,** Calle 15 #48, offers similar rooms with bouncy beds and small windows (singles 80 pesos; doubles 120 pesos; triples 130-150 pesos). Its restaurant offers a well-priced *menú del día* (25 pesos).

FOOD

For daytrips to Chichén Itzá, the **restaurant** on site provides delicious, reasonable dishes (25-30 pesos) with sporadic entertainment. Picnickers can save a few pesos by packing a lunch from one of the **small grocers** that line Calle 15 in Pisté. Lugging fruit and *tortas* up El Castillo won't be too fun, however, and be prepared for your picnic to be as hot and wet as the inner Temple of the Jaguar. For those determined to save *dinero*, Pisté's Calle 15 is lined with restaurants offering cheap *comida yucateca*. **El Carrousel** (tel. 1-00-78) serves three simple meals a day; try eggs any style (10-12 pesos) or enchiladas (15 pesos; open daily 7am-10:30pm). **Restaurant Sayil,** between El Carrousel and the Stardust Inn, is a peaceful place to savor local dishes like *pollo pibil* (chicken cooked in banana leaf, 12 pesos; open daily 7am-10pm).

SIGHTS

As the Mayan name Chichén Itzá (Mouth of the Well) implies, the area's earliest inhabitants were drawn here by the two nearby freshwater *cenotes*, which are not so fresh today. Much of what is known about these sedentary people is based on the pottery shards recovered by diving archaeologists. Later periods in Chichén Itzá's history are illuminated by the **Chilam Balam,** one of the few pre-Hispanic Maya texts to survive the early missionaries' book-burnings. The *Chilam Balam* describes the construction of many buildings visible today, focusing on the period between AD 500 and 800, when construction was purely Maya.

Chichén was mysteriously abandoned at its height in the 7th century AD, and for the next 300 years it remained a crumbling ghost town. Sometime before AD 1000, the Toltec tribes of Tula (see p. 37) infiltrated the Yucatán and overcame peaceful Maya settlements, bringing with them the cult of the plumed serpent Quetzalcóatl (Kukulcán). The Toltecs fortified Chichén, which soon became the most important city on the peninsula. Toltec influence is visible in Chichén's buildings, which became more rounded, and in its iconography. Whereas the Maya depicted only warriors, eagles, and jaguars, the Toltecs brought in long-nosed representations of Chac (the rain god) and elaborate carvings of lesser gods. They also introduced *chac-mool*, reclining figures representing messengers to the gods that were used as altars for human sacrifice. In 1461, Chichén Itzá was again abandoned, this time due to war, but religious pilgrimages to the site continued well after Spanish conquest. Today, the relentless flow of tourists ensures that Chichén will never again stand in solitude.

For a deeper (not to mention air-conditioned) understanding of Chichén and its people, visit the **Centro Cultural Cecijema** (tel. 1-00-04), at Calle 15 #45 in Pisté. The modern gray building houses a small selection of Maya ceramic replicas as well as attractive rotating exhibits, and the well-stocked library offers books in both English and Spanish. A helpful staff will offer what amounts to a one-on-one tutoring session or just leave you alone to browse with a cup of coffee. Get your birthdate converted to Maya calendar format for a small fee (open daily 8am-5pm; free).

The Ruins

The entire site of Chichén Itzá is open daily 8am-5pm (admission 30 pesos; free Sun. and for children under 14). From the main parking lot and visitor's center, the first group of ruins is up the gravel path and to the left. A small **museum** in the **visitor's complex** at the entrance to the site recaps the history of Chichén Itzá and displays some sculptures and objects removed from the **Sacred Cenote**. Its **auditorium** screens documentaries about the ruins in both Spanish and in English (showtimes vary; both open daily 10am-5pm; free).

If you are mainly interested in the architecture of the ruins, hiring a guide at the entrance is unnecessary. A guidebook (or even just a map) and the multilingual explanatory captions on plaques at each major structure are all you need to appreciate the ruins. Free maps are available at the telephone desk around the corner from the ticket counter. You'll need a guide to decipher some of the symbolism of the ruins or to follow the enigmatic recurrence of the number seven throughout the structures. Join one of the guided tours which begin at the entrance (Spanish or English, 6-8 people, 1½hr., 40 pesos per person) or get your own group together and hire a private guide (up to 20 people, 2hr., 150 pesos). Of course, eavesdropping on any of the tours is always free. If you do choose to hire a guide, ask to see identification, which guarantees certification and foreign language ability.

The first sight to meet your eyes is **El Castillo,** Chichén's hallmark. This pyramid, built in honor of Kukulcán, rises in perfect symmetry from the neatly cropped lawn, culminating in a temple supported by pillars in the form of serpents. El Castillo stands as tangible evidence of the astounding astral understanding of the ancient Maya: the 91 steps on each of the four faces, plus the upper platform, total 365 (the number of days in the non-leap year); the 52 panels on the nine terraced levels equal the number of years in a Maya calendar cycle; and each face of the nine terraces is divided by a staircase, yielding 18 sections representing the 18 Maya months. Even more impressive is the precise alignment of El Castillo's axes, which, in coordination with the sun and the moon, produce a bi-annual optical illusion. At sunrise during the spring and fall equinoxes, the rounded terraces cast a **serpentine shadow** on the side of the northern staircase. The sculpted serpent head at the bottom of the staircase completes the illusion. In March, the serpent appears to be sliding down the stairs precisely in the direction of the Sacred Cenote, while in September the motion is reversed. A light-and-shadow lunar serpent-god, identical to that of the equinoxes, creeps up and down the pyramid at the dawn of the full moon following each of the equinoxes. Twice a year people from all over the world converge on Chichén to see this incredible phenomenon, crowding accommodations with calendrical precision.

Climbing El Castillo is easier than coming down; many tourists do the entire descent on their behinds. That sight might elicit a chuckle, but the ambulance blatantly parked at El Castillo each day will sober you a bit. Nestled within El Castillo is an early Toltec **temple** which can be entered at the bottom of the north staircase on the western side. After climbing up steps whose walls sweat as much as you do, you'll be grimacing like the *chac-mool* located in the ceremonial chamber. Behind the chamber is a fanged, molding jaguar throne with jade eyes (open daily 11am-3pm and 4-5pm; free). West of El Castillo, or to the left of the entrance, lies the **ballcourt.** The enormous "I"-shaped playing field is bounded by two high, parallel walls with a temple at each end. The largest ballcourt in Mesoamerica, it also has an amazing side-to-side echo that repeats seven times and making it easy to catch free tidbits from tour guides going by. The game played here was called **pok-ta-pok**. Players of the two contending teams tried to keep a heavy rubber ball in constant motion by using only their hips, knees, and elbows. They scored by knocking the ball through the stone rings still visible today, high up on the walls in the middle of the "I". The elaborate game fascinated the Spanish so much that in 1528 Cortés took two entire teams back to Europe to perform before the crowned heads. After that, European ball games replaced their unyielding, dead wooden balls with lively, rubber ones.

The ball game was much more than just a cultural pastime for the Maya; it was a contest of **good** versus **evil** linked to a game of the gods. The Maya legend in the *Popol Vuh* tells that every harvest **Hun Hunahpu**, god of corn, was decapitated; his head was planted in the ground and became the seed of all corn plants. Every year, the evil gods of the netherworld stole the buried head in an attempt to destroy the Maya. The hero-twins **Xbalanque** and **Hunahpú** (the sun and Venus respectively) would then descend to **Xilbalba** (the netherworld) and challenge the evil gods to an epic game of ball, using the god's head instead of a ball. Invariably, the twins were successful and the seed was recovered. The new crop symbolized the god's resurrection and the Maya's salvation. In response to the legend, after a ball game (according to some historians) the captain of the victorious team would be decapitated and his head offered to honor the gods. The losers were left to live in shame.

A short distance from the ballcourt toward the grassy open area is the **Tzompantli,** Aztec for Platform of the Skulls. When the Spaniards conquered the Aztecs, they were shocked to find ritualized human sacrifice and horrified by the racks in Tenochtitlán designed to display the skulls of the sacrificed. Chichén's Toltec-designed structure served a similar macabre purpose. Today, eerie rows of skulls in bas-relief decorate the low platform's walls. Next to the Tzompantli stands the **Platform of Jaguars and Eagles,** named after the military men bearing the names of these ferocious animals and who were charged with obtaining prisoners from other tribes for human sacrifice. To either side of the feathered serpent heads on the balustrades, reliefs of jaguars and eagles clutch human hearts in their claws. East of the platform is the **Temple of Venus,** decorated with a feathered serpent holding a human head in its mouth. The temple's reliefs symbolize stars and give information on their motion.

The dirt path leading directly north from El Castillo, over the ancient Maya roadway, links the ceremonial plaza with Chichén Itzá's most important religious center, the **Sacred Cenote,** 300m away. The roughly circular sink-hole, about 60m across, induced vertigo in the sacrificial victims perched on the platform before their 25m plunge into the murky depths. The rain god Chac supposedly dwelt beneath the water's surface and needed frequent gifts to grant good rains. Human remains recovered by divers suggest that children and young men were the victims of choice. If they could keep afloat until noon, they were fished out and forced to tell what they had witnessed during the ordeal. With a snack shack nearby and lots of shade, the cenote is a great place to take a bathroom break, cool off, and watch iguanas go by.

A red dirt path on the south side of El Castillo leads to the less photogenic **South Group** of ruins. Beyond the cafeteria and bathrooms, the first pyramid on the right is the **Ossuary,** or **High Priest's Grave,** its distinctive serpent heads mimicking El Castillo. A natural cave extends from within the pyramid 15m into the earth. The human bones and votive offerings found in this cavern are thought to have belonged to an ancient high priest. Past the Ossuary, the road forks, presenting two different routes to the second set of ruins in the South Group, often missed by tourists but well worth the visit. The most interesting structure in this group is the **Observatory,** the large circular building on the left-hand side. This ancient planetarium consists of two rectangular platforms with large, west-facing staircases and two circular towers. Because of the tower's interior spiral staircase (not open to the public), this structure is often called **El Caracol** (the Great Conch). The slits in the dome of the Observatory can be aligned with the important celestial bodies and cardinal directions. El Caracol was built in several stages by Maya and Toltec architects. Notice the small red handprints on the wall of the building just as you come up the stairs; these were supposedly the hands of the sun god Itzamná. Walking south from El Caracol, toward the Nunnery at the other end of the clearing, you will pass a tiny, ruined **sauna** and then the **Temple of the Sculptured Wall Panels** behind it. Though difficult to decipher, the panels on the exterior walls contain emblems of Toltec warriors—jaguars, eagles, and serpents—in three rows.

The largest structure in this part of Chichén is the misnamed **Nunnery,** on the south side of the quadrangle. Although it was probably a Maya royal palace, its stone rooms reminded Spaniards of a European convent—thus the misnomer. After several superimpositions and some decay, the building is now almost 20m high on a base 65m long and 35m wide. Above the entrance on the eastern side of the building, you can still see Maya hieroglyphs. Also on the eastern side, a smaller annex built at an angle is visible. Grab a flashlight and go exploring—many rooms in the nunnery have doorways that lead to dark corridors and small inner rooms. Play Indiana Jones by risking dirty clothes and abrasions to uncover bats, frogs, and, unfortunately, water bottles left by other daring adventurers.

A poorly maintained path (which is sometimes closed during rainy months) runs about 130m east from the nunnery group, past the chapel, to the long **Akab-Dzib.** The oldest parts of this structure are believed to be Chichén's most ancient constructions. The two central rooms date to the 2nd or 3rd century AD, while the annexes on either side and to the east were added later. Inside the rooms, it is possible to make out the small, rose-red handprints of Itzamná on the ceiling. On the path is another cave, partly hidden by trees, whose narrow mouth yields more bats and water bottles nestled in its belly.

The overgrown **Cenote Xtoloc** hides in a dip behind the South Group ticket office. To reach it from the office, take the first left 20m into the site. The cenote is in the hollow, beyond the small, ruined temple of Xtoloc, the lizard god. There is no path down the steep slope through the undergrowth, and swimming is prohibited because of the harsh currents. Follow **sacbé No. 5,** which becomes a winding trail, to get to the back of the observatory.

As if Chichén Itzá couldn't muster enough daytime spectacle, those green panels (whose purpose you've been contemplating all day) pop open for the evening **light and sound show.** The buildings are splashed in red, blue, green, and yellow lights while booming voices detail the history of the site (Spanish version daily at 7pm, 12 pesos; English version daily at 9pm, 18 pesos). Avoid the poorly lit and bug-infested nighttime walk from Pisté and cab it to and from the show (15 pesos each way).

QUINTANA ROO

■ Tulum

Although the architecture of the ruins here may be less impressive than that at Uxmal and Chichén Itzá, the backdrop is stunning. Tulum's graying temples and nearly intact watchtowers rise above tall, wind-bent palm trees, clinging to a cliff above white sand pummeled by the steely-blue Caribbean Sea. Tulum brings together two of the best aspects of the Yucatán: archaeological wonders and Caribbean waters. First settled in the 4th century AD, Tulum was the oldest continuously inhabited city in the New World when the Spanish arrived.

ORIENTATION AND PRACTICAL INFORMATION

Located 42km southeast of Cobá, 63km south of Playa del Carmen, and 127km south of Cancún, Tulum (pop. 12,000) is the southernmost link in the chain of tourist attractions on the Caribbean coast of Quintana Roo, and the eastern extreme of the major Maya archaeological sites. Although few people live here, Tulum sprawls out over three separate areas: **el crucero** (the crossroads), the beach **cabañas,** and

Pueblo Tulum. Arriving in Tulum from Cancún on Rte. 307, buses first stop at *el crucero,* a few kilometers before town. Here, a couple of restaurants, hotels, and overpriced minimarts huddle together 800m west of the ruins. The well-paved access road turns south at the ruins, leading to food and lodging at *cabañas* 2km farther down the road. Pueblo Tulum, 4km south of *el crucero,* offers travelers a handful of roadside restaurants, minimarts, and some services.

The few services available in Pueblo Tulum are on Rte. 307, which serves as the tiny town's main street. There's no tourist office, though a few stands at the ruins can provide sketchy maps. Those desperate to exchange money can do so at the *crucero* or next to the bus office in Pueblo Tulum. New public phones line Rte. 307 in Pueblo Tulum. **Caseta de Tulum** (tel./fax 1-20-09) is a block from the bus station (open daily 7am-9pm). Buses leave from a small waiting room sandwiched between 2 currency exchange booths opposite the Hotel Maya. **ADO** runs to Coatzacoalcos (8am, 11hr., 260 pesos), Córdoba (8am, 12hr., 390 pesos), Escárcega (8am, 4hr., 140 pesos), Mexico City (8am, 22hr., 480 pesos), San Andrés (4:30pm, 9hr., 300 pesos), Veracruz (4:30pm, 12hr., 340 pesos), and Villahermosa (4:30pm, 9hr., 221 pesos). Various **2nd-class buses** run to Cancún (14 per day, 2hr., 24 pesos), Chetumal (12 per day, 4hr., 44 pesos), Chichén Itzá (6 per day, 3½hr., 42 pesos), Cobá (9 per day, 30min., 10 pesos), Escárcega (4:30pm, 8hr., 130 pesos), Mérida (4 per day, 5hr., 60 pesos), Ocosingo (4:30pm, 15hr., 180 pesos), Palenque (4:30pm, 14hr., 163 pesos), Playa del Carmen (14 per day, 1hr., 14 pesos), San Cristóbal (4:30pm, 16hr., 200 pesos), and Valladolid (5 per day, 25hr., 30 pesos). **Súper Farmacia** is just past the post office (open daily 8am-9pm). English-speaking **Dr. Arturo Ventre** is available just in case (Mon.-Sun. 8am-noon and 6-9pm). **Police** (tel. 1-20-55) are in the Delegación Municipal, 2 blocks past the post office. The **Post Office** is a about 100m into town on Rte. 307 (open Mon.-Fri. 9am-1pm and 3-6pm). **Postal Code:** 77780. **Phone Code:** 987.

ACCOMMODATIONS AND FOOD

Tulum offers two lodging options: hotels at *el crucero* in town, or beachside *cabañas.* Don't be afraid to ask for help with a hammock if it's (blush!) your first time. (Hint: protect your back by sleeping crosswise, not lengthwise.) Both the Pueblo and the *crucero* have satisfying and authentic restaurants as well as *mini-súpers;* the former are slightly cheaper and provide filling sustenance for daytrips.

Cabañas Santa Fe, just off the paved road 1km south of the ruins. Follow the signs to Don Armando's and turn left. Shack up here with backpackers from all over the world. Bare *cabaña* with sand floor and small hammock 40 pesos. 1-bed *cabaña* with cement floor 70 pesos; 2-bed *cabaña* 140 pesos; hammock rental 20 pesos per night. Mosquito-net rental 5-10 pesos per night.

Don Armando Cabañas (tel. 4-76-72 or 1-13-54), on the paved road 1km south of the ruins. A humble paradise with a volleyball court. *Cabañas* are solid and safe; the communal facilities are spotless. *Cabaña* with 1 bed and 1 hammock 80 pesos, with 2 beds 100-120 pesos. Deposit 50 pesos. Camp for 20 pesos per person.

Restaurante El Crucero, in Hotel El Crucero. Comfortable and shady interior provides respite from all that Maya sun. Get intimate with that old standby, *pescado al mojo de ajo* (35 pesos). Breakfast (fruit salad, orange juice, toast, and coffee) 19-30 pesos. Open daily 7am-9pm.

Restaurante Santa Fe, at the campground on the beach. Mellow reggae tunes, the rumble of surf, the newly reconstructed *palapa,* the *cabaña*-like sand floor, the fresh fish (30-40 pesos), and quesadillas (18 pesos) are the 6 hallmarks of the Restaurante Santa Fe experience. Restaurant and bar open daily 7am-11pm.

SIGHTS

The Ruins

The ruins would offer a great view of the sea, if only you could climb them (they're roped off). The murals would be beautiful, if only you could see them (they too are roped off). While all you can do is walk around the bases and stare at the ocean, the dramatically situated site certainly still merits a visit. The first thing you see in Tulum will be the still-impressive **dry-laid wall** that surrounded the city center's three land-locked sides. The wall was originally 3.6m thick and 3m high. It shielded the city from the aggression of neighboring Maya city-states and prevented all but the 150 or so priests and governors of Tulum from entering the city for most of the year. After Tulum's defeat at the hands of the Spanish in 1544, the wall fended off English, Dutch, and French pirates and, in 1847, gave rebel Maya refuge from government forces during the Caste War. Magnificent representations of a **figure diving into the water** cover the western walls. The images, depicting the Maya sunset god, are lit every evening by the rays of the setting sun.

Just inside and to the left of the west gate stand the remains of platforms which once supported huts. Behind these platforms are the **House of the Halach Uinik** (the House of the Ruler); the **Palacio,** the largest residential building in Tulum; and the **Temple of the Paintings,** a stellar example of post-Classical Maya architecture. Well-preserved 600-year-old murals inside the temple depict deities intertwined with serpents, as well as fruit, flower, and corn offerings. Masks of Itzamná, the Maya Creator, occupy the northwest and southwest corners of the building.

El Castillo looms behind the smaller buildings and over the rocky seaside cliff. Serving as a pyramid and temple, it commands a view of the entire walled city. It also served as a lighthouse, allowing returning fishermen to find the only gap in the barrier reef just offshore. Its walls, like those of many buildings in Tulum, slope outward, but the doorposts slope inward. The castle's architectural and structural eccentricities are due to its numerous rebuildings. In front of the temple is the sacrificial stone where the Maya held battle ceremonies. Once the stars had been consulted and a propitious day determined, a warrior-prisoner was selected for sacrifice. At the climax of the celebration, attendants painted the warrior's body blue—the sacred color of the Maya—and the chief priest cut his heart out and poured the blood over the idols in the temple. The body was given to the soldiers below, who were thought to acquire the strength to overcome their enemies through cannibalism.

To the right of El Castillo on the same plaza is the **Temple of the Initial Series.** Named after a stela found here, the temple bears a date that corresponded to the beginning of the Maya religious calendar in the year 761 AD. The **Temple of the Descending God,** with a fading relief of a feathered, armed deity diving from the sky, stands on the other side of El Castillo's plaza. Perched on its own precipice on the other side of the beach, the **Temple of the Winds** was acoustically designed to act as a storm-warning system. Surely enough, before Hurricane Gilbert struck the site in 1988, the temple's airways dutifully whistled their alarm (site open daily 8am-5pm; admission 16 pesos, free Sun.; guided tours about 150 pesos for 1-5 people, 200 pesos for groups up to 25 people).

Getting There: Tulum's ruins lie a brisk eight-minute walk east of Rte. 307 from the *crucero.* For the supremely lazy, a dinky **train** (7 pesos) covers the distance in slightly less time. Admission tickets are sold at a booth to the left of the parking lot.

The Beach

Hanging out on the beach in *cabañas* is a popular way to end a day at the ruins. Expect the Europeans to turn it into a topless affair; some even strip to their bare butts. *Cabaña* managers complain if you drift into the campgrounds in the buff.

Offshore, you can see the waves mysteriously breaking on Tulum's **barrier reef,** the largest in the Americas; it runs the full length of the Yucatán peninsula, including Belize. To enjoy the fish below, you can rent scuba and snorkeling equipment from the **dive shop** (tel. 1-20-96) at **Cabañas Santa Fe** (35 pesos per day for snorkeling; open daily 8am-3:30pm). The shop plans trips to the reef and a nearby *cenote* (US$15, including rental, *antojitos,* and *refrescos*). You can also get scuba certified here (US$30) or go diving in the Cenote Dos Ojos (you must be an experienced diver; US$50). Get fins if you snorkel; the 500m swim to the reef is often a struggle against a north-south current.

APPENDIX

HOLIDAYS AND FESTIVALS

Tourist offices can advise you where and when local festivals take place. Expect banks, museums, and other public buildings to close for the following national holidays: **January 1** (New Year's Day); **Thursday and Friday of Holy Week** (the week before Easter); **May 1** (Labor Day); **December 24-25** (Christmas Eve and Christmas); and **December 31** (New Year's Eve). **Patron saint festivals,** replete with parades, dances, food and drink, are also hosted by each country. **Semana Santa** (Easter Week) is the biggest party of the year; if you plan to join in, you'll need to reserve rooms well in advance and expect higher prices. For more details about holidays in each country, check the **Essentials** section at the beginning of each chapter.

CLIMATE

The following chart gives the average high and low temperatures in degrees centigrade (Celsius) and the average yearly rainfall in centimeters during four months of the year. Keep in mind that in Central America, altitude rather than latitude is the main determinant; the lowlands are hot and humid, while a few thousand feet up, both days and nights get downright chilly.

Temp in °C Rain in cm	January Temp	Rain	April Temp	Rain	July Temp	Rain	October Temp	Rain
Guatemala City	20/11	1.0	24/14	3.0	23/14	19.5	22/14	16.5
Belize City	25/17	13.5	27/21	5.0	28/22	17.0	27/21	28.5
San Salvador	32/17	1.0	35/19	4.5	32/19	29.0	31/19	24.5
Tegucigalpa	25/18	1.7	30/19	3.0	28/19	8.5	27/19	13.5
Managua	31/21	0.5	35/24	1.0	31/24	12.5	31/23	26.0
San José	22/13	1.0	27/18	4.5	25/18	20.0	25/18	29.5
Panama City	31/22	3.5	32/23	6.0	31/23	19.0	30/23	26.5

To convert from °C to °F, multiply by 1.8 and add 32. For an approximation, double the Celsius and add 25. To convert from °F to °C, subtract 32 and multiply by 0.55.

°C	-5	0	5	10	15	20	25	30	35	40
°F	23	32	41	50	59	68	77	86	95	104

TELEPHONE COUNTRY CODES

Guatemala	502
Belize	501
El Salvador	503
Honduras	504
Nicaragua	505

Costa Rica	506
Panama	507
Ireland	353
U.K.	44
U.S.	1

Canada	1
Australia	61
New Zealand	64
South Africa	27

TIME ZONES

Belize, El Salvador, Honduras, and Costa Rica are all six hours behind Greenwich Mean Time (in other words, they keep U.S. Central Time). Panama is five hours behind GMT (the same as U.S. Eastern Standard Time). Nicaragua and Guatemala both have loose versions of daylight savings, so the countries are either 5 or 6 hrs. behind GMT, depending on the season. The rest of Central America does not have daylight savings, so add an hour for this part of the year.

MEASUREMENTS

The metric system is used almost universally throughout Central America, with the exception that U.S. gallons are used to measure gasoline. Although you may encounter miscellaneous other terms for weight (including *libra*, or pound) and distance (such as the Honduran *vara*, about .8 meters), someone should be able to convert back to metric upon request.

1 ounce = 28.35 grams (g)	1 gram = 0.04 ounce
1 pound = .454 kilograms (kg)	1 kilogram = 2.21 pounds
1 kilometer (km.) = .612 miles	1 mile = 1.61 kms.
°C = 5/9(°F-32)°	F = 9/5(°CG32)
1 inch = 2.54 centimeters (cm)	1 centimeter = 0.4 inches
1 liter = .264 U.S. gallons	1 U.S. gallon = 3.79 liters
1 foot = .305 meters (m)	1 meter = 3.29 feet

Electrical Current

110 volts, the same as the U.S., is standard voltage in Central America. Ask first, though, as some places might have alarm-clock-melting 220 volt outlets. If you're planning to rely heavily on electricity, bring ample adapters, and converters, including one for converting three prongs to two. Many hotel rooms won't have outlets, or will have only one (which is taken by the fan).

LANGUAGE

Even if you speak no Spanish, a few basics will help you along. Any attempts at Spanish are appreciated and encouraged, and you'll find that many people in larger cites understand some English. You are likely to hear *indígena* languages as well as Spanish. Those who already know peninsular Spanish will find that many common nouns and expressions are different in Central America.

Pronunciation is straightforward. Vowels are always pronounced the same way: a ("ah" in father); e ("eh" in escapade); i ("ee" in eat); o ("oh" oat); u ("oo" in boot); y, by itself, is pronounced like i. Most consonants are the same as English. Important exceptions are: j, pronounced like the English "h" in "hello"; ll, pronounced like the English "y" in "yes"; ñ, which is pronounced like the "gn" in "cognac"; rr, the trilled "r"; h is always silent; x has a bewildering variety of pronunciations.

Let's Go provides approximations for particularly tough town names. Stress in Spanish words falls on the second to last syllable, except for words ending in "r," "l" and "z," in which it falls on the last syllable. All exceptions to these rules require a written accent on the stressed syllable.

No offense is meant if you are called a *gringo/a* (GREEN-goh/gah). You may offend, however, if you call yourself an *americano/a;* as part of the Americas, Central and South Americans resent monopolization of the term by the U.S. Instead, refer to yourself as a *norteamericano/a*. The most appropriate term for the descendants of the Maya and other groups varies from country to country and person to person. *Let's Go* uses *indígena* (in-DEE-heh-nah) or indigenous; the only term that is guaranteed to be universally *offensive* is *indio*.

PHRASEBOOK

English	Spanish	English	Spanish
			Phrases
Hello	Hola	**How are you?**	¿Cómo está? (formal)
			¿Cómo estás? (informal)
Good morning	Buenos días	**Good afternoon**	Buenos tardes
Good evening/night	Buenas noches	**Pleased to meet you**	Mucho gusto
Sorry/Forgive me	Lo siento/Perdóname	**Yes/No/Maybe**	Sí/No/Quizás
Thank you	Gracias	**No thanks**	No, gracias
Thank you very much	¡Muchas gracias!	**You're welcome**	De nada
Please	Por favor	**My name is...**	Me llamo...
I'm fine, thanks	Estoy bien, gracias	**What is your name?**	¿Como se llama? (form.)
			¿Como te llamas? (inf.)
Good-bye	Adiós or Hasta luego	**No problem**	No problema
Excuse me	Con permiso/perdón	**I don't know**	No sé
I don't speak Spanish	No hablo español	**Idon'tunderstand**	No entiendo
Do you speak English?	¿Habla inglés?	**In Spanish, how do you say...?**	¿Cómo se dice...en español?
Could you speak more slowly, please?	¿Podría hablar más despacio, por favor?	**Could you tell me...?**	¿Podría decirme...?
When(what time)?	¿Cuándo?	**What?**	¿Qué?
O.K.	O.K.	**Where is...?**	¿Dónde está...?
Who?	¿Quién?	**Why?**	¿Por qué?
I would like...	Quisiera.../me gustaría	**No smoking**	No fumadores/no fumar
How do you say?	¿Cómo se dice...?	**When is it open?**	¿A qué horas está abierto?
What did you say?	¿Qué dijo?/¿Mande?	**Can you help me?**	¿Puede Usted ayudarme?
No poking	No empujar	**I like Shakira**	Me gusta Shakira
Where is the bathroom?	¿Dónde está el baño?	**What time is it?**	¿Qué hora es?
			Days
Sunday	Domingo	**Today**	Hoy
Monday	Lunes	**Tomorrow**	Mañana
Tuesday	Martes	**Day after tomorrow**	Pasado mañana
Wednesday	Miércoles	**Yesterday**	Ayer
Thursday	Jueves	**Day before yesterday**	Antes de ayer/Anteayer
Friday	Viernes	**Week**	Semana
Saturday	Sábado	**Weekend**	Fin de semana

Numbers

0	cero	15	quince
1	uno	16	dieciseis
2	dos	17	diecisiete
3	tres	18	dieciocho
4	cuatro	19	diecinueve
5	cinco	20	veinte
6	seis	21	veinte-uno
7	siete	30	treinta
8	ocho	40	cuarenta
9	nueve	50	cincuenta
10	diez	60	sesenta
11	once	70	setenta
12	doce	80	ochenta
13	trece	90	noventa
14	catorce	100	cien

GLOSSARY

A
abanico	fan
aduana	customs
aeropuerto	airport
agua purficada	purified water
aire acondicionado	air-conditioning
amigo/a	friend
avenida	avenue
¡ay!	ouch!

B
balneario	spa or resort on the water
baño	bathroom
barrio	neighborhood

C
cabina	a class of transportation ticket which provides a room and bed
calle	street
cambio	change
camioneta	small, pickup sized truck
campamento	campground
cantina	drinking extablishment, usually male dominated
caro/a	expensive
carretera	highway
carro	car, or sometimes a train car
casa de cambio	currency exchange extablishment
casado/a	married
catarata	waterfall
centro	city center
cerveza	beer
colectivo	municipal transit bus
comida corrida	multi-course *á la carte* meal

	consulado	consulate
	cruz roja	Red Cross
D	desayuno	breakfast
	descompuesto	broken, out of order; or spoiled/rotten food
	de turno	a 24-hour rotating schedule for pharmacies
E	embajada	embassy
	emergencia	emergency
	enfermo/a	sick
	estrella	star
	extranjeros	foreigners
F	farmacia	pharmacy
	fiesta	party, holiday
	finca	a plantation-like agricultural enterprise
G	ganga	bargain
	gaseosa	soft drink
	gorro	hat
H	hacienda	ranch
	hervido/a	boiled
	hombre	man
	hospedaje	youth hostel
I	iglesia	church
	indígena	indigenous
L	ladrón	thief
	lago/laguna	lake
	larga distancia	long distance
	lavandería	laundromat
	legos	far
	lista de correos	the general delivery system in most of Central America
M	medico	doctor
	mercado	market
O	oficina de turismo	office of tourism
	oreo	breeze, fresh air
P	payaso	clown
	playa	beach
	peligroso/a	dangerous
R	rana	frog
	restaurante	restaurant
	ropa	clothes
S	sala	room
	salida	exit
	semana	week
	señor/a	sir/madam
T	taqueria/taqueteria	a taco stand or vendor
	tienda	store
	tipo de cambio	exchange rate
V	vino	wine
Z	zapatos	shoes

ndex

INDEX

INDEX

★Let's Go 1998 Reader Questionnaire★

Please fill this out and return it to **Let's Go, St. Martin's Press,** 175 Fifth Ave., New York, NY 10010-7848. All respondents will receive a free subscription to **The Yellowjacket,** the Let's Go Newsletter.

Name: _____

Address: _____

City: _____ **State:** _____ **Zip/Postal Code:** _____

Email: _____ **Which book(s) did you use?** _____

How old are you? under 19   19-24   25-34   35-44   45-54   55 or over

Are you (circle one) in high school   in college   in graduate school   employed   retired   between jobs

Have you used Let's Go before? yes no **Would you use it again?** yes no

How did you first hear about Let's Go? friend   store clerk   television   bookstore display   advertisement/promotion   review   other

Why did you choose Let's Go (circle up to two)? reputation budget focus   price   writing style   annual updating   other: _____

Which other guides have you used, if any? Frommer's $-a-day   Fodor's   Rough Guides   Lonely Planet   Berkeley   Rick Steves   other: _____

Is Let's Go the best guidebook? yes no

If not, which do you prefer? _____

Please rank each of the following parts of Let's Go 1 to 5 (1=needs improvement, 5=perfect). packaging/cover   practical information   accommodations   food   cultural introduction   sights   practical introduction ("Essentials")   directions   entertainment   gay/lesbian information   maps   other: _____

How would you like to see the books improved? (continue on separate page, if necessary) _____

_____

How long was your trip? one week   two weeks   three weeks   one month   two months or more

Which countries did you visit? _____

What was your average daily budget, not including flights? _____

Have you traveled extensively before? yes no

Do you buy a separate map when you visit a foreign city? yes no

Have you seen the Let's Go Map Guides? yes no

Have you used a Let's Go Map Guide? yes no

If you have, would you recommend them to others? yes no

Did you use the Internet to plan your trip? yes no

Would you use a Let's Go: recreational (e.g. skiing) guide   gay/lesbian guide   adventure/trekking guide   phrasebook   general travel information guide

Which of the following destinations do you hope to visit in the next three to five years (circle one)? South Africa   China   South America   Russia   Caribbean   Scandinavia   other: _____

Where did you buy your guidebook? Internet   chain bookstore   independent bookstore   college bookstore   travel store   other: _____